Chronology of
WORLD
SLAVERY

Chronology of
WORLD
SLAVERY

Junius P. Rodriguez

Foreword by Orlando Patterson

ABC-CLIO

Santa Barbara, California
Denver, Colorado
Oxford, England

Library of Congress Cataloging-in-Publication Data

Rodriguez, Junius P.
     Chronology of world slavery / Junius P. Rodriguez ; foreword by
Orlando Patterson.
          p.   cm.
     Includes bibliographical references and index.
     ISBN 0-87436-884-7 (alk. paper)
     1. Slavery—History—Chronology. 2. Slave trade—History—
Chronology. I. Title.
     HT861.R63   1999
     306.3'62'09—dc21   99-23170

ABC-CLIO, Inc.
130 Cremona Drive, P.O. Box 1911
Santa Barbara, California 93116-1911

This book is printed on acid-free paper ∞.

Manufactured in the United States of America

To the memory of

Gary E. Gammon
(1942–1998)

colleague & friend

*". . . but now you are light in
the Lord; walk as children of
light."*
Ephesians 5:8

FOREWORD
Orlando Patterson
HARVARD UNIVERSITY

In spite of the vast outpouring of works on slavery in recent decades, it is still remarkable how unaware the proverbial educated layman is of its extent and significance in human history. Students and even academics often assume that slavery was largely confined to the U.S. South and Latin America and that the only slaves were people of color. It comes as a shock to many of my students when I inform them that the typical slave throughout the Middle Ages was a blond, blue-eyed Slav and that slavery persisted in Eastern Europe right down to the early nineteenth century.

The *Chronology of World Slavery* should disabuse all its readers of such a mistaken view. It makes clear that slavery was a worldwide institution. It has existed in some form in every region of the world, at all levels of sociopolitical development, and among all major ethnic groups. All peoples had ancestors who at some time suffered the ultimate inhumanity, the social death that was slavery. And nearly all peoples can count slaveholders among their ancestors.

While universal, slavery varied considerably in its level of structural significance. In most areas of the world it was economically marginal, demographically no more than 5 percent of the population, and confined to the household. Slavery was important in the Islamic world, although mainly for military, administrative, and household purposes. It was also sociologically important for ritual and honorific purposes among advanced premodern groups such as the ancient Carthaginians, the Aztecs of Mexico, and several of the more centralized precolonial African states such as Dahomey, Benin, and Ashanti.

However, it is in Western civilization that slavery attained its greatest structural and cultural significance. With the possible exception of medieval Korea, it is only in the West that slavery became a major economic institution. It is remarkable that at all the watershed periods in Western history slavery played a key role in the transition process. Ancient Greece, the source culture of the West, rose to prominence on the basis of slave labor. By the late fifth century B.C., one in three adults in Athens was a slave, a proportion similar to the U.S. South at the height of its slave order. Rome was even more dependent on the institution, not only for its vast latifundia—the

ancient counterpart of the modern plantation—but for its urban economy and for the lower-level clerical staff of its imperial bureaucracy. There was a resurgence of slavery in Europe during the late ninth and early tenth centuries; another during the late medieval and early Renaissance period of the Italian Mediterranean empires where the sugar plantation originated; and, of course, the rise of the modern state and capitalism went hand in hand with the rise of the slave plantation system and the vast intercontinental enslavement of some 12 million Africans in the New World.

But slavery's impact went well beyond the economic in the Western world. It profoundly influenced all the key cultural institutions of the West. Thus the social construction of freedom in ancient Greece and Rome was intimately linked to the centrality of the institution in these societies. Christianity, the very foundation of Western civilization, emerged in the slave society of ancient Rome, and its theology—especially its central doctrine of Christ as the redeemer (literally, one who purchases a slave out of slavery) of mankind from the thralldom of slavery, was a powerful introjection of the most important event in the secular life of most members of the primitive church. In modern times, it has been shown that the movements to abolish slavery were themselves strongly linked socially and symbolically to the rise of liberalism and the reinvigoration of the idea of freedom as the absence of constraint on persons and property.

It has been difficult for those who cherish the Western heritage to admit to its long and constitutive relationship with slavery. We prefer to see it as an anomaly confined to the U.S. South, Latin America, and the Caribbean. And persons of European ancestry would like to believe that only people of African ancestry were enslaved. The *Chronology of World Slavery* not only dispels these myths, but presents a wealth of evidence demonstrating the institution's antiquity, universality, and disproportionate impact on Western history and culture. This book is an invaluable resource, not only for students of slavery but for all who wish to understand the West, the extent of man's inhumanity to man, and the often paradoxical ways in which many of the values and ideals we most cherish emerged from the struggles to overcome and change the evils that we most abhor.

CONTENTS

SIDEBARS

~THE CONTRIBUTORS~

Jim Baugess
Ohio State University
Columbus, Ohio

Beverly A. Bunch-Lyons
Virginia Polytechnic Institute &
State University
Blacksburg, Virginia

Joseph P. Byrne
Belmont University
Nashville, Tennessee

Charles W. Carey, Jr.
Central Virginia Junior College
Lynchburg, Virginia

Henry Y. S. Chan
Moorhead State University
Moorhead, Minnesota

Dallas Cothrum
University of Texas–Tyler
Tyler, Texas

Charles A. D'Aniello
State University of New York–Buffalo
Buffalo, New York

James di Properzio
Emory University
Atlanta, Georgia

Clifford R. Dickinson
St. Christopher's School
Richmond, Virginia

Francis A. Dutra
University of California–Santa Barbara
Santa Barbara, California

Peter Eardley
University of Toronto
Toronto, Canada

James C. Foley
University of Mississippi
Oxford, Mississippi

Daniel L. Fountain
University of Mississippi
Oxford, Mississippi

Dan R. Frost
Dillard University
New Orleans, Louisiana

Marti J. Gastineau
Brown University
Providence, Rhode Island

John C. Gibson
University of Toronto
Toronto, Canada

Jennifer Lynn Himelstein
University of New Mexico
Albuquerque, New Mexico

Claude F. Jacobs
University of Michigan–Dearborn
Dearborn, Michigan

Mark L. Kamrath
University of Central Florida
Orlando, Florida

Frances Richardson Keller
San Francisco State University
San Francisco, California

Mary L. Kelley
Texas Christian University
Fort Worth, Texas

Stephen C. Kenny
John Moores University
Liverpool, England

Yitzchak Kerem
Hebrew University
Jerusalem, Israel

Yasue Kuwahara
Northern Kentucky University
Highland Heights, Kentucky

David J. Libby
Wake Forest University
Winston-Salem, North Carolina

Richard D. Loosbrock
University of New Mexico
Albuquerque, New Mexico

Jennifer Margulis
Emory University
Atlanta, Georgia

James D. Medler
Old Dominion University
Norfolk, Virginia

Liliana Mosca
Frederico II University
Naples, Italy

Beatrice Nicolini
Catholic University of the Sacred Heart
Milan, Italy

Onaiwu W. Ogbomo
Allegheny College
Meadville, Pennsylvania

Michael Polley
Columbia College
Columbia, Missouri

Remco Raben
Netherlands State Institute for War
Documentation
Amsterdam, The Netherlands

Maria Elena Raymond
Robbins, California

Manisha Sinha
University of Massachusetts–Amherst
Amherst, Massachusetts

Gene A. Smith
Texas Christian University
Fort Worth, Texas

Richard D. Starnes
Western Carolina University
Cullowhee, North Carolina

Torrance T. Stephens
Emory University
Atlanta, Georgia

Stephen A. Stertz
Dowling College
Oakdale, New York

Carol J. Terry
Texas Christian University
Fort Worth, Texas

Eric Tscheschlok
Auburn University
Auburn, Alabama

Peter M. Voelz
Eastern Illinois University
Charleston, Illinois

Judith Ann Warner
Texas A & M International University
Laredo, Texas

Michael Washington
Northern Kentucky University
Highland Heights, Kentucky

❧ PREFACE ❧

The *Chronology of World Slavery* is designed as a complementary volume that expands the breadth of knowledge about world slavery initiated in *The Historical Encyclopedia of World Slavery* (1997). Like the *Encyclopedia,* the *Chronology* examines the institution of slavery throughout history and across cultures, but by using the methods of a chronological framework, detailed sidebar articles, and a collection of primary documents, this reference tool provides a unique perspective for identifying historical patterns and cause-and-effect relationships that relate to a more complete understanding of slavery in human history. Taken together, these two reference works constitute the most complete examination of slavery as a phenomenon in world history available today.

The chronological method employed in this volume offers a vivid and compelling documentary record of slavery's place in the annals of human history. This work serves as an educational tool, but it also exists to convey a more intrinsic message about human history that should find resonance at many levels. This work is testimony to the tragedy and triumph of the human condition, and its words speak to us of deeds that must not be forgotten.

A reference work that seeks to document the presence of slavery throughout human history should touch two aspects of the human consciousness—one effective, and the other affective. It is the nature of history to educate in the hope that past errors are not replicated by those who are either unaware of prior misdeeds or unwilling to learn from such bygone experiences. The very process of education is one that is designed to facilitate change—to effect transgenerational reform that holds the potential for bettering society at large. It is such a belief that positions progress as a unifying theme in history when the discordant threads of continuity and change are evaluated over time. But works such as this one must also educate at a more visceral level. It is the affective power that these pages command that affords the opportunity for the reader to move beyond mere knowledge and to be stirred to action. Rather than being only passive observers of the historic present, we might become activists who are stirred by a more fundamental calling. This affective response is equally important—and equally valid—as we recount the presence of slavery in the human experience.

Slavery is an issue that troubles the human spirit. Our better angels seem to focus upon the triumph of abolitionism rather than concentrating upon the dark past of human subjugation, but despite such efforts, the fact remains that abolitionism would have been unnecessary had peoples not been enslaved in the first place. We cannot boast of a holier-than-thou morality because of abolitionism without reckoning with the troubling reality that the recessive gene of a slaveholding past still haunts the social consciousness of many. Even still, in a world poised to enter a new millennium, we must ask where is the outrage today as instances of slavery persist in a modern world that finds it increasingly difficult to recognize that the most easily marginalized are often the most easily victimized by the practice of enslavement.

In a 1995 speech South African President Nelson Mandela stated, "The struggle for freedom, equality and dignity is an on-going one in which one must have the modesty to learn from the past and from each other, as well as the courage to meet the future." It is in this historical process where the past touches the present and influences the future that we must struggle to learn and to adapt new behaviors that redefine our understanding of human dignity. All too often in times of crisis society surrenders itself to political, economic, or religious exigencies that serve to devalue the worth of the individual, making the practice of enslavement an acceptable, if not invisible, part of the human experience. It is indeed ironic that those who trace historical progress over time often find it difficult to explain how liberty and the lash have coexisted across cultures throughout time. Mandela's call for the attributes of modesty and courage have special meaning here.

It is important that we study the chronology of slavery throughout human history. This somber reminder should serve to educate, to challenge, and even to inspire. We can learn from the past only if we are willing to examine all elements—even the most unpleasant—as we strive to make sense of our historical legacy and redirect the energies of our human potential. The chronology of slavery in history offers ample evidence of both tragedy and triumph, but how this information is received and to what extent it moves us must be the measure by which we judge the success or failure of this work. If we can read and learn and, in the process, find ourselves moved to action we will have transformed our historical modesty into moral courage. It is a goal that is worthy of our most essential humanity; it is an affective response that is needed in our time.

ACKNOWLEDGMENTS

Undertakings like the *Chronology of World Slavery* mean that many people must offer their time, talents, and skills to a project that calls them to a higher purpose. To all who in any way aided the development and production of this book I am deeply indebted and forever grateful. It has been a singular honor to work with so many colleagues and friends in preparing the world's first chronological history of slavery across cultures and times, and I believe we have created a product we can all be proud of.

Alicia Merritt, Todd Hallman, and Susan McRory of ABC-CLIO have supported my efforts in producing *The Historical Encyclopedia of World Slavery* (1997) and the *Chronology of World Slavery*. Their guidance and cheerful encouragement have provided me with direction and vision as these two reference works have come to fruition over the past three years. I thank them for their support and for the confidence they placed in me throughout this extended project.

This book was made possible by the contributions and advice offered by hundreds of scholars of slavery worldwide. I am certainly appreciative of all who offered their assistance and helped to make this a better work and a more valuable scholarly contribution. Over the course of the three years, many people who started working on this book as professional acquaintances have become good friends, and I have relied quite frequently upon their insight in completing this project.

I am especially grateful to a team of assistants who worked on various components of the manuscript as it came together. Nathan Meyer served as the research assistant for this volume, and his efforts have been tremendous. I am certain that I would not have met important deadlines had he not worked tirelessly to see this work through to completion. His expertise has been invaluable. I also wish to thank several student assistants and interns who have had a hand in helping to develop this project through the years. Sarah Lunt Ewart, Shannon Wettach, Jill Zielinski, Byron Painter, David Steinbeck, and Ryan Tompkins all assisted in the endeavor. Joy Kinder offered secretarial assistance and always helped to make sure that important mailings went out on time. Lynne Rudasill, Paul Lister, Ann Shoemaker, Peg Toliver, Ginny McCoy, Dana Dempsey, Eldrick Smith, and Kathy Whitson all pitched in to help when glitches of varying types appeared, and I appreciate their kind assistance.

I must also thank the Eureka College Faculty Status and Development Committee, which provided funding for this project when it was in its early developmental stages. I am also deeply indebted to Dr. Gary E. Gammon, Academic Dean of Eureka College, who encouraged my work on the world slavery volumes. Gary's tragic death in May 1998 as I was completing the work on this book was a shocking occurrence, but it was also the impetus for a renewed dedication on my part to complete the work in his honor. As a bereaved friend and colleague, I dedicate this volume to him.

I am proud to have been associated with the development of the *Chronology of World Slavery* and take responsibility for its inevitable shortcomings. I hope that the work will be valuable to students and researchers alike and that this labor of love will serve as a valuable reference tool for years to come.

❧ *INTRODUCTION* ❧

If thou suffer injustice, console thyself; the true unhappiness is in doing it.
—Democritus (460–370 B.C.)

Slavery is a practice that seemingly defies logic and human understanding, yet it is an indelible part of our heritage and something that challenges us still today. It is ancient yet modern—that is the paradox of slavery—and in exploring the complexities of this societal institution, we learn more about ourselves as the glories and failures of our past become the foundations upon which we measure the human potential for good and evil. Slavery is the dark mirror that allows us to reflect upon past episodes of social injustice as we trace the events, both great and small, that have defined the meaning of civilization for peoples in bondage throughout the ages.

The pages in this volume chronicle the institution of slavery in its various manifestations through time and across cultures. This powerful testimony reminds us that man's inhumanity to man is limited by neither spatial nor temporal boundaries and that, perhaps not surprisingly, such evil is with us still today. Not all stories conclude with happy endings.

Social scientists maintain that slavery somehow evolved during the era when man's social acculturation had developed to a point that could be deemed civilized. The practice was born out of a benign benevolence that spared the lives of war captives by granting them the right to live—to live a life proscribed by the dictates and the occasional whims of one's conqueror. Our most ancient historic forebears bequeathed to us a cultured past but also left behind less noble legacies amid their ancient grandeur. We, the inheritors of this enigmatic birthright, have been bedeviled by slavery, that recessive gene that waxes and wanes but wears upon us still.

It is not an easy task to study slavery in human history. Our better angels, which call upon the nobility in humans, find it often incomprehensible that so many sagacious minds of the past have defended slavery and found it compatible with natural law and God's will. It is indeed shocking to modern sensibilities to discover that the antislavery impulse is a relatively new concept in human thought and can be traced back only two centuries to the era of the Enlightenment. Since who we *are* is directed in large measure by who we *were,* we sift through the chronological record of the past hoping to find some rational explanation of how a social system like slavery could have evolved and endured among civilized peoples. Although various historical threads abound,

they all become meshed into a social fabric that accepted slavery as a protected institution and shrouded it with legal sanction and popular condonement so that it might endure. We must first be able to expose slavery if we desire ever to understand it.

Historians use facts to tell the story of the past, but facts alone are often insufficient to comprehend past reality. The historian must interpret upon the basis of what is known, to postulate upon the interrelationships between often discordant details, and historical revisionism is born when later scholars, unsatisfied with the original interpretation offered, develop alternative models based once more upon interpretation of the known facts. In such a scholarly milieu one, two, three, or perhaps an endless number of "truths" are possible as historical interpretation brings the past alive when the facts do not speak. Reality, or the postmodern multiple realities, are born of this creative process as we struggle to find a usable past from our scant historical records.

The nature of historical facts themselves becomes particularly burdensome when we contemplate the history of slavery. We mark the historic era by man's development of techniques whereby written records might be kept. Unfortunately, written records have been both the boon and the bane of the historical profession. Written records imply a certain degree of literacy on the part of the record keepers, but often through history the classes that were enslaved were kept illiterate as a means of keeping them subdued. Although there were certainly exceptions to this policy—for example, Greek slaves were often well-educated tutors to their Roman masters—many slaves were ahistorical creatures who left no documentary record of their lives. The work of recording their story was relegated to the literate classes, often the master class, which viewed the lives of slaves from a different, and certainly unique, perspective. Their facts, however imperfect, are the documents with which we must work.

There is a tremendous difference in the worldview held by masters and the one held by slaves. The ability to hold dominion over another and the feeling of abject powerlessness provide rather distinct perspectives from which to interpret one's place in the world as well as the place of others. Friedrich Nietzsche even postulated that separate master and slave moralities exist in the world with ramifications that touch all aspects of the human condition. The manner in which we define "other," that which is different from us, is especially telling in that it often says much about how we comprehend ourselves in relation to that which we are not. Slaves became the mirror by which a ruling class defined itself and formed its own cultural ethos. Nebulous concepts like freedom are defined by the absence of freedom; leisure, by the absence of work. It was such a class, the mirror image of the nonslave, that produced the documentary record by which we must study the past and make value judgments about the historical record.

Despite the often one-sided nature of the documentary record regarding slavery, there is another concern that generally makes the factual record woefully incomplete. Left to their own devices, historical facts seldom impart an affective meaning or response. Although it is important to know that an event occurred, the modern reader expects more from the text than the certitude of detail—larger questions must be answered as well. It is difficult for the facts alone to present a sensory record of the past, but that is what we often desire as we scour the pages of history to find a greater understanding of the institution and practice of slavery. Facts may speak of labor, but facts alone cannot replicate the weariness of Roman slaves toiling in the silver mines of the ancient Mediterranean rim or African slaves struggling in the cotton fields of Georgia. The historical record does not permit us to feel the bleeding fingers wrought from excessive work or the bruised body and spirit of one who has been savagely flogged for alleged misdeeds. The facts alone are silent when we try to comprehend the anguished thoughts of a young mother who has smothered her own child rather than have the baby grow up to become the property of another as a slave. Just as the ancient Greeks knew that sometimes the gods were silent, sometimes the facts leave much unspoken.

Given these genuine limitations, what then is the value of a chronological study of slavery across cultures and throughout history? Facts and details presented in the order of their occurrence do have a powerful effect in helping us to understand the magnitude of slavery's impact upon history and the extent to which our world still reels from this bitter legacy. The chronological record clearly demonstrates that the practice of enslaving others is a custom that has existed from time immemorial, and recent experiences with contemporary slavelike practices reveal a disturbing awareness that great evil can endure when good people remain silent. Knowledge about the past—even when it is a painful lesson—is empowering and can be therapeutic if the greater awareness of injustice moves one to become a stronger advocate of freedom for all. Many slaveowners throughout history denied their slaves the right to an education because they knew that knowledge was power and that empowered bondsmen are the antithesis of a slave society. Yet it was this same awareness that persuaded many abolitionists to be patrons of higher education because they understood the intrinsic power of the biblical dictum, "You will know the truth, and the truth will set you free" (John 8:32). Certainly, today we can learn much from the hard task of trying to reckon with slavery.

There is an additional benefit that we can gain from viewing the history of slavery in chronological form, as doing so helps us fathom a greater understanding of how the practice endured and the noble efforts of many people to abolish it. History is a rather inexact social science that does not easily lend itself to quantitative analysis or empirical research, but it does have tools and methodologies that allow the enlightened reader to make informed judgments on the basis of the available evidence. One of the most basic methods of historical presupposition—the observation of cause and effect—can help us understand the history of slavery if we look at individual decisions and events in the greater context of the times in which these events occurred.

Elie Wiesel, who experienced firsthand the horrors of the Nazi Holocaust and has observed the grim reality of slave labor in the modern world, has spent much of his lifetime teaching others about the importance of remembering the past. Wiesel has stated: "That is my major preoccupation—memory, the kingdom of memory. I want to protect and enrich that kingdom, glorify that kingdom and serve it" (Wiesel, 1995). History is the collective cultural memory of a people, and its lessons should impart values that sustain and nurture even when the topics are particularly difficult. There are those people who see slavery as something that took place in the ancient past—a bitter chapter in societal development yet something that should be relegated to the archives and the curious antiquarianism of scholarly discourse—but they are misguided and they are wrong. We must study slavery to sustain our memory, to comprehend our world, and to explore the nature of our humanity. As Malcolm X stated, "History is a people's memory, and without a memory man is demoted to the lower animals" (Malcolm X, 1964).

Amid the disturbing details and potent images of slavery one can find hope in the pages that follow. Despite society's inclination to enslave throughout much of human history there has been resistance to the practice of slavery as captive peoples have fashioned and used the weapons of the weak and as free individuals with liberty of conscience and moral conviction have agitated for an end to the practice. Heroes do abound in slave societies, for not only do slave rebels and abolitionists deserve such recognition but all who toiled under the burden of forced labor were also ennobled. To endure life as a slave and to maintain a sense of human decency in a senseless world that has thrust abject powerlessness upon you evokes a special sense of bravery.

This chronology of slavery is a testament to the men, women, and children who have gone before us and to those who live among us today who have experienced and do experience the "social death" of enslavement. For most of human history such people have been a nameless, faceless mass, but these unfortunate brethren share a common kinship with us in the human family. We need to attempt to understand their history if we ever hope to comprehend our own, because both stories are inextricably intertwined. If they could speak—if they could scream—perhaps we could hear and begin to comprehend the lives that they endured, but in so many respects their story is silent. As you read these chronologies and allow the historical record to "tell the story" of slavery, listen for the silences—and interpret their meaning. Sometimes even the gods are silent.

❦MAPS❧

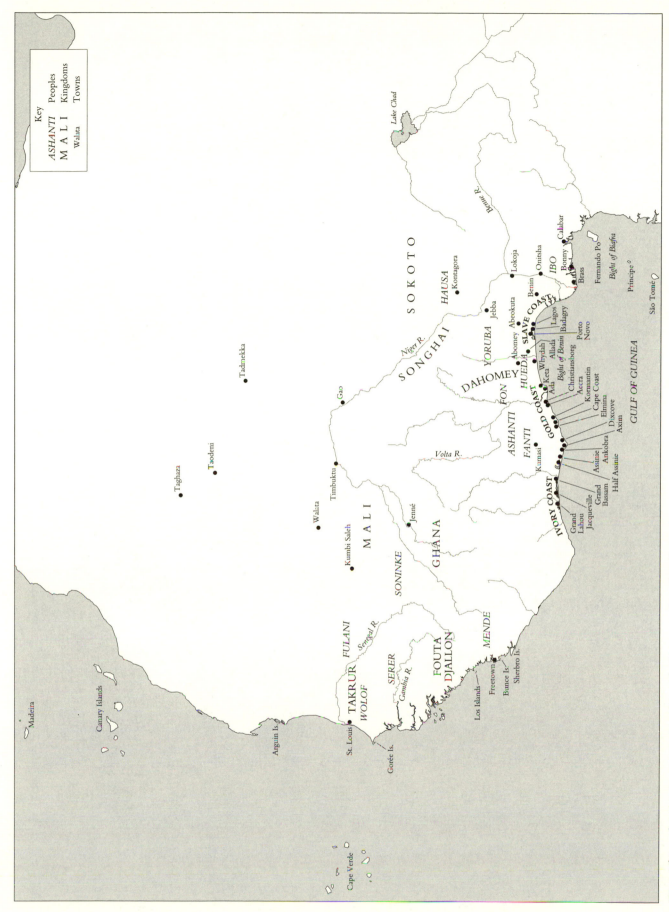

West Africa, showing important peoples and places mentioned in the text.

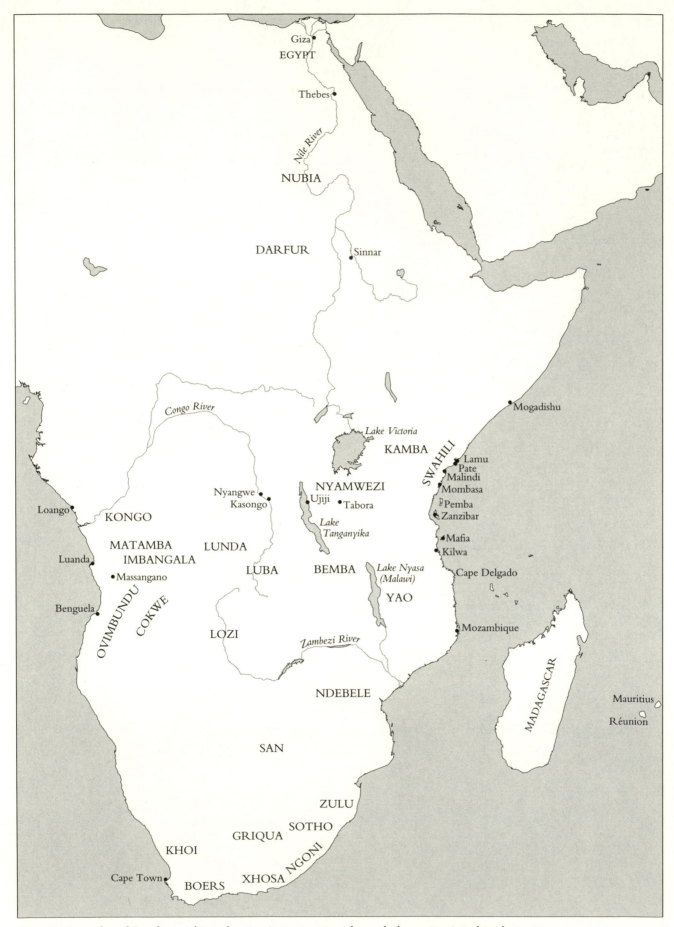

Eastern, Central, and Southern Africa, showing important peoples and places mentioned in the text.

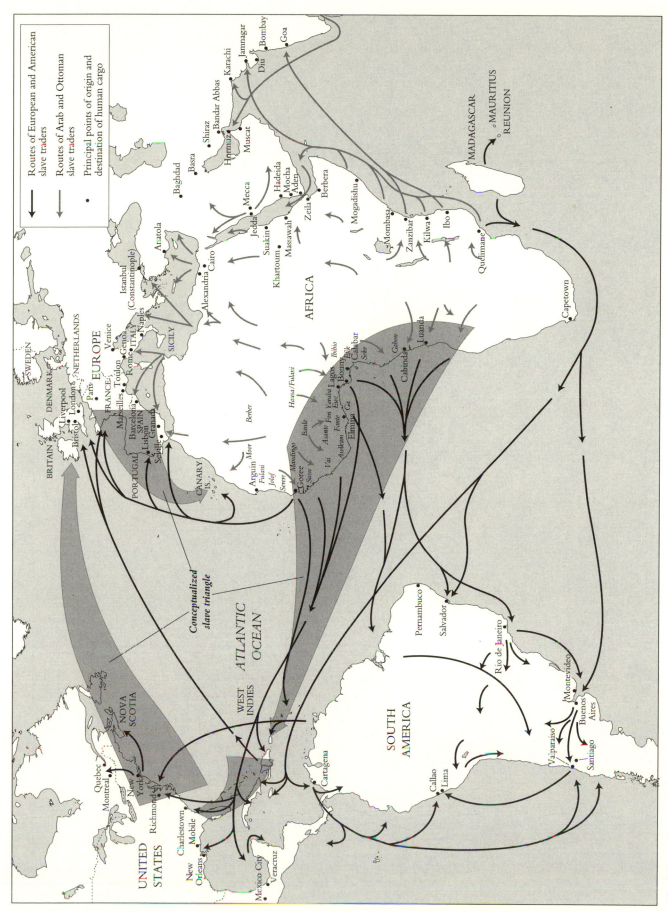

The African Diaspora. Courtesy of Joseph E. Harris.

Routes of European and American slave traders

Routes of Arab and Ottoman slave traders

Principal points of origin and destination of human cargo

BRITAIN
SWEDEN
DENMARK
NETHERLANDS
Liverpool
Bristol
London
Paris
FRANCE
Marseilles
Toulon
Barcelona
SPAIN
Lisbon
Seville
Granada
PORTUGAL
Venice
Genoa
Rome
ITALY
Naples
SICILY
Istanbul (Constantinople)
Anatola
Alexandria
Cairo
EUROPE

CANARY IS.

Arguin
Moor
Fulani
Jolof
Serere
Mandingo
Goree
Susu
Vai
Bullom
Baule
Aukam
Fante
Elmina
Avikam
Ga
Ewe
Fon
Yoruba
Asante
Lagos
Bonny
Benin
Ibibio
Efik
Calabar
Seke
Gabon
Cabinda
Luanda

Berber

Hausa/Fulani

AFRICA

Baghdad
Basra
Shiraz
Bandar Abbas
Hormuz
Muscat
Karachi
Jamnagar
Diu
Bombay
Goa

Mecca
Jedda
Suakin
Khartoum
Massawah
Zeila
Hadeida
Mocha
Aden
Berbera
Mogadishu
Mombasa
Zanzibar
Kilwa
Ibo
Quelimane

MADAGASCAR
MAURITIUS
REUNION

Capetown

ATLANTIC OCEAN

Conceptualized slave triangle

UNITED STATES
Quebec
Montreal
New York
Richmond
Charlestown
Mobile
New Orleans
Mexico City
Veracruz
NOVA SCOTIA

WEST INDIES

Cartagena

SOUTH AMERICA
Callao
Lima
Valparaiso
Santiago
Buenos Aires
Montevideo
Rio de Janeiro
Salvador
Pernambuco

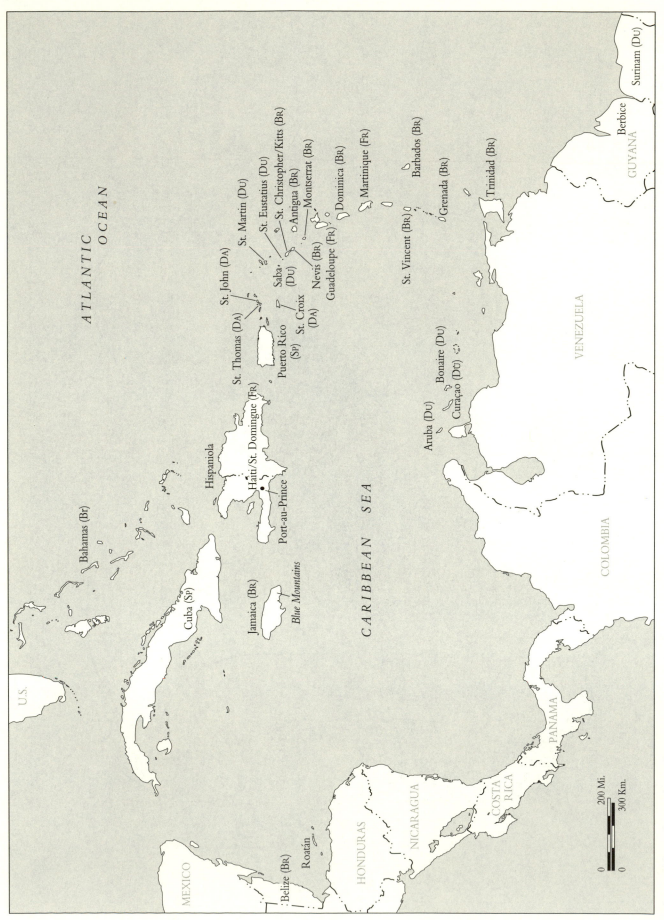

The Caribbean, late eighteenth century (present-day boundaries of countries in Central and South America shown for reference).

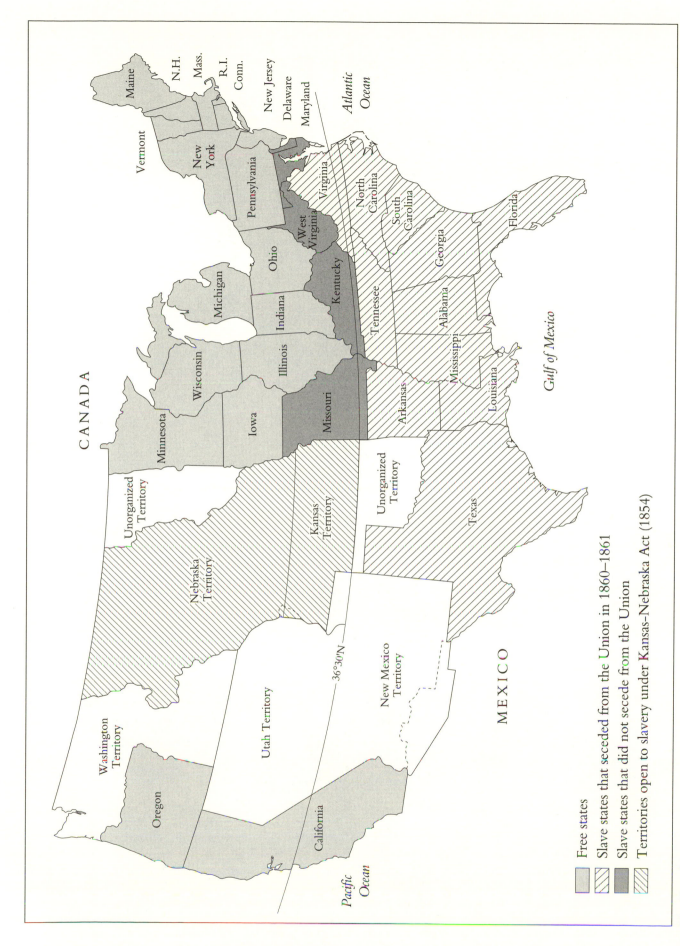

CANADA

MEXICO

Maine
N.H.
Mass.
R.I.
Conn.
New Jersey
Delaware
Maryland

Atlantic
Ocean

Vermont

New York

Pennsylvania

Virginia

West
Virginia

North
Carolina

Ohio

South
Carolina

Michigan

Indiana

Kentucky

Georgia

Tennessee

Wisconsin

Illinois

Alabama

Minnesota

Iowa

Missouri

Arkansas

Mississippi

Louisiana

Florida

Gulf of Mexico

Unorganized
Territory

Kansas
Territory

Unorganized
Territory

Texas

Nebraska
Territory

Washington
Territory

Utah Territory

36°30′N

New Mexico
Territory

Oregon

California

Pacific
Ocean

Free states

Slave states that seceded from the Union in 1860–1861

Slave states that did not secede from the Union

Territories open to slavery under Kansas–Nebraska Act (1854)

The United States, 1860–1861.

❧Ancient World❧

Un paysage quelconque est un état de l'âme.
(Any sort of landscape is a condition of the soul.)
—H. F. Amiel, *Journal Intime*, October 31, 1852

Any effort to divide the world into distinct historical regions or eras that can be distinguished either by geographical certitude or chronological coherence is affected by the inexact nature of the social sciences. Trying to map the history of slavery in specially defined areas and periods further exacerbates the difficulty inherent in these somewhat arbitrary and artificial segments of human history. Fluid terms like *ancient* and *contemporary* convey different meanings within the scholarly community, and even the exact meanings of geographical place-names are often debated in public discourse. Thus, the landscapes of time and place used in this chronology must be defined before they can be accepted upon blind faith.

The ancient world encompasses the period that began with the Neolithic revolution and ended in A.D. 476 with the fall of the Roman Empire in the West. The regions included in this chronology are those that are largely found along the rim of the Mediterranean Sea, including the societies and cultures that arose in Mesopotamia and Egypt as well as the civilizations that developed in Greece, the Hellenistic world, and Rome. The ancient cultures that arose in India, China, Japan, and other parts of Asia are included in the Asian chronology.

Slavery was a characteristic of all societies that developed in the Mediterranean region, but the inexact nature of the historical record often affords only a scant reflection of the true nature of the servile peoples in these early cultures. Also, the realization that the records were maintained by social classes that often held slaves helps us to evaluate the manner in which slaves are depicted (or sometimes ignored) in the extant historical record. In such a setting, we must often consider the absence of evidence to be evidence.

The civilized peoples who coalesced into the first sedentary urban communities represent an important moment in our global humanity. Many of the characteristics that we hold dear—the essence of our civility—find their origins among these early peoples, yet the bane of our culture—war and slavery—also stem from these ancient roots. Later, the classical cultures that arose in Greece and Rome offered much to the world, yet they retained the ignominy of having slavery, and the high rhetoric of those societies seldom matched the social reality of the times.

As we study the chronology of slavery throughout ancient history, we must seek a greater understanding of two meaningful questions. First, how did slavery arise in these ancient societies and become a part of the natural social order of the times? Second, how did civilized peoples find moral justification in their cultural ethos to support such a practice? The search for answers to these questions is meaningful, and each of the chronologies in this volume demonstrates the enduring effects that slavery has had on our world. Across the globe—from ancient to modern times—the staying power of this institution has been remarkable, and we must deal with its legacy even today.

c. 6800 B.C.

Neolithic (New Stone) Age peoples had congregated in the region of Jericho and established the world's first town. The town was surrounded by a protective wall, which indicates that the region was susceptible to enemy raids and that warfare may have been common. The oldest slaves were war captives whose lives were spared so they might endure "social death" and become the servants of the victors who had defeated and captured them. One of the great ironies of the beginnings of civilization is that the ownership of land and other goods made one a target of enemies who desired the property of others. Civilization bred warfare, and warfare created the institution of slavery; thus, from the dawn of civilization, one of the most barbaric human practices—slavery—was institutionalized.

c. 6000 B.C.

Archaeological evidence suggests that the island of Crete was settled by Neolithic (New Stone) Age peoples. These early peoples would have needed seaworthy vessels that could have sailed on the Mediterranean in order to establish these initial settlements.

c. 4200 B.C.

Ancient Sumerian peoples had begun to settle in the marshy delta region where the Tigris and Euphrates Rivers emptied into the Persian Gulf. Also, archaeological evidence suggests that the ancient Egyptians established their first towns along the Nile River during this period.

c. 3600 B.C.

The ancient city of Ur (Uruk) was established in Sumer. The birth of the earliest cities marks the birth of civilized society. Unfortunately, the birth of those cities also led to warfare, which, in turn, produced slavery.

c. 3500 B.C.

In Sumer, the first war chariot was developed. Such an innovation in warfare has had a destabilizing effect upon societies both ancient and modern. The war chariot represented an implement of war that could easily change the tide of battle and result in more military victories and more war captives.

c. 3200 B.C.

There is evidence of a division of labor in the primitive societies that developed in both Sumer and in Egypt. Slavery would eventually become an established part of the social hierarchy that evolved in each of the regions.

c. 2750 B.C.

Probable date for the founding of Troy in Asia Minor.

c. 2600 B.C.

Burial of Queen Shub-ad, whose grave was later discovered by archaeologists, in the city of Ur. This location and other royal graves of Ur suggest the social structure of society in ancient Sumer. The queen was buried along with 74 other persons, probably slaves and retainers who took poison to follow their queen into the next world, where they could continue to serve her.

c. 2575 B.C.

Cheops (or Khufu), the Egyptian pharaoh, sent expeditions up the Nile River into Nubia to capture slaves. In Egypt itself, the construction of the pyramids reflected the powerful belief in life after death that was an important concept in polytheistic Egyptian religion. The pyramids were probably constructed by free laborers, who worked on a corvée system when they were not tending their crops, rather than by slave laborers. Still, much of the art in the pyramids reflected the great triumphs of the pharaoh, which included victory in warfare and the taking of many captives who could become slaves.

c. 2465–2323 B.C.

Egyptian records on the Palermo Stone (one of the historical artifacts that tells us much about Egyptian society and culture) describe military campaigns during the reign of the pharaoh Snofru that resulted in the taking of 7,000 Nubian and 1,100 Libyan captives and making them slaves of the state.

c. 2250 B.C.

In Egyptian pyramids and tombs, the image of a slave-manned boat was a symbolic representation that one could expect a happy and prosperous afterlife.

A drawing made from an impression of a cylinder seal dating from the second half of the fourth millennium B.C., found at Uruk in Babylonia. It is the earliest known depiction of war captives. (British Museum)

C. 2134–1785 B.C.
Egyptian papyrus records from the Middle Kingdom constitute the first evidence of slave ownership by private individuals in Egypt. Previously, the slaves in Egypt had been the property of the pharaoh and the gods.

C. 2100 B.C.
Society in Sumer was based upon the maintenance of law and order. King Ur-Nammu proclaimed a code of laws in which he declared, "By the laws of righteousness of Shamash [a god] forever, I establish justice."

C. 2000 B.C.
Sumerian documents indicate that the cost of a healthy male slave was 11 silver shekels at this time. That amount of money could have also purchased 1,276 square feet of agricultural ground (less than 3 percent of a square acre).

C. 1962 B.C.
Evidence found in the tomb of an Egyptian leader at Kerma (in modern-day Sudan) suggests that wives, slaves, and other attendants were commonly buried with the body of a dead leader. This practice was also common in Sumerian society.

C. 1929–1892 B.C.
Egyptian records from the Middle Kingdom show that during the reign of Pharaoh Amenemhet II, a slave-raiding expedition conducted in Syria resulted in the capture of 1,554 slaves.

These slaves were needed as laborers for public works projects that were under way, including the construction of the pharaoh's pyramid.

C. 1800 B.C.
Abraham, the patriarch of the Hebrew people, left the Sumerian city of Ur and wandered westward, perhaps as far as Egypt. Eventually, Abraham and his Semitic followers settled in the "land of milk and honey" in the region of modern-day Palestine. According to the Old Testament (Gen. 11:31), they settled in the region of Haran (Hebrew) in the land of Canaan.

C. 1790 B.C.
Hammurabi developed a code of laws to govern the city-kingdom of Babylon. Several of the laws related specifically to the rights of slave-owners in maintaining their property in slaves. The detailed laws that Hammurabi decreed demonstrate the complexities of administration that had evolved in the Babylonian state by this time. The preamble to the laws stated Hammurabi's reason for issuing the code of laws—to establish justice in the land. Each of the laws in the code was constructed with a protasis and an apodosis (i.e., "if this shall happen, then this shall happen"), and the measures related to all the classes of people who lived in Babylonian society. [See Document 1.]

C. 1700 B.C.
The horse was introduced into Babylonia by the Kassites and into Egypt by the Hyksos. Like the

Slavery has existed as a social institution in different societies all over the world from classical antiquity to the modern day. Throughout history, peoples with widely varying types of social organization have held slaves. Slavery thrived in medieval Europe, pagan and Islamic Arabia, sub-Saharan Africa, Asia, Scandinavia, the pre-Colombian New World, eighteenth- and nineteenth-century Americas, and elsewhere. Although European thinkers have debated the legal and moral dilemmas evoked by slavery since classical times, the fundamental premise of slavery—that a human could be both property and a human being—and the morality of the institution itself were not called into question until relatively recently. The Stoic philosopher Seneca (c. 4 B.C.–A.D. 65), for example, urged that slaves be treated as human beings without ever mentioning that the system itself was either immoral or should be abolished.

Although the definition of slavery proves a debated topic among historians, sociologists, and economists, most theorists agree that the slave is a social outsider, a person who is considered to be someone else's property, cannot hold property himself, is denied a cultural and social identity outside of being a slave. In addition to being classified as the property or chattel of another human being and being socially ostracized, the slave has little or no authority and is generally denied the human dignity accorded free members of society. Slaves have been alternately described throughout history as ideal servants—loyal, faithful, and servile—on the one hand and as brutes in need of domination on the other hand—lazy, conniving, rebellious, untrustworthy, and sexually promiscuous. Slaves have generally fallen into two categories: those who are taken in war or are captured from an outside culture and those who, although not culturally "other," voluntarily sell themselves or are forced to become slaves because of debt, destitution, or criminal behavior.

Including slavery of "barbarians" in his description of an ideal state, the Greek philosopher Plato (c. 427 B.C.–347 B.C.) might have been the first to argue the natural inferiority of slaves. Aristotle (384 B.C.–322 B.C.) believed, too, that there was a universal logic to slavery. From birth, asserted Aristotle, "some men are marked out for subjugation, others for rule" (Davis, 1966). Echoing Plato and Aristotle, proslavery thinkers, including the best-known American defender of slavery, philosopher and southern politician John C. Calhoun (1782–1850), have argued that no advanced society has existed without a disequilibrium of labor and that some people are naturally unfit for freedom.

Some social theorists, such as Auguste Comte, Karl Marx, and Friedrich Engels, have believed that slavery represented a progressive step in human history. Instead of being sacrificed in war by death, the slave was taken into captivity and forced to work. However, despite the prevalence of slavery, and its socioeconomic importance in many different cultures, Western thought early posited that slavery was contrary to man's natural state. Seeking universal norms in nature, philosophers contrasted the corruption of civilized society with a simpler, purer, more natural, and more primitive state. When England's King Henry VII (1457–1509) asserted that nature made all men free but the "law of nations reduced some under the yoke of servitude" (Davis, 1966), he was echoing an already well-established medieval belief.

Philosophers who early defended man's freedom and inalienable rights, the best known of whom was the Englishman John Locke (1632–1704), were not, however, staunch critics of slavery. Although Locke believed in equality and man's right to "life, health, liberty, [and] possessions" (Davis, 1966), he placed slavery outside the social contract, considering it a lawful state of war between conqueror and captive. Yet Locke's thinking also urged philosophers to question past assumptions and to subject ideas to the test of reason. As European Enlightenment thinking gained ground, proslavery arguments began to lose their force. Indeed, in the eighteenth century, slavery took a more central position in philosophical, moral, legal, and economic debates. The French philosopher Jean-Jacques Rousseau (1712–1778) attacked the institution of slavery, championing the emancipation of all mankind and insisting that slavery contradicted man's liberty. Rousseau rejected Locke's analysis of slavery as being outside the social contract and asserted instead that no man had the right to claim mastery over another.

One of the first eighteenth-century thinkers to analyze the institution of slavery in terms of economics, Benjamin Franklin (1706–1790) calculated the financial cost of American slavery and concluded that Negro slavery as an institution was more costly than free labor in England, that it encouraged sloth in the white population, and that it was detrimental to both rich and poor. Olaudah Equiano, who published *The Interesting Narrative of the Life of Olaudah Equiano, or Gustavus*

Vassa, the African (1789) a year before Franklin's death, in which he claimed to have been kidnapped as a child from Igboland, similarly argued against the institution of slavery for economic reasons. Equiano believed that Africa could be more effectively exploited for mutual financial gain if allowed to participate freely in a market system.

As public sentiment became increasingly critical of the institution of slavery, some philosophers became interested in explaining the role of the master, and the German philosophers Georg Wilhelm Friedrich Hegel (1770–1831) and Friedrich Wilhelm Nietzsche (1844–1900) both explored slavery theoretically from the perspective of its influence on the master. Hegel argued that slavery produced a dependency between master and bondsman. Mediated through the slave's consciousness, the master's consciousness could not exist outside of the slave's; indeed, both the master's lordship and his very existence became, for Hegel, dependent on the slave, which in turn forced the master into a subservient role at the height of his power. Lordship then, in Hegel's thinking, was necessarily "the reverse of what it wants to be" (Davis, 1975). Unlike Hegel, Nietzsche identified a master's morality that was supreme over the slave's. Positing his theory in abstract terms, Nietzsche argued that slave morality, akin to Christian ethics, was perverse and debilitating because it aimed to preserve the herd whereas master morality demanded that its members expend their power to excel over one another.

The expansion of the slave trade to the New World and the reliance of the American South on slave labor in the late eighteenth and early nineteenth centuries coincided with a widespread growth of antislavery sentiment and an increasing international awareness of the evils of slavery. By the 1760s, an unprecedented revolution was taking place in Western thought—the belief in the evil of slavery and its ability to destroy man's destiny. Working with escaped slaves, antislavery champions used public forums, private newspapers, and the publication of slave narratives to convince the public of the evils of slavery. Slave narratives by escaped slaves such as Harriet Jacobs, Frederick Douglass, Solomon Northup, William and Ellen Craft, and William Wells Brown were popular in the nineteenth century and elaborated theoretical, humanistic, religious, and economic arguments against slavery. These firsthand testimonies of the experience of slavery insisted on the humanity of the slave, the brutality of the slave system, and the hypocrisy of professed Christian slaveholders who treated their slaves with the antithesis of Christian kindness, debasing them sexually and morally as well.

Many of the most outspoken American abolitionists, including Lucretia Mott and Lydia Maria Child, were women who came increasingly to identify their lot with that of the slaves. With the Emancipation Proclamation and the end of the American Civil War, slavery as an institution no longer existed legally in the United States. However, the language of slavery was still used long afterward to describe everything from the plight of the newly emancipated slaves to dependency on alcohol in America's immigrant Irish communities.

Although slavery is not as prevalent as it was in the past, there continues to be widespread scholarly interest in the institution. The twentieth century has seen a plethora of literary, historical, and theoretical works about slavery, some of which look at the broad historical and cross-cultural contexts of slavery. The most eminent contemporary scholars of slavery include Orlando Patterson and David Brion Davis.

—*Jennifer Margulis*

For Further Reading
Davis, David Brion. 1966. *The Problem of Slavery in Western Culture.* Ithaca, NY: Cornell University Press; Davis, David Brion. 1975. *The Problem of Slavery in the Age of Revolution 1770–1823.* Ithaca, NY: Cornell University Press; Davis, David Brion. 1984. *Slavery and Human Progress.* New York: Oxford University Press; Foner, Laura, and Eugene D. Genovese. 1969. *Slavery in the New World: A Reader in Comparative History.* Englewood Cliffs, NJ: Prentice Hall; McKitrick, Eric L., ed. 1963. *Slavery Defended: The Views of the Old South.* Englewood Cliffs, NJ: Prentice Hall; Patterson, Orlando. 1982. *Slavery and Social Death.* Cambridge: Harvard University Press.

Hammurabi stands before the sun-god Shamash on this engraved Babylonian stele dating from the eighteenth century B.C. (Erich Lessing/Art Resource)

war chariot, the use of the horse in battle made warfare more intense, and the number of captives taken in battle probably increased. Such innovations in warfare tended to increase the number of war captives who could be enslaved.

C. 1650 B.C.
The Hittites established a law code containing nearly 200 edicts in their capital at Bogazköy in Asia Minor. Like the Code of Hammurabi, each of the Hittite laws was constructed with a protasis and an apodosis, and the measures related to all classes of people in Hittite society.

C. 1650 B.C.
A famine struck in the land of Canaan (the region of Palestine), and the Hebrew people became nomads wandering in search of food. One group, led by Joseph, entered Egypt in search of sustenance, and its members eventually became enslaved as laborers on the pharaoh's public works projects. The Hebrews remained in this

condition for nearly four centuries until Moses led them out of captivity during the Exodus. According to the Old Testament (Exod. 2:12), Moses killed an Egyptian for oppressing a Hebrew slave.

C. 1570 B.C.
The Hyksos had dominated Egypt for nearly 150 years, but the rulers of Egypt were finally able to overthrow their foreign overlords, and the Egyptians then enslaved all foreigners within the country. The Hebrew people, who had wandered into Egypt to escape a famine in Canaan, became enslaved by the pharaoh and were put to work on various public works projects. Among other things, Hebrew slaves helped to build the Egyptian cities of Pithom and Ramses.

C. 1550 B.C.
The Egyptian pharaoh Ahmose I revised his nation's foreign policy and decided to extend the country's boundaries southward. He began to subdue and colonize the region of Nubia, an area where previously, the Egyptians had conducted slaving raids.

1524 B.C.
The Egyptian pharaoh Thutmose I returned to Egypt from an expedition to conquer the region of Nubia. He carried the dead body of the Nubian king back to Egypt as proof that the region had been subdued.

C. 1501–1447 B.C.
During the reign of the Egyptian pharaoh Thutmose III, military campaigns into Syria and Palestine were regularly conducted, and large numbers of slave captives were carried back to Thebes in Egypt. These slaves were considered to be the property of the gods and the pharaohs and were not offered for sale to private citizens.

C. 1500–1450 B.C.
The Hittites established a law code in their capital at Bogazköy in Asia Minor. This code was an abridged version of the older one established c. 1560 B.C., but it did include some modifications. Each of the laws in the code was still constructed with a protasis and an apodosis and related to all classes of people

Men carry grain as slave girls fight over the leftovers in this wall painting from an Egyptian tomb dating from the eighteenth dynasty (sixteenth to fourteenth centuries B.C.). (Erich Lessing/Art Resource)

who lived in Hittite society. In this code, defiance on the part of a slave was deemed to be a capital crime punishable by death, but the code also included provisions that required slaveholders to discipline their slaves without use of excessive violence.

C. 1450 B.C.

A volcanic eruption destroyed the island of Santorin (Thíra) off the coast of Crete. Both Crete and Santorin were at the center of the Minoan civilization, a culture that was known for its expertise in seafaring and trade, including the trading of slaves. After the volcanic eruption at Santorin, the Minoan culture of Crete never recovered its former level of greatness.

C. 1415 B.C.

An Egyptian wall painting found in the tomb of Menena, a scribe, depicts a large number of slaves participating in the agricultural harvest.

C. 1350 B.C.

A carving on the limestone walls of the tomb of the Egyptian pharaoh Horemheb depicts an Egyptian scribe registering a group of African captives who had recently become Egyptian slaves.

C. 1306 B.C.

The Israelites begin to infiltrate into the region of Palestine.

1290 B.C.

The Egyptian pharaoh Rameses II (the Great) built the city of Per-Ramesse. Much of the labor for the building of this city was provided by Hebrew slaves in Egypt.

C. 1235 B.C.

Probable date for the Exodus, the departure of the Hebrew people from Egypt. Led by Moses, the Israelites fled from the slavery that had been

Abraham was told by God that his descendants would be strangers in a land that was not their own and that they would be enslaved and oppressed for 400 years. In biblical times, Joseph was beaten by his brothers, thrown in a pit, and sold to the Ishmaelites, who took him to Egypt. Joseph was bought from the Ishmaelites by Potipher, an officer of the pharaoh and captain of the guard. In Egypt, Joseph interpreted the dreams of the pharaoh's chief of butlers, chief of bakers, and captain of the guard and requested that they tell the pharaoh about him and that he be freed from the dungeon, but they forgot about him. Joseph had correctly interpreted one dream to mean that the pharaoh would hang the chief baker.

Two years later, the pharaoh had a dream that none of his wise men could solve. The chief butler told the pharaoh that he, the captain of the guard, and the chief baker had had dreams and that Joseph, a Hebrew servant belonging to the captain of the guard, had correctly interpreted each man's dream. The pharaoh requested that Joseph be quickly brought to him. He told Joseph that he had dreamed about seven bad and starved cows eating seven fat healthy cows and seven meager ears of corn eating seven fat ears of corn. Joseph interpreted the dream as meaning that God was telling the pharaoh that Egypt would have seven good years of plenty and then seven bad years of famine. Joseph went throughout Egypt for seven years and collected all the food of the land. Then, there was famine in all the lands, but in Egypt there was bread. The people of Egypt cried to the pharaoh for food, and he sent them to Joseph, who opened all the storehouses and sold the Egyptians food. Because of the famine in Canaan, all the people went to Egypt to buy corn from Joseph, and Jacob told his sons to go to Egypt to buy corn. Joseph became governor, and the children of Israel came to buy food.

Jacob himself went to Egypt when the famine in Canaan was very severe. Jacob's son Joseph requested permission for Joseph and his brethren to settle in Goshen, and the pharaoh willingly gave Joseph and his brethren the right to settle in Rameses, the best of the land. Later, when there was famine in Egypt, Joseph gave the Egyptians bread in exchange for their animals. The Jews dwelled in Goshen, were fruitful, and multiplied. Jacob lived in Egypt for 17 years and told his son Joseph to take his body back to Machpelah in Hebron after his death. Joseph and his brothers had numerous descendants, who continued to prosper in Egypt.

A new pharaoh, who did not know Joseph, was very cruel to the Jews. He envied their strength and numbers and decided that the Jews need to be dealt with wisely to prevent them from multiplying and joining Egypt's enemies. So, he set upon the Jews taskmasters who afflicted them with burdens. But the more the Jews were afflicted, the more they multiplied and spread abroad. The Jews were forced to work with rigor, their lives were "bitter in hard service, in mortar and in brick, and in all manner of service in the field; in all their service" (Exod. 1:14).

The king of Egypt commanded two Jewish midwives, Shiphrah and Puah, to kill all the Jewish sons and allow the daughters to live. Fearing God, they disobeyed orders and saved the male children. Then the pharaoh decreed to all of his people that every son born should be cast into the river and daughters should be saved. Moses and Aaron went to the pharaoh and told him that the God of Israel said he should "let my people go." The pharaoh responded that he did not recognize the Lord and refused to let the children of Israel go. Accusing Moses and Aaron of trying to cause the Jews to break loose from their work, the pharaoh instructed the taskmasters to make the Jews get and gather their own straw to make bricks, and they made the Jews wander throughout Egypt to get the needed straw.

God then told Moses that he had established a covenant with the Jews to give them the land of Canaan and that he heard the groaning of the children of Israel in their bondage at the hand of the Egyptians. God reaffirmed his covenant and instructed Moses to tell the children of Israel, "I am the Lord, and I will bring you out from under the burdens of the Egyptians, and I will deliver you from their bondage, and I will redeem you with an outstretched arm, and with great judgments; and I will take you to me for a people, and I will be to you a God; and ye shall know that I am the Lord your God, who brought you out from under the burdens of the Egyptians. And I will bring you unto the land which I swore to give to Abraham, to Isaac, and to Jacob" (Exod. 6:6–8).

God commanded Moses and Aaron to request that the pharaoh let the children of Israel go out of the land of Egypt. Aaron took his rod before the pharaoh, and it turned into a serpent. The pharaoh called his wise men and sorcerers to cast down their rods, and they became serpents. However, Aaron's rod swallowed their rods. The pharaoh's heart turned hard, and God commanded Aaron to lift the rod above the waters in the sight of the pharaoh, and when he did, the waters turned to blood. When the pharaoh refused to let the Jews go free, God smote the rivers and homes with frogs. Each time the pharaoh hardened his heart, Aaron was commanded by God to use his rod to issue another plague against the Egyptians. Next came gnats, then swarms of flies. Then God killed the cattle, horses, camels, herds, and flocks of the Egyptians. The next plague was boils; then hail and thunder. The Egyptians were then plagued by locusts, darkness, and the death of the firstborn human males and cattle. The children of Israel were ordered by God not to eat leavened bread for seven days and to kill the Passover lamb and put its blood on doorposts so that when God passed he would not smite the Jews. The pharaoh ordered the Jews to take their flocks and herds and leave Egypt.

The children of Israel journeyed from Rameses to Succoth east of the Nile Delta. There were some 600,000 adults on foot. God took the children of Israel out of Egypt and led them through the Sinai Desert and wilderness for 40 years until they reached the land of Israel. When the pharaoh learned that the children of Israel had fled, he sent 600 chariots to chase the Israelites. The children of Israel cried out to God for protection, and God instructed Moses to lift up his rod and stretch it over the sea. When the waters divided, the children of Israel went into the midst of the sea on dry ground, and when the Egyptians pursued the Jews into the sea, God set up a pillar of fire and cloud to separate the Jews from the Egyptians. God then instructed Moses to stretch his hand out over the sea, and the waters came back upon the Egyptians and their chariots, destroying all of them. "But the children of Israel walked upon dry land in the midst of the sea; and the waters were a wall unto them on their right hand, and on their left" (Exod. 14:29).

The Jews were slaves in Egypt for 430 years. According to biblical law, a Hebrew could not become a slave unless the court deemed so or one voluntarily volunteered to enter bondage—which was prevalent in cases of debt. In general, slaves for the Israelites were to be acquired from outside the Hebrew nation. Jewish paupers were forbidden to volunteer for bondage, but some did so anyway. Prisoners of war could be taken into bondage, but it has been thought that no prisoners of war were taken into private slavery. A Jewish father could sell his daughter into slavery—usually for household obligations and marriage. Hebrew slaves only had to serve for six years and had to be freed in the seventh year. Alien slaves were to serve the Israelites for eternity and could be passed down to children as part of their inheritance. The same applied to prisoners of war. Paupers and debtors had to be freed after the first Jubilee year (in the seventh year). Female slaves sold by their fathers into bondage were to go free if their master's sons did not want to marry them, and slaves were to be released if their masters caused them grave physical damage, like gouging their eyes or knocking out teeth.

The slaves of Israelites were to be part of the master's home and enjoy and observe the Sabbath and holidays; they had to be circumcised and take part in the Passover sacrifices after circumcision; and they were able to receive inheritance from their masters. Slaves could acquire property and even buy their freedom if they acquired enough assets. Killing a slave was punishable in the same way that killing a freeman was. Masters were obligated to not mistreat slaves, injure them, or obligate them to work beyond their physical strength. A fugitive slave was to be given refuge and not returned to his master.

In the Bible a slave was called an *eved* from the Hebrew verb *laavod*, meaning "to work." Under Talmudic law, a Hebrew slave, *eved ivri*, was a thief who was unable to pay restitution and was sold or sold himself into bondage. A Hebrew slave could not be resold. It is forbidden by Talmudic law for a Hebrew woman to sell herself into slavery. Female Hebrew slaves could only be under 12 and sold by her father into bondage when he had no other means of subsistence remaining, and he was obligated to buy her back as soon as he could obtain the necessary means. According to the Talmud, non-Hebrew slaves could be bought by paying money, the delivery of a deed of sale, or after three years of undisturbed possession. These slaves were to be later bartered or exchanged or taken possession of physically.

A slave could be released if he bought his ransom or if a court compelled the master to deliver a deed. The slave could also be released if the master caused him grave physical harm and permanent disfigurement. A slave would have also been released if his master bequeathed him all of his property. Marriage to a freewoman in the presence of the master would also guarantee a slave freedom. Additionally, marriage to the master's daughter was a means to freedom. Slaves could not be sold to non-Jews. In such a case, the court could order the seller to repay the buyer at a price that could be as much as 10 times the initial price. The slave would also go free in such a case. Any slave, except a pauper who had sold himself into bondage, could be married by his master to a non-Jewish female slave.

—*Yitzchak Kerem*

For Further Reading
Leibovitch, Nehama. 1967. *Studies in Genesis.* Jerusalem: World Zionist Organization, Department for Torah Education and Culture in the Diaspora.

imposed upon them for four centuries. During the reign of Pharaoh Rameses II (the Great), according to the Old Testament, Moses brought his people out of captivity in Egypt after he had killed an Egyptian for oppressing a Hebrew slave (Exod. 2:12).

C. 1200 B.C.

Probable date of the Trojan War, which was memorialized in Homer's epic, the *Iliad* (probably composed in the eighth century B.C.), but accounts of it are highly fictionalized with mythological references. In the thirteenth century B.C., there was economic rivalry in the Aegean world between the Achaean Greeks and the residents of Troy, a city in Asia Minor. Homer's work suggests that Greeks of the archaic period believed that conquest in battle entitled the victors to the spoils of war, including the right to take war captives and make slaves of them. In effect, the prevailing attitude in the *Iliad* is that the right to take slaves was a privilege granted by the gods. Other references to slavery appear in Homer's *Odyssey*, which contains insight about Greek attitudes toward the proper behavior of slaves. Slaves in the *Odyssey* are depicted as being faithful to their masters' interests; those who did not live up to that standard were tortured or killed.

C. 1195 B.C.

Probable date of the death of Moses and the entrance of the Israelites into the region of Palestine under the leadership of Joshua.

C. 1120–950 B.C.

According to Greek tradition, an invasion by the Dorian peoples (Hylleis, Dymanes, and Pamphyloi tribes), who used iron weapons, took place about 80 years after the Trojan War (c. 1200 B.C.). The Dorians attacked central Greece and the Peloponnesus both by land and by sea and ushered in "the dark age" of Greek history (1120–800 B.C.). The iron weapons of the Dorians enabled them to overcome the bronze weapons of the Mycenaeans and Achaeans, who had previously occupied Greece. As the victors, the Dorians acquired land and slaves.

C. 1000 B.C.

Among the Hebrew people, the custom of rule by various judges (chiefs) changed as the Twelve Tribes of Israel decided to form a kingdom. Saul was selected as the first king of the Hebrews.

C. 970 B.C.

King Solomon of the Hebrews began to construct the temple at Jerusalem and other royal palaces. In order to obtain the labor needed for these projects, Solomon raised a levy of laborers and also reduced the Canaanites to serfdom. Most slaves of the Hebrews were captives of war, but occasionally the Hebrews purchased slaves from Phoenician slave traders.

C. 945 B.C.

Probable date of the encounter between Solomon and the queen of Sheba (the latter located in the southern part of the Arabian peninsula). Solomon maintained a vast harem of foreign women, many of whom were traded as slaves.

C. 925–914 B.C.

The Israelites divided into two kingdoms. The 10 northern tribes became known as Israel and maintained a capital at Samaria. The 2 southern tribes became known as Judah and maintained a capital at Jerusalem.

C. 900 B.C.

In the *Odyssey,* Homer describes the household of Odysseus and claims that he held 50 female slaves at his palace and also had 30 herdsmen in bondage. When the island of Lesbos was captured, Homer records that Odysseus took 7 women from the island as slaves. References such as these would indicate that slavery was accepted as a regular part of life in Greece during the archaic period.

C. 884–859 B.C.

Reign of Ashurnasirpal II, king of Assyria. Assyrian records describe one of the military expeditions that King Ashurnasirpal II conducted against his enemies. Besides capturing vast amounts of copper, iron, silver, gold, grain, wool, and linen, Ashurnasirpal was also able to seize 15,000 captives and used them as slaves.

C. 827–800 B.C.

The Chinese began to drive the nomadic Huns out of China toward the west. This event set in motion a chain reaction of migrations as other groups started to move westward through the interior of the Eurasian landmass.

☙ PRISONERS OF WAR AS SLAVE LABORERS ☙

Prisoners of war (POWs) were the earliest known slaves. Evidence indicates that the Sumerians enslaved enemy soldiers captured in battle in the third millennium B.C., and Mesopotamian rulers also placed captured POWs under their authority. The state used these men to work in various tasks including the construction of fortifications, irrigation systems, roads, and temples. The use of prisoners as slave labor developed throughout the Fertile Crescent, including the Babylonian, Egyptian, and Assyrian empires.

The practice of enslaving POWs also served as the basis for the development of slavery in the city-states of ancient Greece—though Greek soldiers frequently failed to give mercy to a defeated enemy on the battlefield. Likewise, a Roman triumph required that 5,000 enemy soldiers be killed in battle, which dampened the zeal of the generals for too many prisoners. Nevertheless, the enslavement of POWs spurred the growth of slavery in Rome.

Throughout antiquity, enslaved POWs worked in a variety of fields as administrators, agricultural laborers, domestics, miners, and swineherds among others. Not all prisoners were enslaved, however. The families of politically important or wealthy prisoners frequently paid a ransom to retrieve their captive relatives, and this practice continued in Europe even as slavery declined there over the centuries following the collapse of Roman authority.

As late as the nineteenth century, European and American governments ransomed prisoners seized by Islamic pirates. The rulers of the states lining the coast of northern Africa—Algiers, Tripoli, and Tunis—commissioned corsairs to ply the Mediterranean and the Atlantic for ships in order to seize their cargoes and enslave their crews.

Islam sanctioned the enslavement of non-Muslims though it exempted other monotheists, particularly Christians and Jews, from slavery except for POWs. Over time, Muslim slavers increasingly extended the practice to include all non-Islamic captives—not just POWs but noncombatants as well—as being suitable for slavery. Muslim rulers acquired slaves from all the lands they conquered, including central Asia, North Africa, and Eastern Europe. In addition to using slaves in traditional occupations, Muslim rulers frequently used their bondsmen as soldiers, which allowed some POWs to continue to practice their profession.

Islamic traders also penetrated the sub-Saharan slave trade. West African domains, including those of the Ashanti and the Dahomeans, traditionally acquired slaves through raiding and warring against their neighbors. Frequently, however, male prisoners were executed instead of enslaved.

During the American Civil War, free blacks and former slaves who served in the Union army faced potential execution and enslavement if captured by Confederate forces. The rebels compelled many black POWs to work as laborers for the army, and the use of POWs as slave laborers continued into the twentieth century. The Nazis required many Soviet POWs to labor involuntarily during the World War II in industries supporting the German military. Now, international agreements reached during the twentieth century prohibit signatories from forcing POWs to work in military industries or without compensation.

—*Dan R. Frost*

For Further Reading
Hopkins, Keith. 1978. *Conquerors and Slaves: Sociological Studies in Roman History. Vol. 1.* Cambridge: Cambridge University Press; Mendelsohn, Isaac. 1949. *Slavery in the Ancient Near East.* New York: Oxford University Press; Smith, Robert S. 1989. *Warfare and Diplomacy in Pre-colonial West Africa.* Madison: University of Wisconsin Press; Westwood, Howard C. 1992. *Black Troops, White Commanders, and Freedmen during the Civil War.* Carbondale: Southern Illinois University Press.

C. 765 B.C.

In the region of Judah, the prophets Amos and Hosea began to speak out against the social ills of their community. They became public spokesmen for the poor and downtrodden as they denounced the social injustices of the kingdom. In their preaching against the evil of their time, the two prophets began to describe the god Jehovah as a god of righteousness for all people.

C. 753 B.C.

The city of Rome was founded along the banks of the Tiber River on the Italian peninsula.

C. 735–715 B.C.

In the First Messenian War on the Greek Peloponnesus, the Spartans defeated the Laconians and then conducted a 20-year campaign to subjugate the Messenians and make them Helots (serfs). The Spartans were descendants of the Dorians, who had invaded the Peloponnesus (c. 1120–950 B.C.) and settled in the Lacedaemon Valley in the eastern part of the peninsula. The Laconians and the Messenians occupied the rich agricultural Stenyclarus plain in the western part of the peninsula, which the Spartans desired. Led by the legendary King Theopompus, the Spartans were able to subjugate the indigenous inhabitants of the region and force them to surrender one-half of their annual produce to Sparta. Thus, as Helots, the Messenians became virtually enslaved to the Spartans.

721 B.C.

Assyrian forces under King Sargon II captured the region of Samaria and made Israel a vassal state. The Assyrians took 27,000 Israelites into eastern Syria—these were the legendary 10 lost tribes of Israel.

705 B.C.

In Greece, the author Hesiod wrote *Works and Days*. This work was a treatise on agriculture and proper farming techniques, but it also portrayed the social classes of the Greek countryside. Hesiod, himself a farmer, revealed that slaves constituted an important part of the labor force on large Greek farms. Hesiod did not describe the slave as a commodity, and he depicted the life of the slave as being not unlike that of a freeman— one filled with hard agricultural labor. The slaves that Hesiod described were generally foreigners who were captives of war or the children of such foreigners who were held in bondage.

689 B.C.

The forces of the Assyrian king Sennacherib launched a military campaign to punish the residents of Babylon who had rebelled against Assyrian rule. The city was besieged by the Assyrians for nine months until it was destroyed. The Assyrians diverted the Arakhatu Canal so that its waters flowed over the ruins of the city and completely obliterated them.

C. 670 B.C.

Greece faced an internal conflict caused by commercial rivalries during the Lelantine War. The city-state of Chalcis (Khalkís), assisted by Corinth, Samos, and the Thessalian League, fought against the city-state of Eretria, which was assisted by Aegina, Miletus, and Megara.

The two sides engaged in land battles on the Lelantine Plain, which was located in the region of Boeotia, and Chalcis eventually emerged victorious from the conflict.

C. 669–630 B.C.

One Assyrian inscription that dates to the reign of King Ashurbanipal includes a contract for the sale of a slave on Cyprus. Another inscription from the same era includes a judicial ruling from a suit involving slave trading on Cyprus.

C. 650–630 B.C.

Having been subjugated as Helots by the Spartans for more than 70 years, the Messenians revolted on the Greek Peloponnesus. During this Second Messenian War, the Messenians, under the leadership of the semilegendary Aristomenes, waged a 20-year-long insurrection against the Spartans. In order to overcome this massive revolt of the Helots, the Spartans turned to the legendary ruler Lycurgus, who turned Sparta into a military state. Although the Spartans were able to suppress the insurrection and restore the Messenians to their status as Helots, the Spartans had learned that a militarized society was needed if they were to maintain a slave society among the Messenians.

C. 600 B.C.

Gladiator fights became popular among the ancient Etruscans on the Italian peninsula. The gladiators, who were generally slaves, fought one another to the death before an audience as part of a public spectacle.

597 B.C.

Under the leadership of King Nebuchadrezzar II, the New Babylonians (Chaldeans) exacted revenge upon a king of Judah who had refused to pay tribute to the Babylonians. Nebuchadrezzar invaded Judah and installed Zedekiah as a puppet ruler over the Hebrew people. The Babylonians also enslaved 3,000 Hebrews and took them to Mesopotamia as laborers. During the time of King Nebuchadrezzar II, the average sale price for a healthy male slave was 40 shekels of silver. The price rose by 50 percent during the following century.

594–560 B.C.

As the leader of Athens, Solon instituted many reforms. One of his more notable contributions

A Babylonian warrior guards Hebrew slave musicians as they play the kinnor (harp). (Tozzer Library, Harvard University)

was the prohibition of enslavement for debt—many Athenian citizens had seen their wives and children enslaved because they were the collateral for family debts that had not been paid. Another of Solon's reforms called for a compulsory reduction in all debts that were owed by Athenian citizens. Some scholars maintain that the class of bondsmen who were imprisoned for debt at Athens (*hektemoroi*) were treated in much the same way as the Spartans treated the Messenians as Helots.

C. 590 B.C.

The First Sacred War was fought in Greece as dwellers from the region around the shrine of Apollo at Delphi fought against the Phocian city of Crisa, which had attempted to impose a toll on all pilgrims who traveled to Delphi. The residents of Delphi and Thermopylae formed the Amphictyonic League and made war upon Crisa. With naval support offered by Cleisthenes of Sicyon, the league was able to defeat Crisa and assume control of the shrine and the Pythian games, which were held there every fourth year.

C. 590 B.C.

King Zedekiah decreed that all slaves held by the Hebrews should be freed. Those Hebrews who were slaveholders complied with the request initially but later found ways to enslave their former slaves once again. The prophet Jeremiah said that Israel would be punished for its failure to keep its pledge to free the slaves.

586–538 B.C.

At the direction of King Nebuchadrezzar II, the Babylonian Captivity began after an 18-month siege of Jerusalem by the New Babylonians (Chaldeans). After the walls of the city were breached, Jerusalem was burned and its walls were demolished. Most of the citizens of Jerusalem were deported 800 miles away to Babylon where they remained as captives until King Cyrus II (the Great) of Persia conquered Babylon in 539 B.C. and allowed the Hebrew people to return to their homeland in 538 B.C.

C. 563 B.C.

Siddhārtha Gautama (known as the Buddah) was born in northern India near modern-day Nepal. He eventually became one of the leading religious figures of southern Asia and, later, much of the world.

C. 560 B.C.

Aesop, the famous Greek teller of fables, was a freed Greek slave who lived in Samos around this time. Though his stories have been handed down through the ages, Aesop himself, almost certainly a legendary figure, never wrote them down. Some of his fables were later put into verse by Socrates, and they were written down many years later. Many of the common phrases associated with Aesop's fables, such as "United we stand, divided we fall" and "Better to die once for all than live in continual terror," perhaps give great insight into the mentality of a former Greek slave.

C. 560 B.C.

Images on a Greek vase dating from this time depict slave women involved in the entire process of textile manufacturing—carding, spinning, weaving, and stacking the finished cloth.

522–486 B.C.

Reign of King Darius I (the Great) of Persia who began to enlarge the borders of his empire after he had consolidated power within Persia. He extended the empire eastward toward the Indus Valley, northward toward the Caspian Sea, and westward into the region of Asia Minor. According to Herodotus, Darius subdued the Scythians in eastern Thrace and eventually moved his army across the Bosporus and entered Europe. After withdrawing his army, Darius directed the governors (satraps) that he left behind to continue the subjugation of Thrace and the Ionian Greek city-states that had been established along the coast of Asia Minor.

530 B.C.

In India, Siddhārtha Gautama (the Buddha) withdrew from his worldly life and became an ascetic seeking answers to the great mysteries of life.

C. 530 B.C.

In the region of Mesopotamia, the average sale price for a healthy male slave was 60 shekels of silver.

509 B.C.

The Roman Republic was established when the last of the Tarquin kings was ousted in a coup.

C. 500–493 B.C.

Ionian Greek city-states revolted against Persian rule and attempted to overthrow the tyrants whom the Persians had assigned as rulers in the region. Led by the actions of the port city of Miletus, other Ionian Greek city-states joined the struggle against Persian authority and deposed the Persian governor (satrap) who ruled at Sardis in Lydia. Darius I (the Great) responded to this insurrection by besieging the port city of Miletus, defeating the Ionians in the Battle of Lade, and eventually sacking the city of Miletus. Darius displayed his wrath with the Ionians by ordering that all the males of Miletus be killed.

500–448 B.C.

Because Athens aided the Ionian Greek city-states in Asia Minor during their revolt against Persian authority (c. 500–493 B.C.), King Darius I (the Great) attacked the Greek mainland. This war between the Persians and the Greeks was viewed as a monumental conflict between the East (barbarism) and the West (civilization), and the Greek historian Herodotus believed the conflict to be the greatest historical event of the ancient world.

497 B.C.

In China, Confucius began to wander through the countryside teaching the people ethics.

496 B.C.

Diplomats from Rome and Carthage agreed to a treaty whereby the Romans would not send ships into the Mediterranean Sea west of Carthage and the Carthaginians promised not to attempt colonization in any part of Roman territory. This agreement, and modifications that followed, helped to avoid open warfare between the two city-states for more than two centuries.

494 B.C.

The Greek city-states of Sparta and Argos competed for supremacy in the Peloponnesus. The Spartans were able to defeat the Argive forces in the Battle of Sepeia.

494 B.C.

In Rome, the Secession of the Plebs was a strike staged by the Roman plebeians when they walked out of the city of Rome and retired to a

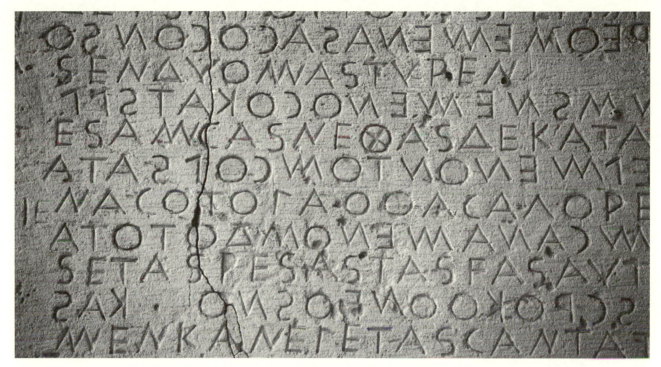

Detail from the Law Code of Gortyn, inscribed in the city walls of Gortyn, Crete. (Kevin Schafer/Corbis)

sacred mountain outside the city. The strike was called to force Roman political leaders to grant greater concessions to the plebeian class, particularly a greater representation in civic matters. The Roman Senate conceded somewhat by creating the position of tribune, which was an office especially created to represent the concerns of Roman plebeians.

490 B.C.

Greek historians maintain that Hanno, a Carthaginian navigator, traveled beyond the Mediterranean Sea along the western coast of Africa. According to a Greek version of Hanno's account of the expedition, Hanno sailed as far as the Cape Verde Islands and as many as 60 ships and 30,000 sailors were involved in the expedition. In September, the Greeks defeated Persian invaders in the Battle of Marathon.

C. 480–460 B.C.

The laws of Gortyn were carved into the walls of the town on the island of Crete. The laws were primarily a civil code and reflected the many social classes that existed in Cretan society as well as the inequality of justice that members of different classes received. For example, the fine for raping a free woman was 50 times more severe than the fine for raping a slave woman.

480 B.C.

The Persian king Xerxes I (the Great), son of King Darius I, invaded Europe by crossing the Hellespont and defeated the Greeks at Thermopylae. In the same year, the Greek city-states defeated the Persian fleet at Salamis. The Persian fleet was destroyed the following year off of Mycale.

478 B.C.

Under the leadership of Athens, several Greek city-states united to form the Delian League for defensive purposes.

C. 468 B.C.

The Athenian admiral Cimon, who had earlier commanded a fleet against the Persians during the Greco-Persian Wars, captured 20,000 prisoners who were sold into slavery in Greece.

C. 464–455 B.C.

The Messenian Helots of the Greek Peloponnesus used the occasion of a severe earthquake in Sparta as an opportunity to rebel and try to overthrow the Spartan overlords who had controlled them for nearly 250 years. In this Third Messenian War, the Messenian rebels entrenched themselves into positions on Mt. Ithome and were able to resist initial Spartan attempts to besiege them. Eventually, however, the Spartans, led by the semilegendary ruler King Archidamus, defeated the Messenians—after having appealed for aid to the Athenians who provided 40,000 hoplites (foot soldiers) to assist the Spartan cause (although the Spartan leader rejected the troops that were offered by Athens). Many Messenians were exiled from the Peloponnesus after this conflict.

460–445 B.C.

The First Peloponnesian War was fought because the Delian League had gradually made Athens into a maritime power, which angered both Sparta and Corinth. After Sparta had rejected the aid of Athens during the Third Messenian War (c. 464–455 B.C.), Athens offered assistance to the enemies of Sparta. By 455 B.C., the Athenians had received the vassalage of many of the Helots who had formerly served Spartan overlords.

451 B.C.

The Roman Senate established a committee of 10 (decemviri) and charged it with the task of codifying Roman law. The Twelve Tables were eventually formulated and put on display so that all Romans would know the laws by which they were governed. Primarily a civil code, the Twelve Tables reflected the many social classes that existed in Roman society and the inequality of justice that members of different classes received. For example, the fine for breaking the bone of a freeman was twice the fine imposed for injuring a slave.

449 B.C.

Pericles began refortifying Piraeus, the port of Athens. Athens enjoyed a brisk business in the manufacturing of pottery, and many slaves were involved in this task. It is believed that half of the population in Athens at this time may have consisted of slaves.

448–437 B.C.

The Parthenon was constructed in Athens as a temple to Athena, the patron goddess of the city. Slave craftsmen assisted the master artisans who built and embellished the structure. They also assisted in the completion of the Erechtheion on the Acropolis as a storage place for sacred religious treasures such as Athena's olive tree and the trident of Poseidon.

445 B.C.

In Rome, the Senate enacted Lex Canuleia (Law of Canuleius, a Roman tribune), which removed all prohibitions concerning intermarriage between plebeians and patricians. The reform did not affect the condition of slaves in Roman society.

C. 440 B.C.

The Athenian general Nicias reportedly leased 1,000 of his slaves to the owner of a mine at Laurion in Thrace. The operator of the mine paid Nicias one obol per slave per day and was responsible for replacing any slaves who died while they worked in the mines. The mining shafts at Laurion were only two feet square, and the slaves who worked in these tight quarters wore iron shackles. As one might expect, the death rate was exceptionally high.

431–404 B.C.

The Second (Great) Peloponnesian War was fought between Athens and Sparta for supremacy in Greece. Athens was primarily a naval power whereas Sparta had an impressive army, but the conflict had the effect of weakening the entire Greek region so that invasion from outside enemies, particularly the Macedonians, became more likely. Sparta was eventually victorious in the conflict.

C. 430 B.C.

Until the time of the Second Peloponnesian War, slaves were generally the captives of war, but during that conflict, the situation began to change. The need for slaves in Greece was so great during the war that the Greeks began to purchase slaves from barbarian slave traders, and soon there were brisk slave markets on the Aegean islands of Chios and Delos. Large numbers of slaves from non-Greek lands were purchased, including many from Phrygia, Colchis, Malta, Syria, Caria, Paphlagonia, Illyria, and Scythia. Many different peoples sold their criminals into slavery, and some residents of Thrace sold their children. Eventually, as the demand for slaves continued to increase, the slave markets in the Aegean islands were selling slaves from Persia, Egypt, and Libya. The estimated population of Attica (the part of Greece where Athens was located) totaled 315,500 individuals as the Second Peloponnesian War began. Of this total, 172,000 were citizens, 28,500 were resident aliens (*metics*), and 115,000 were slaves. At the time, Athens, the birthplace of democracy, was the largest slaveholding city-state in all of Greece.

427 B.C.

In his *History of the Peloponnesian War*, the Greek historian Thucydides remarked that in this year, the slaves in the city-state of Kérkyra (Corfu) sided with the democrats as opposed to the oligarchs when both sides appealed to the slaves for support.

423–403 B.C.

The Greek historian Thucydides wrote his *History of the Peloponnesian War*, in which he commented that many slaves commonly ran away to join the enemy camp during that conflict. He maintained that in the final decade of the war, 20,000 slaves fled Athens and escaped to the Spartans occupying a position near the city of Decelea in Attica. The Spartans had encouraged the slaves to run away from their Athenian masters by promising them freedom, but more than likely, the Spartans sold these fugitive slaves back into captivity in Thebes.

415–413 B.C.

Under the leadership of Alcibiades, the Athenians mounted an ill-fated excursion to conquer the city of Syracuse on the island of Sicily during the Second Peloponnesian War. The city-state of Athens lost 40,000 men and 240 vessels during this failed invasion, and all Athenians who were captured were made slaves.

414 B.C.

Slave trading in ancient Greece took place in the central market (agora) of each city-state. The records of one slave auction held at Athens reveal that a slave child sold for 72 drachmas, a female slave sold for 170 drachmas, and a male slave sold for 301 drachmas.

411 B.C.

The Greek playwright Aristophanes used humor in his plays *Lysistrata* and *Women at the Thesmophoria* to refer to "the Scythian archers"—the police force at Athens that was composed of slaves. Aristophanes had his characters who represent the police force appear as ignorant outsiders who have a poor understanding of Greek and difficulty communicating effectively in the language.

409 B.C.

The Carthaginian general Hannibal (d. 406 B.C.) avenged the death of his grandfather Hamilcar, who had died in battle at Himera on the coast of Sicily in 480 B.C., by laying siege to Himera and eventually destroying the city-state. Hannibal ordered that 3,000 of the region's inhabitants be slain to avenge the death of Hamilcar, and the remaining captives were sold as slaves.

C. 408 B.C.

In the play *Ion*, the Greek playwright Euripides did not believe that slavery was a part of the natural order of things, writing, "The name alone is shameful to the slave—in all things else an honest man enslaved falls not below the nature of the free."

406 B.C.

The Athenians promised both freedom and citizenship to slaves and *metics* (resident aliens who were non-Athenian Greeks) who fought on Athenian ships in the Battle of Arginusae. This special privilege was noted by the playwright Aristophanes in *Frogs*.

405–396 B.C.

Roman forces besieged the Etruscan city of Veii irregularly for a period of 10 years, but an attack upon the Romans by the residents of Capua and Valerii stymied the Roman efforts. When the siege was renewed by the Roman dictator Marcus Furius Camillus, the city of Veii was destroyed, and its citizens were sold into slavery.

405 B.C.

The tyrant Dionysius I (the Elder) came to power at Syracuse on the island of Sicily and soon dominated much of western Greece. In a series of wars against Carthage, he would conquer a city and then demand ransom for its inhabitants. If the ransom were not paid, Dionysius would sell the entire captive population into slavery and thereby have his enemies finance his military campaigns. It was Dionysius who introduced large-scale enslavement practices into the western Mediterranean region.

401–400 B.C.

A group of 10,000 Greek mercenaries who were fighting in Persia retreated 1,000 miles while

The societies and economies of the classical world were built upon the institution of slavery, and female slaves suffered an additional burden because of their sex. As Cato the Elder summarized it, "Our fathers have willed that women should be in the power of their fathers, of their brothers, of their husbands" (Pomeroy, 1975). In many ways, classical women of all classes shared some of the disabilities of slavery, and female slaves thus found themselves at the very nadir of society. Generally relegated to domestic duties, the female slave was usually overseen by the household's mistress but subjected to the sexual whims of the master and those to whom he offered hospitality. Female slaves are rarely mentioned in Greek and Roman sources, and many aspects of their lives remain hidden to us. The Homeric canon presents Bronze Age female slaves as war captives, prizes whose duties centered on serving the noble class. Chores connected to the processing of wool and grain, carrying water, and caring for guests dominate, though some women were important concubines. Later, military conquests by Greek city-states entailed the enslaving of entire populations (e.g., the Messenians by Sparta), which then became the self-reproducing property of the city-state rather than of individuals. In such cases, women lived and served within the existing social structure rather than within an owner's household.

Most slaves in classical Greece were non-Hellenic, acquired as chattel through piracy, war, and external trade or through breeding and internal trade. Exposed infant girls of unknown or slave status were also likely to become slaves. A wealthy household might own from 10 to 20 domestic slaves, mostly female, in addition to many more male farmhands or industrial workers. Females were housed separately from males, and astute masters attempted to control their sexuality. Xenophon wrote that "slaves should not breed without our approval" but that "good slaves are generally more loyal if they have children." He went on to warn, however, that "if bad ones cohabit together, they are more resourceful at devising mischief" (Pomeroy, 1975).

Women raised as slaves from childhood learned domestic skills including working with wool—the most common attribute mentioned in surviving manumission documents—and light agricultural work. Women who served food were sometimes required to wear a throat-choke (*pausikape*, "gulp-preventer") to keep them from eating the master's delicacies. Masters had full sexual access to their slaves and could share them with whomever they pleased. Lactating women were often used or rented out as wet-nurses. Brothel whores and streetwalkers were generally slaves and were prominent in port cities like Corinth. Higher-class slave prostitutes (*hetairai*) were often skilled musicians and dancers and sometimes highly cultured courtesans, such as the famous Aspasia, companion of the Athenian leader Pericles. In the later Hellenistic courts, such sophisticated and ambitious women played important cultural and political roles.

We learn of Roman female slaves from sepulchral inscriptions, wills, and legal and literary works. The sources of Roman female slaves and the outlines of their domestic duties were similar to those of the Greek slaves. Major differences included the scale of the Roman households, which commanded hundreds rather than dozens of slaves, and the resulting specialization of labor. The legal code's *Digest* (33.7) specifically mentioned slave women who made the household's clothes, baked bread, and prepared relishes; maidservants and kitchen maids; the overseer's wife; and the villa's custodian. A list of the female servants of Emperor Augustus's wife Livia added midwife and wet-nurse, personal attendant, dresser, clothes mender, and masseuse; other sources indicate women slaves served as cooks, laundresses, singers, barbers, tailors, and children's nurses. The moralist and historian Tacitus lamented the fact that "in our day we entrust the infant to a little Greek slave-girl who is attended by one or two others, commonly the worst of all slaves, creatures utterly unfit for any important work" (*Dial.* 28–29). Romans were of two minds regarding the Greekness of such a slave nurse, since they thought that her culture (and status) undermined a male child's Roman *virtus* ("superiority in human achievement") while simultaneously introducing him to the superior Greek culture.

Marriage between slaves (*contubernium*, literally, "sharing a tent") was not uncommon, but it was legally invalid. Children (*vernae*) shared the mother's status and might have been exposed or nursed and raised outside the household (perhaps to avoid parental distraction and bonding). Some sources suggest that breeding was encouraged, perhaps especially after the closing of Roman expansion in the third century. Regarding his own slaves, Columella (first century A.D.) wrote that "for a mother of three sons exemption from work was granted; to a mother of more, her freedom as well" (Pomeroy, 1975). Instability within slave "families," however, resulted from the fact that a slave woman was most likely to be sold during her fertile years (a virgin commanded the highest price), and a male slave was more likely to be sold during his most vigorous years. A male slave could purchase a female slave *(vicaria)* to serve as a personal attendant, but ultimately, the woman (and any offspring) belonged to his master. In any case, children born to a slave woman were the property of her master.

Sexual relations between a master (or his sons, male relatives, and friends) and slave women were accepted and did not carry the stigma of adultery. As in the Greek world, this practice may have alleviated some of a wife's burden of perennial childbearing, but there is evidence that in smaller households, there was tension between the wife and female slaves. Additional problems could spring from female slaves' interest in nontraditional, Eastern religions such as the cult of Isis and Christianity. The latter's appeal to the lowly and its messages of human equality and freedom of the spirit were thought to threaten the hold of master over slave, though its indifference to human bondage ensured no real social impact.

Manumission was legally possible after age 30, with exceptions for slave women who validly married, bought their own freedom, or were freed by provisions in a testament. After manumission, the unmarried woman remained under the tutelage of a master as a servant or concubine, as the concubine of a young man between the onset of puberty and marriage, or as the concubine of an older man with children. Since Roman males, especially freedmen, sought socially advantageous marriages, the freedwoman was very unlikely to marry above her station.

—*Joseph P. Byrne*

For Further Reading
Bradley, Keith. 1994. *Slavery and Society at Rome.* Cambridge: Cambridge University Press; Joshel, Sandra. 1986. "Nurturing the Master's Child: Slavery and the Roman Child-nurse." *Signs* 12: 3–22; Pomeroy, Sarah. 1975. *Goddesses, Whores, Wives, and Slaves.* New York: Schocken Books; Rawson, Beryl. 1986. *The Family in Ancient Rome: New Perspectives.* Ithaca, NY: Cornell University Press.

---

being pursued by Persian troops. Xenophon, a general and a future historian, recorded the adventure, known as the March of the 10,000, in *Anabasis.* Only 6,000 of the mercenaries survived the march.

C. 400 B.C.
The earliest books of the Hebrew Bible, the Pentateuch, had been written by this time. These early books present a historical overview of the Hebrew people and their relationship with Yahweh (God). Included are references to slavery and the process of manumission that was established by Hebraic law. According to custom, slaves were to be freed after 7 years of service, and every 50 years, in the year of the Jubilee, all slaves were to be set free. [See Document 2.]

399 B.C.
The teacher and philosopher Socrates was condemned to death in Athens for "corrupting the youth" of the city.

C. 387–347 B.C.
As part of his writings during this period, the Greek philosopher Plato tried to create a model of the ideal state in his work *The Republic,* and slavery would have been a part of this perfect state. Plato saw nothing wrong with the enslavement of foreigners and believed that slavery should be confined to barbarians; he did not believe that freed slaves should be allowed to become citizens of the ideal state.

370 B.C.
The Thebans were able to defeat the Spartans in the Battle of Leuctra during the Theban-Spartan War (379–370 B.C.). As a result of this victory, the Spartans were no longer able to maintain hegemony over the Messenians, whom they had held in virtual slavery as Helots for centuries. Upon the emancipation of the Helots from Spartan subjugation, the rest of the Greek world recognized the Messenians as free people. This case represents the ease with which the transition from slavery to freedom was possible in the ancient world.

C. 366 B.C.
The Greek author Isocrates wrote the rhetorical exercise called *Archidamus* as a speech that the Spartan leader Archidamus III should have given when the Thebans demanded the emancipation of the Messenians. The "speech" presented a clear expression of the Spartan right to enslave the Messenians as Helots.

C. 361 B.C.

In his *Messenian Oration,* the Greek sophist philosopher Alcidamas taught his students that "God created us all free; nature makes no slaves." This oration may well have been Alcidamas's effort to counter the arguments made by Isocrates in *Archidamas.*

C. 360 B.C.

Like most Greeks of his time, the historian Xenophon was a slaveowner. In *Oeonomicus* (Economics), he shared his thoughts on selecting the most trustworthy housekeeper, saying that he always sought "the woman who seems least inclined to gluttony, drink, sleep, and running after men; she must also have an excellent memory, and she must be capable of either foreseeing the punishment which neglect will cost her or thinking of ways of pleasing her masters and deserving their favor."

347 B.C.

The Greek philosopher Plato died and left five domestic slaves in his will.

C. 338 B.C.

The Greek author Isocrates noted in *Trapeziticus* (For the banker) that a former Greek slave named Pasion had been a banker in Greece and that he had been given Athenian citizenship. Pasion had been purchased by two bankers, and they made the slave a partner in the Antisthenes and Archestratus Banking and Loan Company, which was located in Piraeus, the port city near Athens.

335 B.C.

The philosopher Aristotle was in Athens teaching at the Lyceum and writing his treatises on philosophy, science, and logic. In his *Politics,* Aristotle argued, "From the hour of their birth some are marked out for subjection, others for rule."

335 B.C.

In September, the city of Thebes was destroyed during the conquest of Greece by the Macedonian general Alexander the Great. Alexander's forces killed 6,000 of the city's inhabitants, and another 8,000 were captured and sold into slavery.

333–332 B.C.

The forces of Alexander the Great besieged the city of Tyre, which was located on an island off the coast of Phoenicia. Alexander's forces constructed a causeway and built siege towers to effect the surrender of Tyre, but the siege still lasted nine months. All Tyrians who were captured during this conflict were sold into slavery.

333 B.C.

Alexander the Great fought against the Persian forces of King Darius III at the Battle of Issus in Asia Minor. Although his forces were outnumbered, Alexander was able to defeat the Persian force, losing only several hundred men while the Persians reportedly suffered 110,000 casualties. Many of the captives who were taken in the battle were later sold as slaves.

326 B.C.

The Roman Senate enacted Lex Poetelia Papiria (Law of Gaius Poetelius Libo Visolus and Lucius Papirius Cursor, the two consuls) to prohibit debt-bondage and imprisonment for debt within the Roman Republic. This reform marked a tremendous victory for the plebeians, and it was described by the historian Livy in his history of Rome *(Annals of the Roman People)* as "a new beginning of freedom." Although creditors could still require debtors to work for them in order to pay off their debts *(addictio),* such labor was not to be a permanent condition of servitude. Anyone who desired to keep someone in permanent servitude had to purchase a foreign slave.

324 B.C.

The world's first known system of insurance was established on the island of Rhodes. The purpose of the insurance was to protect one's investment in the event that slaves escaped.

323 B.C.

Alexander the Great died. In the years following his death, wars of succession were fought throughout Greece, Asia Minor, Syria, and Egypt, and during these conflicts, many Hellenic captives were taken and sold into slavery. In the Roman world, these well-educated, Greek-speaking slaves were highly prized, and many of them became tutors and government administrators.

❧ALCIDAMAS'S MESSENIAN ORATION❧

The rhetorician and sophist Alcidamas, born in Elaea in Aeolis (in modern-day Greece), taught in Athens in the fourth century B.C. A few of his writings have come down to us, but one that is lost—surviving only in quotations in Aristotle's *Rhetoric* and in anonymous commentaries on Aristotle—the *Messenian Oration,* is reported to have included statements that the divinity made everyone free and that nature made no one a slave: in other words, everyone is born free, and slavery is an artificial human invention. Earlier Greek thinkers had established a distinction between the natural and the artificial; according to some modern scholars, Alcidamas was referring to this distinction and was making a universally valid statement, despite the historical context of the oration.

More recently, such scholars as Keith Bradley and Giuseppe Cambiano have taken the viewpoint that the use of the terms "everyone" and "no one" in the quotation from Alcidamas, which itself is incomplete and may or may not have been cited out of context by Aristotle and the anonymous commentators, must be viewed more narrowly and contextually. The slaves referred to by Alcidamas, according to this viewpoint, were Helots, a group of Greeks who had been conquered and enslaved by the Spartans at a much earlier date. Some of these Helots were Messenians who had been liberated after the Thebans defeated the Spartans in 370 B.C. The oration was written after this victory when Alcidamas was living at the time in Athens, a traditional enemy of Sparta. The Athenians saw Sparta's defeat as revenge for the Spartan defeat of Athens in the Second (Great) Peloponnesian War, which had ended in 404 B.C.—within living memory when the oration was written.

Alcidamas may have been replying to his professional rival, the orator Isocrates (436–338 B.C.), who had written a work, *Archidamas,* a few years earlier that had defended the legitimacy of the enslavement of the Helots and asserted the consequent illegitimacy of their liberation and subsequent treatment as equals who were allowed to own land by other Greeks. The validity of this particular enslavement was, as Plato said in the *Laws,* a frequently debated topic in Athens in this period. Thus, Alcidamas was not attacking the legitimacy of slavery in general. On the other hand, in the *Politics* Aristotle mentioned unnamed thinkers who opposed slavery in general as unnatural, a statement that appears in a number of Greek authors of the fourth and third centuries B.C.

Alcidamas was an orator, not a philosopher, but given the extremely fragmentary nature of his extant writings, it is impossible to determine how much philosophical material appears in his works.

—*Stephen A. Stertz*

For Further Reading
Bradley, Keith. 1994. *Slavery and Society at Rome.* Cambridge: Cambridge University Press; Cambiano, Giuseppi. 1987. "Aristotle and the Anonymous Opponents of Slavery." In *Classical Slavery.* Ed. Moses I. Finley. London: Frank Cass.

---

322 B.C.
The Greek philosopher Aristotle died and left 14 domestic slaves in his will.

312 B.C.
The Roman censor Appius Claudius declared that freed slaves had the right to hold office in the Roman Republic.

C. 300 B.C.
The Athenian orator Demosthenes inherited slaves upon the death of his father. These slaves were artisans and craftsmen who earned an income for Demosthenes—32 of them made knives and swords, and another 20 were bed manufacturers. The ancient Greeks called such slaves "paybringers" because they could be a lucrative source of income for their owner.

C. 300 B.C.
The Stoic school of philosophy was founded. Believing in the brotherhood of man, the Stoics did not support the notion that slavery was a part of the laws of nature.

C. 290 B.C.
Greek historians note that a slave insurrection occurred on the island of Chios in the Aegean Sea.

C. 287 B.C.
The Greek philosopher and naturalist Theophrastus died and left seven domestic slaves in his will. Theophrastus had inherited Aristotle's library and had continued his teaching at the Lyceum in Athens.

The Mediterranean Sea both divides and unites the continents of Africa, Asia, and Europe. Its roughly 970,000 square miles of generally navigable surface is punctuated by the major islands of Sicily, Crete, Cyprus, Majorca, Corsica, Sardinia, and Rhodes. The Nile, Rhone, and Po Rivers allow deep penetration into their respective continents, and access through the Dardanelles opens the Black Sea and its great hinterland to trade and travel. Most important, perhaps, direct access to the Atlantic has provided an enormous stage on which patterns of slavery nurtured along Mediterranean shores would play their part.

Until only recently, slavery was a structural element of Mediterranean society. Trade in slaves required a supply of unfree people, a demand for labor—usually found in hierarchical, settled agricultural or urban communities with a high land-to-labor ratio—and a means of acquiring the unfree labor. When war captives, debtors or their families, or the offspring of slaves proved insufficient, the purchase of slaves, often from nomadic or piratical peoples who did not themselves utilize slaves, augmented the supply. When huge numbers were enslaved simultaneously, as in 167 B.C. when the Romans so reduced some 150,000 inhabitants of Epirus in a single day, an efficient market proved invaluable. Race and ethnicity meant little in the trade, which easily followed the developing sea lanes and caravan routes that flowed into the Mediterranean basin from the interiors of all three continents. Important marketplaces likewise developed, their locations generally determined by the dominant maritime power of the region.

The slave trade among the ancient Near Eastern empires seems to have only brushed the Mediterranean, and the Hebrew and Egyptian demand for slaves was consistently fairly low. The Phoenicians, however, developed along the central North African littoral (Carthage) agricultural, ranching, and shipbuilding operations that were slave labor intensive. This large-scale application of unfree labor required an internal market and drew unfortunates from well outside the bounds of the empire. Early Greeks utilized relatively few slaves in their households and fields, but classical Greek advances in colonization and trade in manufactured goods increased the demand for agricultural and industrial slaves. Alexander the Great's conquests, the later wars among his successors, and general economic prosperity increased both supply and demand in the Hellenistic eastern Mediterranean.

The traditional Rome of small farmers and sub-

ject villages had limited use for slaves, but the Punic Wars of the third and second centuries B.C. devastated the Italian population and introduced Rome to Carthage's system of agricultural slave gangs. The development of latifundia and further imperial expansion in the second century B.C. both increased and fed the Roman hunger for slaves—up to 500,000 new slaves per year. As the Roman Republic collapsed, pirates and their markets—for instance, Delos in the Aegean—thrived despite Roman control of *mare nostrum* ("our sea") and supplied the many hungry Roman markets for field slaves and domestic and industrial slaves, many of whom were highly skilled or educated. The city of Rome had one market for common slaves in the Roman Forum and a second for more sophisticated slaves in the Saepta Julia. In the Black Sea region, slave traders obtained human beings in exchange for grain and salt, and in Gaul, perhaps 15,000 individuals per year were purchased for coins and metal objects. Traders sold both to other traders and to ultimate customers, who themselves might sell or trade their slaves in the highly regulated Roman marketplaces.

The slave economy thrived into the early Roman Empire, but as Roman conquests subsided, the supply of slaves shriveled. Tenantry, sharecropping, and eventually serfdom replaced large-scale agricultural slavery as the empire crumbled. Although early Christians (and later adherents of Islam) counseled humane treatment of slaves, neither religion inveighed against either slavery or the slave trade. In the Byzantine Empire, slaves were imported, especially Slavs from the Black Sea region—often transported by the Scandinavian Rūs—and a market developed in Constantinople that flourished until the eleventh century A.D.

In the chaotic early medieval period, pagans, Jews, Christians, Arians, and Muslims were all targets of slavers from both belligerent or indifferent faiths as the enslavement of coreligionists was forbidden. Trade was usually dominated by the strongest naval power—in turn, Vandal, Byzantine, Muslim, and Italian. Unlike in the manorial north, there was continued slaving activity in the more highly urbanized seacoasts of the Christian and Muslim Mediterranean. From the east flowed Russians, Serbs, Bulgars, Caucasians, Tatars and, later, Turco-Mongols, generally through Constantinople. Blacks—the males often castrated—filtered north along the caravan routes from central Africa and the Sudan to the Islamic entrepôts of North Africa (Tunis, Tripoli, Fez, Algiers) and Iberia. An estimated 7,500,000 enslaved blacks traveled this route between 650 and 1900. Unbaptized captive Germans and Slavs were forced across the Alpine passes to Venice or to the southern French coast where Jewish merchants (*radaniya*) ferried them to Spain. Seville boasted a brisk trade in slaves, who were paraded through the streets and then bought by townspeople as servants and industrial laborers, and tenth-century Córdoba contained about 14,000 slaves. At the same time, Amalfi and Naples emerged as important centers of the Italian trade.

By the thirteenth century, Italians (Venetians, Genoese) handled much of the Mediterranean slave trade, and soon Italian colonies in the eastern basin (Phocaea, Cyprus, Crete) and Majorca were establishing the patterns of estate or plantation slavery that would travel to the Canary Islands and later the Western Hemisphere. Trade in the Black Sea ports of Kaffa (Feodosiya) and Tana, the Spanish Reconquista (the reconquering of the Iberian Peninsula from the Muslims, 711–1492), and random raids fueled their needs while the Genoese illicitly supplied the Egyptian slave armies with non-Muslim slaves from the Black Sea. With the Turkish conquest of the eastern basin in the fifteenth century, black and North African slaves became more important in the Christian West, the former increasingly supplied by the Portuguese (after 1444), while piracy and raiding continued to feed Christians to the Muslim markets in North Africa. Although Venice's public auctions ended as early as 1366, domestic slavery in Italy continued into the seventeenth century.

Christian-Muslim rivalry and antagonism had fueled the supply of slaves, but the demand diminished as the Mediterranean's importance waned. Christian Mediterranean countries abandoned slavery piecemeal and without fanfare during the seventeenth and eighteenth centuries, and the Turks ceased international trade, which left only the western North African areas of "Barbary" as active pirate dens of slavers, dens successfully subdued by American and British naval efforts to protect their shipping and citizens in the early nineteenth century. Ironically, liberal European imperialism and Turkish modernization eradicated the last remnants of the slave trade in the Mediterranean basin during the nineteenth and early twentieth centuries.

—*Joseph P. Byrne*

For Further Reading
Boese, Wayne E. 1973. "A Study of the Slave Trade and Sources of Slaves in the Roman Republic and the Early Roman Empire." Ph.D dissertation, University of Washington; Bradley, Keith R. 1986. "Social Aspects of the Slave Trade in the Roman World." *Münsterische Beiträge zur antike Handelsgeschichte* 5(1): 49–58; Fisher, Alan W. 1978. "The Sale of Slaves in the Ottoman Empire." *Bogaziçi Universitesi Dergisi* 4: 149–171; Heers, Jacques. 1981. *Esclaves et domestiques au moyen âge dans le monde mediterranéen*. Paris: Fayard; Verlinden, Charles. 1969–1970. "Medieval 'Slavers.'" *Explorations in Economic History* 7: 1–14.

280 B.C.

Under the leadership of the Seleucids, several cities in Asia Minor regained prominence as commercial centers. In Miletus, there was large-scale production of textiles, which involved mass production on the part of a slave labor force.

264–241 B.C.

During the First Punic War, Rome fought against the Phoenician city of Carthage for control of trade, colonization, and navigation in the Mediterranean. The Romans became concerned when the North African city of Carthage threatened to take Messina on the island of Sicily, which would have limited Roman navigation of the Mediterranean. Most of the fighting in this war took place on the island of Sicily. The Romans defeated Carthage, and the Carthaginians were forced to pay a huge indemnity to Rome. The Romans began to acquire large numbers of slaves as a result of this conflict.

264 B.C.

Gladiator games first became popular in Rome. Gladiators, who were generally slaves, would fight one another to the death before an audience as part of a public spectacle. The abundance of Punic War captives who were made into slaves in Rome made such a form of public entertainment possible. Many Romans who could not fight the Carthaginians in the war experienced vicarious pleasure by watching their enemies murder one another in these public games.

C. 263 B.C.

The Greek comic playwright Philemon did not believe that slavery was a part of the natural order of things. He wrote: "Though one is a slave, he is a man no less than you, master; he is made of the same flesh. No one is a slave by nature; it is fate that enslaves the body" (Meltzer, 1993).

254 B.C.

During the First Punic War (264–241 B.C.), the Romans sold 13,000 captives into slavery after capturing the Carthaginian naval base located at Panormus (modern-day Palermo) in Sicily. Another 13,000 captives were able to escape certain enslavement by being ransomed.

240 B.C.

The Greek slave Livius Andronicus, a noted poet and playwright in Rome, produced his first tragedy in Rome. Later, he translated Homer's *Odyssey* into Latin.

219–218 B.C.

The residents of Saguntum (Sagunto in modern-day Spain) were allies of Rome, which was enough to stir the wrath of the Carthaginian general Hannibal (247–183 B.C.). Hannibal laid siege to the city for more than a year, and after he had captured it, thousands of the city's inhabitants were sold into slavery.

218–202 B.C.

The Second Punic War again matched the forces of Rome against the North African city of Carthage. The Romans had become concerned about colonies that the Carthaginians had established in the area of Spain, and Hannibal raised a Carthaginian army that was assisted by troops from Gaul and crossed the Alps to invade Italy from the north. The Romans were unable to defeat Hannibal's forces, and his army roamed freely throughout Italy for several years. Hannibal had hoped that there would be an internal rebellion in Italy from which he could draw support, but such an insurrection never occurred. Hannibal returned to Carthage when an army led by the Roman general Scipio Africanus threatened to attack that city and was defeated in the Battle of Zama. Carthage paid a huge indemnity to Rome, the Romans acquired Spain as a province, Romans enslaved in North Africa were emancipated and allowed to return to Rome as free people, and Rome acquired additional numbers of slaves as a result of this war. After the Battle of Zama, Scipio Africanus sold 50,000 Carthaginian captives into slavery.

207 B.C.

In Sparta, a Syrian slave named Nabis rose to power and started a social revolution to free the Helots, destroy the ruling oligarchy, redistribute land, and cancel debts. He was defeated by the Achaean League and was later assassinated.

200 B.C.

Writings from this period indicate that Greek slaves were commonly employed as teachers in the Roman Republic.

198 B.C.

After the Second Punic War (218–202 B.C.), Roman authorities had to suppress a slave revolt that began among many of the North African slaves who had belonged to Carthaginian captives who had been taken to Rome.

196 B.C.

A Roman legion had to suppress a revolt among the slaves of Etruria (modern-day Tuscany). Once the rebellion was suppressed, the leaders of the uprising were crucified.

190?–159 B.C.

The former slave Terence Afer (Terence the African) lived in Rome where he was a respected playwright. He is credited with coining the phrase *Homo sum; humani nihil a me alienum puto* ("I am a man and nothing human is alien to me").

188 B.C.

In the Greek Peloponnesus, Philopoemen, the leader of the Achaean League, marched into Sparta and restored order after a revolt that had been led by Nabis, a Syrian slave. All of the remaining followers of Nabis were sold into slavery.

187 B.C.

By this date, the senatorial class in the Roman Republic had been barred from any type of commercial activity, but the practice was common. Many Roman patricians began to invest in land in Italy in the hope that intensive agricultural production from the land might produce enough food to feed a growing urban population and yield impressive profits. In order to make such a system work, the patrician class needed a sufficient labor force to work the vast estates that they purchased in the countryside. This need was satisfied by the massive influx of foreign slaves into the Roman Republic.

Slaves were transported along Mediterranean trade routes in vessels like this Assyrian ship. (The Granger Collection)

185 B.C.

A serious revolt occurred among the slave shepherds of Apulia, who rose in rebellion to try to effect their freedom. Roman forces were sent into the mountainous region to quell the revolt, and 7,000 of the slave rebels were condemned to work in the mines.

176 B.C.

The Roman general Tiberius Gracchus (senior) crushed a revolt that occurred on the island of Sardinia. Gracchus later boasted that in the process of quelling the unrest, 80,000 people were either killed or captured. Those who were captured became slaves of the Romans.

170 B.C.

The Roman statesman Cato the Elder wrote *De re rustica* (On farming). On the subject of slavery in the Roman Republic, Cato noted that it was more efficient for Roman slaveholders to work their slaves to death and then replace them than it was for the owners to be kind to their slaves and get less productivity out of them. There were so many slaves in the Roman Republic at this time that the value of a slave's

life was exceptionally cheap. Cato's advice to the slaveholder was to "sell the old work oxen, the blemished cattle, the blemished sheep, the wool, the skins, the old wagon, the worn-out tools, the aged slave, the slave that is diseased, and everything else that he does not need." In another passage, Cato advised the owners of large estates (latifundia) that slaves would be most productive if they were "working in chains" upon the land. Cato the Elder himself made many profitable investments in slaves. In *Parallel Lives,* Plutarch wrote that "Cato purchased a great many slaves out of captives taken in war, but chiefly bought up the young ones, who, like whelps and colts, were still capable of being reared and trained." According to Plutarch, Cato often boasted that he never paid more than 1,500 drachmas for a slave.

168–166 B.C.

A freed slave from Carthage named Terence (Publius Terentius Afer) was given recognition at Rome for his play *Andria*. The play was produced at Rome despite jealous opposition from some Roman playwrights. Terence's plays were an important commentary on the social issues of

African elephants were employed in Carthaginian general Hannibal's invasion of Italy, as depicted in this sixteenth-century painting by Italian artist Jacopo Ripanda. Carthage was ultimately defeated in the Second Punic War, and Romans enslaved in North Africa were freed. (Gianni Dagli Orti/Corbis)

his time, including slavery. In one play, he described a Greek merchant who carried women and other trade goods from Greece to Cyprus and feared the possibility of a financial loss.

167 B.C.
The Roman general Lucius Aemilius Paulus took revenge upon the inhabitants of Epirus because they had joined Macedonia in the Third Macedonian War (172–167 B.C.) against Rome. Aemilius destroyed 70 of the Epirot towns in Greece and sold 150,000 of its citizens into slavery.

166 B.C.
The Roman Senate declared the Aegean island of Delos to be a free port—meaning that no customs duties were to be collected there—after Rome destroyed the power of Rhodes. This special economic privilege made Delos an attractive location for trading slaves, and the island soon became a center of much of the trade in captives who had been taken in pirate raids in the eastern Mediterranean. In *Geographical Sketches,* the Greek geographer Strabo claimed that the

port facilities at Delos were capable of sending and receiving 10,000 slaves per day.

166 B.C.
In the Apocrypha, there is the story that King Antiochus of Syria attempted to get the Israelites to abandon their God but they chose death rather than violate their holy covenant. This is the first recorded episode of martyrdom in the history of religious persecution.

153 B.C.
Cato began the practice of ending all of his speeches in the Roman Senate with the expression *Delenda est Carthago* ("Carthage must be destroyed"). It was the Punic Wars (264–146 B.C.) that were responsible for transforming the Roman Republic into a slave-based society.

C. 150 B.C.
Although the enslavement of war captives was the most common way to acquire slaves in the ancient world, other methods were used. Pirate raids became common in the eastern Mediter-

ranean as the demand for vast numbers of slaves made such raiding a potentially lucrative enterprise. Two centers of the pirate slave trading were the Aegean island of Delos and the port city of Side in Pamphylia. The Romans had declared Delos to be a free port in 166 B.C., which meant that no customs duties were collected there, and this special economic privilege made Delos an attractive location for trading slaves.

149–146 B.C.

The Third Punic War resulted in the complete destruction of Carthage at the hands of the Romans. Ninety percent of the residents of Carthage died either in battle or of disease, and the survivors of the city were sold into slavery in Rome. By the end of this conflict, Rome had truly developed into a slave-based society.

146 B.C.

War between the Achaeans and the Romans broke out after the Achaeans of south-central Greece formed the Achaean League with other city-states on the Peloponnesus and tried to force Sparta, which was under Roman protection, to join the league. A Roman army commanded by Lucius Mummius Achaicus defeated the Achaean army, which consisted primarily of ill-equipped slaves, in a battle near Corinth. The Romans sacked and burned Corinth, dissolved the Achaean League, and took possession of Greek territory. Mummius slaughtered all the males of Corinth and sold the women and children into slavery. The fall of Corinth greatly enhanced commerce on the Aegean island of Delos, commerce that was especially active in the slave trade.

140 B.C.

Popillius Laenas, a Roman praetor, returned 917 fugitive slaves from Sicily to their masters on the Italian mainland. Many of the slaves of the Roman Republic who attempted to escape their servitude were able to make their way to Sicily; many tried to live in freedom, but some chose a life of brigandage.

137–133 B.C.

During the Celtiberian wars, the Roman forces attempted to subjugate the Celtic peoples who lived on the Iberian Peninsula. Celtic forces in the town of Numantia (Soria in modern-day Spain) defeated a 20,000-man Roman army commanded by Gaius Hostilius Mancinus. The Romans later returned to Numantia and conducted an eight-month siege. The town was destroyed by the Romans, and its 4,000 inhabitants were either killed or enslaved.

135–132 B.C.

A Syrian slave named Eunus led a large slave revolt (First Servile War) against Roman overlords in Sicily. Angered by the mistreatment that they received on the large agricultural estates, Eunus and an army of 70,000 rebel slaves won several victories against the Romans. Eunus proclaimed himself Antiochus, the king of the Syrians, and fought bravely against the Roman forces. The slave rebels terrorized the island of Sicily until they were defeated. The Romans crucified 20,000 slaves after suppressing this revolt. Eunus was not crucified, but he was locked into a cell and left to rot to death. According to the Greek historian Diodorus of Sicily, who wrote about the conditions that precipitated the First Servile War in *Historical Library:* "The Sicilians, being grown very rich and elegant in their manner of living, bought up large numbers of slaves. They brought them in droves from the places where they were reared, and immediately branded them with marks on their bodies. . . . Oppressed by the grinding toil and beatings, maltreated for the most part beyond all reason, the slaves could endure it no longer."

134 B.C.

The Roman historian Paulus Orosius recorded that the Roman consul Piso captured the town of Mamertium in Sicily during the First Servile War (135–132 B.C.) and killed 8,000 fugitive slaves. Piso crucified those fugitive slaves that he was able to capture alive.

134 B.C.

Inspired by the early success of Eunus and the rebel slaves on the island of Sicily, as many as 4,000 slaves on the Italian mainland attempted to revolt in the cities of Rome, Minturnae, and Sinuessa, but the Roman authorities were able to suppress these attempted rebellions. A similar uprising occurred among the slave miners in the region around Mount Laurium in Greece, which was noted for its vast silver mines.

133 B.C.

Tiberius Sempronius Gracchus was elected tribune of the people in Rome but was assassinated

Food has been one of the slave's primary concerns throughout history. In many systems of slavery, one of the servant's few rights was that of sustenance. Greek city-states of the pre-Christian era, Judea (200 B.C.), Sicily (135–132 B.C.), and the Roman prefecture in Egypt (A.D. 46) all mandated food rations. The Chinese, and later the Spanish, expressed concern about provisioning slaves, and Islam went further and leveled sanctions: owners unable to feed their vassals were obligated to sell them.

Since antiquity, cereal grains—rice, maize, wheat, millet, sorghum, oats, rye, and barley—played a significant role in the diet of slave populations. Comparing favorably with protein-rich foods in energy value, cereals were inexpensive to produce and rich in carbohydrates, and they may have exceeded 80 percent of slave food intake. Eaten in raw grain form, or as ingredients in various dishes (gruel and porridge), cereals were most commonly baked into bread. Vegetables, fruits, and nuts were the chief articles of sustenance in the ancient and Mediterranean worlds after grains while meat was a rare luxury.

Prior to the sixteenth century, the African diet was based largely on taro (bull yam), the smaller African yam, imported Asian bananas, millet, and rice. Most of the high-yield plants grown today—manioc (cassava) and maize (corn)—were introduced into the Mediterranean culture after 1500. Portuguese traders carried New World crops to Africa and later utilized them on the slave ships during the Middle Passage between Africa and the Western Hemisphere. Manioc and corn rapidly became important parts of the slave diet on both sides of the Atlantic, which led to protein deficiencies, particularly in areas where animal protein was excluded from the diet. Symptoms of vitamin-deficiency diseases associated with eating habits—scurvy, rickets, beriberi, nyctalopia (night blindness), xerophthalmia, and pellagra—are well chronicled, and there were also many African taboos regarding the eating of fruit (vitamin C), vegetables (vitamins A, C, B_1, B_2, B_3), eggs (protein), and milk products (calcium).

Increasing the quantity and expanding the range of foods necessitated great ingenuity on the part of slaves. Many masters expected their servants to provision themselves, at least partially, by raising fruits, vegetables, and livestock. Even in regions of intensive agriculture and sizable slave populations, where owners considered every mouthful of food in terms of cash, the bulk of the slave diet consisted of salt fish, pork, and corn.

In the southern part of the United States, rations allocated to slaves were more protein-laden than those consumed in West Africa and the Caribbean. Weekly food allotments generally included a peck of cornmeal and two and a half to four pounds of pork or bacon. Abundance and variety of foods in the slave diet, however, depended heavily on seasonal variation, economic standing, and the liberality of the owners. Nevertheless, the diet of antebellum slaves in the United States represented a nutritional improvement over that of colonial slaves and counterparts laboring in Central and South America. Before 1850, six southern states required owners to provide servants with adequate provisions, and current research suggests that American slave diets were quantitatively adequate but deficient qualitatively. A general ignorance of nutritional principles, more a state of antebellum medical knowledge than the nature of the institution of slavery, produced unbalanced diets for both masters and slaves.

—*Clifford R. Dickinson*

For Further Reading
Hilliard, Sam Bowers. 1972. *Hogmeat and Hoecake: Food Supply in the Old South 1840–1860.* Carbondale: Southern Illinois University Press; Kiple, Kenneth F., and Virginia H. King. 1981. *Another Dimension to the Black Diaspora: Diet, Disease, and Racism.* Cambridge: Cambridge University Press; Owens, Leslie H. 1976. *This Species of Property: Slave Life and Culture in the Old South.* New York: Oxford University Press; Stutch, Richard. 1975. "The Treatment Received by American Slaves: A Critical Review of the Evidence Presented in *Time on the Cross.*" *Explorations in Economic History* 12: 335–448.

BLOSSIUS OF CUMAE (?–C. 129 B.C.)

Gaius Blossius of Cumae, who lived in the second century B.C., supported the policies of the Roman reformer Tiberius Sempronius Gracchus, a personal friend. Although tradition states that the very patriotic Cornelia, mother of Tiberius Gracchus, had employed Blossius to teach her sons Stoic philosophy, which was popular in Roman senatorial circles at the time, there is no evidence for this belief. After Gracchus, whose reforms had nothing to do with slavery, was killed in 133 B.C., Blossius fled to Pergamum in Asia Minor and joined the revolt of Aristonicus, pretender to the throne of that country. Blossius committed suicide after Aristonicus's defeat in 129 B.C.

Blossius was an adherent of the Stoic philosophy, which had first been taught by a former slave (Epictetus), and some supporters of that philosophy preached the equality of all human beings, including, at least theoretically, slaves. Blossius seems to have supported democracy in theory and the revolt of the slaves in parts of western Asia Minor (132–129 B.C.) in practice. For these reasons, earlier scholars put him forward as an opponent of slavery and even as a sort of proto-Marxist revolutionary theoretician, although his writings have not come down to us. More recent scholarship has taken the position that Blossius supported the slave revolt only because he was a supporter of Aristonicus, who was merely using the slaves against the Romans (Aristonicus gathered slaves and the poor around him, calling them "citizens of the sun," [heliopolitani]), and there is no evidence that Blossius inspired the movement. In fact, Aristonicus appears to have begun the movement long before Blossius's arrival.

Blossius, a strong supporter of local autonomy, came, it is believed, from a family that had long supported democracy (which in antiquity had nothing to do with opposition to slavery) and opposed Roman expansion. He joined Aristonicus and thus supported the slave revolt because he was opposed to the centralizing policies of the senatorial faction in Rome that had had Tiberius Gracchus assassinated— and, not incidentally, had presumably had similar plans for Blossius himself. It has been noted that had Blossius in fact been a radical opponent of slavery, he would have joined the slave rebels in Sicily, who were led, not by a royal pretender, but by a slave. To what extent Blossius's Stoic ideas influenced his political views is unknown.

—*Stephen A. Stertz*

For Further Reading
Dudley, D. R. 1941. "Blossius of Cumae." *Journal of Roman Studies* 31: 94–99; Garlan, Yvon. 1995. *Les esclaves en grece ancienne*. Rev. ed. Paris: Editions la Decouverte; Vogt, Joseph. 1974. *Ancient Slavery and the Ideal of Man*. Oxford: Basil Blackwell.

---

before he was able to finish enacting the drastic land reforms he had promised the Roman poor. As a result of his land reforms, more than 80,000 Roman citizens were able to resettle on land in the republic.

132–129 B.C.
Roman forces intervened when slaves at Pergamum in Asia Minor, inspired by the Stoic philosopher Aristonicus and others, rose in rebellion and attempted to establish a "city of the sun" in which all "citizens of the sun" (*heliopolitani*) would live on an egalitarian basis. This revolt was supported by the Roman Stoic Gaius Blossius of Cumae.

131 B.C.
The Roman historian Paulus Orosius recorded that the Roman consul Rutilius captured the towns of Tauromenium and Henna (modern-day Taormina and Enna, respectively), which had been strongholds of fugitive slaves during the First Servile War (135–132 B.C.). Rutilius re-portedly killed more than 20,000 slaves when these towns were taken.

C. 130 B.C.
The Greek historian Polybius noted in his writings that approximately 40,000 slaves worked each day in the silver mines that were located near Carthago Novo (Cartagena in modern-day Spain).

121 B.C.
When his fellow Romans turned against his reforms, Tribune Gaius Sempronius Gracchus convinced one of his own slaves to kill him. In the rioting that followed, more than 3,000 supporters of Gracchus were murdered.

120–56 B.C.
In his *Annals,* the Roman historian Tacitus described the extent of slavery in the Roman Republic: "Segregate the freed and you will only show how few free-born there are."

105 B.C.

The Roman practice of holding gladiator games became sanctioned by Roman authorities when Rome's two consuls authorized the year's entertainment. Gladiators, who were generally slaves, fought one another to the death; the number of war captives who became slaves in Rome made this form of public entertainment possible.

104–99 B.C.

A large force of 6,000 slaves led by Salvius, Tryphon, and Athenion, angered by the mistreatment they received on the large agricultural estates, rebelled against their Roman overlords on the island of Sicily. The insurrectionists gained control of most of the rural areas of Sicily and laid siege to the island's cities. The slave rebels defeated the first Roman army that was sent against them but were defeated by a second army that was put into the field against them. The Roman Senate reported that it cost the lives of 100,000 Roman citizens to suppress this uprising. In *Historical Library,* the historian Diodorus claimed that the captives taken when the rebellion ended were shipped to Rome where they were to die fighting beasts in a public arena. Many of the captured slave rebels chose to die by suicide or by killing one another rather than submit to being entertainment for the Roman masses.

104 B.C.

When the Roman Republic was threatened by Germanic invaders, the Roman Senate requested that the Roman ally state of Bithynia in Asia Minor provide soldiers to assist the Roman forces. The leaders of Bithynia complained that all of their young men had been carried off as slaves by pirates who operated with the blessing of Rome. The Roman Senate decreed that all slaves that were held by allies of Rome should be emancipated so they might help defend Rome against the potential Germanic threat.

C. 104 B.C.

In the wake of Germanic barbarian invasions of the Roman Republic, slave unrest occurred in several different regions of the Italian peninsula, and there were slave revolts in Nuceria and Capua. Near the town of Capua, one slave revolt began when a Roman *eques* ("middle-class citizen") armed his own slaves. Roman authorities were able to quell all of these disturbances.

102–101 B.C.

The Roman general Gaius Marius engaged in battle against Germanic invaders and defeated his foes in the Battle of Vercellae in the Po Valley. An estimated 120,000 of the Germanic invaders were killed in the fighting, and Marius also captured 90,000 Teutons and 60,000 Cimbri; they were sold into slavery in Rome.

95 B.C.

Increasing numbers of rural residents flocked to Rome seeking the benefits of Roman citizenship. The transformation occurred in the countryside, and Rome changed from being a society of freeholding small independent farmers to one of large landed estates farmed by slave laborers, a pattern that would continue and become more common.

91–88 B.C.

Marcus Livius Druses, tribune of the people, introduced a measure to extend Roman citizenship to the rural Italians but was killed before action was taken on the measure. The rural Italian residents rose up against the Romans in the Social War of 91–88 B.C., seeking the benefits of Roman citizenship. Social and economic pressures since the end of the Third Punic War (146 B.C.) and the rise of a slave-based economy had put great pressure on the rural Italians. Roman citizenship would have provided prestige, redress against injustice, the privilege of fighting in the Roman legions, and relief from burdensome taxation.

88 B.C.

The Aegean island of Delos was sacked by Mithridates VI (the Great), king of Pontus, a region that bordered on the Black Sea. Delos had operated as a free port for nearly 75 years and had become the center of the slave trade in the Aegean Sea and eastern Mediterranean regions.

82 B.C.

The Roman general Marcus Licinius Crassus became a very wealthy man by investing in slaves. Crassus obtained slaves through military conquest and educated them before selling them at high prices. Crassus believed that it was his responsibility to treat slaves as necessary implements for effective household management, and he became immensely wealthy by selling his trained skilled slaves to Roman buyers.

In the center of the Cyclades, strategically located in the southern Aegean Sea within easy trading distance of mainland Greece, Asia Minor, the Black Sea, and North Africa, the very small (2 square miles), barren, nearly waterless island of Delos derived its economic importance in antiquity from trading and pilgrimages to its shrine of Apollo. Although agricultural goods grown elsewhere were traded, the most important trading activity was in slaves. Although slavery seems to have existed on the island from its earliest habitation by the Carians, a non-Greek people, the importance of the island as a center of the slave trade dates from the Hellenistic Age, especially after the establishment of the Roman province of Asia (modern-day western Asiatic Turkey) in 133 B.C., when the permanent population of the island was only about 4,000, mostly Greeks but also Italians and other non-Greeks, mainly slave traders.

According to the Greek geographer Strabo, at the height of the island's importance in about 100 B.C., 10,000 slaves might have been sold on the island in a single day. At that time, when Delos was the greatest slave market of the Mediterranean, the majority of slaves came from lands bordering the eastern end of that sea, although others came from Gaul, Spain, and all parts of North Africa. Historically, the island was at its height commercially between 166 B.C., when the Romans made the island a free port and populated it with Athenians, and 88 B.C., when it was sacked by soldiers from Rome's enemy, the kingdom of Pontus. Pirate raids, while supplying slaves when other islands were raided, caused the final decline of the island when Delos itself was raided in 69 B.C. The recovery from warfare of other islands, such as Rhodes, was also a factor.

By 100 B.C., many people important in the politics of Athens had made their fortunes as slave traders on Delos. The slaves included prisoners of war and victims of raids; many were literate, according to archaeological evidence. One graffito written by a slave expresses regret at the barrenness of the island and nostalgia for his vegetation-rich native land. Inscriptions by freed slaves express thanks to Zeus. Other inscriptions indicate that an organization of slaves and freedmen celebrated games, apparently including boxing. Other less-fortunate slaves were castrated, becoming eunuchs. A great slave revolt in 130 B.C. was brutally put down by the Delians themselves according to the historian Diodorus Siculus. An inscription of the time curses those, including pirates, who helped the slaves flee the island and asserts that certain government officials were given police powers against the "thieves and pirates."

—Stephen A. Stertz

For Further Reading
Bruneau, Phillippe. 1968. "Contribution à l'histoire urbaine de Délos à l'époque hellénistique et a l'époque impériale." *Bulletin de correspondance hellenique* 92: 633–709; Déonna, Waldemar. 1948. *La vie privée des Déliens.* Paris: E. de Boccard; Laidlaw, W. A. 1933. *A History of Delos.* Oxford: Oxford University Press.

81 B.C.

The Roman dictator Sulla developed a list of political enemies he wished to have murdered. He maintained a personal bodyguard consisting of former slaves of all the enemies on the list.

78–77 B.C.

The Roman consul Marcus Aemilius Lepidus was a champion of the Roman poor and the dispossessed. When his efforts to alleviate the suffering of these groups failed, the peoples of west-central Italy revolted, and Lepidus supported their cause. He raised an army and attempted to march on Rome but was defeated by the forces of Quintus Lutatius Catalus and Pompey the Great. Lepidus and some of his supporters were able to escape to Sardinia; those who remained in Italy were destroyed by the Roman forces.

76 B.C.

Julius Caesar was enslaved briefly when Cilician pirates captured him while he was sailing to Rhodes to study law. Caesar was freed after a ransom was paid, and he later returned to capture and crucify the pirates who had captured him.

73–71 B.C.

The Thracian gladiator Spartacus led a large slave revolt (Third Servile War) against Roman authority. Spartacus's primary lieutenants in this well-organized insurrection were Crixus and Oenomaus, slaves from Gaul. Beginning in Capua when a group of 70 slave gladiators took refuge on Mt. Vesuvius and became the leaders of an army of 10,000 rebel slaves, the insurrectionists won several victories and terrorized the

Italian countryside. Eventually, Spartacus commanded a rebel force that was estimated to include 70,000 rebel slaves. The rebel forces defeated four Roman armies sent into the field against them, and they were able to plunder much of southern Italy. Eventually, the forces of Roman general Marcus Licinius Crassus defeated Spartacus's army at the Battle of Brundisium (Brindisi) and were able to suppress the rebellion and restore order in the region. The Romans crucified 6,000 of the captured slave rebels along the Appian Way between Capua and Rome. In 71 B.C., the Roman historian Paulus Orosius, in *Adversus paganos historiarum* (History against the pagans) wrote of the Third Servile War: "As soon as Crassus began the fighting against the runaways, he killed 6,000 of them, and captured 900 alive. Then before taking on Spartacus himself, who was menacing the camp at the head of the Silaris River, he defeated his Gallic and German auxiliaries, of whom he killed 30,000 together with their leaders. Finally he smashed Spartacus himself, who had come against him in a pitched battle, together with the majority of his army of runaway slaves . . . the remainder, who had gotten away from this battle and were wandering around, were wiped out thanks to constant hunting parties under various leaders."

69 B.C.
The Aegean island of Delos was sacked by pirates, and the island never recovered its original prominence as a slave-trading center. After the sack of Delos, the city of Rome became the greatest slave-trading market in the Mediterranean world.

67–66 B.C.
The Roman Senate declared war upon the pirates who roamed the Mediterranean Sea. Many Roman citizens had been enslaved by pirates who attacked both coastal communities and ships at sea. The Roman Senate authorized Gnaeus Pompeius Magnus (Pompey the Great) to conduct a three-month campaign against the pirates. The results were quite impressive as 10,000 pirates were killed and nearly 400 pirate vessels were either captured or surrendered to the Romans.

63–62 B.C.
The Roman politician Lucius Sergius Cataline hoped to be elected a Roman consul, but he was not chosen for the position. Cataline decided to seize power by force and organized an army while his supporters conspired with slaves in Apulia to stage a revolt as a diversionary tactic. Many rural slaves and gladiators were said to have been a part of Cataline's army. Marcus Tullius Cicero, the consul, learned of the plot and exposed Cataline's plans in blistering attacks in the Senate. The revolt was suppressed as Cataline and his conspirators were eventually executed or killed in battle with Roman forces.

59 B.C.
Julius Caesar, Gnaeus Pompeius Magnus (Pompey the Great), and Marcus Licinius Crassus formed the First Triumvirate to govern Rome. Caesar and Pompey were both generals, and Pompey was also a wealthy merchant. It was said that Pompey owned 20,000 slaves that he hired out as laborers in various types of manufacturing and industry within the Roman world.

58–51 B.C.
During the Gallic War, the Roman general Julius Caesar reportedly captured 500,000 inhabitants of Gaul and sold them into slavery. In one town alone, Caesar was able to take 53,000 captives.

C. 55 B.C.
The Roman writer Marcus Tullius Cicero discussed the condition of slaves in his ethical treatise *On Duties*: "Let us also remember that justice ought to be preserved even toward the lowest level of persons. The lowest level is the condition and fortune of slaves. Those who advise us to use them as we would hired workers don't give bad advice: work must be done; but justice must be shown." In his treatise *On the Laws*, Cicero considered the nature of justice in a slave-based society. [See Document 3.]

C. 50 B.C.
The Roman poet Lucretius commented upon the enormous number of slave laborers who were employed in mining operations and ruthlessly exploited throughout the Roman world. In *On the Nature of Things*, Lucretius noted that the mortality rate among these laborers was excessively high: "Know you not by sight or hearsay how they commonly perish in a short time and how all vital power fails those to whom the hard compulsion of necessity confines in such an employment."

Death of Spartacus. A Thracian slave and gladiator, Spartacus led a significant revolt against Roman authority but was defeated and killed by the forces of the Roman general Crassus. (Corbis-Bettmann)

c. 50 B.C.

The Greek historian Diodorus Siculus (fl. first century B.C.) wrote a 40-volume *Historical Library* and was one of the few historians to write a sympathetic account of the suffering of slaves in the Roman world. In describing the condition of slaves in the Spanish mines, Diodorus wrote: "The workers in these mines produce incredible profits for the owners, but their own lives are spent underground in the quarries wearing and wasting their bodies day and night. Many die, their sufferings are so great. There is no relief, no respite from their labors. The hardships to which the overseer's lash compels them to submit are so severe that, except for a few, whose strength of body and bravery of soul enables them to endure for a long time, they abandon life, because death seems preferable."

44 B.C.

On March 15, assassins murdered Julius Caesar in Rome. Conspirators within the Roman Senate, led by Gaius Cassius Longinus and Marcus Junius Brutus, feared that Caesar wished to become king and claimed they killed Caesar in order to preserve what remained of the Roman Republic. When the Roman general Sextus Pompeius Magnus (Pompey the Younger) promised freedom to slaves who joined him in a campaign against Cassius and Brutus, thousands of slaves abandoned their masters and volunteered their service to help apprehend the conspirators. Later, after Pompey had been defeated by forces loyal to Octavian (the future emperor Augustus Caesar), 30,000 of the slave soldiers were given back to their masters and 6,000 of them were impaled upon orders of Octavian.

c. 40 B.C.

The Roman scholar Marcus Terentius Varro wrote a treatise on agriculture entitled *De re rustica* (On farming, the same title Cato the Elder had used a century earlier). Varro devoted much attention in his work to the proper treatment of slaves in order to maximize profitability but also maintain order. Varro maintained that slaves "should be neither cowed nor high-spirited," and he warned prospective slaveholders to "avoid having too many slaves of the same nation, for this is a fertile source of domestic quarrels."

38 B.C.

Concerning the siege of Perugia in Italy, the Roman historian Appian (fl. second century A.D.) described the brutal means employed by Romans against their slaves during that siege. In *Civil Wars*, Appian wrote: "Lucius collected the remaining provisions and forbade them to be given to the slaves; but he took care that the slaves should not escape to inform the enemy of the city's extremity. The slaves then collected in crowds and lay down within the city, or between the city and the defending wall, feeding on any grass or green leaves which they could find. Lucius buried those who died in long trenches, so that he might not inform the enemy of the fact by burning the bodies, nor allow stenches and disease to arise if they were left to rot."

34 B.C.

The Roman lyric poet and satirist Horace maintained a small farm in the Sabine Valley near Rome that had been given to him by a wealthy patron named Maecenas. Horace had eight slaves who farmed his land, and he rented five plots to tenant farmers. One can discern Horace's attitude as a slaveowner in his dialogue *My Slave Is Free to Speak Up for Himself*. [See Document 4.]

c. 30 B.C.

In *De vita contemplativa* (About the contemplative life), the Hellenistic Jew Philo Judaeus of Alexandria wrote about the Jewish sect known as the Essenes. Philo said of this group, "There is not a single slave among them, but they are all free, serving one another; they condemn masters not only for representing a system of unrighteousness in opposition to that of equality, but as personifications of wickedness in that they violate a law of nature which made us all brethren, created alike." Philo also wrote about the antislavery community of Therapeutae, which was located near Alexandria: "They do not have slaves to wait upon them as they consider that the ownership of servants is entirely against nature. For nature has borne all men to be free, but the wrongful and covetous acts of some who pursued that source of evil—inequality—have imposed their yoke and invested the stronger with power over the weaker."

Cyprus, the largest island in the Mediterranean east of Sicily, is within easy sailing distance of the Greek islands farther west, Anatolia (modern-day Asiatic Turkey) to the north, the Syrian-Palestinian coast to the east, and Africa to the south. Consequently, in antiquity Cyprus was an important center for trading, including slave trading, and other contacts among all parts of the eastern Mediterranean. In particular, it was an important point of contact between the ancient Near Eastern and Greek civilizations.

The island, rich in natural harbors, traded with Egypt in the second millennium B.C., and Egyptian, Mesopotamian, and Hittite texts refer to raids, in which captives were enslaved, and tribute, including slaves of both sexes. During the Minoan-Mycenaean period, from about 1700 to 1050 B.C., warfare and invasion resulted in the enslavement of much of the population of Cyprus, and Greeks settled on the island, which enjoyed prosperity. During the subsequent "Greek dark ages" at the beginning of the Iron Age (after 1050 B.C.), warfare between local rulers on the island resulted in further enslavement, and tribute to Assyrian and later Persian kings included slaves in the first half of the first millennium B.C. Such cities as Salamis became important centers for the international slave trade. One Assyrian inscription dating from the reign of Ashurbanipal (669–630 B.C.) records a contract for the sale of a slave on Cyprus, and another gives the judge's decision in a civil suit regarding slave trading on the island. In the early Greek period, one local Cypriot ruler was said, by the later Greek writer Athenaeus, to have been fanned by pigeons that were shooed off by special slaves.

After the time of Alexander the Great, in the fourth century B.C., the island lost its independence. Ruled by the Ptolemaic kings of Egypt and then by the Romans, Cyprus enjoyed prosperity, and its cities continued to be important centers for the slave trade. The Roman playwright Terence, writing in the second century B.C., referred to a Greek trader bringing a cargo of "women and other goods" to export from mainland Greece to Cyprus while fearing a financial loss (Hill, 1972). Those women were at least more fortunate than the slaves quarrying gypsum and other stones found on Cyprus; there, as elsewhere in the Greek world, slaves in mines and quarries received the worst treatment. The medical writer Galen mentioned the miserable treatment of slaves who tun-neled deep into the island's earth to collect minerals used for medicinal purposes; he had seen them naked because of the heat and able to tolerate the tunnel's unhealthy air for only short periods, and he had heard that on one occasion, a tunnel collapsed, killing numerous slaves. On the other hand, the philosopher Persaeus had been a slave of the famous philosopher Zeno, the founder of Stoicism.

During the last two centuries before the beginning of the Christian era, there was considerable trading in slaves between Cyprus and the islands of Delos and Rhodes farther west. During this period, pirates in the Aegean and eastern Mediterranean dealt in slaves, or pretended to be slave dealers; the Romans gradually wiped out piracy in the first century B.C., but the slave trade remained legal. In A.D. 115–116, the Jews of Cyprus, together with Jews in parts of Roman North Africa, revolted against Rome, and after the revolt was defeated, many were enslaved and sent to Italy.

Slave traders occupied some important political posts in the island's cities under the Roman Empire, but this phenomenon was less pronounced in Cyprus than in other centers of the slave trade such as Rhodes. There were associations of freedmen who, as elsewhere, held minor priesthoods. Under the Christian emperors, slavery continued to exist on Cyprus, as elsewhere in the Roman Empire. Arab invasions in the seventh to the ninth centuries again resulted in the enslavement of much of the population. Under restored Byzantine rule in the tenth century, slavery continued, with many of the slaves engaging in crafts. After 1192, the Lusignan family, of French origin, ruled the island, and under circumstances not fully understood by modern scholars, rural slavery, perhaps under Western European influence, gradually gave way to serfdom. For several centuries thereafter, female slaves were employed as maids. In 1570, the Turks invaded Cyprus and enslaved the captured inhabitants of several cities, but a few years afterward, serfdom was abolished. Until the early nineteenth century, the Turkish rulers of the island kept a few slaves brought from Africa, Circassia, and elsewhere.

—*Stephen A. Stertz*

For Further Reading
Geneva, University of. 1975. *Chypre des origenes au moyen-age: Seminaire interdisciplinaire.* Geneva: Université de Geneve; Hill, G. 1972. *A History of Cyprus.* Cambridge: Cambridge University Press.

C. 27 B.C.–A.D. 14

During the reign of Emperor Augustus Caesar, large numbers of war captives continued to be sold into slavery. When the Salassi, an Alpine tribe, was subdued, the Romans sold 5,000 captives as slaves. Later when the Bessii tribe of Thrace was conquered, the entire tribe was enslaved.

22 B.C.

The Roman emperor Augustus Caesar organized a fire brigade for the city of Rome, and this public service was provided by slaves who were owned by the state.

8 B.C.

The estates (latifundia) that were owned by many Roman patricians were quite extensive. Pliny the Elder mentioned one individual who died leaving behind an estate that contained 4,117 slaves, 7,200 oxen, and 257,000 other animals.

4 B.C.

Possible date of the birth of Jesus Christ.

2 B.C.

The emperor Augustus Caesar formed the Praetorian Guard to serve as the imperial bodyguard. He also proclaimed the Lex Furia Caninia (the Furian Caninian Law, named after P. Furius Camillus and C. Caninius Gallus, two Roman consuls), which restricted the number of slaves that could be freed upon the death of a master. Augustus was concerned that the emancipation of slaves was occurring too rapidly.

A.D. 4

The emperor Augustus Caesar proclaimed the Lex Aelia Sentia (the Aelian Sentian Law, named after Roman consuls Sex. Aelius Catus and C. Sentius Saturninus), which imposed further restrictions upon the manumission of slaves. Roman leaders noted public concern that there was too much alien blood coming into Roman citizenship.

A.D. 9

The emperor Augustus Caesar proclaimed the Lex Papia Poppaea (the Papian Poppaean Law, named for two Roman consuls), which encouraged strictly moral procreation. In 18 B.C., the Lex Julia de Adulteriis Coercendis (Julian Law on the Orders Permitted to Marry) had encour-

aged procreation within the family and had attempted to restrict unions between free persons and slaves.

A.D. 19

The Roman geographer Strabo expanded his *Geography* by incorporating new material acquired during the reign of Tiberius Caesar. Part of the supplementary material included economic data from the Roman province of Britain, as Strabo provided data on the amount of wheat, cattle, gold, silver, iron, brides, slaves, and hunting dogs to be found in Britain.

A.D. 30

Probable date of the crucifixion of Jesus Christ in Jerusalem.

A.D. 40

In *De vita contemplativa* (About the contemplative life), the Hellenistic Jew Philo Judaeus of Alexandria wrote: "Behave well to your slaves, as you pray to God that he should behave toward you. For as we hear them so shall we be heard, and as we treat them, so shall we be treated. Let us show compassion for compassion, so that we may receive like for like in return."

A.D. 41–54

During the reign of Roman emperor Claudius I, an imperial decree prohibited masters from arbitrarily killing sick and aged slaves or turning them out so they would become a social and economic burden to the empire. Claudius's action also freed those slaves who previously had been abandoned by their masters because of age or infirmity. Also during Claudius's reign, two former slaves served with distinction in the administration of the emperor: Narcissus as secretary of state and Pallas as treasurer. Both of these ex-slaves were among the wealthiest men of their time.

C. A.D. 50

The Roman writers Apion and Aulus Gellius told the story of the semilegendary fugitive slave Androclus (Androcles). According to legend, Androclus was spared from death by a lion during one of the Roman spectacles in which captives were fed to the beasts for public entertainment. The legend maintains that Androclus had removed a thorn from the paw of the lion many years earlier in Africa and that the beast would therefore not harm the slave. As a result, Androclus was reportedly emancipated.

A.D. 52

Roman emperor Claudius I proclaimed that any woman who chose to be the concubine of a slave effectively became a slave herself regardless of her prior status.

A.D. 54–68

During the era when Nero was the Roman emperor, an organized slave market existed in the Roman Forum near the Temple of Castor. War captives were brought to the market and sold at public auction.

C. A.D. 55

During Nero's reign (A.D. 54–68), the Spanish-born Roman author Columella wrote his *De re rustica* (On farming, both Cato and Varro had written similar works). Columella mentioned slavery throughout this treatise on agriculture, and his references give an indication of the status of agricultural slaves at the time: some slaves were employed in chain gangs, some were fettered, and others were imprisoned underground. Columella's advice to slaveholders was they should avoid excessive cruelty when disciplining their slaves.

A.D. 56

In Roman society, it was possible for a freed slave to achieve a position of status within society. One Roman senator commented that "most of the knights [a class of Roman businessmen], and many of the Senators, are descendants of slaves" (Meltzer, 1993).

A.D. 61

One of the slaves belonging to the Roman prefect Pedanius Secundus killed his master. The Roman Senate vowed to set an example that such action would not go unpunished in Rome, and thus 400 other slaves belonging to Pedanius were put to death. This type of retributive justice was meant to discourage slaves from rising up against the authority of their masters.

A.D. 64–67

Major public works projects were initiated under the direction of the Roman emperor Nero. A canal was cut from Ostia to Lake Avernus on the Italian peninsula, and an abortive attempt was made to cut a canal across the isthmus of Corinth in Greece. The Roman general Vespasian gave 6,000 war captives to Nero, who used them as slave laborers on these public works projects.

C. A.D. 64

The apostle Peter was in Rome trying to spread the good news of Christianity. In his letters, he addressed the question of slavery and wrote, "Servants, be subject to your masters with all fear; not only to the good and gentle, but also to the froward [harsh]" (1 Pet. 2:18).

C. A.D. 65

Following the mysterious fire that had destroyed Rome one year earlier, Emperor Nero began the first wave of persecutions against Christians in the Roman Empire. Many Christians were enslaved and subjected to the brutal forms of blood sport that had become institutionalized as public entertainment in Rome.

C. A.D. 65

The Roman philosopher Seneca, who had been a tutor and adviser to Emperor Nero, did not approve of the Roman practice of killing slaves as a part of the entertainment in gladiator games. In *Letters* (7.4.1), Seneca wrote of these events: "I come home more greedy, more cruel and inhuman, because I have been among human beings. . . . Man, a sacred thing to man, is killed for sport and merriment." In an essay that he wrote on the nature of anger, Seneca speculated on why slaves might rise up in revolt against their masters and believed that "wooden racks and other instruments of torture, the dungeons and other jails, the fires built around imprisoned bodies in a pit, the hook dragging on the corpses, and many kinds of chains, the varied punishments, the tearing of limbs, the branding of foreheads" were sufficient reason for slaves to revolt (*On Anger*).

A.D. 66–73

A Jewish revolt against Rome occurred when Jewish zealots tried to remove all foreigners from Palestine. Roman legions were sent into Palestine to restore authority, and many of the war captives were sold as slaves by the Romans.

A.D. 69–79

During the reign of the Roman emperor Vespasian, production from the gold mines in Spain was at its peak, an estimated $44 million (modern figures) per year. The mines were operated primarily by slave laborers, and the mortality rate in this enterprise was said to have been extremely high. The vast profits acquired from these mines and the callous disregard for the health and safety of those who worked in them reflect the cheapness of and the utter disregard for the lives of slaves in the Roman world. However, also during Vespasian's reign, an imperial decree prohibited masters from selling slaves into prostitution.

A.D. 71–73

In the aftermath of the Jewish revolt of A.D. 66–73, the Roman emperor Vespasian sold 97,000 Jews into slavery. Some of these Jewish slaves were able to purchase their freedom, and a community of these ex-slaves was eventually established at Cologne (in modern-day Germany).

A.D. 75–80

Under the direction of the Roman emperors Vespasian and Titus, the Roman Colosseum was built. The facility was used for various forms of public entertainment, including gladiator games and the feeding of slave captives to wild beasts. The Colosseum could seat 45,000 individuals, and there was standing room for an additional 5,000 observers. Similar structures were constructed throughout the Roman Empire (with the exception of Greece) so that Roman citizens in the provinces could experience the same types of public entertainment.

A.D. 77

The Roman scientist Pliny the Elder's *Historia naturalis* (Natural history) presented his scientific philosophies, which were based upon observation of the natural world. One of the comments in the work is that Pliny regretted the discovery of iron since that innovation had made warfare more horrid. Since slaves in the ancient world were generally the captives of war, any device that made warfare more likely, or its effects more horrible, would have a direct bearing upon the expansion of slavery.

A.D. 81–88

During the early years of his reign (A.D. 81–96), the Roman emperor Domitian was almost puritanical in his enforcement of the moral laws that had been enacted by his predecessors. He enforced the Lex Julia de Adulteriis Coercendis (Julian Law on the Orders Permitted to Marry), which had encouraged procreation within the family and had attempted to restrict unions between free persons and slaves. Additionally, Domitian also ended the creation of eunuchs, banned the mutilation of slaves, and canceled all tax debts that were more than five years old.

A.D. 95

During the later years of his reign (A.D. 81–96), the Roman emperor Domitian ordered that all philosophers be banned from Italy. One of the philosophers forced into exile was the Stoic philosopher Epictetus, who was a freed Greek slave. Epictetus moved to Epirus in northwestern Greece where he continued to teach. Epictetus, who had been born a slave in Phrygia, was an opponent of slavery. In *The Golden Sayings,* he offered his own version of the Golden Rule, "What you shun to suffer, do not make others suffer."

A.D. 97

Sextus Julius Frontinus was a Roman soldier and historian. He had previously served as the Roman governor of Britain (A.D. 75–78) and had become the superintendent of the water supply for Rome. In his history of Rome, Frontinus stated that it was slaves—240 belonging to the Roman state and 460 belonging to the imperial household—who were responsible for the upkeep of the Roman water supply. These slaves were responsible both for maintaining the 280 miles of channels and aqueducts (most of which were located underground) and for smelting and manufacturing the lead pipes that were used to carry water into the cities and homes.

C. A.D. 98–117

During the reign of the Roman emperor Trajan, the frequency and duration of the gladiator games were increased to satisfy popular demand for the blood sport. One particular game during Trajan's reign reportedly lasted for 117 days and involved matches in which 4,941 pairs of gladiators fought to the death. War captives who had been made into slaves generally were trained to fight as gladiators in the public spectacles, which were sponsored by the Roman government.

C. A.D. 100

An anonymous author from Alexandria in Egypt wrote the *Periplus of the Erythraean Sea*. This navigator's guide to the eastern coast of Africa suggests that slave trading in that region was an active enterprise at the time. The author mentioned that the region produced "the better sort of slaves" who were brought into Egypt on a regular basis.

A.D. 110–113

The Column of Trajan was constructed in Rome to commemorate the emperor's military victory against the Dacians. The depiction of warfare on the column is powerful, and some scenes show slaves and people who are about to become enslaved.

A.D. 115–116

A revolt occurred among the Jews of Cyprus and North Africa. Roman forces were able to quell the uprising, and large numbers of captives were sold into slavery.

A.D. 117–138

The Roman emperor Hadrian used public funds to provide games and gifts to the people of Rome, thus initiating the "bread and circuses" system that later evolved into a Roman welfare state. Additionally, Hadrian canceled all debts for tax arrears and had the tax records burned publicly, thus eliminating the chance that someone might become enslaved for failing to pay a debt to the state. He also abolished the right of slaveholders to kill their slaves (unless by judicial authority) and instituted the recommended policy of *patria potestas in pietate debet, non atrocitate consistere* ("paternal power must consist of love, not cruelty").

A.D. 127

Hadrian's Wall was completed in Roman Britain. The structure was constructed "to divide the barbarians from the Romans" and served, among other purposes, to reduce the likelihood of slave raids on Roman Britain from the north. Occasional slave raids along the coast did occur periodically.

C. A.D. 130–201

The Roman physician Galen wrote many medical treatises that constitute an authoritative view of medical theory and practice in the an-

The Column of Trajan, erected to commemorate a Roman victory over the Dacians. Scenes depict slaves and captives about to be enslaved. (Vittoriano Rastelli/Corbis)

cient world. In some of his writings, Galen mentioned that he often treated patients who had incurred severe bruises while they were disciplining their slaves. He also made many references to the practice of mutilation, which was used to discipline slaves. Galen wrote, "Such are they who punish their slaves for some error by burning, slitting, and maiming the legs of runaways, the hands of thieves, the bellies of gluttons, the tongues of gossipers—in short by punishing each offender on that part of the body by which he has offended" (Meltzer, 1993).

A.D. 130

The Arch of Constantine was constructed in Rome as a military monument to celebrate recent conquests. The monument is unique in that on it, slaves are depicted as being much smaller than those who are free. This artistic representation says much about the perceived social status that existed among the different classes in the Roman world.

A.D. 132

Rabbi Akiba ben Joseph (A.D. c. 40–c. 135) recognized the growing social and economic crisis that had developed in Israel because many of the poor had sold themselves and their children into slavery in payment of debts. Akiba tried to convince the wealthy to consider the poor "a patrician who has lost his possessions; for they are all descendants of Abraham, Isaac, and

The Arch of Constantine in Rome, a monument to Roman conquests. Uniquely, in the relief sculpture on the arch, slaves are depicted as smaller than free people. (Historical Picture Archive/Corbis)

Jacob" (Meltzer, 1993). According to Leviticus 25:42, God had promised Moses after the Exodus that the Hebrews "shall not be sold as bondmen."

A.D. 138–161

The reign of the Roman emperor Antoninus Pius was noted for a high level of humanitarian concern for all inhabitants of the Roman Empire. Antoninus Pius directed all governors and client kings within the empire to punish those masters of slaves who resorted to harsh violence as a means of disciplining their slaves. Under these reforms, a slave could appeal to a municipal judge if he believed that he had been disciplined too harshly, and in certain circumstances, the Roman authorities might require that slaves who had been mistreated be sold to other masters.

A.D. 151

Later discovered by archaeologists, a papyrus document contained a bill of a sale for a slave girl. The document, written in both Latin and Greek stated, "Sambatis, changed to Athenais, or by whatever other name she may be called, by nationality a Phrygian, about twelve years of age . . . in good health as required by ordinance, not subject to any legal charge, neither a wanderer nor a fugitive, free from the sacred disease [epilepsy]" (Meltzer, 1993).

A.D. 161

Roman emperor Marcus Aurelius continued to spend public funds to provide games and gifts to the people of Rome, a policy that had been initiated by his predecessors. Rome continued to maintain the "bread and circuses" system that evolved into an institutional welfare state over the course of several centuries.

A.D. 166

In a meeting of East and West, Chinese records indicate that Roman emperor Marcus Aurelius

⚕TRANSITION FROM SLAVE LABOR
TO FREE LABOR IN THE ANCIENT WORLD⚕

In the Roman Empire, the economy, especially the agricultural economy, was based on slavery. In the early Middle Ages, large agricultural estates in the empire were first worked by landless laborers known as *coloni* (singular *colonus*) and later by serfs who primarily differed from slaves in that they could not be sold apart from the land. Scholars, particularly those influenced by Marxism, have believed that the transition from slavery to free labor toward the end of the ancient world was primarily the result of the barbarian invasions of the Roman Empire. At first, the dislocations caused by the barbarian threat were said to have disrupted markets and the value of slaves. Later, small farmers, seeking security from the invaders, sought the protection of large landowners and gradually declined to the status of totally dependent tenants and eventually into serfdom.

More recent scholarship has characterized the transition as more complicated than previously believed and emphasized the incomplete and problematical nature of the evidence. In the Byzantine Empire, which occupied much of southeastern Europe, slavery continued to be a recognized and ubiquitous institution for 1,000 years, and in some Western European countries, slaves composed as much as 10 percent of the population even in the late Middle Ages—some domestic servants were slaves even as late as the sixteenth century. In fact, large estates worked by large numbers of slaves in the Roman Empire were confined to a few areas, of which central Italy was the largest, and even in those areas, farms worked by free tenants existed in large numbers. There is no evidence of any substantial change in this situation in any period of Roman imperial history.

In Italy in late antiquity, one type of slave was a sharecropper working his own piece of land, the *residens*, apparently the forerunner of the *colonus* while another type of slave, the *manualis*, worked the master's central domain. In the East, there were several types of agricultural slaves, the exact definitions of which have not come down to us although some undoubtedly corresponded to the two Roman types. Much of the evidence is vague and ambiguous, since slavery was not a literary topic and is either referred to in passing in works on other topics or mentioned in business documents with the terms being understood and thus undefined.

Any shift to tenant farming in the age of the barbarian invasions is now believed by scholars to have been very gradual. In many Roman provinces, agricultural laborers were free and paid wages, the same was true of urban unskilled workers, and skilled workers were often self-employed. Not all the barbarian invaders of the Roman Empire were successful. Some were defeated and enslaved, and according to St. Augustine (Letter 10), other slaves were villagers who had been kidnapped by slave dealers.

The earliest laws concerning *coloni,* in the law code compiled by order of Emperor Theodosius in 450 B.C., defined their status as very similar to that of slaves, but later law codes drawn up in the East stated that *coloni* were in full control of their property. The status of rural slaves and free tenants seems to have gradually increased in similarity until the two groups were assimilated together, but this process seems to have been a very slow, gradual one. The collapse of central authority caused by the barbarian invasions, which placed the tenant farmer totally at the mercy of the landlord, was the primary factor in this transformation.

Well before the fall of the Roman Empire, the power of local rich men had supplanted that of the government in many areas. In the early Middle Ages, there was a lease in which the tenant had no rights whatsoever. Details regarding the transformation of the *coloni* into serfdom are lacking owing to a lack of records from the period of anarchic disorder following the barbarian invasions, a period traditionally known as the Dark Ages. Thus, it is impossible to characterize a "slave society" as immediately or even gradually giving way in identifiable stages to a "feudal society." The disappearance of serfdom itself was a much later development, occurring as late as the nineteenth century in some parts of Europe; only in England did it occur as early as the late Middle Ages.

—*Stephen A. Stertz*

For Further Reading
Brockmeyer, Norbert. 1979. *Antike Sklaverei.* Darmstadt: Wissenschaftliche Buchgesellschaft; Finley, Moses I. 1980. *Ancient Slavery and Modern Ideology.* New York: Penguin Books; Whittaker, C. R. 1987. "Circe's Pigs: From Slavery to Serfdom in the Later Roman World." In *Classical Slavery.* Ed. Moses I. Finley. London: Frank Cass.

Slaves attending their owner in a drapers' shop. This bas relief dates from the second century A.D. *(British Museum)*

sent a diplomatic representative to meet with the Chinese at Tongking (Tonkin).

A.D. 167
A plague affected Rome and cities in the eastern part of the Roman Empire. It is believed that the disease (perhaps bubonic plague) was carried into the empire by soldiers who had traveled into Asia.

A.D. 174
During the reign of Emperor Marcus Aurelius (A.D. 161–180), the Romans began to settle captured Germanic "barbarian" peoples on Roman imperial estates. These Germanic agricultural cultivators became known as *coloni*, tenant farmers on the Roman estates, and some were actually slaveholders themselves. Some Roman writers referred to quasi-*coloni*, who were probably slaves on the Roman estates.

C. A.D. 175
The Roman jurist Florentinus wrote of slavery in one of his judicial rulings, saying, "Slavery is an institution of the law common to all peoples by which, in violation of the law of nature, a person is subjected to the mastery of another" (Meltzer, 1993).

A.D. 177
Roman emperor Marcus Aurelius issued an order calling for the punishment of those religious sects that "excite the ill-balanced minds of men." In response to this decree, 47 Christians were killed in an attack at Lyons (in modern-day France); the dead included a slave girl, Blandina, who had become a Christian.

A.D. 181
The Roman emperor Commodus was notorious for his life of debauchery and legendary excesses. It was reported that during his reign (A.D. 180–192) he maintained a harem of 300 women and a separate collection of 300 young boys. The sexual exploitation of women and children was a common aspect of enslavement during this era.

A.D. 185
The former slave Cleander became the leader of the Praetorian Guard and the favorite of the Roman emperor Commodus. Much like Commodus, Cleander was notorious for his corruption.

A.D. 190
When Roman citizens rose up to oppose the corruption of Cleander, the former slave who had become the leader of the Praetorian Guard and a favorite of Roman emperor Commodus, the emperor had Cleander put to death to appease the Roman mobs.

A.D. 193–211
The Roman emperor Lucius Septimius Severus continued the practice of settling captured Germanic "barbarian" peoples on Roman imperial estates. These Germanic agricultural cultivators became known as *coloni*. This practice was replicated by many Roman landowners throughout the Roman Empire, who noted there was a labor shortage because of a scarcity of slaves. Since slaves were commonly the captives of war, the apparent policy of Pax Romana (Roman peace) during this era had the unforeseen consequence of reducing the available number of war captives who could be enslaved.

A.D. 212–216
The Roman emperor Marcus Aurelius Antoninus (called Caracalla) issued the Constitutio Antoniniana (Constitution of Antonius), which extended the rights of Roman citizenship to all free male adults throughout the Roman Empire.

A.D. 217–222
The former slave Calixtus (Callistus) became a Christian and eventually became Pope Calixtus I.

His accession to the office of bishop of Rome (the papacy) demonstrated the levels to which freed slaves could rise in the Roman world.

A.D. 223
The Roman jurist Ulpian was an adviser to Emperor Severus Alexander, who ended the persecution of all Christians in the Roman Empire. In writing upon the subject of slavery, Ulpian said, "As far as Roman law is concerned, slaves are regarded as nothing, but not so in natural law as well: because as far as the law of nature is concerned, all men are equal."

A.D. 239
The elder Roman statesman Timesitheus (Misethueus) served as a counselor to the young emperor Gordian III (his son-in-law) and helped him escape the power and the intrigues of the eunuchs (many of whom were slaves) who dominated the imperial court.

A.D. 271–275
Roman emperor Aurelian had new walls built around Rome and other major cities of the empire. The emperor also tried to stabilize a struggling economy by regulating trade, directing labor within the empire, and fighting rising inflation. Under the economic directives of Aurelian, the Roman state became more regimented.

A.D. 283–284
The first of the so-called Bacaudae insurrections occurred in Gaul as peasants, slaves, and other lower-class elements rose up in rebellion against Roman authority. The rebellion was suppressed by Roman forces under the command of Maximian, who later became co-emperor with Diocletion (293–305).

A.D. 284–305
The Roman emperor Diocletian had been born a slave in Dalmatia in A.D. 245. His skills as a soldier had allowed him to rise through the ranks of the Roman legions, and his accession to the office of emperor demonstrated the levels to which freed slaves could rise in the Roman world.

C. A.D. 285
The Roman emperor Diocletian decreed that slaveholders were prohibited from abandoning infant slaves and allowing them to die from ex-

Slave badge, which instructed the reader to seize the slave and return him or her to the master, served as an arrest warrant for a runaway slave. (British Museum)

posure to the elements. Increasing financial burdens during a time of economic decline had caused large numbers of slaveholders to practice infanticide by abandonment as a means of reducing their household costs.

A.D. 293
Emperor Diocletian created a vast bureaucracy within the Roman Empire and ushered in the beginnings of a managed economy under state socialism. Among the economic reforms that Diocletian instituted was one that took away the freedom of Roman citizens to change their jobs. The emperor also created a new agency of tax police, who used torture to prevent tax evasion within the empire.

A.D. 301
As part of his continuing efforts to stabilize the Roman economy, Emperor Diocletian issued the *Edictum de pretiis* (Edict of prices), which instituted wage and price controls throughout the Roman Empire. These policies were not popular among the Roman citizens, who found ways to work around them.

A.D. 313
The Roman emperor Constantine I (the Great) issued the Edict of Milan, which ended the

The Roman emperor Constantine transformed the town of Byzantium into his eastern capital city in the A.D. 320s. From then until its conquest by the Muslim Ottoman Turkish sultan Mehmed II in 1453, Constantinople was the capital of the eastern Roman, or Byzantine, Empire. After 1453, it was the Ottoman sultan's capital until the dissolution of the Turkish empire after World War I. Located on a narrow strip of water connecting the Black Sea and the Mediterranean, the city controlled all passing trade and served as a market for goods that arrived by overland routes from the Balkans and Anatolia (Turkey). Since slavery was a vital feature of Roman, Byzantine, and Turkish life, this administrative center also served as a central marketplace for slaves in the eastern Mediterranean for almost 1,600 years.

During the Byzantine millennium, the Christian city followed traditional Roman patterns of slave trade and usage, relying primarily on prisoners of war and the children of slaves as laborers. Emperor Leo VI forbade the selling of oneself into slavery, but the effect of the prohibition was short-lived. The trade apparently languished in the eighth and ninth centuries but seems to have picked up in the tenth century, as evidenced in the *Life* of St. Basil the Younger, who mentioned slaves serving in imperial workshops and as assistants to goldsmiths and weavers. Other documents mention Jewish merchants who transported slaves from Turkistan through Constantinople to as far away as Spain and France. Although sources are scanty, it seems that the trade declined again in the eleventh and twelfth centuries. Exchanges of slaves took place in "the valley of lamentations," a fitting name for the slave market for which captives from Slavic Europe and the Black and Caspian Sea regions provided the bulk of supply.

Although the Byzantine use of slaves for other than domestic purposes declined from the eleventh to the thirteenth centuries, trade accelerated when Russian merchants sold their Caucasian and Turco-Tatar slaves in Constantinople to the dominant Venetian and later Genoese merchants who shipped them to Chios, Crete, Sicily, Venice, and Spain as well as to the Mamluks in Egypt. In the 1290s, the Genoese established themselves along the Black Sea itself, but their colony in the Constantinople neighborhood of Pera continued to thrive. Black African slaves appeared sporadically, and Muslim merchants traded in the city in the fourteenth century and again in the 1430s.

Following the Ottoman conquest, Constantinople's population was enslaved, and Italian merchants lost their markets in the Black Sea and much of the eastern Mediterranean. In rebuilding Constantinople, the sultan located the slave market (Esir Pazari) south of the huge bazaar (Bedestan). As the sultan's armies marched, they took huge numbers of captives as slaves: 60,000 from the Greek isthmus and over 200,000 from Serbia in the 1450s and 10,000 from Kiparissia on the Ionian Sea in the 1460s. Many of these captives were bought by merchants (*esirdjis*) who herded them back to Constantinople (now Istanbul) for sale. They augmented the continued flow of Circassian, Caucasian, and Polish slaves from the north and east. Turkish successes in North Africa opened the market for black Africans, and they began to appear in great numbers.

Tax records reveal that in the 1550s, about 25,000 slaves were sold each year in the city, and in the seventeenth century, the average was 20,000. In the mid-1800s, between 11,000 and 13,000 slaves were shipped in from Africa each year with young black women dominating. Young women were often bought by other women who taught them basic domestic skills and resold them at a profit. Other slaves reentered the market through their judicial petition to be resold because of mistreatment.

The sultan himself controlled an increasing number of slaves, including administrators, soldiers, eunuchs, and women of the harem. From around 20,000 in the 1400s, their number grew to nearly 100,000 in 1609. Throughout the Ottoman period, perhaps 20 percent of the city's population was unfree. Domestic service was most common, but slaves also worked in luxury goods production and as business factors and hired laborers.

Beginning in the seventeenth century, the number of young Christians (*devshirme*) who served as soldiers and administrators (*kul*) declined as free Muslims vied for these places. Domestic slavery remained popular, however, and was challenged only in the nineteenth century under pressure from Great Britain to abolish first the slave trade, then the institution of slavery. The period of the Ottoman *Tanzimat* ("reform") from the 1830s to the 1880s saw the closing of the public slave market in 1847, but slaves continued to be exchanged in private houses. The empire's 1909 ban on slavery satisfied the British but did not abolish the practice or the trade, and only after 1926 did the government effectively shut down the slave trade.

—*Joseph P. Byrne*

For Further Reading
Bon, Ottaviano. 1996. *The Sultan's Seraglio.* London: Saqi Books; Frances, E. 1969. "Constantinople Byzantine aux XIVe et Xve siècles. Population-Commerce-Métiers." *Revue des Etudes Sud-Est Européennes* 7: 405–412; Mansel, Philip. 1995. *Constantinople: City of the World's Desire,* 1453–1924. London: John Murray; Toledano, Ehud. 1983. *The Ottoman Slave Trade and Its Suppression.* Princeton: Princeton University Press; Verlinden, Charles. 1963. "Traite des esclaves et traitants italiens à Constantinople (XIIIe–XVe siècles)." *Moyen Age* 69: 791–804.

persecution of Christians in the Roman Empire. According to this declaration, all property that had been seized from Christians was to be restored, and Christianity was declared to be on a par with other religions within the Roman Empire.

A.D. 330

Officials in Rome were concerned about a population decline that was occurring throughout the empire. Contributing factors to this demographic change were infanticide and other efforts to limit the size of families because of economic distress and the large number of eunuchs throughout the empire.

A.D. 341

The Council of Gangra condemned any Roman citizen who, under the pretext of Christianity, taught slaves to resist the authority of their masters or to flee from their life of servitude. Much of this concern had resulted from the rise of the Donatists, members of a North African heretical Christian sect who were known for their proclivity for violence and fanatical self-immolation practices. It was common practice among the Donatists to attack the people who had wealth and privilege in order to benefit the poor.

A.D. 345

Julian and Gallus, the two young sons of the Roman emperor Constans I, were kept isolated as virtual prisoners for their own protection because their father feared for their safety. An aged slave who served as a teacher to the young boys was their only companion during this captivity.

A.D. 362

Christian leaders meeting in council at the Synod of Alexandria denounced as sinful "anyone who under the pretence of godliness should teach a slave to despise his master, or to withdraw himself from his service" (Meltzer, 1993).

C. A.D. 370

In letters addressed to fellow churchmen, Basil the Great, bishop of Caesarea, advocated social justice for the poor and the oppressed, and he urged masters to use kindness toward their slaves. Although Basil recognized the social inequalities of his time, he argued that there was a greater spiritual force that united all men despite any secular divisions.

A.D. 377

Roman emperor Valentinian I issued an imperial decree stating that those slaves who were held as quasi-*coloni* could not be sold separate from the land they cultivated. This decree shows the gradual transformation from slavery to serfdom that was beginning to occur in the later centuries of the Roman Empire.

C. A.D. 380

According to the historian Gregory of Nyssa, during religious festivals of the early fourth century in Rome it was common for Christians to manumit deserving slaves.

A.D. 380

The Roman emperor Theodosius I (the Great) was baptized a Christian. During his reign (A.D. 379–395), Christianity became the official religion of the Roman Empire.

A.D. 387

Libanius of Antioch delivered an oration *On Slavery* in which he depicted slavery as an ordinary aspect of life in the Roman Empire and speculated that all individuals, in one respect or another, could consider themselves slaves to some type of occupation or controlling force in their lives.

A.D. 395–405

Roman-occupied Britain was attacked along the western coast from Strathclyde southward to Wales by pirate bands of marauding Scots (as

At or after the middle of A.D. 387, Libanius (314–c. 392) of Antioch in Syria, one of the most famous orators of his time, wrote and probably delivered orally an oration, *On Slavery*. Although, in accordance with the rhetorical conventions of the time, the theme of the oration was each man's "slavery" to his passions as well as the professional orator's "slavery" to the demands of his work, the work gives us information that is unavailable elsewhere about agricultural slavery in the eastern part of the later Roman Empire.

According to Libanius, there were numerous types of slaves, some of whom were, in effect, sharecroppers tending their own pieces of land while others tended only or primarily their master's land, and there were several types of slaves (or serfs), the definitions of which are not now exactly known. Mention of these social classes is also made in Libanius's Oration 47, *On the Protection Rackets,* which he delivered a few years after *On Slavery*. In neither oration, nor anywhere else in the extensive writings of Libanius, is slavery depicted as anything but a fully accepted part of life. Slave markets are spoken of as normal parts of life, and elsewhere (Oration 66) Libanius complained that his poor students could afford only two or three slaves who, being too small a household, were insolent.

In the oration *On Slavery,* people in a large number of occupations are successively characterized as slaves of the more-onerous aspects of their work and sometimes compared with particular kinds of slaves. Thus, teachers are slaves of their students as well as their students' parents and grandparents. When teachers travel, they are slaves of doorkeepers and the city gates and innkeepers. *Curiales,* certain part-time local officials who had to contribute out of their own pockets to the public expense and who were given that duty against their will, as was Libanius himself, were slaves, not only of the city magistrates but even of their lowly assistants, who had to be flattered. Some of the people to whom everyone in various occupations was "enslaved" were actually slaves themselves. Everyone with hands and a tongue was, in fact, a slave. Libanius strongly implied that he himself, a professional orator and a *curialis,* was subject to the most onerous form of slavery.

On Slavery was not intended to be taken literally or even, in some respects, very seriously. Libanius's message was merely that life is hard. As was customary, the orator was straining for effects; he was trying to impress his hearers more with the form than with the content of his words, using clever variations on old and well-known rhetorical conventions like a musician performing improvisations.
—*Stephen A. Stertz*

For Further Reading
Festugière, A. J. 1959. *Antioche paienne et chretienne: Libanius, Chrysostome, et les moines de Syrie.* Paris: E. de Boccard; Petit, Paul. 1955. *Libanius et la vie municipale à Antioche au IVe siècle après J.C.* Paris: Paul Geuthner.

they were called) from Ireland. Thousands of British slaves were carried off during these raids, including a young Briton named Patricius, the son of a Roman official living along the Severn estuary. Patricius later escaped from slavery but returned to Ireland as the missionary (Saint Patrick) who carried Christianity to the people of Ireland.

A.D. 407–417
The second of the so-called Bacaudae insurrections occurred in Gaul as peasants, slaves, and other lower-class elements rose up in rebellion against Roman authority. The rebellion was suppressed by the Roman forces of Flavius Honorius, the emperor of the West.

A.D. 409–410
Alaric, the king of the Visigoths, besieged the city of Rome during the reign of the Western emperor Honorius, and the Romans were unable to placate him with bribes of gold, which had worked twice in the past. The situation was grave, and many Romans nearly starved. A large number of barbarian slaves escaped to Alaric's lines and joined the Visigoth forces. In August of 410, King Alaric and the Visigoths were able to enter Rome when a slave opened the gates to the city, which allowed the Germanic "barbarians" to enter. Since Alaric was an Arian Christian, a sect that had been outlawed in the Roman Empire in 379, he did not allow the churches of the city to be destroyed, but the rest of the city was sacked by the Visigoths.

A.D. 411
The Donatists, members of a North African heretical Christian sect, were known for their

proclivity for violence and fanatical self-immolation practices. Members of the sect formed a group called the circumcellions (or prowlers) and began to steal from the wealthy in North Africa in order to benefit those who were in need. St. Augustine of Hippo was one of the biggest opponents of the Donatist cause. In his *Epistles* (185), Augustine questioned, "What master was there who was not compelled to live in dread of his own slaves, if the slave had put himself under the protection of the Donatists?"

C. A.D. *412*

St. Augustine of Hippo wrote *De civitate Dei* (The city of God) sometime after this date. In the work, St. Augustine maintained that slavery was something that "has been imposed by the just sentence of God upon the sinner."

A.D. *476*

Traditional date for the fall of the Roman Empire in the West. Emperor Romulus Augustulus resigned his position, and the Germanic commander Odoacer became the king of Italy.

~Europe~

*All ambitions are lawful except those that climb upward
on the miseries or credulities of mankind.*
—Joseph Conrad, *A Personal Record* (1912)

Europe's place in the story of world slavery looms large as the competing attributes of enslaver/oppressor and abolitionist/emancipator can be used to characterize the people who first established and later abolished the transatlantic slave trade. Notions of virtue and vice appear in this chronology as Europeans struggled with the issue of slavery throughout the centuries and eventually formulated a philosophical basis upon which to challenge an institution that had long been condoned socially and appreciated economically. The modern abolitionist tradition that developed in this setting challenged long-held beliefs of Western thought and heralded the demise of transatlantic slavery.

Western traditions originated among the classical civilizations of ancient Greece and Rome, and those slave-based societies certainly influenced the manner in which later generations of Western Europeans viewed the status of the individual in society. Even after the Mediterranean-based cultures had been influenced by northern Germanic peoples, the social ideology that endorsed enslavement as a proper sanction for war captives, debtors, or the socially dispossessed did not abate. Although European peoples struggled for centuries to establish political hegemony in the form of nation-states, their concept of the social hierarchy gelled more quickly. The position of slave, and that of serf, remained an integral part of the social and economic structure of Western European society into the late feudal era.

Shortly after the notion of enslaving fellow Europeans fell out of disfavor (around the eleventh century), the practice of enslaving Muslims who were captured in battle found ready acceptance by the largely Christian population of Western Europe. The notion of a *just war* was used to excuse such a practice, and this policy was also later applied to the capture of African peoples when European sailors encountered them on fifteenth-century voyages. After the discovery of the Americas, the indigenous populations of that region suffered the same fate. The tragedy of this policy, and its repercussions, still haunt the memory of modern peoples.

To their credit, European philosophers were the first to challenge the basic assumptions upon which the slave economy rested, and Enlightenment thinkers fomented the movement that turned words into deeds. The moral crusade against slavery that was led by William Wilberforce and Thomas Clarkson inspired the beginning of an abolitionist movement in North America and in parts of Latin America as well. By the late-nineteenth century, the transatlantic slave system had been broken, but such success did not mean that slavery had ended.

European nations used their desire to end the indigenous practices of slavery that existed within Africa as a high moral pretense when they launched a renewed era of colonization during the late-nineteenth century. Although the results of this crusading zeal did eliminate enslavement practices in some areas, the type of bonded labor practices that often arose in other regions seemed to counterbalance the effects of this missionary activism. Again, the disparity between virtue and vice found expression as the upward climb of misery caused many people to question the merits of such policies.

This section of the chronology traces the history of a people who were of two minds concerning the issue of slavery. The European dilemma teaches us much about the depths of human depravity and also about the amazing power of human redemption.

━━━━◆━━━━

527–532

The Justinian Code (Corpus Juris Civilis) was prepared by Byzantine jurists at the direction of Emperor Justinian I. Slavery was recognized in the code as a condition that arose from "the law of the nations" *(Iuris Gentium)* rather than being a feature of natural law. In the code, a slave was viewed as property and not as an individual capable of possessing rights.

570

Muhammad, the Prophet of Islam, was born in Arabia.

582

Leaders of the Roman Catholic Church gathered at the First Council of Macen, called by Pope Pelagius II, and issued a statement that no Christian should be obligated to remain a slave.

591

In his *Pastoral Rule,* Pope Gregory I (the Great) echoed the earlier writings of Saint Paul when he urged slaves to recognize their lower status and to obey their masters.

595

In a deed of manumission that freed two Roman slaves, Pope Gregory I (the Great) declared that no heathen who wished to become a Christian should continue to be held as a slave.

c. 610

Isidore, bishop of Seville, wrote extensive histories of Visigothic Spain. In his writings, Isidore criticized people who abused slaves and urged slaveowners to consider manumission of their captives. Isidore did not question the feudal foundation upon which Visigothic society was based, but he did view the ownership of slaves as commodities to be unacceptable and contrary to God's will. Isidore wrote: "Because of the sin of the first man the punishment of slavery was divinely imposed on the human race, so that He might inflict slavery more mercifully on those who He perceived are not suited to liberty. Although original sin was remitted for all the faithful by the grace of baptism, yet God in His justice has so ordered the lives of men, establishing some as slaves, others as masters, that the power of slaves to do evil is restrained by the power of those who rule them. For if all were without any fear, who could restrain anyone from evil?" *(Historiae Gothorum* [History of the Goths]*).

622

The Hegira occurred as Muhammad, the Prophet of Islam, fled Mecca and traveled to Medina in Arabia.

711

North African Moors crossed the Strait of Gibraltar and began the Muslim conquest of Visigothic Spain.

726

Byzantine Emperors Leo III and Constantine V issued the *Ecloga,* a body of laws intended to supplement the Justinian Code (Corpus Juris Civilis). The *Ecloga* provided clear instructions on how and why a slave might be manumitted. The revisions to the code reflect the growing influence of the Orthodox Church in Byzantine life.

732

In October, Charles Martel and a Frankish force halted the advance of the Saracen Muslims (North African Moors) into Western Europe at the Battle of Tours. A very slow process of gradual reconquest now began in Western Europe and continued until Muslim occupation of the Iberian Peninsula finally ended with the fall of Granada in 1492.

798

The Byzantine monastic leader Theodore of Studius urged his fellow monks to avoid the use

⦿THEODORE OF STUDIUS (759–826)⦿

Theodore of Studius, or Studium, as his name is sometimes transliterated, was a major Byzantine monastic leader and reformer canonized by the Greek church after his death. Born into a family of wealthy government officials, he became a monk in 780, and in 794, he became head of the monastery of Sakkoudion, in Bithynia (modern Turkey). In about 798, he became head of the important monastery of Studius in Constantinople. He actively participated in civil disputes and was exiled several times. In his extensive works and in his political activity, Theodore emphasized the independence of the monasteries from the emperor and the government, and he stressed monastic reform, emphasizing hard labor and moral courage.

Like a number of other Byzantine religious figures (for example, Gregory of Nazianzus and Eustathius of Thessalonica), Theodore strongly opposed slavery, especially in monasteries. In his rules for the reform of monasteries expressed in a letter to one Abbot Nicholas, he stated: "Do not obtain any slave nor use in your private service or in that of the monastery over which you preside, or in the fields, man who was made in the image of God. For such an indulgence is only for those who live in the world" (Herzog du Sachsen, 1929). Theodore went on to say that the abbot should himself be like a servant to the other monks, even if in outward appearance he is thought to be master and teacher.

Immediately afterward, Theodore forbade the use of female animals in monasteries since the monks had renounced the female sex, a practice still followed in the great monastic center at Mount Athos in Greece. Thus, the context is one of monastic austerity and also of reform, since Byzantine monasteries are known to have had slaves, especially agricultural slaves. Since such practices continued long after Eustathius's time in the twelfth century, Theodore's reforms were not completely successful.

Opposition to slavery per se does not characterize Theodore's writing. He seems to have regarded it, as did St. Basil (c. 330–379), the founder of Byzantine monasticism, whom Theodore greatly admired, as an unavoidable evil in the secular world but a luxury forbidden to monks, who must be humble and therefore should not have slaves to order around doing the manual, especially agricultural, labor that the monks themselves should be doing. Although Theodore had received the best available classical and philosophical education, his arguments respecting slavery, like those of other Byzantine religious figures, are based entirely on Christian theology.

—*Stephen A. Stertz*

For Further Reading
Herzog du Sachsen, Max. 1929. *Der heilige Theodor, Archimandrit von Studion.* Munich: Georg Muller; Schneider, G. A. 1900. *Der Hl. Theodor von Studion.* Münster: Heinrich Schoningh.

---

of slave laborers within the monasteries. In a letter to a fellow monk, Theodore argued that "such an indulgence is only for those who live in the world" (Herzog zu Sachsen, 1929).

800
Pope Leo III crowned Charlemagne the king of the West.

826–829
Census figures from the community of Villemeux (near Chartres) in France indicate that 10 percent of the heads of households in the region were identified as *servi* ("slaves").

862
Varangian princes began to govern the region of Kievan Rūs, and a brisk slave trade began between Kiev and Constantinople along the route of the Dnieper River and the Black Sea. On their way to the Constantinople slave market, these Slavic captives served as porters who carried other commodities to markets.

862
The arrival of African slaves was recorded in the *Annals of Ireland.* The "blue men," as they were called, had been captured during Viking raids on Spain and North Africa.

870
The Vikings (Norsemen) raided Alt Clut (modern-day Dumbarton) in Scotland and took most of the inhabitants into captivity. Many of these captives were sold as slaves the following year in other European cities.

913
The bishop of Armagh in Ireland intervened to ransom a Welsh slave who was being held captive in the Irish province of Munster.

950

Slavery began to disappear gradually on the Italian peninsula, and the process was completed by 1000. Within the following century, however, the institution of serfdom would arise in its place.

972

Death of the Varangian prince Sviatoslav of Kievan Rūs who had invaded the territory of the Danube Bulgarians. Prince Sviatoslav was quoted by chroniclers as saying: "I want to live in Pereiaslavets for here is the center of my dominions, and here are gathered together all kinds of merchandise. From the Greeks come gold, textiles, wines, and fruits; from the Czechs and Hungarians come silver and horses; and from Russia come furs, wax and honey, and slaves" (Meltzer, 1993).

988–989

Christianity was established in the area of Kievan Rūs. Prior to this period—in the pagan era—society was divided among the free and the slaves. The free were called *muzhi* ("men") and had rights within the state, but slaves were called *cheliad* ("menials") and had no rights. Slaves were treated like work animals, and their masters had the right to punish them to death.

997

In France, serfs and peasants revolted against feudal masters in a series of uprisings in the region of Normandy.

C. 1000

The Vikings (Norsemen) established the port of Dublin as a base of operations for attacks on England, Scotland, and the European coast. The Norse invaders captured many of the indigenous Celts in the region of Dublin and sold them into slavery.

C. 1000

Slavery began to disappear gradually in Catalonia, a process that was completed by 1035. Within the following century, however, the institution of serfdom would arise in place of slavery.

1016–1030

Grand Prince Iaroslav Vladimirovich developed a law code, the *Russkaia Pravda* (Russian truth)

for Kievan Rūs. Three of the 18 sections in the code outline the rights of slaveowners with respect to disciplining their slaves. The right of slaveowners to recapture fugitive slaves was also protected in the code.

1086

In England, King William I (the Conqueror) ordered government officials to collect statistical data that would identify the wealth of the realm. This census of people and property resulted in the document known as the *Domesday Book*. The records show that there were male slaves *(servi)* and female slaves *(ancillae)* in England at the time, but the patterns of ownership indicate that the use of slave labor had been declining since the Norman Conquest (1066).

1087

The Church of St. Gwynllyw in Wales was plundered during a slave-raiding expedition conducted by the Vikings (Norsemen).

1095

Pope Urban II issued the call for the First Crusade, calling upon the Christian knights of Europe to recapture the Holy Land from the Muslims who occupied the region.

1098

Vikings (Norsemen) hired as mercenaries by a Welsh prince attempted to conduct a slave-raiding expedition on the Anglo-Welsh border.

1145

The German historian Otto of Freising first wrote of the legendary Prester John, a Nestorian king who was said to be a descendant of the Magi and who ruled a large kingdom beyond Persia. During the age of exploration, European navigators would search for the legendary Christian king in Africa.

1159

The English clergyman John of Salisbury completed work on his *Policratius*. In the work, which was addressed to Thomas à Becket, John attempted to define the status of the individual classes that made up the society of Latin Christendom. John saw slavery and serfdom as legitimate institutions through which God curbed the excesses of human vice.

~EUSTATHIUS OF THESSALONICA (c. 1115–1195/6)~

Eustathius, who was born and died in Thessalonica (Thessaloníki), became archbishop of that city, the second most important city of the Byzantine Empire, in 1174. Although Eustathius is best known as a scholar and commentator on ancient texts, he wrote a number of sermons and treatises and was an important political figure. His attempts to reform monastic life, noted in his sermons, were like others in earlier years unsuccessful but included emphases on manual labor, which Eustathius glorified, and opposition to the use of slave labor, which he thought unnatural to do the agricultural work of the monasteries. Slavery, according to Eustathius, was contrary to nature and evil; therefore, slaves should be liberated, especially by monks, as manual labor had been enjoined on freemen by God in the time of Adam. Eustathius used sarcasm and irony in support of these and other arguments, seeing the monks' use of slave labor as an example of the sin of sloth.

Centuries earlier, Gregory of Nazianzus had expressed opposition to slavery, although it remained an established institution throughout the Byzantine Empire's 10 centuries of existence. Large agricultural estates owned by temples had existed in Asia Minor since long before the coming of Christianity, and the tradition seems to have continued when monasteries took the place of temples. Arguably, the practice was not so widespread in the European part of the empire, where Eustathius was active. Al-

though Eustathius had the best available classical and philosophical education, his arguments against slavery are based primarily on Christian beliefs.

Eustathius also referred to slavery in his history of the Norman invasion of Thessalonica in 185. There are references to royalty disguising themselves as slaves and to people being enslaved by the invaders, the atrocious behavior of whom is described in detail. Here, slavery is associated with hated, barbaric foreigners, as it is alien to Greek civilization, and the theme of historical progress from barbarism to civilization found elsewhere in Eustathius's writings is echoed at least by implication. It would, however, be anachronistic to characterize Eustathius as an advocate of the outright abolition of slavery since he merely characterized it as evil and unnatural, not a new idea; favored individual emancipation of slaves; and opposed slave labor for monasteries. Several passages in his writings imply that slavery is an accepted, if deplorable, institution: he apparently never suggested to the Byzantine emperor Manuel I Comnenus, of whom he was a not uncritical supporter, that something radical be done about slavery.

—*Stephen A. Stertz*

For Further Reading
Hunger, Herbert. 1955. *Die Normannen in Thessalonike*. Graz, Aus.: Verlag Styria; Wirth, Peter. 1980. *Eustathiana*. Amsterdam: Adolf M. Hakkert.

1165

The French historian Alberic of Trois Fontaines claimed that a letter from the legendary Christian king Prester John had appeared in Europe.

1174

The Byzantine monastic leader Eustathius of Thessalonica (Thessaloníki) urged his fellow monks to avoid the use of slave laborers within the monasteries.

1181

Pope Alexander III issued a bull that proclaimed the emancipation of all slaves.

1212

Thousands of French boys who had gathered together to participate in the Children's Crusade were instead boarded onto ships by slave traders and sold as slaves in Egypt.

1215

On June 15, English nobles forced King John to sign the Magna Carta. In addition to stating that the king was not above the law, this historic document also guaranteed citizens a trial by a jury of one's peers and protection against loss of life, liberty, or property except in accordance with the law.

1224

The English government of King Henry III declared as official a policy that could be used for the recovery of fugitive serfs within the kingdom.

1229

King James I of Aragon reconquered the island of Majorca from Muslim control, and all inhabitants who resisted Christian domination were sold into slavery.

Nineteenth-century woodcut depicting the launching of the Children's Crusade. Many of the would-be crusaders were tricked into boarding slave ships bound for Egypt. (Dover Pictorial Archives)

1256

The Dominican monk and scholastic theologian Thomas Aquinas began to teach at the University of Paris. He later wrote *Summa theologica* (Summary of theology) the most systematic exposition of his scholastic theological beliefs.

1263–1265

The Castilian monarch Alfonso X was responsible for the collection of the law code Las Siete Partidas (Seven-Part Code). In this code, slavery was recognized as an institution that was based upon the custom among nations rather than upon natural law.

1271–1292

The Venetian merchant Marco Polo lived in Cathay (China) where he was employed in the service of the Chinese ruler Kublai Khan.

1282

The Germanic king Rudolf I ruled that the condition of children who are born of unions between free peasants and the unfree shall follow the condition of the lower-status parent.

1287

King Alfonso III of Aragon enslaved the entire Muslim population of the island of Minorca even though the island's inhabitants had surrendered to Christian control 60 years earlier.

1314

Rulers in Sweden freed all slaves still held within the province, but the number of individuals affected by the proclamation seems to have been quite small.

1337

The beginning of the Hundred Years War between England and France—a war that would not end until 1453. One of the effects of this extended conflict was that neither England nor France was able to become involved in the age of exploration and discovery that was inaugurated by the Portuguese navigators.

1344

Pope Clement VI issued a bull that awarded the Canary Islands to Castile over the objections of the Portuguese.

1348–1349

The Black Death, the bubonic plague, ravaged Western Europe, and one-third of the population perished.

1358

In France, serfs and peasants revolted against their feudal masters in a series of uprisings known collectively as the *Jacquerie*.

1381

In England, the rebellion of serfs and peasants against their feudal masters was known as the Peasants' Revolt.

1388

In Catalonia, serfs and peasants began a series of uprisings against their feudal masters that lasted sporadically until 1486.

1415

A military operation organized by Prince Henry of Portugal captured the city of Ceuta (in modern-day Morocco). This event marked the beginning of the European exploration and conquest of the African coast.

1416

The Chinese slave eunuch Admiral Zheng He (Cheng Ho) sailed to the coast of East Africa on an expedition of discovery. In China, it was possible for royal eunuchs (slaves) to hold positions of power and influence within the governmental bureaucracy.

1434

On December 17, Pope Eugene IV issued the bull Creator Omnium, which excommunicated anyone who tried to enslave natives from the Canary Islands who had converted to Christianity.

1437

Reports indicate that peoples from East Africa were being traded as slaves in western India.

1441–1442

Portuguese merchants carried 10 captives from West Africa to Portugal where they were traded as slaves.

1442

On December 19, Pope Eugene IV issued the bull Illius Qui, in which he proclaimed that the

A scholastic theologian of the Middle Ages and doctor of the Roman Catholic Church, Thomas Aquinas was born into nobility at Roccasecca in the Kingdom of Naples and was sent at an early age to study with the Benedictines at the ancient abbey of Monte Casino. In 1244, he entered the Order of Preachers (the Dominicans) and subsequently studied at Cologne and Paris. In 1256, he received his licence to teach and commenced his remarkable career as a master of theology at the University of Paris. Sent by his order to found a school of theology at Naples in 1272, Aquinas died two years later while en route to the Council of Lyons. Despite some controversy regarding several propositions Aquinas had defended during his lifetime, he was eventually canonized by the Catholic Church in 1323. Even today, his influence continues to be considerable among certain academic philosophers and theologians.

It may be said that Aquinas had a certain ambivalence toward the institution of slavery *(servitus)*, partly because he had inherited two rival and incompatible traditions: that of Aristotle, who taught that some human beings are slaves by nature, and that of the fathers of the church and the medieval canonists, who held that all humans are naturally equal and that the existence of slavery was a punishment for sin. In attempting to reconcile the two traditions, Aquinas can be seen to take a compromise position.

According to Aquinas, the existence of slavery—by which he meant the dominance of one person over another so that the latter does not exist for himself *(causa sui)*, as does a freeman, but is geared to the benefit or purposes of another—is a direct result of the Fall. Since freedom is an inherent good, an absence of freedom must be the consequence of sin. Therefore, slavery could not have existed in the state of innocence: humanity's natural, prelapsarian state. However, that should not be taken to mean that no form of dominance of some persons over others would not have existed in the state of innocence, for since man is a social animal, it follows that at least some people must have had authority over the majority in order to direct the community to the end of life, in other words, to the common good. Furthermore, even in the prelapsarian state there would have existed, according to Aquinas, differences in natural ability: some people would have been wiser or more righteous than others, and it would have been wrong if such people had not employed their talents in the service of others.

Because slavery would not have existed in the state of innocence, it is tempting to conclude that Aquinas did not believe it to be natural. That is not so, for even though Aquinas regarded slavery as belonging to the positive law *(jus gentium)* because slavery is punitive, he nonetheless regarded the positive law as being founded on natural law *(jus naturale)*. In other words, Aquinas was anxious not to depart too widely from Aristotle, arguing that slavery is natural according to the "second intention" of nature, that is, that part of the natural law that is applicable to fallen humanity.

This notion of "intentions" marks a distinction between the ideal and the actual. Thus, in the ideal state, the first intention of nature is that all men should be equal. But in the actual state of humanity, the second intention of nature is that since man has in reality fallen from grace, he should be punished for his sins. Slavery is a consequence of the second intention of nature and only "natural" in the sense that while not strictly speaking a part of the natural law, neither is it a violation of the natural law but something "superadded" to it. This distinction may also be regarded as roughly equivalent to the distinction between natural law and positive law, the latter making specific what the former, because framed in general terms, leaves unspecified. In this way, Aquinas reconciled his position with both of the traditions he inherited, patristic and Aristotelian, and thus remained true to his predecessors.

On a more practical level, Aquinas believed that the power of a master over a slave is not absolute but qualified to the extent that the relationship ought to be one of mutual advantage: the master acting in a paternalistic fashion over the one who is seen to be incapable of taking care of himself because he is naturally inferior. Moreover, the master's power is limited in that the slave has the rights of marriage, personal life, and the means of subsistence, areas in which the master may not interfere since it is enjoined by the first intention of the natural law that all persons be allowed to preserve themselves and procreate. As Aquinas put it, while the master is superior in matters superadded to nature, in natural things—by which he meant sleeping, eating, and reproduction—all people are equal. Lastly, since the relationship of master to slave exists for mutual benefit, Aquinas argued that there is no reason, apart from individual inferiority, why one man should be under bondage rather than another. It is only when looked at case by case, as it were, that it becomes expedient for one person to become subject to another. Aquinas thus implicitly ruled out the possibility of there existing an institution of slavery based on race or religion.

—Peter Eardley

For Further Reading
Foster, Kenelm. 1959. *The Life of St. Thomas Aquinas: Biographical Documents.* London: Longmans, Green, Helicon Press; and Taylor, Alfred E. 1924. *St. Thomas Aquinas as a Philosopher.* London: Macmillan.

act of enslaving Africans had the blessing of a crusade and that all who perished in the enterprise would have full remission of sin. With this declaration, the African slave trade fell within the limits of a "just war" that could be waged with papal blessing.

1445

A large slave auction was held at Lagos, Portugal, in which African captives were sold to the highest bidder. One contemporary chronicler described the event as "a terrible scene of misery and disorder" (Meltzer, 1993).

1447

As a result of the African slave trade, there were 900 slaves in Portugal.

C. 1450

In England, the government of King Henry VI decreed that Gypsies (Roma) who escaped from servitude could legally be branded with a "V" on their breast and enslaved for two years when recaptured. The punishment for a second similar offense was to be branded with an "S" and enslaved for life.

1452

On June 18, Pope Nicholas V issued the bull Dum Diversas, which he addressed to King Alfonso V of Portugal. This edict gave the Portuguese the right to attack pagans and other enemies of Christ wherever they might be found. The bull also allowed the Portuguese to enslave people who were taken as captives in such a "just war."

1453

The Ottoman Turks captured the city of Constantinople (Istanbul) and established the Ottoman Empire. Slavery was practiced within the empire until the abolition of slavery in 1857, and even then, some practices persisted until the empire dissolved in 1918.

1455

On January 8, Pope Nicholas V issued the bull Romanus Pontifex, which granted the Portuguese a commercial monopoly in the newly discovered areas of West Africa. Hoping that the inhabitants of these regions might be converted to Christianity, the pope extended to the Portuguese the right to subdue and convert the inhabitants of Africa.

1456

Pope Calixtus III reconfirmed the earlier declarations of Dum Diversas (1452) and Romanus Pontifex (1455) granting special trading privileges to the Portuguese crown.

1460–1474

In India, the sultan of Bengal, Rukn ud Din Barbak Shah, purchased 8,000 African slaves in this period. Many of these captives served in his army, and some attained positions of prominence.

1462

Pope Pius II issued a bull in which he declared the Roman Catholic Church's opposition to the slave trade. The pope's primary concern was that prisoners captured during European wars should not be enslaved by the victorious powers.

1473

An exchange of ambassadors took place between the government of Portugal and Emperor Mamoud of the Mandingo people in West Africa.

1474

A historical account by Ortiz de Zuniga noted that large numbers of African slaves resided in Lisbon, Portugal. The Portuguese government generated revenue for the royal treasury by imposing a duty upon the purchase of slaves. At the same time, large numbers of African slaves lived in Seville, Spain, and King Ferdinand and

Sir William Walworth, Lord Mayor of London, kills Wat Tyler, leader of the Peasants' Revolt, as King Richard II looks on. (The Granger Collection)

Queen Isabella nominated an African named Juan de Valladolid (El Conde Negro) to be the mayor of Africans living there.

1479

On September 4, Spain and Portugal signed the Treaty of Alcaçovas to end the Castilian Civil War (1474–1479). Ferdinand of Aragon and Isabella of Castile recognized the Portuguese crown's monopoly on trade "from the Canary Islands down toward Guinea." The government of Portugal recognized the right of the Spanish to possess the Canary Islands.

1481

On June 21, Pope Sixtus IV issued the bull Æterni Regis, which approved of the agreements made in the Treaty of Alçacovas signed some two years earlier. The pope divided the known world into northern and southern

realms and gave the northern realm to the Spanish and the southern to the Portuguese.

1486

In a rebellion in India, African slaves killed the sultan of Bengal and imposed the leader of the rebellion as the new sultan. Many of the rebels were later punished by being exiled to the Deccan region of the Indian subcontinent.

1488

The king of Portugal presented Pope Innocent VII with a gift of 100 African slaves captured among the Moro people.

1493

On May 4, Pope Alexander VI issued the papal bull Inter Caetera, which created a line of demarcation that separated all newly discovered lands between the Spanish and the Portuguese.

The Portuguese crown was given hegemony in developing trade and building colonial outposts in lands east of the line, including Africa; the Spanish crown received the same rights in lands west of the line, which included practically all of North and South America. Since Spain was barred from direct commercial activity with Africa, the Portuguese were the middlemen who first conducted the transatlantic slave trade and carried Africans to the Americas where they were sold in the Spanish colonies as slaves. [See Document 9.]

1493

On September 26, Pope Alexander VI issued the papal bull Dudum Siquidem, which gave the Spanish crown the right to occupy heathen lands of Asia that were reached by Spanish navigators. The papal bull allowed the Spanish to "take corporal possession of the said islands and countries and to hold them forever." [See Document 10.]

1494

Spain and Portugal signed the Treaty of Tordesillas, which revised the papal line of demarcation by moving it slightly west. This treaty had the effect of making Africa a commercial sphere of the Portuguese, and Portuguese sailors would come to dominate the African slave trade.

1496

The English king Henry VII refused to acknowledge the legality of the Treaty of Tordesillas and authorized an official expedition by the navigator John Cabot (Giovanni Caboto) to seek new lands for the English people.

1497

The Sudebnik of 1497, which was a part of the Muscovite law code (in the region that corresponds to modern-day Russia), limited the movement of indebted peasants to a two-week period around St. George's Day in November. Eventually, indebted peasants were made into serfs who had no freedom of movement.

1498

Spanish explorers in the Americas shipped 200 Carib Indians to Spain where they were sold into slavery. The Carib were considered to be cannibals.

1499

Moors in Granada revolted because the Spanish inquisitor-general, Francisco Jiménez de Cisneros, tried to force religious conversion to Christianity upon the Muslim Moors.

1500

Scottish historical accounts show that several Africans served the Scottish court. These Africans were probably introduced to Scotland by the Portuguese.

1503

On May 3, Pope Alexander VI issued two bulls directed to the government of Ferdinand of Aragon and Isabella of Castile. The first edict gave the Spanish the right to attack pagans and other enemies of Christ wherever they might be found and allowed the Spanish to enslave people taken as captives in such a "just war." The second edict granted the Spanish a commercial monopoly in the areas that they discovered.

1512

On December 27, the Spanish crown enacted the Laws of Burgos in response to protests from Dominican friars who claimed that the indigenous peoples of the Americas had been mistreated. These guidelines gave some additional protection to the indigenous peoples, but they could still be legally enslaved by the Spanish. In 1510 the Spanish crown had also instituted the practice of reading "the Requirement" in order to justify enslaving captives who were taken as the result of a "just war." [See Document 11.]

1513

Ships carrying 565 African slaves from the Guinea coast arrived in Portugal.

1514

When the population of African slaves in Spain reached 25 percent of the nation's inhabitants, King Ferdinand restricted further importation of African slaves into Spain. It was the king's belief that additional imports would threaten the national security of Spain.

1515

Ships carrying 1,423 African slaves from the Guinea coast arrived in Portugal.

Throughout the history of slavery, one constant was the impact of religion on the institution of human bondage. Europe's advance into the New World brought colonialism, slavery, and imperialism under the guise of Christianity, which according to Sipe Mzimela, was nothing more than variations of European culture, specifically German (Lutheranism), English (Anglicanism and Methodism), Scottish (Presbyterianism), French, Belgian, and Portuguese (Catholicism). European or Western religions operated differently from other religions, such as Islam, with respect to slavery. One difference between the involvement of Christians and Muslims in African slavery was that Islam mandated that people read the Qur'an while European missionaries felt that teaching Africans to read was problematic. Christian missionaries preached that all men are equal in the eyes of God but ridiculed Africans and forced them to accept slavery as part of the Christian concept of suffering and because of their failure in racial terms.

From the earliest days of the slave trade, churches and religious views regarding the capture and enslavement of Africans and other nonwhite peoples were dominant. The decree of Pope Alexander VI in 1493, which meant that almost all of the Americas were to be ruled by Spain, basically established that it was appropriate for Europeans to use nonwhites in the name of God. Eventually, the enslavement of human beings was such a way of life in the New World that religious institutions had a vested interest in converting non-Europeans to Christianity. Bartolomé de Las Casas, the apostle of the Indies, argued that African slaves were needed in Hispaniola because the Spanish colonists had killed many of the indigenous people by working them to death.

Missionaries taught Africans that it was the will and desire of God for them to suffer oppression, discrimination, and exploitation, and the scope of the evangelic effort was evident by the number of missions remaining in Africa after colonialism. For instance, in the Congo, there were 669 Catholic missions alone, and history is replete with accounts of missionaries from various denominations and countries actively implementing national policy objectives under the guise of religion. The Portuguese built a fortress on Arguin, an island off the coast of Mauritania, to hold slaves who were taken from the mainland purportedly as part of an effort to gain Christian converts. In 1663, Frenchmen representing the Lazarist missionaries tried to convert one of the rulers of Madagascar to Christianity, but the attempt eventually resulted in the loss of Fort Dauphin and the death of a missionary. But the policy was continued in 1664 when the French government encouraged mixed marriages—but only if the wife were baptized and had accepted the Christian faith.

In many ways, the church, through its clergy and as an institution, supported and encouraged the very onset of the European slave trade. Churches also encouraged the attitude that Africans were heathens without knowledge of a supreme being. A Christian understanding of slavery involved absolute obedience and submission, which both the clergy and the slave masters tried to instill. Some clergy even claimed to be possessed by the Holy Ghost, as was the case with one Father Vernaud, a Swiss. Others, like Juan Ginés de Sepulveda, suggested that some people were inferior and needed the protection of slavery under the direction of gentle Christians. This position was based on the dialectics of Aristotle and matched the Puritans' view of Africans as people more likely to be controlled if they accepted the Christian way.

The religious attitude concerning slavery in the colonies was no less overwhelming. Given that many expeditions were set forth by the Dutch, Portuguese, French, and English, it is not unexpected that, collectively, these white explorers became associated with other philosophical perspectives. Some scholars have suggested that in colonial America, the terms *Christian, European, free,* and *white* were synonymous. Laws in many cases supported this idea and continued to justify slavery since many were based on biblical laws. Puritan slave codes in New England were modifications of an Old Testament version of slavery, and in other colonies, acts such as a Maryland statute passed in 1649 stated all rights of the colony's Christians with the exception of slaves, and in 1667, the Virginia House of Burgesses said that baptism did not remove the condition of slavery. There was heavy Quaker involvement in the slave trade—William Penn owned slaves who had been transported to the colonies on a Quaker ship called *Society*—and Puritans were also intimately involved in the institution of slavery for profit. The Puritans' western Caribbean activities are best represented by New Providence Island, which was well known for the pirating of illegal cargo in the form of slaves. Frank Tannenbaum (1946) noted that 1,000 slaves were sold from two haciendas owned by religious institutions and that the Convent of St. Theresa owned a ranch that had more than 30 slaves.

Some people may have expected that the church, as a bastion of religious humility, would speak out against the violence of perpetuating human bondage and degradation, but the fact is that it did not because the labor of African slaves resulted in commercial, industrial, and financial wealth from which many religions collected proceeds. This is not to say that, over the centuries, churches did not actively speak out against the institution. Popes Pius II, Paul III, and Urban VIII, among others, condemned the practice between 1462 and 1639, and eventually, many religious institutions saw and could no longer ignore how brutal and inhumane slavery was. Many of these institutions began to stand alongside the slave in support of abolition and antislavery, but it was too late since many people had already become wealthy from the trade and still had the blood of those they considered savage and inferior on their hands.

—*Torrance T. Stephens*

For Further Reading
Hanke, Lewis. 1949. *The Spanish Struggle for Justice in the Conquest of America.* Philadelphia: University of Pennsylvania Press; Mzimela, Sipe E. 1988. *Whither South Africa: A Manifesto for Change.* New York: Martin Luther King Fellow Press; Tannenbaum, Frank. 1946. *Slave and Citizen.* Boston: Beacon Press.

1517

Martin Luther began the Protestant Reformation in Europe by posting his 95 theses on the cathedral door in Wittenberg (in modern-day Germany).

1518

Pope Leo X granted special permission to Portuguese bishops to baptize any indigenous peoples of Africa or the Americas who had the educational and moral standards that would make them good candidates for the priesthood.

1518

Emperor Charles V of Spain established the system of the *asiento* and thus legalized the slave trade to the Spanish colonies in the Americas. In any one year, according to the terms of this contract, no more than 4,000 Africans were to be transported as slaves to the Americas (the number increased later).

1518

The Spanish-born explorer and chronicler Leo Africanus (al-Hasan ibn Muhammad al-Wazzān al-Zaiyātī) had visited Africa before he was captured by pirates while traveling on the Mediterranean. The pirates were impressed with his knowledge of Africa, and they presented him as a gift to Pope Leo X. The pope emancipated the captured Moor and bestowed the name "Leo" upon him.

1526

The Spanish government issued the Real Cedula (Royal Decree), which prohibited the introduction of *Negros ladinos* into the Spanish colonies in the Americas (*Negros ladinos* were Africans who had lived for at least two years on the Iberian Peninsula).

1537

Pope Paul III issued a bull in which he declared the Roman Catholic Church's opposition to the slave trade. The pope's primary concern was that prisoners captured during European wars should not be enslaved by the victorious powers.

1538

The Spanish government decreed that Gypsies (Roma) who attempted to escape servitude could legally be enslaved for life when captured.

1539

The Spanish scholar Francisco de Vitoria presented a series of lectures in Spain in which he argued that the indigenous peoples of the Americas were freemen who should be exempt from slavery.

1547

Juan Gines de Sepulveda published *Democrates alter* in which he argued that the Spanish crown had the legal and moral right to conquer and subdue the indigenous peoples of the Americas. Sepulveda's argument ran counter to the ideas put forth by the Dominican friar Bartolomé de Las Casas, who argued that the Spanish were attempting to destroy the indigenous peoples by enslaving them.

1549

On February 22, the Spanish king Charles I (Holy Roman Emperor Charles V) issued a

Pope Leo X, who emancipated the Spanish-born chronicler Leo Africanus, enslaved by Mediterranean pirates in 1518. The explorer later wrote an influential report for the pope about his visit to several West African states and empires in 1507. (Corbis-Bettmann)

proclamation that prohibited the personal servitude of Indians to those Spanish colonists who held *encomienda* (special rights and privileges) rights in the American colonies. [See Document 12.]

1550

The report that Leo Africanus presented to Pope Leo X was published *(History and Description of Africa),* which gave many Europeans their first opportunity to learn more about the continent of Africa and its peoples. The Spanish-born explorer and chronicler had visited the Songhai Empire, the Empire of Mali, and the Hausa States in West Africa in 1507.

1562

The Englishman John Hawkins carried 300 slaves from West Africa to Hispaniola, and because of the profit potential of this trade, he inspired the English government to pursue the possibility of further involvement in this enterprise. England's Queen Elizabeth I later allowed Hawkins to include the image of a bound African in his family coat of arms.

1562

The French writer Etienne de La Boétie published *Discourse on Voluntary Servitude (Discours de la servitude volontaire)* in which he addressed the problems caused by slave ownership. In Part 1, La Boétie wrote: "Where did he get so many eyes to spy on you with, if you didn't lend them to him? How did he come by so many hands to beat you with, if he didn't take them from you? The feet with which he tramples on your cities—where did he get them from, if they're not yours? How can he have any power over you except by your own doing? What could he do to you if you didn't protect the thief who robs you, if you weren't the accomplice of the murderer who kills you, if you weren't traitors to your own cause?" (translation by Harry Kurz, 1975).

1563

The English Parliament enacted the Statute of Artificers. This measure made all English citizens eligible to serve as apprentices, and masters were forced to accept them and put them to work. The measure was enacted to reduce a nationwide unemployment problem by putting the idle to work.

1568

Spanish King Philip II ordered the enslavement of the Morisco minority when Muslims in Granada rebelled against Spanish rule. The Moriscos were sold into slavery in parts of Castile.

1571

The French government of King Charles IX decreed that "all persons are free in this kingdom; as soon as a slave has reached these frontiers and becomes baptized, he is free" (Meltzer, 1993)

1571

Galley slaves were used by both the Spanish Christians and the Ottoman Muslims in the Battle of Lepanto. Many of the Christians who served as galley slaves in the Muslim vessels were able to turn against their masters and assist the Spanish in the battle. At the end of the battle, 15,000 Christian slaves were freed.

1573
The African-born scholar Juan Latino published the historical poem *Austuriad*, which was written to commemorate the Spanish victory in the Battle of Lepanto (1571).

1575
Tatars conducted a massive slave raid in which they captured 35,000 Ukrainians. The captives were taken to the slave markets in Constantinople (Istanbul) and Kaffa (Feodosiya) and were sold there to buyers from Arabia, India, Persia, Syria, and Turkey.

1576
In his work *Six Books of the Commonwealth*, the French jurist Jean Bodin noted: "As for the cruelty visited upon the slaves, however, what we read is incredible: and what would we say if what we read were only the thousandth part of what actually occurred? For the authors to keep their silence on this subject unless the occasion to speak presents itself. Slaves were made to work the earth in chains, as they still do in Barbary, and to sleep in ditches from which the ladders were withdrawn lest they run away, or set the house afire, or kill the masters" (Book 1, chapter 5).

1588
The defeat of the Spanish Armada marked the beginning of England's rise as a major maritime and colonial power.

1592
The Russian czar Ivan IV decreed that indebted peasants in Russia were no longer free to move about during the St. George's Day holiday in November as they had been since 1497. Additionally, the Russian government attempted to register all inhabitants; in time, the indebted peasants were made into serfs.

1596
Queen Elizabeth I sought to have all blacks deported from England as the nation faced a severe economic crisis. The queen also considered Africans to be "infidels, having no understanding of Christ or his Gospel" (Meltzer, 1993).

A sixteenth-century Morisco. (Art Reference Bureau)

1596
The Dutch East India Company began to gain a dominant role in parts of the Indonesian archipelago and to introduce forced labor there.

1602
The Netherlands established the Dutch East India Company to conduct trade between Asia and the Netherlands. The company eventually established a colonial outpost at the Cape of Good Hope, and the Cape Colony became a way station for the trade between Asia and Europe.

1604
William Shakespeare wrote *Othello*. The play was remarkable in that the main character was an African Moor who was depicted as a general in the Venetian army. Additionally, Othello was married to the beautiful Desdemona, a white woman.

1606

In Russia, a major uprising of peasants and serfs was led by Ivan Bolotnikov during "the time of troubles." The insurrection was caused by rising economic distress as agricultural productivity was stagnating during an era in which one's obligations to the landlord and the state were increasing. The Russian government was able to suppress the uprising.

1607

The French government of King Henry IV reconfirmed a 1571 decree which stated that all people in the kingdom were free, including any slave who had reached the frontier and was baptized.

1611

The Spanish king Philip III dedicated a new shrine at the church in Palermo to house the remains of Benedict the Black (d. 1589). Pope Benedict XIV later beatified Benedict the Black, the protector of Palermo and the patron saint of African slaves, and Pope Pius VII canonized him in 1807.

1615

Michalonis Litvani (Michael of Lithuania) published *De moribus Tartarorum fragmina*, which provided a vivid historical account of the Crimean slave trade.

1618

The Company of Royal Adventurers of London established Fort James at Bathurst, Gambia. King James I granted exclusive monopoly rights to this company to explore opportunities for engaging in the African slave trade. The English had limited involvement with the African slave trade during the seventeenth century, but this situation changed during the eighteenth. In the same year, another monopoly charter was granted to Sir Robert Rich to create a company that would trade along the Guinean coast of West Africa.

1621

The Dutch West India Company was formed, a corporation that would be much involved in establishing colonial outposts and in conducting the transatlantic slave trade. Willem Usselinx and other Dutch merchants chartered this corporation to organize trade and to encourage further colonization efforts by the Netherlands in the New World. The Dutch West India Company received a trading monopoly in its charter and soon established the colony of New Netherlands (New York) as the headquarters for its colonial enterprises. [See Document 13.]

1625

Dutch jurist and diplomat Hugo Grotius wrote *De jure belli ac pacis* (Rights of war and peace) in which he categorized 160 types of incomplete slavery. He defined slavery by stating, "That is complete slavery which owes lifelong service in return for nourishment and other necessaries of life; and if the condition is accepted within natural limits it contains no element of undue severity" (Book 3).

1627

In a daring slave-raiding expedition, four Algerian vessels attacked several coastal communities of Iceland and carried some 380 Icelanders into slavery in North Africa.

1634

The Russian czar Michael Romanov issued a royal proclamation declaring that fugitive peasants (and slaves) had to be returned if captured in order to complete their terms of service. [See Document 14.]

1637

The Huguenot synod in France announced that slavery was not condemned by the laws of God.

1639

Pope Urban VIII issued a papal encyclical to the Apostolic Chamber of Portugal (Cámara Apostólica de Portugal) in which he excommunicated all Roman Catholics who continued to engage in the African slave trade. Following a tradition that had been established by his predecessor Pius II in 1462, Urban VIII declared the slave trade to be a crime, and he criticized people who dared to enslave the Africans. One of the pope's primary concerns was that prisoners captured during European wars should not be enslaved by victorious powers.

1648

George Fox founded the Society of Friends (Quakers) in England. This religious denomination was the earliest group to state its opposition to the slave trade and to slavery itself. Many of the early abolitionists in England and in North America were members of the Society of Friends.

1649
The English Parliament incorporated the Society for Propagating the Gospel in New England. Established by John Eliot, this missionary effort had had success in converting Native Americans, and Eliot now expanded the society's efforts into educating blacks and converting them to Christianity.

1649
In Russia, the Ulozhenie of 1649 effectively bound peasants to the land and thus created a class of serfs.

1651
In passing the English Navigation Act, Parliament attempted to stem the commercial influence of the Dutch West India Company in England's North American colonies by limiting the colonial slave trade to English merchants only. England later fought two colonial wars with the Netherlands in an effort to win winning greater concessions in the African slave trade.

1652
The Netherlands granted the Dutch West India Company specific permission to import African slaves into the colony of New Netherlands. Colonial laws prohibited the mistreatment of slaves, and whippings were not allowed without specific permission from the colonial authorities.

1654
The civil code established by Vasile (Basil the Wolf) of Moldavia defined the status of Gypsies (Roma) as that of slaves.

1663
On July 27, the English Parliament approved the second Navigation Act which provided that most imports were to be carried to the colonies on English vessels. Some imports, including servants, were not bound by this act. At the time, the English were not yet actively involved in the African slave trade.

1664
The French government of King Louis XIV chartered the French West Indies Company (Compagnie des Indes Occidentales). French Finance Minister Jean-Baptiste Colbert urged the creation of this enterprise to advance the development of colonies that would support a mercantilist economy for France.

1664
The English Puritan Richard Baxter published his *Christian Directory* in which he described the African slave trade as "one of the worst kinds of thievery in the world." Baxter maintained that it was sinful to purchase slaves unless you intended to free them, and he called slave traders "common enemies of mankind" (Baxter, 1990).

1665
The Dutch cartographer Jan Blaeu produced the map "Africa novae descriptio" (New description of Africa), which incorporated much of the knowledge of the African interior that could be drawn from the travel writings of Leo Africanus.

1667
The English Parliament passed the Act to Regulate the Negroes on the British Plantations, and in it, persons of African descent were described as possessing a "wild, barbarous and savage nature, to be controlled only with strict severity."

1670
In Russia, a major uprising of the peasants and serfs, led by Stenka Razin, was caused by rising economic distress as agricultural productivity stagnated during an era in which one's obligations to the landlord and the state were increasing. The Russian government was able to suppress the uprising.

Stenka (Stepan) Razin, leader of an ultimately unsuccessful revolt of Russian serfs and peasants. (Austrian Archives/Corbis)

1672

The English Parliament passed enabling legislation that chartered the Royal African Company and granted it a monopoly in conducting the English slave trade between Africa and the Americas. The English were eager to acquire profits from the slave trade, which previously had enriched other rival European powers. The Royal African Company held an exclusive monopoly status until 1698 when Parliament opened the slave trade to all English subjects.

1676

Tatars conducted a massive slave raid in which they captured 40,000 Ukranians. The Ukranian captives were taken to the slave markets in Constantinople (Istanbul) and Kaffa (Feodosiya) for sale to buyers from Arabia, India, Persia, Syria, and Turkey.

1677

The Dutch philosopher Benedictus (Baruch) de Spinoza's work *Ethics* was published posthumously. In this work Spinoza speculated that "if men were born free, they would, so long as they remained free, form no conception of good or evil" (Proposition 68 in Part 4).

1682

The Dutch East India Company acquired a trading monopoly in the islands of the East Indies.

1684

Pope Innocent XI attempted to diminish the worst characteristics of the African slave trade, but his efforts had little real effect. At the pope's direction, the Holy Office and the General Congregation of Propaganda Fide issued decisions designed to lessen the brutal effects of the trade. The African Lorenzo de Silva e Mendoza, the procurator-general of a religious association, deserved much of the credit for these initiatives. Unfortunately, neither the English nor the Dutch, who dominated the slave trade at this time, were obligated to enforce any papal decrees.

1685

The French government enacted the Code Noir (Black Code) in all of its colonial settlements. This code required religious instruction for slaves, permitted intermarriage, and outlawed the working of slaves on Sundays and holidays. It also forbade the liberation of mulatto children when they reached the age of 21 if their mothers were still enslaved.

1688

Tatars conducted a massive slave raid in which they captured 60,000 Ukrainians; they were taken to the slave markets in Constantinople (Istanbul) and Kaffa (Feodosiya) and sold to buyers from Arabia, India, Persia, Syria, and Turkey.

1689

The English political philosopher John Locke published his *Second Treatise on Civil Government* in which he condemned the institution and practice of slavery. Locke maintained that to be a slave was to become "subject to the inconstant, uncertain, unknown, arbitrary will of another" ("Of Slavery" in second treatise), which, he argued, was unlawful because one could not voluntarily surrender one's right to self-preservation to another.

1698

The Royal African Company lost its monopoly status for conducting the English slave trade between Africa and the Americas. As a result, participation in the African slave trade was opened to all English subjects, and many New Englanders became involved in extensive slave trading as they realized the potential lucrative profits of the enterprise. Parliament considered the slave trade to be "highly beneficial and advantageous to this kingdom and to the Plantations and Colonies" (Meltzer, 1993). Private traders could enter into the enterprise once they paid a 10 percent duty to the Royal African Company for the maintenance of the West African forts and factories. It is from this date onward that the so-called triangular trade developed as slaves, sugar and molasses, and rum became the dominant trade goods exchanged between Africa, the West Indies, and the colonies of English North America.

1699

The Portuguese government received 3,000 pounds of gold that had been extracted from the colony in Brazil.

1700

In August, *The Blessing* sailed from Liverpool, England, to West Africa to participate in the

❧ BENEDICTUS DE SPINOZA (1632–1677) ❧

Benedictus (Baruch) de Spinoza was born in Amsterdam in 1632, the son of Jewish Marrano immigrants fleeing from the Inquisition in Spain and Portugal. He is generally regarded as one of the most important philosophers in the Western tradition. Although Spinoza had no particular philosophy regarding slavery, his importance lies in the difficulties his philosophy presents when applied to issues of this sort. His ethical thought has a long legacy as an intense object of controversy, widely criticized on the grounds that it renders blatantly corrupt actions and institutions impervious to principled philosophical criticism.

The root of Spinoza's ethical philosophy is his doctrine of necessitarianism, which posits that not only is every action and event determined by prior, external causes but that the causal nexus itself operates as it does, and is what it is, *necessarily*. In the realm of psychology, this doctrine amounts to a denial of free will, for it denies that an agent could have not performed an action that he or she in fact *did* perform. Since social and political institutions are just products of human action, and since human action flows necessarily from an eternal causal nexus, our social and political history is *necessarily* the history we in fact have—it could not be other than it is. Thus, any claim that a certain existing practice (such as slavery) *ought not exist* is metaphysically meaningless if it presupposes that it is possible that it *not* exist.

Spinoza's thesis of necessitarianism is as much a theological principle as it is metaphysical. As Spinoza states: "In nature there is nothing contingent, but all things have been determined from the necessity of the divine nature to act and produce an effect in a certain way" (*Ethics,* 1.29). The causal determination of every action and event, then, issues from nothing short of God himself.

To be sure, Spinoza believed in what is usually referred to as "substance monism," the doctrine that there is only one substance in the universe, and without a change in meaning it can be called either God or nature *(Deus sive natura)*. Everything that exists in the natural world (including social and political institutions), then, is a mode of divine existence. That idea implies that the traditional theological arguments against institutions of human bondage—arguments to the effect that such institutions contradict divine law or will—are without foundation, for it means there is no possibility of placing a wedge between existence and divine will to show that a feature of the former is in contradiction to the latter. If a practice exists, no matter how apparently immoral or evil, it is *by the very fact of its*

existence theologically justified. Should this concept make us uneasy, Spinoza asks us to view these institutions *sub specie aeternitatis* ("in the context of eternity"), in which case we can see that these institutions must have existed when they did. If we fail to achieve this vision, it is for Spinoza merely an indication of the limits of human understanding.

According to Spinoza, this argument implies that right is coextensive with power (his version of the might-is-right thesis). God is the supreme power and thus has a right to do whatever he has the power to do. But (1) if God has the right to do whatever he has the power to do and (2) if whatever occurs in nature is just a manifestation of divine power, then *whatever* occurs in nature must occur *with right*. There are thus no transcendental ethical standards by which practices and institutions can be judged unjust, for the very fact that a practice has the power to exist entails that it exists with right.

Although Spinoza's philosophy offers no necessary or absolute reason why institutions such as slavery ought not exist, it should be pointed out that he did believe there is a perfectly simple empirical argument against institutions of this sort. Spinoza was interested in the descriptive question of how states maintain their power. A sovereign (the form of rule Spinoza was interested in) rules with right only to the extent that he has the power to rule. A successful sovereign, then, will take measures to ensure the stability of his power to rule. This criterion of stability reveals practices such as slavery to be politically self-defeating: violent rule foments violent rebellion. The most rational state will guarantee the basic personal freedoms of those ruled in constitutional arrangements, if for no other reason than they protect the state from insurrection by promoting the willing obedience of its subjects. For Spinoza, only if we treat the problem of slavery (and of blatantly corrupt institutions in general) as a practical question can we offer an adequate statement of its undesirability, for philosophy can say nothing more against it than that it frustrates the underlying goal of any form of rule, the preservation of its power.

—*John C. Gibson*

For Further Reading
Shahan, Robert W., and J. I. Biro, eds. 1978. *Spinoza: New Perspectives*. Norman: University of Oklahoma Press; Spinoza, Baruch. 1982. *The Ethics, and Selected Letters*. Ed. and trans. Samuel Shirley. Indianapolis, IN: Hackett; Spinoza, Baruch. 1958. *Political Works*. Ed. A. G. Wernham. Oxford: Clarendon Press.

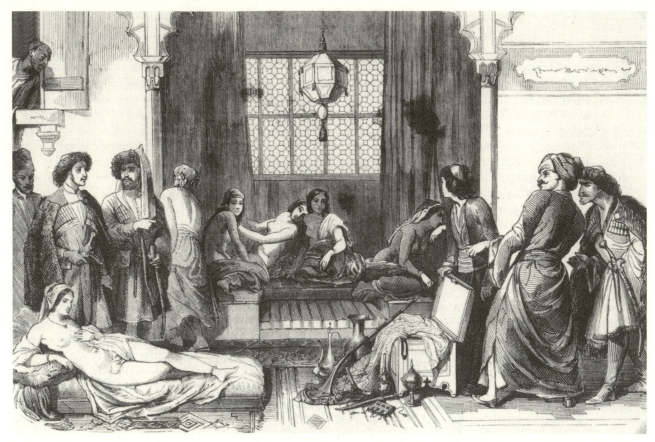

Scene from a Constantinople slave market dealing in Circassian women, 1849. (Corbis-Bettmann)

African slave trade. This was the first vessel from Liverpool to participate in the enterprise, but in time, Liverpool became one of the most active ports in Europe involved in the slave trade.

1701
The Society for the Propagation of the Gospel in Foreign Parts was established as the missionary arm of the Anglican Church.

1701–1714
The French government established the French Guinea Company (French Royal Senegal Company) to provide slaves to the Spanish colonies during the War of the Spanish Succession (Queen Anne's War). During these years, the French held the *asiento* ("contract") and were charged with delivering 38,000 slaves per year to the Spanish colonies in the Americas. [See Document 17.]

1704
English merchants became increasingly involved in the African slave trade during the War of the

Spanish Succession (Queen Anne's War) of 1701–1714. William Snelgrave, an English merchant who was actively involved in the slave trade, witnessed an abortive uprising during one voyage on which slaves were being taken from Africa to the Americas. Such an event was one of the hazards frequently associated with the lucrative slave trade. [See Document 19.]

1706
The Russian czar Peter I (the Great) purchased an African slave at Constantinople and took him back to the Russian court where he was raised. The slave, Abram Petrovich Hannibal, had been a prince in Abyssinia (Ethiopia), and he reached positions of prominence at the Russian court and in the Russian army.

1711
The English South Sea Company received the right to transport Africans to the Americas where they could be sold as slaves.

1713
On March 26, during the negotiation of the

SOCIETY FOR THE PROPAGATION OF THE GOSPEL IN FOREIGN PARTS

The Society for the Propagation of the Gospel in Foreign Parts (SPG) was formed in London in 1701 as a missionary arm of the Church of England. It was established on the request of the Reverend Dr. Thomas Bray, who had become concerned about the spiritual welfare of English subjects in the North American colonies during a six-month stay in Maryland. Between 1702 and 1785, the society sent missionaries, catechists, and teachers as well as Bibles, Common Prayer Books, and official church publications to the Western Hemisphere.

Although the SPG's main focus was the "pastoral care of Europeans" (Wood, 1990), it did not take long for Anglican missionaries to take notice of Native Americans and enslaved Africans. Their efforts to convert these uncivilized heathens began with Native Americans, but few ministers were able to endure the harsh life of the frontier. After unsuccessful attempts, therefore, the SPG missionaries focused their efforts on educating enslaved Africans and improving their living conditions.

Although the SPG was able to accomplish its goals of education and improved living conditions in some cases, the missionaries were never successful in converting non-Europeans to Christianity. First, not only did the number of ministers never exceed a dozen at any one time, but the physical conditions of the colonies, such as long-distance travel and poor weather, made any meaningful contact with Native Americans and slaves extremely difficult. Second, the SPG was not well received by the Puritans in New England, who were fearful of the established church and did everything to prevent SPG ministers from having contact with Africans and Native Americans. In the southern colonies, on the other hand, the SPG met the opposition of slaveowners, who seldom permitted conversion of slaves. Since the SPG depended on the financial contributions of affluent planters, the missionaries made it a priority to maintain a good relationship with the planters, and, moreover, some ministers even became slaveowners themselves. Also, the missionaries in the southern areas had to operate under colonial legislation that guaranteed that baptism would not change the status of slaves. Consequently, the missionaries preoccupied themselves with the salvation of Africans, not their emancipation, by assuring them that baptism promised freedom in the next world, not the present one.

The SPG missionaries' view of slavery reflected that of the Church of England, which formalized a no-emancipation policy in 1727 prior to other Protestant denominations. This view, in turn, reflected British imperialism in the eighteenth century and the white supremacist attitudes that Africans did not deserve humane treatment because they lacked history and culture and that slavery was the only way to save them. Thus, SPG missionaries not only justified slavery by proclaiming that Christianity was completely compatible with the enslavement of Africans but also cultivated the racist culture in the American colonies. Their activities ensured black bondage and set the basis for the proslavery argument of the nineteenth century.

—*Yasue Kuwahara*

For Further Reading
Bellot, Leland J. 1971. "Evangelicals and the Defense of Slavery in Britain's Old Colonial Empire." *Journal of Southern History* 37(1): 19–40; Lincoln, C. Eric. 1984. *Race, Religion, and the Continuing American Dilemma*. New York: Hill and Wang; Wood, Forest G. 1990. *The Arrogance of Faith: Christianity and Race in America from the Colonial Era to the Twentieth Century*. Boston: Northeastern University Press; Wood, Peter H. 1974. *Black Majority: Negroes in Colonial South Carolina from 1670 through the Stono Rebellion*. New York: Knopf.

Treaty of Utrecht, which ended the War of the Spanish Succession (Queen Anne's War) of 1701–1714, the British South Sea Company received the *asiento*, a contract that permitted the South Sea Company to carry 4,800 slaves per year to the Spanish colonies in the Americas for a period of 30 years (144,000 total). Additionally, the British were allowed to send one merchant ship per year to the Spanish colonies for trading purposes.

1716

On September 16, the Portuguese government decreed that any black who set foot on Portuguese soil would be considered free (the policy did not apply to the Portuguese colony of Brazil).

1717

All African slave-trading operations maintained by the government of Brandenburg-Prussia were sold to the Netherlands.

1720

The Portuguese crown issued an order ordering all colonial administrators to have no involvement with the African slave trade.

1721

In Russia, the government of Czar Peter I (the Great) prohibited the sale of slaves unless they were sold as complete families.

1722

In Russia, Czar Peter I imposed the Table of Ranks, which created a form of virtual "slavery" or involuntary servitude as Russian noblemen were obligated to perform compulsory state service during certain times of the year.

1723

In Russia, Czar Peter I transferred the status of all slaves who remained in Russia to the status of serfs.

1729

Attorney General Sir Philip Yorke and Solicitor General Charles Talbot issued what became known as the Yorke-Talbot decision in Britain, which declared that neither entering Great Britain nor accepting Christian baptism made a slave free. This policy was reversed in 1772.

1734

The emancipated slave Ayuba Suleiman Diallo (Job en Solomon) was presented to the royal court of King George II of Great Britain. A British philanthropist named Thomas Bluett had rescued Ayuba from a Maryland tobacco plantation, educated him, and eventually repatriated him to Africa.

1741

Pope Benedict XIV issued a bull in which he declared the Roman Catholic Church's opposition to the slave trade as it was practiced in Brazil. As had been the case with many of his predecessors, one of the pope's primary concerns was that prisoners captured during European wars should not be enslaved by the victorious powers.

1742

Jacobus Eliza Johannes Capitein published several proslavery essays in Holland that defended slavery as a social institution and argued that slavery itself was not contrary to Christian beliefs. Capitein had been educated in the Netherlands by a Dutch merchant after having been kidnapped as a child from the coast of West Africa.

1743

Pope Benedict XIV beatified Benedict the Black, the protector of Palermo and the patron saint of African slaves. Pope Pius VII later canonized him.

1744

Fifty percent of the trade at Liverpool, England, involved ships that participated in the African slave trade.

1748

The French political philosopher Charles Louis de Secondat, baron de la Brède et de Montesquieu, published *The Spirit of the Laws*. Montesquieu was critical of slavery in this work, writing, "The state of slavery is bad of its own nature: it is neither useful to the master nor the slave" (Vol. 10, chapter 1).

1752

The British Parliament chartered the Company of Merchants Trading to Africa. When Parliament had ended the Royal African Company's monopoly on the African slave trade in 1698, it had opened the enterprise to other English corporations (syndicates) that were willing to pay a set duty in order to participate in the trade. In this year, a modification allowed private individuals to engage in the slave trade provided they paid the duty to the Royal African Company (or its successors) for the maintenance of the West African forts and factories. The net result was that more people became involved in the African slave trade, and the business became more notorious at the same time that increased calls to end the trade were heard in many British colonies.

1752

The Scottish-born political philosopher David Hume, who saw a connection between demographics and slavery, published *Political Discourses* in which he argued that the high costs of maintaining a slave society were the primary

❧DAVID HUME (1711–1776)❧

The Scottish-born Enlightenment philosopher, historian, and man of letters David Hume spent his life writing on philosophical, moral, political, and literary questions. Although nowhere in his philosophy is slavery a focal point, Hume's comments on domestic slavery in the ancient world and in modern Europe have had a profound influence on subsequent philosophical and practical debates about slavery and freedom. Hume's position is somewhat paradoxical: while he proved himself staunchly prejudiced against the Negro, he was also vehemently opposed to the slave system. In fact, some historians believe that Hume's antislavery arguments anticipated the reasoning of the growing abolition movement in Britain and colonial America.

Hume's status as a moral, economic, and political philosopher made his a prominent voice in the complicated dialogue of the Enlightenment. His emphasis on personal liberty and self-determination led him to advocate small-scale, direct-representation democracies confederated into a democratic commonwealth that could cooperate in the mutual defense of the local bodies. He found that a great disparity of wealth among the populace hindered equable democracy but doubted that the powerful wealth of some and the disenfranchising poverty of others could be avoided in a free economy without invasive governmental interference in the freedom of the citizens. Thus, parts of his political philosophy were used in the American Revolution, parts were used to oppose the practice of slavery, and parts were used to support the local autonomy and loose confederation of the Confederate South.

Hume published his most important commentary on slavery, "Of the Populousness of Ancient Nations," in a volume of essays entitled *Political Discourses* (1752). This essay responded to writers like Isaac Vos (1618–1689) and Charles Louis Montesquieu (1689–1755) and the clergyman Robert Wallace (1697–1771), who claimed that the ancient world had been more populous than modern Europe. Hume pointed out that the chief difference between the ancient and modern economic systems was the presence of slaves, and to disprove the popular belief that the ancient world was more populous, Hume pointed to the detrimental effects of the ancient slave system.

Hume not only exposed the deleterious moral impact of the ancient system of slavery but also argued that the slave system did not lend itself to fecundity among the slaves, nor to population growth in general. Rather, Hume insisted that the cost of rearing a slave in a city was too high to be profitable and pointed out that the Romans had imported adult slaves to replenish their slave populations. In addition, Hume quoted from numerous classical texts to refute the prevailing notion that slaves were highly fertile and bred often. Drawing from his theory that population growth attends the happiness of any given society, Hume concluded that the severity of the slave system caused population decline. The practice of slavery, Hume asserted, being disadvantageous to both populousness and human happiness, should be replaced with hiring servants.

Hume detailed many of the horrible practices of the ancient slave system, including the torture and whipping of slaves, the practice of putting chained slaves to labor in underground dungeons, and the custom of exposing old or infirm slaves to starvation. He opposed slavery on humanitarian grounds, both because of the injustices done to the slaves and also for the damage the slave system does to the humanity of the master. Accustomed to trampling other human beings, masters become petty tyrants who rule their slaves with arbitrary cruelty and unquestioned authority.

In arguing against slavery, Hume was partly debunking the supposed superiority of the classical world. In the context of the moral and political crisis facing the eighteenth-century thinkers of Hume's time—from Gottfried Wilhelm Leibniz (1646–1716), Jean-Jacques Rousseau (1712–1778), and François-Marie Arouet Voltaire (1694–1778) to Jonathan Edwards (1703–1758) and Benjamin Franklin (1706–1790)—Hume's ideas were both widely influential and vehemently rebutted. Some of his critics, like Scottish philosopher James Beattie (1735–1803) and English theologian John Wesley (1703–1791), stridently objected to Hume's atheistic, antireligious statements while they, too, criticized slavery and, unlike Hume, further defended Africans on religious grounds.

Hume's opinions about the Negro race were not very generous. In a footnote to his essay "Of National Characters" added in 1754, 12 years after the essay was first published in *Essays Moral and Political* (1741–1742), Hume elaborated on his observation of Negro inferiority. While arguing that association, not climate, is responsible for the general characteristics observable in people of different nations, Hume suggested that people living above the polar circle and in the tropics were naturally inferior to the rest of the species of man. Hume found evidence for the inferiority of Negroes by claiming that there had been no civilized nations among them, no eminent individuals, no arts, and no sciences. In comparing Negroes with the rude and barbarous white races (the ancient Germans and the present Tatars), Hume found the Negroes sorely lacking and claimed that no slave in Europe or the British colonies had ever shown signs of exceptional intelligence. These sweeping observations led Hume to posit that nature originally made a distinction between whites and Negroes.

Despite his overt and articulated prejudice against Africans, Hume could not condone the system of slavery. He railed against some Enlightenment thinkers who, while labeling submission of the individual to the government a form of slavery, failed to condemn the ancient and modern institution of actual slavery. Although Hume himself could not rightly be described as an abolitionist and although he did not dwell extensively on slavery in his writings, he found fault with and exposed the irony of partisans of civil liberty who championed slavery. Hume's political essays influenced the authors of the U.S. Constitution, who themselves showed an inconsistency in reconciling the ideals of civil freedom and the domestic slave system. Yet Hume's empiricist philosophical doctrine, and especially his emphasis on moral sentiment, altruism, and sympathy in the work that he regarded as his greatest achievement, *An Inquiry concerning the Principles of Morals* (1752), provided some of the theoretical grounding of the later abolition movement. Hume died the year the American Revolution began. Had he lived longer, he would have been disappointed to see the flourishing of slavery in the newly independent nation.

—*Jennifer Margulis and James di Properzio*

For Further Reading
Davis, David Brion. 1966. *The Problem of Slavery in Western Culture.* Ithaca, NY: Cornell University Press; Miller, Eugene F., ed. 1987. *David Hume: Essays, Moral, Political, and Literary.* Indianapolis, IN: Liberty Fund.

---

reason for the limited populations that existed in the ancient world. In the same year, he also published *An Inquiry Concerning the Principles of Morals.* [See Document 24.]

1759
Birth of William Wilberforce, who later became one of the most prominent abolitionists in Great Britain.

1760
Birth of Thomas Clarkson, who also became a prominent abolitionist in Great Britain.

1762
On January 18, one form of "slavery" was abolished in Russia by a royal decree from Czar Peter III, but this announcement was not immediately publicized throughout the countryside. Noblemen in Russia were no longer obligated to perform compulsory state service, which had been expected of them since 1722.

1763
Several European powers signed the Treaty of Paris (1763), which ended the Seven Years War (French and Indian War) of 1756–1763. Having defeated the French in this conflict, the British acquired the former French colonies of Senegal and Gambia in West Africa. The British province of Senegambia became one of the primary regions exploited by British merchants involved in the African slave trade.

1764
In Russia, the government of Catherine II (the Great) freed 900,000 peasants who lived on church lands. Additional reforms instituted during her reign prohibited freemen and freed peasants from being made serfs, and another statute prohibited the sale of peasants during military conscriptions.

1764
Twenty-five percent of the shipping through the port of Liverpool consisted of vessels involved in the African slave trade, half of the British trade with Africa.

1765
An article entitled "Traite des Negres" (Traits of the Negroes) was included in Diderot's *Encyclopédie.* The article stated: "There is not a single one of these hopeless souls . . . who does not have the right to be declared free, since he has never lost his freedom; . . . since neither his ruler nor his father nor anyone else had the right to dispose of his freedom; . . . this [individual] does not divest himself, indeed cannot under any condition divest himself of his natural rights; he

carries them everywhere with him, and he has the right to demand that others allow him to enjoy those rights. Therefore it is a clear case of inhumanity on the part of the judges in those free countries to which the slave is shipped not to free the slave instantly by legal declaration." The article was written by Chevalier Louis de Jaucourt.

1770

Abbé Guillaume-Thomas-François Raynal published *Histoire philosophique et politique du commerce et des établissements des Européens dans les deux Indies* in Paris. In this work, Raynal predicted that a black Spartacus would soon rise in the New World to avenge the many injustices of man's inhumanity to man. Some people have credited this historic antislavery work with inspiring the Haitian Revolution.

1770

The *Oxford English Dictionary* included the word "race" for the first time.

1771

The practice of serfdom was abolished in the Kingdom of Savoy.

1771

The government of King Louis XV decreed that persons of African descent in the French colonies would not be granted the same rights and privileges as white citizens, and the French minister of colonies refused a request to grant citizenship to mulattoes in the French colonies.

1772

In a landmark judicial ruling in May, in the case of *Knowles v. Somersett*, the decision of Chief Justice Lord Mansfield (William Murray, first earl of Mansfield) abolished slavery within England. In this decision, Mansfield declared that "the air of England has long been too pure for a slave, and every man is free who breathes it. Every man who comes to England is entitled to the protection of English law, whatever oppression he may heretofore have suffered, and whatever may be the color of his skin." [See Document 26.]

1773

In Russia, a major uprising of the peasants and serfs was led by one Emelian Pugachev. This in-

Emelian Pugachev chained inside a cage after the failure of the peasant and serf insurrection he led. (Corbis-Bettmann)

surrection, like others before it, was caused by rising economic distress as agricultural productivity stagnated just as one's obligations to the landlord and the state were increasing. The Russian government was again able to suppress the uprising.

1773

On January 16, under the leadership of the marquis of Pombal, Sebastião José Carvalho e Melo, the government of Portugal abolished slavery within Portugal itself but continued the practice in the Portuguese colonies. It was Portugal that had first transported Africans as slaves to Europe in 1442.

1774

John Wesley, the founder of English Methodism, published *Thoughts upon Slavery*. In the work, Wesley attacked the moral foundation upon which slaveowners used biblical justification to defend their ownership of slave property. Wesley maintained that slaveowners continued to live in sin until the moment they emancipated their slaves.

1776

The British Parliament briefly debated a measure that called for an end to the African slave trade, the first time Parliament had considered this question. In the same year, the House of Commons defeated a resolution that condemned slavery as being contrary to the laws of God.

1776

The political economist Adam Smith published *An Inquiry into the Nature and Causes of the Wealth of Nations,* and in it, he wrote: "The pride of man makes him love to domineer, and nothing mortifies him so much as to be obliged to condescend to persuade his inferiors. Wherever the law allows it, and the nature of the work can afford, therefore, he will generally prefer the service of slaves to that of freemen" (Book 3).

1777

The French government issued a decree expressly prohibiting blacks or mulattoes, whether slave or free, from emigrating to France.

1778

In the British Parliament, the House of Commons created a special committee to investigate the African slave trade. In the same year, Joseph Knight, a slave who had been taken from Jamaica to Scotland, sued for his freedom in the Edinburgh Court of Session. The Scottish court based its ruling upon the judicial precedent established in *Knowles v. Somersett* (1772) and declared Knight to be free.

1779

The British abolitionist Granville Sharp appealed to Anglican bishops to voice their opposition to the African slave trade.

1780

The British political leader Edmund Burke, who was an antislavery supporter, wrote "Sketch of a Negro Code" as a means of preparing slaves for a future life of "civilization and gradual manumission." As a member of the British Parliament, Burke supported efforts by abolitionist William Wilberforce to end the African slave trade.

1780

In France, Marie-Jean-Antoine-Nicolas Caritat, marquis de Condorcet, wrote *Réflexions sur l'esclavage des nègres* (Reflections on the enslavement of Negroes) under the pseudonym Joachim Schwartz. In this antislavery tract, Condorcet urged the initiation of a program to abolish slavery gradually throughout the French colonies.

1781

On November 29, 133 slaves were thrown from the English slave ship *Zong* into the Atlantic Ocean. The captain, Luke Collingwood, had ordered the Africans thrown overboard because the vessel lacked sufficient provisions for the completion of a successful voyage. The resulting court case, *Gregson v. Gilbert,* did not involve murder charges but was, rather, a case involving property rights and insurance fraud. [See Document 30.] The British abolitionist Granville Sharp used the *Zong* incident to rally antislavery supporters in the cause of ending the African slave trade.

1783

The London Meeting for Sufferings, a special committee established by the Society of Friends (Quakers) in Great Britain, published the tract *The Case of Our Fellow Creatures, the Oppressed Africans, Recommended to the Serious Consideration of the Legislature of Great Britain, by the People Called Quakers.* This antislavery pamphlet was distributed among prominent citizens in the hope that Parliament could be convinced to take action on ending the African slave trade. In the same year, British abolitionists published *Letters of the Late Ignatius Sancho, an African,* who had been a slave in the British West Indies before being taken to England as a child.

1783

On September 3, the Treaty of Paris officially ended the American Revolution and recognized the independence of the United States of America. In other terms of this treaty, the French, who had allied themselves with the Americans, recovered lost colonial possessions in the West Indies and in India. The French also regained control of Senegal and Gorée Island in West Africa, which they had lost to the British in 1763.

1784

The British abolitionist James Ramsay published *Essay on the Treatment and Conversion of African Slaves.*

ADAM SMITH (1723–1790)

Adam Smith, a Scottish Enlightenment philosopher, laid the foundations for the free market economic theory, a theory that replaced mercantilism and dominated British and American thinking during the nineteenth century. Under the mercantilist system, states either regulate, tax, or subsidize trade in order to promote the flow of gold and silver into their country. In his consequential book, *An Inquiry into the Nature and Causes of the Wealth of Nations* (1776), Smith focused on the production of rather than the transfer of wealth. He promoted free markets and free labor and proposed that the value of the products of land and labor rather than the amount of specie determines a country's true wealth. Thus, Smith predated Karl Marx by developing an early version of the labor theory of value.

Slavery figured in Smith's theory as an enemy to the production of national wealth and the development of a progressive population. Land, he argued, provided the most stable form of national wealth, but its full value could not be achieved through slave labor. Slaves could not expect to gain more than their maintenance, regardless of the effort they expended, and thus would not be motivated to increase the soil's yield. Freemen, however, who work the land as tenants or sharecroppers possess the necessary spirit and innovativeness for improvement. In a sharecropper or lease system, the landowner receives a portion of the produce in exchange for land and supplies allotted to the laborer, so the freeman works to make the soil as productive as possible to increase his own profit as well as that of the owner.

As a second factor, Smith proposed that buying and maintaining slaves proved more costly than using freemen. Not only did an owner fail to reap the full value from his land, but he had the extra expenses of purchase and upkeep. Given the high mortality rate of slaves (particularly on sugar plantations), owners frequently had to procure replacements. Except in the United States, proprietors seldom elected to buy females for purposes of propagation, choosing instead to replenish their stock through the slave market. Also, marriage and families were not options for slaves, so Smith considered slavery morally unacceptable as well.

Smith's theory concerning the dispersal of wealth took into account the role of slave labor. Wealth should exist in descending order, because great riches controlled by a few pose a threat to the economic advancement of the community. Proper disbursement can be accomplished only if the rich invest their accumulated capital in free labor, thereby providing an opportunity to create new wealth. Men who controlled great fortunes, perhaps motivated by pride to dominate and extort all possible from those they perceived to be lower than themselves, Smith argued, preferred to use slaves to carry out every function in agriculture, trade, and commerce. When the nature of the work allowed it, and the law did not prevent it, the rich chose slaves over freemen. Thereby, according to Smith, wealth became a detriment to the community. But if a rich man were persuaded to employ free labor, he would serve the entire community by using his capital to promote trade and industry.

Smith used the example of the sugar and tobacco plantations in the West Indies to illustrate the ill effects of mercantilist monopolies. Because these industries were protected from competition, they were able to amass exorbitant profits even when relying on the expensive system of slave labor. In countries dominated by extensive plantations and large numbers of slaves, however, masters felt compelled to use harsh measures to prevent insurrection, and Smith argued that these countries would never develop a growing and healthy population that could produce a surplus of free laborers and new capital.

Smith suggested that individual self-interest drives the economic order. Because of this, he reasoned, slavery and serfdom had gradually disappeared in Western Europe. In countries governed by monarchs, kings and clergymen had found it in their joint interest to weaken the power of the great nobles by freeing the slaves. Proprietors, particularly in England and France, had discovered the more profitable system of free tenancy. By contrast, elective or democratic governments seldom initiated the abolition of slavery, Smith argued, because slaveowners served as the legislators, and these self-interested masters created laws to strengthen their authority and protect their property.

Smith's economic theories had far-reaching significance, and his book is considered a milestone of the Enlightenment. His encouragement of free trade over mercantilism and free labor over slave labor in the *Wealth of Nations* contributed to the eventual demise of slavery.

—*Carol J. Terry*

For Further Reading
Campbell, R. H., and A. S. Skinner, eds. 1981. *Adam Smith, an Inquiry into the Nature and Causes of the Wealth of Nations.* Indianapolis, IN: Liberty Classics; O'Driscoll, Gerald P., Jr. 1979. *Adam Smith and Modern Political Economy.* Ames: Iowa University Press; Raphael, D. D. 1985. *Adam Smith.* New York: Oxford University Press.

1786

A group of British abolitionists known as the Clapham Sect established the Committee for Relieving the Black Poor. The group was especially concerned about the social and economic well-being of those freed slaves who lived as beggars in London and other cities. The British abolitionist Dr. Henry Smeathman, who had visited the region of Sierra Leone in West Africa, first proposed that a settlement be established there for those freed blacks living in Great Britain who might wish to return to Africa. In the same year, the British abolitionist Thomas Clarkson published *An Essay on the Slavery and Commerce of the Human Species, Particularly the African.*

1787

British abolitionists established the Association for the Abolition of Slavery; Peter Peckard published the tract *Am I not a Man? And a Brother?* an antislavery pamphlet specifically addressed to members of the British Parliament; and Granville Sharp chaired a committee that was formed by antislavery supporters in Great Britain who wished to promote the abolition of slavery through parliamentary action. Abolitionists in Great Britain also established the Society for Effecting the Abolition of the Slave Trade. The society's goals were to raise funds to support the abolitionist cause and to collect information that could be used to sway Parliament. Thomas Clarkson assumed the task of gathering data and collecting research material to support the work of the society.

1787

The former slave Quobna Ottobah Cugoano published *Thoughts and Sentiments on the Evil and Wicked Traffic of the Slavery and Commerce of the Human Species, Humbly Submitted to the Inhabitants of Great Britain, by Ottobah Cugoano, a Native of Africa.* This antislavery narrative, which was probably written in collaboration with Olaudah Equiano (Gustavus Vassa), refuted the arguments advanced by proslavery apologists.

1787

The British potter Josiah Wedgwood created a famous antislavery cameo of an African slave in chains kneeling in supplication. The caption on the cameo read, "Am I not a man and a

Antislavery author Gustavus Vassa (Olaudah Equiano). (New-York Historical Society)

brother." The cameos were sold by abolitionists to raise funds to support the antislavery crusade, but Wedgwood preferred to give them away—claiming he did not want it said that he had ever sold a slave.

1788

The British abolitionist Thomas Clarkson published *An Essay on the Impolicy of the African Slave Trade,* and abolitionist James Ramsey published *Objections to the Abolition of the Slave Trade with Answers.* Abolitionists in Great Britain organized a petition campaign throughout the nation to have Parliament outlaw the African slave trade, and leading British abolitionists such as William Pitt, William Wyndham Grenville, and William Wilberforce addressed Parliament demanding an end to the African slave trade. For its part, Parliament enacted a statute regulating the conditions permitted in conducting the African slave trade, but the measure fell far short of abolition, which the antislavery supporters were demanding. In addition, the Privy Council Committee for Trade and Plantations began to investigate the state of British commercial relations with Africa.

1788

On January 9, the Association for Promoting the Discovery of the Interior Parts of Africa was established in London, England.

1788

On February 19, a group of antislavery supporters in France established the Société des Amis des Noirs (Society of the Friends of Blacks), and the French abolitionists began to correspond with like-minded reformers in Great Britain and the United States.

1789

In France, the Société des Amis des Noirs tried to petition the Estates General to abolish slavery in the French colonies, and as a secondary goal, the group sought to end the African slave trade. British abolitionist Thomas Clarkson shared some of the evidence against the slave trade that he had collected with the French abolitionists. The free mulattoes Julian Raymond and Jacques Vincent Ogé traveled to France to request that the National Assembly grant the rights of citizenship to free blacks in the colony of Saint Domingue (modern-day Haiti) and also requested the right to be seated as colonial representatives. The National Assembly did not respond favorably to either request.

1789

Gustavus Vassa (Olaudah Equiano) published *The Interesting Narrative of the Life of Olaudah Equiano, or Gustavus Vassa, the African, Written by Himself*. The narrative was extremely popular among British abolitionists who were waging a strong national campaign to have the British Parliament abolish the African slave trade. [See Document 34.] In the same year, the British abolitionist William Wilberforce introduced 12 resolutions into the House of Commons that called for the abolition of the African slave trade. Rather than acting upon the issue, the Members of Parliament requested additional information before making a decision on the matter.

1789

The storming of the Bastille in Paris on July 14 marked the beginning of the French Revolution. The revolutionary events that shook France during the following decade would have international implications as slavery was abolished,

then reinstituted, in French colonies. On August 26, the French National Assembly issued the Declaration of the Rights of Man and Citizen, the most important document of the French Revolution. The declaration stated: "Men are born and remain free and equal in rights." [See Document 33.]

1790

The French Constituent Assembly decided to accept a report that had been issued by its Committee on Colonies, which meant that the assembly did not act upon abolition of the African slave trade, as the French abolitionists had urged.

1790

The British Parliament and Queen Charlotte received a petition from the former slave Gustavus Vassa (Olaudah Equiano) urging that action be taken to end the African slave trade. In the British Parliament, a select committee of the House of Commons conducted hearings and interviewed witnesses on the subject of the African slave trade.

1790

The Spanish crown abolished the Casa de Contratacion (House of Commerce), which had regulated all aspects of colonial commerce, including the slave trade, in the Spanish colonies since its creation in 1510.

1790

On October 21, Vincent Ogé and Jean-Baptiste Chavanne led an uprising of mulattoes in Saint Domingue (modern-day Haiti) against French control of the colony; the revolt was put down, and both leaders were executed in February 1791.

1791

In an open letter to the colonists of Saint Domingue, Abbé Henri-Baptiste Grégoire of France declared "You were men, you are now citizens" (Blake, 1861). On August 22, what had begun as a civil war evolved into a slave revolt in the French colony, and the fighting would last for more than a decade.

1791

The French National Assembly abolished slavery in all French colonial possessions, but the action proved to be only temporary as Napoleon Bonaparte reinstituted slavery in all French dominions in 1802. On May 15, the assembly voted to extend the suffrage to all free colonists, regardless of color, who met the requisite property qualifications. However, the assembly rescinded this measure after violence erupted in the colony of Saint Domingue.

1791

In Great Britain, the House of Commons rejected an attempt by the abolitionist William Wilberforce to introduce a resolution calling for the abolition of slavery. Parliament did charter the Sierra Leone Company and charge it with the responsibility of transporting free blacks and former slaves to West Africa and providing supplies to aid the settlers already repatriated to Sierra Leone.

1792

British abolitionists published a pamphlet entitled *Trial of Captain John Kimber, for the Murder of a Negro Girl, on Board the Ship* Recovery. This tract attempted to show the horrors of the African slave trade by concentrating upon the brutal means used to enforce discipline on board slaving vessels. The abolitionists also published an antislavery tract entitled *No Rum! No Sugar! or, The Voice of Blood*. This work included a fictional dialogue between Englishmen and Africans in which possible methods for ending the African slave trade were discussed.

1792

A new Legislative Assembly in France declared that free blacks and mulattoes in the colonies had equal rights with white citizens.

1792

The British Parliament received 499 petitions from Quakers and other abolitionists against the African slave trade and slavery itself. The House of Commons approved of a resolution to end the African slave trade, but the House of Lords rejected the measure.

1792

The Danish crown issued an order demanding that the importation of African slaves into Danish colonies be ended by 1803. With this action, the government of Denmark hoped to end both the African slave trade and the practice of slavery itself in all Danish possessions within a decade.

1793

In Europe, France was at war with England and Spain, and the conflict spread into the racial conflict in the colony of Saint Domingue (modern-day Haiti) when Spanish and English forces invaded the colony and assisted Toussaint Louverture's forces against the French. French Commissioner Léger Félicité Sonthonax emancipated the slaves in Saint Domingue's North Province in the hope that the freed slaves would then support his efforts to defeat the rebel forces of Louverture.

1794

When the government of the French Republic abolished slavery in the colonies without compensating the slaveowners and extended universal citizenship to all regardless of color, the rebel slave leader Toussaint Louverture joined the forces of the French Republic.

1795

In Great Britain, the House of Commons rejected a bill to abolish the African slave trade that abolitionist William Wilberforce had introduced.

1797

The British Parliament endorsed a proposal made by Charles Rose Ellis to encourage colonial assemblies to promote the idea that slave populations should be enlarged through natural increase. This idea, which was endorsed by planter interests, would make it more feasible to consider ending the African slave trade.

1799

The Anglican Church established the Society for Missions in Africa and the East. This organization, which later changed its name to the Church Missionary Society, was active in the development of missions in Sierra Leone and other areas.

1802

On May 12, Napoleon Bonaparte reinstituted slavery and the African slave trade in all areas within the French empire where it had been outlawed by the French National Assembly in 1791.

The abolition of slavery in the French empire by the Convention of February 4, 1794. (Bibliothèque National, Paris; Giraudon/Art Resource)

1803

The government of Denmark became the first modern nation to ban the African slave trade.

1804

In Great Britain, the House of Commons approved a bill to end the African slave trade that had been proposed by abolitionist William Wilberforce, but Prime Minister William Pitt's government delayed a vote in the House of Lords. In the same year, the British Foreign Bible Society was established. Many of the members of this organization were activists who were also involved in other reform movements, including the abolitionist movement, and one of the goals of the new society was to send missionaries into colonial regions where they could mount a moral campaign against slavery.

1804

Victorious blacks declared the independence of Haiti, the first black republic in the Western Hemisphere.

1805

In Great Britain, the House of Commons defeated a bill to end the African slave trade that had been proposed by the abolitionist William Wilberforce, but the government of Prime Minister William Pitt did issue an order in council aimed at slightly reducing the volume of the African slave trade. According to this declaration, the slave trade was prohibited in any new foreign colonies the British established, and slave imports in such areas could not exceed 3 percent annually of the existing slave population in the region.

1805

The Russian government of Czar Alexander I allowed slaveholders in Russia to liberate their slaves if they chose to do so, but few Russian slaveholders liberated their slaves at this time.

1806

Following the death of Prime Minister William Pitt on June 10, the British Parliament approved a resolution introduced by Charles James Fox calling for the abolition of the African slave trade, but specific measures for enacting this policy were not considered. [See Document 38.]

1807

The British Parliament defeated a measure introduced by Earl Percy calling for the abolition of slavery in the colonies. British abolitionists did not support this proposal. The British abolitionist Thomas Clarkson published *Three Letters to the Planters and Slave Merchants*, and the African Institution was established to monitor the effectiveness of efforts to abolish the African slave trade and to promote the development of alternative types of commerce between Great Britain and Africa.

1807

Pope Pius VII canonized Benedict the Black, the patron saint of African slaves and the protector of Palermo.

1807

On March 25, with the backing of Lord Grenville's government, Great Britain enacted statutes that abolished the African slave trade, which became effective the next year. The slave trade having been abolished through parliamentary action, abolitionists next turned their attention to the abolition of slavery itself.

1808

The British abolitionist Thomas Clarkson published *History of the Rise, Progress, and Accomplishment of the Abolition of the African Slave Trade by the British Parliament*.

1808

On March 1, the General Abolition Act approved by the Parliament in 1807 took effect. With this action, Great Britain officially ended its involvement in the African slave trade. [See Document 38.]

1810

British abolitionists were unable to win the emancipation of Venus, an enslaved woman of the South African Khoi people who had been brought to England by her owner for purposes of sexual exploitation. Abolitionists could not effect her freedom through legal means, and Venus did not seek to be liberated from her scandalous life. She died of alcoholism five years later in Paris.

1811

The colonial government in India enacted the Abolition Act of 1811, which specifically prohibited the importation of any additional African slaves into India. The practice of slavery would continue in British India, however, until it was outlawed in 1838. The British Parliament enacted a statute that made participation in the African slave trade a felony for all British citizens.

1813

On March 3, Great Britain ceded the island of Guadeloupe to Sweden, and in exchange, the Swedish government promised not to import additional African slaves onto the island and officially abolished Swedish involvement in the African slave trade.

1814–1815

During discussions held at the Congress of Vienna, the British tried to convince the French government to abolish the slave trade. The 1814 Treaty of Paris provided the French with a five-year period before the question of the slave trade would be addressed. Other maritime nations attending the Congress of Vienna agreed to a rather vague proclamation that condemned the African slave trade but failed to impose any collective sanctions against it.

1814

British abolitionists published *The Narrative of the Most Remarkable Particulars in the Life of James Albert Ukawsaw Gronniosaw, an African Prince.* Like most nineteenth-century slave narratives, this work was designed to present a firsthand view of the horrible realities of slavery.

1814

On January 15, the government of the Netherlands officially ended Dutch involvement in the African slave trade.

1815

British abolitionists attempted to get Parliament to support a law calling for a centralized registration of all slaves in the West Indies, but the measure was not supported by Parliament. The registry would have allowed antislavery supporters to make sure that new Africans and free blacks were not being enslaved in the British colonies there.

1815

Upon his triumphant return from exile in Elba on March 29, former French emperor Napoleon Bonaparte proclaimed the abolition of the African slave trade.

1815

On July 30, after the final defeat of Napoleon at Waterloo, the French government of Louis XVIII enacted a weak measure to end the slave trade, but it was not effectively enforced.

1816

British abolitionists published *Remarks on the Insurrection in Barbadoes.*

1817

On September 23, the government of Great Britain compensated the Spanish government with £400,000 for Spain's promise to end the African slave trade north of the equator.

1817

On December 19, the government of Portugal signed a treaty with Great Britain in which the Portuguese promised to abolish the African slave trade in the waters north of the equator. The trade was permitted to continue in the region south of that line.

1818

During the Congress of Aix-la-Chapelle (today's Aachen), British diplomats were unsuccessful in getting the major powers of Europe to agree to permit the British navy to search suspected slave ships in international waters.

1819

The British Parliament authorized the creation of Courts of Mixed Commission to be established in Sierra Leone. The purpose of these tribunals was to decide the fate of slave vessels seized in the waters off West Africa.

1819

The French government officially ended its involvement with the African slave trade.

1820

Antislavery advocates in Britain encouraged Parliament to support a registration system for all slaves in the British colonies. It was argued that such a system would decrease the likelihood that illegal African slaves would be imported into the British colonies. In the same year, British diplomats attempted to negotiate

Thomas Clarkson addressing the Anti-Slavery Society Convention. (National Portrait Library, London)

an agreement with the Persian Gulf sheiks in an effort to suppress the Arab slave trade along the East African coastline.

1820
On May 30, the Spanish government abolished the slave trade in the region south of the equator.

1821
The British Parliament terminated the charter of the Royal African Company, which had been actively involved in conducting the slave trade since the company was formed in 1672. All of the company's assets were transferred to the government.

1821
French abolitionists established the Société de la Morale Chrétienne (Society of Christian Morals) to agitate for the abolition of the African slave trade and the abolition of slavery in French colonies. The French Chamber of Deputies refused consideration of a petition by one Joseph Morénas that called for an end to the African slave trade.

1822
During the Congress of Verona, British diplomats were unsuccessful in efforts getting the major powers of Europe to agree to permit the

British navy to search suspected slave ships in international waters.

1822
The Russian government of Czar Alexander I allowed slaveholders in Russia to deport their slaves to Siberia if they exhibited any mutinous behavior.

1823
British abolitionists established the Society for the Mitigation and Gradual Abolition of Slavery, better known as the Anti-Slavery Society. William Wilberforce was elected to serve as the first president of this new abolitionist organization.

1824
The British Parliament officially declared that participation in the African slave trade was to be considered an act of piracy.

1824
Elizabeth [Coltman] Heyrick published *Immediate, Not Gradual Abolition, or, An Inquiry into the Shortest, Safest, and Most Effectual Means of Getting Rid of West Indian Slavery.* Heyrick, one of the most active female abolitionists in Great Britain, believed in the concept of immediate abolition because she viewed slavery as a moral issue rather than as an economic or political concern.

≈GEORGE CANNING (1770–1827)≈

George Canning was a Member of Parliament from 1794 until 1822, British foreign minister from 1822 to 1827, and prime minister in 1827 and a leading spokesman for the abolition of the international slave trade and the amelioration of existing slave conditions. Although England had outlawed slavery in 1772, the slave trade remained an integral part of Britain's colonial empire. Early in his political career Canning supported the abolition of the slave traffic based on his moral and humanitarian beliefs. In a parliamentary motion to abolish the practice on April 3, 1798, he successfully proposed a resolution to limit the cultivation of new lands in the West Indian colonies, which, it was believed, would help curb the extension of the slave trade. The abolition motion, however, failed, and Canning's resolution did not attain the force of law.

In 1799, Canning delivered his first speech on the slave issue, attacking the people who defended the practice based on its longevity and traditional eighteenth-century property rights. He characterized the slave trade as "that scandal of the civilised world" (Temperley, 1968), and over his lifetime, Canning issued over 1,000 dispatches on the issue and lobbied foreign governments to curb the trade. On May 27, 1802, he introduced a motion in Parliament to use the newly acquired island of Trinidad as an experiment in abolition. The bill, however, contained no provision for compensation for the slaveowners, and it was ultimately rejected. Eventually, Parliament did outlaw the slave trade on March 25, 1807, but Canning dissented on grounds that the policy would be impossible to enforce in international waters.

Following the successful campaign to abolish the slave trade, Foreign Minister Canning applied diplomatic pressure and utilized the Royal Navy to enforce the ban. He persuaded the Dutch and Spanish to confiscate vessels containing prima facie evidence of slave-trading activities and complained to Madrid about the continued slave trade in the Spanish colony of Cuba. He urged France to enforce its ban against slavers, and he sought the right of the Royal Navy to search and detain foreign slave ships. As a result, by 1822 most of the leading maritime nations had followed suit and had abolished the slave trade. Additionally, in March 1824, Canning sought agreement with the United States for a bilateral convention on the suppression of the slave trade. However, the U.S. Senate refused to approve the agreement, citing the issues of the right of search and encroachment on its power to ratify treaties.

In 1823, Parliament recommended the abolition of slavery throughout the empire, but Canning believed enforcement would be difficult. As a practical statesman he recognized that the resistance of landed interests would be resolute and might lead to possible violence and bloodshed. Therefore, on March 24, 1824, he introduced an Order in Council for the gradual improvement of the slaves' condition. He insisted that through gradualism, "not only may the individual slave be set free, but his very status may be ultimately abolished" (Hinde, 1973). Although the colonial governments protested interference by the home government, Parliament enacted partial improvements. The new measures called for the establishment of schools and churches for slaves; the legalization of slave marriage; the recognition of certain legal rights such as the holding and transferring of property and the right of access to banks; the limitation of the use of the whip for discipline; a ban on the separation of slave families; and the right of slaves to purchase their freedom.

Only those possessions under direct rule by London—Trinidad, St. Lucia, and Demerara—were immediately affected, but Canning hoped that the local legislatures of other colonies would enact similar legislation. England later abandoned its policy of gradualism and abolished slavery throughout the British Empire in 1833.

—*Mary L. Kelley*

For Further Reading
Hinde, Wendy. 1973. *George Canning.* New York: St. Martin's Press; Temperley, Harold W. V. 1925. *The Foreign Policy of Canning, 1822–1827.* London: G. Bell and Sons; Temperley, Harold W. V. 1968. *Life of Canning.* New York: Haskell House.

1824

On March 24, the British House of Commons gave its support to a resolution introduced by George Canning calling for an improvement in the conditions of slavery found in the British colonies. Colonial authorities were encouraged to made specific changes as a result of the passage of this measure.

1825

British abolitionists published *A Narrative of Some Remarkable Incidents in the Life of Solomon Bayley, Formerly a Slave in the State of Delaware, North America, Written by Himself and Published for His Benefit to Which Are Prefixed a Few Remarks by Robert Hurnard.* Like other nineteenth-century slave narratives, this work was designed to present realities of slavery.

1826

Members of the British Parliament received a packet of documents pertaining to the condition of the African slave trade in the years since the British and U.S. governments had outlawed the practice in 1807.

1828

David Barclay, a London merchant and an abolitionist, published *A Practical View of the Present State of Slavery in the West Indies, or, An Examination of Mr. [James] Stephen's "Slavery in the British West Indies Colonies."*

1831

Mary Prince published *The History of Mary Prince, a West Indian Slave, Related to Herself, with a Supplement by the Editor, to Which Is Added the Narrative of Asa-Asa, a Captured African.* This narrative, published in London with the support of British abolitionists, was the first slave narrative written by a female slave.

1831

Diplomatic representatives from Great Britain and France signed a treaty aimed at cooperative efforts between the two nations to abolish the African slave trade in international waters.

1833

William Wilberforce died in July. For the previous generation, Wilberforce had been the most prominent abolitionist in Great Britain, and he had worked tirelessly to end the slave trade and slavery itself from all British possessions.

1833

On August 1, the British Parliament enacted the Emancipation Act, which effectively ended slavery in all British colonial possessions. The system of gradual abolition would free all slaves in the British colonies within five years.

1834

In Great Britain, the *Anti Slavery Reporter* began publication. This abolitionist periodical addressed the progress of efforts to abolish the institution of slavery within the British Empire, and many of the writings and speeches of Thomas Clarkson and other prominent abolitionists were reprinted in it.

1834

On August 8, the Kingdom of Sardinia entered into a treaty with Great Britain and France in which the African slave trade was outlawed.

1836

The British Parliament received a report from the select committee of Parliament that had investigated the status of the apprenticeship system in the colonies. As a part of the gradual abolition law enacted in 1833, slaves in the colonies became apprentices for a period of years before they became totally free. In the same year, British abolitionists published *A Narrative of Travels, etc., of John Ismael Augustus James, an African of the Mandingo Tribe, Who Was Captured, Sold into Slavery, and Subsequently Liberated by a Benevolent English Gentlemen.* Proslavery apologists described the narrative as a mere "pious hoax" that was published to be used as abolitionist propaganda.

1836

In December, the Portuguese crown declared it illegal to export slaves from any Portuguese colonial possession to any other location. Despite this proclamation, Africans taken from Angola and Mozambique continued to be shipped as slaves to Brazil. Bernardo di Sá da Bandeira had tried to prohibit the practice of importing and exporting slaves into Portuguese colonies south of the equator, but he was unable to win approval of the proposal.

In Supremo was a papal letter of 1839 that condemned Christian participation in or support of enslavement and the slave trade. Pope Gregory XVI (Bartolomeo Alberto Cappellari, pope from 1831 to 1846) was a Camaldolese monk and theologian with a reactionary nature who generally set himself against liberalism and threats to ecclesiological traditions. A patron of the era's missionary revival, he created over 70 new dioceses and apostolic vicariates and named 195 missionary bishops. For over half his reign, however, he remained silent on the issues of slavery.

In the 1830s, European antislavery movements were active if usually ineffectual. In 1838, Spain unsuccessfully ordered colonial authorities to enforce existing laws (in effect since 1825) against the trade, and the government of nominally Catholic France remained cool toward abolition. Few members of the Roman Catholic Church hierarchy anywhere had recently spoken out against either slavery or the trade in slaves, and many people felt that an official statement from the pope was necessary to give shape to Catholic opinion. In July 1839, the prime minister of Great Britain, Lord Palmerston, openly suggested that the pope speak out against slavery, and in November, Palmerston sent Thomas Buxton to Rome as a secret envoy of Queen Victoria to negotiate a "Christian league" to combat the slave trade and establish schools, railroads, and Christian civilization in Africa. Buxton, however, reported reluctance on Gregory's part—owing at least in part to Buxton's and Britain's Protestant affiliations.

Nevertheless, on December 3, 1839, the pope issued the apostolic letter In Supremo, in which he formally condemned the act of enslavement and the traffic in slaves and forbade Christians from participating in or defending that traffic, publicly or privately. His 1,000-word statement accepted St. Paul's desire that the slave be obedient and the master kindly but happily noted that since the first century, many slaves had been freed and many Christian nations had abandoned slavery entirely. The letter mentioned the unsuccessful attempts of the pope's predecessors to eliminate the practice altogether—previous papal condemnations had been issued by Urban VIII in 1639, Benedict XIV in 1741, and Pius VII in 1815—and Gregory lamented that many Christians still participated in the inhuman enslavement, molestation, and despoliation of Indians and blacks and bought and sold blacks as though they were animals. Although neither the English nor the Vatican admitted to any British influence on the pope, the queen's Foreign Office did see to it that the papal letter was circulated in capitals that supported Anglo-French agreements to the right of inspection for illicit slaves on the high seas.

The statement spurred wider participation by European Catholic clergy in abolitionist movements and is credited with the decision of eight bishops and archbishops to join the Institut d'Afrique, an international society (active 1842–1848) that sought to aid Africa through European colonization and the abolition of slavery. Spanish authorities published the letter in the *Gaceta de Madrid* on January 1, 1840, apparently to little effect in Hispanic cultural areas that still retained the slave trade. Like other attempts at moral or spiritual suasion, the pope's seems to have had limited effect.

In America, Catholic bishops gathered at the Fourth Provincial Council of Baltimore (1840) formally accepted the letter. Led by Bishop John England of Charleston, South Carolina, they insisted, however, that Gregory had carefully avoided censuring slavery itself while condemning the same trade that U.S. law forbade. Bishop England's denominational newspaper, *United States Catholic Miscellany*, correctly reported: "His Holiness speaks of reducing Indians, negroes and such others, into slavery; of assisting those who engage in that inhuman traffic, and through the desire of gain, go so far as to excite quarrels and wars among them in their native country. . . . Domestic slavery, as it exists in the Southern States, and in other parts of the Christian world, he does not condemn" (December 9, 1843).

—*Joseph P. Byrne*

For Further Reading
Daget, Serge. 1980. "A Model of the French Abolitionist Movement and Its Variations." In *Anti-Slavery, Religion, and Reform.* Ed. Christine Bolt and Seymour Drescher. Hamden, CT: Archon Books; Messmer, S. G., ed. 1908. *The Works of the Right Reverend John England, First Bishop of Charleston.* Vol. 5. Cleveland, OH: Arthur H. Clark Company; Shearer, Donald C. 1933. *Pontificia Americana.* New York: J. F. Wagner.

1837

On June 9, the cities of the Hanseatic League of the Baltic region entered into a treaty with Great Britain and France in which the African slave trade was outlawed.

1837

On November 24, the Kingdom of Tuscany entered into a treaty with Great Britain and France in which the African slave trade was outlawed. Vessels flying the Tuscan flag had not been used in the transatlantic slave trade, but they had been used to transport African captives from the Barbary Coast of North Africa to the slave market in Constantinople.

1838

In keeping with the British government's pledge to abolish slavery within the empire, slavery was officially abolished in India (Hindustan). By this date, all slaves in the British colonies had been freed. British diplomats also attempted to negotiate an agreement with the Persian Gulf sheiks to help suppress the Arab slave trade that was occurring along the East African coastline.

1838

On February 14, the Kingdom of Naples entered into a treaty with Great Britain and France in which the African slave trade was outlawed.

1839

The Spanish government filed a diplomatic protest against the United States when the Spanish slaver *Amistad* was captured off the coast of Long Island, New York, and the Africans aboard the vessel were jailed until their ownership and status could be determined in a court of law.

1839

The British Parliament enacted the Palmerston Act, which permitted British vessels to search Portuguese ships and other vessels suspected of carrying African slaves to the Americas. This unilateral measure was enacted as a coercive device to hasten an end to the African slave trade, but despite the measure, Brazil imported an estimated 20,000 slaves in 1845.

1839

On December 3, Pope Gregory XVI issued the bull In Supremo. In this document, the Roman Catholic Church stated its opposition to both slavery and the slave trade. [See Document 50.]

1840

The British artist J. M. W. Turner painted *Slave Ship*. The British abolitionist Sir Thomas Fowell Buxton published *The African Slave Trade and Its Remedy*, which suggested further measures that should be taken by the Royal Navy to prevent the continuation of the illegal African slave trade. In June, Buxton established the African Civilization Society. Among other projects, this organization attempted to establish a model agricultural community in the Niger River valley in order to help spread European technology, civilization, and Christianity. The experiment was not successful and was abandoned during its first year of operation.

1841

On December 20, the government of Austria entered into a five-power treaty with Great Britain, France, Russia, and Prussia in which the African slave trade was outlawed. Vessels flying the Austrian flag had not been used in the transatlantic slave trade, but they had been used to transport African captives from the Barbary Coast of North Africa to the slave market in Constantinople (Istanbul). On the same date, the governments of Russia and Prussia entered into the same five-power treaty.

1842

Czar Nicholas I decreed the abolition of slavery in Russia, but the statement had little effect. Millions of Russians continued to be held in a virtual form of enslavement as serfs.

1843

With encouragement from the British government, the colonial government of India enacted the Indian Government Act of 1843, which abolished the legal status of slavery in India.

1846

The British missionary David Livingstone began his first expedition into the interior of the African continent. In addition to exploring the uncharted regions of Africa, Livingstone also hoped to convince African leaders to end the slave trade by encouraging the development of other types of trade.

The cutter of H.M.S. Daphne *capturing an Arab slave dhow off the coast of East Africa, part of the British campaign to put an end to the slave trade. (Archive Photos)*

1848

In February, Karl Marx and Friedrich Engels published *The Communist Manifesto*. This radical work called upon the workers of the world to revolt against the wage slavery that was imposed upon them by the industrial bourgeoisie of the world. According to Marx and Engels in the closing words of the *Manifesto,* "The proletarians have nothing to lose but their chains!"

1848

On April 27, the French government abolished slavery in all French colonies.

1850

Karl Marx published *Grundrisse* in which he addressed the question of slavery, writing that "slavery . . . is always secondary, derived, never original, although [it is] a necessary and logical result of property founded on the community and labor in the community" (McLellan, 1971).

1850

The British political economist John Stuart Mill published the essay "The Negro Question" to respond to a racist tract that Thomas Carlyle had published criticizing the abilities of blacks in the British West Indies.

1851

British diplomats attempted to negotiate an agreement with the kings of Somalia in an effort to suppress the Arab slave trade that was occurring along the East African coastline.

1853

British efforts to get Portugal to end the African slave trade had proved unsuccessful even though, by this date, the British government had paid £2,850,965 in bribes to try to convince the Portuguese government to end the slave trade.

1855

British diplomats attempted to negotiate an agreement with the shah of Persia in an effort to suppress the Arab slave trade that was occurring along the East African coastline.

The British philosopher, economist, and social critic John Stuart Mill was born into a progressivist intellectual family, his father, James Mill, having been the foremost disciple of the founder of utilitarianism, Jeremy Bentham. Widely considered the most famous British philosopher of the nineteenth century, John Stuart Mill is said to have exerted an influence on Oxford and Cambridge similar to Aristotle's influence on education in the Middle Ages. However, if Mill's theories on logic and economics were influential and widely respected, many of his progressive views on social, gender, and racial questions were held in contempt by many of his peers. For much of his life, Mill was employed by the East India Company, although later he was briefly a Member of Parliament. His written output was prodigious and varied, ranging from topics on politics and economics to topics on logic and literature. He died at Avignon, France, in 1873 of a local fever.

Mill's attitude toward slavery, like his attitude toward any form of social oppression based on nonessential qualities, was consistent with his overall commitment to social justice and reform. A passionate defender of the rights and abilities of persons of African descent, Mill proved an outspoken critic of the nineteenth-century British ruling classes, whose outlook tended to exhibit little in the way of sympathy for racial equality. However, by the time Mill started taking an interest in questions regarding race relations, slavery had already been abolished in the British Empire (1833). Yet it is hardly surprising that not 20 years after that event there were still intellectuals, such as Mill's onetime friend Thomas Carlyle, who continued to harbor proslavery sentiments. Indeed, Mill's break with his former friend was occasioned precisely by Carlyle's unabashed racism.

Mill's "The Negro Question" (1850) was his response to Carlyle's "Occasional Discourse on the Negro Question" (1849), in which Carlyle portrayed the black population of the West Indies as lazy and naturally inferior to whites, their laziness the result of British public opinion, which had, according to Carlyle, become soft and sentimental toward Negroes. In Mill's critique of Carlyle, Mill first accused Carlyle of being not merely racist but proslavery and of therefore undermining the work of the great abolitionists of the previous generation. But Mill's most persuasive argument against Carlyle was directed toward the latter's belief in African racial inferiority. Carlyle had argued that since Negroes were inferior, they should be the ser-

John Stuart Mill (Library of Congress)

vants of whites who were the wiser of the races, a doctrine Mill called "damnable." He argued that any doctrine that advances essentialist doctrines of racial superiority and inferiority can only be the result of an ignorance of human nature. According to Mill, if Carlyle had examined the issue carefully, he would have seen that the development of human character is clearly a function, not of nature, but of historical circumstance, and Mill went so far in his defense of African abilities as to argue that the Greeks had learned their first lessons in civilization from the Egyptians.

But if Carlyle thought British public opinion too soft and philanthropic when it came to race relations in the West Indies, Mill took a diametrically opposed position. He argued that, far from being too humanitarian in their regard for Negroes, the opinions of the British ruling classes in this matter—in contrast to those of the French—were positively retrograde, a fact that could be seen in their tacit support of the Confederacy in the American Civil War. Indeed, from the beginning, Mill was a keen observer of the U.S. experiment in democracy, and when war broke out in 1861, he took the occasion to chastise the implicit proslavery sentiments of the British opinion makers, many of whom championed the confederate cause as being primarily one of self-determination and only secondarily as one having to do with slavery.

In "The Contest in America" (1862), Mill's most sustained analysis of the nature and causes of the American Civil War, he argued not only against the immorality of slavery and the secessionist cause in general but also against the viability of slavery as an economic institution. He cautioned those who defended southerners on the grounds of their right to independence and autonomy against equating a fight for self-determination in resisting oppression with that of the Confederacy, which, if indeed motivated by the noble cause of autonomy, was nonetheless attempting to achieve it in the name of oppression. For Mill, the mere desire for autonomy was not a sufficient condition for international sympathy: a nation's motives had also to be morally worthy. In contrast to many of his contemporaries, therefore, Mill argued that it was the very existence of slavery that was at issue in this war, and he predicted its eventual demise if the North could only keep it contained within the borders of the southern states. Mill saw clearly (with the help of his friend, the Irish economist John Elliot Cairnes, who demonstrated the futility of southern slavery as an economic institution in his work *The Slave Power*) that unless the southern states could ensure their expansion to new and fertile areas, slavery would eventually undermine its own ability to exist owing to its insatiable tendency to deplete natural resources.

Mill therefore characterized the Confederacy as an aggressively expansionist and somewhat imperialist entity, an emerging rogue state that Britain and the other European states would eventually have to confront if it were left to its own devices and allowed to become an autonomous member of the community of nations. He sided with the unionist Republican Party, for while he knew that its members were not committed to the cause of outright abolition, he saw clearly that their motive was the containment of slavery, something that, if successfully accomplished, would ultimately have the same result.

—*Peter Eardley*

For Further Reading
Britton, Karl. 1969. *John Stuart Mill: His Life and Philosophy.* New York: Dover Publications.

1857
British diplomats attempted to negotiate agreements with the kings of Somalia and the Persian Gulf sheiks to suppress the Arab slave trade along the East African coastline.

1860
The Dutch government abolished slavery throughout its possessions.

1861
The British government issued a proclamation of neutrality, stating that it had no intention of becoming involved in the American Civil War.

1861
On February 19, the Russian czar Alexander II issued a decree that freed all the serfs in Russia.

1863
British diplomats negotiated an agreement with the king of Mukalla (Al Mukallā in modern-day Yemen) in an effort to suppress the Arab slave trade along the East African coastline.

1863
The government of the Netherlands officially abolished slavery in all Dutch colonies.

1866–1868
The Russian government conquered the khanate of Bukhara in central Asia and made it a Russian protectorate. One of the important changes that the Russian government imposed upon the region was the abolition of slavery.

1870
The British government gave Sir Samuel Baker the task of ending the slave trade in the sudanic region of the upper Nile from Khartoum to Gondokoro.

1873
British diplomats negotiated an agreement with the sultan of Zanzibar in an effort to suppress the Arab slave trade along the East African coastline.

1877
In October, Great Britain negotiated a treaty of commerce with the Hova government of Madagascar and convinced the island's leaders to proclaim the liberation of all slaves there.

1878
The German philosopher Friedrich Nietzsche

There are hundreds of references to slavery scattered throughout the work of Friedrich Nietzsche, though none constitutes a theory except those that refer to what he called "slave morality." Nietzsche had no social philosophy as such, no prescription for a particular arrangement of society, so actual chattel slavery was not immediately relevant to his work. He was not a systematic or literal-minded philosopher either, so when one culls from throughout his writings, as one must to weigh the consequences of his thought on slavery, one must do so with caution. His thought does have some possible ramifications for slavery, and one of his most important ideas is a way of understanding every morality as being either a "master morality" or a "slave morality."

Trained as a classical philologist, Nietzsche loved the world and literature of classical and Homeric Greece and the values and culture of its noble citizens. His interpretation of those values, however, was much grimmer than the Renaissance's nostalgic revision of the classical period. Nietzsche approved of the stratification of Greek society, not only the slavery but also the rank and struggle for prominence of the wellborn citizens. "Order of rank" in society is important in his thought; he disapproved of instituted assumptions of an equality he saw as untrue to the differences among individuals and not conducive to the improvement of the society. This improvement—a sort of evolution of the society—he thought was necessary to a living society and part of the natural order of life. Strife and suffering he believed to be inevitable in life and the source of all that is healthiest and best, whether in a person, a society, or a species. The best members of a group exercise their will to power—living creatures' universal desire to exert themselves and impose their own effect on the world—to improve themselves and to strive against others in order that the best and the whole may flourish.

Master morality values all that serves that dynamic—pride of place, struggle, vengeance, etc.—and deems things "good" (noble, sublime, tasteful) or "bad" (base, mediocre, ugly). Slave morality values all that helps "the herd" survive together—pity, industry, humility, etc.—and deems things good or evil in the senses common to Christian morality (the slave morality par excellence). Thus, slave morality inverts the morality of the masters, and Nietzsche, in his "revaluation of all values,"

sought to turn it back to the master morality. This thinking does not support the masters of modern societies, who are part of the dynamic of the slave morality and are really prisoners of the herds they rule. Both moralities are manifestations of will to achieve power, but the slave morality is a perverse and debilitating one because it aims at the preservation of the herd whereas the master morality demands that its members expend their power striving to excel one another. One cannot "excel," intransitively, for Nietzsche; the moral implication is that one cannot excel in equality with one's fellows. Nevertheless, while subjugating others is always a manifestation of will to power, it is as often an unhealthy manifestation as a beneficial one, and the best exercise of will to power is in overcoming one's self.

Nietzsche made a number of brief claims, in various contexts, about historical slavery. Greek slavery, which was based not on race but on capture (often of wellborn Greek citizens from other cities), is spoken of favorably in several places scattered throughout his work, but elsewhere he suggests that Greek society perished from it. His use of the term *slavery* is often broad and also covers Christianity, which he saw as the slavery of his day, and as the sickest possible manifestation of will to power. In the notes collected as *Will to Power,* slave morality, as a manifestation of the will to power, is seen as the worst possible perversion. Nietzsche saw slavery in the broadest sense as having been changed in form, rather than abolished, from institutional slavery to the institutional slave morality of the Christian church.

Slave morality is not imposed upon "slaves"—be they the working poor, Christians, or literal slaves. They create it out of their resentment of their condition and use it (unconsciously) both to pervert the values of their masters and to perpetuate their own herd condition. Adherents of slave moralities, in fact, demand masters, even if they are tamed, transformed masters who are kept in their positions and resented nevertheless.

Nietzsche was not a proponent of the Enlightenment, and we ought not dress him up to seem more acceptable to our sympathies. However, he did not find these "truths"—always, for Nietzsche, his truths—to be easy to face, but he did find them to be part of the cruel dynamic of the natural world, which must be embraced, in a healthy manifestation, if a person or a society is to thrive. He did not seek for society to return to any former state or to take up any previous morality, nor did he prescribe any *specific* values or practices. Thus, he did not suggest the institution of an underclass or of slavery. He saw the social effect of his thought as assisting an incipient liberation from slave morality and a stale social order.

—*James di Properzio*

For Further Reading
Nietzsche, Friedrich. 1966. *Beyond Good and Evil*. Trans. Walter Kaufmann. New York: Random House; Nietzsche, Friedrich. 1974. *The Gay Science*. Trans. Walter Kaufmann. New York: Random House; Nietzsche, Friedrich. 1996. *Human, All Too Human*. Trans. R. J. Hollingdale. Cambridge: Cambridge University Press.

first articulated the ideas that became known as "master morality" and "slave morality" in his work *Human, All Too Human*. He would later explore these concepts in greater detail in a later work, *Beyond Good and Evil*.

1880

The Spanish government enacted the Law of Patronato, which began a process of gradual emancipation in all of the country's colonial dominions over an eight-year period.

❧Asia❧

There is no silence in the East.
—W. Somerset Maugham, *The Gentleman in the Parlour* (1930)

Some of the world's most ancient civilizations originated in remote river valleys of the vast Asian landmass. Great distances served to isolate these cultures from the peoples who populated the Mediterranean rim at the time, and a self-desired detachment later perpetuated the isolation that physical geography had created earlier. The twin attributes of distance and detachment have characterized Asia's relationship with other world regions throughout most of the region's long history.

Despite the physical and cultural separation that distanced Asian peoples from the other ancient peoples of Europe and Africa, slavery still developed in the Orient. It is quite telling that the symbolism of a scientific model—with its use of an isolated control group and an experimental group exposed to social variables—did not apply in Asia because of the spontaneous origin of slavery in the region. Since neither induction nor deduction explains the development of slavery in Asia, one must assume that the social practice may be inherently human rather than culture-specific. Such an awareness speaks volumes about the pervasive nature of slavery in human history—indeed, we find "no silence in the East."

There were subtle differences between the type of slavery that developed in Asia and the types in other regions of the world. Slavery within Asia tended to be associated with questions of caste and class, which tended to differentiate between the lowborn and the wellborn, to form a social hierarchy. For the most part, there seems to have been little regard for ethnic distinctiveness in identifying those of slave status in Asia. Within each culture, there was a social stratum that, either through tradition or popular sanction, formed a servile population who attended to their social betters. It was these lowborn people who performed the less-than-desirable occupations that were essential to their communities.

In this chronology, the history of slavery in Asia is traced from its earliest origins in the Huang Ho (Yellow) River region to the modern horrors of the *laogai* system (forced labor camps) established in the People's Republic of China in the twentieth century. From the trade along the ancient Silk Road to the more modern *mui tsai* ("little younger sister") trade, various forms of enslavement and servitude are examined in their historical context. One significant geographical note is that materials regarding slavery in the region of southwestern Asia—generally described today as the Middle East—are also included in this chronology.

In *Non-Violence in Peace and War* (1948), the Indian nationalist leader Mohandas (Mahatma) K. Gandhi wrote: "The moment the slave resolves that he will no longer be a slave, his fetters fall. He frees himself and shows the way to others. Freedom and slavery are mental states." This chronology of slavery in Asia clearly demonstrates the extent to which "mental states" have influenced the self-definition of Asian peoples and cultures throughout history. In spite of distance and detachment, Asia's history is not silent on the question of slavery.

C. 4500 B.C.
Archaeological records indicate the beginnings of a civilization along the Huang Ho (Yellow) River in China. The culture that evolved in this ancient settlement was named the Tang-shao, and it maintained an agricultural economy based upon the cultivation of millet, pigs, goats, and dogs.

C. 2205 B.C.
According to Chinese chroniclers, Yu the Great established the Hsia (Xia) dynasty, a semi-legendary dynasty said to have been governed by benign and exemplary kings, which ruled over the Huang Ho (Yellow) River region and marked the beginning of Chinese civilization.

C. 1900 B.C.
Chinese civilization experienced the Chalcolithic Age in which local copper ore was smelted and used along with stone in the manufacture of tools and ornaments. An archaeological site at Yang Shao (Zhengzhou) in the northwestern part of Henan Province revealed the presence of wheelmade pottery, and other evidence suggests that pigs and dogs had already been domesticated by the Chinese.

C. 1557 B.C.
The tyrant Chieh, the last ruler of the Hsia (Xia) dynasty, was deposed in China by the victorious forces of T'ang who established the Shang dynasty. The Shang were able to argue convincingly through warfare that the Hsia had lost "the mandate of heaven," which had entitled them to rule. In ancient China, as in other world cultures, war captives generally became the slaves of the victors.

C. 1395 B.C.
The city of Anyang was established along the Huan River in China. Located to the north of the Huang Ho (Yellow) River valley, this great city of the Shang dynasty was supposedly founded by the tribal chief Pan-Keng. It was in this location that the cultivation of silkworms and the making of silk cloth began. The kings who were buried at Anyang were generally buried along with a large number of their attendants, which means that the practice of taking one's slaves into the next life was common among the Chinese rulers, as it was among the Egyptian pharaohs.

C. 1200 B.C.
During this century, the Chinese book of divination, *I Ching* (The book of changes), was written.

C. 1027 B.C.
The Chou (Zhou) dynasty came to power in China and ushered in a period, which lasted for three centuries, during which China became unified into one feudal kingdom.

841 B.C.
The oppressive reign of the Chinese king Li ended when he was removed from power and the Kung Ho (Public Harmony) regency assumed control of the government. Li was forced from power during a citizens' revolt when armed slaves and commoners ejected him from the royal palace. From this point onward in Chinese history, the chronological record is more authentic because the historical record is more complete than for earlier centuries. Under the Kung Ho regency, China endured as a feudal state until the rise of the Han dynasty.

827–800 B.C.
The Chinese were successful in driving the nomadic Huns west out of Chinese territory. The westward migration of the Huns would force a similar migration of the Scythians, and eventually, Western Europe would feel the effects of this demographic shift on the Eurasian landmass.

771 B.C.
King Yu of the Chou (Zhou) dynasty was deposed, thus ending the original unified feudal reign of the Chou. The dynasty would survive for another five centuries with a different capital city, but the form of government became a decentralized regime of warring barons who were loosely unified under a symbolic leader known as "the king of heaven." As the Chinese barons made war upon one another during this period, the enslavement of war captives was a common occurrence.

C. 660 B.C.
Invaders who were ethnically Mongolian entered the Japanese islands by way of the Korean peninsula and subjugated the indigenous Ainu people. With this event, the semilegendary Jimmu became the first emperor of Japan. From this point on until the Nara period (A.D.

710–794) in Japanese history, the term *yakko* was used to refer to a male slave. Slaves in early Japan were either war captives or criminals.

C. 600–321 B.C.

In India during the Vedic period, the ownership of hired laborers and slaves *(dasa-bhritaka)* was a common practice among landowners who needed cultivators to work their fields.

C. 600 B.C.

The sixth century B.C. inaugurated one of China's most productive periods of literary and philosophic creativity. This formative period of Chinese cultural life would continue until the end of the Chou (Zhou) dynasty in 256 B.C.

594 B.C.

In China, officials in the state of Lu began the system of collecting a land tax. One of the results of this new policy was that the system of agricultural slavery in the region became transformed into a system of feudal tenancy.

500 B.C.

Iron was used for the first time in China though bronze continued to be the metal of choice for weapons for several more centuries.

497 B.C.

The Chinese philosopher Confucius began his period of wandering through China as a teacher who moved from one court to another.

C. 490

The Chinese philosopher Mo-tzu (Mo Ti), who taught a message of love and pacifism, was active in China at this time.

483 B.C.

The Chinese philosopher Confucius ended his period of wandering and began working on his dialogues. He also wrote appendixes to *I Ching* (The book of changes) at this time.

470 B.C.

The disciples of the Chinese philosopher Confucius collected and recorded his teachings. Rather than espousing a clear religious dogma, Confucius's teachings were more ethical in nature and were based upon the proper social relationships that grow out of a life based upon the Golden Rule.

403–222 B.C.

China, which was already a decentralized feudal state, experienced greater deterioration of central control as the Warring States period began. During this period of anarchy, large numbers of war captives were taken and made into slaves.

350 B.C.

The nature of Chinese warfare changed as horses, which had previously been used to pull war chariots, were now used as part of cavalry charges during battle. Innovations in military techniques and strategy tend to make warfare more frequent and more brutal. Captives of war generally became slaves in ancient China.

332 B.C.

The Chinese philosopher Mencius began to travel as an itinerant teacher from court to court as Confucius had done. Mencius's teachings also were based upon ethical concepts rather than upon any strict religious dogma.

307 B.C.

King Wu Ling of the state of Chao in northern China was actively involved in fighting against the Huns. Based upon pragmatism and wartime necessity, Wu Ling transformed his entire army from one that used war chariots to one that used cavalry.

C. 300 B.C.

The *Arthashastra,* a treatise on society, economics, and political life, was supposedly written by Kautilya, an adviser to Candragupta (emperor c. 321–c. 297 B.C.) in India. The work recognized four ways that one might become a slave: by birth, by voluntarily selling one's self, by being captured in warfare, or as the result of judicial punishment. A slave in India was able to purchase his own freedom, and many others were emancipated by their owners.

259 B.C.

In the battle of Ch'ang P'ing, which occurred near the great bend in the Huang Ho (Yellow) River in China, the forces of the Ch'in (Qin) were able to defeat the forces of the Chao state. During this period of Chinese history, as in other world cultures, war captives generally became slaves of the victors.

Archaeologists at the site of a Chinese copper mine dating from the Warring States period (403–222 B.C.), during which many war captives were permanently enslaved. (© Liu Xinning/Sovfoto/Eastfoto/PNI)

256 B.C.

The last of the Chou (Zhou) emperors in China abdicated as the forces of the Ch'in (Qin) continued to make war upon the Chou state. The Ch'in were able to argue convincingly through warfare that the Chou had lost "the mandate of heaven," their entitlement to rule.

246 B.C.

Cheng adopted the title Shih Huang Ti (first august emperor) as the Ch'in (Qin) dynasty was established in China.

240 B.C.

The Chinese emperor Shih Huang Ti fought against the Huns and pushed them west.

225 B.C.

In China, construction began on the Great Wall, and the project was completed in 214 B.C. Emperor Shih Huang Ti constructed this enormous barrier, which stretched for 2,000 miles, to pro-

tect China against any further encroachment of the Huns. A prophet had warned the emperor that the wall would be successful only if it were built over the bodies of 10,000 men, but rather than kill 10,000 slaves to satisfy this purpose, the wall was built over the body of one man whose name meant "ten thousand."

210 B.C.

Chinese laborers built a magnificent tomb for the emperor Shih Huang Ti. Reportedly, the workmen who built the structure, many of them slave laborers, were buried alive in the tomb.

206 B.C.

The short-lived Ch'in (Qin) dynasty ended as Liu Pang, a self-described man of the people, formed the Han dynasty and claimed "the mandate of heaven."

C. 200 B.C.

The Han dynasty consolidated its power

A system akin to slavery in Southeast Asia has flourished since ancient times. Both ancient texts of high culture and stories handed down by the oral tradition of different Southeast Asian nations mention various forms of slavery and servitude and comment upon relationships between servants and masters. Yet in these texts, as well as in sixteenth-, seventeenth-, and eighteenth-century accounts by Europeans, the system of slavery in Southeast Asia is depicted as mild and the practice is sometimes even celebrated. Although slavery differed in Southeast Asian societies from place to place, three characteristics remained fairly constant: slaves and masters often entered into close, quasi-familial relationships, not unlike the dependency of less fortunate family members on their richer relatives; slaves were often allowed to hire themselves out to generate independent income; and there was a tendency to manumit second-generation slaves or to assimilate them into a less rigidly defined form of bondage.

The sources of slaves in Southeast Asia were mainly war captives and men and women who were sold or who sold themselves into slavery because of a debt obligation. Weddings, loans, gambling debts, and other financial obligations were often paid by pawning oneself or a family member into servitude.

Unlike in Europe, in most Southeast Asian societies, land was abundant and the source of power and the indicator of prestige came instead from having control over large numbers of bondsmen. Slavery thrived during periods of Southeast Asian urban expansion and successful international trade. In cities with populations of over 100,000—such as Angkor, Ayodhya (Ajodhya), Malacca (Melaka), Banten, Aceh, and Makasar—large labor forces were needed and were provided by bondsmen. Slaves worked in various capacities, including as domestic servants, entertainers, concubines, messengers, interpreters, traders, soldiers, seamen, craftsmen, construction workers, and scribes. Agricultural slaves (rice farmers, cash croppers, etc.) usually had their own houses and tended to be assimilated into a kind of serfdom where they would have to pay some part of their crop to the landlord. Unlike in the American South, urban, not rural, slaves were responsible for slave modes of production in Southeast Asia.

Although the system is often dubbed debt-bondage, it is appropriate to call the relationship between the master and the bondsman slavery for several reasons. The initial debt, instead of being reduced by the labor of the bondsman, often became permanent and was inherited by the bondsman's children. Bonded laborers could be bought, sold, and traded in the marketplace. They were considered property by masters and often given away, sold, or inherited. For example, bondsmen and bondswomen could be given to others as gifts, donated to monasteries, or offered as loan security.

European traders and colonists (most especially the Portuguese and the Spanish in the sixteenth century and the British, Dutch, and French in the seventeenth century) tended to distinguish between "debt-bondage" and "true slavery," but these distinctions overlooked the fact that in most Southeast Asian cultures (Thailand, which had a nineteenth-century law explicitly differentiating debtors and slaves, being the notable exception), the link between debt and bondage was inherent and clear. The indigenous demarcation made a distinction between captives from other cultures and native debtors.

A number of Southeast Asian states became prominent because of their trafficking in slaves: in the sixteenth century, Aru (Sumatra) and Onin (New Guinea); in the seventeenth century, Sulu, Buton, and Tidore; and in the eighteenth century, Sulu again. Most slave trafficking was from smaller, more divided states to wealthier nations, from east to west, and from non-Muslim to Muslim states. However, after the British abolition of the slave trade (1807), the Treaty of Vienna (1815), and the slave trade abolition in the Dutch colonies (1818), only Southeast Asian countries that were outside the realm of European domination (for example, Nias, Bali, and Sulu) still furnished slaves.

With the rise in the seventeenth and eighteenth centuries of a class of penurious landless workers and the increasing of centralized state control, as well as the spread of a religion that espoused benevolent treatment, slavery in its most severe form began to decline in Southeast Asia, and extreme forms of bondage were reconfigured into hierarchical systems of obligation. Although there was a marked decline in some forms of slavery, it is misleading to assume that a complete abolition of slavery in Southeast Asia has been effected. For example, the Tharu people in western Nepal still live in an extreme form of servitude that arose as late as the 1950s, and the selling of Burmese and Thai women and girls into brothels in Thailand has been cited by human rights organizations as a modern form of slavery. In addition, debt-bondage continues to be prevalent in Southeast Asia in the twentieth century, and the result is a system not unlike earlier forms of slavery.

—Jennifer Margulis

For Further Reading
Reid, Anthony, ed. 1983. *Slavery, Bondage, and Dependency in Southeast Asia*. New York: St. Martin's Press; Watson, J. L., ed. 1980. *Asian and African Systems of Slavery*. Berkeley: University of California Press.

throughout China during the second century B.C. and eventually established trade and commercial ties with the West. The Han dynasty endured for four centuries, and its period of rule coincided with the age of the Roman Republic and the Roman Empire's Pax Romana.

180 B.C.

The western part of the Mauryan empire in India was taken over by a line of kings known as the Indo-Greeks. These rulers eventually formed an alliance with the leaders of Han China.

150 B.C.

Faced with the territorial expansion of the Han state in China, the Huns began a westward migration that initiated a chain reaction as other tribal peoples were also pushed west because of the advancing Huns. The Yüeh-Chi tribe moved into the Aral Sea region around modern-day Turkestan, which affected the Scythians (Sakas).

140 B.C.

Emperor Wu Ti, the greatest of the Han leaders in China, came to power and ruled for 50 years. He initiated many social reforms during his long reign, including the creation of state monopolies in which socialized industries were formed. Other economic reforms regulated both incomes and prices in Han China.

138 B.C.

Han China attempted to form a diplomatic alliance with the Yüeh-Chi tribe to make war upon the Huns, but the negotiations were not successful and the alliance never formed.

122 B.C.

Chang Ch'ien was sent on an exploratory mission to the West by the leaders of Han China. One of the primary discoveries of his mission were the fine horses that were found in Sogdiana, a province of the Persian Empire.

111 B.C.

Emperor Wu Ti of Han China conquered and annexed the kingdom of Nan Yüeh (southern China and northern Vietnam) to China proper. The region of northern Vietnam was named Annam, which means "pacified south," and the Chinese subjugated the region, taking captives in the process.

C. 100 B.C.

Dong Zhongshu (Tung Chung-shu), a famous follower of Confucius, advised Emperor Wu that reforms were necessary if an agricultural crisis that threatened China's well-being was to be averted. Dong specifically argued that "slavery and the right to execute servants on one's own authority should be abolished" (Meltzer, 1993). His reforms included the limitation of ownership of both land and slaves, but these suggestions were never implemented because of strong opposition from China's wealthy families.

40 B.C.

Despite having been supported by China, Hermaeus, the last of the Indo-Greek kings of India, was dethroned by the Yüeh Chi tribe.

32 B.C.

The gradual decline of the Han dynasty in China began with the accession to the throne of Emperor Cheng Ti. He, like many of his successors, was controlled by a court clique, which held the real power in China during this extended period of decline, and many ministers within the bureaucracy were slave eunuchs who had reached positions of prominence in the Chinese government.

A.D. 17

During "the Red Eyebrow rebellion," the chief minister, Wang Mang, was able to usurp the throne and introduce sweeping reforms into Chinese society. Wang Mang abolished slavery in China and imposed an income tax—actions that provoked the wrath of Chinese landlords.

A modern painting depicting the Red Eyebrow rebels storming Changan, the imperial capital, in A.D. 17. During this rebellion, the reforming chief minister, Wang Mang, came to power for a short period and outlawed slavery, but the abolition was only temporary. (The Purcell Team/Corbis)

When flooding along the Huang Ho (Yellow) River caused economic distress, a peasant revolt led by one Mother Lu spread through the countryside. The combined effect of opposition from the wealthy and the poor eventually forced Wang Mang from power.

A.D. 23

In China, "the usurper," Wang Mang, was assassinated. After his death, his reforms were invalidated, and slavery was soon reestablished in China.

A.D. 39–43

During the Trung Sisters rebellion, the aristocratic families in northern Vietnam attempted to throw off Chinese control and restore the previous feudal society that had existed in the region. The Trung Sisters did not receive the support of the local peasants, however, and the Chinese were able to quell the rebellion.

A.D. 57

The Chinese court received an envoy who had been sent by a Japanese chieftain.

A.D. 65–67

The Chinese emperor sent envoys to India in order to learn about Buddhism, and soon thereafter, Buddhist missionaries began to visit China.

C. A.D. 81

The weakened Han dynasty in China struggled against renewed pressure by the Huns. This warfare threatened the security of the Silk Road, which had become a lucrative commercial artery linking China to the West.

A.D. 150

The Chinese began to store state documents, which were written on good rag paper, in the Great Wall, and it became a de facto archival repository. Consequently, the documentary record for Chinese history is exceptionally good from this point on.

A.D. 166

Chinese records indicate that Roman Emperor Marcus Aurelius sent a diplomatic representative to meet with the Chinese at Tongking (Tonkin), a historical meeting of East and West.

A.D. 173

China suffered from a plague that lasted for 11 years. The epidemic, which may have been the bubonic plague, was probably the result of a visit by Roman soldiers as a similar outbreak of the plague had occurred a few years earlier in the Roman Empire.

A.D. 184–204

China suffered through a period of anarchy and division as a result of a rebellion of the Daoist-inspired Yellow Turbans. The weakened Han dynasty was suffering because of the misrule of a court clique of eunuch ministers (many eunuch slaves had become officials in the Chinese bureaucracy through the years), and the rebellion was inspired by the Taiping, a sect of Taoist mystics that had suffered great persecution at the hands of the bureaucratic eunuchs. The rebellion was cruelly suppressed, and many of the Taiping mystics were made slaves of the state.

A.D. 190

A child by the name of Hsien-Ti ascended the throne in China. The last of the Han emperors, he was deposed in the following year by a usurper who destroyed the power of the slave eunuchs who had dominated the imperial court. Although Hsien-Ti was allowed to serve as a puppet ruler until A.D. 221, this action effectively ended the Han dynasty in China.

A.D. 200

A portion of the Korean peninsula was invaded and subdued by Japanese forces of the warrior empress Jingō. In keeping with the common practice of ancient warfare, captives of war were sold into slavery.

A.D. 221

In China, the fall of the Han dynasty, which had governed for four centuries, was followed by a 45-year period of anarchy and violence known as the period of the Three Kingdoms.

C. A.D. 241

Diplomats from the state of Wu in southern China were sent to Funan (modern-day Cambodia), and Japan received diplomatic envoys sent by the state of Wei in northern China. Wu and Wei were two of the Three Kingdoms.

A.D. 265

Northern China's kingdom of Wei was able to exert some authority over surrounding states, and its leaders proclaimed the creation of the Tsin (Chin) dynasty.

A.D. 304

Led by the Chinese-educated Liu Yüan, the Huns in northern China began to identify themselves as the Hun Han dynasty.

C. A.D. 311

China continued to be invaded by the Huns despite the presence of the Great Wall. During this era, the influence of the Huns extended into Siberia.

A.D. 316

In China the Tsin dynasty withdrew its support from all Hun kings in northern China.

A.D. 369

Japan invaded the Korean peninsula and established a colony there.

A.D. 379

Buddhism was declared the state religion of China.

A.D. 387

A Chinese victory in the battle of Fei Shui saved the region of southern China from a Hun invasion, but northern China was still prey to attack by the Huns.

A.D. 399

The Chinese traveler Fa-hsien embarked upon a mission to India to learn more about the country and its inhabitants.

A.D. 431

A group of Nestorian Christians, a heretic sect who were persecuted in the West, wandered into Persia and eventually reached China.

A.D. 549

The city of Nanjing (Nanking), established as an impressive cultural center by the Buddhist emperor Wu Ti (Hsiao Yen) who governed southern China, was destroyed by invaders.

A.D. 552

Buddhism, which would eventually become the state religion, was first introduced into Japan.

A.D. 589

China became tenuously unified under the short-lived Sui dynasty when the warlord Yang Chien (reign name, Wen Ti) came to power.

A.D. 592

In Japan, the ruler Shōtoku created a written constitution based upon Buddhist ethical beliefs. Shōtoku imported artists and scholars from China and Korea in an effort to encourage the arts and sciences in Japan.

A.D. 618

The T'ang dynasty began in China with its capital at Ch'angan (modern-day Xi'an) in east-central China. This new dynasty, which combined Hun blood and Buddhist ideas, ushered in a new period of greatness in Chinese history.

A.D. 622

The Hegira occurred as the prophet Muhammad fled Mecca and traveled to Medina in Arabia.

A.D. 628–635

China's trade and prosperity increased under the T'ang rulers as China was visited by envoys from Byzantium, Persia, and Arabia. After having endured an extended period of warfare, the leaders of T'ang China advocated a policy of diplomacy and peace in 626.

A.D. 645

Japan went through a period called "the Taika reform," or "great reform," and emerged as a more unified state with an autocratic, monarchial government. As a part of that reform, the *Danjo no Hō* (Rules for men and women) was enacted. This was the first time in Japanese history that *nuhi* ("slaves") were distinguished from *ryōmin* ("free commoners"). In Japan, slaves were generally either war captives or criminals.

A.D. 701

In Japan, the Taihō Code better defined the condition and rights of slaves in Japanese society. The code divided the *semmin* ("lowborn" or "base people") into five different social categories. The *kunuhi* ("public slaves," owned by the government) and the *shinuhi* ("private slaves," owned by individuals) made up two of the five classes of the lowborn. The code stipulated that slaves could marry only within their class. Although the possibility did exist that public slaves might be elevated to a higher status as the result of amnesty, that privilege did not apply to the private slaves. *Shinuhi* were considered to be private property, and as such, they could be sold, donated, or bequeathed.

A.D. 713

In China, Emperor Hsüan Tsung Li (Lung-chi) encouraged a "second blossoming" of T'ang culture during his reign and became a patron of poets, artists, and writers.

A.D. 751

Muslim (Saracen) forces encountered Chinese forces in a battle near Samarkand. The victorious Muslims enslaved the Chinese prisoners taken in the battle.

A.D. 755

A rebellion against the T'ang occurred in China when a military governor attempted an uprising against the government of the emperor. Muslim (Saracen) forces were sent into China to aid the emperor in putting down the rebellion.

A.D. 765

A revolt of African slaves occurred in the city of Medina on the Arabian peninsula.

A.D. 766

A rebellion in China that had lasted for a decade was finally quelled. Some accounts claim that 36 million lives were lost during the conflict. China was weakened as a result of the rebellion, but the T'ang dynasty would survive for another two centuries.

A.D. 833–842

Previously, many Turks captured in warfare had become the slaves of the Abbasid caliphs, and the practice intensified during the reign of Caliph al-Mu'tasim. Hundreds of young boys were purchased from slave traders in central Asia and transported to Baghdad, where they were converted to Islam. These young Turkish captives were eventually trained to be soldiers in the armies of the Abbasid caliphs.

A.D. 869

The most serious of the of the Zanj slave revolts occurred as African slaves who labored in the

Slavery existed in the pre-Islamic societies of the Mediterranean basin, Asia, and Africa even before the life of Muhammad (570–632), the spread of Islam, and the rise of the influence of the Arab world. The Qur'an itself, the sacred scripture of Islam regarded by Muslims as the word of God revealed to the prophet Muhammad, presupposes the existence of slavery. In the Qur'an, the manumission of a slave is a penalty for misconduct such as accidentally killing a believer or breaking an oath. Although the Qur'an repeats in several different passages that freeing a slave, like feeding and clothing the needy, is an act of benevolence, it also explicitly condones sexual relations between male masters and female slaves. For example, while sexual intercourse with a married woman is explicitly forbidden, it is accepted if that woman is a slave. The Qur'an emphasizes the restraint of carnal desire, except with one's wife and one's slave girls; in those cases, fulfillment of that desire is deemed "lawful" for practicing Muslims.

Although slavery is not condemned by the Qur'an, a strict interpretation of the *shari'a*, the religious laws of Islam, forbade Muslims to enslave each other. At the same time, a jihad (struggle) against non-Muslims was explicitly condoned by the *shari'a* and was generally considered a holy duty. This interpretation of the religious law led, after the rise of Islam in the Arab world, to slave raids upon the non-Muslim world, seen by those who embarked upon them as jihads. Captured slaves were generally not used by the Arabs for the large-scale production of goods, and because there were no extensive cotton, tobacco, or sugarcane fields in Arabia, as there were in the New World, slaves in the Arab world were used primarily as servants and soldiers.

Under Abbasid rule (749–1258), the dynasty of the Arab caliphs descended from Abbas, uncle of the Prophet Muhammad, the use of slave military forces was common. The slave soldier was the property of his master and could be bought or sold. However, the social position of the slave was determined by the status of his master, not his personal servitude. Therefore, a sultan's slave could be a general or a minister of the state, and a general's slave could be an army officer or an administrator. Military slaves were almost always eventually manumitted and given limited legal rights. In the tenth century, for instance, a slave governor, Alptigin, who ruled the capital of Ghazna (a city in modern-day Afghanistan), seized power in the region by establishing a slave soldier regime. The slaves themselves overtook Khurasan (999–1040) and conquered territory from Iran to India, replacing ruling elites with slave governments.

Slave armies like Alptigin's became one of the salient factors of Middle Eastern Arab governance. As the Abbasid empire declined (between 950 and 1258), regimes were buttressed by often nomadic armies that usually consisted of ethnic minorities. These regimes followed a policy of positioning slave regiments against each other in order to maintain the authority of the ruler.

During the Mamluk era throughout the Arab region (1250–1517), slave soldiers had exclusive rights to the military establishment. On the premise that the alien slave belonged only to the state and had no family or local ties that would compromise his devotion to his master and military service, no native Egyptian or Syrian, in principle, could belong to the military elite. Foreign (mostly Turkish and Circassian) slaves were bought when they were 10 or 12 years old, converted to Islam, raised as slaves, and trained in military techniques and loyalty.

Like previous Middle Eastern leaders, when the Ottomans rose to power, they replaced their independent followers with slave troops. New troops were first recruited from volunteers or prisoners, but in 1395, a human tax system was implemented that provided manpower from Christian populations in the Balkans. Unlike the Mamluks, who were by necessity taken from outside the native population, the Ottomans took slaves for the sultan's army from their own subject populations. At one point during the Ottoman Empire, the slave infantry was estimated to number 28,000 men.

When the Muslims began their campaign to conquer Iberia in 711, they raided Christian lands and took slaves as booty from Christian Europe. Warlike princes like Abū 'Amir al-Mansūr (938–1002) took vast numbers of captives; in one campaign against the Kingdom of Léon, it is reported that 30,000 slaves were taken. Captured in the long wars between Muslims and Christians in the lands bordering the Mediterranean, most of the white slaves were Spaniards, Portuguese, and Italians. The most famous white slave, Spanish novelist Miguel de Cervantes (1547–1616), was captured in 1575 and ransomed five years later. During the sixteenth and seventeenth centuries, there were an estimated 25,000–40,000 white slaves in Algiers. Another significant source of white slaves was from shipwrecked vessels captured and raided by Arab privateers. The threat of enslavement by the Barbary pirates increased for

Americans in the 1790s after the citizens of the newly formed United States lost the protection of the more powerful British fleet.

Although the export slave trade from Africa remained relatively small until the nineteenth century, Arab traders and explorers still captured and bought thousands of slaves, using the women in their harems and the men for military service and menial labor. African slaves were also shipped to Arabia, Persia, and other lands in the Arab world. As African leaders converted to Islam they, too, profited from cooperating with the invaders in the exportation of slaves.

With the decline of the West African slave trade, the conquest by the Russians of the Caucasus, and the rising need for slaves for private armies in the Arab world, the slave trade from East Africa to Arabia increased. Although Arabs had maintained control of the main East African coastal trade routes since 200 B.C., the trade in slaves had not been of major economic or social significance. The most developed trade was in highly prized Ethiopian youths. Young Abyssinian (Ethiopian) women were reputed for their beauty and sensuality while young Abyssinian men, noted for their honesty and belligerence, were important to Arabian rulers who used them in vast numbers in private armies. The demand for slaves in the early- and middle-nineteenth century became so extreme that Muslim traders began raiding the interior, traveling as far as Lake Victoria and the upper Congo. They gathered large numbers of slaves and marched them in huge coffles (chained groups of slaves) for transport to Zanzibar where they were used as plantation hands or shipped to Arab lands, Iraq, Persia, and Turkey.

European colonial expansion checked the spread of Islam in sub-Saharan Africa at the beginning of the twentieth century, and the end of the slave trade in Europe brought European, mostly British, disapprobation of the Arab practice. After the abolition of slavery in Europe, Britain used its powerful navy to enforce laws against the slave trade. In 1841, the British appointed a consul to Zanzibar, and by 1873, they were able to effectively force the sultan of Zanzibar to prohibit the slave trade. British diplomats also sought to end

A mounted Mamluk archer in battle, c. 1300. (The Granger Collection)

the slave trade in the Ottoman Empire, and in 1890, the Ottoman government signed the Brussels Act which prohibited the slave trade in Africa. By the middle of the twentieth century, slavery as a widespread institution had greatly declined in the Arab world as a whole. However, in several Islamic countries, including Mauritania, Sudan, and Pakistan, chattel slavery and bonded labor continue to exist. Most recently, the civil war that erupted in the Sudan in 1983 between the north and the south led to a widespread revival of chattel slavery.

—*Jennifer Margulis*

For Further Reading
Clissold, Stephen. 1977. *The Barbary Slaves.* London: Elek Books; De Jong, Garrett E. 1934. "Slavery in Arabia." *Moslem World* 24 (April): 126–144; Fisher, Allan G. B., and Humphrey J. Fisher. 1970. *Slavery and Muslim Society in Africa.* London: C. Hurst and Company; Lapidus, Ira M. 1988. A *History of Islamic Societies.* Cambridge: Cambridge University Press; Lovejoy, Paul E. 1983. *Transformations in Slavery: A History of Slavery in Africa.* Cambridge: Cambridge University Press; Rutter, Eldon. 1993. "Slavery in Arabia" *Journal of the Royal Central Asian Society* 20: 315–332.

salt flats southeast of Baghdad in lower Mesopotamia rose up against their Muslim overlords. The slaves attempted this revolt during a time of weakened enforcement while the Muslim civil war (A.D. 861–870) was taking place. Forces of the local caliph were able to restore order to the region.

A.D. 874

The second of the Zanj slave revolts began when African slaves who labored in the salt flats southeast of Baghdad again rose up against their Muslim overlords. Led by Riyah, "the lion of the Zanj," the rebels attracted many followers and defeated initial efforts by Abbasid caliph al-Mu'tamid's forces to end the insurrection.

Central Asia, the vast area stretching from the Caucasus Mountains in the west to Mongolia in the east, and from Kazakhstan in the north to Afghanistan and the Indo-Tibetan plateau in the south, incorporates terrain ranging from mountain to desert to steppe. It is also one of the most ethnically complex regions in the world, a complexity that has been compounded by the historical ease of mobility across the steppes. Traditionally, there was a heavy emphasis on the raiding of sedentary peoples by the mounted nomads of the steppes, of which the taking of slaves, especially women, was an integral component. This density of competing ethnic groups is rivaled only by that of sub-Saharan Africa; perhaps it is no coincidence that both have historically served as major sources of slaves.

During the early period of Islamic expansion, institutionalized military slavery grew as well, often in an attempt by central governments to balance the influence of constituent tribal elites. Central Asia quickly became known for producing some of the finest military slaves, most likely owing in no small part to the warrior ethos of the steppes. With the spectacular early Arabian conquests, slaves were more often than not gained as booty without any particular effort. By the time of the Abbasid caliphate (750–1258), slaves had become more of an issue of trade rather than of conquest per se. In addition to the purchase or capture of slaves, many were given as tribute while others appear to have taken on the status voluntarily.

Marginal central Asian peoples were still subject to slave raids. Samarkand (in modern Uzbekistan) became renowned as a slave-trading center, although many slaves from central Asia found their way to the slave market of Baghdad, the Abbasid capital. Eventually, Turks came to predominate as military slaves because of their numbers, martial qualities, and religious zeal. These slaves, known as *ghilman*, were purchased individually and then grouped as regiments that were trained, supplied, and paid by their own leaders. This trend eventually led to virtual autonomy and a greater loyalty to regimental commanders than to the caliph, which accelerated the disintegration of the Islamic world into competing political units.

It is interesting to note that within the Islamic context, the social position of all classes of slaves did not necessarily reflect personal servitude but was linked instead to the status of the master. It was not at all uncommon for a slave to reach a high position in administration or the military, and military slaves especially were almost always manumitted at the close of their active careers.

Almost every major Islamic dynasty depended on military slavery to varying degrees, up to and including outright control of the government by the slaves themselves. Most notable in the use of military slaves from central Asia were the Ghaznavids (977–1186), whose dynasty had in fact been founded by a former slave and served as something of a template for later institutions of military slavery. The Seljuks (1038–1194) were initially founded by free tribal steppe warriors but gradually came under increasing control of their own military slaves; the Ayyubids (1169–1250) were founded by Saladin using free Kurdish and Turkish soldiers but were eventually overthrown by the slave dynasty of the Mamluks (1250–1571), who were recruited primarily from the steppe regions of central Asia and from the Black Sea coast; the Safavids (1501–1732) depended on military slaves from the Caucasus to balance the various internal tribal influences. In northern India, military slaves from central Asia were the norm, as opposed to those in the south and east, who largely came from Africa.

The rise of the Mongols under Genghis Khan had an understandably immense impact on the region, but the trade in slaves remained virtually intact. This fact may be explained by the Mongol emphasis on administration through existing institutions to maintain steady tribute, although if any administrative unit became restive, retribution was swift and harsh. The various Mongol successor states maintained this practice, and in the course of time most were Islamized. However, during one episode in 1307, the Kipchak khan expelled a colony of Genoese merchants from his capital, Sarai, located on the lower Volga River, on the grounds that they were selling too many local Turkish military slaves to the then-rival Mamluks.

For the most part, the practice of slavery continued as it had for centuries until the late-nineteenth century. Russian imperial expansion used the abolition of the slave trade as one of its major pretexts for the establishment of a protectorate over the khanate of Khiva in 1873 and the annexation of the khanate of Khokand (later Fergana Province), which formally ended the practice of slavery in central Asia.

—*James D. Medler*

For Further Reading
Grousset, Rene. 1970. *The Empire of the Steppes: A History of Central Asia.* New Brunswick, NJ: Rutgers University Press; Lapidus, Ira M. 1988. *A History of Islamic Societies.* New York: Cambridge University Press; Pipes, Daniel. 1981. *Slave Soldiers and Islam.* New Haven, CT: Yale University Press.

The Zanj rebels disrupted commerce for nearly 15 years before they were defeated by the forces of the caliph's brother, al-Muwaffaq. When slaves in the region attempted to renew the insurrection, Muslim forces massacred 10,000 slaves near Monsul in northern Mesopotamia.

A.D. C. 900

Buzurg, a merchant in and navigator of the Persian Gulf region, wrote *Kitab al-Ajaib al-Hind*. This collection of sailing adventures includes references to slave-trading ventures on the coast of eastern Africa. [See Document 6.]

A.D. 907

Slave status was abolished by law in Japan with the *Engi Kyaku* (Penal procedures of the Engi era), but *nuhi* ("slaves") continued to constitute a large part of the agricultural labor force during the later Heian period (794–1185). Slaves would eventually merge with the *genin* ("serf") class so that *nuhi* became indistinguishable as a separate class.

A.D. 956

The Koryŏ dynasty in Korea freed all slaves on the Korean peninsula who had been impressed into servitude unfairly.

C. 1000

The Chinese called the coast of eastern Africa Po-Pa-Li. Regular trade, including the transportation of Africans as slaves, occurred between Mo Lin (Malindi) and Canton (Guangzhou). [See Document 5.]

1178

The Chinese author Chou Ch'u-fei wrote the travel account *Ling-wai-tai-ta*, which described eastern Africa and the slave-trading activities that occurred there. [See Document 7.]

1185–1333

Even though slavery had been abolished in Japan, it was common during the Kamakura era for *nuhi* ("slaves") to be employed as household servants.

1206–1526

In India, the Delhi sultanate is sometimes called "the slave sultanate" or "the slave dynasty" because the period was dominated by Turkish slaves (mamluks) who served as military leaders, provincial governors, and court officers in the region. Only three of the sultans—Qutb-ud Dīn Aybak (r. 1206–1210), Iltutmish (r. 1210–1236), and Balaban (r. 1266–1286)—were slaves themselves, but many of the other officers and leaders of the Delhi sultanate were slaves.

C. 1240–1438

Slavery was practiced during the rule of the Sukhothai kingdom in Siam (modern-day Thailand). Most of the people who were enslaved were the victims of warfare or natural disasters.

1271–1292

The Venetian traveler Marco Polo lived in Cathay (China) where he was employed in the service of the Chinese ruler, Kublai Khan.

1279–1368

While the Yuan Mongols controlled China, they regularly dealt with Arab merchants engaged in the trans-Eurasian slave trade. Peoples of various ethnic minorities who were held under the Yuan Mongols often found themselves the victims of this trade when they were traded as commodities along the Silk Road between China and Europe.

1307

A group of Genoese merchants were expelled from Sarai (in modern-day Russia) when the Kipchak khan in the Volga River region believed they were trading too many Turkish military slaves to his rivals.

1333–1568

Even though slavery had been abolished in Japan, *nuhi* ("slaves") were still employed as household servants during the Muromachi era.

1368–1398

The Chinese emperor T'ai Tsu (Chu Yüanchang) founded the Ming dynasty and overthrew the Yuan Mongols who had imposed their rule upon China. One of the reforms that T'ai Tsu introduced was the abolition of all forms of slavery, which the Yuan Mongols had introduced during their period of domination.

1382

The Circassians of central Asia became the primary group of people to supply their own children to the Muslim sultans and emirs as slaves. Young boys were sold to become mamluks (sol-

T'ai Tsu, literally meaning "grand progenitor," was the posthumous designation of Emperor Hung-wu, whose original name was Chu Yüan-chang (1328–1398). Founder of the Ming dynasty (1368–1644), T'ai Tsu is one of the controversial figures in Chinese history. He was revered for liberating the Chinese from Mongol oppression in the fourteenth century but criticized for his despotic rule.

Forty-nine years before Chu Yüan-chang's birth, Kubilai Khan (1215–1294) had established the Yuan dynasty (1279–1368) in China. The Yuan government freely expropriated land for its garrisons, and officials and soldiers arbitrarily kept war captives, including Chinese peasants, as slaves. Throughout the Yuan period, the enslavement of free people *(liangmin)* continued unabated. Contemporary records testify to the existence of slave markets in Dadu (Beijing) and other large cities.

Chu Yüan-chang was born in the twilight years of the Yuan dynasty when the Mongol government was losing its grip on the empire. The son of itinerant peasants of Anhui Province in central China, Chu Yüan-chang lived in poverty during his early years. When a plague took the lives of his parents and brothers in 1344, he became a lay novice in a Buddhist monastery and for the next three years wandered through east-central China as a mendicant monk, coming into contact with men of all walks and learning about the terrain and culture of the region. His experience helped prepare him for his subsequent political career.

In 1352, Chu Yüan-chang joined one of the rebellious groups as the Mongol empire began to fall apart. In the civil war, he quickly proved himself a distinguished general, and his ascendency from commoner to emperor began. In 1356, Chu subdued his rivals in the Yangtze Valley and captured the city of Nanjing (Nanking). Two years later, the Mongols were decisively defeated by his forces in the northeast. With the fall of the Yuan, Chu proclaimed the establishment of the Ming dynasty in 1368.

Once the Mongols were expelled from China, T'ai Tsu worked conscientiously toward rebuilding the country. With the assistance of his advisers, he created a centralized government, codified the law, and reopened the civil service examination. In order to restore social stability, he abolished all forms of slavery that had been imposed on the Chinese by the Mongols and subsidized the resettlement of the depopulated north by freehold farmers. His policies and programs laid the foundation of the Ming dynasty, which lasted over two and a half centuries. In his last years, he became increasingly suspicious of his subordinates, and in a series of purges, he exterminated tens of thousands of people. Although modern Chinese historians praise T'ai Tsu as a great dynasty founder, they are critical of his cruelties.

—*Henry Y. S. Chan*

For Further Reading
Ebisawa, Tetsuo. 1983. "Bondservants in the Yuan." *Acta Asiatica* 45: 27–48; Hucker, Charles. 1978. *The Ming Dynasty: Its Origins and Evolving Institutions.* Ann Arbor: Center for Chinese Studies, University of Michigan; Mote, Frederick W., and Denis Twitchett, eds. 1988. *The Ming Dynasty, pt. 1.* Vol. 7, *The Cambridge History of China.* Cambridge: Cambridge University Press.

diers) of the Muslims, and young daughters were sold into harems. On some occasions, the children were not sold, but used in lieu of tribute payments. Prior to the ascendancy of the Circassians, this enterprise had been dominated by the Kipchaks, another central Asian group.

1392

The Choson (Yi) dynasty came to power on the Korean peninsula and freed many of the slaves who belonged to the largest landlords in Korea. It seems that this action was taken to maintain a proper balance between the number of commoners and slaves in the region. Still, there remained a class of "base people" *(ch'ŏnmin),* who were public and private slaves. Many of these individuals served in certain prescribed areas as butchers, actors, and female entertainers *(kisaeng),* the last similar to later Japanese geisha.

1416

The Chinese slave eunuch Admiral Zheng He (Cheng Ho) sailed to the coast of East Africa on an expedition of discovery. In the system of slavery that existed in China at the time, royal eunuchs could hold positions of power and influence within the Chinese governmental bureaucracy.

1437

Reports indicate that peoples from East Africa were being traded as slaves in western India.

1460–1474

In India, the sultan of Bengal, Rukn ud Din Bar-bak Shah, purchased 8,000 African slaves during this period. Many of these captives served in the sultan's army, and some rose to positions of prominence.

1484

The Choson (Yi) dynasty, which governed the Korean peninsula, reportedly owned 350,000 public slaves.

1486

In a rebellion in India, African slaves killed the sultan of Bengal and installed the leader of the rebellion as the new sultan. Many of the rebels were later punished by being exiled to the Deccan region of the Indian subcontinent.

1493

On September 26, Pope Alexander VI issued the papal bull Dudum Siquidem, which granted to the Spanish crown the right to occupy heathen lands in Asia when they were reached by Spanish navigators. The papal bull granted the Spanish the right to "take corporal possession of the said islands and countries and to hold them forever." [See Document 10.]

1497

On December 25, the Portuguese navigator Vasco da Gama became the first Portuguese sailor to navigate the eastern coastline of Africa when he sailed along the region that he named Natal. From this region, da Gama later embarked upon the final part of his expedition, which took him to India.

1498

On May 20, the Portuguese navigator Vasco da Gama arrived in Calicut, India, and thus became the first European to reach the Indies by a sea route.

1514

Portuguese sailors reached the coast of southeastern China. Though the Chinese had maintained overland commercial contact with the Europeans for several centuries, this was the first time that Europeans had reached China proper by sea.

1575

European Tatars conducted a massive slave raid in which they captured 35,000 Ukrainians. The captives were taken to the slave markets in Constantinople (Istanbul) and Kaffa (Feodosiya) and sold to buyers from Arabia, India, Persia, Syria, and Turkey.

1603–1868

During the Edo (Tokugawa) period of Japanese history, the term *yakko* was used to refer to women who were forced into slavery as a form of punishment. Many of these women were the wives and daughters of criminals who had been either executed or sent into exile.

1644

When the Manchu established the Ching (Qing) dynasty, they enslaved large numbers of Chinese, and many of the newly enslaved bondsmen became personal retainers *(bugu)* of their new imperial lords. Since the Ching were outsiders, they tried to rely upon the cooperation of the indigenous Chinese to bolster the image of the new dynasty. Thus, many Chinese slaves rose to positions of power in the administrations of the Ching emperors.

1655

The Choson (Yi) dynasty, which governed the Korean peninsula, now owned about 190,000 public slaves, down from the larger numbers held earlier.

1676

European Tatars conducted a massive slave raid in which they captured 40,000 Ukrainians. As had been done earlier, the captives were taken to the slave markets in Constantinople (Istanbul) and Kaffa (Feodosiya) to be sold to buyers from Arabia, India, Persia, Syria, and Turkey.

1688

European Tatars again conducted a massive slave raid, this time capturing 60,000 Ukrainians. Again, the captives were taken to the slave markets in Constantinople and Kaffa and sold to buyers from Arabia, India, Persia, Syria, and Turkey.

1736

King Yongjo of the Choson (Yi) dynasty in Korea reduced the tribute tax on slaves by 50 percent. He would later make the tax identical for both slaves and commoners.

C. 1750
The number of public slaves reported owned by the Choson (Yi) dynasty had dropped to 27,000.

1775
The beginnings of emancipation on the Korean peninsula can be traced to the actions initiated by King Yongjo. By reducing the tax on slaves to the point where it was equal to the tax paid by commoners, the king created a condition whereby in economic status at least there was no longer a difference between a slave and a commoner.

1785–1808
In the Ottoman Empire, slavery was often a way to rise to a position of authority within the state. Five of the 12 Ottoman grand viziers who ruled during this era had begun their careers as slaves of pashas.

1801
The Korean government freed all agricultural slaves who belonged either to the central government or to the royal family.

1811
The colonial government in India enacted the Abolition Act of 1811, which specifically prohibited the importation of any additional African slaves into India. The practice of slavery would continue in British India, however, until it was outlawed in 1838.

1818
On January 15, the government of the Netherlands officially ended Dutch involvement in the African slave trade, which ended the practice in all Dutch colonies, including the region of modern-day Indonesia.

1837
In keeping with the British government's pledge to abolish slavery within the empire, slavery was officially abolished in India (Hindustan).

1839–1842
The first Opium War was fought between Great Britain and China. In the aftermath of China's defeat in this conflict and the gradual decline of the Ching (Qing) dynasty, the conditions of life for many of the commoners in China sank to slavelike conditions.

1843
With encouragement from the British government, the colonial government of India enacted the Indian Government Act of 1843, which abolished the legal status of slavery in India. Still, in many parts of India, practices of indigenous slavery continued. One British colonial official commented upon this practice when he remarked that "the lower classes are glad to bind themselves and their posterity to such perpetual service in order to be secure of subsistence in sickness and in old age" (Meltzer, 1993).

C. 1845
As European nations ended the African slave trade, the demand for Asian laborers increased dramatically. Chinese coolies were exported in large numbers as a replacement labor force in many areas that had previously depended upon African slave labor. By the late 1840s, substantial numbers of Chinese male laborers were being shipped under contract, mainly from Amoy (Xiamen) but also from Macao and other ports. These laborers were shipped to locations such as Cuba, Peru, Hawaii, Sumatra, and Malaya.

1848
The Dutch abolitionist W. R. van Hoëvell believed that the Dutch government should end the practice of slavery in its colonies, but he was concerned about what might happen if the Dutch tried to end the various forms of indigenous slavery that existed there. He argued against a blanket abolition policy because such indigenous practices "could not be removed without bringing about a total revolution of the society and emasculate the state" (Meltzer, 1993).

1850–1864
During the Taiping Rebellion, the rebel leader Hung Xiuquan (Hung Hsiu-ch'üan) implemented a far-reaching plan of social reforms that included the abolition of slavery, prostitution, and the trading of wives. The defeat of the rebel movement and the suicide of its leader brought an end to the proposed reforms.

1856–1860
The second Opium War was fought between Great Britain and China.

Discussions about the desirability or condemnation of slave labor were seldom heard in the Asian colonies. On the one hand, colonial realities obstructed Christian idealism, which pervaded many metropolitan societies. On the other hand, slavery was not a cornerstone of colonial society and economy. On the whole, slavery began declining in Asia in the eighteenth century, and slavery was not vital to the economic interests of Europeans in the colonies. Only in a few isolated cases in South and Southeast Asia were slaves employed in the large-scale production of market crops or in mining activities for the world market. Moreover, the "soft" character of household slavery in Asia seldom aroused strong indignation about the lot of slaves. Indigenous slavery, which formed by far the greatest majority of the servitude, hardly touched the conscience of European administrators.

Consequently, a proslavery argument was seldom mentioned by colonial writers on nineteenth-century Asia, and little hampered the growing anti-slavery sentiment in Europe, where abolitionism carried the day. Most discussions in government circles and the press concerned the method and pace of abolition; they never questioned emancipation itself. However, in a sense, a proslavery attitude did find expression in the silent acceptance of the state of being in the colonies, and in particular of the indigenous forms of slavery. This passiveness dominated most colonial governments in the early- and mid-nineteenth century.

Colonial arguments to leave indigenous slavery untouched ranged from indifference to economic and political pragmatism. One British official in India remarked that "the lower classes are glad to bind themselves and their posterity to such perpetual service, in order to be secure of subsistence in sickness and in old age" (Klein, 1993). An additional argument concerned the cost of paying indemnities to former slaveowners. Besides, fear concerning an upheaval of the indigenous social structure strongly influenced some colonial administrators to defer the abolition of servitude existing outside the European realm. The Dutch minister of religion, W. R. van Hoëvell, the strongest spokesman for the abolitionist cause, remarked in 1848 that slavery in the indigenous society should not be affected and "could not be removed without bringing about a total revolution of the society and emasculate the state" (Hoëvell 1848).

Initially, only the slavery in European circles was dealt with, and the worst excesses elsewhere were banned. Only later during the nineteenth century, when ideas of a European civilizing mission gained force, did pressure increase to ban slavery altogether, which, given the atmosphere of mounting colonial intervention, met with hardly any resistance in European circles. Still, there were marked differences between colonial powers in their eagerness to abolish slavery in indigenous societies. Whereas the British were fairly swift in discarding slave practices from newly occupied territories, Dutch policies in the Indonesian archipelago took a more pragmatic and reluctant course.

For the local elites, emancipation entailed nothing less than a total upheaval of their vested interests and rights, and conflicts over slavery crystallized into an opposition between central governments—whether colonial or indigenous—and local rulers and members of the aristocracy. The abolition of slavery was forced upon the Asian ruling classes by the colonial powers and by expanding and modernizing regimes as in Siam (Thailand). Although the elites seldom vented their conservatism on the issue in an explicit proslavery argument, they understandably fiercely resented and resisted the course of events. The signing of contracts with colonial governments by which local rulers agreed to ban slavery did not in most cases put an end to servitude. For the owners and many of the slaves, the mutual obligations of service and maintenance were a strong bond and formed a well-entrenched proslavery sentiment. Formal abolition in the late-nineteenth and early-twentieth centuries may have removed the legal basis for slavery, but personal attachments through bondage were a deeply felt fact of life that no abolitionist movement could easily dispel.

—*Remco Raben*

For Further Reading
Hoëvell, W. R. van. 1848. *De emancipatie der slaven in Neerlands-Indië: Eene verhandeling.* Groningen: C. M. von Bolhuis Hoitsema; Klein, Martin A., ed. 1993. *Breaking the Chains: Slavery, Bondage, and Emancipation in Modern Africa and Asia.* Madison: University of Wisconsin Press.

Mutiny of Chinese coolies, who with the ending of the African slave trade began to be exported in large numbers to areas previously dependent on African slaves. Conditions in many respects were little different from those suffered by slaves. (Corbis-Bettmann)

1859
British colonial officials in India enacted the Workman's Breach of Contract Act, which gave employers the right to put workers into a virtual system of indentured servitude. Although slavery had been abolished in India in 1843, servitude and debt bondage remained quite common.

1860
Large number of indentured servants from India were introduced to the Cape Colony in South Africa.

1860
The colonial government of the Dutch East Indies officially abolished slavery by statute.

1863
The government of the Netherlands officially abolished slavery in all Dutch colonies. This declaration ended the practice of slavery in the region of modern-day Indonesia.

1868
King Mongkut (Rama IV) of Siam (Thailand), concerned about a growing problem of slavery in his country that resulted from gambling debts, issued an edict requiring that a husband obtain his wife's consent before selling her or their children into slavery.

1873
The practice of slavery was officially abolished in the khanate of Khiva.

1874
Under the direction of Rama V, better known as King Chulalongkorn, the government of Siam (Thailand) began to initiate administrative reforms that would officially abolished the practice of slavery in the region by 1905.

1877
The colonial government of Cambodia began the process of abolishing slavery in the region.

The importance of the khanate of Khiva in the history of slavery lies in its role as a major center for the slave trade, even until the late-twentieth century. Khiva is located near the banks of the Amu Dar'ya River south of the Aral Sea in what is now Uzbekistan, near the border with Turkmenistan. Like other important cities along the Silk Road and other major trading routes, the history of slavery in Khiva lies in that city's status as an oasis town (a rest area for caravans and other related trade). The various struggles to form empires and conquer territory naturally came to target these rich, settled areas. Cities like Khiva, Samarkand, Bukhara, and Merv (now Mary) all functioned as nodes for the slave trade, and for most other commercial activities, but as often as not their own people were also victimized by invasion and siege.

Reaching a peak of power in the late-twelfth and early-thirteenth centuries, the shahs of Khwārzim (Khwarezm), as the region encompassing Khiva was then known, expanded their domains to comprise, by 1217, the area bounded in the north by the Syr Dar'ya River, the east by the Pamir Mountains, the west by Azerbaijan, and the south by the majority of Afghanistan and Persia. It was a great misfortune that this fledgling empire, held together by the personality of one man, Muhammad of Kwariszm, should have run afoul of Genghis Khan and the Mongols. By eliminating any form of buffer state between the two rulers, and by condoning the robbing and killing of a Mongol caravan without offering restitution, Muhammad precipitated the Mongol wrath, and his empire was utterly destroyed in 1220. Following the death of Genghis Khan, Kwariszm passed to the house of his eldest son Jochi (khanate of Kipchak), in keeping with the Mongol tradition that the oldest son's holdings should be the farthest away from the paternal residence. Eventually, the territory would pass to the control of the khanate of Jagatai (Chagatai), descended from Genghis Khan's second son, in a round of fraternal warfare between 1262 and 1265. Kwariszm formed an integral part of the Timurid empire in the late-fourteenth century.

As successors to the Timurids, the Shaybanids, descended from a grandson of Genghis Khan through the house of Jochi, were in possession of Khiva by 1506. During the middle of the fourteenth century, the hordes subject to the Shaybanids had taken the name of Uzbek, by which their descendants are still known. Around 1613, the tra-

City gate, Khiva. (Wolfgang Kaehler/Corbis)

ditional Kwariszmian capital of Urganch was abandoned owing to the drying up of its tributary of the Amu Dar'ya River, and Khiva became the formal seat of power as well as a primary commercial center in its own right. The relative decline of Khiva and the other oasis cities was tied to the rise of alternate routes between East and West, especially the sea routes, which were completely inaccessible to this landlocked region. The Shaybanids ruled in fact until the establishment of the Russian protectorate in 1873 and were retained as figureheads until 1920.

The establishment of the Russian protectorate, while primarily an imperial grasp for territory, was predicated on the grounds of finally stamping out the slave trade once and for all by occupying its last major remaining center. As a background to this imperialism was "the great game," which began during the mid-nineteenth century, in which the British in India and the Russians in northern Eurasia competed for influence in central Asia, Afghanistan, northern India, and Tibet. Tales abound of intrepid British agents risking the traveling slave raiders to visit Khiva and becoming embroiled in its quarrels with Khokand and Bukhara in an attempt to get the three to cooperate in the face of the Russian threat and to abolish slavery, which would thus remove the grounds for Russian intervention.

A major Russian invasion force was decimated by the climate in 1839, and in 1840, a British emissary, Lt. Richard Shakespear, managed to persuade the khan to release all Russian slaves. However, the days of independence for the khanate were still numbered, even though slavery in the region was at least officially abolished in 1873. The imperial issues were finally settled at the Congress of Berlin in

1878 and by the Anglo-Russian Convention of 1907. The khanate's history was inextricably linked with the slave trade, but the time of both city and institution had passed.

—James D. Medler

For Further Reading
Grousset, Rene. 1970. *The Empire of the Steppes: A* *History of Central Asia.* New Brunswick, NJ: Rutgers University Press; Hopkirk, Peter. 1992. *The Great Game: The Struggle for Empire in Central Asia.* New York: Kodansha International; Lapidus, Ira M. 1988. *A History of Islamic Societies.* New York: Cambridge University Press.

Additional legislation was passed to complete the abolition of slavery in 1884.

1880
The U.S. Congress conducted hearings and prepared a report regarding the conditions of slavery in China after concerns were raised about the circumstances faced by Chinese-Americans who were being repatriated to China.

1884
The colonial government of Cambodia officially abolished slavery by statute.

1886
The Korean government proclaimed that servitude in Korea would be limited to one generation only. This action effectively abolished hereditary slavery in Korea.

1894–1895
The First Sino-Japanese War was fought between China and Japan. The Japanese defeated China in this conflict and won certain island territorial concessions, but Japan did not acquire any territory on the mainland of China.

1895
Following the First Sino-Japanese War, the Choson (Yi) court abolished slavery on the Korean peninsula. This proclamation of uncompensated emancipation was enacted at the urging of the Japanese government, which wished to modernize Korea before annexing the region.

1900
Reports from American observers indicated that the practice of slavery in the Philippine Islands was growing extinct and that acts of piracy in the region had become quite rare.

1904–1905
In the Russo-Japanese War, fought between Russia and Japan, the Japanese defeated the Russians and thus became the first Asian power in history to defeat a European power.

1905
The government of Siam (Thailand) officially abolished the practice of slavery.

1909
During the final years of imperial rule in China, the Ching (Qing) leaders decreed that slavery was abolished in the country, but despite this change in official policy, the practice persisted well into the twentieth century.

1915
The colonial government of Malaya officially abolished slavery by statute.

1926
The colonial government of Burma officially abolished slavery by statute.

1929–1939
Officials in Hong Kong and Malaya began an intense campaign to reduce the number of young girls who were enslaved for purposes of prostitution. In the decade before World War II began, it was estimated that the numbers of young girls who were enslaved had been reduced by two-thirds. However, large numbers of *mui tsai* ("little younger sister") were still available in China for prices as low as $5, and some of these children were sold for $500 in the flesh markets of Singapore.

1929
The government of Burma instituted a program of compensated emancipation to encourage slaveholders to liberate their slaves. As many as 9,000 slaves were reported to be freed as a result of this policy.

Old forms of slavery persisted in Asia until well into the twentieth century. Two men of Kageros, Central Sulawesi (Celebes), were photographed in 1902 with their slave (on left). (Exclusive News Agency)

1930

An estimated 4 million Chinese children were enslaved in China as part of the *mui tsai* ("little younger sister") system even though China had abolished slavery in 1909. Many of these enslaved children were branded and beaten regularly.

1931

On September 19, the Mukden, or Manchurian, incident marked the beginning of conflict between Japan and China in the Far East. The Japanese occupation of Manchuria began the hostilities that would develop into the Pacific theater of World War II.

1937

On July 7, without a formal declaration of war, hostilities between Japan and China commenced in an incident at Lugouqiao (Lu-kou-ch'iao). This event was soon followed by a full-scale invasion of China.

1937

In December, the world learned of "the rape of Nanking," which occurred when Japanese forces attacked that Chinese city and raped and murdered many innocent civilians in the process. Stung by the international criticism, the Japanese military decided to establish comfort stations as a sexual outlet for Japanese troops. Many thousands of Korean and Chinese women were forced into sexual slavery during the years of World War II as military comfort women (*jugun ianfu*).

1945

September 2, VJ (Victory in Japan) Day marked the end of World War II in the Pacific theater.

1949

Shortly after his victory over Nationalist forces in China, the Communist leader Mao Tse-tung proclaimed the abolition of all slavery in mainland China.

1951

Two years after the successful Communist revolution, the People's Republic of China instituted a system of forced labor camps (*laogai*) that were designed to introduce "reform through labor." Many of the prisoners who were assigned to these labor camps were put to work on massive public works projects to benefit the Chinese state.

1953

The Japanese Ministry of Labor estimated that 40,000 Japanese children had been sold into slavery for purposes of prostitution in the previous year. Poverty and overpopulation had forced many parents to sell their children, and in the slave market, the owners of brothels were able to purchase children for prices ranging between $25 and $100.

1954

Having established the forced labor camps (*laogai*) in 1951, the government of the People's Republic of China enacted State Regulations on the Reform Through Labor. This statute authorized the use of prisoners as laborers in any type of work for 9–10 hours per day.

1957

A report filed by the Committee on Forced Labor of the International Labour Organization investigated charges that slave labor practices were in place in China. The report concluded that "the People's Republic of China had set up a very highly organized system of forced labor, in prisons and labor camps, for the purpose of political coercion and education and for economic purposes" (Meltzer, 1993).

1958

British journalist Alan Winnington traveled into southwestern China and observed the continuing enslavement of individuals by Narsu slave-owners in Yunnan Province even though the

The concepts of both slave and free labor refuse to be unequivocally applied in Asia. In ancient times, many forms of bonded labor had abounded in most regions of the area, ranging from personal attachment to debt-bondage and forms of saleable human property. Unless the American plantation model was used, slaves were seldom systematically employed in the mass cultivation of market crops; many were part of the family household or had relative freedom of action. Moreover, the transition from slave to free labor was not a linear process. The abolition of slavery gave rise to the development of different forms of bonded labor, which only slowly gave way to a free labor market.

Western pressure and increasing state intervention gradually pushed back slavery in South and Southeast Asia during the nineteenth and early-twentieth centuries, but "abolition" came at a time when slavery was already on the decline. After a ban on slave trade in the beginning of the nineteenth century (1807 in the British colonies, 1818 in the Dutch), the East India Company in India abolished slavery in 1843 (10 years after abolition in the British colonies in the Americas) but did not make the act fully effective until 1860. In that latter year, slavery was also abolished in the Dutch East Indies. However, these measures were only directed against slavery in areas under direct colonial rule.

Generally speaking, the abolition of "colonial" slavery went without many problems. Numbers of officially registered slaves were small, and they were mainly employed in household tasks and not vital to European economic interests. The official figure of slaves liberated by government decree on January 1, 1860, in the Dutch East Indies turned out to be only 4,735, including 514 slaves emancipated on the plantations of the Banda Islands, one of the few places where slavery had assumed a form similar to that of the plantation colonies in the Caribbean. As the nutmeg industry had gradually petered out by the mid-nineteenth century, however, even there the manumission of the slave population was carried out without much disturbance.

More fundamental were the changes in indirectly ruled and newly conquered areas where the process of abolition was accompanied by an increasing intervention of the colonial state. Abolition followed the expansion of the European colonies during the last decades of the nineteenth century. Through contracts and legislation, the slave trade, slavery, and debt-bondage were gradually phased out from the colonial centers outward.

In the late-nineteenth and early-twentieth centuries, the establishment of colonial authority or suzerainty often went hand in hand with a ban on slave taking and slavery. It wasn't until well into the twentieth century—in eastern Burma, for instance, not before 1926—before all regions in the colonial states were brought under colonial dominion, and slavery and debt-bondage were abolished.

Interestingly, a similar process of change occurred in the independent state of Siam (Thailand). Change in labor relations was accompanied by a transition in the system of land ownership and the development of free commerce. In Siam, decrees to alter the lot and later to abolish forms of saleable human property stretched over the second half of the nineteenth century. Pivotal in the change were the cautious policies of Rama V, known as King Chulalongkorn (r. 1868–1910), who strove to gradually dissolve slavery and guide the economy toward a free labor market. Although humanitarian motives were instrumental and were partly inspired by foreign advisers and European examples, a wish to curb the power of the elite, increase taxation, and preclude the jurisdiction of neighboring elites over Siamese "subjects" through personal bonds were equally powerful incentives.

Political motives and changing ideas of the state buttressed the wish to dissolve slavery and servitude. In the countries under colonial rule, formal abolition was pushed forward more abruptly, but it was equally related to the extension of central power over all sections of society. Thus, French policies in Indochina were motivated less by the liberal ideas of metropolitan moral advocates than by the practical aim of disempowering local elites.

Economic motives behind abolitionism were scanty. Administrators did not explicitly set out to establish a free labor market. Consequently, the end of slavery did not necessarily or immediately effect free labor relations. In fact, the assessment of labor in terms of wages came slowly. Only in densely populated areas, like Java, did wage labor became fairly common during the nineteenth century, especially in areas of intensive foreign (Chinese and European) economic activity. Colonial governments, businesses, and indigenous elites turned to other institutions to exploit labor reserves, and many of the methods had existed previously alongside slavery. Thus, the Dutch government on Java continued to use corvée labor in several forms. Later in the nineteenth century, entrepreneurs began systematically granting credits to bind contract coolies to the plantations and mines. Only with the advent of humanitarian labor legislation, the establishment of free enterprises, a large increase in population—and thus, in labor mobility—did a "free" wage labor system develop.

The abolition of slavery and other forms of bondedness was only one part in a slow evolution of labor relations. In many places a "free" labor market did not crystallize until well into in the twentieth century. In isolated parts of Asia, servitude still persists.

—*Remco Raben*

For Further Reading
Klein, Martin A., ed. 1993. *Breaking the Chains: Slavery, Bondage, and Emancipation in Modern Africa and Asia.* Madison: University of Wisconsin Press; Knaap, Gerrit J. 1995. "Slavery and the Dutch in Southeast Asia." In *Fifty Years Later: Antislavery, Capitalism, and Modernity in the Dutch Orbit.* Ed. Gert Oostindie. Leiden: KITLV Press; Lasker, Bruno. 1950. *Human Bondage in Southeast Asia.* Chapel Hill: University of Carolina Press; Reid, Anthony, ed. 1983. *Slavery, Bondage, and Dependency in Southeast Asia.* St. Lucia, London, and New York: University of Queensland Press.

government of the People's Republic of China was trying to end the practice through a form of compensated emancipation.

1959

The Chinese government of Mao Tse-tung proclaimed the end of the feudal system of serfdom that had been practiced in Tibet, thereby officially ending all forms of slavery in China. In the same year, however, the International Labour Organization, which continued to monitor labor practices in China, concluded that Mao's government had expanded its previous forced labor policies to include "vagrants, persons who refuse to work, persons guilty of minor offenses, and those who, for various reasons, have no means of existence" (Meltzer, 1993).

1960

In April, Harry Wu, a Chinese student and son of a well-to-do Shanghai banker, was jailed by Chinese authorities for making statements against the government of Mao Tse-tung. Wu was sentenced to 19 years of labor in "the bamboo gulag," a slave labor camp that was part of the elaborate system of forced labor camps *(laogai)* that had been established and were operated by the Chinese Communists.

1967

A group of Pakistani brickkiln workers founded the Bhatta Mazdor Mahaz (Brickkiln Workers Front) to try to fight against bonded labor that was used in the brick-making industry. This group eventually became known as the Bonded Labor Liberation Front, and it had continued to fight against the forced labor of adults and children in Pakistan.

1973

Bao Ruo-wang published *Prisoner of Mao,* the first work to present an insider's knowledge of the Chinese forced labor system. The work recounted Bao's years spent in the forced labor camps *(laogai)* of Mao Tse-tung's government.

1990

On November 16, Professor Yun Chong-ok established the Korean Council for the Women Drafted for Military Sexual Slavery by Japan during World War II. Established to bring forward the facts surrounding the use of "comfort women" as sexual slaves during the war, the group seeks a redress of grievances related to this massive human rights violation and hopes to obtain an official apology from the Japanese government.

1991

Anti-Slavery International, a British-based organization, instituted the Anti-Slavery Award to recognize those individuals or groups that are working to eradicate all forms of slavery from the modern world, and the Bonded Labour Liberation Front of India was the first organization to be so recognized.

1991

In August, Kim Hak-sun gave the first public testimony about the life of a comfort woman, the women who were used as sexual slaves by the Japanese military during World War II.

1992

The Korean Council for the Women Drafted for Military Sexual Slavery by Japan took the issue of comfort women to the UN Human Rights

Mui tsai, a Cantonese term meaning "little younger sister," perhaps best translated as maidservant, was a common practice of female servitude throughout China before the 1950s. Since women were considered outsiders in the Chinese kinship system, they were not a matter of concern in the traditional family, and in times of destitution, desperate parents were prone to present their daughters to rich families to work as domestic servants.

Usually *mui tsai* were small children at the time of transfer. In the transaction, a deed of gift was prepared and signed by both sides in the presence of a mediator. The parents would agree to give up their rights to the child in return for a sum of money. Generally, they had the right to visit her at the owner's house, but in practice, the connection ended if the young girl moved with her master's family to a distant place.

The *mui tsai*'s work varied from attending to her mistress to performing all forms of household drudgery. Although the master provided her food and shelter, she received no wages and enjoyed no freedom of movement. A marriage would be arranged when she reached puberty. After marriage, the *mui tsai* retained ritual ties to her former household in a position akin to that of an adopted daughter.

As China fell into political disintegration at the beginning of the twentieth century, war and famine produced a steady supply of *mui tsai*. The wealthy Chinese patronized the institution, for it was considered an act of charity to save poor girls from starvation and misfortune. The custom soon spread to the treaty ports along the South China coast, and even some European and Indian merchants owned Chinese *mui tsai*. Problems of child abuse and human traffic later caught the attention of some European humanitarians and administrators. The *mui tsai* system became an issue under examination by the British Parliament in the 1920s and the League of Nations' slavery committees in the 1930s. Each investigation reached the conclusion that the system was a form of child slavery, because the girls were sold for money and they lost their freedom and rights as a result. Recent research has further unveiled a more negative side of the institution. The *mui tsai* were often ill-treated by their owners, they were sometimes sold to dealers and changed hands several times, and they suffered a social stigma because they had been sold by their parents.

Before World War II, the colonial authorities in Hong Kong and Singapore passed regulations to control the institution, but they were ineffective. The social revolution of the Chinese Communists in the 1950s did eventually put an end to this form of female servitude in China. As the supply of poor girls from China stopped and the rural economy improved, the *mui tsai* custom also disappeared in Hong Kong and Singapore.

—Henry Y. S. Chan

For Further Reading
Jaschok, Maria. 1988. *Concubines and Bondservants: The Social History of a Chinese Custom.* Hong Kong: Oxford University Press; Miers, Suzanne. 1994. "Mui Tsai through the Eyes of the Victim: Janet Lim's Story of Bondage and Escape." In *Women and Chinese Patriarchy: Submission, Servitude, and Escape.* Ed. Maria Jaschok and Suzanne Miers. Hong Kong: Hong Kong University Press; Watson, James L. 1980. "Transactions in People: the Chinese Market in Slaves, Servants, and Heirs." In *Asian and African*

Commission. Recently discovered documents showed that the Japanese government had been heavily involved in setting up the comfort woman system.

1993
Harry Wu published his autobiographical account, *Bitter Winds: A Memoir of My Years in China's Gulag,* which recounted the 19 years that he had spent in the forced labor camps of Mao Tse-tung's government.

1994
In December, the Reebok Foundation presented the 1994 Youth-in-Action Award to Iqbal Masih of Pakistan, a young international activist who spoke out against the enslavement of children in the carpet mills of Pakistan.

1995
Liu Zongren published *Hard Time: 30 Months in a Chinese Labor Camp,* which described the author's experiences as a slave laborer on China's Chadian Labor Reform Farm No. 583 during China's Cultural Revolution (1967–1976).

1995
In April, Iqbal Masih, the 12-year-old Pakistani youth who had become an international spokesperson for the plight of child laborers,

was murdered. Having been a slave laborer in the carpet mills of Pakistan for eight years, Masih was an outspoken advocate for reforms aimed at ending the abuse of children in Pakistan and around the world.

1995

On September 8, the U.S. House Subcommittee on International Operations and Human Rights heard testimony regarding the practice of slave labor in the forced labor camps *(laogai)* operated by the People's Republic of China. Many members of the U.S. Congress wished to make the continuation of China's most-favored-nation trade status contingent upon real reforms in the area of human rights abuses.

1995

On November 16, Anti-Slavery International presented the 1995 Anti-Slavery Award to Chi-

nese dissident Harry Wu. Wu had been imprisoned in China for speaking out against his government, and since his release from prison, he has been critical of the use of forced labor in Chinese prison camps.

1996

On February 6, Radhika Coomaraswamy, the UN special investigator on violence against women, presented her report on the comfort women question to the United Nations. Her recommendations on this matter were that the government of Japan should apologize for this human rights violation, compensate the victims, punish those who were responsible, and teach the story of this crime in Japanese history classes.

⚍Africa⚌

So geographers in Afric-maps
With savage-pictures fill their gaps;
And o'er unhabitable downs
Place elephants for want of towns.
—Jonathan Swift, On Poetry (1733)

A lack of knowledge about Africa was characteristic of early maps of the continent, which largely considered the region to be little more than a blank canvas that required creative solutions. The geographers Swift satirized tried to hide their ignorance of the "dark continent" by placing creatures that existed only in their imaginations upon the vacant landscapes. Scholars therefore viewed Africa as a historical region that was still in the process of development—a work in progress—unfinished and certainly misunderstood.

Historians rely upon primary sources—consisting of written records, artifacts, memory—to fashion the basis of their interpretations. Although traditional African societies do not have extensive archival written documents, the creative interpretation of African material culture and the oral tradition can often form the factual basis for a rather sophisticated understanding of the peoples who lived in preliterate societies.

In order to fashion a complete understanding of much of the history of Africa, social scientists other than historians, from disciplines as varied as sociology, anthropology, and linguistics, have helped in the formulation of an understanding of the complex civilizations that developed throughout the continent over time. Evidence that comes to us from these various disciplines indicates that the institution of slavery has a long history among African peoples.

Indigenous forms of slavery between and among African peoples began very early, but the nature of this form of slavery was substantially different from the practice that arose in the fifteenth century when Europeans arrived along the coast of western Africa. Indigenous slaves tended to be captives taken in war, orphans, and people who were traded as payment for debt. In most African societies, the form of slavery imposed was not a lifetime status as social mechanisms for manumission did exist.

Even before the arrival of the Europeans and the beginnings of the transatlantic slave trade, there was a well-developed trans-Saharan slave trade between West African states and the Berbers to the north. Some of the African captives who were traded in this market were later sent to slave markets in the ancient Greek and Roman worlds. The four centuries of the transatlantic slave trade that occurred later had terrible social, economic, political, and demographic effects upon the African continent as the diaspora wreaked havoc on the African peoples who were victimized for the economic gain of others. No other peoples in the history of the world have been exploited in such a fashion.

The history of early Egypt and the first African experiences with slavery appear in the section on ancient chronology. This section mostly chronicles the history of African slavery from the time of the European arrival in the fifteenth century to the "scramble for Africa" at the end of the nineteenth century. African slavery in the twentieth century is dealt with in the section on contemporary chronology.

In dealing with slavery, historians have tended to avoid viewing the institution in terms of its psychological impact on slaves, masters, and the entire social fabric of the Western world, but if one does focus on these elements, one is better able to evaluate the behaviors associated with slavery. By looking at one's behavior, environment, and the antecedents involved with daily existence, it is easier to understand the dynamics involved in being a slave. The problem is that many scholars tend to limit their interpretation exclusively to the Western mind and body dualism. Consequently, historians fail to address the fact that Africans in the colonial world were held in bondage to white owners, which resulted in an incessant disenfranchisement from their social, collective, and cultural identity. Therefore, expected behavior was based on definitions that the slaves had no part in making.

The impact of Europeans on Africans can best be reflected in the relationship of one culture dominating another. In slavery, the views, beliefs, and practices of Europeans were imposed on individuals of African origin. As a result, through the slave experience, Africans developed a disoriented self-image based on standards set and described by Europeans. Thomas Jefferson wrote of this conundrum and questioned the acceptance of the ideas proclaimed by the Declaration of Independence when one owned slaves.

Behavior toward enslaved Africans was basically vile and uncivilized. Many injustices occurred during the Middle Passage as slaves who succumbed to disease were thrown into the ocean and some were murdered by ship captains when supplies were perceived to be low. It has been advanced that approximately 2 of every 10 slaves en route to the New World died aboard ship during the voyage. These voyages saw men, women, and children chained to each other by their wrists and ankles and also chained to the floor. Ship captains used both loose and tight methods of quartering the slaves. The loose method was, in theory, supposed to limit the number of deaths owing to disease and unsanitary conditions. The tight method was based on the assumption that more slaves on the ship would offset the number of slave deaths on the journey. Neither approach was effective in providing the psychosocial support required for a healthy human existence. A documented instance of the loose method being used occurred on a British ship called *Zong* in 1791, and an example of the tight method is recorded in Frank Tannenbaum's *Slave and Citizen*.

Slaves were to respond to all demands of the master without choice or question, even though in many cases, slaves were unwilling to go along with their master's requests. However, slaves were either beaten into shape or "seasoned" and "broken in" before they reached North America. From a psychological perspective, behavior is defined in a general sense to include observable behavior as well as internal feelings. Thus, given the description of many slaves as being on one of two extremes, docile or recalcitrant, it was more likely than not that those considered docile exhibited the behavior expected of slaves.

Since the main reason for slavery was an economic one, it was essential for Europeans to develop a rationale in support of slavery, which resulted in an attached stigma to African people in the colonies. The logic was based on the view that Africans were savage and not human and that it was the duty of whites to make Africans worthwhile. Thus, the legal discrimination of Africans preceded and led to a status of physical and psychological inferiority being attached to slaves in the American South. This attitude may have best been evinced in the disposition of the people involved with slavery at all levels.

An examination of the collective and social elements involved in the slave-master relationship seems to suggest that the stress factors faced by Africans were very different from those faced by their European counterparts. Compared to whites, the total sum of stressful events was much greater for African slaves, a condition that was especially true for those events that were the result of racism, which resulted in feelings of anger, worthlessness, helplessness, alienation, and inferiority. During the nineteenth century, for example, it was common for whites to kill slaves who resisted being "corrected" for a given offense.

Since the business of slave trading was situational, a race-slavery linkage was formed because of the large numbers of non-Europeans involved. Racial attitudes that developed as a by-product of slavery were eventually manifest in every institutional structure of governance in the United States as well as the greater portion of group and individual behavior. In tracing these processes, it is essential to recognize that slavery as a practice was basically the same across the United States but somewhat different when slavery in the United States was compared to slavery in the West Indies or South America or to that practiced on the continent of Africa. Slaves in African society had certain rights. For example, among the Ashanti, slaves could marry free people, and they could not be killed without the king's permission. In the kingdom of Benin, children could earn enough money to buy their freedom. In Brazil, there was no law preventing slaves from learning to read or write.

When Europe started to expand during the fifteenth century, the Europeans came in contact with peoples of different cultures. The accepted assumption that Africans and other non-Europeans were inferior grew from slavery and was promulgated by scientists. Resulting categories and classifications became attached to behavioral dispositions, which may or may not exist, and express some anthropological connection to ability and intellect solely in racial terms. Systematic rules based on biology and natural history were supported via the scientific method to canonize differences in identity as discrimination, domination, and exclusion. These ideas found expression in the works of Carl von Linné, Francis Galton, Charles Darwin, and Sigmund Freud—the last, in *Totem and Taboo*, referred to Africans as savage and primitive. Edward Thorndike suggested using sterilization programs to eliminate Africans because they had bad genes.

Psychology has even affected modern metaphors that always equate black with evil. The terms "blackball," "black market," and "blackmail"—not to mention the color black as the representation of evil—symbolize the impact of slavery and the subordination of a human because of race. Institutional parameters like the post-Reconstruction-era black codes extended the psychological control of former slaves by equating the status of peonage with being black.

Behavioral research covering the psychology of slavery is important and requires a clear focus on all individuals involved and the environment of the participants. Despite the lack of pure objective research on the subject, it is evident that the behavior of all participants, especially African slaves, was complex and that any valid examination of slavery requires an evaluation of the relations in which slaves were considered as being unable to survive as free persons. This is the only approach to use if we are to refute antebellum proslavery apologists like Samuel Cartwright who said that, from a behavioral perspective, African slaves were childlike and completely dependent on whites.

—*Torrance T. Stephens*

For Further Reading
Bradley, Michael. 1978. *The Iceman Inheritance; Prehistoric Sources of Western Man's Racism, Sexism, and Aggression.* New York: Kayode; Goldberg, David. 1993. *Racist Cultures: Philosophy and the Politics of Meaning.* Oxford: Blackwell; Nobles, Wade. 1986. *African Psychology.* Oakland, CA: Black Family Institute; Tannenbaum, Frank. 1946. *Slave and Citizen.* Boston: Beacon Press.

915

Historical evidence of a slave trade on the eastern coast of Africa appears in the writings of the Arabian geographer Masoudi (Abu'l-Hasan Ali al-Mas'udi). According to his sources, slaves were traded at Kilwa and Mombasa and were transported to Arab settlements.

c. 922

Buzurg ibn Shahriyar, a merchant and navigator of the Persian Gulf region, wrote *Al-Kitab al-Ajaib al-Hind* (The book of the south and India). This collection of sailing adventures includes references to slave-trading ventures on the coast of eastern Africa. [See Document 6.]

c. 1000

The Chinese were aware of the coast of eastern Africa, which they called Po-Pa-Li, and regular trade, including the transportation of Africans as slaves, occurred between Mo Lin (Malindi) and Canton. [See Document 5.]

1178

The Chinese author Chou Ch'u-fei wrote the travel account *Ling-wai-tai-ta*, which described eastern Africa and the slave-trading activities that occurred in the region. [See Document 7.]

1324

The Mali empire was at the height of its power in western Africa. Mansa Kankan Musa made a pilgrimage to Mecca in the years 1324–1325 and returned to his empire with Muslim teachers and architects. The city of Timbuktu later become the center of culture and learning in West Africa.

1341

Portuguese navigators reached the Canary Islands, known in ancient times as the Fortunate Islands.

1344

Pope Clement VI issued a bull that gave Castile jurisdiction over the Canary Islands; the Portuguese objected.

1352–1353

Ibn Battuta, a Moroccan traveler, visited the Mali empire and the coastal areas of Somalia and Kenya in eastern Africa. Battuta described the Africans that he encountered as "those who most abhor injustice." [See Document 8.]

1402

Jean de Bethencourt led the first Castilian expedition to the Canary Islands. He returned to the region in 1405 and captured the island of Lanzarote for the Kingdom of Castile.

1415

A military operation organized by Prince Henry of Portugal captured the city of Ceuta in modern-day Morocco, an event that marked the beginning of the European exploration and conquest of the African coast. In the same year, the island of Tenerife in the Canary Islands was captured by an expedition sent by the Kingdom of Castile.

1416

The Chinese eunuch (and slave), Admiral Cheng Ho (Zhenghe) sailed to the coast of East Africa on an expedition of discovery. In the system of slavery that existed in China at the time, royal eunuchs could find positions of power and influence within the government bureaucracy.

1417

The Florentine merchant and traveler Benedetto Dei reportedly visited the Mali empire in western Africa and observed trading in the city of Timbuktu.

1418

Portuguese navigators landed on the Madeira Islands off the coast of North Africa and claimed the region for Portugal. Within a short time, Portuguese settlers began to cultivate sugarcane in the islands.

1421

A school of navigators financed by Prince Henry the Navigator was established at Sagres in Portugal. New innovations in sailing and cartography came out of this school, innovations that set the stage for the European age of exploration.

1425

A Portuguese force captured the Canary Islands from the Castilians, who had occupied the islands since 1405.

1425

Nyatsimba Mutota (Mwanamutapa), the king of the Shona-speaking Karanga people, conquered the entire plateau between the Limpopo and Zambezi Rivers in eastern Africa. This conquest led to the creation of the Mwanamutapa dynasty and the establishment of the city of Great Zimbabwe.

1430

Granite walls were constructed around Great Zimbabwe.

1431

The Portuguese navigators Diogo de Seville and Gonçalo Cabral visited the uninhabited Azores and claimed them for Portugal.

1433

Berber forces led by Akil captured the city of Timbuktu, the cultural center of the Mali empire. This expansion of the North African Berbers into sudanic Africa resulted in the enslavement of many peoples of sub-Saharan Africa, and a thriving trans-Saharan slave trade followed the conquest.

1433

The Portuguese navigator Gilianes (Gil Eanes) became the first European to reach Cape Bojador (located directly south of the Canary Islands in modern-day Morocco).

1437

The Portuguese abandoned their settlement at Ceuta after an expedition meant to resupply the colony was destroyed.

1437

Reports indicate that peoples from East Africa were being traded as slaves in western India.

1440

The Benin Kingdom in West Africa started to grow in power and influence under the leadership of Oba Ewuare.

1441

The Portuguese navigator Antam Gonçalvez captured 10 Africans and transported them to Lisbon where they were sold in the market as slaves.

1443

The Portuguese established their first trading outpost in western Africa when they founded a settlement on the island of Arguin. The settlement was located to the south of Cape Blanc in the modern-day nation of Mauritania. At the time, the Portuguese were able to trade one horse for 25–30 slaves in the Senegambia region.

1444

Portuguese navigators continued their exploration of the western coastline of Africa. During the expedition of Nino Tristram, the Portuguese finally reached the mouth of the Senegal River.

1445

The Portuguese navigator Dinís Dias reached Cap Vert in modern-day Senegal.

1445

A large slave auction was held in Lagos, Portugal. One contemporary chronicler described the event as "a terrible scene of misery and disorder" (Meltzer, 1993)

1447

An estimated 900 African slaves were in Portugal.

1448

Prince Henry the Navigator of Portugal established a slave market and a fort at Arguin Bay in West Africa.

1450

Portuguese ships carried 200 Africans from Arguin Bay to Lisbon, Portugal, where they were sold as slaves.

1455

Recognizing that there were abuses present in the slave trade, Prince Henry the Navigator tried to forbid the capture of Africans, but the enterprise had become well established in Portuguese society and its profits were quite lucrative. On average, 800 Africans were carried to Portugal as slaves each year.

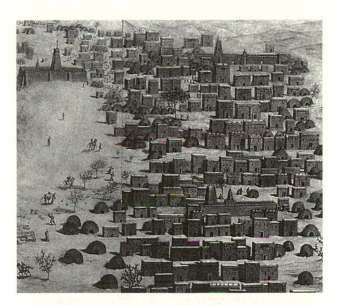

Timbuktu as it appeared in 1830 to the French explorer René Caillié. (The Granger Collection)

1459

A Venetian monk by the name of Fra Mauro produced a map of Africa that identified the kingdom of a legendary African ruler named Prester John. Many Europeans believed that somewhere within Africa they could find this mythical Christian ruler, and the search for Prester John became one of the goals of the European exploration of the African coastline.

1462

The Portuguese established a slave-trading center at Cacheu in modern-day Guinea-Bissau. After the discovery and colonization of New World settlements, this region became one of the prime centers for the slave-trading enterprise that developed in the seventeenth and eighteenth centuries.

1464

Sunni Ali became the leader of the Songhai Empire in western Africa and soon began a campaign of conquest that enlarged his empire and brought many tribute peoples under his control.

1466

Portugal officially sanctioned action that had already begun by chartering trading agreements for commercial enterprise in Guinea and the Cape Verde Islands.

Rice (*oryza sativa*) belongs to the oryzoid group of the grass family Gramineae, and more than 20 species and 7,000 varieties of rice have been identified. Three water systems regulate rice production: the upland system, which relies entirely on rainfall; inland swamps; and tidal irrigation, which allows rice to be cultivated along river estuaries and floodplains. Historically, rice raised in the United States has depended on irrigation.

The origins of domesticated rice in Asia are still undetermined. Archaeological evidence suggests rice cultivation in China as early as 4000 B.C. and in India by the third millennium. By the eleventh century A.D., China boasted an extensive interregional rice trade, and rice was grown commercially along the Yangtze River and along other large rivers on the east coast. Large-scale overseas export of rice from the Far East was limited by poor access to markets. Rice was imported from India to the Mediterranean long before it was cultivated in Europe, and Arab traders introduced rice to the Middle East and Africa. In A.D. 700, Moors carried the seed to southern Europe during their conquest of Spain, and between 1400 and the early 1600s, Spaniards transported rice seed to Italy and then overseas to Central and South America. The Dutch introduced rice into the West Indies, and the Portuguese took rice to Brazil. It appears, however, that the establishment of rice culture in these areas had little influence on the rice industry that developed in North America.

Rice played a significant role in the economic development of the U.S. South. The earliest accounts of rice culture in colonial America are varied and inconsistent, but experimental plantings were made in Virginia as early as 1622, and by 1690, rice was an established commercial staple along the South Atlantic seaboard near what is now Charleston, South Carolina. In 1698, 10,407 pounds of rice were exported from South Carolina; 10 years later, the total was 1,510,679 pounds, and colonial American rice exports had skyrocketed to 27,372,500 pounds by 1750. On the eve of the Revolution, rice cultivated in South Carolina and Georgia accounted for about 20 percent of American commodity exports. After 1820, rice exports showed little appreciable gain as cotton succeeded rice as the primary southern agricultural staple. The largest American rice crop, in 1849, totaled 215 million pounds, and it was not until the eve of the Civil War that rice agriculture along the Atlantic seaboard showed any indication of decline.

American rice production became profitable with the introduction of new seed varieties and skilled slave labor. Carolina Gold seed, the most highly esteemed and cultivated seed, became the basis of the southern rice trade. Recent scholarship suggests that many African slaves, already conditioned to labor in coastal lowlands, were experienced rice growers. On the coast of sub-Saharan West Africa, which is where many of the slaves in the U.S. South came from, seed varieties from the species *Oryza glaberrima* had been harvested since 1500 B.C. By 1860, the greatest concentration of slaves in the United States was to be found in the rice-producing region along the South Carolina–Georgia coast.

—*Clifford R. Dickinson*

For Further Reading
Bray, Francesca. 1986. *The Rice Economies: Technology and Development in Asian Societies.* New York: Basil Blackwell; Carney, Judith A. 1993. "From Hands to Tutors: African Expertise in the South Carolina Rice Economy." *Agricultural History* 67: 1–30; Dethloff, Henry C. 1988. *A History of the American Rice Industry, 1685–1985.* College Station: Texas A&M University Press; Gray, Lewis Cecil. 1933. *History of Agriculture in the Southern States to 1860. Vol. 2.* Gloucester, Mass.: Peter Smith.

1468

The Songhai under Sunni Ali captured the city of Timbuktu, which had been held by Berber peoples (Tuaregs) since 1433.

1471

Portuguese navigators, who had continued to explore the African coastline, reached the Gold Coast (modern-day Ghana).

1471

The Portuguese established a trading center at Elmina in modern-day Ghana. At this trading center, African gold was traded for Portuguese goods.

1472

Portuguese navigators finally crossed the equator and reached the Bight of Benin.

1473

Sunni Ali and the Songhai captured the city of Jenné, and the power and influence of the Empire of Mali began to diminish. As Mali declined, its territory was absorbed into the Songhai Empire.

1475

On December 21, the Portuguese navigator Ruy de Sequeira reached the island of São Tomé off the coast of West Africa near modern-day Gabon.

1476

The Spanish occupied the Canary Islands and suppressed a revolt there the following year.

1479

On September 4, Spain and Portugal signed the Treaty of Alçacovas to end the Castilian Civil War (1474–1479). Ferdinand of Aragon and Isabella of Castile recognized Portugal's monopoly status concerning trade "from the Canary Islands down toward Guinea," and the government of Portugal recognized the right of the Spanish to the Canary Islands.

1481

Representatives of the declining Mali empire sought to form an alliance with the Portuguese against the Songhai, who threatened the security of Mali. The unstable political situation in western Africa helped lead to the expansion of the slave trade by the Europeans. Many of the trade goods that were introduced by the Portuguese became used as implements of war, which only exacerbated the political destabilization of the region. Since war captives fueled the slave trade, conditions in West Africa produced a vicious cycle that led to a large-scale depopulation through the slave trade.

1481

On June 21, Pope Sixtus IV issued the bull Æterni Regis, which approved the agreements made in the Treaty of Alçacovas (1479). The pope divided the known world into northern and southern realms, which he distributed to the Spanish and the Portuguese, respectively.

1482

The Portuguese constructed a castle, São Jorge da Mina, at Elmina along the Gold Coast in modern-day Ghana. This location became one of the largest slave-trading centers used by the Portugese in all of West Africa.

1482

An expedition led by the Portuguese navigator Diogo Cão reached the mouth of the Congo River. The leaders of the Kongo people collaborated with the Portuguese in order to bring Christianity and technology into their kingdom.

1485

The Portuguese began the colonization of São Tomé. They developed sugarcane plantations on the island, and by 1490, they had imported slaves from Benin to cultivate the plantation lands.

1486

The Benin Kingdom began to trade regularly with Portugal, and one of the common exchanges was Benin trading slaves for European-made firearms.

1487

The Portuguese explorer Pero da Covilhão was sent to the Middle East to try to locate Prester John. During his expedition, Covilhão traveled as far as India and Madagascar and returned to Portugal with the insight that Portuguese ships could reach these locations if they were able to round the continent of Africa.

1488

The Portuguese navigator Bartolomeu Dias reached the Cape of Good Hope at the southern tip of the African continent. In the same year, the king of Portugal presented Pope Innocent VII with a gift of 100 African slaves captured among the Moro people.

1490

The Portuguese traveled 200 miles into the interior of the Congo River basin. They converted Mani Nzinga Nkuwu, the leader of the Kongo Kingdom, to Christianity, but he later reverted to local animist beliefs.

1493

Upon the death of Sunni Ali, one of his lieutenants, Mohammed Toure, became the new leader of the Songhai Empire and adopted the

∽DIOGO CÃO (fl. 1480–1486)∽

Although little is known of his early life, according to tradition Diogo Cão was born in Vila Real in northern Portugal. His grandfather Gonçalo Cão had been a backer of John I of Portugal in the struggle against Castile in the 1380s. During the second half of the 1470s, Diogo saw action along the African coast in the war against Castile, and he captured one of that kingdom's ships, the *Mondanina,* in early 1480. Diogo made two important voyages of discovery, during the course of which he advanced Portuguese knowledge of the African coast south of the equator almost 20 degrees of latitude.

On the first voyage, Diogo left Portugal in spring 1482 in an effort to find a passage to the Indian Ocean, and he had returned home by mid-April 1484. During this voyage, he sailed along the West African coast, stopping at São Jorge da Mina for supplies. After passing Cape Catarina (2 degrees below the equator), the southernmost point then known to the Portuguese, he became the first known European to see the Congo (Zaïre) River, and he planted at its mouth a *padrão,* or stone column, inscribed with the Portuguese crown's coat of arms—one of a dozen or so planted by the Portuguese along Africa's coasts before 1500. His men explored the river upstream about 100 miles, reaching as far as Yelala (near today's river port of Matadi in Congo [formerly Zaïre]). Although the details and chronology of Diogo Cão's encounters with the Kongo Kingdom are hazy, it is clear that contact was made, and it marked the beginning of a long relationship between the two kingdoms. On both voyages he seems to have brought back to Portugal some of that kingdom's inhabitants. He continued southward along the coast of present-day Angola to Cape Santa Maria, or Cabo do Lobo, 13 degrees south latitude, where he planted

another *padrão* before returning to Lisbon, erroneously thinking that he had reached the southernmost part of Africa.

Upon his return to Portugal in 1484, he was granted a patent of nobility and a coat of arms for his discoveries. In 1485 Pope Innocent VIII was informed by the Portuguese ambassador that Cão's ships had sailed "to near the Promontory Prasso at the beginning of the Arabian Gulf (Diffie and Winius, 1977)." The maps of Cristóforo Sóligo (c. 1485–1490) and Henricus Martellus Germanus (c. 1489) reported Cão's discoveries to a wider world.

On his second voyage of 1485–1486, Cão stopped off at the Kongo Kingdom, leaving off some of the Kongolese he had gotten on his first voyage and continued south to Cape Cross (22 degrees south in present-day Namibia where he left another *padrão,* by this time realizing that he had not reached the southernmost part of Africa. He may have even sailed as far as Walvis Bay (22 degrees 59 minutes south). Although some people believe that Cão died in that region, others suggest that he returned to Portugal but lived in obscurity because of King John's displeasure at having been misled by the erroneous reports of Cão's first voyage.

—*Francis A. Dutra*

For Further Reading

Albuquerque, Luis de. 1987. *Navegadores, Viajantes, e Aventureiros Portugueses, Séculos XV e XVI.* 2 vols. Lisbon: Caminho; Cordeiro, Luciano. 1971. *Diogo Cão.* Lisbon: Agencia-Geral do Ultramar; Diffie, Bailey W., and George D. Winius. 1977. *Foundations of the Portuguese Empire, 1415–1580.* Minneapolis: University of Minnesota Press; Peres, Damião. 1983. *História dos Descobrimentos Portugueses.* Porto, Portugal: Vertentes.

---

name Askiya Muhammad Turay I. The new emperor ruled the Songhai Empire at its height, and he strongly promoted the introduction of Islam into all Songhai territory.

1494

Spain and Portugal signed the Treaty of Tordesillas, which revised the papal "line of demarcation" by moving it slightly farther west. This agreement had the effect of making Africa a commercial sphere of the Portuguese, and Por-

tuguese sailors came to dominate the African slave trade.

1497

Askiya Muhammad Turay I, the emperor of the Songhai, made a pilgrimage to Mecca where he received the title of caliph of the Sudan.

1497

On December 25, Vasco da Gama became the first Portuguese sailor to navigate the eastern

~DUARTE PACHECO PEREIRA (C. 1460-1533)~

Duarte Pacheco Pereira was a Portuguese explorer, navigator, conquistador, cosmographer, and author of *Esmeraldo de situ orbis,* a treasure trove of information about the peoples, customs, flora, and fauna of Western Africa in the late-fifteenth century.

During the reign of King John II (1481–1495), Pereira made several voyages to the Guinean coast of Africa and explored the region around the Senegal River and the Benin Kingdom, the capital of which he visited four times. Because of his navigational experience, he was a technical adviser to the Portuguese delegation that was given the task of negotiating the Treaty of Tordesillas (1494) and signed that document as a witness. He sailed for India in 1503 and distinguished himself there, especially in the defense of Cochin, and returned to Portugal in June or July 1505.

About 1505, he began writing *Esmeraldo de situ orbis,* which he described as "a book of cosmography and navigation," but that project seems to have been interrupted in early 1508. Later that year, King Manuel I (r. 1495–1521) put him in charge of a coastguard expedition to track down French corsairs. In early 1509, Pereira captured Mondragon, one of the most notorious of the corsairs, seizing a total of three pirate vessels and sinking one. In 1511, he headed a fleet that was sent to the rescue of the besieged Portuguese North African outpost of Tangier. In 1519, Pereira was named governor of São Jorge da Mina for three years. In 1522, he was arrested and brought back to Portugal at the orders of King John III (r. 1521–1557), but after a period of imprisonment, he was released by John and granted a pension.

Duarte Pacheco Pereira's *Esmeraldo de situ orbis,* which was first published in 1892, almost four centuries after being penned, combines a partial chronicle of Portuguese overseas discoveries and a cosmography of the world. His projections regarding latitude were some of the most accurate of his day, and his account gives detailed sailing instructions for sailing along the western coast of Africa, with descriptions of that region.

—*Francis A. Dutra*

For Further Reading

Carvalho, Joaquim Barradas de. 1983. *À la recherche de la spécificité de la renaissance Portugaise: L'"Esmeraldo de situ orbis" de Duarte Pacheco Pereira et la littérature portugaise de voyages à l'époque des grandes découvertes.* 2 vols. Paris: Fondation Calouste Gulbenkian Centre Culturel Portugais; Pereira, Duarte Pacheco. 1937. *Esmeraldo de situ orbis.* Trans. and ed. G. H. T. Kimble. London: Hakluyt Society; Pereira, Duarte Pacheco. 1991. *Esmeraldo de situ orbis.* Critical ed. by Joaquim Barradas de Carvalho. Lisbon: Fundação Calouste Gulbenkian.

---

coastline of Africa when he sailed along the region that he named Natal. From this area, da Gama embarked upon the final part of his expedition, which took him to India.

1498

On May 20, the Portuguese navigator Vasco da Gama arrived in Calicut, India, and thus became the first European to reach the continent of Asia by a sea route.

1500

The price of slaves generally rose as the demand for them increased. In the Senegambia region, the Portuguese were able to trade one horse for six to eight slaves.

1505

The Portuguese established a slave-trading post at Sofala, Mozambique, and began to sell Africans captured in the region as slaves. In the same year, a Portuguese expedition commanded by Francisco de Almeida continued Portugal's efforts to establish commercial hegemony in East Africa. The Portuguese forces attacked the cities of Kilwa (in modern-day Tanzania) and Mombasa (in modern-day Kenya) and established Fort Santiago at Kilwa. Also in the same year, the navigator Duarte Pacheco Pereira, who had sailed along the coastline of West Africa on several Portuguese expeditions, began writing *Esmeraldo de situ orbis,* which he described as "a book of cosmography and navigation."

1506

The Portuguese landed on Madagascar.

1507

The traveler and chronicler Leo Africanus visited the Songhai Empire, the Empire of Mali, and the Hausa states in West Africa.

Since earliest times, different but well-interacting communities, trade goods, peoples, ideas, and cultures contributed to build a global system in the Indian Ocean. There were two main slave routes—one from East Africa and the Red Sea to Arabia, India, and Southeast Asia; the other from the opposite direction—which meant that slaves in the Indian Ocean region were not only black peoples of Africa but also of Asian origin. Religious elements—such as Hinduism in India, Buddhism in the Malaya-Indonesian archipelago, and, beginning in the seventh century, the spread of Islam through short- as well as long-distance trade routes—strongly influenced, and in many cases modified, the concept and use of slavery. The social, political, and economic functions of slaves were domestic-patriarchal, productive-agricultural (bonded labor directed into intensive wet-crop agriculture), and military-administrative.

Nevertheless, the trans–Indian Ocean slave trade was minimal and incidental at most. Within the Islamic world, slave soldiers came from central Asia, mainly Turkish peoples from the Caucasus and from the steppes until their Islamization, while domestic slaves came chiefly from the coastal strip of East Africa. In the late ninth century, the Zanj, black slaves from East Africa who were employed on sugarcane plantations, revolted against the Abbasid caliph, al-Mu'tawid, and became masters of southern Iraq and Basra. Toward the end of the tenth century, 200 slaves were imported yearly from East Africa to Oman, traveling on Arab dhows. By the mid-eleventh century, there was extensive commerce of slaves from Ras Asir ("the cape of slaves") and Pemba to China in exchange for ceramics and luxury goods.

During the twelfth and thirteenth centuries, many African peoples were bought on the islands of Zanzibar and Pemba and then transported to the Arabian peninsula, where they mainly engaged in pearl fishing in the Persian Gulf. Slaves also became lords of Indian and African reigns, as their masters considered them more loyal than anybody in their clans and tribes. Omani Arabs used to recruit mercenary troops from the Baluchi tribes, and these troops developed a long-lived military tradition and represented a real element of power within Omani areas of influence in Africa.

With the arrival of the Europeans at the end of the fifteenth century, the slave trade grew considerably. Portuguese colonial rulers taxed Asian vessels and goods in Portuguese-controlled ports, and those merchants who could not pay or those who refused to bow to the Portuguese commercial hegemony were enslaved. The Portuguese also bought slaves in India, the Comoros, and Madagascar, and they purchased unwanted Chinese girls from their parents in Macao. Of the 3,000 rounded up annually, some were sold to European merchants, and some were kept in the Indian Ocean region as laborers, craftsmen, and soldiers (the women as maids, mistresses, and prostitutes). Beginning in 1596, parts of the Indonesian archipelago lost their economic autonomy to the Dutch East India Company, which introduced ruthless methods of forced labor in the cultivation of crops and nutmeg in Amboina and in the working of gold mines in Sumatra and the colony of the Cape of Good Hope. In the mid-seventeenth century, the French East India Company bought slaves in Zanzibar and sold them in Oriental markets or transported them to French commercial and strategic outposts on the Mascarene Islands as well as in India.

In the early 1730s, the conversion of the Mascarenes to a plantation economy generated an escalating demand for labor, and the French began to seek slaves from Kilwa south of the mouth of the Zambezi River. The Mascarene Islands' demand for slaves supplemented a larger and older slave trade from the Swahili coast and Red Sea ports to Muslim markets in Arabia, the Persian Gulf, and India. During the reign of Said ibn Sultan (Said Sayyid, r. 1806–1856) in the Mascarenes, the Swahili coast, the Brava coast, and Portuguese East Africa became the commercial centers of an external trade. From the north, Kilwa blacks were exported to the Arabian peninsula, India, Madagascar, and the Mascarenes; from Mozambique, blacks were chiefly exported to Madagascar, the Mascarenes, Brazil, and Cuba. The export trade from East Africa reached nearly 30,000 per year in the first half of the nineteenth century.

The British government, under heavy pressure from abolitionist and humanitarian groups, developed a policy of signing anti-slave-trade treaties with both European and Afro-Asiatic powers as well as a policy of promoting British commercial and strategic interests in the Indian Ocean. Treaties with Zanzibar in the 1820s restricted the destinations of slave exports but did not reduce the number. The peak of the African slave trade came after 1850, partly because of the free emigration system to the French sugar islands of Réunion, Mayotte, and Nosy Be. From 1870 onward, the slave trade penetrated from the East African coast to the African hinterland. In 1873, the British government succeeded in getting the sultan of Zanzibar to abolish the slave trade within his domain.

The banning of slavery required a century and a half: the British abolished slavery throughout the empire in 1833, and by 1843, the legal status of slavery in British India had been abolished. The French abolished slavery in 1848, and the Dutch abolition of slavery in 1860 increased the effectiveness of the attacks of the liberal opposition against a system of forced cultivation as another form of slavery and a denial of the rights of economic liberty to Dutch residents as well as to Indonesians. The last vestige of compulsory labor was abolished in 1865. In 1870, a new agrarian law was enacted and the system of forced cultivation abolished in Java. Despite the abolition treaties, the most important years in the Oriental slave trade were from 1750 to 1900.

—*Liliana Mosca and Beatrice Nicolini*

For Further Reading
Economics of the Indian Ocean Slave Trade in the Nineteenth Century. 1989. Ed. William Gervase Clarence-Smith. London: Frank Cass.

1512
The Portuguese dismantled Fort Santiago at Kilwa (Tanzania).

1513
The Portuguese took control of the city of Azemmour in Morocco and enslaved most of the city's residents.

1513
The Hausa states joined into an alliance with the Songhai Empire but were later able to regain their autonomy.

1514
Manuel I, king of Portugal, received a formal protest from Afonso I, the Christian king of the Kongo, concerning the disruption that the slave trade was causing within his kingdom. Despite Afonso's pleas for assistance, he was not able to change the attitude of Portugal regarding the slave trade.

1518
Portuguese forces attacked and destroyed the city of Berbera (in modern-day Somalia).

1519
The historian Mahmoud Kati wrote the *Ta'rikh el-Fettach* in Timbuktu. This book, the oldest West African literary work, records many of the oral records and histories of the Songhai, Mandingo, and Sarakole peoples.

1522
In Egypt, mamluks (military slaves) in the areas of El Faiyûm and West Delta revolted against Turkish rule.

1526
In writing to his brother in Lisbon, Afonso I, the ruler of Kongo, remarked upon the effects of the slave trade in his kingdom: "We cannot reckon how great the damage is . . . and so great . . . is the corruption and licentiousness that our country is being completely depopulated" (Meltzer, 1993)

1528
The Portuguese put down an uprising against their slave-trading activities in eastern Africa and then sacked the city of Mombasa (in modern-day Kenya) in retaliation against those who had revolted.

1530
An English sailor, William Hawkins, became the first Englishman to become involved in African trade and commerce. Hawkins visited Brazil after visiting the Guinea coast of West Africa, but he did not engage in the slave trade.

1540
The Ottoman Turks, who had extended their commercial interests down the Red Sea corridor, began to attack coastal kingdoms in eastern Africa. Some of the African rulers appealed to the Portuguese for assistance against the Ottoman threat.

1541
Responding to several calls for aid, the Portuguese dispatched troops to Ethiopia to prevent the Ottoman Turks from conquering the region.

1544
The Portuguese established a slave-trading post at Quelimane (in modern-day Mozambique). This location was operational until the late-nineteenth century and was one of the most

The figure at the top of this seventeenth-century Kongo staff represents Christ, an early example of the incorporation of Christian symbolism into African sculpture. (Musée Royale Afrique Centrale, Tervuren, Belgium; Werner Forman Archive/Art Resource)

notorious slave-trading locations in all of East Africa.

1548
The Portuguese began the colonization of the island of Madagascar.

1550
The Songhai Empire began to show signs of decline. The Hausa states were successful in a revolt to gain more autonomy, and the Kingdom of Kanem-Bornu captured the trans-Saharan trading-center of Air.

1553
Ships from the Netherlands arrived in West African waters, and the Dutch began to participate in the African slave trade.

1562
The Englishman John Hawkins carried 300 slaves from West Africa to Hispaniola. His recognition of the lucrative profits that could be made from this slave trade inspired the English Crown to pursue the possibility of further English involvement in the enterprise. England's Queen Elizabeth I allowed Hawkins to include the image of a bound African in his family coat of arms.

1563
Father Gouveia, a Jesuit missionary who served in Africa, recommended that the Portuguese government annex Angola so that its inhabitants could be Christianized.

1565
The Portuguese proclaimed East Africa to be Portuguese territory.

1569
The government of Portugal began construction of a fort at Mombasa.

1571
Idris Alooma, the leader of Kanem-Bornu, first introduced firearms into warfare between African peoples. The social destabilization caused by war and the higher likelihood of increased conflict wrought by firearms combined to make the incidence of slave trading more intense in West Africa.

1574
The Portuguese fortress at Mozambique was attacked and burned by African forces; in the same year, the Portuguese established a colony in Angola.

1576
The Portuguese fortress at Accra (in modern-day Ghana) was attacked and destroyed by African forces.

1579
In Angola, a war began between the Ngola people and the Portuguese, but the Portuguese used an army composed of other African peoples to fight the Ngola.

1584
The Portuguese admiral Thomé de Sousa Coutinho defeated a Turkish force that sought to dislodge the Portuguese from East Africa.

Eighteenth-century French representation of a European commercial settlement on the West African coast, with four compounds—one each for the British, French, Dutch, and Portuguese. (The Granger Collection)

1585

Several Swahili towns along the coastline of East Africa revolted against Portuguese rule.

1587

A group of Zimba warriors attacked Kilwa and killed 3,000 of the city's 4,000 inhabitants. Some of the dead were eaten. The Portuguese sent forces into the region to restore order.

1588

The government of Portugal established several new slave-trading centers in West Africa at Cacheu, Lagos, Warri, New and Old Calabar, and along the Cameroon River.

1591

In the Battle of Tondibi, forces of the Songhai Empire were defeated by a Moroccan army, which included 3,000 Spanish mercenaries who carried firearms into battle. The superiority of firepower decided the battle and resulted in the destruction of the Songhai Empire.

1593

The Portuguese began construction of Fort Jesus at Mombasa (Kenya), but the citadel was not completed until 1639. This military outpost was the largest fortification the Portuguese constructed in East Africa.

1595

The Spanish monarch, Philip II, authorized a slave-trading agreement with Gómez Reynal in which Reynal was given the right to transport 38,250 Africans to the Spanish colonies over a nine-year period. As a part of the arrangement, Reynal had to ship Africans directly from Africa to the Americas, and he could not supply mulattoes, mestizos, Turks, or Moors as slaves.

1598

The Dutch established the first of their slave-trading centers in West Africa. During the seventeenth century, the Dutch were very active participants in the African slave trade.

1602

The Netherlands established the Dutch East

Portuguese invaders in East Africa, seventeenth century. Opposition from African peoples as well as other European powers confined the Portuguese to a few coastal settlements such as Fort Jesus in Mombasa and Mozambique Island. (Bojan Brecelj/Corbis)

Indies Company to conduct trade between Asia and the Netherlands. The company eventually established a colonial outpost at the Cape of Good Hope, and this Cape Colony became a way station for conducting the trade between Asia and Europe.

1607
Dutch forces attacked the Portuguese fortification at Mozambique. Although the attack was unsuccessful, it signaled that the Portuguese now had other European rivals in the Indian Ocean region.

1618
The English established Fort James at Bathurst (now Banjul), Gambia. The English had very little initial involvement with the African slave trade, but this situation changed during the eighteenth century.

1621
The Dutch established a slave-trading center at Gorée Island off the coast of Senegal.

1626
France established a settlement at Saint-Louis along the Senegal River. This outpost was the first settlement that the French established in West Africa.

1628
France established a center for trade purposes at Saint Luce in Madagascar.

1637
France established Fort Saint-Louis along the Senegal River, and the French merchants of Dieppe were able to win trading privileges in the region for a 10-year period.

1637
The Dutch took control of Elmina Castle along the Gold Coast (modern-day Ghana). The site, constructed and occupied by the Portuguese since 1482, was one of the largest slave-trading centers on the coast of West Africa.

Cape Coast Castle, originally a Dutch fort, was captured in 1655 by the English, who made it their West African administrative center. (© 1990 Dwight R. Cendrowski, MIRA)

1640

A slave trader named Captain Smith carried a group of Africans to Massachusetts after he had illegally attacked their village in West Africa. Massachusetts authorities refused to accept the cargo of Africans and ordered that they be returned to Africa at the colony's expense. Smith was arrested for capturing Africans who had not been taken as a result of a "just war" situation, in which enslavement would have been morally acceptable.

1640

The government of Sweden became involved in the African slave trade.

1642

France chartered the Compagnie de l'Orient for the specific purpose of establishing a French colony in Madagascar.

1645

The *Rainbowe,* which was the first slave ship ever constructed in England's North American colonies, sailed for Africa and began to operate in the transatlantic slave trade.

1652

The Dutch government established a colony at the Cape of Good Hope to assist the work of the Dutch East India Company, which was trading between Asia and Europe. The Dutch also took control of a Portuguese fort at Axim and began to seize English forts along the West African coast. The only English fort the Dutch did not capture was Fort Carolusburg (Cape Coast Castle) in the Gold Coast region.

1655

The Khoi people, indigenous inhabitants of South Africa, attempted to resist the seizure of their land by the Dutch, but the Dutch forces were able to subdue the resistance.

1657

In South Africa's Cape Colony, the Dutch East India Company allowed some settlers, known as Boers, to move inland and settle the Liesbeeck Valley.

1658

A war erupted between the indigenous Khoi people and the Boer settlers in South Africa.

1660

The English government rechartered the Royal Adventurers (a group that had originally been formed in 1618) for the purpose of expanding English commercial interests in West Africa, and the group conducted an extensive campaign against Dutch possessions in West Africa.

1662

The Danish government constructed Fort Christiansborg along the Gold Coast in West Africa. This location became the commercial center of Denmark's involvement in the slave trade.

1663

The English established their first colonial settlement in Africa at Sierra Leone. In time, as the antislavery sentiment developed in England, the region of Sierra Leone became a colony that was used to repatriate former slaves from the English colonies who wished to return to Africa.

1663

John Barbot, an agent of the French Royal African Company, wrote, "The trade of slaves is . . . the business of kings, rich men, and prime merchants." [See Document 17.]

1665

The English seized Cape Coast Castle from the Dutch and made it the administrative center of English operations in West Africa.

1671

The French government proclaimed the island of Madagascar to be French royal property; also, French forces constructed a fort at Why-dah (Ouidah in modern-day Benin).

1672

The English Parliament passed enabling legislation that chartered the Royal African Company and granted it a monopoly in conducting the English slave trade between Africa and the Americas. The English were eager to acquire profits from the slave trade, which previously had enriched other rival European powers. The Royal African Company held its exclusive monopoly status until 1698 when Parliament opened the slave trade to other traders.

1673

The French government chartered the French Senegal Company to operate the slave trade and to provide slaves to French colonies in the Americas.

1676

Slave traders from the English colonies in North America began to operate along the eastern coast of Africa and the island of Madagascar. Competition between the English Royal African Company and the Dutch West India Company prevented the New England traders from operating in West African waters.

1678

The French seized the fort located at Arguin Island in Mauritania from the Portuguese.

1679

The Dutch East India Company began recruiting potential settlers in France, the Netherlands, and the Germanic states for resettlement in the Cape Colony in South Africa.

1687

Settlers from Brandenburg-Prussia founded a settlement on Arguin Island in Mauritania and established a slave market there.

1690

A slave revolt occurred at Stellenbosch in the Cape Colony, but the Dutch settlers were able to restore order in the region.

1698

The Royal African Company lost its monopoly status for conducting the English slave trade between Africa and the Americas. As a result, participation in the slave trade was opened to all English subjects, and many New Englanders became involved in extensive slave trading as they realized the lucrative profits that the enterprise afforded.

1698

The Portuguese lost Fort Jesus at Mombasa (Kenya) to the Omanis, which effectively ended Portuguese rule in that part of East Africa.

1700

Franciscan missionaries in the Guinea coast region protested against the African slave trade.

The slave trade appears to have existed in Madagascar "from time immemorial," and there seems to be no major ethnic group that did not have some members participating in the trade as dealers or purchasers. The Madagascar external slave trade began well before the arrival of the Europeans, as there are some indications in medieval accounts, although scarce, that blacks from Madagascar were taken to the markets of Arabia and the Middle East. Western intrusion in the Indian Ocean region in the sixteenth century marked a revolution in the existing system and brought much change.

From the mid-seventeenth century on, the Malagasy people, in particular the northern and southern Sakalawa, had a flourishing trade with European merchants. The Portuguese, Dutch, Americans, British, and French took black captives to the Americas, to the Cape Colony, to Batavia, and to the Mascarene Islands. By the mid-eighteenth century, the French had established sugar and coffee plantations on the Mascarene Islands using slave labor. The closest and cheapest source of slaves was Madagascar, from which the Mascarenes imported 40 percent of the 80,000 to 90,000 slaves introduced between 1722 and 1810. The French usually traded at the eastern ports—Île Sainte Marie (modern-day Nosy Boraha), Mahavelona, Toamasina, Sainte Lucie, and Toalanoro—and occasionally at Mahajanga on the northwest coast where they could buy Malagasy captives from the Sakalawas or blacks from Arab traders coming from the East African coast. Slaves were obtained by raiding neighboring peoples or were exchanged for guns, ammunition, and other commodities.

The rise of the Menabe and Boina kingdoms on the western part of the island, of the Betsimisáraka Confederation on the east coast, and of the Merina kingdom in the central highlands of Madagascar were all connected with the slave trade. After the late-eighteenth century, Merina traders had a virtual monopoly of the east coast slave trade, supplanting the Sakalawas, but the trade was irregular or interrupted because of the Merina wars of conquest. Thus, from 1785 to 1820, Betsimisáraka and Sakalawa peoples, with the Antalaotse or sea people (the Antaloatra in Merina), made slave raids on the Comoro Islands and on Kilwa, Ibo, Mozambique Island, and Querimba.

By 1820, when a British-Merina treaty banned all slave sales from the Merina-controlled regions of Madagascar, the Malagasy external slave trade to the Mascarenes had receded, but the internal slave trade had not. The growth of the Merina kingdom required a large amount of manpower, and the Merina kings satisfied the labor shortage by launching several expeditions to gather slaves. In the late 1840s, they started to buy large quantities of East African slaves imported through the ports of western Madagascar by Arab middlemen from Zanzibar, the Comoro Islands, Nosy Be, and Oman. In the late 1850s, the westward trade in humans resumed and became greater than ever before. The need for more field labor on Réunion, Mayotte, and Nosy Be stimulated French merchants to trade with the Sakalawas as well as with the Swahili Arab communities all along the west coast. Indeed, the island was exporting Malagasy slaves from the west coast at the same time it was importing East African blacks for the interior market as well as for reexport to French colonies.

During the 1860s and until the mid-1870s, slave importations into Madagascar dramatically increased, mainly from the African coast between Kilwa and Sofala. In 1877, international pressure and internal problems led the Merina government to prescribe the emancipation of all imported slaves—the so-called Mozambiques—but the emancipation did not halt either the interior slave market or the slave trade in the distant seaports of the west coast. Merina authority in the central and southwestern parts of Madagascar was just theoretical, and despite the British anti-slave-trade patrols in the Mozambique Channel, the Swahili Arabs and the Indian traders succeeded in maintaining and implementing their slave networks in the main Malagasy shipping points: Soalala, Maintirano, and Nosy Be.

The trade in Malagasy captives from the Merina and Betsileo regions and in blacks largely from the southern coast of East Africa continued throughout the 1880s and 1890s in Malagasy in Arab dhows flying French colors. A number of these slaves continued to be transshipped to the French colonies or to the Persian Gulf region, the latter mainly to the Omani port of Masqat. Some degree of slave trading persisted after the French conquest of Madagascar in 1882–1883 and even after the French abolished slavery there in 1896.

—*Liliana Mosca*

For Further Reading
Campbell, Gwyn. 1989. "Madagascar and Mozambique in the Slave Trade of the Western Indian Ocean, 1800–1861." In *Economics of the Indian Ocean Slave Trade in the Nineteenth Century.* Ed. William Gervase Clarence-Smith. London: Frank Cass.

1700

The slave trader James Barbot noted, "With an assortment of sundry goods amounting to about fourteen hundred pounds sterling, it may be reasonably expected to get about three hundred slaves or more, which brings them to near the rate of five pounds a head" (Meltzer, 1993)

1702

The French government chartered the French Guinea Company to help facilitate the slave trade and provide slaves to French colonies in the Americas.

1706

In Cairo, Egypt, there were disturbances caused by unrest among the Janissaries. Members of these elite troops of the Ottoman sultan had been enslaved from childhood and trained as soldiers.

1711

On June 18, a group of Janissaries was massacred in a battle near Cairo, Egypt.

1714

Slave-trading factories were constructed in Guinea by the French Senegal Company.

1715

The French occupied the island of Mauritius, which the Dutch had abandoned in 1710, and renamed it Île de France.

1717

All African slave-trading operations maintained by the government of Brandenburg-Prussia were sold to the Dutch.

1720

The Dutch East India Company established a slave-trading post at Delagoa Bay in South Africa for captives taken from Madagascar and East Africa.

1721

The French settled the island of Île de France (Mauritius) and introduced African slaves to work in the colony.

1737

A group of Moravian missionaries began working in the Gold Coast region of West Africa.

1744

Ibrahim became the ruler of Egypt. He had previously served as the commander of the Ottoman Janissary corps, an elite group of soldiers who had been enslaved as children and trained as warriors.

1752

English missionaries from the Society for the Propagation of the Gospel in Foreign Parts arrived in the Gold Coast region. They conducted their missionary activities from Cape Coast Castle.

1753

Dutch settlers in the Cape Colony in South Africa enacted a number of statutes that codified the laws governing slavery within the colony.

1756

The African Olaudah Equiano was captured from the Ibo region (modern-day Nigeria) and sold into slavery in the British colonies.

1763

Angola had become one of the prime slave markets used by the Portuguese, who were transporting many slaves to Brazil.

1765

Having defeated the French in the Seven Years War (1756–1763), the British acquired the areas of Senegal and Gambia in West Africa. The British province of Senegambia became one of the primary regions exploited by British merchants involved in the African slave trade.

1770

Alafin Obiudun became the leader of the Oyo Kingdom, an influential Yoruban state in West Africa. Obiudun earned great profits by trading with various European merchants and providing captives, who were traded as slaves.

1775

In South Africa, the Xhosa people crossed the Fish River, which had been the boundary between Dutch and African settlements in the region. The two groups encountered each other the following year along the Zeekee River, and a series of wars was fought between these two groups for control of the region.

A nineteenth-century representation of Janissaries seizing Christian children. The Janissaries, who were originally formed from Byzantine prisoners of war, were the Ottoman Empire's elite body of infantry and themselves enslaved children from among the empire's non-Muslim subjects. (The Granger Collection)

1776

On December 14, the French government concluded an agreement with the sultan of Kilwa in eastern African (modern-day Tanzania) authorizing the French to conduct slave-trading operations from that site. The agreement gave the French the right to build a fort, but they did not do so. [See Document 29.]

1777

The Spanish colonies in the Americas required a steady supply of slaves, and the Spanish government established a slave factory on the island of Fernando Po in the Bight of Biafra in order to provide those slaves. In previous years, the Spanish had depended upon other nations who held the *asiento* (contract or agreement) to ac-quire slaves for the Spanish colonies, but the Spanish now entered the slave trade on their own.

1787

The British government began the process of repatriating former slaves to Africa by sending them to Sierra Leone. A settlement called Granville Town, named after the English abolitionist Granville Sharp, was the first community established by those former slaves who were sent to the colony.

1789

The African Olaudah Equiano published *The Interesting Narrative of the Life of Olaudah Equiano, or Gustavus Vassa, the African, Writ-*

≈COMORO SLAVERY≈

The Comorian word *mrumwa* is generally translated as "slave." The word however did not apply to the *wazalia*, who were slaves born in the Comoros (Comoro Islands) who were fully Islamized and culturally integrated, but rather to the *wamakwa*, who were traded as slaves to the islands from Mozambique in the nineteenth century. In the island society, slaves were members of a subordinate stratum, but not all slaves had the same status. Slaves were obtained by trade, in warfare and raiding, and through inheritance.

Although there is still some scholarly debate about the date (eighth through tenth centuries A.D.) of the arrival of the first settlers of the Comoros, it seems that the origin and growth of the institution of slavery in the archipelago predates the coming of Islam (c. eleventh to twelfth centuries). During the pre-Islamic period, slave labor was employed in the iron industry (Allibert, 1996). Arab settlers, according to the historian al-Hamawi Yaqut imported slaves to the Comoros from the East African coast, and archaeological work has revealed the presence of black Africans among the people of the Comoros in the thirteenth century (Allibert and Verin, 1996). By the fourteenth century, the Comorans had started an external slave trade, as the Arab historian Ibn Battuta recounted that slaves from the Comoros were exported to Red Sea ports. Western accounts dating from the mid-sixteenth century confirm the existence of a large number of slaves in the archipelago, employed mainly in agricultural tasks, as well as of a flourishing trade in the export of slaves to the Oriental markets by Arab, Swahili, and European merchants.

Throughout the seventeenth and late-eighteenth centuries, the Comoros were an important port of call for freshwater and provisions, which transformed the economy. The ruling families and the nobility increased their control over the land, and there was a corresponding intense demand for slaves to do the cultivating. The Europeans also had a political impact on the archipelago when they conferred their favors on one sultan rather than another. Internecine strife and trade disputes

were overwhelmed by Malagasy slave raids from 1795 to 1820. The Sakalawa and Betsimisáraka peoples periodically attacked the Comoros for slaves to export to the Mascarene Islands, which left the Comorans in a state of great poverty.

Just a few decades later, however, the Comorans were able to regain their former prosperity because of a growing demand for blacks from the French islands of Réunion, Nosy Be, and Mayotte and from the Merina kingdom in the central highlands of Madagascar. The archipelago became a slave entrepôt, despite anti-slave-trade treaties signed in 1844, 1854, and 1882, and both upper and lower classes made large profits from the slave trade. Slavery and the slave trade gave the Comorans wealth and social standing. Slaves were attached to their masters in a symbiotic relationship and performed most of the manual labor associated with slavery. Even after the French abolished slavery in the colony in 1904, many freedmen remained in their master's house, and others continued to fulfill their traditional service obligations. The old social order did not collapse, and ex-slaves remained at the bottom of the society.

—*Liliana Mosca*

For Further Reading

Allibert, Claude. 1996. "Métallurgie, traite, et ancien peuplement du Canal de Mozambique aux Xe–XIIe siècles. Eléments historiques pour un essai de compréhension du début du peuplement austro-africaine de Madagascar." Paper presented at the conference on Fanandevozana or Slavery, held in Antananarivo, Madagascar, September; Allibert, Claude, and Pierre Verin. 1996. "The Early Pre-Islamic History of the Comoros Islands: Links with Madagascar and Africa." In *The Indian Ocean in Antiquity*. Ed. Julian Reade. London: Kegan Paul International; Newitt, Malyn. 1984. *The Comoro Islands: Struggle against Dependency in the Indian Ocean.* Boulder, CO: Westview Press; Shepherd, Gill. 1980. "The Comorians and the East African Slave Trade." In *Asian and African Systems of Slavery.* Ed. James L. Watson. Berkeley: University of California Press.

ten by Himself. The narrative was extremely popular among British abolitionists who were waging a strong national campaign to have the British Parliament abolish the African slave trade. [See Document 34.]

1791

The community of Freetown was established in

Sierra Leone. Also, the British Parliament chartered the Sierra Leone Company and charged it with the responsibility of transporting additional settlers and providing trade goods to aid the repatriated settlers already in the region.

1794

French colonists on Île de France continued to

Freetown, the capital of Sierra Leone, founded in 1791. The town became the home of many slaves captured from slave-trading vessels and freed by the British. (Church Mission Society)

maintain slavery even though the French National Convention had decreed the abolition of the practice throughout the French colonies.

1795

The British took control of the Cape Colony in South Africa. The legal transfer of colonial authority would come in 1815 with the decisions made at the Congress of Vienna.

1800

Portuguese exports of slaves from Mozambique were estimated to be 15,000 per year. Most of these slaves were transported to Brazil. [See Document 43.]

1800

A group of 550 Jamaican Maroons requested repatriation to Sierra Leone and were transported to Freetown, Sierra Leone. After they had been captured by the British at the end of the Second Maroon War (1795–1796), these Maroons had first been deported to Nova Scotia.

1804

The African ruler Uthman dan Fodio (1754–1817) began a jihad that would result in Fulani domination of northern Nigeria. The Sokoto caliphate that he formed was one of the most influential states in nineteenth-century Africa.

1807

The English Parliament officially ended the slave trade, and the English governor of the Cape Colony in South Africa ended the slave trade in the region.

1808

The British government proclaimed Sierra Leone and Gambia to be British colonies.

1810

Shaka, the famous leader of the Zulu people, began his military career in battle against the Buthelezi people.

1812

James Prior, a surgeon in the British navy, visited Kilwa (in modern-day Tanzania) and noted,

Samuel Ajayi Crowther (c. 1806–1891), who was settled in Sierra Leone by the British after they freed him from a Portuguese slaver. In the 1840s he returned to his native Nigeria as an Anglican missionary and rose to become the first bishop of West Africa. (Church Mission Society)

"The people were formerly said to be numerous, civilised and wealthy; the city extensive and fortified, its habitations elegant and public buildings numerous . . . but whither have they gone?" (Meltzer, 1993).

1814
On August 13, the Dutch ceded the Cape Colony in South Africa to the British as a result of terms reached at the Congress of Vienna.

1817
The French took possession of the former British settlements in Senegal.

1818
The Zulu leader Shaka defeated the Ndwandwe people, and this event marked the beginning of the Mfecane (also known as the Wars of Wandering). In his wars of conquest, Shaka depopulated the region of Natal by death and migration to such a great extent that

the Boers encountered little resistance when they took "the great trek" in 1834. Modern scholarship suggests that disease, famine, and slave trading also contributed to this demographic change.

1819
In an effort to suppress the African slave trade, the British navy regularly intercepted slave ships in African waters. One route that continued to be used by the slave traders went from East Africa to Mauritius. [See Document 41.]

1820–1824
The Egyptian ruler Muhammad 'Ali Pasha purchased 20,000 slaves from the Sudan. He hoped to use these slaves to supplement his army, but the plan failed when 17,000 of the captives died.

1820
On February 6, the *Mayflower of Liberia* (previously the brig *Elizabeth*) sailed from New York City to Sierra Leone on the western coast of Africa with 86 blacks who had agreed to return to Africa as part of a colonization scheme. The ship arrived in Sierra Leone on March 9. The British had established Sierra Leone as a colony where former slaves could be repatriated to Africa, and the colony had been accepting freed blacks and fugitive slaves for three decades.

1821
The British government united Sierra Leone, Gambia, and the Gold Coast (modern-day Ghana) into a reorganized administrative unit called British West Africa.

1822–1824
The British naval captain W. F. Owen visited the coast of East Africa as part of a cartographic surveying expedition and observed the level at which the African slave trade continued to operate in spite of British efforts to suppress it. [See Document 44.]

1822
The American Colonization Society settled its first group of repatriated Africans in a settlement at Monrovia, Liberia, in West Africa. Eventually, about 15,000 people were settled in the colony. Much of the success of the Liberian

Portuguese Government House at Mesuril, in Mozambique harbor. Portuguese slave traders exported slaves from this area to Brazil until well into the nineteenth century. (From Henry Salt, A Voyage to Abyssinia . . . in the Years 1809 and 1810, in which are included, An Account of the Portuguese Settlements on the East Coast of Africa, visited in the Course of the Voyage, *London, 1814.)*

colony was owing to the efforts of one Jehudi Ashmun, who was sent to Liberia by the American Colonization Society to direct efforts there.

1826

Legislators in the Cape Colony in South Africa refused to publish the British Slave Ordinance of 1826, and many slaveowners in the colony indicated that they would resist any British efforts to emancipate the slaves in the Cape Colony.

1826

Jehudi Ashmun published *History of the American Colony in Liberia, from Dec. 1821 to 1823.*

1830

In an effort to curb the slave trade, the British government placed slave trade commissioners on the island of Fernando Po in order to monitor activities in West Africa.

1831

The French government prohibited the slave trade in Senegal.

1834

The Great Trek began in South Africa as Boers left the Cape Colony and made their way to interior settlements in the Orange Free State and Transvaal.

1838

The Portuguese government removed the governor of Angola from his position because of his involvement in the African slave trade.

1841

On March 9, the U.S. Supreme Court upheld a lower court's decision by finding that the Africans from the ship *Amistad* had been illegally kidnapped and ordered them set free and

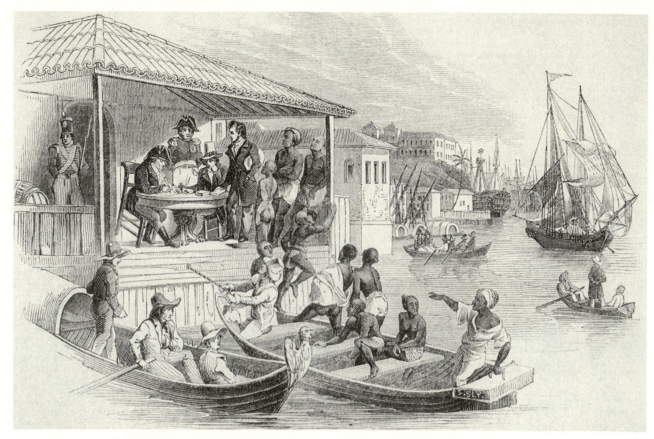

Laborers arriving in the British colony of Mauritius. Once slavery was outlawed, plantation owners resorted to labor systems resembling slavery in many ways. Imported workers, known as "hill coolies," had little legal protection once they had been brought to the island. (Illustrated London News/Corbis)

returned to Africa as soon as possible. Former president John Quincy Adams defended the Africans before the Supreme Court.

1842

The United States and Great Britain agreed to maintain a naval force called the African Squadron off the coast of West Africa in order to patrol the coast to prevent the continuation of the slave trade. Whenever vessels were captured by the African Squadron, captives on board were taken to colonies like Liberia or Sierra Leone where they were freed.

1842

Joseph Jenkins Roberts, who had once been a free black resident of Virginia, became president of the colony of Liberia.

1843

One Lieutenant Barnard, who commanded a British vessel as part of the African Squadron, seized the notorious slaver *Progresso* off the coast of East Africa. [See Document 52.]

1844

Arabs established a slave-trading center along the East African coast at Unyamwezi (near Tabora in modern-day Tanzania). During the era when the West African slave trade was in decline and Western nations sought to suppress it, a large-scale network of slave trading existed in the Indian Ocean region in which East African peoples were captured, enslaved, and transported.

1845

Oba Kosoko, a notorious slave trader of West Africa, became the ruler of the Yoruba kingdom of Lagos. His failure to submit to the antislavery pressures of the British government prompted British intervention in the Bight of Benin region in 1851.

1847

On July 26, President Joseph Jenkins Roberts, who had been born a free black in Petersburg, Virginia, declared the West African nation of Liberia to be an independent republic.

≈OBA KOSOKO (1815–1872)≈

Oba Kosoko (r. 1845–1851) was a renowned ruler, slave trader, and diplomat of the precolonial West African kingdom of Lagos. His international recognition can be attributed to his involvement in the Atlantic slave trade and his resistance to British control of trading activities along the West African coast in the nineteenth century. Born in 1815, he was the son of Oba Esilogun (Osinlokun in some sources), who ruled Lagos from 1780 to 1819. From youth, Kosoko was considered to be an intelligent, bold, courageous, and defiant prince. This aspect of his personality featured prominently in his relations with the missionaries and British colonial officials.

As a result of being passed over in the kingdom's succession process, Kosoko attempted to overthrow his cousin Oluwole. The failure of the coup attempt, called "the Ewe Koko war," forced Kosoko and his followers to flee Lagos. While his followers relocated to Epe (in modern-day Nigeria) and other towns, Kosoko moved down the Bight of Benin to Porto-Novo and subsequently to Whydah (Ouidah in modern-day Benin). In both locations, he became involved in slave-trading activities with the Portuguese and Brazilians. Following the death of Oba Oluwole in 1841, Kosoko was again passed by the kingmakers in favor of his uncle Akitoye. Following the accession of Akitoye to the throne, Kosoko was recalled to Lagos and made a chief of Ereko, a part of Lagos Island, where he had his own court.

By 1845, with the assistance of his slave-trading friends, Kosoko had masterminded a revolt and overthrew Akitoye. Akitoye then tried to persuade John Beecroft, the British consul for the Bights of Benin and Biafra, to reinstate him on the throne of Lagos. In November 1851, using gunboat diplomacy, Beecroft tried to persuade Kosoko to sign a treaty with the British abolishing the slave trade in the kingdom. Kosoko refused, which led to a British attack on the kingdom. "After he had expelled King Akitoye from the throne, and made himself King of Lagos, Her Majesty the Queen of England sent an English consul to convey to him, that it would be Her Majesty's great pleasure to see that he put down the 'Slave-trade' in his Kingdom; and to sign such a treaty, pleading as an excuse he was under the King of Benin, to whom the treaty should be first submitted by Her Majesty's Consul and he would follow. This message was conveyed to the British Officers through his War-Captain Osodi" (Losi, 1914).

On December 27, 1851, the town of Lagos was seized by the British, and Akitoye was restored to the throne. In explaining their intervention in Lagos politics in 1851, the British argued that they were trying to stamp out the slave trade and institute "legitimate commerce" in palm produce, cotton, indigo, shea-butter, and other local goods. There is no doubt that there was more to it than meets the eye. As J. F. A. Ajayi has written, "It is essential to remember that the dispute between Akitoye and Kosoko was not a dispute between slave-traders and anti-slave traders but a struggle for power between two rival branches of the ruling dynasty of Lagos" (Ajayi, 1961).

The dynastic crisis provided the British the opportunity to intervene in the internal affairs of Lagos. More important, the British colonial officials were invited by English missionaries and traders who were determined to utilize Lagos as a corridor to the interior of Yoruban land. Again according to Ajayi: "The missionaries and British traders saw Lagos as the gateway to the thickly populated, prosperous Yoruba country, full of great potentialities for the missionary and the trader. Together, they began to urge the British Government to take Akitoye under their protection and use him to establish British interests in Lagos. In order to get the British Government to act, they publicised the picture of Lagos as the 'notorious slave depot' and of Kosoko as the arch-slave trader who had determined to wipe out English traders and missionaries in the interest of the slave trade. At the same time, they built up Akitoye as confirmed anti-slave trader" (Ajayi, 1961).

Following the British intervention, Kosoko and his followers escaped from Lagos and settled at Epe with the consent of the ruler. Through the support of about 300–400 warriors and a Lagos chieftain, Kosoko established Epe as rival kingdom to Lagos. From Epe, he extended his influence to Leki (also in modern-day Nigeria) and Palma, where he engaged in an export trade, presumably in slaves and palm produce. He succeeded through the support of European slave merchants and Portuguese and Brazilian associates. In addition: "The most important factor in explaining Kosoko's success in establishing himself almost at once as an independent territorial power was his military strength. He is remembered in Lagos and Epe as a leader of courage and energy, and his career shows that he inspired loyalty in his followers. He had been brought up to warfare, and was especially experienced in the naval form which obtained among the lagoon peoples" (Smith, 1969).

Fearing Kosoko's power would disrupt political and economic activities in Lagos, the British, represented by Consul Benjamin Campbell, entered into a treaty with Kosoko on September 28, 1854. The Treaty of Epe, as it was called, contained seven articles, providing, among other things, that Kosoko and his chiefs would refrain from attempting to seize Lagos, renounce the slave trade, and promise to protect merchants and traders who wanted to trade. On the other hand, the British agreed to recognize Palma as Kosoko's port and pay him an annual salary of 10,000 heads of cowries or $1,000 at his option for life. Kosoko then conducted legitimate trade until he ceded his lands to the British in 1862. He died in 1872.

—*Onaiwu W. Ogbomo*

For Further Reading
Ajayi, J. F. A. 1961. "The British Occupation of Lagos, 1851–1865: A Critical Review." *Nigeria Magazine* 69: 96–105; Burns, A. C. 1929. *History of Nigeria.* London: George Allen and Unwin; Geary, Sir William N. M. 1927. *Nigeria under British Rule.* London: Frank Cass and Company; Losi, John B. 1914. *History of Lagos.* Lagos: Tika-Tore Press; Matheson, Jane D. 1974. "Lagoon Relations in the Era of Kosoko, 1845–1862: A Study of African Reaction to European Intervention." Ph.D. Thesis, Boston University; Smith, Robert. 1969. "To the Palaver Islands: War and Diplomacy on the Lagos Lagoon in 1852–1854." *Journal of the Historical Society of Nigeria.* 5(1): 3–25.

1849

As the newly appointed British consul to Benin and Biafra, John Beecroft worked tirelessly to try to end the African slave trade.

1851

British forces attacked and occupied the city of Lagos (in modern-day Nigeria). John Beecroft had previously described Lagos as "a nest for slave traders" (Dike, 1956), but the British hoped to encourage more legitimate commerce in the region.

1853

The British explorer David Livingstone began his expedition into Africa's interior.

1855

The Egyptian government established an outpost at Fashoda (modern-day Kokok) in the Sudan to monitor slave-trading activities in the region.

1857

The Portuguese captured a French slaver, the *Charles et Georges,* in the waters off of Mozambique. France protested the seizure even though the French government had officially banned all French citizens from participating in the African slave trade in 1831.

1858

Msiri established a trading post in Katanga (modern-day Shaba in Congo), where slaves and other commodities were traded.

1860

A significant trade in slaves was reported in the northern and eastern parts of the Congo River basin. In the same year, a large number of indentured servants from India were introduced to the Cape Colony in South Africa.

1865

Treaty signed between Great Britain and the

Arab slaver Tippu Tip, who from the 1850s through the 1870s built up a powerful but short-lived state in Central Africa through his slave, ivory, and copper trading. (Bodleian Library)

References to slavery in Madagascar are common, and most accounts of the country's history and culture mention the institution. Several authors speak of its existence since "time immemorial," but it is probably more correct to imagine that slavery there goes back to the tenth or eleventh century. The origin of slavery in Madagascar is not clear, but it is likely that the institution was brought to Madagascar by the earliest Malagasy immigrants. The interaction between these and later immigrants probably accounts for the difference between Malagasy and African slavery: in the former, marriages between free and slave persons were customarily disapproved because of well-established descent groups in the Malagasy social system.

The Malagasy word *andevo,* or *ondevo,* is generally translated as "slave." Slaves were generated by warfare and raiding enemies, and they could be obtained through various "customary" ways: persons might be condemned to slavery, generally together with their families, for crime or political offenses; other peoples were sold for debt, and their descendants also remained slaves. In the late-fifteenth century, when the first Malagasy kingdoms began to develop, wealth and power largely depended on the capture and use of slaves as labor. The Sakalawa kingdoms, whose economy originally was dominated by herding and hunting, partially converted to a slave mode of production after the mid-seventeenth century. The Sakalawa raided peoples from the neighboring tribes and enslaved them as payment for tribute or for exchange for arms and commodities with Arab, Swahili, and European traders.

In the 1770s, slaveowning was common in the expanding Merina kingdom in the central highlands. Slaves were engaged in household, agricultural, and commercial tasks, and slaves were also a form of capital accumulation and social prestige. The majority of the slaves were Merina subjects, but by the end of the eighteenth century, owing to King Andrianampoinimerina's wars of conquest, captives began to predominate in the slave population, and the kings of Antananarivo became the first large-scale slave exporters of Madagascar. The Sakalawa tried to regain control of this trading activity and sent a series of raiding expeditions along the southern coast of East Africa during the first two decades of the nineteenth century. However, they were unable to challenge the primacy of the Merina traders, who instead increased their supply of slaves to the French merchants of the Mascarene Islands—Île de France (Mauritius) and Île Bourbon (Réunion)—in exchange for firearms and European goods. Thus, the Merina monarchy established a quasi-monopoly of the slave trade on the east coast of Madagascar, mainly in the harbors of Foulpointe and Toamasina.

A treaty banning the export of slaves, signed on October 23, 1817, between King Radama I and Great Britain and enforced in 1820, caused a recession in the Madagascar external slave trade but an increase in the slave population of the Merina kingdom. Despite the treaty, the Merina kingdom launched slaving campaigns through the mid-1850s because of the new patterns of its economic system. Slave labor and the unremunerated forced labor of freemen were linked to agricultural, commercial, and semi-industrial exploitations. Cheap labor also continued to be in great demand following the antislavery British-Merina Treaty of 1865. The monarch, the aristocracy, and the ruling class continued to resort to slave labor, and slaves were imported into Madagascar from Mozambique by Antalaotra and Karany merchants with the connivance of Sakalawa chiefs.

The British campaign against the slave trade in East Africa had the effect of committing the Merina authorities to anti-slave-trade provisions. A royal proclamation in October 1874 liberated the slaves imported since the British-Merina Treaty of 1865, and three years later, on June 20, 1877, all Mozambique slaves were liberated by an edict of Queen Victoria. Approximately 150,000 slaves were manumitted. Still, the slave markets in the Merina kingdoms remained active, and by the end of the 1870s, 17,000 slaves were being imported annually. The demand for slave labor also increased after the Franco-Merina War of 1882–1885, and by the mid-1880s, perhaps as many as 12,000 slaves were traded per year in the Merina kingdom. The main slave market in Antananarivo, near the French residence, was closed on September 27, 1896, following the French declaration that abolished slavery throughout Madagascar. Although the French outlawed slavery on the island, undoubtedly the manumission did not change the Malagasy social system.

—*Liliana Mosca*

For Further Reading
Bloch, Maurice. 1980. "Modes of Production and Slavery in Madagascar: Two Case Studies." In *Asian and African Systems of Slavery.* Ed. James L. Watson. Berkeley: University of California Press; Campbell, Gwyn. 1988. "Slavery and Fanampoana: The Structure of Forced Labour in Imerina (Madagascar), 1790–1861." *Journal of African History* 29(3): 463–486.

Sir Samuel Baker, an explorer whose efforts to extinguish slavery in the Upper Nile ultimately helped promote British interests in the region. (Hulton-Deutsch Collection/Corbis)

Merina kingdom in the central highlands of Madagascar.

1870

The British government gave Sir Samuel Baker the task of ending the slave trade in the sudanic region of the upper Nile from Khartoum to Gondokoro.

1873

The sultan of Zanzibar signed a treaty with Great Britain in which he pledged to stop the East African slave trade.

1874

A royal proclamation in October liberated the slaves imported into the Merina kingdom since the treaty was signed between that kingdom and the British in 1865.

1877

On June 27, all Mozambique slaves were liberated by an edict of Queen Victoria.

1882

In a case heard before the Egyptian Court of Appeal, British jurist John Scott argued that the form of slavery that existed in Africa was not sanctioned by the Qur'an. [See Document 70.]

1884–1885

European powers met at the Berlin Conference to determine the future of the Congo basin and settle other questions related to colonial expansion in Africa. Participants condemned the slave trade but took no unified action to abolish it. Instead, each nation that developed a colonial sphere in Africa pledged to work toward the end of the slave trade in their respective regions. [See Document 71.]

1884

The Congo Free State was formed and became the personal fiefdom of King Leopold of Belgium.

1896

The French abolished slavery throughout Madagascar.

1897

Once the supply of African slaves began to decline, the emir of Bida (Doha in modern-day Qatar) noted, "To be a king means to have plenty of slaves, without which you are nothing" (Meltzer, 1993).

❧Latin America❧

Must I dwell in slavery's night
And all pleasure take its flight
Far beyond my feeble sight,
Forever?
—Juana Ines de la Cruz, "The Slave's Complaint"

The Mexican educator José Vasconcelos used the expression "cosmic race" to define the complex cultural milieu that formed in Latin America as Europeans, Africans, and indigenous peoples of the Americas came into contact with one another and created "a new man for a new world." Slavery played no small part in the formation of this social amalgam as the power that Europeans and American-born Creoles exerted over indigenous groups and Africans contributed to the subjugation of peoples, cultures, and identity through nearly four centuries of enslavement. For the millions who endured servile status on the large estates of Latin America—those forced to "dwell in slavery's night . . . Forever?"—the experience was both disheartening and often deadly.

Perhaps more than in any other setting, slavery in Latin America demonstrates the degree to which a slave's life was subject to the vagaries of economic pursuit. The desire of Europeans to seek handsome profits either through mining or the large-scale cultivation of cash crops led to massive demographic shifts that altered the social and cultural landscape of the region. The initial use of indigenous peoples as slave laborers by the Spanish and Portuguese prompted a decline in populations among many native groups as the effects of forced labor and widespread epidemics decimated many parts of Latin America. The later importation of Africans prompted a cultural transformation in the region as they brought many indigenous beliefs, customs, values, and traditions to the new environment where they were forced to labor as slaves.

The pages that follow trace the origins of slavery in Latin America from the arrival of the Spanish explorers in the late-fifteenth century through the formal abolition of the practice in Brazil in 1888. Information pertaining to certain modern forms of slavery and bonded labor that persist in the region are to be found in the Contemporary section of this chronology. It is also important to note that certain forms of slavery were practiced between and among indigenous peoples of the Americas prior to the arrival of the Europeans, but since the knowledge of such practices comes from disciplines within the social sciences that do not lend themselves to chronological documentation, it is not possible to include these instances in this chronology.

1492

On October 12, the Genoan-born Spanish navigator Christopher Columbus landed on an island in the Bahamas that he named San Salvador. Columbus commanded three ships and 88 men who were attempting to reach the Orient by sailing west across the Atlantic. On October 28, Columbus reached Cuba, and on December 6, his expedition landed on the island of Hispaniola.

1493

On May 4, Pope Alexander VI issued the papal bull Inter Caetera, which created a line of demarcation that divided all newly discovered lands between the Spanish and the Portuguese. The Portuguese crown was given hegemony in lands east of the line, including Africa, and the Spanish crown received the same right in lands west of the line, which included practically all of North and South America. Since Spain was barred from direct commercial activity with Africa, the Portuguese became the middlemen in the first transatlantic slave trade. [See Document 9.]

1494

Spain and Portugal signed the Treaty of Tordesillas, which revised the papal line of demarcation by moving it further west.

1494

On his second voyage to the Americas, Christopher Columbus landed on the island of Jamaica on May 14. On his return to Spain, Columbus carried several hundred indigenous Arawak people to be sold as slaves in Spain.

1495

Christopher Columbus began a large-scale campaign to capture the indigenous Arawak (who he mistakenly called Indians) and of the 1,500 captured and imprisoned, several hundred were shipped to Spain and sold as slaves. Many of these slaves died, and the business of transporting the Arawak across the sea was soon deemed an unprofitable commercial venture. With the demise of this Indian slave trade, the Spaniards in the Americas began searching for gold in the islands that they had "discovered" and used Indian laborers in this effort.

1495

Although Columbus had shipped five vessels filled with Arawak peoples to Spain, Isabella, queen of Castile, refused to permit the sale of nearly 500 indigenous people into slavery in Spain because Bishop Juan Rodriguez de Fonseca, president of the Council of the Indies, and other theological advisers to the queen were uncertain as to the legality of enslaving the Indians.

1498

The Spanish explorers in the Americas shipped 200 Carib Indians, who were considered to be cannibals, to Spain where they were sold into slavery.

1498

The Spanish had already begun to use indigenous peoples of the Caribbean islands as slaves in the mining industry. Accounts from this era suggest that the feeble constitution of these peoples and the level of mistreatment that they received at the hands of the Spanish contributed to a high death rate among the slaves. Additionally, the introduction of European diseases like smallpox caused epidemics that rapidly decimated the indigenous populations because most of the natives had no natural immunity to such diseases.

1500

The Portuguese gained a colonial claim to Brazil when the explorer Pedro Alvares Cabral landed in Brazil in April after being blown off course by a storm while sailing near the west coast of Africa.

1501

On September 3, the Spanish crown signed documents officially authorizing the introduction of African slaves into the newly established colonies in the Americas. It was understood that all Africans who were to be shipped to the Americas had to be shipped first to Spain where they could be Christianized.

1502

The first African slaves were introduced into the Spanish colonies in the New World after they were transported across the Atlantic on a Portuguese vessel.

1505

Governor Nicolas Ovando of the colony at Hispaniola took 17 African slaves from Seville to work in the copper mines on the island, and King Ferdinand of Spain wrote to the governor of Hispaniola and promised to send as many as 100 slaves to the island to be used in the collection of gold.

1510

According to a Spanish historian, King Ferdinand of Spain ordered that 50 African slaves be sent to Hispaniola to work in the gold mines on the island. According to the king, the indigenous laborers on the island were naturally weak and would make poor laborers.

1510

The Spanish crown established the Casa de Contratacion (House of Commerce), which regulated colonial commerce, including the slave trade, and this body authorized the sending of more Africans as slaves to work in the sugarcane fields and gold mines of Hispaniola.

1510

The Spanish crown instituted the practice of reading "the Requirement" in order to justify that captives who were enslaved had been taken as the result of a "just war." [See Document 11.]

1511

In December, Father Antonio Montesinos delivered a sermon in which he criticized the Spanish settlers on Hispaniola for their abuse of the indigenous peoples. Many of the indigenous Arawak had been enslaved by the Spanish colonizers.

1512

The Dominican friar Bartolomé de Las Casas became a missionary among the indigenous people of Cuba. He became the best-known defender of the indigenous peoples against the mistreatment of the Spanish—he was known as "the protector of the Indians"—but his efforts to defend one group against mistreatment would result in the enslavement of Africans for several centuries.

1512

The Spanish crown enacted the Laws of Burgos on December 27. These guidelines gave some additional protection to the indigenous peoples, but they could still be legally enslaved by the Spanish.

1513

The Spanish government began to earn revenue through the slave trade, partly because colonial settlers had to purchase licenses in order to import slaves into Cuba and Hispaniola. In the same year, the Spanish crown authorized the use of African slave labor on the island of Cuba.

1514

Bartolomé de Las Casas began to speak out against the enslavement of indigenous peoples in the Americas and urged the Spanish king Ferdinand to authorize the use of Africans as slaves in the Americas rather than indigenous peoples.

1516

The Spanish established the first sugar mill on Hispaniola.

1516

Cardinal Francisco Ximenes de Cisneros, archbishop of Toledo, briefly suspended the importation of Africans to the New World colonies.

1518

Emperor Charles V of Spain established the system of the *asiento*, which legalized the slave trade to the Spanish colonies in the Americas. According to the terms of this contract, no more than 4,000 Africans were to be transported per year as slaves to the Americas, but that number increased later.

1521

A revolt of African slaves occurred on Hispaniola on Christmas Day. The slaves who organized and led the rebellion were owned by the colony's governor, Diego Colón, the son of Christopher Columbus. The Spanish used great cruelty to suppress the revolt, and order was restored within one week. Many of the captured slaves were castrated by the Spanish. This is the first recorded incident of a slave revolt in the history of the Western Hemisphere, but many more episodes would occur.

1524

In Spain, the Council of the Indies was organized. This group took over the responsibility of governing the New World colonies, which had previously been handled by royal advisers, and it would attempt to standardize policies for all colonies in the Spanish domain.

1527

A revolt of African slaves and indigenous Arawak peoples occurred on the island of Puerto Rico. In the same year, Spanish officials in Mexico reported slave unrest in that region as well. A commander in Mexico City reported that slaves "had chosen a King, and had agreed . . . to kill all the Spaniards . . . and that the Indigenous Mexicans were also with them" (Jenkins, 1996). The Spanish temporarily halted any further importation of African slaves into Mexico until the security of the Spanish colonists there had been restored.

1528

Estimates suggest that 10,000 Africans were working as slaves in the New World settlements.

1529

Slave arsonists burned Santa Marta, the capital of Magdalena, in modern-day Colombia.

1530

An English sailor named William Hawkins became the first Englishman to become involved in African trade and commerce. Hawkins traveled to Brazil after visiting the coast of West Africa, but he did not engage in the slave trade.

1530

The Portuguese crown established a system of captaincies in Brazil to try to encourage settlement of the colony.

1530

Emperor Charles V tried to have Spain's Casa de Contratacion (House of Commerce) restrict Berbers (North African Arabs) and Wolofs (Africans from the West African region of the Senegal and Gambia Rivers) from being transported as slaves to the Spanish colonies, for it was believed that slaves from these groups had been leaders in the revolt that took place in Puerto Rico in 1527.

1531

By royal order, the Spanish government declared it illegal to enslave indigenous peoples in the American colonies.

1532

The Portuguese established a colony at São Vicente in Brazil, the first real effort to colo-

nize Brazil on the part of the Portuguese government.

1533

Slaves working in the mines at Jobabo on the island of Cuba revolted.

1537

Pope Paul III issued the bull Veritas Ipsa, which decreed that indigenous peoples in the Americas were not to be enslaved.

1537

Restrictions on slaves in the Americas were often severe. The *cabildo* (municipal governing council) of Lima issued an order that slaves could not cut down trees or collect fruit or corn. Slaves could receive 100 lashes for a first offense, and a second offense was punished by castration. [See Document 22.]

1538

On July 10, the Spanish government decreed that any slave who married a free person remained a slave. The crown also maintained that children born to such a union were also slaves.

1538

The first African slaves were introduced to Brazil in the area around Bahia. The slaves were transported from West Africa's Guinea coast by Jorge Lopes Bixorda, a Portuguese landowner in Brazil.

1542

Estimates placed the number of slaves on Hispaniola at 30,000, and as many as 3,000 were said to be Maroons, fugitives who had established communities in the interior.

1542

The Spanish crown issued the New Laws of the Indies. These regulations were designed to make it more difficult for Spaniards to enslave indigenous peoples through the *encomienda* system, a system for extracting labor and tribute in kind from conquered Indians. Despite these new restrictions, the Spanish colonists found ways to avoid the laws and continue to maintain the system.

1543

The Spanish government issued a decree that prohibited any African Moor who had con-

❧NEW LAWS OF THE INDIES❧

The New Laws of the Indies (*Leyes y ordenanzas nuevamente hechas por S. M. para la governación de las Indias y buen tratamiento y conservación de los Indios*), drafted in 1542 during the reign of the Spanish king, Charles V, proclaimed that the indigenous peoples of the Americas within the Spanish Empire were free. In addition, the laws clarified the indigenous peoples' relationship to both the Spanish crown and the colonists. Although humanitarian in their wording, the New Laws reflected the crown's self-interest and attempted to check the growing power of the settlers.

Following the conquest of the Indies, Spaniards on both sides of the Atlantic began a vigorous debate concerning the indigenous peoples of the New World. Who the "Indios" were and what relationship Spaniards should have with them were primary concerns, and the views of the conquistadors and the crown differed greatly. The former saw the Indians as a natural source of labor in their search for wealth, and the latter feared that a growing concentration of land and Indians in the hands of settlers would lead to the establishment in the Americas of feudal lords who would, in time, become independent of royal authority.

On Hispaniola, Spanish colonists revived the *encomienda*, or "entrustment," a policy that had been used earlier during the reconquest of the Iberian Peninsula from the Moors. Elsewhere in the New World, settlers used the policy to distribute the Indians among themselves in order to have a right to their labor and to receive tribute. For a while, the crown wavered on the issue, but, in 1503 Ferdinand II of Aragon formally recognized the *encomienda* system, and consequently, this form of Indian slavery spread rapidly throughout the rest of the Spanish Empire. Hernán Cortés, for example, allotted himself an *encomienda* of 100,000 Indians in Mexico.

Attacks on the cruelties of the *encomienda* system became a part of the teachings and writings of Dominican priests such as Antonio de Montesinos and Bartolomé de Las Casas. As a consequence of such criticism, Charles V issued the Laws of Burgos in 1512, the first general code regulating Indian-Spanish relations. These laws called for humane treatment of the Indians and limited the power of the *encomenderos*, the holders of *encomiendas*. In addition, the *encomenderos* had a responsibility to Christianize and Hispanicize the Indians.

In the culmination of its efforts to control the *encomienda* system, the Spanish crown issued the New Laws. After a long, formal introduction, the New Laws prohibited further enslavement of Indians for any reason, including rebellion. Compulsory personal service of Indians was also forbidden, but when Indian laborers were essential, their life and health were not to be put at risk. The use of Indians, or Africans, was banned in pearl fishing, given the high number of casualties that had ensued from that activity. Although the New Laws permitted any of the original conquistadors who were without an allotment of Indians to receive tribute in order to ensure themselves a moderate measure of support and maintenance, it prohibited the creation of any new *encomiendas*. Moreover, the code prohibited *encomenderos* from passing on their entrustments to heirs. Finally, the New Laws declared the Indians to be free persons, possessed of their own free will, and vassals of the crown. As such, the code called for the Indians' good care and instruction in the Roman Catholic faith. Anyone found guilty of their mistreatment was to be brought to justice.

In the New World, the colonists' reaction to the New Laws was angry and swift. *Encomenderos*, along with some clergy who depended on Indian labor for the construction and maintenance of churches and monasteries, rallied against the limitations of the code, especially the one pertaining to passing *encomiendas* on to their heirs. In the face of these protests, the crown modified its position and reissued a weakened version of the New Laws in 1552. Although this version reaffirmed that Indians were free people, it recognized the right of inheritance of and *encomienda* through as many as five generations, after which it reverted to the crown.

As the *encomienda* system began to wane in the mid-sixteenth century throughout Spanish America, new forms of exploitation of Indian labor and enslavement emerged, including the *repartimiento*, the crown's temporary allotment of Indians to colonists for a specified task and period of time, and the *haciendas* (large estates). The latter were originally conceived as using paid, free Indian labor, but in time, that became debt-peonage.

—*Claude F. Jacobs*

For Further Reading
Haring, C. H. 1947. *The Spanish Empire in America*. New York: Oxford University Press; Simpson, Lesley Byrd. 1950. *The Encomienda in New Spain: The Beginning of Spanish Mexico*. Berkeley: University of California Press; Stevens, Henry, ed. 1893. *The New Laws of the Indies*. London: Chiswick Press.

verted from Islam to Christianity from being imported to a colony in the Americas.

1547

The Spanish humanist Juan Ginés de Sepúlveda published a tract entitled *Democrates alter* in which he defended the Spanish policy of conquering the Americas and subduing the indigenous peoples by force. Sepúlveda's arguments were written to counter the writings of Bartolomé Las Casas, the Dominican friar who had criticized the horrible mistreatment that the Spanish inflicted upon the indigenous peoples of the Americas.

1548

A serious slave revolt occurred in the mining region of Colombia, and 20 Spanish settlers were killed in the incident.

1549

On February 22, King Charles I of Spain (Holy Roman Emperor Charles V) issued a proclamation that prohibited the personal servitude of Indians to those Spanish colonists who held *encomienda* rights (the right to extract labor and tribute in kind from conquered Indians) in the New World colonies. [See Document 12.]

1550

A slave revolt in Peru resulted in the burning of the settlement at Santa Marta. Spanish colonial officials responded to the incident by issuing a strict curfew on all slaves in the region.

1552

Bartolomé de Las Casas published *Brief Relations of the Destruction of the Indies* in which he attacked the Spanish system that had allowed the destruction of the indigenous peoples of the Americas to continue.

1553

Estimates placed the number of African slaves in Mexico at 20,000.

1553

As many as 800 fugitive slaves lived in a Maroon (fugitive slave) community near Nombre de Dios in Panama.

1555

Spanish authorities conducted three military ex-
peditions against the Maroons (fugitives who established their own communities) of Panama.

1555

A slave named Bayano led a slave revolt against the Spanish settlers in Peru.

1557

The Jesuit Manuel de Nobrega denounced using indigenous peoples as slaves when he arrived in Brazil, but he accepted the use of black slaves as an economic necessity.

1562

The Englishman John Hawkins carried 300 slaves from West Africa to Hispaniola, and his recognition of the lucrative profits that could be made from the slave trade inspired the English government to pursue the possibility of further English involvement in this enterprise.

1568

The Spanish government enacted a measure making it illegal for mulattoes to carry weapons in the Spanish colonies.

1571

In Cuzco, Peru, Spanish colonial authorities executed a rebel leader, Tupac Amaru, who claimed to be the last of the Incas. He was executed because the colonial officials wanted to prevent all efforts at insurrection that the indigenous peoples might attempt.

1573

Bartolomé de Albornoz, a law professor at the University of Mexico, wrote an essay attacking the legal foundation upon which the enslavement and sale of African peoples was based in Spanish custom and practice.

1576

It was estimated that there were 40,000 African slaves laboring in South America.

1580

The Spanish crown issued the first *asiento* (slave trading contract) authorizing the introduction of African slaves into Mexico.

1580

During the 1580s, sugar producers on *fazendas* (plantations) in Brazil began to shift increas-

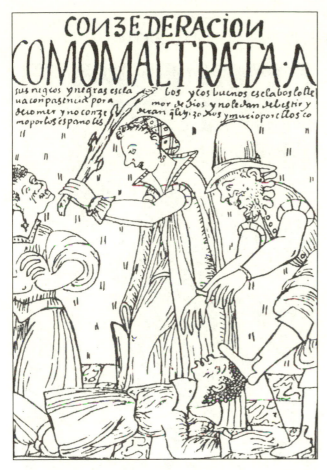

An early seventeenth-century depiction of the mistreatment of slaves in Peru by the Spanish. (The Granger Collection)

ingly to using African slaves as field laborers. The sugar revolution transformed the agricultural and industrial economy of Brazil as thousands of Africans were imported each year to plant, maintain, and harvest the sugar crop. [See Document 16.]

1584

Richard Hakluyt wrote *A Discourse Concerning Western Planting* in order to encourage Englishmen to create colonial outposts in the Americas, but the first permanent English colony, at Jamestown, Virginia, was not established until 1607.

1585

Estimates placed the population of Brazil at 57,000 inhabitants, of whom 14,000 were slaves.

1595

The Spanish monarch Philip II authorized a slave-trading agreement with one Gómez Reynal, giving him the right to transport 38,250 Africans to the Spanish colonies over a nine-year period. As a part of the arrangement, Reynal had to ship Africans directly from Africa to the Americas, and he could not supply mulattoes, mestizos, Turks, or Moors as slaves.

1600

By the end of the sixteenth century, 900,000 Africans had been transported as slaves to the New World colonies. In the seventeenth century, the sugar revolution would triple the demand for slaves in the Americas.

1607

In June, Conde da Ponta, the governor of Bahia in Brazil, reported to Portuguese officials in Lisbon that Hausa slaves in the colony had recently revolted. The Hausa, who were Muslim, continued to stage periodic revolts throughout the history of colonial and early-national Brazil.

1609

A slave named Yanga led a group of 80 Maroons (fugitive slaves) in an uprising against Spanish authority in Mexico. When a force of 600 Spanish troops was unable to subdue the rebels, the colonial authorities negotiated with Yanga, and the Maroons were granted their freedom. The independent town of San Lorenzo de los Negros was eventually founded by some of these Maroons.

1610

The Jesuit Peter Claver arrived in Colombia to minister to the slaves. During his 40 years in the New World, Claver baptized as many as 300,000 slaves. He was eventually canonized a saint in the Roman Catholic Church and is historically known as "the friend to the blacks."

1610

The Maroons (fugitive slaves) of Brazil begin to form the African state of Palmares within the Portuguese colony of Brazil. Palmares operated as a semiautonomous community until it was finally attacked and destroyed in 1697.

1612

Wild rumors of a pending slave insurrection led authorities in Mexico City to execute 30 slaves.

Slavery arose in Latin America for economic reasons with ideological justification based upon religion and a legacy of bondage in Europe. The Iberian kingdoms of Spain and Portugal had a preexisting legal tradition regulating slavery, and upon colonization, the indigenous populations of Spanish and Portuguese America were enslaved. In the early sixteenth century, Juan Ginés de Sepúlveda, a Spanish proslavery advocate, wrote a treatise attempting to prove the innate inferiority of the Indians, arguing that Indians were incapable of the ability to reason and fit Aristotle's category of barbarians or "natural slaves." This application of an ideology built on European Christian thought and social norms resulted in the devaluation of indigenous culture and practices.

Sepúlveda characterized the Indians as innately cruel, sexually promiscuous and deviant, and practitioners of cannibalism and human sacrifice. His racist discourse stigmatized Indians as a group of *gente inhumana* ("inhuman people") who did not recognize God's natural laws and were cowardly and inferior. Sepúlveda stated that Indians were "in prudence, talent, virtue and humanity as inferior to Spaniards as children are to adults and women to men. There is as much difference between them as there is between wild and cruel and very merciful people, between those who are intemperate and those who practice self restraint and are moderate, and I am saying monkeys and men" (Sepúlveda, 1941). He considered Indians to be "subordinate to their superior ones, defined as Spaniards, men and human" (Sepúlveda, 1941).

Laura Lewis (1995) argues that the proslavery argument among Spanish colonizers of Latin America relied on dehumanizing metaphors. These highlighted racial difference, social and cultural nonconformity, and a social definition of the indigenous as "outsiders" in the Spanish colonial social structure, and these contrasts were used to justify enslavement of the indigenous population under terms of the *encomienda* system, which gave the Spanish rights to the labor of Indians. Yet clerical reaction to the mistreatment of Indians under the *encomienda* system, especially Bartolomé de Las Casas's *Brevissima relacion de la desstruicion de las Indias* (The destruction of the Indies) inverted Sepúlveda's social metaphors by describing the inhumane behavior of the Spanish as unchristian and animalistic. Las Casas rejected the racist ideology that indigenous groups were destined for natural slavery and argued that Indians possessed reason and were exemplary spiritual Christians.

Spanish humanist Juan Ginés de Sepúlveda (c. 1490– 1574), who defended Spain's policies toward indigenous peoples in the Americas. (The Granger Collection)

The Spanish crown, thinking of its own priorities and attempting to control both the colonizers and the clergy, then instituted the *repartimiento* (a form of forced labor draft), which was issued by crown decree. Although the *repartimiento* failed as a measure to free the indigenous peoples, as the institution of debt-peonage on haciendas (landed estates) evolved to replace it, the legal position of the Indians improved.

Difficulties in maintaining the servitude of the indigenous population in the face of crown reforms resulted in the importation of African slaves. Spanish colonizers stressed the need to import African slaves to work in mines and agriculture and emphasized that blacks could alleviate the Indian population's burden in producing goods as they could do more work than Indians. The *encomienda* system's harsh conditions had resulted in the decimation of the Indian population and a need for relief. Similarly, Portuguese colonialists in Brazil were faced with a reduction in the Indian population and Indian rebellion and flight.

Las Casas and many Spanish clerics accepted black slavery, despite the practice of Christian baptism and the teaching of slaves. Lewis (1995) considers that two dichotomous forms of thinking were employed to justify slavery: (1) emergent concepts of racial groupings and racist beliefs distinguishing conquered and conquerors and (2) a polarization between barbarism and civilization that was incompletely connected to ideas about cultural and technological evolution. A binary opposition valorized being Spanish, civilized and white, as against being a "natural slave." Indians moved toward the category of "civilized" as they became Christianized, but Africans, despite extensive cultural differentiation, were considered a homogenous people capable of being enslaved.

Both the Portuguese and the Spanish colonial elite attempted a biblical rationalization of black slavery. Tannenbaum (1975) indicated that slaveholders believed that whites were descended from Adam and that Negroes were descended from Cain, who was black and died cursed by God himself. This belief was used to support the idea that blacks were born to serve solely as slaves.

Portuguese slaves are said to have benefited from Las Siete Partidas (Seven-Part Code), a legal code which specified that slaves were human beings with moral and legal rights (Tannebaum, 1975). Portuguese Catholicism asserted that master and slave were equal in the eyes of God and brothers in Christ. Materialist theorists have challenged this thesis, arguing that legal codes will be violated by people in search of profit and that the Latin American slaveholders, whether Spanish or Portuguese, were not necessarily more humane than slaveholders in other regions.

Spanish justifications of black slavery included treating dark skin color as a sign of past sins and paganism. In temperament, Africans were viewed as untamable and aggressive. St. Clair Drake (1990) identified "black" as a master symbol after the fifteenth century and thought that racist ideologies justified a distinction between Indians and blacks, with Indians being viewed as more physically acceptable and less "savage." The church supported black slavery because it considered slavery a condition that would be overcome by equality in Christ. Slaveholders were considered to have a Christian duty toward slaves, and the church legitimized a Spanish social order based on enslavement.

In the 1880s, Brazilian abolitionist-era arguments in support of slavery described the paternalistic master-slave relationship in glowing terms. Proslavery people argued that slaves were fed, clothed, and sheltered while the poor of Europe were left to starve. Atrocity stories were denied, and instances of manumission highlighted. Yet slave proprietors did not try to justify slavery as more humane than freedom or more cost-effective than free labor. No argument based on moral principles was advocated. Instead, slaveholders asserted that property rights required respect for legal ownership, which should not be taken away without indemnification. The issues of legal ownership and indemnification were ideological camouflage in the attempt to preserve the servile institution. After Brazil's abolition law of 1888, slaveholders initiated an organized effort for indemnification. Thus, the economic basis of slavery was laid bare before the abolitionist's gaze.

—*Judith Ann Warner*

For Further Reading

Davis, David Brion. 1975. "Slavery: The Continuing Contradiction." In *The African in Latin America*. Ed. Ann M. Pescatello. New York: Random House; Drake, St. Clair. 1990. *Black Folk Here and There*. 2 vols. Los Angeles: University of California Center for Afro-American Studies; Lewis, Laura A. 1995. "Spanish Ideology and the Practice of Inequality in the New World." In *Racism and Anti-Racism in World Perspective*. Ed. Benjamin B. Bowser. Thousand Oaks, CA.: Sage; Sepulveda, Juan G. 1941. *Tratado sobre las justas causas de la guerra contra los Indios*. Mexico City: Fondo de Cultura Economica; Tannenbaum, Frank. 1975. "Slave or Citizen: A Problem of Semantics?" In *The African in Latin America*. Ed. Ann M. Pescatello. New York: Random House.

1613

The English began to establish a colonial settlement in Bermuda.

1614

In an effort to discourage theft among slaves, colonial authorities in the Americas enacted regulations making it a crime to purchase goods from a slave.

1616

The Dutch began to establish a colony in Guiana in South America and imported slaves from the East Indies to labor in the colony.

1621

The Dutch government established the Dutch West India Company, a corporation that was involved in establishing colonial outposts and conducting the transatlantic slave trade. Willem Usselinx and other Dutch merchants chartered the corporation to organize trade and encourage further colonization efforts by the Netherlands in the New World. [See Document 13.]

1623

Colonial authorities in Cuba passed legislation that protected the status of free blacks (morenos) on the island. Free blacks were used by colonial authorities to help defend the colony against potential violence, which included the possibility of defending Cuban colonists against a slave revolt.

1624

St. Christopher was established as an English colony, the first in the West Indies.

1625

After Spanish colonists had evacuated the western portion of the island of Hispaniola, the French established the colony of Saint Domingue (Haiti) in the region. The Spanish recognized the legality of this settlement in the Treaty of Ryswick in 1697.

1627

St. Kitts was established as a French colony, the first in the West Indies. By 1629, there were African slaves in the colony.

1630

The British introduced sugarcane cultivation into their colony on Barbados.

1630

The Dutch attempted to seize control of the Portuguese colony of Brazil and were able to obtain control of the cities of Olinda and Recife in the region of Pernambuco.

1634

A colonial census revealed that there were 6,000 slaves on the island of Barbados.

1639

Pope Urban VIII issued a papal encyclical to the Apostolic Chamber of Portugal (Cámara Apostólica de Portugal) in which he excommunicated all Roman Catholics who continued to engage in the African slave trade. Urban VIII declared the slave trade to be a crime, and he criticized anyone who dared to enslave Africans.

1641

The French established the colonial settlement of Port Margot in Saint Domingue (Haiti), and African women were introduced into the settlement to help populate the French colony. In time, there was a significant mulatto population in Saint Domingue.

1642

The French government established a colony on the island of Martinique and introduced slavery into the region.

1645

Since the Dutch had seized control of the prime slave-exporting region of Angola in Africa, slaves from the East African region of Mozambique were imported into the colony of Brazil by the Portuguese.

1646

Mexican authorities estimated there were 35,000 Africans living in Mexico and 100,000 Afro-mestizos (zambos) in the colony.

1647

In Santiago, Chile, an African slave proclaimed himself to be the king of Guinea in West Africa.

1648

The English government under Oliver Cromwell began shipping Irish political prisoners to Barbados where they were supposed to work as indentured servants. By 1655, 12,000 Irish political prisoners had been transported into forced servitude in the Americas.

1648

The Portuguese general Henrique Dias used a group of black soldiers during an engagement against Dutch forces in the first battle of Guararapes near Recife, Brazil.

1650

The production of tobacco and sugarcane led to a rapid increase in the slave population of many Caribbean islands, and by this date, Barbados's population included 18,000 slaves. [See Document 28.]

1650

French settlers began cultivating sugarcane on the island of Martinique, and within a century,

The word *Creoles* (Portuguese *crioulos,* Spanish *criollos,* French *créoles*) refers to various people and languages created by African slaves. The meaning of the word and its use varies and often conflicts from one region to another, and within regions, people have redefined it to fit with changes in social structure, culture, and notions of race.

The earliest use of the word is attributed to the Portuguese *crioulo,* which denoted a black person born *(criado)* in the house of a master, especially in Brazil. Over time, the meaning was extended to refer to American-born Europeans as well, particularly those of French and Spanish descent. In Louisiana and elsewhere along the Gulf Coast of the United States, people whose descent is both African and European use the term to emphasize their French or Spanish ancestry and cultural traditions.

In the Spanish colonial empire, Creole slaves were distinguished from *bozales,* slaves born in Africa, and *ladinos,* slaves regardless of their place of birth who had learned Spanish, become Christian, and adopted the Hispanic culture. In the British colonies, a similar distinction was made between slaves who were "country born," equivalent to Creole, and "saltwater Negroes," equivalent to *bozales.*

Although slaveowners may have preferred household slaves who were Creoles, since some degree of acculturation was useful in those positions, many looked down on them otherwise. Compared to what was seen as the more docile and sober nature of the African-born slaves, which was possibly owing to the trauma of the Middle Passage, Creoles were at times considered untrustworthy, undisciplined, immoral, and too knowledgeable of European ways.

As succeeding generations of slaves were born in the New World, they developed their own cultural traditions. Therefore, the origins of the Creole culture are to be found in the ways the earliest slaves came to grips with their slave status, and once in place, these patterns formed the "host culture" for succeeding new arrivals from Africa. The relationship between Creole and African-born slaves was often complex, and which group was dominant varied over time and depended on the adjustment that individual slaves made to the system. In Jamaica, the two groups had distinct forms of holiday celebrations, funeral customs, eating habits, and dress. In Spanish America, *confradías,* religious brotherhoods, began to divide along the lines of Creole and *bozal.* Creole cultural patterns and the way Creoles were socialized into the slave system have been credited with producing a distinct personality type, referred to as "quashie" in the West Indies and "sambo" in the United States.

No matter what differences developed between the Creole and African-born slaves, both were part of a system in which they were viewed as subordinate, used as a source of labor, and denied their full rights as human beings. Consequently, members of both groups were prone to run away. Although Maroon (fugitive slave) communities in the West Indies prior to the eighteenth century were often headed by African-born slaves and composed of people who spoke the same African languages, marronage after that period increasingly involved Creole slaves and leaders. The same was true for slave rebellions. If highly acculturated Creoles were less likely to form a part of the relatively isolated Maroon communities, they were more likely to flee to urban areas, or from one urban area to another, where they might use their skills in various crafts to pass themselves off as free people. In other instances, such Creoles bought their own freedom.

—*Claude F. Jacobs*

For Further Reading
Bowser, Federick P. 1974. *The African Slave Trade in Colonial Peru, 1524–1650.* Stanford, CA: Stanford University Press; Patterson, Orlando. 1967. *The Sociology of Slavery.* London: McGibbon and Kee.

the island's population included 60,000 slaves.

1654
The Jesuit father Diego Ramirez Farina took over the missionary work among the slaves that Father Peter Claver had begun in the area of Cartagena, Colombia.

1654
The Dutch were driven out of the area around Pernambuco in Brazil, and once again, the entire colony of Brazil was in the hands of the Portuguese.

1655
Colonial officials in Brazil enacted legislation on April 9 that provided greater protection to the indigenous peoples of the colony. This legislation had been urged by the Jesuit Antônio Vieira, who did missionary work among the indigenous peoples of Maranhão from 1652 to 1661. [See Document 15.]

Caribbean pirates became involved in the lucrative slave trade. (Archive Photos)

1655

On May 10, the British took over the Spanish colonies on Jamaica and the Cayman Islands. English forces then mounted an unsuccessful campaign to defeat the 1,500 Maroons (fugitive slaves) who occupied the interior mountains of Jamaica.

1663

English colonial officials on Jamaica announced that freedom had been granted to the Maroons in the interior of the island. Juan de Bolas, the leader of the Maroons, became a colonel in the colonial militia.

1667

The Spanish government was informed by the *cabildo* (municipal governing council) of Buenos Aires that epidemics in the region of Argentina had resulted in the death of many slaves and that additional imports were needed.

1670

The French crown authorized Frenchmen to participate in the African slave trade to the islands of the French Caribbean. The order stated that "there is nothing that does more to help the growth of those colonies" (Jenkins, 1996) than the importation of Africans as slaves.

1670

The Spanish government signed a treaty acknowledging that the English government had effective control and possession of Jamaica.

1671

The English Quaker George Fox visited Barbados and ministered to the slaves on the island.

1671

The Danish West India Company received permission from the Danish crown to colonize the island of St. Thomas. By 1673, 100 African slaves had been introduced into the colony.

1672

The English Parliament passed enabling legislation that chartered the Royal African Company and granted it a monopoly on the English slave trade between Africa and the Americas. The company generally supplied 3,000 slaves per year to the English colonies in the West Indies.

1674

A harsh slave code was enacted on Barbados, and slaves on the island responded with a series of revolts in 1674, 1692, and 1702.

1680

The Spanish crown issued the Recopilación de las Leyes de los Reinos de las Indias (Recompilation of the Laws of the Kingdoms of the Indies) in an effort to develop a unified framework of Spanish law for the colonies. The body of law included provisions regulating slavery and the slave trade.

1685

The French crown issued the Code Noir (Black Code) to regulate the practice of slavery in the French colonies in the Americas.

1685

The Spanish crown issued an *asiento* (slave trading contract) to one Baltasar Coyman that authorized him to transport 10,000 slaves to the Spanish colonies in the Americas.

1685

Fugitive slaves in Surinam (Suriname) began to

establish a Maroon (fugitive slave) community in the interior. Eventually, this community attracted indigenous peoples of the region, and the cultural mixture that resulted from this association became known as the Saramakan people.

1688

The volume of the slave trade from Angola to Brazil was estimated to be 6,000 per year.

1688

The Barbados colonial legislature enacted statute No. 82 as an addendum to the slave code that had taken effect in 1674. Regulations in Barbados were exceptionally harsh to the slaves on the island.

1693

Gold was discovered in Brazil's Minas Gerais region, and vast numbers of slaves were soon imported to conduct mining operations in the area.

1694

Gold was discovered in Taubaté, Brazil, which meant that vast numbers of slaves were imported to work in the mines there.

1697

The Portuguese finally succeeded in overthrowing the Republic of Palmares in Brazil. Palmares had existed since 1610 as one of the most successful and durable Maroon (fugitive slave) communities in the history of the Americas.

1697

Major European powers signed the Treaty of Ryswick, which ended the War of the Grand Alliance (War of the League of Augsburg, 1688–1697). One of the terms of this treaty required that Spain recognize French control of the western third of the island of Hispaniola. The French had established the colony of Saint Domingue there in 1625 after Spanish colonists had evacuated the area. Saint Domingue eventually became known as Haiti.

1699

The Portuguese government received 3,000 pounds of gold that had been extracted in the colony in Brazil.

1701

Colonial officials in Guinea made it compulsory for all slaves to learn the catechism, for many of the officials believed that teaching slaves to be Christians would make them less likely to revolt.

1701

The War of the Spanish Succession (1701–1714) began in Europe. When the war ended, England acquired the *asiento* (slave trading contract) and thus held the right to ship slaves to the Spanish colonies for a period of 30 years.

1702

The French government established the French Guinea Company (French Royal Senegal Company) to provide slaves to the Spanish colonies during the War of the Spanish Succession (1701–1714). During the years of the war, the French held the *asiento* (slave trading contract) and were charged with delivering 38,000 slaves per year to the Spanish colonies in the Americas.

1710

There were fears of a slave insurrection in Brazil as rumors spread that Muslim slaves in the colony had conspired.

1710

Colonel Christopher Codrington died on Barbados and willed two plantations to the Society for the Propagation of the Gospel in Foreign Parts. It was Codrington's wish that the land should be used to build a college to educate the island's slaves. He hoped such a college would prove that slavery and Christianity could coexist, but his wish was ignored by the society.

1711

A mulatto named Audrestoe led a slave insurrection in Venezuela.

1711

The Spanish government granted an *asiento* (slave trading contract) to the French West Indies Company to provide slaves to the Spanish colonies in the Americas for an unspecified number of years.

1712

A census on Jamaica revealed that 3,500 Euro-

Branding slaves. (Corbis-Bettmann)

pean colonists inhabited the island along with 42,000 slaves.

1713
French colonial policy for Guadeloupe and the Leeward Islands allowed the manumission of slaves only with the specific permission of the governor general of the colony.

1713
During the negotiation of the Treaty of Utrecht, which ended the War of the Spanish Succession (Queen Anne's War) of 1701–1714, the British South Sea Company received the *asiento,* a contract that permitted the company to carry 4,800 slaves per year to the Spanish colonies in the Americas for a period of 30 years (144,000 total). Additionally, the British were allowed to send one merchant ship per year to the Spanish colonies for trading purposes.

1714
Gold was discovered in Villa Nova do Principe, Brazil. This community was located in the midst of a Maroon community that had been established by slaves who had abandoned plantations in Brazil's interior regions.

1715
The Spanish crown authorized the introduction of slaves onto the island of Puerto Rico.

1715
Ricardo O'Farrill created a slave market in Havana, Cuba, that was used to sell incoming Africans to potential buyers. This market operated for nearly 150 years, and in time, it became known as one of the most notorious slave markets in the Western Hemisphere.

1716
On September 16, the Portuguese government decreed that any black who set foot on Portuguese soil would be considered free. The fact that the policy did not apply to Brazil reflects the different attitudes toward slavery with regard to the mother country and its large slave-based colony.

1719
A slave revolt occurred in Brazil.

1720
The French introduced coffee as another potential plantation crop in their colony of Martinique.

1720

The Portuguese crown issued an order preventing all colonial administrators from any involvement with the African slave trade.

1723

Coffee became a major plantation crop of Brazil, and large numbers of slaves were imported into the coffee-producing regions of the colony. The crop was also introduced into the French colony of Saint Domingue (Haiti), where it quickly became a viable cash crop.

1726

A serious slave revolt occurred in the Dutch colony of Suriname (formerly Surinam).

1728

Portuguese colonists discovered diamonds in Minas Gerais, Brazil. Since slaves were used as laborers in the diamond mines, the number of slaves in the region increased dramatically.

1729

In Montevideo, Uruguay, city officials prohibited mulattoes from serving as aldermen or councilmen.

1730

The First Maroon War began in Jamaica, and British colonial forces struggled against the Maroons (fugitive slaves) who occupied the island's interior until a negotiated settlement was reached in 1739.

1731

A slave rebellion occurred in Cuba at Santiago del Prado. In the same year, slave revolts took place in the regions of Berbice and Essequibo in the region of the Berbice and Essequibo Rivers in the Dutch colony of Guiana.

1732

The Moravian Church established its first missionary outpost on Jamaica as it attempted to bring Christianity to the slaves. The Moravians would eventually expand their missionary work to the islands of Antigua, St. Christopher, and Barbados.

1734

A war took place between British colonial forces and the Maroons (fugitive slaves) of Jamaica. One Captain Cudjoe, who commanded the Maroons, used guerrilla tactics to prevent the British from destroying the Maroon settlement.

1738

Although the British held the *asiento,* a contract that authorized them to take all slaves to the Spanish colonies, the military governor of Uruguay sought permission from Spanish authorities to acquire three shiploads of slaves from Brazil.

1739

The British signed the first treaty with the Maroons (fugitive slaves) who had established themselves in the interior of Jamaica. One Captain Cudjoe of the Trelawney Town Maroons negotiated a settlement with the British that allowed the Maroons to maintain autonomy within the colony of Jamaica.

1741

The Spanish crown granted an *asiento* (slave trading contract) to one Tomas Navarro to supply slaves to the regions of Buenos Aires and Montevideo.

1741

Pope Benedict XIV issued letters to King John V of Portugal and the bishop of Brazil in which he condemned the practice of slavery in Brazil. Specifically, Benedict XIV was opposed to the enslavement of the indigenous peoples of Brazil.

1743

Toussaint Louverture, who became the revolutionary liberator of slaves in Saint Domingue (Haiti), was born a slave on a sugar estate near Cap Français on the island of Hispaniola on May 20.

1750

By this date, the Jesuits in Rio de Janeiro had established a music conservatory in order to teach music to slaves.

1750

The legal practice of *contratacion,* a method to allow slaves to purchase their own freedom by establishing a prearranged sale price, was common on the island of Cuba.

Coffee refers to the beans or seeds of several tropical evergreen shrubs of the species *Coffea*. These beans are used primarily to produce a beverage, although they may also be used to create flavorings, extracts, and ingredients in other products. The coffee tree is believed to have originated in either Ethiopia or Arabia, and its beans first became valuable as a trade item in the thirteenth century when the beverage, also known as coffee, came into being. Over the next several centuries, demand for the beverage increased as its popularity spread across the Mediterranean into Europe.

Coffee was first introduced as a slave-produced product on Saint Domingue (Haiti) in 1723, where it quickly became a substantial cash crop. The crisis of the Haitian slave revolt (1791–1804) caused many planters to flee that island for other areas of the Caribbean and Latin America, and when they did so, they took their capital and knowledge of coffee cultivation with them to places such as Jamaica, Cuba, and Brazil. That revolution, together with a steady rise in North American and European demand for coffee after 1815, helped to establish it as a slave-produced cash crop in each of those areas.

Cuba was the first to benefit from coffee cultivation. The crop became important there in 1791, and the crop's cultivation and trade then experienced a substantial growth period until the 1830s. The tremendous expansion of coffee agriculture in Cuba led to significant, simultaneous growth in slave imports and the overall slave population. In addition, the expanding economy led to an increase in the entire Cuban population across racial categories and created new opportunities for these additional people, especially among those classified as free coloreds. Despite all of this growth and success, however, Cuban coffee plantations followed the West Indian estate model, which meant that the amount of land and number of field laborers involved in the coffee production remained relatively low.

Brazil did not take on a significant role in the world coffee market until the 1830s, although the crop had been known there since the early-eighteenth century. Once established, however, the cultivation of coffee by slaves had a remarkable impact on Brazilian society. From the beginning, coffee was produced by slaves, and its production was, therefore, critically linked to the growth of slave imports and the Atlantic slave trade. Production began on a small scale in the central valleys. Virgin soil was needed for successful cultivation, and when the soil became exhausted, cultivation moved into the interior highlands. It was there, in regions such as Vassouras, that coffee production and slavery in Brazil took on a new fervor and character. Some plantations employed 300–400 slaves to care for the coffee trees and harvest the beans, although a workforce of 70–100 slaves was more typical for most plantations in the area. Nevertheless, even the smaller estates were twice the size of those that used the West Indian model of cultivation.

Such large-scale production led to a significant demand for more slave labor. In the early decades of the nineteenth century, Brazil imported nearly 15,000 African slaves per year, and by the last two decades, that number had increased to 20,000 per year. This increase and continued demand were no doubt linked to the expansion of coffee cultivation and trade, as more slaves were employed in its production than in any other activity in those last two decades. With the abolition of the slave trade, Brazil's internal trade of slaves increased dramatically as workers were shifted from other regions to the coffee-producing areas of São Paolo, Vassouras, and Rio de Janeiro. Consequently, a large portion of Brazil's black population was concentrated in those areas at the time of emancipation in 1888.

—*Marti J. Gastineau*

For Further Reading
Dean, Warren. 1976. *Rio Claro: A Brazilian Plantation System, 1820–1920.* Stanford, CA: Stanford University Press; Holloway, Thomas H. 1977. "Immigration and Abolition: The Transition from Slave to Free Labor in the Sao Paulo Coffee Zone." In *Essays concerning the Socioeconomic History of Brazil and Portuguese India.* Ed. Dauril Alden and Warren Dean. Gainesville: University Presses of Florida; Klein, Herbert S. 1986. *African Slavery in Latin America and the Caribbean.* New York: Oxford University Press; Stein, Stanley J. 1985. *Vassouras: A Brazilian Coffee County, 1850–1900.* Princeton, NJ: Princeton University Press.

Slaves harvesting coffee in the Brazilian highlands. Coffee became an important cash crop in Brazil in the eighteenth century. (By permission of the Houghton Library, Harvard University)

1751

A period of unrest began in Saint Domingue (Haiti) as Maroons (fugitive slaves) from the interior led a sustained resistance effort against the French. A chief by the name of Mackandal, a Maroon leader who had developed a plot to poison the white slaveholders in the colony, led organized resistance against the French for six years until he was betrayed and arrested.

1753

The Cunliffe family of Liverpool, England, was actively involved in the slave trade to the West Indies. The family operated 12 vessels that made as many as three trips per year to the Americas. In 1753, the Cunliffe family transported 1,210 slaves to the West Indies.

1754

Colonial estimates of the population of Saint Domingue (Haiti) suggest that the colony included 14,000 white colonists, 4,000 mulattoes, and 172,000 slaves.

1755

The colonial government in Brazil emancipated all indigenous Brazilians who were held as slaves, which made the demand for African slaves even greater in the colony.

1756

On Saint Domingue (Haiti), the free black Jasmin Thomassam opened a charitable home for poor and indigent free backs in the colony. Thomassam operated this home for 40 years.

1756

On April 15, a plot was discovered in Brazil in which slaves of the Minas Gerais region planned an insurrection on the evening of Good Friday when all of the Portuguese colonists would be at Mass. The plans had called for the indiscriminate murder of all white and mulatto men; women were to be spared.

1758

Manuel Riberro de Rocha published *The Ethiopian Ransomed, Indentured, Sustained, Corrected, Educated, and Liberated*. In this work, Rocha argued that Brazil should do away with the practice of slavery and adopt instead a system in which indentured servants provided the colony's labor force.

1760

Tacky's Rebellion began on the island of Jamaica on April 7 when a group of Akan slaves attacked the English fort at Port Maria. The fighting spread across the island, and the rebellion was not suppressed until October 1761.

1761

The Dutch acknowledged the freedom of the Saramakan people of Suriname (Surinam). For nearly 80 years, a Maroon community composed of these fugitive slaves and indigenous peoples had resisted Dutch efforts to destroy it.

1761

The British settled the island of Dominica and introduced slaves into the region.

1761

At the urging of the marquis of Pombal, the Portuguese government decreed on September 19 that slaves could no longer be brought into Portugal from Africa, Asia, or Brazil.

1763

The British settled the islands of Grenada and St. Vincent and introduced slaves into both colonies.

1763

A great rebellion began in the region of Berbice, in the Dutch colony that later became British Guiana (Guyana), and lasted until 1764. This massive slave revolt may have included half the slaves in the colony, who were led into revolt by charismatic leaders known as Coffy and Accara. Once the rebellion had been suppressed, there were many slave executions in the colony.

1764

A colonial census estimated that 140,000 slaves were used as laborers in Jamaica.

1764

The British Parliament enacted the Sugar Act, which placed a duty upon West Indian sugar imported into Britain's North American colonies. This duty had an adverse effect upon the sugar-plantation-based economy of the West Indies.

1767

The Spanish government expelled the Jesuits from all Spanish colonies in the Americas, and any slaves belonging to the Jesuits were turned over to the Spanish government.

1768

Spanish settlers in Cuba began to cultivate coffee as a plantation crop. The successful cultivation of this new cash crop required greater imports of African slaves to Cuba.

1770

Abbé Guillaume-Thomas-François Raynal published *Histoire philosophique et politique des établissements et du commerce des Européens dans les deux Indies* (Philosophical and political history of the establishment of European commerce in the Indies) in Paris. In this work, Raynal predicted that a black Spartacus would soon rise in the New World to avenge the many injustices of man's inhumanity to man, and some people have credited this historic antislavery work with inspiring the Haitian Revolution (1792–1804).

1772

King Charles III of Spain publicly condemned slavery and announced that any fugitive slave who sought refuge in Spanish territory would be set free, but the king still allowed slavery to persist in Spanish colonies throughout the Americas.

1772

The colony of Guyana again faced a serious slave uprising as slaves in the Demerara region revolted against Dutch colonial rule.

Engraving by David of the 1760 Jamaican slave uprising known as Tacky's Rebellion. (Bibliothèque Nationale, Paris, Giraudon/Art Resource)

"A Rebel Negro Armed and on His Guard," illustration from John G. Stedman, Narrative of a Five Years' Expedition against the Revolted Negroes of Surinam *(London, 1796). (Tozzer Library, Harvard University)*

1772
In May, Chief Justice Lord Mansfield (William Murray, first earl of Mansfield) decided the case of *Knowles v. Somersett* and thereby abolished slavery in England. However, the practice of slavery in colonies throughout the British Empire was not affected by the decision. [See Document 26.]

1773
British colonial officials on the island of St. Vincent reached an agreement with the Black Caribs who had resisted British rule for nearly 75 years, and as a result, the Black Caribs received control of one-third of the island.

1773
The Spanish government granted permission to the marquis of Case Eirle to sell African slaves in Cuba.

1773
Under the leadership of the marquis of Pombal,

the government of Portugal abolished slavery within Portugal on January 16, but the practice continued in the Portuguese colonies.

1780
French colonial officials in Saint Domingue (Haiti) negotiated a peace treaty with Maroons on the island who had been fighting the French for nearly eight years.

1783
Simón Bolívar, the future liberator of much of the South American continent, was born in Caracas, Venezuela, on July 24.

1784
The branding of slaves was prohibited by legislative act in the Rio de la Plata region of Argentina.

1784
The Virginia-born African-American missionary George Liele traveled to Jamaica as a missionary. During his seven years in the region, he baptized 400 slaves.

1788
Ninety-eight slave ships carrying 29,500 Africans arrived in the colony of Saint Domingue (Haiti). In the 10-year period from 1782 to 1792, the island's slave population doubled.

1788
City officials in Buenos Aires expressed concern at the growing number of free blacks in the city.

1788
A group of antislavery supporters in France established the Société des Amis des Noirs (Society of the Friends of the Blacks) on February 19, and abolitionists in France began to correspond with like-minded reformers in Great Britain and the United States.

1789
In France, the Société des Amis des Noirs tried to petition the Estates General to abolish slavery in the French colonies. As a secondary goal, the group sought to end the African slave trade.

1789
Julian Raymond and Vincent Ogé traveled to

Revolt in St. Domingue in 1790. (Corbis-Bettmann)

France to request that the National Assembly grant the rights of citizenship to free blacks in the colony of Saint Domingue (Haiti).

1789

The Spanish king, Charles III, issued the Real Cédula (Spanish Slave Code). In this official pronouncement, the monarch demanded that accurate record keeping of all slave-related demographic data should be maintained by colonial officials.

1789

On August 26, the French National Assembly issued the Declaration of the Rights of Man and Citizen, the most important document of the French Revolution. The declaration stated that "men are born and remain free and equal in rights." [See Document 33.]

1790

The Spanish government abolished the Casa de Contratacion (House of Commerce).

1790

In Saint Domingue (Haiti), Vincent Ogé and Jean-Baptiste Chavanne led an uprising of mulattoes against French control of the colony on October 21, but the revolt was put down and both leaders were executed in February 1791.

1791

Coffee became a major plantation crop in Cuba, and large numbers of slaves were imported into the coffee-producing regions in the eastern mountains.

1791

In an open letter to the Haitians, Abbé Henri-Baptiste Grégoire of France declared, "You were men, you are now citizens" (Jenkins, 1996).

1791

A slave named Farcel led a slave uprising in Dominica, an event that forced the British to postpone their efforts to end the slave trade.

The West India regiments were units of black soldiers in the British army from 1795 until World War I. They were formed in the British West Indies at the beginning of the Napoleonic Wars to combat the black forces being used by the French in the Caribbean, where white troops on both sides were dying in great numbers from malaria and yellow fever. Europeans in the Americas found black forces to be loyal, skilled, and effective in many kinds of military uses. Very often race consciousness, whether pertaining to African or native background, and color prejudice took a back seat to military emergencies and the need to arm slaves, free blacks, mulattoes, and Indians in military campaigns that found whites, blacks, and Indians fighting on all sides.

The British West India regiments were the logical result of the military slave tradition in the Americas that started during the conquest period when armed native slaves were used as auxiliary troops by the Spanish conquistadors. Later, African slaves and free blacks were employed as bodyguards, police, sailors, pirates, military construction workers, and in paramilitary roles as spies, agents, cowboys, slave hunters, and watchmen. Many became regular soldiers, some serving in cavalry and artillery units, and a few even became officers. The military experience provided a way of upward social mobility and freedom for many blacks, and for some of them, it led to high civil and military positions.

From the sixteenth century on, thousands of slaves and free blacks served in the colonial militias throughout Latin America and the Caribbean and eventually became the mainstay of the militia in some colonies like Cuba, Brazil, Saint Domingue, and some British islands. By the end of the eighteenth century, many British and French colonies had formed special black corps made up of armed slaves. In the American Revolution, both sides benefited from the use of black auxiliaries.

After observing the loyal, skilled, and effective fighting of such units of armed slaves, the British military devised the West India regiments, which took slave corps a step further by putting them on a regular footing with white English troops, and thus under the complete control of the British army, and allowing them to be stationed on any island in the Caribbean and eventually in Africa. It would take years of pressure to obtain the cooperation of the islands' planters and experimenting with many different methods of recruitment to raise such slave regiments, but the British military

persisted because it had little choice. The French were conquering some of the British Caribbean colonies using almost totally black forces led by the great mulatto general Victor Hugues. The English military was bogged down fighting in Europe, and most of the British troops sent to the West Indies were sickening and dying from tropical diseases. The Caribbean had become a second major front in the Napoleonic Wars, and the lucrative sugar colonies and their strategic location demanded a powerful defense.

Britain had also experienced the wide use of slave and free black and mulatto forces on Saint Domingue (Haiti) during a six-year occupation of parts of that island in the 1790s. There the British had responded to the thousands of freed slaves being employed by the French and native revolutionaries by forming free and slave corps of their own. Under pressure from commanders on the spot, the English king approved the formation of black units as part of the British army, and eventually some 5,000 black troops were used there. Many were part of French loyalist forces fighting the revolutionaries, and about 3,000 of the armed slaves were formed into the Seventh and Tenth West India Regiments, some with their own French officers, after leaving the island in 1799.

The deadly effect of the tropical climate was the main reason the British army resorted to a massive and official formation of black forces. Normally, over half the English troops in the West Indies died within a year or two from malaria and yellow fever, compared to 1 in 50 in North America. In a four-month English invasion of Havana in 1762, over one-third of the white troops died from disease whereas few of their black auxiliaries even got sick. During the occupation of Saint Domingue, the English lost 630 of 980 men of the Eighty-second Regiment from disease in 10 weeks, and in a few months, all of the Ninety-sixth Regiment died. But Africans were mostly immune to malaria and yellow fever, partly because of the effects of anemia, and thus the vast slave population was seen as a potential pool of soldiers for the British army. After pressure from the army, the king approved the raising of black West India regiments in 1795.

Yet such an idea was anathema to the planters and assemblies of the colonies, who not only valued their most soldierly slaves but also had a great dread of arming slaves they could not control, especially when their main fear was, not of French invasion, but of slave revolt. Would not armed slaves become the very leaders of such a slave insurrection? These fears proved false with time, but the military would have to find many ways to raise the slave regiments in opposition to the colonial leaders.

At first, the army simply requisitioned some of the islands' slave corps that had already been formed and also trained the slave pioneer corps to be soldiers. These military laborers were attached to regular units to do various chores. During the American Revolution, the English had found one such unit, the South Carolina Corps, so useful that they shipped the slaves to the islands and employed them in pioneer functions for several years, eventually forming them into part of a West India regiment. The army tried to attract free blacks to the regiments, but very few agreed to join. A few slaves were bought by the assemblies from local planters and sold to the army, and the army bought a few more outright from the planters, but slave prices were high and usually jacked up for the army. The regiments filled up slowly.

The army finally decided to recruit slaves fresh off the ships from Africa. The army discovered these slaves could be trained as regular British soldiers, and they became the main troops of the West India regiments for a decade. After the passage of the act ending the slave trade, the regiments were recruited from "prize Negroes"—those captured from foreign ships that were smuggling slaves. Many of these were returned to Sierra Leone on the West African coast and enlisted there. Later on in the nineteenth century, enlistees came from free blacks in both the West Indies and Africa, and some 20,000 blacks served in 12 regiments, sometimes outnumbering white forces stationed in the British Caribbean.

Unlike any other black military units in the New World, the West India regiments were treated on an equal footing with British white units, receiving the same pay, food, pensions, and general treatment. There was different treatment in the posting of black corps to sites with higher rates of sickness in order to spare the lives of white troops, and the black units were led by white officers until the mid-1800s when some black officers were commissioned. There had been black noncommissioned officers in the regiments since 1800 as they proved beneficial in translating African languages and ensuring the loyalty of the black soldiers. The troops were given basic education and religious instruction and were baptized.

The units proved very loyal and useful through the years, although there were two mutinies in the beginning. In 1802, several hundred members of the Eighth West India Regiment on Dominica mutinied when they were used for nonmilitary purposes and some concluded they were being made into slaves. The mutiny was put down by both black and white troops in one day. In 1808, several dozen "new Negro" trainees mutinied while parading in Jamaica, but about 1,000 other members of the Second West India Regiment captured or killed the mutineers, some giving their lives to protect their white officers. The military concluded that the loyalty and effectiveness of those in the regiments who had not mutinied showed the overall benefit of the units.

Through the years, the regiments received high praise from their officers and the army. They fought in almost all engagements and garrisoned most of the West Indies for over a century. By the mid-1800s, the West India regiments were also serving in Africa, helping to suppress the slave trade and conquer colonies for Britain. The slave troops were manumitted after their service until 1807 when Parliament freed all 10,000 of the black soldiers in one act. Many regimental retirees became leaders in their communities, most being discharged in Trinidad, British Honduras, or Sierra Leone, and by 1862, about one-eighth of Trinidad's population consisted of black soldier retirees. It has been estimated that using black troops instead of white troops in the West Indies and Africa probably saved the lives of some 60,000 or more British soldiers.

—*Peter M. Voelz*

For Further Reading
Buckley, Roger N. 1979. *Slaves in Red Coats: The British West India Regiments, 1795–1815.* New Haven, CT: Yale University Press; Caulfield, James E. 1896. *One Hundred Years' History of the Second West India Regiment.* London: Forster Groom; Ellis, Alfred Burden. 1885. *The History of the First West India Regiment.* London: Chapman and Hall; Voelz, Peter M. 1993. *Slave and Soldier: The Military Impact of Blacks in the Colonial Americas.* New York: Garland.

1791

The Spanish crown declared that the only port of entry for slaves in the southern region of South America was Montevideo.

1791

On May 15, the French National Assembly granted mulattoes the right to serve in colonial assemblies. Additionally, all mulattoes in Haiti who had been born of free parents were granted the suffrage.

1791

What began as a civil war on August 22 evolved into a slave revolt in the French colony of Saint Domingue (Haiti), and after more than a decade of fighting, victorious blacks would declare the independence of Haiti in 1804. Haiti was the first black republic in the Western Hemisphere.

1791

On December 4, the freed slave known as Toussaint de Bréda (later Toussaint Louverture) joined the efforts of slave insurrectionists on Saint Domingue (Haiti) to take control of the colony from the French.

1792

The Danish crown issued a royal order demanding that the importation of African slaves into Danish colonies be ended by 1803.

1792

Colonial authorities in Jamaica enacted a statute requiring owners to care for all slaves who were disabled or otherwise infirm. Some slaveowners had previously attempted to use manumission as a means of avoiding such responsibility by making disabled free blacks wards of the state.

1792

On April 4, the French legislative assembly decreed that free blacks had the right to vote in elective assemblies and to hold public office.

1793

In Saint Domingue (Haiti), the rebel leader Toussaint Louverture began an insurrection against French colonial rule. Toussaint proclaimed the creation of the Republic of Haiti and gathered an army to win independence from the French. In the same year, French com-missioner Léger Félicité Sonthonax emancipated the slaves in Saint Domingue's North Province in the hope that the freed slaves would then support his efforts to defeat the rebel forces of Toussaint Louverture.

1794

Portuguese authorities expelled the Capuchin friar Jose de Bolonha after he questioned the legality of slavery in Brazil.

1794

In France, the National Assembly abolished slavery in all French colonial possessions, instituting immediate, noncompensated emancipation of all slaves in the French colonies. Napoleon Bonaparte later reversed this decision.

1794

The English took control of the former French possessions of Martinique, St. Lucia, and Guadeloupe.

1795

British colonial officials began fighting the Second Maroon War against the fugitive inhabitants of Jamaica's interior. Several hundred Maroons were captured and were transported to Nova Scotia when the war ended in 1796.

1795

On the island of Grenada, the free black planter Julien Fédon rallied the island's population in March to oppose the British, who had acquired the French colony in 1763. Fédon's forces consisted of slaves, free blacks, and whites, all of whom were motivated by their dislike of the British and inspired by the rhetoric of the French Revolution. The rebellion was finally suppressed in July 1796.

1795

On August 17, slaves on the island of Curaçao in the Dutch West Indies staged an insurrection that lasted for one month before it was suppressed by colonial authorities. The rebellion was led by slaves named Tula and Carpata, and colonial officials used a force of free black militia to put down the insurrection.

1796

The British faced a serious slave revolt on the island of St. Lucia and promised freedom to those

The Spanish Slave Code of 1789 (Real Cédula de Su Majestad sobre la educación, trato, y ocupaciones de los esclavos, en todos sus dominios de Indias, e islas Filipinas), drafted during the reign of Charles III, was a product of the Bourbon reform movement that was intended to foster reason and humanity in the Spanish Empire. Before the formulation of this code, Spanish laws regarding slavery had proliferated and often conflicted with each other. The 1680 Recopilación de las Leyes de los Reinos de las Indias (Recompilation of the Laws of the Kingdoms of the Indies), which was the crown's attempt to form a comprehensive legal framework for its New World colonies, contained slave provisions, but changes in the scope of the slave trade and shifting attitudes toward slavery made it necessary to reformulate those provisions.

The significance of the 1789 code is twofold. First, unlike the Código Negro Carolino (Negro code of Charles II), the 1785 Bourbon reform code formulated specifically for the Spanish colony of Santo Domingo, the Real Cédula was the first code dedicated exclusively to African slavery that was to be applied to the entire Spanish Empire. Second, in addition to the ideas of the thirteenth-century Spanish-Catholic tradition reflected in the Siete Partidas (Seven-Part Code), the Real Cédula reflected the ideas of the eighteenth-century Enlightenment.

Guided to a great extent by the Council of the Indies, the Spanish crown dictated the Real Cédula. In the preamble and provisions, which were divided into 13 chapters, the code set out the duties that slaves had to masters and, strikingly, the obligations that masters had to slaves. First, slaves were to be instructed in the Catholic religion; second, the slaves were to receive proper food and clothing; third, working conditions for slaves were to be regulated by age, gender, and occupation; fourth, slaves were to be freed from work on festival days; and fifth, they were to be properly housed, as well as hospitalized and buried at the owner's expense. Sixth, owners were expected to maintain aged and infirm slaves rather than manumit them; seventh, slaves had a right to marriage; and eighth, slaves who were properly maintained were to obey and respect their masters and overseers.

Ninth, punishment of slaves, when needed, was limited to 25 lashes, and any punishment over 25 lashes was to be administered by the state, but only after the slave had been tried before local justices. In all cases, the punishment was to be exactly the same as that administered to people who were free. Tenth, masters found guilty of failing to carry out the provisions of the code were to be fined up to 200 pesos; in cases where punishment caused dismemberment or great bodily harm to slaves, the master was to be held liable, just as if the injury had been inflicted on a free person; a maltreated slave was to be sold to another master or, if incapacitated, was to be maintained by the master for life. Eleventh, only masters could punish slaves; twelfth, masters were to give the local authorities a notarized list of their slaves as a way for the state to check on owners and prevent them from causing the disappearance or death of slaves; and thirteenth, the local authorities were to make triennial visits to plantations to see that masters were abiding by the provisions of the code.

Although the Real Cédula was silent on the issue of manumission and did not protect families from separation, it concentrated on the slaves' physical welfare and the state's protection of their basic human rights, treating them as equal to free people in some instances. Consequently, the code has been characterized as an advance in humane legislation and superior to the codes that either preceded or followed it.

When the Real Cédula was sent to the colonies on January 19, 1790, slave masters in the Caribbean and Louisiana reacted quickly to prevent it from being put into effect. Complaints focused on the requirements related to food, housing, and basic welfare of slaves since owners thought they were already meeting those needs adequately. In addition, owners resented the code's restrictions on their authority to punish slaves, given the owners' perceptions of what was needed to build and maintain a disciplined workforce.

Even though the 1789 code was never promulgated in the areas of the Spanish Empire where slaves were most numerous—the Caribbean and Louisiana—it did influence the less liberal legislation that followed, including an 1806 free-marriage decree and the 1842 Cuban Regiamento de Esclavos (Rules for Slaves).

—*Claude F. Jacobs*

For Further Reading
Carrancá y Trujillo, Raúl. 1938. "El Estatuo Jurídico de los Esclavos en las *Postrimerías de la Colonización Española.*" *Revista de Historia de América* 3: 20–60; Hall, Gwendolyn Midlo. 1971. *Social Control in Slave Plantation Societies: A Comparison of St. Domingue and Cuba.* Baltimore, MD: Johns Hopkins University Press; Klein, Herbert S. 1967. *Slavery in the Americas: A Comparative Study of Virginia and Cuba.* Chicago: University of Chicago Press.

rebels who would lay down their weapons and surrender.

1798

On October 1, Toussaint Louverture and his forces entered the city of Mole St. Nicholas in Saint Domingue as conquerors, and English forces on the island of Hispaniola recognized the independence of Haiti.

1800

The Portuguese were exporting 10,000 Africans per year from Mozambique and transporting them as slaves to Brazil.

1800

Fears of an impending slave revolt in Montevideo, Uruguay, prompted defensive measures by Spanish colonists in the region.

1800

A group of 550 Jamaican Maroons (fugitive slaves) were transported to Freetown, Sierra Leone, at their request. After they had been captured by the British in 1796, these Maroons had been deported to Nova Scotia.

1801

Napoleon Bonaparte sent General Charles-Victor-Emmanuel Leclerc to the rebellious colony of Saint Domingue (Haiti) to try to restore French authority there. Napoleon reportedly told Leclerc to "remember that blacks are not human beings" (Jenkins, 1996).

1801

Toussaint Louverture became the governor general for life in Saint Domingue (Haiti), and his government officially abolished slavery in the region.

1802

On May 12, Napoleon Bonaparte reinstituted slavery and the slave trade in all areas within the French empire where it had been outlawed by previous action of the French National Assembly.

1802

After agreeing to the terms of a peace treaty with the French, Toussaint Louverture was captured and taken to France where he was imprisoned. He died in his prison cell at Fort de Joux.

Jean-Jacques Dessalines. (Corbis-Bettmann)

1803

The government of Denmark became the first modern nation to ban the African slave trade.

1804

The independence of Haiti was declared on January 1 after Jean-Jacques Dessalines and his forces captured Port-au-Prince and forced the expulsion of the French from the region.

1804

The former slave Jean-Jacques Dessalines became governor general for life in Haiti and soon proclaimed himself Emperor Jacques I. As ruler of the black republic, Dessalines ordered the massacre of many whites and mulattoes who he believed were enemies of the state.

1806

The Haitian leader Jean-Jacques Dessalines was assassinated by his own troops on October 17. The Afro-Haitian leader Henri Christophe was named his successor, but mulattoes on the island who had been greatly oppressed by the Dessalines regime resisted Christophe and civil war ensued in Haiti.

1807

In Haiti, the forces of mulatto General Alexandre Pétion defeated the armies of the Afro-Haitian Henri Christophe, and Haiti became a divided nation. Christophe continued to govern the northern part of the country, and Pétion established a government in the southern part of the country near Port-au-Prince. [See Document 40.]

1807

The governments of Great Britain and the United States both enacted statutes to prohibit their citizens from participating in the African slave trade.

1897

When the British navy helped Portuguese ruler John VI escape from Lisbon to Brazil, he promised to work toward ending the African slave trade to Brazil.

1809

The colonial government in Brazil dedicated a public square named Plaza Fidelidad (Fidelity Square) in Buenos Aires to commemorate the loyalty of the area's slaves during the British invasion of 1806.

1809

Placido (Gabriel de la Concepción Valdés), one of the greatest Afro-Cuban poets, was born in Mantanzas, Cuba. He became know for his writings, which protested Spanish oppression on the island, and in 1844, he was executed because he was suspected of being involved in a "racial conspiracy" against Spanish authority.

1809

The population of New Orleans increased dramatically as 6,000 new immigrants arrived in the Louisiana colony. These immigrants were originally from the French colony of Saint Domingue (Haiti), but they had left that island when a slave insurrection began in 1791. They had initially moved to Cuba but were expelled from that island in 1809 after Napoleon's forces invaded Spain and relations between France and Spain grew cold.

1810

The Supreme Junta of Caracas, Venezuela, ordered the end of the African slave trade.

1810

In Mexico, Father Miguel Hidalgo y Costilla issued an emancipation decree before his rebellion was put down by royalist forces.

1811

Officials in Cuba protested matters the Spanish Cortes (legislature) was debating that would have ended the slave trade and initiated gradual abolition in the colonies.

1811

Brazil enacted a new militia law that allowed only those individuals who were white, who had grandfathers who were white, and who had parents who had been born free to qualify for militia service.

1811

In Chile, a statute was enacted decreeing that children born to slaves were born free, but this measure did not change the status of the child's parents, who remained slaves.

1811

In Haiti, Henri Christophe declared himself to be King Henri I.

1812

A large insurrection took place among the slaves of Venezuela.

1814

Pope Pius VII addressed a letter to the French king, Louis XVIII, in which Pius condemned any assertion made either by the church or by a Christian that the slave trade was a legal practice.

1815

President Alexandre Pétion of Haiti gave refuge to Simón Bolívar during the Latin American wars of independence.

1816

Simón Bolívar acquired military supplies from the government of Haiti after promising that he would work to crush slavery in South America. He also issued a proclamation promising freedom to slaves who helped him fight the royalist troops in Venezuela.

1816

José de San Martín issued a proclamation

The Supreme Junta of Caracas, also known as the Junta Suprema Conservadora de los Derechos de Fernando VII, was formed by Venezuelan creoles (Spaniards born in the Americas) in Caracas, Venezuela, on April 19, 1810. The junta declared Venezuela's independence and enacted many decrees, including the end of the slave trade.

Venezuelan creoles desired to form a junta following the abdication of Ferdinand VII of Spain in 1808 when Spain fell to Napoleon, and the *creole cabildo* ("town council") finally formed the Supreme Junta to rule in the name of Ferdinand in 1810. The *cabildo* of Caracas called itself into session as a *cabildo abierto,* an extraordinary meeting of the governing council (which could only be called by the governor), and took political authority as a revolutionary junta. Thus began the movement for independence in Venezuela. In March 1811, a three-member junta replaced the first Supreme Junta, and it declared Venezuelan independence on July 5, 1811.

Reforms of the Supreme Junta included a decrease in taxes and a declaration of free trade. The junta also abolished Indian tribute and promised economic changes. However, many decrees were symbolic and not enforced. The Supreme Junta abolished the slave trade by decree on August 14, 1810, but slavery as an institution remained. The decree stated that no one could introduce slaves to the colony, but this action was not controversial because the slave trade to Venezuela was not really active, having reached its peak in 1730–1780 with the cacao boom and declined after 1780. By 1810, few slaves were being brought into Venezuela because of the Napoleonic Wars and the worsening economic situation of planters. From 1500 to 1810, Venezuela received 12 percent (121,168) of the slaves that arrived in the Spanish-American colonies. From 1780 to 1790, approximately 5,410 slaves entered Venezuela; from 1800 to 1810, only 2,343 slaves.

The Venezuelan population in 1810 consisted of white and indigenous peoples, each composing about 23 percent of the population. Almost half the population were *pardos* (people of mixed descent), and only one-fifteenth of the population was made up of slaves. By 1810, the slave population amounted to less than 5 percent of the population, and in agricultural regions, it made up no more than 10 percent. At this time, cacao plantations dominated Caracas Province, and *hacendados* (owners of large estates) employed free labor on cacao plantations. Slavery was not seen as a labor system that would last forever, but planters did not argue about the end of the slave trade; instead, there was indifference.

The banning of the slave trade by the Supreme Junta was the first of a series of laws that led to the abolition of slavery. The 1821 Cúcuta slave law declared slave children free after service to their master for 18 years, but the 1830 manumission law was a reactionary law that raised the age at which a slave could receive manumission to 21. Venezuela faced an agricultural crisis in the 1840s, which also lessened the need for slave labor, and as the value of land decreased, making slaves and coffee trees major investments, slaves were no longer profitable. The Venezuelan congress abolished slavery in 1854.

—*Jennifer Lynn Himelstein*

For Further Reading
Lombardi, John. 1971. *The Decline and Abolition of Negro Slavery in Venezuela, 1820–1854.* Westport, CT: Greenwood; McKinley, P. Michael. 1985. *Pre-Revolutionary Caracas: Politics, Economy, and Society, 1777–1811.* Cambridge: Cambridge University Press; Parra-Pérez, Caracciolo. 1992. *Historia de la primera república de Venezuela.* Caracas: Biblioteca Ayacucho.

promising freedom to slaves who helped him fight royalist troops during his invasion of Chile.

1816
A slave named Washington Franklin led a major slave insurrection on the island of Barbados, and planters in the region suffered vast property losses. The colony's harsh slave code was abolished as a result of this uprising.

1816
The government of Argentina enacted a statute that prohibited the exportation of slaves from Argentina to any other nation.

1817
The government of Great Britain compensated the Spanish government with £400,000 in exchange for a promise to end the African slave trade north of the equator.

Mexican mural depicting a scene from the Hidalgo Rebellion featuring the independence leaders Morelos and Father Miguel de Hidalgo y Costilla. Before the suppression of the rebellion Hidalgo had issued an emancipation decree. (National Palace, Mexico City, Charles and Josette Lenars/Corbis)

1819

In December, Simón Bolívar's efforts to have his proclamations of emancipation ratified were unsuccessful at the Congress of Angostura. Bolívar had liberated slaves as a matter of military necessity, but the congress decided that the slaves had to be prepared for freedom before a blanket emancipation decree could be issued.

1820

Henri Christophe (Henri I), the self-declared king of Haiti, committed suicide.

1820

The Spanish government abolished the slave trade in the region south of the equator.

1821

The Congress of Cúcuta adopted a program of gradual abolition of slavery for the Republic of Gran Colombia.

1821

General José de San Martín outlawed the African slave trade and began a program of gradual abolition in Peru. At his urging, Peru enacted a free birth law on July 28 to begin the abolition of slavery within the nation. According to the statute, children born to slaves after that date were called *libertos* ("freemen") and would serve their master until 20 (if female) or 24 (if male).

1822

Brazil declared its independence from Portugal.

1823

In Chile, the practice of enslaving Africans was outlawed.

1823

José Bonifácio de Andrada e Silva noted that the aggregate slave population in Brazil did not increase despite the importation of 40,000 new slaves per year, which Bonifácio believed suggested the level of mistreatment that existed within Brazilian society. He argued that the abolition of the slave trade would have the effect of

~JOSÉ DE SAN MARTÍN (1778–1850)~

José de San Martín, an Argentine general and a patriot commander in the wars of Spanish American independence, recruited slaves to his forces and ordered the emancipation of children of slave mothers. While he was governor of Cuyo Province in the Río de la Plata region, he recruited and trained the Army of the Andes. He promised to free blacks and mulattoes who volunteered to serve, and one-third of his army was African or of African descent.

He called for the liberation of Chile and then Peru. After victories in Chile, he headed to Lima where he recruited slaves and promised them freedom if they enlisted. In Peru, he desired to gain the support of the Creoles (Spaniards born in the Americas) for independence. He wanted to negotiate with the Spanish instead of engaging in an armed struggle, which he feared could result in an Indian and slave revolt. The Creole elite was divided, but in June 1821, the Spanish army left, and in July 1821, San Martín was given power and named "the protector of Peru."

With Peru's independence, San Martín abolished the tribute system and *mita* (Indian labor conscription) and ordered that the word Peruvian replace Indian in official documentation. He also called for the gradual emancipation of slaves. On August 12, 1821, he decreed the Law of the Free Womb, which declared that children born of slave mothers after July 28, 1821, were free. This was a move toward abolition, but limitations existed. The freed slave would become a *liberto* (a free child born of slave parents) and would serve the master until the age of 20 for females and 24 for males. In October, he prohibited the use of the lash, and on November 20, he prohibited the slave trade, which had been declared illegal in 1817, making any slave entering Peru free.

San Martín's laws marked the beginning of the end of slavery. In September 1821, he freed slaves who had served in the patriot army and slaves whose owners had left the country during the wars of independence. Many owners disliked San Martín because he enlisted their slaves, but he needed the support of the owners and thus declared that if any had left the country for business reasons, they could retrieve their slaves. The Creole elite of Lima opposed his reforms.

Slavery was not abolished, and slaves did not

José de San Martín. (Corbis-Bettmann)

become citizens in Peru under San Martín because he needed Creole support, and at the time of independence, there were 50,000 black slaves in the country. Some slaves achieved the status of *liberto*, which meant they were free but still had to serve their owners. After a meeting with Simón Bolívar in Guayaquil, Ecuador, in July 1822, San Martín resigned and went to Europe. Slavery was finally abolished in Peru in 1854.

—*Jennifer Lynn Himelstein*

For Further Reading
Blanchard, Peter. 1992. *Slavery and Abolition in Early Republican Peru*. Wilmington, DE: Scholarly Resources; Lynch, John. 1986. *The Spanish American Revolutions, 1808–1826*. New York: W. W. Norton.

improving the condition of slaves already in Brazil because owners would want to sustain their labor force. [See Document 42.]

1823
Brazil failed to ratify a proposed constitution that contained a clause critical of slavery.

1824
A legislator in Dominica wrote *An Appeal and a Caution to the British Nation* in which he expressed concern that if the British government took action to abolish slavery within the colonies, such action should include some form of compensation to the slaveowners affected.

1824
On April 24, the National Constituent Assembly of the Central American Federation emancipated the slaves held in the United Provinces of Central America. This measure was relatively easy to enact because there were very few slaves who were held in these states—only 100 in Costa Rica and 800 in Guatemala.

1825
Programs of gradual abolition of slavery went into effect in Argentina, Peru, Chile, Bolivia, and Paraguay.

1825
José Bonifácio de Andrada e Silva, known to many as the patriarch of Brazilian independence, wrote a treatise critical of slavery in Brazil and argued that a free labor force would allow Brazil to develop more modern techniques of mechanical production. Although Bonifácio lost political influence because of his antislavery views, later abolitionists would view him as an early supporter of the movement to end slavery in Brazil.

1825
A group of Venezuelans were captured and charged with involvement in the African slave trade. The Venezuelan government treated the infraction as a case of piracy.

1826
Negotiations were held between diplomatic representatives of Great Britain and Brazil. As a result of these talks, Brazil abolished slavery north of the equator and agreed to end its involvement with the African slave trade in regions south of the equator by 1830.

1826
The program of gradual abolition of slavery that Chile had initiated in 1825 was completed.

1826
Simón Bolívar wrote the constitution for the new independent nation of Bolivia. The document abolished slavery, which Bolívar described as a crime that represented the "negation of all law." [See Document 46.]

1826
In June, the U.S. president, John Quincy Adams, requested Senate confirmation of two delegates to go to the Panama Conference of Latin American States organized by Simón Bolívar. Although some senators opposed participation because international involvement ran counter to American diplomatic tradition, Vice-President John C. Calhoun, who presided over the Senate, opposed it because nations that were governed by blacks would participate in the conference. After partisan debate, the Senate eventually approved the appointments, but the delay meant that neither of the diplomats made it to Panama in time for the conference.

1827
Cuba contained a population that was 55.9 percent Afro-Cuban. Of this group, 106,494 free blacks lived on the island, and the other 286,492 were slaves.

1828–1837
Muslim slaves in Brazil revolted periodically.

1829
Under the leadership of President Vincente Guerrero, the government of Mexico abolished slavery on September 15.

1829
On December 2, after protests by slaveowning settlers from the United States who had emigrated to Texas, the Mexican president Vincente Guerrero exempted Texas from Mexico's antislavery proclamation of September 15, 1829.

1830
The British colonies of Trinidad, Saint Lucia,

Nineteenth-century slave market in Brazil. Slavery remained legal there until 1888; Brazil was the last country in the Americas to outlaw the institution. (Corbis-Bettmann)

Demerara, and Berbice formed the Four Orders in Council to regulate slavery within their collective region.

1830

Luiz Gama, who became one of Brazil's best-known black abolitionists, was born a freeman in Bahia. By 1840, Gama's white father had sold his mulatto son into slavery in São Paulo, and during his lifetime, Gama would help 500 slaves escape from their servitude in Brazil.

1830

The governments of Great Britain, Portugal, and Brazil signed a treaty in which Brazil promised to end the African slave trade south of the equator. In addition, legislation in Brazil decreed that participation in the African slave trade was deemed an act of piracy; this legislation was not enforced for many years.

1831

The French government officially banned all French citizens from participating in the African slave trade.

1831

On November 7, the Brazilian government enacted a measure to end the African slave trade, but despite the law, the practice of importing Africans continued unabated for many more years.

1831

A serious slave rebellion in Jamaica on December 27 caused $3.5 million in property damage and brought economic ruin to many planters on the island. Known variously as the Jamaica Rebellion, the Christmas Rebellion, the Baptist War, and Samuel Sharpe's Rebellion, the event was one of the largest slave insurrections to occur in the British West Indies, and it helped the British Parliament decide the monumental question of whether or not slavery should be maintained in British colonial possessions.

1832

The British government received a report from the Select Committee on the Extinction of Slavery, which had been appointed by the Anti-Slavery Society, that suggested the government should enact a program of gradual abolition of slavery at the earliest possible convenience and should ensure the safety of all inhabitants of the British colonies as the program was put into effect.

1833
In keeping with the British government's pledge to abolish slavery within the empire, slavery was abolished on the island of Antigua.

1833
Two Uruguayan slaves, Joaquín Artigas and Dionisio Oribe, were members of the Treinta y Tres (the Thirty-Three) who fought with one Captain Lavalleya to win independence for Uruguay.

1833
In Brazil, the antislavery newspaper *O Homem de Cor* (The Colored Man) began publication. The paper's masthead included a statement from Brazil's constitution that stated, "Every citizen may be admitted to civil, political, and military public offices, with no qualifications except those of his talents and virtues" (Jenkins, 1996).

1833
The British Parliament enacted the Emancipation Act on August 1 and thus effectively ended slavery in all British colonial possessions. By 1838, the system of gradual abolition had freed all slaves in the British colonies.

1834
In keeping with the British government's pledge to abolish slavery within the empire, slavery was abolished in British Guiana and Jamaica.

1835
The island of Cuba faced serious slave revolts in the cities of Jaruco, Havana, and Matanzas.

1835
In Brazil, an insurrectionary force of 400–600 slaves nearly seized control of the community of Bahia on January 25. Known as the Hausa uprising or the great Malê uprising, this insurrection was the last major slave revolt in Brazil before emancipation.

1835
In Mexico, President Antonio López de Santa Anna announced his intention to establish a unified constitution for Mexico on December 15. This decision meant that the exemption from Mexico's antislavery proclamation granted to Texas in 1829, which allowed the continuation of slavery in the region, would now be invalidated. American settlers in Texas who were slaveholders vowed they would fight a war of secession from Mexico rather than surrender their right to hold slaves in Texas.

1836
The Portuguese crown declared it illegal to export slaves from any Portuguese colonial possession to any other location. Despite this proclamation, Africans from the Portuguese colonies of Angola and Mozambique continued to be shipped as slaves to Brazil. The viscount of Sá da Bandeira tried to prohibit the practice of importing and exporting slaves into Portuguese colonies south of the equator, but he was unable to win approval of the proposal, and the Portuguese continued to participate in the slave trade.

1836
Texas, which had declared itself an independent republic, drafted a constitution on March 17 that legalized slavery in the Republic of Texas. Texas settlers then fought Mexico in order to win their independence. Shortly after achieving that independence, Texans sought annexation to the United States.

1837
By legislative action, the importation of slaves into Uruguay was prohibited.

1837
The government of Mexico enacted its second decree abolishing slavery within the nation. This measure provided for a system of compensated emancipation to indemnify those who still owned slaves within Mexico.

1838
John Gabriel Stedman published *Narrative of Joanna: An Emancipated Slave of Surinam.*

1838
In keeping with the British government's pledge to abolish slavery within the empire, slavery was abolished in British Honduras (Belize).

The most highly organized slave revolt in Brazil, the Hausa uprising (also known as "the great Malê uprising") began in the early morning of January 25, 1835, in the province of Bahia. The slaves of Bahia, one of the most turbulent areas of the country, had a reputation for being restive and difficult to control, and slaves and freemen in Bahia had had a long history of revolt. The Portuguese brought Africans into Brazil as early as 1538, and the introduction of sugar cultivation at about the same time spurred slave imports in vast numbers. By the turn of the nineteenth century, Bahia had become an extremely prosperous sugar-producing region, and hundreds of thousands of African slaves were imported annually.

Quilombos, or runaway slave (Maroon) communities, had existed at least as early as 1603 when a group of mostly Bantu-speaking runaway African slaves established an African state, the Republic of Palmares in Alagoas in northeastern Brazil. Palmares successfully resisted invasion by the Portuguese and the Dutch until it was overtaken by Portuguese troops in 1697. In the early decades of the nineteenth century, slave uprisings, in the form of both minor pockets of violence and impromptu resistance and more organized rebellions, became more frequent because of the growth of the sugar economy, the vast numbers of Africans imported into the New World, the increased work burden on African slaves, and food shortages, which led to widespread hunger. As the number of slaves taken from the west coast of Africa increased, there was an influx of Africans from the same ethnic groups or from neighboring tribes. Consequently, Africans in Bahia maintained their African identities and remained strongly connected to the practices of their homeland.

Practicing Muslims from Africa or of African descent were known as Malês in Brazil. Although Malê was often synonymous with Hausa, the term also included Muslim peoples of Yoruba descent (known as Nagôs) and others from neighboring West African tribes. Like many of the numerous rebellions that had occurred earlier, the 1835 uprising is often attributed to Hausa organization and ingenuity. However, although there is no question that religion played an important part in the uprising, the extent to which the 1835 rebellion can be called a Muslim jihad is unclear.

Rebels had planned the uprising for Sunday, January 26, when many whites would be celebrating the feast day of Our Lady of Guidance and hence outside of the city, but on Saturday, the air was rife with rumor about a rebellion—so much so that a freed slave and an ex-slave couple both independently informed the authorities that a widespread rebellion was being planned for the next day. The authorities began searching African-owned houses in Bahia, and justices of the peace were attacked by a band of about 60 Africans meeting at No. 2 Ladeira da Praça. Although the Africans easily dispersed the Brazilian soldiers, the element of surprise was greatly diminished, and that fact has been cited as the reason the uprising failed. A group of rebels took to the streets of Salvador, the capital of Bahia, and fought for three hours with soldiers. The facts that the rebels opted for one-on-one combat and did not resort to indiscriminate violence or looting have led historians to believe that the leaders who organized the uprising had political goals, perhaps even a takeover of the entire power structure, in mind. However, the rebellion of between 400 and 600 Africans was thwarted by security forces. Approximately 70 people died in the fighting—most of them Africans killed by Brazilian armed forces.

Many of the rebels who fought in the uprising wore white prayer garments (which authorities called "war garments"), and police found that many of the rebels also wore amulets (or charms) containing passages from the Qur'an written in Arabic. Although the fighting had ended by dawn of January 26, police continued rounding up both slaves and freemen considered suspicious for several days. Over 230 people were tried for the uprising, and many of them were formerly freed slaves while the majority were Nagôs or Hausa. Several of the alleged leaders of the rebellion were sentenced either to death or to deportation, and some of the slaves found guilty were flogged and then sent back to work. Subsequently, Africans were treated with suspicion and hostility, and a law was passed in Bahia making it a crime to own anything overtly African in nature. The 1835 rebellion was the last noteworthy uprising of slaves and freemen in Brazil.
—*Jennifer Margulis*

For Further Reading
Goody, Jack. 1986. "Writing, Religion, and Revolt in Bahia." *Visible Language* 20: 318–343; Kent, Raymond K. 1970. "African Revolt in Bahia." *Journal of Social History* 3 (Summer): 334–356; Reis, Joao José. 1993. *Slave Rebellion in Brazil: The Muslim Uprising of 1835 in Bahia*. Trans. Arthur Brake. Baltimore, MD: Johns Hopkins University Press.

1838

In the northern Brazilian province of Maranhão, a large-scale slave revolt known as the Balaiada Movement began when a group of poor rural settlers and a group of fugitive slaves began to terrorize the countryside. The uprising continued until it was finally suppressed by government forces in 1841.

1838

André Rebouças, who became one of the most prominent black abolitionists in Brazil, was born in Bahia, Brazil, on January 13.

1839

The government of Haiti reaffirmed its opposition to the African slave trade and vowed to do what it could to suppress the trade.

1839

Pope Gregory XVI issued the bull In Supremo in which the Roman Catholic Church stated its opposition to both slavery and the slave trade. [See Document 50.]

1839

The British Parliament enacted the Palmerston Act, which permitted British vessels to search Portuguese ships suspected of carrying African slaves to the Americas. Even so, the Portuguese continued to be active in the African slave trade. [See Document 58.]

1839

The government of Venezuela enacted legislation that outlawed the African slave trade.

1839

In July, the Spanish slave ship *Amistad* was seized off the coast of Cuba when the 54 Africans on board, led by Joseph Cinqué, revolted and killed the captain. The Africans demanded that the remaining crewmen return the vessel to Africa, but later in the summer, the vessel was captured off the coast of Montauk, Long Island. After a series of trials in the United States, 35 *Amistad* survivors won their freedom and were returned to Africa when they were defended before the U.S. Supreme Court by former president John Quincy Adams.

1840s

During this decade, legislative programs of gradual abolition were enacted in Colombia, Venezuela, and Ecuador. Slavery finally ended in Colombia and Ecuador in 1852 while Venezuela ended the practice in 1854.

1840

A U.S. slave ship carrying 38 slaves from Richmond, Virginia, to New Orleans, Louisiana, wrecked in the Abaco Islands of the Bahamas where, as in the rest of the British Empire, slavery had been abolished in 1833. British colonial officials removed the cargo of the slaver *Hermosa* and freed the slaves who were being transported. The United States protested this matter in diplomatic channels, and 15 years later, the British government agreed to compensate the owners of the slaves from the *Hermosa* who had been freed.

1840

Juan Manzano published *Poems by a Slave in the Island of Cuba Recently Liberated*. This collection of verse contained vivid descriptions of slavery in Cuba and disturbing reminders of the African slave trade, which continued to operate.

1841

Cuba's population was 58.5 percent Afro-Cuban. Of this group, 152,838 were free blacks, and 436,495 were slaves.

1841

Great Britain, France, Russia, Prussia, and Austria signed the Quintuple Agreement, which declared slave trading to be the equivalent of piracy. According to the terms of this agreement, ships suspected of carrying slaves could be stopped and searched at sea.

1841

While they were being transported from Hampton Roads, Virginia, to New Orleans, Louisiana, slaves on board the *Creole* revolted on November 7 and took control of the vessel. They sailed to Nassau in the Bahamas where all of the slaves on board the vessel, except those accused of murder, were granted asylum and eventually freed.

1842

The government of Uruguay enacted a partial

emancipation program that liberated some of the slaves in the nation. Complete emancipation of all slaves in Uruguay did not come until 1854.

1842

Paraguay enacted the Law of the Free Womb and thus began the process of ending the practice of slavery. Although the measure stated that slavery would be abolished within the country in 1843, it was not until 1862 that all slaves in the country were finally liberated.

1842

Colonial authorities in Cuba issued the Regiamento de Esclavos (Rules for Slaves) as a harsher version of the Real Cédula (Spanish Slave Code) issued in 1789.

1843

A slave revolt occurred on a sugar plantation near Alcancia, Cuba. The slave population of the whole island was estimated to be 436,000.

1843

A series of slave revolts occurred in the gold-mining region of the Cauca River valley in Venezuela and Colombia.

1844

Cuban colonial authorities suppressed a large-scale "racial conspiracy" (called "the conspiracy of the ladder") involving Afro-Cubans and mestizos on the island. The Cuban general Leopoldo I. O'Donnell authorized a massacre of Afro-Cubans suspected of involvement in the conspiracy, and one of the casualties was Placido (Gabriel de la Concepción Valdés), an Afro-Cuban poet.

1845

The governments of Chile and of Portugal both declared the slave trade to be a form of piracy.

1845

José Ferreira de Menezes, who eventually became one of the most prominent black abolitionists in Brazil, was born in Rio de Janeiro.

1845

The British Parliament enacted the Aberdeen Act, which permitted British vessels to search Brazilian ships and other vessels suspected of carrying African slaves to the Americas. This

General Leopoldo O'Donnell (1809–1867), who brutally suppressed an alleged conspiracy of Afro-Cubans in Cuba in 1844. (The Granger Collection)

unilateral measure was enacted as a coercive device to hasten an end to the African slave trade.

1845

Spanish colonial officials in Cuba passed a law that was designed to reduce the slave trade to (and within) Cuba. The measure had little effect in reducing the island colony's dependence upon slave labor.

1847

The Danish king, Christian VIII, issued a law of free birth for the children of slaves born in the

Danish West Indies. The king also promised the complete abolition of slavery in the islands by 1859.

1847

Castro Alves, "the poet of the slaves," was born in Bahia, Brazil, on March 14. Alves became one of Brazil's leading abolitionists, and he used his poetry to speak out against the great injustice of slavery.

1848

The French government abolished slavery in all French colonies on April 27.

1848

The government of Denmark had promised to abolish slavery in the Danish West Indies by 1859, but a crowd of 8,000 slaves who were unwilling to wait demanded and received their freedom from the colonial governor on July 2. Planters responded to the decision with looting, but colonial authorities were able to restore order.

1850s

The government of Peru began to import large numbers of Chinese coolies to serve as indentured laborers.

1850

On September 4, the government of Brazil enacted the Queirós Law, which effectively ended the African slave trade to Brazil. By the terms of this law, the government declared the slave trade to be a form of piracy, and all Brazilian nationals were prohibited from taking part in the enterprise. [See Documents 55 and 61.]

1851

Cuban authorities executed Narciso Lopez in September after he had been captured during his third attempt to seize control of the island of Cuba. Lopez, a Venezuelan, had become associated with proslavery expansionists in the United States who desired the annexation of Cuba as a potential slave state.

1852

The government of Ecuador enacted a statute that liberated all slaves in the country. This action completed the program of gradual emancipation that the nation had begun in the previous decade.

Statue of Brazilian poet and abolitionist Antonio de Castro Alves, Salvador, Bahia, Brazil. (Jeremy Horner/©Corbis)

1852

On January 1, the program of gradual abolition of slavery that Colombia had initiated in the early 1840s was completed when all remaining slaves in the country were emancipated.

1854

The program of gradual abolition of slavery that Argentina had initiated in 1825 was completed. With the adoption of the new national constitution, which had been written in 1852, there no longer were any slaves in the nation of Argentina.

1854

The program of gradual abolition of slavery that Venezuela had initiated in the early 1840s was completed.

1854

José do Patrocíno, who eventually became a famous Afro-Brazilian abolitionist, was born.

Umbanda is an Afro-spiritist religion that originated in Brazil and is related to a religion known as Candomble, which was developed by descendants of enslaved Africans and originally combined African and indigenous beliefs. An increasingly popular religion in Brazil, contemporary Umbanda represents a syncretic fusion of Afro-Brazilian beliefs, religious practices, and Brazilian Catholicism. Today, the religious beliefs of Umbanda encompass a global vision for the interpretation of reality, a moral ethic, and universalistic values. Charity is especially valued and, as a form of religious expression, Umbanda has attracted middle-class adherents.

Umbanda has functioned as a vehicle for the popularization and rationalization of Afro-spiritist beliefs, as individuals from all social classes and of all races or ethnicity practice it, and Umbanda is losing its identification as its African slave origins become less emphasized. Diana DeGrout Brown's ethnographic research on Umbanda (Brown, 1994) identifies it as a religion of the middle class, yet many practitioners are members of Brazil's immense lower-class population. Lindsay Lauren Hale (1997) stresses that although Cardist spiritism and Catholic symbolism have been incorporated into Umbanda, the degree to which it has become de-Africanized varies considerably according to the racial and social-class backgrounds of the cult's members.

Afro-spiritist religions, including Umbanda, emphasize subjective spiritual experiences. Visions, hearing voices, emotionalism, and the expression of psychosomatic symptoms are accepted elements of spirituality. Afro-spiritist beliefs provide a vehicle for the interpretation of personal suffering and the role of powerful saints as helpers in solving life's problems. These saints, who possess mediums, include the spirits of *pretos velhos* ("old blacks") like Father Joaquim, Indians, cowboys, and other symbols of Brazilian identity that relate to personal problems (Hale, 1997). Hale's semiotic analysis of *preto velho* stories emphasizes that the imagery of old slave spirits and their stories provide an indictment of the cruelty of slavery and the perpetuation of racism in Brazilian society for people who identify as the spiritual descendants of the *preto velhos*. Their suffering is linked to the martyrdom of Christ and the Catholic saints, who are also incorporated into Umbanda. After the end of military rule in the mid-1980s, when Brazilian society became more open, valorization of African heritage and a critique of slavery became a part of the voices of the mediums of the *pretos velhos*. For white, middle-class Umbanda practitioners, however, the linkage to an African past is downplayed or discarded, and other issues, even racist themes, become important instead.

Umbanda is similar to traditional Afro-spiritism in that vows, obligations, and promises are exchanged with saints and spirits, but Umbanda departs from the Afro-spiritist tradition by emphasizing a belief in charity, which is channeled to needy individuals rather than simply supporting a center.

Cecilia Loreto Mariz (1994) characterizes Umbanda as a more rationalized form of Afro-spiritist belief owing to its development of an intellectualized belief system, a moral ethic that includes an emphasis on charity, and the bureaucratization of its institutions. The religious belief has had a social and economic impact as Umbanda provides religious careers for some individuals, permitting survival and even upward mobility. Brown (1994) considers that through both the support of religious leaders and the reliance on the help of the saints, Umbanda reproduces the social relations of patronage that characterize the Brazilian system of social stratification. Brazil has very small upper and middle classes, and the vast majority of the population lives in various degrees of poverty. The various groups encompassed by Umbanda represent these strata and a variety of orientations that reflect racial, social class, and Brazilian identity in a mode of religious expression that permits an emotive expression of one's personal problems.

—*Judith Ann Warner*

For Further Reading

Brown, Diana DeGrout. 1994. *Umbanda: Religion and Politics in Urban Brazil*. New York: Columbia University Press; Hale, Lindsay Lauren. 1997. "*Preto Velho*: Resistance, Redemption, and Engendered Representations of Slavery in a Brazilian Possession-Trance Religion." *American Ethnologist* 24(2): 392–414; Mariz, Cecilia Loreto. 1994. *Coping with Poverty: Pentecostals and Christian Base Communities in Brazil*. Philadelphia: Temple University Press; Prandi, R. 1991. *Os Candombles de Sao Paulo: Velha Magia na Metropole Nova*. São Paulo: HUCITEC and Editora da Universidada de São Paulo.

1854

The program of partial abolition of slavery that Uruguay had initiated in 1842 was completed, and all slaves within the country were liberated.

1854

The Portuguese government emancipated all of the slaves in the Portuguese empire who were held on royal lands.

1854

On October 18, U.S. diplomats Pierre Soulé (minister to Spain), John Y. Mason (minister to France), and James Buchanan (minister to Great Britain) met in Ostend, Belgium, to discuss a strategy that the United States might follow in order to purchase Cuba from Spain or to seize the island by force if necessary. The resulting Ostend Manifesto proposed that the United States offer the Spanish government no more than $120 million for Cuba and that should Spain reject the offer, the United States should take the island by force. Expansionists, who tended to be proslavery supporters, hoped that Cuba might eventually form two additional slave states.

1854

In December, General Ramón Castilla proclaimed the abolition of slavery in Peru and promised a program of compensated emancipation to indemnify all slaveholders.

1856

Portugal had continued shipping captives from Angola and Mozambique to Brazil as slaves throughout the early-nineteenth century, but in this year, the last recorded shipload of Africans arrived as slaves in Brazil.

1856

The Portuguese government freed all slaves in its empire who belonged to town councils, religious brotherhoods, and Portuguese churches.

1857

Mexico adopted a new constitution as a part of the La Reforma movement led by Benito Juarez. According to the new constitution, a fugitive slave became free the moment he or she set foot on Mexican soil. Between the years 1857 and 1865, a large number of fugitive slaves from the United States made their way to Mexico seeking emancipation.

1858

The slave ship *Echo,* which was transporting 300 Africans to Cuba where they were to be sold as slaves, was captured at sea by the USS *Dolphin.* After the crew of the *Dolphin* had brought the *Echo* into port at Charleston, South Carolina, the Africans were returned to Liberia, but a Charleston grand jury refused to indict the captain and crew members of the *Echo.*

1861

James Theodore Holly led a group of 2,000 free blacks from New York City who had decided to emigrate to Haiti. Two-thirds of the emigrants died on the voyage to Port-au-Prince.

1861

Cuba contained a population that was 43.2 percent Afro-Cuban. Of this group, there were 232,493 free blacks on the island and 370,553 slaves.

1862–1863

Because of a labor shortage that was worsened by the closing of the African slave trade, the government of Peru sought alternative methods of acquiring laborers. In less than 12 months, 38 ships arrived in Peru transporting 3,600 Pacific Islanders who were technically contract laborers but were treated as slaves. The Peruvian government suspended this practice on April 28, 1863.

1862

The U.S. Congress authorized the president to appoint diplomatic representatives to Haiti, which had declared its independence in 1803.

1862

The program of gradual abolition of slavery that Paraguay had initiated in 1825 was completed.

1863

The Netherlands officially abolished the slave trade and prohibited Dutch citizens from taking part in this commercial activity.

1863

The Netherlands abolished slavery in the Dutch West Indies on July 1. On the same date, slavery was also officially abolished in Surinam (Suriname), but the freed slaves were required to remain on their plantations and work as wage laborers for an additional 10 years.

The Ostend Manifesto of 1854, which proclaimed that the United States should acquire Cuba, by force if necessary, fanned the flames of sectional discord over the issue of slavery expansion. The Democratic administration of President Franklin Pierce had come into office in March 1853 committed to a policy of territorial aggrandizement and intent upon acquiring Cuba from Spain. Southerners enthusiastic about Manifest Destiny coveted Cuba, for they hoped to make the island, with its bountiful sugar plantations, an additional slave state. So strong was the southern longing for Cuba, in fact, that it helped give rise to a dangerously militant form of proslavery expansionism. Mississippi senator Albert Gallatin Brown, for example, flatly declared that he wanted Cuba, as well as other Latin American regions, for one reason—"the planting or spreading of slavery" (May, 1989). Mississippi's fire-eating governor, John A. Quitman, went further, backing several illegal filibustering expeditions to Cuba and other Caribbean areas.

Northern antislavery interests denounced American designs on Cuba but had no influence upon administrative policy. Though from New Hampshire, President Pierce was a known "dough-face"—a northerner with prosouthern views. His cabinet contained a number of southern proslavery zealots, including the future president of the Confederacy, Jefferson Davis of Mississippi. Similarly, the northern members of Pierce's cabinet were vociferous opponents of abolitionism. Secretary of State William L. Marcy, for example, led the Hunker wing of New York's Democratic Party, which decried its rival Barnburner faction as a horde of antislavery fanatics.

Pierce's selections for top diplomatic posts also conformed to this pattern. For minister to Great Britain he chose James Buchanan of Pennsylvania, an accomplished statesman but a confirmed doughface. John Y. Mason of Virginia, another competent statesman, was named minister to France, and although he was no great apologist for slavery, Mason nonetheless advocated the purchase of Cuba. To head the U.S. mission to Spain, Pierce selected Pierre Soulé of Louisiana, a proslavery extremist and leader of the Cuban annexation movement in the Senate. This last appointment would prove disastrous, for Soulé had no ambassadorial experience, was prone to rash judgment, and had a caustic demeanor.

Soulé estranged himself from his Spanish hosts soon after arriving in Madrid. After abortive attempts to negotiate the cession of Cuba in mid-1854, Soulé tried to bully the Spanish monarchy with threats and ultimatums. Madrid rebuffed all these overtures. To help Soulé get his stalled mission back on track, Pierce and Marcy suggested that the Louisianan meet with Buchanan and Mason in the hope that the three envoys could arrive at a resolution to the impasse in Madrid. Marcy also instructed the ministers to draft a confidential report outlining their recommendation for further action.

Accordingly, Soulé summoned Buchanan and Mason from their London and Paris legations to Ostend, Belgium, where the three statesmen conferred in early October. On October 12, they repaired to Aix-la-Chapelle (Aachen), and following a week of discussions, the American ministers drafted a memorandum subsequently known as the Ostend Manifesto. In this document, the three diplomats recommended another attempt to purchase Cuba from Spain. The manifesto declared, however, that the United States should consider seizing Cuba by force if this effort failed. In the view of the Ostend trio, American security might require U.S. possession of the island, in which case "we will be justified in wresting it from Spain" (May, 1989). In a separate letter attached to the memorandum, Soulé made clear that he supported the swift and forceful annexation of Cuba.

The Ostend Manifesto was meant to be a confidential dispatch to Marcy, but in yet another blunder, Soulé leaked news of the "secret" Ostend conference to the European press. A New York newspaper soon broke the story and published a roughly accurate version of the Ostend communiqué in November 1854, placing the Pierce administration in an awkward position. America's flagrant disregard of Spanish sovereignty threatened to spark an international incident, and moreover, the Ostend Manifesto was made public shortly after Congress had approved the controversial Kansas-Nebraska Act. Northern antislavery forces, already infuriated over the administration-sponsored passage of the Kansas-Nebraska bill, roundly denounced the Ostend affair as a savage and illegal plot to extend slavery. Likewise, northern Whigs and free soil Democrats joined in condemning Pierce and his administration as minions of the southern slavocracy. The uproar against the Ostend Manifesto enervated the movement to obtain Cuba, but the episode left a lasting legacy to the sectional conflict over the expansion of slavery.

—Eric Tscheschlok

For Further Reading
Gara, Larry. 1991. *The Presidency of Franklin Pierce.* Lawrence: University Press of Kansas; Learned, H. Barrett. 1958. "William L. Marcy." In *The American Secretaries of State and Their Diplomacy.* Ed. Samuel Flagg Bemis. 17 vols. New York: Pageant Book Company; May, Robert E. 1989. *The Southern Dream of a Caribbean Empire, 1854–1861.* Athens: University of Georgia Press; Moore, J. Preston. 1955. "Pierre Soulé: Southern Expansionist and Promoter." *Journal of Southern History* 21 (May): 203–223.

1864

The United States finally recognized Haiti as an independent republic, and the Haitian general Fabre Geffrard announced a plan to move "industrious men of African descent" from the United States to Haiti.

1865–1870

The War of the Triple Alliance was fought between Paraguay and the allied nations of Brazil, Argentina, and Uruguay. One effect of this war was the end of slavery in the upper Plata region of Paraguay, but the conflict also caused Brazil to reconsider its efforts to maintain slavery.

1867

The last recorded shipload of Africans arrived as slaves in Cuba. This event officially marked the end of the Middle Passage, which had been in operation since 1502.

1868–1878

The Ten Years War was fought in Cuba as the Cuban people sought their independence from Spain. The question of emancipation for the Cuban slaves was raised during this conflict.

1868

All children born to slave mothers in Cuba were considered to be born free after 1868, but their mothers remained slaves.

1869

During the Ten Years War (1868–1878) in Cuba, an assembly of the insurrectionists met and proclaimed the abolition of slavery in Cuba.

1869

In Lisbon, Portugal, the legislative assembly declared that all slaves held in Portuguese possessions were considered to be *libertos* ("freemen"). As such, these individuals were paid wages and treated as other colonial workers until they were finally emancipated.

1869

As the War of the Triple Alliance (1865–1870) came to an end, the government of Paraguay was persuaded to enact legislation in October freeing all remaining slaves within the country.

1870

Additional legislation adopted in Cuba freed all slaves who had once performed military service under the Spanish flag and all slaves who were over 60 years of age.

1870

In Spain, a bill that called for the gradual abolition of slavery throughout all Spanish colonies was introduced into the Cortes (legislature).

1870

On June 23, the Spanish government enacted the Moret Law, which effectively began the process of abolishing slavery on the island of Cuba. By the terms of this statute, all children born to slaves in Cuba after the law went into effect were considered to be free.

1871

On September 28, the Brazilian government enacted the Law of Free Birth (also known as the Rio Branco Law), which effectively began the process of abolishing slavery in Brazil. By the terms of this statute, all children born to slaves in Brazil after the passage of the measure were considered to be free, but these free children were expected to serve as apprentices until they reached the age of 21. In spite of this reform, 1.5 million individuals continued to labor as slaves in Brazil. [See Document 69.]

1872

A bill calling for the implementation of a compensated emancipation plan was introduced into the Cortes (legislature) in Puerto Rico.

1873

Slavery was abolished in Puerto Rico.

The slave's diet varied by geography, climate, season, method of food preparation, period, and, of course, master. Often slaves ate a poorer version of the foodstuffs available to masters or poorer whites, and to various degrees, they supplemented their diet by hunting, fishing, trapping, raising poultry, or tilling private plots. It appears that slave children were significantly less well nourished than adults, that men were better nourished than women, and that American slaves were better nourished than Africans, poor Europeans, and Caribbean slaves but not white Americans. Although the slave diet did not differ significantly from that of poor whites, genetic factors such as lactose intolerance, difficulty in acquiring vitamin D, and heavy work that required a high calorie intake (3,200–4,000 calories daily) made the slaves far more susceptible to consequences of their diet's nutritional inadequacies than were whites.

Central to the diet of American slaves were a daily pound of cornmeal and a daily half-pound of salted or pickled hog meat (rice instead of corn served as a staple in the Carolinas). Corn was used to make cornbread; hominy, bleached and hulled kernels of corn, was used to make grits; and cornmeal was used to make hoecakes and cornpone. Some planters substituted molasses for meat. The diet was supplemented by peas, beans, and red peppers, common foods in West Africa, and some planters supplied a daily portion of vegetables. Drinking pot liquor, the liquid produced by cooking vegetables, may have enabled some slaves to benefit from the vitamin-rich fluid that whites normally discarded, but some scholars believe that the extensive consumption of "greens" and pot liquor occurred only after emancipation. Okra was introduced from West Africa, and the sweet potato, or yam, was popular with planters. The type of potato or yam used, however, was light in color and provided little vitamin A. Seasonable vitamin C deficiency was a regular problem. The quality of the meat varied, but it usually consisted of fatty, second-rate pieces like fatback or sowbelly. Lactose intolerance prevented milk products from becoming an important part of the slave diet. To the dismay of planters who wished to feed slaves communally to ensure what they perceived as good nutrition, American slaves generally insisted on eating as a family and enjoying a special Sunday meal.

Many slaves were undoubtedly niacin deficient because of the reliance on corn, and because the vegetables consumed were overwhelmingly white, many slaves certainly suffered from vitamin A defi-ciency. What vitamin A there was would have been destroyed because of the custom of cooking with rancid fat. The manner of cooking vegetables, simmering them for long periods, also reduced vitamin C yield, and the oxidation from cooking in iron pots further reduced the vitamin. As a consequence of lactose intolerance and their skin color, which inhibited vitamin D production, calcium absorption among slaves was a problem. B complex vitamin deficiency, even when vegetables were a part of the diet, was caused by boiling and frying and ultimately led to niacin deficiency and the poor metabolizing of carbohydrates, fats, and proteins. As Kenneth Kiple and Virginia King point out, the slave diet was most deficient in calcium, vitamin C, riboflavin, and niacin; seriously deficient in iron and protein; and, seasonally, deficient in thiamine and vitamin A.

Deficiency diseases among slave populations are well documented. Bleeding gums and scurvy indicate vitamin C deficiency. Poor and deformed teeth indicate deficiencies of vitamins D and C and calcium. Eye problems and night blindness can be linked to vitamin A deficiency, and pellagra symptoms resulted from a diet seriously low in niacin. Diarrhea was caused by vitamin B deficiency. Dietary deficiencies affect the quantity and quality of breast milk produced, and poorly nourished mothers passed along little of nutritional value to their children. Rickets, caused by vitamin D deficiency, was especially common among slave children as was energy-protein malnutrition—formerly classified as protein-calorie malnutrition—as is evidenced by the distended stomachs referred to in numerous accounts.

Worms were a serious problem for slave children because of the children's already weakened physical condition—nutritionally healthy children can generally tolerate worms with few negative consequences. Even the smothering deaths common among slave children (the supposed suffocation of children while sleeping with their parents) may actually have been examples of sudden infant death syndrome (SIDS), which seems to correlate with nutritional deficiencies. Thiamine deficiency was passed on to children through their mother's milk, and the nearly always fatal illness infantile beriberi was common. Insufficient fat intake caused problems as well. Pellagra, resulting from B complex deficiencies, was regularly endured, with negative gastrointestinal and nervous system consequences. The eating of dirt was prompted by the need to assuage mineral deficiencies. In addition to physical consequences, Kiple and

King suggest that the persistent lack of B vitamins may explain the negative behaviors that were frequently reported by planters such as lethargy, apathy, and melancholia. Most, if not all of these problems, appear to have been more pronounced in areas other than North America.

—*Charles A. D'Aniello*

For Further Reading
Dilday, Kenya, and Jonathan Gill. 1996. "Food." In *Encyclopedia of African-American Culture and History.* New York: Macmillan Library Reference USA and Simon and Schuster Macmillan; Finkelman, Paul, ed. 1989. "Medicine, Nutrition, Demography, and Slavery." In *Articles on American Slavery, Vol. 15.* New York: Garland Publishing; Kiple, Kenneth F. 1984. *The Caribbean Slave: A Biological History.* Cambridge: Cambridge University Press; Kiple, Kenneth F. 1988. "Diet." In *Dictionary of Afro-American Slavery.* Ed. Randall M. Miller and John David Smith. New York: Greenwood Press; Kiple, Kenneth F., and Virginia H. King. 1981. *Another Dimension to the Black Diaspora: Diet, Disease, and Racism.* Cambridge: Cambridge University Press.

1878

In Cuba, the Ten Years War ended with the Peace of Zanjón, and the Spanish liberated those slaves who had fought with the royalist forces during the war.

1880

The Spanish government enacted the Law of Patronato, which began a process of gradual emancipation in all of its colonial dominions over an eight-year period. All of the slaves in Cuba had been freed by 1886.

1880

The Brazilian Anti-Slavery Society was established in Rio de Janeiro on September 7. The first meeting of the society took place in the home of the abolitionist Joaquim de Araujo Nabuco.

1880

In November, the Brazilian Anti-Slavery Society published the first issue of its antislavery journal *O Abolicionista* (Abolitionism).

1883

The Brazilian abolitionist Joaquim de Araujo Nabuco wrote *O abolicionismo* (Abolitionism), a work that helped galvanize public opinion in Brazil against the perpetuation of slavery. Nabuco argued that social and economic progress could only be achieved in Brazil under a system of free labor.

1883

In August, José do Patrocíno and other leading Brazilian abolitionists, including André Rebouças, Joaquim de Araujo Nabuco, and Joaquim Serra, established the Abolitionist Confederation. This group of antislavery advocates issued the manifesto *Confederacao abolicionista* (Abolitionist confederation), which called for an immediate end to slavery in Brazil.

1884

On March 25, the northern province of Ceará abolished slavery within its borders even though slavery remained legal in Brazil.

1884

On May 24, the northern province of Amazonas abolished slavery within its borders even though slavery remained legal in Brazil.

1885

The Brazilian government enacted the Sexagenarian Law, which freed all slaves in Brazil who were 65 or older. Those slaves who were 60 years old were to work only three more years before being freed by their masters.

1886

The Spanish government abolished slavery in all colonial dominions where it still existed. This action officially ended slavery in Cuba.

1886

The government of Brazil pledged to enact a plan of gradual abolition of slavery according to the enabling legislation that had been enacted in 1885.

1888

Pope Leo XIII issued an encyclical in which he proclaimed that the Roman Catholic Church offered support for people who were enslaved throughout the world.

1888

Slavery officially ended in Brazil on May 13

ANTÔNIO CONSELHEIRO (1830–1897)

Antônio Conselheiro (original name, Antônio Vicente Mendes Maciel) was a religious leader, critic of slavery, and founder of the community of Canudos, a refuge for many ex-slaves in the *sertão* ("backlands") of northeastern Brazil.

Before emerging as a religious leader in northeastern Brazil, Antônio Maciel worked as a tutor, shop clerk, traveling salesman, and peddler. Later, he accompanied itinerant evangelical lay-Catholic missionaries and then began a ministry of his own in the *sertão*. By the mid-1870s, he had become known as Brother Antonio; he later was known as Antônio Conselheiro ("wise counselor").

Contemporary writers generally referred to Conselheiro as "white," but his birth certificate listed him as *pardo,* a generalized term at that time for anyone of mixed ancestry. No matter what his ancestry, many of Brazil's ex-slaves were among the people who flocked to Conselheiro. Although there is no evidence that he was an abolitionist, he denounced slavery in his sermons and especially in his writings. He declared that Brazil's Golden Law of 1888, which freed the slaves, was divine will and that God punished the country for its long delay in enacting emancipation by allowing the empire to become a republic in 1889.

In 1893, Conselheiro established Canudos. At its height in 1895, the community may have had 35,000 residents, making it the second-largest city in the state of Bahia. Canudos attracted a wide range of people including blacks, who despite the end of legal slavery, were still de facto slaves and lived far from certain lives as free laborers. Some blacks in Canudos built housing of their own design clustered along what was called "the street of the Negroes," and black women dressed and styled their hair in an African fashion. Members of the local landholding elite described Canudos as being composed of "miserable ex-slaves" who were often referred to as *O povo 13 de Maio* ("the people of May 13"), the date of the Golden Law. Of the 88 people baptized in Canudos in 1896, all but one were listed as *pardos.* Consequently, Canudos has been called Brazil's last *quilombo,* a settlement established by fugitive slaves.

Like other Brazilian *quilombos,* such as Palmares in the seventeenth century, Canudos developed into an agrarian settlement with links to the surrounding population. The basic needs of food and shelter were met, and antisocial behaviors, such as drunkenness and prostitution, were absent. The size of the community and Conselheiro's teachings shook local landowners, church authorities, and government leaders.

In an attempt to arrest Conselheiro and disband Canudos, the Brazilian government failed to take into account the residents' organization, strength, and determination. Only after four campaigns, using modern armaments and causing countless deaths, did the Brazilian military destroy the settlement. Although some of the residents fled into the surrounding countryside before the final battle took place on October 5, 1897, others refused to give up, preferring to fight to the end. Medical examiners determined that Conselheiro had died, probably of dysentery, two weeks before the fall of Canudos. Soldiers exhumed his body, severed the head, and displayed the latter on a pike in military parades on the coast of Bahia.

—*Claude F. Jacobs*

For Further Reading
da Cunha, Euclydes. 1944. *Rebellion in the Backlands.* Chicago: University of Chicago Press; Levine, Robert M. 1992. *Vale of Tears: Revisiting the Canudos Massacre in Northeastern Brazil, 1895–1897.* Berkeley: University of California Press.

---

when the legislative assembly enacted the Lei Aurea (Golden Law). The measure was supported by Imperial Princess Isabel who acted as regent while her brother, Pedro II, was out of the country receiving medical treatment in Europe. This act of emancipation effectively liberated 725,000 slaves in Brazil. [See Document 72.]

1891
On May 13, the government of the Republic of Brazil ordered the burning of all documents related to the institution of slavery in Brazil.

1893
Antônio Conselheiro established the community of Canudos in the *sertão* ("backlands") of Brazil. Many of the recently freed slaves in Brazil moved to this settlement, and by 1895, it boasted a population of 35,000 residents. Considering the settlement to be all too similar to a *quilombo* (Maroon, or fugitive slave) settlement, the Brazilian government destroyed the site in a battle on October 5, 1897.

❧United States❧

The sunlight that has brought life and healing to you has brought
[slave] stripes and death to me. This Fourth of July is yours, not mine.
— Frederick Douglass, "What to the Slave Is the Fourth of July?" (1852)

For two and a half centuries, slavery dominated the social, economic, and political life of the United States. Throughout the formative years of the colonial period, slavery was an ever-present reality that influenced the budding American republic to define freedom by recognizing its absence. During the early generations of America's democratic experiment, it was the divisive issue of slavery that bedeviled a nation seeking noble pursuits but confronted by the reality of its own deep-rooted injustices. In a perverse sense, both liberty and the lash helped to define a nation that was founded upon freedom but was uncertain of the fullest meaning of the term. Frederick Douglass's heartfelt lament foretold that freedom for *all* would have to await the "new birth of freedom" that Lincoln prophesied at Gettysburg in 1863.

A chronological study of slavery's presence in the history of the United States offers a unique opportunity to try to make sense out of a custom and practice that became so ingrained in the American cultural consciousness that its residual effects still influence the modern national dialogue. Slavery and racism have left such indelible imprints upon American life that it is imperative for us to examine the history of these practices in order to discover the essence of a national self-identity. We are confronted by the reality that one cannot elevate the abolitionist self without bearing witness to the demons of the slaveholding self. Seeking to understand the historical American self is a painful exercise that is often easier to dismiss than to assess.

Slavery in the United States was not unlike the other forms of chattel slavery that existed in Latin America and the Caribbean region at the same time. Yet somehow, the polarization of ideology concerning slavery that found expression in American political life set the U.S. experience apart from other slave-based societies. The realization that the slavery question could foment (or at least strongly influence) fratricidal civil war is a condition that is without parallel throughout the historical era. We must struggle to find clues to explain such madness—we must search incessantly to discover the historical national self that eludes us.

History does not allow us to erase the past; at best it allows us to find understanding and to have a chance to avoid in our own time the pitfalls of former generations. The historical process relies heavily upon the act of remembering, and progress results only when we can use historical memory to effect positive change in our time. This section can help us remember the historical reality of slavery in the United States, but how we use this knowledge in our time is our challenge.

1619

African American history and the approximate start of slavery in the American colonies all began on August 20 when a Dutch ship delivered "twenty and odd" Africans to the English settlement at Jamestown, Virginia, where they were sold by bid as indentured servants. Although they did not become slaves immediately, these 20 individuals represented the first permanent involuntary Africans immigrants in the region that eventually became the United States. According to the contemporary records of John Rolfe, "About the last of August came in a dutch man of warre that sold us twenty Negars" (Rolfe, 1951). Most indentured servants were released after serving a term, generally four to seven years, and then were allowed to become property owners and participate in civic affairs. Within the first generation of their arrival in Virginia, most of the initial African servants had had their period of indenture extended to the point where they became servants for life.

1620

A public school that taught both blacks and Indians was established in the Virginia Colony. As time went by, most of the colonies enacted restrictions that prohibited the right to an education to most nonwhite inhabitants.

1621

The Dutch West India Company, a corporation that would be much involved in establishing colonial outposts and in conducting the transatlantic slave trade, was created by Willem Usselinx and other Dutch merchants to organize trade and to encourage further colonization efforts by the Netherlands in the New World. The Dutch West India Company received a trading monopoly in its charter and soon established the colony of New Netherlands (New York) as the headquarters for its colonial enterprise. [See Document 13.]

1622

Virginia colonial court records from Old Accomack (Northampton) County indicate that the first free blacks in the colony were Anthony and Mary Johnson. Anthony Johnson eventually became an owner of African slaves. In the same year, the Virginia House of Burgesses enacted a law fining anyone who had an improper relationship with a black in an effort to prevent interracial liaisons within the colony (Virginia would not adopt an antimiscegenation law until 1691). The primary justification for laws of this type was that colonial assemblies were particularly concerned about the problems that arose in determining the legal status of children who were born of interracial parents.

1624

Church records indicate that William Tucker, the first black child to be born in England's North American colonies, was baptized at Jamestown, Virginia. Although this child's parents were likely to have been indentured servants, it is probable that the young man grew up to be a slave in the Virginia Colony. Throughout the colonial and early national periods, churches continued to record significant genealogical information about the lives of those slaves who were Christians.

1626

The Dutch introduced 11 Africans as indentured servants into the newly established colony of New Netherlands. Dutch colonial records identify Paul d'Angola, Simon Congo, Anthony Portuguese, and John Francisco as 4 of these early servants who were imported to serve as laborers on Hudson Valley farms. As in Virginia, many of the African servants saw their period of indenture extended to the point where they became servants for life. According to Dutch law as applied within the colony, children who were born to manumitted (freed) slaves were still bound to slavery in New Netherlands.

1629

Africans were imported as slaves into the region that became the colony of Connecticut.

1630

The Massachusetts Bay Colony enacted a fugitive law that protected slaves who fled owners because of ill treatment. According to the language of the statute, those fugitive slaves who sought self-protection because of abuse were protected until their circumstances could be remedied.

1630

In Virginia, the white colonist Hugh Davis was publicly whipped as punishment for his being

The first black indentured servants arrive in Jamestown, Virginia, in 1619. (Library of Congress)

guilty of "defiling his body by lying with a Negro" (Jenkins, 1996).

1634
Africans were imported as slaves into the Massachusetts Bay Colony.

1634
Slavery was first introduced into the colony of Maryland.

1634
In the French colony of Louisiana, Catholic settlers urged colonial authorities to provide educational opportunities for blacks in the colony, including those blacks who were slaves.

1636
Slavery was first introduced into the colony of Delaware.

1638
On December 12, Governor John Winthrop of the Massachusetts Bay Colony reported that Boston had received its first shipment of black slaves from Barbados with the arrival of the slave ship *Desire*. The slaves were transported as cargo along with other commodities, including cotton and tobacco. Captain William Pierce of Salem, Massachusetts, who commanded the *Desire*, regularly traded indigenous Pequot Indians as slaves in the West Indies in exchange for Africans whom he transported as slaves to Boston.

1639
Virginia's House of Burgesses enacted a statute that prohibited blacks from carrying firearms within the colony.

1640
A slave trader named Captain Smith illegally attacked a village in West Africa and carried some of the villagers to Massachusetts. However, Massachusetts authorities refused to accept the cargo of Africans and ordered that they be returned to Africa at the colony's expense, and Captain Smith was arrested for the offense of capturing individuals who were not taken as a result of a "just war" situation, in which case enslavement would have been morally acceptable.

1640
In July, a Virginia black indentured servant, one John Punch, was sentenced to lifetime service for having run away. Two other white indentured servants who had run away with John Punch were given lesser punishment. This episode makes it clear that black indentured servants were quickly becoming enslaved in the colony of Virginia. Also in Virginia, events demonstrated the extent to which racial distinctiveness had already affected crime and punishment within the colony. A Virginia court charged that a white man and a black woman had been "associated" in an inappropriate manner and meted out the punishment deemed necessary. The man was ordered to do penance while the woman was publicly whipped.

1641
In December, Massachusetts became the first colony to legalize slavery by giving statutory recognition to the practice in section 91 of the *Body of Liberties,* but added a caveat that forbade capture by "unjust violence." This provision was later incorporated into the Articles of the New England Confederation, and all of the other New England colonies eventually added the provision to their statutes regarding the institution of slavery. The Massachusetts law recognized the slave trade as a legal enterprise and allowed for the enslavement of blacks and Indians.

1642
The Virginia House of Burgesses passed a law imposing fines upon anyone who harbored runaways—the penalty assessed was 20 pounds of tobacco per night of refuge granted—and the same measure authorized the branding of slaves

The *Oxford English Dictionary* offers more than 60 usages for the word "pass." One of these meanings suggests the sense in which the word relates to slavery, although it scarcely encompasses the ramifications that have come to be associated with the concept: "To be accepted," the fifteenth meaning says, to be "received or held in repute, often with the implication of being something else."

Many of the examples provided in the other usages also verge, if sometimes remotely, on conditions relevant to consequences of slavery. In 1662, an English character cried, "God made him and therefore let him passe for a man." Another early writer mused, "Had Lucretia been only a poet, this might have passed for a handsomely described fable." Martin Gil said to a stranger, "You pass for a kind-hearted gentleman." Another Englishman, a political commentator, remarked, "Something happened which at least passed for a regular election," while still another and later speaker said, "Most of those who now pass as Liberals are Tories of a new type."

In the modern American sense, however, "passing" can carry the dimension of color, usually with reference to persons of at least partial African-American descent whose skin color is light and who, therefore, could seem to be white. This sense also has the implication that the person who passes wishes to hide his or her true origins.

There are many variations of meaning associated with the term in literature and in law, especially in the period from the close of the American Civil War into the late-nineteenth century. As the American South rushed to pass laws ensuring white supremacy, it became legally possible to declare persons known to have some African-American heritage to be white persons, that is, legally to be permitted to pass. For instance, the Mississippi code of 1885 drew the line at one-fourth Negro blood, and by 1890, all persons of one-eighth Negro blood were legally white in Mississippi. In Louisiana, a descendant of a white person and a quadroon (a person of one-quarter black ancestry) was a white person. Before the American Civil War, a person was legally white in Ohio if he or she were more than half white. South Carolina concluded that "where color or feature is doubtful," a jury must decide by reputation, by reception into society, and by the exercise of the privileges of a white man as well as by admixture of blood. But in Georgia, "person of color" meant "all such as have an admixture of Negro blood." Clearly, these varying distinctions and prohibitions reflected the desire of white politicians to maintain control in areas where blacks outnumbered whites.

The problem, however, has not been an exclusively American problem. Never within memory have two races existed side by side in whatever circumstances without intermingling. In some instances, in ancient Egypt and some other societies, accommodation has progressed at a less harrowing, even beneficial pace. In the United States, however, the coexistence of two races has proved divisive and the consequences recurrent. The effects of "passing" have given rise not only to legal complexities but to a poignant literature.

Several patterns of "passing" can be discerned in American literature of the nineteenth and twentieth centuries. In his novel *The House behind the Cedars* (1900) Charles W. Chesnutt, a writer of partial African-American descent, told the story of Rena. Beautiful, complex, sensitive, and possessed a deep emotional nature, Rena lived the tragedy of the outcast struggling to discover an acceptable style of life. The daughter of a white father and a light-skinned Negro mother of pre–Civil War days, Rena grew up at the edge of town. Because Rena's mother could never hope for marriage, she and her children lived as lonely exiles in a house provided by her white paramour. Rena's older brother John learned the law while working as office boy for a white man and then left to go to South Carolina where he passed as a white person. Despite his success, he felt some discomfiture and returned to offer Rena a home. Moved by Rena's beauty and her natural dignity, George Toyon, one of John's clients, asked her hand in marriage. But because Rena could not forget her mother, Toyon learned of her Negro blood and rejected her. He still desired her, but only for what he knew to be the supreme insult, a liaison without marriage. Sick at this vindication of her worst fears, Rena returned to her childhood home where she was driven into the dangerous cypress swamps of the North Carolina lands abutting Cape Fear River and met her death.

The story touches several situations that frequently arose in the pre–Civil War South. In some instances, white families lived close to second black families. Sharing the same father, sisters and brothers who might resemble one another came into contact. Some people who successfully "passed" suffered mental distress from the loss of family connections, or they felt the embarrassment of daily denials on one level or another. Many variations of these situations have provided literary themes.

In another facet of the situation, some people made conscious choices and lived with them. Charles Chesnutt himself was a light-skinned Negro child born to free Negro parents. Though some of his relatives left the circumstances in which they were born and effectively lost connection with the past, and though he could himself have "passed," Chesnutt decided his life project would be to champion black people, and he always made a point of his own racial connections. On the other hand, the twentieth-century writer Anatole Broyard, who was for many years an editor and book reviewer for the *New York Times* and who could also "pass," went to great lengths to conceal his heritage. Broyard, a gifted intellectual, resolved in the words of Henry Louis Gates, Jr., "to pass so that he could be a writer, rather than a Negro writer" (*New Yorker,* June 17, 1996). Whatever the individual means of dealing with the situation of being born into one race in the United States yet looking more like members of another race, built-in mental and social cruelties generally provided a sure accompaniment.

—*Frances Richardson Keller*

For Further Reading
Chesnutt, Charles W. 1988. *The House behind the Cedars.* Athens: University of Georgia Press; Gates, Henry Louis, Jr. 1996. "White Like Me." *New Yorker,* June 17, 66–81; Keller, Frances Richardson. 1978. *An American Crusade: The Life of Charles Waddell Chesnutt.* Provo, UT: Brigham Young University Press; Monfredo, Miriam Grace. 1993. *North Star Conspiracy.* New York: Berkley Publishing Group.

who attempted a second escape. This law is viewed as the precursor of other fugitive slave acts imposed later.

1643

An intercolonial agreement drafted for the New England Confederation stated that mere certification by a local magistrate could serve as enough evidence to convict a runaway slave. This decision formed the basis for many of the fugitive slave acts that would be enacted in the eighteenth and nineteenth centuries.

1643

The Virginia House of Burgesses took action to standardize the period of service for indentured servants to a span of four to seven years (previously, a range of two to eight years had been common). Colonial records do indicate that the period of indenture assigned to African servants tended to be longer than that assigned to white servants. By 1661, Virginia authorities would consider black servants to be servants for life.

1644

The first recorded marriage of blacks in the region that eventually became the United States occurred at the Boulweire Chapel on Manhattan Island in the New Netherlands Colony when Antony van Angola and Lucie d'Angola were married. In the same year, Dutch authorities in colony presented land grants to the first 11 blacks who had been introduced into the colony in 1626. The land grants were located in the areas that today comprises Brooklyn and Greenwich Village.

1645

The *Rainbowe,* the first slave ship constructed in the American colonies, sailed for Africa to begin operation in the transatlantic slave trade.

1645

Slavery was introduced into the colony of New Hampshire.

1648

Governor William Berkeley of Virginia began to plant rice on his plantation. Some of Berkeley's slaves had suggested the crop because they noted the similarity between Virginia and their former homeland in West Africa.

1649

A colonial census found there were 300 indentured servants of African descent in Virginia.

1649

A Maryland statute stated all rights of the colony's Christians except for baptized slaves.

1649

The English Parliament incorporated the Society for Propagating the Gospel in New England. This missionary effort, established by John Eliot, had had much previous success in con-

Former slaves at work on a North Carolina rice plantation on the Cape Fear River, 1866. Rice had been grown in the southern United States since the seventeenth century; slaves from West Africa were already familiar with the crop. (Library of Congress/Corbis)

verting Native Americans, and Eliot now expanded the society's efforts into areas of educating blacks and converting them to Christianity.

1650

Connecticut Colony legally recognized the institution of slavery by passing statutes to regulate the practice.

1651

In Northampton, Virginia, Anthony Johnson, a free black man, imported five servants, which entitled him to receive a 200-acre land grant along the Pugoteague River. Johnson and a group of other free blacks attempted to establish an independent black community, and at one point, the community contained 12 homesteads.

1651

With passage of the English Navigation Act of 1651, Parliament attempted to limit the commercial influence of the Dutch West India Company in England's North American colonies as the act limited the colonial slave trade to English merchants only.

1652

The government of the Netherlands granted the Dutch West India Company specific permission to import African slaves into the Dutch colony of New Netherlands. Colonial laws prohibited the mistreatment of slaves, and whippings were not allowed without specific permission from the colonial authorities.

1652

On May 18, the colonial assembly of Rhode Island enacted the first legislative measure in the American colonies to declare slavery illegal, but legislation enacted in 1700 would reverse this decision.

1652

Also on May 18, Quakers meeting in Warwick, Pennsylvania, approved a resolution that black slaves should be afforded the same status as white indentured servants within the colony of Pennsylvania. The language of the resolution stipulated that no one could be enslaved for a term of more than 10 years.

1654

In Northampton County, Virginia, Anthony Johnson, himself a free black, filed suit in court to make his black indentured servant John Casor a servant for life. This is the first recorded case in a Virginia civil court in which an indentured servant was essentially transformed into a slave.

1657

Quaker founder George Fox encouraged his American brethren in "the duty of converting

Engraving, The Modern Medea, *depicting Margaret Garner, a slave who escaped from Kentucky to Ohio but was recaptured by four pursuers. Two of her children lie dead on the floor—she killed them to prevent them from being reenslaved. (Library of Congress/Corbis)*

the slaves" and demonstrated his personal commitment to this ideal by ministering to slaves in the West Indies.

1658
A group of black and Indian slaves revolted in the area of Hartford, Connecticut.

1660
The English political philosopher John Locke drafted a constitution for the Carolinas that gave every freeman in the colony complete power and authority over his slaves. Locke's constitution was never enacted, but subsequent colonial and state charters would grant slaveowners much power over their slaves.

1660
The colonial assembly in Connecticut enacted a statute that prohibited blacks from serving in the militia.

1660
On March 13, the Virginia House of Burgesses enacted a measure limiting the amount of tax that could be charged upon the sale of a slave.

1661
Virginia Colony passed a law that recognized the condition in which some blacks were assumed to serve their masters for life. Although white indentured servants who committed an offense might be punished by an extended period of indenture, the law described blacks as "persons incapable of making satisfaction by addition of time" (Jenkins, 1996). This measure suggests that a gradual transformation had occurred between 1619 and 1661 whereby the condition of indentured labor for black servants had become transformed into a condition of enslavement.

1661
Administrators of the Dutch colony of New Netherlands received a petition for freedom presented by a slave.

1662
The House of Burgesses in Virginia passed a law

The study of slavery is incomplete unless one considers the consequences slaves suffered while yielding to the human tendency to want to be free. Slavery is the condition in which one human is the personal property of another. The European form of slavery differed from other world slavery systems in that the master held absolute property rights and the slaves had little protection by law. In addition, slave marriages were not recognized as being legally binding, and slaves were typically viewed as tools. African slaves, on the other hand, were considered to be members of their master's family and to be workers with rights. Slavery under Islam was also quite different from European slavery as Muslims had to abide by a religious code of treatment for slaves as ordered by the Qur'an.

Since the role of slaves in the Western world was clearly demarcated by the master's successful ability to strip them of their active, collective, and individual personalities by treating and thinking of them as less than human, the punishment of slaves evolved into a significant part of the institution of slavery. The psychological benefits to the master class included the maintenance of the system as well as the lucrative profits generated by free labor. However, such psychological and physical oppression could be neither implemented nor maintained without the use of brute force, mob violence, and punishment. The basic historical picture of the punishment of slaves has focused on the lash. The lash in the hands of white masters embodied the concept of slavery, and public floggings were used to degrade, discipline, and deter slaves from engaging in activities that masters perceived of as disrupting the public good. The practice of punishing slaves seemed to have less relationship to the crime than to the ability to maintain control and embed fear.

Extending the boundaries of the European worldview to the colonies through the transatlantic slave trade led to the conception of Africans being distinctly inferior creatures, and because of this belief, Africans and other indigenous populations were treated like chattel in the New World. Workhouse irons and brands were commonly applied as were laws that reinforced the inferiority of slaves and justified cruel and unusual punishment for minor offenses. For example, slaves were not allowed to leave their master's property without passes, and they could not meet in large groups, carry weapons, or strike a white person. At the same time, masters were free to impart punishment whenever and however it was deemed necessary without legal prosecution. In areas where large numbers of slaves were concentrated, white men formed patrols. Slaves were also punished for playing with white children, running away, being disobedient, and committing crimes against the Sabbath such as selling liquor on Sunday. A common punishment for slaves who had learned to read or write was amputation—slave narratives indicate that the removal of a finger at the joint was considered a warning for stealing a book and that beheading was punishment for a repeat offense. Slaves could also be punished by death if they attempted to harm others, but the basic punishment for most offenses was based on Hebraic law and involved a whipping of approximately 39 lashes.

In one case that occurred in 1640 in Virginia, three slaves (one white) were punished for running away. The white slave had the term of his labor extended for four years, but one of the Africans, one John Punch, was sentenced to work for his master for the remainder of his life. In Richmond, Virginia, a slave could receive nearly 40 lashes for stealing a pair of boots, and there are countless accounts of burning slaves on selected parts of the anatomy as well. After the New York rebellions of 1741, slaves were denied legal counsel, and the authorities expressed regret that nothing more extreme was available than hanging or burning the rebellious Africans at the stake: 18 were hanged and 13 were burned alive at the stake. After an 1800 Virginia slave conspiracy, said to have been organized by one Gabriel Prosser, the Virginia courts ordered that at least 25 slaves be put to death. In addition to actual punishment of slaves, history is rife with accounts of random murder. The twentieth-century historian Gilberto de Mello Freyre frequently wrote about rampant murders of African slaves by colonialists in Brazil.

The historical records are also replete with evidence regarding the psychological aspect of the punishment of slaves. As mentioned, neither slave fatherhood nor slave marriage was recognized by whites because doing so would impinge upon their concept of property rights. Slave narratives contain an abundance of descriptions of slave punishments. One woman recalled that a slave boy who had killed his master received a swift trial by six white men who, upon his confession, took an ax and cut off his head. Another tells of whites taking slaves to a bridge in South Carolina, lining the slaves up, and shooting them off of the bridge. Still another makes reference to her mother being punished by 50 lashes for refusing to obey her white master.

It is obvious that the punishment of slaves in the New World by their masters was brutal and inhumane in most respects. Punishment was a means by which slaveowners maintained the institution of slavery to maximize its economic context, and punishment was implemented for a range of so-called crimes to facilitate the slaveowners' ability to hold other men and women in perpetual bondage.
—*Torrance T. Stephens*

For Further Reading
Bancroft, Frederick. 1931. *Slave Trading in the Old South.* Baltimore, MD: J. H. Furct; Cornelius, Janet. 1983. "We Slipped and Learned to Read: Slave Accounts of the Literacy Process, 1830–1865." *Phylon* 44(3): 171–186; Freyre, Gilberto. 1966. *The Masters and the Slaves: A Study in the Development of Brazilian Civilization.* 2d. English language edition. New York: Alfred A. Knopf; Hurmence, Belinda. 1989. *Before Freedom: When I Just Can Remember.* Winston-Salem, NC: John Blair.

that declared that the status of all children—whether bound or free—should be determined by the condition of the mother only. With the passage of this measure, the condition of slavery became hereditary in the colony.

1663

Laws in the English colony of Maryland made all imported black servants within the colony servants for life (slaves). A law passed in this year further declared that free white women who married slaves became slaves themselves during the lifetime of their spouse and that children born of such a union were also slaves. This measure was later repealed in order to prevent the forced marriages of white servant women to slaves. In the same year, Governor Charles Calvert of Maryland wrote to Lord Baltimore in England and suggested that the colony had a great need for African slaves and that he was concerned that the Company of Royal Adventurers might not be interested in providing slaves to Maryland since the colony was too poor to purchase large numbers of Africans.

1663

As settlement of the Carolina Colony began, settlers were promised 20 acres of land for each male slave they brought into the colony and 10 acres for every female slave.

1663

On July 27, the English Parliament approved the second Navigation Act, which developed a stronger mercantile arrangement between the mother country and its colonies. According to this legislation, all imports were to be carried to the colonies on English vessels, but an exception was made for certain imports, including servants. At this time, the English were not yet actively involved in the African slave trade, but this situation eventually changed.

1663

On September 13, a house servant named Berkenhead in Gloucester County, Virginia, betrayed a planned uprising that involved a conspiracy between black slaves and white indentured servants. This episode is believed to be the first serious slave conspiracy in England's North American colonies. Throughout the colonial and early national periods, local authorities maintained a careful vigilance to suppress all episodes of organized resistance by slaves.

1664

Maryland passed a law stating that Christian baptism did not affect the slave status that was imposed upon black servants within the colony—effectively, blacks were considered servants for life. This measure was necessitated because certain precedents in English common law allowed for the emancipation of slaves who became converts to Christianity and then established a legal domicile within the colony. Eventually, similar laws were enacted by the colonial assemblies in New York, New Jersey, North Carolina, South Carolina, and Virginia, but Pennsylvania and Delaware did not institute such policies. On September 20, the colonial assembly in Maryland enacted an antimiscegenation statute to prevent "freeborn women from . . . shameful matches." The assembly was particularly concerned about problems that arose in determining the legal status of children who were born of interracial parents.

1664

The two colonies of New York and New Jersey legally recognized the institution of slavery by passing statutes to regulate the practice. Slavery had existed in both of these colonial regions prior to this time, when the area was still under Dutch control, but the statutes marked the first time that English authorities in these colonies officially recognized the legal status of slavery.

1665

The laws that the Duke of York (the future King James II of England) developed for governing the colony of New York recognized the legality of slavery within the colony and did not prevent the enslavement of Native American peoples or Christian Africans.

1667

In England, Parliament passed the Act to Regulate the Negroes on the British Plantations, which described persons of African descent as possessing a "wild, barbarous and savage nature, to be controlled only with strict severity."

1667

Virginia authorities declared that it was not to be considered a felony if one's slave died while being corrected. On September 23, Virginia repealed an earlier statute that had enfranchised blacks who had converted to Christianity. The new law stated that Christian baptism did not affect the slave status that was imposed upon black servants within the colony—effectively, blacks were considered servants for life. In the Preamble to the statute, Virginia lawmakers urged the colony's slaveowners to be more diligent in converting slaves to Christianity.

1668

The Virginia House of Burgesses enacted a measure that declared that free black women in the colony should not receive the same privileges and rights as English women.

1669

In October, the Virginia House of Burgesses enacted a statute that acquitted slaveowners who killed their slaves. The law, which stated that "it cannot be presumed that premeditated malice (which alone makes murder a felony) should induce any man to destroy his own estate" (Jenkins, 1996) was based upon the assumption that a slave's value as an item of property superseded the slave's value as a person.

1670

Statutes in the Body of Liberties for the colony of Massachusetts were revised so that the enslavement of a slave woman's offspring was legalized. According to this policy, the status of the child was viewed as the same as the status of the mother in all circumstances. Previous language had created a legal loophole which the children of certain slaves had used in attempting to sue for their freedom.

1670

The settlement of South Carolina began in earnest when 2,000 emigrants from the island of Barbados in the English West Indies moved to the mainland colony and brought their slaves with them.

1670

On October 13, the Virginia House of Burgesses passed legislation asserting that all non-Christian servants who were imported by sea were thereafter to be considered as servants for life and that the condition of all issue should follow the status of the mother. Because of moral concerns raised by the possible enslavement of Christians, the law stipulated that blacks who were Christians before their arrival in Virginia could not be enslaved for life, but this provision was repealed in 1682. The law also stated that servants who entered the colony by land were to serve until they reached the age of 30 if they were adult men or women when their period of servitude began.

1671

Virginia Governor William Berkeley believed there were 2,000 blacks and 6,000 white indentured servants in the colony out of a total population of 40,000 inhabitants. Slaves therefore constituted about 20 percent of the colony's population.

1671

The colonial assembly in Maryland enacted a measure declaring that the conversion of blacks to Christianity, either before or after their enslavement in the colony, did not affect their condition of service for life. This measure was necessitated by the apprehension of slave traders who believed that their economic welfare was dependent upon such a declaration. With the passage of the measure, slave importers felt free to encourage the conversion of slaves to Christianity.

Although the institution of slavery robbed African Americans of their freedom, it did not strip them of their creativity and artistic abilities. From the beginning of their forced migration from Africa until emancipation, African-American slaves made significant contributions to the American tradition of arts and crafts. Indeed, a select cohort of slave artists left a memorable legacy within the fine and decorative arts while even greater numbers of their enslaved brethren created functional yet equally beautiful pieces of art within the craft tradition. Much of the artwork produced by slaves exhibits both African and European characteristics and thus reflects the cultural diversity and synthetic nature that defines African-American culture.

Slave contributions to the fine and decorative arts mostly reflect the significant role played by slave artisans within colonial America and the early U.S. economy. Slave artisans produced a wide range of luxury items that required the delicate blend of the craftsman's skillful hand and the artist's eye. The slaves' refined artistic abilities appear in the gold and silver work, furniture, wood carvings, and ironwork produced by their hands. The wrought iron fences and balconies of Charleston, South Carolina, and New Orleans are an excellent example of the slaves' considerable talent for high art. However, slave contributions to the fine and decorative arts were not limited to the work of artisans. Small numbers of slaves also demonstrated their artistic abilities through portraiture. In fact, the notable American painter Gilbert Stuart drew early inspiration from watching Neptune Thurston, a slave, sketch faces on barrels. Similarly, the work of the slave painter Scipio Morehead inspired the African-American poet Phillis Wheatley to dedicate a poem to his ability as an artist.

Although some slaves exhibited their artistic talent through high art, a far greater percentage of African Americans revealed similar skills through handicrafts. Unlike the luxury items created by slave artisans, the artistic items produced by the typical slave were not purchased primarily by white consumers but remained within the creator's community where they served day-to-day needs. The most common handicrafts produced by slaves were wood carvings, baskets, quilts, and pottery. Each of these slave craft forms reveals the persistence of African culture within the slave community as age-old skills combined with New World circumstances to create articles of utility and beauty.

Slaves used their carving skills to create useful items like bowls, spoons, forks, and walking sticks out of wood. These items often featured anthropomorphic images that resembled decorative forms used in Africa, and African cultural continuity also appears through the variety of split wood, palmetto, and grass baskets made by slaves. Used in fanning rice, picking cotton, and storing food, the baskets strongly resembled forms found throughout the continent of Africa. In addition to keeping people warm inside the typically drafty slave quarters, slave-made quilts maintained African decorative and textile traditions through their creators' use of similar colors, patterns, and iconography. Finally, slave-made pottery forms such as face jugs and Colono Ware (low-fired handmade pottery) resemble West African ceramic styles and may demonstrate the continuation of African religious beliefs in America.

—*Daniel L. Fountain*

For Further Reading
Fry, Gladys-Marie. 1990. *Stitched from the Soul: Slave Quilts from the Ante-bellum South.* New York: Dutton Studio Books; Peek, Phil. 1978. "Afro-American Material Culture and the Afro-American Craftsman." *Southern Folklore Quarterly* 42(2-3): 109–134; Vlach, John. 1978. *The Afro-American Tradition in Decorative Arts.* Cleveland: Cleveland Museum of Art; Vlach, John. 1991. *By the Work of Their Hands: Studies in Afro-American Folklife.* Ann Arbor, MI: UMI Research Press.

1672

The English Parliament chartered the Royal African Company and granted it a monopoly in conducting the English slave trade between Africa and the Americas. The company's exclusive monopoly lasted until 1698 when the Parliament opened the slave trade to all English subjects.

1672

In Virginia, a law was enacted that placed a bounty on the head of Maroons—black fugitives who formed independent communities in the mountains, swamps, and forests of the colony. These communities were viewed with disdain as occasionally, the residents of Maroon communities would raid towns and plantations in order to obtain needed provisions.

1674

After having had success with Native American

peoples, John Eliot and the Society for Propagating the Gospel in New England began to support the education of persons of African descent throughout the English colonies in North America.

1676
Dutch slave traders carrying Africans to the Americas found the business lucrative. Africans purchased in Angola cost the Dutch traders 30 florins each, and they sold the slaves in the Americas for prices ranging between 300 and 500 florins. At this time, the Dutch traders transported approximately 15,000 Africans per year for sale as slaves in the Americas.

1676
An English Quaker, William Edmondson, addressed a general letter to the slaveholders of England's North American colonies. In the letter, Edmondson argued that Christianity was incompatible with slaveholding, and he urged his colonial brethren to separate themselves from the vile institution of slavery.

1676
Colonial legislators in New Jersey prohibited the practice of slavery in the western portion of that colony.

1680
A Virginia law prohibited blacks from gathering together in large groups or carrying weapons of any type.

1680
On October 31, the General Court of Massachusetts imposed fines and prohibited any ship from sailing from a Massachusetts port with "any servant or Negro" aboard without the governor's specific permission.

1681
A colonial census estimated that 3,000 blacks resided in Virginia.

1681
A slave girl named Maria was burned alive in the colony of Massachusetts after she was convicted of burning her master's home. This case of arson was especially disturbing because it had caused the death of a child in the home.

1681
A Maryland colonial law declared free those black children who were born either of European mothers or of free black mothers. With the passage of this measure, the status of slaves in the colony of Maryland effectively followed the status of the father. Legislators enacted this measure because many colonial planters had been encouraging white indentured women to marry slaves so their offspring would become slaves.

1682
The English colony of South Carolina legally sanctioned the practice of slavery within its borders, thus giving statutory recognition to the institution.

1682
The Virginia House of Burgesses passed a law that reduced all non-Christian bond servants to permanent status as slaves regardless of any future religious conversion. The new law also allowed slaves who were Christians at the time of their arrival in Virginia to be enslaved for life. This measure reversed existing policies that had been established in 1670, probably because previous legislation had caused economic distress by limiting the number of slave imports into the Virginia colony.

1682
The colonial assembly of Pennsylvania chartered the Free Society of Traders in Pennsylvania, which recognized the legality of slavery in the colony but sought to introduce a new commercial scheme. The society established a system of slave apprenticeship in which slaves would be freed after 14 years provided they continued to cultivate plots allotted to them and they submitted two-thirds of their agricultural produce annually to the society.

1685
The French government enacted the Code Noir (Black Code) in all of its colonial settlements. In the case of North America, this involved the French colony of Louisiana, but settlers often ignored the provisions of the decree. The Code Noir required religious instruction for slaves, permitted intermarriage, and outlawed the working of slaves on Sundays and holidays. The Code Noir also forbade the liberation of mulatto children when they reached the age of 21 if their mothers were still enslaved.

Slave artisans composed a major component of the colonial and early-American skilled labor force. Typically male, American-born, and English-speaking, slave artisans worked in countless occupations throughout the colonies and much of the United States. Although there were slave artisans of Native American descent during the colonial period, the overwhelming majority of enslaved skilled labor was of African descent. This steady pool of skilled slave labor helped provide a young American economy plagued by chronic labor shortages with the necessary ingredient for it to grow, diversify, and ultimately industrialize.

Slave artisans served two primary functions within the American economy. First, slave artisans provided urban centers with a captive and capable labor supply that their fledgling industries desperately needed and could readily exploit. Second, slave artisans enabled rural plantation managers to improve and diversify their operations' productive capacity by increasing the range of money-saving or cash-producing activities that took place on site. Thus, the labor of slave artisans helped transform plantations into increasingly efficient, self-sufficient units of production.

An abbreviated list of slave artisan occupations helps to illustrate the importance of this diverse labor source for both urban and rural localities. Slave artisans worked as barbers, blacksmiths, carpenters, coopers, draftsmen, hatters, joiners, potters, printers, shipbuilders, shoemakers, silversmiths, and wood carvers. Historians believe that the tradition of skilled artisans in Africa augmented this wide range of occupations both quantitatively and qualitatively as African knowledge meshed well with the demands of familiar tasks in the New World. The fine ironwork of slave-built, antebellum homes in Charleston, South Carolina, and New Orleans attests to this historic transfer of talent.

The slave artisans' value to master and community often allowed these skilled individuals greater autonomy and privileges than what was allowed average slaves. Many slave artisans worked without daily supervision or the constant threat of physical coercion, and the demands of skilled occupations such as printing allowed slave artisans greater access to the empowering tool of literacy. Masters often permitted slave artisans to hire out their own time within the community upon the condition that the master receive a designated percentage or specified amount of the money earned. Particularly industrious slaves could receive material incentives to find extra work. For example, masters might permit slave artisans to retain the surplus portion of money earned in excess of an agreed amount. In addition to using these earnings to improve their material conditions, many such artisans used this money to buy their own or a family member's freedom.

The ability to negotiate and improve the conditions of their bondage elevated many artisans to positions of leadership within the slave community. Occasionally, slave artisans like Gabriel Prosser used their leader status to organize and incite rebellion against the institution of slavery, and for this reason and because of their success in competing against free artisans, the white community viewed slave artisans with suspicion and resentment. Accordingly, cities like Philadelphia and Charleston sought to limit the number and activities of slave artisans through restrictive legislation.

—*Daniel L. Fountain*

For Further Reading
DuBois, W. E. B., ed. 1902. *The Negro Artisan.* Atlanta, GA: Atlanta University Press; Newton, James, and Ronald Lewis, eds. 1978. *The Other Slaves: Mechanics, Artisans, and Craftsmen.* Boston: G. K. Hall; Peek, Phil. 1978. "Afro-American Material Culture and the Afro-American Craftsman." *Southern Folklore Quarterly* 42(2-3): 109–134; Vlach, John. 1991. *By the Work of Their Hands: Studies in Afro-American Folklife.* Ann Arbor, MI: UMI Research Press.

1685
The Virginia House of Burgesses passed a statute that prohibited slaves in the colony from participating in any Quaker meetings that were held for educational purposes.

1687
In Westmoreland County, Virginia, rumors of a planned slave insurrection abounded. Public gatherings of slaves in the region were banned by local authorities, and slaves were not allowed to hold public funerals for other slaves.

1687
In New England, fugitive slaves were often captured and returned to slavery by various people who served as slave catchers and were paid a

small bounty by colonial slaveowners to perform this service.

1688

On February 18, the famous Germantown Protest occurred when a group of Pennsylvania Mennonite Quakers declared openly at their monthly meeting that slavery was contrary to Christian principles and signed an antislavery resolution to that effect. This antislavery document, prepared by Francis Daniel Pastorius and his fellow brethren, is viewed as the first public condemnation of the institution and practice of slavery in the Western Hemisphere, and it is also viewed as one of the first examples of nonviolent protest in American history. [See Document 18.]

1690

The colonial assembly in Connecticut enacted a pass law that made it unlawful for black and Indian servants to travel freely in the colony without having specific written permission from their masters or some other person of authority. Anyone guilty of violating this policy was deemed a fugitive and could be disciplined accordingly.

1691

Virginia's House of Burgesses enacted an antimiscegenation law to prevent intermarriage between races. Virginia officials also sought to restrict the practice of manumission within the colony and ordered any blacks who had been freed to leave the colony within a six-month period. If a slaveowner did free a slave under this new policy, it was the responsibility of the owner to pay all necessary costs for transporting the freed slave beyond the borders of Virginia. Officials did not want to have a large free black population in the colony because they feared that such a group might endanger regional security "by their either entertaining . . . slaves or receiving stolen goods or being grown old and bringing a change upon the country" (Jenkins, 1996).

1692

The colonial assembly in Maryland imposed a penalty of seven years of indenture upon any white man who either married or fathered a child with a black woman. The law also imposed penalties upon any white women who were "associated" with blacks and upon the black men themselves.

1692

Virginia law stated that a fugitive slave might be legally killed and that the owners who experienced such a loss would be compensated by the colony with 4,000 pounds of tobacco. [See Document 28.]

1692

Pennsylvania statutes imposed strict penalties upon any slave loitering in an unauthorized area without a pass from his owner. Such a slave could be imprisoned without food or drink and could receive 39 lashes in a public whipping.

1692

In Salem, Massachusetts, a witch craze swept the community, and 20 citizens were executed after having been accused and convicted of being witches. Much of the initial fear had grown from stories of black magic that a slave woman named Tituba had shared with a group of adolescent girls in the home of the Reverend Samuel Parris. Tituba was not executed for her role in Salem's witchcraft hysteria, but she did remain a slave.

1693

Quaker George Keith published *An Exhortation and Caution to Friends Concerning Buying or Keeping of Negroes,* which had been presented as a paper at the Quaker annual meeting in Philadelphia. It was Keith's desire that those Quakers who owned slaves should free them as soon as possible.

1693

In Boston, Puritan minister Cotton Mather prepared the "Rules for the Society of Negroes." This group represented the first black religious association known to have been formed in the American colonies.

1695

In Goose Creek Parish, South Carolina, the Reverend Samuel Thomas established a school where he taught black children.

1696

During their annual meeting, American Quakers (Society of Friends) admonished the mem-

A nineteenth-century engraving of a meeting of the Society of Friends (Quakers), who were the first organized body to oppose the institution of slavery in the North American colonies. (Library of Congress)

bership for participating in the importation of slaves and threatened those who continued to import slaves with possible expulsion from the Society of Friends.

1698
Blacks composed 12 percent of the population in the colony of New York.

1698
Pennsylvania Quaker William Southeby petitioned Quakers in Barbados to stop shipping blacks to Pennsylvania as slaves. Because of his sustained efforts to fight against slavery, Southeby was eventually expelled from the Society of Friends, which had not yet adopted the position of antislavery.

1698
The Royal African Company lost its monopoly for conducting the English slave trade between Africa and the Americas. As a result, participation in the slave trade was opened to all English subjects, and many New Englanders became involved in extensive slave trading as they realized the lucrative profits the enterprise afforded. Parliament considered the slave trade to be "highly beneficial and advantageous to this kingdom and to the Plantations and Colonies" (Jenkins, 1996). Private traders could enter into the enterprise once they had paid a 10 percent duty to the Royal African Company for the maintenance of the West African forts and factories. From this date onward, the so-called triangular trade developed as slaves, sugar and molasses, and rum became the dominant trade goods exchanged between Africa, the West Indies, and the colonies of English North America.

1698
Officials in Massachusetts changed the colonial tax codes so that "all Indian, mulatto, and Negro servants be estimated as other personal estate" (Jenkins, 1996). Prior to 1698, Massachusetts listed slaves as people on the tax lists, but this action changed their legal status to property.

Slavery was permitted in the Bible, and Jews as freemen in different historical periods owned slaves. A small number of them were active in the slave trade at various times. Middle- and upper-class Jews, primarily urban dwellers, frequently had domestic slaves or help, but since they were usually not farmers or agricultural landowners, they did not own large numbers of slaves. In the Byzantine Empire, slave trading was forbidden to people belonging to other religions, like the Jews, who were considered to be infidels, but even though legislation forbidding Jews to trade in slavery was promulgated by several emperors, some Jews were able to discreetly buy and sell slaves. Explicit legislation forbade Jews from owning and circumcising Christian slaves, but there were noted exceptions. Some Jews purchased slaves in Bulgaria and later sold them in Venice in 885 to an envoy of Basil I. According to Joshua Starr (1939), at the end of the eleventh century, the Jews of Cherson appear to have bought and possibly sold slaves with impunity.

The thirteenth-century codification of the law of the Siete Partidas (Seven-Part Code) sponsored by Alfonso X of Castile and León typified the Catholic position toward slavery. No Jew, Moor, or heretic was to own a Christian slave, but in practicality, the code of laws had little connection to Castilian reality and law. Slaves had few rights, and the masters could punish them as they saw fit. Even though there was a promulgation prohibiting owners from punishing slaves with death, there were many exceptions in history, and the treatment of Moorish slaves was known to be the worst in the world. The Jews were exempt from the *devshirme* (levy of Christian children to be enslaved) since they were *zimmis,* protected minority religious groups and people of the Scriptures who accepted the supremacy of Islam. However, the historian Yosef Hacker noted that after the fall of the Byzantine Empire, Jews were taken captive and children were subjected to the *devshirme.*

From 1567 until 1575, Jews and other *zimmis* from Naxos, Sakis-Adasi (Chios), and other Aegean islands were enslaved by Christian pirates and sold in slave markets in Anatolian cities. In response to this widespread problem, the Ottoman authorities ordered their release. Those Jews who had been taken on Naxos were returned to their Jewish families, but in general, enslaved *zimmis* who had accepted Islam could not be returned to the "unbelievers." In the Ottoman Empire, Jewish slave traffic was permitted until Murad III prohib-

ited the Jews from engaging in slave trading in 1575. In the war between the Ottoman Empire and Cyprus in 1571, Jews were permitted by the sultan to keep Christian slaves they captured in the war and those that the soldiers had brought from the war and had been purchased by Jews in Safed (Zafat) and Damascus. In the slave markets set up in Constantinople, Salonika (Thessaloníki), Brusa (Bursa), and other cities consisting of Christian captives from wars waged by Turkey against Christian countries, Jewish participation in slave trade was minimal.

Even though it was forbidden for Jews and Christians to own slaves, they continued to do so. According to the historian Morris Goodblatt, the Jews circumvented the prohibition against owning Muslim slaves by claiming they were only hiring domestic servants for a limited period of time. Jews often had household slaves, and the latter also observed the Sabbath. Female slaves often converted to Judaism and married their masters or other Jews. The conversion of slaves to Judaism apparently did not encounter opposition from the Ottoman authorities. The historian Y. Hakan Erdem showed that Jews, Armenians, Greeks, and other Christians continued to employ slaves from the seventeenth through the nineteenth centuries, citing a November 4, 1796, document showing how *zimmis* were allowed to own slaves and paid a tax for this privilege to the government. The Jewish traveler, J. J. Benjamin of Moldavia, observed between 1846 and 1855 the feudal Kurdish in which Jews and Nestorian peasants were held in bondage, but Tanzimat centralist reforms of 1856 led to the disruption of the local feudal system in the southeastern corner of Anatolia where Yazdi, Nestorians, and Jews were sold into slavery to Kurdish feudal chiefs.

According to the *Encyclopaedia Judaica,* the Jews of Dutch Brazil (1630–1654) appear to have been among the major retailers of slaves since they had available money and were willing to trade slaves for sugar. The bylaws of the Jewish congregations in Recife and Mauricia in 1648 included a tax of 5 soldos for each slave that a Brazilian Jew bought from the Dutch West India Company. The Jews of colonial America were slaveowners, just as many white Christians were, and most of the Jews lived in cities and primarily used their slaves as domestics. Since more Jews lived along the northeastern seaboard, in cities like Newport, New York, and Philadelphia, most of the Jewish slaveowners were there and not in the South. Few Jews had plantations in the South, and those who were planters, had small plantations and only a handful of slaves.

Jewish farmers in mid-eighteenth-century Georgia had at most a few hundred acres of land and only a few slaves. When Abraham De Lyon, a Portuguese Jew who had grown up in the vineyards of Portugal, wanted to produce a refined wine comparable to that of Porto or Málaga in Georgia, Governor James Oglethorpe rejected his appeal for a grant for the enterprise on the grounds that they could not afford white laborers and slave labor would not be tolerated. When the colony declined in 1741, De Lyon left the colony and left his vines to one of the German Protestant newcomers. The Jews of South Carolina occupied themselves only sporadically in planting, but one who dealt with farming on a large scale was Francis Salvador, who grew indigo on his 6,000-acre plantation and had some 30 slaves.

In colonial America, the most noted and active Jewish slave traders in the 1770s were Aaron Lopez and his father-in-law, Jacob Rivera of Newport, Rhode Island. Beginning in 1764, Lopez and Rivera sent at least one slave ship a year to the West African coast, and in 1772 and 1773, they had a total of eight such ships at sea. David Franks of Philadelphia was involved in the profession in the early 1760s. Isaac Da Costa of Charleston was also a large-scale importer of slaves. The Montsanto brothers in Natchez and New Orleans were slave traders on a modest scale on the lower Mississippi and were surprisingly tolerated by the Spanish colonial officials there despite their Jewish identity and the expulsion of their ancestors from Spain in 1492. Under both the French and Spanish in Louisiana, the brothers frequently bought and sold slaves—in 1787, for example, they purchased 44 blacks.

When slave trading was abolished at the end of the eighteenth and the beginning of the nineteenth century, northern Jews abandoned their old activities, but slavery continued in the South and most southern Jews continued to own slaves. By the middle of the eighteenth century, slavery was an important factor in the development of the South's economy, and Jacob Cardoza, of Portuguese Jewish descent and editor of the Charleston, South Carolina, *Southern Patriot,* and also the most prominent economic theoretician of the South, had developed the idea of a model economy motivated by slavery and low tariffs.

However, southern Jewish involvement in slave trading was very minimal in relation to the white Christian population. Levy Jacobs was an active slave trader in New Orleans and Mobile in the 1820s. According to the eminent deceased historian of American Jewry, Jacob Marcus (1970), Jews composed 3 of the 74 slave traders in Richmond, 4 of 44 in Charleston, and 1 out of 12 in Memphis. The largest Jewish slave traders were members of the Davis family of Petersburg and Richmond, Virginia, who went on the road to sell gangs of slaves in the lower states of the South beginning around 1838. Marcus further commented that "sales of all Jewish traders lumped together did not equal that of one Gentile firm dominant in the business" (Marcus, 1970). In 1860, the few Jewish brokers and auctioneers of slaves in Charleston, South Carolina, made a great deal of money from their activities. A superior slave was priced between $1,000 and $1,200, and one B. Mordecai owned large slave pens adjacent to his warehouses and purchased $12,000 worth of slaves in one sale in 1859. But all the slave-dealing activities of the southern Jews combined did not come close to matching the turnover of the largest single non-Jewish firm specializing in slaves, Franklin and Armfield.

In 1820, over 75 percent of all Jewish families in Charleston, South Carolina; Richmond, Virginia; and Savannah, Georgia owned slaves, usually as domestic servants. Marcus cited that at this time, almost 40 percent of all Jewish householders in the United States owned one slave or more. In 1830, there were only 1,500 Jews in the South, and only 23 Jews out of a total of 59,000 slaveowners owned 20 or more slaves. Out of 11,000 slaveholders who owned 50 or more slaves, only 4 were Jews. On the other hand, according to the 1839 census, more than 3,500 free blacks, mainly in the South, owned 12,000 slaves; a figure much higher than Jewish slave ownership. According to Marcus, Jewish businesses imported less than 2 percent of the black slaves brought to the United States; a ratio far less than the role of Muslims, Protestants, and Catholics.

Preceding the American Civil War in 1861, there were 20,000 Jews living in the South, and a quarter of them, similar to the percentage of their white Christian neighbors, owned at least one slave. In the 1850s, Jacob Levin of Columbia, South Carolina, and Israel I. Jones of Mobile, Alabama, were both leaders of their respective Jewish communities and merchants who bartered slaves. Most of the Jews in the South were patriotic to the Confederacy. Many of the original Sephardim remembered their ancestors' trials and tribulations in the inquisitions of the Iberian Peninsula, and they cherished freedom from the British and later the United States. They were naturally conservative, and southern Jews, in general, outnumbered 100 to 1 by Gentiles, were very cautious not to divert from societal norms and used great discretion. Consequently, they refrained from protest and did not voice opposition to slavery, an important part of the economy of the Confederacy. The Sephardic Jew Judah Benjamin, a former Louisiana senator and secretary of state and secretary of war for the Confederacy, continuously took the brunt of the public's ire after battle losses to the Union, but he continued his devotion to the Confederacy until its defeat when he was forced to flee to England.

Slavery was so integral to southern life that even though the naval captain, and later commodore, Uriah P. Levy expressed a desire to abolish slavery, he continued to operate his Virginia plantation with slave labor. Rabbi David Einhorn of Baltimore was outspoken in condemning slavery and supporting the abolitionists. In the pages of the newspapar *Sinai,* he supported the founding of a black Republican Party to resist slavery, and in the midst of proslavery riots in the city in 1861, incited by seeing Union soldiers in the streets and believing there were threats to his life, he fled to Philadelphia. The New York newspaper, the *Jewish Messenger,* accused Einhorn of forsaking the role of rabbi by "making the pulpit the vehicle for political invective" (Berson, 1971).

Most of the rabbis in the North took a proabolitionist position, one exception being Rabbi Morris J. Raphall of New York City who defended slavery because it existed in biblical times and viewed it, not as a sin, but as protected under the Ten Commandments and practiced by Abraham, Isaac, Jacob, and Job. Raphall did not actually support the slavery system and the mistreatment of slaves in the South, but he felt that the abolitionists misconstrued the biblical view of slavery. He noted that the slaveowners acted in accordance with the Bible but that their treatment of slaves as "things" without rights and privileges negated the Bible, and he advocated that the slaveowners of the South treat their slaves mercifully. His words appealed to the proslavery public, southern politicians, and fundamentalist ministers but not to most of the German Jewish immigrants of his time who had experienced anti-Semitism in Europe and did not accept any exploitation of others or intolerant bigotry.

The German Jewish political liberals were interested in manumission and the protection of blacks, but manumission advocates were not always sympathetic to the condition of slaves and not all of them were abolitionists. Solomon Etting, of Baltimore, himself a slaveowner, was a member of the Maryland Colonization Society, which sought to ship freedmen back to Africa. In general, Jews in Philadelphia and New York City were active in the early abolition movement. Jacob I. Cohen and Isaac Isaacs, noted Richmond merchants, manumitted slaves in their wills, and the deceased David Brandon of Charleston, whose will was probated in 1838, requested that his family be kind to his servant, a free black, who was "the best friend he ever had." The New Orleans philanthropist Judah Touro was generous to a freewoman of color and appointed his good friend Pierre Destrac Cazenave, a descendant of blacks, as one of the executors and beneficiaries of his will.

There were a few rare Jewish individuals in the South, like the Friedman brothers of Tuscumbia, Alabama, who clandestinely dared to help blacks free themselves. Others were not as courageous. In 1860, Marx E. Lazarus, a socialist, opposed slavery but joined the Confederate army when the Civil War broke out because, as a southern nationalist, he opposed what he saw as the evil tyranny of the North. Many Jews treated their slaves well and fairly, which is witnessed by some former slaves adopting their owner's name after liberation. On the other hand, some Jews, like some Gentile slaveowners, were cruel to their slaves—in particular, in response to rebellion and escape. American Jews did not encourage their slaves to adopt Judaism.

In Jamaica, Jews were not allowed to trade slaves, and in Jamaica and Barbados, the authorities limited Jews to owning only one or two slaves. In the Caribbean, Jews were forbidden to own numerous slaves, so they did not maintain plantations. Only in the Guianas, in Surinam under the Dutch, did Jews have plantations and employ large numbers of slaves.

In Curaçao, Jews generally could not engage in the slave trade since the Dutch West India Company had a monopoly on that trade. Don Manuel Belmonte (Isaac Nunez) of Amsterdam was appointed by the Dutch governor to ship slaves to Curaçao, and Philipe Henriquez (Jacob Senior) was the only Jew to receive a concession to obtain slaves in Africa and transport them by ship to Curaçao—the brothers David and Jacob Senior had gone to Curaçao in about 1685 from Amsterdam. In the late-seventeenth and early-eighteenth centuries, Jews began to conduct large-scale purchases of slaves for the Dutch West India Company. In addition to the Senior bothers, who occasionally were given permission by the company to conduct independent transactions in slaves, another Jew of the island, Manuel Alvares Correa (1650–1717), was active in the local slave trade for many years. According to the *Encyclopaedia Judaica,* in 1699, he served as an intermediary for both the Dutch and the Portuguese West Indies companies for the transfer of a shipment of slaves from Africa to Mexico via Curaçao.

Jews were slandered when it was said they controlled the slave trade business and reduced prices. Although Jews consisted of more than half the population of Curaçao, they had only a third of the landholdings of the Protestants, who owned large plantations and maintained hundreds of slaves. According to the 1675 slave tax list, the Jews on Curaçao owned barely 25 percent of the slaves, and the Protestants owned 75 percent. In 1720, the six active Jewish slave masters had only 165 slaves compared to the six largest Protestant slaveholders, who owned 497 slaves. In 1744, the Protestants owned 1,788 slaves, and the Jews owned only 310. According to the 1765 slave census, Jews owned only 860 of 5,534 slaves on the island.

—*Yitzchak Kerem*

For Further Reading
Bancroft, Frederic. 1964. *Slave Trading in the Old South*. New York: Frederick Ungar; Berson, Lenora E. 1971. *The Negroes and the Jews*. New York: Random House; Davis, David Brion. 1966. *The Problem of Slavery in Western Culture*. Ithaca, NY: Cornell University Press; Emmanuel, Isaac S., and Suzanne A. Emmanuel. 1970. *History of the Jews of the Netherlands Antilles*. 2 vols. Cincinnati: American Jewish Archives; Marcus, Jacob R. 1970. *The Colonial American Jew, 1492–1776*. Detroit, MI: Wayne State University Press; Starr, Joshua. 1939. *The Jews in the Byzantine Empire, 641–1204*. New York: Columbia University Press.

1699

Virginia's House of Burgesses imposed an import duty of 20 shillings on each slave imported into the colony.

1700

The slave population in England's North American colonies was estimated at 27,817 with 22,611 living in the southern colonies and 5,206 living in the northern colonies. As a group, slaves constituted 10 percent of the total population in the English colonies.

1700

The English colonies of Pennsylvania and Rhode Island passed legislation legally sanctioning the practice of slavery within their respective borders. In Pennsylvania, William Penn organized a monthly meeting for blacks as Quakers began to make an effort throughout the colonies to provide religious instruction to slaves.

1700

Judge Samuel Sewall organized an antislavery organization known as the Boston Committee of 1700, which lobbied for the implementation of a high duty upon slave imports. The group believed that excessive taxation might be one means of destroying the slave trade in Massachusetts, but its efforts were unsuccessful.

1700

On June 24, Judge Samuel Sewall published *The Selling of Joseph* in Boston, Massachusetts. This antislavery tract based its arguments against the institution and practice of slavery upon biblical sources and questioned those people who used biblical interpretation to condone the practice of slavery.

1701–1714.

England fought two colonial wars with the Netherlands in the hope of winning greater concessions in the African slave trade. By the end of the War of the Spanish Succession (Queen Anne's War), England had wrested control of the slave trade away from the Dutch.

1701

The Society for the Propagation of the Gospel in Foreign Parts was founded in England by Thomas Bray. One of the primary concerns of the society was the religious conversion of Native American peoples and persons of African descent in the English colonies.

1702

New Jersey colonial legislators enacted statutes that gave legal recognition to the practice of slavery in the colony.

1703

Colonial legislators in South Carolina imposed a duty on all slave imports into the colony.

1703

A work entitled *John Saffin's Tryall* was published in Boston. This work initiated the literary genre of the slave narrative, which would be popular throughout the rest of the colonial and

The institution of slavery has seldom been humane. Although some historians like Robert Fogel and Stanley Engerman in *Time on the Cross: The Economics of American Negro Slavery* (1974) argue that white slave masters treated their slaves with respect and kindness, the documentary evidence suggests that slavery was a horrible practice. Thus, it was not unusual for slaves to be subjected to cruel and unusual punishment—including mutilation.

The mutilation of slaves was often implemented under the guise of punishment or for the purpose of doing something for the slave's personal well-being. Punishment through mutilation is well recorded, and it was more often an act of brutality rather than one of rehabilitation. The record shows, for example (in the case of one Captain Philippe Loit), that a common practice was to break the teeth of female slaves who were considered to be recalcitrant. Other accounts show that mutilation was no different than death. For many ship captains on the Middle Passage, one means of trying to prevent slaves from jumping ship was to recapture those who had jumped and to behead them in front of other slaves.

Documents also show that on the Middle Passage, ship captains would make use of a tool called "speculum oris," an instrument shaped like a pair of scissors with serrated blades, to force open the mouths of captives who refused to eat. On sugar plantations in the West Indies, slaves who fell asleep in the mill because of the long work hours might have a limb cut off as an example to other slaves of the dangers of falling asleep on the job. Slaves were also placed in cast-iron weights or boots in which it was not unusual for them to lose an appendage. Even those practices were not nearly as horrendous as other acts practiced by slave- and plantation owners. In Grenada, slaves were taken to open forums for punishment in which mutilation was not out of the ordinary. One female slave taken to St. George's, Grenada, in 1789 was supposed to have her finger removed as punishment, but, instead, she was suspended from a crane and her thighs, breast, and back were split open. In Jamaica, it was not extraordinary for female slaves to have their skin peeled off from heel to back and breast to waist. One 1692 account tells of a freed slave whose master and mistress had cut off her ears.

Moses Roper, who had lived as a slave in the Carolinas and Georgia, recalls in her narrative that her master poured tar on her head and face and set her on fire before placing the fingers of her hand in a vise and removing her fingernails and having another man smash her toes with a sledgehammer. Other tools of mutilation included the thumbscrew and pickets, the latter being used so extensively in Jamaica that slaves who were forced to stand on them often had to have their feet amputated. Some accounts indicate that nails were inserted or hammered into body parts, such as appendages and ears, and hammers were used to knock out teeth. Some slaves who accidentally touched whites had their hands or the body part involved in the touching cut off. Breaking legs in piecemeal fashion, removing sensory organs, and castration were additional means masters used to emphasize their control to captives.

A broad range of activities were used to justify acts of maiming and mutilation. Frederick Douglass in his *Narrative* stated that looking at a person in the wrong way, saying certain words, making a simple mistake, or running away could result in permanent injury or death for slaves. The mutilation of slaves was so bad in the French colonies that Louis XIV signed the Code Noir (Black Code) in 1685 to curtail cruelty.

Since slaves in most parts of the New World were under the complete control of their masters, it is difficult to gauge the true extent of mutilation practices. Moreover, slave codes in the United States were developed and implemented in all slave states to maintain and enhance the master's absolute control and to justify the power of whites to treat Africans as they willed. Consequently, the slave patrols created to enforce the codes often employed mutilation to discipline slaves.

The system of slavery was an inhuman institution that enabled descendants of European ancestry to maintain control over slaves through brutish actions against slaves. Although slavery was practiced by Africans, the Chinese, and Arabs, it was European slavery that was replete with atrocities that often resulted in the mutilation of slaves. This difference may be why many people have noted that the slavery practiced in the Americas was quite unlike the slavery in prior civilizations.

—*Torrance T. Stephens*

For Further Reading
Blake, W. O. 1860. *The History of Slavery and the Slave Trade, Ancient and Modern*. Columbus, OH: H. Miller; Douglass, Frederick. 1845. *Narrative of the Life of Frederick Douglass, an American Slave*. London: Leeds; Jordan, Winthrop. 1974. *The White Man's Burden: Historical Origins of Racism in the United States*. London: Oxford University Press; Stein, Robert L. 1979. *The French Slave Trade in the Eighteenth Century: An Old Regime Business*. Madison: University of Wisconsin Press.

early national periods. Many of the slave narratives were published and used by antislavery supporters as powerful propaganda tools to agitate for an end to the slave trade and, eventually, to slavery itself.

1703

Rhode Island's colonial legislators enacted statutes that gave legal recognition to the practice of slavery in the colony.

1704

The first school to educate black children in what eventually became the United States was founded when Elias Neau, a French Huguenot immigrant, opened the Catechism School for Negroes at Trinity Church in New York City.

1704

In Connecticut, a mulatto slave named Abda sued his owner, Thomas Richards of Hartford. Abda maintained that he should be free because of his white blood, and a Connecticut court agreed and set him free. The colony's general assembly reversed the court's decision and returned Abda to slavery.

1705

Following the lead taken by other colonies, legislators in Massachusetts imposed a duty of four pounds upon all slaves imported into the colony. However, this customs imposition was not severe enough to tax the slave trade out of business as Samuel Sewall and the Boston Committee of 1700 had desired. In the same year, the colonial legislature enacted an antimiscegenation law designed to prevent intermarriage between races. The goal of the Act for the Better Preventing of a Spurious and Mist Issues was to ensure that problems arising from determining the legal status of such offspring would be reduced in colonial Massachusetts. This prohibition was not repealed until 1843.

1705

The colonial legislature in New York developed a measure to reduce the number of slaves running away from their owners by enacting stiff punishments for fugitives. The legislation called for the death penalty to be imposed against any fugitive slave who was captured in the region beyond a line 40 miles north of Albany, New York, as capture within that area was sufficient evidence of the fugitive slave's desire to reach Canada.

1705

Virginia's black code placed severe restrictions upon slave mobility and also authorized heavy penalties to discourage the practice of miscegenation within the colony. The measure also recognized slaves as being real estate rather than people, thus dehumanizing the status of the slave to nothing more than chattel property that could be bought, sold, and traded at will. On October 23, the colonial assembly declared that "no Negro, mulatto, or Indian shall presume to take upon him, act in or exercise any office, ecclesiastic, civil, or military" (Jenkins, 1996). Blacks were also forbidden by law to serve as witnesses in court cases, and they were condemned to lifelong servitude unless they had previously been Christians in their native land or freemen in a Christian country. Additionally, slavery was defined as a legal condition that was limited to blacks only with the exception of "Turks and Moors in amity with her majesty."

1706

A statute enacted by the colonial legislators in New York prohibited the testimony of a slave against a freeman in both civil and criminal cases.

1707

In Massachusetts, selected free blacks were allowed to join the colonial militia. On the other hand, colonial legislators in Massachusetts imposed a fine of five shillings upon any free black who helped to harbor a fugitive slave. A significant number of slaves were being imported into Massachusetts at this time, and the problem of slave runaways was becoming acute in the colony. [See Document 20.]

1707

In Philadelphia, a group of mechanics and artisans banded together into a guild to protest the economic competition that their crafts faced because of the amount of work performed by slaves who were hired out in the city. The mechanics and artisans believed they faced unfair competition from the labor performed by slaves.

1708

Virginia officials estimated that 12,000 blacks resided in the colony.

A contentious issue in the antebellum South, southern whites were ambivalent on the question of slave education. Prominent leaders such as James Henry Hammond and John C. Calhoun warned of dire consequences for white southern society if slaves were taught to read and write, but despite these warnings, and for various social, economic, and religious reasons, some whites chose to teach their slaves. Slave education, perhaps more than any other issue, represented the ideological duplicity of the South's slaveowning class. Slaves themselves recognized the importance of education, perhaps because it was normally kept from them. Knowledge, especially for those in bondage, represented empowerment and a type of freedom.

Organized efforts at slave education began as early as the seventeenth century. A minority of masters, realizing that literate slaves would be more useful and worth more in the event of sale, took a keen interest in teaching slaves to read and write. Others had more altruistic motivations. Christian missionaries, usually Anglicans, believed that education was a key component of a slave's religious salvation. Unless slaves were educated, they could not read the Bible, understand and appreciate the liturgy, and never be truly saved.

Through organizations like the Society for the Propagation of the Gospel in Foreign Parts, Anglican missionaries established schools, trained slave teachers, and taught hundreds of slave students basic literacy and the tenets of the Christian faith. These efforts met with some success. One such school in Charleston had an enrollment of 70 slaves in 1755 and enjoyed the support of several prominent leaders despite legal prohibitions against such activities. Other denominations shared Anglican views on slave education. Puritans in New England and Quakers in Pennsylvania agreed that literacy was a key component in the religious indoctrination of slaves and made some organized attempts to educate them. Therefore, before the American Revolution, some masters and religious leaders called for the education for slaves, but these whites were definitely in the minority.

The majority of slaveowners believed that slaves lacked the ability to absorb formal education. African slaves were believed to be ignorant, primitive, and unworthy to receive formal education, and by educating them, masters believed they were acknowledging that slaves were more than chattel to be bought and sold like livestock. Slaves, in their view, were meant for work and little else, and a life of the mind was unnecessary in the rice, cotton, and tobacco fields. Moreover, many people feared that literacy would make slaves more difficult to control, for it was believed that literate slaves would become leaders in the slave quarters and would use their skills to foment rebellion.

The 1739 Stono Rebellion in South Carolina led to severe restriction of slave activities in that colony. Laws were passed that prohibited slaves from assembling, traveling without written permission, possessing firearms, and other actions that were, from the perspective of many whites, threatening. Teaching slaves to read and write was also prohibited, though this section of the law was enforced sporadically. Georgia enacted similar a similar law against slave education in 1770, and all southern states had followed suit by 1803. In some ways, this fear of slave empowerment through education was justified. Many of the future leaders of slave rebellions, such as Denmark Vesey and Nat Turner, were literate.

Slaves themselves thirsted for knowledge and the intellectual liberation literacy provided, but relatively few slaves were afforded the opportunity to learn to read. Masters most often taught favorite slaves, usually house servants, sometimes this included teaching their own mulatto children. White children, who received instruction from private tutors or at local academies, might also impart their newly found knowledge to slave playmates. Such cases were the exception, however, as only about 5 percent of the southern slave population was functionally literate. Usually, slaves were educated if it was in the master's economic interest to do so, though some masters felt a moral obligation to educate their slaves. This small cadre of educated slaves provided ministers, artisans, and other leaders of the slave community. In some cases, slaves kept account books, tracked crop production, and managed plantations, tasks they ascended to because of their literacy. After 1865, these educated slaves became the first generation of black politicians.

More slaves acquired vocational skills as a result of the work their masters assigned them. Male slaves became forge operators, blacksmiths, woodworkers, tanners, and stockmen as well as other skilled and semiskilled trades. Women had more limited opportunities, but many became seamstresses, weavers, or midwives. This type of vocational education allowed some slaves to earn cash with which to purchase their freedom, and to develop trades that helped them adapt to harsh economic realities following emancipation.

Despite the relatively small number of literate slaves, virtually all desired to learn to read. Religion was one of the most important forces driving this quest for literacy. Religion, as historians such as Eugene Genovese and John Blassingame have demonstrated, was one of the key elements of life in the slave community. Although slave preachers were sometimes literate, many were not, and they wanted to be able to read the Bible so as to better minister their congregations. The laity wanted to read the Bible for themselves in order to partake of God's word firsthand. Literacy allowed blacks to free themselves from a theology imposed by whites and to interpret the Scriptures for themselves.

Like so many other areas of life, education was severely proscribed for slaves in the South before the Civil War. Masters might occasionally teach a favorite slave, but as often as not such instruction was thought to be as more for the master's benefit than for the slave's. Slaves desired education and the intellectual and religious freedom it provided.

Nevertheless, educated slaves remained a small, though important, segment of the slave population. After emancipation, the lack of literacy among former slaves was a serious problem, one that was addressed in part by northern philanthropic organizations. Although former slaves never received an educational level equal to that of whites, emancipation afforded them the opportunity for an education, a right denied them so long by law and custom.

—*Richard D. Starnes*

For Further Reading
Blassingame, John. 1972. *The Slave Community: Plantation Life in the Antebellum South*. New York: Oxford University Press; Cornelius, Janet. 1991. *"When I Can Read My Title Clear?" Literacy, Slavery, and Religion in the Antebellum South*. Columbia: University of South Carolina Press; Genovese, Eugene. 1974. *Roll, Jordan, Roll: The World the Slaves Made*. New York: Pantheon Books; Webber, Thomas. 1978. *Deep Like the Rivers: Education in the Slave Quarter Community, 1831–1865*. New York: W. W. Norton.

1708
A census in the Carolina Colony showed that the combined total of black and Indian slaves in the region surpassed the white population.

1708
Pennsylvania authorities responded to the protest of white mechanics and artisans and moved to restrict the further importation of slaves into the colony; the English government invalidated this restrictive policy.

1708
In an October slave uprising in the Long Island community of Newton, New York, seven whites were killed. The event was suppressed, and four blacks were executed. The legislature responded to this event by enacting a new law aimed at preventing slave conspiracies.

1709
Colonial authorities in Virginia discovered and suppressed a conspiracy of black and Indian slaves who were planning to revolt.

1710
The slave population in England's North American colonies was estimated at 44,866 with 36,563 living in the southern colonies and 8,303 living in the northern colonies.

1710
Virginia's House of Burgesses agreed to manumit a slave named Will because he had informed colonial authorities of a planned slave conspiracy. The practice of rewarding slave informants with freedom was a common practice during the colonial and early national periods as local authorities sought to maintain peace and security in the plantation districts by discouraging conspiracies. In the same year, Governor Alexander Spotswood tried to discourage the further importation of slaves into Virginia as white residents were becoming alarmed at the growing number of blacks in the colony.

1711
The South Sea Company, organized in England, received the right to transport Africans to the Americas where they could be sold as slaves.

1711
At the insistence of Quakers and Mennonites, the Pennsylvania colonial assembly outlawed slavery, but the action was immediately overruled by the British Crown.

1711

In South Carolina, Governor Robert Gibbes and other colonial authorities struggled to combat a sustained campaign of slave resistance inspired by a large community of Maroons led by a fugitive slave named Sebastian. The people of the colony were fearful of the Maroon attacks until Sebastian was killed by an Indian hunter.

1711

The Tuscarora Indians, alarmed because English colonists were moving into their lands in the Carolinas in the region of the Roanoke and Chowan Rivers, engaged in a series of skirmishes with the colonists on September 22. A number of slaves were able to take advantage of the chaos to escape from their owners.

1712

The colonial assembly in South Carolina enacted an Act for the Better Ordering and Governing of Negroes and Slaves, a comprehensive measure that became the model used by many other slave codes developed in the South during the colonial and national periods.

1712

Nine white residents were killed and seven wounded in a slave revolt that occurred in New York City on April 7–8. Once the tumult had subsided, 21 were convicted and sentenced to death for their roles in the uprising. Six other blacks committed suicide. [See Document 21.] In response to the revolt, the colonial assemblies of New York and Massachusetts enacted measures designed to prevent, suppress, and punish slave conspiracies and insurrections within their colonies.

1712

On June 7, the colonial assembly in Pennsylvania banned the further importation of slaves into the colony, which meant that Pennsylvania was the first of the English colonies to prohibit the slave trade. This action followed efforts by William Sotheby to have the assembly abolish slavery within the colony.

1713

After Great Britain withdrew from the War of the Spanish Succession (Queen Anne's War) of 1701–1714, the Treaty of Utrecht (1713) awarded the British South Sea Company with the *asiento,* the contract to supply slaves to the Spanish colonies in the Americas. Awarded on March 26, the contract permitted the South Sea Company to carry 4,800 slaves per year to the Spanish colonies in the Americas for a period of 30 years (144,000 total). Additionally, the British were allowed to send one merchant ship per year to the Spanish colonies for trading purposes.

1714

Rhode Island's colonial legislators enacted a measure to limit the mobility of slaves within the colony by not permitting slaves to travel on a ferry without the specific written permission of their owners.

1714

Colonial legislators in New Hampshire enacted statutes that recognized the legality of slavery in the colony.

1715

A census taken in the New England colonies revealed that 2,000 blacks lived in the region. Estimated imports of slaves into all of England's North American colonies was 2,500 per year. The population of the English colonies was estimated to be 434,600, and the total population of slaves was 58,850 (13.5 percent) at this time.

1715

The colony of North Carolina enacted legislation that legalized the practice of slavery within its borders. The legislature also enacted an antimiscegenation law designed to prevent intermarriage between races. Slaves in the colony were also denied the right to have their own religious meetinghouses.

1715

Virginia officials estimated that 24 percent of the colony's population consisted of slaves.

1715

Quaker John Hepburn published a tract entitled *The American Defence of the Christian Golden Rule* in which he presented many arguments against slavery but stressed that most importantly, slavery was a practice that robbed individuals of the freedom of choice. The Quaker Elihu Coleman published the tract *A Testimony against That Anti-Christian Practice of Making Slaves of Men.*

1715

On April 15, encouraged by agitators from Spanish Florida, the Yamassee Indians attacked colonial settlements in South Carolina and killed hundreds of white settlers. During the conflict, the Yamassee freed many South Carolina slaves.

1716

An antislavery tract appeared in the Massachusetts Colony that argued that the presence of slavery in the English colonies had a debilitating effect upon encouraging the immigration of additional white settlers. The tract argued that slavery reduced the number of occupations that remained open to white settlers and that this type of economic competition did not encourage whites to immigrate to the English colonies.

1716

On June 6, the large-scale importation of slaves into the French colony of Louisiana began when two slave ships belonging to John Law's Company of the West carried Africans to that colony.

1717

In Boston, Massachusetts, Cotton Mather established an evening school in order to educate Indian and slave youth.

1717

The colonial legislature in South Carolina enacted an antimiscegenation law designed to prevent intermarriage between races. Many colonies adopted similar measures because of problems associated with determining the legal status of children born of interracial unions.

1717

The colonial legislature of Maryland enacted a measure designed to discourage interracial marriage within the colony. According to the provisions of this statute, if a free black married a white colonist, the black spouse became the slave of the white spouse.

1719

The first large shipment of slaves arrived at New Orleans in the French colony of Louisiana when the ships *Grand Duc du Maine* and *Aurora* delivered approximately 500 Africans to the colony. John Law, then the proprietor of the colony through his Company of the West, built a slave-trading station along the Mississippi River directly across the river from New Orleans. At this Plantation of the Company, Africans were sold and distributed to the Louisiana colonists.

1720

The population of the English North American colonies was estimated to be 474,000, and the total population of slaves was 68,839, 14.5 percent. In the same year, it was estimated that 2,000 slaves resided in the colony of Pennsylvania.

1720

A slave insurrection in May, described as "a very wicked and barbarous plott" (Jenkins, 1996), occurred in Charleston, South Carolina, Put down by local authorities, 23 slaves were arrested in conjunction with the incident, and 3 were eventually executed for their role in the revolt.

1721

The colonial legislature in Delaware enacted an antimiscegenation law designed to prevent intermarriage between races. According to this statute, a child born to a white mother and a slave father was legally bound to the county court until the mixed-race child reached the age of 31.

1721

In Boston, Massachusetts, the first smallpox inoculations in America were administered by Zabdiel Boylston on May 21 to his son and to two African slaves. Cotton Mather had recommended the experiment after one of his slaves, Onesimus, had informed him that various African tribes used inoculations successfully. This African medical knowledge helped save the lives of many Boston residents during the smallpox epidemic of the same year.

1722

In Virginia, authorities detected a conspiracy among slaves from several counties. The leaders of the plot were imprisoned, and several others associated with the plan were sold and transported out of the colony.

1722

The colonial assembly in Pennsylvania denounced the "wicked and scandalous practice" of blacks cohabiting with white colonists. In the same year, Pennsylvania officials responded to the protest of white mechanics and artisans by declaring that the practice of hiring slaves into the trades was "dangerous and injurious to the republic and not to be sanctioned" (Jenkins, 1996). Pennsylvania's action applied to both slaves and free blacks, and several other colonies followed the lead of Pennsylvania and enacted similar prohibitions designed to protect white mechanics and artisans against "unfair" competition from blacks.

1723

The Virginia legislature disenfranchised free blacks and Native Americans in the colony and also discriminated heavily against them in the imposition of colonial taxes. With its reliance upon race as a controlling factor, this law represented a departure from policies in effect since 1670 that had only restricted the suffrage on the basis of property qualifications. Additionally, free blacks were denied the right to carry weapons of any sort within the colony. In May, seven slaves from Middlesex and Gloucester Counties were sold and transported out of Virginia because of their involvement in a planned slave uprising.

1723

On April 13, after an extensive arson campaign in the colony, the acting governor of the Massachusetts Colony, William Dummer, issued a proclamation announcing that fires "have been designedly and industriously kindled by some villainous and desperate negroes or other dissolute people as appears by the confession of some of them" (Jenkins, 1996). Apprehension was high for many weeks as the white citizens of Boston feared that blacks planned to destroy the city.

1724

A religious tract published in Virginia, *The Present State of Virginia* by Hugh Jones, encouraged slaveowners to baptize and to educate their slaves. Jones suggested that owners should be exempt from paying taxes on baptized slaves who were under the age of 18.

1724

In March, the Code Noir (Black Code) went into effect in the French colony of Louisiana. Instituted by Governor Jean-Baptiste Le Moyne, sieur de Bienville, the code contained 55 provisions that regulated the life of slaves within the colony of Louisiana. Though this code primarily affected the slaves of the colony, certain provisions also directed the liberties afforded to free blacks. Additionally, the code ordered that all Jews leave the colony and prohibited "the exercise of any other religion than the Catholic."

1725

The population of slaves in England's North American colonies was estimated to be 75,000.

1725

After many years of pressure by white settlers, the colonial assembly in Pennsylvania enacted an antimiscegenation law designed to prevent intermarriage between races. The assembly was particularly concerned about problems that arose in determining the legal status of children born of interracial encounters.

1725

The Virginia House of Burgesses granted permission for free blacks in Williamsburg to establish the first Church of Colored Baptists.

1725

The colonial assembly in South Carolina imposed a £200 fine on slaveowners who took slaves to the western frontier of the colony. It was believed that such close proximity to the wilderness beyond the frontier would prompt slaves to escape. The law also sought to diminish the likelihood that slaves might conspire with Native Americans to harm the frontier settlements.

1726

Colonial Governor William Burnet of New York requested that the chiefs of the Six Nations of the Iroquois Confederacy surrender all fugitive slaves who had sought asylum among the Iroquois. Although the chiefs agreed to comply with Burnet's request, no fugitives were ever returned to colonial authorities.

1726

Peter Vantrump, a free black, was kidnapped and sold into slavery in North Carolina by one Captain Mackie who had promised to take Vantrump to Europe. When Vantrump sued for his freedom,

The history of slavery in Louisiana falls in two periods: a colonial period alternating between French and Spanish rule from 1699 until 1803 and an American period from 1803 until emancipation at the end of the American Civil War. Unlike the colonies along the Caribbean and Atlantic coasts of North America, colonial Louisiana was not initially a plantation society. Large-scale slave ownership did not become crucial until after the mid-eighteenth century, when varieties of sugarcane and a method of sugar processing suitable to Louisiana's climate were introduced, and during the American period, when cotton became Louisiana's most widely cultivated crop north of Baton Rouge. As the size of plantations grew and commodity production became more profitable, Louisiana slavery became harsher and legendary.

After claiming Louisiana in 1682, French colonizers established permanent settlements in 1699 at Biloxi, Mississippi, and in 1702 at Fort Louis on Mobile Bay, Alabama. The colony's first slaves were Indians, and they numbered 11 in the 1704 census and 80 in the count four years later. Colonists quickly became dissatisfied with Indian slaves, however, and in 1706 petitioned for Africans instead.

When the first Africans arrived in the colony is unknown, but the first black child was born in 1712, and the black population at that time totaled approximately 20. In 1719, one year after the founding of New Orleans, French ships brought in approximately 500 slaves. The number of slaves increased modestly at first and then dramatically. At the end of the French rule in the 1760s, slaves in the colony numbered approximately 10,000; by the end of the Spanish colonial era, there were about 28,000; and in 1860, under the Americans, the number of slaves reached a peak of 331,726. After the introduction of African slaves, Indian slavery continued on a small scale. Individuals from the two groups sometimes ran off together, held each other in bondage, mated to produce offspring referred to in the colonial records as *grifes*, and on occasion joined in conspiracies against the colonial governments, including the 1729 massacre of the French at Natchez.

Although slaves destined for Louisiana were taken from several regions of Africa, two-thirds of the direct arrivals during the French colonial rule came from the Senegambia, with the Bambara being the largest group and, thereby, the most significant contributors to the formation of the colony's Afro-Creole culture. Under the Spanish, slaves continued to be brought from the Senegambia, but others also came from central Africa, the Bight of Benin, and the Bight of Biafra. The 1791 Revolution in Saint Domingue (Haiti) strengthened French and Afro-Creole culture in Louisiana as many slaveowners and their slaves fled Hispaniola and settled in the colony. In 1808, more Saint Domingue exiles came to Louisiana from Cuba where they had originally sought refuge. Although slaves from elsewhere in the United States were brought into Louisiana during the entire colonial period, the number increased dramatically after 1803, especially when the exhaustion of the soil along the eastern seaboard created a surplus of slaves in that region and the agricultural boom in the lower South and the Southwest created a demand for them. Consequently, Louisiana's Afro-Creole culture became partially Anglicized, and in this form, the culture spread throughout much of the rest of the United States following the Civil War.

Slaves arriving to Louisiana from Africa were often skilled technically and had considerable knowledge of tropical crop production. On plantations, women and men worked in the fields, and in urban areas, such as New Orleans, they worked as domestic servants. Other slaves were skilled laborers, such as blacksmiths, masons, metalworkers, and carpenters, and some were leased out for hire and returned a portion of their earnings to their owners. City authorities responsible for maintaining levees and constructing roads, wharves, and public buildings also purchased the labor of slaves, who might work alongside people who were free. What developed was a relatively flexible situation in which slaves generally had contact with a variety of people and a degree of physical mobility.

Slavery in colonial Louisiana developed along lines similar to French and Spanish societies in the Caribbean and gave rise to cultural patterns that endured, in part, into the American period. These included, first, a tolerance of widespread interracial matings so that large numbers of mulattoes existed alongside pure Africans and frequent manumission meant that a sizable population of free people of color existed alongside slaves. Second, a slave code was instituted that afforded some protection to slave families and permitted manumission; third, a syncretic religious tradition, Voodoo, that drew on Catholicism and traditional African beliefs was created; and fourth, there was a continuation of African language or ethnic communities that facilitated marronage. Fifth, language patterns evolved into a form of widely spoken Creole the General Court of North Carolina denied his petition, and he remained a slave.

1727

In Pennsylvania, Benjamin Franklin, a noted opponent of slavery, established a benevolent association called the Junto. Upon joining the organization, members pledged that they would work toward the abolition of slavery and other forms of inhumanity to man.

1727

In the French colony of Louisiana, Roman Catholic Ursuline nuns began to educate black children in New Orleans.

1729

In Rhode Island, the colonial assembly required slaveowners to post a £100 bond to ensure that their slaves would not become a public charge because of sickness, lameness, or other reasons.

1729

Quaker Ralph Sandyford (Sandiford) published an antislavery tract entitled *A Brief Examination of the Practice of the Times, by the Foregoing and the Present Dispensation.* The work was published in Philadelphia by Benjamin Franklin, who supported efforts to abolish the institution of slavery.

1729

The Society for the Propagation of the Gospel in Foreign Parts was reorganized, and the group changed its name to Dr. Bray's Associates. Thomas Bray had worked since 1701 to support the religious education of blacks in the English colonies.

1730

Slaves constituted 13.9 percent of the total inhabitants of the British North American colonies. Of the 91,021 slaves who lived in the colonies, 17,323 lived in the northern colonies, and 73,698 lived in the southern colonies.

1730

In Virginia, white residents were placed on heightened alert when slave conspiracies were detected in Norfolk and Princess Anne Counties. Governor William Gooch authorized white males in the affected region to carry weapons with them when attending church services. In Williamsburg, Virginia, slaves planned a rebellion as a rumor spread that the former colonial governor, Alexander Spotswood, had returned to the colony from London with authority to free all persons who were baptized as Christians. Authorities in the colony crushed the conspiracy and executed four of the slaves who were believed to be the leaders of the planned rebellion.

1730

On August 15, authorities in South Carolina discovered a plot that involved as many as 200 slaves who were planning to revolt. Part of the plan allegedly included a planned attack upon a church at the mouth of Virginia's Rappahannock River.

1731

The British monarch, George II, issued royal instructions to all colonial governors that specifically prohibited the imposition of any customs duties on slave importations. This action was consistent with British mercantile policy and reflected the Crown's concern with the well-being of the slave-trading enterprise, which was quite lucrative for British merchants.

1732

The Virginia House of Burgesses imposed a 5 percent import duty on all slaves brought into the colony, and this provision remained in effect for many years. In 1759, colonial authorities attempted to raise the duty to 20 percent, but the British Crown thought that amount excessive.

1733

Georgia was founded as the last of the 13 British colonies in North America. Georgia was viewed as an experimental colony in that slavery was not permitted when the colony was founded, but eventually authorities within the colony relaxed that prohibition. The philanthropist James Oglethorpe who founded the colony was a slaveholder himself in the Carolinas, and he also served as the deputy governor of the Royal African Company, which was actively involved in the slave trade.

1733

Because of persistent attacks by Maroons on plantations and farms in South Carolina, Governor Robert Johnson announced a reward of £20 for anyone who assisted in apprehending fugitives who operated as Maroons within the colony.

1733

Slaveowners in several southern colonies feared that slaves might conspire and organize an exodus to Spanish Florida, as Spanish officials in Florida had promised to liberate any slave who escaped from a Protestant colony and sought refuge in Catholic Florida. This call was, in large part, responsible for much of the unrest that rocked South Carolina in 1739.

1735

In New York, the Dutch burgher John Van Zandt whipped a slave to death for the offense of being picked up outside of his quarters after curfew. A coroner's jury heard the case and declared that the slave was killed "by the visitation of God" rather than the actual beating. Van Zandt was found innocent of any criminal wrongdoing.

1736

Virginia planter William Byrd II commented upon the hypocrisy of New England Puritans who criticized slavery but, nonetheless, participated actively in the African slave trade. Byrd commented that "the Saints of New England" were responsible for importing so many Africans into Virginia that "the Colony will some time or other be Confirmed by the name of New Guinea" (Jenkins, 1996).

1737

The Quaker author Benjamin Lay published a radical antislavery work entitled *All Slave-Keepers That Keep the Innocent in Bondage; Apostates*. The controversial tract, which blended biting satire and advocacy of nonviolent resistance, was printed by Benjamin Franklin, who was himself an opponent of slavery.

1738

In Nantucket, Massachusetts, authorities discovered a well-planned conspiracy among Native American peoples to attack the community in the night and kill all the white settlers while sparing the blacks.

1738

The Moravian Church established a mission in Bethlehem, Pennsylvania, specifically to minister to blacks in the region.

1739

The trustees of Georgia Colony received petitions from two groups, one supporting the introduction of slavery into the colony and the other opposing such action. For the time being, the trustees decided it was better to keep slavery out of the colony.

1739

Fugitive slaves who escaped to Spanish Florida and thus liberated themselves built a fort at St. Augustine to protect their own self-earned freedom and to prevent the British from sending expeditions into Spanish Florida to try to recapture fugitives.

1739

On September 9, a slave named Cato led a severe slave revolt along the Stono River in South Carolina in a region where blacks constituted a very large majority of the population. The group of slaves involved reportedly sought to leave South Carolina and travel to St. Augustine, Florida, where Spanish missionaries had reputedly promised liberation. Anyone who tried to prevent the migration was targeted as a victim. Thirty white residents and 44 blacks died during the Stono Rebellion and its eventual

Dominated by slavery and its legacies, the history of South Carolina—as experience and example—has clearly influenced the broader historiographical twists and turns of North American slavery. There are several good reasons why this particular state figures so largely in the literature of involuntary servitude. Most obviously, there is the morbid appeal of the state's unique history of ultraconservative reactionism. Such episodes include the period of states' rights radicalism and the drafting of the ordinance of nullification in 1832, a leading role in the increasingly fanatical and racial justifications and defenses of southern slavery in the 1850s, and finally, the unilateral decision to secede in December 1860, which made the American Civil War an imminent and tragic inevitability. Together with the other great "mountain of conceit," Virginia, South Carolina has been frequently mythologized as a spiritual center of the antebellum southern aristocracy—a sentimental image still profitably employed by the region's tourist industry. Scholars of slavery on their grand tours of great southern cities, finding traces of "unofficial," neglected, and marginalized sources, have perhaps felt impelled to counter such romantic chimera by documenting some of the state's less apocryphal, but equally important, historical moments.

South Carolina was first successfully colonized by migrants from Barbados in 1670. They brought with them their well-established practice of plantation slavery and fundamental constitutions that left no doubt as to the intended status of their imported slave labor. These founding documents gave white freemen "absolute power and authority over Negro Slaves" and determined that, even allowing for a Christian conversion, Negro slaves would remain "in ye same State and Condition"—in other words, lifelong bondage (Wood, 1974). Other forms of enforced labor were tested in the early years of the colony, most notably white indentured servitude and the enslavement of Native Americans. The former group proved both costly and unreliable while the latter option was found to be damaging to trade and seriously threatened the safety of the settlers. By contrast, African slaves allegedly posed fewer problems. Cheaply and easily secured, initially from the Caribbean, Africans were seen as an attractive source of labor because of their invaluable frontier skills. When rice cultivation began to develop in the low country, West African knowledge of the planting and processing of this profitable staple crop further stimulated slave imports and eventually led to the formation of a black majority in the colony.

Outnumbered by slaves from around 1708, the white population began to show clear signs of insecurity and enacted a series of harsh and prohibitive statutes (in particular, the acts of 1712, 1722, and 1740), allegedly "for the better ordering and governing of Negroes and Slaves" (Wood, 1974), which set the general pattern of repressive "white over black" race relations in South Carolina for the next 250 years. Despite being legally confirmed in their chattel status, subject to close social control, and exposed to the constant surveillance and arbitrary justice of white patrollers, black slaves stubbornly refused to submit to the white colonial regime. The 1739 Stono Rebellion and the mass of documentary evidence in Lathan A. Windley's third volume of *Runaway Slave Advertisements* (collected from South Carolina newspapers between the years 1730 and 1790 and published in 1983) demonstrate that point emphatically and irrefutably.

With Charleston prospering as a key area in international and interregional slave-trading systems and as a major exporter of staple crops, the low country dominated South Carolina's economy and society throughout the eighteenth century. Large-scale plantation operations and planter wealth proliferated in this area, as did slave numbers and a constant concern for their "management." Furthermore, it was this region that first gave rise to a clearly distinctive African-American folk culture. From the collision of a plethora of African and European influences and in response to the demands of a new working environment, the black population creatively developed a range of composite or syncretic cultural forms. For example, a new language, Gullah, evolved, and it enabled slaves to communicate both in the language of authority and, more important, in code (Joyner, 1984).

From 1800 onward, as cotton began to take a firm hold in the up-country part of South Carolina, the whole state became both more economically dependent on slave labor and more marked by the rituals and tensions of the master-slave/aristocrat-yeoman social roles. Fearful of black revolt after the Denmark Vesey conspiracy of 1822 and coming under increasing attack from northern abolitionists, the South Carolina elite set about strengthening the Charleston militia and actively deploying the "positive good" proslavery defense pioneered by John C. Calhoun. However, the armor and ideology of the plantocracy failed to win the battles of the Civil War, and thereafter the state had to deal with the difficulties of Reconstruction.

For Further Reading
Dusinberre, William. 1996. *Them Dark Days: Slavery in the American Rice Swamps.* New York: Oxford University Press; Faust, Drew Gilpin. 1982. *James Henry Hammond and the Old South: A Design for Mastery.* Baton Rouge: Louisiana State University Press; Joyner, Charles. 1984. *Down by the Riverside: A South Carolina Slave Community.* Urbana: University of Illinois Press; Wood, Peter H. 1974. *Black Majority: Negroes in Colonial South Carolina from 1670 through the Stono Rebellion.* New York: W. W. Norton.

suppression. This revolt was the most intense of three outbreaks that plagued South Carolina during the year. The other two events took place at Stone Creek and in St. John's Parish in Berkeley County.

1740

Of the 149,664 slaves who lived in the British North American colonies, 23,598 lived in the northern colonies, and 126,066 lived in the southern colonies.

1740

The colonial legislature in South Carolina imposed a harsh slave code that prohibited slaves from raising livestock, provided that any animals previously owned by slaves be forfeited, and set very high penalties for slaves who made "false appeals" to the governor on the grounds that they had been enslaved illegally.

1740

Georgia's colonial governor, James Oglethorpe, mounted a limited incursion into Spanish Florida and captured Forts Picolata and San Francisco de Pupo, but his small force was eventually pushed out of the area. The Spanish forces were assisted by Seminole Indians and nearly 200 fugitive slaves who had escaped to Florida and found refuge there.

1740

An insurrectionary panic swept New York City when it was believed that slaves in the city had poisoned the water supply in an effort to kill their masters and win their freedom.

1740

In January, in response to concerns raised by the Stono Rebellion the previous year, 50 blacks were put to death by hanging when there were rumors of another slave conspiracy in Charleston, South Carolina.

1741

After a series of arsonist acts in New York City in February, March, and April, wild rumors spread that there was a unified conspiracy between slaves and poor whites to either burn or seize control of the city. Though the evidence of such a plot was slight, a general hysteria developed, and 18 blacks were hanged, 11 were burned alive at the stake, and 70 were banished from the colony. The white backlash against slaves stemmed from their presence in the city rather than from any hard evidence of their connection with a criminal conspiracy.

1742

Spanish officials in Florida mounted an invasion of Georgia Colony in retaliation for Oglethorpe's raid in 1740. The Spanish troops that fought in Georgia included a regiment of black troops commanded by black officers.

1742

On April 15, the General Court of Massachusetts granted a divorce to a slave named Boston. Boston had charged that his wife Hagar had had an adulterous affair with a white man and had given birth to a mulatto child.

1743

In New Jersey Colony, John Woolman, an itinerant Quaker clergyman, preached a series of sermons that called for an end to slavery and urged greater consideration of racial equality. Woolman published his ideas in 1754 and carried his antislavery message to Quaker meetings in several colonies.

Two slaves being burned at the stake in New York City in 1741 as a result of rumors of a conspiracy between slaves and poor whites. In the general hysteria among whites, 11 other slaves were burned and 18 hanged. (Archive Photos)

1743

In Charleston, South Carolina, Mr. Garden's School was established. This institution was created to teach black youth in the city, and the school was supported by both the free black and the white residents of Charleston. In the same year, another school, one specifically designed to train black missionaries, was established in Charleston by the Society for the Propagation of the Gospel in Foreign Parts (now known as Dr. Bray's Associates).

1744

The colonial assembly in Virginia revised a 1705 law regarding the rights of blacks to serve as witnesses in court proceedings. The amended statute entitled "any free Negro, mulatto, or Indian being a Christian" (Jenkins, 1996) the right to serve as a witness in criminal or civil suits involving another Negro, mulatto, or Indian.

1744

The Anglican missionary Samuel Thomas established a school for free blacks in South Carolina.

1745

Thomas Ashley published *A New General Collection of Voyages and Travels* in which he responded to those proslavery supporters who said that slavery was beneficial to the African. Ashley challenged that if slavery were indeed beneficial, then it would follow that Africans should be allowed to choose for themselves whether or not they wanted to be enslaved.

1746

Lucy Terry, a slave poet, wrote "Bars Fight," a commemorative poem that is considered to be one of the best accounts of an Indian massacre that occurred in Deerfield, Massachusetts. Terry, who is generally considered to be the first black poet in America, later tried unsuccessfully to convince the board of trustees at Williams College to admit her son to that school.

1746

In New Jersey, the colonial assembly met at Perth Amboy and authorized John Hamilton, the commander of the colonial militia, to raise a regiment of 500 free blacks and Native Americans to be used as soldiers against the French in Canada.

1747

The South Carolina colonial assembly thanked black slaves for demonstrating "great faithfulness and courage in repelling attacks of His Majesty's enemies" (Jenkins, 1996). The assembly also made cautious provision for using black troops in times of dire emergency but warned that black recruits should never constitute more than one-third of the colony's troop strength.

1748

The Virginia Militia Act became law within the colony of Virginia. According to this measure, free blacks and Native Americans were prohibited from carrying weapons. During the years of the American Revolution this provision was revised so that free blacks could serve as soldiers in the Continental army.

1749

On October 26, the trustees of Georgia Colony repealed their initial prohibition against the importation of slaves into the colony. This measure was later approved by the British Parliament, which amounted to an effectual endorsement by Parliament of slavery within the British colonies in North America. The same measure also attempted to protect slaves from being hired out and from cruel treatment that might be imposed upon them. Legislation within Georgia Colony stipulated that four slaves could be kept in the colony for every white servant. [See Document 23.]

1750

Estimated imports of slaves into the British North American colonies was 7,500 per year. The slave population was estimated to be 236,420, with 206,198 living in the southern colonies and 30,222 living in the northern colonies. Although slaves composed roughly 20 percent of the population of all colonies combined, they formed more than 40 percent of the population of Virginia Colony.

1750

In Philadelphia, Anthony Benezet and a group of his Quaker brethren established an evening school for free blacks in the city.

1750

By this date, the French had established five colonial villages in the western territory that eventually became the state of Illinois. The population in this region was indeed sparse, but the 1,100 white settlers in the five communities owned 300 black slaves and 60 Native American slaves. Although the Northwest Ordinance of 1787 would later prohibit slavery in this region and Illinois would eventually join the Union as a free state in 1818, a strong proslavery element remained active in some of the region's older French communities.

1750

The British Parliament enacted a modification to its slave trade policies that had far-reaching implications for the enterprise. When Parliament had ended the Royal African Company's monopoly on the trade in 1698, lawmakers had opened the enterprise to other English corporations (syndicates) that were willing to pay a set duty in order to participate in the trade. The 1750 modification allowed private individuals to engage in the slave trade as well, provided

A slave revolt on board ship. Slave rebellions, both on the high seas and on land, were a constant fear of whites. (Corbis-Bettmann)

they paid duty to the Royal African Company for the maintenance of the West African forts and factories. As a result, more people became involved in the African slave trade and the business became more notorious just as increased calls to end the trade were coming from many British colonists.

1750

In Framingham, Massachusetts, Crispus Attucks escaped from his master, Deacon William Browne, in the fall. Attucks would later become a heroic figure for his role in the Boston Massacre of 1770.

1751

Benjamin Franklin, who was an opponent of slavery, wrote a pamphlet entitled *Observations concerning the Increase of Mankind and the Peopling of Countries* in which he argued that slave labor represented one of the most inefficient forms of production that was used in the world.

⤳ TRIANGULAR TRADE ⤳

In the triangular trade, a ship would depart from Newport, Rhode Island, for the west coast of Africa with New England rum. In Africa, most of the rum would be sold, and slaves would be purchased; a small amount of the rum would be used as currency to purchase slaves from tribal chiefs in the African interior. The slave-castle governors of the foreign powers of England, France, Holland, Portugal, and Denmark obtained the slaves from tribal chieftains and other brokers and housed the slaves in the castles until they were shipped abroad. The slaves would be chained down on small packed boats and taken to the West Indies for sale. The voyage was rough, and many slaves died en route from the terrible conditions. In the West Indies, the slaves would be sold for large sums of money, and the sugar needed for molasses and rum production would be purchased; the sugar would then be taken to New England.

In Newport, there were some 22 stills that converted sugar into rum as early as 1730. In 1764, there were more than 30 distilling houses in Rhode Island. In the 1770s, some 184 vessels in Rhode Island were involved in the slave trade—surpassed in quantity in the colonies only by South Carolina. Most owners never set foot on their ships and had no physical contact with the slaves. The owners hired slaver captains to organize the ships and conduct price negotiations with the resident governors in Africa.

For example, two New England merchants, Aaron Lopez and his father-in-law, Jacob Rivera of Newport, were active in sending ships to Africa with rum and other goods in exchange for slaves. They sent their first ship, the *Grayhound,* in 1761 to Africa to buy slaves and sell them in the Caribbean. Lopez sent at least 18 ships to Africa to purchase slaves, and after Lopez had terminated his activities in this area in about 1774 or 1775, Rivera continued to send ships to Africa. Lopez owned at least 26 ships and was a major, if not the foremost, merchant in Newport. The clergyman Ezra Stiles, first president of Yale University, praised Lopez by describing him as "a Merchant of the first Eminence; for Honor and Extent of Commerce probably surpassed by no Merchant in America" (Marcus, 1970). A ship of slaves could yield between £1,500 and £2,000, making the slave trade a lucrative business. The ship owners had virtually no contact with their ships or the slaves, and the slave trade was but one component of this monetary transaction connected with the triangular trade.

—*Yitzchak Kerem*

For Further Reading
Birmingham, Stephen. 1971. *The Grandees, America's Sephardic Elite.* New York: Harper and Row; Chyet, Stanley F. 1962–1963. "Aaron Lopez: A Study in Buenafama." *American Jewish Historical Quarterly* 52: 295–309; Marcus, Jacob R. 1970. *The Colonial American Jew 1492–1776.* Detroit: Wayne State University Press.

1751

The Jesuits introduced the cultivation of sugarcane into the French colony of Louisiana. The large-scale cultivation of that commodity which ensued necessitated a more massive importation of slaves into the region, just as "the sugar revolution" of the previous century had caused enormous numbers of slaves to be taken to Brazil and the islands of the West Indies.

1752

Maryland became the first of the English colonies to enact a manumission statute.

1752

There were 18 slaves on the estate of Mount Vernon in Virginia when George Washington inherited the property in July upon the death of his half brother. During Washington's ownership of the estate, the number of slaves grew to 200. Washington was concerned with the physical well-being of his slaves, but he was never certain about his willingness to grant them freedom or to do without their services. Upon Washington's death in 1799, he did manumit his slaves in his final testament.

1753

Phillis Wheatley, the future child prodigy poet, was born in West Africa.

1754

In Philadelphia, John Woolman published *Some Considerations on the Keeping of Negroes: Recommended to the Professors of Christianity of Every Denomination,* a tract designed to challenge his fellow Quakers to manumit their slaves on moral grounds. Woolman was one of

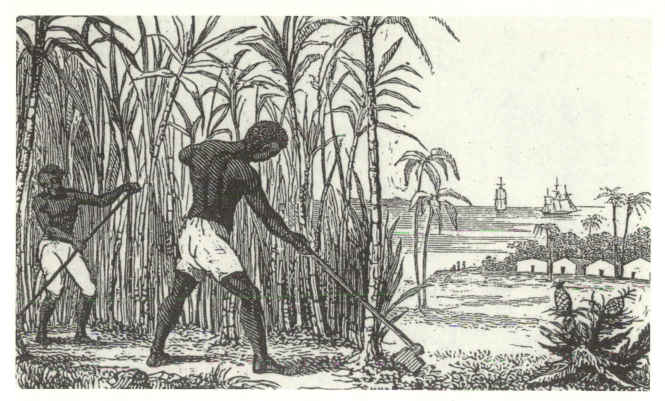

Slaves cultivating sugarcane in Louisiana. (Library of Congress)

the most influential Quaker abolitionists of the eighteenth century. He published a second part of the tract in 1762.

1754
In Baltimore, Maryland, a 22-year-old free black named Benjamin Banneker became the first person in the English North American colonies to build a clock. Though Banneker had never before seen a clock, the device he created worked accurately for 20 years.

1754
In Charleston, South Carolina, two female slaves belonging to an owner named Croft were burned alive because they had burned some of the buildings on the owner's estate.

1755
Having previously made a denominational stand against the practice of slavery, American Quakers (Society of Friends) excluded from their denomination all members who continued to import slaves.

1755
Two slaves belonging to John Codman of Charlestown, Massachusetts, were executed after they conspired and poisoned their owner. The slaves, Mark and Phillis, had learned that they were to be freed upon the death of Codman and had decided to expedite the date of their liberation. Authorities tried to set an example to other slaves with swift and certain punishment. Mark was hanged and disemboweled while Phillis was burned to death.

1755
The colonial assembly in Georgia enacted statutes that made slavery legal in the colony.

1756
The population of Virginia Colony was estimated to have reached 250,000, of which 40 percent consisted of slaves.

1757
The English writer Edmund Burke wrote *An Account of the European Settlements in America* (which was published in 1760). In this work, Burke encouraged methods of increasing colonial productivity and warned of the danger of possible slave insurrections if steps were not taken to improve the conditions of slaves in the colonies.

A slave coffle crossing the Rapidan River on their way to be sold. (New-York Historical Society)

1758

In Mecklenburg, Virginia, William Byrd II established the Bluestone African Baptist Church on his plantation located near the Bluestone River.

1758

Antislavery supporter Anthony Benezet and other Pennsylvania Quakers began meeting yearly to discuss and plan strategies for the abolition crusade. The group formed the basis of the Society for the Relief of Free Negroes Unlawfully Held in Bondage that was organized in Philadelphia in April 1775.

1760

The slave trade was banned completely in South Carolina by the colonial assembly, but the British Crown disallowed the measure because it conflicted with British mercantile interests.

1760

In Boston, Briton Hammon published a pamphlet entitled *A Narrative of the Uncommon Sufferings and Surprising Deliverance of Briton Hammon, a Negro Man*. This work is considered to be the first prose work to be published by a black author in America.

1760

On February 14, Richard Allen, who would eventually become a religious leader and founder of the African Methodist Episcopal Church, was born a slave in Philadelphia.

1760

On December 25, the black poet Jupiter Hammon published *Salvation by Christ with Penitential Cries* in New York City.

1761

The colony of Virginia tried to impose an importation duty of 20 percent on slaves who were brought into the colony, but the British Crown did not allow this action to stand. Such a measure was viewed by the British government as an excessive tax that was contrary to the economic interests of the British mercantile system.

1761

The Society of Friends (Quakers) voted to exclude slave traders from church membership, but many Quakers continued to be slaveowners.

1761

An eight-year-old African child named Phillis Wheatley arrived in Boston, Massachusetts, as a slave. She became known as a poet of the late-colonial period.

1762

James Derham, who was recognized as the first black physician in America, was born a slave in Philadelphia. In the same year, Anthony Benezet, a Pennsylvania Quaker who was an opponent of slavery, published *A Short Account of That Part of Africa Inhabited by the Negroes*. Although the work was ostensibly a study of African life and culture, Benezet also included a clear antislavery message.

1763

In Massachusetts, free blacks formed a significant social group as they constituted 2.2 percent of the colony's inhabitants. Out of a total population of 235,810 residents, there were 5,214 free blacks in Massachusetts.

1764

After the British Parliament's passage of the Sugar Act, New England merchants and slave-ship captains protested the increase in the prices of sugar and molasses, declaring these items to be indispensable to the slave trade, which they described as "vital commerce" for the region. A group of merchants published a pamphlet entitled *A Statement of the Massachusetts Trade and Fisheries* in which they protested that the increased duties on such essential commodities might bring economic disaster to the region. In the same year, James Otis published *The Rights of the British Colonies Asserted and Proved* to protest Parliament's imposing the Sugar Act. Otis maintained that the British action represented "taxation without representation," and he further claimed that slaves had a right to be free. Sensing an inconsistency between coercive action and liberalism, Otis saw a connection between the infringement upon colonists' liberties by the British and the institu-

Anthony Benezet, a Quaker antislavery supporter shown here teaching black children, helped establish a school for blacks in Philadelphia and left the school an endowment at his death in 1783. (The Granger Collection)

tion of slavery, and he criticized slavery as an evil that "threatens one day to reduce both Europe and America to the ignorance and barbarity of the darkest ages" (Jenkins, 1996).

1765

The population of the British North American colonies was estimated to be 1,750,000, and slaves constituted approximately 20 percent of the total.

1766

Negro Tom, one of George Washington's slaves at Mount Vernon, was punished for running away. Washington ordered that the unruly slave be sold to the West Indies for a hogshead of rum and other goods, including molasses, limes, tamarinds, sweetmeats, and spirits. Washington ordered the ship's captain who carried Tom away to keep the slave chained until the ship was at sea.

1766

On November 6, a group of Massachusetts slaves tried to initiate court action against their owners by citing a violation of trespass laws; the colonial courts did not support the claim.

1767

"A Poem by Phyillis, a Negro Girl, on the Death of Reverend Whitefield" was written by Phillis

RUN away from the subscriber in *Albemarle*, a Mulatto slave called *Sandy*, about 35 years of age, his stature is rather low, inclining to corpulence, and his complexion light; he is a shoemaker by trade, in which he uses his left hand principally, can do coarse carpenters work, and is something of a horse jockey; he is greatly addicted to drink, and when drunk is insolent and disorderly, in his conversation he swears much, and in his behaviour is artful and knavish. He took with him a white horse, much scarred with traces, of which it is expected he will endeavour to dispose; he also carried his shoemakers tools, and will probably endeavour to get employment that way. Whoever conveys the said slave to me, in *Albemarle*, shall have 40 s. reward, if taken up within the county, 4 l. if elsewhere within the colony, and 10 l. if in any other colony. from
THOMAS JEFFERSON.

An advertisement placed by Thomas Jefferson in the September 14, 1769, Virginia Gazette seeking the return of his runaway slave. (Virginia Historical Society)

Wheatley, a 14-year-old slave girl in Boston. The poem was published in 1770, and Wheatley was soon recognized internationally as a prodigy.

1769

Thomas Jefferson was elected at the age of 26 to the Virginia House of Burgesses. His first action as an elected official was to lead an unsuccessful attempt to pass a bill that would emancipate slaves within the colony of Virginia.

1770

The population of the British North American colonies was estimated at 2,312,000, which included 462,000 slaves, approximately 20 percent of the colonial population.

1770

In Virginia, George Washington was one of several planters to sign a petition circulated by the Association for the Counteraction of Various Acts of Oppression on the Part of Great Britain. Washington and the others who signed promised not to purchase slaves who had not been in North America for at least one year. This measure was designed to create economic distress for the British government by not supporting the African slave trade.

1770

The colonial assembly in Rhode Island enacted a statute that prohibited the further introduction of slaves into the colony.

1770

The colonial assembly in Massachusetts debated a proposed bill that would have prohibited the further introduction of slaves into the colony, but legislators defeated the measure. On March 5, Crispus Attucks, a slave who had escaped from his owner in 1750, was the first to fall in the Boston Massacre.

1770

On June 28, Anthony Benezet led a successful campaign among the Quakers to establish a school for blacks in Philadelphia. When Benezet died in 1784, he left his personal fortune to endow the school, known as Binoxide House.

1771

The Massachusetts colonial assembly approved of a resolution calling for an end to the importation of Africans as slaves in the colony, but the colonial governor, Thomas Hutchinson, refused to support the measure.

1771

For the first time in many years, the average annual number of Africans imported as slaves into the American colonies declined. This statistical change reflected the growing opposition to the slave trade by many people in the British colonies.

1771

The colonial assembly in Connecticut enacted a statute that prohibited the African slave trade within the colony.

1772

In Virginia, the colonial House of Burgesses placed a substantial tariff on slave imports in an effort to curtail the practice within the colony. Officials in Virginia requested that the British government support this action against "a Trade of great Inhumanity" (Jenkins, 1996), but the Crown did not allow the action to stand because it was contrary to the economic interests of the British mercantile system. The House of Burgesses enacted 33 different measures that called for an end to the slave trade, primarily in defiance of Parliament's passage of the Townshend Acts in 1767 rather than as sincere support for abolishing the slave trade upon moral grounds.

1772

In Boston, the Reverend Isaac Skillman published *Oration upon the Beauties of Liberty.* Skillman used a philosophical natural rights argument in this pamphlet to support the slaves' right to rebellion, and he called for an immediate end of slavery in the British colonies.

1772

In a landmark judicial ruling in May, the decision of Chief Justice Lord Mansfield (William Murray, first earl of Mansfield) in the case of *Knowles v. Somersett* abolished slavery in England. Mansfield declared: "The air of England has long been too pure for a slave, and every man is free who breathes it. Every man who comes to England is entitled to the protection of English law, whatever oppression he may heretofore have suffered, and whatever may be the color of his skin." [See Document 26.]

1773

The idea of colonizing West Africa with free blacks was first discussed and promoted publicly by Ezra Stiles, the president of Yale College, and Samuel Hopkins, a Congregational minister. The idea of colonization would continue to be popular, and in the early-nineteenth century, the American Colonization Society supported such a program, but some white abolitionists and many free blacks were opposed to this strategy. Stiles and Hopkins also sent a circular to many New England churches urging their opposition to the slave trade.

1773

The slave Phillis Wheatley published her first book of poetry, *Poems on Various Subjects, Religious and Moral.* It was the second book to be published by an American woman. Wheatley was manumitted shortly after the publication of the book of verse.

1773

In Savannah, Georgia, David George, George Lisle, and Andrew Bryan established the first Negro Baptist Church in the colony. Another black church was established in Silver Bluff, South Carolina, in the same year.

1773

In Philadelphia, Dr. Benjamin Rush published *An Address to the Inhabitants of the British Settlements on the Slavery of the Negroes in America.* This tract was perhaps the most significant

Dr. Benjamin Rush (1746–1816) in 1773 published what is perhaps the most important American antislavery tract of the eighteenth century. (Library of Congress)

expression of the American antislavery position to be published in the eighteenth century.

1773

Residents of Leicester, Massachusetts, urged their elected representatives to enact legislation against slavery and the slave trade. On January 6, a group of slaves in Massachusetts petitioned the colonial legislature for their freedom—during the years of the American Revolution, eight petitions of this type were presented to the legislature of Massachusetts. Much of why the slaves' sought liberation from their enslavement in the colonies was inspired by the 1772 *Somersett* case, which had effectively ended slavery in England. [See Documents 26 and 27.]

1774

During the First Continental Congress Thomas Jefferson and Benjamin Franklin convinced delegates to approve a measure that called for an end to the slave trade effective December 1, 1775, and sought to impose economic sanctions upon those countries that continued to participate thereafter in the slave trade. These pledges were included in the Articles of Association that were adopted by the Continental Congress. In the same year, Thomas Jefferson wrote *A Summary View of the Rights of British America,* his

Broadside dated July 25, 1774, Savannah, Georgia. At the top a sale of African slaves is advertised; the last item seeks the return of runaway slaves. (Library of Congress)

first published work. In the pamphlet, Jefferson argued that the British colonists supported the abolition of slavery, writing that "the abolition of slavery is the great object of desire in those colonies where it was unhappily introduced," but he also cautioned that it would first be necessary "to exclude all further importations from Africa."

1774

After a slave conspiracy was discovered in Boston, Abigail Adams wrote to her husband John, who was attending the Continental Congress, and discussed the matter: "I wish most sincerely there was not a slave in the province. It always appeared a most iniquitous scheme to me—fight ourselfs for what we are daily robbing and plundering from those who have as good a right to freedom as we have" (Jenkins, 1996).

1774

In Philadelphia, the Society of Friends (Quakers) adopted rules at the society's annual meeting that prohibited Quakers from buying or selling any additional slaves. Those Quakers who owned slaves were advised that they should prepare their slaves for emancipation.

1774

The colonial legislatures of Rhode Island and Connecticut forbade the continuation of slave imports into each colony. The Rhode Island legislation declared that any new slave who was brought into the colony would be made free, but the legislation did not emancipate the slaves who were already laboring in the colony.

1774

Delegates met at a convention in New Berne, North Carolina, for the purpose of organizing a provincial congress. It was the belief of the delegates who gathered that the colonies should immediately end the importation of African slaves.

1774

In St. Andrews Parish, Georgia, a slave revolt resulted in the death of four white colonists and the injury of three others. The two slaves who led the revolt were punished by being burned to death.

1774

On December 1, George Washington chaired a meeting at which delegates from several Virginia counties approved of the Fairfax Resolves, authored by George Mason, which condemned the slave trade. Resolution number 17 stated, "It is the opinion of this meeting that during our present difficulties and distress, no slaves ought to be imported into any of the British colonies on this continent; and we take this opportunity of declaring our most earnest wishes to see an entire stop forever put to such a wicked, cruel and unnatural trade" (Jenkins, 1996). As a result of this action, the Virginia Association suspended further importation of slaves into the colony and threatened a boycott of all English exports.

1775

On the Natural Variety of Mankind (Humani Varietate nativa) was published in Germany by Johan Friedrich Blumenback. This work was the first of its kind to challenge the prevailing racist assumptions that viewed blacks as racially inferior and thus prone to be enslaved by superior peoples. Blumenback's work challenged the ideas of "enlightened" thinkers such as François-Marie Arouet Voltaire, David Hume, and Carl von Linné who had argued that blacks were somehow related to apes. Blumenback proved that both the skulls of blacks and Europeans and the brain size of each were similar.

1775

Sally Hemings, a two-year-old child, arrived as a slave at Monticello, Thomas Jefferson's home in Virginia.

1775

The colonial assembly in Delaware approved a measure that would have prohibited the introduction of any additional slaves into the colony, but Governor John McKinly vetoed the bill.

1775

Thomas Paine published his first antislavery essay, "African Slavery in America," in the *Pennsylvania Journal*. Paine signed the article "Humanus" and argued that slavery should be abolished and that land and other economic opportunities should be offered to freed slaves.

1775

On April 14, a group of Quakers in Philadelphia organized the Society for the Relief of Free Negroes Unlawfully Held in Bondage, the first secular antislavery society in the American colonies. Benjamin Franklin and Benjamin Rush were among the founding members of this group. The society suspended its operations during the years of the American Revolution, but it was reorganized in 1787.

1775

The American Revolution began on April 14 when shots were fired at Lexington and Concord in Massachusetts. Free blacks were among the men who took part in these opening battles for American freedom.

1775

On May 10, black soldier-patriots Lemuel Haynes, Primas Black, and Epheram Blackman fought with Ethan Allen and the Green Mountain Boys during the capture of Fort Ticonderoga, generally considered to be the first aggressive action taken by American forces during the American Revolution.

1775

On June 17, during the Battle of Bunker Hill, several black soldier-patriots, including Peter Salem and Salem Poor, fought and distinguished themselves.

1775

General Horatio Gates, in his capacity as adjutant general of the Continental Army, issued a general order on July 10 that banned free blacks from serving in the Continental army.

1775

In a decision made by the Council of General Officers on October 8, it was determined that neither slaves nor free blacks would be allowed to fight in the Continental army.

1775

On October 23, the Second Continental Congress specifically prohibited blacks from joining the American Continental army.

1775

In an effort to raise a local Loyalist army, John Murray, fourth earl of Dunmore, the British governor of Virginia Colony, promised on November 14 to free any male slaves who deserted their plantations or farms and joined British forces in an effort to suppress the rebellion that had been begun by the American patriot forces. Approximately 800 Virginia slaves accepted Dunmore's invitation and joined the king's forces, but Dunmore lost the support of many loyalist planters by initiating this policy.

1775

A general order issued on November 12 by General George Washington, commander of the Continental army, prohibited all recruiting officers from enlisting blacks, both slave and free, into the service of that army.

1775

On December 31, apparently alarmed by the action taken by John Murray, fourth earl of Dunmore, George Washington, who had originally opposed the use of black troops, modified his initial position on the matter and ordered his recruiting officers to enlist any free blacks who offered their services to the Continental cause; Washington continued to resist the use of slaves as soldiers.

SOCIETY FOR THE RELIEF OF FREE NEGROES UNLAWFULLY HELD IN BONDAGE

The Society for the Relief of Free Negroes Unlawfully Held in Bondage was the first secular antislavery organization in the United States. Led by Philadelphia area Quakers such as Anthony Benezet, who had met yearly as early as 1758, the society was organized in April 1775 when twenty-four men, including sixteen Quakers, met at the Sun Tavern on Second Street in Philadelphia to discuss the plight of an Indian mother who claimed that in the eyes of the law, she and her four children were free. Believing that the egalitarian and humanitarian principles of the Quakers ought to be extended to others, the men attempted to remedy the situation by organizing and denouncing slavery both as an injustice to the slave and as a temptation to sin for the owner.

The American Revolution resulted in the suspension of meetings until 1784, when the society attempted to build a broader base of support. Although the impetus for reorganizing was a situation involving two free black men accused of being runaway slaves, reluctance on the part of many Quakers to give up their slaves and the concern that Quaker pacifism might discredit the society's antislavery testimony led to a new rationale for abolishing slavery. Relying less on moral arguments, the society now used the philosophy of the Revolution, which allowed the members to portray slavery as a contradiction of American political values. Slavery, they argued, not only violated the law of God, but in an age of liberation and enlightenment, it undermined the rights of man. Accordingly, during its April 23, 1787, meeting, the society revised its constitution, elected Benjamin Franklin honorary president, and renamed itself the Pennsylvania Society for Promoting the Abolition of Slavery, for the Relief of Free Negroes Unlawfully Held in Bondage, and for Improving the Condition of the African Race. Strengthened, the society's membership now included non-Quakers and such well-known individuals as Thomas Paine, John Jay, Noah Webster, and Dr. Benjamin Rush.

Pursuing a more pragmatic agenda, the society became a model for similar organizations in other states, such as New York. Toward the end of the eighteenth century, the Pennsylvania Abolition Society mounted a more aggressive attack against the slave trade and slavery itself and sought to improve the existing social order and to bring about justice by more rigorously enforcing existing laws. As part of its efforts, the society promoted the development of other societies, sent petitions to Congress, publicized state laws regarding slavery, printed and distributed antislavery literature, corresponded with prominent antislavery leaders in England and France, and began a policy of assisting free blacks and people illegally held in bondage. In addition to forbidding members to own slaves and backing the antislavery movement, the society also sought to improve the general social and economic conditions of blacks.

Although the Society for the Relief of Free Negroes Unlawfully Held in Bondage evolved into an effective state society, its importance in the antislavery movement lies in the way early Quakers initiated antislavery thought and action and attempted to curtail the growth of slavery in colonial America. As such, the society contributed to the development and success of later abolitionist groups.

—*Mark L. Kamrath*

For Further Reading
Bumbrey, Jeffrey Nordlinger. 1976. "Historical Sketch of the Pennsylvania Abolition Society." In *A Guide to the Microfilm Publication of the Papers of the Pennsylvania Historical Society*. Philadelphia: Pennsylvania Abolition Society and Historical Society of Pennsylvania; Dumond, Dwight Lowell. 1961. *Antislavery: The Crusade for Freedom in America*. Ann Arbor: University of Michigan Press; Needles, Edward. 1848. *An Historical Memoir of the Pennsylvania Society, for Promoting the Abolition of Slavery; Relief for Free Negroes Unlawfully Held in Bondage, and for Improving the Condition of the African Race. Compiled from the Minutes of the Society and Other Official Documents*. Philadelphia: Pennsylvania Abolition Society; Turner, Edward Raymond. 1912. "The First Abolition Society in the United States." *Pennsylvania Magazine of History and Biography*. 36: 92–109.

The Reverend Lemuel Haynes (1753–1833), noted Revolutionary War veteran and abolitionist, shown here in the pulpit in a nineteenth-century tray painting. (The Granger Collection)

1776

The marquis de Lafayette praised the efforts of black troops for their role in covering Washington's retreat to Long Island. In the same year, Thomas Jefferson drafted a plan proposing a colonization plan to return former slaves to Africa, and the Reverend Samuel Hopkins, a Congregational minister in Newport, Rhode Island, published an antislavery tract entitled *A Dialogue Concerning the Slavery of the Africans.* Hopkins forwarded a copy of his work to the Second Continental Congress in the hope that his argument might help to sway the officials there to abolish slavery within the colonies.

1776

In Delaware, a new constitution was drafted, and it included a provision that prohibited the further importation of slaves into the region.

1776

In Philadelphia, the Society of Friends (Quak-ers) approved of a measure at their annual meeting that urged other Quakers to shun fellow Quakers who refused to manumit their slaves.

1776

In Williamsburg, Virginia, a group of free blacks organized the African Baptist Church.

1776

The Second Continental Congress gave its approval on January 16 to George Washington's policy of accepting enlistments from free blacks who wished to join the Continental army.

1776

By resolution on April 9, the Second Continental Congress called for an eventual end to the importation of slaves from Africa. During the course of the American Revolution, it is estimated that 5,000 slaves supported the American forces in their efforts against the British.

An African American soldier, Peter Salem, at the Battle of Bunker Hill shoots British Major Pitcairn, who had shed the first blood at the earlier Battle of Lexington. (Corbis-Bettmann)

1776

The Declaration of Independence, penned by Thomas Jefferson while serving as a delegate to the Second Continental Congress, was adopted on July 4. Jefferson was swayed by the protest of delegates from South Carolina and Georgia and finally deleted lines critical of the slave trade and denouncing slavery from the final draft of the declaration. The deleted passage stated that King George III encouraged "cruel war against human nature itself, violating its most sacred rights of life and liberty in the persons of a distant people who never offended him, captivating and carrying them into slavery in another hemisphere" (Jenkins, 1996).

1776

In December, two black soldiers, Prince Whipple and Oliver Cromwell, took part in Washington's crossing of the Delaware River in order to attack British forces and their Hessian mercenaries at Trenton, New Jersey.

1777

In North Carolina, the assembly readopted an older colonial statute that had prohibited the manumission of slaves by private citizens except for cases of meritorious service that were documented and verified by a local magistrate. It was the intention of North Carolina officials to make "the evil and pernicious practice of freeing slaves" more difficult.

1777

Schools in the colony/state of New Jersey began to segregate black and white students.

1777

On July 2, Vermont's state constitution abolished slavery within its borders. Vermont had declared itself to be an independent state on January 16, 1777, but it was not yet an official part of the United States. Therefore, Pennsylvania's action against slavery in 1780 is generally considered to be the first time that a state abolished the institution of slavery in the United States.

1778

In Maryland, Quakers decided that the continued ownership of slaves by fellow Quakers after the Society of Friends had recommended manumission was a moral offense that warranted disownment.

1778

Upon the motion of Thomas Jefferson, the House of Burgesses enacted a statute that prohibited the importation of additional slaves into Virginia.

1778

In an unprecedented act made necessary by wartime exigencies, a black battalion of 300 slaves was formed in Rhode Island in February after they had been promised freedom upon the successful conclusion of the war. This group eventually engaged in battle and was responsible for killing 1,000 Hessian mercenaries. The same group eventually took part in the battle at Ponts Bridge in New York State.

1779

In the Continental Congress, South Carolina representative Henry Laurens proposed that 3,000 slaves be used as soldiers in the southern colonies. The proposal was contested by many of the southern representatives, but Alexander Hamilton of New York supported the idea. Hamilton stated, "I have not the least doubt that the Negroes will make very excellent soldiers . . . for their natural faculties are as good as ours" (Jenkins, 1996). Although the Continental Congress approved the recommendation, the proposal was rejected by the South Carolina legislature.

1779

On November 12, the New Hampshire colonial assembly received a petition from 20 slaves urging that body to abolish slavery. The petition requesting emancipation argued that "the God of nature gave them life and freedom upon the terms of most perfect equality with other men; that freedom is an inherent right of the human species, not to be surrendered but by consent" (Jenkins, 1996).

1780

It was estimated that there were 575,420 slaves in the United States, with 56,796 in the northern states and 518,624 in the southern states.

1780

There were rumors of a slave conspiracy in and around the city of Albany, New York, and a combined force of slaves and a few white associates did plot and burn the Half-Moon Settlement near that city.

1780

In Newport, Rhode Island, Newport Gardner and his associates formed the African Union Society, which was a mutual benefit organization designed to assist free blacks in the region. In 1803, the society merged with the African Benevolent Society.

1780

On February 10, Paul Cuffe, a free black merchant, led a group of seven free blacks in Dartmouth, Massachusetts, in petitioning against the Continental Congress for imposing taxation without representation because they were denied the benefits of citizenship.

1780

On March 1, Pennsylvania's legislature passed a measure aimed at the gradual abolition of slavery within the state's borders. According to this legislation, no child born after its enactment would be a slave in the state of Pennsylvania, and children who were born to slaves after 1780 would be considered to be bond servants until they reached the age of 21. With this action, Pennsylvania effectively became the first state to abolish slavery (Vermont had not yet become a state when action was taken there in 1777).

1780

In Botecourt County, Virginia, a slave named Jack was hanged in April because he had threatened to lead a group of slaves to the British army of Lord Cornwallis in an effort to escape.

1781

On July 20, shortly after the defeat of British General Charles Cornwallis at Yorktown, Virginia, there were reports of Maroon attacks upon plantations in the region, and a report of a planned slave uprising near Williamsburg surfaced when slaves burned several buildings there, including the capitol. One white colonist was killed in the incident.

1782

Thomas Jefferson completed his *Notes on Virginia* (published in 1785) in which he presented a mixed view of slavery and the role of blacks in society. Jefferson wrote that "the whole commerce between master and slave is a perpetual exercise of the most boisterous passions," but he later penned the strange assessment that blacks' "griefs are transient." [See Document 31.] At the time, Virginia's slave population was estimated to be 260,000. In the same year, as a result of Thomas Jefferson's insistence, the Virginia legislature enacted a measure making emancipation of slaves by private citizens through manumission legal in the state. According to this measure it was permissible for one "by last will and testament or other instrument in writing sealed and witnessed, to emancipate and set free his slaves" (Jenkins, 1996). It is ironic that when Jefferson died in 1826 he freed some, but not all, of the slaves that he had held in bondage.

1782

The state legislature of Rhode Island freed the slave Quaco Honeyman because of services he had rendered as a spy during the American Revolution.

1782

British ships carried off an estimated 5,000 slaves when they sailed from Savannah, Georgia. Many of these "black loyalists" would eventually settle in the Canadian provinces of New Brunswick and Nova Scotia. The following year, British ships left the New York City area carrying 3,000 slaves, and other ships left Charleston, South Carolina, transporting 6,500 slaves out of the region.

1782

In the state of Massachusetts the legislature received a petition from a 70-year-old slave woman named Belinda requesting freedom and protection for herself and her daughter from their owner. This petition seeking freedom from slavery is believed to be the first to be filed by a slave in the United States of America.

1783

By the end of the American Revolution, at least 10,000 blacks had served in the Continental armies. Nearly half of these served as regular soldiers.

1783

Diplomats in Paris signed the Treaty of Paris, which officially ended the American Revolution. Article 7 of the treaty included a provision in which the British government agreed to return all slaves that had been taken from their American owners. The British government did not comply with this provision.

1783

Shortly before his death in 1784, Anthony Benezet published *A Serious Address to the Rulers of America*. In this antislavery pamphlet, Benezet chided the American people for having presented the American Revolution as a struggle against British tyranny and slavery while keeping thousands of people in bondage as slaves in a land that claimed to love liberty.

1783

Legislative action in Maryland prohibited involvement in the African slave trade, but not the institution of slavery, within the state.

1783

In Louisiana, the slave James C. Derham purchased his freedom from his owner, Dr. Robert Dove. Derham remained in New Orleans as a free black and established his own practice there as a doctor.

1783

A Massachusetts court heard a case brought by Paul Cuffe and his brother John. The judges ruled that free blacks who paid taxes to the state of Massachusetts were entitled to suffrage rights within the state.

1783

The county court in Great Barrington, Massachusetts, heard a case brought by a fugitive slave woman named Elizabeth (Mumbet) Freeman who had escaped her abusive master in 1742. Freeman was fighting against reenslavement, which had been threatened, and she appealed to Thomas Sedgwick, an attorney, to defend her. Freeman won her case, and her former

James Derham, the first registered African-American physician in the United States, began life as a slave, bought his own freedom, and went on to establish a successful medical practice in New Orleans. Derham was born in Philadelphia, but very little is known of his early years except that he was a slave of a Dr. John Kearsley who taught him to compound medicines and to assist in the treatment of patients. At Kearsley's death, Derham was sold, possibly several times, and eventually wound up as the slave of Dr. George West, a surgeon of the Sixteenth British Regiment during the American Revolution. Under West, Derham received additional training in medicine. At the end of the war, he was sold to Dr. Robert Dove of New Orleans, who made him an assistant in his practice.

In 1783, Derham purchased his freedom from Dr. Dove for 500 pesos, a practice known as *coartación* (process by which slaves purchased their freedom) in Spain's New World colonies. In the act of emancipation, written in Spanish, Derham was given, in addition to his freedom, all rights and privileges with respect to buying and selling, appearing in court, entering into contracts, and performing acts, judicial or otherwise, that free persons might perform.

Speaking English, French, and Spanish, Derham established his own medical practice and became a well-known New Orleans physician serving people of all races. By 1800, it is said that he netted an annual income of $3,000 from his work. Like most individuals who entered medicine at the time, Derham's preparation had come through apprenticeship rather than university education.

On a trip to Philadelphia in 1788, Derham met Dr. Benjamin Rush, the noted physician, author, and signer of the Declaration of Independence. In commenting on James Derham to the Pennsylvania Abolition Society, Rush wrote: "I have conversed with him upon most of the acute and epidemic diseases of the country where he lives and was pleased to find him perfectly acquainted with the modern simple mode of practice on these diseases. I expected to have suggested medicines to him; but he suggested many more to me" (Miller, 1916).

Details concerning Derham's date of death and burial are unknown. In his honor, New Orleans established the James Derham Middle School in 1960.

—*Claude F. Jacobs*

For Further Reading
Miller, Kelly. 1916. "The Historic Background of the Negro Physician." *Journal of Negro History* 1(2): 99–109; Morais, Herbert M. 1969. *The History of the Negro in Medicine*. New York: Publishers Company; Tureaud, A. P., and C. C. Haydel. 1935. *The Negro in Medicine in Louisiana*. New Orleans: Amistad Research Center.

master was ordered to pay damages in the amount of 30 shillings.

1783
By the end of 1783, all states north of Maryland had taken effective legislative action to ban the further importation of Africans for use as slave laborers.

1783
In a landmark judicial decision on July 8, slavery was abolished in Massachusetts by action of the Massachusetts Supreme Court in the case of *Commonwealth v. Jennison*, which involved efforts of a slave, Quock Walker, to obtain his freedom. The decision was based upon an interpretation of the Massachusetts Declaration of Rights, included in the Massachusetts state constitution of 1780, which stated that all men were "born free and equal." Chief Justice William Cushing and other Massachusetts jurists interpreted this phrase to be a repudiation of slavery. Many opponents of slavery believed that the Massachusetts ruling signified the removal of any judicial sanction for the institution and practice of slavery.

1783
On October 7, the Virginia House of Burgesses passed a measure that granted freedom to those Virginia slaves who had served in the Continental army during the American Revolution.

1784
Congress, as part of the Articles of Confederation government, considered a "Report of Government for the Western Territory" drafted by Thomas Jefferson. Before enacting the measure, Congress deleted certain controversial provisions, including, by a vote of seven to six, a proposal that would have prohibited slavery and involuntary servitude from all western territories after 1800.

1784

The Pennsylvania Abolition Society was organized in Philadelphia.

1784

Members of the Methodist Episcopal Church meeting at a conference in Baltimore, Maryland, adopted proposals that Methodists owning slaves must begin manumitting them or face the possibility of excommunication from the church.

1784

The states of Connecticut and Rhode Island enacted legislative bills aimed at providing for the abolition of slavery within their respective states.

1784

In Virginia, the Society of Friends (Quakers) required all Quakers in the state who owned slaves to manumit them.

1784

Phillis Wheatley, the black American poet, died in Boston on December 5.

1785

John Marrant published *A Narrative of the Lord's Wonderful Dealings with J. Marrant, a Black . . . Taken Down from His Own Relation.* This work was the first autobiography of a person of African descent to be written in the English language.

1785

The New York state legislature took action making slavery illegal within the state. An effort to enact a program of gradual emancipation failed to win legislative approval because the measure would have denied civil and political rights to free blacks living in the state. In the same year, the New York Society for Promoting Manumission was chartered, and John Jay was selected to serve as the first president of the group.

1785

The general committee of Virginia Baptists took action within their denomination to condemn the institution of slavery as being "contrary to the word of God."

1785

The Methodist Conference, meeting in Baltimore, voted to suspend the 1784 ruling that required Methodists to manumit their slaves.

1785

The future black abolitionist David Walker was born on September 28, as a free child, in Wilmington, North Carolina.

1786

George Washington wrote a letter to the marquis de Lafayette, the young Frenchman who had assisted him during the American Revolution, in which he shared some of his views on the question of slavery. Washington wrote: "To set the slaves afloat at once would, I believe, be productive of much inconvenience and mischief; but, by degrees it certainly might, and assuredly ought to be, effected, and that too, by legislative authority" (Jenkins, 1996). On the basis of this statement, it would seem that Washington endorsed a plan of gradual emancipation to bring an end to slavery.

1786

The New Jersey state legislature declared slavery illegal in the state and adopted a program of gradual emancipation.

1786

The Massachusetts legislature enacted a measure that prohibited interracial marriage.

1786

The state legislature of Virginia freed a slave named James, who had been owned by William Armstead, because of the services James rendered as a spy during the American Revolution.

1787

John Cabot and Joshua Fisher established the first cotton factory in the United States at Beverly, Massachusetts. As the factory system spread throughout New England, textiles became a major item of manufacture, and northern-based production of cotton cloth became increasingly dependent upon southern-based cotton production.

1787

In a detailed proposal quite comparable to the Underground Railroad that would arise in the nineteenth century, Quaker Isaac T. Hopper of Philadelphia promoted a plan in which northerners could aid slaves who tried to escape from the southern states.

1787

In response to numerous Quaker petitions, the legislature of Rhode Island enacted a law that specifically prohibited Rhode Island citizens from participating in the slave trade.

1787

The South Carolina legislature approved of a temporary halt to slave importations into the state.

1787

On April 12, Richard Allen and Absalom Jones formed the Free African Society in Philadelphia, which they described as "the first wavering step of a people toward a more organized social life (Jenkins, 1996)."

1787

Benjamin Franklin and Benjamin Rush were among the members of the Pennsylvania Society for Promoting the Abolition of Slavery, the Relief of Free Negroes Unlawfully Held in Bondage, and Improving the Condition of the African Race, which was reorganized on April 23. Franklin served as the honorary president of the organization.

1787

On July 13, slavery was prohibited from all territories north of the Ohio River (the Old Northwest Territory) when the Congress, as part of the Articles of Confederation government, approved passage of the Northwest Ordinance. [See Document 32.]

1787

Prince Hall, who had participated in military service during the American Revolution, established African Lodge No. 459, the first black Masonic lodge in America, on September 12. The charter for this new group was granted by the Grand Lodge of England.

1787

The U.S. Constitution was signed on September 17. This document included a "three-fifths clause," which meant that only three of every five slaves were counted for purposes of representation and taxation. The document also stipulated that Congress could not act to prohibit the African slave trade until 1808.

1787

On September 24, the black poet Jupiter Hammon published *An Address to Negroes in the State of New York* in which he urged slaves to be obedient and faithful to their masters. Hammon wrote, "Now whether it is right, and lawful, in the sight of God, for them to make slaves of us or not, I am certain that while we are slaves, it is our duty to obey our masters, in all their lawful commands, and mind them unless we are bid to do that which we know to be sin, or forbidden in God's word."

1787

Boston blacks under the leadership of Prince Hall petitioned the Massachusetts legislature on October 17 to establish equal educational facilities for black students in the state.

1787

On November 1, the New York Manumission Society established the African Free School in New York City.

1788

In Newport, Rhode Island, the Negro Union Society advocated a campaign of repatriating free blacks to Africa through an emigration program, but the Free African Society of Philadelphia opposed the strategy.

1788

Legislative actions taken in Connecticut, Massachusetts, New York, and Pennsylvania prohibited citizens of those states from participating in the African slave trade.

1788

A group of free blacks led by Prince Hall petitioned the Massachusetts state legislature after a shocking incident in Boston in late February. A number of free blacks were seized on the streets of Boston, kidnapped, and transported as slaves to the French colony of Martinique in the West Indies. Governor John Hancock used his influence to win the release of the blacks who had been captured illegally, and legislators in Massachusetts enacted a measure in March declaring

Founded in April 1787 by Richard Allen (1760–1831) and Absalom Jones (1746–1818), both free blacks in Philadelphia, the Free African Society was a benevolent organization started to promote the positive treatment of people of color. The society espoused moral reform, self-help, self-improvement, and black unity. The Free African Society members believed in making the United States hospitable to blacks, advocated abolition, and condemned prevalent repatriation schemes. Although the membership maintained close ties to both the Methodist Church and the Quakers, the Free African Society was nondenominational. Members of the society insisted upon the humanity and equality of blacks and on their right to fair treatment. They petitioned both state and federal governments and issued broad appeals to the white community and to enslaved and freed blacks to end the inhumane practice of slavery in the United States.

Members contributed money to the general treasury that was then used to help widows and orphans and others in need, they attended regular meetings, and they were further required to adhere to the society's articles of association. These articles were guidelines for sobriety, decorum, and good moral conduct. Infractions of the rules were judged by a committee of members, and anyone found guilty was either fined or suspended.

During the Philadelphia yellow fever epidemic of 1793, members responded to the public solicitation for colored people to help care for the sick. Under the guidance of Absalom Jones and William Gray, and encouraged by the belief that people of color were not liable to succumb to the infection, black people from the Free African Society visited over 20 families a day, removed the dead bodies that whites refused to touch, buried corpses, administered to the needs of the dying, and even fulfilled duties such as bloodletting for white physicians.

Meetings of the society, which were held for the first year at 150 Spruce Street in the home of Richard Allen and for three years subsequent at the Willings Alley School House, were used in part to plan for the establishment of an independent African church. The free black community in Philadelphia was rudely awakened to the necessity of establishing their own church when they were forced to sit in segregated areas in St. George Methodist Episcopal Church, where there were a growing number of black worshipers. After several black worshipers had been forcibly removed by white deacons while kneeling in prayer in the church, the black community withdrew its membership completely from the church. Afterward, the Free African Society as an organization became increasingly hostile to Methodism and began showing a tendency toward Quaker thought. Among other reforms, they adopted a simple, Quaker-like marriage ceremony and began each meeting by observing 15 minutes of silence. Richard Allen maintained that the Quaker message of detachment and introspection was not as relevant to the needs of free blacks as Methodism, and he broke with the society in the spring of 1789, leaving its leadership in the hands of the less dynamic but also less confrontational Absalom Jones.

Jones and other members of the Free African Society began a public subscription to raise money for a church building that, on July 17, 1794, became the African Episcopal Church. At the same time, Richard Allen and several former members of the society created a Methodist society and worked to establish their own church. They began public worship services toward the end of July 1794 and secured a charter from the Pennsylvania legislature in 1796 for the Mother Bethel Church, the African Methodist Episcopal Church that later played an active role in the Underground Railroad and the abolition movement. With increasing attention to the establishment of individual African churches of different denominations, the Free African Society disbanded in the early 1790s.

—*Jennifer Margulis*

For Further Reading
Allen, Richard. 1983. *The Life Experience and Gospel Labors of the Rt. Rev. Richard Allen.* Nashville, TN: Abingdon Press; DuBois, W. E. B. 1899. *The Philadelphia Negro.* Philadelphia: University of Pennsylvania Press; George, Carol V. R. 1973. *Segregated Sabbaths: Richard Allen and the Emergence of Independent Black Churches, 1760–1840.* New York: Oxford University Press; Nash, Gary B. 1988. *Forging Freedom: The Formation of Philadelphia's Black Community, 1720–1840.* Cambridge, MA: Harvard University Press.

Absalom Jones (1746–1818), one of the founders of the Free African Society, who became the first black minister to be ordained in America. (The Granger Collection)

the slave trade illegal and establishing a fund to pay for compensatory damages to the victims of such kidnapping incidents.

1788

"An Essay on Negro Slavery" was published in the November-December issue of the journal *American Museum*. The anonymous author of the essay used the pen name "Othello of Maryland."

1789

The Delaware state legislature approved a resolution that prohibited citizens of Delaware from participating in the African slave trade.

1789

In Rhode Island, the Providence Society for Abolishing the Slave Trade was established.

1789

Having been ratified by a sufficient number of states, the Constitution of the United States became effective on March 4, and the first session of the U.S. Congress was called into session. At the time, the nation consisted of 13 states, 7 of which were free states, and 6 of which remained slave states.

1790

The first census of the United States revealed that 757,181 blacks, 19.3 percent of the total population, resided in the 13 states—59,557 were identified as free blacks, and 697,624 were slaves. Only Massachusetts (and Maine) reported having no slaves.

1790

The U.S. government entered into its first treaty with the Creek nation. The treaty included a provision requiring the Creek to return any fugitive slaves who sought protection in Creek territory.

1790

The Virginia Abolition Society was organized at a meeting in Richmond.

1790

In early February, Congress received its first formal petition calling for the emancipation of slaves. The petition was presented by the American Quakers (Society of Friends) and the Pennsylvania Abolition Society. Benjamin Franklin had signed the memorial and urged Congress to remove "this inconsistency from the character of the American people" (Jenkins, 1996).

1790

On March 23, "Historicus" (Benjamin Franklin) published "An Essay on the African Slave Trade" in the *Federal Gazette*. In the essay, Franklin used biting satire to parody the prevailing proslavery view in Congress and presented a Muslim argument that could be used for justifying the enslavement of Christians.

1790

In Charleston, South Carolina, a group of free blacks organized the Brown Fellowship Society on November 1. The organization was limited to emancipated blacks of good character who paid annual dues. The group served as a benevolent organization, supported schools, and operated a clubhouse and a private cemetery for society members.

1791

At the request of Thomas Jefferson, Benjamin Banneker was appointed to the surveying commission that would establish plans for the new national capital of Washington, D.C. In the

The rules and regulations of the Brown Fellowship Society record that the organization was established on November 1, 1790, by five "free brown" men (James Mitchell, George Bampfield, William Cattel, George Bedon, and Samuel Saltus) who sought to relieve "the wants and miseries" and promote "the welfare and happiness" of the free mulatto population of Charleston, South Carolina, by founding a charitable and benevolent association. As the earliest and the "preeminent mulatto organization in antebellum Charleston" (Johnson and Roark, 1982), the society's membership was restricted to 50 of the city's wealthiest free mulatto (brown) men. Perhaps as a consequence of such self-conscious class and complexional exclusivity, several other free black and free mulatto mutual aid societies later formed in Charleston, most notably the Humane Brotherhood and the Friendly Moralist Society.

The Brown Fellowship Society levied a sizable $50 initiation fee and regular monthly dues to insure members for times of illness and indigence, providing "a decent funeral for any deceased member who did not leave in his estate sufficient funds for that purpose" (Harris, 1981), and furnishing financial support for widows and educating any remaining children when necessary. The purchase of a lot to be used as a burial ground was achieved soon after the society's formation, a necessity no doubt made more urgent by the difficulties of burying brown bodies in such a color-conscious Christian city. Although the Brown Fellowship Society included affluent tailors, carpenters, shoemakers, a nationally known hotelier (Jehu Jones, Sr.), and even some slaveholders, its relatively well-heeled members were not shielded from the growing force of racially oppressive and proscriptive white supremacist legislation. In the wake of Denmark Vesey's conspiracy (1822), Nat Turner's revolt (1831), and the growing sectional crisis, the free black and free mulatto populations of Charleston found themselves facing new controls on their education and mobility, which added to the burden of special "capitation" taxes and subaltern status under South Carolina's "Negro law."

Questions of status and identity have been the key issues occupying most scholarly analyses of Charleston's free mulatto aristocracy and its organizations. Although most historians agree that the free brown elite managed to occupy a middle ground between the broader free black and slave populations and the city's white residents, there has been some dispute as to the degree of exclusivity, color consciousness, or caste discrimination as evidenced by the correspondence and official records of mulattoes affiliated to self-help groups such as the Brown Fellowship Society. In addition to the organization's name having often been taken too "literally by many scholars as *prima facie* evidence of mulatto exclusiveness" (Harris, 1981), perhaps too little has been made of the achievement of the free brown elite's mindful policy of public accommodation and simultaneous exploitation of the personalism of the dominant culture (Johnson and Roark, 1984). Although members of the Brown Fellowship Society did not enjoy the dubious comforts of the third racial space occupied by the mulattoes of New Orleans, they successfully maintained their organization beyond the difficult years of the Civil War by judiciously eluding political controversy and by carefully cultivating white patronage. Just when the society disbanded is uncertain, but it continued to own the burial ground until 1957.

—Stephen C. Kenny

For Further Reading
Harris, Robert L., Jr. 1981. "Charleston's Free Afro-American Elite: The Brown Fellowship Society and the Humane Brotherhood." *South Carolina Historical Magazine* 81: 289–310; Johnson, Michael P., and James L. Roark. 1982. "'A Middle Ground': Free Mulattoes and the Friendly Moralist Society of Ante-bellum Charleston." *Southern Studies* 21(3): 246–265; Johnson, Michael P., and James L. Roark, eds. 1984. *No Chariot Let Down: Charleston's Free People of Color on the Eve of the Civil War.* Chapel Hill: University of North Carolina Press; Wikramanayake, Marina. 1973. *A World in Shadow: The Free Black in Ante-bellum South Carolina.* Columbia: University of South Carolina Press.

same year, Pierre Charles L'Enfant, the architect who designed the original plans for the District of Columbia, hired slaves from owners in Maryland and Virginia to begin construction of the new federal buildings in the national capital.

1791

The U.S. Congress enacted a measure that prevented blacks and Indians from serving in the peacetime militia.

1791

After some of President George Washington's slaves were taken to Pennsylvania, officials there claimed that they could not be returned to Virginia as slaves. Washington asked Tobias Lear to offer his assistance so that the slaves might be returned in a fashion that would "deceive both the slaves and the public" (Jenkins, 1996).

1791

On January 5, free blacks in Charleston, North Carolina, presented a petition to the state legislature protesting recent legislation that prohibited black-initiated lawsuits in the courts and disallowed the testimony of blacks in the courts. The state legislature rejected the petition, and the condition of inequality before the law remained in effect.

1792

George Mason, a noted Virginia statesman, spoke out in opposition to slavery, saying that the institution of slavery was a disgrace to mankind and comparing it to a slow poison that, in time, would corrupt future politicians. In the same year, Joshua Bishop, a free black preacher in Portsmouth, Virginia, was appointed to be the new pastor of the First Baptist Church, which served a white congregation.

1792

The Virginia Quaker Warner Mifflin sent an antislavery memorial to the U.S. Congress, and the petition created a contentious debate. One South Carolina congressman questioned whether the First Amendment's right to petition expressly included the "mere rant and rhapsody of a meddling fanatic" (Jenkins, 1996).

1792

In April, Presbyterian clergyman David Rice attempted unsuccessfully to have the Kentucky constitutional convention exclude slavery from that state. A later legislative attempt to achieve the same objective failed in 1799. On June 1, Kentucky, which had previously been a part of Virginia's western territory, entered the Union as a slave state. At this point, the United States consisted of 15 states, 8 of them free states and 7 of them slave states.

1793

The New Jersey Abolition Society was organized.

1793

The General Committee of Virginia Baptists reached the conclusion that since emancipation was a political question, it should be addressed by legislative action and not through pronouncements agreed upon by church convocations. In the same year, the Virginia legislature passed a law making it illegal for any free black to enter the state.

1793

Free blacks in South Carolina petitioned the state legislature in opposition to the state's poll tax.

1793

The Georgia legislature enacted a measure prohibiting the importation of any slaves from the West Indies or Spanish Florida, but the importation of slaves directly from Africa was still allowed.

1793

On February 12, the U.S. Congress enacted a federal Fugitive Slave Act, which made it a criminal offense for anyone to harbor a slave or to prevent the arrest of a fugitive. The law based its legality upon Article 4, Section 2 of the U.S. Constitution, which established a legal mechanism for the recovery of fugitive slaves. The measure remained in effect until Congress passed a stronger Fugitive Slave Act in 1850.

1793

On October 28, Eli Whitney invented the cotton gin in Mulberry Grove, Georgia. This invention revolutionized southern agriculture as it made short-staple (upland) cotton easier to process, and as the planting of upland cotton increased

Short-staple cotton pertains to cultivated strains of *Gossypium hirsutum* that are domesticated as a cash crop, with "short-staple" referring to the short length of the fibers of this species in comparison to other domesticated species of cotton. It is native to Central America but has been grown intensively in the southern United States since the 1790s. Like all cottons, *G. hirsutum* is a perennial in the wild, but in cultivation it is grown as an annual. As it was the chief cash crop of the South by the mid-nineteenth century, most southern slaves worked on plantations and farms that produced short-staple cotton.

Before it became a major cash crop in the 1790s, short-staple cotton was grown only for household consumption. Its fibers clung tightly to the seeds, which made seed removal a lengthy process that occupied evenings and rainy days along with spinning and weaving. Thus, short-staple cotton was an integral part of the household economy in the late-eighteenth century, but it was the cotton gin, which automated the separation of the fibers from the seeds, that allowed for the cultivation of short-staple cotton as a cash crop.

Prior to the development of the cotton gin, only longer-staple cottons, with seeds that were easily separated, could be grown commercially in the New World. However, these long-staple cottons (primarily *G. barbadense*) had a lengthy growing season that could only be accommodated on the Caribbean islands and the coastal islands of South Carolina and Georgia. *G. hirsutum,* however, had a shorter growing season and grew in virtually any soil, thus it was also referred to as upland cotton.

The introduction of the cotton gin along with more productive and easily cultivated strains of *G. hirsutum* at the end of the eighteenth century spurred the reopening of the Atlantic slave trade before its final ban in the United States in 1808, and the demand for slaves suddenly grew after a period of several decades of decline. Cotton cultivation also postponed the inevitable resolution that Americans faced concerning slavery by creating a new market for the domestic slave trade. The debate over the expediency of slavery as an economic system became a moot point as cotton's economic potential became apparent. Questions concerning slavery's morality were hushed as the revitalized domestic trade increased the value of all slaveholders' property.

The cultivation of short-staple cotton also sped the migration of planters and yeomen, as well as their slaves, to the southwestern territories and states as lands there were prime for cotton production. Virginia planters who had turned away from labor-intensive tobacco toward wheat readily sold their excess slaves to cotton planters in the Deep South, and many of them took their entire plantation populations with them and relocated to the Southwest. Easy credit and plentiful lands made the wealth to be generated from cotton planting seem boundless, but such reckless investments in frontier lands and slaves contributed to several economic downturns throughout the first half of the nineteenth century.

Although southern planters were not often noted for widespread efforts at agricultural reform, the selective breeding of strains of short-staple cotton illustrates one exception to that generalization. As early as the first decade of the nineteenth century, southerners were looking for hardier and more productive strains of *G. hirsutum*. In 1807, for instance, William Dunbar first cultivated a sample of a productive Mexican strain in Mississippi, and throughout the 1820s and 1830s, Dr. Rush Nutt crossbred that strain with several others to develop the hardy and productive Port Gibson (Mississippi) strain, which became a very popular variety throughout the South. In the 1840s and 1850s, southerners developed several other new strains of *G. hirsutum*, but none were as popular as the Port Gibson strain.

For the slaves who cultivated the cotton, the specific strain mattered little as all involved the same labor patterns, although short-staple cotton cultivation was generally less labor intensive than long-staple cotton production. In almost all circumstances, the short-staple cotton routine employed the gang (rather than the task) system of labor. Cotton growing began with the clearing of the fields in late February and March; planting began after the last frost, usually on April 1; and as the young plants grew up, repeated passes with the plow killed grasses and weeds that competed with the cotton plants and thinned out all but the strongest plants. By late May and early June, the slaves continually went through the fields with hoes, scraping weeds and grasses and pushing dirt around the base of the plant. Scraping passes continued until the lay-by time, in midsummer, when the slaves tended to livestock, food crops, and plantation maintenance. The picking season began as soon as the bolls opened, usually in September, and as the bolls opened faster than they could be picked, the harvest ran into December and even January. At the height of the harvest, slaves often picked 100 or more pounds of cotton in a day, but earlier and later in the season, individual totals amounted to 15 or 20 pounds. A separate "trash gang" of children and elderly slaves followed the main gangs of pickers.

Once collected, the trash gang cleaned the cotton as it dried on scaffolds while waiting to be ginned. After the gin removed the seeds, the cotton awaited baling in a separate magazine. Baling involved the use of a cotton press and the labor of six to eight slaves as well as a horse or mule to compress as much as 500 pounds of cotton into a squared-off bale.

The production of short-staple cotton tied the southern slave economy to the Industrial Revolution and an international economy. Raw southern cotton became finished yarn and cloth in northern and European cotton mills, and some of that cloth became clothing worn by both planters and slaves. Many plantations forsook food crops to raise cotton and thus became consumers of food grown in the northwestern states. Wealthy planters also purchased European luxury goods as displays of their wealth and elegance.

Short-staple cotton is still a major cash crop in many southern states, and its cultivation was the agricultural basis for the sharecropping economy of the "new South." The cultivation processes described here remained virtually intact until the 1950s when planters began to invest in machinery to automate cotton production.

—*David J. Libby*

For Further Reading
Gray, Lewis C. 1933. *History of Agriculture in the Southern United States to 1860.* 2 vols. Washington, DC: Carnegie Institution; Moore, John Hebron. 1958. *Agriculture in Ante-Bellum Mississippi.* New York: Bookman Associates; Moore, John Hebron. 1988. *The Emergence of the Cotton Kingdom in the Old Southwest: Mississippi, 1770–1860.* Baton Rouge: Louisiana State University Press.

in the old Southwest, the region of slaveholding also increased. Whitney received a patent for his invention on March 14, 1794.

1793

In Albany, New York, a slave revolt took place on November 25 when a group of insurrectionists rebelled and burned several buildings. The property damage caused by the arsonists was estimated to be $250,000, and three slaves were eventually executed.

1794

The Connecticut legislature considered a bill that provided for immediate emancipation, but the measure failed to win final approval. Additional provisions of this measure would have required masters to care for old and infirm blacks and provide for the education of black children.

1794

In Philadelphia, the first meeting was held of the Convention of Delegates from the Abolition Societies. Delegates representing nine antislavery societies from several states discussed long-range strategies that should be employed to advance the cause of abolition.

1794

George Washington wrote a letter to Alexander Spotswood in which he shared some of his views on slavery. Washington wrote: "Were it not then, that I am principled against selling *African Americans*, as you would cattle at a market, I would not in twelve months from this date, be possessed of one as a slave. I shall be happily mistaken if they are not found to be a very troublesome species of property ere many years pass over our heads" (Jenkins, 1996).

1794

On March 22, Congress prohibited the slave trade to all foreign ports and also prohibited the outfitting of any foreign vessels in any American port for the purpose of slave trading.

1794

In Philadelphia, Pennsylvania, Absalom Jones and his associates dedicated the First African Church of St. Thomas on July 17. It was the first black Episcopal congregation in the United States, and Jones became the first black minister to be ordained in America.

1794

On July 29, Richard Allen and his followers established the Mother Bethel Church in Philadelphia, the first African Methodist Episcopal church established in the United States. The church is also the oldest piece of property in the United States that has been continuously been owned by blacks.

The cotton gin is a device for separating cottonseed from the fiber. In the United States, the first profitable variety of cotton produced consisted of long fibers grown in the Sea Islands and coastal South Carolina, Georgia, and Florida. Introduced in 1786, the plant's black seeds were easily separated from the lint by hand or gins, which made it cost effective for landowners to use African and African-American slaves in processing the fiber. Environmental factors, however, prevented this variant from being cultivated inland.

In the southern uplands, a plant with short fibers and green seeds grew abundantly, but the extreme difficulty of extracting the seeds from the fibers made it unprofitable to process. Gins used for separating black seeds from the long-staple cotton proved ineffective when applied to the shorter fibers. Those gins were patterned on a device used for centuries in India consisting of two grooved wooden rollers that rotated conversely when turned by a handle. The grooves captured the seeds of the long-staple cotton as it was pulled through the rollers, thereby cleaning it for spinning. The seeds from the upland variety, however, clung so tightly to the fiber that the rollers could not remove them.

Planters in Georgia brought this problem to the attention of Eli Whitney (1765–1825), a mechanically inclined graduate of Yale University from Massachusetts. In 1792, Whitney accepted a position as tutor for a family in South Carolina, and on his journey south, he met Catherine Littlefield Greene (1755–1814) and accepted an invitation to stay at her plantation in Georgia. Following discussions with Greene and others regarding the problems of ginning upland cotton, Whitney chose not to proceed to South Carolina. Instead, he remained at Greene's plantation and worked on a means of separating green seeds from the upland cotton.

Whitney constructed a model for a cotton gin in 10 days in November 1792 and then spent six months building a working machine, which he finished in April 1793. Whitney based his design on the gins used in cleaning lowland cotton, but his apparatus consisted of one roller with iron pins attached that pulled the lint through a metal grid, which caught the seeds and dropped them into a box below. A second cylinder rotated a brush that removed the fibers from the toothed roller. Supposedly, it was Greene who suggested employing the brush, which solved the problem of how to prevent the lint caught on the pins from accumulating and choking the gin.

Whitney's device cleaned 50 times more fiber than could be accomplished by hand and made it profitable to put slaves to work picking short-staple cotton, thereby encouraging the expansion of slavery throughout the southeastern United States. The gin also enabled the United States to become the world's leading producer of cotton by 1825. The boom in the production of cotton encouraged white southerners to demand the removal of Native Americans from their lands so that planters could acquire more land for cultivation.

Whitney profited little from his invention. Although he and a business associate received a federal patent, other mechanics easily varied the basic design, which allowed for the proliferation of gins while ensuring the near impossibility of Whitney's collecting either damages or royalties.

—*Dan R. Frost*

For Further Reading
Green, Constance McLaughlin. 1956. *Eli Whitney and the Birth of American Technology.* Boston: Little, Brown; Mirsky, Jeannette, and Allan Nevins. 1952. *The World of Eli Whitney.* New York: Macmillan; Ogilvie, Marilyn Bailey. 1986. *Women in Science: Antiquity through the Nineteenth Century.* Cambridge, MA: MIT Press.

1795
The average price of a slave laborer who worked as an agricultural field hand was $300.

1795
George Washington published an advertisement calling for the return of one of his slaves who had escaped from Mount Vernon. Washington stipulated that the notice not be run in any state north of Virginia.

1795
In April, colonial officials in Spanish Louisiana put down a slave revolt in Pointe Coupee Parish, hanged 23 slaves who were implicated in the conspiracy, and deported three white sympathizers from the colony. Officials in Louisiana believed that this rebellion was related to the insurrection that had rocked the French colony of Saint Domingue (Haiti).

1796
In New York City, the free black community organized the Zion Methodist Church.

Slaves depicted as cheerfully operating the first cotton gin. (Library of Congress/Corbis)

1796

Forty-four free blacks organized the Boston African Society. [See Document 35.]

1796

St. George Tucker, a professor of law and police at the College of William and Mary in Williamsburg, Virginia, published a work entitled *A Dissertation on Slavery: With a Proposal for the Gradual Abolition of It, in the State of Virginia*, which put forward the view that slavery was inconsistent with the high moral purpose of the Bill of Rights. Tucker called for Virginia to adopt a program of gradual abolition of slavery that would end the practice within a century.

1796

Tennessee was admitted to the Union as a slave state on June 1, but the state's constitution did not deny the suffrage to free blacks. At this point, the United States consisted of 16 states, which were evenly divided between free and slave states.

1797

Sojourner Truth (born Isabella Baumfree) was born a slave on an estate near Hurley, New York.

1797

The Polish general Tadeusz Kosciuszko received a land grant in the Ohio Valley as compensation for his service to the American cause during the American Revolution. Kosciuszko requested that his land grant be sold and that the revenues raised be used to establish a school for black children.

1797

In Kentucky, a young lawyer named Henry Clay urged the state legislature to enact a program of gradual abolition of slavery. Clay often defended slaves who sued for their freedom.

I SELL THE SHADOW TO SUPPORT THE SUBSTANCE.
SOJOURNER TRUTH.

Sojourner Truth, born a slave in New York State, became an influential figure in the abolitionist and women's rights movements. (Library of Congress)

1797

On January 30, a group of free blacks petitioned Congress protesting against a North Carolina law requiring that even though slaves had been freed by their Quaker masters, they must be returned to the state and to their former condition; the petition was rejected by the Congress.

1798

During an undeclared naval war with France, Secretary of the Navy Benjamin Stoddert refused to allow the deployment of blacks on American naval vessels, thus overturning the nonracial policy that the navy had used previously. Despite this ban, blacks like William Brown and George Diggs did manage to serve on board American naval vessels.

1798

A school for black children was established in the home of Primus Hall, a free black in Boston, Massachusetts.

1798

The Georgia legislature enacted a measure that prohibited the further importation of slaves into the state.

1798

The U.S. Congress debated a resolution that would have prohibited slavery from Mississippi Territory, but the measure was defeated.

1798

A collection of stories was published with the title *A Narrative of the Life and Adventures of Venture*. The stories were based upon the life of Venture Smith, a Connecticut slave, who had been the son of a West African prince. [See Document 25.]

1799

In his last will and testament George Washington declared, "It is my will and desire that all the slaves which I hold in my right, shall receive their freedom."

1799

In Boston, the first minstrel performance occurred when Gottlieb Graupner performed a repertoire of songs that he had learned from blacks in Charleston, South Carolina. The young German immigrant would later form the Boston Philharmonic Society.

1799

A bill that provided for the gradual abolition of slavery was enacted by the legislature of New York on March 29.

1800

The second census of the United States recorded that there were 1,002,037 blacks, both slave and free, 18.9 percent of the national population.

1800

The Virginia Assembly enacted legislation that supported development of a colonization plan to return former slaves to Africa. The assembly enacted similar nonbinding resolutions on colonization in 1802, 1805, and 1816.

1800

On January 2, the U.S. House of Representatives rejected a petition advanced by a group of free blacks from Philadelphia who sought to end slavery in the United States through a system of gradual emancipation. The petition also protested against the slave trade and the enforcement of the Fugitive Slave Act of 1793. The measure was defeated by a margin of 85 to 1. [See Document 36.]

1800

John Brown, the white abolitionist who participated in antislavery activities in Kansas and attempted to seize the Harpers Ferry arsenal in 1859, was born in Torrington, Connecticut, on May 9.

1800

On August 30, Virginia authorities discovered and suppressed the plot of Gabriel Prosser and Jack Bowler to capture Richmond and the surrounding area in a large-scale slave insurrection involving thousands of slaves. Prosser and 15 of his associates were hanged on October 7 for their role in the conspiracy after the betrayal of the plot by two slaves. Governor James Monroe requested that federal troops be sent into the region to quell any further efforts at insurrectionary violence.

1800

On a plantation in Southampton County, Virginia, a slave child named Nat Turner was born on September 2. He would eventually become a slave preacher and would organize and lead a slave insurrection in the region in 1831.

1801

In the aftermath of Gabriel Prosser's conspiracy in Virginia, the American Convention of Abolition Societies issued a public statement which stated that "an amelioration of the present situation of the slaves, and the adoption of a system of gradual emancipation . . . would . . . be an effectual security against revolt" (Jenkins, 1996).

1802

Residents of Indiana Territory met in a convention at Vincennes called by Territorial Governor William Henry Harrison. The convention forwarded a memorial to Congress asking that the Northwest Ordinance of 1787 be suspended so that slaves might be introduced into Indiana. Congress did not support Governor Harrison's recommendation, but a measure was later enacted that did allow indentured servants to be brought into the territory.

1802

The U.S. Congress considered a proposed bill that would have strengthened the Fugitive Slave Act of 1793, but the measure was defeated.

1802

In Mississippi Territory, the legislature considered a bill that would have prohibited the importation of male slaves into the region, but the measure was defeated.

1802

Authorities in North Carolina were on alert throughout the year as several rumors of revolt surfaced in Charlotte, Elizabeth, Hertford, Wake, Warren, and Washington Counties. In May, a disturbance near Elizabeth City was organized by Tom Cooper, a fugitive slave who lived in the swamps as a Maroon. Local authorities restored order in the county, and 15 slaves were executed for their role in the plot.

1803

South Carolina's legislature, which previously had tried to limit slave imports, authorized the importation of slaves from South America and from the West Indies. This move was especially controversial as many people feared that slaves who had been "tainted" by the insurrection in Saint Domingue (Haiti) would carry seeds of discontent into the American South. With the expansion in cultivation of upland cotton that had followed Eli Whitney's invention of the cotton gin, however, states like South Carolina soon realized the economic pressure for greater numbers of slaves to work the new lands that were brought under cotton cultivation.

1803

Lunsford Lane was born a slave on a plantation in North Carolina. By 1839, Lane was a well-known lecturer for the American Anti-Slavery Society, and in 1842, he published a narrative of his life.

1803

In February, free blacks and slaves in York, Pennsylvania, rioted and attempted to burn the town to protest the conviction of Margaret Bradley on the charge that she had attempted to poison two white citizens. Governor Thomas McKean ordered the state militia into the city to restore order, and the legislature funded a $300

Gabriel Prosser (also referred to as Prosser's Gabriel), a slave, a highly skilled blacksmith, and a literate black, was born in 1776 when the United States was fighting to rid itself of British hegemony. The historical event that historians refers to as Gabriel's plot or rebellion was an abortive slave revolt in half a dozen counties of Virginia, and it was organized against the backdrop of the changing circumstances during the Revolutionary era in America. The rhetoric that all men were created equal and had certain natural and inalienable rights, including "life, liberty, and the pursuit of happiness," unfortunately did not apply to slaves. Although the American War of Independence did not lead to freedom for blacks, it gave the slaves a lasting impression of the importance of liberty and freedom. Some slaves used the war to escape as runaways, and all slaves took to heart the lesson that the possibility of freedom existed. One of the regions in which this hope was played out was postwar Virginia.

In 1800, Richmond, Virginia, was inhabited by about 5,700 people, and about half were slaves and free blacks. As a growing port city, Richmond had a thriving merchant class that benefited from the new wealth of which slave labor contributed a substantial amount. One of the conditions that prepared a fertile ground for the slaves to revolt was the collapse of control over slaves in Virginia and, more important, in the city of Richmond. Economic and social factors arising from the changes occurring in the post–Revolutionary War era were also significant.

The major economic development of the period was the production of such crops as wheat, hemp, flax, and cotton and the introduction of small-scale, local manufacturing industries. These industries relied on skilled slave labor to effect the changes and chart new directions for the economy. In addition to economic changes, a new evangelical movement (the First Great Awakening, 1720–1770) challenged both the religious and the social order in Virginia—the Baptists and the Methodists, especially, were motivated by this new evangelism. This new wave of Christianity emphasized an unusual fellowship between the preachers, the congregation, and the slaves. The humanity of the slaves was recognized, and they were accepted as equals in the sight of God. Emancipation and freedom became the slaves' creed.

It was in this climate that Gabriel and his co-conspirators planned the destruction of Richmond in 1800. Gabriel belonged to the Prosser plantation of Brookfield, which was about six miles north of Richmond. The plantation was owned by Thomas Prosser, who owned 53 slaves, including Gabriel, his parents, and two of his brothers, Martin and Solomon. Prosser and his wife, Ann, had two children, Elizabeth and Thomas Henry, the latter born on November 5, 1776. Since Thomas Henry and Gabriel were born the same year; and because they grew up on the same plantation, they were said to have been playmates in their childhood. In spite of the close companionship, their fortunes turned out to be quite different because of the accident of their birth—one a slave and the other a freeborn. It has also been speculated that Gabriel in his early years might have been taught to read either by Thomas Henry or by Ann Prosser. Whoever did so gave Gabriel a head start over most slaves of his time and age. As Gabriel grew older, the class differences between him and Thomas Henry became more apparent, and while Thomas Henry was being trained by his father to take over as the master of the plantation, Gabriel and his brother were learning a trade, blacksmithing.

Owing to his size, courage, and intellect, Gabriel was respected by both whites and blacks. He was never afraid to fight back if he felt he was wronged—for example, in 1799 it was reported that he bit off one Absalom Johnson's left ear in an argument over a stolen hog. For this action, Gabriel spent a month in jail. In order to avoid any possible confrontation with Gabriel, his master, Thomas Prosser, was said to have granted him considerable freedom and autonomy. For instance, Prosser never subjected Gabriel's wife, Nanny, to abuse as he might have done. Following the death of Thomas Prosser on October 7, 1798, the leadership of Prosser's plantation passed to Thomas Henry who was then 22. Having inherited the plantation, Thomas Henry was determined not only to keep it solvent but to also increase its profit margins.

In order to secure productivity from his slaves, it is said that the young Prosser was harsh to them. More important, he adopted the strategy of hiring out surplus slaves to people who needed their services. The slaves worked either on farms or as house help or craftsmen in urban centers. This highly profitable practice of hiring out slaves without doubt freed the bondsmen from the control of their masters. Consequently, Gabriel and such other insurrectionists, known as Martin, Solomon, Jack Ditcher (also called Jack Bowler), Sam Byrd, Jr., and George Smith, took advantage of the relaxed control to plot their insurrection. Douglas

Egerton argues that in addition to the practice of hiring out slaves, the cash that they earned "conferred a degree of psychological and social independence on the wage-earning bondsman" (Egerton, 1993). In the process of being hired out, slaves like Gabriel were either underpaid or cheated by wicked employers. This injustice violated Gabriel's and others' sense of justice and fair play, and they felt the unscrupulous employers had to be taught a lesson. Also subjected to harsh economic and social discrimination were free blacks and poor unskilled whites, and in time, slaves formed an alliance with them to challenge the status quo.

Gabriel and his fellow accomplices chose 1800 to strike back. The year was unique in other ways—it was the year Nat Turner and John Brown were born and the year Denmark Vesey bought his freedom. The plot began early in the spring of 1800. Initially, the leadership of the plot was uncertain. A number of sources have pointed out that in spite of Gabriel's early involvement with the plot, it was not his brainchild and he first heard of the scheme from Jack Ditcher. Gabriel, however, emerged as the leader of the group at age 24, and Gerald Mullin contends that "more than any other organizer he sensed the narcotic and self-justifying effects of revolutionary rhetoric and organization. Because he was able to make decisions, delegate responsibilities, and pursue routine tasks to their completion in order to avert the strong possibility of disaster, the rebellion came to be his. And it bore his own quietly methodical, businesslike character" (Mullin, 1972). Although Gabriel may have been a methodical, businesslike, and skillful leader, it is debatable if he really averted "the strong possibility of disaster" as Mullin claims. From what we know, the plot was nipped in the bud.

The level of success the conspiracy achieved depended on the recruitment strategy and effort. The main recruiters were Gabriel, Jack Ditcher, George Smith, Sam Byrd, Jr., and Ben Woolfolk, and they employed various strategies and locations to recruit potential participants. The enlistment of a slave was for the most part based on the test, "Was he willing to fight the white people for his freedom?" More often than not, the leaders of the plot found slaves who in addition to hating whites were willing to kill to secure their freedom. The goal of the plot was a coup that would result in an insurrection. The number of insurrectionists was estimated at about 1,000, and it was this core group that was expected to launch the attack on Richmond and subsequently count on the support of slaves, free blacks, and lower-class whites in the region. The conspirators believed that the capture of Richmond would result in the end of slavery in Virginia and "subdue the whole country where slavery was permitted" (Dillon, 1990). In carrying out their plan, Gabriel cautioned his co-conspirators not to hurt the Quakers, Methodists, or French people. Nonetheless, they planned to enter Richmond carrying a flag with the inscription, "Death or liberty."

The insurrectionists had planned to strike at midnight on August 30, 1800, but a violent storm at about noon of that day prompted the postponement of the rebellion until the following night. Meanwhile, two slaves had broken their oath of secrecy, and Virginia state authorities, led by Governor James Monroe, acted swiftly by calling out about 600 troops. The slaves were subsequently arrested, tried, and executed, Gabriel being arrested in late September 1800 while trying to escape in the schooner *Mary*. Governor Monroe tried to interview Gabriel as to his motives, but to no avail. Gabriel along with others was executed on October 7, 1800. Although Gabriel and his co-conspirators failed to achieve their ultimate goal of ending slavery, they undoubtedly drew attention to the plight of the slaves. More important, they made it clear that slaves were anything but docile.

—*Onaiwu W. Ogbomo*

For Further Reading
Dillon, Merton L. 1990. *Slavery Attacked: Southern Slaves and Their Allies, 1619–1865*. Baton Rouge: Louisiana State University Press; Egerton, Douglas R. 1993. *Gabriel's Rebellion: The Virginia Slave Conspiracies of 1800 and 1802*. Chapel Hill: University of North Carolina Press; Mullin, Gerald W. 1972. *Flight and Rebellion: Slave Resistance in Eighteenth Century Virginia*. New York: Oxford University Press; Mullin, Michael. 1992. *Africa in America: Slave Acculturation and Resistance in the American South and the Caribbean, 1736–1831*. Chicago: University of Chicago Press.

reward for information that would aid in the capture of the revolt's leaders.

1803

On February 19, Ohio became the seventeenth state to be admitted to the Union. At this point in the nation's history there were nine free states and eight slave states. Since Ohio was part of the Old Northwest Territory, it was the first state to join the Union in which slavery was prohibited by law from the beginning of statehood.

1803

On February 28, the U.S. Congress enacted An Act to Prevent the Importation of Certain Persons into Certain States, Where, by the Laws Thereof, Their Admission is Prohibited. This measure was thought necessary because many people feared that slaves who had been "tainted" by the insurrection in Saint Domingue (Haiti) would carry the seeds of discontent into the American South if they were permitted into the region. [See Document 37.]

1804 February-March

In February and March, the U.S. Congress debated legislation that organized Louisiana Territory. In keeping within the guidelines of the Louisiana Purchase, the federal government agreed to recognize and protect the property of Louisiana slaveowners who had been protected by Spanish and French laws. Additionally, Congress voted to restrict the slaves that could be brought into the territory to those slaves who were the actual property of settlers moving into the region. Congress defeated a proposal that would have limited the period of servitude of slaves in the territory to one year.

1804

Thomas Branagan, who had been a slave trader himself, published *A Preliminary Essay on the Oppression of the Exiled Sons of Africa*. This work was a brutally frank denunciation of the African slave trade from the vantage point of someone who had experienced the enterprise directly.

1804

On January 5, Ohio, a state that was carved from the Old Northwest Territory, enacted black laws that restricted the rights and movement of free blacks within the state. Illinois, Indiana, and Oregon later adopted similar policies or inserted anti-immigration provisions into their respective state constitutions.

1804

The legislature of New Jersey enacted a bill on February 15 that provided for the abolition of slavery in the state. After the passage of this measure, all states north of the Mason-Dixon line had taken some type of step to prohibit slavery within their borders or to provide for its gradual demise.

1804

The Lewis and Clark expedition left St. Louis on May 14 on a two-year-long journey to explore the upper portion of the territory of the Louisiana Purchase. A slave named York accompanied the expedition and served as William Clark's valet.

1805

The Virginia state legislature approved a resolution, which was forwarded to the U.S. Congress, that called for the establishment of a new territory in the upper portion of the Louisiana Purchase where free blacks could be settled.

1805

A Kentucky court decided the case of *Thompson v. Wilmot*. Will Thompson, who was a slave in Maryland, had been taken to Kentucky to serve a specified number of years as an indentured servant. When his period of indenture expired, his master, Thomas Thompson, had attempted to enslave Will. The court ruled that Will had been illegally enslaved and ordered him freed. The verdict was sustained upon appeal in 1809.

1805

Benjamin Banneker, the noted mathematician and astronomer who had helped to survey the District of Columbia when the new national capital was established, died on October 9.

1805

William Lloyd Garrison was born on December 10 in Newburyport, Massachusetts. Garrison became the most famous of all the abolitionists in the United States, and he published and edited the *Liberator*, an abolitionist weekly, from 1831 to 1865.

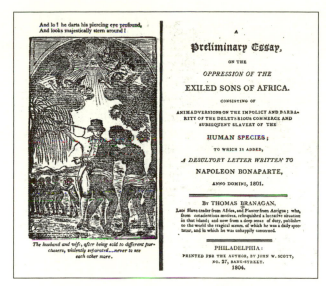

The frontispiece and title page of Thomas Branagan's denunciation of the African slave trade, published in 1804 and written from the vantage point of someone who had experienced the enterprise directly. (Library of Congress)

1806

The Virginia Assembly enacted legislation requiring that anyone who was manumitted after May 1 leave the state within one year.

1806

On December 2, President Thomas Jefferson sent a message to Congress urging the passage of legislation ending all slave importation to the United States effective January 1, 1808. When the Constitution of the United States was written in 1787, a 20-year moratorium on any legislative action regarding the suppression of the African slave trade (Article 1, Section 9) had been included.

1807

In Charleston, South Carolina, two boatloads of Africans who had been brought to the Americas as slaves starved themselves to death rather than submit to slavery.

1807

Although slavery had been prohibited in the region by the Northwest Ordinance of 1787, legislators in Indiana Territory enacted a measure that established a strict indenture system in the region. This de facto form of slavery remained in effect for three years until the law was repealed in 1810. [For more on the Northwest Ordinance, see Document 32.]

1807

New Jersey amended its 1776 state constitution to limit the right of suffrage so that only free white males could vote.

1807

In Kentucky, several antislavery supporters established a new abolitionist society called Friends of Humanity. Even though Kentucky was considered a slave state, active abolitionists remained there right up to the time of the American Civil War.

1807

On March 2, the U.S. Congress passed landmark legislation that prohibited the importation of African slaves into any region within the jurisdiction of the United States effective January 1, 1808, and President Thomas Jefferson signed the measure into law. Despite efforts of the U.S. government to enforce this measure, violations of the law occurred until the time of the American Civil War. [See Document 39.]

1808

Judges in the District of Columbia heard the case of *United States v. Mullany* and declared that free blacks were competent to testify as witnesses in court proceedings.

1808

The General Conference of the Methodist Episcopal Church decided to remove the church's rules on slavery from copies of its *Discipline* that were sent to states in the U.S. South.

1808

The ban on the importation of Africans as slaves took effect on January 1. It is estimated that there were 1 million slaves in the United States at the time. Many people believed that the elimination of external imports would set the stage for the gradual elimination of slavery within the country, but by 1860, there were nearly 4 million slaves in the southern states.

1809

The population of New Orleans increased dramatically when 6,000 new immigrants arrived in the colony of Louisiana. These immigrants were originally from the French colony of Saint Domingue (Haiti), but they had left that island when a slave insurrection took place in 1791.

The image of Sambo as a smiling, happy-go-lucky, and accommodating black man, usually portrayed with big eyes and thick lips, has a long and complex role in American race relations. The origin of the name is ambiguous. Some scholars believe it is derived from the Spanish word for monkey *(mono)*, but it also could have been derived from Tambo or Pompey, names occasionally assigned to black slaves in the Americas. John Blassingame (1972) states that it was a term used by slaveowners to designate slaves who were one-quarter white. Regardless of the origin of the name, the image has proved to be persistent and troubling for Americans.

In antebellum society, Sambo was contrasted with images of rebellious and surly slaves. Sambo was assumed to be intensely loyal to his master, and his image justified the slaveowners' point of view that white masters were needed to watch over such childish creatures. Sambo also seemed to refute the charge of abolitionists that slaves were miserable in bondage, and as folklore, Sambo gave slaveholders a powerful image to use in justifying the institution of slavery.

After emancipation, the Sambo image not only survived but actually gained much wider circulation. Sambo was a frequent figure in minstrel shows, postcards, folk art, and commercial art, and the Sambo image played a major role in the portrayal of blacks in film and on the radio. The most widely recognized version of Sambo had an unlikely source. Helen Bannerman, a Scottish woman living in India, published an illustrated children's book featuring Sambo in 1899. The narrative is actually very positive and shows Sambo using his wits to vanquish powerful tigers, but the illustrations show Sambo in a most unflattering way. Because of the illustrations, the book disappeared from American schools and libraries in the 1950s and 1960s.

The Sambo image has not been restricted to white art and literature as Sambo appears frequently in poetry, novels, and stories written by black authors. The most well-known example is *The Invisible Man* (1952) by Ralph Ellison, in which a young black man grows disenchanted with radical politics and begins selling Sambo dolls on the streets of Harlem. Although Sambo was a white creation, the image became a symbol all Americans have struggled with.

In historiography, Stanley Elkins (1959) used his psychological study to elevate Sambo to a powerful metaphor to describe how slaves coped with their situation. John Blassingame (1972), Winthrop Jordan (1969), and Eugene Genovese (1972) criticized Elkins for uncritically accepting the Sambo image promoted by white writers. No one denied that Sambo existed, but the emerging version of Sambo stressed the strategy of "putting on Massa"—that slaves could achieve their goals by manipulating the Sambo image to their advantage. This historiographical dispute is likely to continue.

Despite widespread disapproval, the image of Sambo persists in American society, and despite disputes over the origin, accuracy, and appropriateness of the image, Sambo remains a constant reminder of the troubled history of American slavery and its impact on race relations.

—*Michael Polley*

For Further Reading
Blassingame, John W. 1972. *The Slave Community: Plantation Life in the Antebellum South.* New York: Oxford University Press; Boskin, Joshua. 1986. *Sambo: The Rise and Demise of an American Jester.* New York: Oxford University Press; Elkins, Stanley M. 1959. *Slavery: A Problem in American Institutional and Intellectual Life.* Chicago: University of Chicago Press; Genovese, Eugene. 1972. *Roll, Jordan, Roll: The World the Slaves Made.* New York: Pantheon books; Jordan, Winthrop D. 1969. *White over Black: American Attitudes toward the Negro, 1550–1812.* New York: Penguin Books.

They had initially moved to Cuba but were expelled from that island in 1809 after Napoleon's forces invaded Spain and relations between France and Spain grew cold. Many people in Louisiana feared the introduction of these immigrants and the slaves that they introduced.

1809
A Louisiana court heard the case of *Girod v. Lewis.* Judges decided that the marriages of slaves had no binding civil effect while the individuals involved remained slaves but upon manumission, such a marriage had the same legal standing as white marriages.

1809
Abraham Lincoln was born in Hardin County, Kentucky, on February 12. In 1860, Lincoln became the nation's sixteenth president. Because of his decision to issue the Emancipation Procla-

An 1859 painting by Eastman Johnson entitled Old Kentucky Home, Life in the South *typifies the image southerners hoped to project of slaves who were happy with their lot in life and satisfied to be subject to whites. (New-York Historical Society)*

mation, Lincoln became known as the Great Emancipator.

1810
The third census of the United States documented that 1,377,808 blacks, both slave and free, constituted 19 percent of the national population.

1810
A Louisiana court heard the case of *Adelle v. Beauregard* and declared that a black was considered free unless it was otherwise proven that the person in question was a slave. Another Louisiana court would issue a similar ruling in the case of *State v. Cecil* in 1812.

1810
Lewis Dupre published an antislavery tract enti-

tled *An Admonitory Picture and a Solemn Warning Principally Addressed to Professing Christians in the Southern States.* Published in Charleston, South Carolina, this pamphlet urged southern slaveowners to adopt an enlightened view and work to bring about an end to slavery.

1810
The future black abolitionist Charles Lenox Remond was born in Salem, Massachusetts, on February 1. In 1838, he was the first black to be hired as a lecturer by the Massachusetts Anti-Slavery Society.

1811
Paul Cuffe (1759–1818) sailed with 38 blacks to the colony of Sierra Leone in West Africa, spending $4,000 of his own funds to finance the expedition. Cuffe favored a program of

The only known portrait of Paul Cuffe (1759–1818) is this silhouette with his brig Traveller on the Sierra Leone coast in 1812. Cuffe financed an expedition to repatriate thirty-eight free blacks to the West African colony. (The Granger Collection)

colonization in which free blacks would be repatriated to Africa and used this voyage to promote that position. In subsequent decades, many other individuals and organizations would take up the cause of colonization.

1811
The Delaware state legislature enacted a law that prohibited free blacks from moving into the state. Any free black who arrived in Delaware was given a 10-day grace period to leave. After that time, free blacks were fined $10 per week until they removed themselves from the state.

1811
The North Carolina militia attacked a Maroon community in Cabarrus County that contained several fugitive slaves. Two slaves were killed, one was wounded, and most of the Maroons were captured and returned to slavery.

1811
A Maryland court heard the case of *Commonwealth v. Dolly Chapple* and decided that blacks

were permitted to testify against whites in those cases where a white defendant stood accused of having committed an act of mayhem upon a black person.

1811
On January 8–10, a massive slave revolt occurred along the River Road plantations 35 miles west of New Orleans (a region commonly called the German Coast) in the parishes of St. Charles and St. John the Baptist. Nearly 500 slaves were estimated to have been involved in the uprising, which was organized and led by Charles Deslondes. A combined force of planter militia and U.S. Army troops quelled the rebellion and restored order, apparently with great bloodshed. It is estimated that 100 slaves were either killed in the suppression of the revolt or executed as a result of the trials that followed.

1811
Harriet Beecher (Stowe), the author of *Uncle Tom's Cabin*, was born in Litchfield, Connecticut, on June 14.

1812
Paul Cuffe wrote *A Brief Account of the Settlement and Present Situation of the Colony of Sierra Leone.*

1812
The General Conference of the Methodist Church met in New York City and decided that slaveowners were no longer eligible to be elders in the Methodist Church.

1812
Louisiana entered the Union as a slave state on April 30. According to the state's constitution, freedmen were allowed to serve in the state militia. At this point the United States consisted of 18 states, which were evenly divided between free and slave.

1813
Judges in the U.S. Circuit Court for the District of Columbia heard the case of *United States v. Douglass* and declared that free blacks were competent to testify as witnesses in court proceedings against whites.

1813
Letters from a Man of Color on a Late Bill was

Cabins of ex-slaves a few years after the Civil War in the parish of St. John the Baptist, Louisiana, site of a massive slave revolt in 1811. (Archive Photos)

published anonymously in Philadelphia; it is believed that James Forten was the author. In this tract, the author criticized a bill the Pennsylvania state legislature was considering that would have prohibited the introduction of additional free blacks into the state. The legislature did not enact the measure.

1814

A Louisiana court heard the case of *Davenport v. the Commonwealth*. In their decision, the judges fined and imprisoned a white man who had kidnapped a free black woman and sold her as a slave.

1814

Charles Osborn and other antislavery associates established the Manumission Society of Tennessee.

1814

The territorial legislature in Illinois passed enabling legislation that allowed settlers to hire slaves from outside the territory and bring them into Illinois as laborers.

1814

In September, authorities in Louisiana tried to end the slave trading and other business ventures of Jean Laffite and his pirates in the Barataria Bay region south of New Orleans. Naval commander Daniel Patterson and army colonel George T. Ross conducted an amphibious assault upon the pirate's compound and disrupted the activities of Laffite. Eventually, the pirates relocated their illegal activities to the area of Galveston Island, Texas.

1814

In an emergency proclamation issued from Mobile, Alabama, on September 21, General Andrew Jackson called upon free blacks "to rally around the standard of the eagle" and help to defend the American cause during the War of 1812.

1814

On December 18, General Andrew Jackson issued a proclamation to the free black troops at New Orleans in which he stated: "TO THE MEN OF COLOR.—Soldiers! From the shores of Mobile I collected you to arms; I invited you to share in the perils and to divide the glory of your white countrymen. I expected much from you, for I was not uninformed of those qualities which must render you so formidable to an invading foe. I knew that you could endure hunger and thirst and all the hardships of war. I knew that you loved the land of your nativity, and that like ourselves, you had to defend all that is most dear to you. But you surpass my hopes. I have found in you, united to these qualities, that noble enthusiasm which impels to great deeds" (Jenkins, 1996).

1814

In the Treaty of Ghent, which ended the War of 1812 between the United States and Great Britain, both nations agreed on December 24 to cooperate in naval efforts to suppress the African slave trade.

1815

The Quaker abolitionist Benjamin Lundy organized the Union Humane Society in St. Clairsville, Ohio. This organization was one of the first abolitionist societies to be formed in the Midwest.

1815

In the Battle of New Orleans on January 8, two battalions of free blacks (about 600 soldiers) served alongside Andrew Jackson's forces to defend the city from an attack by British forces.

1815

In October, George Boxley, a white man, failed in an attempt to foment a slave rebellion in Spotsylvania and Orange Counties, Virginia. Boxley and his fellow conspirators had planned to attack the community of Fredericksburg during the harvest season, but a slave woman reported the conspiracy to authorities and the leaders of the planned attack were arrested before they could commence their plans. Boxley was never captured, but six slaves were executed for their role in the affair.

1815

Henry Highland Garnet, who later became a minister, abolitionist, and diplomat, was born a slave on a plantation in Kent County, Maryland, on December 23.

1816

The Book and Slavery Irreconcilable was published by George Bourne. The work is considered to be one of the most radical antislavery tracts to be published in America.

1816

The Virginia state legislature asked the federal government to establish a colony in the Pacific Northwest where free blacks from Virginia might be resettled as part of a colonization scheme. In the same year, Virginia Congressman John Randolph of Roanoke proposed a resolution requesting that Congress halt the "infamous traffic" of slaves in the nation's capital. Even though Washington, D.C., was a southern city, located in a federal district carved out of Maryland and Virginia, two slave states, the presence of the slave trade in the nation's capital was disturbing to many people who opposed slavery. Congress continued to receive many memorials (petitions) urging the end of the slave trade in the District of Columbia until the practice was finally abolished as a part of Henry Clay's Compromise of 1850.

1816

Louisiana law prohibited slaves from testifying in court against whites or free blacks unless the case in question involved a slave insurrection.

1816

North Carolina Quakers who supported the abolition of slavery established a manumission society in that state.

1816

The Bethel Charity School for Negroes was founded in Baltimore by Daniel Coker.

1816

The first convention of the African Methodist Episcopal Church (AME) was held on April 9–11 in Philadelphia, and Richard Allen was ordained as the first bishop of the church. The first black church in the United States to be totally free and independent of any white church, the AME established a policy of denying membership to anyone who was a slaveowner.

1816

In June, South Carolina authorities discovered a slave conspiracy that involved a planned attack upon Camden on July 4. A slave who had learned of the plot alerted his master before the violence began, and local authorities were able to arrest the leaders of the plot. The state legislature eventually emancipated the slave who betrayed the plot and gave him a lifetime pension for his services to the state.

The War of 1812, also known as the Second War for American Independence or the War for American Economic Independence, was a conflict between the United States and Great Britain, declared by the U.S. Congress on June 18, 1812, and concluded by the Treaty of Ghent on December 24, 1814. Considered by many people to have been an outgrowth of the Napoleonic conflict in Europe, the war's notable highlights included failed invasions of Canada by U.S. generals William Hull, Stephen Van Rensselaer, and Henry Dearborn in fall 1812; U.S. naval victories on Lake Erie by Oliver Hazard Perry in 1813 and on Lake Champlain by Thomas Macdonough in 1814; British general Robert Ross's August 1814 raid and burning of Washington, D.C., and his unsuccessful September attack against Baltimore, Maryland; Andrew Jackson's spring 1814 defeat of the Creek at Horseshoe Bend and his victory against the British at New Orleans in January 1815, after the war had officially ended.

Although there were several immediate causes for the conflict, its antecedents can be traced to as early as 1789. The beginnings of the French Revolution initiated a generation of warfare between Great Britain and France, and the fighting placed all neutral nations, especially the new republic of the United States, in a precarious position. President James Madison's war message to Congress in June 1812 identified four major reasons for the conflict: (1) British impressment of American seamen; (2) violation of American neutral rights on the high seas and in U.S. territorial waters; (3) the British blockade of U.S. ports; and (4) Britain's refusal to revoke or modify its orders in council dealing with the rights of neutral powers regarding trade. Although these points have been considered the official justification, other equally important causes included the British encouragement of Native American attacks in the U.S. Northwest Territory; the principles of Manifest Destiny—the desire by American war hawks to acquire Canadian and western Native American lands and perhaps even Spanish East and West Florida; an agricultural depression, which prompted some southern congressmen to view war as a means to revive the U.S. economy; and an intense American Anglophobia created by the years of humiliation at the hands of Great Britain.

It has been estimated that more than 5,000 African Americans, both free and slave, participated in the U.S. Army and Navy, British forces, and even the Spanish military during the conflict in the hopes of bettering their material conditions or to fight for causes in which they believed. They provided notable service to the United States with Perry at Lake Erie, General Samuel Smith at the Battle of Baltimore, and Jackson at New Orleans. British Colonial Marines, or runaway slaves, participated in the burning of Washington, D.C., on August 24, 1814. Runaway slaves and some free blacks also joined renegade mulatto and Indian communities in the Gulf South in an unsuccessful attempt to maintain their freedom against aggressive American frontiersmen and southern slaveholders.

As a part of their policy of destroying the American economy, British military forces liberated and carried off slaves during their operations in the Chesapeake Bay and along the Gulf Coast. This practice, combined with fears of a British-sponsored slave insurrection, prompted repressive measures against African Americans, which included destroying armed mulatto communities in Spanish Florida that were viewed as a threat to peace and a challenge to the established white status quo. The War of 1812 ultimately strengthened slavery in the American old Southwest, for after the war, the opening of new farmlands in Mississippi Territory and western Georgia, the destruction of mulatto communities along the frontier, and the ultimate removal of Native Americans east of the Mississippi River provided an impetus to the growing southern plantation system and continued slavery. In the end, the War of 1812 helped accelerate the American Civil War as the former strengthened the foundations for African American slavery in an ever-expanding agricultural South.

—*Gene A. Smith*

For Further Reading
Altoff, Gerard T. 1996. *Amongst My Best Men: African-Americans and the War of 1812.* Put-in-Bay, OH: Perry Group; Hickey, Donald R. 1989. *The War of 1812: A Forgotten Conflict.* Urbana: University of Illinois Press; Horsman, Reginald. 1962. *The Causes of the War of 1812.* Philadelphia: University of Pennsylvania Press; Stagg, J. C. A. 1983. *Mr Madison's War: Politics, Diplomacy, and Warfare in the Early Republic.* Princeton, NJ: Princeton University Press.

Begun by Benjamin Lundy in 1815, the Union Humane Society aimed primarily at extending humanitarian assistance to blacks in Ohio, but it also had the distinction of seeking to embrace all existing antislavery organizations. Resembling the Quaker antislavery societies that had operated for decades in Pennsylvania to aid free blacks and fugitive slaves, the efforts of the Union Humane Society to abolish slavery would eventually involve almost 1,000 antislavery societies.

Lundy, a 26-year-old New Jersey Quaker, organized the society in St. Clairsville, Ohio, when after much reflection over the "sad condition of the slave" he called a small number of friends to his house (Earle, 1847). Deeply affected by the frequent slave coffles (trains of slaves shackled together) he witnessed in Wheeling, Virginia, he expressed his desire to relieve those held in bondage. The society quickly grew to include nearly 500 members, among whom were most of the influential preachers and lawyers in the state of Ohio. On January 4, 1816, Lundy (under a pseudonym) published a circular on the subject of slavery in which he appealed to the philanthropists of the whole country, urging them to organize themselves in a similar manner. He also proposed that societies should be formed wherever "a sufficient number of persons could be induced to join them," that a name should be adopted that would be common to all societies, and that in addition to a uniform constitution, correspondence should be kept up between all societies (Earle, 1847).

In promoting "gradual emancipation," the constitution of the society, which was drafted on April 20, 1816, relied on the Golden Rule and on statements from the Declaration of Independence asserting the inalienable rights of man. In addition, its stated goals were to remove legal restrictions, to assist blacks illegally held in bondage, and to protect the rights of free blacks entering Ohio. Beyond working for the abolition of slavery, members of the society also promised to vote only for political leaders who opposed slavery and to erase racial prejudice and various forms of discrimination. Lundy's publication of the *Genius of Universal Emancipation,* the only exclusively antislavery journal in the country at the time, aided in this cause. However, as discussion of slavery increased, Lundy discovered that any plan to abolish slavery had to deal with a range of complexities. This need became evident with the founding of the American Colonization Society and Thomas Hedges Genin's attack at the semiannual meeting of the Union Humane Society at Mount Pleasant of its plan to send blacks back to Africa. Lundy did not initially agree with Genin, but the latter's views were part of a message delivered on behalf of the Union Humane Society at the 1819 American Convention for Promoting the Abolition of Slavery in Philadelphia.

Such internal disputes aside, the inability of the Union Humane Society to spread ideas and to limit slavery eventually led to disinterest and, ultimately, its disbanding. However, despite the society's declining effectiveness in promoting the abolition of slavery, the impact of Lundy and his organization can be seen in the effectiveness of other antislavery advocates, such as William Lloyd Garrison.

—*Mark L. Kamrath*

For Further Reading
Adams, Alice. 1908. *The Neglected Period of Anti-Slavery in America.* Gloucester, MA: Peter Smith; Dillon, Merton L. 1966. *Benjamin Lundy and the Struggle for Negro Freedom.* Urbana: University of Illinois Press; Dumond, Dwight Lowell. 1961. *Antislavery: The Crusade for Freedom in America.* Ann Arbor: University of Michigan Press; Earle, Thomas, ed. 1847. *The Life, Travels, and Opinions of Benjamin Lundy, including His Journeys to Texas and Mexico; with a Sketch of Contemporary Events, and a Notice of the Revolution in Hayti.* Philadelphia: William D. Parrish. Reprinted 1969. New York: Negro Universities Press.

1816

As part of the U.S. Army's efforts to stem the anarchy and lawlessness in Florida, army forces attacked and destroyed Fort Blount on Apalachicola Bay on July 27. The fort had been renamed Negro Fort after it was manned by nearly 300 escaped slaves and 20 Creek Indian allies who had sought asylum in the Spanish colony of East Florida. During the attack upon the fort, the fugitive slaves who defended the site suffered tremendous casualties—only 40 defenders were still alive when the fort was surrendered to the American forces. U.S. troops also conducted an expedition against a large fugitive settlement in South Carolina.

1816

The American Colonization Society (ACS) was

A meeting of the American Colonization Society. (Corbis-Bettmann)

founded in Washington, D.C., on December 28 in the hall of the House of Representatives. The purpose of the organization was to help former slaves return to Africa, and the ACS was instrumental in establishing the colonial outpost of Liberia on the West African coast as a homeland for repatriated Africans.

1817
The New York state legislature enacted a second gradual abolition bill. According to this measure, all blacks who had not yet been emancipated by the first gradual emancipation act of 1799 would become free effective July 4, 1827.

1817
A Maryland court heard the case of *Burrows Admiralty v. Negro Anna* and decided that a master provided freedom to a slave by implication if he granted the slave a gift of property. This decision was based upon the understand-

ing that a slave could not own property; therefore, if property were given, it was apparent the owner desired that the slave be emancipated.

1817
Most abolitionists did not support the colonization plans that had started returning freed blacks to Africa. At the yearly meeting of the American Convention of Abolition Societies, delegates approved a resolution stating "the gradual and total emancipation of all persons of colour, and their literary and moral education, should precede their colonization" (Jenkins, 1996).

1817
In January, James Forten led a protest meeting of 3,000 free blacks in Philadelphia who opposed the work of the American Colonization Society. The group that met at the Bethel AME Church believed that the society sought to remove them from America, the land of their birth.

1817

Frederick Douglass was born a slave on a plantation near Tuckahoe, in Talbot County, Maryland, on February 14. He would eventually escape from slavery and become the best-known black abolitionist in the United States.

1817

A revolt involving as many as 200 slaves occurred in St. Mary's County, Maryland, on April 7.

1817

On August 29, the white abolitionist Charles Osborn began publishing an antislavery newspaper, the *Philanthropist,* in Mt. Pleasant, Ohio.

1817

Samuel Ringgold Ward, who became a noted abolitionist, minister, and author, was born a slave on Maryland's Eastern Shore, on October 17. In 1855 he published *The Autobiography of a Fugitive Negro.*

1817

Mississippi entered the Union as a slave state on December 10. At this point, the United States consisted of 20 states, which were evenly divided between free and slave states.

1818

A Mississippi court heard the case of *Harvy and Others v. Decker* and determined that slaves who were transported from Virginia into Indiana and later taken into Mississippi were legally free. The Mississippi judges ruled that according to the Northwest Ordinance of 1787, the slaves had made been free when they were taken into the free territory of Indiana. [For more on the Northwest Ordinance, see Document 32.]

1818

Action by the state legislature disenfranchised blacks in the state of Connecticut.

1818

A South Carolina court decided the case of *Arthur v. Wells,* declaring that the killing of a fugitive slave was lawful only if the fugitive resisted recapture and thus threatened the safety of the slave catcher.

1818

In Philadelphia, a group of free blacks estab-

James Forten (1766–1842), a leader of Philadelphia's African American community and a prominent abolitionist, opposed the efforts of the American Colonization Society to repatriate free blacks to Africa. (The Granger Collection)

lished the Pennsylvania Augustine Society in order to provide educational opportunities for free black children.

1818

Judges in the U.S. Circuit Court for the District of Columbia heard the case of *Sarah v. Taylor* and declared that children who were born between the date of promised manumission and the date of actual manumission were entitled to be freed at the same time their mother was freed.

1818

New York Congressman James Tallmadge, Jr., tried to stall the admission of Illinois into the Union because he was concerned that the proposed state constitution did not contain a clear and strong prohibition of slavery.

1818

A Delaware court heard the case of *Meunier v. Duperrow,* and the judges convicted two free black women of the charge that they had been kidnapping other free blacks and selling them into slavery.

1818

In the Battle of Suwannee in Spanish Florida on April 18, General Andrew Jackson defeated a combined force of Indians and blacks, thus ending the First Seminole War. Jackson had called the conflict "this savage and negro war" in his communications during the war (Jenkins, 1996).

1819

The U.S. Congress granted authority to President James Monroe to dispatch armed vessels to the coast of West Africa. These American warships became a part of the African Squadron, which was a joint British and U.S. venture to try to suppress the illegal African slave trade.

1819

Attorney Roger B. Taney defended the Reverend Jacob Gruber, who was accused of inciting slaves to riot. In his defense of Gruber, Taney cited slavery as a great evil that had to be destroyed. Years later, Taney, as chief justice of the U.S. Supreme Court, sat in judgment in the case of *Dred Scott v. Sandford*.

1819

The white abolitionist Charles Osborn began publishing an antislavery newspaper entitled the *Manumission Intelligencer* in Tennessee.

1819

Former president James Madison promoted a plan that slavery should end through gradual abolition with freed slaves being allotted western homesteads. Although Madison wanted slavery to end, he believed that racial separation would have to exist in the United States if civil order were to be maintained.

1819

On January 26, Congress considered a measure to create Arkansas Territory out of Arkansas County in Missouri Territory. This action was approved, but not before Congress defeated an amendment, proposed by New York Representative John W. Taylor, that would have prohibited slavery in Arkansas Territory.

1819

When Missouri Territory sought admission to the Union as a slave state on February 13, the action was challenged by New York Representative James Tallmadge, Jr., who proposed that an antislavery amendment be attached to the bill proposing Missouri statehood. The amendment would have prevented the further importation of slaves into Missouri and also emancipated all children born to slaves in Missouri, after its admission as a state, when they reached the age of 25. Although the House of Representatives approved both of these amendments, the Senate defeated both measures.

1819

Even though Congress had legally ended the African slave trade, a lucrative illegal trade continued as slave ships tried to smuggle shiploads of Africans into American coastal waters. In order to end these smuggling efforts, Congress enacted a measure on March 3 creating a reward of $50 per slave to be given to any informer who provided reports that helped stem the illegal importation of slaves into the United States. The measure also gave the president the power to return any Africans who were captured in this fashion back to Africa.

1819

In the spring, a slave named Coot was captured and executed for having organized a slave conspiracy to burn the city of Augusta, Georgia.

1819

Alabama entered the Union as a slave state on December 14, but the state's constitution did give the legislature the ability to abolish slavery and compensate slaveowners should it see fit to take such action. At this point, the United States consisted of 22 states, which were evenly divided between slave and free.

1820

According to the fourth census of the United States, the black population of the country, both slave and free, was 1,771,656—18.4 percent of the nation's population.

1820

Free blacks organized the New York African Society as a benevolent association to assist the needs of the free black population. The success of this organization spawned the creation of other such groups in New York City, including

The Tallmadge Amendment, an antislavery provision attached to the Missouri statehood bill of 1819, initiated the first sectional clash over slavery in the territories. In February 1819, a bill came before Congress calling for an enabling act to allow Missouri Territory to petition for statehood. As Missouri was a slaveholding territory embracing 10,000 bondsmen, the common assumption was that Missouri would enter the Union straightaway as a slave state. Congressman James Tallmadge, Jr., of New York thought otherwise. He attached to the proposed enabling act an amendment closing Missouri to the further ingress of slavery and stipulating that slave children born in Missouri after its admission to the Union should be manumitted at age 25. The amendment proposed no regulations concerning slaves already present in the territory, but the Tallmadge proviso did effectively prescribe a program of gradual emancipation that would ultimately extinguish the peculiar institution in Missouri.

The Tallmadge Amendment caused great alarm in the South. Some slave-state politicians, such as Nathaniel Macon of North Carolina and future president John Tyler of Virginia, denied the authority of Congress to interfere with slavery in the territories. Others predicted disunion and civil war unless northern antislavery agitation ceased. Virginia's chief justice, Spencer Roane, suggested that the South, "if driven to it," could form with the slaveholding West a "great nation" apart from the "northern Yankies [*sic*]" (Roane, 1906). Georgia Senator Freeman Walker went further, suggesting that Tallmadge's crusade would lead to "civil wars," to "a brother's sword crimsoned with a brother's blood" (Moore, 1953).

Congress debated the Tallmadge Amendment for a full year. Reintroduced several times, the measure repeatedly passed in the House of Representatives, where northern delegates formed a majority. The amendment continually failed in the Senate, however, where southern representation equaled that of the North owing to an exact balance between slave and free states. Illinois Senator Jesse B. Thomas broke the deadlock in February 1820 when he offered an amendment to the Missouri bill that resulted in the Missouri Compromise. The Thomas proviso called for the admission of Missouri as a slave state without the Tallmadge restrictions and proposed the admission of Maine as a free state in order to preserve the sectional balance. Additionally, the Thomas Amendment excluded slavery from the remainder of the old Louisiana Territory north of 36 degrees 30 minutes north latitude.

Both sections grudgingly accepted the Thomas compromise. Southerners preferred an immediate short-term victory while free-state leaders feared for the safety of the Republic if they clung to the Tallmadge plan. As antislavery Congressman Charles Kinsey of New Jersey explained, he opted for compromise because an antislavery victory in Missouri would be "gained at the hazard of the Union" (Fehrenbacher, 1980). Yet the Missouri Compromise solved little. It left the slavery question to a future generation of Americans, who revisited the Tallmadge controversy time and again before ultimately fulfilling Freeman Walker's prophesy of a bloody civil war between American brothers-in-arms.

—*Eric Tscheschlok*

For Further Reading
Brown, Richard H. 1966. "The Missouri Crisis, Slavery, and the Politics of Jacksonianism." *South Atlantic Quarterly* 65 (Winter): 55–72; Fehrenbacher, Don E. 1980. *The South and Three Sectional Crises*. Baton Rouge: Louisiana State University Press; Moore, Glover. 1953. *The Missouri Controversy, 1819–1821.* Lexington: University of Kentucky Press; Roane, Spencer. 1906. "Letters of Spencer Roane, 1788–1822." *New York Public Library Bulletin* 10: 167–180.

the Union Society, the Clarkson Association, the Wilberforce Benevolent Society, and the Woolman Society of Brooklyn.

1820

The American Colonization Society established Liberia on the coast of West Africa. The site was to be used as an outpost for colonization efforts aimed at returning free blacks to Africa, and many antislavery advocates like Margaret Mer-

cer worked tirelessly to support the colonization efforts of the society. In 1847, Liberia declared it was an independent republic.

1820

The premise that slaves received their freedom when they were transported from a slave state to a free state or territory was confirmed by two legal decisions. Kentucky courts upheld the principle in the case of *Rankin v. Lydia,* and Vir-

MARGARET MERCER (1791–1846)

As an antislavery advocate, teacher, and author, Margaret Mercer is considered to have been Virginia's preeminent female supporter of Negro colonization. Driven by religious motives, Mercer entered into altruistic activities as a young woman, beginning by supporting church activities as well as giving money and time during the Greek war of independence from Turkey (1821–1832). Her main focus, however, was her interest in antislavery causes, specifically those embodied by the American Colonization Society (ACS). The goal of the ACS was to provide funds for free Negroes to emigrate to Africa and to encourage the emancipation of slaves by asking slaveowners to send their slaves to the newly created colony of Liberia. The ACS believed that this manner of dealing with slavery would ultimately rid the United States of the practice. ACS supporters also clearly stated that the removal of free slaves to Africa would open up job opportunities for white citizens and would eventually accomplish the creation of a white (and therefore more acceptable) populace.

Mercer, the daughter of a Maryland governor (John F. Mercer served 1801–1802), emancipated the 15 slaves she inherited from her father, diligently worked on fund-raising for the colonization project, sponsored education projects in the Liberian colony, and was a forthright voice in the argument for Liberian colonization. Eventually, enthusiasm for the ACS began to wane among some of its leading members, who felt the ACS was ineffective and divisive among abolitionists. The American Union for the Relief and Improvement of the Colored Race was organized in its stead, and Mercer, deeply offended, turned her efforts to teaching. She was the author of two books published in 1837: *Studies for Bible Classes* and *Popular Lectures on Ethics or Moral Obligation for the Use of Schools*. Mercer died of tuberculosis in Virginia.

—*Maria Elena Raymond*

For Further Reading
Malone, Dumas, ed. 1933. *Dictionary of American Biography*. New York: Charles Scribner's Sons; Staudenraus, P. J. 1961. *The African Colonization Movement 1816–1865*. New York: Columbia University Press.

---

ginia courts reached the same decision in the case of *Griffith v. Fanny*.

1820

In February, President James Monroe signed a presidential order that allowed the U.S. Army to enact a policy depriving blacks or mulattoes of the right to serve in the U.S. military.

1820

The *Mayflower of Liberia* (previously the brig *Elizabeth*) sailed from New York City on February 6 to Sierra Leone on the western coast of Africa with 86 blacks who had agreed to return to Africa as part of a colonization scheme. The ship arrived in Sierra Leone on March 9. The British had established Sierra Leone as a colony where former slaves could be repatriated to Africa, and the colony had been accepting freed blacks and fugitive slaves for three decades.

1820

The U.S. Senate passed the measure known as the Missouri Compromise on February 17. In this measure, it was understood that Missouri would enter the Union as a slave state and Maine would enter as a free state, thus maintaining the delicate balance of votes that existed in the Senate chamber. Senator Jesse B. Thomas of Illinois introduced an amendment to this measure calling for the prohibition of slavery in those areas within Louisiana Territory that were north of the line 36 degrees 30 minutes north latitude, and the measure passed as amended in the Senate.

1820

The House of Representatives defeated the Senate version of the Missouri Compromise legislation on February 28. Members of the House attempted to pass a modified version of the bill, which included a controversial Taylor Amendment that would have barred slavery from the western territories. Taylor had earlier tried to introduce this measure on January 26, 1819, but the proposal had been defeated at that time.

1820

Congress agreed to the Missouri Compromise on March 3, allowing Missouri to enter the Union as a slave state and Maine to enter as a free state. The measure also prohibited slavery

The Missouri Compromise (1820) raised the important question of whether or not slavery would be allowed to expand into the Louisiana Territory that the United States had purchased from France in 1803. Although the territory in question was west of the Mississippi, the most important debate over the issue occurred in the nation's capital. Representatives and senators from North and South clashed over the sensitive issue of slavery in heated debate, the likes of which would not be seen again until the 1850s.

The long-term cause of the Missouri crisis was the gradual evolution of slavery in the United States. Following the American Revolution, the northern states began to abolish slavery, and many northerners began to question the place of slavery in a country that had fought a war for liberty and which professed in its Declaration of Independence that all men were created equal and possessed inalienable rights to life, liberty, and the pursuit of happiness. Many southerners, however, retained slavery despite the inconsistency between slavery and a war fought for independence. Southerners defended slavery by stating that the Revolution had preserved liberty, including the protection of private property, which included slaves. Although they clung to slavery, many southerners often professed the wish to be rid of slavery, which kept hopes alive in the North that the institution of slavery could be abolished.

Little seemed unusual when the territory of Missouri applied to Congress in 1818 for the right to form a state government and draft a constitution. Henry Clay presented the petition to Congress on December 18, 1818, and little happened until February 13, 1819, when James Tallmadge, a Republican congressman from New York, introduced an amendment that sought "the further introduction of slavery or involuntary servitude be prohibited, except for the punishment of crimes" (*Annals of Congress*, 15th Cong., 2d sess.). His amendment also provided that all children born into slavery in Missouri were to freed when they reached the age of 25. After furious debate on February 15, 1819, the House passed the Tallmadge Amendment, but the Senate rejected it. Northerners supported the measure while southerners opposed it.

Congress resumed its debate over slavery in Missouri in December 1819, and one of the main questions was whether Congress had the authority to regulate slavery. Northerners tended to argue that Congress did by pointing to the Northwest Ordinance of 1787 as precedent; southerners replied that slavery was a state institution and Congress could not regulate it. The debates also featured northern attacks on slavery and southern defenses of it. Northerners criticized slavery as an unrepublican institution and stated that it blighted the southern landscape and made a mockery of national values. Southern defenders of slavery counterattacked with their own readings of the Constitution and the Declaration of Independence and defended the right of slaveholders to move their property, slaves, to Missouri. Southerners also charged that efforts to exclude slavery from Missouri would make the residents of that state second-class citizens, unable to share in the common rights enjoyed by other Americans.

Following months of venomous debate, Congress, led by Henry Clay of Kentucky, decided to effect a compromise. Maine, currently a province of Massachusetts, had also sought admission to the Union as a state, and southern members of Congress held up the admission of Maine, in effect using Maine as a bargaining chip in the dispute over Missouri's admission into the Union. The compromise resulted in the admission of Maine into the Union as a free state and allowed the Missouri legislature to decide the future of slavery in that state, although most observers expected Missouri to enter as a slave state. Through this arrangement, the balance of power in the Senate would be maintained. Another part of the compromise called for a line to be drawn on the map of the United States at 36 degrees 30 minutes north latitude, a line that represented the southern border of Missouri. Lands north of this line in the remaining territory of the Louisiana Purchase would be free territory, except for Missouri; territory south of the line would be considered open to settlement by slaveholders.

In the second 1820 congressional session, there was an episode that nearly scuttled the agreement reached only months earlier. Missouri's legislature voted to prohibit the immigration of free blacks into that state, an action that raised the thorny question of black citizenship. Northern opponents of the measure stated that the Constitution made no mention of color as a prerequisite for citizenship, and southern supporters of the measure pointed to custom for evidence. The latter noted that states in both the North and the South denied suffrage to free blacks, prohibited interracial marriage, and prohibited free blacks from joining the militia. These southern arguments proved powerful because they expressed a common belief that blacks were inferior to whites, and no northern opponent of Missouri's constitutional stipulation expressed any sentiments that contradicted such a belief.

As a result of this Missouri constitutional provision, Congress delayed the admission of Missouri into the Union. Competing resolutions for and against the offending clause in the state's constitution lacked majorities in Congress, and once again, Henry Clay managed to create a compromise. This one required the Missouri legislature, in a public act, to ignore the principles of their state's constitution and not pass laws that contradicted the federal Constitution. The Missouri legislature responded by passing a law stating that Congress lacked the right to order such a bill and that the order of Congress lacked binding authority on the state. President James Monroe accepted this law, and Missouri became a state on August 10, 1821.

The Missouri Compromise revealed an important lesson to the political generation of that day. Slavery must not become a topic of debate in Congress. The heated passions expressed during the debates revealed a growing antislavery sentiment in the North and a growing commitment to slavery in the South. Slavery in the territories provoked a crisis in 1819; its status would later provoke a civil war.

—*James C. Foley*

For Further Reading
Ashworth, John. 1995. *Slavery, Capitalism, and Politics in the Antebellum Republic.* Vol. 1, *Commerce and Compromise, 1820–1850.* New York. Cambridge University Press; Dangerfield, George. 1952. *The Era of Good Feelings.* New York: Harcourt Brace and Company; Freehling, William. 1990. *The Road to Disunion.* New York: Oxford University Press; Moore, Glover. 1953. *The Missouri Controversy, 1819–1821.* Lexington: University Press of Kentucky.

from being allowed in any territories north of the 36-degree 30-minute parallel line. (The Thomas Amendment had been incorporated, and the Taylor Amendment had been rejected.)

1820

In April, the Quaker Elihu Embree began publishing the *Emancipator,* an antislavery newspaper, in Jonesboro, Tennessee. The previous year, Embree had published the short-lived *Manumission Intelligencer,* probably the first antislavery newspaper published in the United States.

1820

In an effort to stop the illegal importation of African slaves to America, the Congress of the United States declared on May 15 that hereafter the involvement in the African slave trade would be considered an act of piracy. Punishments for those found guilty of such action included forfeiture of all vessels and cargo and the execution of any American citizens found to be participating in the illegal activity.

1820

Missouri Territory drafted a constitution for the proposed state of Missouri on July 19, but it included a discriminatory prohibition keeping mulattoes and free blacks from entering the future state. This controversial provision presented problems when Congress reviewed the constitution on November 14, 1820.

1821

In New York State, the constitutional convention altered provisions made in the state's 1777 constitution by increasing property and residence requirements for blacks. This action effectively limited the suffrage to fewer free blacks.

1821

U.S. Attorney General William Wirt advised port officials in Norfolk, Virginia, that blacks could not legally command naval vessels. Wirt claimed that maritime law required that all naval commanders be citizens of their country and that this provision prevented free blacks from such service because they were not considered to be citizens of the United States.

1821

Harriet Tubman was born a slave on a plantation in Dorchester County, Maryland. She escaped from slavery in 1849 and became one of the most celebrated "conductors" on the Underground Railroad as she assisted hundreds of other slaves in their escape from slavery in the southern states.

1821

Benjamin Lundy, a Quaker, began publication of the *Genius of Universal Emancipation* in Mount Pleasant, Ohio, in January. This publication was one of the earliest abolitionist newspapers in the United States. Although Lundy relocated his

Published monthly in Jonesboro, Tennessee, from April to October 1820, the *Emancipator* was the second newspaper in the United States devoted solely to the abolition of slavery. The paper was a one-man effort, written by and funded by Quaker Elihu Embree (1782–1820), but its subscription list of over 2,000 carried it beyond Tennessee. It succeeded Embree's earlier weekly *Manumission Intelligencer* established in Jonesboro, probably the first American antislavery periodical, which had ceased publication in December 1819. After Embree's death, and the fiscal difficulties of the iron businesses in which he had been involved, the *Emancipator* ceased publication. Another abolitionist newspaper, *The Genius of Universal Emancipation*, might not have been published had Embree's father, Thomas, been successful in convincing Benjamin Lundy to continue publishing the *Emancipator* after Elihu's death.

In the *Emancipator*, Embree sought to encourage manumission by applying Christian principles and exposing the behavior of slaveowners. Embree advocated neither immediate manumission nor the use of violence; he urged gradual emancipation and colonization. He distributed the paper to legislators, advised antislavery voters to use the ballot, and encouraged petitions. He also celebrated the slaveowners who had freed their slaves; published pertinent letters from one individual to another; traced the history of slavery; declared that northern farms were more prosperous than southern farms; published the speeches of people who opposed slavery; and argued that slavery was not economically advantageous, that it destroyed family ties, and that it fostered unrepublican attitudes among slaveowners and the general populace.

Embree complained that unsympathetic postal workers interfered with distribution of his paper. When he sent complimentary copies to several southern governors, the copies were returned in a manner that required him to pay postage. Also, Governor George Poindexter of Mississippi denounced him as a paid stooge of northern agitators.

Embree resigned from the Manumission Society of Tennessee because its constitution might have interfered, in his view, with the publication of his paper. The eleventh article of the society's constitution required that an inspection committee approve the publications of members, but the irregular gatherings of the society would have made it difficult for Embree to publish his writings regularly. Ironically, the society's articles had been written in 1815 by Embree to ensure consensus decision making. Despite his resignation, he regularly published the society's addresses, proceedings, and tracts. Above all, he believed that God would punish the unjust and declared (in the second issue of the *Emancipator*): "My creed is universal and equal liberty," and I "endeavor to know what is right, and do it, dreading no consequences."

In 1813 or 1814, Embree had been converted to abolition after having been compelled to sell a family of slaves to cover a debt, but he remained a slaveowner until his death when, in his will, he freed his "faithful servant and slave black Nancy together with her children Frames a yellow boy or young man Abegil & Sophea her two black daughters and Mount her yellow daughter and John her son nearly black" (Blassingame and Henderson, 1980). Not only did he free Nancy's children, he made provision for their education as well. Manumission laws made any other course difficult because of the ages of the children.

—*Charles A. D'Aniello*

For Further Reading
Blassingame, John W., and Mae G. Henderson, eds. 1980. *Antislavery Newspapers and Periodicals*. Vol. 1, *(1817–1845): Annotated Index of Letters in the Philanthropist, Emancipator, Genius of Universal Emancipation, Abolition Intelligencer, African Observer, and the Liberator*. Boston: G. K. Hall; Embree, Elihu, and Robert H. White. 1932. *The Emancipator*. Nashville, TN: B. H. Murphy; Goodheart, Lawrence B. 1982. "Tennessee's Antislavery Movement Reconsidered: The Example of Elihu Embree." *Tennessee Historical Quarterly* 41(3): 224–238.

publication to Baltimore (1824), Washington, D.C. (1830), and Illinois (1838), the newspaper remained in print rather regularly from 1821 to 1839 except for a brief hiatus in 1835–1836.

1821

On March 2, Speaker of the House Henry Clay negotiated a last-minute compromise when Congress balked at discriminatory provisions in the proposed constitution of Missouri that would have barred free blacks and mulattoes from the state. Congress voted to approve statehood for Missouri provided state officials did not attempt to limit the rights of citizens, espe-

❧GENIUS OF UNIVERSAL EMANCIPATION❧

During the 1820s, under Benjamin Lundy's editorship, the *Genius of Universal Emancipation* was the nation's major antislavery newspaper and linked together abolitionist groups across the nation. It was first published in Lundy's hometown of Mount Pleasant, Ohio, in January 1821. Elihu Embree's father had hoped that Lundy would continue the *Emancipator* after Elihu's death in 1820 and move to Jonesboro, Tennessee, but Lundy moved to Greeneville, Tennessee, a few months later instead. However, the *Genius of Universal Emancipation* was continued using the same printing equipment as the earlier newspaper. Then, in the summer of 1824, the paper was moved to Baltimore, where a Baltimore slave dealer, Austin Woolfolk, assaulted Lundy in 1827 because of comments published in the paper. The paper was moved to Washington, D.C., in 1830, where it was published until 1834. Between 1835 and 1836, publication of the *Genius of Universal Emancipation* ceased, and Lundy began publishing another newspaper in Philadelphia, the *National Enquirer,* which opposed the annexation of Texas. This paper became the *Pennsylvania Freeman* in 1838. That May, Lundy lost all his papers in a mob attack on Pennsylvania Hall, and he moved to Illinois and reestablished the *Genius of Universal Emancipation.* The 12 issues that preceded his death had the dateline of Hennepin, Illinois, but they were actually printed in Lowell, Illinois.

Lundy is credited with bringing William Lloyd Garrison into the national spotlight. In 1829, Garrison became associate editor after Lundy had met him during a six-month lecture tour, but Garrison's militancy led to a separation with Lundy. In 1830, while Lundy was away, Garrison libeled a Newburyport, Massachusetts, slave dealer in the paper, and both he and Lundy were sued and physically attacked. Garrison even spent seven weeks in jail for the libel. In 1831, Garrison moved to Boston and founded the *Liberator,* and this paper quickly replaced the *Genius of Universal Emancipation* as the nation's major antislavery newspaper. As early as 1829, Garrison had openly recanted "gradual abolition" in the *Genius of Universal Emancipation,* which he noted in the prospectus for the *Liberator.*

Lundy's approach was different as he advocated a gradualist voluntary approach to abolition. He believed that demonstration of the productivity of free black labor would lead to the gradual extinction of slavery through voluntary manumission, and although he believed free blacks had a right to stay in the United States, he thought it would be easier for them to prove the superiority of their labor in emigrant colonies. To find a suitable location for a colony for freed blacks, he traveled to Haiti (1825 and 1829), Upper Canada (1832), and Mexico's Texas (1830–1831, 1833–1834, 1834–1835). He published both evangelical appeals, expressed largely by southerners, and secular arguments against slavery and condemned only violence as a means for ending the institution. Lundy denounced slavery for nurturing aristocratic and undemocratic attitudes among slaveowners. Ahead of his time, he advocated political action as an appropriate antislavery strategy. The types of material he published included reports of law cases, proceedings of abolition societies, biographical and historical sketches, and summaries of pertinent foreign and domestic news.

—*Charles A. D'Aniello*

For Further Reading
Blassingame, John W., and Mae G. Henderson, eds. 1980–1984. *Antislavery Newspapers and Periodicals.* Vol. 1, *(1817–1845): Annotated Index of Letters in the Philanthropist, Emancipator, Genius of Universal Emancipation, Abolition Intelligencer, African Observer, and the Liberator.* Boston: G. K. Hall; Dillon, Merton L. 1966. *Benjamin Lundy and the Struggle for Negro Freedom.* Urbana: University of Illinois Press; Dillon, Merton L. 1986. "Benjamin Lundy: Quaker Radical," *Timeline* 3(3): 28–41.

---

cially free black citizens, as guaranteed by the U.S. Constitution. On June 26, 1821, the Missouri legislature approved this stipulation.

1821
In New York City, James Varick was installed as the first bishop of the newly established African Methodist Episcopal Zion (AMEZ) Church on June 21.

1821
Missouri entered the Union as a slave state on August 10. At this point, the United States consisted of 24 states, 12 free and 12 slave.

1821
In December, the Maryland State Supreme Court ruled in the case of *Hall v. Mullin,* deciding that a master provided freedom to a slave by implication if he left a bequest of property to

A ship carrying freed slaves from the United States is shown arriving in Liberia under the sponsorship of the American Colonization Society in this 1832 engraving. (The Granger Collection)

that slave in a will or final testament. This decision was based upon the understanding that since a slave could not own property, if property were willed, it was apparent that the former owner wanted the slave to be emancipated.

1822

The American Colonization Society settled its first group of repatriated Africans in Monrovia, Liberia, in West Africa. Eventually, about 15,000 persons were settled in the colony. Much of the success of the Liberian colony was owing to the efforts of Jehudi Ashmun, who was sent to Liberia by the American Colonization Society to direct efforts there.

1822

Free blacks were disenfranchised in Rhode Island.

1822

Judges in the U.S. Circuit Court for the District of Columbia heard the case of *Matilda v. Mason* and declared that it was not necessary to remove all antislavery supporters from a potential jury pool if a case involved questions regarding slaveowners and their property. Evidently, this discriminatory practice was common in many of the southern states.

1822

A struggle began in Illinois as proslavery supporters tried to create a state constitution that would legalize slavery there. The debates raged in the state until the proposal was effectively defeated in 1824 when Governor Edward Coles refused to call a constitutional convention that, most likely, would have drafted a proslavery document.

1822

The premise that slaves received their freedom when they were transported from a slave state to a free state or territory was again confirmed in a state court. A Pennsylvania court heard the case of *Commission v. Robinson* and held that transporting a slave from a slave state to a free state did in fact make a slave free.

1822

The Tennessee Manumission Society addressed a memorial to the U.S. Congress calling for an end to slavery in Washington, D.C.

1822

A New York court heard the case of *Overseers of Marbletown v. Overseers of Kingston* and decided that a marriage between a free black and a slave did not change the status of either party.

The judge further ruled that the children of such a union would be born free only if the mother were free.

1822
The abolitionist John Finely Crowe began publishing the *Abolition Intelligencer* in Shelby, Kentucky.

1822
On May 30, authorities in Charleston, South Carolina, detected a slave insurrection that was planned by a free black, Denmark Vesey, when a house servant alerted authorities to the wide-ranging conspiracy. Vesey, a sailor and carpenter, had organized one of the most elaborate slave conspiracies in the history of the United States. He was eventually hanged along with 36 of his conspirators while 130 blacks and 4 whites were arrested during the intensive investigation that followed the discovery of the plot. South Carolina and several other southern states took immediate action to restrict the mobility of and education afforded blacks in light of this plot.

1822
Denmark Vesey and five of his principal accomplices were hanged at Blake's Landing in Charleston, South Carolina, on July 2.

1823
A decision in a U.S. circuit court in South Carolina regarding the case of *Elkison v. Deliesseline* asserted that the removal of a slave from a slave state to a free state effectively bestowed freedom.

1823
The Mississippi state legislature enacted a measure that made it illegal to teach a slave to read or write. Additionally, any gathering that consisted of more than five slaves or free blacks was deemed illegal by legislative action.

1823
Judges in the U.S. Circuit Court for the District of Columbia heard the case of *United States v. Brockett*. In rendering their decision, the judges declared that "to cruelly, inhumanely, and maliciously cut, slash, beat and ill treat one's own slave is an indictable offence at common law."

1824
In Illinois, Iowa, Indiana, and Michigan, state laws required that blacks must post bond to guarantee good behavior in order to be qualified for suffrage rights.

1824
The Louisiana state legislature enacted a new slave code that updated some of the provisions of the older Code Noir (Black Code), which had been in operation since 1724. [See Document 45.]

1824
The Missouri Supreme Court decided the case of *Winny v. Whitesides,* and in their decision, the justices declared that a slave did indeed become free by residing for a time in Illinois or any other free jurisdiction.

1824
In December, the Indiana state legislature enacted a measure that made enforcement of the Fugitive Slave Act of 1793 more difficult. The new Indiana law allowed justices of the peace to settle cases in fugitive slave cases, but both the fugitive and the claimant had the right to demand a trial by jury. This action made the work of reclaiming a fugitive more time consuming and, in effect, more expensive. The Indiana law was eventually invalidated when the Fugitive Slave Act of 1850 was passed.

1825
The legislatures in 8 of the 12 free states approved resolutions calling upon the federal government to enact a program of compensated emancipation to end the practice of slavery in the United States. Southern politicians in the Congress blocked efforts to consider these proposals.

1825
The slave Josiah Henson, who was later used as the prototype for Uncle Tom in Harriet Beecher Stowe's *Uncle Tom's Cabin,* led a group of slaves from Maryland to freedom in Kentucky. He later crossed the border into Ontario (Upper Canada), where he headed a community of former slaves.

1826
Frances Wright established Nashoba Plantation,

Denmark Vesey, a former slave, a skilled carpenter, a literate free black, and a man of imposing strength, was the leader of an abortive slave rebellion in Charleston, South Carolina, in 1822. Born about 1767, it is not clear whether his birth occurred in Africa or on the island of St. Thomas in the Caribbean. It is known that he lived as a slave boy on the island in the 1700s. In 1781, Denmark and 390 other slaves were transported to Saint Domingue (Haiti). The ship's master, Captain Joseph Vesey, took an interest in the boy, dressed him up, and took him to his cabin. On arrival at Cape Français, Saint Domingue, Denmark was sold along with other slaves.

On Captain Vesey's next trip to Saint Domingue, he was told that the French sugar planter who had bought Denmark had rejected him, complaining that Denmark was "unsound and subject to epilepsy" (Lofton, 1948). According to the slave trading practice of the time, Captain Vesey had to take Denmark back, and between 1781 and 1783, Denmark sailed with his master on slave-trading voyages to different ports in the Caribbean and once to Africa. As a consequence of his travels, Denmark learned to speak English, French, Danish, and Spanish.

In 1783, Captain Vesey decided to settle in Charleston, South Carolina, which, at the time, was a growing urban center and ranked as the fourth-largest city after New York, Philadelphia, and Boston. One of the reasons Captain Vesey abandoned the slave trade was that in the 1780s, the market for slaves in the United States began a downward slide. More important, in 1783, the state of South Carolina imposed heavy duties on slave imports, and beginning in 1787, it prohibited trafficking in slaves. Thus, the economic climate did not favor slave trading. The suspension of the trade was only temporary, however, because in 1803, a boom in cotton production led to an increased trade in slaves. Captain Vesey having given up trading in slaves, began a business in Charleston as a ships' chandler, and for the next 17 years, Denmark served his master in Charleston.

As a result of the cosmopolitan character of Charleston, external influences were bound to permeate the society. For instance, the ideological rhetoric of the French Revolution gradually crept into the city, and Denmark and others were later to borrow a leaf from the rebelling slaves of Saint Domingue. As a slave in Charleston, Denmark was like most urban bondsmen who worked as domestics for the urban elites, which included ship-builders, lawyers, doctors, engineers, merchants, and businessmen. Because of Denmark's skills as a carpenter, he was hired out by his master, which provided Denmark ample opportunity not only to earn extra cash but also to educate himself through learning about current events in Charleston and elsewhere. The freedom to move around aided Denmark in establishing a network with slaves and free blacks, and this circle of friends became the pivot around which he later organized his plot.

Another significant development in Denmark's life occurred in December 1799 when he won a lottery prize of $1,500. In January 1800, Denmark met his master, Joseph Vesey, to negotiate his freedom and used $600 of the prize money to buy his freedom. As a freeman, Denmark used the $900 he had left to establish a carpenter's workshop. From then on, he joined the ranks of free blacks who lived in Charleston and worked as carpenters, tailors, hairdressers, barbers, cooks, seamstresses, shoemakers, blacksmiths, bricklayers, painters, contractors, merchants, coal and wood dealers, and artisans. Many of them, including Denmark, were successful in their chosen profession.

Despite the successes of the free blacks, their social status in antebellum Charleston was only a level above that of slaves, as even with manumission, free blacks never achieved total freedom. For instance, despite Denmark Vesey's wealth, the law still required that he carry his manumission papers wherever he went, and until 1783, when a law was enacted against the abduction and selling of free blacks, they could be kidnapped and sold into slavery all over again. Free blacks were tried in the same manner as slaves, and they lacked legal representation. By about 1820 there were 3,165 free blacks living in Charleston whose privileges were thus circumscribed; it was only a matter of time before they reacted.

Based on external influences and his own conviction, Denmark became dissatisfied with the status of African Americans in the United States, and he felt that the degradation of African Americans in Charleston cast an aspersion on his race. He was, therefore, impatient with blacks whom he considered servile and worked strenuously to galvanize those blacks who thought there was no way to change their subservient status. With time, Denmark became a strong critic of the institution of slavery. His intellectual crusade was informed by reading about slavery; the American, French, and Haitian revolutions; and about abolitionists and their activities. His extensive knowledge enabled him to understand the hardships inherent in the institution of slavery, and he was not afraid to express his views.

Denmark began his program for freedom by preparing potential participants in his plot to overthrow the slave system. He felt it was his responsibility to inform blacks in Charleston that whites were neither superior nor were they God, and he also prepared his followers psychologically to dislike whites. He used the Bible as a basis to criticize the evils of slavery—reading from the Bible how the children of Israel were delivered out of Egypt from bondage—and he made references to the success of the Haitians in their bid to acquire independence from the French.

In December 1821, Denmark Vesey took a major step in achieving his objectives by picking able and trusted confidants. Among them was Peter Poyas (a slave belonging to one James Poyas), a literate ship's carpenter whose job allowed him to move freely, which meant that he could coordinate communication between rural and urban slaves. Other confidants included Rolla and Ned Bennett, slaves of Governor Thomas Bennett, and their closeness to the governor meant they were able to spy and inform on the white community of Charleston. Another important associate of Denmark was Jack Glenn, a literate and skilled slave whose occupation was painting. Glenn acted as the group's treasurer, collecting money from hired-out slaves who had disposable income for the purchase of weapons and horses. Monday Gell, a skilled harness maker, was also a member of Denmark's circle of confidants. Gell managed a shop on Meeting Street and was well regarded by whites, who considered him intelligent, steady, and dependable. Among Denmark Vesey's lieutenants, Jack Pritchard (Gullah Jack) was deemed the most effective. He was said to possess supernatural powers and was therefore considered a conjurer. He commanded considerable respect among rural Gullah slaves who lived in the coastal sea islands. Denmark relied on Gullah Jack to rally the cowardly and hesitant slaves by using his assumed powers.

Once Vesey's team was in place, the business of extensive recruitment began. A number of meetings were held in Vesey's house, in Monday Gell's shop, and at Bulkley's farm on Charleston Neck at which the leaders compared notes, exchanged information, and planned strategies for the operation. The recruitment effort went beyond Charleston. Recruiters went as far as the coastal islands to the east, Georgetown to the north, the Combahee River to the south, and John's Parish in Berkeley County to the west. Denmark Vesey and his co-conspirators took the utmost care to prevent any possible leaks, but their efforts in this regard were unsuccessful.

July 14, 1822, the second Sunday of the month, was set as the date for the rebellion. A summer month was chosen because the majority of whites would have traveled out of town, and a Sunday was picked because on that day, many blacks could visit Charleston without being suspected of any sinister motive. Before the plan could be executed, a house servant who was a target of recruitment informed his master of the planned insurrection on May 30. Vesey then attempted to move the date of the uprising forward to June 16, but unfortunately, more revelations of the plot had been made by other slaves who were acting as spies. The mayor of Charleston and the governor of South Carolina acted swiftly, and the insurrectionists were arrested.

Following a long trial, of the 130 African Americans who had been apprehended, 36 were hanged, 43 were banished from the state, and the charges against 51 were discharged. Peter Poyas; Ned, Rolla, and Batteau Bennett; Jessy Blackwood; and Denmark Vesey were executed on July 2, 1822.

—*Onaiwu W. Ogbomo*

For Further Reading

Aptheker, Herbert. 1943. *American Negro Slave Revolts.* New York: Columbia University Press; Edwards, Lillie J. 1990. *Denmark Vesey.* New York: Chelsea House Publishers; Killens, John Oliver. 1970. *The Trial Record of Denmark Vesey.* Boston: Beacon Press; Lofton, John M., Jr. 1948. "Denmark Vesey's Call to Arms." *Journal of Negro History* 33(4): 395–417.

a utopian community near Memphis, Tennessee, that was designed to train blacks for eventual settlement outside the United States. In the same year, Wright also published *A Plan for the Gradual Abolition of Slavery in the United States without Danger of Loss to the Citizens of the South.*

1826

Upon his death in Virginia, Thomas Jefferson freed only five of his slaves and bequeathed the rest to his heirs.

1826

An antislavery newspaper called the *African Observer* began publication in Philadelphia, Pennsylvania.

1826

The Reverend Samuel E. Cornish, a free black

JOSIAH HENSON (1789–1883)

The Reverend Josiah Henson was born a slave in Charles County, Maryland. Henson's earliest recollections of slavery were of the selling of his father to a planter in Alabama and the auctioning off of himself, five siblings, and his mother after the death of their master, one Dr. Mcpherson. Henson described himself in his youth as one who was full of energy and thrived on competition. Such characteristics were probably the reasons Henson's master Isaac Riley chose him to serve as the plantation overseer after a white overseer was fired for stealing. Henson's mother saw to it that her son regularly received lessons in Christian ethics, which were taught by her.

Around the age of 18, Henson experienced a religious conversion, which he attributed to a sermon he had heard preached by John McKenny, a Christian man who lived in Georgetown in Washington, D.C. McKenny had preached that all could receive spiritual salvation through Jesus Christ, and moved by the sermon, Henson began to think of his own salvation and that of other slaves. His belief in the possibility of personal salvation, even for slaves, probably influenced his decision to carry out a task for his master that he would later regret.

Mounting debt led Henson's master, Isaac Riley, to hide some of his slaves to prevent their seizure by debt collectors. Riley charged Henson with escorting 18 of his bondspeople to his brother's home in Kentucky, and Henson carried out the task, arriving in Kentucky with the slaves in April 1825. He later witnessed many of the same slaves being sold on a Kentucky auction block, and this event, which had a transformative effect on Henson, made him obsessed with freedom.

In 1828, Henson met privately with a white preacher who was opposed to slavery. The two developed a plan for Henson to obtain his freedom by purchasing it from Riley, but the plan was unsuccessful because Riley reneged on his part of the agreement. Henson eventually obtained his freedom by escaping to Canada with his wife and children in October 1830. Henson later helped over 100 slaves escape to freedom in Canada.

After arriving in Canada, Henson worked as a farm laborer while continuing his efforts to spread the gospel. Financial support from northern philanthropists assisted him in establishing the British American Manual Labor Institute, located near Chatham, Upper Canada (currently known as Ontario), in 1842. Henson envisioned the institute as a place where black boys could learn mechanical arts and black girls could learn domestic arts. Over the next several years, Henson toured England to raise funds to support the British American Manual Labor Institute, which eventually closed in 1868 amid claims of mismanagement.

Henson was thrust into the limelight when Harriet Beecher Stowe's work *Uncle Tom's Cabin* was published in 1852. Many people believed the book was based on Henson's life, especially since Stowe had indeed interviewed Henson. In 1876, Henson took his last tour of England and was received by Queen Victoria. After returning to the United States, he met with President Rutherford B. Hayes to discuss Henson's travels abroad. He then returned to his home in Canada, where he died in 1883 at the age of 94.

—*Beverly A. Bunch-Lyons*

For Further Reading
Hartgrove, W. B. 1918. "The Story of Josiah Henson." *Journal of Negro History* 3(1): 1–21; Lobb, John, ed. 1971. *"Uncle Tom's Story of His Life": An Autobiography of the Rev. Josiah Henson.* London: Frank Cass.

---

from New York, published an antislavery tract entitled *A Remonstrance against the Abuse of the Blacks.*

1826

In an effort to weaken enforcement of the Fugitive Slave Act of 1793, the Pennsylvania legislature passed a law making the crime of kidnapping a felony and requiring slave catchers to obtain a special "certificate of removal" before fugitive slaves could be removed from the state. The United States would eventually strike down this law in the case of *Prigg v. Pennsylvania* (1842).

1826

In June, President John Quincy Adams requested Senate confirmation of two delegates he wished to send to the Panama Conference of Latin American States organized by Simón Bolívar. Although some senators opposed participation because international involvement ran counter to the U.S. diplomatic tradition, Vice-President John C. Calhoun, who presided over

The word *communitarians* refers to various communal groups formed in the nineteenth century, primarily between the American Revolution and the Civil War. Although the groups varied widely in their motives, all of them sought to create ideal communities that would serve as models for the rest of American society. Their lifestyles and values were usually at odds with the norms of the day, as they generally advocated egalitarianism and communal property holding and were often critical of capitalism and individualism. Members were often involved in the many other social reform movements of the day, including the abolitionist movement.

The combination of communitarianism and abolitionism occurred most notably in the work of Frances Wright. As a young woman, Wright traveled extensively throughout the United States and met and became well acquainted with Robert Owen, the wealthy Scottish director of the New Harmony settlement in Indiana. She was quite interested in his utopian efforts and wished to combine those ideals with her own notions about emancipating American slaves. Wright believed that education was essential for slaves if they were to find employment and protect themselves once they became free.

With these ideas in mind, she and George Flower, the leader of an English utopian community in Illinois, drew up plans for a communitarian settlement based upon Owen's theories. Their approach, however, was a great deal more fantastic. In this community, black slaves would provide manual labor while receiving an occupational education, working 5–10 years to earn their eventual freedom. In 1825, Wright purchased a plantation in Tennessee as the site for her settlement and named it Nashoba.

She hoped that her experiment would serve as a model for several such farms throughout the southern states. To publicize her theories and solicit financial support, she published a pamphlet entitled *A Plan for the Gradual Abolition of Slavery in the United States without Danger of Loss to the Citizens of the South*. Despite Wright's grand plans, Nashoba harbored only a handful of slaves and never became much more than a rough, backwoods settlement. By 1830, the plantation was bankrupt, and the remaining slaves were freed and sent to Haiti.

—*Marti J. Gastineau*

For Further Reading
Stewart, James Brewer. 1976. *Holy Warriors: The Abolitionists and American Slavery*. New York: Hill and Wang; Tyler, Alice Felt. 1962. *Freedom's Ferment: Phases of American Social History from the Colonial Period to the Outbreak of the Civil War*. New York: Harper and Brothers; Walters, Ronald G. 1978. *American Reformers: 1815–1860*. New York: Hill and Wang.

---

the Senate, opposed the appointment because nations that were governed by blacks would participate in the conference. The Senate eventually approved the appointments, but because of the delay the partisan debate had caused, neither of the diplomats made it to Panama in time for the conference.

1827
Abolitionist editor Benjamin Lundy was attacked in Baltimore by Austin Woolfolk, a slave dealer who was angered by remarks that Lundy had published in his newspaper, the *Genius of Universal Emancipation*.

1827
A North Carolina court heard the case of *Trustees of the Quaker Society of Contentnea v. Dickenson*. The judge in this case ruled that ownership of slaves by Quakers was illegal in North Carolina because it was tantamount to emancipation. Since the state of North Carolina permitted manumission only in specialized cases, the courts held that the ownership of slaves by Quakers, who were obligated by their faith to manumit their slaves, would be contrary to North Carolina law.

1827
The abolitionist William Goodell began publication of the *Investigator,* an antislavery newspaper, in Providence, Rhode Island. In 1829, the paper merged with the *National Philanthropist*.

1827
The first black newspaper to be published in the United States, *Freedom's Journal,* began publication in New York City on March 16. The paper was cofounded and coedited by John B. Russwurm and the Reverend Samuel Cornish, who stated: "We wish to plead our own cause. Too long have others spoken for us." In the newspaper's prospectus, Russwurm and Cornish stated, "In the spirit of candor and humility we

FREEDOM'S JOURNAL

" RIGHTEOUSNESS EXALTETH A NATION."

NEW-YORK, FRIDAY, MARCH 16, 1827.

The masthead of the first black newspaper in the United States, cofounded and coedited by John B. Russwurm and the Reverend Samuel Cornish. (The Granger Collection)

intend to lay our case before the public with a view to arrest the progress of prejudice, and to shield ourselves against its consequent evils." [See Document 47.]

1827

Slavery was officially abolished in the state of New York on July 4 when 10,000 slaves were set free after passage of the New York State Emancipation Act.

1828

The practice of performers using blackface during minstrel shows was first popularized by Thomas Dartmouth Rice, "the father of American minstrelsy," who danced and sang to a tune called "Jim Crow." Over the course of the nineteenth century, the term Jim Crow became synonymous with blacks in the United States.

1828

An antislavery newspaper called the *Liberalist* began publication in New Orleans, Louisiana. Milo Mower, the publisher of the paper, was imprisoned in 1830 for circulating advertisements of his abolitionist newspaper in New Orleans.

1828

An antislavery newspaper called the *Free Press* began publication in Bennington, Vermont. Also in Bennington, an abolitionist writer named William Lloyd Garrison began to publish a series of articles attacking slavery in the *National Philanthropist*.

1828

On December 19, Vice-President John C. Calhoun wrote *South Carolina Exposition and Protest,* anonymously, to decry what he believed to be unjust and oppressive action by the federal government upon the state of South Carolina. Calhoun used the states' rights argument to defend his position, and he endorsed the right of individual states to nullify federal law. Calhoun

did not speak for all South Carolinians as James Louis Petigru, South Carolina's attorney general, and others did not agree with Calhoun's doctrine.

1829

In New York City, a free black, Robert Alexander Young, wrote and published *The Ethiopian Manifesto, Issued in Defense of the Black Man's Rights in the Scale of Universal Freedom*. Young used passages from the Bible to condemn the institution of slavery, and he predicted the coming of a black messiah who would smite slaveholders and bring emancipation to the black masses.

1829

After John B. Russwurm emigrated to Liberia, the Reverend Samuel E. Cornish continued to publish the antislavery newspaper *Freedom's Journal* under a new masthead, *The Rights of All*.

1829

A book of poetry entitled *The Hope of Liberty* was published by George Moses Horton, a North Carolina slave. Horton's work, which included the poem "The Slave's Complaint," was the first book of poetry by a black author to be published since the time of Phillis Wheatley. Horton published this book of verse in an effort to raise funds in order to purchase his freedom, but sales of the book were poor.

1829

A serious race riot erupted in Cincinnati, Ohio, on August 10 in which whites attacked black residents and burned and looted their homes. As a result of this attack, 1,200 black residents fled the area and started a new life in Canada.

1829

The government of Mexico abolished slavery on September 15.

1829

On September 28, David Walker, a free black who lived in Boston, published *An Appeal to the Colored Citizens of the World*. This militant antislavery publication advocated resistance by blacks to the institution of slavery. The pamphlet was distributed throughout the United States and greatly disturbed southern slaveowners, who believed its message would incite unrest among the slave populace.

~JAMES LOUIS PETIGRU (1789–1863)~

Historians have traditionally portrayed prominent white southerners as monolithic in their support of slavery and states' rights during the antebellum period. Although most of them were of like mind concerning such issues, an important minority criticized slavery and supported the Union, attacking the social and economic foundations of southern life. No southern dissenter was more important than James Louis Petigru.

Petigru was born near Abbeville, South Carolina, on May 10, 1789, the first of eight children. His father, William Petigrew, soon lost his land to gambling and drinking and came to rely on his wife's brother to support his family. James grew up doing farm chores much as any youth of the period. However, his mother imbued him with a deep intellectual curiosity and schooled him at home until he was 15, when he entered a local academy. Two years later, he entered South Carolina College in Columbia. Graduating in 1809, James read law with Beaufort attorney William Robertson and was admitted to the bar in 1812. During this time, he also changed the spelling of his name to "Petigru," a reflection of his poor relationship with his father. Then he embarked on one of the most brilliant and controversial legal careers in the history of southern jurisprudence.

Petigru's legal practice was initially lackluster, but he found success after David Hugen, a prominent South Carolina lawyer and politician, took an interest in his career. In rapid succession, Petigru became a state solicitor, a partner in a powerful Charleston firm, and state attorney general. In court, he often made arguments that were unpopular with other white southerners, and on several occasions, he took cases brought by slaves against their masters, arguing for the extension of basic human rights for slaves. As attorney general, he argued that South Carolina's Negro Seaman Law, which prohibited black sailors from coming ashore in the state, was unconstitutional. These actions do not mean that Petigru was a racial egalitarian. Rather, he believed that slavery was an impediment to the South, one that prevented social reform and economic development. To end the practice, he favored manumission, a controversial practice that involved owners freeing their slaves by bequest.

Petigru's opposition to slavery was not the only view that placed him in conflict with prominent leaders in his state and region. He also opposed nullification, a stand that placed him at odds with powerful politicians such as John C. Calhoun, arguing that nullification was an unconstitutional act. In Petigru's view, federal law superseded state laws, and if a state took issue with a federal act, it should seek relief through the judicial and legislative channels established by the Constitution. Armed confrontation, according to Petigru, was not a viable solution. For many of the same reasons, he later opposed secession, becoming a vocal unionist until his death in 1863. His views of slavery, nullification, and secession set James Louis Petigru at odds with the prevailing opinions of the day and made him one of the great southern dissenters of the antebellum period.

—*Richard D. Starnes*

For Further Reading
Degler, Carl. 1974. *The Other South: Southern Dissenters in the Nineteenth Century.* New York: Harper and Row; Eaton, Clement. 1964. *The Freedom of Thought Struggle in the Old South.* New York: Harper and Row; Pease, William, and Jane Pease. 1995. *James Louis Petigru: Southern Conservative, Southern Dissenter.* Athens: University of Georgia Press.

1829

After encountering the protests of slaveowning American settlers who had emigrated to Texas, on December 2, Mexican President Vincent Guerrero exempted Texas from the Mexican antislavery proclamation of September 15, 1829.

1830

According to the fifth census of the United States, 3,777 black heads of families were listed as slaveowners, most of them being found in Louisiana, Maryland, Virginia, North Carolina, and South Carolina. Blacks, both slave and free, constituted 18.1 percent of the national population, or 2,328,642 people.

1830

In North Carolina, slaveowners manumitted more than 400 slaves and turned them over to Quakers living in the state. The Quakers retained legal ownership but allowed the "slaves" to live in virtual freedom until the Quakers could afford to transport them to a true life of freedom in the North.

1830

The state legislature of Louisiana petitioned

~EDWARD BEECHER (1803–1895)~

A noted preacher, abolitionist, and educator, Edward Beecher was the third child and second son of Lyman and Roxanna Beecher. He was born on Long Island in East Hampton, New York, and when Edward was seven, his family moved from East Hampton to Litchfield, Connecticut. In his early years, Edward received religious instruction in orthodox Protestant Christianity, taught to him by his father, Lyman, and these early lessons greatly influenced the future direction of Edward's life.

In 1818, Edward Beecher began his education at Yale College. Four years later, in 1822, he graduated from Yale as valedictorian. For Beecher, 1822 was a year filled with momentous occasions, of which his conversion to abolitionism may have been the most significant. It was also in 1822 that Beecher became the headmaster of the Hartford Grammar School, a position he held for two years. After tiring of his efforts to impart knowledge in the heads of unwilling young boys at the grammar school, Beecher decided he was ready to become a minister and enrolled in Andover Theological Seminary in 1824. Discontented with the Andover curriculum, his stay there was short-lived, but he soon accepted a tutorship at Yale.

In 1826, Beecher accepted the pastorship of the Park Street Church in Boston, which was widely recognized for its strict adherence to orthodoxy. Beecher spent four years at Park Street before he was dismissed from his post by parishioners who were not satisfied with his preaching. Beecher then accepted an invitation to become president of Illinois College in Jacksonville, Illinois, in 1830.

The 1830s saw Beecher thrust into the abolition movement. He was an advocate of abolition but supported gradual emancipation or African colonization. Events witnessed by Beecher in the mid-1830s, however, convinced him that gradual emancipation was not the answer to slavery. Rioting mobs composed of leading citizens often violently attacked vocal supporters of abolition. Beecher established a close relationship with the militant abolitionist Elijah Lovejoy and eventually became a staunch supporter of those who advocated immediate emancipation. In spite of his eventual support of immediate emancipation, though, Beecher continued to view William Lloyd Garrison and his supporters as extremists.

Over the next few years, Beecher worked closely with Lovejoy to spread the abolitionist message. In November 1837, Lovejoy was murdered by rioters protesting his outspoken stance on slavery. Several years later, in 1844, worn out from his antislavery efforts and neglect of his theological work, Beecher returned to Boston, this time as the pastor of the Salem Street Church. Beecher spent the next several decades of his life engaged in both theological work and antislavery activities.

—*Beverly A. Bunch-Lyons*

For Further Reading
Merideth, Robert. 1968. *The Politics of the Universe: Edward Beecher, Abolition, and Orthodoxy.* Nashville, TN: Vanderbilt University Press; Rugoff, Milton. 1981. *The Beechers: An American Family in the Nineteenth Century.* New York: Harper and Row.

Congress complaining that slaves from the state were escaping to Mexico. The state legislature also enacted a measure that made it a criminal offense to teach a slave to read or write.

1830
Massachusetts abolitionist Edward Beecher became president of Illinois College in Jacksonville, Illinois. While in the Midwest, Beecher became a friend and supporter of the antislavery work of editor Elijah Lovejoy. Shortly after the murder of Lovejoy in 1837, Beecher returned to Massachusetts to accept the position of pastor at the Salem Street Church in Boston.

1830
On January 21, municipal authorities in Portsmouth, Ohio, forcibly deported all black residents from the community.

1830
Mexican authorities prohibited the further colonization of Texas by U.S. citizens on April 6. This action also prohibited those American settlers who were already in Texas from importing additional slaves into the region.

1830
Much of the debate between the North and the South over slavery was based upon the states' rights views of the political leaders who represented the interests of their regions. Occasionally, these views were articulated in a less-than-subtle fashion. At the Jefferson Day Dinner on

April 30, President Andrew Jackson presented the toast, "Our Federal Union—It must be preserved!" Jackson's vice-president, John C. Calhoun of South Carolina, responded to Jackson's remarks with his own toast, "The Union—Next to our liberty, the most dear!"

1830
Richard Allen chaired the first National Negro Convention, which met in Philadelphia at the Bethel AME Church from September 20 to September 24. The purpose of the gathering was to launch a church-affiliated program to uplift and improve the status of American blacks.

1830
In December, the *Comet,* an American schooner transporting slaves between Alexandria, Virginia, and New Orleans, Louisiana, as part of the domestic slave trade, was wrecked off the Bahamas. British officials in the Bahamas set the slaves on board the vessel free, much to the chagrin of the Americans who owned the slaves. The manner in which the *Comet* episode was handled was a matter of diplomatic contention between the United States and Great Britain for more than a decade.

1831
The term Underground Railroad was used for the first time to describe the system in the northern states whereby whites and free blacks who were sympathetic to the abolitionist cause helped fugitive slaves make their way to freedom.

1831
Residents of Mississippi formed the Mississippi Colonization Society to establish a colony for the purpose of repatriating former slaves from that state to Africa.

1831
The Georgia state legislature announced a reward of $5,000 to anyone who would capture William Lloyd Garrison and turn him over to Georgia authorities. It was the belief of the Georgia legislators that the abolitionist editor of the *Liberator* should face criminal prosecution and conviction in a Georgia courtroom.

1831
In Philadelphia, the first annual meeting of the Convention of the People of Color was held at the Wesleyan Church. Delegates discussed the possibility of creating Canadian settlement communities but voiced strong opposition to the African emigration policies of the American Colonization Society.

1831
John E. Stewart, a black abolitionist, began publication of an antislavery newspaper entitled the *African Sentinel and Journal of Liberty* in Albany, New York.

1831
Alexis de Tocqueville, the French bureaucrat who wrote the seminal study *Democracy in America,* toured the United States for several months as he tried to learn about American culture. At a dinner party in Boston, de Tocqueville sat next to former president John Quincy Adams and had an opportunity to question Adams about his views on slavery. When asked, "Do you look on slavery as a great plague for the United States?" Adams responded saying, "Yes, certainly that is the root of almost all the troubles of the present and the fears for the future" (Jenkins, 1996).

1831
Maria W. Stewart published *Religion and the Pure Principles of Morality—The Sure Foundation on Which We Must Build.* Stewart, a free black who opposed slavery, is considered to be the first African American political writer in the United States.

1831
Virginia state legislator and college professor Thomas Roderick Dew described his state as a "Negro-raising state" for the remainder of the South. During the following three decades, nearly 300,000 slaves were exported from Virginia to other states as part of the internal slave trade.

1831
William Lloyd Garrison, one of America's more radical abolitionists, began publication of the *Liberator* in Boston on January 1. It continued publication weekly through December 1865, which made it the longest-running, most successful, and best known of all antislavery newspapers. In establishing this organ for the abolitionist cause, Garrison declared, "I am in

∽SOUTH CAROLINA EXPOSITION *AND* PROTEST∽

The *South Carolina Exposition* and *Protest,* publications against federal tariff laws, were introduced in the state legislature in 1828 and mark the start of the nullification crisis. Although the *Exposition* failed to pass the legislature, its 1829 publication by the state government and John C. Calhoun's authorship of the document, even though that was initially concealed, vested it with more authority than the shorter and less confrontational *Protest.* The *Exposition* established Calhoun as a preeminent southern political theorist as it recast states' rights theory for the defense of slavery. Citing the precedent of the 1798 Virginia and Kentucky resolutions in response to the Alien and Sedition Acts, Calhoun sought to evoke state power against the actions of the federal government. But instead of an appeal to local majorities to check an undemocratic federal government, the *Exposition* devised ways and means to secure the interests of the slaveholding minority against the voice of the majority. The theory of nullification, or state veto, of federal laws outlined in the *Exposition* also violated the cardinal tenet of the states' rights theory, strict interpretation of the Constitution, as it was nowhere mentioned in the Constitution and circumvented the amendment process laid out in it.

The *Exposition* contended that the policy of protection, or the levying of tariffs, was unconstitutional and oppressive to the slave South. Calhoun made the startling and unique claim that import duties equaled export duties, which meant that the main burden of such a tariff fell on southerners, the nation's main exporters. According to this logic, the South, rather than all consumers, paid import duties. In an interesting if implausible discovery of political economy, Calhoun claimed that producers, not consumers, paid duties levied on foreign goods—and not all producers but producers of exported crops, that is, mainly the slaveholding planter class. He claimed that this policy was the cause of the South's economic woes and felt the tariff should be lowered and should mainly be a source of revenue for the government rather than protection for northern manufacturing. Calhoun concluded with the pet claim of the South Carolina nullifiers that the federal government, which now acted against the profits of the slave South, would soon attack the South's system of labor, slavery.

Calhoun's championship of slaveholders' interests influenced his minority-versus-majority theory of politics, and he referred to another venerable precedent, James Madison's *Federalist* No. 10, to legitimize the grievances of southern slaveholders.

For Calhoun, the minority in question was synonymous with a particular class and section, and the only solution to majority domination was state sovereignty. The state as representative of the minority would have the power to veto a federal law that it considered unconstitutional. Calhoun's notion of state sovereignty justified nullification by a single state but was contradicted by his assertion that after a state veto, the supreme power to decide the question at issue would lie with the constitution-amending authority, three-fourths of the states. Furthermore, a minority, little more than one-fourth of the states, could make or break federal law. Calhoun's theory of nullification was not only an undemocratic prescription for minority rule but could act as an ironclad protection for southern slaveholders against any federal attempt to regulate or abolish slavery. Later, Calhoun would use the term *concurrent majority* to characterize his theory and to answer accusations that he favored minority rule. He would also claim that the nullifying state had a choice either to accede to the wishes of three-fourths of the states or to secede from the Union, thereby laying the foundations for the southern notion of an allegedly constitutional right to secession.

Calhoun had injected a new issue into the traditional fears of propertied minorities in majoritarian republics, and that was the specific dilemma of the southern slaveholding minority. He would have no qualms about dispensing with minority rights when it came to northern abolitionists or the unionists in his own state. A state veto or minority check that he saw epitomized in the state government of South Carolina would lead to similar undemocratic, planter-dominated politics. His concept of nullification was profoundly conservative, designed to check what South Carolinian nullifiers saw as the excesses of democracy and majoritarianism.

—*Manisha Sinha*

For Further Reading
Ellis, Richard E. 1987. *The Union at Risk: Jacksonian Democracy, States' Rights and the Nullification Crisis.* New York: Oxford University Press; Ford, Lacy, Jr. 1988. "Recovering the Republic: Calhoun, South Carolina, and the Concurrent Majority." *South Carolina Historical Magazine* 89 (July): 146–159; Freehling, William W. 1965. *Prelude to Civil War: The Nullification Controversy in South Carolina, 1816–1836.* New York: Harper; Sinha, Manisha. 1994. "The Counter-Revolution of Slavery: Class, Politics, and Ideology in Antebellum South Carolina." Ph.D. dissertation, Department of History, Columbia University, New York.

earnest—I will not equivocate—I will not excuse—I will not retreat a single inch—AND I WILL BE HEARD!" Garrison promised he would continue to publish his newspaper until slavery had been abolished in the United States. [See Document 48.]

1831

In Southampton County, Virginia, a large-scale slave insurrection was led by Nat Turner, a literate slave preacher who claimed that voices inspired him to lead the revolt. Turner's owner, Joseph Travis, and his family were among the 57 whites who were killed by Turner and his 70 associates during the rampage on August 21–22, and the entire South experienced panic because of the shocking violence. Turner was captured in the swamps on October 30 after an exhaustive search, and he was convicted and sentenced to death by hanging in Jerusalem, Virginia, on November 11.

1831

In the U.S. House of Representatives on December 12, Congressman John Quincy Adams of Massachusetts began a pro-abolition campaign against slavery that he would maintain until his death in 1848. Adams introduced 15 petitions organized by Pennsylvania residents that called for the abolition of slavery in the District of Columbia. Although Congress abolished the slave trade in the nation's capital as a part of the Compromise of 1850, it was not until 1862 that slavery itself was abolished there.

1831–1832

In Virginia, a state convention used the winter session to debate the issue of slavery within the state. Various plans of gradual emancipation and colonization were considered, but in the end, all of the measures to change the state's involvement with slavery were defeated by the proslavery element that attended the convention. On January 21, 1832, Thomas Jefferson Randolph, grandson of the former president Thomas Jefferson, presented the assembly with a proposal for gradual emancipation that his grandfather had promoted nearly 40 years earlier. The plan did not sway the convention, and the proposal was defeated.

1832

In Canterbury, Connecticut, Prudence Crandall, a white teacher, admitted a black student named Sarah Harris to the school that she ran and suffered public admonishment for this action. Crandall was eventually arrested on June 27, 1833, for teaching black children. The school was targeted by vandals and was eventually demolished.

1832

A serious academic debate between students and faculty began at Lane Theological Seminary in Cincinnati, Ohio, on the topics of abolition and colonization. When the trustees of the seminary ordered an end to the discussion in May 1833, many of the students left the seminary and eventually moved to the more open educational setting of Oberlin College.

1832

Thomas Roderick Dew, a professor of political economy at William and Mary College in Virginia, published his *Review of the Debate in the Virginia Legislature of 1831 and 1832.* Dew was a southern apologist for slavery, and his presentation represented a one-sided view that emphasized the proslavery perspective. In the same year, Dew also published an essay entitled "The Pro-slavery Argument" in which he provided an intellectual foundation for the racist assumptions that southern slaveholders used to justify the institution and practice of slavery.

1832

On January 6, a group of 12 white abolitionists met at the African Baptist Church on Boston's Beacon Hill to organize the New England Anti-Slavery Society. William Lloyd Garrison played an important role in the founding of this organization, and the group supported the concept of "immediatism" because it believed that gradual abolition was an inadequate response to the sin of slavery.

1832

In November, using the defense of a states' rights argument, the legislature of South Carolina nullified the federal tariff acts of 1828 and 1832, an action that precipitated a showdown between the state of South Carolina and the executive authority of President Andrew Jackson. The question of states' rights and the doctrine of nullification were divisive issues in the decades leading up to the American Civil War.

Founded by William Lloyd Garrison in 1832, the New England Anti-Slavery Society distinguished itself from other antislavery societies by resisting colonization and openly promoting "immediatism," the belief that immediate, determined measures must be adopted for the emancipation of every slave. Although the society was short-lived and its role and impact were limited in a national sense, it played a pivotal role in advancing later, more broadly effective antislavery activity.

After initially meeting in Samuel Sewall's law office on November 13, 1831, to hear Garrison's proposal, about a dozen Bostonian men assembled again on December 16, 1831, and then on January 6, 1832, in the basement schoolroom of the Boston African Baptist Church to discuss formation of the abolitionist society. Seeing that British societies succeeded only after they adopted the principle of immediate emancipation, the group accepted immediatism as the new organization's guiding principle. It appointed Arnold Buffum as its first president and Garrison as its corresponding secretary.

In drafting the society's constitution, which was published in Garrison's *Liberator* on February 18, 1832, Sewall, Garrison, and others made the society's objectives clear. As stated in the second article, the purpose of the New England Anti-Slavery Society was to "endeavor, by all means sanctioned by law, humanity and religion, to effect the Abolition of Slavery in the United States, to improve the character and condition of the free people of color, to inform and correct public opinion in relation to their situation and rights, and obtain for them equal civil and political rights and privileges with the whites" (New England Anti-Slavery Society, 1832). In the *Address to the Public,* which the society sent to editors of newspapers in New England, they affirmed that the object of the society was "neither war nor sedition" and that the "fun-

damental principle" of their constitution was "OUR SAVIOR'S GOLDEN RULE," that is, the idea that *"all things whatsoever ye would that men should do to you, do ye even so unto them"* (New England Anti-Slavery Society, 1832). Unlike the constitution, the *Address* outlined what was meant by "immediate abolition" and critiqued the objectives of the American Colonization Society, a society Garrison criticized more heavily in his pamphlet *Thoughts on African Colonization* (1832). Although blacks were not involved in the initial founding of the society, they later had substantial numbers in its ranks. When the society's constitution was approved, for instance, about one-fourth of the 72 signers were of African descent.

Membership increased slowly, and after three years, the name was changed to the Massachusetts Anti-Slavery Society. As indicated in the annual report for 1835, the formation and designs of the larger and recently organized American Anti-Slavery Society were making an impact. Also, the fact that state societies had already been established in Maine, New Hampshire, and Vermont caused the New England Anti-Slavery Society, which already was confining its activities to Massachusetts, to become a state society only. By 1837, the American Anti-Slavery Society had taken the lead nationally in promoting immediate emancipation. Despite these later developments, the New England Anti-Slavery Society played a vital role in encouraging debate and discussion concerning the antislavery movement and in persuading people to take up the cause.

—*Mark L. Kamrath*

For Further Reading
Barnes, Gilbert Hobbs. 1933. *The Anti-Slavery Impulse 1830–1844.* New York: Harcourt Brace; Dumond, Dwight Lowell. 1961. *Antislavery: The Crusade for Freedom in America.* Ann Arbor: University of Michigan Press.

1833

From its founding, Oberlin College in Ohio was an integrated institution and took a leading role in the growing abolitionist movement. By the time of the American Civil War, one-third of Oberlin's students were black. Many black abolitionists like John Mifflin Brown were strong advocates of the institution because of its antislavery heritage.

1833

The white abolitionist David Lee Child pub-

lished *The Despotism of Freedom—Or, The Tyranny and Cruelty of American Republican Slavemasters.*

1833

Eliza Lee Cabot Follen and other female abolitionists organized the Boston Female Anti-Slavery Society, which remained active until 1840.

1833

John Rankin, a Presbyterian minister and Tennessee abolitionist, published *Letters on Ameri-*

An important approach to constitutional interpretation, the doctrine of nullification played a significant role in the debate over slavery in the United States. Nullification was founded on the premise that sovereignty resided with the people but was exercised by the states with the people's consent. Believing that the Tenth Amendment justified such action, advocates of nullification believed states could declare null and void any federal law they deemed unconstitutional.

Nullification had its roots in protests arising in 1798 in response to the Alien and Sedition Acts and previously proposed Hamiltonian banking measures. Fearing such federal laws could stifle free speech, James Madison and Thomas Jefferson articulated their beliefs concerning the right of states to limit the power of the federal government. In the Virginia Resolution of 1798, Madison argued that the federal government possessed only those powers specifically granted to it by the U.S. Constitution. Therefore, Madison believed that individual states could interpose their authority between the federal government and the citizenry to prevent the enforcement of oppressive or inequitable legislation. In the Kentucky Resolution of the same year, Jefferson took Madison's idea of interposition one step further and argued that states could nullify federal laws that were deemed by the state legislature to be unconstitutional. In Jefferson's argument, states became the final arbiters of the Constitution. These important documents firmly asserted the supremacy of state sovereignty.

This strict construction of the Constitution with regard to states' rights became one of the fundamental principles of the Democratic-Republican Party in 1792, and the doctrine of nullification resurfaced in a firestorm of debate surrounding the tariff of 1828. In an effort to decrease public debt and protect American manufacturers, Congress passed the highest protective tariff to date in 1827, and southern politicians, most notably from Virginia and South Carolina, vehemently opposed it. Labeling it "the tariff of abominations," they protested the increase in the cost of manufactured goods in the South. When Andrew Jackson was elected in 1828, southerners were confident the new chief executive would identify with their cause. Their confidence was misplaced, however, as Jackson had never made his position on the tariff clear. In fact, he saw the protective tariff as a way to garner support for the Democratic Party in the North.

However, southern antitariff leaders did have a vocal, articulate champion in the administration.

Vice-President John C. Calhoun considered the tariff to be an unconstitutional act that favored one section of the country over another, and in 1828, the South Carolina legislature published anonymously Calhoun's *South Carolina Exposition* and *Protest,* in which he resurrected a remedy for such blatantly oppressive legislation: nullification. Drawing on the ideas of Madison and Jefferson, Calhoun argued that the Union was a compact of individually sovereign states and these states had the authority to nullify federal laws they deemed oppressive. This action could not be taken arbitrarily. In order to nullify a law, a special state convention had to be elected to consider the question, thereby following the same procedures as the ratification of the Constitution. If a law was determined to be unconstitutional by this body, the state could prevent its enforcement within state boundaries. The federal government would then be forced to repeal the law or to seek a constitutional amendment to guarantee its validity.

In October 1832, the South Carolina legislature endorsed Calhoun's doctrine and called for a convention to consider nullifying the tariff of 1828. Meeting the following month, the convention adopted an ordinance that nullified both the 1828 and the 1832 tariffs, reasoning that these duties placed an unfair economic hardship on the citizens of South Carolina.

Jackson reacted swiftly. In December, he declared his intention to continue collecting the tariff in South Carolina as well as his belief that nullification was both unconstitutional and detrimental to the Union. To demonstrate federal resolve, Jackson dispatched troops and naval vessels to Charleston; in response, the South Carolina legislature mobilized the state militia. In January, Jackson asked Congress to formalize his authority to use troops to enforce federal law in South Carolina. While this act, called the force bill, was being debated, moderates in Congress, led by Henry Clay of Kentucky, were formulating a compromise that lowered tariff rates gradually until 1842. This solution allowed both Jackson and the nullifiers to claim victory—and it was hoped it would avoid an armed confrontation. Jackson signed both the force bill and the new tariff into law on March 2, 1833. In response, the South Carolina convention rescinded the ordinance of nullification, and, in an effort to assert the supremacy of states' rights, nullified the force bill. Thus ended the nullification crisis, but nullification, and the corollary doctrine of states' rights, remained important themes in antebellum politics.

As historian Richard Ellis has argued, while not directly involved in the nullification crisis itself, slavery was linked to this important doctrine in the minds of northerners and southerners alike. Many northerners, and even Jackson himself, believed that the nullification crisis had raised divisive sectional issues that the Missouri Compromise had merely masked. Southerners, in many ways for the first time, began to view themselves as a minority within the nation whose interests were considered secondary by the majority. Nullification, while unsuccessful in 1833, offered an important course of action for the South. Faced with abolitionist attacks on the slave system, and fearing federal intervention, nullification was a doctrine that offered white southerners a measure of protection to the two things they cherished most: state sovereignty and slave property.

After 1833, a vocal, influential minority of southern politicians, the fire-eaters, embraced the idea of nullification to the ultimate extreme. They reasoned that states could do more than nullify oppressive federal legislation; when faced with a national government that was detrimental to their interests and the interest of their citizens, states could also dissolve the bonds that held them in the Union. Secession, therefore, can be seen as the most extreme example of nullification in practice.

—*Richard D. Starnes*

For Further Reading
Ellis, Richard. 1987. *The Union at Risk: Jacksonian, States' Rights and the Nullification Crisis.* New York: Oxford University Press; Freehling, William. 1966. *Prelude to Civil War: The Nullification Controversy in South Carolina, 1818–1836.* New York: Harper and Row; Potter, David. 1976. *The Impending Crisis, 1848–1861.* New York: Harper and Row.

can Slavery. Rankin was forced to leave the South because of his antislavery views, but his book became a handbook for abolitionist speakers around the country.

1833
Quaker abolitionist Elijah P. Lovejoy began to publish the *Observer,* an antislavery newspaper, in St. Louis, Missouri.

1833
Abolitionist editor Joshua Leavitt and others organized the New York City Anti-Slavery Society.

1833
Justice and Expediency, a popular antislavery tract, was published by the American poet John Greenleaf Whittier.

1833
The British Parliament enacted a measure on August 28 that provided for the compensated, gradual abolition of slavery in all British colonial possessions. This action energized the abolitionist movement in the United States as that country was increasingly viewed as a pariah nation because it maintained the practice of slavery. In future decades, a true transatlantic abolitionist movement formed as British and American abolitionists worked together to try to bring an effective end to slavery in the United States. Also on August 28, the British Parliament appropriated £20 million to be used for com-

pensated emancipation for slaveholders in the British West Indies who would suffer economic losses as a result of Britain's policy of abolishing slavery within the empire. In all, 700,000 slaves were emancipated in the British colonies.

1833
In December, the Quaker Lucretia Mott became the first president of the Philadelphia Female Anti-Slavery Society, which she helped organize.

1833
William Lloyd Garrison, Theodore Dwight Weld, Arthur Tappan, Lewis Tappan, and several other black and white abolitionists met in Philadelphia on December 4 to establish the American Anti-Slavery Society, the first national abolitionist society to form in the United States.

1834
The South Carolina legislature enacted a measure making it a crime to teach black children, slave or free, to read.

1834
In New Orleans, a riot developed when authorities there discovered a torture chamber in the home of one Madame Delphine Lalaurie in which slaves were horribly abused. City residents rose in righteous indignation over the alleged cruelty that had occurred in the home, but Madame Lalaurie was able to escape the mob's wrath and flee to France.

⚬JOHN MIFFLIN BROWN (1810–1876)⚬

The abolitionist, educator, and eventually the eleventh bishop of the African Methodist Episcopal (AME) Church, John Mifflin Brown, was born in Cantwell's Bridge (currently known as Odenta), Delaware, on September 8, 1810. Details of his early life are sketchy, but it is probable that his future close involvement with the AME Church was owing to the influence of his mother and grandfather, both of whom were Methodists.

Prior to reaching his teens, Brown left Cantwell's Bridge for Wilmington, Delaware, where he resided with the Quaker family of William A. Seals. While in Wilmington, Brown attended Sunday school and church services at the Presbyterian Church, where he and all the other blacks were forced to sit in black pews located in the gallery of the church. Unwilling to accept this seating arrangement, Brown began attending Sunday school at the Roman Catholic Church, where he was welcomed. The next few years of Brown's life were spent serving as an apprentice, first to attorney Henry Chester and then to Frederick H. Hinton, a barber.

In January 1836, Brown became a member of the Bethel AME Church in Philadelphia. After working as a barber in New York for a short while, Brown enrolled in Wesleyan Academy in Wilbraham, Massachusetts, in order to prepare for college, but failing health forced him to return to Philadelphia in summer 1840. During fall 1841, he enrolled at Oberlin College but did not complete a degree. Brown was an avid supporter of Oberlin, an institution that was known for its abolitionist tradition and a place where Brown found an environment that welcomed abolitionist lecturers and activists. Brown praised Oberlin College for its liberal tradition and encouraged blacks to attend because of this tradition and because of the college's reasonable tuition. In 1844, Brown opened the first school for black children living in Detroit, Michigan, and during the same year, he began serving as acting minister of the AME Church there, a position he held until 1847.

After joining the Ohio Conference of the AME Church in 1849, Brown was given the pastorship of the AME Church in Columbus, Ohio. That same year, he was appointed principal of Union Seminary, the first school owned and operated by the AME Church. Although enrollment at Union Seminary grew dramatically under Brown's leadership, the future of the school was tenuous, and in 1856, the assets from the then-defunct Union Seminary were merged with the newly established Wilberforce University.

Brown was committed to abolition and spreading the gospel, and as a result, he was imprisoned on several occasions for allowing slaves to attend worship services. In 1858, he became the pastor of Bethel AME Church in Baltimore, where he was instrumental in increasing church membership and also raising significant funds to remodel the building. In 1868, Brown was elected bishop, was consecrated, and was assigned to the Seventh Episcopal District, which included several southern states. Brown was instrumental in organizing conferences and increasing church membership. He died at his Washington, D.C., home on March 16, 1876.

—*Beverly A. Bunch-Lyons*

For Further Reading

Angell, Stephen Ward. 1992. *Bishop Henry McNeal Turner and African-American Religion in the South.* Knoxville: University of Tennessee Press; Murphy, Larry G., J. Gordon Melton, and Gary Ward, eds. 1993. *Encyclopedia of African American Religions.* New York: Garland.

1834

Rioting rocked the city of New York for eight days (July 4–12) after a proslavery mob attacked an antislavery society meeting being held in New York's Chatham Street Chapel on Independence Day. The proslavery group was angered because black and white abolitionists were sitting together in the audience. In the rioting, several churches and homes were destroyed by fire.

1834

In October, the homes of nearly 49 free blacks in Philadelphia were destroyed when a proslavery mob went on a riotous rampage through the city.

1835

Theodore Dwight Weld began to train abolitionist agents for the American Anti-Slavery Society who would spread the antislavery message as disciples throughout rural communities of the northern states and the border states. Members of this group, known as "the Seventy," were physically attacked by proslavery supporters in many communities.

⤳ELIZA LEE CABOT FOLLEN (1787–1860)⤳

Eliza Lee Cabot Follen was overshadowed by her husband, Dr. Charles Follen, during her adult years, but she received a strong education as a young woman. Her mother saw to it that her daughter's interests were directed toward religious and social problems, and even before her marriage to Follen, she was well connected to Boston society and known for her firm and verbal convictions.

Follen is considered more of a footnote in the development of the abolition movement than many of her female acquaintances. For several years she concentrated on writing religious tracts, books, and a monthly teachers' manual for Christian teachers. In the early 1830s, Follen was part of a group of men and women who organized the Unitarian Federal Street Church in Boston. By the late 1830s, it was clear to true abolitionists that the Federal Street Church was no more supportive of the antislavery movement than most churches, and it appears that Follen's connection with the church ended at that time.

The Boston Female Anti-Slavery Society was also formed during the 1830s. The mixture of members included middle-class African-American women, some of the wealthiest white women in the city, and self-supporting women abolitionists and activists who had jobs in the religious community or in other social reform movements. Follen was among the members who voted to send regular monetary support to a Boston school for young black girls in 1833, but the school eventually lost the support of radical abolitionists and closed in 1839. Through her extensive travels in England and France, Follen was able to strengthen ties with foreign abolitionists, a move that strongly aided the antislavery movement both in the United States and abroad.

In the early 1840s, the Boston Female Anti-Slavery Society deteriorated because of a struggle among members over the methods of operation and the personalities involved in the society. In addition to her work with the Boston organization, Follen also served on the executive committee of the American Anti-Slavery Society and as a counselor of the Massachusetts Anti-Slavery Society. After the decline of the Boston Female Anti-Slavery Society, Follen focused her energies on the American Anti-Slavery Society. She died in Boston of typhoid fever during the occasion of the organization's annual meeting in 1860.

—*Maria Elena Raymond*

For Further Reading
Hansen, Debra Gold. 1993. *Strained Sisterhood: Gender and Class in the Boston Female Anti-Slavery Society*. Amherst: University of Massachusetts Press; Malone, Dumas, ed. 1931. *Dictionary of American Biography*. Vol. 6. New York: Charles Scribner's Sons; Sterling, Dorothy. 1993. *Ahead of Her Time: Abby Kelly and the Politics of Antislavery*. New York: Norton.

1835

North Carolina became the last southern state to deny the suffrage to free blacks by making changes to its state constitution. Additionally, the state legislature made it illegal for whites to teach free blacks.

1835

The Georgia state legislature enacted a measure that provided for the death penalty for anyone convicted of publishing abolitionist tracts that might foment insurrection among the slaves in the state.

1835

The state of South Carolina, like most of the southern states, made an effort to keep abolitionist literature out of the hands of slaves and free blacks. In a report to the state legislature, South Carolina Governor George McDuffie commented that "the laws of every community should punish this species of interference by death without benefit of clergy" (Jenkins, 1996).

1835

Unitarian minister William Ellery Channing, pastor of Boston's Federal Street Church, published *Slavery*, an antislavery tract in which he openly promoted abolitionist sentiments. In the same year, the poet and abolitionist John Greenleaf Whittier published the poem "My Countrymen in Chains."

1835

Elizabeth Buffum Chace and other antislavery supporters organized the Ladies' Anti-Slavery Society of Fall River, Massachusetts.

1835

One of the recommendations to come out of the

⮘JOSHUA LEAVITT (1794–1873)⮚

Joshua Leavitt was a prominent American antislavery newspaper editor and political activist. In 1825, he became a supporter of the American Colonization Society's efforts to end slavery by transplanting freeborn blacks and emancipated slaves to Africa and began writing antislavery articles for the *Christian Spectator,* an evangelical magazine with close ties to Yale Theological Seminary. In 1831, he became editor of the New York *Evangelist,* a weekly newspaper devoted to several reform causes, including abolition. In 1833, he helped to found the New York City Anti-Slavery Society and became the recording secretary of the American Anti-Slavery Society. He also bought the *Evangelist* and, having rejected colonization as an effective means of ending slavery, began to thunder out his unmitigated support for immediate abolition via voluntary emancipation. His enunciations of this position, forceful to the point of being blunt and tactless, engendered much hard feeling among his readers, many of whom were more interested in other reform movements. By 1837, he had alienated so many subscribers that he was forced to sell the paper in order to avoid bankruptcy.

Later that year, Leavitt became editor of the *Emancipator,* the official weekly newspaper of the American Anti-Slavery Society. Under his editorship, the struggling paper revived and became a major forum for the expression of abolitionist sentiment. Although earlier he had espoused voluntary emancipation as the best way to end slavery, he now became convinced that political action was required to coerce the slave states into outlawing human bondage. This position brought him into direct opposition to the prominent abolitionist William Lloyd Garrison, who declared that voting in a federal election implicitly gave support to the proslavery clauses of the U.S. Constitution. Undeterred by the opposition of Garrison and others in the society, in 1839, Leavitt called for the nomination of independent antislavery candidates, a move that cost him many subscribers and engendered much rancor among politically minded abolitionists, most of whom preferred to agitate against slavery within the ranks of the Whig Party.

In 1840, Leavitt played a prominent role in the establishment of the abolitionist Liberty Party by enthusiastically supporting James G. Birney, its candidate for president, and by traveling extensively to build a party organization at the grassroots level. Shortly after the election, he opened a lobbying agency in Washington, D.C., and for the next five years provided abolitionists with firsthand accounts of congressional action on matters pertaining to slavery. His editorials helped to bring the slavery question to the floor of the House of Representatives, despite its rules against such debate. Having become the sole owner of the *Emancipator* in 1840, the next year he moved its offices to Boston, where he merged it with the *Free American* and began publishing under the auspices of the Massachusetts Abolition Society. From 1844 to 1847, he served as chairman of the Liberty Party's national committee. In 1848, he sold the *Emancipator* and then worked privately for abolition.

—*Charles W. Carey, Jr.*

For Further Reading
Davis, Hugh. 1990. *Joshua Leavitt, Evangelical Abolitionist.* Baton Rouge: Louisiana State University Press.

National Negro Convention meeting in Philadelphia, held June 1–5, was that blacks remove the word "African" from all of their organizations and institutions.

1835
On July 6, Alfred Huger, the local postmaster in Charleston, South Carolina, requested that Postmaster General Amos Kendall prohibit antislavery tracts from the U.S. mail. Huger's request was denied by Kendall, who maintained that he did not have the authority to make such a decision, but he did suggest that Huger might act on his own initiative. Kendall stated, "We owe an obligation to the laws, but a higher one to the communities in which we live" (Schlesinger, 1983). On July 29, antislavery pamphlets and other abolitionist literature were removed from the public mail in Charleston and burned in the streets.

1835
Mob violence forced the closure of Noyes Academy in Canaan, New Hampshire, on August 10. The school was burned to the ground because it had operated on an integrated basis with 14 black students.

1835
In a letter to abolitionist Gerrit Smith dated

Abolitionist and women's rights activist Lucretia Coffin Mott (1793–1880). (Library of Congress)

September 13, James G. Birney wrote: "The antagonist principles of liberty and slavery have been roused into action and one or the other must be victorious. There will be no cessation of strife until slavery shall be exterminated or liberty destroyed."

1835

A scheduled address by British abolitionist George Thompson to the Female Anti-Slavery Society in Boston on October 21 was disrupted by a proslavery mob. On the same day, efforts to organize an antislavery society in Utica, New York, were also disrupted by a proslavery mob, and William Lloyd Garrison, the radical abolitionist editor of the *Liberator,* was attacked by a mob in Boston that was estimated to include 2,000 people. Garrison was delivering a speech on the theme that "all men are created equal" when the enraged mob turned against the antislavery orator. Garrison was rescued and lodged in Boston's Leverett Street Jail for his own personal safety.

1835

In December, just before the Second Seminole

War began in Florida, John Caesar organized an attack of hundreds of slaves upon plantations in the region of St. Johns River. Many fugitive slaves took part in the fighting of the Second Seminole War.

1835

On December 7, bowing to pressure from states' rights advocates, President Andrew Jackson considered measures that would give southern postmasters the right to restrict the mailing and distribution of abolitionist tracts in the southern states. Jackson asked Congress to consider enacting a law that would prohibit the circulation of antislavery literature through the mail.

1835

On December 15, President Antonio López de Santa Anna announced his intention to establish a unified constitution for Mexico, which would mean that the exemption granted to Texas in 1829 allowing the continuation of slavery there would be invalidated. American settlers in Texas who were slaveholders vowed they would fight a war of secession from Mexico rather than surrender their right to hold slaves in Texas.

1836

In a tract entitled *An Appeal to the Christian Women of the South,* the South Carolina–born abolitionist Angelina Grimké urged the abolition of slavery and advocated social equality for free blacks. Copies of her pamphlet were burned at several South Carolina post offices when they were found in the mail. In the same year, Sarah Moore Grimké published a tract entitled *An Epistle to the Clergy of the Southern States* in which this South Carolina–born abolitionist called for the overthrow of the institution of slavery. Copies of her pamphlet received the same treatment at several South Carolina post offices.

1836

The Missouri Supreme Court decided the case of *Rachael v. Walker,* declaring that a slave did indeed become free by residing at a northern military base or in a territory where slavery had been prohibited.

1836

The white abolitionist Lydia Maria Child pub-

Lydia Maria Child (1802–1880), a passionate and accomplished writer on behalf of the antislavery cause. (Library of Congress)

lished *An Appeal in Favor of That Class of Americans Called Africans.*

1836

The Massachusetts Supreme Court ruled that any slave who was brought within the state's borders by a master became legally free.

1836

Richard Hildrith, a white historian, published the novel *The Slave: Or, Memoirs of Archy Moore.* Hildrith attempted to write this novel in the style of a slave autobiography.

1836

Softening its previous antislavery tone, the Methodist Church stated its intention to avoid interfering in the civil and political relationships that existed between master and slave.

1836

In Granville, Ohio, a meeting of the Ohio Anti-Slavery Society was disrupted by ruffians who had been hired by community leaders.

1836

In January, James G. Birney began publishing a new antislavery newspaper called the *Philanthropist* in Philadelphia.

1836

On January 11, Congress received several petitions from abolitionists calling for the abolition of slavery in the District of Columbia. Senator John C. Calhoun of South Carolina described these petitions as a "foul slander" upon the South (Schlesinger, 1983).

1836

On March 11, the U.S. Senate began the practice of hearing antislavery petitions that were presented to the body and then rejecting them.

1836

Texas, which had declared itself an independent republic, drafted a constitution on March 17 that legalized slavery in the Republic of Texas. Texan settlers fought the Texas Revolution against Mexico in order to win their independence, and shortly after achieving that goal, Texas sought annexation to the United States.

1836

The U.S. Congress began using the so-called gag rule on May 26, a rule that prevented the reading and circulation of all antislavery petitions received by Congress. As a parliamentary maneuver, the House of Representatives had to renew the gag rule at the start of every year's congressional session until the rule was repealed in 1844.

1836

Arkansas entered the Union as a slave state on June 15. At this point, the United States consisted of 26 states, of which 12 were free states and 13 slave states. This was the first time in the nation's history that the number of slave states surpassed the number of free states.

1836

After James G. Birney relocated his abolitionist press to Cincinnati, Ohio, a proslavery mob that was upset with him for publishing the *Philanthropist*, an antislavery newspaper, attacked Birney's press on July 12 and destroyed the type that he used to publish the newspaper.

The American Anti-Slavery Society became the single largest and most influential organization against slavery up to the end of the American Civil War. Arguing that slavery was a sin of national proportions, not just a southern one, the society drew support from a range of racial, social, and economic backgrounds and produced millions of newspapers, pamphlets, and books as part of its effort to abolish slavery. In addition to drawing heavily from interdenominational developments within the evangelical movement, the society published the *Emancipator* and the *National Anti-Slavery Standard*. It also had former slaves such as Frederick Douglass give speeches in an attempt to expose the wrongs of slavery.

Begun in Philadelphia on December 4, 1833, at a three-day organizational meeting, the American Anti-Slavery Society was a diverse, national organization formed by 63 delegates from 10 states and was devoted exclusively to promoting immediate emancipation. Led by William Lloyd Garrison, the meeting joined New Englanders such as John Greenleaf Whittier with financially successful, conservative abolitionists such as Arthur and Lewis Tappan and William Jay, men who were not necessarily in complete agreement with Garrison's notion of "immediatism" but who nevertheless joined the society's ranks. The society also included 21 Quakers, 4 women, and 3 black participants—James G. Barbadoes of Boston, Robert Purvis, and James Mc-Crummell of Philadelphia. Although the last were involved in the proceedings and later signed various documents relating to the society's purpose and organization, they were not considered delegates.

The delegates to the Philadelphia conference opposed the colonization movement, which aimed at relocating blacks to Liberia, and denounced gradual antislavery movements as false or ineffective. As stated in the constitution drafted in Philadelphia, the primary object of the society was "the entire abolition of slavery in the United States" (AASS, 1838). Although the society recognized the right of states to legislate with regard to abolition, it nevertheless sought the "immediate abandonment" of the practice and to influence Congress in constitutionally appropriate ways.

In a "Declaration of Sentiments" delivered to the public on December 6, 1833, the delegates outlined more specifically the principles that informed their efforts to emancipate "one-sixth part of our countrymen" (AASS, 1838). As part of their moral and political imperatives, they proposed organizing antislavery societies, sending forth individuals to raise the voice of "warning and rebuke," circulating "antislavery tracts and periodicals," and enlisting "the pulpit and the press in the cause of suffering and the dumb" (AASS, 1838). Although the document did not call for complete social equality, it declared that "all persons of color" should have the same "privileges" as whites (AASS, 1838). It also revealed the depths of Garrison's pacifism and his dislike for political abolitionism.

The following year, at the society's annual convention in New York, Robert Purvis and eight fellow black abolitionists were elected to the board of managers, which consisted of about 10 percent of the society's membership. Although there was similar participation in 1835, the appointment of blacks to leadership positions after 1837 lessened owing to efforts to streamline the organization of the society. During the rest of the decade, black attendance at the society's annual meetings was minimal.

Despite repeated acts of violence against supporters like Lewis Tappan, whose house in New York was vandalized, the decision by the Reverend William Ellery Channing, a leader in the Unitarian Church, to publish *Slavery* (1835) was an indication that antislavery agitation had become more acceptable in American society. His willingness to denounce the evils of slavery legitimized, especially for northerners, antislavery arguments and appeals. Indeed, such was the acceptance of antislavery sentiment that by 1838, the American Anti-Slavery Society had 1,350 affiliated societies with a membership of about 250,000, a clear signal that the antislavery movement in the United Stated had become more mainstream. Yet despite this increase in its ranks, there was also growing disagreement. Ideological controversy became more heated between Garrison and his followers and less-radical abolitionists like the Tappans and the Reverend William Goodell, who could not support the Garrisonians' attacks on the clergy as being proslavery.

The growing rift between Garrison and the more conservative members of the society, such as the Tappans, became particularly evident at the New England Anti-Slavery Convention held in May 1838 when "the woman question" divided the abolitionist movement. Garrison's backing of Angelina and Sarah Moore Grimké, southern women who testified against the institution of slavery, reached a turning point at the annual meeting of the American Anti-Slavery Society in New York in 1840 when those aligned with Garrison nominated Abby Kelley for a position on the executive committee. Upset about the way Garrison allowed his sympathies for women's rights to influence his politics and policymaking concerning abolition, a large contingent of the society (approximately 300 members) led by Arthur and Lewis Tappan, Henry B. Stanton, Theodore Dwight Weld, and others walked out of the convention and set up the short-lived American and Foreign Anti-Slavery Society. They later threw their support to the Liberty Party, which many people consider was the first political party based on antislavery.

Continued debate over the antislavery nature of the U.S. Constitution and dissent during the late 1840s and 1850s between Gerrit Smith, Lysander Spooner, and the Tappans in one camp and Garrison in the other prevented unity even when the Fugitive Slave Act of 1850 was considered. Financial problems and dwindling numbers also hurt the society's cause. Black abolitionists criticized the actions of white abolitionists, who wrangled over nonresistance and other esoteric antislavery theories, and because black leaders continued to be marginalized with regard to leadership positions, many moved to rival societies, joined black-sponsored associations, or simply worked on their own. Douglass, for example, eventually went his own way, founded *North Star* and, much to Garrison's dissatisfaction, embraced the political ideas of abolitionists from western New York State. In an 1851 meeting of the American Anti-Slavery Society, Douglass shared his new views, which later prompted Garrison to denounce Douglass as "destitute of every principle of honor, ungrateful to the last degree and malevolent in spirit" (Garrison, 1851).

The American Anti-Slavery Society lasted through the Civil War, but even after the enactment of the Thirteenth Amendment, when Garrison's supporters attempted to discontinue the society, Wendell Phillips and others argued for its continued existence to preserve black rights and freedom. In 1869, after Congress proposed the Fifteenth Amendment and submitted it to states for ratification, the society resolved at its annual meeting in May that in giving blacks the vote, the amendment represented the effective completion of the antislavery movement. The ratification process was completed in March 1870, and in April of that same year, the American Anti-Slavery Society held its last meeting, a move that other smaller societies quickly followed.
—*Mark L. Kamrath*

For Further Reading
American Anti-Slavery Society. 1838. *The Constitution of the American Anti-Slavery Society.* New York: American Anti-Slavery Society; Barnes, Gilbert Hobbs. 1933. *The Anti-Slavery Impulse 1830–1844.* New York: Harcourt Brace; Bracey, John H., August Meier, and Elliott Rudwick, eds. 1971. *Blacks in the Abolitionist Movement.* Belmont, CA.: Wadsworth Publishing; Dumond, Dwight Lowell. 1961. *Antislavery: The Crusade for Freedom in America.* Ann Arbor: University of Michigan Press; Friedman, Lawrence J. 1982. *Gregarious Saints: Self and Community in American Abolitionism, 1830–1870.* New York: Cambridge University Press; Garrison, William Lloyd. 1851. *The Liberator,* Oct. 1.

1836

By December of 1836, it was estimated that 500 different abolitionist societies were active in the northern states.

1837

William Whipper, a free black from Philadelphia, Pennsylvania, published "An Address on Non-Resistance to Offensive Aggression." This article was published 12 years before Henry David Thoreau's essay on nonviolence, and it may have been the first literary reference in United States history to the concept of nonviolent protest. Also in Philadelphia, Quaker Richard Humphreys established the Institute for Colored Youth. In 1902, the school moved to Cheney, Pennsylvania, where it became known as Cheney University.

1837

In Boston, the Reverend Hosea Eaton published *A Treatise on the Intellectual Character and Political Condition of the Colored People of the United States.*

1837

John Greenleaf Whittier published *A Narrative of Events since the First of August, 1834,* which he believed to be the true narrative of a slave named James Williams. Impressed by the powerful message of this narrative, the American Anti-Slavery Society distributed a copy of the work to every member of the U.S. Congress. It was later discovered that the story that Williams told, however powerful, was untrue.

1837

The Panic of 1837, a serious economic recession, affected the institution of slavery. Prior to the economic downturn, a prime field hand in Virginia might have sold at auction for $1,300, but such prices declined significantly during the recession.

☙ELIZABETH BUFFUM CHACE (1806–1899)☙

Elizabeth Buffum Chace was a leader of the anti-slavery movement in Massachusetts and Rhode Island. Her paternal grandfather was a member of the Rhode Island Society for the Gradual Abolition of Slavery and harbored runaway slaves from New York; her father, Arnold Buffum, became the first president of the New England Anti-Slavery Society in 1832. A supporter of William Lloyd Garrison's demands for immediate abolition, in 1836 Elizabeth Chace cofounded the Ladies' Anti-Slavery Society of Fall River, Massachusetts, and became its vice-president. She was elected president in 1837 when it changed its name to the Female Anti-Slavery Society of Fall River, and she was a delegate to the 1838 Female Anti-Slavery Convention in Philadelphia. However, because she was profoundly reluctant to speak in public, even before a small group, she mostly worked quietly for abolition by hosting many of the society's meetings in her home, circulating petitions demanding that the Massachusetts legislature grant more civil rights to blacks, contributing items she had sewn to proabolition fund-raising events, and maintaining a small lending library of antislavery books.

In 1839, when her husband closed his business in Fall River and opened a new one in Valley Falls, Rhode Island, she accompanied him and continued to work behind the scenes for abolition. She organized antislavery meetings across the state and made the necessary arrangements for establishing a Sunday series of proabolition lectures in Providence while continuing to raise money, circulate petitions, write letters, contribute articles to Garrison's newspaper the *Liberator*, serve as secretary of the Rhode Island antislavery conventions, and house visiting abolitionist speakers. She also took an active role by turning her home into a station on the Underground Railroad. Runaway slaves who had hidden aboard vessels bound from Virginia would sneak ashore at one of Cape Cod's many ports, make their way or be sent to New Bedford, Massachusetts, and go from there to Fall River where they were harbored by Elizabeth's sister and brother-in-law. Chace and her husband received fugitives from Fall River and sent them by train to Worcester, Massachusetts, where they boarded another train that carried them through Vermont to Canada and freedom.

Chace spoke out publicly against slavery only once, when she said a handful of sentences at a Society of Friends' meeting. Although this stand occasioned hard feelings among some of her fellow Quakers, it was the continued refusal of the New England Yearly Meeting to open the doors of local meetinghouses to antislavery gatherings that compelled her to renounce the Quaker faith in 1843. That same year she adopted Garrison's policy of refusing to vote because voting implicitly sanctioned the proslavery provisions of the U.S. Constitution. In 1860, she served as vice-president of the New England Anti-Slavery Convention and remained a member of the American Anti-Slavery Society after Garrison's retirement in 1865, serving as vice-president from 1865 to 1870 in an effort to assist the freedmen.

—*Charles W. Carey, Jr.*

For Further Reading
Salitan, Lucille, and Eve Lewis Perera, eds. 1994. *Virtuous Lives: Four Quaker Sisters Remember Family Life, Abolitionism, and Women's Suffrage.* New York: Continuum; Wyman, Lillie Buffum Chace. 1913. *American Chivalry.* Boston: W. B. Clarke; Wyman, Lillie Buffum Chace, and Arthur Crawford Wyman. 1914. *Elizabeth Buffum Chace, 1806–1899: Her Life and Its Environment. Vol. 1.* Boston: W. B. Clarke.

1837
In Canada, blacks received the right to vote.

1837
On February 6, a resolution approved in the U.S. House of Representatives asserted that slaves did not possess the right of petition that was guaranteed to citizens by the U.S. Constitution.

1837
The *Weekly Advocate,* the first black newspaper published in the United States, was first published in New York City on May 10.

1837
In August, a planned slave conspiracy was detected in Rapides Parish, Louisiana, when a slave, Lewis Cheney, alerted authorities to the plot. Cheney earned his freedom for this action even though he was the person who had first initiated the planned uprising. In the aftermath of this episode, U.S. troops were sent into Alexandria, Louisiana, to put an end to the vigilante-based hangings of suspected black conspirators.

This illustration of a mistress whipping a slave woman tied to a post, from Bourne's Picture of Slavery *(1834), is typical of antislavery publications of the time, which emphasized the barbarity of the institution of slavery. (Library of Congress)*

1837

In Alton, Illinois, the antislavery newspaper publisher Elijah Lovejoy was murdered by an antiabolition mob on November 7 when he refused to stop publishing antislavery material and defended his press from mob attack. Lovejoy's press had been attacked on two previous occasions and had been smashed and thrown into a river, but it had been replaced by the Ohio Anti-Slavery Society.

1837

On December 4, during a brief moment when the gag rule was not in effect, Vermont Congressman William Slade presented a series of antislavery petitions to Congress. The angry debate that followed prompted Congress to enact an even stronger gag rule on December 19. The measure remained in effect until 1844 but had to be renewed each year at the start of the congressional term.

1837

Motivated by the brutal lynching of the Quaker abolitionist Elijah Lovejoy, Wendell Phillips delivered his first abolitionist address at Faneuil Hall in Boston, Massachusetts, on December 8. In this oration, Phillips declared "my *curse* be on the Constitution of the United States" (Jenkins, 1996) because the document protected slavery as a legal and permissible institution.

1837

During the Second Seminole War, American forces defeated a Seminole party under the command of the black chief, John Horse, in the Battle of Okeechobee on December 25. Chief John Horse shared his command responsibilities with Alligator Sam Jones and Wild Cat.

1838

Throughout the South, slaveowners became increasingly suspicious of the ways in which religious services might sway the passions of slaves. Black preachers found it more and more difficult to conduct services, and slaves were required to worship in settings where they could be under the direct supervision of the slaveowners.

1838

Robert Purvis published *Appeal of Forty Thousand Citizens Threatened with Disenfranchisement to the People of Pennsylvania.*

1838

The Massachusetts Anti-Slavery Society hired Charles Lenox Remond to serve as a lecturer for the organization. Remond was the first black abolitionist to be employed in this capacity.

1838

On January 3–12, South Carolina Senator John C. Calhoun, alarmed by efforts of northern abolitionists to have slavery outlawed in the District of Columbia and to prohibit the domestic slave trade, presented a series of proposals to the Senate that were designed to bolster the legal protection of slavery. The Senate approved one of Calhoun's measures, which affirmed that the national government should "resist all attempts by one portion of the Union to use it as an

By the 1850s, the issue of slavery, particularly the expansion of slavery into new territories, had come to dominate the American political scene. As the nation moved toward disunion and civil war, the dividing line was clearly drawn between those groups and people who would preserve the institution and those who would eradicate it. This division affected most institutions in American life, as political parties, religious denominations, and even families split between pro- and antislavery factions. For the Whig Party, internal divisions over slavery proved fatal.

The Whig Party originated as a political coalition against the Jacksonian Democrats in 1834. Led by Henry Clay, Daniel Webster, and William Henry Harrison, the emergence of the Whigs inaugurated the second-party system in the United States. The Whigs adopted a loose construction of the Constitution, believing that the federal government should take an active role in the nation's economic life. Initially, the party was made up of a loose coalition of disaffected Democrats and others united by a hatred of Jackson and their support of a national bank, a high protective tariff, and federal aid to internal improvements. Although united on these economic issues, the Whigs were divided on other policy matters, particularly slavery. This division led to the formation of two internal factions during the debates over the Wilmot Proviso in 1846.

One faction, called the Conscience Whigs, opposed the expansion of slavery into the territories. Led by Turlow Weed and William H. Seward, Conscience Whigs believed that slavery was a moral blight upon the nation and should not be expanded. More radical members of this group called for immediate and uncompensated abolition. Abraham Lincoln, elected to Congress in 1846, can be described as a Conscience Whig. Although strongest in New England and in New York, this faction was present in most northern and midwestern states. In 1848, many of these Whigs left the party altogether and merged with antislavery Democrats and remnants of the Liberty Party to form the Free Soil Party. Conscience Whigs who remained in the Whig ranks continued to push for antislavery legislation and the adoption of antislavery planks in the national party platform.

Though originally attributed to proslavery Whigs in Massachusetts, the term Cotton Whigs can be used to describe another faction of the party. Made up of southern Whigs and northerners from states with a vested interest in the continued vitality of southern agriculture, Cotton Whigs supported the institution of slavery on social, economic, and constitutional grounds. Prominent Cotton Whigs included Alexander H. Stephens, Henry Clay, and Daniel Webster. Though labeled by Charles Sumner a partnership between "the lords of the lash and the lords of the loom," members of this faction varied considerably in their ideology concerning slavery (Brauer, 1967). Although southerners like Stephens defended the legality of slavery under the Constitution and emphasized the perceived inferiority of blacks, Webster argued that slavery should not be expanded into the territories and would die a natural death without legislative intervention. Despite these differences, Cotton Whigs agreed that the moral tone injected into the slavery debate by the 1840s heightened what to them was essentially a political issue.

The internal division over slavery was the death knell of the Whig Party. By 1856, the party had imploded, with Cotton Whigs gravitating to the Democratic or American (Know-Nothing) Parties, both of which refused to take a definitive stand on slavery. Many Conscience Whigs joined the Republicans, who staunchly opposed slavery expansion. In many ways, the dissolution of the Whig Party mirrored the deepening sectional tension in the nation as a whole during the 1840s and 1850s. By failing to resolve party differences over slavery, the Whigs could no longer wield meaningful political power. The split, largely along sectional lines, was an important precursor to the bloody national epoch that began in 1861.

—*Richard D. Starnes*

For Further Reading
Brauer, Kinley. 1967. *Cotton versus Conscience: Massachusetts Whig Party Politics and Southwestern Expansion, 1843–1848*. Lexington: University of Kentucky Press; Freehling, William. 1990. *The Road to Disunion*. New York: Harper and Row; Potter, David. 1976. *The Impending Crisis, 1848–1861*. New York: Harper and Row.

A lynch mob attacking the warehouse of Godfrey Gilman and Elijah Lovejoy in Alton, Illinois, on the night of November 7, 1837. Lovejoy, an antislavery publisher, was murdered by the mob. (Library of Congress/Corbis)

instrument to attack the domestic institutions of another" (Schlesinger, 1983).

1838
On February 15, Massachusetts Congressman John Quincy Adams introduced 350 antislavery petitions in defiance of the gag rule that the House of Representatives had instituted. The petitions opposed slavery and the annexation of Texas.

1838
Led by Robert Purvis, free blacks in Philadelphia, Pennsylvania, held a mass meeting on March 14 to protest the disenfranchisement of blacks in the state.

1838
Philadelphia's Pennsylvania Hall was burned to the ground by a proslavery mob on May 17. The group was angered that the building had been used to host recent antislavery meetings.

1838
In August, the black abolitionist David Ruggles

began publication of the *Mirror of Liberty* in New York City, the first black magazine to be published in the United States.

1838
Frederick Douglass escaped from slavery in Baltimore, Maryland, on September 3 and made his way to New York City.

1838
Ohio Representative Joshua Giddings, the first abolitionist to be elected to the U.S. Congress, took his seat in the House of Representatives on December 3. Among other issues, Congressman Giddings worked tirelessly to do away with the gag rule, which prohibited Congress from considering any antislavery petitions that were submitted.

1838
On December 11, the U.S. House of Representatives voted to renew the gag rule, adopted in 1836, which prohibited the consideration of any antislavery petitions received by Congress. The 1838 renewal became known as "the Atherton gag" because the measure had been

Antiabolition mobs and riots became an important feature of the social landscape of Jacksonian America. Such mobs represented the most violent reaction to abolitionism, a movement that gained strength throughout the 1830s and 1840s, and most of the behavior occurred in the North because the abolitionist movement never took firm root in the South. There were episodes in the South, however, when opponents of slavery found themselves dunked in water, ridden out of town on a rail, or tarred and feathered. Such crowd actions shared the ritualized violence of the charivari (raucous European peasant celebrations) with their northern counterparts, but there was less destruction of property than there was in the North, such as in the New York City riot of 1834. In the South, such actions represented punishment for those people who transgressed lines of family honor and questioned the institution of slavery. Southerners thus responded with the creation of "lynch law" and vigilance committees that controlled the expression of dissent by antislavery southerners and ejected northern abolitionists. There was little physical violence; rather, the ritualized violence served to maintain racial solidarity among whites, protect slavery from criticism, and prevent servile rebellion.

Antiabolition riots occurred in the North between 1833 and 1845, especially in New England, New York, and Ohio, which were areas of sustained abolitionist activity. Opposition to the antislavery movement in the North occurred for several different reasons. Antiabolitionists from the propertied classes feared that antislavery activities might disrupt the Union because of the anger that the abolitionist movement created in the South. They also feared the loss of profitable southern business, such as the exporting of southern agricultural products or acting as middlemen or agents for such products. Finally, antiabolitionists from the working classes often disliked blacks and feared they would take jobs from whites, and such fears became acute during hard economic times, such as the depression that followed the Panic of 1837. Whites also feared that interaction with blacks would lead to miscegenation and the amalgamation of the races. Such racist fears suffused the antiabolitionist movement and were especially prominent among the working classes, who lived nearest to the free black communities in the North.

The most common form of antiabolition mob action in the North was rioting. Paul Gilje defines a riot as "any group of twelve or more people attempting to assert their will immediately through the use of force outside the normal bounds of law" (Gilje, 1996). Mobs sought to enforce their will through "coercion or compulsion based upon violence, or based on the threat of violence" (Gilje, 1996). Thus, mobs blocked entrances to halls used by abolitionists; threw eggs, paint, and ink at abolitionists; and played drums and horns to drown out abolitionist speakers. Greater destruction of property took place when mobs attacked the presses of abolitionist newspapers and destroyed machines, threw away type, and burned buildings. Occasionally, mobs stoned or clubbed abolitionists, but such physical violence was rare. The worst violence occurred in race riots such as that in New York City when from July 4–12, 1834, white mobs attacked black sections of the city and destroyed homes, churches, and a school.

There is still much debate about who composed the antiabolition mobs. Leonard Richards asserts that most mobs consisted of "gentlemen of property and standing" (Richards, 1970), that is, merchants, lawyers, doctors, bankers, and politicians. In his study, Richards demonstrates that over 70 percent of each mob came from the commercial and professional ranks whereas fewer than 20 percent came from the ranks of tradesmen and manufacturers. The mobs tended to be native-born and attracted sizable percentages of Episcopalians. The mobs differed greatly from the abolitionists, who attracted far fewer numbers of high-ranking professional or commercial men and Episcopalians, tending to attract instead more foreign-born people and more men from the ranks of tradesmen and manufacturers. Antiabolitionists thus often perceived the abolitionists as threats to their elite status, moral leadership, and values and traditions. Antiabolitionists also feared miscegenation and amalgamation should southern slaves be freed and head north. Paul Gilje, on the other hand, sees antiabolition mobs as tradesmen expressing opposition to black encroachment into their professions and to the de-skilling of labor, which was a side effect of the industrialization of the North.

Antiabolition rioting began to decrease dramatically after 1845 as northern newspapers began to decry the destruction of property and lawless behavior of the mobs. Abolitionists pointed to southern vigilance committees as the first step toward the loss of free speech for northern white men, and mob action against northern antislavery efforts led more people into the antislavery movement because of the perceived threat to northern civil liberties.

—James C. Foley

For Further Reading
Gilje, Paul. 1996. *Rioting in America*. Bloomington: Indiana University Press; Nye, Russel. 1949. *Fettered Freedom: Civil Liberties and the Slavery Controversy, 1830–1860*. East Lansing: Michigan State College Press; Richards, Leonard. 1970. *Gentlemen of Property and Standing: Anti-Abolition Mobs in Jacksonian America*. New York: Oxford University Press; Wyatt-Brown, Bertram. 1982. *Southern Honor: Ethics and Behavior in the Old South*. New York: Oxford University Press.

introduced by Congressman Charles G. Atherton, a New Hampshire Democrat.

1839

American Slavery As It Is: Testimony of a Thousand Witnesses was published by Theodore Dwight Weld. This work was an attempt to present a documentary history—based upon southern newspaper accounts and eyewitness testimony—that would identify the true condition of slaves in the American South. Weld was assisted in this project by South Carolina abolitionist Angelina Grimké, and the two abolitionists were married later the same year.

1839

The U.S. State Department declared that blacks were not considered citizens and therefore denied a black applicant's request for a passport.

1839

In a papal letter, Pope Gregory XVI declared the official opposition of the Roman Catholic Church to the slave trade and to slavery. In the United States, Catholic slaveholders generally ignored the papal pronouncement and continued to participate in the institution of slavery. [See Document 50.]

1839

Antislavery advocate Elizur Wright became the editor of the abolitionist newspaper *Massachusetts Abolitionist* and used the paper as a forum to advocate political action to bring an end to slavery. Wright was also active in efforts to establish the Liberty Party.

1839

The American Anti-Slavery Society hired Presbyterian minister Samuel Ringgold Ward to serve as an abolitionist lecturer.

1839

Senator Henry Clay of Kentucky planned to run for the presidency in 1840 as a candidate of the Whig Party, but Clay believed that many Americans associated the Whigs with the abolitionist cause. In a Senate debate on slavery on February 7, Clay criticized the abolitionists and said they had no legal right to interfere with slavery in those areas where it already existed. Clay hoped that he could gain support among northern and southern conservatives by speaking out against abolitionists, who were considered the extremists of their day. Despite his efforts, Clay was unable to secure the Whig Party's nomination in 1840, but the Whig standard-bearer, General William Henry Harrison, was elected president.

1839

In late February, during the Second Seminole War, captured Seminoles along with their black allies were shipped from Tampa Bay, Florida, to a new home in the Indian Territory of Oklahoma.

1839

Robert Smalls, who later became a hero during the American Civil War and eventually served as a Reconstruction-era congressman from South Carolina, was born into slavery in Beaufort, South Carolina, on April 5.

1839

In July, the Spanish slave ship *Amistad* was seized off the coast of Cuba when the 54 Africans on board, led by Joseph Cinqué, revolted and killed the captain. The Africans demanded that the remaining crewmen return the vessel to Africa, but later in the summer, the vessel was captured off the coast of Montauk, Long Island. After a series of trials, the *Amistad* captives won their freedom when they were

CHARLES LENOX REMOND (1810–1873)

Charles Lenox Remond was born in Salem, Massachusetts, to John and Nancy Remond, both noted abolitionists. His mother played a significant part in establishing the Salem Antislavery Society in the early 1830s, and in 1835, his father became a lifetime member of the Massachusetts Anti-Slavery Society. John and Nancy Remond's involvement in antislavery activities greatly influenced the future direction of their son's life.

Charles began participating in activities of the American Anti-Slavery Society at an early age and became a staunch supporter of white abolitionist William Lloyd Garrison. In his early years, Remond found Garrison's philosophy of nonresistance appealing, but his own abolitionist philosophy would eventually become much more radical as he came to the conclusion that white abolitionists did not fully understand the problems facing African Americans.

In 1838, Remond was hired by the Massachusetts Anti-Slavery Society to lecture—the first black to hold the position. For the next two years, he traveled throughout New England delivering antislavery speeches and organizing new antislavery societies. In summer 1838, two new antislavery societies were established in Maine shortly after a visit from Remond.

Remond also spoke out in favor of women's involvement in antislavery activities. In most cities, women were encouraged to create their own auxiliary societies, rather than work alongside men. When women delegates were refused seating at the World Anti-Slavery Convention in London in 1840, where Remond was serving as one of four representatives from the American Anti-Slavery Society, he voiced his disapproval and proceeded to remove himself from the assembly. Remond's trip to London had been financed by several female antislavery societies.

Remond continued on the lecture circuit for the next year, returning to the United States in 1841. His speeches were well received, especially in London and Ireland, but that was frequently not the case in the United States. Remond became increasingly disillusioned with Garrison's belief that voting constituted tacit support of a proslavery government operating in compliance with a proslavery constitution. In 1848, Remond cast his ballot for Free Soil candidate Stephen C. Phillips, who, if elected governor of Massachusetts, pledged greater appropriations for the support of black schools.

By 1850, Remond was supporting a more radi-

Charles Lenox Remond (Library of Congress)

cal approach to abolition. At a convention held in New Bedford, Massachusetts, to discuss the *Dred Scott* decision, Remond stated he was prepared to write an address encouraging slaves to revolt. He also suggested that change in the South would likely be the result of violence. He believed that the efforts of abolitionists had been a failure, because conditions for most blacks remained dismal.

During the American Civil War, Remond recruited soldiers for the Union army, further evidence of his growing discontent and radicalism. He eventually become less involved in public life owing to failing health that was exacerbated by the death of his second wife. Remond died in Boston in 1873.

—*Beverly A. Bunch-Lyons*

For Further Reading
Quarles, Benjamin. 1969. *Black Abolitionists.* New York: Oxford University Press; Ripley, C. Peter, ed. 1992. *The Black Abolitionist Papers.* Vol.5, *The United States, 1859–1865.* Chapel Hill: University of North Carolina Press; Salzman, Jack, David Lionel Smith, and Cornel West, eds. 1996. *Encyclopedia of African-American Culture and History.* New York: Macmillan.

❧JOSHUA REED GIDDINGS (1795–1864)❧

A powerful opponent of slavery for 21 years in the U.S. House of Representatives, Joshua Reed Giddings's uncompromising attitude on slavery earned him the title "lion of Ashtabula" (name of the county in Ohio he was from). Giddings went to Congress from one of the nation's most fervent abolitionist strongholds, Ohio's Western Reserve (northeastern Ohio), and never one to be obsessed with party regularity, Giddings did not compromise on principle.

Giddings fought against slavery on the basis of its denationalization, i.e., taking the federal government out of the slavery controversy. He argued that one of the rights all states could cherish was the right not to support slavery by law or federal appropriation. From the official protection of slavery in the District of Columbia (1795) to the *Dred Scott* decision (1857), the federal government sought to protect slavery, but Giddings believed that the great expense of and the moral blight wrought upon the nation by this policy were staggering. He made his mark in Congress his first term, when, in partnership with John Quincy Adams, he tried to circumvent the infamous gag rule, which denied any discussion of slavery or petitions against it on the floor of the House.

The greatest expression of Giddings's opposition to slavery and the federal government's protection of it came as a result of the *Creole* case. Several slaves aboard the brig *Creole* bound for New Orleans from Virginia mutinied and killed the owner of 39 of the slaves aboard. The ship docked in the Bahamas, and the British gave the mutineers (except for the murderers) haven. The southern leadership wanted the slaves returned for trial. On March 21–22, 1842, Giddings offered in the House of Representatives "the municipal theory," encased in nine resolutions largely written by Theodore Dwight Weld, to solve the *Creole* crisis. The House interpreted his resolutions as justification for slave rebellion and murder. Giddings was censured for his efforts and resigned the next day, but he was returned to the Congress by an overwhelming margin the following month.

When the Whigs nominated slaveowner Zachary Taylor for president in 1848, Giddings bolted and joined the Free Soil Party, and when the Kansas-Nebraska Act passed in 1854, he helped organize the new Republican Party. Whatever party Giddings was affiliated with, he was always its most radical member. Though many admired him, there were scores of legislators who avoided him.

Joshua Giddings (Corbis-Bettmann)

In his later years he was known as "father Giddings" by his admirers. As the years passed and slave power became more entrenched in the federal government, Giddings grew more radical. He abandoned his trust in political abolition and came out for "higher law" ideas and declared that "powder and ball" should be issued to the slaves if they were ever to be free.

Giddings's influence on Abraham Lincoln was considerable. Lincoln listened intently to Giddings's impassioned speeches during the Mexican War congress of 1847–1849, and Giddings had Lincoln's ear during and after the campaign of 1860. Giddings died in Montreal while serving as U.S. consul to Canada on May 27, 1864.

—*Jim Baugess*

For Further Reading
Gamble, Douglas A. 1979. "Joshua Giddings and the Ohio Abolitionists: A Study in Radical Politics." *Ohio History* 88(1): 37–56; Miller, William Lee. 1996. *Arguing about Slavery: The Great Battle in the United States Congress*. New York: Knopf; Stewart, James Brewer. 1970. *Joshua Giddings and the Tactics of Radical Politics*. Cleveland: Case Western University Press.

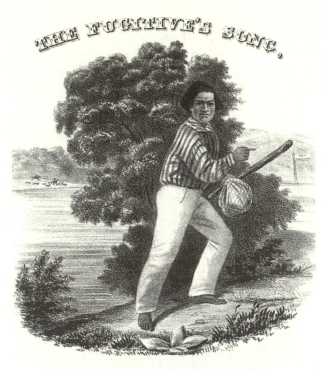

THE FUGITIVE'S SONG,

The cover page for the sheet music to "The Fugitive's Song," "composed and respectfully dedicated . . . to Frederick Douglass, A Graduate of the 'Peculiar Institution,' for his fearless advocacy, signal ability, and wonderful success in behalf of his brothers in bonds (and to the fugitives from slavery in the Free States and Canada) by their friend, Jesse Hutchinson, Junr." (Corbis-Bettmann)

defended before the U.S. Supreme Court by former president John Quincy Adams.

1839

The Liberty Party, the first antislavery political party in the United States, was established by James G. Birney at a convention in Warsaw, New York, on November 13. Some of the leading supporters of this new political party included the black abolitionists Samuel Ringgold Ward and Henry Highland Garnet. Prominent white supporters included Gerrit Smith and Salmon P. Chase. The convention nominated Birney for the presidency, and Francis J. Lemoyne was nominated for vice-president. As part of the party's political activism, members urged boycotts of southern-made products and crops.

1840

The Unitarian minister William Ellery Channing, pastor of Boston's Federal Street Church, published *Emancipation,* an antislavery tract that urged the U.S. government to follow the same path as the British Parliament and abolish slavery. Channing believed that the success demonstrated in the British government's experience at ending slavery throughout its vast empire proved that the abolition of slavery was indeed a real possibility in the United States.

1840

Theodore Dwight Weld, a non-Garrisonian abolitionist, broke with the Garrisonians concerning the tactics that should be used in the abolitionist movement. Weld eventually established the American and Foreign Anti-Slavery Society.

1840

Both New York and Vermont instituted a new judicial policy of holding a jury trial in all cases involving fugitive slaves who had been captured within their respective states. In the case of Vermont, the law creating this new procedure was rescinded in 1843, but the policy was reestablished in 1850 upon passage of the new Fugitive Slave Act.

1840

The Reverend Samuel E. Cornish and Theodore S. Wright published *The Colonization Scheme Considered in Its Rejection by the Colored People,* which outlined the reasons why free blacks in the United States should oppose all efforts to recolonize them in West African locations like Liberia and Sierra Leone.

1840

A group of abolitionists from the United States traveled to London to attend the World Anti-Slavery Convention but were dismayed by a convention policy that denied seats to the female abolitionists who had planned to participate in the event. American abolitionists Elizabeth Cady Stanton and Lucretia Mott walked out of the convention in protest when they were denied seats as delegates, and William Lloyd Garrison showed his solidarity with the female abolitionists by leaving the meeting as well. In some respects, the poor treatment afforded the female abolitionists helped to encourage the eventual development of an American women's rights movement.

1840

On April 1, the Liberty Party held its first national convention in Albany, New York, and confirmed the candidacy of James G. Birney for

~ELIZUR WRIGHT (1804–1885)~

Elizur Wright played a prominent role in establishing the American Anti-Slavery Society and creating the abolitionist Liberty Party. Taught to abhor slavery by his father, who sheltered runaway slaves in their Ohio home, he became a vocal advocate of immediate abolition in 1832 after reading William Lloyd Garrison's "Thoughts on African Colonization," a persuasive condemnation of efforts to end slavery by relocating freed slaves to Africa. In 1833, Wright became recording secretary of the New York City Anti-Slavery Society, and later that year he was appointed secretary of domestic correspondence of the newly created American Anti-Slavery Society, which favored immediate emancipation rather than a gradualist approach.

As secretary, he functioned as the de facto office manager of the society's American headquarters in New York for the next six years and supervised its field agents, corresponded with its several hundred state and local affiliates, mailed out thousands of antislavery tracts, and raised money. He also edited many of the society's publications, including *Anti-Slavery Reporter, Anti-Slavery Record, Human Rights,* and *Quarterly Anti-Slavery Magazine,* and from time to time he contributed to its official newspaper, the *Emancipator.* In 1837, the society increased the number of its auxiliary societies to over 1,000, so Wright relinquished his editorial duties the next year to concentrate on coordinating the activities of what had become the nation's largest organization devoted to immediate abolition. However, his blunt personality, his vociferous opposition to the Fugitive Slave Act of 1793, and his virulent anticlericalism—he once declared that immediacy's most formidable opponents were ordained Christian ministers—made it increasingly difficult for him to work with the society's conservative executive board, which was firmly devoted to upholding the U.S. Constitution and achieving abolition by working through the churches.

In 1839, Wright resigned as secretary of the American society to become editor of the *Massachusetts Abolitionist,* the official voice of those abolitionists opposed to Garrison's increasingly radical views, particularly his insistence that political action in general (and voting in particular) implicitly sanctioned the proslavery clauses of the Constitution. As editor, Wright argued forcefully and repeatedly for the creation of a third party devoted to abolishing slavery, and he enthusiastically endorsed the fledgling Abolitionist Party when it nominated a presidential ticket that same year. In 1839, he attended the convention of the Liberty Party (new name of the Abolitionist Party) at which James G. Birney was nominated to run for the presidency and trumpeted the merits of Birney's candidacy as an abolitionist in his editorials. However, half of the paper's subscribers, whose political sentiments favored the election of William Henry Harrison, a northern Whig, canceled their subscriptions in protest, and Wright was forced to step down as editor that same year.

From 1846 to 1850, he edited the *Chronotype,* a Boston daily newspaper that espoused several reforms including immediacy. He remained on its editorial staff after the paper became the *Commonwealth,* a Free Soil Party organ, but resigned in 1852 after being falsely charged for harboring a runaway slave. Shortly thereafter he faded from the abolitionist scene.

—*Charles W. Carey, Jr.*

For Further Reading
Goodheart, Lawrence B. 1990. *Abolitionist, Actuary, Atheist: Elizur Wright and the Reform Impulse.* Kent, OH: Kent State University Press.

---

the presidency. Birney was the first antislavery candidate to seek that office.

1840
In an effort to prevent the kidnapping of free blacks that resulted in their being sold into slavery in the South, on May 14 the legislature of New York enacted An Act More Effectually to Protect the Free Citizens of This State from Being Kidnapped, or Reduced to Slavery.

1840
In June, the American Anti-Slavery Society began publishing the *National Anti-Slavery Standard* as its official organ to support immediate emancipation. The publication remained in operation under various titles until April 1870.

1840
The New York State Convention of Negroes was held in Albany, New York, August 18–20.

1841
Thornton Stringfellow, a proslavery apologist from Virginia, published *A Brief Examination*

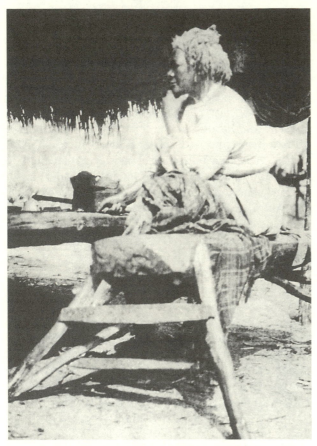

"Hannah," believed to be 105 years old at the time this photograph was taken in 1925, when she was "discovered" in a Seminole camp in the Florida Everglades and was considered to be the only unfreed slave in the country. (UPI/Corbis-Bettmann)

of *Scripture Testimony on the Institution of Slavery*. Stringfellow believed that the number of references supporting slavery that were to be found in the Bible were sufficient proof of the moral legitimacy of the practice.

1841
In New York, the state legislature gave public schools the authority to segregate students by race in all educational facilities.

1841
In March, the free black Solomon Northup was kidnapped in Washington, D.C., and sold into slavery in the South. Northup spent the next 12 years of his life as a slave on several Louisiana cotton plantations. Abolitionists in the North would work to win his eventual release. [See Document 51.]

1841
Blanche K. Bruce was born a slave on a planta-

tion in Prince Edward County, Virginia, on March 1. During the Reconstruction era, Bruce represented the state of Mississippi in the U.S. Senate, the only black to serve a full term in the Senate during Reconstruction.

1841
On March 9, the U.S. Supreme Court upheld a lower court's decision and found that the Africans from the ship *Amistad* had been illegally kidnapped and ordered them set free and returned to Africa as soon as possible. Former president John Quincy Adams had defended the Africans in legal arguments before the Supreme Court.

1841
In August, Frederick Douglass began to speak on the abolitionist lecture circuit on behalf of the Massachusetts Anti-Slavery Society.

1841
The Pennsylvania State Convention of Negroes was held in Pittsburgh, Pennsylvania, August 23–25.

1841
While they were being transported from Hampton Roads, Virginia, to New Orleans, Louisiana, slaves on board the *Creole* revolted on November 7 and took control of the vessel. They sailed to Nassau in the Bahamas where all the slaves on board the vessel, except those accused of murder, were granted asylum and eventually set free by British officials. This event sparked an international diplomatic incident between the United States and Great Britain. Secretary of State Daniel Webster put forth the argument that slaves on board an American vessel were bound by American law, but the British maintained that the seizure took place in international waters and that American law did not apply in this instance.

1842
William G. Allen, a free black abolitionist, began publication of the *National Watchman*, an antislavery newspaper, in Troy, New York.

1842
The Rhode Island legislature granted the suffrage to free blacks living within the state.

African slaves on the Amistad *rebel and kill Captain Ramón Ferrer; Don José Ruiz and Don Pedro Montes, the slaves' owners, look on in horror. (Library of Congress/Corbis)*

1842

On January 24, Congressman John Quincy Adams of Massachusetts presented Congress with a petition drafted by the citizens of Haverhill, Massachusetts, that called for the peaceful dissolution of the Union.

1842

The U.S. Supreme Court issued a ruling in the case of *Prigg v. Pennsylvania* on March 1 stating that a Pennsylvania statute which interfered with the enforcement of the Fugitive Slave Act of 1793 was unconstitutional. A state court had previously convicted Edward Prigg of kidnapping when Prigg, a slave catcher, had tried to take the fugitive slave Margaret Morgan from Pennsylvania back to slavery in Maryland. The Supreme Court upheld the validity of the Fugitive Slave Act of 1793 and the primacy of federal law over state efforts to block enforcement, but most of the northern states found means to avoid assisting the efforts of southerners to have fugitive slaves recaptured and returned to the South. The decision stated, however, that it was a federal responsibility to enforce the Fugitive Slave Act since the states could not be obliged to enforce federal laws through state officers, and many northern states used this interpretation as a judicial loophole. Most northern states soon thereafter enacted personal liberty laws, which helped state officials circumvent enforcement of the federal Fugitive Slave Act.

1842

On March 21 and 22, Congressman Joshua Giddings, an Ohio Whig, introduced a series of measures, collectively called "the Giddings resolutions," in which he attacked the federal sanction of slavery and the coastal slave trade. Giddings's actions were largely a response to a controversy that had been caused by the *Creole* incident, and his measures went so far as to encourage resistance like that which had taken place on board the *Creole* the previous year when slaves mutinied and took control of the vessel. Giddings was censured by his colleagues on March 23 and resigned, but he was reelected by his district and returned to Congress the following month.

1842

In Boston, George Latimer, an escaped slave, was captured in October. The case surrounding his efforts to avoid being returned to slavery in the South sparked an intense North-South struggle over the effective enforcement of existing fugitive slave laws and northern attempts to circumvent those measures by passing personal liberty laws. In the case of Latimer, a Boston abolitionist eventually forced Boston authorities to allow him to purchase Latimer from his southern owner on November 17, thereby allowing the fugitive to become free. The debates regarding this case prompted Frederick Douglass to publish his first printed articles on behalf of the abolitionist movement.

1843

Diplomats of the United States and Great Britain met in Washington, D.C., to negotiate the Webster-Ashburton Treaty. As a result of one of the articles of this treaty, the African Squadron was formed, and naval officials of the United States and Great Britain agreed to cooperate and patrol the waters off the coast of West Africa in an effort to intercept ships that might

∾NATIONAL ANTI-SLAVERY STANDARD∾

The *National Anti-Slavery Standard* was the official journal of the American Anti-Slavery Society from June 1840 to April 1870. The society then published, from May to July 1870, the *Standard: A Journal of Reform and Literature;* from July 30, 1870, to December 23, 1971, the *National Standard: An Independent Reform and Literary Journal;* and, from January to December 1872, the *National Standard: A Temperance and Literary Journal.* The *National Anti-Slavery Standard* was published weekly, and except between July 1854 and November 1865, when it was published in Philadelphia, it was published in New York City. The *Standard* was well served by a distinguished succession of editors, among them, most notably, Lydia Maria Child, who was technically a coeditor with husband, David L. Child, from May 1841 to May 1843.

Immediate emancipation was the goal of the American Anti-Slavery Society, and the *Standard* made a strong religious appeal for abolition. Chastising the American church and calling God abolition's "most efficient ally," it also initially recognized the value of political action. The year of its founding saw the American Anti-Slavery Society torn apart over tactics (specifically William Lloyd Garrison's nonresistant contention that governments are by nature immoral, which offended the politically minded abolitionists) and over the rights of women. Some dissenters founded the American and Foreign Anti-Slavery Society, and others founded the Liberty Party. Consequently, the language of that party's prospectus was inclusive and appropriate for an umbrella organization, in regard to both gender and tactics. But in 1844, David Lee Child, now serving as editor after charges of meek editorial style had prompted his wife to resign, resigned himself after disunionism and nonresistance (a form of Christian anarchism) became the official creed of the society. Modes of action were no longer to be left up to individual members. Later, the American Civil War brought the society firmly behind the president and the Republican Party.

Recruited in 1840 by William Lloyd Garrison, who supported women's rights, Lydia Maria Child

(1802–1880), appointed with her husband, first served alone because of his poor health. She gave the *Standard* a literary flavor that made it appealing to educated readers. The *Standard,* in fact, was the first American journal to publish William Blake's poetry ("The Little Black Boy" on March 10, 1842), which appealed to the Unitarian circle that contributed to the society. Child's "Letters from New York," describing life in the city and commenting on current events and reforms such as nonresistance and the woman question, were published in the *Standard* and then published in two volumes in 1843 and 1844. First, however, they were refused by the publisher because of the letters' abolitionist assertions, which had already been muted by the author in an act of self-censorship.

The *Standard* published material from the American Anti-Slavery Society and from other abolitionist groups in America and abroad; letters from frequent correspondents such as Charles K. Whipple, "D.Y.," Samuel J. May, Jr., Henry C. Wright, Harriet Beecher Stowe, and Wendell Phillips; extracts from a wide range of newspapers; and material from various religious denominations. A miscellany of news, not always focused on reform, was regular, along with excerpts of works by prominent authors. Reform causes other than slavery were discussed, and after the onset of the Civil War, the focus of coverage changed from abolition to prospects and potentialities for the life of the slaves as freemen and freewomen.

—*Charles A. D'Aniello*

For Further Reading
Blassingame, John W., Mae G. Henderson, and Jessica M. Dunn, eds. 1980–1984. *Antislavery Newspapers and Periodicals.* Vol. 4 *(1840–1860)* and Vol. 5 *(1861–1871). Annotated Index of Letters in the National Anti-Slavery Standard.* Boston: G. K. Hall; Karcher, Carolyn L. 1994. *The First Woman in the Republic: A Cultural Biography of Lydia Maria Child.* Durham, NC: Duke University Press; Mills, Bruce. 1994. *Cultural Reformations: Lydia Maria Child and the Literature of Reform.* Athens: University of Georgia Press.

be engaging in the slave trade. When ships were captured by the squadron, Africans on board were repatriated either to Liberia or to Sierra Leone. Treaty negotiations did not reach a final agreement as to how the slave trade within the Western Hemisphere might be best restricted.

1843

In light of the recent Supreme Court decision in the case of *Prigg v. Pennsylvania* (1842), the state legislatures in Massachusetts and Vermont specifically forbade any state officials from aiding and abetting anyone, including federal authorities, in efforts to remove fugitive slaves from their respective states and return them to the condition of enslavement in the South.

1843

In March, in an action that ran counter to the prevailing national trend, the Massachusetts legislature decriminalized miscegenation by repealing a 1786 law that had prohibited interracial marriage. As a result, intermarriage between whites, blacks, mulattoes, or Indians was legalized by Massachusetts state law.

1843

On June 1, Sojourner Truth (Isabella Baumfree), who had been born a slave in New York State, became the first black woman to join the abolitionist lecture circuit and speak openly from a public platform on behalf of antislavery and women's causes.

1843

At the annual meeting of the National Convention of Colored Men in Buffalo, New York, on August 22, Henry Highland Garnet called for slaves in the South to rise up and revolt and urged free blacks to participate in a general strike to improve conditions for blacks in the country. Other delegates, including Frederick Douglass, disapproved of the message Garnet delivered. [See Document 53.]

1843

The Liberty Party held a national convention in Buffalo, New York, on August 30–31, and Samuel Ringgold Ward, Henry Highland Garnet, and Charles B. Ray participated, thereby becoming the first blacks to take an active role in a national political gathering. Ward led the convention in prayer, Garnet served on the nominating committee, and Ray was one of the convention secretaries. The convention nominated James G. Birney for president and Thomas Morris for vice-president. The party platform opposed the extension of slavery into any western territories, but it did not take a stand on the question of Texas annexation.

1843

Free blacks in Michigan held their first statewide convention in Detroit, Michigan, October 23–27.

Blanche K. Bruce (1841–1898), who was born a slave and became the first African American to serve a full term in the U.S. Senate. (Library of Congress)

1843

Black abolitionist David Jenkins founded the antislavery newspaper *Palladium of Liberty* in Columbus, Ohio, on December 27.

1844

The slavery question began to cause a schism in many American religious communities. For instance, the Methodist Episcopal Church of the United States divided over the question of whether or not bishops in the church could hold slaves. This schism grew out of the decision by Georgia Bishop James O. Andrews to continue holding his slaves after church authorities had told him to manumit them or else to give up his bishopric. As a result of this division, white southerners formed the Methodist Episcopal Church, South.

1844

Proslavery forces in South Carolina were energized by a speech supporting disunion that fire-eater Robert Barnwell Rhett delivered in Bluffton, South Carolina. "The Bluffton movement" was a short-lived effort to stir the political passions of South Carolina residents over the issues of states' rights and nullification.

Joshua Giddings, an antislavery congressman from Ohio's Western Reserve (northeastern Ohio), secured a place in history by offering controversial resolutions in the House of Representatives on March 21–21, 1842. He paid a substantial political price for presenting the resolutions, but in doing so, he began to destroy the infamous gag rule, which denied discussion of (or the presentation of) antislavery petitions on the floor of the House of Representatives.

The occasion for presenting the resolutions was the *Creole* incident of 1841, in which 19 slaves aboard the brig *Creole* mutinied, murdered the owner of 39 of the slaves, and wounded 2 crew members. The mutineers commandeered the ship into Nassau in the Bahamas on the morning of November 9, 1841, and sought sanctuary.

The politicians of the American South were appalled at the British response to the *Creole* incident and argued that the response encouraged both slave rebellion and murder. John C. Calhoun agreed, but further stated that national honor and property rights had also been violated by the British. Northern abolitionists wanted the British to stand their ground and neither indemnify the slaveowners nor return the slaves to the United States.

During the period of delicate negotiations over the *Creole* incident and other Anglo-American issues, Giddings offered his resolutions in the House. The congressman proposed nine resolutions (written largely by the committee's researcher, Theodore Dwight Weld) that presented the state theory of slavery's status as it applied to international law. Giddings argued that if some states could elect to support slavery, then free states could elect not to support it as well. He declared that prior to the adoption of the U.S. Constitution, the states exercised "full and exclusive" jurisdiction over slavery within their territory, and they could continue or abolish it at will. The moment a ship left the area where slavery was law, the people on board ceased to be under the subjection of those state laws and were governed "in their own relations to each other by, and are amenable to the laws of the United States" (Miller, 1996).

Southern congressmen were outraged because they believed that Giddings was supporting mutiny, slave rebellion, and murder. The House reacted by censuring Giddings by a vote of 125–69, with all Democrats and most Whigs voting against him. Giddings resigned the next day, but was returned by his district in a landslide reelection victory the following month. His arguments, nevertheless, remained part of the slavery discussion until the adoption of the Emancipation Proclamation in 1863. His view was that slavery may be legal but it was not moral; he also felt that the true state of nature for all humanity was that of freedom and liberty.

The remaining slaves on the *Creole* were freed, except for two murderers, who were executed. Twelve years later, the British, valuing peaceful relations with the United States, paid the slaveowners $119,330 for their loss of "property." After Giddings returned to the House of Representatives, he boldly offered his resolutions in a long speech, but he was not censured. The resolutions marked the beginning of the end for the gag rule, and they exposed the slavery issue as both a national and an international problem.

—*Jim Baugess*

For Further Reading
Gamble, Douglas A. 1979. "Joshua Giddings and the Ohio Abolitionists: A Study in Radical Politics." *Ohio History* 88(1): 37–56; Miller, William Lee. 1996. *Arguing about Slavery: The Great Battle in the United States Congress*. New York: Knopf; Savage, Sherman W. 1938. "The Origins of the Giddings Resolutions." *Ohio Archaeological and Historical Quarterly* 48 (October): 28–39; Stewart, James Brewer. 1970. *Joshua Giddings and the Tactics of Radical Politics*. Cleveland: Case Western University Press.

1844

The Baptist Church suffered a schism in regard to the slavery question that was reflective of society at large. The church divided into northern and southern conventions over the question of whether or not slaveowning missionaries should be sent into the territories of the expanding Southwest.

1844

On June 8, the U.S. Senate rejected a treaty that would have provided for the annexation of the Republic of Texas and its admission to the Union as a slave state. Antislavery forces within the Senate were able to convince a majority that the sectional division that would be caused by admitting another slave state to the Union outweighed any possible benefits that might come from such action.

1844

Free blacks in Massachusetts held a series of

The Bluffton movement, led by secessionists and former nullifiers (South Carolina political figures who tried to nullify federal laws in the 1830s) like Robert Barnwell Rhett and Governor James Henry Hammond, was a short-lived attempt to make South Carolina provoke disunion. It began when Rhett gave a fire-eating speech in Bluffton, South Carolina, on July 31, 1844 (hence the name of the movement) calling for nullification or secession. "The Bluffton boys" sought to nullify the Whig tariff of 1842, called for the annexation of Texas as a slave state, and threatened to secede from the Union if southern demands were not met. "Texas or disunion" became a popular phrase in the state and as during nullification debates, the tariff was portrayed as a part of a northern antislavery plot. The repeal of the gag rule against abolitionist petitions by Congress in 1844 further aggravated the secessionist-minded slaveholding Carolinian aristocracy. Moreover, during the same year, Samuel Hoar ventured into this stronghold of slavery to remonstrate against the unjust treatment of African-American citizens of Massachusetts under South Carolina's notorious Negro Seamen's Act. Hoar was summarily expelled from the state and barely escaped the ire of the Carolina slave oligarchy with his body intact. The Bluffton movement received added support from Governor Hammond when, in his annual message, he recommended state action to address southern grievances.

John C. Calhoun, who dominated state politics, headed off the revolt by Rhett and Hammond and nipped the movement in the bud. His faithful lieutenants, Francis W. Pickens and Franklin Harper Elmore, and former unionists like Benjamin F. Perry and Christopher G. Memminger led the counterattack against the Bluffton boys. The ill-fated movement was, according to most historians, a victim of Calhoun's plans to win the Democratic Party presidential nomination. The Carolinian leader, after the bitter experience of nullification, was probably also convinced of the inadvisability of precipitous and lone action by his state. More important for Calhoun, through much of the 1840s, southern redemption lay not in secession but in his own elevation to the presidency.

Rhett and the Bluffton boys, unlike many before them, emerged unscathed from their temporary falling out with Calhoun. He and Franklin Harper Elmore, president of the Bank of South Carolina, had led the Calhoun political machine, which controlled the state after nullification. In fact, Rhett quickly reemerged as a Calhoun confidant and was enlisted to check local criticism of Calhoun's advocacy of internal improvements on the Mississippi. On the other hand, Pickens, who helped Calhoun contain the Bluffton movement, soon became estranged from him over the issue. Moreover, some of Calhoun's closest followers, George McDuffie and Armistead Burt, had flirted with Blufftonism. Calhoun's private correspondence reveals that he, like the Bluffton boys, was acutely suspicious of the Van Buren northern wing of the Democratic Party and saw northern opposition to the annexation of Texas as extremely dangerous for the future of the slave South. Calhoun also played an instrumental role in fulfilling one of the major demands of the Bluffton movement, namely, the annexation of Texas. The Carolina leader differed with the Bluffton boys in policy but not principles.

—*Manisha Sinha*

For Further Reading
Boucher, Chauncey S. 1919. "The Annexation of Texas and the Bluffton Movement in South Carolina." *Mississippi Valley Historical Review* 4 (June): 3–33; Rayback, Joseph G. 1948. "The Presidential Ambitions of John C. Calhoun, 1844–1848." *Journal of Southern History* 14(3): 331–356; Sinha, Manisha. 1994. "The Counter-Revolution of Slavery: Class, Politics, and Ideology in Antebellum South Carolina." Ph.D. dissertation, Department of History, Columbia University, New York.

protest meetings on June 24 in opposition to the state's segregated school policy.

1844

On December 3, after eight years of difficult enforcement, the House of Representatives lifted the gag rule, which had prohibited the discussion of any antislavery petitions received by Congress. Much of the agitation against the rule had been led by Congressman John Quincy Adams of Massachusetts and Congressman Joshua Giddings of Ohio. The resolution calling for repeal of the gag rule passed by a vote of 108 to 80.

1845

Frederick Douglass published the *Narrative of the Life of Frederick Douglass, an American Slave.* The autobiographical slave narrative

Fugitive slaves from Norfolk, Virginia, are shown arriving in Philadelphia in 1856 in this illustration from William Still's The Underground Railroad *(1872). (Library of Congress)*

included a preface written by William Lloyd Garrison and a supporting letter by Wendell Phillips. [See Document 49.]

1845

Les Cenelles, the first anthology of African American verse, was published. Several of the poems included were written by Camille Thierry, a New Orleans Creole.

1845

In the state of New York, the Democratic Party found itself divided over the question of slavery, and two factions formed to run slates of candidates for statewide office. The Barnburners were considered the more radical antislavery wing of the party, and the Hunkers were the more traditional Cotton Democrats (northern Democrats with prosouthern views) who did not share antislavery sentiments. The Barnburners would eventually leave the Democratic Party and join the Free Soil Party because of their views on slavery.

1845

Free blacks in the New England region organized the Freedom Association. The purpose of this group was to assist fugitive slaves in their efforts to escape from the southern states and find freedom in the North.

1845

Florida was admitted to the Union as a slave state on March 3. At this point, the United States consisted of 27 states, of which 13 were free states and 14 slave states, which meant that the number of slave states continued to surpass the number of free states.

1845

Texas was admitted to the Union as a slave state on December 29, which meant that of the 28 states, 13 were free states, and 15 were slave states. The imbalance between the number of slave and free states caused many antislavery supporters to ponder the fate of the nation as new territories prepared for statehood.

1846

Antislavery supporters in Great Britain paid £150 ($711) to purchase the freedom of Frederick Douglass. After Douglass had gained celebrity as an abolitionist lecturer, his former owner had sought to have him returned under the terms of the Fugitive Slave Act of 1793.

∼HENRY CLAY (1777–1852)∼

Henry Clay's efforts to defuse sectional tensions earned him acclaim as "the great compromiser," but his statecraft made little impact on the elimination of slavery. At the age of 20, Clay moved from his native Virginia to Kentucky and became a leading politician and plantation owner. Clay first gained national acclaim in 1812 as a leading "war hawk," concluding that war with Britain was necessary to maintain American commercial and political sovereignty. His primary political concerns were the development of the Whig Party and pursuit of the presidency. The Whig Party, formed in opposition to the principles of Andrew Jackson, advocated Clay's "American system" with a national bank, a protective tariff, and the government offering economic aid for internal improvements. Clay's leadership, which resulted in five unsuccessful presidential efforts, helped define national policies for over four decades but failed to preserve the solidarity of the Union.

Throughout his career, Clay opposed slavery, argued against it, and practiced it on a large scale. He believed slavery was an evil institution and knew slaves lived in physical and mental anguish. Nonetheless, he bought, sold, and leased slaves for his Ashland estate in Kentucky and firmly believed that slaves were unprepared to succeed as freemen because they lacked education. He concluded that emancipation would be injurious to the slave and the master and would result in a bloody racial war.

His solution was to remove African Americans to colonies in Africa, compensating slaveowners for their loss of property, and from 1836 until his death in 1852, Clay served as the president of the American Colonization Society. Although the effort colonized former slaves in Liberia, it failed to gain support of state or federal governments, and Clay turned to politics in an effort to solve the problem.

Although a nationalist and a proponent of a vigorous federal government, Clay deferred to the states on the issue of emancipation. Maintaining public opinion would eventually result in the elimination of slavery, and he urged Congress to solve the dilemma with the Missouri Compromise in 1820. His proposal resulted in Maine entering the Union as a free state while Missouri entered as slave state, but sectional strife continued. Southerners argued that Congress had no authority to regulate slavery, and northerners abhorred the introduction of slaves into the area acquired by the Louisiana Purchase.

In 1844, the Whigs nominated Clay for president, but he was defeated by the lesser-known Democratic nominee, James Polk. As a result of

Henry Clay (Library of Congress)

Clay's opposition to the annexation of Texas, a republic permitting slavery, the South refused to support his candidacy. During the hostilities between Mexico and the United States in 1846–1848, Clay denounced the Polk administration and predicted that any territories acquired from the conflict would challenge the solidarity of the nation. He criticized Polk's prosecution of the "most unnecessary and horrible war" (the Mexican War, 1846–1848), claiming that it was too costly—in lives and dollars (Remini, 1991). Clay also maintained that Polk had exceeded the bounds of the executive office, and when aiming for the presidency in 1848, Clay claimed that if he had been elected in 1844, war would have been averted.

Returning to the Senate in 1849, Clay hoped to forge a lasting compromise that would defuse the arguments in Congress regarding the western territories and slavery. Concerned about Senator John C. Calhoun and other intemperate southern politicians who favored disunion if slavery were banned in the territories, Clay drafted a compromise calling for the admission of California as a free state, the organization of New Mexico as a territory without restrictions on slavery, and the payment of the debts incurred by the Republic of Texas in exchange for a significant reduction of eastern lands claimed by that state. The compromise, however, passed only as separate measures, revealing the disparate interests of North and South. After leaving the Senate, Clay briefly returned home to Kentucky before returning to Washington, D.C., to speak about the need to curb sectional strife. Clay did not witness the turbulence of the American Civil War as tuberculosis claimed him on June 29, 1852, at his Washington residence.

His compromises in 1820 and 1850 proved inadequate, but his principles shaped the nation from 1810 through Reconstruction. Although Clay never enjoyed the public approval of his rival An-drew Jackson, his vision for the future of the United States was incorporated by the Republican Party, and Abraham Lincoln declared Clay the ideal statesman and his guiding influence.

—*Dallas Cothrum*

For Further Reading
Eaton, Clement. 1957. *Henry Clay and the Art of American Politics.* New York: Little, Brown; Peterson, Merrill. 1987. *The Great Triumvirate: Webster, Clay, and Calhoun.* New York: Oxford University Press; Remini, Robert. 1991. *Henry Clay: Statesman of the Republic.* New York: W. W. Norton.

With the purchase of his freedom, Douglass was legally free when he returned to the United States after conducting a successful lecture tour in England and Scotland.

1846
The Reverend Moses Dickson and 11 other free black leaders met in St. Louis, Missouri, and organized the Knights of Liberty. The purpose of the secret militant group was to gain a national following that would make the violent overthrow of slavery a real possibility. A decade later, the organization claimed to have 47,240 members.

1846
In Louisiana, the multiple-effect vacuum evaporation process for processing sugar was patented by Norbert Rillieux, a mulatto. This process revolutionized the sugar industry as it created a more efficient means of processing refined sugar from cane juice.

1846
In Lynn, Massachusetts, a convention of New England workingmen adopted an antislavery resolution on January 16 in which they urged their elected representatives to continue the fight against slavery until abolition had been achieved.

1846
Many workers in the North felt a particular kinship with the slaves of the antebellum South, and the labor newspaper *Voice of Industry* published a poem entitled "What It Is to Be a Slave" on January 23. [See Document 54.]

1846
On August 8, Democratic Congressman David Wilmot of Pennsylvania introduced the Wilmot Proviso, which proposed that slavery should be excluded from any territory that might be acquired from the war with Mexico. Wilmot borrowed part of the language for his proviso from the Northwest Ordinance of 1787, which stated that "neither slavery nor involuntary servitude shall ever exist in any part of" the territory that the United States might acquire from the war with Mexico. Since the Mexican government had abolished slavery in 1829, many people feared the message the United States would send if slavery were reintroduced into free territory. The Senate defeated the proviso, but the measure reappeared before Congress many times over before the beginning of the American Civil War. Votes on this measure did not follow a party line but were based upon a clear geographical delineation between northern and southern representatives. [For more on the Northwest Ordinance of 1787, see Document 32.]

1847
William Wells Brown published the *Narrative of William W. Brown, a Fugitive Slave, Written by Himself,* one of the few slave narratives written by the subject and not dictated to white abolitionists. The book quickly became a best-seller.

1847
Antislavery advocate Gamaliel Bailey became the editor of the *National Era,* a weekly newspaper published by the American and Foreign Anti-Slavery Society. It was Bailey's *National Era* that would begin publication of Harriet Beecher Stowe's *Uncle Tom's Cabin* in serial form in 1851.

≈GAMALIEL BAILEY (1807–1859)≈

Gamaliel Bailey was a prominent American anti-slavery newspaper editor who became involved in Lane Theological Seminary's famous debate over slavery in 1832–1833 and who became convinced of the rightness of immediate abolition via voluntary emancipation. In 1835, he helped to found and served as secretary of the Cincinnati Anti-Slavery Society, and in 1836, he became corresponding secretary of the Ohio Anti-Slavery Society and an assistant to James G. Birney, editor of the *Philanthropist*, the society's official organ and the first abolitionist newspaper in Ohio.

In 1837, Bailey became the paper's coeditor, and although he continued to espouse moral suasion as the best way to abolish slavery, he also began promoting political action against slavery by calling on abolitionists to vote only for antislavery candidates. He further demanded that the federal government outlaw slavery in the District of Columbia and federal territories and stop enforcing the Fugitive Slave Act of 1793. In 1838, he began to formulate "the slave power" theory by arguing that because proslavery forces controlled the apparatus of both major political parties and therefore the government, they threatened the liberties of free whites as well as bound blacks and must be opposed in both the political and the moral arenas. He insisted that the best way to end slavery was to eliminate the slave power influence in the federal government, after which the people of the South would voluntarily repeal the oppressive and inefficient labor system that was slavery. To this end, he called for the creation of a third party devoted to immediate abolition.

In 1847, Bailey moved to Washington, D.C., to become editor in chief of the weekly *National Era*, the official organ of the American and Foreign Anti-Slavery Society. He sought to appeal to a wide readership by printing national and international news items as well as literary pieces, articles on religion, and abolitionist editorials. The most important literary piece he published was Harriet Beecher Stowe's *Uncle Tom's Cabin*. Originally scheduled to appear in serial form in 10 issues in 1851, its immediate popularity caused Stowe to lengthen it significantly so that it ran well into 1852, thereby greatly enhancing the paper's reputation and helping to increase circulation to its mid-1853 peak of 28,000. However, Bailey's main purpose was to inform the South's nonslaveholding majority that slavery was an economic and political evil and that abolitionism was a class struggle, not a sectional one, and he appealed to those southerners to voluntarily throw off the oppression of slave power. His cogent editorials and the paper's moderate tone gained enough of a readership among nonabolitionists in both North and South so that in 1850, the proslavery *Southern Press* was started in Washington, D.C., to counter the *National Era*'s rising popularity.

Bailey's moderate position, necessitated in large part by his situation as the only abolitionist editor publishing in slave territory, drew constant criticism from radical abolitionist editors safely ensconced in the North. It also made the *National Era*, one of the country's most influential antislavery papers.

—*Charles W. Carey, Jr.*

For Further Reading
Harrold, Stanley. 1986. *Gamaliel Bailey and Antislavery Union*. Kent, OH: Kent State University Press.

1847
Free blacks constituted a sizable and somewhat affluent segment of Philadelphia's population; the collective taxable income of all free blacks in that city was estimated at $400,000.

1847
New York abolitionist Gerrit Smith attempted to form a community of free black farmers by dividing his sizable land holdings in New York State and making land available to prospective black farmers. Unfortunately, the poor quality of the land and the inability of black farmers to afford such a purchase diminished the effectiveness of this experimental community. In the same year, New York voters defeated an amendment to the state constitution that would have granted the suffrage to free blacks in the state.

1847
On January 16, the U.S. House of Representatives passed the Oregon bill, which excluded slavery from Oregon Territory on the basis of the Northwest Ordinance of 1787. On March 3, 1847, the Senate tabled the measure. [For

more on the Northwest Ordinance of 1787, see Document 32.]

1847

The U.S. Senate approved passage of the army appropriations bill on February 19 after defeating the Wilmot Proviso, which had been attached as an amendment. During the debates on this matter, South Carolina Senator John C. Calhoun had made an impassioned argument that it was the duty of Congress to protect slavery, using the property rights argument to suggest that Congress had no right to limit the expansion of slavery into any state or territory. Essentially, Calhoun's arguments questioned the legality of measures like the Missouri Compromise of 1820. Although the Senate did not endorse Calhoun's position, in 1857, the Supreme Court in the case of *Dred Scott v. Sandford* would state the same basic positions that Calhoun supported at this time.

1847

On June 30, the slave Dred Scott filed the initial lawsuit seeking his freedom in the Circuit Court of St. Louis, Missouri. This case traveled through several judicial venues for a decade until the U.S. Supreme Court decided the case of *Dred Scott v. Sandford* in 1857.

1847

President Joseph Jenkins Roberts, who had been born a free black in Petersburg, Virginia, declared the West African nation of Liberia to be an independent republic on July 26.

1847

In November, the Liberty Party held a convention in New York City and nominated John P. Hale of New Hampshire as the party's candidate for president and Leicester King of Ohio for vice-president. Hale later declined the nomination in deference to former president Martin Van Buren when the Liberty Party merged with the Free Soil Party in 1848.

1847

On December 3, Frederick Douglass and Martin Delany started publishing the *North Star,* an antislavery newspaper, in Rochester, New York. This abolitionist newspaper opposed the methods and strategies advocated by William Lloyd Garrison and Wendell Phillips.

1847

On December 14, the concept of popular sovereignty as a possible solution to the question of slavery's expansion into the western territories first entered the national political vocabulary when New York Senator Daniel S. Dickinson, a Democrat, introduced a resolution that would have allowed territorial legislatures to determine whether or not slavery would be permitted in each respective territory.

1847

Michigan Senator Lewis Cass, a Democrat who intended to seek his party's nomination for president in 1848, lent his support to the idea of popular sovereignty that New York Senator Daniel S. Dickinson had proposed two weeks earlier. In a letter written to Alfred O. P. Nicholson, a Tennessee politician, on December 29, Cass argued that the question of reaching a decision regarding slavery in the territories should be left up to the territorial legislatures. The idea received serious consideration in national political discourse, and it was employed later as part of the Kansas-Nebraska Act (1854). Many politicians were attracted to the idea of popular sovereignty because it allowed them to avoid the moral and legal implications of any decision regarding slavery by turning the issue over to the will of the majority.

1848

Fellow abolitionists Frederick Douglass and John Brown met for the first time in Springfield, Massachusetts.

1848

Captains Daniel Drayton and Edward Sayres who operated the *Pearl,* a small coastal vessel, attempted to transport 76 slaves valued at $100,000 from Washington, D.C., to freedom in the northern states. The vessel was seized in Chesapeake Bay, and Drayton and Sayres were arrested and charged with attempted slave stealing. The two men were convicted and were sentenced to prison in Maryland.

1848

The legislature of the state of Vermont supported a resolution calling for the prohibition of slavery in the western territories and its outright abolition in the District of Columbia. The measure was nonbinding and largely symbolic, but

The Alabama Platform, an important statement of the southern perspective on slavery in the territories, was first presented to the Alabama Democratic Party Convention in 1848. Facing attacks on the institution of slavery in the form of the Wilmot Proviso and the idea of popular sovereignty, Alabama Democrats set forth the southern view of the sanctity of slave property under the Constitution.

In an impassioned speech to the assembled delegates, William Lowndes Yancey set forth the principles of the Alabama Platform, arguing that no territory that outlawed slavery could prevent citizens from the slave states from removing to or settling in such territory with his property, be it slave property or other (Potter, 1976). Furthermore, Yancey believed that Congress had a constitutional responsibility to protect the property of slaveowners nationwide. Therefore, "territory acquired by common suffering, blood, and toil" could not be restricted by either Congress or territorial legislatures (Potter, 1976). If the national Democratic Party Convention did not support these principles, Yancey called for Alabama delegates to leave the convention. The platform gained wide support across the South, was officially supported by the Democratic conventions of Florida and Virginia, and was sanctioned by the Georgia and Alabama legislatures.

Sectional tensions were high at the Democratic Convention in Baltimore, and the party adopted a platform that did not directly address slavery. Yancey interpreted this silence to mean that party leaders were not concerned about southern interests. The convention also nominated Michigan Senator Lewis Cass, one of the foremost advocates of popular sovereignty, for the presidency. When that occurred, Yancey left the convention, but the remainder of the Alabama delegation remained, in defiance of its instructions.

At the 1860 Democratic Convention in Charleston, South Carolina, the Alabama Platform again contributed to internal party debates on the future of slavery. Again, Alabama Democrats, as well as those from other lower South states, had been instructed to leave the convention if a plank safeguarding slavery and slave property were not included in the platform. When the convention adopted a platform without such a provision, dele-

William L. Yancey (1814–1863), prominent and eloquent advocate of the extreme white southern position. (Campbell Papers, Southern Historical Collections, Library of University of North Carolina–Chapel Hill)

gates from Alabama, Texas, Florida, Louisiana, Mississippi, Arkansas, Georgia, and South Carolina left in protest. In a subsequent convention, the southern wing of the party united behind John C. Breckinridge of Kentucky. Adherence to the Alabama Platform in 1860 split the Democratic Party and served as warning to the nation that secession over the issue of slavery was imminent.

—*Richard D. Starnes*

For Further Reading
Freehling, William. 1990. *The Road to Disunion.* New York: Harper and Row; Potter, David. 1976. *The Impending Crisis, 1848–1861.* New York: Harper and Row.

it reflected the growing spirit of the free soil position in American national life.

1848

Virginia enacted a law requiring postmasters to inform the local police whenever any proabolition literature arrived at a post office in the state. The law further stipulated that such literature must be surrendered to state authorities for burning.

1848

The legislature of the state of Alabama supported a resolution calling upon Congress to do its duty and protect the rights of all people and their property in the western territories. In the same year, the southern fire-eater, William Lowndes Yancey of Alabama, drafted the Alabama Platform, a proslavery missive created to counter the arguments supporting the Wilmot Proviso. Yancey believed that it was the duty of the national government to protect the life and property, including slaves, of all citizens who lived in the western territories. Several other southern states adopted the stand enunciated by Yancey's Alabama Platform.

1848

The black abolitionist Henry Highland Garnet published *The Past and Present Condition and the Destiny of the Colored Race*.

1848

In Rochester, New York, an abolitionist organization called the Liberty League held a national convention on June 2 and nominated a slate of antislavery candidates for national office. The group nominated Gerrit Smith of New York for president and Charles E. Foot of Michigan for vice-president.

1848

On July 27, the U.S. Senate approved the Clayton Compromise, named after Senator John M. Clayton, a Whig from Delaware. The measure proposed that slavery be excluded from Oregon, and it would have prohibited any legislation regarding slavery by the territories of California and New Mexico and would have had the Supreme Court hear the appeal of all territorial slave cases. The measure was tabled by the House of Representatives the day after it was approved by the Senate.

1848

A coalition that included various abolitionists and Conscience Whigs (northern Whigs who opposed slavery) gathered in Buffalo, New York, on August 9 and 10 to organize the Free Soil Party. Several black abolitionists took part in this gathering. The antislavery party nominated Martin Van Buren for president and Charles Frances Adams for vice-president. "Free soil, free speech, free labor, and free men" was adopted as the campaign slogan of the Free Soil Party.

1848

On August 14, President James K. Polk signed the bill that established Oregon Territory without slavery. Southern political leaders did not challenge this point as they were willing to have a free Oregon with the implied understanding that other western territories would be open to the possible expansion of slavery.

1848

In Washington, D.C., a group of southern congressmen held a caucus on December 22 to discuss the slavery question and to determine a strategy that could be used to protect slaveholders' rights.

1848

On December 26, in one of the most dramatic slave escapes of the antebellum era, William and Ellen Craft made their way from slavery in Georgia to freedom in Philadelphia. Ellen impersonated a white slaveowner who was traveling north to seek medical treatment, and William acted as his "master's" trusted servant. The Crafts lived in England for a number of years before returning to the United States in 1868. While in England, they published their story in the book, *Running a Thousand Miles for Freedom; or, The Escape of William and Ellen Craft from Slavery* (1860).

1849

James William Charles Pennington, an American fugitive slave who became a noted black abolitionist, published *The Fugitive Blacksmith* in London. Pennington hoped that his autobiographical narrative would help expose the true horrors of slavery in the United States.

1849

The Wisconsin state legislature enacted a statute that disenfranchised free blacks within the state.

A controversial approach to the problem of slavery in the territories, popular sovereignty was envisioned as a democratic solution to this divisive issue. Popular sovereignty did not solve the problem of slavery expansion, however; in many ways, it heightened sectional tensions and brought the nation closer to civil war.

By the 1840s, the issue of slavery in the territories was as old as the Union itself. Congress first attempted to regulate slavery in newly acquired lands through the Northwest Ordinance of 1787. Prohibiting the extension of slavery north of the Ohio River, this legislation set an important precedent. Congress assumed the role of regulating slavery in the territories, and this role became important in 1820 when a conflict over the admission of Missouri to the Union brought the issue to the forefront. A compromise brokered by Speaker of the House Henry Clay provided for the admission of Missouri and Maine, thereby preserving the numerical balance between slave and free states in Congress. More important, the Missouri Compromise established that slavery would be prohibited in the Louisiana Purchase north of 36 degrees 30 minutes north latitude. This agreement defused the immediate conflict over the admission of Missouri, but it was merely a temporary solution to the question of slavery in the territories.

Slavery in the territories was the most divisive issue in American politics by the 1840s, and this single issue split both political parties and threatened to dissolve the Union itself. Several important factors contributed to this tension. During the previous decade, northern abolitionists such as Theodore Weld, William Lloyd Garrison, and Lyman Beecher had become increasingly vocal and politically influential. Moreover, they had begun to attack the morality of southern slaveowners, not simply the institution itself. As a result of these attacks, a high protective tariff, and other factors, southerners came to believe that their social and economic interests were not being served by the federal government. Southerners became vocal proponents of states' rights in an effort to protect these interests, which in reality was a thinly veiled euphemism for slavery.

This sectional debate over the future of the institution became more pronounced after the Mexican War (1846–1848) when Congress debated the future of slavery expansion. Abolitionists, some northern Democrats, and antislavery Whigs demanded that slavery be excluded from the lands acquired from Mexico because that nation had previously abolished the institution. The most famous articulation of this position was the 1846 Wilmot Proviso. Southern slaveowners and proslavery Whigs argued that any attempt to regulate slavery in the territories, even the Missouri Compromise line, was unconstitutional, as territories were a collective possession of the states and the federal government was obliged by the Constitution to protect the property of any citizen taken there.

These extreme positions threatened to dissolve the Union, but Michigan senator Lewis Cass offered a solution to the problem. Cass, who had previously served as territorial governor of Michigan, secretary of war, and minister to France, was a moderate who believed that the extreme positions of David Wilmot and John C. Calhoun would never satisfactorily settle the question of slavery expansion. Therefore in 1848, Cass offered a proposal that would transfer the political burden of deciding the issue from Congress to the territorial legislatures. Cass argued that the federal government should not decide such internal matters, as such action was both corrosive to the bonds of Union and fundamentally undemocratic. Therefore, he proposed that the territorial legislatures, as the elected representatives of the people, decide the slave question in each individual territory. According to Cass, Congress had no constitutional authority to regulate slavery in the territories, and popular sovereignty, or squatter sovereignty as it was sometimes known, offered the best solution to the problem of slavery expansion.

Popular sovereignty had many political benefits. It was a democratic solution to a pressing national issue; it also, at least on the surface, had something to offer both southern slaveowners and northern abolitionists. Southerners and their property would be protected if they chose to migrate to a territory, where they would have an equal voice in the final determination of slavery through the electoral process. Northern free soil advocates understood that much of the land in the territories was unsuitable for slave-based agriculture. Moreover, it was assumed that the new territories would be quickly populated by midwestern farmers, who would dominate the legislature and ban slavery in the territories. Despite these theoretical appeals to both sides, the ambiguity of popular sovereignty undermined its popularity. Cass was never clear on the precise point at which a territory could act on slavery, nor on the proper method for taking this action. Southerners realized their property would never be truly protected in the territories, and free soil activists would not entertain a proposal that might protect the institution of slavery.

Despite this initially lackluster appeal, popular sovereignty was destined to have far-reaching political implications. Cass won the 1848 Democratic presidential nomination, but the debate over popular sovereignty deepened the gap between the northern and southern wings of the party. Though Cass lost the election to Zachary Taylor, popular sovereignty continued to have political resonance. The Compromise of 1850 allowed territorial legislatures broad legislative powers, which some people interpreted as an unstated endorsement of popular sovereignty. However, the most important manifestation of the concept arose in 1854 during debates over the Kansas and Nebraska Territories.

Stephen A. Douglas, a U.S. Senator from Illinois, was one of the most influential converts to popular sovereignty. He used this approach to appeal to southern Democrats whose support Douglas needed for the establishment of a transcontinental railroad with an eastern terminus in his native state. In 1854, he sponsored a bill that created two new territories, Kansas and Nebraska, both of which were north of 36 degrees 30 minutes north latitude. According to the bill, the territorial legislatures would have full authority to determine the future of slavery within their respective borders. More important, Douglas agreed to an amendment that repealed the Missouri Compromise altogether, arguing that popular sovereignty was the best method for deciding the future of slavery in the territories.

The Kansas-Nebraska Act had far-reaching implications. The Whig Party ceased to exist as a cohesive political entity, as its members split into proslavery and free soil factions over this issue. The Republican Party, which embraced free soil ideology, united its members by its stand on the Kansas-Nebraska Act, and Douglas's own presidential hopes were dashed by this sponsorship of his controversial bill. More immediately, and more important, violence erupted in Kansas, as proslavery and free soil interests literally fought for the power to determine the future of slavery in the territory. This division and violence were important steps toward, and in many ways a rehearsal for, the American Civil War.

—*Richard D. Starnes*

For Further Reading
Freehling, William. 1990. *The Road to Disunion.* New York: Harper and Row; Potter, David. 1976. *The Impending Crisis, 1848–1861.* New York: Harper and Row; Rawley, James. 1969. *Race and Politics: "Bleeding Kansas" and the Coming of the Civil War.* Philadelphia: Lippincott.

1849

The Connecticut State Convention of Negroes was held in New Haven, Connecticut, January 10–13; at the same time, the Ohio State Convention of Negroes was held in Columbus, Ohio.

1849

On March 10, the state legislature of Missouri approved a resolution declaring that "the right to prohibit slavery in any territory belongs exclusively to the people thereof" (Schlesinger, 1983). The language of this measure indicated support for the concept of popular sovereignty.

1849

On March 29–30, the Virginia slave Henry "Box" Brown ingeniously obtained his emancipation by hiding in a box that was mailed to abolitionists in Philadelphia. Two years later, Brown told his story in his *Narrative of the Life of Henry Box Brown.* [See Document 57.]

1849

Harriet Tubman escaped from slavery in Maryland in the summer, and after her escape, she became active in the Underground Railroad, which helped fugitive slaves make their way to freedom in the northern states and eventually to Canada. Tubman is reported to have made 19 trips back into the states of the upper South in order to help more than 300 slaves escape to freedom. As a result of her heroic actions, she became known as "the Moses" of her people.

1849

From September 1 to October 13, a statehood convention, called by Territorial Governor Bennett Riley, was held in Monterey, California. Without waiting for congressional sanction to begin the statehood process, the gathering created a state constitution that prohibited slavery, and the measure was approved by California voters on November 13.

1849

In November, Massachusetts attorney Charles Sumner broke new ground by introducing the legal concept of equal protection under the law in a racial controversy in the case *Sarah C.*

Harriet Tubman (far left) with a group of slaves she had helped to escape. (Corbis-Bettmann)

Roberts v. the City of Boston. This foundational legal principle would later be introduced into the U.S. Constitution with the passage of the Fourteenth Amendment after the Civil War. In the Massachusetts case, Benjamin Roberts had filed the first school integration lawsuit on behalf of his daughter Sarah, who had been denied admission to a white school. The Massachusetts Supreme Court rejected the lawsuit and established the controversial "separate but equal" precedent that would later reappear in the case of *Plessy v. Ferguson* (1896).

1849

On December 4, President Zachary Taylor recommended that Congress accept California's request to join the Union as a free state. There was considerable opposition to this action by southern politicians, who did not desire to create another free state and thus upset the delicate political balance between northern and southern states. The level of political bickering caused by this debate is reflected in the difficulty of Congress to choose a new speaker. After 63 ballots

and three weeks of debate, Georgia Congressman Howell Cobb was selected as Speaker of the House of Representatives.

1850

During contentious debates associated with passage of the Compromise of 1850, Senator Henry Clay remarked, "I would rather be right than be president" (Schlesinger, 1983).

1850

In New York City, a group of black and white abolitionists rushed into a courtroom to rescue James Hamlet, a fugitive slave.

1850

The seventh census of the United States revealed that 37 percent of the free black population was identified as mulattoes. Also, the entire black population, slave and free, was 3,638,808 persons, 15.7 percent of the national population.

1850

Samuel R. Ward became the first president of

the American League of Colored Laborers, an organization that was a union of skilled black workers seeking to encourage free black artisans to develop black-owned businesses.

1850

In his last great speech before the U.S. Senate on February 5–6, Henry Clay argued that the Senate should enact the compromise measures he had proposed as a means of preserving the Union that was so threatened by sectional discord. Extremists from both sides of the issue questioned Clay's actions and motives. New York Senator William Seward declared, "There is a higher law than the Constitution which regulates our authority," and South Carolina Senator John C. Calhoun, near the end of his life, said that abolitionists in the North must "cease the agitation of the slavery question" (Schlesinger, 1983).

1850

On January 29, dismayed by the rhetoric of extremists on both sides of the slavery issue, Senator Henry Clay began work on obtaining passage of a series of resolutions known collectively as the Compromise of 1850. It was Clay's wish that the Union be preserved, and he believed that the give-and-take of good-faith compromise was the only way to achieve this end.

1850

Sensing the extreme levels of discontent in the preceding debate, on March 7 Senator Daniel Webster offered his support for Senator Henry Clay's efforts to enact the series of compromise resolutions that eventually became law as the Compromise of 1850. In a speech to the Senate, Webster supported the provisions of the fugitive slave bill, which to many northern lawmakers was the most odious part of Clay's package. The poet John Greenleaf Whittier later immortalized Webster's "fall" in the poem "Ichabod": "All else is gone from those great eyes / The soul has fled; / When faith is lost when honor dies / The man is dead." [See Document 56.]

1850

On May 8, a Senate committee composed of seven Whigs and six Democrats worked with the series of resolutions that Henry Clay had in-troduced to the Senate. The committee refined the measures into two bills: the first, an omnibus bill, affected slavery in the western territories, and the second bill outlawed the slave trade in the District of Columbia. Eventually, the omnibus bill was broken down into five separate measures, and Congress voted on each individually.

1850

Debate over Henry Clay's compromise resolutions dominated the affairs of Congress during June. In an impassioned speech in the House of Representatives, Georgia Congressman Robert A. Toombs used a classical allusion and likened himself to Hamilcar, the father of the Carthaginian general Hannibal, a mortal enemy of Rome. Toombs warned his northern colleagues, "I will . . . bring my children and my constituents to the altar of liberty, and like Hamilcar I would swear them to eternal hostility to your foul domination" (Jenkins, 1996).

1850

The Nashville Convention took place from June 3 to 12 as delegates from nine southern states met in Nashville, Tennessee, to discuss the issues of slavery and states' rights. Some of the most radical delegates, the so-called fire-eaters, favored immediate secession as the only means of preserving southern traditions and rights, but the moderates prevailed at this meeting. Delegates approved of several resolutions, including one that would have extended the Missouri Compromise line of 36 degrees 30 minutes north latitude all the way across the western territories to the Pacific Ocean.

1850

The Underground Railroad had been operational for nearly two decades as antislavery supporters in the northern states assisted fugitives who had made their escape from slavery in the South. Unfortunately, there are no accurate numbers of how many fugitives were assisted by this method. On August 2, the black abolitionist William Still, who was an active "conductor" on the Underground Railroad, began keeping statistical records of how many fugitives escaped. The passenger records that Still kept are some of the best source materials available today for determining the effectiveness of the railroad. Many white abolitionists, like John

The Compromise of 1850 emerged out of President Zachary Taylor's attempt to resolve problems related to territorial expansion and slavery following the Mexican War (1846–1848). When Taylor was inaugurated in 1849, four compelling issues faced the nation. First, the rush of some 80,000 miners to California qualified that territory for admission to the Union, but California's entry as a free state would upset the balance between slave and free states that had prevailed since 1820.

The unresolved status of the territory acquired from Mexico in the Southwest posed a second problem. The longer the area was left unorganized, the louder local inhabitants called for an application of either the Wilmot Proviso, which prohibited slavery in the newly acquired territories, or the Calhoun doctrine, which protected the extension of slavery. The boundary between Texas and New Mexico Territory was also in dispute, with Texas claiming lands all the way to Santa Fe. This claim increased northern fears that Texas might be divided into five or six slave states. A third problem was the existence of slavery and slave trading in the nation's capital, one of the largest slave markets in North America. Fourth, southerners resented lax federal enforcement of the Fugitive Slave Act of 1793 and called for a stronger act that would end the protection northerners gave runaway slaves.

President Taylor attempted to sidestep the conflict over slavery in the territories by inviting California and New Mexico to bypass the territorial stage and apply immediately for statehood, presumably as free states. The residents could then decide the slavery question for themselves without embarrassment to Congress. Southerners, seeing that California had already prohibited slavery and expecting New Mexico to do the same, realized that Taylor's plan was as effective as the Wilmot Proviso in keeping slavery out of that area. When they protested, Taylor drew a firm line, threatening to use force if necessary to preserve the Union.

The southerners decided that Taylor had betrayed them, and in late 1849, 69 congressmen and senators from the South convened a special caucus in Washington, D.C. John C. Calhoun emerged as leader of the caucus and accused the North of numerous "acts of aggression" against the South. According to Calhoun, and the 48 congressmen who eventually signed the caucus petition, the North was out to destroy the South's way of life. As proof he cited the laws prohibiting slavery in various territories and the problems southerners were having in recapturing fugitive slaves in the North. Calhoun insisted that the only way out of the impasse was to restore to southerners their Fifth Amendment property rights, which he interpreted to mean that slaveowners should be able to take their slaves anywhere in the United States and should be afforded adequate legal assistance in repossessing escaped slaves.

The main spokesman for the northern antislavery forces was William H. Seward of New York. Seward and those who sided with him in the long and heated debate insisted that the former Mexican territories should not be surrendered to slavery, that the fugitive slave law could not be enforced, and that the agitation in the North against slavery was impossible to suppress. With disunion threatening, the aged Senator Henry Clay of Kentucky, author of the famous Missouri Compromise of 1820, offered another compromise that he hoped would settle for good the territorial crisis and other disputed issues between the two sections of the country. Clay's plan, which was introduced in Congress in January 1850 as an omnibus bill, contained five key provisions: immediate admission of California as a free state; organization of the rest of the area acquired from Mexico into two territories, Utah and New Mexico, without restrictions on slavery, the matter to be decided by the constitutions of the territories; assumption of the Texan national debt by the federal government; abolition of the slave trade in the District of Columbia; and a tough new fugitive slave law. When Clay's package of compromise measures came to a vote, opponents of the individual measures defeated it. His bill and his health in ruins, Clay withdrew into retirement.

Stephen A. Douglas of Illinois assumed Clay's place in steering the compromise through Congress. Douglas devised a new strategy of introducing Clay's measures separately, relying on sectional blocs and a few swing votes to form majorities for each of the separate laws, which became known as the Compromise of 1850. The first was the Texas and New Mexico Act of September 9, 1850, which established the borders of Texas and a payment of $10 million to that state. The act provided that when New Mexico entered the Union, the state would make its own decision on slavery. The Utah Act of September 9, 1850, provided that this territory, too, should decide for itself the legal status of slavery within its borders. On that same date, California was admitted as a free state. The District of Columbia Act of September 20, 1850, abolished the slave trade, but not slavery, in that area. The slaveholders won their most cherished victory with the passage of the Fugitive Slave Act in September 1850. This act, far more stringent than the 1793 law, authorized slaveholders to pursue runaways into other states and imposed heavy fines on people who aided runaway slaves.

The immediate response to the Compromise of 1850 was an enthusiastic welcome with celebrations held in many cities, but events soon revealed that the compromise had settled nothing at all, only delayed more serious sectional conflict. In its aftermath, political parties appeared to realign more along sectional lines. In addition, northern-

ers, in response to the Fugitive Slave Act, increased Underground Railroad activity and passed personal liberty laws, which prohibited the use of state officials and institutions in recovering fugitive slaves.

—*Michael Washington*

For Further Reading
Holt, Michael F. 1978. *The Political Crisis of the 1850s*. New York: Norton; Miller, William Lee. 1996. *Arguing about Slavery: The Great Battle in the United States Congress*. New York: Knopf.

and Hannah Peirce Cox of Pennsylvania, were actively involved.

1850
With the voting taking place in September, the Compromise of 1850 admitted California to the Union as a free state; adjusted the borders of Texas; established the territories of Utah and New Mexico with the understanding that popular sovereignty would decide the fate of slavery in those regions; prohibited the slave trade, but not slavery, in the District of Columbia; and provided for the passage of a newer and stronger Fugitive Slave Act. As a result of the New Fugitive Slave Act, thousands of fugitive slaves in the northern states crossed the international boundary and entered Canada. [See Document 56.]

1850
Vermont became the first state to enact a personal liberty law, which was designed to circumvent enforcement of the federal Fugitive Slave Act enacted in the same year.

1850
The city council in Chicago, Illinois, passed a resolution on October 21 that criticized recent congressional approval of the Fugitive Slave Act as a part of the Compromise of 1850.

1850
The Southern Rights Association was established on October 25 to provide united opposition to all antislavery efforts mounted by abolitionist groups.

1850
Southern delegates held a second Nashville Convention, November 11–15, and again con-

sidered the possibility of seceding from the Union.

1850
A Georgia state convention, held December 13–14, declared the intention of the state of Georgia to remain in the Union but warned that this action was contingent upon the northern states' willingness to enforce all of the measures recently enacted in the Compromise of 1850, especially the new federal Fugitive Slave Act.

1851
A group of black abolitionists rushed into a Baltimore, Maryland, courtroom to rescue the fugitive slave Rachel Parker.

1851
The U.S. Supreme Court decided the case of *Strader v. Graham,* and in their decision, the justices declared that three slaves who had returned to Kentucky after visiting Indiana and Ohio were to be governed by the laws of Kentucky. In what was viewed as a proslavery ruling, the Court maintained that it was the states themselves that determined the status of all persons living within their respective jurisdictions.

1851
Services of Colored Americans in the Wars of 1776 and 1812 was published by the abolitionist William C. Nell. This work is considered to be the first extended study of the history of African Americans.

1851
In Boston, Massachusetts, Thomas Simms, a fugitive slave who had been captured, was returned to his owner in Georgia. Abolitionists

A small but powerful group of antebellum southern politicians, the fire-eaters were an important force during the sectional crisis in the United States. Although they represented a minority of southern leaders, the fire-eaters were vocal, articulate advocates for their region and the cause of states' rights.

Fire-eaters believed that by the 1840s, the South's social, political, and economic interests were under attack by outside forces. Vocal northern abolitionists seemed to wield significant influence in both houses of Congress, and more important, the abolitionists had begun to attack the character and morality of slaveowners, not simply the institution itself. By the 1850s, proposals like the Wilmot Proviso and agreements like the Compromise of 1850 led many southern leaders to conclude that the South's interests would no longer be protected by the national government. In fact, to many fire-eaters, the government itself appeared to be doing the bidding of northern abolitionists by attempting to legislate slavery—and thereby the social and political organization of southern society—out of existence.

Faced with these apparent attacks, a minority of southern politicians began actively to champion the cause of states' rights. Drawing on the ideological legacy of Thomas Jefferson, this group, called the fire-eaters by people of both the North and the South, went beyond traditional rhetoric concerning state sovereignty. These leaders believed that the U.S. Constitution represented a compact of states that had agreed to unite in 1787 for certain purposes. The federal government established by this compact was charged with national defense, international diplomacy, regulation of interstate commerce, and very little else.

Fire-eaters like Jefferson and John C. Calhoun before him believed that the powers of the federal government were limited to those specified by the Constitution, with all remaining powers reserved for the states or individual citizens. These reserved powers included the power to regulate slavery. Furthermore, they believed that the Union existed to protect the interests and rights of individual states. Over time, the Union had been transformed, gradually assuming more power, and according to the fire-eaters, this transformation had led to federal policies that were contrary to southern interests. Therefore, as southern rights were no longer being honored and protected, the slave states should dissolve the bonds that held them in the Union. This belief went beyond earlier notions of interposition and nullification. Through secession, the fire-eaters reasoned that the southern states would retain their sovereignty and protect their slave-based economic system. Secession was a panacea designed to protect what the fire-eaters viewed as the fundamental social, political, and economic underpinnings of southern society.

Fire-eaters were most powerful in South Carolina, Alabama, and Mississippi, but they existed in smaller numbers in other southern states. United in their belief in immediate secession as a way to protect southern rights and slavery, the fire-eaters had few other things in common. Most were political leaders in their respected states with a gift for oratory, and fire-eaters were almost universally from planter families or had risen to such status through their own labor. Though small in number, several fire-eaters were particularly influential. Robert Barnwell Rhett edited the bombastic *Charleston Mercury,* which became the voice of the fire-eater cause. John A. Quitman, though born in Ohio, served as military governor of Mexico and as governor of Mississippi. A vocal proponent of states' rights, Texan Louis T. Wigfall later became a severe critic of Jefferson Davis and the Confederate government. Agriculturalist and editor Edmund Ruffin of Virginia fired the first shot at Fort Sumter, and subsequently committed suicide after Appomattox. In Alabama, William Lowndes Yancey articulated the fire-eaters' position in the Alabama Platform and generally served as the faction's most eloquent orator in Congress and at Democratic Party conventions.

Although the fire-eaters did not cause the dissolution of the Union in 1861, their ardent defense of states' rights and protectionist attitudes toward slavery certainly helped create a political climate in which secession could be considered. Ironically, many went on to criticize the Confederate government for usurping the rights of individual states. These vocal defenders of states' rights and slavery, though representing an extreme minority view in the South, wielded tremendous influence and helped lead the nation to civil war.

—*Richard D. Starnes*

For Further Reading
Heidler, David. 1994. *Pulling the Temple Down: The Fire-Eaters and the Destruction of the Union.* Mechanicsburg, PA: Stackpole Books; Potter, David. 1976. *The Impending Crisis, 1848–1861.* New York: Harper and Row; Walther, Eric. 1992. *The Fire-Eaters.* Baton Rouge: Louisiana State University Press.

⧽HANNAH PEIRCE (PEARCE) COX (1797–1876)⧽

As an abolitionist and partner in operating the first Underground Railroad station in Pennsylvania, Hannah Peirce (variously spelled Pearce) Cox is considered one of America's premier abolitionists. She grew up on her family's farm in Pennsylvania, part of the fifth generation of her family to be born in America. Her Quaker upbringing shaped her sympathy for people held captive by slavery, and her marriage to John Cox, a like-minded Quaker, served to reinforce her antislavery beliefs.

Hannah Cox was reportedly stirred by reading William Lloyd Garrison's *Liberator* and by attending a lecture at which John Greenleaf Whittier's poem "Our Fellow Countrymen in Chains" was read. She became an ardent supporter of immediate emancipation and felt the idea of a gradual extermination of slavery to be ridiculous. She agreed with fellow abolitionists like Garrison that the gradual release of slaves was "to tell a man to moderately rescue his wife from the hands of the ravisher, or tell the mother to gradually extricate her babe from the fire" (Smedley, 1969). The burning of Philadelphia's Pennsylvania Hall in 1838 by proslavery advocates further spurred her activity in the antislavery cause.

Hannah and John Cox eagerly joined the Underground Railroad, providing their home as the first station north of Wilmington, Delaware, on the way to the Canadian border. Their children also aided in the almost nightly activities: feeding everyone, clothing those who needed clothes, conveying people to the next safe house along the route, or giving them directions for their flight northward. The Coxes carried on these duties quietly for many years, and slaves were not the only people welcomed at the Cox home. Fellow abolitionists Lucretia Mott, William Lloyd Garrison, Sarah Pugh, Abby Kelley, Lucy Stone, John Greenleaf Whittier, and many others always found comfort at the Cox homestead.

Hannah and John Cox were frequently chosen as delegates to antislavery state and national conventions over the years, and from the antislavery movement, Hannah Cox went on to support many other social causes. She died in her home in Pennsylvania in the same house where she had been born and lived her entire life.

—*Maria Elena Raymond*

For Further Reading
Hanaford, Phebe A. 1883. *Daughters of America; or, Women of the Century*. Augusta, ME: True and Company; Malone, Dumas, and Allen Johnson, eds. 1930. *Dictionary of American Biography*. New York: Charles Scribner's Sons; Smedley, R. C. 1969. *History of the Underground Railroad*. New York: Arno Press.

---

had considered an attempt to rescue Simms by force but were unable to carry out such a plan.

1851
The Colored Man's Journal, an antislavery newspaper operated by free blacks, began publication in New York City.

1851
The Virginia legislature enacted a measure requiring free blacks who had been recently manumitted to leave the state within one year of their emancipation or else face the possibility of renewed enslavement in Virginia.

1851
A group of black abolitionists rushed into a Boston, Massachusetts, courtroom on February 15 to rescue the fugitive slave Shadrach.

1851
Frederick Douglass and William Lloyd Garrison split over disagreements concerning the tactics and strategies to be employed in the antislavery movement during the eighteenth annual meeting of the American Anti-Slavery Society (May 7–9). It was the issue of moral force versus political force that caused the rift.

1851
On May 28, the black abolitionist and former slave Sojourner Truth (born Isabella Baumfree) attended a Women's Rights Convention in Akron, Ohio. Her presence at the gathering helped to demonstrate the illogical underpinnings of sex discrimination as she compared those views to the racism that justified slavery. According to later biographers, Truth's declaration that "ar'n't I a woman?" became a powerful testimony to the twin evils of racism and sexism in American society.

1851
The National Era, a Washington-based aboli-

Black abolitionist William Still (1821–1902). His book on the Underground Railroad was effective testimony to the daring and ingenuity of fugitive slaves. (Library of Congress)

tionist newspaper, began publishing a story called "Uncle Tom's Cabin" by Harriet Beecher Stowe in serial form on June 5.

1851

In the so-called Christiana riot, a group of free blacks and antislavery whites dispersed a party of slave catchers at Christiana, Pennsylvania, on September 11. In the melee, one white man was killed and three wounded. This episode represents the heightened levels of passion that were caused by passage of the new Fugitive Slave Act, as the Christiana riot was the most violent instance of civil disobedience and outright resistance to this unpopular legislation.

1851

In Syracuse, New York, a group of black and white abolitionists rushed into a courtroom on October 1 to rescue Jerry M'Henry, a fugitive slave.

1851

By December, the results of recent congressional elections indicated that southerners approved of the Compromise of 1850, and unionists were elected to office in several of the southern states over more radical fire-eaters who supported se-

cession. In the northern states, the opposite seemed to be the case. The state of Massachusetts, for example, elected the abolitionist Charles Sumner to the U.S. Senate.

1852

The Pro-Slavery Argument was published by a group of southern apologists, including William Harper, Thomas R. Dew, and James Henry Hammond. This work contained a collection of essays, many of which had been previously published, that used a wide range of theoretical justification based upon biblical and classical sources to defend the institution of slavery as it existed in the American South.

1852

In deciding the case of *Scott v. Emerson,* the Missouri Supreme Court declared that Dred Scott was a slave. This decision reversed Missouri precedents that had been in place since the *Winny v. Whitesides* (1824) decision.

1852

In response to the passage of the Fugitive Slave Act, the black abolitionist Martin Delany published *The Condition, Elevation, Emigration, and Destiny of the Colored People of the United States Politically Considered.*

1852

Sojourner Truth (Isabella Baumfree) spoke before a gathering of the National Women's Suffrage Convention meeting in Akron, Ohio.

1852

There were 3,500 free blacks living in Cincinnati, Ohio. Among this group, 200 were identified as prosperous property owners who had an aggregate wealth of $500,000. Despite this fact, free blacks were often the target of violent, racially motivated episodes.

1852

During a speech that he delivered on January 28 before the Massachusetts Anti-Slavery Society, abolitionist Wendell Phillips first spoke the oft-quoted phrase, "Eternal vigilance is the price of liberty."

1852

On March 20, the first edition of *Uncle Tom's Cabin, or, Life among the Lowly* was published

Physician, newspaper editor, and army officer Martin R. Delany (1812–1885) wrote the book that later earned him the sobriquet "the father of black nationalism" in response to the Fugitive Slave Act of 1852. (Archive Photos)

by Harriet Beecher Stowe. This work offered a moving account of the brutality of the institution of slavery in its many forms. The work was considered to be a literary classic in the nineteenth century, and it was one of the seminal works that influenced American attitudes about the institution and practice of slavery. The story had first been published in serial form in 1851 by the *National Era*, but in its first year of publication as a novel, over 1 million copies were sold.

1852

In Rochester, New York, city officials invited Frederick Douglass, the city's most famous resident, to deliver the July 4 oration to commemorate the nation's independence. Douglass delivered "What to the Slave is the Fourth of July?" speech, in which he noted, "To him your celebration a sham; your boasted liberty an unholy license, your national greatness, swelling vanity; your sounds of rejoicing are empty and heartless; your denunciation of tyrants, brass-fronted impudence; your shouts of liberty and equality, hollow mockery; your prayers and hymns, your

sermons and thanksgivings, with all your religious parade and solemnity, are to him mere bombast, fraud, deception, impiety, and hypocrisy—a thin veil to cover up crimes which would disgrace a nation of savages (Aptheker, 1951)."

1852

The Free Soil Party held its first national convention in Pittsburgh, Pennsylvania, on August 11 and nominated John P. Hale of New Hampshire for president and George W. Julian of Indiana for vice-president. The party platform condemned slavery and decried the recent enactment of the Compromise of 1850 by stating, "Slavery is a sin against God and a crime against man."

1852

In Troy, New York, a dramatic version of *Uncle Tom's Cabin* was performed for the first time on September 27 by George L. Aiken, an actor and playwright. The performance was judged a huge success, and the play ran for 100 nights.

1852

Abolitionist Senator Charles Sumner of Massachusetts delivered a four-hour speech in the Senate chamber on October 26 in which he chastised Congress for passing the Fugitive Slave Act as a part of the Compromise of 1850.

1853

Clotel; or, The President's Daughter: A Narrative of Slave Life in the United States, the first novel to be written by an African American author, was published in London by William Wells Brown. The story was based loosely upon the rumored affair between Thomas Jefferson and his slave Sally Hemings.

1853

Frederick Douglass published the short story "The Heroic Slave." The story was based upon the exploits of Madison Washington, who had participated in the seizure of the slave ship *Creole* in 1841 when it was traveling from Virginia to Louisiana. The slaves on board the vessel sailed the *Creole* to the Bahamas where they gained their freedom.

1853

James Dyson, an Englishman who ran a school

Wendell Phillips (1811–1884), an outstanding orator of the abolitionist movement. (Library of Congress)

in New Orleans, was arrested and charged with conspiracy for trying to organize a slave insurrection.

1853

There seemed to be growing nationwide support for a large-scale campaign to deport free blacks to colonial settlements on the coast of West Africa. In Virginia, a poll tax was imposed upon free blacks in order to generate funds to support such a project, and the *New York Herald* supported the idea of emigration and stated that "racial inferiority" made such a program desirable.

1853

In January, Solomon Northup, a free black who had been illegally kidnapped and held as a slave for 12 years, was freed from his enslavement in Louisiana after an extended campaign on his behalf conducted by northern abolitionists. In March, Northup published his story in the book *Twelve Years a Slave*. [See Document 51.]

1853

The National Council of Colored People met and was founded in Rochester, New York, on July 6–8. This organization, established by delegates from several states who wished to encourage the mechanical training of blacks, grew out of the Negro Convention movement, which had been active in several states for more than a decade.

1853

Free blacks in Massachusetts petitioned the state legislature on August 1 for permission to join the state militia.

1853

By December, Harriet Beecher Stowe's book *Uncle Tom's Cabin* had sold more than 1.2 million copies. Criticized by many people who claimed that Stowe had exaggerated the true condition of slaves in the South in order to create a sympathetic antislavery propaganda tract, she responded by publishing the *Key to Uncle Tom's Cabin* in which she defended her work and outlined the factual basis upon which the novel was written.

1854

Sociology for the South; or, The Failure of Free Society by George Fitzhugh, a southern apologist, was published. In the same year, William Grayson published "The Hireling and the Slave" in an effort to counter Harriet Beecher Stowe's dark portrayal of southern life in *Uncle Tom's Cabin*. Grayson's long, didactic poem tried to contrast the benefits of the slave's ideal life in the South with the wretched conditions experienced by "wage slaves" in the industrial North. Also, *Sociology for the South* was published by George Fitzhugh, a southern proslavery polemicist. The work contained a series of proslavery newspaper articles that Fitzhugh had previously published in the *Richmond Examiner*.

1854

Connecticut and Rhode Island each enacted personal liberty laws, which were designed to circumvent enforcement of the federal Fugitive Slave Act of 1850.

1854

The Ashmun Institute was founded at Oxford in Chester County, Pennsylvania, on January 1. Known today as Lincoln University, it was the first black college established in the United States.

❧GEORGE WASHINGTON JULIAN (1817–1899)❧

Throughout his 40-year public career, George Washington Julian consistently stood at the forefront of antislavery politics and battles for black civil rights in the United States. Perhaps owing to his Quaker upbringing in Indiana, Julian demonstrated a moral disgust for human bondage at an early age. A devoted abolitionist, Julian began practicing law in 1840 and quickly joined such antislavery lawyers as Salmon P. Chase. In 1845, Julian entered the Indiana legislature as a Whig, but when the Whig Party chose slaveholder Zachary Taylor as its 1848 presidential candidate, Julian bolted the organization and allied himself with the nascent Free Soil Party. In 1849, Indiana voters elected Julian to the U.S. House of Representatives, where the Free Soilers opposed the Compromise of 1850 because of its fugitive slave provisions and its noninterventionist posture regarding slavery in the territory received following the Mexican War (1846–1848).

Julian lost his congressional seat in 1851 and did not hold another public office for a decade, though he remained politically active throughout the 1850s. He ran for the vice-presidency on the Free Soil ticket in 1852, and he consistently strove to build free soil coalitions at the state and regional levels, hoping to unite disparate antislavery elements into a single party of liberty. To this end, Julian joined and promoted the Republican Party when it evolved in the wake of the Kansas-Nebraska conflict, and he helped the fledgling antislavery party gain a firm foothold in the Midwest. Julian's tireless activism commanded attention from ally and adversary alike. His antiabolitionist opponents, for example, assigned him the deprecatory moniker, "orator of free dirt" while the black abolitionist Frederick Douglass once praised Julian as "one of the truest and most disinterested friends of freedom whom [antislavery activists] have ever met" (Sewell, 1976).

In 1861, Julian began the first of five consecutive terms in Congress, where he emerged as a leading radical Republican spokesman. From the outset of the Civil War, Julian pressed President Abraham Lincoln to issue an emancipation proclamation, to enlist black troops, and to guarantee equal citizenship rights for blacks. After the war, Julian joined other radicals in denouncing President Andrew Johnson's prosouthern plan of restoration, which contained no safeguards for black enfranchisement or civil rights. A leading figure in the implementation of congressional Reconstruction in 1866–1867, Julian supported the Thirteenth and Fourteenth Amendments to the Constitution, backed the Reconstruction acts, and even tried to introduce legislation guaranteeing women's suffrage.

After 1868, Julian turned his attention to matters of civil service reform. A vocal critic of President Ulysses S. Grant's graft-ridden administration, Julian soon fell out of favor with the Republican Party. He failed to win reelection to Congress in 1871 and quickly faded out of the political limelight.

—Eric Tscheschlok

For Further Reading
Blue, Frederick J. 1973. *The Free Soilers: Third Party Politics, 1848–54.* Urbana: University of Illinois Press; Riddleberger, Patrick W. 1966. *George Washington Julian, Radical Republican.* Indianapolis: Indiana Historical Bureau; Sewell, Richard H. 1976. *Ballots for Freedom: Antislavery Politics in the United States, 1837–1860.* New York: Oxford University Press.

1854

As Congress debated the merits of the Kansas-Nebraska Act on January 16, Senator Archibald Dixon, a Kentucky Whig, introduced a resolution that would have repealed the Missouri Compromise of 1820, which had established the line of 36 degrees 30 minutes north latitude as the boundary between potential slave and free territory in the territory of the Louisiana Purchase. The following day, Massachusetts Senator Charles Sumner introduced a resolution that reaffirmed the Missouri Compromise.

1854

On January 24, six prominent abolitionists from the northern states signed their names to a document entitled "The Appeal of the Independent Democrats in Congress, to the People of the United States." The appeal was allegedly written by Salmon P. Chase of Ohio, and it was signed by Charles Sumner of Massachusetts, Joshua Giddings of Ohio, Gerrit Smith of New York, Edward Wade of Ohio, and Alexander De Witt of Massachusetts. The manifesto voiced strong opposition to the Kansas-Nebraska Act, which it described as a plot by slaveholders, and is credited with galvanizing public sentiment in favor of creating the Republican Party. [See Document 59.]

❧ "APPEAL OF THE INDEPENDENT DEMOCRATS" ❧

The "Appeal of the Independent Democrats," issued in January 1854 by northern antislavery Democrats, was a protest against the terms of the Kansas-Nebraska bill. In late 1853, Illinois Senator Stephen A. Douglas introduced a bill to organize the Nebraska Territory. According to the Missouri Compromise of 1820, which prohibited slavery in the Louisiana Purchase north of latitude 36 degrees 30 minutes, Nebraska was to be free territory. A senatorial group of proslavery southerners, however, coerced Douglas into amending his bill so as to create two new territories—Kansas and Nebraska—and to provide for the repeal of the Missouri Compromise restriction, thereby leaving the status of slavery in the new territories to be decided according to the principle of popular sovereignty. The issue became a bitter debate over slavery expansion. Southern Democrats and Whigs alike backed the bill while northern Whigs and Free Soil Party members fought the measure. Northern Democrats, meanwhile, including President Franklin Pierce, generally bowed to pressure from leading southerners and supported the bill.

A few northern free soil Democrats, however, opposed the rescission of the 36-degree 30-minute ban on slavery. Calling themselves Independent Democrats, these anti-Nebraska dissenters counted among their leaders Senators Salmon P. Chase of Ohio and Charles Sumner of Massachusetts as well as Representatives Gerrit Smith of New York and Joshua R. Giddings of Ohio. In January 1854, these congressmen and two colleagues published the "Appeal of the Independent Democrats" protesting the Kansas-Nebraska proposition. Mostly Chase's work, the appeal warned the nation of a great slave-power conspiracy bent upon reopening to slavery territories previously consigned to freedom. It assailed the Nebraska bill as "a criminal betrayal of precious rights; as part and parcel of an atrocious plot" to convert Nebraska into "a dreary region of despotism, inhabited by masters and slaves" (Foner, 1970). The Independent Democrats attributed this plot not only to a cabal of sinister southern slavemongers but to their northern "doughface" accomplices as well. The appeal singled out Douglas for especially harsh arraignment, accusing him of pandering to the slave power to advance his own political fortunes.

The "Appeal of the Independent Democrats" failed to prevent the passage of the Kansas-Nebraska Act, which became law in May 1854. Nevertheless, the protest deserves a prominent place among the list of speeches, tracts, and events that galvanized northern public opinion against the proliferation of slaveholding territory. Equally important, the appeal prefigured the coalescence of Conscience Whigs (northern Whigs who opposed slavery), Free Soilers, and anti-Nebraska Democrats into a single antislavery party—the Republican Party, which took shape in the wake of the Kansas-Nebraska controversy.

—*Eric Tscheschlok*

For Further Reading
Blue, Frederick J. 1987. *Salmon P. Chase: A Life in Politics.* Kent, OH: Kent State University Press; Foner, Eric. 1970. *Free Soil, Free Labor, Free Men: The Ideology of the Republican Party before the Civil War.* New York: Oxford University Press; Gienapp, William E. 1987. *The Origins of the Republican Party, 1852–1856.* New York: Oxford University Press; Potter, David M. 1976. *The Impending Crisis, 1848–1861.* New York: Harper and Row.

1854

In response to the political discord caused by debates over the Kansas-Nebraska bill, a group of 50 disillusioned Whigs, Free Soilers, and northern Democrats held a preliminary meeting in Ripon, Wisconsin, on February 28 to discuss the possibility of creating a new political party, one that was opposed to the expansion of slavery into the western territories. This meeting represents the earliest beginnings of the Republican Party.

1854

In Worcester, Massachusetts, the Massachusetts Emigrant Aid Society was established on April 26 by the abolitionist Eli Thayer. The purpose of this organization was to send at least 2,000 free blacks and antislavery supporters to Kansas in order to prevent the territory from opening to slavery. In 1855, the organization changed its name to the New England Emigrant Aid Company, and under its auspices, many free soil communities were established in Kansas.

1854

On May 24, a U.S. deputy marshal arrested the fugitive slave Anthony Burns in Boston and began the process of returning him to his owner in the South as stipulated by the Fugitive Slave Act of 1850. Black and white abolitionists, including Wendell Phillips, rallied to Burns's cause but were unable to prevent his extradition. Burns's owner in Virginia had rejected an offer by northern abolitionists to purchase Burns for $1,200 in order to set him free.

1854

With the support of Illinois Senator Stephen A. Douglas, Congress passed the Kansas-Nebraska Act on May 30. This measure repealed the clause in the Missouri Compromise (1820) that prohibited slavery in the territories north of 36 degrees 30 minutes north latitude and instead allowed popular sovereignty to determine the status of slavery in those regions. The measure was responsible in large part for the founding of the Republican Party, which opposed the expansion of slavery into any of the western territories.

1854

The U.S. government spent $100,000 to return one fugitive slave to the South. In Boston, hundreds of state militia and 2,000 federal troops were required to maintain order as the fugitive slave Anthony Burns was escorted from his jail cell on June 3 through the streets of Boston to Long Wharf to be returned to his owner in Virginia. It was estimated that 50,000 Bostonians lined the streets in protest at this event, and during the dramatic march to the dock, Boston church bells tolled and buildings along the route were draped in black. One year later, Boston abolitionists were able to purchase Burns from his owner and grant Burns the freedom that had eluded him in the Massachusetts courts. The citizens of Massachusetts were so aroused by this unpleasant episode that the state of Massachusetts never returned another fugitive slave to the South.

1854

In response to the political discord caused by passage of the Kansas-Nebraska Act, a group of disillusioned Whigs, Free Soilers, and northern Democrats met in Jackson, Michigan, on July 6 and formed the Republican Party.

1854

On July 19, the Wisconsin State Supreme Court decided the case of *In re Booth and Rycraft* and declared the Fugitive Slave Act of 1850 to be un-constitutional. Sherman Booth and John Rycraft, who had rescued the fugitive Joshua Glover from extradition back to slavery in the South, were ordered freed by the court. The case was appealed to the U.S. Supreme Court, and in the *Ableman v. Booth* (1859) decision, that Court ruled that state courts did not have the authority to declare federal laws unconstitutional.

1854

The Negro Emancipation Convention, with delegates from 11 states, was held in Cleveland, Ohio, August 24–26.

1854

In October, Abraham Lincoln made his first public statement on slavery in a speech given in Peoria, Illinois. In it, Lincoln stated that he opposed the extension of slavery into the western territories.

1854

On October 18, American diplomats Pierre Soulé (minister to Spain), John Y. Mason (minister to France), and James Buchanan (minister to Great Britain) met in Ostend, Belgium, to discuss what strategy the United States might follow in order to purchase Cuba from Spain or to seize the island by force if necessary. The Ostend Manifesto, a confidential diplomatic dispatch written primarily by Soulé, proposed that the United States offer the Spanish government no more than $120 million for Cuba and that should Spain reject that offer, the United States should take the island by force. The document was made public by enemies of President Franklin Pierce who wanted to discredit the proslavery Pierce administration. Expansionists, who tended to be proslavery supporters, hoped that Cuba might eventually form two additional slave states.

1854

After an estimated 1,600 border ruffians crossed from Missouri into Kansas on November 19 to influence an election by voting for a proslavery candidate, that candidate, J. W. Whitfield, was elected to be Kansas Territory's representative to the Congress. This event established the pattern for subsequent elections in Kansas Territory that would be fraught with intimidation and fraud. It was in this setting that Kansas used the system of popular sovereignty to settle the slavery question in that territory.

The Kansas-Nebraska Act, passed by the U.S. Congress on May 30, 1854, repealed the Missouri Compromise of 1820, which had specifically excluded slavery from the region north of latitude 36 degrees 30 minutes. Illinois senator Stephen A. Douglas introduced the bill, which organized the two territories of Kansas and Nebraska in such a way that each could determine the status for slaves via "popular sovereignty," i.e., whether or not slavery was instituted in the state would be decided by popular vote.

In addition to repealing the Missouri Compromise, the popular sovereignty portion of the act abrogated certain portions of the Compromise of 1850, which had stipulated that northern Texas, California, and Oregon were to be free territories and the remaining part of Texas was to be settled by proslavery southerners. The problem was that if the Kansas-Nebraska Act nullified parts of the Compromise of 1850, then slavery could be extended to other territories. Later, during the Lincoln-Douglas debates of 1858, Abraham Lincoln criticized Douglas by stating that popular sovereignty did nothing to address the moral and ethical concerns of slavery. Whig Congressman Samuel P. Benson of Maine noted during the 1854 congressional debate that the Northwest Ordinance of 1787 indicated that slavery was not to be extended for any reason. In other words, the prohibition of slavery in the Northwest Territory was a compact against the extension of slavery.

Not surprisingly, the Kansas-Nebraska Act was unacceptable to those traditionalists who supported slavery vehemently. It upset many people in the North who considered the Missouri Compromise a long-standing binding agreement, and it was also strongly opposed in the proslavery South. Still others felt that the agitation caused by Douglas was only to guarantee that the transcontinental railroad would be built westward from Chicago. The problem was that any such plan would need the support of southerners, and thus encompass the issue of slavery. Although Douglas had no personal stance on the issue of slavery, congressional "nonintervention" may have led to the conflict between rival factions in what was called Bleeding Kansas.

After the act was passed, pro- and antislavery supporters hurried to Kansas in an attempt to influence the outcome of the first election held after the law went into effect. When the final results indicated that proslavery settlers had won the election, a charge of fraud was made by antislavery proponents, who argued that the results were unjustified. When a second election was held, proslavery settlers refused to vote. This refusal re-sulted in the establishment of two opposing factions of the Kansas legislature. It also led some historians to contend that the American Civil War began when proslavery and antislavery forces began to debate whether land north of latitude 36 degrees 30 minutes should be slave or free territory.

The disagreement escalated until 1861. People's opinions about the Kansas-Nebraska Act were so vehement that it was not uncommon for premeditated attacks, which often led to death, to be waged against the opposing faction. Georgia native Charles A. Hamelton, the leader of the proslavery forces in the region, had gone to Kansas to garner support for making it a slave state but had been forced to leave by antislavery supporters. He gathered a group of men, and on their way to Missouri, they captured 11 free-state supporters, lined them up on the side of a road, and fired their weapons at them in what became known as the Marais des Cygnes massacre. Five of the 11 men died. The irony of this incident was that many of these men were Hamelton's former neighbors. Only one of his group, William Griffith, was caught and hanged.

Public sentiment over the incident was intense and horrified. The event was so troubling that John Greenleaf Whittier wrote a poem, "Le Marais du Cygne," about the act which was published in the September 1858 *Atlantic Monthly*. President Franklin Pierce, in support of the proslavery settlers, sent in federal troops to stop the violence and disperse the antislavery legislature. Another election was called. However, Congress did not recognize the constitution adopted by the proslavery settlers and consequently did not allow Kansas into the Union at that time.

Feelings over the situation in Missouri and Kansas even prompted violence on the floor of the Senate. In the end, antislavery supporters, who composed the majority, won an election, and a new constitution was penned. President Franklin Pierce supported the new antislavery constitution, which was eventually adopted. Both Kansas and Nebraska chose to be free states. On January 29, 1861, prior to the start of the Civil War, Kansas was admitted to the Union as a free state; Nebraska did not qualify for admittance until after the war had ended.

—*Torrance T. Stephens*

For Further Reading
Morrison, Michael A. 1997. *Slavery and the American West: The Eclipse of Manifest Destiny and the Coming of the Civil War.* Chapel Hill: University of North Carolina Press.

1855

My Bondage and My Freedom was published by Frederick Douglass. In this autobiographical account, Douglass described himself as a self-proclaimed graduate of the institution of slavery. Frederick Douglass was also nominated by the antislavery-based Liberty Party as a candidate for secretary of state in New York, the first time a black was nominated for a statewide office in the United States.

1855

William Wells Brown published *The American Fugitive in Europe: Sketches of Places and People Abroad,* an account of Brown's travels as a publicist for the antislavery cause.

1855

The legislatures of Maine, Massachusetts, and Michigan all enacted personal liberty laws, which prohibited state officials from assisting in the capture or return of fugitive slaves who might be found within their borders. These measures polarized northern-southern attitudes as they were designed specifically to enable state officials to circumvent the mission and purpose of the Fugitive Slave Act of 1850 by failing to assist federal marshals in enforcing a federal law. [See Document 60.]

1855

John Mercer Langston, who had been born a slave on a Virginia plantation, became the first African American to win elective office in the United States when he was elected clerk of Brownhelm Township in Lorain County, Ohio. Langston later served in the Freedman's Bureau, as the first dean of Howard University Law School, and as U.S. minister to Haiti.

1855

In Ohio, abolitionist Senator Salmon P. Chase was elected governor. Many people in the Republican Party believed that Chase would make an excellent presidential candidate. Also in Ohio, Peter H. Clark, a black abolitionist, began publishing the *Herald of Freedom,* an antislavery newspaper.

1855

On January 9, the United States and Great Britain finally agreed to a monetary settlement in regard to the *Creole* incident of 1841. The

In a long and distinguished career, John Mercer Langston (1829–1897) served as the first dean of the Howard University Law School and as U.S. minister to Haiti. Born a slave on a Virginia plantation, he was the first African American elected to public office in the United States. (Library of Congress/Corbis)

British had freed a shipload of slaves who had mutinied at sea and found refuge in the Bahamas, and for years, that action had caused a diplomatic rift between the two nations. Joshua Bates, an American-born British banker, negotiated the settlement in which the British government agreed to compensate the owners of the slaves, who had been emancipated by Bahamian authorities in 1841, in the amount of $119,330.

1855

Eureka College was chartered on February 6 after a group of Kentucky abolitionists moved to central Illinois and established the educational institution in the hope of continuing the antislavery struggle.

1855

The first territorial elections were held in Kansas Territory on March 30. A group of border ruffians, estimated at 5,000, entered Kansas from Missouri and forced the election of a proslavery legislature in an election that was wracked by fraud. There were many more votes cast than there were eligible voters in the territory, but despite irregularities, Territorial Governor Andrew H. Reeder allowed the election results to stand because he feared that an escalation of violence would occur if he failed to do so.

1855

On April 28, the Massachusetts legislature abolished racial segregation in all Massachusetts public schools, and integration proceeded without incident.

1855

In Pawnee, Kansas, the new proslavery territorial legislature met on July 2 and enacted a series of measures that protected slavery in Kansas. The proslavery majority in the legislature went so far as to expel the members of the antislavery faction (known as "jayhawkers") who had been elected in the spring.

1855

On July 31, President Franklin Pierce ordered the removal of Andrew H. Reeder as territorial governor of Kansas Territory. Pierce cited a conflict of interest as his reason for making the change because Reeder was speculating in Kansas lands, but in reality, Reeder's greatest offense to President Pierce was that he did not support the proslavery legislature that had been elected in March. Pierce replaced Reeder with Wilson Shannon, a proslavery supporter from Ohio.

1855

In Lawrence, Kansas, a free soil community that had been founded by the New England Emigrant Aid Company, a group of antislavery supporters (jayhawkers) gathered together on August 4 to call for their own constitutional convention since the sitting proslavery legislature had come to power through election fraud.

1855

A convention was held at Big Springs, Kansas, on September 5 in which antislavery supporters (jayhawkers) repudiated the results of the fraudulent election of March 30. The antislavery supporters formed the free-state forces and soon started to receive shipments of arms from the northern states. John Brown eventually arrived in Kansas and became a leader of these forces.

1855

On October 1, J. W. Whitfield was again elected as the Kansas territorial representative to Congress when proslavery men in Kansas and border ruffians from Missouri again manipulated the balloting. In response to this fraud, the antislavery supporters (jayhawkers) of Kansas held their own election on October 9 and elected former territorial governor Andrew H. Reeder as the territory's representative to Congress. In Washington, D.C., faced with representatives elected from each side in the Kansas dispute, Congress refused to seat either Whitfield or Reeder.

1855

In Kansas Territory, free-state forces met from October 23 to November 12 to draft the Topeka Constitution, which outlawed slavery, and to elect a governor and legislature supportive of that position. The Topeka Constitution also included a curious provision that barred all blacks from Kansas. For nearly two years, Kansas Territory operated with two governments: a proslavery government seated in Lecompton and an antislavery government (jayhawkers) seated in Topeka. The political repercussions of the situation in Kansas forced battle lines to form in Congress as the rhetoric over the situation intensified.

1855

The first California Negro Convention was held in Sacramento, California, November 20–22.

1855

In Kansas Territory, the Wakarusa war (November 26–December 7) erupted when a group of 1,500 border ruffians from Missouri entered Kansas and fought a series of skirmishes with antislavery groups (jayhawkers) in the Wakarusa River region. The border ruffians had intended to attack the community of Lawrence but refrained from doing so when they learned that the town was well defended. The fighting diminished when Territorial Governor Wilson Shannon intervened and sent the territorial militia into the affected region.

1855

Free soil supporters in Kansas Territory held a referendum on December 15 and approved the Topeka Constitution, which outlawed slavery in Kansas and also prohibited blacks from the region.

The jayhawkers of Kansas became, in the 1850s, a major obstacle to the expansion of slavery in the United States. In the contest to determine the status of slavery in the territory, partisan bands engaged in frequent violent episodes that foretold the future civil war. The antislavery forces were called "jayhawkers"—the origins of the term are obscure, and there are numerous conflicting explanations. The jayhawkers' resistance to the proslavery forces, or border ruffians, eventually helped make Kansas a free state.

The Kansas-Nebraska Act, signed in 1854, opened two new territories with no reference as to the status of slavery in either of them. The residents of the territories were to vote on slavery prior to the formation of state constitutions, a practice called popular sovereignty. Kansas's close proximity to Missouri, a slave state, virtually ensured conflict since most of the early settlers of Kansas Territory were antislavery farmers from free states in the Midwest.

After slavery advocates from Missouri flooded across the border to cast fraudulent votes in the 1855 territorial elections, the region exploded in violence. In the polarized political climate of the 1850s, Bleeding Kansas became a national issue, since many people perceived the territory to be a crucial test over the future of slavery.

The jayhawkers were the frontier vanguard of the American antislavery movement, but they differed from their high-minded eastern abolitionist counterparts in important ways. Most jayhawkers wanted to exclude not only slaves but all blacks from settlement in Kansas although most of them were content to allow the institution to remain in Missouri. By and large they had little love or sympathy for blacks—free or slave—as they saw them as competitors for land and jobs.

The key leaders of the jayhawkers were James Lane, James Montgomery, and Charles R. Jennison. During the American Civil War, the jayhawkers formed Union bands that roamed the Kansas-Missouri area and engaged proslavery forces in fierce guerrilla fighting. The jayhawkers and their proslavery counterparts often matched each other in violence.

—*Richard D. Loosbrock*

For Further Reading
Castel, Albert. 1958. A *Frontier State at War: Kansas, 1861–1865.* Ithaca, NY: Cornell University Press; Monaghan, Jay. 1955. *Civil War on the Western Border, 1854–65.* Boston: Little, Brown.

Jayhawkers from Kansas Territory help themselves to horses belonging to proslavery Missouri farmers. (Library of Congress)

1856

David Christy published *Cotton Is King, or, The Economical Relations of Slavery*. It is from this work that the popular expression "king cotton" came into use.

1856

Free blacks in Ohio were granted the right to control their own schools.

1856

The Knights of Liberty, a secret society of free blacks, claimed to have a membership of 47,240 throughout the country. The purpose of this secret militant group was to bring about the end of slavery through violent action.

1856

Governor James H. Adams of South Carolina called for the reopening of the African slave trade, which had been illegal since 1808. Adams believed that South Carolina planters were having a difficult time obtaining sufficient numbers of slaves through the domestic slave trade, and he feared what the economic implications of a shortage of slave laborers might mean to his state. Adams's apprehension seems somewhat dubious, for according to census figures, slaves constituted 57.6 percent of South Carolina's population in 1850 and in 1860, slaves made up 57.2 percent of the state's population.

1856

On January 15, free soil supporters in Kansas Territory elected Charles Robinson as their territorial governor, and they also elected an anti-slavery legislature. The free soil Kansans took this action in behalf of the Topeka Constitution, which they had ratified in a December 1855 referendum. In Washington, D.C., President Franklin Pierce looked upon the actions taken by the free soil Kansans as an act of rebellion against federal authority because the national government had already recognized the proslavery legislature that had been elected in March 1855.

1856

On January 24, a proslavery address was delivered at the Tremont Temple in Boston, Massachusetts, by Georgia Senator Robert A. Toombs.

1856

The polarization that the country faced regarding the issue of slavery was greatly exacerbated by the Kansas-Nebraska Act, and nowhere was this more apparent than in the U.S. Congress. It took the House of Representatives more than two months to decide upon a Speaker of the House of Representatives; eventually, Congressman Nathaniel P. Banks of Massachusetts was elected to that post on February 2.

1856

On February 11, President Franklin Pierce, who supported the proslavery element in Kansas, issued a special proclamation to the residents of Kansas Territory in which he called upon both the border ruffians and the free soil supporters to cease all hostilities.

1856

Members of the Republican Party held their first national meeting in Pittsburgh, Pennsylvania, on February 22.

1856

The free soil government in Kansas Territory, with its legislature seated in Topeka, petitioned the U.S. Congress on March 4 to admit Kansas to the Union as a free state. Although the proposal was popular among many of the Republicans in Congress, Illinois Senator Stephen A. Douglas proposed a bill that would make Kansas statehood contingent upon the promulgation of a new state constitution.

1856

Booker Taliaferro Washington was born into slavery in Franklin County, Virginia, on April 5.

1856

On May 19, after delivering a "Crime against Kansas" speech, Senator Charles Sumner of Massachusetts was savagely beaten with a cane by Congressman Preston Brooks of South Carolina. The attack took place in the U.S. Senate chamber, and Sumner would require three years of recuperation before he could return to his position there. The state of Massachusetts kept the position vacant for this period, which meant that Sumner's empty chair in the Senate chamber was a symbolic reminder of the attack. In his speech, Sumner had insulted the aged Senator Andrew Butler of South Carolina, the uncle

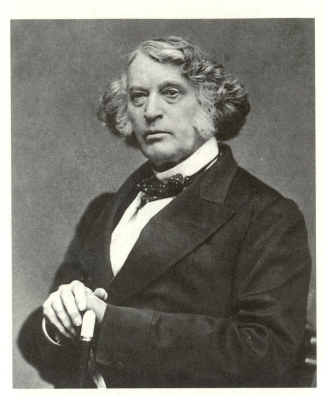

Radical abolitionist Charles Sumner (1811–1874), U.S. senator from Massachusetts. (Library of Congress)

of Congressman Brooks, and Preston Brooks believed that his action in attacking Sumner was justified as he defended both the honor of his family and the interests of his state and region.

1856
On May 21, a group of proslavery forces attacked and sacked the town of Lawrence, Kansas, which had acquired the reputation of being an abolitionist, free soil stronghold and was reputedly a station on the Underground Railroad. One antislavery supporter was killed in the attack, and the radical abolitionist John Brown led a group of antislavery men (jayhawkers) in a nighttime attack on May 24 that killed five proslavery settlers at Pottawatomie Creek in retaliation for the attack on Lawrence. These episodes began the two-year struggle, known as Bleeding Kansas, over the issues of slavery and popular sovereignty; more than 200 Kansas settlers died in the struggle.

1856
On June 2, an antislavery faction within the American Party (Know-Nothing Party) held its own nominating convention in New York City. At this meeting, John C. Frémont of California was nominated as candidate for the presidency

and W. F. Johnston of Pennsylvania for the vice-presidency.

1856
The Republican Party held its first national nominating convention on June 17–19. John C. Frémont was nominated as the first Republican candidate for the presidency, and William L. Dayton was nominated for vice-president. Frémont ran on a platform that did not support the expansion of slavery into the western territories, and the slogan "Free soil, free speech, free men, Frémont" was used throughout the campaign. In November, Frémont lost the election to the Democrat James Buchanan.

1856
On July 3, although the House of Representatives voted to accept Kansas as a state with its Topeka Constitution, which prohibited slavery, the Senate rejected the measure. The question of Kansas statehood, and the nature of whether Kansas would become slave or free, remained undecided at the conclusion of the Thirty-fourth Congress.

1856
With the support of the administration of President Franklin Pierce, federal troops from Fort Leavenworth in Kansas Territory were dispatched to Topeka on July 4 to break up the free-state legislature that was convened there. Since the national government had gone on record as recognizing the proslavery government in Kansas Territory, President Pierce believed that the legislature convening in Topeka represented a challenge to federal authority in the region.

1856
In August, Kansas Territory experienced the horror of civil war as the specter of Bleeding Kansas resulted in nearly 200 deaths and more than $2 million in property damage. During the struggle between proslavery and antislavery (jayhawker) forces, two different governments were seated simultaneously in Kansas Territory, and Congress refused to seat representatives from either government. The matter was not completely resolved until October 1857.

1856
In Kansas Territory, Governor Wilson Shannon

The contest over slavery in the United States broke into open conflict in the border war of 1854–1859, also known as Bleeding Kansas. The Kansas-Missouri border erupted into armed combat seven years in advance of the American Civil War as southerners tried to advance slavery in the newly formed Kansas Territory.

The long-term causes of the border war were rooted in the westward expansion of slavery and the Missouri Compromise of 1820. The compromise had allowed Missouri to enter the union as a slave state but prohibited slavery from any future states in Louisiana Purchase territory above the 36-degree 30-minute line, the southern border of Kansas. Although the agreement seemed to quell the sectional tensions of 1820, it was, as Thomas Jefferson said, a "firebell in the night" (Nichols, 1954), and the development of industry in the northern states and the rise of abolitionism, among other factors, in the next three decades polarized the nation over the issue of slavery.

In the short term, the border war was the product of the Kansas-Nebraska Act of 1854. That act organized two territories west and northwest of Missouri, and the bill's author, Illinois Senator Stephen A. Douglas, invoked the doctrine of popular sovereignty, which meant the status of slavery in each territory would be decided by a vote of the citizens of the territories. Since these territories lay north of the 36-degree 30-minute line, the act effectively nullified the Missouri Compromise. The bill narrowly passed Congress but raised the ire of the increasingly antislavery North. Out of this dispute rose the Republican Party, a sectional party dedicated to stopping the expansion of slavery in the territories.

Popular sovereignty was seen by many people as a panacea for the ills of sectionalism, but events in Kansas Territory soon destroyed that illusion. When the territory was officially opened for settlement in mid-1854, many of the early inhabitants were nonpartisans who cared little for the slave issue, but others saw Kansas as the next great battleground over slavery. In the territorial elections of March 1855, several thousand proslavery Missourians, called "border ruffians," flooded across the boundary to cast fraudulent votes. Even though free soil settlers were in the majority, they lost by a count of 5,247 to 797. It was later determined that 4,968 of the proslavery votes were fraudulent, but the proslavery forces had the territorial government thoroughly intimidated.

The dispute soon erupted into violence. A November 1855 killing of a free soil settler by a proslavery man triggered a series of events that led to the formation of large partisan bands that resembled armies. In May 1856, a federal marshal gathered a posse of 700 proslavery men to arrest some free soil officials at their headquarters in Lawrence. The posse went well beyond the arrests and looted the town, destroying two presses of antislavery newspapers and burning the Free State Hotel. The "sack of Lawrence" led to a series of violent reprisals. John Brown, the man who later tried to incite a slave insurrection on the eve of the Civil War, led his sons in a brutal attack along Pottawatomie Creek in which five men were taken from their homes in a small proslavery community and hacked to death with swords.

Some 200 men died in Kansas during 1856 alone, and the violence continued unabated. The national press covered each murder and skirmish with intense scrutiny, fueling sectional tensions. The Missourians' hopes of making Kansas a slave state were ultimately swamped by a sea of settlers from the free states. The instability of the territory made the prospect of taking slaves there a very risky proposition, and for many people the Kansas prairie seemed to represent the natural limits of the institution of slavery. By 1857, the Free State Party was in firm control of territorial political life, and in 1859, the Topeka Convention drafted a free soil constitution. Still, Kansas did not enter the Union until after the first southern states had seceded in the winter of 1860–1861.

The border war technically ended in 1859, but the local fighting was merely subsumed by the larger Civil War. The Kansas-Missouri border area witnessed some of the most brutal guerrilla conflict as the border ruffians and the antislavery supporters (jayhawkers) continued their bitter contest. The border war was a dress rehearsal for the American Civil War.

—*Richard D. Loosbrock*

For Further Reading
Monaghan, Jay. 1955. *Civil War on the Western Border, 1854–1865*. Boston: Little, Brown; Nichols, Alice. 1954. *Bleeding Kansas*. New York: Oxford University Press; Rawley, James A. 1969. *Race and Politics: "Bleeding Kansas" and the Coming of the Civil War*. Philadelphia: J. B. Lippincott.

One of the bloodiest incidents of the Border War was the Marais des Cygnes massacre in Lynn County, Kansas, May 19, 1858, in which Missourians murdered five Free Staters. John Greenleaf Whittier honored the dead in his poem "Le Marais du Cygne." (Library of Congress)

resigned his position on August 18 and was replaced by John W. Geary.

1856
The Methodist Episcopal Church founded Wilberforce University in Ohio on August 30. The African Methodist Episcopal Church later purchased the university.

1856
In Kansas Territory, Governor John W. Geary used federal troops to prevent an army of 2,500 border ruffians from Missouri from marching into Kansas on September 15.

1857
Legislators in Maine and New Hampshire granted freedom and citizenship to all persons of African descent residing within their respective borders. This action represents further evidence of efforts by the northern states to negate the effects of the Fugitive Slave Act of 1850.

1857
Hinton Rowan Helper of North Carolina, an abolitionist who despised blacks, published *The Impending Crisis of the South: How to Meet It.* Helper based his arguments upon statistical information he had garnered from the seventh census of the United States taken in 1850 and asserted that slavery had caused great economic distress to nonslaveholders and poor whites of the South. He urged the South's poor whites to rise up and overthrow slavery, but he also advocated the deportation of freed blacks to Africa. Sixty-eight members of the House of Representatives endorsed the book, most without having read it, and the Republican Party distributed 100,000 copies of it in the northern states. Once the book was published, it was banned in the southern states, and Helper was considered such a pariah in the region that he was forced to flee to New York for his personal safety.

1857
George Fitzhugh of Virginia, a noted proslavery polemicist, published *Cannibals All!: or, Slaves without Masters,* in which he presented the argument that northern "wage slaves" were essentially worse off than slave laborers in the South. Fitzhugh believed that the exploitative nature of industrial capitalism did not provide a system of economic security to northern workingmen similar to the benevolence found in the paternalistic institution of slavery that existed in the South. Fitzhugh lived until 1881, and in the

Hinton Rowan Helper's most famous book, *The Impending Crisis of the South: How to Meet It,* published in 1857, was probably the harshest condemnation of slavery ever to be written by a southerner. Helper's argument, buttressed by statistical evidence and written in a combative style of prose, ensured that the book could never be published in the South. In fact, a New York publisher, A. B. Burdock, published it only after Helper had guaranteed that the publisher would not suffer any financial loss.

Helper's main theme was that slavery retarded the economic growth of the South as slavery caused great suffering not only for slaves but also for millions of poor white southerners. This latter group was Helper's intended audience. Helper himself came from a yeoman family in North Carolina; however, he tended to lump yeoman farmers and poor whites together into one category he called "poor whites." He cast slaveholders as the enemies, not the friends, of the poor whites and referred to slaveholders disparagingly as "the lords of the lash."

To prove his point about economic underdevelopment, Helper contrasted the North and the South in both 1790 and 1850. Using statistical evidence culled from the census for each decade, Helper showed that after starting out equal to or even surpassing the northern states, by 1850 the southern states were woefully behind the North in commerce and agricultural and industrial output. He used his statistics to reveal that supposed southern superiority in agricultural production did not exist; rather, his numbers revealed that the North was superior in agricultural production and other key indexes such as livestock holdings, value of farm implements, and land values. Furthermore, southern backwardness extended into the realms of education and literature, with the North exceeding the South in literacy, libraries, colleges, and writers. To explain these phenomena, Helper placed the blame squarely on the South's devotion to slavery and the slaveholders' political, economic, and oratorical manipulation of the poor whites.

The proper remedy for this situation was the abolition of slavery, which would encourage free white labor—heretofore assigned a degraded status—raise land values, and destroy the slaveholding aristocracy's grip on power in the South. To effect the abolition of slavery, southern nonslaveholding whites must unite in organized, independent political action. Slaveholders must be rendered ineligible for political office. No political cooperation with slaveholders should occur, nor should there be religious fellowship or social affiliation with them.

Poor whites should refuse to patronize slaveholding merchants. In fact, proslavery men should not be recognized, except as the criminals or ruffians they actually were. Poor whites should discontinue subscriptions to proslavery newspapers, and to help encourage free white labor, nonslaveholders must refuse to hire slaves for work.

Finally, there must be an immediate emancipation of slaves. It appears that Helper actually envisioned gradual emancipation because he recommended a tax of $60 per slave with an additional $40 tax levied for each slave held after July 4, 1863. This tax money would be given to the slaves as recompense for their years of unpaid labor as well as to cover the cost of their colonization to Africa, Latin America, or elsewhere in the United States. Helper had genuine pity for the slaves despite his thoroughgoing racism; he called the slaves "cowards" and "pitiable," yet he called slavery "the most barbaric relic of the most barbarous age" (Helper, 1857). He saw both slaves and poor whites as victims of tyrant slaveholders.

In effect, what Helper advocated, though not explicitly, was class conflict in the South. He hoped change would be peaceful and stated that he sought "fair play, [to] secure to us the right of discussion, the freedom of speech, and we will settle the difficulty at the ballot box, not on the battle-ground—by force of reason, not by force of arms" (Helper, 1857). Slaveholders however were not convinced of Helper's pacific intentions, especially when he noted that 9 out of 10 slaves "would be delighted with an opportunity to cut their masters' throats" (Helper, 1857). Such violent rhetoric brought up the ever-present fears of another Nat Turner and servile rebellion. As Clement Eaton (1964) notes, Helper's message had little impact in the Old South. Most poor whites rallied around slaveholders when war broke out in 1861, and racial antipathy toward blacks proved stronger than class interest.

—*James C. Foley*

For Further Reading
Degler, Carl. 1974. *The Other South: Southern Dissenters in the Nineteenth Century.* New York: Harper and Row; Eaton, Clement. 1964. *The Freedom-of-Thought Struggle in the Old South.* Baton Rouge: Louisiana State University Press; Fredrickson, George M. 1988. *The Arrogance of Race: Historical Perspectives on Slavery, Racism, and Social Inequality.* Middletown, CT: Wesleyan University Press; Helper, Hinton. 1857. *The Impending Crisis of the South: How to Meet It.* New York: A. B. Burdock.

years following the American Civil War, he supported efforts to attract northern industry to the New South.

1857

Kansas Territory's proslavery legislature held a session in Lecompton, Kansas, that lasted from January 12 to February 15 and issued a call for a territorial census and a constitutional convention. Governor John W. Geary vetoed the measures, but the legislature overrode the governor's actions.

1857

Delegates who favored the peaceful separation of the North and South met in Worcester, Massachusetts, at the State Disunion Convention on January 15. Abolitionist William Lloyd Garrison addressed the crowd that had gathered for the meeting, and in an impassioned speech, he declared, "No union with slave holders!" This phrase became the slogan of the organization.

1857

On March 6, the U.S. Supreme Court, by a vote of seven to two, decided the case of *Dred Scott v. Sandford* and declared that blacks were not citizens of the United States but property that had no right to sue for freedom in a court of law. In the words of Chief Justice Roger B. Taney, slaves had "no rights a white man need respect." The court also asserted that the Congress had no power to exclude slavery from any of the territories—in effect, declaring the Missouri Compromise to be unconstitutional.

1857

The state of Massachusetts adopted a literacy test as a requirement for voting on May 1.

1857

In Kansas Territory, Robert J. Walker of Mississippi was appointed governor on May 26, and he pledged he would make sure that any proposed state constitution was offered to the voters would be presented in a fair election.

1857

In June, the California state legislature narrowly defeated a proposal that would have prohibited the further immigration of free blacks into the state.

1857

In Kansas Territory, Governor Robert J. Walker supervised elections on October 5 to ensure that fraudulent votes were not cast. Frederick P. Stanton of Tennessee, who served as territorial secretary, saw to it that several thousand fraudulent proslavery ballots were rejected by election officials. When the votes were finally counted, the Free State Party had won a majority in both houses of the territorial legislature. The struggle that Kansas had endured demonstrated the difficulties that could arise if popular sovereignty became the means employed to settle the issue of slavery's expansion into the western territories.

1857

Proslavery forces in Kansas hold a constitutional convention in Lecompton on October 19–November 8 and drafted a document that legalized slavery in Kansas. Upon realizing that passage of this document was unlikely, delegates to the convention drafted a separate article on slavery that would be put before the voters in a referendum. Regardless of how the vote turned out on the slavery article, the constitution would still protect the institution in Kansas. Although Kansas Territorial Governor Robert J. Walker opposed the efforts of the delegates at Lecompton, President James Buchanan, who hoped to maintain a strained sense of unity within the Democratic Party, endorsed the work of the Lecompton Convention.

1857

When antislavery supporters (jayhawkers) in the Kansas Territory refused to take part in the December 21 referendum on the proslavery Lecompton Constitution, the proslavery document was approved for the territory.

1858

William Wells Brown published *The Escape; or, A Leap for Freedom*, the first play to be written by an African American. Brown had previously written an unpublished antislavery drama entitled "Experience, or, How to Give a Northern Man a Backbone."

1858

Kansas and Wisconsin each enacted personal liberty laws, which were designed to circumvent enforcement of the federal Fugitive Slave Act of 1850.

JAMES BUCHANAN (1791–1868)

As the fifteenth president of the United States, James Buchanan pushed the sectional controversy over slavery practically to the point of no return. Graduating from Dickinson College in 1809, Buchanan joined the bar of his native Pennsylvania three years later. He entered his state's legislature following the War of 1812, commencing a long political career in which he held some type of public trust almost continuously until 1861. In 1820, he won election to Congress as a Federalist, though by the end of his 10-year tenure in the House of Representatives, he had adopted the Jacksonian faith. Consequently, Andrew Jackson named Buchanan minister to Russia (1832–1833). Returning from St. Petersburg, Buchanan spent the next 10 years in the U.S. Senate (1835–1845), where he showed traces of being a "doughface"—a northerner who sympathized with the South on the slavery question. For instance, he supported the annexation of Texas as a slave state.

In 1844, Buchanan worked hard to carry Pennsylvania for the Democratic presidential candidate, James K. Polk, who returned the favor by bringing Buchanan into his cabinet as secretary of state (1845–1849). In this office, Buchanan showed skill and tact in handling the Texas and Oregon boundary crises, but at the same time, his prosouthern tendencies came into sharper focus. He supported Polk's aggression against Mexico and joined southerners in opposing the Wilmot Proviso, which aimed to bar slavery from all territory acquired as a result of the Mexican War (1846–1848). Moreover, Buchanan headed the unsuccessful efforts of the Polk administration to buy Cuba from Spain. These overtures alarmed northern opponents of slavery, who knew that southern proslavery zealots coveted Cuba as an additional slave state.

Buchanan emerged as a contender for his party's presidential nomination in 1848. As a solution to the controversy over slavery expansion, Buchanan advocated extending the Missouri Compromise line to the Pacific coast, thereby dividing the territory acquired from Mexico into clearly delineated free and slaveholding spheres. But party chieftains rejected this formula, as well as Buchanan's candidacy, and instead turned to Michigan senator Lewis Cass, who adopted the doctrine of popular sovereignty as his solution to the territorial problem—that is, he supported the idea of territorial self-determination of the slavery question.

After Buchanan failed in another presidential bid in 1852, he joined Franklin Pierce's administration as minister to Great Britain (1853–1856). In this post, he again became involved in plans for the annexation of Cuba. In 1854, Buchanan helped draft the Ostend Manifesto, which sanctioned the American conquest of Cuba if Spain refused to sell the island. This action endeared Buchanan to southern slavery expansionists, who were clamoring for Cuba louder than ever, but it earned him the wrath of northern free soilers, who became convinced that Buchanan was a thoroughgoing ally of the slave power. Nevertheless, the Ostend affair paled in comparison with the Kansas-Nebraska controversy, which also exploded in 1854 and which helped make Buchanan the Democratic presidential nominee in 1856. Rising anti-Nebraska sentiment in the party caused Democratic leaders to pass over Buchanan's chief rivals, the incumbent Pierce and Stephen A. Douglas of Illinois. Buchanan won the party's candidacy because he was overseas when the Nebraska trouble broke and thus seemed untainted by the affair. With strong southern backing, he won the election of 1856.

Sectional discord over slavery plagued Buchanan throughout his term, and he did much to fuel the antagonisms. Tensions began mounting days after his inauguration, when the Supreme Court issued its decision in the Dred Scott case (1857) and thus denied the authority of Congress and territorial legislatures to prohibit slavery in the territories. Seeing the ruling as a final solution to the territorial debate, Buchanan endorsed it. In fact, he privately, and improperly, pressured a northern justice to rule with the Court's southern majority against congressional or territorial regulation of slavery. The president's southern supporters appreciated his stance, but it placed northern Democrats in an untenable position because since 1848, Democrats had embraced popular sovereignty as their formula for dealing with slavery in the territories. Yet, the Dred Scott decision seemed to invalidate that doctrine and to do so with the president's blessing. Buchanan thus helped precipitate a sectional rift in the party.

Buchanan disrupted his party completely in 1857 when the proslavery legislature in Lecompton, Kansas, submitted a slave-state constitution to Congress in petitioning for admission to the Union. It was well known that the Lecompton assembly was a "bogus" legislature, owing its existence solely to rigged elections, and that most Kansans were free staters. Nonetheless, Buchanan advocated the admission of Kansas under the Lecompton Constitution. He hoped that a speedy admission, even under an illegitimate regime, would bring closure to the sectional struggle in the territory. Once again, though, he failed to see the consequences of his blatantly prosouthern policies. Led by Stephen Douglas, several anti-Lecompton Democrats broke with the regular party and joined Republicans in denouncing the proslavery constitution as an undemocratic violation of the will of the free soil majority in Kansas. Buchanan's course, therefore, shattered the northern Democrats and thus virtually ensured a Republican presidential victory in 1860 and the resultant secession in the winter of 1860–1861.

Buchanan approached southern secession with equivocation. He denied the right of any state to withdraw from the Union, but concurrently, he denied the power of the federal government to coerce states to remain in the Union. He spent his final days as president attempting to avert civil war, happily transferring the reins of government to Abraham Lincoln in early 1861. He retired to Pennsylvania, where died in 1868.

Buchanan fancied himself "the old public functionary," a reference to the many offices he held during his long public career. Yet, for all his political experience, Buchanan approached the sectional conflicts of the 1850s with gross ineptitude. Indeed, his policies helped sunder the Union to which he had devoted his life.

—*Eric Tscheschlok*

For Further Reading
Klein, Philip S. 1962. *President James Buchanan: A Biography*. University Park: Pennsylvania State University Press; Nichols, Roy F. 1948. *The Disruption of American Democracy*. New York: Macmillan; Potter, David M. 1976. *The Impending Crisis, 1848–1861*. New York: Harper and Row; Smith, Elbert B. 1975. *The Presidency of James Buchanan*. Lawrence: University Press of Kansas.

1858

The decision was made that slaves could not patent an invention because they were not considered citizens of the United States. Additionally, Jefferson Davis was unable to obtain a patent on a type of boat propeller that his slave Benjamin Montgomery had invented as it was ruled that slaves could not assign any of their inventions to their owners.

1858

In Kansas Territory, the Lecompton Constitution appeared on the ballot for a second time in a popular referendum held on January 4. In a reversal of the initial vote, proslavery voters boycotted the election, and the free soil supporters were able to defeat the measure.

1858

In February, the radical abolitionist John Brown, who was wanted by federal authorities for murder charges in Kansas Territory, spent a month living in the home of Frederick Douglass in Rochester, New York. During this time, Brown began to develop the plan for his raid on the Harpers Ferry arsenal in Virginia.

1858

On February 2, President James Buchanan urged Congress to admit Kansas to the Union with the Lecompton Constitution, which allowed slavery, even though Kansas voters had rejected the document in January. Buchanan was strongly criticized by Illinois Senator Stephen A. Douglas, who believed the Lecompton Constitution did not represent the true wishes of Kansas voters as expressed through the system of popular sovereignty.

1858

Illinois Senator Stephen A. Douglas was unable to find the votes to block President James Buchanan's wishes, and on March 23, the U.S. Senate voted to allow Kansas to enter the Union under the Lecompton Constitution, which permitted slavery, even though the voters of Kansas had previously rejected this constitution. In the House of Representatives, it was decided that the people of Kansas should again vote on the constitution through a third popular referendum, and on April 1, the House of Representatives passed a resolution requiring voters in the Kansas Territory to vote again on the Lecompton Constitution.

1858

In California's most celebrated fugitive slave case, the Mississippi-born fugitive Archy Lee won the right to his freedom on April 14 and then moved to Victoria, British Columbia. Several other fugitive slaves living in California also moved to British Columbia to avoid the possibility that California courts might be used to try to return them to a condition of slavery in the southern states.

1858

In an effort to find a compromise that could settle the impasse concerning Kansas statehood, on May 4, Indiana Congressman William B. English proposed that Congress provide statehood to Kansas in the event that the voters there approved of the Lecompton Constitution. Congress agreed to the compromise proposed in the English Act.

1858

On May 8, the American abolitionist John Brown held an antislavery convention in Chatham, Canada, and 12 whites and 34 blacks attended the gathering.

1858

Abraham Lincoln delivered "the house divided" speech as he accepted the Republican Party's nomination for senator from Illinois on June 16. In the speech, Lincoln declared: "A house divided against itself cannot stand. I believe this government cannot endure permanently half *slave* and half *free*. I do not expect the Union to be *dissolved*. I do not expect the house to *fall*, but I do expect it will cease to be divided." [See Document 62.]

1858

On August 2, voters in Kansas rejected the Lecompton Constitution, and the territory became a free (nonslaveholding) territory. In rejecting this constitution and the stipulations attached in the English Act of May 4, Kansans turned away from the notion of immediate statehood and opted instead for an opportunity to keep the region free of slavery. Kansas did not enter the Union as a state until 1861, when it joined the Union as a free state.

1858

Abraham Lincoln and Stephen A. Douglas conducted a series of seven debates in conjunction with the race for the U.S. Senate seat for Illinois. These debates were held in the communities of Ottawa (August 21), Freeport (August 27), Jonesboro (September 15), Charleston (September 18), Galesburg (October 7), Quincy (October 13), and Alton (October 15). During the debates, Douglas made statements that alienated many of his southern supporters, thus making his chances of a successful presidential bid less likely. Lincoln used the debates to state his opposition to slavery, but he also declared his belief that it would be impossible to achieve racial equality in the United States.

1858

In September, a group of several hundred Oberlin College students led by one of their professors, local abolitionists, and free blacks rescued a fugitive slave named (Little) John Price in Wellington, Ohio, and helped him escape to Canada. This action was in direct violation of the Fugitive Slave Act of 1850, and the federal government brought charges against 37 of the alleged rescuers.

1858

New York Senator William H. Seward, who hoped that he might be the Republican Party's nominee for the presidency in 1860, spoke at a public rally in Rochester, New York, on September 25 during the midterm elections and stated, "It is an irrepressible conflict between opposing and enduring forces, and it means that the United States must and will, sooner or later, become either entirely a slaveholding nation or entirely a free-labor nation" (Schlesinger, 1983). Though the Republicans did gain additional congressional seats in 1858, Seward's "irrepressible conflict" statement had made him a radical within the party, and his chances of securing the Republican Party's presidential nomination in 1860 diminished.

1859

The American sculptor John Rogers created a group sculpture called "The Slave Auction." The work was featured at an art showing in New York City from 1859 to 1860.

1859

A group of Maryland slaveholders held a convention in Baltimore at which businessmen complained that many of the jobs in the service industries were monopolized by free blacks. Despite these reservations, the convention did not support a resolution to deport free blacks from the state of Maryland.

1859

In February, the Arkansas legislature presented free blacks with the choice of choosing between exile or enslavement.

In the summer and fall of 1858, two candidates for the U.S. Senate from Illinois, Republican Abraham Lincoln and Democrat Stephen A. Douglas, faced each other in a series of seven debates. This in itself was unusual, because since the state legislature would decide who would fill the Senate seat, a campaign for this office was unprecedented. The tense political climate of the period made these debates even more significant, as they represented an articulate statement of conflicting views on slavery and its expansion, a capstone of a generation of controversy during which these issues dominated the American political scene.

The participants were polar opposites, both physically and politically. Senator Stephen A. Douglas was one of the most powerful politicians in the United States. Nicknamed "the little giant" because of his small stature and oratorical prowess, Douglas had extensive political experience. After serving several terms in the House of Representatives, he had been elected to the U.S. Senate in 1846. While a member of that body, he rose to chair the important Committee on Territories, and as such, he sponsored the Kansas-Nebraska Act (1854), which brought the debate over slavery in the territories and the idea of popular sovereignty to the political forefront.

Douglas believed that allowing the settlers of each territory decide the slavery question for themselves, popular sovereignty, was the solution to a persistent political problem. First, he believed that under the Constitution, states, not the federal government, had the authority to enact legislation dealing with slavery. Second, he believed the institution would die out without any federal intervention. Third, he understood that his political future, and that of his party, rested on a fragile coalition of northern and southern Democrats, which a strong stand on either side of the issue would dissolve. So Douglas, the consummate politician, chose what he believed to a safe, moderate position. When Kansas erupted in civil war over the issue of slavery, Douglas's critics argued that popular sovereignty was merely another way to protect slavery's westward expansion. One of his most vocal opponents was a former Whig, Abraham Lincoln.

In 1858, Lincoln was not a politician of national stature. He had served several terms in the Illinois legislature and a single term in Congress. A successful Springfield lawyer, he had left the Whigs over the issue of slavery in 1856 and joined the fledgling Republican Party. Lincoln believed slavery was a moral wrong and opposed its expansion.

He argued that the institution was a corrosive force in American society, and he felt it should be eliminated as quickly as possible. Therefore, Lincoln and Douglas represented the two opposing views on the expansion of slavery that dominated American politics before the Civil War.

The debates themselves were a departure from political tradition because Senate candidates normally did not campaign, as the state legislatures elected senators and the party that controlled the state assembly usually elected powerful party leaders to such a post. In 1858, the controversy over the expansion of slavery and the resulting political turmoil meant that for the first time, the Senate election was an important issue in the Illinois legislative races. It was, in fact, a referendum on the future of slavery in the United States.

The voters had an unprecedented opportunity to evaluate the Senate candidates after the Chicago *Times* suggested that Lincoln and Douglas debate across Illinois. Lincoln quickly agreed and was followed, somewhat more reluctantly, by Douglas. As the incumbent, Douglas realized that he had much more to lose than his relatively unknown Republican challenger. Seven debates were scheduled, all similar in content and form to modern political forums.

The first debate, in Ottawa, Illinois, on August 21, set the tone for the debates that followed as the issue of slavery expansion came to the forefront. Douglas declared that it was "the sovereign right of each State to decide the slavery question . . . for themselves, without interference from any other states or power whatsoever" (Jaffa, 1959). According to Douglas, this right also extended to territories, which should be allowed to decide the question through the democratic process. He went on to accuse Lincoln and the Republican Party of being "in favor of the citizenship of the negro" (Jaffa, 1959). Lincoln denied that he favored black equality, but he admitted that he believed the institution was a moral blight upon the nation and argued that "we shall not have peace upon the question until the opponents of slavery arrest the further spread of it" (Donald, 1995). During the second debate in Freeport, Illinois, Lincoln questioned Douglas's support of the *Dred Scott* decision, as it seemed to contradict the continued endorsement of a popular sovereignty position. Douglas's response, which thereafter became known as the "Freeport doctrine," was to assert that slavery could effectively be prohibited from any region if local police regulations were not in place to enforce it.

Lincoln addressing the crowd in the famous debates (from a lantern slide). (Corbis-Bettmann)

The debates had far-reaching effects, the least of which was the outcome of the 1858 Illinois legislative races. Voters, to some degree, cast their ballots for legislators based on the senatorial candidates. Although the Democrats carried both houses of the state legislature and reelected Douglas to the Senate, the Republicans showed impressive strength. Also, Douglas, who had been reluctant to enter the debates, lost much of his national prestige. Southern Democrats questioned his view of the use of the federal government to protect slave property, and northerners accused him of pandering to slave interests. In attempting to take a moderate position, Douglas became something of a pariah in an increasingly polarized political climate. Lincoln, the heretofore unknown, emerged from the debates with a national political reputation.

Most important, the debates brought increased attention to the issue of slavery and its expansion. Two years later, in the presidential campaign of 1860 in which Lincoln and Douglas were both can-

didates, the debates took on increased political importance. Douglas, whose earlier positions had angered southerners, could not unite the Democratic Party. Lincoln, on the other hand, was able to use his speeches to attract free soil Democrats and former Whigs to win the election. So this series of debates, which began as a forum for senatorial candidates in Illinois, contributed in no small way to the course of American history during its most trying time.

—*Richard D. Starnes*

For Further Reading
Donald, David. 1995. *Lincoln*. New York: Simon and Schuster; Jaffa, Harry. 1959. *Crisis of the House Divided: An Interpretation of the Lincoln-Douglas Debates*. Garden City, NJ: Doubleday; Johannsen, Robert. 1989. *The Frontier, the Union, and Stephen A. Douglas*. Urbana: University of Illinois Press; Johannsen, Robert. 1973. *Stephen A. Douglas*. New York: Oxford University Press.

Like many other "doctrines" throughout history, Stephen Douglas's Freeport doctrine was the result of political expediency, but despite its humble origins, the Freeport doctrine illuminated a great deal about Abraham Lincoln's political ascent in the late-1850s and Douglas's decline. Douglas's reply to Lincoln's question about the future of slavery in the territories during the debate of August 27, 1858, says volumes about the breakdown of national consensus at that time.

Stephen Douglas and Abraham Lincoln's second debate of the 1858 Senate campaign occurred at Freeport, Illinois, a town close to the Wisconsin border. Most accounts agree that Lincoln had been placed on the defensive during the first debate, and in order to regain momentum, Lincoln decided to ask Douglas several questions at Freeport, including Douglas's opinion on whether residents of a territory could decide to prohibit slavery before a state constitution was drafted. This ostensibly straightforward question was based on the background of the Kansas-Nebraska Act, the recent turmoil in Kansas, and the *Dred Scott* decision. Lincoln hoped to portray Douglas as a leader preaching a contradiction between the popular sovereignty philosophy behind the Kansas-Nebraska Act and the proslavery attitudes of James Buchanan and the Supreme Court. However Douglas replied, his stand would cost him much needed political support. To oppose slavery in the territories would lose southern support for Douglas; to support *Dred Scott* and the proslavery Lecompton Constitution in Kansas would cause northern Democrats to desert him. Douglas opted for consistency and denied that *Dred Scott,* presidential pressure, or any other obstacle would keep people in a territory from prohibiting slavery.

Douglas's reply became known as the Freeport doctrine, despite the fact that he had frequently taken the same stand in several previous public speeches. The exchange may have won Lincoln some momentum, although the heavily Republican composition of the crowd may have accounted for much of it, but Lincoln still lost the election to Douglas, despite the points he scored getting his opponent to commit to the Freeport doctrine.

While Lincoln was still alive, a heated debate about his motives in getting Douglas to state the Freeport doctrine arose, and the debate continued into the twentieth century. Lincoln admirers developed an elaborate legend that Lincoln asked a question of minimal interest to Illinois voters because he intended to run for president in 1860. Lincoln scholars have meticulously debunked the legend, but its persistence is a tribute to the compulsion of Americans to posthumously endow great leaders with superhuman powers of foresight.

A balanced historical understanding of the Freeport doctrine should place it in the context of the debate strategies of Lincoln and Douglas. For Lincoln, the goal was to focus on slavery and to prevent Douglas from dodging the issue. For Douglas, the goal was to portray Lincoln as a black Republican (i.e., he was pro-abolitionist) committed to legal and political equality with white Americans. Both candidates hammered away at these issues during the 1858 debates, and it was only in retrospect, when viewed by people who knew the outcome, that Douglas's remarks at Freeport were elevated to the status of a doctrine.

All debunking aside, the Freeport doctrine still offers valuable insights into what was happening in the United States at that time. What happened at Freeport was part of each candidate's strategy to portray himself as a moderate on the divisive issue of slavery. Unfortunately, by 1858 moderation was no longer admired or emulated in American politics, and it would take more than a series of debates to confront the legal and moral implications of slavery for the Union.

—*Michael Polley*

For Further Reading
Donald, David, H. 1995. *Lincoln.* New York: Simon and Schuster; Fehrenbacher, Don E. 1987. *Lincoln in Text and Context: Collected Essays.* Palo Alto, CA: Stanford University Press; Holt, Michael. 1978. *The Political Crisis of the 1850s.* New York: Norton.

1859

The U.S. Supreme Court decided the case of *Ableman v. Booth* on March 7. The case had begun in 1854 when the Wisconsin Supreme Court had freed Sherman M. Booth, an abolitionist editor, after he had been convicted in a federal court of violating the federal Fugitive Slave Act. The Supreme Court maintained that states did not have the right to interfere in federal cases and upheld the constitutionality of the Fugitive Slave Act of 1850. In light of the ruling, the Wisconsin state legislature declared that "this assumption of jurisdiction by the federal judiciary . . . is an act of undelegated power, void, and of no force" (Schlesinger, 1983). In an unusual twist of fate, it was a northern antislavery state that used the argument of states' rights to defend its actions.

1859

In Vicksburg, Mississippi, southern delegates gathered on May 12 to participate in the annual Southern Commercial Convention. Delegates to the convention approved a resolution stating, "In the opinion of this Convention, all laws, State or Federal, prohibiting the African Slave Trade, ought to be repealed" (Schlesinger, 1983), and the measure was approved despite the opposition of several delegates from Tennessee and Florida.

1859

In Kansas Territory, delegates gathered at Wyandotte on July 5 to hold a constitutional convention. The primary issue debated concerned whether or not Kansas should allow slavery. On October 4, 1859, Kansas voters ratified a constitution that contained antislavery provisions, approving the measure by a nearly two-to-one margin.

1859

The New England Colored Citizens' Convention was held in Boston, Massachusetts, August 1–2.

1859

On August 20, John Brown held a secret meeting with Frederick Douglass at a stone quarry near Chambersburg, Pennsylvania. Brown told Douglass of his planned raid at Harpers Ferry in the hope of gaining Douglass's support of the project. Douglass cautioned Brown that the plan was ill-advised and refused to offer his support.

1859

Harriet E. Wilson, a free black woman, published the novel *Our Nig; or, Sketches from the Life of a Free Black* in Boston on September 5. The work was the first novel to be written by an African-American woman and the first novel to be published by an African American author in the United States. It was also the first work to explore the exploitation and race-based abuse that free blacks faced in the North.

1859

John Brown and his associates (13 whites and 5 blacks) raided the U.S. Army arsenal at Harpers Ferry, Virginia, on October 16 and 17 hoping to seize weapons that would help foment a massive slave uprising. During the attack, 2 blacks were killed, 2 were captured, and 1 escaped. Brown was captured by forces led by Colonel Robert E. Lee and transported to Charleston, Virginia, where he was tried for treason, convicted, and executed by hanging. As a result of his death on December 2, Brown became a martyr of the abolitionist cause for many people. Four black coconspirators—Shields Green, Dangerfield Newby, Sherrard Lewis Leary, and John A. Copeland—were also hanged. [See Document 63.]

1859

A speech about the death of John Brown was delivered at the Tremont Temple in Boston, Massachusetts, by the abolitionist editor William Lloyd Garrison on December 2. [See Document 64.]

1859

The House of Representatives took two months to settle the question of who would serve as Speaker of the House. Ohio Congressman John Sherman had hoped to win the post, but his earlier endorsement of Hinton Rowan Helper's book, *The Impending Crisis,* made him an unacceptable candidate to southern congressmen. In the end, on December 5 the House elected New Jersey Congressman William Pennington as the Speaker of the House of Representatives for the Thirty-sixth Congress.

1859

On December 14, the Georgia state legislature enacted a measure that made it illegal for a slaveowner to manumit slaves through a final will or testament.

1859

Two black accomplices of John Brown, John A. Copeland and Shields Green, were hanged on December 16 at Charleston, Virginia, for their role in the failed raid on the Harpers Ferry arsenal.

1859

On December 17, the Georgia state legislature enacted a measure that said that any free black

An illustration from William Still's classic Underground Railroad *(1872) depicting slavecatchers invading a barn that served as a station on the Underground Railroad. (Library of Congress)*

in the state of Georgia who was indicted for vagrancy could be sold as a slave.

1859

President James Buchanan used the occasion of his annual message to Congress on December 19 to state his opposition to any effort to reestablish the African slave trade. Although Buchanan pledged to use the government's resources to stop the illegal slave trading that had persisted, he also criticized the detention and search of American merchant vessels by British patrols off the coast of West Africa.

1860

The results of the eighth census of the United States revealed that of the more than 8 million white residents of the South, only 383,637 were identified as slaveowners. The black population, both slave and free, was recorded at 4,401,830, 14.1 percent of the nation's population. Of this total, 448,070 were identified as free blacks, and 3,953,760 were slaves.

1860

Free blacks in New York State petitioned the legislature to grant them equal suffrage rights with white citizens.

1860

Although involvement in the African slave trade had been illegal since January 1, 1808, *The Clothilde,* the last recorded slave ship to carry slaves to the United States, landed a shipment of Africans at Mobile, Alabama.

1860

The approximate price of a slave field hand was between $1,200 and $1,800.

1860

Skilled slave artisans could earn $500–$600 per year by hiring their services out in the community. They had to have the approval of their owners to do so, and the owners generally received a portion of the money earned.

1860

The legislature of the state of Virginia enacted a measure that made it possible for free blacks to be sold into slavery as punishment for committing acts that would otherwise lead to imprisonment.

1860

Legislators in Maryland outlawed the practice of manumission in the state.

1860

Abraham Lincoln, in a speech prior to his nomination as a presidential candidate, identified slavery "as an evil not to be extended, but to be tolerated and protected only because of and so far as its actual presence among us makes that toleration and protection necessary" (Jenkins, 1996).

1860

In the U.S. Senate, Senator Jefferson Davis of Mississippi introduced a series of resolutions on February 2 that maintained the federal government did not have the authority to prevent the expansion of slavery into the western territories and said the government must actually protect slaveholders and their property in those regions. Although Davis was aware that the Senate would not support these measures, his effort was more of a calculated political move that was aimed at swaying the Senate's Democrats to this position. Davis hoped to derail the presidential aspirations of Illinois Senator Stephen A. Douglas, who was an advocate of the popular sovereignty position.

1860

On February 27, Abraham Lincoln delivered an address to the Young Men's Central Republican Union at the Cooper Institute in New York City. In the speech, Lincoln outlined the principles of the Republican Party and stated his no-compromise position on the issue of slavery. The publicity attained from this address helped to make Lincoln a frontrunner for the Republican Party's presidential nomination.

1860

The Democratic Party held its national nominating convention in Charleston, South Carolina, on April 23–May 3. The party rejected a proslavery plank in its platform, a decision that caused the delegates from eight southern states to walk out. The convention adjourned without selecting a presidential nominee for the Democratic Party.

1860

The Constitutional Union Party was formed at a convention in Baltimore, Maryland, on May 9 as southern unionists, former members of the Whig Party, and former members of the American (Know-Nothing) Party came together in an effort to preserve national unity through effective compromise. These like-minded delegates believed that secession was a greater evil than slavery. The platform of the Constitutional Union Party did not mention slavery, but the party pledged loyalty to the Union, support for the Constitution, and a willingness to enforce all national laws. The party nominated John Bell of Tennessee for the presidency and Edward Everett of Massachusetts for vice-president.

1860

The Republican Party held its nominating convention in Chicago, Illinois, on May 16–18 and nominated Abraham Lincoln of Illinois as its presidential candidate and Hannibal Hamlin of Maine as the vice-presidential candidate. The Republican platform stated the party's opposition to the expansion of slavery into the western territories but pledged that the party would not interfere with slavery in the states where it already existed.

1860

As a result of their failed convention in Charleston, South Carolina, the Democratic Party held a second nominating convention in Baltimore, Maryland, on June 18–23. Southern delegates again stormed out of the convention in protest of the party's unwillingness to include a strong proslavery plank in its platform. After the southern delegates left the convention, the remaining delegates selected Illinois Senator Stephen A. Douglas to be the party's presidential nominee and Herschel V. Johnson of Georgia as the vice-presidential nominee.

1860

The southern delegates who had walked out of the Democratic Party conventions in Charleston and Baltimore held their own rump convention in Baltimore on June 28 and drafted a party platform that demanded federal protection of the right to own slaves. The delegates nominated the current vice-president, John C. Breckinridge of Kentucky, as their presidential nominee and Senator Joseph Lane of Oregon for the vice-presidency.

1860

On November 6, Abraham Lincoln was elected

The Democratic Party was one of the two major political parties in pre–Civil War United States. Although historians debate whether the party came into being to protect the interests of slaveholding southerners, the party had become identified by 1860 as the staunch defender of slavery. The Democratic Party, which for so long had supported the right of slaveholding southerners to move their property into the disputed western territories, ended up a casualty of the sectional discord that engulfed the nation in 1860. In that year, the party split into two wings, northern and southern, with each wing running its own presidential candidate.

The Democratic Party came into being around 1826. Its principal architect was the veteran New York politician Martin Van Buren, and the principal reason for the creation of this party was to help elect Andrew Jackson president in 1828. In lining up newspaper editors in various states, which offered Jackson the opportunity to spread his message to potential voters, Van Buren laid the groundwork for the first mass political party. Though not explicitly formed to protect slavery, this new party, with a Tennessee slaveholder as its first presidential candidate, did not offend any slaveholder or threaten the right to hold slave property, and Democratic Party ideology reinforced this sense of security among slaveholders. The party carried on the Jeffersonian tradition of advocating a limited national government, promoting states' rights, and making the primary task of the national government the maintenance of order and the protection of private property. The Democratic Party, particularly its southern wing, viewed the ownership of slaves not only as the right to own constitutionally protected private property but also as an example of liberty.

From 1830 to 1860, the Democratic Party upheld the rights of slaveholders as the abolitionist movement gained strength in the North. In 1835, President Jackson responded to the burning of abolitionist literature that had been seized from a South Carolina post office by instructing his postmaster, Amos Kendall, not to forward this type of material to the South. Jackson viewed such abolitionist tactics as threats to the sanctity of the Union. In 1836, the Democratic Party–controlled House of Representatives approved the gag rule, which laid aside, without opportunity for debate, abolitionist petitions sent to Congress. The gag rule lasted until 1844, when the House repealed the measure. Thus, to a large degree, the politics of slavery negated freedom of speech.

In 1846, the first sign of a split in party unity appeared. During the Mexican War, David Wilmot, a freshman representative from Pennsylvania, introduced a resolution that would forbid the introduction of slavery into any territory acquired from Mexico as a result of the war. Though the House repeatedly passed the proviso, the Senate never approved the measure and Wilmot's proposal died in Congress. The Compromise of 1850 resolved the issue, though neither satisfactorily nor for very long.

The issue of the expansion of slavery into the territories introduced a North-South sectional division not only into American politics generally but also into the Democratic Party. The Fugitive Slave Act of 1850 proved to be highly unpopular in the North and strengthened the abolitionist movement. In 1854, Congress approved the Kansas-Nebraska Act, the brainchild of Democratic senator Stephen A. Douglas, which effectively repealed the Missouri Compromise of 1820. Slavery could now spread to the territories if the residents of a territory, through popular sovereignty, decided to allow slavery in that territory. A sense of outrage swept across the North, and in 1854, voters elected not to return most Democrats to the House of Representatives—the number of northern Democrats in the House fell from 91 to 25. As a result, southern Democrats dominated the party in the national government, and northerners came increasingly to identify the Democratic Party as the party of the South and of slavery.

New political parties that favored the exclusion of slavery from the territories, such as the American (Know-Nothing) Party and the Republican Party, fostered such a policy through their campaign rhetoric, and abolitionists and their political allies accused northern Democrats who supported southern interests of being tools of "the slave power." By 1860, the breach between the two wings of the Democratic Party had become irreparable, and the party split at the conventions held in Charleston, South Carolina, and Baltimore, Maryland, and each section ran a candidate agreeable to its position on slavery.

—*James C. Foley*

For Further Reading
Cooper, William. 1978. *The South and the Politics of Slavery, 1828–1856*. Baton Rouge: Louisiana State University Press; Freehling, William. 1990. *The Road to Disunion*. New York: Oxford University Press; Holt, Michael. 1978. *The Political Crisis of the 1850s*. New York: John Wiley and Sons; Potter, David. 1976. *The Impending Crisis, 1848–1861*. New York: Harper and Row.

to the presidency of the United States on a platform that opposed the extension of slavery into the western territories. Lincoln garnered only 40 percent of the popular vote in a race that featured four prominent candidates, but he won handily in the Electoral College.

1860

In December, President James Buchanan urged Congress to pass constitutional amendments that upheld the fugitive slave acts.

1860

On December 18, Senator John J. Crittenden of Kentucky chaired a special Senate committee that sought to find an eleventh-hour compromise that might prevent the secession of the southern states and the possibility of civil war. Among other things, Crittenden's compromise measures included the call for a constitutional amendment that would have taken the 36-degree 30-minute north latitude boundary, first used in the Missouri Compromise of 1820, and applied it across all of the western territories. The efforts of Crittenden's committee were ineffective. President-elect Abraham Lincoln had been elected on a platform that called for prohibiting the expansion of slavery into the western territories, and Lincoln could not support a measure that would have granted the possibility of slavery expanding into those lands. [See Document 65.]

1860

On December 20, South Carolina became the first southern state to secede from the Union by declaring itself to be an "independent commonwealth." By February 1, 1861, six other southern states had followed South Carolina out of the Union—Mississippi (January 9), Florida (January 10), Alabama (January 11), Georgia (January 19), Louisiana (January 26), and Texas (February 1).

1861

Harriet Jacobs published *Incidents in the Life of a Slave Girl*. The work, considered to be one of the most important slave narratives, presents a vivid portrayal of the multifaceted exploitation faced by women who were slaves.

1861

Delegates from the seven southern states that

Stephen A. Douglas (Library of Congress/Corbis)

had seceded from the Union met at Montgomery, Alabama, on February 4–9 and adopted the provisional constitution of the Confederate States of America. On February 9, the body elected Senator Jefferson Davis of Mississippi as the provisional president of the Confederacy.

1861

On February 18, Confederate President Jefferson Davis described slavery as a practice "as necessary to self-preservation" in his inaugural address (Jenkins, 1996).

1861

In March, Alexander Stephens, vice-president of the Confederate States of America, stated that his government "rests upon the great truth that the Negro is not equal to the white man, that slavery, subordination to the superior race, is a natural and normal condition . . . our new Government, is the first in the history of the world, based upon this great physical, philosophical, and moral truth" (Jenkins, 1996).

❧STEPHEN A. DOUGLAS (1813–1861)❧

Despite being of small stature, Stephen A. Douglas cast a long shadow in the tumultuous political period before the American Civil War. Intelligent, charismatic, and politically astute, Douglas's belief in the indissolubility of the Constitution and the importance of political compromise in order to preserve the Union placed him at the forefront of the debate over slavery in the United States.

Born on a farm in Brandon, New York, on April 23, 1813, Stephen Arnold Douglas had a very typical childhood for youth of the period even though his father, a physician, died shortly after Stephen's birth and his mother was forced to move in with her brother. As a child, he did farm chores, attended the local common school, and aspired to a better, more secure future. At 15, he apprenticed himself to a local cabinetmaker, a trade he practiced for two years before physical disability and a love of politics led him in new directions. He entered the Canandaigua Academy in 1830 and obtained a classical education at his own expense. He began to read law, recognizing that that profession was the traditional route to political office, but stringent requirements for the New York bar and rumors of opportunity in the west led him to Illinois in 1833. Once there, he was quickly admitted to the bar and became active in Democratic Party politics.

An avid Jacksonian, Douglas was more adept at politics than law. In rapid succession, he was elected a state attorney, legislator, secretary of state, and superior court judge, and all the while, he honed his oratorical skills and strengthened his political connections. Elected to the U.S. Congress in 1843, he soon became a powerful force in national politics. Dubbed "the little giant," a dual reference to his powerful oratory and his small stature, one of Douglas's most common political themes was a strong belief in popular democracy. Douglas believed strongly in the ability of the people to make proper decisions through the electoral process. By the end of the Mexican War (1846–1848), he had realized that slavery's westward expansion was the most volatile issue in American politics. In 1846, he voted against the Wilmot Proviso, which would have banned slavery in territory acquired from Mexico, because he believed that the question of whether or not to exclude slavery would be best made by voters through their territorial legislatures. This, according to Douglas, was the most democratic and least divisive way to cope with the issue.

Thus, popular sovereignty, as the concept was called, came to dominate, and in some ways haunt, Douglas's political philosophy for the rest of his life. Initially, this position gave him widespread popularity, as many voters and politicians were ambivalent on the issue of slavery expansion and appealing to the democratic ethos of the electorate seemed to be the best and least divisive solution. In 1854, Douglas, as chairman of the important Committee on Territories, used this principle as the basis of the controversial Kansas-Nebraska Act, which allowed each individual territory to determine its slavery status. Although the debates surrounding the bill were bitterly divisive, the Kansas-Nebraska Act passed by a narrow margin. Through this important legislation, Douglas repealed the Missouri Compromise, which had regulated slavery's expansion since 1820. Douglas argued that popular sentiment, not accidents of geography, should determine the future of slavery in a newly admitted state.

That faith in democracy worked well in theory but poorly in practice. Nebraska voted to remain free, but Kansas erupted in civil war. The conflict in Kansas between free- and slave-state advocates resulted in the destruction of property, many deaths, and two different constitutions. Slavery proponents produced the controversial Lecompton Constitution, which legalized slavery in Kansas, and soon gained the support of President James Buchanan and southern Democrats in Congress. Douglas, however, opposed the Lecompton Constitution, believing correctly that it did not represent the majority of Kansans. This stand tarnished Douglas in the eyes of many southern Democrats.

Although the crisis in Kansas occupied much of his time, Douglas faced political opposition at home. Free soil Democrats criticized Douglas for what they perceived as a willingness to sacrifice morality in pursuit of higher office. To them, popular sovereignty was a veiled mechanism to protect slave interests. In Illinois, the Republican Party quickly gained political power after 1856, uniting former Whigs and Free soil Democrats to fight slavery's expansion, and Douglas became the target of the Republicans during the legislative race in 1858. The Senate seat, which the legislature would fill, became an important campaign issue, and candidates campaigned actively for this office. This unusual campaign for the seat pitted Republican Abraham Lincoln against Douglas, and the race was defined by the issue of slavery. In a series of seven debates, the two candidates offered opposing views of slavery and slavery expansion. Lincoln favored restricting slavery's westward movement, realizing that the institution would eventually die out. Douglas held firm to the theory of popular sovereignty as the most democratic means to address slavery expansion. Although Lincoln condemned slavery on moral grounds, Douglas refused to do so, hoping to revive his reputation among disaffected southern Democrats. Douglas returned to the Senate, but the issue remained in the forefront of his activities.

In 1860, Douglas sought the Democratic presidential nomination. His opposition to the proslavery Lecompton Constitution made southerners suspicious of his true beliefs, and they nominated John C. Breckinridge for the presidency while northerners backed Douglas. This sectional split destroyed Democratic hopes and allowed the Republican Abraham Lincoln to win the election. Douglas's belief in popular sovereignty as a remedy for slavery expansion, while true to his belief in popular democracy, dashed his hopes for national office. He died in 1861, shortly after Lincoln's inauguration.

—*Richard D. Starnes*

For Further Reading

Johannsen, Robert. 1989. *The Frontier, the Union, and Stephen A. Douglas.* Urbana: University of Illinois Press; Johannsen, Robert. 1973. *Stephen A. Douglas.* New York: Oxford University Press.

1861

On March 2, the U.S. Congress adopted a proposed constitutional amendment to be sent to the states for ratification. The proposed amendment stated that the federal government would have no right to subsequent action that would "abolish or interfere . . . with the domestic institutions" of the states (Jenkins, 1996). As a result of the outbreak of the American Civil War in April 1861, the proposal was not ratified by the states.

1861

Abraham Lincoln was inaugurated as the nation's sixteenth president in Washington, D.C., on March 4. In his inaugural address, Lincoln stated unequivocally, "I have no purpose . . . to interfere with the institution of slavery." Nonetheless, Lincoln cautioned the southern states: "In *your* hands, my dissatisfied fellow countrymen, and not in *mine,* is the momentous issue of civil war. The government will not assail *you.* You can have no conflict, without being yourselves the aggressors. *You* have no oath registered in Heaven to destroy the government, while *I* shall have the most solemn one to 'preserve, protect and defend' it" (Schlesinger, 1983).

1861

Confederate forces began the bombardment of the federal garrison at Fort Sumter in Charleston Harbor, South Carolina, on April 12. This incident marked the beginning of the American Civil War.

1861

On April 15, President Lincoln issued a national call for 75,000 troops for three months. Rather than describing the situation as one of war, he used the word "rebellion." Free black troops sought to respond to Lincoln's call but were rejected.

1861

On May 20, North Carolina became the eleventh, and final, southern state to secede from the Union. Other states of the upper South had waited until after the incident at Fort Sumter before deciding upon secession, but once it was clear that Abraham Lincoln would use force against the South, four additional states seceded, joining the seven that had left the Union earlier. Besides North Carolina, the other three states were Virginia (April 17), Arkansas (May 6), and Tennessee (May 6).

1861

On May 24, Union General Benjamin F. Butler put a group of fugitive slaves to work at Fort Monroe, Virginia. Butler described the fugitives as "contraband of war."

1861

In the summer, slaves on several plantations located along Second Creek in Adams County, Mississippi, planned an uprising that was to coincide with the arrival of Union troops in the region. Local planters discovered the plot, executed nearly 40 slaves who were suspected of involvement, and then kept silent about the extent of the plot in the hope that other slaves might not be inspired to similar acts by the episode.

1861

On July 22, the U.S. Senate declared that "this

Contrabands, as slaves liberated during the Civil War were known, follow a railroad track to work in this 1862 engraving. Freed slaves were paid a small wage to work for the Union army. (Library of Congress)

war is not waged . . . for any purpose . . . of overthrowing or interfering with the rights or established institutions of . . . southern States." The resolution further stated that the specific aim of the war was "to preserve the Union," not the abolition of slavery in the southern states (Schlesinger, 1983).

1861
With the passage of the first Confiscation Act on August 6, Congress authorized the freeing of those slaves who were in regions under Union army control and who had previously been employed to aid the Confederate cause.

1861
Acting upon his own initiative and without the backing of officials in Washington, D.C., Major General John C. Frémont invoked martial law on August 30 and issued a proclamation that freed the slaves of all disloyal owners in Missouri. Lincoln effectively nullified the order by asking Frémont to revise his proclamation so it would not overstep congressional laws regarding emancipation. Lincoln later reassigned Frémont to a different department.

1861
In September, the Union army officially rejected the application of free black volunteers who had offered their services to fight in the war, even though black volunteers had already fought on behalf of the Confederacy both on land and at sea.

1861
On September 11, General John C. Frémont refused to comply with President Lincoln's request that he revise his proclamation that freed the slaves of disloyal owners in Missouri. Using his power as commander in chief of the nation's armed forces, Lincoln ordered Frémont to comply.

1861
Mary Peake, a black teacher, established a school at Fort Monroe, Virginia, on September 17. This school marked the beginning of what eventually became the Hampton Institute.

1861
The secretary of the navy authorized the enlistment of black slaves on September 25.

1861

At President Lincoln's request, Secretary of War Simon Cameron deleted several controversial clauses from his annual report to Congress on December 1. The passages in question had advocated the use of emancipation as a wartime necessity and related to the use of former slaves as military laborers and soldiers. Lincoln would soon removed Secretary Cameron from the War Department by naming him minister to Russia and appointed Edwin M. Stanton as his replacement as secretary of war.

1862

In Memphis, Tennessee, the Lincoln School for Negroes was established as an elementary school for black children. The institution eventually grew and developed into LeMoyne-Owen College.

1862

The First Regiment Louisiana Heavy Artillery and the Massachusetts Fifty-fourth and Fifty-fifth Infantry Regiments were formed. These units were the first authorized black combat units to be used in the Civil War.

1862

The National Freedmen's Relief Association was established in New York City in March. The purpose of this organization was to help former slaves to make the transition from slavery to freedom. Similar freedmen's societies were eventually established in Boston, Philadelphia, Cincinnati, and Chicago, and these groups were later consolidated into the American Freedmen's Aid Commission under the leadership of James Miller McKim.

1862

On March 6, Abraham Lincoln sent a message to the Congress in which he proposed that a plan of gradual, compensated emancipation be enacted.

1862

With the adoption of a new article of war on March 13, Congress prohibited northern military commanders from capturing any fugitive slaves or helping to return any fugitives to their owners.

1862

On April 3, Union General David (Black David) Hunter requested permission from the War Department to recruit blacks in the South Carolina Sea Islands and arm them for military service. When officials in Washington, D.C., failed to respond to his request, Hunter initiated the plan on his own accord.

1862

On April 10, the U.S. Congress agreed to cooperate with any state that sought to establish a plan of gradual abolition of slavery with compensated emancipation.

1862

Congress ended slavery in the nation's capital on April 16 when a program of compensated emancipation for slaves in the District of Columbia was enacted into law. Congress appropriated $1 million to compensate the owners of slaves freed by this measure and also appropriated $100,000 for the resettlement of freed blacks in Liberia, Haiti, or other locations that were deemed appropriate. [See Document 66.]

1862

Without prior approval of Union military authorities, General David (Black David) Hunter organized the First South Carolina Volunteers on May 9, the first all-black regiment to be formed during the Civil War. (Later, when the War Department failed to pay or equip the regiment, Hunter was forced to disband it.) On the same day, and again without the backing of officials in Washington, D.C., Hunter issued a proclamation that freed the slaves owned by all rebels in Georgia, Florida, and South Carolina.

1862

On May 13, the slave Robert Smalls commandeered a Confederate steamer, *The Planter*, and surrendered it to the Union navy as war booty in Charleston Harbor, South Carolina. Smalls would later serve as a congressman during the Reconstruction era.

1862

On May 19, President Lincoln revoked the proclamation issued by General Hunter on May 9. Lincoln feared that an emancipation edict instituted in any setting might be sufficient cause to encourage the border states to leave the

First South Carolina Volunteers, the first all-black regiment formed during the Civil War, 1862. (Library of Congress)

Union. Lincoln urged the border states (Missouri, Kentucky, Maryland, and Delaware) to adopt a program of gradual, compensated emancipation.

1862
The U.S. Congress approved a resolution on June 19 that prohibited slavery from all federal territories, but not the states.

1862
On July 12, President Lincoln lobbied the senators and congressmen from the four border states to support a plan of gradual, compensated emancipation, which would be followed by the systematic colonization of freed slaves to points outside the United States. Lincoln cautioned that if the political leaders failed to act, slavery "will be extinguished by mere friction and abrasion—by the mere incidents of the war" (Jenkins, 1996). On July 14, the political leaders from the border states voted to reject Lincoln's proposal.

1862
On July 17, Congress enacted the second Confiscation Act, which granted freedom to slaves of masters who supported the Confederacy but did not provide for universal emancipation. With the passage of this measure, the president was also authorized to employ "persons of African descent" in any fashion deemed necessary, including their use as armed troops in military service. On the same day, Congress also enacted the Militia Act, which permitted the employment of blacks in "any military or naval service for which they may be found competent." The measure also bestowed freedom upon any slave who was employed in this capacity.

1862
Abraham Lincoln first submitted a working draft of the Emancipation Proclamation to his cabinet on July 22. It was the decision of the cabinet that the president should wait until a major Union victory was achieved on the battlefield before making the proclamation public.

Consequently, Lincoln postponed announcement until after the Union victory in the Battle of Antietam on September 17.

1862
Acting upon his own initiative, General Jim Lane began to organize the First Kansas Colored Volunteers in August.

1862
Abraham Lincoln held a meeting with prominent black leaders on August 14 in which he urged them to support a colonization plan either to Central America or to Africa. Although this was the first time an American president had conferred with black leaders on a matter of public policy, many free blacks in the North were highly critical of President Lincoln's suggestions.

1862
Shortly after the capture of New Orleans, General Benjamin F. Butler, acting on his own initiative, issued a call on August 22 for the free blacks of New Orleans to organize a military unit in support of the Union cause. On the same date, President Lincoln responded to Horace Greeley's editorial "A Prayer of Twenty Millions," which had appeared in the August 20 edition of the *New York Tribune*. Greeley's editorial was, in effect, an open letter to the president calling for action on the issue of emancipation. Despite having previously drafted the Emancipation Proclamation, Lincoln responded to Greeley's challenge by stating: "My paramount object in this struggle *is* to save the Union, and it is *not* either to save or to destroy slavery. If I could save the Union without freeing *any* slave I would do it, and if I could save it by freeing *all* the slaves I would do it; and if I could save it by freeing some and leaving others alone I would also do that." [See Document 67.]

1862
On August 25, Secretary of War Edwin M. Stanton authorized General Rufus Saxton, commander of the Southern Department, to arm up to 5,000 slaves and to train them as guards for plantations and settlements in the South Carolina Sea Islands.

1862
On September 22, Abraham Lincoln issued the preliminary draft of his Emancipation Proclamation shortly after the Union victory in the Battle of Antietam on September 17. In this statement, President Lincoln warned the southern states that he intended to free the slaves in all regions that remained in rebellion against the national government on January 1, 1863. Lincoln also used this occasion to pledge financial support to any border state that adopted a program of gradual, compensated emancipation. He also stated his support for the colonization of freed slaves to points outside the United States, such as Liberia and Haiti. [See Document 67.]

1862
On September 23, only one day after publicly announcing the Emancipation Proclamation and stating his intention to end slavery, Abraham Lincoln met with his cabinet to discuss the acquisition of new territory that might be used for the deportation of free blacks upon the abolition of slavery.

1862
The First Louisiana Native Guards, the first black regiment to receive officially sanctioned recognition by the U.S. government, was mustered into service on September 27 to assist the Union army. Free blacks from New Orleans composed most of the membership of this regiment.

1862
Fearing the potential for unrest on plantations that might arise because of the absence of proper supervision, the Confederate Congress enacted a measure on October 11 that exempted from military service those slaveowners who held more than 20 slaves. Many cynics observed that this action was another example of how the American Civil War was a rich man's war but a poor man's fight.

1862
On October 28, black troops took part in battle for the first time during the American Civil War. The First Kansas Colored Volunteers, which had been organized by General Jim Lane, engaged and repulsed a large rebel force at Island Mound, Missouri.

1862
Still supporting a plan of compensated emancipation, Abraham Lincoln sent a message to Congress on December 1 urging that federal

Artist's rendering of a Union soldier reading the Emancipation Proclamation to a group of slaves in their home. In fact the proclamation initially applied only to slaves in areas still under Confederate control. (Library of Congress)

bonds be used to fund a compensation scheme for those states that agreed to abolish slavery before 1900.

1862
Confederate President Jefferson Davis signed an order on December 23 immediately mandating that any black Union troops and the white officers who commanded them when captured in battle were not to be treated as prisoners of war but rather were to be turned over to state authorities and prosecuted as criminals.

1863
With the support of President Abraham Lincoln, an American vessel carried 500 black settlers to Cow Island off the coast of Haiti, but the colonization attempt failed.

1863
On January 1, the Emancipation Proclamation

became effective, and all slaves were declared free except those in states, or parts of states, that were no longer in rebellion. The proclamation did not apply in the border states, nor did it apply in areas that were already under control of the Union army. These areas included 13 parishes in southern Louisiana (including the city of New Orleans), the 48 counties that made up West Virginia, 7 counties in eastern Virginia (including the city of Norfolk), and the state of Tennessee. President Lincoln also announced the Union's intention of recruiting blacks as sailors and soldiers. [See Document 67.]

1863
On January 26, Secretary of War Edwin M. Stanton authorized the governor of Massachusetts, John A. Andrew, to organize a company of black troops. The Fifty-fourth Massachusetts Volunteers, under the command of Colonel

Provost Guards attack draft rioters in New York. Opposition to the draft combined with hostility to blacks prompted mobs of mostly poor whites to riot, July 13–17, 1863. (Corbis-Bettmann)

Robert Gould Shaw, was the first black regiment to be raised in the North.

1863

In February, Pennsylvania Congressman Thaddeus Stevens pushed a bill through Congress that called for the enlistment of 150,000 U.S. Colored Troops.

1863

The city of Jacksonville, Florida, was captured and occupied on March 10 by the First and Second South Carolina—two black regiments. The fear of white communities being occupied by black troops caused great distress in many parts of the South.

1863

On March 16, Secretary of War Edwin M. Stanton established the American Freedmen's Inquiry Commission within the War Department. This commission was charged with investigating the conditions faced by freed slaves and making recommendations that would aid their future welfare and potential for employment.

1863

The Confederate Congress, responding to the worst fears of white southerners, declared on May 1 that all black troops, and the white officers who commanded them, would thereafter be considered criminals in the South. For blacks, this action meant that black troops captured in battle would either be executed or forced into slavery. If the white officers who commanded blacks were captured, they would be executed.

1863

The U.S. War Department issued General Order No. 143 on May 22, which placed control of black troops under the U.S. Colored Troops. An aggressive recruiting campaign to attract black troops who were willing to fight for the cause of freedom began.

1863

In July, 30 regiments of U.S. Colored Troops were armed and equipped.

1863

Draft riots occurred in New York City on July

Storming Fort Wagner, an 1890 lithograph depicting the famous assault by the 54th Massachusetts (Colored) Regiment, July 18, 1863, in which over 1,200 men were killed or wounded. (The Granger Collection)

13–17, and white mobs displayed a vast amount of antiblack sentiment in perhaps the bloodiest race riot in American history—1,200 deaths, mostly blacks, were reported. The combined effects of fearing the economic competition of free blacks, the new cause of freedom for which the war was being waged, and hostility to the draft all contributed to the rage among poor white immigrant mobs in New York City.

1863
On July 18, the Fifty-fourth Massachusetts Volunteers, an all-black regiment, made its famous assault upon Fort Wagner at Charleston Harbor, South Carolina.

1863
On July 30, Abraham Lincoln announced that the U.S. government would "give the same protection to all its soldiers, and if the enemy shall sell or enslave anyone because of his color, the offense shall be punished by retaliation upon the enemy's prisoners in our possession" (Jenkins, 1996). The immediate result of this eye-for-an-eye policy was that the Confederate government backed away from its May 1 position—but individual commanders continued to execute captured black troops.

1863
On October 3, the War Department began recruiting blacks for military service in the border states of Maryland and Missouri and also in the state of Tennessee, which was effectively under Union control. Congress appropriated funding to compensate owners of these slaves, provided the owners had remained loyal unionists throughout the rebellion.

1863
President Abraham Lincoln issued his Proclamation of Amnesty and Reconstruction on December 8, in which he outlined the basis of his Ten Percent Plan, the percentage of voters needed to swear an oath of allegiance to the government. Should southerners take an oath of allegiance to the Union and promise to accept emancipation, Lincoln was willing to offer a

federal pardon and restore all property, except slaves, that had been taken during the rebellion. Lincoln's proposal also outlined the procedure by which the southern states could begin the process of gaining readmission to the Union.

1864
A new federal law enabled northern states to recruit black soldiers in the South.

1864
Sergeant William Walker of the Third South Carolina Regiment was shot by order of a court-martial for protesting against the inequality in pay received by black troops during the Civil War.

1864
Pro-Union voters in occupied Arkansas ratified a new state constitution on March 16 that abolished slavery in the state.

1864
On April 8, the U.S. Senate approved, by a vote of 38 to 6, a proposed constitutional amendment that would abolish slavery in the United States.

1864
On April 12, during the Battle at Fort Pillow, near Memphis, Tennessee, nearly 300 blacks were massacred by Confederate troops under the command of Nathan Bedford Forrest. Confederate troops had been told that black troops used in battle would not be taken as prisoners of war.

1864
On June 7, the U.S. War Department began enlisting blacks into the Union military in the border state of Kentucky whether or not the slaves had the permission of their owners to do so. As was the case in other regions, loyal owners who had maintained unionist sympathies during the rebellion were compensated for the slaves who were taken for military service.

1864
On June 15, the U.S. House of Representatives failed to approve the proposed constitutional amendment abolishing slavery in the United States that the Senate had approved on April 8. There were 95 votes for the measure and 66

against, but the proposed amendment failed because it was 13 votes shy of the two-thirds majority needed for approval before the measure could be sent to the states for ratification. On the same date, Congress equalized the bounties that were paid for enlistment of white and black soldiers with the passage of the army appropriations bill. The same measure equalized pay, arms, equipment, and medical services that were provided to black troops. The adjustment in pay, from $10 per month to $13 per month, was made retroactive to January 1, 1864, for slaves who served in the military, and it was made retroactive to the time of enlistment for all free blacks who served.

1864
On June 20, the U.S. Congress enacted a pay increase for all Union soldiers, black and white alike. Privates would now earn $16 a month.

1864
In July, Congress authorized that families of black troops who had been killed in the war were entitled to receive government pensions.

1864
The Wade-Davis bill, a measure for the radical reconstruction of the South, was passed by both houses of the U.S. Congress on July 2, but Lincoln refused to sign the bill before Congress adjourned.

1864
On July 5, Horace Greeley, editor of the *New York Tribune,* received a letter from Canada suggesting that Confederate diplomats in that country were prepared to negotiate a peaceful settlement to the Civil War. Greeley informed President Lincoln of this correspondence, and on July 9 Lincoln informed Greeley that anyone who wanted to negotiate should contact the proper authorities in Washington, D.C. Nonetheless, Lincoln did allow Greeley to travel to Niagara Falls, Canada, on July 18 to meet with the Confederate diplomats. The negotiations proved to be unsuccessful as the southern negotiators would accept nothing short of southern independence.

1864
In occupied Louisiana, prounionist delegates drafted a new reunion constitution on July 23 at

The Wade-Davis bill, passed by both houses of Congress in 1864, expressed the vision of radical Republicans for the reconstruction of the Confederate states. Drafted by Congressman Henry Winter Davis of Maryland and Senator Benjamin F. Wade of Ohio, two radicals who chaired the Committee on the Rebellious States in their respective chambers, the bill articulated radical opposition to President Abraham Lincoln's own plan of restoration. In December 1863, Lincoln had issued a proclamation declaring that any seceded state could resume its proper position in the Union if 10 percent of its qualified electorate swore an oath of allegiance to the United States and formed a civil government accepting the terms of the Emancipation Proclamation. Lincoln believed that the largely Union-occupied states of Louisiana, Arkansas, and Tennessee would prove receptive to this plan within a short period. Congressional radicals, though, deemed the 10 percent plan too lenient. They wanted, not a simple restoration of the former slave states, but revolutionary measures that guaranteed freedom and civil rights for blacks and that excluded treasonous Confederates from the democratic process. Accordingly, the radical-led Congress passed the Wade-Davis bill as an alternative to Lincoln's program.

The Wade-Davis provisions were more restrictive and punitive than the president's proposals. Unlike the Ten Percent Plan, the former disallowed the wartime formation of popular governments in the South and enjoined the president to assign provisional governors to the states that were in revolt for the duration of the war. Only after hostilities ceased could the rebel states move to regain self-government, and only when a majority of a state's voters swore an "ironclad" oath affirming their loyalty to the Union throughout the entire war. In addition, the Wade-Davis measure denied suffrage rights to former Confederates and proscribed them from holding public office. Finally, the bill required the southern states to adopt new constitutions expressly outlawing slavery.

Congress finalized the Wade-Davis bill on July 2, 1864. Two days later, just hours before the congressional session expired, radical Senators Charles Sumner of Massachusetts and Zachariah Chandler of Michigan rushed the bill to the president for a hurried signature. To their surprise, Lincoln declined to endorse the legislation. Though he agreed with several of the bill's points, he feared its harsh tone would jeopardize the erection of loyal governments in Union-held areas of the South. Moreover, Lincoln objected on constitutional grounds to the provisions mandating the abolition of slavery as a requisite for the readmission of states to the Union. When Chandler insisted that the bill's essential point was "that one prohibiting slavery in the reconstructed states," Lincoln retorted, "That is the point on which I doubt the authority of Congress to act" (Oates, 1977). As the president noted, the Republican Party had always conceded the inability of the federal government to regulate slavery in the states. Of course, Lincoln had done precisely that with the Emancipation Proclamation, but he justified the decree as a wartime measure flowing from the executive powers vested in the nation's commander in chief. Congress, however, possessed no such constitutional authority and thus could not pass upon the issue of slavery in the states. Consequently, Lincoln did not sign the bill before Congress adjourned.

Lincoln's pocket veto of the Wade-Davis bill incensed the radical wing of his party, and radicals generally denounced his position. Wade and Davis, for example, published an incendiary tract accusing Lincoln of usurping legislative prerogatives and disregarding the human rights of blacks. The Wade-Davis manifesto did little to alter Lincoln's stance on Reconstruction, however. Nevertheless, the ideas embodied in the Wade-Davis bill ultimately served as the core principles of congressional guidance of Reconstruction after 1867.

—*Eric Tscheschlok*

For Further Reading
Henig, Gerald S. 1973. *Henry Winter Davis: Antebellum and Civil War Congressman from Maryland.* New York: Twayne; Oates, Stephen B. 1977. *With Malice toward None: The Life of Abraham Lincoln.* New York: Harper and Row; Paludan, Phillip Shaw. 1994. *The Presidency of Abraham Lincoln.* Lawrence: University Press of Kansas; Trefousse, Hans L. 1963. *Benjamin Franklin Wade: Radical Republican from Ohio.* New York: Twayne.

a state constitutional convention that had been called by Governor Michael Hahn. This new constitution abolished slavery, but it did not grant the suffrage to blacks immediately (the new constitution did allow the legislature to extend the franchise to blacks at a later date). The new state constitution was approved on September 5 by prounionist voters who had taken an oath of allegiance to the federal government.

1864

In New Orleans, the *New Orleans Tribune (La Tribune de la Nouvelle Orleans)* began publication on October 4. It was the first black daily newspaper and was published both in French and in English. Louis Charles Roudanez and his brothers operated the newspaper, and for many years it was one of the most influential black newspapers in the United States.

1864

On October 10, President Abraham Lincoln wrote to Henry W. Hoffman, a Maryland political leader, urging ratification of the proposed state constitution that would abolish slavery in the state. Maryland voters were scheduled to vote upon the measure in an October 13 referendum, and many people believed that the passage of the constitution was doubtful. Lincoln wrote: "I wish all men to be free. I wish the material prosperity of the already free which I feel sure the extinction of slavery would bring. I wish to see, in process of disappearing, that only thing which ever could bring this nation to civil war" (Jenkins, 1996).

1864

In the border state of Maryland, a new state constitution that abolished slavery went into effect on November 1. The measure had been approved by state voters in an extremely close vote on October 13.

1864

On November 8, President Abraham Lincoln was reelected to a second term in office as he defeated his Democratic rival, General George B. McClellan. In many respects, the election was a referendum on Lincoln's conduct of the war effort and his decision to issue the Emancipation Proclamation. The Republican Party also increased its majority in the House of Representatives and the Senate.

1865

The American Missionary Association established Atlanta University in Georgia as an institution of higher education for African Americans. The institution later merged with Clark College and changed its name to Clark-Atlanta University.

1865

The Baltimore Association for the Moral and Educational Improvement of Colored People established Baltimore Normal School in order to educate free black children. The institution eventually grew and developed into Bowie State University.

1865

On January 9, prounionist delegates attending a constitutional convention in occupied Tennessee adopted an amendment to the state constitution that abolished slavery in Tennessee. Prounionist voters ratified the proposed amendment in a referendum on February 22.

1865

On January 11, General Robert E. Lee recommended that the Confederacy begin arming slaves as a means of filling the ranks of the Confederate army. On the same date, delegates attending a constitutional convention in St. Louis ratified a new constitution that abolished slavery within the border state of Missouri.

1865

Secretary of War Edwin M. Stanton traveled to Savannah, Georgia, on January 12 to confer with General William T. Sherman and 20 black leaders to discuss the welfare of freed slaves in the aftermath of the rebellion. On the same date, in a speech before the House of Representatives, Congressman Thaddeus Stevens of Pennsylvania described slavery as "the worst institution upon earth, one which is a disgrace to man and would be an annoyance to the infernal spirits" (Jenkins, 1996). During the Reconstruction era, which followed the American Civil War, Congressman Stevens became one of the most influential radical Republican leaders to direct Reconstruction policy.

1865

General William T. Sherman issued Special Field Order 15 on January 16. This measure set aside

40-acre plots on the coastal islands of Georgia, South Carolina, and Florida to be distributed to freed slaves who would receive "possessory title" to the lands. The property in question had constituted large plantation estates in the years prior to the Civil War, but the lands had been seized when Union forces entered the region.

1865
Realizing the difficult conditions he faced, General Robert E. Lee said on January 17 that it was "not only expedient but necessary" (Jenkins, 1996) that slaves be used as soldiers by the Confederate government to fill the ranks of the Confederate army.

1865
On January 31, the House of Representatives, by a vote of 119 to 56, finally approved a proposed constitutional amendment that would abolish slavery in the United States. The election of more Republicans to Congress in the November 1864 elections had made it easier for the measure to obtain the two-thirds majority that was necessary for approval. The Senate had approved the measure on April 8, 1864, but the initial vote in the House of Representatives had failed on June 15 of that year. After ratification by the states, this measure became the Thirteenth Amendment to the Constitution of the United States. [See Document 68.]

1865
On February 3, President Abraham Lincoln met with Confederate Vice-President Alexander Stephens at an abortive peace conference off the coast of Hampton Roads, Virginia. Continuing Confederate demands that the South be granted autonomy as a sovereign independent republic resulted in the failure of the negotiations.

1865
Henry Highland Garnet became the first black minister to preach in the U.S. Capitol building on February 12. Garnet delivered a memorial sermon on the abolition of slavery.

1865
On March 3, in anticipation of the work that would have to take place after the Civil War ended, Congress authorized the creation of the Bureau of Refugees, Freedmen, and Abandoned Lands, a government agency that became the first public welfare program in the history of the United States. The Freedmen's Bureau was designed to assist freedmen and refugees as they made the difficult social and economic transition from slavery to freedom after the war. On the same day, by a joint resolution, Congress emancipated the wives and children of all blacks who served in the Union military during the Civil War.

1865
On March 13, the government of the Confederate States of America authorized the filling of military quotas by using slaves, with the permission of their owners. The government did stipulate, however, that the number of slaves was not to exceed 25 percent of the able-bodied male slave population between the ages of 18 and 45. This last-ditch effort was enacted too late to assist the Confederate war effort.

1865
Confederate General Robert E. Lee surrendered to Union General Ulysses S. Grant at Appomattox Court House, Virginia, on April 9. This event marked the end of the American Civil War.

1865
On April 11, Abraham Lincoln recommended that Congress consider granting the suffrage to black veterans and other blacks who were considered to be intelligent.

1865
President Abraham Lincoln died on April 15 after having been shot on the evening of April 14 by John Wilkes Booth, a southern sympathizer. Upon the death of Lincoln, Vice-President Andrew Johnson of Tennessee became the nation's seventeenth president.

1865
On May 11, blacks in Norfolk, Virginia, held mass meetings to demand the suffrage and equal rights with whites.

1865
President Andrew Johnson publicly announced his plans for the reconstruction of the southern states on May 29. Johnson believed that the states of the defeated Confederacy had to ratify the Thirteenth Amendment to the Constitution,

Starting in about 1862, the U.S. Congress began planning to take part in determining the terms of Reconstruction once the American Civil War ended, and on March 3, 1865, Congress passed an act to establish a Bureau of Refugees, Freedmen, and Abandoned Lands. Subsequently known as the Freedmen's Bureau Act, the agency it created was to focus on issues that distressed a torn nation. Designed to provide relief and medical attention, to establish schools, and to aid former slaves and white refugees in the exigencies of their situations, the bureau functioned influentially but precariously. To this time, such services as were available had been furnished more or less haphazardly by a few groups, some public, some private. In its brief existence, the Freedmen's Bureau operated as the first broadly conceived welfare program of the federal government of the United States.

A compelling need for such a program had arisen when, at the termination of hostilities and without preparation, 4 million black slaves were released from bondage and many white people were wounded or displaced. Lands had been "abandoned" or seized. Medical needs had become urgent. Education had been forbidden for slaves and neglected for whites throughout the antebellum era, just as industrial advance had recommenced. Yet no agency had been designated to deal with the desperate social problems that ensued.

The bureau also came into being because of the consequences that followed the introduction of human slavery in Virginia in 1619. From the acceptance of the Articles of Confederation in 1783 to the military conclusion of the Civil War in 1865, struggles over slavery had characterized the republic, and states had been admitted or rejected according to arrangements regulating legal black bondage. In 1865, when many freedmen and freedwomen joined the ranks of the displaced, the question of whether the federal government should assist all Americans who lacked survival resources became acute. The Freedmen's Bureau was intended to address this problem, the largest part of which resulted from black slavery.

Despite observations of some people that the bureau was only a mere beginning in the effort to meet the needs of former slaves and white clients, it did bring substantial, if often temporary, relief. During its brief four-year existence, the bureau distributed 21 million parcels of food to former slaves and white refugees, or 140,000 rations per day. It set up more than 40 hospitals, treated 450,000 ill and wounded individuals, and helped resettle as many as 30,000 displaced persons. The bureau achieved its most lasting success in the area of education. In the years 1866 and 1867, it established 1,200 new day and night schools in the South and found 1,700 teachers, many of them from the North. All of the schools met crucial needs, especially the needs of former slaves, and many later became important institutions.

It had taken two years, however, to secure the passage of the first bureau bill, and conceived of as a wartime measure, the agency was situated in the War Department and designed to last for only one year after the close of hostilities. Congress allowed no operating appropriation, intending that the bureau would be financed by the sale of abandoned lands. Upon the finding of a joint committee of Congress that the work of the bureau was indeed valuable, a second bill was introduced and passed by Congress in 1866, this time with some arrangement for financial support.

President Lincoln chose Union General Oliver O. Howard to administer the agency, and from the start, General Howard and agents of the bureau experienced difficulties of every description with the governments being established in the states of the former Confederacy. Appeals to southern Union supporters proved useless, nor could the bureau's efforts bring about any degree of cooperation.

The bureau's activities also produced disturbing harbingers of continued racial alienation. Supporters had intended that the agency would work on behalf of the Negroes, but the bureau had little success in promoting civil rights for all or in dealing with the state governments that President Andrew Johnson favored. According to George Bentley's early *History of the Freedmen's Bureau* (1955), the sponsors in point of fact only cared about furnishing the North with some economic benefits through constructing the new state governments and through securing votes. But more recently, William McFeely provided a less censorious interpretation in *Yankee Stepfather: General O. O. Howard and the Freedmen's Bureau* (1968).

Whatever the reasons for establishing a federal agency, it is nearly impossible to portray the unforgiving degree of opprobrium heaped upon the bureau, its agents, and northern teachers in bureau schools. People were ostracized. They were persecuted. Some were driven from the South, and some were even lynched. This aspect of the bureau's efforts is sensitively treated in Charles W. Chesnutt's little-known but poignant short story "The Bou-

Freedmen line up to receive rations from the Freedmen's Bureau, set up in 1865 to help freedmen make the transition from slavery to freedom. (Library of Congress)

quet" (1899) and in William Faulkner's novel *Light in August* (1932).

President Andrew Johnson opposed a second Freedmen's Bureau bill in 1866, and in rendering the first of his many vetoes, he thus brought to the attention of Congress the connected issues of welfare for the destitute and civil rights for all Americans. The president argued that federal programs for aid were unconstitutional and that they ought to be considered, if at all, at the state level of government. Johnson, a southerner, said the bill would establish military control over the defeated territories, something southerners vehemently denounced, and insisted that the framers of the Constitution never contemplated federal aid for destitute people. He concluded that the positions of the former slaves were not desperate because their labor was necessary and would function as a bar-

gaining tool. The president's refusal to modify his position led in part to his impeachment. His confrontation with the nation's representatives over welfare and the civil rights implications of the Freedmen's Bureau Act and the repeated resurgence of these issues demonstrate that these issues had connections to historical precedents.

—*Frances Richardson Keller*

For Further Reading
DuBois, W. E. B. 1995. *Black Reconstruction in America.* New York: Simon and Schuster; Franklin, John Hope. 1994. *Reconstruction after the Civil War.* Chicago: University of Chicago Press; Litwack, Leon. 1979. *Been in the Storm So Long: The Aftermath of Slavery.* New York: Vintage Books; Woodward, C. Vann. 1966. *Reunion and Reaction: The Compromise of 1877 and the End of Reconstruction.* Boston: Little, Brown.

which repudiated slavery, but he did not believe that the suffrage should be extended to freedmen. [See Document 68.]

1865

On June 6, blacks in Petersburg, Virginia, held mass meetings to demand the suffrage and equal rights with whites.

1865

Blacks in Vicksburg, Mississippi, held mass meetings on June 19 to demand the suffrage and equal rights with whites. On the same date, news about the Emancipation Proclamation finally reached slaves in Texas when Union general Gordon Granger arrived in Galveston Bay, Texas, and liberated nearly 200,000 slaves. The

CHARLES WADDELL CHESNUTT (1858–1932)

Charles Waddell Chesnutt confronted perils of slavery and its reaches through imaginative literature and then through political action. An artistic innovator, he combined fiction with social history in the hope of awakening white Americans and attaining social justice and produced a distinctive genre of American literature. Disappointed in his purpose, however, he turned to other literary categories—biography, letters, essays, articles, speeches—and to politics. He became a foremost expository protagonist for African Americans and a formidable antagonist of racism in the United States.

Although he could have passed as a white person, Chesnutt determined to honor his black heritage and to throw his talents into the balance. His collections of short stories *(The Conjure Woman and Other Conjure Tales, The Wife of His Youth and Other Stories)* established him as a superlative writer of short fiction, and his novels *(The House behind the Cedars, The Marrow of Tradition, The Colonel's Dream)* drew their themes from his own experience and the experiences of his ancestors as well as from the drama being played out in the long shadow of black slavery in the United States. The novels examine "passing" (blacks passing for whites), race riots, and the lingering powers of the landed families of the antebellum era. Critics as eminent as William Dean Howells applauded Chesnutt's work, but because the South was rushing toward white supremacy, his books never reached a substantial public.

Turning to expository writing and political action, Chesnutt addressed subjects of concern to African Americans and to white contemporaries. He wrote a life of Frederick Douglass, the black abolitionist-orator-journalist born in slavery, and through many publications and speeches Chesnutt confronted racial issues of the American experience: laws affecting former slaves and reinstating limits on their opportunities; problems of lynching and race rioting; political alignments that reinstituted slave conditions; and African American civil rights, their abrogation, and the consequences to the nation of their denial. He corresponded with figures of influence in the white world.

Chesnutt conducted extensive dialogues with Booker T. Washington and W. E. B. DuBois, African American leaders who, in the wake of American slavery, set courses for interracial relations. In widely read articles, Chesnutt delineated a third racial posture: Washington believed vocational education and the interlacing of black energy with white business would eventually achieve resolution; DuBois believed militant insistence on every right, especially education, would bring results; Chesnutt thought the vote should be secured immediately regardless of education or previous servitude. He concluded that in the end, intermarriage of the races would prove the only answer to cruelties attendant on slavery.

—*Frances Richardson Keller*

For Further Reading

Andrews, William L. 1980. *The Literary Career of Charles W. Chesnutt*. Baton Rouge: Louisiana State University Press; Chesnutt, Helen. 1952. *Charles Waddell Chesnutt: Pioneer of the Color Line*. Chapel Hill: University of North Carolina Press; Keller, Frances Richardson. 1978. *An American Crusade: The Life of Charles Waddell Chesnutt*. Provo, UT: Brigham Young University Press; Render, Sylvia Lyons. 1979. *Charles Waddell Chesnutt: Eagle with Clipped Wings*. Washington, DC: Howard University Press.

---

celebration of "Juneteenth" as a commemoration of Emancipation Day became popular among African Americans within the state of Texas, and the celebration is now recognized in communities all across the United States.

1865

Blacks in Nashville, Tennessee, held mass meetings on August 7–11 to demand the suffrage and equal rights with whites.

1865

On September 16, Pennsylvania Congressman Thaddeus Stevens urged the confiscation of all estates belonging to former Confederate leaders, believing that these lands should be redistributed to adult freedmen. This was the basis of the "40 acres and a mule" method of providing freedmen with the economic means to survive in a world after slavery.

1865

On September 18, blacks in Richmond, Virginia, held mass meetings to demand the suffrage and equal rights with whites.

In compliance with the "black codes" enacted in former Confederate states, African Americans considered vagrants were forced into labor or jailed until they chose to work. Here a free man is auctioned off for such a purpose. (Library of Congress)

1865
Blacks in Raleigh, North Carolina, held mass meetings on September 29–October 3 to demand the suffrage and equal rights with whites.

1865
On October 7, blacks in Jackson, Mississippi, held mass meetings to demand the suffrage and equal rights with whites.

1865
Blacks in Charleston, South Carolina, held mass meetings from November 20 to November 25 to demand the suffrage and equal rights with whites.

1865
In the fall and winter, legislatures in states that constituted the former Confederate States of America enacted black codes, which were designed to restrict the civil rights and liberty of movement of the newly emancipated freedmen.

1865
On December 18, the Thirteenth Amendment, which abolished slavery, became a part of the U.S. Constitution. [See Document 68.]

❧Contemporary History❧

Let us listen to the voices of our
Forebears . . .
In the smoky cabin, souls that
wish us well are murmuring.
—Léopold Sédar Senghor, "Nuit de Sine"

As the twentieth century draws to a close, many people will attempt to assess the larger meaning and historical significance of our time. In so doing, the advancements of technology, the marvels of modern science, and the benefits of economic prosperity will have to be weighed against two world wars, the twin horrors of the Holocaust and the atomic age, and the ever-widening gap between the rich and the poor. Yet we must not forget slavery—for however far we believe our world has advanced, this age-old practice reminds us of the darkest nature of ourselves as a world people. The ancient souls that murmur from our past soothe the captive but chide the well-to-do and the complacent for their obliviousness. Slavery has survived.

Is it that difficult to notice the effects of slavery upon modernity? During the imperialistic generation that marked the end of the nineteenth century, European powers took pride in their high moral sense of trusteeship that sought to end indigenous practices of slavery in "the scramble for Africa" that ensued. The record of these efforts was not completely effective as less-than-noble effects often resulted. Although some practices were ended, other horrors, like the forced labor imposed in the Congo Free State, instituted methods and practices that defy the civilized imagination. Eventually, international bodies like the League of Nations and the United Nations had to reckon with the issue of slavery in the mod-

ern world. World War II demonstrated that even modern-industrial nations like Germany and Japan can resort to barbarous practices of enslavement in a moment of nationalistic fervor. The Cold War taught us that slave labor was the punishment of choice in the Soviet *gulag* and the Chinese *laogai* as a host of people lost their lives to an ideology that professed the equality of all. Even today, at the end of the twentieth century, Anti-Slavery International estimates that millions of people are still enslaved worldwide.

History operates within a fluid continuum where past, present, and future are inexact indicators of change through the course of time. The word *contemporary* is a relative term which marks those events of the recent past that share attributes of the present era. For the purposes of this section of the chronology, the contemporary era of slavery begins in the late-nineteenth century with "the scramble for Africa" that marked the beginning of the age of imperialism. The practice of slavery is traced to the present day where a beckoning future holds forth the likelihood that customs and traditions rooted in the ancient past shall still endure.

In viewing slavery as an institution of an earlier time, many people fail to see the lingering vestiges of this institution that punctuate the modern era. The particular lessons of enslavement that appear in these pages suggest that much of the modern world is too absorbed by its own affairs to recognize the modern face of slavery. As a result, benign indifference and callous disregard often reign supreme, and both are reprehensible behaviors that characterize the savage inequalities of modern life. In the self-created noise of our existence, we do not hear the murmuring of the forebears, we do not hear the cries of the oppressed, and the echoes of the forlorn seldom move us. We condone through our silence, and by design we share a degree of complicity in the world about us. Much like an original sin that is borne by all, the stigma of slavery permeates history and touches all who seek to find a larger meaning in our humanity.

1880
The U.S. Congress conducted hearings and prepared a report regarding the conditions of slavery in China after concerns were raised about the circumstances faced by Chinese-Americans who had been repatriated to China.

1884–1885
European powers met at the Berlin West African Conference to determine the future of the Congo basin and to settle other questions related to colonial expansion in Africa. Participants condemned the slave trade but took no unified action to abolish it. Instead, each nation that had developed a colonial sphere in Africa pledged to work toward the end of the slave trade in its respective region. [See Document 71.]

1884
The Congo Free State was formed in central Africa and became the personal fiefdom of King Leopold II of Belgium.

1884
The colonial government of the Dutch East Indies officially abolished slavery by statute, however some forms of indigenous slavery persisted in the region even after this proclamation was issued.

1885
Diplomatic representatives of Great Britain and Germany met in London to negotiate an agreement that officially recognized each nation's sphere of influence in eastern Africa. Both nations pledged to suppress the slave trade that existed within their spheres in Africa and to move the region toward an economic system based upon free labor.

1885
The Brazilian government enacted the Sexagenarian Law, which freed all slaves in Brazil aged 65 or older. Slaves who were 60 years old were to work only three more years before being freed by their masters.

1885
Charles George Gordon (called Chinese Gordon) died in battle at Khartoum in the Sudan on January 26. The British government had sent Gordon into the Sudan to restore order after the Egyptian government requested assistance in suppressing the Mahdist war (Sudanese War of 1881–1885). Its leader, Muhammad Ahmad, who called himself "the Mahdi," had once been a slave trader, but as a charismatic religious leader he launched a jihad against Egyptian influence in the Sudan.

1886
The Spanish government abolished slavery in all colonial dominions where it still existed. This action officially ended slavery in Cuba.

1886
The Korean government proclaimed that servitude in Korea would be limited to one generation only. This action effectively abolished hereditary slavery in Korea.

1886
The government of Brazil pledged to enact a plan of gradual abolition of slavery according to enabling legislation that had been enacted in 1885.

1887
The German philosopher Friedrich Wilhelm Nietzsche published *Towards a Genealogy of Morals,* in which he outlined his thoughts on "master morality" and "slave morality."

1888
Charles-Martial-Allemand Lavigerie, the cardi-

Peonage is a labor practice in which individuals and families are forced into an involuntary state of servitude because of debt. Entrapment originates when people hire out their services to raise crops, which is known as sharecropping, or contract to pick crops, harvest natural resources, or perform a specified nonagricultural task. Peons work under conditions in which wage fraud, force, or impossible contract terms make it impossible for them to leave employment.

Peonage emerged in the Americas as a neocolonial form of maintaining the stability of indigenous labor, the labor of formerly enslaved Africans and their descendants, and that of ethnoracial immigrants, such as the Chinese. It was a method employed by capitalists to maintain profitability after the loss of slave labor through legal emancipation. Debt-peonage cases have survived into the twentieth century in labor-intensive ventures in many world regions and reemerged with the formation of a global economy in the late-twentieth century when economic restructuring placed pressure on the weaker sectors of the North American economy. In the United States, peak periods for the practice of peonage occurred after Emancipation and in the late-twentieth century.

After the emancipation of the African-American population in the nineteenth century, southern planters in the United States established a sharecropping system in which blacks signed annual contracts that gave them an advance on the anticipated crop share. The cost of supplies would exceed the crop share, however, placing the sharecropper in debt as a way of compelling workers to continue to labor for their employers. African Americans often signed on again, in hope of getting ahead, but often moved on, if permitted, in search of better farming opportunities. A portion of the planters, however, refused to allow sharecroppers to leave until they had contributed sufficient labor to clear the debt, thus keeping them in bondage. Both coercion and violence were used to maintain peonage.

Peonage differs from independent sharecropping in the degree to which labor is extracted by compulsion. Daniel (1990) considers that "inflated" and "partially fictitious" bills that stabilized workers in debt do not constitute true peonage. Debts can be both real and fictitious. The 1867 federal peonage statute defines peonage as debt servitude under conditions of coercion. A worker needs to establish that "restraint" has occurred, and many debt-related complaints have been dismissed because of lack of evidence.

Peonage of African Americans has been made possible by corrupt law enforcement in which jailing and the setting of bail have been used as a means of establishing debt. At the turn of the twentieth century, most southern states had contract labor laws which specified that workers who signed agricultural labor contracts and left employment were criminally liable and could be arrested. State and local laws were reinforced by custom, and peonage was supported by unconstitutional formal laws and pseudolaws that illiterate laborers could not challenge. Violence, in the form of severe beatings and death, has also been used to intimidate African-American laborers.

Three patterns of concentration of peonage emerged in the southern United States. Cotton plantations, from South Carolina to Texas and the Mississippi Delta, were the major source of peonage charges. Turpentine harvesting in northern Florida, South Georgia, Alabama, and Mississippi was another source of numerous complaints and also involved the use of foreign immigrants for forced labor owing to indebtedness. Railroad construction camps were another location of immigrant peonage. In the case of turpentine stills and the railroads, commissary costs were a mechanism of compulsory indebtedness. Thousands of immigrants were placed in debt-bondage, but court action was later able to stop this practice.

Daniel (1990) believes that the federal peonage statute was not an adequate tool as indebtedness had to be proved. Although the Alabama contract labor law was abolished in 1911, contract labor laws persisted in many southern states until the 1940s. In 1948, a revision of the Justice Department code provided three legal options for combating peonage: a peonage statute (1581 USC), a slave-kidnapping law (1583 USC), and a sale-into-involuntary-servitude law (1584 USC). In the United States, charges of peonage still continue, now often involving immigrant and native agricultural workers.

—*Judith Ann Warner*

For Further Reading

Acuna, Rodolfo. 1981. *Occupied America: A History of Chicanos*. New York: Harper and Row; Chepesiuk, Ron. 1992. "Peonage for Peach Pickers." *Progressive* 56(12): 22–24; Daniel, Pete. 1990. *The Shadow of Slavery: Peonage in the South, 1901–1969*. Urbana: University of Illinois Press; Potts, Lydia. 1990. *The World Labour Market: A History of Migration*. New York: Zed Books; Vigil, James Diego. 1997. *From Indians to Chicanos: The Dynamics of Mexican American Culture*. Prospect Heights, IL: Waveland Press.

nal primate of Africa and founder of the missionary order the Society of Our Lady of Africa, rallied support among Europeans to launch a crusade against slave traders in Africa. Many abolitionist groups were established in European cities as a result of Lavigerie's efforts.

1888
Pope Leo XIII issued an encyclical in which he proclaimed that the Roman Catholic Church offered support to people who were enslaved throughout the world.

1888
Slavery officially ended in Brazil on May 13 when the legislative assembly enacted the Lei Aurea (Golden Law). The measure was supported by Imperial Princess Isabel, who acted as regent while her brother, Pedro II, was receiving medical treatment in Europe. This act of emancipation effectively liberated 725,000 slaves in Brazil. [See Document 72.]

1889
The sultan of Zanzibar (modern-day Tanzania) issued a proclamation declaring the emancipation of all children born to slaves after 1890. Despite the antislavery rhetoric of this proclamation, the decree was never publicly announced, nor was it enforced.

1890
On July 2, all major European colonial powers signed the Brussels Act, or the General Act of the Repression of the African Slave Trade. This measure had been prepared during the Brussels Conference (1889–1890), which had been called to prepare the first comprehensive, unified campaign to abolish the slave trade within Africa.

1891
On May 13, the government of the Republic of Brazil ordered the burning of all documents related to the institution of slavery in Brazil.

1892
Frederick John Dealtry Lugard published *The Rise of Our East African Empire*. As a British colonial administrator in Africa, Lugard had formed strong opinions on the topic of slavery. He believed that the majority of Africa's indigenous slaves were content with their social posi-

A young Moroccan man with his African slave, c. 1900. (Michael Maslan Historic Photograph/Corbis)

tion, but he argued that the British should not recognize the legal status of slaves within its colonies in Africa. [See Document 73.]

1893
Antônio Conselheiro established the community of Canudos in the *sertão* ("backlands") of Brazil. Many of the recently freed slaves in Brazil moved to this settlement, and by 1895, it boasted a population of 35,000 residents. Considering the settlement to be all too similar to a *quilombo* (Maroon or fugitive slave) settlement, the Brazilian government destroyed the site in a battle on October 5, 1897.

1895
Efforts of the European powers to end the slave trade within Africa as well as the practice of slavery itself were often stymied by the defense of the practices drawn from indigenous beliefs and sometimes from Muslim beliefs. [See Document 74.]

1895

Following the Sino-Japanese War (1894–1895), the Choson (Yi) court abolished slavery on the Korean peninsula. The proclamation of uncompensated emancipation was enacted at the urging of the Japanese government, which wished to modernize Korea before it annexed the region.

1897

Once the supply of African slaves began to decline, the emir of Bida (located in modern-day Qatar along the Persian Gulf) noted, "To be a king means to have plenty of slaves, without which you are nothing" (Jenkins, 1996).

1897

Faced with mounting pressure by the British government, the sultan of Zanzibar (modern-day Tanzania) formally abolished slavery in Zanzibar and on the island of Pemba.

1900

Reports from American observers indicated that the practice of slavery in the Philippines was becoming extinct and that acts of piracy in the region had become quite rare.

1901

Colonial officials in German East Africa issued the Decree Respecting Domestic Slavery in German East Africa. This measure indicated that although the European colonial powers wished to end the type of chattel slavery that existed in Africa, they were not willing to change the indigenous beliefs that allowed domestic slavery to exist. [See Document 75.]

1905

The government of Siam (Thailand) officially abolished the practice of slavery.

1909

During the final years of imperial rule, the Ching (Qing) leaders decreed that slavery was abolished in China, but despite this change in official policy, the practice persisted well into the twentieth century.

1909

On June 19, the government of the Dominican Republic signed an extradition convention with the United States. Among several other items, the Dominican Republic promised to extradite any-

Slaves in the Congo, early twentieth century. Under the brutal rule of Belgium's King Leopold, many Congolese were victims of a slave labor system and other abuses; when these practices came to light, the Belgian Parliament took over Leopold's private fiefdom, which became known as the Belgian Congo. (Snark/Art Resource)

one who committed "crimes and offenses against the laws of both countries for the suppression of slavery and slave trading" (Jenkins, 1996).

1913

On March 26, the government of Paraguay signed an extradition treaty with the United States in which Paraguay promised to extradite anyone who committed "crimes and offenses against the laws of both countries for the suppression of slavery and slave trading" (Jenkins, 1996).

1914–1918

The major powers of Europe were engaged in World War I.

1915

The colonial government of Malaya officially abolished slavery by statute. In spite of this proclamation, reports indicate that the practice endured in some parts of Malaya for several more years.

~ANNA JULIA COOPER (C. 1858–1964)~

Anna Julia Cooper was a controversial educator who demanded standards of excellence as well as equal opportunity for black schools. Late in life she headed one of the first community colleges, Freylingshuysen University in Washington, D.C. An early black feminist, Cooper lectured widely on behalf of the "doubly enslaved" black woman while insisting on the right to higher education for all women. In the nineteenth century, she became a founder and one of those who nourished the National Association of Colored Women's Clubs and other organizations. As a crowning achievement, her 1925 Sorbonne doctoral thesis expressed a seminal interpretation of international slavery and its repercussions (L'Attitude de la France a l'égard de l'esclavage pendant la revolution [Slavery and the French revolutionists]).

Anna Cooper's mother was Hannah Stanley, a slave, the property of Dr. Fabius J. Haywood in Raleigh, North Carolina—Haywood was also Cooper's owner and probably her father. Emancipation occurred in 1865. After the death of her young husband, Cooper, along with Mary Church Terrell and Ida A. Gibbs, was among the first women to receive a bachelor's degree from Oberlin College in 1885; in 1887, she received a master's degree; and 38 years later, she received her doctorate from the Sorbonne in Paris, France.

In 1892, Cooper published her first book, A Voice from the South by a Black Woman of the South. In this feminist work, she discussed the discouragements she had encountered in growing up in the post–Civil War South. For much of her life, she wrote and lectured on women's rights and on justice for former slaves, and for many years, she taught Latin and Greek and mathematics to students at the M Street Colored High School in Washington, D.C. A gifted linguist, she later translated from ancient to modern French a classic epic, Le Pelerinage de Charlemagne (The pilgrimage of Charlemagne).

Her least-known and probably most important work was her study of the relations between the assemblies of the French Revolution and the slaves of their richest colony, Saint Domingue (Haiti). Cooper believed that slavery anywhere affects slavery everywhere, that it encapsulates a world labor problem, and that slave labor thus becomes a matter of international concern. She thought that denial of freedom to the slaves of Saint Domingue severely limited the freedom of the French and negated hope of democratic progress through the French Revolution. She thus showed the inevitable involvement of darker peoples with the Western world. Cooper wrote this study in French when she was 67 years old, and the Sorbonne published it. Until 1988, it was never published in any language in her native land, but toward the end of her 105 years, Cooper did see major scholars advance the issues that she had raised in her scholarship.

—Frances Richardson Keller

For Further Reading
Cooper, Anna Julia. 1988. *Slavery and the French Revolutionists (1788–1805)*. Trans. from French with an introductory essay by Frances Richardson Keller. Lewiston, NY: Edwin Mellen Press; Hutchinson, Louise Daniel. 1981. *Anna J. Cooper: A Voice from the South*. Washington, DC: Smithsonian Institution Press.

1918–1921

During the Russian Civil War, the Soviet government established a dual system of state-operated prisons that used forced labor as a means of "rehabilitating" inmates. One system existed to punish common criminals; the other was operated by the secret police (Cheka) and detained only political enemies of the Soviet state.

1918

The British governor of Hong Kong informed his superiors in London that in his estimation, nearly every household in the colony that had the financial means held a young child as a domestic slave.

1918

Although the rhetoric of the Bolshevik Revolution in Russia proclaimed the freedom of workers from the exploitation of the bourgeoisie, a labor code issued by the Soviet state recommended that "all citizens be subject to compulsory labor" (Meltzer, 1993).

1919

In the aftermath of World War I (1914–1918), the victorious Allied powers abrogated as no longer necessary both the Berlin Act of 1885 and the Brussels Act of 1890, which had been established to end the slave trade in Africa.

1919

In the covenant of the League of Nations, the signatory powers pledged to "secure and maintain fair and humane conditions of labor," and they voiced support for "just treatment of the native inhabitants under their control" (Jenkins, 1996). Article 23 of the covenant bound member states to provide "fair and humane conditions of labor for men, women, and children."

1919

The victorious Allied powers signed a treaty at St. Germain, France, on September 10 in which they promised to supervise their colonial peoples to ensure their moral and material well-being. The Allied powers also pledged to work toward the suppression of slavery in all of its forms.

1922

In September, John Harris, the secretary of the British-based Anti-Slavery and Aborigines Protection Society, persuaded Sir Arthur Steel-Maitland, New Zealand's delegate to the League of Nations, to introduce a resolution calling for an international investigation into practices of slavery worldwide.

1922

On November 10, the government of Costa Rica signed an extradition treaty with the United States. Among several other items, Costa Rica promised to extradite anyone who committed "crimes and offenses against the laws of both countries for the suppression of slavery and slave trading" (Jenkins, 1996).

1923

In February, the British colonial government in Hong Kong adopted an ordinance that officially outlawed the selling of little girls (mui tsai) into domestic service in Hong Kong, but the practice continued despite efforts to restrict it.

1923

Ethiopia was admitted to membership in the League of Nations on September 28 over the objection of Great Britain but with the support of Italy and France. The government of Ethiopia pledged to take steps to abolish slavery.

1924

The government of Ethiopia officially abolished slavery, but the practice still continued for many more years.

1924

After an intensive lobbying campaign mounted by the British and Foreign Anti-Slavery Society and the Aborigines Protection Society, the League of Nations appointed an eight-member Temporary Slavery Commission, which consisted of experts who were charged with investigating "slavery in all its forms."

1926–1930

The governments of Afghanistan, Iraq, Nepal, Kalat (a former Indian state, now part of Baluchistan, Pakistan), Trans-Jordan, and Iran officially abolished slavery during this period, but the practice still continued for many more years.

1926

The colonial government of Burma officially abolished slavery by statute. Eventually, the government of Burma had to institute a system of compensated emancipation to end the continuing practice of slavery in the region.

1926

At the urging of its Temporary Slavery Commission, the League of Nations approved the Slavery Convention on September 25. More than thirty nations signed this document, which defined slavery as "the status or condition of a person over whom any or all of the powers attaching to the right of ownership are exercised." Member nations were charged with working to suppress all forms of slavery. [See Document 76.]

1927

On September 22, the government of Sierra Leone officially abolished slavery by statute. Sierra Leone had been founded as a colony by the British in the eighteenth century to serve as a homeland for freed slaves who wished to be repatriated to Africa.

1929–1939

Officials in Hong Kong and Malaya began an intense campaign to reduce the number of young girls who were enslaved for purposes of prostitution. In the decade before World War II began, it was estimated that the number of young girls (mui tsai) who were enslaved had

Members of the League of Nations White Slave Commission, which was authorized to conduct an inquiry into the traffic in women and children in East Asia, visit a geisha school in Tokyo in 1931. (UPI/Corbis-Bettmann)

been reduced by two-thirds. Still, large numbers of *mui tsai* were available in China for prices as low as $5, and these children could be sold for $500 in the flesh markets of Singapore.

1929

The government of Burma instituted a program of compensated emancipation to encourage slaveholders to liberate their slaves. It was reported that as many as 9,000 slaves were freed as a result of this policy.

1930

An estimated 4 million Chinese children *(mui tsai)* were enslaved in China even though China had abolished slavery in 1909. Many of these enslaved children were branded and beaten regularly.

1930

The rights of colonial laborers were protected under the terms of the Forced Labor Convention. This document was negotiated and drafted under the auspices of the League of Nations with the cooperation of the International Labour Organization.

1930

On March 8, the Johnson-Christy Commission to Liberia was authorized as a joint effort between the U.S. government and the League of Nations. The commission investigated the condition of the indigenous laborers, and on September 8, it reported that conditions of slavery still existed within Liberia, which had been founded as a colony by the American Colonization Society in the nineteenth century to serve as a homeland for freed slaves who wished to be repatriated to Africa.

1930

On April 7, the Soviet Union established a new network of forced labor camps that were operated under the auspices of the secret police. This network of detention facilities was known as the State Administration of Camps, or Gosudarstvennoe Upravlenie Lageriami, commonly called the Gulag.

1931

At the urging of the United States, the nation of Liberia requested that the League of Nations investigate charges that slavery persisted within Liberia. After the League of Nations made specific recommendations, however, Liberia rejected them as an affront to national sovereignty.

1931

The Mukden incident on September 19 marked the beginning of conflict between Japan and China in the Far East as the Japanese occupation of Manchuria began the hostilities that would develop into the Pacific Theater of World War II.

1932

The League of Nations appointed the Committee of Experts on Slavery to investigate ways in which slavery might be suppressed in colonial regions. The committee met for only one year.

1933

The Nazis began to construct concentration camps throughout Germany as preparation for an elaborate slave labor system. The first of these camps was constructed at Dachau near Munich.

1933

Adolf Hitler became the chancellor of Germany on January 30. Later, in addressing the historical topic of slavery, Hitler said: "Such a thing once almost ruled the world! The peoples of the world mastered it in the end, but don't let anyone sing too soon of victory: the womb from which it crawled can still bear fruit" (Meltzer, 1993).

1934

The League of Nations appointed the Advisory Committee of Experts on Slavery to investigate continuing charges that forced labor practices continued to exist in many colonial regions.

1936

Benito Mussolini's Italian government conquered the African nation of Ethiopia. One of the reforms that the Italians introduced there was the abolition of slavery in 1942.

1936

The Muslim leader Ibn Saud conquered the Hejaz (western Arabian peninsula) and entered into a treaty with Great Britain to end the importation of new slaves into the region. Ibn Saud also promised to encourage the sale and manumission of all slaves already in Saudi Arabia.

1936

The colonial government of British Bechuanaland (modern-day Botswana) officially abolished slavery by statute.

1937

Without a formal declaration of war, hostilities between Japan and China commenced in an incident at Lukouchiao on July 7. This incident was soon followed by a full-scale invasion of China.

1937

In December, the world witnessed "the rape of Nanking" when Japanese forces attacked that Chinese city and raped and murdered many innocent civilians. Stung by international criticism, the Japanese military decided to establish comfort stations as a sexual outlet for Japanese troops. Many thousands of Korean and Chinese women were then forced into sexual slavery during the years of World War II as *jugun ianfu*, "military comfort women."

1938

The Nazi government of Germany began to realize that its system of concentration camps could serve an additional purpose beyond that of punishing political prisoners. German leaders recognized the economic value of slave laborers, who could be employed in German industries, and large companies like I. G. Farben, Krupp, A.E.G., Siemens, and Rheinmetall established factories near concentration camps so they could exploit that resource.

1939

World War II began in Europe when German forces invaded Poland on September 1 and Great Britain and France honored their commitments to protect Poland from Nazi aggression.

1942

Fritz Sauckel was named plenipotentiary general for the allocation of labor and was placed in charge of the slave labor operations for the Nazi government. Sauckel maintained that the foreign workers were "to be treated in such a

In the World War II death camps of Auschwitz-Birkenau, Treblinka, Chelmno, Maidonick, Sobibor, and Belzec, the German army compelled mostly Jews but also Gypsies, homosexuals, and political prisoners to engage in hard labor in the camps themselves and factories with no rights and little food. Political prisoners were Communists, political dissidents, opponents of Germany, captured partisans, and citizens of countries occupied by the Germans were coopted or lured into forced labor. People who had volunteered for well-paid positions in German war factories ended up as slave prisoners of the Germans once Germany began losing the war, evacuating concentration and labor camps, and moving prisoners and installations in every direction because of intense Allied bombings and advances.

The *Fremdarbeiter* ("foreign workers") came from Germany's satellites or occupied territories to work for the German Reich. As early as March 1938 when Germany invaded Austria, some 100,000 Austrian civilians were taken to work in Germany, and by August 31, 1939, 70,000 workers from the Protectorate of Bohemia and Moravia had been taken to work in Germany. After Germany attacked Poland in September 1939 and the Soviet Union in 1941, harsh methods were used to recruit workers to work for the German war effort as replacements for the millions of Germans who had been drafted and were fighting in the army. In opposition to international law, Germany also used prisoners of war (POWs) to help support the German economy. As early as fall 1939, 340,000 Polish prisoners of war were being compelled to work the land, and in August 1942, Germany enacted a decree that made possible forced labor in all occupied countries and POW camps. In Western Europe, local authorities cooperated with the Germans in recruitment in an effort to have their own POWs released or to have the status of their POWs changed to that of foreign workers in Germany. Although Germany recruited millions of workers between 1942 and 1944, there were never enough for the country's needs, partly because Germany encountered difficulties in recruiting since the word had spread about the terrible working conditions in Germany and the treatment of foreign workers and partly because of Germany's impending defeat.

Most foreign workers in Germany came from Poland and the Soviet Union. In early 1941, there were 800,000 Polish foreign workers in Germany, and after Germany invaded the Soviet Union in

Prisoners in a German labor camp, 1935. The Nazis began to construct such concentration camps in preparation for their slave labor system as soon as they came to power in 1933. (Library of Congress/Corbis)

June 1941, German-occupied areas of the country became the major area for recruiting foreign laborers. In September 1944, when there were 5.5 million foreign laborers in Germany and 2 million POWs, 38 percent of the laborers were Soviets and 20 percent were Poles. The rest of the foreign workers had been drafted in France, Czechoslovakia, the Netherlands, Belgium, Norway, and as far away as Greece. Italy, Germany's Axis partner, supplied significant numbers of workers to Germany. By late 1944, there were 9 million foreign workers (including POWs) in Germany. One out of every five workers was a foreigner, and one out of every four tanks and every four aircraft manufactured in Germany were made by foreign workers.

Although foreign workers were at first to be paid and treated well, in most instances they were supervised by the Sicherheitspolizei (Security Police), and the Auslandische Arbeiter (Foreign Worker) section of the Gestapo, and members of these groups were guided by racism, xenophobia, and arbitrary decisions. Workers from Western Europe were treated better those from elsewhere, and Poles and Russians were regarded as inferior and subhuman beings. The Eastern European workers were subjected to hard physical labor, put under harsh control, humiliated, and severely penalized for misdeeds. They received very low pay, and they had to wear special signs on their clothes—P for Poles and Ost (East) for the Russians—and they had to remain in their living quarters after work and could not socialize or mix with German society in any way. Germans who had sexual intercourse with foreign workers could be sentenced to death. Even though Western European workers were treated better, they also complained that they were treated like slaves, and millions of Russian POWs faced starvation, ill-treatment, and intentional murder.

Jews who were taken as POWs or became foreign workers tried to avoid being identified as being Jewish. When the British were overcome by the Germans in Greece and on Crete, many of the Jews of the Palestine units of the British army became POWs and were sent to Dachau and other concentration camps.

Most of the 6 million Jews annihilated in the Holocaust were gassed immediately upon arriving by train at one of the six Nazi death camps in Poland. Only a small minority was selected for labor in the death camps or for work in other labor camps. When Germany invaded Poland in September 1939, army units recruited Jews at random for forced labor, forcing them to remove roadblocks and pave roads. Not only were the Jews mistreated, but their work was specifically chosen to degrade them. Jews were subject to beatings and harassment like cutting off part or all of their beards.

From October to December 1939 in Poland, the Germans issued decrees drafting into compulsory labor Jewish men and women aged 14–60 and children aged 12–14. Jews had to register with the Judenrat, the German-imposed local Jewish councils, and they had to carry out temporary work assignments such as removing snow, loading goods the Nazis had confiscated from other Jews, and building walls around the Jewish ghettos. Eventually, special labor camps were set up for the Jews—in the Lublin district in Poland alone there were 29 such camps by July 1940. In August 1940, 20,000 Jews from the ages of 19 to 35 were ordered to report to the labor camps. Many defied the recruitment despite the danger involved in doing so.

Conditions in the labor camps were horrific. Often the men had no sleeping quarters and had to sleep outside. Sometimes they were not fed even their meager rations, and they were humiliated and persecuted by dogs, Nazi threats, and beatings. Those working on land amelioration projects sometimes had to stand in water to work. Out of 6,000 men sent from the Warsaw Ghetto to labor camps, 1,000 were no longer fit for labor after only two weeks. In Poland's Lodz Ghetto, the entire Jewish population had to partake in forced labor as the ghettos themselves became labor camps.

Large numbers of Jews worked in German factories in Poland and in ghetto "shops" (workshops) during the last years of the ghettos. At the end of 1940, over 700,000 Jews were engaged in forced labor in Poland. The figure dropped to 500,000 in 1942 and to little more than 100,000 in mid-1943 owing to the high death rate in the ghettos and to deportations of the Jews from the ghettos to the death camps for extermination. In most work camps, the Jews had to work 10–12 hours a day and received no benefits or vacations. If Jews were paid, they were paid less than the minimum or meager wage that people of other nationalities received. Jewish wages did not enable them to purchase food on the black market, so most of the workers starved. Those working in the ghetto shops sorted the possessions of the Jews who had been deported to the death camps. Factories using Jewish labor had to pay sizable sums to the German secret police. The Jews had to pay bribes in order to obtain such employment, which they naively believed would exempt them from being deported to the concentration camps.

In mid-1942 and in April and May 1943, some of the Jews in the ghettos were taken to the Trawniki and Poniatowa labor camps in Poland, and in November 1943, the Germans murdered 40,000 Jews in those camps. In Lodz, forced labor was used longer than elsewhere and existed until the ghetto was liberated in August 1944.

In Greece, the Germans compelled Jews to be recruited to forced labor. In Thessaloníki, when 9,000 Jewish males aged 18–45 had to register for German forced labor on July 11, 1942, they were forced to stand all day in the hot sun and were tortured by the German soldiers. Over 4,000 had to work on the roads; many died because of the terrible conditions. When the Jewish community was unable to raise the total ransom sum of 3.5 billion drachmas, the Germans ordered the destruction of the ancient Jewish cemetery in December 1942, but the Jewish male laborers were released. Most of those liberated were deported to Auschwitz-Birkenau from March to July 1943.

Jews were also made to engage in forced labor in North Africa. In Libya, many Jews died in terrible conditions in Italian labor camps, and over 500 Jews died from the inhumane conditions in the Italian-run Giado camp. In Tunisia, the Nazis operated some nine labor camps during the short Nazi occupation in 1942. Over 2,000 Tunisian Jews died in the Holocaust. The causes of death ranged from dying while engaged in forced labor in German concentration camps in Europe or in labor camps in Tunisia to disease to being victims of Allied bombings. Jews also died in southern Tunisia in labor camps run by the Italians and the French Vichy government.

Jews arriving in Auschwitz-Birkenau who were selected for labor and not death faced the horrors of forced labor. Eating only a small piece of bread and watery soup either before or after a long, tough workday, most Jewish prisoners lost weight very fast and succumbed to diseases like typhus. Health conditions in the camps were primitive and the water undrinkable, and epidemics spread quickly. The Germans kept the Jews in a constant state of terror. People could be shot anytime and for any reason.

Jewish males had to operate the gas chambers and crematoria, and Jews had to do the dirty work in the Nazi-instigated death camps against their fellow Jews, often even relatives or fellow Jewish community members. Unlucky men and women were selected for the most hideous medical experiments. Jewish prisoners had to clear rocks, fill trains full of dirt, dig trenches and tunnels, sort the possessions of new arrivals (which were confiscated by the Germans), and work in ammunition factories. Mostly, Jews were slave laborers in factories for the German military effort. Whether Jews were making or putting together airplane parts or ammunition, working in coal mines, or working in machine shops, they were abused by the Germans. Jews were compelled to steal in order to survive, some Jews had to discipline other Jewish inmates

with great cruelty and inhumanity, and Jewish women were forced into prostitution.

Toward the end of World War II, Jewish prisoners were often shot in forests or on long marches by foot or journeys by train after camps were evacuated because of Allied bombings. Many Jewish prisoners ended up in Bergen Belsen, where they were neglected and left to die of typhus. In the last days before liberation, the Germans poisoned potato storehouses so that many Jews died when eating this food, the only food to be found. After liberation, the Allies were not always careful to limit eating, and many prisoners died from overeating. Most Jews selected for labor in the death camps did not survive until liberation.

—*Yitzchak Kerem*

For Further Reading
Ben, Yosef. 1985. *Greek Jewry in the Holocaust and Resistance 1941–1944*. Tel Aviv: Saloniki Jewry Research Center; Kerem, Yitzchak. 1986. "Rescue Attempts of Jews in Greece in the Second World War." *Pe'amim* 27: 77–109 (in Hebrew); Landau, Zbigniew. 1990. "Forced Labor: Jews in Occupied Poland." In *Encyclopedia of the Holocaust*. Ed. Israel Gutman, pp. 500–502. New York: Macmillan Publishing.

way as to exploit them to the highest possible extent at the lowest conceivable degree of expenditure" (Meltzer, 1993).

1943
In June, the German industrial giant Krupp built a factory to manufacture parts for automatic weapons at Auschwitz. Slave labor from that prison camp provided workers for the factory.

1945
By the end of World War II, the Krupp industrial works had used 100,000 slave laborers in 100 factories all across Germany.

1945
On January 17, the German government ordered the evacuation of the concentration camp at Auschwitz, and the prisoners began their "death march" as the Nazi government attempted to relocate the slave laborers to other locations within Germany. Soviet troops liberated Auschwitz on January 27.

1945
VE (Victory in Europe) Day on May 8 marked the end of World War II in Europe.

1945
On August 8, representatives of the United States, the Soviet Union, and Great Britain met in London and signed the London Agreement for the Prosecution and Punishment of the Major War Criminals of the European Axis. The international military tribunal that heard such cases later met in Nuremberg, Germany, and the trials were completed by October 1, 1946. Twelve of the Nazi defendants were sentenced to death, three to life imprisonment, and four to lesser prison sentences; three were acquitted of all charges. Fritz Sauckel, the plenipotentiary general for the allocation of labor who was in charge of the slave labor operations for the Nazi government, was one of the war criminals who was hanged.

1945
VJ (Victory in Japan) Day on September 2 marked the end of World War II in the Pacific.

1948
The United Nations ratified the Universal Declaration of Human Rights. This document states that "no one shall be held in slavery or servitude; slavery and the slave trade shall be prohibited in all their forms." [See Document 77.]

Slaves of the pasha (ruler) of Taoudeni, Mali, stack slabs of salt in the desert, c. 1950. (Hulton-Deutsch/Corbis)

1948

The Afrikaner National Party (Herstigte) won elections in South Africa and began to institute a race-based system of apartheid in South Africa.

1948

Trials of Japanese accused war criminals began in Tokyo on August 15. The Allies eventually executed 900 Japanese war criminals out of the more than 5,000 who were put on trial. Most of those who were executed were convicted of crimes against humanity that stemmed from the wartime mistreatment of Allied prisoners of war. Seven of the 25 major Japanese officials who were convicted of war crimes were sentenced to death and hanged on December 23.

1949

In an international effort to enforce basic human rights around the world, several nations signed the Convention for the Suppression of the Traffic in Persons and the Exploitation of the Prostitution of Others. The purpose of this measure was to end the so-called white slavery that existed in many regions of the world.

1949

Shortly after his victory over Nationalist forces in China, the Communist leader Mao Zedong proclaimed the abolition of all slavery in mainland China.

1950–1951

The United Nations established the United Nations Ad Hoc Committee on Slavery to continue the antislavery activities that had been begun by the League of Nations.

1951

In an international effort to enforce basic human rights around the world, 103 nations signed the Convention on the Prevention and Punishment of the Crime of Genocide. This agreement provided for international prosecution of those who committed acts that were intended to destroy, in whole or in part, members of any national, ethnic, or religious group.

1951

Two years after the successful Communist revolution, the People's Republic of China instituted a system of forced labor camps *(laogai)*, which were designed to introduce "reform through labor." Many of the prisoners who were assigned to these labor camps were put to work on massive public works projects to benefit the Chinese state.

1953

The Japanese Ministry of Labor estimated that 40,000 Japanese children had been sold into slavery for purposes of prostitution in the previous year, partly because poverty and overpopulation had forced many parents to sell their children. In the slave market, the owners of brothels were able to purchase children for prices ranging between $25 and $100.

1953

After the death of Soviet leader Joseph Stalin in March, Lavrenty Pavlovich Beria, the director of the Soviet secret police, released a number of political prisoners from the gulags. The Communist Party's central committee challenged Beria's action and approved the resolution On the Violation of the Law by State Security Organs. Beria was then arrested, convicted, and executed for his role in Stalin's crimes against the Soviet state.

1953

The United Nations Protocol of December 7 condemned the practice of forced labor as being contrary to the spirit of the UN Charter and the Universal Declaration of Human Rights. [See Document 78.]

1954

Having established the *laogai* system of labor camps in 1951, the government of the People's Republic of China now enacted State Regulations on the Reform Through Labor. This statute authorized the use of prisoners as laborers in any type of work for 9–10 hours per day.

1956

The United Nations enacted its Supplemental Convention on the Abolition of Slavery, the Slave Trade, and Institutions and Practices Similar to Slavery. This measure was viewed as the first major revision of the Slavery Convention of 1926 prepared by the League of Nations. In addition to slavery, this later convention also recognized the problems of child slavery, bonded labor, enforced prostitution, and the servitude of indigenous peoples as matters that must be suppressed by the United Nations. [See Document 79.]

1956

As a result of Nikita Khrushchev's "De-Stalinization Speech" (or "the secret speech") some of the political prisoners in the Soviet gulags were granted amnesty on February 24–25. Although the Gulag was "reformed," it continued to operate until the fall of the Soviet Union in 1991.

1957

The British and Foreign Anti-Slavery Society changed its name to the Anti-Slavery Society for the Protection of Human Rights. During the 1990s, the organization changed its name again to Anti-Slavery International.

1957

In an effort to enforce basic human rights around the world, several nations signed the Abolition of Forced Labor Convention.

1957

The Committee on Forced Labor of the International Labour Organization had investigated charges that slave labor practices were being used in China, and its report concluded that "the People's Republic of China had set up a very highly organized system of forced labor, in prisons and labor camps, for the purposes of political coercion and education and for economic purposes" (Meltzer, 1993).

1958

British journalist Alan Winnington traveled in southwestern China and observed the continuing enslavement of individuals by Narsu slave-owners in Yunnan Province. The government of the People's Republic of China was trying to end the practice through a form of compensated emancipation.

1959

The Chinese government of Mao Zedong proclaimed the end of the feudal system of serfdom that had been practiced in Tibet, thereby officially ending all forms of slavery in China.

1959

The International Labour Organization, which continued to monitor labor practices in China, concluded that Mao Zedong's government had expanded its previous forced labor policies to include "vagrants, persons who refuse to work, persons guilty of minor offenses, and those who, for various reasons, have no means of existence" (Meltzer, 1993).

1960

Harry Wu, a Chinese student and the son of a well-to-do Shanghai banker, was jailed by Chinese authorities for making statements against the government of Mao Zedong. Wu was sentenced to 19 years of labor in "the bamboo gulag," a slave labor camp that was part of the elaborate *laogai* system established and operated by the Chinese Communists.

1962

The nations of Yemen and Saudi Arabia officially abolished slavery by statute. In spite of the latter's abolition decree, reports in the 1990s indicated that some practices of slavery persisted.

1962

The Soviet author and dissident Aleksandr I. Solzhenitsyn published *One Day in the Life of Ivan Denisovich,* a fictionalized account of the author's eight-year imprisonment in a Soviet gulag. In the work, Solzhenitsyn wrote, "Condemned to die of starvation, we were forgotten by society."

1962

In Saudi Arabia, King Faisal issued a decree that made slavery illegal, and since then, chattel slavery, as distinguished from the ownership of women and girls, has been limited in extent in that country. Until the decree was issued, slave-owning and the slave trade had flourished in Arabia, with Saudi Arabia being the center for both activities.

1966

The United Nations ratified the International Covenant on Civil and Political Rights, a document designed to prohibit the use of forced labor as a tool for political (re)education or as punishment for one's political views.

1967

A group of Pakistani brick kiln workers founded the Bhatta Mazdor Mahaz (Brickkiln Workers Front) to try to fight against the bonded labor being used in the brick-making industry. Later known as the Bonded Labor Liberation Front (BLLF), this group continued to fight against the forced labor of adults and children in Pakistan.

1969

In an international effort to enforce basic human rights around the world, 132 nations signed the International Convention on the Elimination of All Forms of Racial Discrimination. The intent of this measure was to prohibit both discrimination and the dissemination of hate-based ideas that support notions of racial superiority.

1970

The nation of Oman officially abolished slavery by statute.

1970

The Soviet author and dissident Aleksandr I. Solzhenitsyn was awarded the Nobel Prize for Literature but was unable to travel to Stockholm to receive the award.

1973

The Soviet author and dissident Aleksandr I. Solzhenitsyn published *The Gulag Archipelago.* A prisoner in a gulag for eight years and an exile for three during the reign of Stalin, this work by Solzhenitsyn presents a firsthand view of the realities of the slave labor system used for punishing political prisoners and other dissidents in the Soviet Union. In this work, Solzhenitsyn identifies one of the great paradoxes of a slave society: "If only there were evil people somewhere insidiously committing evil deeds and it were necessary only to separate them from the rest of us and destroy them. But the line dividing good and evil cuts through the heart of every human being. And who is willing to destroy a piece of his own heart?"

1973

Bao Ruo-wang published *Prisoner of Mao,* the first work to present an insider's view of the Chinese forced labor system. The work recounts the years Bao spent in the forced labor camps of Mao Zedong's government.

1973

The United Nations ratified the International Convention on the Suppression and Punishment

The only nonprofit organization in Pakistan dedicated entirely to freeing bonded laborers, the Bonded Labor Liberation Front (BLLF) has successfully liberated over half a million slaves during its 30-year existence. Following the motto "Freedom from slavery through education," the BLLF has implemented a system of primary schools across the country. Many of the 250 established schools, called Apna (*Our* in Urdu) schools, have only one or two teachers and a dozen or so students. Since primary education is not compulsory in Pakistan, and Christians, as well as low-caste people, are often prohibited from educating their children, the Apna schools provide the only viable education for thousands of freed child slaves.

The BLLF, originally called Bhatta Mazdor Mahaz (Brickkiln Workers Front), was founded in 1967 by a small group of brick kiln workers with the help of a 19-year-old Muslim journalist, Ehsan Ullah Khan. The original mission was limited to providing legal aid to bonded brick kiln workers and appealing to the federal government to outlaw bonded brick kiln labor. After the Pakistani Supreme Court ruled in September 1988 that the use of bonded labor in the brick kilns violated the country's constitution in response to lobbying from the group, other groups of disenfranchised bonded laborers petitioned Bhatta Mazdor Mahaz to expand its mandate to include laborers held in debt-bondage in other industries. These workers joined Bhatta Mazdor Mahaz, and the Bonded Labor Liberation Front was created.

The BLLF is a nondenominational, nonprofit organization that has as its mandate the abolishing of all contemporary forms of slavery, bondage, and forced labor in all sectors of Pakistani industry, including in brick making and carpet weaving, the manufacturing of leather and medical instruments, agriculture, stone quarrying, mining, and domestic servitude. There are an estimated 20 million bonded laborers in Pakistan who have become enslaved either because they inherited a family debt or because they were sold into servitude. In the *peshgi* (debt) system, which is prevalent all over Pakistan, children are loaned or apprenticed to factory owners in return for a certain sum of money. Their labor is then used to repay the debt incurred. However, the debt typically increases over time as it is added to each time the laborer makes a mistake. The BLLF insists on the illegality of the *peshgi* system, and when its members free bonded laborers, they refuse to repay the initial debt to the landlord or factory owner.

The main activities of the BLLF include freeing bonded laborers, building community schools to educate freed slaves, lobbying the government, and reporting violations to the international human rights community. The BLLF has proved that bonded families and children are subjected to frequent physical and psychological abuse by both factory owners and police. Torture is used to prevent laborers from registering legal complaints against their masters, and workers have reportedly been beaten with sticks, hanged upside down from ceiling fans, and scalded with hot oil. Abuses can be carried out with impunity because the factory owners are often related to the local police or are able to bribe them to look the other way.

The BLLF has been the subject of controversy and has faced opposition in Pakistan from industrialists, businessmen, factory owners, government officials, and religious leaders who defend the debt-bondage system. In April 1995, after the highly publicized slaying of the group's youngest activist, a 12-year-old former carpet weaver named Iqbal Masih, the Federal Investigation Agency, a secret police force, raided BLLF offices; detained 11 employees; confiscated office equipment, computers, fax machines, and files; and took cash money. The government of Pakistan put a freeze on BLLF bank accounts and registered a sedition case, the sentence for which is the death penalty, against BLLF president Ehsan Ullah Khan and against the BLLF's press secretary, a prominent journalist named Zafar Yab Ahmed. Forced into involuntary exile since May 1995, Ehsan Ullah Khan has continued the work of the BLLF from Sweden. The government of Pakistan still denies the Bonded Labor Liberation Front access to its bank accounts, but the village schools have continued to function, and the BLLF has continued its work of freeing adults and child bonded laborers from involuntary servitude.

—*Jennifer Margulis*

For Further Reading
Karim, Farhad. 1995. *Contemporary Forms of Slavery in Pakistan*. New York: Human Rights Watch; U.S. Congress. 1994. *By the Sweat and Toil of Children: The Use of Child Labor in American Imports*. July 15. Report to the Committees on Appropriations. Washington, DC.: Government Printing Office.

of the Crime of Apartheid, a measure intended to put international pressure on the government of South Africa to reform its race-based system of apartheid, which had been in effect since 1948.

1974

The Soviet author and dissident Aleksandr I. Solzhenitsyn was expelled from the Soviet Union. He settled in Switzerland and later moved to the United States.

1975

The UN Commission on Human Rights established the Working Group on Contemporary Forms of Slavery of the Sub-Commission on the Protection of Minorities to collect information on a wide range of slavelike practices that persisted in the modern world.

1979

In keeping with its charge to end all forms of servitude, the United Nations ratified the Convention on the Elimination of All Forms of Discrimination against Women. This measure was enacted in an effort to abolish the practice of servile marriage throughout the world.

1980

The Islamic Republic of Mauritania abolished slavery on July 5. Reports from the region maintained that the practice of slavery persisted despite the government's official abolition proclamation.

1981

In an international effort to enforce basic human rights around the world, 120 nations signed the Convention on the Elimination of All Forms of Discrimination against Women, a measure to protect women from discrimination in public life, education, employment, health, marriage, and the family.

1987

Seventy-one nations signed the Convention against Torture and Other Cruel, Inhuman, or Degrading Treatment or Punishment, which holds signatory nations responsible for preventing torture and for punishing torturers. Even those individuals who are acting as torturers under orders are not protected from prosecution under this measure.

1989

The United Nations also ratified the Convention on the Rights of the Child, a document designed to protect children from bonded labor by stating that the work of children should not be "hazardous," should not "interfere with [their] education," and should not "be harmful to the child's health or physical, mental, spiritual, moral or social development."

1990

In another effort to enforce basic human rights around the world, 126 nations signed a new Convention on the Rights of the Child. This measure defines the rights that are basic to all children and includes primary health care and education as rights that nations must strive to provide for children around the world.

1990

F. W. De Klerk, president of South Africa, tried to begin the process of reforming South Africa's apartheid system when he removed the ban that had outlawed the African National Congress, the Pan African Congress, and the Communist Party. De Klerk was also responsible for releasing Nelson Mandela from prison in the same year.

1990

The India-based Bonded Labor Liberation Front (BLLF) organized the first National Workshop on Eradication of Child Labor in the Carpet Industry in Delhi, India.

1990

On November 16, Professor Yun Chông-ok established the Korean Council for the Women Drafted for Military Sexual Slavery by Japan to bring forward the facts surrounding the use of comfort women as sexual slaves during World War II. The group seeks a redress of grievances related to this massive human rights violation and hopes to obtain an official apology from the Japanese government.

1991

Anti-Slavery International, a British-based organization, instituted the Anti-Slavery Award to recognize those individuals or groups who are working to eradicate all forms of slavery from the modern world. The first organization to be so recognized was the Bonded Labor Liberation Front of India.

Immigrants who enter the United States to work without legal documentation are vulnerable to enslavement. Sasha Lewis (1979) argues that forced confinement of undocumented workers and coercion to remain are primary for conditions fostering contemporary U.S. slavery. The high cost of being smuggled in, the threat of deportation by the Immigration and Naturalization Service, and low wages, which do not permit illegal workers to better their lot, are predisposing conditions for alien enslavement. In the 1990s, unfavorable contracts for immigrants who work in agriculture, sweatshops, and domestic service often provided little or no economic return for their labor. Labor-intensive crops, garment contracting, and private households employing maids were periodically reported as sites of labor law violation and enslavement.

In the United States, a person is considered to be legally enslaved if he or she is unable to leave employment voluntarily owing to coercion. Overt coercion occurs when workers are obliged to repay excessive smuggling fees for entry, purchase food and housing at inflated costs, or are forcibly confined under threat of deportation. Below-minimum-wage pay, poor working conditions, and exploitative charges for often substandard room and board are not legally considered to constitute enslavement although they are covertly coercive. The implication is that a humanitarian standard for determining enslavement would extend to a structure of substandard labor conditions. Terms of labor involving overt or covert coercion maintain individuals in a state of *virtual slavery* bound to a system of unequal exchange relations.

The enslavement process can begin by someone arranging for an immigrant's illegal entry through an alien smuggling ring. Unpaid fees for illegally smuggling individuals into the United States are a means of holding workers in captivity until they can pay off their debts, and estimates are that smuggling entry debts can run up to $45,000 for a long-distance international migrant (Bolz, 1995). In the 1990s, Jennifer Bolz (1995) indicated that transnational Chinese-organized criminal groups, known as triads, were smuggling up to 100,000 aliens per year out of the People's Republic of China with multibillion-dollar profits. After a down payment, aliens worked off their debt in addition to sending remittances to China. Immigrants who were unable to repay their debt were enslaved in manufacturing sweatshops. In 1995, 74 Thai immigrant workers were released from indentured servitude in a boarded-up garment sweatshop that

was encircled with barbed wire. Some of those workers had sought to repay smuggling fees and had had to pay exorbitant fees for room and board for up to seven years (*Economist*, 1995).

In the late-twentieth century, a time of economic restructuring, covert coercion of labor occurred when labor-intensive, dangerous industries like meat-packing, which had a high rate of employee injury, replaced unionized citizens with an imported labor force. Low wages and substandard working conditions for a mixture of Mexican, Somalian, and other noncitizen workers, with and without documents, were offered by some processors. Major garment manufacturers subcontracted work to employers who broke labor laws, including failure to pay the minimum wage or overtime, withholding wages from workers, and providing unacceptable working conditions, including lack of ventilation. Covert coercion occurred when Levi Straus and The Gap subcontracted work to employers on the U.S. commonwealth of Saipan who had confiscated the passports of Chinese workers and made them labor 84-hour weeks for subminimum wages.

In 1997, the *New York Times* reported that an alien smuggling ring operated by an extended family from Mexico City had enslaved 44 undocumented Mexicans, most of whom were deaf, in New York, Chicago, and Los Angeles. They were put to work peddling trinkets in the informal economy and poorly housed. Although slavery is considered to be formally abolished in the United States, one deaf Mexican immigrant reported that individuals had actually been auctioned off to bosses who then forced them to peddle trinkets.

Private householders may attempt enslavement based on differences in citizenship status ranging from exploiting undocumented status to, in Canada, a virtual indentured servitude that is legally mandated by the state. The Live-in Caregiver Program requires workers to engage in compulsory labor for two years. Their rent is deducted from their wages, and they are dependent on their relationship with a particular employer that cannot be changed without their being subject to deportation. Working conditions include long hours, low wages, and little control over time and energy demands. A domestic worker must endure social isolation, separation from family, and potential exposure to employer abuse. This is a government-supported labor practice that severely limits the rights of alien workers.

In the United States, undocumented domestics

Police escort Mexican nationals living in a house in Queens, New York, where they were reportedly being held against their will. (Associated Press)

are subject to immediate deportation, which further undermines labor conditions. In 1997, in Kerrville, Texas, it was revealed that a woman had been kept against her will in debt-peonage, forced to perform domestic labor by day and locked in a garage at night. The debt she owed to the smugglers was $1,400.

Although the United Nations is debating human rights codes, there is a lack of full agreement over what constitutes *contemporary forms* of enslavement. In 1990, the UN General Assembly passed the International Convention on Protection of the Rights of All Migrant Workers and Members of Their Families, a document which specifies that migrant workers are to be treated on equal terms with native workers, using national or international labor standards, but does not fully protect workers, such as migrants in domestic service, who are covered by national legislation. In contrast, the International Labour Organization (ILO) sets minimum international labor standards, for nations rat-

ifying its agreements, that place far greater limitations on the ability of employers to practice covert coercion of workers. Through ratification of ILO minimum standards, emergent forms of contemporary enslavement can be better contained than by using existing the laws of nation-states.

—*Judith Ann Warner*

For Further Reading

Boltz, Jennifer. 1995. "Chinese Organized Crime and Illegal Alien Trafficking: Humans as a Commodity." *Asian Affairs* 22(3): 147–158; Crosette, Barbara. 1997. "What Modern Slavery Is, and Isn't." *New York Times,* July 27; Lewis, Sasha Gregory. 1979. *Slave Trade Today: American Exploitation of Illegal Aliens.* Boston: Beacon Press; "The Profits of Sin." 1995. *Economist,* August 12, pp. 23–24; Udesky, Laurie. 1994. "Sweatshops behind the Labels." *Nation* 258(19): 665–668; UN General Assembly. 1990. *"International Convention on Protection of the Rights of All Migrant Workers and Members of Their Families."* Report: A/45/838. New York.

A slave for six years and subsequently an activist for children's rights, Iqbal Masih became recognized in Pakistan and internationally as an eloquent and charismatic spokesperson against Pakistan's system of debt-bondage. Although slavery is unconstitutional in Pakistan and all indentured servitude became illegal after the Abolition of Bonded Labor Act passed by Parliament in 1992, laws against enslaving children have seldom been enforced. At the urging of a factory middleman, Iqbal's father loaned Iqbal at age 4 to a carpet factory for 600 rupees (the equivalent of approximately $12) in order to pay for an elder son's wedding. Iqbal was forced to weave for over 12 hours a day, and he was beaten, verbally abused, and chained to the loom by the factory owner. When he made mistakes in knotting the carpets, his fingers were plunged into boiling oil. At the time of his escape from the factory in 1992, his hands were horribly scarred, he was suffering from tuberculosis and chronic bronchitis, and his growth had been severely stunted from years of malnutrition.

Iqbal ran away from the factory where he worked and sought help from the Bonded Labor Liberation Front (BLLF), a grassroots organization dedicated to freeing illegally enslaved laborers. He was taken in by the BLLF, enrolled in one of its Apna (*Our* in Urdu) schools, and taught to read and write—he was probably 10 years old at the time. Quick-witted and articulate, Iqbal began speaking at local rallies against child slavery. His unusual eloquence and his strikingly small size caught the interest of both local and international media and international human rights organizations. The BLLF estimates that Iqbal's highly publicized speeches and work on behalf of other child slaves helped free over 3,000 other child workers.

In November 1994, Iqbal left Pakistan, traveled to Sweden and the United States, and called for an end to slavery in Pakistan at rallies, in schools, and in front of labor organizations and community groups. He received a $25,000 Youth-in-Action Award from the Reebok Foundation in December and spoke at the nationally televised award ceremony to an audience of over 2,500 people.

In April 1995, four months after his visit to the United States, Iqbal, then about 12 years old, was gunned down while riding a bicycle on a village road in Muridke, Pakistan, with his cousin and his uncle. Activists against bonded labor believed he was killed by "the carpet mafia" and immediately called for a full investigation of his death. However,

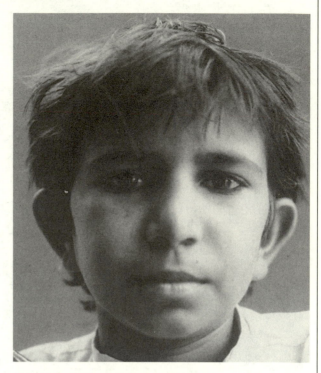

Iqbal Masih (Reebok International)

the facts of the murder were never clarified—the government of Pakistan concluded that Iqbal had been killed by a landless peasant after Iqbal and his relatives had allegedly surprised him as he was fornicating with a donkey. After Iqbal's murder, the government of Pakistan registered a sedition case, the sentence for which is death, against BLLF president Ehsan Ullah Khan and against the BLLF press secretary, a prominent journalist named Zafar Yab Ahmed. The Federal Investigation Agency (FIA), a secret police force, detained Iqbal's mother, his younger sister, and 11 members of the BLLF; confiscated BLLF computer equipment, office supplies, and files; took cash money; and put a freeze on BLLF bank accounts. At the same time, the Pakistan Carpet Manufacturers and Exporters Association reported a $10 million decline in carpet sales.

Iqbal was buried in an unmarked grave in Muridke, his body wrapped in a flag of the BLLF. Over 800 mourners attended his funeral, and thousands of protesters demonstrated in Lahore a week later demanding an end to child slavery. His murder motivated student groups around the world, most notably in the United States, Sweden, and Canada, and sparked international activism against child servitude.

—*Jennifer Margulis*

For Further Reading
Karim, Farhad. *Contemporary Forms of Slavery in Pakistan.* 1995. New York: Human Rights Watch; U.S. Congress. 1994. *By the Sweat and Toil of Children: The Use of Child Labor in American Imports.* July 15. Report to the Committees on Appropriations. Washington, D.C.: Government Printing Office.

1991

In August, Kim Hak-sun gave the first public testimony on the issue of comfort women, women who were used as sexual slaves by the Japanese military during World War II.

1991

In September, *Asiaweek* magazine reported the arrest of a wealthy businessman from Saudi Arabia who had purchased a 10-year-old child in Hyerabad, India, for $240. The Saudi businessman was arrested when he attempted to fly the young girl out of India, supposedly to be his wife.

1992

The Korean Council for the Women Drafted for Military Sexual Slavery by Japan took the issue of comfort women to the UN's Human Rights Commission. Recently discovered documents had shown a pattern of heavy involvement on the part of the Japanese government.

1992

Anti-Slavery International presented the yearly Anti-Slavery Award to Ricardo Rezende of Brazil for his work among the poor of Brazil who have been forced to work as slave laborers on estates in the Amazon basin. [See Document 80.]

1993

Anti-Slavery International presented the Anti-Slavery Award to the organization End Child Prostitution in Asian Tourism (ECPAT), which had organized an international campaign to prevent the commercial sexual exploitation of children.

1993

Harry Wu published his autobiographical account, *Bitter Winds: A Memoir of My Years in China's Gulag.* The work recounts the 19 years that Wu spent in the forced labor camps during the period of Mao Zedong's government.

1993

The Organization of African Unity sponsored a Pan-African Conference on Reparations for African Enslavement, Colonization, and Neo-Colonization. The meeting was held in Abuja, Nigeria, on April 27–29.

1994

Anti-Slavery International presented the Anti-Slavery Award to Father Edwin Paraison, who helped to raise international concern for the enslavement of Haitian cane cutters on the sugarcane plantations of the Dominican Republic.

1994

National elections were held in South Africa with universal suffrage being allowed for the first time. A government of national unity with an African National Congress (ANC) majority was elected, and Nelson Mandela was inaugurated as the president of South Africa.

1994

In December, the Reebok Foundation presented the Youth-in-Action Award to Iqbal Masih of Pakistan, a young boy who had become an international activist speaking out against the enslavement of children in Pakistani carpet mills.

1995

Liu Zongren published *Hard Time: 30 Months in a Chinese Labor Camp* in which he described his experiences as a slave laborer on China's Chadian Labor Reform Farm No. 583 during the Cultural Revolution of the 1960s.

1995

In April, Iqbal Masih, the 12-year-old Pakistani youth who had become an international spokesperson for the plight of child laborers, was murdered.

1995

On September 8, the U.S. House Subcommittee on International Operations and Human Rights heard testimony regarding the practice of slave labor in the *laogai* (forced labor camps) operated by the People's Republic of China.

Maria Rosa Henson, the first Filipino woman to admit publicly that she had been forced into sexual slavery by Japanese soldiers during World War II, displays a 1996 letter of apology on behalf of Japan from Prime Minister Ryutaro Hashimoto. (Associated Press)

1995

On November 16, Anti-Slavery International presented the year's Anti-Slavery Award to the Chinese dissident Harry Wu, who had been imprisoned in China for speaking out against the government and since his release from prison had been critical of the use of forced labor in Chinese prison camps.

1996

Anti-Slavery International presented the Anti-Slavery Award to the Regional Indigenous Organisation of Atalaya (OIRA) in Peru for its work to help liberate thousands of the indigenous Ashaninka who had been enslaved for debt-bondage in the Amazon basin.

1996

Isaac J. Vogelfanger published *Red Tempest:*

The Life of a Surgeon in the Gulag in which he described the eight years he spent in the forced labor camps of the Soviet Union during Stalin's regime in the 1940s.

1996

On February 6, Radhika Coomaraswamy, the UN's special investigator on violence against women, presented her report on the comfort women issue to the United Nations. Her recommendations on this matter were that the government of Japan should apologize for this human rights violation, compensate the victims, punish those who were responsible, and teach the story of this crime in Japanese history classes.

1996

In March, Gaspar Biro, a special UN human rights monitor, testified before a committee of the U.S. Congress and confirmed the existence of modern-day slave markets and chattel slavery in the Sudan.

1997

Anti-Slavery International presented the Anti-Slavery Award to Pureza Lopes Loiola of the state of Maranhão, Brazil, in recognition of her work against the enslavement of Brazil's poor on rural estates throughout the country.

1997

In December, the television news program *60 Minutes* aired an investigative report that exposed the Trokosi system, an indigenous practice of slavery that persists in eastern regions of Ghana. This practice, which is rooted in the custom of atonement for past misdeeds, requires families to dedicate their daughters to the local temples where animist priests use their labor and often sexually exploit them.

1998

On November 18, Anti-Slavery International recognized Cheikh Saad Bouh Kamara of Mauritania with its annual Anti-Slavery Award. Kamara is the first African to receive this honor. As a human rights activist, he has worked tirelessly to end slavery in Mauritania.

☙DOCUMENTS☙

☙DOCUMENT 1☙
EXCERPTS FROM THE CODE OF HAMMURABI (C. 1790 B.C.)

Selected passages from the Code of Hammurabi demonstrate that the status of slave was well established and clearly defined within the laws of ancient Babylonia in the eighteenth century B.C. The distinctions noted within this code of laws show that within Babylonian society, a slave was viewed as a lesser creature than a freedman and that the servile status was hereditary.
[Laws which pertain to those of slave status:]

7. If any one buy from the son or the slave of another man, without witnesses or a contract, silver or gold, a male or female slave, an ox or a sheep, an ass or anything, or if he take it in charge, he is considered a thief and shall be put to death.

15. If any one take a male or female slave of the court, or a male or female slave of a freed man, outside the city gates, he shall be put to death.

16. If any one receive into his house a runaway male or female slave of the court, or of a freedman, and does not bring it out at the public proclamation of the major domus [royal household], the master of the house shall be put to death.

17. If any one find runaway male or female slaves in the open country and bring them to their masters, the master of the slaves shall pay him two shekels of silver.

18. If the slave will not give the name of the master, the finder shall bring him to the palace; a further investigation must follow, and the slave shall be returned to his master.

19. If he hold the slaves in his house, and they are caught there, he shall be put to death.

20. If the slave that he caught run away from him, then shall he swear to the owners of the slave, and he is free of all blame.

116. If the prisoner die in prison from blows or maltreatment, the master of the prisoner shall convict the merchant before the judge. If he was a free-born man, the son of the merchant shall be put to death; if it was a slave, he shall pay one-third of a mina of gold, and all that the master of the prisoner gave he shall forfeit.

117. If any one fail to meet a claim for debt, and sell himself, his wife, his son, and daughter for money or give them away to forced labor: they shall work for three years in the house of the man who bought them, or the proprietor, and in the fourth year they shall be set free.

118. If he give a male or female slave away for forced labor, and the merchant sublease them, or sell them for money, no objection can be raised.

119. If any one fail to meet a claim for debt, and he sell the maid servant who has borne him children, for money, the money which the merchant has paid shall be repaid to him by the owner of the slave and she shall be freed.

129. If a man's wife be surprised (in flagrante delicto) with another man, both shall be tied and thrown into the water, but the husband may pardon his wife and the king his slaves.

146. If a man take a wife and she give this man a maid-servant as wife and she bear him children, and then this maid assume equality with the wife: because she has borne him children her master shall not sell her for money, but he may keep her as a slave, reckoning her among the maid-servants.

171. If, however, the father while still living did not say to the sons of the maid-servant: "My sons," and then the father dies, then the sons of the maid-

servant shall not share with the sons of the wife, but the freedom of the maid and her sons shall be granted. The sons of the wife shall have no right to enslave the sons of the maid; the wife shall take her dowry (from her father), and the gift that her husband gave her and deeded to her (separate from dowry, or the purchase-money paid her father), and live in the home of her husband: so long as she lives she shall use it, it shall not be sold for money. Whatever she leaves shall belong to her children.

175. If a State slave or the slave of a freed man marry the daughter of a free man, and children are born, the master of the slave shall have no right to enslave the children of the free.

176. If, however, a State slave or the slave of a freed man marry a man's daughter, and after he marries her she bring a dowry from a father's house, if then they both enjoy it and found a household, and accumulate means, if then the slave die, then she who was free born may take her dowry, and all that her husband and she had earned; she shall divide them into two parts, one-half the master for the slave shall take, and the other half shall the free-born woman take for her children. If the free-born woman had no gift she shall take all that her husband and she had earned and divide it into two parts; and the master of the slave shall take one-half and she shall take the other for her children.

199. If he put out the eye of a man's slave, or break the bone of a man's slave, he shall pay one-half of its value.

205. If the slave of a freed man strike the body of a freed man, his ear shall be cut off.

215. If a physician make a large incision with an operating knife and cure it, or if he open a tumor (over the eye) with an operating knife, and saves the eye, he shall receive ten shekels in money.

216. If the patient be a freed man, he receives five shekels.

217. If he be the slave of some one, his owner shall give the physician two shekels.

218. If a physician make a large incision with the operating knife, and kill him, or open a tumor with the operating knife, and cut out the eye, his hands shall be cut off.

219. If a physician make a large incision in the slave of a freed man, and kill him, he shall replace the slave with another slave.

221. If a physician heal the broken bone or diseased soft part of a man, the patient shall pay the physician five shekels in money.

222. If he were a freed man he shall pay three shekels.

223. If he were a slave his owner shall pay the physician two shekels.

226. If a barber, without the knowledge of his master, cut the sign of a slave on a slave not to be sold, the hands of this barber shall be cut off.

227. If any one deceive a barber, and have him mark a slave not for sale with the sign of a slave, he shall be put to death, and buried in his house. The barber shall swear: "I did not mark him wittingly," and shall be guiltless.

229 If a builder build a house for some one, and does not construct it properly, and the house which he built fall in and kill its owner, then that builder shall be put to death.

230. If it kill the son of the owner the son of that builder shall be put to death.

231. If it kill a slave of the owner, then he shall pay slave for slave to the owner of the house.

251. If an ox be a goring ox, and it shown that he is a gorer, and he do not bind his horns, or fasten the ox up, and the ox gore a free-born man and kill him, the owner shall pay one-half a mina in money.

252. If he kill a man's slave, he shall pay one-third of a mina.

278. If any one buy a male or female slave, and before a month has elapsed the benu-disease [leprosy] be developed, he shall return the slave to the seller, and receive the money which he had paid.

279. If any one by a male or female slave, and a third party claim it, the seller is liable for the claim.

280. If while in a foreign country a man buy a male or female slave belonging to another of his own country; if when he return home the owner of the male or female slave recognize it: if the male or female slave be a native of the country, he shall give them back without any money.

281. If they are from another country, the buyer shall declare the amount of money paid therefor to the merchant, and keep the male or female slave.

282. If a slave say to his master: "You are not my master," if they convict him his master shall cut off his ear.

Source: "The Code of Hammurabi," trans. L. W. King (New Haven, CT: Yale University, Avalon Project, 1996; www.yale.edu/lawweb/avalon/hamframe.htm).

⮞DOCUMENT 2⮜
VERSES FROM THE OLD TESTAMENT

Several books of the Old Testament include commentary upon the societal structure of the Hebrew people. Although these passages indicate the pervasive nature and extent of slavery within Hebrew society, they also suggest the tolerable limit to which the slaves themselves had rights that had to be respected by their owners.

EXODUS 21:2–11
When you buy a male Hebrew slave, he shall serve six years, but in the seventh he shall go out a free

person, without debt. If he comes in single, he shall go out single; if he comes in married, then his wife shall go out with him. If his master gives him a wife and she bears him sons or daughters, the wife and her children shall be her master's and he shall go out alone. But if the slave declares, "I love my master, my wife, and my children; I will not go out a free person," then his master shall bring him before God. He shall be brought to the door or the doorpost; and his master shall pierce his ear with an awl; and he shall serve him for life.

When a man sells his daughter as a slave, she shall not go out as the male slaves do. If she does not please her master, who designated her for himself, then he shall let her be redeemed; he shall have no right to sell her to a foreign people, since he has dealt unfairly with her. If he designates her for his son, he shall deal with her as with a daughter. If he takes another wife to himself, he shall not diminish the food, clothing, or marital rights of the first wife. And if he does not do these three things for her, she shall go out without debt, without payment of money.

LEVITICUS 25:39–55

If any who are dependent on you be come so impoverished that they sell themselves to you, you shall not make them serve as slaves. They shall remain with you as hired or bound laborers. They shall serve with you until the year of the jubilee. Then they and their children with them shall be free from your authority; they shall go back to their own family and return to their ancestral property. For they are my servants, whom I brought out of the land of Egypt; they shall not be sold as slaves are sold. You shall not rule over them with harshness, but shall fear your God. As for the male and female slaves whom you may have, it is from the nations around you that you may acquire male and female slaves. You may also acquire them from among the aliens residing with you, and from their families that are with you, who have been born in your land; and they may be your property. You may keep them as a possession for your children after you, for them to inherit as property. These you may treat as slaves, but as for your fellow Israelites, no one shall rule over the other with harshness.

If resident aliens among you prosper, and if any of your kin fall into difficulty with one of them and sell themselves to an alien, or to a branch of the alien's family, after they have sold themselves they shall have the right of redemption; one of their brothers may redeem them, or their uncle or their uncle's son may redeem them, or anyone of their family who is of their own flesh may redeem them; or if they prosper they may redeem themselves. They shall compute with the purchaser the total from the year when they sold themselves to the alien until the jubilee year; the price of the sale shall be applied to the number of years: the time they were with the owner shall be rated as the time of a hired laborer. If many years remain, they shall pay for their redemption in proportion to the purchase price; and if few years remain until the jubilee year, they shall compute thus: according to the years involved they shall make payment for their redemption. As a laborer hired by the year they shall be under the alien's authority, who shall not, however, rule with harshness over them in your sight. And if they have not been redeemed in any of these ways, they and their children with them shall go free in the jubilee year. For to me the people of Israel are servants; they are my servants whom I brought out from the land of Egypt: I am the LORD your God.

DEUTERONOMY 15:12–18

If a member of your community, whether a Hebrew man or a Hebrew woman, is sold to you and works for you six years, in the seventh year you shall set that person free. And when you send a male slave out from you a free person, you shall not send him out empty-handed. Provide liberally out of your flock, your threshing floor, and your wine press, thus giving to him some of the bounty with which the LORD your God has blessed you. Remember that you were a slave in the land of Egypt, and the LORD your God redeemed you; for this reason I lay this command upon you today. But if he says to you, "I will not go out from you," because he loves you and your household, since he is well off with you, then you shall take an awl and thrust it through his earlobe into the door, and he shall be your slave forever.

You shall do the same with regard to your female slave.

JEREMIAH 34:8–17

The word that came to Jeremiah from the LORD, after King Zedekiah had made a covenant with all the people in Jerusalem to make a proclamation of liberty to them, that all should set free their Hebrew slaves, male and female, so that no one should hold another Judean in slavery. And they obeyed, all the officials and all the people who had entered into the covenant that all would set free their slaves, male or female, so that they would not be enslaved again; they obeyed and set them free. But afterward they turned around and took back the male and female slaves they had set free, and brought them again into subjection as slaves. The word of the LORD came to Jeremiah from the LORD: Thus says the LORD, the God of Israel: I myself made a covenant with your ancestors when I brought them out of the land of Egypt, out of the house of slavery, saying, "Every seventh year each of you must set free any Hebrews who have been sold to you and have served you six years; you must set them free from your service." But your ancestors did not listen to me or incline their ears to me. You yourselves recently repented and did what was right in my sight by proclaiming liberty to one another, and you made a covenant before me in the house that is called by my name; but then you turned around and profaned my name when each of you took back your male and female slaves, whom you had set free according to their desire, and you brought them again into subjection to be your slaves. Therefore, thus says the LORD : You have not obeyed me by granting a release to your neighbors and friends; I am going to grant a release to you, says the LORD—a release to the sword, to pestilence, and to famine. I will make you a horror to all the kingdoms of the earth.

Source: New Revised Standard Version Bible (Nashville, TN: Thomas Nelson, 1989).

❧DOCUMENT 3❧
AN EXCERPT FROM ON THE LAWS BY MARCUS TULLIUS CICERO

In the writings of the Roman orator Cicero, we often find observations and commentary upon the prevailing social structure of the Roman Empire. In this dialogue taken from On the Laws, *Cicero remarks that "we are born for justice" and "there is no difference in kind between man and man," but the society that he describes was one that rested upon a slave-based economy. The rhetoric and the reality of the Roman world are seemingly inconsistent in this passage.*

M. . . . that animal which we call man, endowed with foresight and quick intelligence, complex, keen, possessing memory, full of reason and prudence, has been given a certain distinguished status by the supreme God who created him; for he is the only one among so many different kinds and varieties of living beings who has a share in reason and thought, while all the rest are deprived of it. But what is more divine, I will not say in man only, but in all heaven and earth, than reason? And reason, when it is full grown and perfected, is rightly called wisdom. Therefore, since there is nothing better than reason, and since it exists both in man and God, the first common possession of man and God is reason. But those who have reason in common must also have right reason in common. And since right reason is Law, we must believe that men have Law also in common with the gods. Further, those who share Law must also share justice; and those who share these are to be regarded as members of the same commonwealth. If indeed they obey the same authorities and powers, this is true in a far greater degree; but as a matter of fact they do obey this celestial system, the divine mind, and the God of transcendent power. Hence we must now conceive of this whole universe as one commonwealth of which both gods and men are members.

And just as in States distinctions in legal status are made on account of the blood relationships of families, according to a system which I shall take up in its proper place, so in the universe the same thing holds true, but on a scale much vaster and more splendid, so that men are grouped with Gods on the basis of blood relationship and descent. For when the nature of man is examined, the theory is usually advanced (and in all probability it is correct) that through constant changes and revolutions in the heavens, a time came which was suitable for sowing the seed of the human race. And when this seed was scattered and sown over the earth, it was granted the divine gift of the soul. For while the other elements of which man consists were derived from what is mortal, and are therefore fragile and perishable, the soul was generated in us by God. Hence we are justified in saying that there is a blood relationship between ourselves and the celestial beings; or we may call it a common ancestry or origin. Therefore among all the varieties of living beings, there is no creature except man which has any knowledge of God, and among men themselves there is no race either so highly civilized or so savage as not to know that it must believe in a god, even if it does not know in what sort of god it ought to believe. Thus it is clear that man recognizes God because, in a way, he remembers and recognizes the source from which he sprang.

Moreover, virtue exists in man and God alike, but in no other creature besides; virtue, however, is nothing else than Nature perfected and developed to its highest point; therefore there is a likeness between man and God. As this is true, what relationship could be closer or clearer than this one? For this reason, Nature has lavishly yielded such a wealth of things adapted to man's convenience and use that what she produces seems intended as a gift to us, and not brought forth by chance; and this is true, not only of what the fertile earth bountifully bestows in the form of grain and fruit, but also of the animals; for it is clear that some of them have been created to be man's slaves, some to supply him with their products, and others to serve as his food. Moreover innumerable arts have been discovered through the teachings of Nature; for it is by a skilful imitation of her that reason has acquired the necessities of life. Nature has likewise not only equipped man himself with nimbleness of thought, but has also given him the senses, to be, as it were, his attendants and messengers; she has laid bare the obscure and none too [obvious] meanings of a great many things, to serve as the foundations of knowledge, as we may call them; and she has granted us a bodily form which is convenient and well suited to the human mind. For while she has bent the other creatures down toward their food, she has made man alone erect, and has challenged him to look up toward heaven, as being, so to speak, akin to him, and his first home. In addition, she has so formed his features as to portray therein the character that lies hidden deep within him; for not only do the eyes declare with exceeding clearness the innermost feelings of our hearts, but also the countenance, as we Romans call it, which can be found in no living thing save man, reveals the character. I will pass over the special faculties and aptitudes of the other parts of the body, such as the varying tones of the voice and the power of speech, which is the most effective promoter of human intercourse; for all these things are not in keeping with our present discussion or the time at our disposal; and besides, this topic has been adequately treated, as it seems to me, by Scipio in the books which you have read. But, whereas God has begotten and equipped man, desiring him to be the chief of all created things, it should now be evident, without going into all the details, that Nature, alone and unaided, goes a step farther; for, with no guide to point the way, she starts with those things whose character she has learned through the rudimentary beginnings of intelligence, and, alone and unaided, strengthens and perfects the faculty of reason.

A. Ye immortal gods, how far back you go to find the origins of Justice! And you discourse so eloquently that I not only have no desire to hasten on to the consideration of the civil law, concerning which I was expecting you to speak, but I should have no objection to your spending even the entire day on your present topic; for the matters which you have taken up, no doubt, merely as preparatory to another subject, are of greater import than the subject itself to which they form an introduction.

M. The points which are now being briefly touched upon are certainly important; but out of all the material of the philosophers' discussions, surely there comes nothing more valuable than the full realization that we are born for justice, and that right is based, not upon men's opinions, but upon Nature. This fact will immediately be plain if you once get a clear conception of man's fellowship and union with his fellow-men. For no single thing is so like another, so exactly its counterpart, as all of us are to one another. Nay, if bad habits and false beliefs did not twist the weaker minds and turn them in whatever direction they are inclined, no one would be so like his own self as all men would be like all others. And so, however we may define man, a single definition will apply to all. This is a sufficient proof that there is no difference in kind between man and man; for if there were, one definition could not be applicable to all men; and indeed reason, which alone raises us above the level of the beasts and enables us to draw inferences, to prove and disprove, to discuss and

solve problems, and to come to conclusions, is certainly common to us all, and, though varying in what it learns, at least in the capacity to learn it is invariable. For the same things are invariably perceived by the senses, and those things which stimulate the senses, stimulate them in the same way in all men; and those rudimentary beginnings of intelligence to which I have referred, which are imprinted on our minds, are imprinted on all minds alike; and speech, the mind's interpreter, though differing in the choice of words, agrees in the sentiments expressed. In fact, there is no human being of any race who, if he finds a guide, cannot attain to virtue.

The similarity of the human race is clearly marked in its evil tendencies as well as in its goodness. For pleasure also attracts all men; and even though it is an enticement to vice, yet it has some likeness to what is naturally good. For it delights us by its lightness and agreeableness; and for this reason, by an error of thought, it is embraced as something wholesome. It is through a similar misconception that we shun death as though it were a dissolution of nature, and cling to life because it keeps us in the sphere in which we were born; and that we look upon pain as one of the greatest of evils, not only because of its cruelty, but also because it seems to lead to the destruction of nature. In the same way, on account of the similarity between moral worth and renown, those who are publicly honoured are considered happy, while those who do not attain fame are thought miserable. Troubles, joys, desires, and fears haunt the minds of all men without distinction, and even if different men have different beliefs, that does not prove, for example, that it is not the same quality of superstition that besets those races which worship dogs and cats as gods, as that which torments other races. But what nation does not love courtesy, kindliness, gratitude, and remembrance of favours bestowed? What people does not hate and despise the haughty, the wicked, the cruel, and the ungrateful? Inasmuch as these considerations prove to us that the whole human race is bound together in unity, it follows, finally, that knowledge of the principles of right living is what makes men better.

Source: Cicero (Marcus Tullius Cicero), *On the Laws*, in *The Humanities*, vol. 1, *Three Cultural Roots*, ed. Mary Ann Frese Witt et al. (Lexington, MA: D. C. Heath and Company, 1989).

☙*DOCUMENT 4*❧
MY SLAVE IS FREE TO SPEAK UP FOR HIMSELF, *BY HORACE*

The Roman author Horace (Quintus Horatius Flaccus) used slavery as a euphemism in this comic dia-

logue in which he asks the perceptive question, "Who, then, is free?" Horace demonstrates that various types of "masters" control the lives of all and that one's status in society results from all of the slave-master relationships by which all are bound.

Davus. I've been listening for quite some time now, wanting to have a word with you. Being a slave, though, I haven't the nerve.

Horace. That you, Davus?

Dav. Yes, it's Davus, slave as I am. Loyal to my man, a pretty good fellow: pretty good, I say. I don't want you thinking I'm too good to live.

Hor. Well, come on, then. Make use of the freedom traditionally yours at the December holiday season. Speak up, sound off!

Dav. Some people like misbehaving: they're persistent and consistent. But the majority waver, trying at times to be good, at other times yielding to evil. The notorious Priscus used to wear three rings at a time, and then again, none. He lived unevenly, changing his robes every hour. He issued forth from a mansion, only to dive into the sort of low joint your better-class freedman wouldn't want to be caught dead in. A libertine at Rome, at Athens a sage, he was born, and he lived, out of season. When Volanerius, the playboy, was racked by the gout in the joints of his peccant fingers (so richly deserved), he hired a man, by the day, to pick up the dice for him and put them in the box. By being consistent in his gambling vice, he lived a happier life than the chap who tightens the reins and then lets them flap.

Hor. Will it take you all day to get to the bottom of this junk, you skunk?

Dav. But I'm saying, you're at the bottom.

Hor. How so, you stinker?

Dav. You praise the good old days, ancient fortunes and manners, and yet, if some god were all for taking you back, you'd hang back, either because you don't really think that what you are praising to the skies is all that superior or because you defend what is right with weak defenses and, vainly wanting to pull your foot from the mud, stick in it all the same. At Rome, you yearn for the country, but, once in the sticks, you praise to high heaven the far-off city, you nitwit. If it happens that no one asks you to dinner, you eulogize your comfortable meal of vegetables, acting as if you'd only go out if you were dragged out in chains. You hug yourself, saying how glad you are not to be forced to go out on a spree. But Maecenas suggests, at the very last minute, that you be his guest: "Bring some oil for my lamp, somebody! Get a move on! Is everyone deaf around here?" In a dither and a lather, you charge out. Meanwhile, your scrounging guests, Mulvius & Co., make their departure from your place with a few descriptive remarks that won't bear repeating—for example, Mul-

vius admits, "Of course, I'm fickle, led around by my stomach, and prone to follow my nose to the source of a juicy aroma, weak-minded, lazy, and, you may want to add, a gluttonous souse. But you, every bit as bad and perhaps a bit worse, have the gall to wade into me, as if you were better, and cloak your infamy in euphemism?"

What if you're found out to be a bigger fool than me, the hundred-dollar slave? Stop trying to browbeat me! Hold back your hand, and your temper, while I tell you what Crispinus' porter taught me.

Another man's wife makes you her slave. A loose woman makes Davus hers. Of us two sinners, who deserves the cross more? When my passionate nature drives me straight into her arms, she's lovely by lamplight, beautifully bare, all mine to plunge into at will, or, turning about, she mounts and drives me to death. And after it's over, she sends me away neither shamefaced nor worried that someone richer or better to look at will water the very same plant. But when you go out for it, you really come in for it, don't you? Turning yourself into the same dirty Dama you pretend to be when you take off your equestrian ring and your Roman robes, and change your respectable self, hiding your perfumed head under your cape?

Scared to death, you're let in the house, and your fear takes turns with your hope in rattling your bones. What's the difference between being carted off to be scourged and slain, in the toils of the law (as a gladiator is), and being locked up in a miserable trunk, where the maid, well aware of her mistress' misconduct, has stored you away, with your knees scrunched up against your head? Hasn't the husband full power over them both, and even more over the seducer? For the wife hasn't changed her attire or her location, and is not the uppermost sinner. You walk open-eyed right under the fork, handing over to a furious master your money, your life, your person, your good reputation. Let's assume that you got away: you learned your lesson, I trust, and will be afraid from now on, and be careful? Oh, no! You start planning how to get in trouble again, to perish again, enslave yourself over and over. But what wild beast is so dumb as to come back again to the chains he has once broken loose from? "But I'm no adulterer," you say. And I'm not a thief when I wisely pass up your good silver plate. But our wandering nature will leap when the reins are removed, when the danger is taken away. Are you my master, you, slave to so many other people, so powerful a host of other things, whom no Manumission could ever set free from craven anxiety, though the ritual were conducted again and again? And besides, here's something to think about: whether a slave who's the slave of a slave is a plain fellow slave or a "sub-slave," as you masters call him, what am I your?

[sic] You, who command me, cravenly serve someone else and are led here and there like a puppet, the strings held by others.

Who, then, is free? The wise man alone, who has full command of himself, whom poverty, death, or chains cannot terrify, who is strong enough to defy his passions and scorn prestige, who is wholly contained in himself, well rounded, smooth as a sphere on which nothing external can fasten, on which fortune can do no harm except to herself. Now which of those traits can you recognize as one of yours? Your woman asks you for five thousand dollars, needles you, shuts the door in your face and pours out cold water, then calls you back. Pull your neck from that yoke! Say, "I'm free, I'm free!" Come on, say it. You can't! A master dominates your mind, and it's no mild master who lashes you on in spite of yourself, who goads you and guides you. Or when you stand popeyed in front of a painting by Pausias, you madman, are you less at fault than I am who marvel at the posters of athletes straining their muscles in combat, striking out, thrusting, and parrying, in red chalk and charcoal, as if they were really alive and handling these weapons? But Davus is a no-good, a dawdler, and you? Oh, MONSIEUR Is an EXPERT, a fine CONNOISSEUR of antiques, I ASSURE you. I'm just a fool to be tempted by piping-hot pancakes. Does your strength of character and mind make much resistance to sumptuous meals? Why is it worse for me to supply the demands of my stomach? My back will pay for it, to be sure. But do you get off any lighter, hankering after delicate, costly food? Your endless indulgence turns sour in your stomach, your baffled feet won't support your pampered body. Is the slave at fault, who exchanges a stolen scraper for a bunch of grapes, in the dark? Is there nothing slavish in a man who sells his estate to satisfy his need for rich food?

Now, add on these items:

(1) You can't stand your own company as long as an hour;

(2) You can't dispose of your leisure in a decent fashion;

(3) You're a fugitive from your own ego, a vagabond soul, trying to outflank your cares by attacking the bottle or making sorties into sleep. And none of it works: The Dark Companion rides close along by your side, keeps up with and keeps on pursuing the runaway slave.

Hor. "Where's a stone?"

Dav. "What use do you have for it?"

Hor. "Hand me my arrows!"

Dav. The man is either raving or satisfying his craving for creative writing.

Hor. If you don't clear out, instanter, I'll pack you off to the farm to be my ninth planter.

Source: Horace (Quintus Horatius Flaccus), *My Slave Is Free to Speak Up for Himself,* in *The Humanities,* vol. 1, *Three Cultural Roots,* ed. Mary Ann Frese Witt et al. (Lexington, MA: D. C. Heath and Company, 1989).

☙DOCUMENT 5☙
TUAN CH'ENG-SHIH DESCRIBES PO-PA-LI (AFRICA) IN YU-YANG-TSA-TSU

This ancient Chinese travel account reveals an early knowledge about the continent of Africa (Po-pa-li). The recognition that inhabitants of this region were kidnapped and sold reveals that the Chinese were aware of an early slave trade in the Indian Ocean region in which captives taken from East Africa were sold as commodities by Persian merchants.

The country of Po-pa-li is in the southwestern sea. (The people) do not eat any of the five grains but eat only meat. They often stick a needle into the veins of cattle and draw blood which they drink raw, mixed with milk. They wear no clothes except that they cover (the parts) below their loins with sheepskins. Their women are clean and of proper behaviour. The inhabitants themselves kidnap them, and if they sell them to foreign merchants, they fetch several times their price. The country produces only ivory and ambergris. If Persian merchants wish to go into their country, they collect around them several thousand men and present them with strips of cloth. All, whether old or young draw blood and swear an oath, and then only do they trade their products. From olden times they were not subject to any foreign country. In fighting they use elephants' tusks and ribs and the horns of wild buffaloes as lances and they wear cuirasses and bows and arrows. They have twenty myriads of foot soldiers. The Arabs make frequent raids upon them.

Source: Tuan Ch'eng-shih, *Yu-yang-tsa-tsu,* in *A Collection of Documents on the Slave Trade of East Africa,* ed. R. W. Beachey (London: Rex Collings, 1976).

☙DOCUMENT 6☙
A TENTH-CENTURY SLAVING VENTURE

Arab merchants from the coast of modern-day Oman regularly plied the waters of eastern Africa in search of captives who might be purchased and traded as slaves. This passage from the tenth century reveals how an African king taken captive along with his retinue was sold into slavery in the Omani market.

When everything was in order, and the king knew of our intention to set sail, he accompanied us to the shore with several of his people, got into one of the boats and came out to the ship with us. He even came on board with seven of his companions.

When I saw them there, I said to myself: In the Oman market this young king would certainly fetch thirty dinars, and his seven companions sixty dinars. Their clothes alone are not worth less than twenty dinars. One way and another this would give us a profit of at least 3,000 dirhams, and without any trouble. Reflecting thus, I gave the crew their orders. They raised the sails and weighed anchor . . . When the day came, the king and his companions were put with the other slaves whose number reached about 200 head. He was not treated differently from his companions in captivity. The king said not a word and did not even open his mouth. He behaved as if we were unknown to him and as if we did not know him. When he got to Oman, the slaves were sold, and the king with them. . . .

We said farewell to him. Go, he said, and if you return, I shall not treat you otherwise than I have done. You will receive the best welcome. And the Muslims may know that they may come here to us, as to brothers, Muslims like themselves. As for accompanying you to your ship, I have reasons for not doing so. And on that we parted.

Source: G. S. P. Freeman-Greenville, "The East African Coast, Select Documents," in *A Collection of Documents on the Slave Trade of East Africa*, ed. R. W. Beachey (London: Rex Collings, 1976).

DOCUMENT 7
DESCRIPTION OF EAST AFRICA (1178)

A Chinese chronicler notes the well-established nature of the African slave trade in this twelfth-century account.

. . . there is an island in the sea on which there are many savages. Their bodies are black as lacquer and they have frizzled hair. They are enticed by food and then captured and sold as slaves to the Arabic countries, where they fetch a very high price. They are employed as gate-keepers, and it is said that they have no longing for their kinfolk . . . thousands of them are sold as foreign slaves.

Source: Chou Ch'u-fei, *Ling-wai-tai-ta*, in *A Collection of Documents on the Slave Trade of East Africa*, ed. R. W. Beachey (London: Rex Collings, 1976).

DOCUMENT 8
FROM THE TRAVELS OF IBN BATTUTA

Some of the earliest historical records of West Africa are found in the travel accounts of Ibn Battuta. This passage includes commentary upon the customs and practices that existed in the indigenous forms of slavery found in sub-Saharan Africa.

WHAT I APPROVED OF AND WHAT I DISAPPROVED OF AMONG THE ACTS OF THE SUDAN

One of their good features is their lack of oppression. They are the farthest removed of people from it and their sultan does not permit anyone to practise it. Another is the security embracing the whole country, so that neither traveller there nor dweller has anything to fear from thief or usurper. Another is that they do not interfere with the wealth of any white man who dies among them, even though it be qintar upon qintar. They simply leave it in the hands of a trustworthy white man until the one to whom it is due takes it. Another is their assiduity in prayer and their persistence in performing it in congregation and beating their children to make them perform it. If it is a Friday and a man does not go early to the mosque he will not find anywhere to pray because of the press of the people. It is their habit that every man sends his servant with his prayer-mat to spread it for him in a place which he thereby has a right to until he goes to the mosque. Their prayer-carpets are made from the fronds of the tree resembling the palm which has no fruit. Another of their good features is their dressing in fine white clothes on Friday. If any one of them possesses nothing but a ragged shirt he washes it and cleanses it and attends the Friday prayer in it. Another is their eagerness to memorize the great Koran. They place fetters on their children if there appears on their part a failure to memorize it and they are not undone until they memorize it.

I went into the house of the qadi [owner] on the day of the festival and his children were fettered so I said to him: "Aren't you going to let them go?" He replied: "I shan't do so until they've got the Koran by heart!" One day I passed by a youth of theirs, of good appearance and dressed in fine clothes, with a heavy fetter on his leg, I said to those who were with me: "What has this boy done? Has he killed somebody?" The lad understood what I had said and laughed, and they said to me: "He's only been fettered so that he'll learn the Koran!"

One of their disapproved acts is that their female servants and slave girls and little girls appear before men naked, with their privy parts uncovered. During Ramadan I saw many of them in this state, for it is the custom of the farāriyya to break their fast in the house of the sultan, and each one brings his food carried by twenty or more of his slave girls, they all being naked. Another is that their women go into the sultan's presence naked and uncovered, and that his daughters go naked. On the night of 25 Ramadan I saw about 200 slave girls bringing out food from his palace naked, having with them two of his daughters with rounded breasts having no covering upon them. Another is their sprinkling dust and ashes on their heads out of good manners. Another is what I mentioned in connection with the comic anecdote about the poets' recitation. Another is that many of them eat carrion, and dogs, and donkeys.

ANECDOTE

Farba Magha informed me that when Mansa Musa arrived at this channel he had with him a qadi, a white man whose kunya [servant] was Abu 'l-'Abbas, known as Al-Dukkali. He bestowed on him 4,000 mithqals for his expenses. When they reached Mima he complained to the sultan that the 4,000 mithqals had been stolen from him from his house. The sultan summoned the emir of Mima and threatened him with death if he did not produce the one who had stolen them. The emir looked for the thief but found nobody, for no thief is to be found in that country, so he entered the qadi's house and coerced his servants and threatened them. So one of Dukkali's slave girls told him: "He hasn't lost anything. He has just buried them with his own hands in that place." She indicated the place to him and the emir got them out and took them to the sultan and told him the tale. He was enraged with the qadi and banished him to the land of the infidels who eat mankind. He stayed among them for four years, then he was returned to his own country. The infidels refrained from eating him simply because he was white, for they say that the eating of a white man is harmful because he has not matured. In their opinion the black man is the matured one.

ANECDOTE

A group of these Sudan who eat human kind came with an emir of theirs to the sultan Mansa Sulayman. It is their custom to attach big ear-rings to their ears, the hole through each ring being half a span across, and envelop themselves in wraps of silk. The gold mine is in their country. The sultan did them honour and gave them a slave girl as part of his reception-gift. They slaughtered her and ate her and smeared their faces and hands with her blood and came in gratitude to the sultan. I was informed that their custom whenever they come in deputation to him is to do that, and I was told of them that they say that the tastiest part of women's flesh is the palms and the breast.

Then we set off from this village which is on the channel and reached the village of Quri Mansa. The camel which I used to ride died there. The man who was pasturing it told me about this so I went out to look into it and found that the Sudan had eaten it according to their custom of eating carrion. So I sent two youths whom I had hired for my service for them to buy me a camel at Zaghari, which was at a distance of two days' journey away. Some of the companions of Abu Bakr b. Ya'qūb stayed with me while he went on to wait for us at Mima. I stayed for six days, during which a certain pilgrim of this village made me his guest, until the two youths arrived with the camel.

Source: Ibn Battuta, in *Corpus of Early Arabic Sources for West African History,* ed. N. Levtzion and J. F. P. Hopkins (Cambridge: Cambridge University Press, 1981).

◈DOCUMENT 9◈
POPE ALEXANDER VI, INTER CAETERA (1493)

European monarchs often sought papal approval to legitimize their expeditions of exploration and conquest. Shortly after Christopher Columbus's voyage of 1492, the rulers of Spain appealed to Pope Alexander VI, and he issued the bull Inter Caetera. According to this papal pronouncement, a "line of demarcation" divided the world between the nations of Spain and Portugal.

Alexander, bishop, servant of servants of God, to illustrious sovereigns, our very dear son in Christ, Isabella, queen of Castile, Leon, Aragon, Sicily, and Granada, health and apostolic benediction. Among other works well pleasing to the Divine Majesty and cherished of our heart, this assuredly ranks highest, that in our times especially the Catholic faith and the Christian religion be exalted and be everywhere increased and spread, that the health of souls be cared for and that barbarous nations be overthrown and brought to the faith itself. Wherefore inasmuch as by the favor of divine clemency, we, though of insufficient merits, have been called to this Holy See of Peter, recognizing that as true Catholic kings and princes, such as we have known you always to be, and as your illustrious deeds already known to almost the whole world declare, you not only eagerly desire but with every effort, zeal, and diligence, without regard to hardships, expenses, dangers, with the shedding even of your blood, are laboring to that end; recognizing also that you have long since dedicated to this purpose your whole soul and all your endeavors—as witnessed in these times with so much glory to the Divine Name in your recovery of the kingdom of Granada from the yoke of the Saracens—we therefore are rightly led, and hold it as our duty, to grant you even of our own accord and in your favor those things whereby with effort each day more hearty you may be enabled for the honor of God himself and the spread of the Christian rule to carry forward your holy and praiseworthy purpose so pleasing to immortal God. We have indeed learned that you, who for a long time had intended to seek out and discover certain islands and mainlands remote and unknown and not hitherto discovered by others, to the end that you might bring to the worship of our Redeemer and the profession of the

Catholic faith their residents and inhabitants, having been up to the present time greatly engaged in the siege and recovery of the kingdom itself of Granada were unable to accomplish this holy and praiseworthy purpose; but the said kingdom having at length been regained, as was pleasing to the Lord, you, with the wish to fulfill your desire, chose our beloved son, Christopher Columbus, a man assuredly worthy and of the highest recommendations and fitted for so great an undertaking, whom you furnished with ships and men equipped for like designs, not without the greatest hardships, dangers, and expenses, to make diligent quest for these remote and unknown mainlands and islands through the sea, where hitherto no one had sailed; and they at length, with divine aid and with the utmost diligence sailing in the ocean sea, discovered certain very remote islands and even mainlands that hitherto had not been discovered by others; wherein dwell very many peoples living in peace, and, as reported, going unclothed, and not eating flesh. Moreover, as your aforesaid envoys are of opinion, these very peoples living in the said islands and countries believe in one God, the Creator in heaven, and seem sufficiently disposed to embrace the Catholic faith and be trained in good morals. And it is hoped that, were they instructed, the name of the Savior, our Lord Jesus Christ, would easily be introduced into the said countries and islands. Also, on one of the chief of these aforesaid islands the said Christopher has already caused to be put together and built a fortress fairly equipped, wherein he has stationed as garrison certain Christians, companions of his, who are to make search for other remote and unknown islands and mainlands. In the islands and countries already discovered are found gold, spices, and very many other precious things of divers kinds and qualities. Wherefore, as becomes Catholic kings and princes, after earnest consideration of all matters, especially of the rise and spread of the Catholic faith, as was the fashion of your ancestors, kings of renowned memory, you have purposed with the favor of divine clemency to bring under your sway the said mainlands and islands with their residents and inhabitants and to bring them to the Catholic faith. Hence, heartily commending in the Lord this your holy and praiseworthy purpose, and desirous that it be duly accomplished, and that the name of our Savior be carried into those regions, we exhort you very earnestly in the Lord and by your reception of holy baptism, whereby you are bound to our apostolic commands, and by the bowels of the mercy of our Lord Jesus Christ, enjoin strictly, that inasmuch as with eager zeal for the true faith you design to equip and despatch this expedition, you purpose also, as is your duty, to lead the peoples dwelling in those islands and countries to embrace the Christian religion; nor at any time let dangers or hardships deter you therefrom, with the stout hope and trust in your hearts that Almighty God will further your undertakings. And, in order that you may enter upon so great an undertaking with greater readiness and heartiness endowed with the benefit of our apostolic favor, we, of our own accord, not at your instance nor the request of anyone else in your regard, but of our own sole largess and certain knowledge and out of the fullness of our apostolic power, by the authority of Almighty God conferred upon us in blessed Peter and of the vicarship of Jesus Christ, which we hold on earth, do by tenor of these presents, should any of said islands have been found by your envoys and captains, give, grant, and assign to you and your heirs and successors, kings of Castile and Leon, forever, together with all their dominions, cities, camps, places, and villages, and all rights, jurisdictions, and appurtenances, all islands and mainlands found and to be found, discovered and to be discovered towards the west and south, by drawing and establishing a line from the Arctic pole, namely the north, to the Antarctic pole, namely the south, no matter whether the said mainlands and islands are found and to be found in the direction of India or towards any other quarter, the said line to be distant one hundred leagues towards the west and south from any of the islands commonly known as the Azores and Cape Verde. With this proviso however that none of the islands and mainlands, found and to be found, discovered and to be discovered, beyond that said line towards the west and south, be in the actual possession of any Christian king or prince up to the birthday of our Lord Jesus Christ just past from which the present year—one thousand four hundred and ninety-three begins. And we make, appoint, and depute you and your said heirs and successors lords of them with full and free power, authority, and jurisdiction of every kind; with this proviso however, that by this our gift, grant, and assignment no right acquired by any Christian prince, who may be in actual possession of said islands and mainlands prior to the said birthday of our Lord Jesus Christ, is hereby to be understood to be withdrawn or taken away. Moreover we command you in virtue of holy obedience that, employing all due diligence in the premises, as you also promise—nor do we doubt your compliance therein in accordance with your loyalty and royal greatness of spirit—you should appoint to the aforesaid mainlands and islands worthy, God-fearing, learned, skilled, and experienced men, in order to instruct the aforesaid inhabitants and residents in the Catholic faith and train them in good morals. Furthermore, under penalty of excommunication *latae sententie* [recently decreed] to be incurred *ipso facto*, should anyone thus contravene, we strictly forbid all persons of whatsoever rank, even imperial and royal, or of whatsoever estate, degree, order, or condition, to dare, without your special permit or that of your aforesaid heirs and successors, to go for the purpose of trade or any other reason to the islands or mainlands, found and to be found, discovered and to be discovered, towards the west and south, by drawing and establishing a line from the Arctic pole to the Antarctic pole, no matter whether the mainlands and islands, found and to be found, lie in the direction of India or toward any other quarter whatsoever, the said line to be distant one hundred leagues towards the west and south, as is aforesaid, from any of the islands commonly known as the Azores and Cape Verde; apostolic constitutions and ordinances and other decrees whatsoever to the contrary notwithstanding. We trust in Him from whom empires and governments and all good things proceed, that, should you, with the Lord's guidance, pursue this holy and praiseworthy undertaking, in a short while your hardships and endeavors will attain the most felicitous result, to the happiness and glory of all Christendom. But inasmuch as it would be difficult to have these present letters sent to all places where desirable, we wish, and with similar accord and knowledge do decree, that two copies of them, signed by the hand of a public notary commissioned therefor, and sealed with the seal of any ecclesiastical officer or ecclesiastical court, the same respect is to be shown in court and outside as well as anywhere else as would be given to these presents should they thus be exhibited or shown. Let no one, therefore, infringe, or with rash boldness contravene, this our recommendation, exhortation, requisition, gift, grant, assignment, constitution, deputation, decree, mandate, prohibition, and will. Should anyone presume to attempt this, be it known to him that he will incur the wrath of Almighty God and of the blessed apostles Peter and Paul. Given at Rome, at St. Peter's, in the year of the incarnation of our Lord one thousand four hundred and ninety-three, the fourth of May, and the first year of our pontificate.

Gratis by order of our most holy lord, the pope. June. For the referendary,

A. De Mucciarellis
For J. Bufolinus
A. Santo severino
L. Podocatharus

Source: Alexander VI (Rodrigo de Borja y Borja), "Inter Caetera," in *New Iberian World: A Documentary History of the Discovery and Settlement of Latin America to the Early 17th Century, Volume I,* ed. John H. Parry and Robert G. Keith (New York: Times Books, Hector and Rose, 1984).

◈DOCUMENT 10◈
POPE ALEXANDER VI, DUDUM SIQUIDEM (1493)

Pope Alexander VI issued the bull Dudum Siquidem to guarantee to the Spanish monarchs the right to take any lands that they might find in or near India as a result of the transatlantic expedition undertaken by Christopher Columbus. With papal approval, the subsequent expeditions were viewed as a type of "just war," in which the spread of Christianity justified the actions taken by the Spanish conquerors.

Alexander, bishop, servant of the servants of God, to the illustrious sovereigns, his very dear son in Christ, Ferdinand, king, and his very dear daughter in Christ, Isabella, queen of Castile, Leon, Aragon, and Granada, health and apostolic benediction.

A short while ago of our own accord and out of our certain knowledge, and fullness of our apostolic power, we gave, conveyed, and assigned forever to you and your heirs and successors, kings of Castile and Leon, all islands and mainlands whatsoever, discovered and to be discovered, toward the west and south, that were not under the actual temporal dominion of any Christian lords. Moreover, we invested therewith you and your aforesaid heirs and successors, and appointed and deputed you as lords of them with full and free power, authority, and jurisdiction of every kind, as more fully appears in our letters given to that effect, the terms whereof we wish to be understood as if they were inserted word for word in these presents. But since it may happen that your envoys and captains, or vassals, while voyaging toward the west or south, might bring their ships to land in eastern regions and there discover islands and mainlands that belonged or belong to India, with the desire moreover to bestow gracious favors upon you, through our similar accord, knowledge, and fullness of power, by apostolic authority and by tenor of these presents, in all and through all, just as if in the aforesaid letters full and express mention had been made thereof, we do in like manner amplify and extend our aforesaid gift, grant, assignment, and letters, with all and singular the clauses contained in the said letters, to all islands and mainlands whatsoever, found and to be found, discovered and to be discovered, that are or may be or may seem to be in the route of navigation or travel toward the west or south, whether they be in western parts, or in the regions of the south and east and of India. We grant to you and your aforesaid heirs and successors full and free power through your own authority, exercised through yourselves or through another or others, freely to take corporal possession of the said islands and countries and to hold them forever, and to defend them against whosoever may oppose, with this strict prohibition however to all persons, of no matter what rank, estate, degree, order, or condition, that under penalty of excommunication *latae sententiae* [recently decreed], which such as contravene are to incur *ipso facto,* no one without your express and special license or that of your aforesaid heirs and successors shall, for no matter what reason or pretense, presume in any manner to go or send to the aforesaid regions for the purpose of navigating or of fishing, or of searching for islands or mainlands—notwithstanding apostolic constitutions and ordinances, and any gifts, grants, powers, and assignments of the aforesaid regions, seas, islands, and countries, or any portion of them, made by us or our predecessors to any kings, princes, infantes, or any other persons, orders, or knighthoods, for no matter what reasons, even for motives of charity or the faith, or the ransom of captives, or for other reasons, even the most urgent; notwithstanding also any repealing clauses, even though they are of the most positive, mandatory, and unusual character; and no matter what sentences, censures, and penalties of any kind they may contain; providing however these grants have not gone into effect through actual and real possession, even though it may have happened that the persons to whom such gifts and grants were made, or their envoys, sailed thither at some time through chance. Wherefore should any such gifts or grants have been made, considering their terms to have been sufficiently expressed and inserted in our present decree, we through similar accord, knowledge, and fullness of our power do wholly revoke them and as regards the countries and islands not actually taken into possession, we wish the grants to be considered as of no effect, notwithstanding what may appear in the aforesaid letters, or anything else to the contrary. Given at Rome, at St. Peter's, on the twenty-sixth day of September, in the year of the incarnation of our Lord one thousand four hundred and ninety-three, the second year of our pontificate.

Gratis by order of our most holy lord the Pope.

JOHANNES NILIS.   P. GORMAZ.

Source: Alexander VI (Rodrigo de Borja y Borja), "Dudum Siquidem," in *New Iberian World: A Documentary History of the Discovery and Settlement of Latin America to the Early 17th Century, Volume I,* ed. John H. Parry and Robert G. Keith (New York: Times Books, Hector and Rose, 1984).

⚘DOCUMENT 11⚘
THE REQUIREMENT (1510)

In an act of legal folly, the Spanish government believed that it could justify making war upon the indigenous peoples of the Americas and capturing them for use as slave laborers. Before going into battle, *Spanish conquerors read "the Requirement" aloud in Spanish. If the indigenous peoples refused to submit to the power of this document, all subsequent actions were viewed as a "just war"—including the capture and enslavement of women and children.*

On the part of the King, Don Fernando, and of Doña Juana, his daughter, Queen of Castile and Leon, subduers of the barbarous nations, we their servants notify and make known to you, as best we can, that the Lord our God, Living and Eternal, created the Heaven and the Earth, and one man and one woman, of whom you and we, all the men of the world, were and are descendants, and all those who come after us. But, on account Of the multitude which has sprung from this man and woman in the five thousand years since the world was created, it was necessary that some men should go one way and some another, and that they should be divided into many kingdoms and provinces, for in one alone they could not be sustained.

Of all these nations God our Lord gave charge to one man, called St. Peter, that he should be Lord and Superior of all the men in the world, that all should obey him, and that he should be the head of the whole human race, wherever men should live and under whatever law, sect, or belief they should be; and he gave him the world for his kingdom and jurisdiction.

And he commanded him to place his seat in Rome, as the spot most fitting to rule the world from; but also he permitted him to have his seat in any other part of the world, and to judge and govern all Christians, Moors, Jews, Gentiles, and all other sects. This man was called Pope, as if to say, Admirable Great Father and Governor of men. The men who lived in that time obeyed that St. Peter, and took him for Lord, King, and Superior of the universe; so also they have regarded the others who after him have been elected to the pontificate, and so has it been continued even till now, and will continue till the end of the world.

One of these Pontiffs, who succeeded that St. Peter as Lord of the world, in the dignity and seat which I have before mentioned, made donation of these isles and Tierra-firme to the aforesaid King and Queen and to their successors, our lords, with all that there are in these territories, as is contained in certain writings which passed upon the subject as aforesaid, which you can see if you wish.

So their Highnesses are kings and lords of these islands and land of Tierra-firme by virtue of this donation: and some islands, and indeed almost all those to whom this has been notified, have received and served their Highnesses, as lords and kings, in the way that subjects ought to do, with good will, without any resistance, immediately, without delay, when they were informed of the aforesaid facts. And also they received and obeyed the priests whom their Highnesses sent to preach to them and to teach them our Holy Faith; and all these, of their own free will, without any reward or condition, have become Christians, and are so, and their Highnesses have joyfully and benignantly received them, and also have commanded them to be treated as their subjects and vassals; and you too are held and obliged to do the same. Wherefore, as best we can, we ask and require you that you consider what we have said to you, and that you take the time that shall be necessary to understand and deliberate upon it, and that you acknowledge the Church as the Ruler and Superior of the whole world, and the high priest called Pope, and in his name the King and Queen Doña Juana our lords in his place, as superiors and lords and kings of these islands and this Tierra-firme by virtue of the said donation, and that you consent and give place that these religious fathers should declare and preach to you the aforesaid.

If you do so, you will do well, and that which you are obliged to do to their Highnesses, and we in their name shall receive you in all love and charity, and shall leave you your wives, and your children, and your lands, free without servitude, that you may do with them and with yourselves freely that which you like and think best, and they shall not compel you to turn Christians, unless you yourselves, when informed of the truth, should wish to be converted to our Holy Catholic Faith, as almost all the inhabitants of the rest of the islands have done. And, besides this, their Highnesses award you many privileges and exemptions and will grant you many benefits.

But, if you do not do this, and maliciously make delay in it, I certify to you that, with the help of God, we shall powerfully enter into your country, and shall make war against you in all ways and manners that we can, and shall subject you to the yoke and obedience of the Church and of their Highnesses; we shall take you and your wives and your children, and shall make slaves of them, and as such shall sell and dispose of them as their Highnesses may command; and we shall take away your goods, and shall do you all the mischief and damage that we can, as to vassals who do not obey, and refuse to receive their lord, and resist and contradict him; and we protest that the deaths and losses which shall accrue from this are your fault, and not that of their Highnesses, or ours, nor of these cavaliers who come with us. And that we have said this to you and made this Requisition, we request the notary here present to give us his testimony in writing, and we ask the rest who are present that they should be witnesses of this Requisition.

Source: Palacios Rubios, "The Requirement," in *New Iberian World: A Documentary History of the*

Discovery and Settlement of Latin America to the Early 17th Century, Volume I, ed. John H. Parry and Robert G. Keith (New York: Times Books, Hector and Rose, 1984).

⮞DOCUMENT 12⮜
DECREE PROHIBITING THE PERSONAL SERVITUDE OF INDIANS (1549)

The Spanish government eventually abolished the practice of enslaving indigenous peoples in the Americas, but unfortunately the forced labor supply was supplanted by importing large numbers of Africans to the Americas as slave laborers. In the following document the Spanish authorities in Peru discontinued the practice of demanding forced labor from the indigenous peoples, labor that had been viewed previously as encomienda (tribute) rights of Spanish colonists.

THE KING.

President and judges of Our Royal *Audiencia,* which is in the City of the Kings in the provinces of Peru.

I am informed that as a result of allowing personal services to be given in that land to be used in the mines or in other things by way of assessment or exchange in place of the tributes that are assessed to pay, there result great problems. Notably, since many of the Indians go to serve more than fifty leagues away from their homes, and others more or less according to where the mines are, and since they go carrying food, blankets, and beds, some of them are taken sick and die. In addition, the Christian teaching they are supposed to receive is interfered with and other offences are commited against Our Lord God and the people of those provinces are reduced, and many other injuries and problems result for the life and health of the Indians and their teaching. In addition to this, many Indian pueblos, both those under Crown administration and those that are granted in encomienda to the settlers, are assessed for more than they can reasonably pay. Thus wishing to make provision in this matter that is important to the service of God and the welfare of that country and its natives, after it was seen and discussed by the members of Our Council of the Indies, it was agreed that We should order the issuance of this My *cedula* [decree] for you, and I agreed with this. Therefore We command you, as soon as you see this, to inform yourself and find out with all care and diligence the pueblos in those provinces in which personal services are given for the mines and for their households and other services and works. You shall make provision that from here on these not be granted by way of assessment or exchange, even if the caciques and Indians of the pueblos agree to it, saying that the personal services are given in place of the tributes that are taken from them and this is the way they wish it. If these commutations of personal services cease, they will have to pay the tributes from the things they grow and make, according to the quality and custom of each pueblo, following what We have commanded with regard to this. We are also informed that the assessments of the said provinces in some pueblos are very excessive, and that their inhabitants cannot reasonably meet or pay them because the number of Indians has declined, so that they do not have the resources they did and for other reasons. Therefore you will look at the assessments that have been made for the tributes that the Indian pueblos have to pay in those provinces, both those that are under Crown administration and those granted in *encomienda* to private individuals, and you shall remove from these assessments all the personal services that may be found in them, whether by way of assessment or commutation. As has been said, it is Our will that in the assessments of the Indians, they not be required to give any personal services, and that tributes not be commuted after they are assessed. You shall review these assessments again where you take away the assessments or commutations of personal services and make a new assessment of what they have to pay, keeping to the tenor and form that is given in this by one of the laws that has been made by Us about the assessment of the tributes that the Indians have to pay. And you shall carry this out in spite of any reclamations that may be made in this, whether by Our officials, by the persons who hold the said Indians in *encomienda,* or any one else, either Indian or Spanish. It is Our will that be well treated and relieved, and that the tribute that they have to give be in those things that they have in their lands and that they can reasonably give, without any impediment to their multiplication and conversion and to their instruction in the things of Our Holy Catholic faith. And you shall do and carry this out without regard for any other *cedulas,* letters, and *provisiones* issued by Us that order something contrary to this. And because as We have understood, the horses, mules, and other beasts of burden have increased to such an extent that with the proper order and diligence they would be enough for all the carrying that is required in that land, since you as persons who are on the spot and in whom We have confidence would look after it as would be expected from your Christian zeal, We have decided to commit this to you, so that in the cases where it may be necessary and where you see that the said mules, beasts, and carts are not adequate, you will make arrangements for the pueblos close to a place where this occurs to assign persons in turns to hire themselves out to engage in this, insuring that the loads they have to carry and the personal labor in which they are occupied be very moderate, for a short time,

and over short distances, and making sure that the persons assigned are those who are least needed in their houses and farms, and especially in the things of Our Holy Catholic faith, and also making provision that [the wages] they receive for their labor be given directly into the possession of each of the individuals who do this work and not to their caciques. And because I am informed that one of the reasons that the said Indians do not come of their own will to hire themselves out is that they are commonly given no more than eight and a half maravedis [Spanish coins of little value] for their labor each day, out of which they have to eat, and this seems so little that it differs little from working for free, I command you from here on in those cases and matters where it may be necessary for the Indians to be forced to hire themselves, as is said, to take particular care to assess a reasonable salary for the Indians who are occupied in this from which they can comfortably maintain themselves and save for other necessities they may have. And because it seems here that the maize and other things that the Indians may have to take for the provision of the mines, where this cannot be done in any other way due to the lack of beasts of burden, would be done with less injury to the health and persons of the Indians if they were paid piece rates at a reasonable level rather than a salary, because it would be taken little by little and at the times that this is less injurious to them and they would not have a person over them to mistreat them. Therefore you shall give orders that it be done in this manner with piece rates, or in some better manner if you find one, always making sure that the price that is given them for this piece work be paid individually to those who do the work and not to their caciques and *principales,* realizing that one of the things in which I will be best served will be if you always act with the intention of bringing about the total abolition of these personal services. We understand that this will be greatly in the service of Our Lord God and will encourage the conservation and increase of the natives of that land.

Done in Valladolid, the 22nd of February, 1549.

Source: Diego de Encinas, "Decree Prohibiting the Personal Servitude of Indians," in *New Iberian World: A Documentary History of the Discovery and Settlement of Latin America to the Early 17th Century, Volume I,* ed. John H. Parry and Robert G. Keith (New York: Times Books, Hector and Rose, 1984).

∽DOCUMENT 13∽
CHARTER OF THE DUTCH
WEST INDIA COMPANY (1621)

The Dutch West India Company was responsible for founding Dutch colonies like New Netherlands and

Suriname in the Americas. The company was also responsible for transporting large numbers of Africans to these colonies where they served as slave laborers. Eventually, the transporting of slaves from Africa became one of the primary mercantile interests of this company.

JUNE 3, 1621

The States-General of the United Netherlands, to all who shall see these Presents, or hear them read, Greeting. Be it known, that we knowing the prosperity of these countries, and the welfare of their inhabitants depends principally on navigation and trade, which in all former times by the said Countries were carried on happily, and with a great blessing to all countries and kingdoms; and desiring that the aforesaid inhabitants should not only be preserved in their former navigation, traffic, and trade, but also that their trade may be encreased as much as possible in special conformity to the treaties, alliances, leagues and covenants for traffic and navigation formerly made with other princes, republics and people, which we give them to understand must be in. all parts punctually kept and adhered to: And we find by experience, that without the common help, assistance, and interposition of a General Company, the people designed from hence for those parts cannot be profitably protected and mantained [*sic*] in their great risque [risk] from pirates, extortion and otherwise, which will happen in so very long a voyage. We have, therefore, and for several other important reasons and considerations as thereunto moving, with mature deliberation of counsel, and for highly necessary causes, found it good, that the navigation, trade, and commerce, in the parts of the West-Indies, and Africa, and other places hereafter described, should not henceforth be carried on any otherwise than by the common united strength of the merchants and inhabitants of these countries; and for that end there shall be erected one General Company, which we out of special regard to their common well-being, and to keep and preserve the inhabitants of those places in good trade and welfare, will maintain and strengthen with our Help, Favour and assistance as far as the present state and condition of this Country will admit: and moreover furnish them with a proper Charter, and with the following Priveleges and Exemptions, to wit, That for the Term of four and twenty Years, none of the Natives or Inhabitants of these countries shall be permitted to sail to or from the said lands, or to traffic on the coast and countries of Africa from the Tropic of Cancer to the Cape of Good Hope, nor in the countries of America, or the West-Indies, beginning at the fourth end of Terra Nova, by the streights [Straits] of Magellan, La Maire, or any other streights and passages situated thereabouts to the straights of Anian, as well on the

north sea as the south sea, nor on any islands situated on the one side or the other, or between both; nor in the western or southern countries reaching, lying, and between both the meridians, from the Cape of Good Hope, in the East, to the east end of New Guinea, in the West, inclusive, but in the Name of this United Company of these United Netherlands. And whoever shall presume without the consent of this Company, to sail or to traffic in any of the Places within the aforesaid Limits granted to this Company, he shall forfeit the ships and the goods which shall be found for sale upon the aforesaid coasts and lands; the which being actually seized by the aforesaid Company, shall be by them kept for their own Benefit and Behoof. And in case such ships or goods shall be sold either in other countries or havens they may touch at, the owners and partners must be fined for the value of those ships and goods: Except only, that they who before the date of this charter, shall have sailed or been sent out of these or any other countries, to any of the aforesaid coasts, shall be able to continue their trade for the sale of their goods, and cosine [trade] back again, or otherwise, until the expiration of this charter, if they have had any before, and not longer: Provided, that after the first of July sixteen hundred and twenty one, the day and time of this charters commencing, no person shall be able to send any ships or goods to the places comprehended in this charter, although that before the date hereof, this Company was not finally incorporated: But shall provide therein as is becoming, against those who knowingly by fraud endeavour to frustrate our intention herein for the public good: Provided that the salt trade at Ponte del Re may be continued according to the conditions and instructions by us already given, or that may be given respecting it, any thing in this charter to the contrary notwithstanding.

II. That, moreover, the aforesaid Company may, in our name and authority, within the limits herein before prescribed, make contracts, engagements and alliances with the limits herein before prescribed, make contracts, engagements and alliances with the princes and natives of the countries comprehended therein, and also build any forts and fortifications there, to appoint and discharge Governors, people for war, and officers of justice, and other public officers, for the preservation of the places, keeping good order, police and justice, and in like manner for the promoting of trade; and again, others in their place to put, as they from the situation of their affairs shall see fit: Moreover, they must advance the peopling of those fruitful and unsettled parts, and do all that the service of those countries, and the profit and increase of trade shall require: and the Company shall successively communicate and transmit to us such contracts and alliances as they shall have made with the aforesaid princes and nations; and likewise the situation of the fortresses, fortifications, and settlements by them taken.

III. Saving, that they having chosen a governor in chief, and prepared instructions for him, they shall be approved, and a commission given by us, And that further, such governor in chief, as well as other deputy governors, commanders, and officers, shall be held to take an oath of allegiance to us and also to the Company.

IV. And if the aforesaid Company in and of the aforesaid places shall be cheated under the appearance of friendship, or badly treated, or shall suffer loss in trusting their money or Goods, without having restitution, or receiving payment for them, they may use the best methods in their power, according to the situation of their affairs, to obtain satisfaction.

V. And if it should be necessary for the establishment, security and defence of this trade, to take any troops with them, we will, according to the constitution of this country, and the situation of affairs furnish the said Company with such troops, provided they be paid and supported by the Company.

VI. Which troops, besides the oath already taken to us and to his excellency, shall swear to obey the commands of the said Company, and to endeavour to promote their interest to the utmost of their ability.

VII. That the provosts of the Company on shore may apprehend any of the military, that have inlisted in the service of the aforesaid company, and may confine them on board the ships in whatever city, place, or jurisdiction they may be found; provided, the provosts first inform the officers and magistrates of the cities and places where this happens.

VIII. That we will not take any ships, ordnance, or ammunition belonging to the company, for the use of this country, without the consent of the said company.

IX. We have moreover incorporated this company, and favoured them with privileges, and we give them a charter besides this, that they may pass freely with all their ships and goods without paying any toll to the United Provinces; and that they themselves may use their liberty in the same manner as the free inhabitants of the cities of this country enjoy their freedom, notwithstanding any person who is not free may be a member of this company.

X. That all the goods of this company during the eight next ensuing years, be carried out of this country to the parts of the West Indies and Africa, and other places comprehended within the aforesaid limits, and those which they shall bring into this country, shall be from outward and home convoys; provided, that if at the expiration of the aforesaid eight years, the state and situation of these Countries will not admit of this Freedom's continuing for a longer time, the said goods, and the merchandises coming from the places mentioned in this Charter, and exported again out of these countries, and the outward convoys and licenses, during the whole time of this Charter, shall not be rated higher by us than they have formerly been rated, unless we should be again engaged in a war, in which case, all the aforesaid goods and merchandises will not be rated higher by us than they were in the last list in time of war.

XI. And that this company may be strengthened by a good government, to the greatest profit and satisfaction of all concerned, we have ordained, that the said government shall be vested in five chambers of managers; one at Amsterdam,—this shall have the management of four-ninths parts; one chamber in Zealand, for two-ninth parts; one chamber at the Maeze, for one-ninth part; one chamber in North Holland, for one-ninth-part; and the fifth chamber in Friesland, with the city and country, for one-ninth part; upon the condition entered in the record of our resolutions, and the Act past respecting it. And the Provinces in which there are no chambers shall be accommodated with so many managers, divided among the respective chambers, as their hundred thousand guilders in this company shall entitle them to.

XII. That the chamber of Amsterdam shall consist of twenty managers; the chamber of Zealand of twelve; the chambers of Maeze and of the North Part, each of fourteen, and the chamber of Friesland, with the city and country, also of fourteen managers; if it shall hereafter appear, that this work cannot be carried on without a greater number of persons; in that case, more may be added, with the knowledge of nineteen, and our approbation, but not otherwise

XIII. And the States of the respective United Provinces are authorized, to lay before their High Mightinesses' ordinary deputies, or before the magistrates of the cities of these Provinces, any order for registering the members, together with the election of managers, if they find they can do it according to the constitution of their Provinces. Moreover, that no person in the chamber of Amsterdam shall be chosen a manager who has not of his own in the fields of the company, the sum of five thousand guilders; and the Chamber of Zealand four thousand Guilders, and the chamber of Maeze, of the North Part, and of Friesland, with the city and country. the like sum of four thousand guilders.

XIV. That the first managers shall serve for the term of six years, and then one-third part of the number of managers shall be changed by lot; and two years after a like third part, and the two next following years, the last third part; and so on successively the oldest in the service shall be dismissed; and in the place of those who go off, or of any that shall die, or for any other reason be dismissed, three others shall be nominated by the managers, both remaining and going oaf [off], together with the principal adventures in person, and at their cost, from which the aforesaid Provinces, the deputies, or the magistrates, shall make a new election of a manager, and successively supply the vacant places; and it shall be held before the principal adventurers, who have as great a concern as the respective managers.

XV. That the accounts of the furniture and outfit of the vessels, with their dependencies, shall be made up three months after the departure of the vessels, and one month after, copies shall be sent to us, and to the respective chambers: and the state of the returns, and their sales, shall the chambers (as often as we see good, or they are required thereto by the chambers) send to us and to one another.

XVI. That evry [sic] six years they shall make a general account of all outfits and returns, together with all the gains and losses of the company; to wit, one of their business, and one of the war, each separate; which accounts shall be made public by an advertisement, to the end that every one who is interested may, upon hearing of it, attend; and if by the expiration of the seventh year, the accounts are not made out in manner aforesaid, the managers shall forfeit their commissions, which shall be appropriated to the use of the poor, and they themselves be held to render their account as before, till such time and under such penalty as shall be fixed by us respecting offenders. And notwithstanding there shall be a dividend made of the profits of the business, so long as we find that term per Cent shall have been gained.

XVII. No one shall, during the continuance of this charter, withdraw his capital, or sum advanced from this company; nor shall any new members be admitted. If at the expiration of four and twenty years it shall be found good to continue this company, or to erect a new one, a final account and estimate shall be made by the nineteen, with our knowledge, of all that belongs to the company, and also of all their expences, and any one, after the aforesaid settlement and estimate, may withdraw his money, or continue it in the new company, in whole or in part, in the same proportion as in this; And the new company shall in such case take the remainder, and pay the members which do not think fit to continue in the company their share, at such times as the nineteen, with our knowledge and approbation, shall think proper.

XVIII. That so often as it shall be necessary to have a general meeting of the aforesaid chambers, it shall be by nineteen persons, of whom eight shall come from the chamber of Amsterdam; from Zealand, four; from the Maeze, two; from North Holland, two; from Friesland, and the city and country, two, provided, that the nineteen persons, or so many more as we shall at any time think fit, shall be deputed by US for the purpose of helping to direct the aforesaid meeting of the company.

XIX. By which general meeting of the aforesaid chambers, all the business of this Company which shall come before them shall be managed and finally settled, provided, that in case of resolving upon a war, our approbation shall be asked.

XX. The aforesaid general meeting being summoned, it shall meet to resolve when they shall fit out, and how many vessels they will send to each place, the company in general observing that no particular chamber shall undertake any thing in opposition to the foregoing resolution, but shall be held to carry the same effectually into execution. And if any chamber shall be found not following the common resolution, or contravening it, we have authorized, and by these presents do authorize, the said meeting, immediately to cause reparation to be made of every defect or contravention, wherein we, being desired, will assist them.

XXI. The said general meeting shall be held the first six years in the city of Amsterdam, and two years thereafter in Zealand. and so on from time to time in the aforesaid two places.

XXII. The managers to whom the affairs of the company shall be committed, who shall go from home to attend the aforesaid meeting or otherwise, shall have for their expences and wages, four guilders a day, besides boat and carriage hire; Provided, that those who go from one city to another, to the chambers as managers and governors, shall receive no wages or travelling charges, at the cost of the company.

XXIII. And if it should happen that in the aforesaid general meeting, any weighty matter should come before them wherein they cannot agree, or in case the vote are equally divided, the same shall be left to our decision; and whatever shall be determined upon shall be carried into execution.

XXIV. And all the inhabitants of these countries, and also of other countries, shall be notified by public advertisements within one month after the date hereof, that they may be admitted into this Company, during five months from the first of July this year, sixteen hundred and twenty one, and that they must pay the money they put into the Stock in three payments; to wit, one third part at the expiration of the aforesaid five months, and the other two-thirds parts within three next succeeding years. In case the aforesaid general meeting shall find it necessary to prolong the time the members shall be notified by an advertisement.

XXV. The ships returning from a voyage shall come to the place they sailed from; and if by stress of weather. the vessels which sailed out from one part shall arrive in another; as those from Amsterdam, or North Holland, in Zealand, or in the Maeze; or from Zealand, in Holland; or those from Friesland, with the city and country, in another part; each chamber shall nevertheless have the direction and management of the vessels and goods it sent out, and shall send and transport the goods to the places from whence the vessels sailed, either in the same or other vessels: Provided, that the managers of that chamber shall be held in person to find the place where the vessels and goods are arrived, and not appoint factors to do this business; but in case they shall not be in a situation for travelling, they shall commit this business to the chamber of the place where the vessels arrived.

XXVI. If any chamber has got any goods or returns from the places included within the Limits of this charter, with which another is not provided, it shall be held to send such goods to the chamber which is unprovided, on its request, according to the situation of the case, and if they have sold them, to send to another chamber for more. And in like manner, if the managers of the respective chambers have need of any persons for fitting out the vessels, or otherwise, from the cities where there are chambers or managers, they shall require and employ the managers, of this company, without making use of a factor.

XXVII. And if any of the Provinces think fit to appoint an agent to collect the money from the inhabitants, and to make a fund in any chamber, and for paying dividends, the chamber shall be obliged to give such agent access, that he may obtain information of the state of the disbursements and receipts, and of the debts; provided, that the money brought in by such agent amount to fifty thousand Guilders or upwards.

XXVIII. The managers shall have for commissions one per cent. On the outfits and returns, besides the Prince's; and an half per cent. On gold and silver: which commission shall be divided; to the Chamber of Amsterdam, four-ninth parts; the Chamber of Zealand, two-ninth parts; the Maeze, one-ninth part; North Holland, one-ninth part, and Friesland, with the city and country, a like ninth part.

XXIX. Provided that they shall not receive commissions on the ordnance and the ships more than once. They shall, moreover, have no commissions on the ships, ordnance, and other things with which we shall strengthn the Company; nor on the money which they shall collect for the Company, nor on the profits they receive from the goods, nor shall they charge the Company with any expenses of traveling or provisions for those to whom they shall commits the providing a cargo, and purchasing goods necessary for it.

XXX. The book-keepers and cashiers shall have a salary paid them by the managers out of their commissions.

XXXI. The manager shall not deliver or sell to the Company, in whole or in part, any of their own ships, merchandise or goods; nor buy or cause to be bought, of the said Company, directly or indirectly, any goods or merchandize nor have any portion or part therein on forfeiture of one year's commissions for the use of the poor, and the loss of Office.

XXXII. The managers shall give notice by advertisement, as often as they have a fresh importation of goods and merchandize, to the end that every one may have seasonable knowledge of it, before they proceed to a final sale.

XXXIII. And if it happens that in either Chamber, an [one] of the managers shall get into such a situation, that he cannot make good what was entrusted to him during his administration, and in consequence thereof any loss shall happen, such Chamber shall be liable for the damage, and shall also be specially bound for their administration, which shall also be the case with all the members, who, on account of goods purchased, or otherwise, shall become debtors to the Company, and so shall be reckoned all cases relating to their stock and what may be due to the Company.

XXXIV. The managers of the respective chambers shall be responsible for their respective cashiers and book-keepers.

XXXV. That all the goods of this Company which shall be sold by weight shall be sold by one weight, to wit, that of Amsterdam; and that all such goods shall be put on board ship, or in store without paying any excise, import or weigh-money; provided that they being sold; shall not be delivered in any other way than by weight; and provided that the impost and weigh-money shall be paid as often as they are alienated, in the same manner as other goods subject to weigh-money.

XXXVI. That the persons or goods of the managers shall not be arrested, attached or encumbered, in order to obtain from them an account of the administration of the Company, nor for the payment of the wages of those who are in the service of the Company, but those who shall pretend to take the same upon them, shall be bound to refer the matter to their ordinary judges.

XXXVII. So when any ship shall return from a voyage, the generals or commanders of the fleets, shall be obliged to come and report to us the success of the voyage of such ship or ships, within ten days after their arrival, and shall deliver and leave with us a report in writing, if the case requires it.

XXXVIII. And if it happens (which we by no means expect) that any person will, in any manner, hurt or hinder the navigation, business, trade, or traffic of this Company, contrary to the common right, and the contents of the aforesaid treaties, leagues, and covenants, they shall defend it against them, and regulate it by the instructions we have given concerning it.

XXXIX. We have moreover promised and do promise, that we will defend this Company against every person in free navigation and traffic, and assist them with a million of Guilders, to be paid in five years, whereof the first two hundred thousand guilders shall be paid them when the first payment shall be made by the members; Provided that we, with half the aforesaid million of Guilders, shall receive and bear profit and risque in the same manner as the other members of this Company shall.

XL. And if by a violent and continued interruption of the aforesaid navigation and traffic, the business within the limits of their Company shall be brought to an open war, we will, if the situation of this country will in any wise admit of it, give them for their assistance sixteen ships of war, the least one hundred and fifty lasts burthen; with four good well sailing yachts, the least, forty lasts burthen, which shall be properly mounted and provided in all respects, both with brass and other cannon, and a proper quantity of ammunition, together with double suits of running and standing rigging, sails, cables, anchors, and other things thereto belonging, such as are proper to be provided and used in all great expeditions; upon condition, that they shall be manned, victualled, and supported at the expense of the Company, and that the Company shall be obliged to add thereto sixteen like ships of war, and four yachts, mounted and provided as above, to be used in like manner for the defence of trade and all exploits of war: Provided that all the ships of war and merchant-men (that shall be with those provided and manned as aforesaid) shall be under an admiral appointed by us according to the previous advise of the aforesaid General Company, and shall obey our commands, together with the resolutions of the Company, if it shall be necessary, in the same manner as in time of war; so notwithstanding that the merchantmen shall not unnecessarily hazard their lading.

XLI. And if it should happen that this country should be remarkably eased of its burthens, and that this Company should be laid under the grievous burthen of a war, we have further promised, and do promise, to encrease the aforesaid subsidy in such a manner as the situation of these countries will admit, and the affairs of the Company shall require.

XLII. We have moreover ordained, that in case of a war, all the prizes which shall be taken from enemies and pirates within the aforesaid limits, by the Company or their assistants; also the goods which shall be seized by virtue of our proclamation, after deducting all expenses and the damage which the Company shall suffer in taking each prize, together with the just part of his excellency the admiral, agreeable to our resolution of the first of April sixteen hundred and two; and the tenth part for the officers, sailors and soldiers, who have taken the prize, shall await the dis-

posal of the managers of the aforesaid Company; Provided that the account of them shall be kept separate and apart from the account of trade and commerce; and that the nett proceeds of the said prizes shall be employed in fitting our ships, paying the troops, fortifications, garrisons, and like matters of war and defence by sea and land; but there shall be no distribution unless the said nett proceeds shall amount to so much that a notable share may be distributed without weakening the said defence, and after paying the expenses of the war, which shall be done separate and apart from the distributions on account of Trade: And the distribution shall be made one-tenth part for the use of the United Netherlands, and the remainder for the members of this Company, in exact proportion to the capital they have advanced.

XLIII. Provided nevertheless, that all the prizes and goods, taken by virtue of our proclamation, shall be brought in, and the right laid before the judicature of the counsellors of the admirality for the part to which they are brought, that they may take cognizance of them, and determine the legality or illegality of the said prizes: the process of the administration of the goods brought in by the Company remaining nevertheless pending, and that under a proper inventory; and saving a revision of what may be done by the sentence of the admirality, agreeable to the instruction given the admiralty in that behalf. Provided that the vendue-masters and other officers of the Admiralty shall not have or pretend to any right to the prizes taken by this Company, and shall not be employed respecting them.

XLIV. The managers of this Company shall solemnly promise and swear, that they will act well and faithfully in their administration, and make good and just accounts of their trade: That they in all things will consult the greatest profit of the Company, and as much as possible prevent their meeting with losses: That they will not give the principal members any greater advantage in the payments or distribution of money than the least: That they, in getting in and receiving outstanding debts, will not favour one more than another: that they for their own account will take, and, during the continuance of their administration, will continue to take such sum of money as by their charter is allotted to them; and moreover, that they will, as far as concerns them, to the utmost of their power, observe and keep, and cause to be observed and kept, all and every the particulars and articles herein contained.

XLV. All which privileges, freedoms and exemptions, together with the assistance herein before mentioned, in all their particulars and articles, we have, with full knowledge of the business, given, granted, promised and agreed to the- aforesaid Company; giving, granting, agreeing and promising moreover that they shall enjoy them peaceably and freely; ordaining that the same shall be observed and kept by all the magistrates, officers and subjects of the United Netherlands, without doing anything contrary thereto directly or indirectly, either within or out of these Netherlands, on penalty of being punished both in life and goods as obstacles to the common welfare of this country, and transgressors of our ordinance: promising moreover that we will maintain and establish the Company in the things contained in this charter, in all treaties of peace, alliances and agreements with the neighboring princes, kingdoms and countries, without doing anything, or suffering any thing to be done which will weaken their establishment. Charging and expressly commanding all governors, justices, officers, magistrates and inhabitants of the aforesaid United Netherlands, that they permit the aforesaid Company and managers peaceably and freely to enjoy the full effect of this charter, agreement, and privilege, without any contradiction or impeachment to the-contrary. And that none may pretend ignorance hereof, we command that the contents of this charter shall be notified by publication, or an advertisement, where, and in such manner, as is proper; for we have found it necessary for the service of this country. Given under our Great Seal, and the Signature and Seal of our Recorder, at the Hague, on the third day of the month of June, in the year sixteen hundred and twenty one.

Was countersigned

J. MAGNUS, Secr.

Underneath was written,

The ordinance of the High and Mighty Lords the States General.

It was subscribed,

C. AERSSEN.

And has a Seal pendant, of red Wax, and a string of white silk.

Source: Government of the Netherlands, "Charter of the Dutch West India Company" (New Haven, CT: Yale University, Avalon Project, 1996; www.yale.edu/lawweb/avalon/westind.htm).

∽DOCUMENT 14∽
CZAR MICHAEL ROMANOV'S DECREE ON RUNAWAY PEASANTS (1635)

Russian serfdom was another form of unfree labor that bore many of the characteristics of slavery. In the following document, Czar Michael Romanov ordered that runaway peasants who were fugitives from the households of their landowners were still legally bound to be returned to their previous condition of servitude if captured within a decade of their escape.

Extracted from the List of Articles:

In the petition of the gentlemen and junior boyars [nobility]: when they learn who has any of their runaway peasants, and although those runaway peasants are still within the term of years, they cannot achieve justice concerning these peasants of theirs and the decree; but [as regards] any which are brought to court, much time is involved in bringing the court case to a conclusion, and some of their runaway peasants pass beyond the term of years, and those peasants are withdrawn from them by the term of years [having expired], even without the court; but in previous years, they say, and under previous Sovereigns there was no term of years for those runaway peasants; and would that the Sovereign would grant a privilege ordering the term of years for peasants who had run away from them to be abandoned, and would that the Sovereign might order that those runaway peasants and labourers of theirs be given back to them in accordance with their service and heritable grants and the inquisition registers and extracts, each man to them by what he is bound, and the people also be given back in accordance with the deeds of bondage.

And the Sovereign Tsar and Grand Prince Mikhail Fedorovich of All Russia decreed and the boyars assented; for the Sovereign Tsar and Grand Prince Mikhail Fedorovich of All Russia in his, the Sovereign's crown villages and in black volosts [provinces] to give [them] back according to justice and the search and the bonds for ten years; also from the Patriarch, metropolitans, archbishops, bishops and the monasteries, and the boyars, chamberlains and people of the council, and the sewers, bearers of insignia, the Moscow gentlemen, the clerks and the attendants, and the in-servants and every rank of Moscow people, and the gentlemen of the towns and junior boyars, and the foreigners, and widows and minors, whoever they are, they are to take away the runaway peasants and labourers who ran away [to those landlords] ten years ago or less and to give them back too; but the claimants are to take suit, simultaneously with [their suit against] the peasants, [against them as] peasants and peasant [chattel] property and the peasant's holding; but if anyone starts to sue for peasant property and holdings not simultaneously with [their suit against] the peasants, but separately, they are to be refused and not given justice.

Source: Michael (Mikhail Fyodorovich Romanov), czar of Russia, "Extract from a List of Articles Containing the Tsar's Decree on the Term for Search for Runaway Peasants," in *The Enserfment of the Russian Peasantry,* ed. R. E. F. Smith (Cambridge: Cambridge University Press, 1968).

∽DOCUMENT 15∽
ANTÔNIO VIEIRA'S SERMON CONDEMNING INDIAN SLAVERY (1653)

Father Antônio Vieira was an outspoken critic of the enslavement of the indigenous peoples in the Por-

At what a different price the devil today buys souls compared to what be offered for them previously. There is no market in the world where the devil can get them more cheaply than right here in our own land. In the Gospel, he offered all the kingdoms of the world for one soul; in Maranhão the devil does not need to offer one-tenth as much for all the souls. It is not necessary to offer worlds, nor kingdoms; it is not necessary to offer cities, nor towns, nor villages. All he has to do is offer a couple of Tapuya Indians and at once he is adored on both knees. What a cheap market! An Indian for a soul! That Indian will be your slave for the few days that be lives; and your soul will be a slave for eternity, as long as God is God. This is the contract that the devil makes with you. Not only do you accept it but you pay him money on top of it.

Christians, nobles, and people of Maranhão, do you know what God wants of you during this Lent? That you break the chains of injustice and let free those whom you have captive and oppressed. These are the sins of Maranhão; these are what God commanded me to denounce to you. Christians, God commanded me to clarify these matters to you and so I do it. All of you are in mortal sin; all of you live in a state of condemnation; and all of you are going directly to Hell. Indeed, many are there now and you will soon join them if you do not change your life.

Is it possible that an entire people live in sin, that an entire people will go to hell? Who questions thus does not understand the evil of unjust captivity. The sons of Israel went down into Egypt, and after the death of Joseph, the Pharaoh seized them and made slaves of them. God wanted to liberate those miserable people, and He sent Moses there with no other escort than a rod. God knew that in order to free the captives a rod was sufficient, even though He was dealing with a ruler as tyrannical as Pharaoh and with a people as cruel as the Egyptians. When Pharaoh refused to free the captives, the plagues rained down upon him. The land was covered with frogs and the air clouded with mosquitos; the rivers flowed with blood; the clouds poured forth thunder and lightning. All Egypt was dumbfounded and threatened with death. Do you know what brought those plagues to the earth? Unjust captivity. Who brought to Maranhão the plague of the Dutch? Who brought the smallpox? Who brought hunger and drought? These captives. Moses insisted and pressed the Pharaoh to free the people, and what did Pharaoh respond? He said one thing and he did an-

other. What he said was, I do not know God and I do not have to free the captives. However, it appears to me proper and I do declare them free. Do you know why you do not give freedom to your illicitly gotten slaves? Because you do not know God. Lack of Faith is the cause of everything. If you possessed true faith, if you believed that there was an eternal Hell, then you would not take so lightly the captivity of a single Tapuya. With what confidence can the devil today say to you: *Si cadens adoraveris me?* ["Do you worship me?"] With all the confidence of having offered you the world. The devil made this speech: I offer to this man everything; if he is greedy and covetous, he must accept. If he accepts, then, he worships me because greed and covetousness are a form of idolatry. It is an idea expressed by St. Paul. Such was the greed of Pharaoh in wanting to keep and not to free the captive sons of Israel, confessing at the same time that he did not know God. This is what he said.

What he did was to take out after the fleeing Israelites with all the power of his kingdom in order to recapture them. And what happened? The Red Sea opened so that the captives could pass on dry land. It did not matter that the Hebrews did not merit this. They were worse than the Tapuyas. A few days later they worshiped a golden calf and of all the six hundred thousand men only two entered into the promised land, but God is so favorable to the cause of liberty that be grants it even to those who do not deserve it. When the Hebrews had reached the other side, Pharaoh entered between the walls of water which were still open, and as he crossed, the waters fell over his army and drowned them all. What impresses me is the way Moses tells this: that the waters enveloped them and the sea drowned them and the earth swallowed them up. Now, if the sea drowned them how could the earth swallow them? Those men, like his, had both a body and a soul. The waters drowned the bodies because they were at the bottom of the sea; the earth swallowed the souls because they descended to Hell. All went to Hell, without a single exception, because where all pursue and all capture, all are condemned. This is an excellent example. Now, let us look at the reasoning.

Any man who deprives others of their freedom and being able to restore that freedom does not do so is condemned. All or nearly all are therefore condemned. You will say to me that even if this were true they did not think about it or know it and that their good faith will save them. I deny that. They did think about it and know it just as you think of it and know it. If they did not think of it nor know it, they ought to have thought of it and to have known it. Some are condemned by their knowledge, others by their doubt, and still others by their ignorance. . . . If only the graves would open and some who died in that unhappy state could appear before you, and in the fire of their misery you could clearly read this truth. Do you know why God does not permit them to appear before you? It is exactly as Abraham said to the rich miser when he asked him to send Lazarus to this world: *Ilabent Moysen et Prophetas* (Luc. 16.29). It is not necessary for one to appear on earth from Hell to tell you the truth because you already have Moses and the Law, you have the prophets and learned men. My brothers, if there are any among you who doubt this, here are the laws, here are the learned men, question them. There are in this State, three religious orders which have members of great virtue and learning. Ask them. Study the matter and inform yourselves. But it is not necessary to question the religious: go to Turkey, go to Hell, because there is no Turk so Turkish in Turkey nor no devil so devilish in Hell who will tell you that a free man can be a slave. Is there one among you with natural intelligence who can deny it? What do you doubt?

I know what you are going to tell me . . . our people, our country, our government cannot be sustained without Indians. Who will fetch a pail of water for us or carry a load of wood? Who will grind our manioc? Will our wives have to do it? Will our sons? In the first place, this is not the state into which I am placing you as you soon will see. But when necessity and conscience require such a thing, I answer yes and repeat again yes. You, your wives, your sons, all of us are able to sustain ourselves with our own labor. It is better to live from your own sweat than from the blood of others! . . .

You will tell me that your slaves are your very feet and hands. Also, you will say how much you love them because you raised them like children and took care of them as you would your very own. It may be so, but Christ said to this land: *Si oculus tuus scandalizat te, erue eum et si manus, vel pes tuus scandalizat te, amputa elum* (Math. 5–29 [5.29]; Marc. 9.42.44). Christ did not mean to say that we should pull out our eyes nor that we ought to cut off our hands and feet. What he meant was that if that which we loved as our eyes harmed us, or that which was as necessary as our hands and feet harmed us, we should cast away from us that source of harm even if it hurts us as if we had cut it off from us. Who amongst you does not love his arm or his hand but should it become gangrenous would not permit its amputation in order to save his life. . . . If, in order to quiet your conscience or save your soul, it is necessary to lose everything and remain as miserable as Job, lose everything.

But take heart, my friends, it is not necessary to arrive at such a state, far from it. I have studied the matter carefully and in accordance with the most lenient and favorable opinions and have come to a conclusion by which, with only minor worldly losses, all the inhabitants of this state can ease their consciences and build for a better future. Give me your attention.

All the Indians of this State are either those who serve as slaves or those who live as free inhabitants in the King's villages, or those who live in the hinterlands in their natural or free condition. These latter are the ones you go upriver to buy or "to rescue," giving the pious verb "to rescue" to a sale so involuntary and violent that at times it is made at pistol point. These are held, owned, and bequeathed in bad faith: therefore they will be doing no small task if they forgive you for their past treatment. However, if after you have set them free, they, particularly those domestics whom you raised in your house and treated as your children, spontaneously and voluntarily wish to continue to serve you and remain in your home, no one will or can separate them from your service. And what will happen to those who do not wish to remain in your service? These will be obliged to live in the King's villages where they also will serve you in the manner which I shall mention. Each year you will be able to make your expeditions into the interior during which time you can really rescue those who are prisoners ready to be eaten. Those justly saved from death will remain your slaves. Also, all those captured in just wars will be made slaves. Upon this matter the proper judges will be the Governor of the State, the Chief Justice of the State, the Vicars of Maranhão or of Para, and the Prelates of the four orders: Carmelite, Franciscan, Mercedarian, and the Company of Jesus. All of these who after judgment are qualified to be true captives, will be returned to the inhabitants. And what will happen to those captured in a war not classified as just? All of them will be placed in new villages or divided among the villages which exist today. There, along with the other village Indians they will be hired out to the inhabitants of this State to work for them for six months of every year alternating two months of hired work with two months devoted to their own labors and families. Thus, in this manner, all the Indians of this State will serve the Portuguese either as legitimate slaves, that is those rescued from death or captured in a just war, or those former slaves who freely and voluntarily wish to serve their old masters, or those from the King's villages who will work half the year for the good and growth of the State. It only remains to set the wages of those village Indians for their labor and service. It is a subject which would make any other nation of the world laugh and only in this land is not appreciated. The money of this land is cloth and cotton, and the ordinary price for which the Indians work and will work each month is seven feet of this cloth which has a market value of about twenty cents. An Indian will work for less than a penny a day. It is an insignificant amount and it is unworthy of a man of reason and of Christian faith not to pay such a slight price to save his soul and to avoid Hell.

Could there be anything more moderate? Could there be anything, more reasonable than this? Whoever is dissatisfied or discontent with this proposal either is not a Christian or has no understanding. To conclude this point, let us look at the advantages and disadvantages of this proposal.

The single disadvantage is that some of you will lose a few Indians. I promise you they will be very few. But to you who question this, I ask: Do not some of your Indians die or flee? Many do. Will death do what reason will not? Will chance do what a good conscience will not? If smallpox strikes and carries off your Indians, what will you do? You will have to show patience. Well, is it not better to lose the Indians to the service of God than to lose them by a punishment of God? The answer is obvious.

Let us look at the advantages of which there are four principal ones. The first is that you will have a clear conscience. You will no longer live in a state of mortal sin. You will live like Christians, you will be confessed as Christians, you will die like Christians, you will bequeath your goods as Christians. In short, you will go to Heaven and not to Hell, which would certainly be a tragic ending.

The second advantage is that you will remove this curse from your homes. There is no greater curse on a home or a family than to be unjustly supported by the sweat and blood of others. . . .

The third advantage is that in this way more Indians will be rescued from cannibal practices. . . . It is important to invade the forest to save Indians from being killed and eaten.

The fourth and last advantage is that henceforth your proposals on the labor problem will be worthy of submission to His Majesty, and worthy of His Majesty's approval and confirmation. Whoever asks for the illegal and unjust deserves to have the legal and just denied him, and whoever petitions with justice, reason, and good conscience deserves the fulfillment of his request. You know the proposal which you made? It was a proposal which vassals could not make in good conscience, nor could ministers consult it in good conscience. And even if the King might have permitted it, what good would it have done you? If the King permits me to steal falsely, will it mean that the false oath is no sin? If the King permits me to steal, will the theft be any less a sin? The same thing applies to the Indians. The King can command the slaves to be free, but his jurisdiction does not extend to the power to order the free to become slaves. If such a request went to Lisbon, the stones of the street would have to rise up against the men of Maranhão. On the other hand, if you submit a just,

legal, and Christian request, those very same stones would take your part. . . .

Source: Father Antonio Vieira, "Vieira's Sermon Condemning Indian Slavery," in *A Documentary History of Brazil*, ed. E. Bradford Burns (New York: Alfred A. Knopf, 1966).

✒DOCUMENT 16✒
A DESCRIPTION OF BRAZIL'S SUGAR INDUSTRY (1654)

The "sugar revolution" transformed the slave-based economy of the Americas. As the cultivation of sugar spread from Brazil to the Caribbean islands, the number of African slaves needed to sustain this agricultural transformation rose accordingly. The dramatic expansion of the African slave trade during the eighteenth century was a direct result of the expansion of sugar as an agricultural commodity in the Americas. In the following passage, an English observer describes Brazil's sugar region in 1654.

I will return to speak of the Riches of the Country, chiefly consisting in their Sugar, which when I have named, I have named all; not that it wants others, but that it can want no others, having that, since that country which abounds with that commodity which all others have need of, can never want any commodity which others abound withall. . . . Now for their Sugar thus it grows, and thus 'tis made; Their Sugar canes are prun'd to the heighth of standing corn: nor need they other culture, but every second year to cut them close by the roots, as we do Osiers, when against the next year they never fail to spring up agen, the flaggs of which Canes are of a pleasant green, and shew a far off just like in a Field of Corn, which being ripe about the month of June, they joint them in pieces some foot long, and carry them to the Mill, turn'd by Oxen, or Water, consisting of two round Cylinders, about the bignesse of Mil-posts, plated with Iron, which turning inwards, and joyning as close together as they can meet so squeez the canes in passing through them, as they come out on th' other side all bruzed and dry as keques, which were all liquid before; which Liquor is conveyed by Troughs to certain Caldrons, where 'tis boyl'd, still retaining its amber colour, till pour'd out at last into their forms or coolers, with a certain Lee 'tis rendered white; And in these Mills they work both day and night, the work of immediately applying the canes into the Mill being so periilous as if through drousiness or heedlessnesse a fingers end be but engag'd betwixt the posts, their whole body inevitably follows, to prevent which, the next Negro has always a Hatchet readie to chop off his Arm, if any such Misfortune should arrive.

Source: Richard Flecknoe, "A Description of the Sugar Industry," in *A Documentary History of Brazil*, ed. E. Bradford Burns (New York: Alfred A. Knopf, 1966).

❦DOCUMENT 17❦
DESCRIPTION OF THE
AFRICAN SLAVE TRADE (1682)

Some of the most damning testimony about the African slave trade comes from accounts by Europeans who were involved in the nefarious business. John Barbot, an agent of the French Royal African Company, recorded these recollections of his visits as a slave trader to the west coast of Africa in 1678 and 1682.

Those sold by the Blacks are for the most part prisoners of war, taken either in fight, or pursuit, or in the incursions they make into their enemies territories; others stolen away by their own countrymen; and some there are, who will sell their own children, kindred, or neighbours. This has been often seen, and to compass it, they desire the person they intend to sell, to help them in carrying something to the factory by way of trade, and when there, the person so deluded, not understanding the language, is sold and deliver'd up as a slave, notwithstanding all his resistance, and exclaiming against the treachery. . . .

The kings are so absolute, that upon any slight pretense of offences committed by their subjects, they order them to be sold for slaves, without regard to rank, or possession. . . .

Abundance of little Blacks of both sexes are also stolen away by their neighbours, when found abroad on the roads, or in the woods; or else in the Cougans, or corn-fields, at the time of the year, when their parents keep them there all day, to scare away the devouring small birds, that come to feed on the millet, in swarms, as has been said above.

In times of dearth and famine, abundance of those people will sell themselves, for a maintenance, and to prevent starving. When I first arriv'd at Goerree, in December, 1681, I could have bought a great number, at very easy rates, if I could have found provisions to subsist them; so great was the dearth then, in that part of Nigritia [Africa].

To conclude, some slaves are also brought to these Blacks, from very remote inland countries, by way of trade, and sold for things of very inconsiderable value; but these slaves are generally poor and weak, by reason of the barbarous usage they have had in traveling so far, being continually beaten, and almost famish'd; so inhuman are the Blacks to one another. . . .

The trade of slaves is in a more peculiar manner the business of kings, rich men, and prime merchants, exclusive of the inferior sort of Blacks.

These slaves are severely and barbarously treated by their masters, who subsist them poorly, and beat them inhumanly, as may be seen by the scabs and wounds on the bodies of many of them when sold to us. They scarce allow them the least rag to cover their nakedness, which they also take off from them when sold to Europeans; and they always go bareheaded. The wives and children of slaves, are also slaves to the master under whom they are married; and when dead, they never bury them, but cast out the bodies into some by place, to be devoured by birds, or beasts of prey.

This barbarous usage of those unfortunate wretches, makes it appear, that the fate of such as are bought and transported from the coast to America, or other parts of the world, by Europeans, is less deplorable, than that of those who end their days in their native country; for aboard ships all possible care is taken to preserve and subsist them for the interest of the owners, and when sold in America, the same motive ought to prevail with their masters to use them well, that they may live the longer, and do them more service. Not to mention the inestimable advantage they may reap, of becoming christians, and saving their souls, if they make a true use of their condition. . . .

Many of those slaves we transport from Guinea to America are prepossessed with the opinion, that they are carried like sheep to the slaughter, and that the Europeans are fond of their flesh; which notion so far prevails with some, as to make them fall into a deep melancholy and despair, and to refuse all sustenance, tho' never so much compelled and even beaten to oblige them to take some nourishment: notwithstanding all which, they will starve to death; whereof I have had several instances in my own slaves both aboard and at Guadalupe. And tho' I must say I am naturally compassionate, yet have I been necessitated sometimes to cause the teeth of those wretches to be broken, because they would not open their mouths, or be prevailed upon by any entreaties to feed themselves; and thus have forced some sustenance into their throats. . . .

As the slaves come down to Fida from the inland country, they are put into a booth, or prison, built for that purpose, near the beach, all of them together; and when the Europeans are to receive them, every part of every one of them, to the smallest member, men and women being all stark naked. Such as are allowed good and sound, are set on one side, and the others by themselves; which slaves so rejected are there called Mackrons, being above thirty five years of age, or defective in their limbs, eyes or teeth; or grown grey, or that have the venereal disease, or any other imperfection. These being set aside, each of the others, which have passed as good, is marked on the breast, with a red-hot iron, imprinting the mark of the French, English, or Dutch companies, that so each nation may distinguish their own, and to prevent their being chang'd by the natives for worse, as they are apt enough to do. In this particular, care is taken that the women, as tenderest, be not burnt too hard.

The branded slaves, after this, are returned to their former booth, where the factor is to subsist them at his own charge, which amounts to about two-pence a day for each of them, with bread and water, which is all their allowance. There they continue sometimes ten or fifteen days, till the sea is still enough to send them aboard; for very often it continues too boisterous for so long a time, unless in January, February and March, which is commonly the calmest season: and when it is so, the slaves are carried off by parcels, in bar-canoes, and put aboard the ships in the road. Before they enter the canoes, or come out of the booth, their former Black masters strip them of every rag they have, without distinction of men or women; to supply which, in orderly ships, each of them as they come aboard is allowed a piece of canvas, to wrap around their waist, which is very acceptable to those poor wretches. . . .

If there happens to be no stock of slaves at Fida, the factor must trust the Blacks with his goods, to the value of a hundred and fifty, or two hundred slaves; which goods they carry up into the inland, to buy slaves, at all the markets, for above two hundred leagues up the country, where they are kept like cattle in Europe; the slaves sold there being generally prisoners of war, taken from their enemies, like other booty, and perhaps some few sold by their own countrymen, in extreme want, or upon a famine; as also some as a punishment of heinous crimes: tho' many Europeans believe that parents sell their own children, men their wives and relations, which, if it ever happens, is so seldom, that it cannot justly be charged upon a whole nation, as a custom and common practice . . .

One thing is to be taken notice of by sea-faring men, that this Fida and Ardra slaves are of all the others, the most apt to revolt aboard ships, by a conspiracy carried on amongst themselves; especially such as are brought down to Fida, from very remote inland countries, who easily draw others into their plot: for being used to see mens flesh eaten in their own country, and publick markets held for the purpose, they are very full of the notion, that we buy and transport them to the same purpose; and will therefore watch all opportunities to deliver themselves, by assaulting a ship's crew, and murdering them all, if possible: whereof, we have almost every year some instances, in one European ship or other, that is filled with slaves.

Source: John Barbot, "A Description of the Coasts of North and South Guinea," in *Collection of Voyages and Travels*, ed. Thomas Astley and John Churchill (London: H. Lintot, 1744).

DOCUMENT 18
THE GERMANTOWN PROTEST (1688)

The first recorded protest against African slavery in what eventually became the United States was issued in Germantown, Pennsylvania, in 1688. Basing opposition to the practice of slavery upon the Golden Rule, a congregation of Mennonite Quakers found the existence of slavery to be inconsistent with Christian principles.

This is to the monthly meeting held at Richard Worrell's:

These are the reasons why we are against the traffic of men-body, as followeth: "Is there any that would be done or handled at this manner" viz., to be sold or made a slave for all the time of his life? How fearful and faint-hearted are many at sea, when they see a strange vessel, being afraid it should be a Turk, and they should be taken, and sold for slaves into Turkey. Now, what is this better done, than Turks do? Yea, rather it is worse for them, which say they are Christians; for we hear that the most part of such negers are brought hither against their will and consent, and that many of them are stolen. Now, though they are black, we cannot conceive there is more liberty to have them slaves, as it is to have other white ones. There is a saying, that we should do to all men like as we will be done ourselves; making no difference of what generation, descent, or colour they are. And those who steal or rob men, and those who buy or purchase them, are they not all alike? Here is liberty of conscience, which is right and reasonable; here ought to be likewise liberty of the body, except of evil-doers, which is another case. But to bring men hither, or to rob and sell them against their will, we stand against. In Europe there are many oppressed for conscience-sake; and here there are those oppressed which are of a black colour. And we who know that men must not commit adultery—some do commit adultery in others, separating wives from their husbands, and giving them to others: and some sell the children of these poor creatures to other men. Ah! do consider well this thing, you who do it, if you would be done at this manner—and if it is done according to Christianity! You surpass Holland and Germany in this thing, This makes an ill report in all those countries of Europe, where they hear of [it], that the Quakers do here handel men as they handel there the cattle. And for that reason some have no mind or inclination to come hither. And who shall maintain this your cause, or plead for it? Truly, we cannot do so, except you shall inform us better hereof, viz.: that Christians have liberty to practice these things. Pray, what thing in the world can be done worse towards us, than if men should rob or steal us away, and sell us for slaves to strange countries; separating husbands from their wives and children. Being now this is not done in the manner we would be done at; therefore, we contradict, and are against this traffic of men-body. And we who profess that it is not lawful to steal, must, likewise, avoid to purchase such things as are stolen, but rather help to stop this robbing and stealing, if possible. And such men ought to be delivered out of the hands of the robbers, and set free as in Europe. Then is Pennsylvania to have a good report, instead, it hath now a bad one, for this sake, in other countries; Especially whereas the Europeans are desirous to know in what manner the Quakers do rule in their province; and most of them do look upon us with an envious eye. But if this is done well, what shall we say is done evil?

If once these slaves (which they say are so wicked and stubborn men,) should join themselves—fight for their freedom, and handel their masters and mistresses, as they did handel them before; will these masters and mistresses take the sword at hand and war against these poor slaves, like, as we are able to believe, some will not refuse to do? Or, have these poor negers not as much right to fight for their freedom, as you have to keep them slaves?

Now consider well this thing, if it is good or bad. And in case you find it to be good to handel these blacks in that manner, we desire and require you hereby lovingly, that you may inform us herein, which at this time never was done, viz., that Christians have such a liberty to do so. To the end we shall be satisfied on this point, and satisfy likewise our good friends and acquaintances in our native country, to whom it is a terror, or fearful thing, that men should be handelled so in Pennsylvania.

This is from our meeting at Germantown held ye 18th of the 2d month, 1688, to be delivered to the monthly meeting at Richard Worrell's.

Garret Henderich,
Derick op de Graeff,
Francis Daniel Pastorius,
Abram op de Graeff.

Source: Daniel Franz Pastorius, "The Germantown Protest, 1688," in *Documents of American History,* ed. Henry Steele Commager (New York: Appleton-Century-Crofts, 1963).

⮞DOCUMENT 19⮜
MUTINY DURING THE MIDDLE PASSAGE (1704)

Occasionally, African captives aboard slave ships revolted in an attempt to liberate themselves from the uncertain future that lay ahead. The following passage provides an account of a mutiny that occurred in 1704 just off of the coast of West Africa.

The first Mutiny I saw among the Negroes, happened during my first voyage, in the Year 1704. It was on board the Eagle Galley of London, commanded by my Father, with whom I was as Pursar. We had bought our Negroes in the River of Old Callabar in the Bay of Guinea. At the time of their mutinying we were in that River, having four hundred of them on board, and not above ten white Men who were able to do Service: For several of our Ship's Company were dead, and many more sick; besides, two of our Boats were just then gone with Twelve People on Shore to fetch Wood, which lay in sight of the Ship. All these circumstances put the Negroes on consulting how to mutiny, which they did at four o'-clock in the Afternoon, just as they went to Supper. But as we had always carefully examined the mens Irons, both Morning and Evening, none had got them off, which in a great measure contributed to our Preservation. Three white Men stood on the Watch and Cutlaces in their Hands. One of them who was on the Forecastle, a stout fellow, seeing some of the Men Negroes take hold of the chief Mate, in order to throw him over board, he laid on them so heartily with the flat side of his Cutlace, that they soon quitted the Mate, who escaped from them, and run on the Quarter Deck to get arms. I was then sick with an Ague, and lying on a Couch in the great Cabbin, the Fit being just come on. However, I no sooner heard the Outcry, That the Slaves were mutinying, than I took two Pistols, and run on the Deck with them; where meeting with my Father and the chief Mate, I delivered a pistol to each of them. Whereupon they went forward on the Booms, calling to the Negroe Men that were on the Forecastle; but they did not regard their Threats, being busy with the Centry, (who had disengaged the chief Mate,) and they would have certainly killed him with his own Cutlace could they have got it from him; but they could not break the Line wherewith the Handle was fastened to his Wrist. And so, tho' they had seized him, yet they could not make use of his Cutlace. Being thus disappointed, they endeavoured to throw him overboard, but he held so fast by one of them that they could not do it. My Father seeing this stout Man in so much Danger, ventured amongst the Negroes, to save him; and fired his Pistol over the Heads, thinking to frighten them. But a lusty Slave struck him with a Billet so hard, that he was almost stunned. The Slave was going to repeat the Blow, when a young Lad about seventeen years old, whom we had been kind to, interposed his Arm, and received the Blow, by which his arm-bone was fractured. At the same instant the Mate fired his Pistol, and shot the Negroe that had struck my Father. At the sight of this the Mutiny ceased, and all the Men-negroes on the Forecastle threw themselves flat on their Faces, crying out for Mercy.

Upon examining into the matters we found, there were not above twenty Men slaves concerned in this Mutiny; and the two Ringleaders were missing, having, it seems, jumped overboard as soon as they found their Project defeated, and were drowned.

Source: William Snelgrave, "Mutiny during the Middle Passage," in *Africans Abroad,* ed. Graham W. Irwin (New York: Columbia University Press, 1977).

❧DOCUMENT 20❧
DESCRIPTION OF SLAVE TRADING IN MASSACHUSETTS (1706)

In the years prior to the American Revolution, slavery existed in all of the 13 colonies on the Atlantic seaboard of North America. This account from the Boston News Letter *reveals many of the prevailing racist attitudes toward slaves in the colony of Massachusetts in the early eighteenth century.*

By last Years Bill of Mortality for the Town of Boston in Numb 100 News Letter, we are furnished with a List of 44 Negroes dead last year, which being computed one with another at 30 l. [pound sterling] per Head, amounts to the Sum of One Thousand three hundred and Twenty Pounds, of which we would make this Remark: That the Importing of Negroes into this or the Neighbouring Provinces is not so beneficial either to the Crown or Country, as White Servants would be.

For Negroes do not carry Arms to defend the Country as Whites do:

Negroes are generaly Eye-Servants, great Thieves, much addicted to stealing, Lying, and Purloining.

They do not People our Country as Whites would do whereby we should be strengthened against an Enemy.

By Encouraging the importing of White Men Servants, allowing somewhat to the importer, most Husbandmen in the Country might be furnished with Servants for 8, 9, or, 10 l. a Head, who are not able to Launch Out 40 or 50 l. for a Negro the now common Price.

A Man then might buy a White Man Servant we suppose for 10 l. to Serve 4 years, and Boys for the same price to Serve 6, 8 or 10 years: If a White Servant die, the Loss exceeds not 10 l. but if a Negro dies 'tis a very great Loss to the Husbandman. Three years Interest of the price of the Negro, will near upon if not altogether purchase a White Man Servant.

If Necessity call for it, that the Husbandman must fit out a man against the Enemy; if he has a Negro he cannot send him, but if he has a White Servant, 'twill answer the end, and perhaps save his Son at home.

Were Merchants and Masters Encouraged as already said to bring in Men Servants, there needed not be such complaint against Superiors Impressing our Children to the War, there would then be Men enough to be had without Impressing.

The bringing in of such servants would much enrich this Province, because Husbandmen would not only be able far better to manure what Lands are already under Improvement, but would also improve a great deal more that now lyes waste under Woods, and enable this Province to set about raising of Naval Stores, which would be greatly advantageous to the Crown of England, and this Province . . .

Suppose the Government here should allow Forty Shillings per head for five years, to such as should Import every of those years 100 White Men Servants, and each to serve 4 Years, the cost would be but 200 l. a year, and a 1000 for the five years: the first 100 servants being free the 4th year, they serve the 5th for Wages, an the 6th there is 100 that goes out into the Woods, and settles a 100 Families to strengthen and Baracade us from the Indians, and so a 100 Families more every year successively.

And here you see that in one year the Town of Boston has lost 1320 l. by 44 Negroes, which is also a Loss to this Country in general, and for a less Loss, (if it may improperly be so called) for a 1000 l. the Country may have 500 Men in 5 years time for the 44 Negroes dead in one year.

A certain person within these 6 years had two Negroes dead computed both at 60 l. which would have procured him six white Servants at 10 l. per head to have Served 24 years, at 4 years a piece, without running such a great risque [risk], and the Whites would have strengthened the Country, that Negroes do not. 'Twould do wel[l] that none of those Servants be liable to be Impressed during their Service of Agreement at their first Landing.

That such Servants being Sold or Transported out of this Province during the time of their Service, the person that buys them be liable to pay 3 l. into the Treasury.

Source: Newsletter, June 19, 1706, "The Importation of Negroes into Massachusetts," in *Documents Illustrative of the History of the Slave Trade to America, Volume III—New England & the Middle Colonies,* ed. Elizabeth Donnan (Washington, DC: Carnegie Institution of Washington, 1932).

❧DOCUMENT 21❧
DESCRIPTION OF A SLAVE CONSPIRACY IN NEW YORK (1712)

A tremendous fear captivated New York City in 1712 as residents feared that a massive slave conspiracy had been discovered. In the following account, colonial governor Robert Hunter provides details about the plot to the Lords of Trade (investors in colonial commerce) in London.

Gov. Robert Hunter to the Lords of Trade, June 23, 1712.

I must now give your Lordships an account of a bloody conspiracy of some of the slaves of this place, to destroy as many of the Inhabitants as they could. It was put in execution in this manner, when they had resolved to revenge themselves, for some hard usage, they apprehended to have received from their masters they agreed to meet in the orchard of Mr Crook the middle of the Town, some provided with fire arms, some with swords and others with knives and hatchets, this was the sixth day of April, the time of meeting was about twelve or one o'clock in the night, when about three and twenty of them were got togeather, one coffee and negroe slave to one Vantilbrugh set fire to an out house of his Masters, and then repairing to the place where the rest were they all sallyed out togeather with their arm's and marched to the fire, by this time the noise of fire spreading through the town, the people began to flock to it upon the approach of severall the slaves fired and killed them, the noise of the guns gave the allarm, and some escaping their shot soon published the cause of the fire, which was the reason, that not above nine Christians were killed, and about five or six wounded, upon the first notice which was very soon after the mischeif was begun, I order'd a detachment from the fort under a proper officer to march against them, but the slaves made their retreat into the woods, by the favour of the night, having ordered centries the next day in the most proper places on the Island to prevt [prevent] their escape, I caused the day following the Militia of this town and of the county of west Chester to drive the Island, and by this means and strict searches in the town, we found all that put the design in execution, six of these having first laid violent hands upon themselves, the rest were forthwith brought to their tryal before ye [the] Justices of this place who are authorized by Act of Assembly, to hold a Court in such cases, In that Court were twenty seven condemned whereof twenty one were executed, one being a woman with child, her execution by that meanes suspended, some were burnt others hanged, one broke on the wheele, and one hung a live in chains in the town, so that there has been the most exemplary punishment inflicted that could be possibly thought of, and which only this act of assembly could justify, among these guilty persons severall others were apprehended, and again acquitted by the Court, for want of sufficient evidence, among those was one Mars a negroe man slave to one Mr Regnier, who was to his tryall and acquitted by the jury, the Sheriffe the next day moving the Court for the discharge of such as were or should be soe acquitted, by reason hee apprehended they would attempt to make their escape but Mr Bickley who yn [then] executed the office of the Atter: Generall, for Mr Rayner opposed his motion, telling the Court that at that time, none but Mars being acquitted, the motion could be only intended in his favour, against whom he should have some thing further to object, and therefore prayed he might not be discharged. so the sheriff did not obtain his motion, Mars was then indicted a second time and again acquitted, but not discharg'd, and being a third time presented was transferr'd to the supream Court, and there tryed and convicted on ye same evidence, on his two former tryals, this prosecution was carried on to gratify some private pique of Mr Bickleys against Mr Regnier, a gentleman of his own profession, which appearing so partial, and the evidence being represented to me as very defective, and being wholly acquitted of ever having known any thing of the Conspiracy by the Negroe witnesses, who were made use of in the tryals of all the criminals before the Justices, and without whose testimonies very, few could have been punished, I thought fit to reprieve him till Her Majesties pleasure be known therein. if this supream court were likewise tryed, one Husea belonging to Mrs Wenham, and one John belonging Mr Vantilbourgh and convicted, these two are prisoners taken in a Spanish prize this war and brought into this Port by a Privateer, about six or seven years agoe and by reason of their colour which is swarthy, they were said to be slaves and as such were sold, among many others of the same colour and country, these two I have likewise reprieved till Her Majesties pleasure be signified. soon after my arrival in this government I received petitions from several of these Spanish Indians as they are called here, representing to me that they were free men subjects to the King of Spain, but sold here as slaves, I secretly pittyed their condition but haveing no other evidence of wt [what] they asserted then their own words, I had it not in my power to releive them, I am informed that in the West Indies where their laws against their slaves are most severe, that in case of a conspiracy in which many are engaged a few only are executed for an example, In this case 21 are executed, and six having done that justice on themselves more have suffered than we can find were active in this bloody affair which are reasons for my repreiving these, and if your Lordships think them of sufficient weight, I beg you will procure Her Majesty's pleasure to be signifyed to me for their pardon, for they lye now in prison at their masters charge, I have likewise reprieved one Tom a Negroe belonging to Mr Van Dam and Coffee a Negroe belonging to Mr Walton these two I have reprieved at the instance of the Justices of the Court, who where of oppinion that the evidence against them, was not sufficient to convict them. . . .

Source: Robert Hunter, "A Slave Conspiracy in New York, 1712," in *A Documentary History of Slavery in*

North America, ed. Willie Lee Rose (New York: Oxford University Press, 1976).

❧DOCUMENT 22❧
DESCRIPTION OF LIMA, PERU (1748)

Many colonies in the Americas developed a complex social hierarchy as a result of racial mixing between Europeans, Africans, and indigenous peoples of the Americas. Over time, a castelike system developed within many of these communities. The following document explores the complexity of race and class in the city of Lima, Peru, in the eighteenth century.

The inhabitants of Lima are composed of whites, or Spaniards, Negroes, Indians, Mestizos, and other casts, proceeding from the mixture of all three.

The Spanish families are very numerous; Lima according to the lowest computation, containing sixteen or eighteen thousand whites, Among these are reckoned a third or fourth part of the most distinguished nobility of Peru; and many of these dignified with the stile of ancient or modern Castilians, among which are no less than 45 counts and marquises. The number of knights belonging to the several military orders is also very considerable. Besides these are many families no less respectable and living in equal splendor; particularly 24 gentlemen of large estates, but without titles, tho' most of them have ancient seats, a proof of the antiquity of their families. One of these traces, with undeniable certainty, his descent from the Incas. The name of this family is Ampuero, so called from one of the Spanish commanders at the conquest of this country, who married a Coya, or daughter of the Inca. To this family the kings of Spain have been pleased to grant several distinguishing honours and privileges, as marks of its great quality: and many of the most eminent families in the city have desired intermarriages with it.

All those families live in a manner becoming their rank, having estates equal to their generous dispositions, keeping a great number of slaves and other domestics, and those who affect making the greatest figure, have coaches, while others content themselves with calashes or chaises, which are here so common, that no family of any substance is without one. It must be owned that these carriages are more necessary here than in other cities, on account of the numberless droves of mules which continually pass thro' Lima, and cover the streets with their dung, which being soon dried by the sun and the wind, turns to a nauseous dust, scarce supportable to those who walk on foot. These chaises, which are drawn by a mule, and guided by a driver, have only two wheels, with two seats opposite to each other, so that on occasion they will hold four persons. They are very slight and airy; but on account of the gildings and other decorations, sometimes cost eight hundred or a thousand crowns. The number of them is said to amount to 5 or 6000; and that of coaches is also very considerable, tho' not equal to the former.

The funds to support these expenses, which in other parts would ruin families, are their large estates and plantations, civil and military employments or commerce, which is here accounted no derogation to families of the greatest distinction; but by this commerce is not to be understood the buying and selling by retail or in shops, every one trading proportional to his character and substance. Hence families are preserved from those disasters too common in Spain, where titles are frequently found without a fortune capable of supporting their dignity. Commerce is so far from being considered as a disgrace at Lima, that the greatest fortunes have been raised by it; those on the contrary, being rather despised, who not being blessed with a sufficient estate, through indolence, neglect to have recourse to it for improving their fortunes. This custom, or resource, which was established there without any determinate end, being introduced by a vain desire of the first Spaniards to acquire wealth, is now the real support of that splendor in which those families live; and whatever repugnance these military gentlemen might originally have to commerce. it was immediately removed by a royal proclamation, by which it was declared that commerce in the Indies should not exclude from nobility or the military orders; a very wise measure, and of which Spain would be still more sensible, were it extended to all its dependencies.

At Lima, as at Quito, and all Spanish America, some of the eminent families have been long since settled there, whilst the prosperity of others is of a later date; for being the center of the whole commerce of Peru, a greater number of Europeans resort to it, than to any other city; some for trade, and others, from being invested in Spain with considerable employments: among both are persons of the greatest merit; and tho' many after they have finished their respective affairs, return home, yet the major part induced by the fertility of the soil, and goodness of the climate, remain at Lima, and marry young ladies remarkable equally for the gifts of fortune as those of nature and thus new families are continually settled.

The Negroes, Mulattoes, and their descendants, form the greater number of the inhabitants; and of these are the greatest part of the mechanics; tho' here the Europeans also follow the same occupations, which are not at Lima reckoned disgraceful to them, as they are at Quito; for gain being here the universal passion, the inhabitants pursue it by means of any trade, without regard to its being followed by Mulattoes, interest here preponderating against any other consideration.

The third, and last class of inhabitants are the Indians and Mestizos, but these are very small in proportion to the largeness of the city, and the multitudes of the second class. They are employed in agriculture, in making earthen ware, and bringing all kinds of provisions to market, domestic services being performed by Negroes and Mulattoes, either slaves or free, though generally by the former.

The usual dress of the men differs very little from that worn in Spain, nor is the distinction between the several classes very great; for the use of all sorts of cloth being allowed, every one wears what he can purchase. So that it is not uncommon to see a Mulatto, or any other mechanic dressed in a tissue, equal to any thing that can be worn by a more opulent person. They all greatly affect fine cloaths, and it may be said without exaggeration, that the finest stuffs made in countries, where industry is always inventing something new, are more generally seen at Lima than in any other place; vanity and ostentation not being restrained by custom or law. Thus the great quantities brought in the galleons and register ships notwithstanding they sell here prodigiously above their prime cost in Europe, the richest of them are used as cloaths, and worn with a carelessness little suitable to their extravagant price; but in this article the men are greatly exceeded by the women, whose passion for dress is such as to deserve a more particular account.

In the choice of laces, the women carry their taste to a prodigious excess; nor is this an emulation confined to persons of quality, but has spread thro' all ranks, except the lowest class of Negroes. The laces are sewed to their linen, which is of the finest sort, though very little of it is seen, the greatest part of it, especially in some dresses, being always covered with lace; so that the little which appears seems rather for ornament than use. These laces too must be all of Flanders manufacture, no woman of rank condescending to look on any other.

Their dress is very different from the European, which the custom of the country alone can render excusable; indeed to Spaniards at their first coming over it appears extremely indecent. Their dress consists of a pair of shoes, a shift, a petticoat of dimity, an open petticoat, and a jacket, which in summer, is of linen, in winter of stuff. To this some add a mantellette, that the former may hang loose. The difference between this dress and that worn at Quito, though consisting of the same pieces is, that at Lima it is much shorter, the petticoat which is usually tied below the waist, not reaching lower than the calf of the leg, from whence, nearly to the ankle, hangs a border of very fine lace, sewed to the bottom of the under petticoat; through which the ends of their garters are discovered, embroidered with gold or silver, and sometimes set with pearls; but the latter is not common. The upper petticoat, which is of velvet, or some rich stuff, is fringed all round, and not less crowded with ornaments, than those described in the first volume of this work. But be the ornaments what they will, whether of fringe, lace, or ribbands, they are always exquisitely fine. The shift's sleeves, which are a yard and a half in length, and two yards in width, when worn for ornament, are covered with rolls of laces, variegated in such a manner as to render the whole truly elegant. Over the shift is worn the jacket, the sleeves of which are excessively large, of a circular figure, and consist of rows of lace, or slips of cambrick or lawn, with lace disposed betwixt each, as are also the shift sleeves, even of those who do not affect extraordinary ornament. The body of the jacket is tied on the shoulders with ribbands fastened to the back of their stays; and the round sleeves of it being tucked up to the shoulders, are so disposed together with those of the shift, as to form what may be term'd four wings. If the jacket be not buttoned or clasped before, it is agreeably fastened on the shoulders; and indeed the whole dress makes a most elegant figure. They who use a close vest, fasten it with clasps, but wear over it the loose jacket, already described. In the summer they have a kind of veil, the stuff and fashion of which is like that of the shift and body of the vest, of the finest cambrick or lawn, richly laced: But in winter the veil worn in their houses is of baize; when they go abroad full dressed, it is adorned like the sleeves. They also use brown baize, finely laced and fringed, and bordered with slips of black velvet. Over the petticoat is an apron of the same stuff as the sleeves of the jacket, hanging down to the bottom of it. From hence some idea may be formed of the expense of a dress, where the much greater part of the stuff is merely for ornament; nor will it appear strange that the marriage shift should cost a thousand crowns, and sometimes more.

One particular on which the women here extremely value themselves, is the size of their feet, a small foot being esteemed one of the chief beauties; and this is the principal fault they find with the Spanish ladies, who have much larger feet than those of Lima. From their infancy they are accustomed to wear straight shoes, that their feet may not grow beyond the size of which they esteem beautiful; some of them do not exceed five inches and a half, or six inches in length, and in women of a small stature they are still less. Their shoes have little or no sole, one piece of Cordovan serving both for that and the upper leather, and of an equal breadth and roundness at the toe and heel, so as to form a sort of long figure of eight; but the foot not complying with this figure, brings it to a greater regularity. These shoes are always fastened with diamond buckles, or something very brilliant in proportion to the ability of the wearer, being worn less for use than ornament; for the shoes are made in such a manner that they never loosen of themselves, nor do the buckles hinder their being taken off. It is unusual to set these buckles with pearls, a particular to be accounted for, only from their being so lavish of them in the other ornaments of dress, as to consider them as of too little value. The shoemakers, who are no strangers to the foible of the sex take great care to make them in a manner very little calculated for service. The usual price is three half crowns a pair, those embroidered with gold or silver cost from eight to ten crowns. The latter, however, are but little worn, the encumbrance of embroidery being suited rather to enlarge than diminish the appearance of a small foot.

They are fond of white silk stockings, made extremely thin, that the leg may appear the more shapely; the greatest part of which is exposed to view. These trifles often afford very sprightly sallies of wit in their animadversions on the dress of others.

Hitherto we have considered only the more common dress of these ladies; the reader will conceive a still higher idea of their magnificence, when he is informed of the ornaments with which they are decorated in their visits, and upon public occasions. We shall begin with their manner of dressing the hair, which being naturally black, and capable of reaching below their waists, they dispose in such a manner as to appear perfectly graceful. They tie it up behind in six braided locks, through which a golden bodkin a little bent is inserted, and having a cluster of diamonds at each end. On this the locks are suspended so as to touch the shoulder. On the front and upper part of the head they wear diamond egrets, and the hair is formed into little curls, hanging from the forehead to the middle of the ear, with a large black patch of velvet on each temple. Their earrings are of brilliants, intermixed with tuffs of black silk, covered with pearls, resembling those already described in the first volume. These are so common an ornament, that besides their necklaces, they also wear about their necks rosaries, the beads of which are of pearls, either separate or set in clusters to the size of a large filbert; and those which form the cross are still larger.

Besides diamond rings, necklaces, girdles, and bracelets, all very curious both with regard to water and size, many ladies wear other jewels set in gold, or for singularity sake, in tombac [an alloy consisting essentially of copper and zinc]. Lastly, from their girdle before is suspended a large round jewel enriched with diamonds; much more superb than their bracelets, or other ornaments. A lady covered with the most expensive lace instead of linen, and glittering from head to foot with jewels, is supposed to be dressed at the expense of not less than thirty or forty thousand crowns. A splendor still the more astonishing, as it is so very common.

A fondness for expense in these people, does not confine itself to rich apparel; it appears no less in the strange neglect, and the small value they seem to set upon them, by wearing them in a manner the most careless, and by that means bringing upon themselves fresh expenses in repairing the old or purchasing new jewels; especially pearls on account of their fragility.

The most common of the two kinds of dresses worn when they go abroad, is the veil and long petticoat; the other is a round petticoat and mantelet. The former for church, the latter for taking the air, and diversions; but both in the prevailing taste for expense, being richly embroidered with silver or gold.

The long petticoat is particularly worn on holy Thursday; as on that day they visit the churches, attended by two or three female Negro or mulatto slaves, dressed in an uniform like pages.

Source: Jorge Juan and Antonio de Ulloa, *A Voyage to South America* (Dublin: printed for William Williamson at Mecana's Head, 1758).

◈DOCUMENT 23◈
REPEAL OF THE ACT EXCLUDING NEGROES (1750)

When English investors first established the colony of Georgia in 1733 they excluded slavery from the colony. In 1750, the charter of the colony was modified so that Africans might be introduced into the colony as slaves.

May it please Your Majesty,
The Trustees for establishing the Colony of Georgia in America in pursuance of the Powers and in Obedience to the Directions to them given by Your Majesty's most Gracious Charter humbly lay before Your Majesty the following Law Statute and Ordinance which they being for that purpose assembled have prepared as fit and necessary for the Government of the said Colony and which They most humbly present under their Common Seal to Your most Sacred Majesty in Council for your Majesty's most Gracious Approbation and Allowance.

Whereas an Act was passed by his Majesty in Council in the Eighth Year of his Reign Intituled by which Act the Importation and Use of Black Slaves or Negroes in the said Colony was absolutely prohibited and forbid under the Penalty therein mentioned and whereas at the time of passing the said Act the said Colony of Georgia being in its Infancy the Introduction of Black Slaves or Negroes would have been of dangerous Consequence but at present it may be a Benefit to the said Colony and a Convenience and Encouragement to the Inhabitants thereof to permit the Importation and Use of them into the said Colony under proper Restrictions and Regulations without Danger to the said Colony as the late War hath been happily concluded and a General Peace established. Therefore we the Trustees for establishing the Colony of Georgia in America humbly beseech Your Majesty that it may be Enacted And be it enacted That the said Act and every Clause and Article therein contained be from henceforth repealed and made void and of none Effect and be it Further Enacted that from and after the first day of January in the Year of Our Lord One thousand seven hundred and fifty it shall and may be lawful to import or bring Black Slaves or Negroes into the Province of Georgia in America and to keep and use the same therein under the Restrictions and Regulations hereinafter mentioned and directed to be observed concerning the same And for that purpose be it Further Enacted that from and after the said first day of January In the Year One thousand seven hundred and fifty it shall and may be lawful for every Person inhabiting and holding and cultivating Lands within the said Province of Georgia and having and constantly keeping one white Man Servant on his own Lands capable of bearing Arms and aged between sixteen and sixty five Years to have and keep four Male Negroes or Blacks upon his Plantation there and so in bearing Arms and of such Age the aforesaid as shall be kept by every Person within the said Province And Be It Further Enacted that every person shall from and after the said first day of January in the Year of Our Lord One thousand seven hundred and fifty have and keep more than four Male Negroes or Blacks, to every such Male Servant as aforesaid contrary to the Intent and true Meaning of this Act shall forfeit the Sum of Ten pounds Sterling Money of Great Britain for every such Male Negroe or Black which he shall have and keep above the said Number and shall also forfeit the further Sum of Five pounds of like Money for each Month after during which he shall retain and keep such Male Negroe or Black the said several Sums of Ten pounds and Five pounds to be recovered and applyed in such manner as is hereinafter mentioned and be it Further Enacted that no Artificer within the said Province of Georgia (Coopers only excepted) shall take any Negroe or Black as an Apprentice nor shall any Planter or Planters within the said Providence lend or let out to any other Planter or Planters within the same any Negroe or Negroes Black or Blacks to be employed otherwise than in manuring and cultivating their Plantations in the Country. . . . And be it Further Enacted that all and every Negroe and Negroes Black and Blacks which shall be imported into or born within the said Province of Georgia shall be registered in a proper Office or Offices to be kept for that Purpose within the said Province and that no Sale of any such Negroe or Negroes Black or Blacks shall be

good or valid unless the same be duly registered as aforesaid. And that Inquisitions shall be made and taken once in every Year (or oftner if need shall be) into the several Registers thereof by juries to be impannelled for that purpose within the several Districts of the said Province who shall immediately after such Inquisition make their several Reports and Returns to the President and Magistrates of the said Province and whereas the permitting Ships with Negroes or Blacks to send them on Shore when ill of contagious Distempers (particularly the Yellow Fever) must be of the most dangerous Consequence Therefore for the Prevention of so great a Calamity be it further enacted that no Ship which shall bring any Negroes or Blacks to the said Province shall land any Negroe or Negroes Black or Blacks within the said Province until such Ship shall have been visited by the proper Officer or Officers of the said Province for that purpose and shall have obtained a Certificate of Health And that no ship which shall come to the said Province with Negroes or Blacks shall come nearer to the said Province than Cockspur at the Mouth of the River Savannah but that every ship shall first anchor and remain there until such Ship shall have been visited by the proper Officer or Officers And if upon Inspection any such Ship shall be found to be infected such Ship shall perform such Quarantine in Tybee Creek in the River Savannah as by the President and Assistants of the said Province shall be from time to time ordered and directed. And to the End that due Care may be taken of the Crews of such infected Ships and of the Negroes brought therein be it further enacted that a Lazaretto be forthwith built within the said Province under the Direction and Inspection of the President and Magistrates thereof on the West Side of Tybee Island in the said River Savannah for the Use and Convenience of the said Colony where the whole Crews of such infected Ships and the Negroes brought therein may be conveniently lodged and assisted with Medecines and accommodated with Refreshments to be provided at the Expence of the Captain of the Ship And in Case any Master of a Ship shall attempt to land any Negroes in any other Part of the Colony except as aforesaid he shall for the said Offence forfeit the Sum of Five hundred pounds Sterling Money of Great Britain And in Case he shall land any Negroes before his Ship is visited and the proper Certificate of Health obtained or not perform the full Quarantine directed he shall for the said Offence not only forfeit the like Sum of Five Hundred pounds but also the Negroes on board the said Ship The said Forfeitures to be recovered and applied in such manner as is herein after mentioned and be it further enacted that if any Person or Persons shall not permit or even oblige his or their Negroe or Negroes Black or Blacks to attend at some time on the Lords Day for Instruction in the Christian Religion in such Place and Places as the Protestant Ministers of the Gospel within the said Province shall be able to attend them contiguous to the Residence of such Negroe or Negroes Black or Blacks such Person or Persons shall for every such Offence forfeit the Sum of Ten pounds Sterling Money of Great Britain to be recovered and applied in such manner as is hereinafter mentioned. . . . To which the Common Seal was affixed the Eighth day of August 1750.

Source: Trustees for Establishing the Colony of Georgia in America, "Repeal of the Act Excluding Negroes," in *Documents Illustrative of the History of the Slave Trade to America, Volume IV—The Border Colonies and the Southern Colonies,* ed. Elizabeth Donnan (Washington, DC: Carnegie Institution of Washington, 1935).

❧DOCUMENT 24❧
FROM DAVID HUME, "OF NATIONAL CHARACTERS" (1754)

Even among British intellectuals, the concept of African inferiority was a commonly accepted belief, which led some to argue that slavery was a morally and culturally uplifting experience. In the following account, the eighteenth-century British philosopher David Hume questions the cultural abilities of African peoples.

I am apt to suspect the Negroes to be naturally inferior to the Whites. There scarcely ever was a civilised nation of that complexion, nor ever any individual, eminent either in action or speculation. No ingenious manufactures among them, no arts, no sciences. On the other hand, the most rude and barbarous of all the whites, such as the ancient Germans, the present Tartars [Tatars], have still something eminent about them in their valour, form of government, or some other particular. Such a uniform and constant difference could not happen, in so many countries and ages, if nature had not made an original distribution between these breeds of men. . . . In Jamaica, indeed, they talk of one Negro as a man of parts and learning; but it is like he is admired for slender accomplishments, like a parrot who speaks a few words plainly.

Source: From David Hume, "Of National Characters, 1753," in *Empire and Slavery,* ed. Patrick Richardson (New York: Harper and Row Publishers, 1968).

❧DOCUMENT 25❧
A NARRATIVE OF THE LIFE AND ADVENTURES OF VENTURE SMITH (1798)

Venture Smith wrote one of the earliest accounts of the African slave trade from the perspective of a captured African. His words offer a unique insight into the practices that were routinely used in the slave trade, and his account helped to inspire the abolitionist movement in Great Britain.

I was born at Dukandarra, in Guinea, about the year 1729. My father's name was Saungm Furro, Prince of the tribe of Dukandarra. My father had three wives. Polygamy was not uncommon in that country, especially among the rich, as every man was allowed to keep as many wives as he could maintain. By his first wife he had three children. The eldest of them was myself, named by my father, Broteer. The other two were named Cundazo and Soozaduka. My father had two children by his second wife, and one by his third. I descended from a very large, tall and stout race of beings, much larger than the generality of people in other parts of the globe, being commonly considerable above six feet in height, and every way well proportioned.

The first thing worthy of notice which I remember was, a contention between my father and mother, on account of my father marrying his third wife without the consent of his first and eldest, which was contrary to the custom generally observed among my countrymen. In consequence of this rupture, my mother left her husband and country, and travelled away with her three children to the eastward. I was then five years old. She took not the least sustenance along with her, to support either herself or children.

I was able to travel along by her side; the other two of her offspring she carried one on her back, and the other being a sucking child, in her arms. When we became hungry, our mother used to set us down on the ground, and gather some of the fruits which grew spontaneously in that climate. These served us for food on the way. At night we all lay down together in the most secure place we could find, and reposed ourselves until morning. Though there were many noxious animals there; yet so kind was our Almighty protector, that none of them were ever permitted to hurt or molest us. Thus we went on our journey until the second day after our departure from Dukandarra, when we came to the entrance of a great desert. During our travel in that we were often affrighted with the doleful howlings and yellings of wolves, lions, and other animals. After five days travel we came to the end of this desert, and immediately entered into a beautiful and extensive interval country. Here my mother was pleased to stop and seek a refuge for me. She left me at the house of a very rich farmer. I was then, as I should judge, not less than one hundred and forty miles from my native place, separated from all my relations and acquaintance. At this place my mother took her farewell of me, and set out for my own country. My new guardian, as I shall call the man with whom I was left, put me into the business of tending sheep, immediately after I was left with him. The flock which I kept with the assistance of a boy, consisted of about forty. We drove them every morning between two and three miles to pasture, into the wide and delightful plains. When night drew on, we drove them home and secured them in the cote. In this round I continued during my stay here. One incident which befel me when I was driving my flock from pasture, was so dreadful to me in that age, and is to this time so fresh in my memory, that I cannot help noticing it in this place. Two large dogs sallied out of a certain house and set upon me. One of them took me by the arm, and the other by the thigh, and before their master could come and relieve me, they lacerated my flesh to such a degree, that the scars are very visible to the present day. My master was immediately sent for. He came and carried me home, as I was unable to go myself on account of my wounds. Nothing remarkable happened afterwards until my father sent for me to return home.

Before I dismiss this country, I must just inform my reader what I remember concerning this place. A large river runs through this country in a westerly course. The land for a great way on each side is flat and level, hedged in by a considerable rise in the country at a great distance from it. It scarce ever rains there, yet the land is fertile; great dews fall in the night which refresh the soil. About the latter end of June or first of July, the river begins to rise, and gradually increases until it has inundated the country for a great distance, to the height of seven or eight feet. This brings on a slime which enriches the land surprisingly. When the river has subsided, the natives begin to sow and plant, and the vegetation is exceeding rapid. Near this rich river my guardian's land lay. He possessed, I cannot exactly tell how much, yet this I am certain of respecting it, that he owned an immense tract. He possessed likewise a great many cattle and goats. During my stay with him I was kindly used, and with as much tenderness, for what I saw, as his only son, although I was an entire stranger to him, remote from friends and relations. The principal occupations of the inhabitants there, were the cultivation of the soil and the care of their flocks. They were a people pretty similar in every respect to that of mine, except in their persons, which were not so tall and stout. They appeared to be very kind and friendly. I will now return to my departure from that place.

My father sent a man and horse after me. After settling with my guardian for keeping me, he took me away and went for home. It was then about one year since my mother brought me here. Nothing remarkable occurred to us on our journey until we arrived safe home.

I found then that the difference between my parents had been made up previous to their sending for me. On my return, I was received both by my father and mother with great joy and affection, and was once more restored to my paternal dwelling in peace and happiness. I was then about six years old.

Not more than six weeks had passed after my return, before a message was brought by an inhabitant of the place where I lived the preceding year to my father, that the place had been invaded by a numerous army, from a nation not far distant, furnished with musical instruments, and all kinds of arms then in use; that they were instigated by some white nation who equipped and sent them to subdue and possess the country; that his nation had made no preparation for war, having been for a long time in profound peace; that they could not defend themselves against such a formidable train of invaders, and must therefore necessarily evacuate their lands to the fierce enemy, and fly to the protection of some chief; and that if he would permit them they would come under his rule and protection when they had to retreat from their own possessions. He was a kind and merciful prince, and therefore consented to these proposals.

He had scarcely returned to his nation with the message, before the whole of his people were obliged to retreat from their country, and come to my father's dominions.

He gave them every privilege and all the protection his government could afford. But they had not been there longer than four days before news came to them that the invaders had laid waste their country, and were coming speedily to destroy them in my father's territories. This affrighted them, and therefore they immediately pushed off to the southward, into the unknown countries there, and were never more heard of.

Two days after their retreat, the report turned out to be but too true. A detachment from the enemy came to my father and informed him, that the whole army was encamped not far out of his dominions, and would invade the territory and deprive his people of their liberties and rights, if he did not comply with the following terms. These were to pay them a large sum of money, three hundred fat cattle, and a great number of goats, sheep, asses, &c.

My father told the messenger he would comply rather than that his subjects should be deprived of their rights and privileges, which he was not then in circumstances to defend from so sudden an invasion. Upon turning out those articles, the enemy pledged their faith and honor that they would not attack him. On these he relied and therefore thought it unnecessary to be on his guard against the enemy. But their pledges of faith and honor proved no better than those of other unprincipled hostile nations; for a few days after a certain relation of the king came and informed him, that the enemy who sent terms of accommodation to him and received tribute to their satisfaction, yet meditated an attack upon his subjects by surprise, and that probably they would commence their attack in less than one day, and concluded with advising him, as he was not prepared for war, to order a speedy retreat of his family and subjects. He complied with this advice.

The same night which was fixed upon to retreat, my father and his family set off about the break of day. The king and his two younger wives went in one company, and my mother and her children in another. We left our dwellings in succession, and my father's company went on first. We directed our course for a large shrub plain, some distance off, where we intended to conceal ourselves from the approaching enemy, until we could refresh ourselves a little. But we presently found that our retreat was not secure. For having struck up a little fire for the purpose of cooking victuals, the enemy who happened to be encamped a little distance off, had sent out a scouting party who discovered us by the smoke of the fire, just as we were extinguishing it, and about to eat. As soon as we had finished eating, my father discovered the party, and immediately began to discharge arrows at them. This was what I first saw, and it alarmed both me and the women, who being unable to make any resistance, immediately betook ourselves to the tall thick reeds not far off, and left the old king to fight alone. For some time I beheld him from the reeds defending himself with great courage and firmness, till at last he was obliged to surrender himself into their hands.

They then came to us in the reeds, and the very first salute I had from them was a violent blow on the back part of the head with the fore part of a gun, and at the same time a grasp round the neck. I then had a rope put about my neck, as had all the women in the thicket with me, and was immediately led to my father, who was likewise pinioned and haltered for leading. In this condition we were all led to the camp. The women and myself being pretty submissive, had tolerable treatment from the enemy, while my father was closely interrogated respecting his money which they knew he must have. But as he gave them no account of it, he was instantly cut and pounded on his body with great inhumanity, that he might be induced by the torture he suffered to make the discovery. All this availed not in the least to make him give up his money, but he despised all the tortures which they inflicted, until the continued exercise and increase of torment, obliged him to sink and expire. He thus died without informing his enemies where his money lay. I saw him while he was thus tortured to death. The shocking scene is to this day fresh in my mind, and I have often been overcome while thinking on it. He was a man of remarkable stature. I should judge as much as six feet and six or seven inches high, two feet across his shoulders, and every way well proportioned. He was a man of remarkable strength and resolution, affable, kind and gentle, ruling with equity and moderation.

The army of the enemy was large, I should suppose consisting of about six thousand men. Their leader was called Baukurre. After destroying the old prince, they decamped and immediately marched towards the sea, lying to the west, taking with them myself and the women prisoners. In the march a scouting party was detached from the main army. To the leader of this party I was made waiter, having to carry his gun, &c. As we were a-scouting we came across a herd of fat cattle, consisting of about thirty in number. These we set upon, and immediately wrested from their keepers, and afterwards converted them into food for the army. The enemy had remarkable success in destroying the country wherever they went. For as far as they had penetrated, they laid the habitations waste and captured the people. The distance they had now brought me was about four hundred miles. All the march I had very hard tasks imposed on me, which I must perform on pain of punishment. I was obliged to carry on my head a large flat stone used for grinding our corn, weighing as I should suppose, as much as twenty-five pounds; besides victuals, mat and cooking utensils. Though I was pretty large and stout of my age, yet these burdens were very grievous to me, being only six years and a half old.

We were then come to a place called Malagasco. When we entered the place we could not see the least appearance of either houses or inhabitants, but upon stricter search found, that instead of houses above ground they had dens in the sides of hillocks, contiguous to ponds and streams of water. In these we perceived they had all hid themselves, as I suppose they usually did on such occasions. In order to compel them to surrender, the enemy contrived to smoke them out with faggots. These they put to the entrance of the caves and set them on fire. While they were engaged in this business, to their great surprise some of them were desperately wounded with arrows which fell from above on them. This mystery they soon found out. They perceived that the enemy discharged these arrows through holes on the top of the dens directly into the air. Their weight brought them back, point downwards on their enemies heads, whilst they were smoking the inhabitants out. The points of their arrows were poisoned, but their enemy had an antidote for it, which they instantly applied to the wounded part. The smoke at last obliged the people to give themselves up. They came out of their caves, first spatting the palms of their hands together, and immediately after extended their arms, crossed at their wrists, ready to be bound and pinioned. I should judge that the dens above were extended about eight feet horizontally into the earth, six feet in height and as many wide. They were arched over head and lined with earth, which was of the clay kind, and made the surface of their walls firm and smooth.

The invaders then pinioned the prisoners of all ages and sexes indiscriminately, took their flocks and all their effects, and moved on their way towards the sea. On the march the prisoners were treated with clemency, on account of their being submissive and humble. Having come to the next tribe, the enemy laid siege and immediately took men, women, children, flocks, and all their valuable effects. They then went on to the next district which was contiguous to the sea, called in Africa, Anamaboo. The enemies' provisions were then almost spent, as well as their strength. The inhabitants knowing what conducts they had pursued, and what were their present intentions, improved the favorable opportunity, attacked them, and took enemy, prisoners, flocks and all their effects. I was then taken a second time. All of us were then put into the castle, and kept for market. On a certain time I and other prisoners were put on board a canoe, under our master, and rowed away to a vessel belonging to Rhode Island, commanded by Captain Collingwood, and the mate Thomas Mumford. While we were going to the vessel, our master told us all to appear to the best possible advantage for sale. I was bought on board by one Robertson Mumford, steward of said vessel, for four gallons of rum, and a piece of calico, and called VENTURE, on account of his having purchased me with his own private venture. Thus I came by my name. All the slaves that were bought for the vessel's cargo, were two hundred and sixty.

Source: Venture Smith, "Taken from the Guinea Coast as a Child," in *Afro-American History, Primary Sources,* ed. Thomas R. Frazier (Chicago: Dorsey Press, 1988).

❧DOCUMENT 26❧
EXCERPT FROM KNOWLES V. SOMERSETT (1772)

In the case of Knowles v. Somersett, *William Murray, first earl of Mansfield, effectively abolished the practice of slavery in England.*

... The only question before us is whether the cause on the return is sufficient. If it is, the negro must be remanded; if it is not, he must be discharged. Accordingly, the return states that the slave departed and refused to serve; whereupon he was kept, to be sold abroad. So high an act of dominion must be recognized by the law of the country where it is used. The power of a master over his slave has been extremely different in different countries. The state of slavery is of such a nature that it is incapable of being introduced on any reasons, moral or political, but only by positive law, which preserves its force long after the reasons, occasion, and time itself from whence it was created is erased from memory. It is so odious that nothing can be suffered to support it but positive law. Whatever inconveniences, therefore, may follow from the decision, I cannot say this case is allowed or approved by the law of England; and therefore the black must be discharged.

Source: "Excerpt from Somersett's Case," in *Selected Speeches and Documents on British Colonial Policy, 1763–1917,* ed. Arthur Berriedale Keith (London: H. Milford, Oxford University Press, 1918).

❧DOCUMENT 27❧
SLAVES PETITION FOR FREEDOM DURING THE REVOLUTIONARY ERA (1773)

The growing spirit of egalitarianism inspired by the coming of the American Revolution encouraged some slaves to petition colonial legislatures for their freedom. In this 1773 petition, a slave named Felix urges the Massachusetts legislature to consider the merits of manumission.

Province of the Massachusetts Bay To His Excellency Thomas Hutchinson, Esq; Governor; To The Honorable His Majesty's Council, and To the Honorable House of Representatives in General Court assembled at Boston, the 6th Day of January, 1773.

The humble PETITION of many Slaves, living in the Town of Boston, and other Towns in the Province is this, namely

That your Excellency and Honors, and the Honorable the Representatives would be pleased to take their unhappy State and Condition under your wise and just Consideration.

We desire to bless God, who loves Mankind, who sent his Son to die for their Salvation, and who is no respecter of Persons; that he hath lately put it into the Hearts of Multitudes on both Sides of the Water, to bear our Burthens, some of whom are Men of great Note and Influence; who have pleaded our Cause with Arguments which we hope will have their weight with this Honorable Court.

We presume not to dictate to your Excellency and Honors, being willing to rest our Cause on your Humanity and justice; yet would beg Leave to say a Word or two on the Subject.

Although some of the Negroes are vicious, (who doubtless may be punished and restrained by the same Laws which are in Force against other of the King's Subjects) there are many others of a quite different Character, and who, if made free, would soon be able as well as willing to bear a Part in the Public Charges; many of them of good natural Parts, are discreet, sober, honest, and industrious; and may it not be said of many, that they are virtuous and religious, although their Condition is in itself so unfriendly to Religion, and every moral Virtue except Patience. How many of that Number have there been, and now are in this Province, who have had every Day of their Lives embittered with this most intollerable Reflection, That, let their Behaviour be what it will, neither they, nor their Children to all Generations, shall ever be able to do, or to possess and enjoy any Thing, no, not even Life itself, but in a Manner as the Beasts that perish.

We have no Property! We have no Wives! No Children! We have no City! No Country! But we have a Father in Heaven, and we are determined, as far as his Grace shall enable us, and as far as our degraded contemptuous Life will admit, to keep all his Commandments: Especially will we be obedient to our Masters, so long as God in his sovereign Providence shall suffer us to be holden in Bondage.

It would be impudent, if not presumptuous in us, to suggest to your Excellency and Honors any Law or Laws proper to be made, in relation to our unhappy State, which, although our greatest Unhappiness, is not our Fault; and this gives us great Encouragement to pray and hope for such Relief as is consistent with your Wisdom, justice, and Goodness.

We think Ourselves very happy, that we may thus address the Great and General Court of this Province, which great and good Court is to us, the best judge, under God, of what is wise, just—and good.

We humbly beg Leave to add but this one Thing more: We pray for such Relief only, which by no Possibility can ever be productive of the least Wrong or Injury to our Masters; but to us will be as Life from the dead.

Signed,
FELIX

Source: Herbert Aptheker, ed., "Slaves Petition for Freedom during the Revolution, 1773–1779," in *A Documentary History of the Negro People in the United States, Volume I* (New York: Carol Publishing Group, 1951).

≫DOCUMENT 28≪
DESCRIPTION OF TOBACCO PLANTERS' EXTRAVAGANCE (1775)

The use of slave labor on plantations and farms in the Americas created a propertied leisure class whose wealth was based upon cash crops produced in a slave-based economy. In the colony of Virginia, the cultivation of tobacco created a class of planter-aristocrats, who were often noted for their extravagance and luxury, and tobacco remained the primary cash crop for Virginia throughout the colonial era and into the period of statehood.

The tobacco planters live more like country gentlemen of fortune than any other settlers in America; all of them are spread about the country, their labour being mostly by slaves, who are left to overseers; and the masters live in a state of emulation with one another in buildings . . . furniture, wines, dress, diversions etc., and this to a degree, that is rather amazing that they should be able to go on with their plantations at all, than that they should not make additions to them. . . . The poverty of the planters here is much talked of, and from thence there has arisen a notion that their husbandry is not profitable: this false idea prevails because of the general luxury and the extravagant way of living that prevails among them . . . for men without some rich article of product cannot afford, even with the assistance of credit, to live in such a manner . . . that will support such luxury, and pay eight per cent on their debts. What common culture in Europe will do this?

Source: "American Husbandry, 1775," in *Empire and Slavery,* ed. Patrick Richardson (New York: Harper and Row Publishers, 1968).

≫DOCUMENT 29≪
DESCRIPTION OF AN ARRANGEMENT TO SUPPLY SLAVES FROM KILWA TO FRENCH POSSESSIONS IN THE INDIAN OCEAN (1776)

African leaders were often involved in the trading of fellow Africans as captives to European slave traders. The following document, negotiated between the king of Kilwa and French merchants, reveals the type of exchanges that were negotiated in slave-trading treaties.

We, King of Kilwa, Sultan Hasan, son of Sultan Ibrahim and son of Sultan Yusuf the Shirazi, Kilwa, give our word to Monsieur Morice, a French national, that we will provide him with 1,000 slaves a year for twenty *piastres* each and that he will give the king a tribute of two piastres per head of slaves. No other than he shall be able to trade for slaves, be he French, English, Dutch, Portuguese, &c., unless and until he shall have received his slaves and requires no more. This contract is made for 100 years between him and us. To guarantee our word we give him the fortress in which he can place the number of cannons he desires and his flag. The French, the Moors and the King of Kilwa will henceforward be one.

Whosoever attacks one of us we two together will attack him.

Made on 14 December 1776 under our signs and seals, signed: Morice.

We the undersigned Captain and Officers of the vessel *L'Abyssinie*, owner Monsieur Morice, certify to all whom it may concern that the present treaty was made in our presence at Kilwa on 14 December 1776.

Signed: Pichard, Pigne, Broüard.

Source: G. S. P. Freeman-Greenville, "The French at Kilwa Island," in A Collection of Documents on the Slave Trade of East Africa, ed. R. W. Beachey (London: Rex Collings, 1976).

❧ DOCUMENT 30 ❧
PRINCE HOARE DESCRIBES THE ZONG CASE (1783)

One of the most infamous of the slave ships was the Zong. In 1781, the captain of that ship ordered that the sick and dying slaves aboard the vessel should be thrown into the ocean so that traders could claim the losses against their insurance company. This incident aboard the Zong was used by British abolitionists as a prime example of the inhumanity associated with the African slave trade.

The ship *Zong*, or *Zung*, Luke Collingwood master, sailed from the island of St. Thomas, on the coast of Africa, the 6th September, 1781, with four hundred and forty slaves (or four hundred and forty-two) and seventeen Whites on board, for Jamaica; and on the 27th November following she fell in with that island; but, instead of proceeding to some port, the master, either through ignorance or a sinister intention, ran the ship to leeward, alleging that he mistook Jamaica for Hispaniola.

Sickness and mortality had by this time taken place, which is almost constantly the case on board slave-ships, through the avarice of those most detestable traders, which induces them to crowd, or rather to pack, too many slaves together in the holds of their ships; so that on board the *Zong*, between the time of her leaving the coast of Africa and the 29th of November 1781, sixty slaves and upwards, and seven White people, died; and a great number of the remaining slaves, on the day last mentioned, were sick of some disorder or disorders, and likely to die, or not to live long.

These circumstances of sickness and mortality are necessary to be remarked, and also the consequences of them—*viz.* that the dead and dying slaves would have been a dead loss to the owners, and, in some proportion, a loss also to the persons employed by the owners, unless some pretence or expedient had been found to throw the loss upon the insurers, as in the case of jetsam or jetson—*i.e.,* a plea of necessity to cast overboard some part of a cargo to save the rest. These circumstances, I say, are necessary to be remarked, because they point out the most probable inducement to this enormous wickedness.

The sickness and mortality on board the *Zong*, previous to the 29th November 1781 (the time when they began to throw the poor Negroes overboard alive), was not occasioned by the want of water; for it was proved that they did not discover till that very day, the 29th November (or the preceding day) that the stock of fresh water was reduced to two hundred gallons: yet the same day, or in the evening of it, "before any soul had been put to short allowance," and before there was any present or real want of water, "the master of the ship called together a few of the officers, and told them to the following effect:—that, if the slaves died a natural death, it would be the loss of the owners of the ship; but if they were thrown alive into the sea, it would be the loss of the underwriters": and, to palliate the inhuman proposal, he the said Collingwood pretended, that "it would not be so cruel to throw the poor sick wretches (meaning such slaves) into the sea, as to suffer them to linger out a few days under the disorders with which they were afflicted, or expressed himself to the like effect." To which proposal the mate (whose name is Colonel James Kelsal) objected, it seems, at the first, and said "there was no present want of water to justify such a measure": But "the said Luke Collingwood prevailed upon the crew, or the rest of them, to listen to his said proposal; and the same evening, and two or three or some few following days, the said Luke Collingwood picked, or caused to be picked out, from the cargo of the same ship, one hundred and thirty-three slaves, all or most of whom were sick or weak, and not likely to live; and ordered the crew by turns to throw them into the sea; which most inhuman order was cruelly complied with." I am informed, by a memorandum from the deposition of Kelsal the chief mate (one of the murderers), that fifty-four persons were actually thrown overboard alive on the 29th of November; and that forty-two more were also thrown overboard on the 1st December. And on this very day, 1st December, 1781, before the stock of water was consumed, there fell a plentiful rain, which, by the confession of one of their own advocates, "continued a day or two, and enabled them to collect six casks of water, which was full allowance for eleven days, or for twenty-three days at half-allowance"; whereas the ship actually arrived at Jamaica in twenty-one days afterwards—*viz.* on the 22d December, 1781. They seem also to have had an opportunity of sending their boat for water no less than thirteen days sooner, viz. on the 9th December, when they "made the west end of Jamaica, distant two or three leagues only," as I am informed by a person who was on board: and yet, notwithstanding this proof of a possibility that they might perhaps obtain further supplies by rain, or that they might be able to hold out with their new-increased stock of water till they might chance to meet with some ship, or be able to send to some island for a further supply, they nevertheless cast twenty-six more human persons alive into the sea, even after the rain, whose hands were also fettered or bound; and which was done, it seems, in the sight of many other unhappy sufferers that were brought up upon deck for the same detestable purpose, whereby ten of these miserable human creatures were driven to the lamentable necessity of jumping overboard, to avoid the fettering or binding of their hands, and were likewise drowned. . . .

Source: Prince Hoare, "Memoirs of Granville Sharp," in *Documents Illustrative of the History of the Slave Trade to America, Volume III—New England & the Middle Colonies,* ed. Elizabeth Donnan (Washington, DC: Carnegie Institution of Washington, 1932).

∾DOCUMENT 31∾
THOMAS JEFFERSON CONDEMNS SLAVERY BUT ASSERTS RACIAL DIFFERENCES (1787)

Thomas Jefferson's views about slavery seem rather inconsistent. A slaveowner himself, Jefferson likely fathered children by a slave mistress, yet he penned the words "all men are created equal" in the Declaration of Independence. He seems to have opposed slavery but felt himself powerless to try to abolish the practice. In the following passage, Jefferson evaluates the racial differences that he viewed between Europeans and Africans.

Query XIV.
The Administration of Justice and the Description of the Laws?

Many of the laws which were in force during the monarchy being relative merely to that form of government, or inculcating principles inconsistent with republicanism, the first assembly which met after the establishment of the commonwealth appointed a committee to revise the whole code, to reduce it into proper form and volume, and report it to the assembly. This work has been executed by three gentlemen, and reported; but probably will not be taken up till a restoration of peace shall leave to the legislature leisure to go through such a work.

The plan of the revisal was this. The common law of England, by which is meant, that part of the English law which was anterior to the date of the oldest statutes extant, is made the basis of the work. It was thought dangerous to attempt to reduce it to a text: it was therefore left to be collected from the usual monuments of it. Necessary alterations in that, and so much of the whole body of the British statutes, and of acts of assembly, as were thought proper to be retained, were digested into 126 new acts, in which simplicity of style was aimed at, as far as was safe. The following are the most remarkable alterations proposed:

To change the rules of descent, so as that the lands of any person dying intestate shall be divisible equally among all his children, or other representatives, in equal degree.

To make slaves distributable among the next of kin, as other moveables.

To have all public expences, whether of the general treasury, or of a parish or county, (as for the maintenance of the poor, building bridges, courthouses, &c.) supplied by assessments on the citizens, in proportion to their property.

To hire undertakers for keeping the public roads in repair, and indemnify individuals through whose lands new roads shall be opened.

To define with precision the rules whereby aliens should become citizens, and citizens make themselves aliens.

To establish religious freedom on the broadest bottom.

To emancipate all slaves born after passing the act. The bill reported by the revisors does not itself contain this proposition; but an amendment containing it was prepared, to be offered to the legislature whenever the bill should be taken up, and further directing, that they should continue with their parents to a certain age, then be brought up, at the public expence, to tillage, arts or sciences, according to their geniusses, till the females should be eighteen, and the males twenty-one years of age, when they should be colonized to such place as the circumstances of the time should render most proper, sending them out with arms, implements of household and of the handicraft arts, feeds, pairs of the useful domestic animals, &c. to declare them a free and independent people, and extend to them our alliance and protection, till they have acquired strength; and to send vessels at the same time to other parts of the world for an equal number of white inhabitants; to induce whom to migrate hither, proper encouragements were to be proposed. It will probably be asked, Why not retain and incorporate the blacks into the state, and thus save the expence of supplying by importation of white settlers, the vacancies they will leave? Deep rooted prejudices entertained by the whites; ten thousand recollections, by the blacks, of the injuries they have sustained; new provocations; the real distinctions which nature has made; and many other circumstances, will divide us into parties, and produce convulsions, which will probably never end but in the extermination of the one or the other race.—

To these objections, which are political, may be added others, which are physical and moral. The first difference which strikes us is that of colour. Whether the black of the negro resides in the reticular membrane between the skin and scarf-skin, or in the scarf-skin itself; whether it proceeds from the colour of the blood, the colour of the bile, or from that of some other secretion, the difference is fixed in nature, and is as real as if its seat and cause were better known to us. And is this difference of no importance? Is it not the foundation of a greater or less share of beauty in the two races? Are not the fine mixtures of red and white, the expressions of every passion by greater or less suffusions of colour in the one, preferable to that eternal monotony, which reigns in the countenances, that immoveable veil of black which covers all the emotions of the other race? Add to these, flowing hair, a more elegant symmetry of form, their own judgment in favour of the whites, declared by their preference of them, as uniformly as is the preference of the Oranootan for the black women over those of his own species. The circumstance of superior beauty, is thought worthy attention in the propagation of our horses, dogs, and other domestic animals; why not in that of man? Besides those of colour, figure, and hair, there are other physical distinctions proving a difference of race. They have less hair on the face and body. They secrete less by the kidneys, and more by the glands of the skin, which gives them a very strong and disagreeable odour. This greater degree of transpiration renders them more tolerant of heat, and less so of cold than the whites. Perhaps too a difference of structure in the pulmonary apparatus, which a late ingenious experimentalist has discovered to be the principal regulator of animal heat, may have disabled them from extricating, in the act of inspiration, so much of that fluid from the outer air, or obliged them in expiration, to part with more of it. They seem to require less sleep. A black after hard labour through the day, will be induced by the slightest amusements to sit up till midnight, or later though knowing he must be out with the first dawn of the morning. They are at least as brave, and more adventuresome. But this may perhaps proceed from a want of forethought, which prevents their seeing a danger till it be present. When present, they do not go through it with more coolness or steadiness than the whites. They are more ardent after their female: but love seems with them to be more an eager desire, than a tender delicate mixture of sentiment and sensation. Their griefs are transient. Those numberless afflictions, which render it doubtful whether heaven has given life to us in mercy or in wrath, are less felt, and sooner forgotten with them. In general, their existence appears to participate more of sensation than reflection. To this must be ascribed their disposition to sleep when abstracted from their diversions, and unemployed in labour. An animal whose body is at rest, and who does not reflect, must be disposed to sleep of course. Comparing them by their faculties of memory, reason, and imagination, it appears to me that in memory they are equal to the whites; in reason much inferior, as I think one could scarcely be found capable of tracing and comprehending the investigations of Euclid; and that in imagination they are dull, tasteless, and anomalous. It would be unfair to follow them to Africa for this investigation. We will consider them here, on the same stage with the whites, and where the facts are not apocryphal on which a judgement is to be formed. It will be right to make great allowances for the difference of condition, of education, of conversation, of the sphere in which they move. Many millions of them have been brought to, and born in America. Most of them indeed have been confined to tillage, to their own homes, and their own society: yet many have been so situated, that they might have availed themselves of the conversation of their masters; many have been brought up to the handicraft arts, and from that circumstance have always been associated with the whites. Some have been liberally educated, and all have lived in countries where the arts and sciences are cultivated to a considerable degree, and have had before their eyes samples of the best works from abroad. The Indians, with no advantages of this kind, will often carve figures on their pipes not destitute of design and merit. They will crayon out an animal, a plant, or a country, so as to prove the existence of a germ in their minds which only wants cultivation. They astonish you with strokes of the most sublime oratory; such as prove their reason and sentiment strong, their imagination glowing and elevated. But never yet could I find that a black had uttered a thought above the level of plain narration; never see even an elementary trait of painting or sculpture. In music they are more generally gifted than the whites with accurate ears for tune and time, and they have been found capable of imagining a small catch. Whether they will be equal to the composition of a more extensive run of melody, or of complicated harmony, is yet to be proved. Misery is often the parent of the most affecting touches in poetry.—Among the blacks is misery enough, God knows, but no poetry. Love is the peculiar cestrum [poisonous flower] of the poet. Their love is ardent, but it kindles the senses only, not the imagination. Religion indeed has produced a Phyllis Whately; but it could not produce a poet. The compositions published under her name are below the dignity of criticism. The heroes of the Dunciad are to her, as Hercules to the author of that poem. Ignatius Sancho has approached nearer to merit in composition; yet his letters do more honour to the heart than the head.

They breathe the purest effusions of friendship and general philanthropy, and shew how great a degree of the latter may be compounded with strong religious zeal. He is often happy in the turn of his compliments, and his stile is easy and familiar, except when he affects a Shandean fabrication of words. But his imagination is wild and extravagant, escapes incessantly from every restraint of reason and taste, and, in the course of its vagaries, leaves a tract of thought as incoherent and eccentric, as is the course of a meteor through the sky. His subjects should often have led him to a process of sober reasoning: yet we find him always substituting sentiment for demonstration. Upon the whole, though we admit him to the first place among those of his own colour who have presented themselves to the public judgment, yet when we compare him with the writers of the race among whom he lived and particularly with the epistolary class, in which he has taken his own stand, we are compelled to enroll him at the bottom of the column. This criticism supposes the letters published under his name to be genuine, and to have received amendment from no other hand; points which would not be of easy investigation. The improvement of the blacks in body and mind, in the first instance of their mixture with the whites, has been observed by every one, and proves that their inferiority is not the effect merely of their condition of life. We know that among the Romans, about the Augustan age especially, the condition of their slaves was much more deplorable than that of the blacks on the continent of America. The two sexes were confined in separate apartments, because to raise a child cost the master more than to buy one. Cato, for a very restricted indulgence to his slaves in this particular, took from them a certain price. But in this country the slaves multiply as fast as the free inhabitants. Their situation and manners place the commerce between the two sexes almost without restraint.—The same Cato, on a principle of economy, always sold his sick and superannuated slaves. He gives it as a standing precept to a master visiting his farm, to sell his old oxen, old waggons, old tools, old and diseased servants, and every thing else become useless. "Vendat boves vetulos, plaustrum vetus, ferramenta vetera, servum senem, servum morbosum, & si quid aliud supersit vendat." *Cato de re rustica*, C. 2. The American slaves cannot enumerate this among the injuries and insults they receive. It was the common practice to expose in the island Aesculapius, in the Tyber, diseased slaves, whose cure was like to become tedious. The emperor Claudius, by an edict, gave freedom to such of them as should recover, and first declared that if any person chose to kill rather than expose them, it should be deemed homicide. The exposing them is a crime of which no instance has existed with us; and were it to be followed by death, it would be punished capitally. We are told of a certain Vedius Pollio, who, in the presence of Augustus, would have given a slave as food to his fish, for having broken a glass. With the Romans, the regular method of taking the evidence of their slaves was under torture. Here it has been thought better never to resort to their evidence. When a master was murdered, all his slaves, in the same house, or within hearing, were condemned to death. Here punishment falls on the guilty only, and as precise proof is required against him as against a freeman. Yet notwithstanding these and other discouraging circumstances among the Romans, their slaves were often their rarest artists. They excelled too in science, insomuch as to be usually employed as tutors to their master's children. Epictetus, Terence, and Phaedrus, were slaves. But they were of the race of whites. It is not their condition then, but nature, which has produced the distinction.—Whether further observation will or will not verify the conjecture, that nature has been less bountiful to them in the endowments of the head, I believe that in those of the heart she will be found to have done them justice. That disposition to theft with which they have been branded, must be ascribed to their situation, and not to any depravity of the moral sense. The man, in whose favour no laws of property exist, probably feels himself less bound to respect those made in favour of others. When arguing for ourselves, we lay it down as a fundamental, that laws, to be just, must give a reciprocation of right: that, without this, they are mere arbitrary rules of conduct, founded in force, and not in conscience: and it is a problem which I give to the master to solve, whether the religious precepts against the violation of property were not framed for him as well as his slave? And whether the slave may not as justifiably take a little from one, who has taken all from him, as he may slay one [who] would slay him? That a change in the relations in which a man is placed should change his ideas of moral right and wrong, is neither new, nor peculiar to the colour of the blacks. Homer tells us it was so 2600 years ago.

'Emisu, ger t' aretes apoainutai europa Zeus
Haneros, eut' an min kata doulion ema elesin.
Od. 17.323.
Jove fix'd it certain, that whatever day Makes man a slave takes half his worth away.

But the slaves of which Homer speaks were whites. Notwithstanding these considerations which must weaken their respect for the laws of property, we find among them numerous instances of the most rigid integrity, and as many as among their better instructed masters, of benevolence, gratitude, and unshaken fidelity.—The opinion, that they are inferior in the faculties of reason and imagination, must be hazarded with great diffidence. To justify a general conclusion, requires many observations, even where the subject may be submitted to the anatomical knife, to optical glasses, to analysis by fire, or by solvents. How much more then where it is a faculty, not a substance, we are examining; where it eludes the research of all the senses; where the conditions of its existence are various and variously combined; where the effects of those which are present or absent bid defiance to calculation; let me add too, as a circumstance of great tenderness, where our conclusion would degrade a whole race of men from the rank in the scale of beings which their Creator may perhaps have given them. To our reproach it must be said, that though for a century and a half we have had under our eyes the races of black and of red men, they have never yet been viewed by us as subjects of natural history. I advance it therefore as a suspicion only, that the blacks, whether originally a distinct race, or made distinct by time and circumstances, are inferior to the whites in the endowments both of body and mind. It is not against experience to suppose, that different species of the same genus, or varieties of the same species, may possess different qualifications. Will not a lover of natural history then, one who views the gradations in all the races of animals with the eye of philosophy, excuse an effort to keep those in the department of man as distinct as nature has formed them? This unfortunate difference of colour, and perhaps of faculty, is a powerful obstacle to the emancipation of these people. Many of their advocates, while they wish to vindicate the liberty of human nature are anxious also to preserve its dignity and beauty. Some of these, embarassed by the question "What further is to be done with them?" join themselves in opposition with those who are actuated by sordid avarice only. Among the Romans emancipation required but one effort. The slave, when made free, might mix with, without staining the blood of his master. But with us a second is necessary, unknown to history. When freed, he is to be removed beyond the reach of mixture. . . .

Query XVIII.
The particular customs and manners that may happen to be received in that state?

It is difficult to determine on the standard by which the manners of a nation may be tried, whether catholic, or particular. It is more difficult for a native to bring to that standard the manners of his own nation, familiarized to him by habit. There must doubtless be an unhappy influence on the manners of our people produced by the existence of slavery among us. The whole commerce between master and slave is a perpetual exercise of the most boisterous passions, the most unremitting despotism on the one part, and degrading submissions on the other. Our children see

this, and learn to imitate it; for man is an imitative animal. This quality is the germ of all education in him. From his cradle to his grave he is learning to do what he sees others do. If a parent could find no motive either in his philanthropy or his self-love, for restraining the intemperance of passion towards his slave, it would always be a sufficient one that his child is present. But generally it is not sufficient. The parent storms, the child looks on, catches the lineaments of wrath, puts on the same airs in the circle of smaller slaves, gives a loose to the his worst of passions, and thus nursed, educated, and daily exercised in tyranny, cannot but be stamped by it with odious peculiarities. The man must be a prodigy who can retain his manners and morals undepraved by such circumstances. And with what execration should the statesman be loaded, who permitting one half the citizens thus to trample on the rights of the other, transforms those into despots, and these into enemies, destroys the morals of the one part, and the amor patriae of the other. For if a slave can have a country in this world, it must be any other in preference to that in which he is born to live and labour for another: in which he must lock up the faculties of his nature, contribute as far as depends on his individual endeavours to the evanishment [destruction] of the human race, or entail his own miserable condition on the endless generations proceeding from him. With the morals of the people, their industry also is destroyed. For in a warm climate, no man will labour for himself who can make another labour for him. This is so true, that of the proprietors of slaves a very small proportion indeed are ever seen to labour. And can the liberties of a nation be thought secure when we have removed their only firm basis, a conviction in the minds of the people that these liberties are of the gift of God? That they are not to be violated but with his wrath? Indeed I tremble for my country when I reflect that God is just: that his justice cannot sleep for ever: that considering numbers, nature and natural means only, a revolution of the wheel of fortune, an exchange of situation is among possible events: that it may become probable by supernatural interference! The almighty has no attribute which can take side with us in such a contest.—But it is impossible to be temperate and to pursue this subject through the various considerations of policy, or morals, of history natural and civil. We must be contented to hope they will force their way into every one's mind. I think a change already perceptible, since the origin of the present revolution. The spirit of the master is abating, that of the slave rising from the dust, his condition mollifying, the way I hope preparing, under the auspices of heaven, for a total emancipation, and that this is disposed, in the order of events, to be with the consent of the masters, rather than by their extirpation.

Source: Thomas Jefferson, "Thomas Jefferson Condemns Slavery but Asserts Racial Differences," in *A Documentary History of Slavery in North America*, ed. Willie Lee Rose (New York: Oxford University Press, 1976).

∼DOCUMENT 32∼
THE NORTHWEST ORDINANCE
(JULY 13, 1787)

By prohibiting slavery in the Old Northwest Territory (i.e., the lands north of the Ohio River), the stage was set for subsequent battles in the U.S. Congress over whether or not slavery would be allowed to spread into territories acquired by the nation. This debate over the expansion of slavery proved to be one of the major causes of the American Civil War.

July 13, 1787
An Ordinance for the government of the Territory of the United States northwest of the River Ohio.

Be it ordained by the United States in Congress assembled,

That the said territory, for the purposes of temporary government, be one district, subject, however, to be divided into two districts, as future circumstances may, in the opinion of Congress, make it expedient.

Be it ordained by the authority aforesaid, That the estates, both of resident and nonresident proprietors in the said territory, dying intestate, shall descent to, and be distributed among their children, and the descendants of a deceased child, in equal parts; the descendants of a deceased child or grandchild to take the share of their deceased parent in equal parts among them: And where there shall be no children or descendants, then in equal parts to the next of kin in equal degree; and among collaterals, the children of a deceased brother or sister of the intestate shall have, in equal parts among them, their deceased parents' share; and there shall in no case be a distinction between kindred of the whole and half blood; saving, in all cases, to the widow of the intestate her third part of the real estate for life, and one third part of the personal estate; and this law relative to descents and dower, shall remain in full force until altered by the legislature of the district. And until the governor and judges shall adopt laws as hereinafter mentioned, estates in the said territory may be devised or bequeathed by wills in writing, signed and sealed by him or her in whom the estate may be (being of full age), and attested by three witnesses; and real estates may be conveyed by lease and release, or bargain and sale, signed, sealed and delivered by the person being of full age, in whom the estate may be, and attested by two witnesses, provided such wills be duly proved, and such conveyances be acknowledged, or the execution thereof duly proved, and be recorded within one year after proper magistrates, courts, and registers shall be appointed for that purpose; and personal property may be transferred by delivery; saving, however to the French and Canadian inhabitants, and other settlers of the Kaskaskies, St. Vincents and the neighboring villages who have heretofore professed themselves citizens of Virginia, their laws and customs now in force among them, relative to the descent and conveyance, of property.

Be it ordained by the authority aforesaid, That there shall be appointed from time to time by Congress, a governor, whose commission shall continue in force for the term of three years, unless sooner revoked by Congress; he shall reside in the district, and have a freehold estate therein in 1,000 acres of land, while in the exercise of his office.

There shall be appointed from time to time by Congress, a secretary, whose commission shall continue in force for four years unless sooner revoked; he shall reside in the district, and have a freehold estate therein in 500 acres of land, while in the exercise of his office. It shall be his duty to keep and preserve the acts and laws passed by the legislature, and the public records of the district, and the proceedings of the governor in his executive department, and transmit authentic copies of such acts and proceedings, every six months, to the Secretary of Congress: There shall also be appointed a court to consist of three judges, any two of whom to form a court, who shall have a common law jurisdiction, and reside in the district, and have each therein a freehold estate in 500 acres of land while in the exercise of their offices; and their commissions shall continue in force during good behavior.

The governor and judges, or a majority of them, shall adopt and publish in the district such laws of the original States, criminal and civil, as may be necessary and best suited to the circumstances of the district, and report them to Congress from time to time: which laws shall be in force in the district until the organization of the General Assembly therein, unless disapproved of by Congress; but afterwards the Legislature shall have authority to alter them as they shall think fit.

The governor, for the time being, shall be commander in chief of the militia, appoint and commission all officers in the same below the rank of general officers; all general officers shall be appointed and commissioned by Congress.

Previous to the organization of the general assembly, the governor shall appoint such magistrates and other civil officers in each county or township, as he shall find necessary for the preservation of the peace and good order in the same: After the general assembly shall be organized, the powers and duties of the magistrates and other civil officers shall be regulated and defined by the said assembly; but all magistrates and other civil officers not herein otherwise directed, shall during the continuance of this temporary government, be appointed by the governor.

For the prevention of crimes and injuries, the laws to be adopted or made shall have force in all parts of the district, and for the execution of process, criminal and civil, the governor shall make proper divisions thereof; and he shall proceed from time to time as circumstances may require, to lay out the parts of the district in which the Indian titles shall have been extinguished, into counties and townships, subject, however, to such alterations as may thereafter be made by the legislature.

So soon as there shall be five thousand free male inhabitants of full age in the district, upon giving proof thereof to the governor, they shall receive authority, with time and place, to elect a representative from their counties or townships to represent them in the general assembly: Provided, That, for every five hundred free male inhabitants, there shall be one representative, and so on progressively with the number of free male inhabitants shall the right of representation increase, until the number of representatives shall amount to twenty five; after which, the number and proportion of representatives shall be regulated by the legislature: Provided, That no person be eligible or qualified to act as a representative unless he shall have been a citizen of one of the United States three years, and be a resident in the district, or unless he shall have resided in the district three years; and, in either case, shall likewise hold in his own right, in fee simple, two hundred acres of land within the same; Provided, also, That a freehold in fifty acres of land in the district, having been a citizen of one of the states, and being resident in the district, or the like freehold and two years residence in the district, shall be necessary to qualify a man as an elector of a representative.

The representatives thus elected, shall serve for the term of two years; and, in case of the death of a representative, or removal from office, the governor shall issue a writ to the county or township for which he was a member, to elect another in his stead, to serve for the residue of the term.

The general assembly or legislature shall consist of the governor, legislative council, and a house of representatives. The Legislative Council shall consist of five members, to continue in office five years, unless sooner removed by Congress; any three of whom to be a quorum: and the members of the Council shall be nominated and appointed in the following manner, to wit: As soon as representatives shall be elected, the Governor shall appoint a time and place for them to meet together; and, when met, they shall nominate ten persons, residents in the district, and each possessed of a freehold in five hundred acres of land, and return their names to Congress; five of whom Con-

gress shall appoint and commission to serve as aforesaid; and, whenever a vacancy shall happen in the council, by death or removal from office, the house of representatives shall nominate two persons, qualified as aforesaid, for each vacancy, and return their names to Congress; one of whom congress shall appoint and commission for the residue of the term. And every five years, four months at least before the expiration of the time of service of the members of council, the said house shall nominate ten persons, qualified as aforesaid, and return their names to Congress; five of whom Congress shall appoint and commission to serve as members of the council five years, unless sooner removed. And the governor, legislative council, and house of representatives, shall have authority to make laws in all cases, for the good government of the district, not repugnant to the principles and articles in this ordinance established and declared. And all bills, having passed by a majority in the house, and by a majority in the council, shall be referred to the governor for his assent; but no bill, or legislative act whatever, shall be of any force without his assent. The governor shall have power to convene, prorogue, and dissolve the general assembly, when, in his opinion, it shall be expedient.

The governor, judges, legislative council, secretary, and such other officers as Congress shall appoint in the district, shall take an oath or affirmation of fidelity and of office; the governor before the president of congress, and all other officers before the Governor. As soon as a legislature shall be formed in the district, the council and house assembled in one room, shall have authority, by joint ballot, to elect a delegate to Congress, who shall have a seat in Congress, with a right of debating but not voting during this temporary government.

And, for extending the fundamental principles of civil and religious liberty, which form the basis whereon these republics, their laws and constitutions are erected; to fix and establish those principles as the basis of all laws, constitutions, and governments, which forever hereafter shall be formed in the said territory: to provide also for the establishment of States, and permanent government therein, and for their admission to a share in the federal councils on an equal footing with the original States, at as early periods as may be consistent with the general interest:

It is hereby ordained and declared by the authority aforesaid, That the following articles shall be considered as articles of compact between the original States and the people and States in the said territory and forever remain unalterable, unless by common consent, to wit:

Art. 1. No person, demeaning himself in a peaceable and orderly manner, shall ever be molested on account of his mode of worship or religious sentiments, in the said territory.

Art. 2. The inhabitants of the said territory shall always be entitled to the benefits of the writ of habeas corpus, and of the trial by jury; of a proportionate representation of the people in the legislature; and of judicial proceedings according to the course of the common law. All persons shall be bailable, unless for capital offenses, where the proof shall be evident or the presumption great. All fines shall be moderate; and no cruel or unusual punishments shall be inflicted. No man shall be deprived of his liberty or property, but by the judgment of his peers or the law of the land; and, should the public exigencies make it necessary, for the common preservation, to take any person's property, or to demand his particular services, full compensation shall be made for the same. And, in the just preservation of rights and property, it is understood and declared, that no law ought ever to be made, or have force in the said territory, that shall, in any manner whatever, interfere with or affect private contracts or engagements, bona fide, and without fraud, previously formed.

Art. 3. Religion, morality, and knowledge, being necessary to good government and the happiness of mankind, schools and the means of education shall forever be encouraged. The utmost good faith shall always be observed towards the Indians; their lands and property shall never be taken from them without their consent; and, in their property, rights, and liberty, they shall never be invaded or disturbed, unless in just and lawful wars authorized by Congress; but laws founded in justice and humanity, shall from time to time be made for preventing wrongs being done to them, and for preserving peace and friendship with them.

Art. 4. The said territory, and the States which may be formed therein, shall forever remain a part of this Confederacy of the United States of America, subject to the Articles of Confederation, and to such alterations therein as shall be constitutionally made; and to all the acts and ordinances of the United States in Congress assembled, conformable thereto. The inhabitants and settlers in the said territory shall be subject to pay a part of the federal debts contracted or to be contracted, and a proportional part of the expenses of government, to be apportioned on them by Congress according to the same common rule and measure by which apportionments thereof shall be made on the other States; and the taxes for paying their proportion shall be laid and levied by the authority and direction of the legislatures of the district or districts, or new States, as in the original States, within the time agreed upon by the United States in Congress assembled. The legislatures of those districts or new States, shall never interfere with the primary disposal of the soil by the United States in Congress assembled, nor with any regulations Congress may find necessary for securing the

title in such soil to the bona fide purchasers. No tax shall be imposed on lands the property of the United States; and, in no case, shall nonresident proprietors be taxed higher than residents. The navigable waters leading into the Mississippi and St. Lawrence, and the carrying places between the same, shall be common highways and forever free, as well to the inhabitants of the said territory as to the citizens of the United States, and those of any other States that may be admitted into the confederacy, without any tax, impost, or duty therefor.

Art. 5. There shall be formed in the said territory, not less than three nor more than five States; and the boundaries of the States, as soon as Virginia shall alter her act of cession, and consent to the same, shall become fixed and established as follows, to wit: The western State in the said territory, shall be bounded by the Mississippi, the Ohio, and Wabash Rivers; a direct line drawn from the Wabash and Post Vincents, due North, to the territorial line between the United States and Canada; and, by the said territorial line, to the Lake of the Woods and Mississippi. The middle State shall be bounded by the said direct line, the Wabash from Post Vincents to the Ohio, by the Ohio, by a direct line, drawn due north from the mouth of the Great Miami, to the said territorial line, and by the said territorial line. The eastern State shall be bounded by the last mentioned direct line, the Ohio, Pennsylvania, and the said territorial line: Provided, however, and it is further understood and declared, that the boundaries of these three States shall be subject so far to be altered, that, if Congress shall hereafter find it expedient, they shall have authority to form one or two States in that part of the said territory which lies north of an east and west line drawn through the southerly bend or extreme of Lake Michigan. And, whenever any of the said States shall have sixty thousand free inhabitants therein, such State shall be admitted, by its delegates, into the Congress of the United States, on an equal footing with the original States in all respects whatever, and shall be at liberty to form a permanent constitution and State government: Provided, the constitution and government so to be formed, shall be republican, and in conformity to the principles contained in these articles; and, so far as it can be consistent with the general interest of the confederacy, such admission shall be allowed at an earlier period, and when there may be a less number of free inhabitants in the State than sixty thousand.

Art. 6. There shall be neither slavery nor involuntary servitude in the said territory, otherwise than in the punishment of crimes whereof the party shall have been duly convicted: Provided, always, That any person escaping into the same, from whom labor or service is lawfully claimed in any one of the original States, such fugitive may be lawfully reclaimed and conveyed to the person claiming his or her labor or service as aforesaid.

Be it ordained by the authority aforesaid, That the resolutions of the 23rd of April, 1784, relative to the subject of this ordinance, be, and the same are hereby repealed and declared null and void.

Source: U.S. Government, "The Northwest Ordinance," in *Documents of American History,* ed. Henry Steele Commager (New York: Appleton-Century-Crofts, 1963).

☙DOCUMENT 33☙
DECLARATION OF THE RIGHTS OF MAN AND OF THE CITIZEN

The language of the Declaration of the Rights of Man and Citizen inspired free blacks in the colony of Saint Domingue to seek the rights they believed they were due as French citizens. The revolt spawned by this issue eventually grew into a massive slave revolt that overthrew French control of the colony and eventually produced the nation of Haiti, the first black republic established in the Western Hemisphere.

Approved by the National Assembly of France, August 26, 1789

The representatives of the French people, organized as a National Assembly, believing that the ignorance, neglect, or contempt of the rights of man are the sole cause of public calamities and of the corruption of governments, have determined to set forth in a solemn declaration the natural, unalienable, and sacred rights of man, in order that this declaration, being constantly before all the members of the Social body, shall remind them continually of their rights and duties; in order that the acts of the legislative power, as well as those of the executive power, may be compared at any moment with the objects and purposes of all political institutions and may thus be more respected, and, lastly, in order that the grievances of the citizens, based hereafter upon simple and incontestable principles, shall tend to the maintenance of the constitution and redound to the happiness of all.

Therefore the National Assembly recognizes and proclaims, in the presence and under the auspices of the Supreme Being, the following rights of man and of the citizen:

Articles:

1. Men are born and remain free and equal in rights. Social distinctions may be founded only upon the general good.

2. The aim of all political association is the preservation of the natural and imprescriptible rights of man. These rights are liberty, property, security, and resistance to oppression.

3. The principle of all sovereignty resides essentially in the nation. No body nor individual may exercise any authority which does not proceed directly from the nation.

4. Liberty consists in the freedom to do everything which injures no one else; hence the exercise of the natural rights of each man has no limits except those which assure to the other members of the society the enjoyment of the same rights. These limits can only be determined by law.

5. Law can only prohibit such actions as are hurtful to society. Nothing may be prevented which is not forbidden by law, and no one may be forced to do anything not provided for by law.

6. Law is the expression of the general will. Every citizen has a right to participate personally, or through his representative, in its foundation. It must be the same for all, whether it protects or punishes. All citizens, being equal in the eyes of the law, are equally eligible to all dignities and to all public positions and occupations, according to their abilities, and without distinction except that of their virtues and talents.

7. No person shall be accused, arrested, or imprisoned except in the cases and according to the forms prescribed by law. Any one soliciting, transmitting, executing, or causing to be executed, any arbitrary order, shall be punished. But any citizen summoned or arrested in virtue of the law shall submit without delay, as resistance constitutes an offense.

8. The law shall provide for such punishments only as are strictly and obviously necessary, and no one shall suffer punishment except it be legally inflicted in virtue of a law passed and promulgated before the commission of the offense.

9. As all persons are held innocent until they shall have been declared guilty, if arrest shall be deemed indispensable, all harshness not essential to the securing of the prisoner's person shall be severely repressed by law.

10. No one shall be disquieted on account of his opinions, including his religious views, provided their manifestation does not disturb the public order established by law.

11. The free communication of ideas and opinions is one of the most precious of the rights of man. Every citizen may, accordingly, speak, write, and print with freedom, but shall be responsible for such abuses of this freedom as shall be defined by law.

12. The security of the rights of man and of the citizen requires public military forces. These forces are, therefore, established for the good of all and not for the personal advantage of those to whom they shall be intrusted.

13. A common contribution is essential for the maintenance of the public forces and for the cost of administration. This should be equitably distributed

among all the citizens in proportion to their means.

14. All the citizens have a right to decide, either personally or by their representatives, as to the necessity of the public contribution; to grant this freely; to know to what uses it is put; and to fix the proportion, the mode of assessment and of collection and the duration of the taxes.

15. Society has the right to require of every public agent an account of his administration.

16. A society in which the observance of the law is not assured, nor the separation of powers defined, has no constitution at all.

17. Since property is an inviolable and sacred right, no one shall be deprived thereof except where public necessity, legally determined, shall clearly demand it, and then only on condition that the owner shall have been previously and equitably indemnified.

Source: French National Assembly, *Declaration of the Rights of Man and of the Citizen* (www.yale.edu/lawweb/avalon/rightsof.htm).

∽DOCUMENT 34∽
OLAUDAH EQUIANO DESCRIBES THE HORRORS OF THE MIDDLE PASSAGE (1789)

Like Venture Smith, Olaudah Equiano was able to write about the African slave trade from a unique perspective—that of a captive African who found himself traded as a commodity by European merchants. In this account, Equiano describes the horrid conditions of life aboard a slave ship during the Middle Passage from Africa to the Americas.

The first object which saluted my eyes when I arrived on the coast was the sea, and a slave ship, which was then riding at anchor, and waiting for its cargo. These filled me with astonishment, which was soon converted into terror, when I was carried on board I was immediately handled, and tossed up, to see if I were sound, by some of the crew; and I was now persuaded that I had got into a world of bad spirits, and that they were going to kill me. Their complexions too differing so much from ours, their long hair, and the language they spoke (which was very different from any I had ever heard) united to confirm me in this belief. Indeed such were the horrors of my views and fears at the moment, that, If ten thousand worlds had been my own, I would have freely parted with them all to have exchanged my condition with that of the meanest slave in my own country. When I looked round the ship too and saw a large furnace or copper boiling, and a multitude of black people of every description chained together, every one of their countenances expressing dejection and sorrow, I no longer doubted of my fate; and, quite overpowered with horror and anguish, I fell motionless on the deck and fainted. When I recovered a little I found some black people about me, who I believed were some of those who had brought me on board, and had been receiving their pay; they talked to me in order to cheer me, but all in vain. I asked them if we were not to be eaten by those white men with horrible looks, red faces, and long hair. They told me I was not; and one of the crew brought me a small portion of spirituous liquor in a wine-glass; but being afraid of him, I would not take it out of his hand. One of the blacks therefore took it from him and gave it to me, and I took a little down my palate, which, instead of reviving me, as they thought it would, threw me into the greatest consternation at the strange feeling it produced, having never tasted any such liquor before. Soon after this the blacks who brought me on board went off, and left me abandoned to despair. I now saw myself deprived of all chance of returning to my native country, or even the least glimpse of hope of gaining the shore, which I now considered as friendly; and I even wished for my former slavery in preference to my present situation, which was filled with horrors of every kind, still heightened by my ignorance of what I was to undergo. I was not long suffered to indulge my grief; I was soon put down under the decks, and there I received such a salutation in my nostrils as I had never experienced in my life: so that with the loathsomeness of the stench, and crying together, I became so sick and low that I was not able to eat, nor had I the least desire to taste any thing. I now wished for the last friend, death, to relieve me; but soon, to my grief, two of the white men offered me eatables; and, on my refusing to eat, one of them held me fast by the hands, and laid me across, I think the windlass, and tied my feet, while the other flogged me severely. I had never experienced any thing of this kind before: and, although not being used to the water, I naturally feared that element the first time I saw it, yet, nevertheless, could I have got over the nettings, I would have jumped over the side, but I could not; and, besides, the crew used to watch us very closely who were not chained down to the decks, lest we should leap into the water: and I have seen some of these poor African prisoners most severely cut for attempting to do so, and hourly whipped for not eating. This indeed was often the case with myself. In a little time after, amongst the poor chained men, I found some of my own nation, which in a small degree gave ease to my mind. I inquired of these what was to be done with us? they gave me to understand we were to be carried to these white people's country to work for them. I then was a little revived, and thought, if it were no worse than working, my situation was not so desperate: but still I feared I should be put to death, the white people looked and acted, as I thought, in so savage a manner; for I had never seen among any people such instances of brutal cruelty; and this not only shown towards us blacks, but also to some of the whites themselves. One white man in particular I saw, when we were permitted to be on deck, flogged so unmercifully with a large rope near the foremast, that he died in consequence of it; and they tossed him over the side as they would have done a brute. This made me fear these people the more; and I expected nothing less than to be treated in the same manner. I could not help expressing my fears and apprehensions to some of my countrymen: I asked them if these people had no country, but lived in this hollow place (the ship)? they told me they did not, but came from a distant one, "Then," said I, "how comes it in all our country we never heard of them!" They told me, because they lived so very far off. I then asked where were their women? had they any like themselves? I was told they had: "And why," said I, "do we not see them?" they answered, because they were left behind. I asked how the vessel could go? they told me they could not tell; but that there were cloth put upon the masts by the help of the ropes I saw, and then the vessel went on; and the white men had some spell or magic they put in the water when they liked in order to stop the vessel, I was exceedingly amazed at this account, and really thought they were spirits. I therefore wished much to be from amongst them, for I expected they would sacrifice me: but my wishes were vain; for we were so quartered that it was impossible for any of us to make our escape. While we stayed on the coast I was mostly on deck; and one day, to my great astonishment, I saw one of these vessels coming in with the sails up. As soon as the whites saw it, they gave a great shout, at which we were amazed: and the more so as the vessel appeared larger by approaching nearer. At last she came to an anchor in my sight, and when the anchor was let go I and my countrymen who saw it were lost in astonishment to observe the vessel stop; and were now convinced it was done by magic. Soon after this the other ship got her boats out, and they came on board of us, and the people of both ships seemed very glad to see each other. Several of the strangers also shook hands with us black people, and made motions with their hands, signifying I suppose, we were to go to their country; but we did not understand them. At last, when the ship we were in, had got in all her cargo, they made ready with many fearful noises, and we were all put under deck, so that we could not see how they managed the vessel. But this disappointment was the least of my sorrow. The stench of the hold while we were on the coast was so intolerably loathsome, that it was dangerous to remain there for any time, and some of us had been permitted to stay on the deck for the fresh air; but now that the whole ship's cargo were confined together, it became absolutely pestilential. The closeness of the place, and the heat of the climate, added to the number in the ship, which was so crowded that each had scarcely room to turn himself, almost suffocated us. This produced copious perspirations, so that the air soon became unfit for respiration, from a variety of loathsome smells, and brought on a sickness amongst the slaves, of which many died, thus falling victims to the improvident avarice, as I may call it, of their purchasers. This wretched situation was again aggravated by the galling of the chains, now become insupportable; and the filth of the necessary tubs, into which the children often fell, and were almost suffocated. The shrieks of the women, and the groans of the dying, rendered the whole a scene of horror almost inconceivable. Happily perhaps for myself I was soon reduced so low here that it was thought necessary to keep me almost always on deck; and from my extreme youth I was not put in fetters. In this situation I expected every hour to share the fate of my companions, some of whom were almost daily brought upon deck at the point of death, which I began to hope would soon put an end to my miseries. Often did I think many of the inhabitants of the deep much more happy than myself, I envied them the freedom they enjoyed, and as often wished I could change my condition for theirs. Every circumstance I met with served only to render my state more painful, and heightened my apprehensions and my opinion of the cruelty of the whites. One day they had taken a number of fishes; and when they had killed and satisfied themselves with as many as they thought fit, to our astonishment who were on the deck, rather than give any of them to us to eat, as we expected, they tossed the remaining fish into the sea again, although we begged and prayed for some as well as we could, but in vain; and some of my countrymen, being pressed by hunger, took an opportunity, when they thought no one saw them, of trying to get a little privately; but they were discovered, and the attempt procured them some very severe floggings. One day, when we had a smooth sea and moderate wind, two of my wearied countrymen who were chained together (I was near them at the time), preferring death to such a life of misery, somehow made through the nettings and jumped into the sea: immediately another quite dejected fellow, who on account of his illness, was suffered to be out of irons, also followed their example; and I believe many more would very soon have done the same if they had not been prevented by the ship's crew who were instantly alarmed. Those of us that were the most active were in a moment put down under the deck, and there was such a noise and confusion amongst the people of the ship as I never heard before, to stop her, and get the boat out to go after the slaves. However two of the wretches were drowned, but they got the other, and afterwards flogged him unmercifully for thus attempting to prefer death to slavery. In this manner we continued to undergo more hardships than I can now relate, hardships which are inseparable from this accursed trade. Many a time we were near suffocation from the want of fresh air, which we were often without for whole days together. This, and the stench of the necessary tubs, carried off many. During our passage I first saw flying fishes, which surprised me very much: they used frequently to fly across the ship, and many of them fell on the deck. I also now first saw the use of the quadrant; I had often with astonishment seen the mariners make observations with it, and I could not think what it meant. They at last took notice of my surprise: and one of them, willing to increase it, as well as to gratify my curiosity, made me one day look through it. The clouds appeared to me to be land, which disappeared as they passed along. This heightened my wonder; and I was now more persuaded than ever that I was in another world, and that every thing about me was magic. At last we came in sight of the island of Barbadoes, at which the whites on board gave a great shout, and made many signs of joy to us. We did not know what to think of this; but as the vessel drew nearer, we plainly saw the harbour, and other ships of different kinds and sizes; and we soon anchored amongst them off Bridge-Town. Many merchants and planters now came on board, though it was in the evening. They put us in separate parcels, and examined us attentively. They also made us jump, and pointed to the land, signifying we were to go there. We thought by this we should be eaten by these ugly men, as they appeared to us; and, when soon after we were all put down under the deck again, there was much dread and trembling among us, and nothing but bitter cries to be heard all the night from these apprehensions, insomuch that at last the white people got some old slaves from the land to pacify us. They told us we were not to be eaten, but to work, and were soon to go on land, where we should see many of our country people. This report eased us much; and sure enough, soon after we landed, there came to us Africans of all languages. We were conducted immediately to the merchant's yard, where we were all pent up together like so many sheep in a fold, without regard to sex or age. As every object was new to me, every thing I saw filled me with surprise. What struck me first was that the houses were built with bricks and stories, and in every other respect different from those I had seen in Africa: but I was still more astonished on seeing people on horseback. I did not know what this could mean; and indeed I thought these people were full of nothing but magical arts. While I was in this astonishment one of my fellow prisoners spoke to a countryman of his about the horses, who said they were the same kind they had in their country. I understood them, though they were from a distant part of Africa, and I thought it odd I had not seen any horses there; but afterwards when I came to converse with different Africans, I found they had many horses amongst them, and much larger than those I then saw. We were not many days in the merchant's custody before we were sold after their usual manner, which is this:—On a signal given, (as the beat of a drum) the buyers rush at once into the yard where the slaves are confined, and make choice of that parcel they like best. The noise and clamour with which this is attended, and the eagerness visible in the countenances of the buyers, serve not a little to increase the apprehension of terrified Africans, who may well be supposed to consider them as the ministers of that destruction to which they think themselves devoted. In this manner, without scruple, are relations and friends separated, most of them never to see each other again. I remember in the vessel in which I was brought over, in the men's apartment, there were several brothers, who, in the sale were sold in different lots; and it was very moving on this occasion to see and hear their cries at parting. O, ye nominal Christians! might not an African ask you, learned you this from your God, who says unto you, Do unto all men as you would men should do unto you? Is it not enough that we are torn from our country and friends, to toil for your luxury and lust of gain? Must every tender feeling be likewise sacrificed to your avarice? Are the dearest friends and relations, now rendered more dear by their separation from their kindred, still to be parted from each other, and thus prevented from cheering the gloom of slavery with the small comfort of being together, and mingling their sufferings and sorrows? Why are parents to lose their children, brothers their sisters, or husbands their wives? Surely this is a new refinement in cruelty, which, while it has no advantage to atone for it, thus aggravates distress, and adds fresh horrors even to the wretchedness of slavery.

Source: Olaudah Equiano, "The Horrors of the Middle Passage," in *Afro-American History, Primary Sources,* ed. Thomas R. Frazier (Chicago: Dorsey Press, 1988).

~DOCUMENT 35~
RULES OF THE BOSTON AFRICAN SOCIETY, AN EARLY NEGRO SOCIETY (1796)

In the years following the American Revolution, the number of free blacks living in the United States grew. These blacks often found themselves in a tenuous situation in which they were not treated as slaves but, nonetheless, were not altogether free. In many communities free blacks organized themselves into fraternal societies "for the mutual benefit of each other."

1st. We, the African Members, form ourselves into a Society ... for the mutual benefit of each other, which may from time to time offer; behaving ourselves at the same time as true and faithful Citizens of the Commonwealth, in which we live; and that we take no one into the Society, who shall commit any injustice or outrage against the laws of the country.

2d. That before any person can become a Member of the Society, he must be presented by three of the Members of the same; and the person, or persons, wishing to become Members, must make application one month at least beforehand, and that at one of the monthly, or three monthly meetings. Person, or persons if approved of shall be received into the Society. And, that before the admittance of any person into the Society, he shall be obliged to read the rules, or cause the same to be read to him; and not be admitted as a member unless he approves them.

3d. That each Member on admittance, shall pay one quarter of a Dollar to the Treasurer; and be credited for the same, in the books of the Society; and his name added to the list of Members.

4th. That each Member shall pay one quarter of a Dollar per month to the Treasurer, and be credited for the same on the book; but no benefit can be tendered to any Member, untill he has belonged to the Society one year.

5th. That any Member, or Members, not able to attend the regular meetings of the Society, may pay their part by appointing one of their brothers to pay the same for them. ...

6th. That no money shall be returned to any one, that shall leave the Society; but if the Society should see fit to dismiss any one from their community, it shall then be put to a vote, whether the one, thus dismissed shall have his money again. ...

7th. That any Member, absenting himself from the Society, for the space of one year, shall be considered as separating himself from the same. ...

8th. That a committee, consisting of three or five persons, shall be chosen by the members every three months; and that their chief care shall be, to attend to the sick, and see that they want nothing that the Society can give. ...

9th. That all monies, paid into the Society shall be credited to the payers ...

10th. When any Member, or Members of the Society is sick, and not able to supply themselves with necessaries, suitable to their situations; the committee shall then tender to them and their family whatever the Society have, or may think fit for them. And should any Members die, and not leave wherewith to pay the expenses of his funeral, the Society shall then see that any, so situated, be decently buried. But it must be remembered, that any Member, bringing on himself any sickness, or disorder, by intemperance, shall not be considered, as entitled to any benefits, or assistance from the Society.

11th. Should any Member die, and leave a lawful widow and children, the Society shall consider themselves bound to relieve her necessities, so long as she behaves herself decently, and remains a widow; and that the Society do the best in their power to place the children so that they may in time be capable of getting an honest living.

12th. Should the Society with the blessing of heaven acquire a sum, suitable to bear interest, they will then take into consideration the best method they can of making it useful.

13th. The Members will watch over each other in their Spiritual concerns. ...

14th. That each Member traveling for any length of time; by Sea or Land, shall leave a Will. ...

Source: Herbert Aptheker, ed., "Rules of an Early Negro Society," in A Documentary History of the Negro People in the United States, Volume I (New York: Carol Publishing Group, 1951).

∾DOCUMENT 36∾
CONGRESSMAN DESCRIBES PETITION TO EASE PLIGHT OF SLAVES (1800)

Throughout the history of the early republic, the U.S. Congress regularly received petitions and memorials calling for an end to the African slave trade and often to slavery itself. In the following document, Congressman Robert Waln of Pennsylvania discusses a petition presented by Absalom Jones.

The petitioners, after mentioning their sense of the bounties of Providence in their freedom, and the happiness they felt under such a form of Government, represent that they cannot but be impressed with the hardships under which numbers of their color labored, who they conceived equal objects of representation and attention with themselves or others under the Constitution. That the solemn compact, the Constitution, was violated by the trade of kidnaping, carried on by the people of some of the Southern States on the shores of Maryland and Delaware, by which numbers were hurried into holes and cellars, torn from their families and transported to Georgia, and there inhumanly exposed to sale, which was degrading to the dignified nature of man. That by these and other measures injurious to the human species, there were 700,000 blacks now in slavery in these States. They stated their application to Congress to be, not for the immediate emancipation of the whole, knowing that their degraded state and want of education would render that measure improper, but they ask an amelioration of their hard situation. They prayed that the act called the fugitive bill, which was very severe on that race of people, might be considered; also that the African slave trade might be put a stop to.

Source: Robert Waln, "A 'Disquieting' Negro Petition to Congress, 1800," in *A Documentary History of the Negro People in the United States, Volume I,* ed. Herbert Aptheker (New York: Carol Publishing Group, 1951).

∾DOCUMENT 37∾
AN ACT TO PREVENT THE IMPORTATION OF CERTAIN PERSONS INTO CERTAIN STATES, WHERE, BY THE LAWS THEREOF, THEIR ADMISSION IS PROHIBITED (1803)

The fear of importing into the United States slaves who were "tainted" with the spirit of insurrection that had arisen in the French colony of Saint Domingue led Congress to pass a special measure placing limitations upon who could be brought into the country for use as slave laborers.

Be it enacted by the Senate and House of Representatives of the United States of America in Congress assembled, That from and after the first day of April next, no master or captain of any ship or vessel, or any other person, shall import or bring, or cause to be imported or brought, any negro, mulatto, or other person of colour, not being a native, a citizen, or registered seaman of the United States, or seamen natives of countries beyond the Cape of Good Hope, into any port or place of the United States, which port or place shall be situated in any state which by law has prohibited or shall prohibit the admission or importation of such negro, mulatto, or other person of colour, and if any captain or master aforesaid, or any other person, shall import or bring, or cause to be imported or brought into any of the ports or places aforesaid, any of the persons whose admission or importation is prohibited, as aforesaid, he shall forfeit and pay the sum of one thousand dollars for each and every negro, mulatto, or other person of colour aforesaid, brought or imported as aforesaid, to be sued for and recovered by action of debt, in any court of the United States; one half thereof to the use of the United States, the other half to any person or persons prosecuting for the penalty; and in any action instituted for the recovery of the penalty aforesaid, the person or persons sued may be held to special bail: Provided always, that nothing contained in this act shall be construed to prohibit the admission of Indians.

Section 2
And be it farther enacted, That no ship or vessel arriving in any of the said ports or places of the United States, and having on board any negro, mulatto, or other person of colour, not being a native, a citizen, or registered seaman of the United States, or seamen natives of countries beyond the Cape of Good Hope as aforesaid, shall be admitted to an entry. And if any such negro, mulatto, or other person of colour, shall be landed from on board any ship or vessel, in any of the ports or places aforesaid, or on the coast of any state prohibiting the admission or importation, as aforesaid, the said ship or vessel, together with her tackle, apparel, and furniture, shall be forfeited to the United States, and one half of the nett proceeds of the sales on such forfeiture shall inure and be paid over to such person or persons on whose information the seizure on such forfeiture shall be made.

Section 3
And be it further enacted, That it shall be the duty of the collectors and other officers of the customs, and all other officers of the revenue of the United States, in the several ports or places situated as aforesaid, to notice and be governed by the provisions of the laws now existing, of the several states prohibiting the admission or importation of any negro, mulatto, or other person of colour, as aforesaid. And they are hereby enjoined vigilantly to carry into effect the said laws of said states, conformably to the provisions of this act; any law of the United States to the contrary notwithstanding.

APPROVED, February 28, 1803.

Source: U.S. Congress, *An Act to Prevent the Importation of Certain Persons into Certain States, Where, by the Laws Thereof, Their Admisson Is Prohibited* (1803; New Haven, CT: Yale University, Avalon Project, 1996; www.yale.edu/lawweb/avalon/statutes/slavery/s1003.htm)

∾DOCUMENT 38∾
AN ACT FOR THE ABOLITION OF THE SLAVE TRADE (1806)

Abolitionists in Great Britain finally succeeded in their efforts to end the African slave trade when Parliament approved a measure abolishing the trade in June 1806. The British government used diplomatic efforts in subsequent decades to convince other European powers to agree to the same statement of principle.

Whereas the Two Houses of Parliament did, by their Resolutions of the Tenth and Twenty-fourth Days of June One thousand eight hundred and six, severally resolve, upon certain Grounds therein mentioned, that they would, with all practicable Expedition, take effectual Measures for the Abolition of the

African Slave Trade, in such Manner, and at such Period as might be deemed adviseable: And Whereas it is fit upon all and each of the Grounds mentioned in the said Resolutions, that the same should be forthwith abolished and prohibited, and declared to be unlawful; be it therefore enacted by the King's most Excellent Majesty, by and with the Advice and Consent of the Lords Spiritual and Temporal, and Commons, in this present Parliament assembled, and by the Authority of the same, That from and after the First Day of May One thousand eight hundred and seven, the African Slave Trade, and all and all manner of dealing and trading in the Purchase, Sale, Barter, or Transfer of Slaves, or of Persons intended to be sold, transferred, used, or dealt with as Slaves, practised and carried on, in, at, to or from any Part of the Coast or Countries of Africa, shall be, and the same is hereby utterly abolished, prohibited, and declared to be unlawful; and also that all and all manner of dealing, either by way of Purchase, Sale, Barter, or Transfer, or by means of any other Contract or Agreement whatever, relating to any Slaves, or to any Persons intended to be used or dealt with as Slaves, for the Purpose of such Slaves or Persons being removed and transported either immediately or by Transhipment at Sea or otherwise, directly or indirectly from Africa, or from any Island, Country, Territory, or Place whatever, in the West Indies, or in any other Part of America, not being in the Dominion, Possession, or Occupation of His Majesty, to any other Island, Country, Territory or Place whatever, is hereby in like Manner utterly abolished, prohibited, and declared to be unlawful; and if any of His Majesty's Subjects, or any Person or Persons resident within this United Kingdom, or any of the Islands, Colonies, Dominions, or Territories thereto belonging, or in His Majesty's Occupation or Possession, shall from and after the Day aforesaid, by him or themselves, or by his or their Factors or Agents or otherwise howsoever, deal or trade in, purchase, sell, barter, or transfer, or contract or agree for the dealing or trading in, purchasing, selling, bartering, or transferring of any Slave or Slaves, or any Person or Persons intended to be sold, transferred, used, or dealt with as a Slave or Slaves contrary to the Prohibitions of this Act, he or they so offending shall forfeit and pay for every such Offence the Sum of One hundred Pounds of lawful Money of Great Britain for each and every Slave so purchased, sold, bartered, or transferred, or contracted or agreed for as aforesaid, the One Moiety thereof to the, Use of His Majesty, His Heirs and Successors, and the other Moiety to the Use of any Person who shall inform, sue, and prosecute for the same.

II. And be it further enacted, That from and after the said First Day of May One thousand eight hundred and seven, it shall be unlawful for any of His Majesty's Subjects, or any Person or Persons resident within this United Kingdom, or any of the Islands, Colonies, Dominions or Territories thereto belonging, or in His Majesty's Possession or Occupation, to fit out, man, or navigate, or to procure to be fitted out, manned, or navigated, or to be concerned in the fitting out, manning, or navigating, or in the procuring to be fitted out, manned, or navigated, any Ship or vessel for the Purpose of assisting in, or being employed in the carrying on of the African Slave Trade, or in any other the Dealing, Trading, or Concerns hereby prohibited and declared to be unlawful, and every Ship or Vessel which shall, from and after the Day aforesaid, be fitted out, manned, navigated, used, or employed by any such Subject or Subjects, Person or Persons, or on his or their Account, or by his or their Assistance or Procurement for any of the Purposes aforesaid, and by this Act prohibited, together with all her Boats, Guns, Tackle, Apparel, and Furniture, shall become forfeited, and may and shall be seized and prosecuted as herein-after is mentioned and provided.

III. And be it further enacted, That from and after the said First Day of May One thousand eight hundred and seven, it shall be unlawful for any of His Majesty's Subjects, or any Person or Persons resident in this United Kingdom, or in any of the Colonies, Territories or Dominions thereunto belonging, or in His Majesty's Possession or Occupation, to carry away or remove, or knowingly and wilfully to procure, aid, or assist in the carrying away or removing, as Slaves, or for the Purpose of being sold, transferred, used, or dealt with as Slaves, any of the Subjects or Inhabitants of Africa, or of any Island, Country, Territory, or Place in the West Indies, or any other Part of America, whatsoever, not being in the Dominion, Possession, or Occupation of His Majesty, either immediately or by Transhipment at Sea or otherwise, directly or indirectly from Africa, or from any such Island, Country, Territory, or Place as aforesaid, to any other Island, Country, Territory, or Place whatever, and that it shall also be unlawful for any of His Majesty's Subjects, or any Person or Persons resident in this United Kingdom, or in any of the Colonies, Territories, or Dominions thereunto belonging, or in His Majesty's Possession or Occupation, knowingly and wilfully to receive, detain, or confine on board, or to be aiding, assisting, or concerned in the receiving, detaining, or confining on board of any Ship or Vessel whatever, any such Subject or Inhabitant as aforesaid, for the purpose of his or her being so carried away or removed as aforesaid, or of his or her being sold, transferred, used, or dealt with as a Slave, in any, Place or Country whatever; and if any Subject or Inhabitant, Subjects or Inhabitants of Africa, or of any Island, Country, Territory, or Place in the West Indies or America, not being in the Dominion, Possession or Occupation of His Majesty, shall from and after the Day aforesaid, be so unlawfully carried away or removed, detained, confined, transhipped, or received on board of any Ship or Vessel belonging in the Whole or in Part to, or employed by any Subject of His Majesty, or Person residing in His Majesty's Dominions or Colonies, or any Territory belonging to or in the Occupation of His Majesty, for any of the unlawful Purposes aforesaid, contrary to the Force and Effect, true Intent and Meaning of the Prohibitions in this Act contained, every such Ship or Vessel in which any such Person or Persons shall be so unlawfully carried away or removed, detained, confined, transhipped, or received on board for any of the said unlawful Purposes together with all her Boats, Guns, Tackle, Apparel, and Furniture, shall be forfeited, and all Property or pretended Property in any Natives of Africa so unlawfully carried away or removed, detained, confined, transhipped or received on board, shall also be forfeited and the same respectively shall and may be seized and prosecuted as herein-after is mentioned and provided; and every Subject of His Majesty, or Person resident within this United Kingdom, or any of the Islands, Colonies, Dominions, or Territories thereto belonging, or in His Majesty's Possession or Occupation, who shall, as Owner, Part Owner, Freighter or Shipper, Factor or Agent, Captain, Mate, Supercargo, or Surgeon, so unlawfully carry away, or remove detain, confine, tranship, or receive on board, for any of the unlawful Purposes aforesaid, any such Subject or Inhabitant of Africa, or of any Island, Country, Territory, or Place, not being in the Dominion, Possession, or Occupation of His Majesty, shall forfeit and pay for each and every Slave or Person so unlawfully carried away, removed, detained, confined, transhipped, or received on board, the Sum of One hundred Pounds of lawful Money of Great Britain, One Moiety thereof to the Use of His Majesty, and the other Moiety to the Use of any Person who shall inform, sue, and prosecute for the same.

IV. And be it further enacted, That if any Subject or Inhabitant, Subjects or Inhabitants of Africa, or of any Island, Country, Territory, or Place, not being in the Dominion, Possession, or Occupation of His Majesty, who shall, at any Time from and after the Day aforesaid, have been unlawfully carried away or removed from, Africa, or from any Island, Country, Territory, or Place in the West Indies or America, not being in the Dominion, Possession, or Occupation of His Majesty, contrary to any of the Prohibitions or Provisions in this Act contained, shall be imported or brought into any Island, Colony, Plantation, or Territory, in the Dominion, Possession, or Occupation of His Majesty, and there sold or disposed of as a Slave or Slaves, or placed, detained, or kept in a State

Of Slavery, such Subject or Inhabitant, Subjects or Inhabitants, so unlawfully carried away, or removed and imported, shall and may be seized and prosecuted as forfeited to His Majesty, by such Person or Persons, in such Courts, and in such Manner and Form, as any Goods or Merchandize unlawfully imported into the same Island, Colony, Plantation, or Territory, may now be seized and prosecuted therein by virtue of any Act or Acts of Parliament now in force for regulating the Navigation and Trade of His Majesty's Colonies and Plantations and shall and may, after his or their Condemnation, be disposed of in Manner herein-after mentioned and provided.

V. And be it further enacted, That from and after the said First Day of May One thousand eight hundred and seven, all Insurances whatsoever to be effected upon or in respect to any of the trading, dealing, carrying, removing, transhipping, or other Transactions by this Act prohibited, shall be also prohibited and declared to be unlawful; and if any of His Majesty's Subjects, or any Person or Persons resident within this United Kingdom, or within any of the Islands, Colonies, Dominions, or Territories thereunto belonging, or in His Majesty's Possession or Occupation, shall knowingly and wilfully subscribe, effect, or make, or cause or procure to be subscribed, effected, or made, any such unlawful Insurances or Insurance, he or they shall forfeit and pay for every such Offence the Sum of One hundred Pounds for every such Insurance, and also Treble the Amount paid or agreed to be paid as the Premium of any such Insurance, the One Moiety thereof to the Use of His Majesty, His Heirs and Successors, and the other Moiety to the Use of any Person who shall inform, sue, and prosecute for the same.

VI. Provided always, That nothing herein contained shall extend, or be deemed or construed to extend, to prohibit or render unlawful the dealing or trading in the Purchase, Sale, Barter, or Transfer, or the carrying away or removing for the Purpose of being sold, transferred, used, or dealt with as Slaves, or the detaining or confining for the Purpose of being so carried away or removed, of any Slaves which shall be exported, carried, or removed from Africa, in any Ship or Vessel which, on or before the said First Day of May One thousand eight hundred and seven, shall have been lawfully cleared out from Great Britain according to the Law now in force for regulating the carrying of Slaves from Africa, or to prohibit or render unlawful the manning or navigating any such Ship or Vessel, or to make void any Insurance thereon, so as the Slaves to be carried therein shall be finally landed in the West Indies on or before the First Day of March One thousand eight hundred and eight, unless prevented by Capture, the Loss of the Vessel, by the Appearance of an Enemy upon the Coast, or other unavoidable Necessity, the Proof whereof shall lie upon the Party charged; any Thing herein-before contained to the contrary notwithstanding.

VII. And Whereas it may happen, That during the present or future Wars, Ships or Vessels may be seized or detained as Prize, on board whereof Slaves or Natives of Africa, carried and detained as Slaves, being the Property of His Majesty's Enemies, or otherwise liable to Condemnation as Prize of War, may be taken or found, and it is necessary to direct in what Manner such Slaves or Natives of Africa shall be hereafter treated and disposed of: And Whereas it is also necessary to direct and provide for the Treatment and Disposal of any Slaves or Natives of Africa carried, removed, treated or dealt with as Slaves, who shall be unlawfully carried away or removed contrary to the Prohibitions aforesaid, or any of them, and shall be afterwards found on board any Ship or Vessel liable to Seizure under this Act, or any other Act of Parliament made for restraining or prohibiting the African Slave Trade, or shall be elsewhere lawfully seized as forfeited under this or any other such Act of Parliament as aforesaid; and it is expedient to encourage the Captors, Seizors and Prosecutors thereof; Be it therefore further enacted, That all Slaves and all Natives of Africa, treated, dealt with, carried, kept or detained as Slaves, which shall at any Time from and after the said First Day of May next be seized or taken as Prize of War, or liable to Forfeiture, under this or any other Act of Parliament made for restraining or prohibiting the African Slave Trade, shall and may for the Purposes only of Seizure, Prosecution, and Condemnation as Prize or as Forfeitures, be considered, treated, taken, and adjudged as Slaves and Property, in the same Manner as Negro Slaves have been heretofore considered, treated, taken, and adjudged, when seized as Prize of War, or as forfeited for any Offence against the Laws of Trade and Navigation respectively; but the same shall be condemned as Prize of War, or as forfeited to the sole Use of His Majesty, His Heirs and Successors, for the Purpose only of divesting and barring all other Property, Right, Title, or Interest whatever, which before existed, or might afterwards be set up or claimed in or to such Slaves or Natives of Africa so seized, prosecuted and condemned; and the same nevertheless shall in no case be liable to be sold, disposed of, treated or dealt with as Slaves, by or on the Part of His Majesty, His Heirs or Successors, or by or on the Part of any Person or Persons claiming or to claim from, by or under His Majesty, His Heirs and Successors, or under or by force of any such Sentence of Condemnation: Provided always, that it shall be lawful for His Majesty, His Heirs and Successors, and such Officers, Civil or Military, as shall, by any general or special Order of the King in Council, be from Time to Time appointed and empowered to re-

ceive, protect, and provide for such Natives of Africa as shall be so condemned, either to enter and enlist the same, or any of them, into His Majesty's Land or Sea Service as Soldiers, Seamen or Marines, or to bind the same, or any of them, whether of full Age or not, as Apprentices, for any Term not exceeding Fourteen Years, to Such Person or Persons, in such Place or Places, and upon such Terms and Conditions, and subject to such Regulations, as to His Majesty shall seem meet, and as shall by any general or special Order of His Majesty in Council be in that Behalf directed and appointed; and any Indenture of Apprenticeship duly made and executed, by any Person or Persons to be for that Purpose appointed by any such Order in Council, for any Term not exceeding Fourteen Years, shall be of the same Force and Effect as if the Party thereby bound as an Apprentice had himself or herself, when of full Age upon good Consideration, duly executed the same; and every such Native of Africa who shall be so enlisted or entered as aforesaid into any of His Majesty's Land or Sea Forces as a Soldier, Seaman, or Marine, shall be considered, treated, and dealt with in all Respects as if he had voluntarily so enlisted or entered himself.

VIII. Provided also, and be it further enacted, That where any Slaves or Natives of Africa, taken as Prize of War by any of His Majesty's Ships of War, or Privateers duly commissioned, shall be finally condemned as such to His Majesty's Use as aforesaid, there shall be paid to the Captors thereof by the Treasurer of His Majesty's Navy, in like Manner as the Bounty called Head Money is now paid by virtue of an Act of Parliament, made in the Forty-fifth Year of His Majesty's Reign, intituled, An Act for the Encouragement of Seamen, and for the better and more effectually manning His Majesty's Navy during the present War, such Bounty as His Majesty, His Heirs and Successors, shall have directed by any Order in Council, so as the same shall not exceed the Sum of Forty Pounds lawful Money of Great Britain for every Man, or Thirty Pounds of like Money for every Woman, or Ten Pounds of like Money for every Child or Person not above Fourteen Years old, that shall be so taken and condemned, and shall be delivered over in good Health to the proper Officer or Officers, Civil or Military, so appointed as aforesaid to receive, protect, and provide for the same; which Bounties shall be divided amongst the Officers, Seamen, Marines, and Soldiers on board His Majesty's Ships of War, or hired armed Ships, in Manner, Form, and Proportion, as by His Majesty's Proclamation for granting the Distribution of Prizes already issued, or to be issued for that Purpose is or shall be directed and appointed, and amongst the Owners, Officers, and Seamen of any private Ship or Vessel of War, in such Manner and Proportion as, by an Agreement in Writing that they shall have entered into for that Purpose, shall be directed.

IX. Provided always, and be it further enacted, That in order to entitle the Captors to receive the said Bounty Money, the Numbers of Men, Women, and Children, so taken, condemned, and delivered over, shall be proved to the Commissioners of His Majesty's Navy, by producing, instead of the Oaths and Certificates prescribed by the said Act as to Head Money, a Copy, duly certified, of the Sentence or Decree of Condemnation whereby the Numbers of Men, Women, and Children, so taken and condemned, shall appear to have been distinctly proved; and also, by producing a Certificate under the Hand of the said Officer or Officers, Military or Civil, so appointed, as aforesaid, and to whom the same shall have been delivered, acknowledging that he or they hath or have received the same, to be disposed of according to His Majesty' s Instructions and Regulations as aforesaid.

X. Provided also, and be it further enacted, That in any Cases, in which Doubts shall arise whether the Party or Parties claiming such Bounty Money is or are entitled thereto, the same shall be summarily determined by the Judge of the High Court of Admiralty, or by the Judge of any Court of Admiralty in which the Prize shall have been adjudged, subject nevertheless to an Appeal to the Lords Commissioners of Appeals in Prize Causes.

XI. Provided also, and be it further enacted, That on the Condemnation to the Use of His Majesty, His Heirs and Successors, in Manner aforesaid, of any Slaves or Natives of Africa, seized and prosecuted as forfeited for any Offence against this Act, or any other Act of Parliament made for restraining or prohibiting the African Slave Trade (except in the Case of Seizures made at Sea by the Commanders or Officers of His Majesty's Ships or Vessels of War) there shall be paid to and to the Use of the Person who shall have sued, informed, and prosecuted the same to Condemnation, the Sums of Thirteen Pounds lawful Money aforesaid for every Man, of Ten Pounds like Money for every Woman, and of Three Pounds like Money for every Child or Person under the Age of Fourteen Years, that shall be so condemned and delivered over in good Health to the said Civil or Military Officer so to be appointed to receive, protect, and provide for the same, and also the like Sums to and to the Use of the Governor or Commander in Chief of any Colony or Plantation wherein such Seizure shall have been made; but in Cases of any such Seizures made at Sea by the Commanders or Officers of His Majesty's Ships or Vessels of War, for Forfeiture under this Act, or any other Act of Parliament made for restraining or prohibiting the African Slave Trade, there shall be paid to the Commander or Officer who shall so seize, inform, and prosecute,

for every Man so condemned and delivered over, the Sum of Twenty Pounds like Money, for every Woman the Sum of Fifteen Pounds like Money, and for, every Child or Person under the Age of Fourteen Years the Sum of Five Pounds like Money, subject nevertheless to such Distribution of the said Bounties or Rewards for the said Seizures made at Sea as His Majesty, His Heirs and Successors, shall think fit to order and direct by any Order in Council made for that Purpose; for all which Payments so to be made as Bounties or Rewards upon Seizures and Prosecutions for Offences against this Act, or any other Act of Parliament made for restraining or abolishing the African Slave Trade, the Officer or Officers, Civil or Military, so to be appointed as aforesaid to receive, protect, and provide for such Slaves or Natives of Africa so to be condemned and delivered over, shall, after the Condemnation and Receipt thereof as aforesaid, grant Certificates in favour of the Governor and Party seizing, informing, and prosecuting as aforesaid respectively, or the latter alone (as the Case may be) addressed to the Lords Commissioners of His Majesty's Treasury; who, upon the Production to them of any such Certificate, and of an authentic Copy, duly certified, of the Sentence of Condemnation of the said Slaves or Africans to His Majesty's Use as aforesaid, and also of a Receipt under the Hand of such Officer or Officers so appointed as aforesaid, specifying that such Slaves or Africans have by him or them been received in good Health as aforesaid, shall direct Payment to be made from and out of the Consolidated Fund of Great Britain of the Amount of the Monies specified in such Certificate, to the lawful Holders of the same, or the Persons entitled to the Benefit thereof respectively.

XII. And be it further enacted, That if any Person shall wilfully and fraudulently forge or counterfeit any such Certificate, Copy of Sentence of Condemnation, or Receipt as aforesaid, or any Part thereof, or shall knowingly and wilfully utter or publish the same, knowing it to be forged or counterfeited, with Intent to defraud His Majesty, His Heirs and Successors, or any other Person or Persons whatever, the Party so offending shall, on Conviction, suffer Death as in Cases of Felony, without Benefit of Clergy.

XIII. And be it further enacted, That the several Pecuniary Penalties or Forfeitures imposed and inflicted by this Act, shall and may be sued for, prosecuted, and recovered in any Court of Record in Great Britain, or in any Court of Record or Vice Admiralty in any Part of His Majesty's Dominions wherein the Offence was committed, or where the Offender may be found after the Commission of such Offence; and that in all Cases of Seizure of any Ships, Vessels, Slaves or pretended Slaves, Goods or Effects, for any Forfeiture under this Act, the same shall and may respectively be sued for, prosecuted and recovered in any Court of Record in Great Britain, or in any Court of Record or Vice Admiralty in any Part of His Majesty's Dominions in or nearest to which such Seizures may be made, or to which such Ships or Vessels, Slaves or pretended Slaves, Goods or Effects (if seized at Sea or without the Limits of any British Jurisdiction) may most conveniently be carried for Trial; and all the said Penalties and Forfeitures, whether pecuniary or specific (unless where it is expressly otherwise provided for by this Act) shall go and belong to such Person and Persons in such Shares and Proportions, and shall and may be sued for and prosecuted, tried, recovered, distributed, and applied in such and the like Manner and by the same Ways and Means, and subject to the same Rules and Directions, as any Penalties or Forfeitures incurred in Great Britain, and in the British Colonies or Plantations in America respectively, by force of any Act of Parliament relating to the Trade and Revenues of the said British Colonies or Plantations in America, now go and belong to, and may now be sued for, prosecuted, tried, recovered, distributed and applied respectively in Great Britain or in the said Colonies or Plantations respectively, under and by virtue of a certain Act of Parliament made in the Fourth Year of His present Majesty, intituled, An Act for granting certain Duties in the British Colonies and Plantations in America; for continuing, amending, and making perpetual an Act passed in the Sixth Year of the Reign of his late Majesty, King George the Second, intituled, an Act for the better securing and encouraging the Trade of His Majesty's Sugar Colonies in America; for applying the Produce of such Duties to arise by virtue of the said Act towards defraying the Expences of defending, protecting, and securing the said Colonies and Plantations; for explaining an Act made in the Twenty-fifth Year of the Reign of King Charles the Second, intituled, An Act for the Encouragement of the Greenland and Eastland Trades, and for the better securing the Plantation Trade, and for altering and disallowing several Drawbacks on Exports from this Kingdom, and more effectually preventing the clandestine Conveyance of Goods to and from the Colonies and Plantations, and improving and securing the Trade between the same and Great Britain.

XIV. And be it further enacted, That all Ships and Vessels, Slaves or Natives of Africa, carried, conveyed, or dealt with as Slaves, and all other Goods and Effects that shall or may become forfeited for any Offence committed against this Act, shall and may be seized by any Officer of His Majesty's Customs or Excise, or by Commanders or Officers of any of His Majesty's Ships or Vessels of War, who; in making and prosecuting any such Seizures, shall have the Benefit of all the Provisions made by the said Act of the Fourth Year of His present Majesty,

or any other Act of Parliament made for the Protection of Officers seizing and prosecuting for any Offence against the said Act or any other Act of Parliament relating to the Trade and Revenues of the British Colonies or Plantations in America.

XV. And be it further enacted, That all Offences committed against this Act may be inquired of, tried, determined, and dealt with as Misdemeanors, as if the same had been respectively committed within the Body of the County of Middlesex.

XVI. Provided also, and be it further enacted, That it shall and may be lawful for His Majesty in Council from Time to Time to make such Orders and Regulations for the future Disposal and Support of such Negroes as shall have been bound Apprentices under this Act, after the Term of their Apprenticeship shall have expired, as to His Majesty shall seem meet, and as may prevent such Negroes from becoming at any time chargeable upon the Island in which they shall have been so bound Apprentices as aforesaid.

XVII. Provided always, and be it further enacted, That none of the Provisions of any Act as to enlisting for any limited Period of Service, or as to any Rules or Regulations for the granting any Pensions or Allowances to any Soldiers discharged after certain Periods of Service, shall extend, or be deemed or construed in any Manner to extend, to any Negroes so enlisting and serving in any of His Majesty's Forces.

XVIII. And be it further enacted, That if any Action or Suit shall be commenced either in Great Britain or elsewhere, against any Person or Persons for any Thing done in pursuance of this Act, the Defendant or Defendants in such Action or Suit may plead the General Issue, and give this Act and the Special Matter in Evidence at any Trial to be had thereupon, and that the same was done in pursuance and by the Authority of this Act; and if it shall appear so to have been done, the jury shall find for the Defendant or Defendants; and if the Plaintiff shall be nonsuited or discontinue his Action after the Defendant or Defendants shall have appeared, or if judgement shall be given upon any Verdict or Demurrer against the Plaintiff, the Defendant or Defendants shall recover Treble Costs and have the like Remedy for the same, as Defendants have in other Cases by Law.

Source: George III, king of England, "An Act for the Abolition of the Slave Trade," in *Documents Illustrative of the History of the Slave Trade to America, Volume II—The Eighteenth Century,* ed. Elizabeth Donnan (Washington, DC: Carnegie Institution of Washington, 1931).

DOCUMENT 39
CLOSING OF THE AFRICAN
SLAVE TRADE (1807)

Following the lead taken by Great Britain and observing the timetable outlined in the U.S. Constitution, the Congress acted in March 1807 to abolish the African slave trade effective January 1, 1808. With the adoption of this legislation, it became illegal for any citizen of the United States to take part in the transatlantic slave trade, but the domestic slave trade in the United States was not affected.

An Act to Prohibit the Importation of Slaves into any Port or Place Within the Jurisdiction of the United States, From and After the First Day of January, in the Year of our Lord One Thousand Eight Hundred and Eight

Be it enacted by the Senate and House of Representatives of the United States of America in Congress assembled, That from and after the first day of January, one thousand eight hundred and eight, it shall not be lawful to import or bring into the United States or the territories thereof from any foreign kingdom, place, or country, any negro, mulatto, or person of colour, with intent to hold, sell, or dispose of such negro, mulatto, or person of colour, as a slave, or to be held to service or labour.

Section 2

And be it further enacted, That no citizen or citizens of the United States, or any other person, shall, from and after the first day of January, in the year of our Lord one thousand eight hundred and eight, for himself, or themselves, or any other person whatsoever, either as master, factor, or owner, build, fit, equip, load or otherwise prepare any ship or vessel, in any port or place within the jurisdiction of the United States, nor shall cause any ship or vessel to sail from any port or place within the same, for the purpose of procuring any negro, mulatto, or person of colour, from any foreign kingdom, place, or country, to be transported to any port or place whatsoever, within the jurisdiction of the United States, to be held, sold, or disposed of as slaves, or to be held to service or labour: and if any ship or vessel shall be so fitted out for the purpose aforesaid, or shall be caused to sail so as aforesaid, every such ship or vessel, her tackle, apparel, and furniture, shall be forfeited to the United States, and shall be liable to be seized, prosecuted, and condemned in any of the circuit courts or district courts, for the district where the said ship or vessel may be found or seized.

Section 3

And be it further enacted, That all and every person so building, fitting out, equipping, loading, or other-wise preparing or sending away, any ship or vessel, knowing or intending that the same shall be employed in such trade or business, from and after the first day of January, one thousand eight hundred and eight, contrary to the true intent and meaning of this act, or any ways aiding or abetting therein, shall severally forfeit and pay twenty thousand dollars, one moiety thereof to the use of the United States, and the other moiety to the use of any person or persons who shall sue for and prosecute the same to effect.

Section 4

And be it further enacted, If any citizen or citizens of the United States, or any person resident within the jurisdiction of the same, shall, from and after the first day of January, one thousand eight hundred and eight, take on board, receive or transport from any of the coasts or kingdoms of Africa, or from any other foreign kingdom, place, or country, any negro, mulatto, or person of colour, in any ship or vessel, for the purpose of selling them in any port or place within the jurisdiction of the United States as slaves, or to be held to service or labour, or shall be in any ways aiding or abetting therein, such citizen or citizens, or person, shall severally forfeit and pay five thousand dollars, one moiety thereof to the use of any person or persons who shall sue for and prosecute the same to effect; and every such ship or vessel in which such negro, mulatto, or person of colour, shall have been taken on board, received, or transported as aforesaid, her tackle, apparel, and furniture, and the goods and effects which shall be found on board the same, shall be forfeited to the United States, and shall be liable to be seized, prosecuted, and condemned in any of the circuit courts or district courts in the district where the said ship or vessel may be found or seized. And neither the importer, nor any person or persons claiming from or under him, shall hold any right or title whatsoever to any negro, mulatto, or person of colour, nor to the service or labour thereof, who may be imported or brought within the United States, or territories thereof, in violation of this law, but the same shall remain subject to any regulations not contravening the provisions of this act, which the legislatures of the several states or territories at any time hereafter may make, for disposing of any such negro, mulatto, or person of colour.

Section 5

And be it further enacted, That if any citizen or citizens of the United States, or any other person resident within the jurisdiction of the same, shall, from and after the first day of January, one thousand eight hundred and eight, contrary to the true intent and meaning of this act, take on board any ship or vessel from any of the coasts or kingdoms of Africa, or from any other foreign kingdom, place, or country, any negro, mulatto, or person of colour, with intent to sell him, her, or them, for a slave, or slaves, or to be held to service or labour, and shall transport the same to any port or place within the jurisdiction of the United States, and there sell such negro, mulatto, or person of colour, so transported as aforesaid, for a slave, or to be held to service or labour, every such offender shall be deemed guilty of a high misdemeanor, and being thereof convicted before any court having competent jurisdiction, shall suffer imprisonment for not more than ten years nor less than five years, and be fined not exceeding ten thousand dollars, nor less than one thousand dollars.

Section 6
And be it further enacted, That if any person or persons whatsoever, shall, from and after the first day of January, one thousand eight hundred and eight, purchase or sell any negro, mulatto, or person of colour, for a slave, or to be held to service or labour, who shall have been imported, or brought from any foreign kingdom, place, or country, or from the dominions of any foreign state, immediately adjoining to the United States, into any port or place within the jurisdiction of the United States, after the last day of December, one thousand eight hundred and seven, knowing at the time of such purchase or sale, such negro, mulatto or person of colour, was so brought within the jurisdiction of the United States, as aforesaid, such purchaser and seller shall severally forfeit and pay for every negro, mulatto, or person of colour, so purchased or sold as aforesaid, eight hundred dollars; one moiety thereof to the United States, and the other moiety to the use of any person or persons who shall sue for and prosecute the same to effect: Provided, that the aforesaid forfeiture shall not extend to the seller or purchaser of any negro, mulatto, or person of colour, who may be sold or disposed of in virtue of any regulation which may hereafter be made by any of the legislatures of the several states in that respect, in pursuance of this act, and the constitution of the United States.

Section 7
And be it further enacted, That if any ship or vessel shall be found, from and after the first day of January, one thousand eight hundred and eight, in any river, port, bay, or harbor, or on the high seas, within the jurisdictional limits of the United States, or hovering on the coast thereof, having on board any negro, mulatto, or person of colour, for the purpose of selling them as slaves, or with intent to land the same, in any port or place within the jurisdiction of the United States, contrary to the prohibition of this act, every such ship or vessel, together with her tackle, apparel, and furniture, and the goods or ef-fects which shall be found on board the same, shall be forfeited to the use of the United States, and may be seized, prosecuted, and condemned, in any court of the United States, having jurisdiction thereof And it shall be lawful for the President of the United States, and he is hereby authorized, should he deem it expedient, to cause any of the armed vessels of the United States to be manned and employed to cruise on any part of the coast of the United States, or territories thereof, where he may judge attempts will be made to violate the provisions of this act, and to instruct and direct the commanders of armed vessels of the United States, to seize, take, and bring into any port of the United States all such ships or vessels, and moreover to seize, take, and bring into any port of the United States all ships or vessels of the United States, wheresoever found on the high seas, contravening the provisions of this act, to be proceeded against according to law, and the captain, master, or commander of every such ship or vessel, so found and seized as aforesaid, shall be deemed guilty of a high misdemeanor, and shall be liable to be prosecuted before any court of the United States, having jurisdiction thereof; and being thereof convicted, shall be fined not exceeding ten thousand dollars, and be imprisoned not less than two years, and not exceeding four years. And the proceeds of all ships and vessels, their tackle, apparel, and furniture, and the goods and effects on board of them, which shall be so seized, prosecuted and condemned, shall be divided equally between the United States and the officers and men who shall make such seizure, take, or bring the same into port for condemnation, whether such seizure be made by an armed vessel of the United States, or revenue cutters thereof, and the same shall be distributed in like manner, as is provided by law, for the distribution of prizes taken from an enemy: Provided, that the officers and men, to be entitled to one half of the proceeds aforesaid, shall safe keep every negro, mulatto, or person of colour, found on board of any ship or vessel so by them seized, taken, or brought into port for condemnation, and shall deliver every such negro, mulatto, or person of colour, to such person or persons as shall be appointed by the respective states, to receive the same, and if no such person or persons shall be appointed by the respective states, they shall deliver every such negro, mulatto, or person of colour, to the overseers of the poor of the port or place where such ship or vessel may be brought or found, and shall immediately transmit to the governor or chief magistrate of the state, an account of their proceedings, together with the number of such Negroes, mulattoes, or persons of colour, and a descriptive list of the same, that he may give directions respecting such Negroes, mulattoes, or persons of colour.

Section 8

And be it further enacted, That no captain, master or commander of any ship or vessel, of less burthen than forty tons, shall, from and after the first day of January, one thousand eight hundred and eight, take on board and transport any negro, mulatto, or person of colour, to any port or place whatsoever, for the purpose of selling or disposing of the same as a slave, or with intent that the same may be sold or disposed of to be held to service or labour, on penalty of forfeiting for every such negro, mulatto, or person of colour, so taken on board and transported, as aforesaid, the sum of eight hundred dollars; one moiety thereof to the use of the United States, and the other moiety to any person or persons who shall sue for, and prosecute the same to effect: Provided however, That nothing in this section shall extend to prohibit the taking on board or transporting on any river, or inland bay of the sea, within the jurisdiction of the United States, any negro, mulatto, or person of colour, (not imported contrary to the provisions of this act) in any vessel or species of craft whatever.

Section 9

And be it further enacted, That the captain, master, or commander of any ship or vessel of the burthen of forty tons or more, On and after the first day of January, one thousand eight hundred and eight, sailing coastwise, from any port in the United States, to any port or place within the jurisdiction of the same, having on board any negro, mulatto, or person of colour, for the purpose of transporting them to be sold or disposed of as slaves, or to be held to service or labour, shall, previous to the departure of such ship or vessel, make out and subscribe duplicate manifests of every such negro, mulatto, or person of colour, on board such ship or vessel, therein specifying the name and sex of each person, their age and stature, as near as may be, and the class to which they respectively belong, whether negro, mulatto, or person of colour, with the name and place of residence of every owner or shipper of the same, and shall deliver such manifests to the collector of the port, if there be one, otherwise to the surveyor, before whom the captain, master, or commander, together with the owner or shipper, shall severally swear or affirm to the best of their knowledge and belief, that the persons therein specified were not imported or brought into the United States, from and after the first day of January, one thousand eight hundred and eight, and that under the laws of the state, they are held to service or labour; whereupon the said collector or surveyor shall certify the same on the said manifests, one of which he shall return to the said captain, master, or commander, with a permit, specifying thereon the number, names, and general description of such persons, and authorizing him to proceed to the port of his destination. And if any ship or vessel, being laden and destined as aforesaid, shall depart from the port where she may then be, without the captain, master, or commander having first made out and subscribed duplicate manifests, of every negro, mulatto, and person of colour, on board such ship or vessel, as aforesaid, and without having previously delivered the same to the said collector or surveyor, and obtained a permit, in manner as herein required, or shall, previous to her arrival at the port of her destination, take on board any negro, mulatto, or person of colour, other than those specified in the manifests, as aforesaid, every such ship or vessel, together with her tackle, apparel and furniture, shall be forfeited to the use of the United States, and may be seized, prosecuted and condemned in any court of the United States having jurisdiction thereof; and the captain, master, or commander of every such ship or vessel, shall moreover forfeit, for every such negro, mulatto, or person of colour, so transported, or taken on board, contrary to the provisions of this act, the sum of one thousand dollars, one moiety thereof to the United States, and the other moiety to the use of any person or persons who shall sue for and prosecute the same to effect.

Section 10

And be it further enacted, That the captain, master, or commander of every ship or vessel, of the burthen of forty tons or more, from and after the first day of January, one thousand eight hundred and eight, sailing coastwise, and having on board any negro, mulatto, or person of colour, to sell or dispose of as slaves, or to be held to service or labour, and arriving in any port within the jurisdiction of the United States, from any other port within the same, shall, previous to the unlading or putting on shore any of the persons aforesaid, or suffering them to go on shore, deliver to the collector, if there be one, or if not, to the surveyor residing at the port of her arrival, the manifest certified by the collector or surveyor of the port from whence she sailed, as is herein before directed, to the truth of which, before such officer, he shall swear or affirm, and if the collector or surveyor shall be satisfied therewith, he shall thereupon grant a permit for unlading or suffering such negro, mulatto, or person of colour, to be put on shore, and if the captain, master, or commander of any such ship or vessel being laden as aforesaid, shall neglect or refuse to deliver the manifest at the time and in the manner herein directed, or shall land or put on shore any negro, mulatto, or person of colour, for the purpose aforesaid, before he shall have delivered his manifest as aforesaid, and obtained a permit for that purpose, every such captain, master, or commander, shall forfeit and pay ten thousand dollars, one moiety thereof to the United States, the other moiety to the use of any person or persons who shall sue for and prosecute the same to effect. APPROVED, March 2, 1807.

Source: U.S. Congress, *Closing of the African Slave Trade* (1807; New Haven, CT: Yale University, Avalon Project, 1996; www.yale.edu/lawweb/avalon/statutes/slavery/s1004.htm.)

DOCUMENT 40
HENRI CHRISTOPHE'S STATE OF HAYTI PROCLAMATION (1810)

Slaves in the French colony of Saint Domingue achieved what many people thought was impossible when they defeated the French government and proclaimed the independence of the black republic of Haiti.

SOLDIERS!
The place of St. Nicholas Mole has just fallen by the success of your arms, rebellion is extinguished in this quarter, and you have planted on every side the colours of the legitimate authority, already so distinguished by the numerous triumphs obtained over the enemies of liberty.

Twenty days of regular siege have sufficed to destroy, to the very foundations, those fortresses which parricidal hands had raised in defence of rebellion. In vain a pretending expedition had flattered itself with the hope of perpetrating intestine dissensions, and sacrificing at the, shrine of error; your arms, strengthened by the most just of causes, have, in a few days, overthrown these edifices, and buried under their ruins the projects and presumptive hopes of a criminal faction.

Weary of temporising measures, that had for their object to spare the effusion of blood, and having perceived that nothing could equal my patience and my kindness, but the, obduracy and the inflexibility of the factious, I decided on the fate of this guilty place. The two chiefs, who successively took the command of it, have bitten the dust; two of their vessels of war being shattered, presented in the roads nothing more than, unavailing skeletons; a considerable pile of cannon, of mortars, of stores, and provisions of every kind, are the results of your toils, and the reward of your valour; while these men, who have issued from the results of the extremity of the South, with the intent to deprive you of the most precious of all blessings, now obliged to surrender at discretion, have experienced that your clemency is equal to your valour.

Such is ever the recompence of true courage! Nothing can resist it, because it is maintained by fidelity to one's chief, guided by honour, and inspired by patriotism.—Soldiers, and you, brave seamen, who have rivalled in all respects the land forces, you whose efforts have braved the winds, the currents,

and the waves, in a cruise which will be the admiration of all who are experienced in naval affairs, the new lustre which your glorious exploits have just reflected upon the arms of your chief is your best eulogium. In truth, the zeal, the constancy, the loyalty, the fidelity, and the intrepidity which you have displayed in a multitude of engagements, which were rendered necessary through the most inconceivable animosity, constitute at once my glory and my pride; yes, I have found in you the most intrepid warriors, who have contributed to the establishment of liberty and independence, and I have, more than once, in this campaign gloried in being at your head. It is indeed Gratifying to me to declare solemnly, that you have all deserved well of the country! and that it will be a satisfaction for my heart to decree honorary rewards to those of you who have most distinguished themselves.

But to acquire distinction in the career of heroes is not all; there is another virtue, another species of glory of which we ought to furnish an example.

You have seen the inveterate supporters of error, the obstinate partisans of a cause revolting to reason as well as to nature; you have seen them, I say, these unhappy children of the south, basely abandoned and betrayed by their comrades, after having experienced all that human misfortunes have in them of extremest bitterness, after having been compelled to lay down their arms, to come and throw themselves at my feet, to acknowledge their errors, and implore my clemency; they thought to find in me an irritated conqueror; they expected to read in my offended front their sentence to die. Ungrateful men! they have only been witnesses of my compassion, and of the tears which their repentance has wrung from me. You too, soldiers, melted at this example, have nobly shared with them your tents, you [*sic*] clothing, and your food; they have found no other than brethren in you, and your arms have carefully borne their sick and wounded to the hospitals, to be treated and attended in the same manner as your own companions. But still more, the 9th regiment, that same one which first raised the standard of revolt, as well as the remains of the 16th, 18th, 21st, 22d, 23d, and 24th, made prisoners, are to-day astonished at taking rank in the army of Hayti; but let their astonishment cease when they know that in punishing, a father is always paternal; and let them remember these words of the common Father mankind: "There is more joy in heaven over that one sheep which is found again, than for the whole flock that hath never strayed."

May this trait of magnanimity soften the hearts of those who still foment or encourage calumny! Let them at length understand that it is good to sacrifice private passions to the general benefit; let them consider that the vile agents of the French government, like greedy vultures, are only watching an opportunity to fall upon their prey; let them reflect, that the vessel of independence in which we are all embarked, must save itself, or perish with the passengers; and that, to enable it to reach the desired port in safety, it is glorious to rally with brethren who know how to fight, to conquer, and forgive. For my part, convinced as I am that our divisions constitute the joy and the hope of our enemies; persuaded that this region is the only one which is still at the service of free minds; assured by experience that the cause of the black and of the yellow is one and indivisible; and acquainted by ample proof of the new plots that are framing by our common tyrants to render our quarrels of endless duration; I call upon God and upon men to witness, that no sacrifice shall be too dear for me that can tend to reunite the children of Hayti under the paternal shield.—Trusting in my own means, and confident of the legitimacy of my cause, which give strength to my ascendancy, I do not hesitate to renew here the *general amnesty* which I have already offered, to promote the welfare of the state, the only object of my ambition.

But, if it be desirable that one portion of the Haytians, who are still under the influence of error, should relinquish that error, and expiate the wrongs of many years by a moment of repentance, it is for the public advantage that the members of the great family should reunite, to the consternation and despair of our tyrants, and not the less necessary to preserve that attitude which befits men, who, having done much, are aware that there still remains much more for them to do.

SOLDIERS,

You are about to return to your respective garrisons and cantonments, to refresh yourselves after the toilsome fatigues you have undergone; carry with you that sense of order, of subordination and discipline which is the sacred pledge of victory.

It is my intention to distribute the rewards of valour to those who have distinguished themselves by their good deeds: your corps are about to be completed, and clothed and equipped anew; enjoy then in peace the fruit of your laurels, and be ready, at the first signal, to complete the triumph of the legitimate authority.

Done at our Palace of Cape Henry, the 8th October 1810, in the seventh year of the independence of Hayti.

HENRY CHRISTOPHE

By the President,
The Field Marshal, and private Secretary of his Serene Highness,

PREVOST

Source: Henri Christophe, "State of Hayti," in *Haytian Papers*, ed. Prince Sanders (Westport, CT: Negro University Press, 1969).

DOCUMENT 41
THE OBSERVER, ON THE EAST AFRICAN SLAVE TRADE, FEBRUARY 22, 1819

Despite the efforts of European powers to end the African slave trade, the practice often seemed to continue unabated, especially in the waters of the Indian Ocean off the eastern coast of Africa.

Philip Caday, alias Phillibert, Amand Clarensac, and Joseph Ann Tregrosse, were arraigned at the Old Bailey on Saturday to take trial for having feloniously taken a number of Negroes from the Mozambique Islands, on the coast of Africa, and carried them to the Isle de France, in the Mauritius, for the purpose of being dealt with as slaves, contrary to the statute etc. The *Magicienne* frigate was stationed off the Isle of France to suppress the traffic in slaves. The captain saw a schooner, of which the prisoners were part of the crew, in the harbour, and suspected it was in the slave trade. He sent some of his men in pursuit and it was discovered that 92 human beings had been landed for the purpose of sale. The prisoners were afterwards apprehended. They were found guilty and sentenced to three years' confinement in the House of Correction, and to hard labour.

Source: "*The Observer,* February 22, 1819," in *A Collection of Documents on the Slave Trade of East Africa,* ed. R. W. Beachey (London: Rex Collings, 1976).

DOCUMENT 42
ROBERT WALSH DESCRIBES CONDITIONS IN A BRAZILIAN SLAVE MARKET (1828)

During the nineteenth century, most European nations declared the end of the African slave trade, but transatlantic importations often continued because of Brazil's seemingly insatiable demand for new slaves. The following document examines the conditions typically found in the nineteenth-century slave market in Brazil.

The place where the great slave mart is held, is a long winding street called the Vallongo, which runs from the sea, at the northern extremity of the city. Almost every house in this place is a large warehouse, where the slaves are deposited, and customers go to purchase. These warerooms stand at each side of the street, and the poor creatures are exposed for sale like any other commodity. When a customer comes in, they are turned up before him; such as he wishes are handled by the purchaser in different parts, exactly as I have seen others feeling a calf; and the whole examination is the mere animal capability, without the remotest inquiry as to the moral quality, which a man no more thinks of, than if he was buying a dog or a mule. I have frequently seen Brazilian ladies at these sales. They go dressed, sit down, handle and examine their purchases, and bring them away with the most perfect indifference. I sometimes saw groups of well-dressed females here, shopping for slaves, exactly as I have seen English ladies amusing themselves at our bazaars.

The warerooms are spacious apartments, where sometimes three or four hundred slaves, of all ages and sexes are exhibited together. Round the room are benches on which the elder generally sit, and the middle is occupied by the younger, particularly females, who squat on the ground stowed close together, with their hands and chins resting on their knees. Their only covering is a small girdle of cross-barred cotton, tied round the waist.

The first time I passed through this street, I stood at the bars of the window looking through, when a cigano [street person] came and pressed me to enter. I was particularly attracted by a group of children, one of whom, a young girl, had something very pensive and engaging in her countenance. The cigano observing me look at her, whipped her up with a long rod, and bade her with a rough voice to come forward. It was quite affecting to see the poor timid shrinking child standing before me, in a state the most helpless and forlorn, that ever a being, endued, like myself, with a reasonable mind and an immortal soul, could be reduced to. Some of these girls have remarkably sweet and engaging countenances. Notwithstanding their dusky line, they look so modest, gentle and sensible, that you could not for a moment hesitate to acknowledge, that they are endued with a like feeling, a common nature, with your own daughters. The seller was about to put the child into all the attitudes, and display her person in the same way, as he would a man; but I declined the exhibition, and she shrunk timidly back to her place, and seemed glad to bide herself in the group that surrounded her.

The men were generally less interesting objects than the women; their countenances and hues were very varied, according to the part of the African coast from which they came; some were soot black, having a certain ferocity of aspect that indicated strong and fierce passions, like men who were darkly brooding over some deep-felt wrongs, and meditating revenge. When any one was ordered, he came forward with a sullen indifference, threw his arms over his head, stamped with his feet, shouted to show the soundness of his lungs, ran up and down the room, and was treated exactly like a horse, put through his paces at a repository; and when done, he was whipped to his stall.

The heads of the slaves, both male and female, were generally half shaved; the hair being left only on the fore part. A few of the females had cotton handkerchiefs tied round their heads, which with some little ornaments of native seed or shells, gave them a very engaging appearance. A number, particularly the males, were affected with eruptions of a white scurf which had a loathsome appearance, like leprosy. It was considered, however, a wholesome effort of nature, to throw off the effects of the salt provisions used during the voyage; and, in fact, it resembles exactly a saline concretion.

Many of them were lying stretched on the bare boards; and among the rest, mothers with young children at their breasts, of which they seemed passionately fond. They were all doomed to remain on the spot, like sheep in a pen, till they were sold; they had no apartment to retire to, no bed to repose on, no covering to protect them; they sit naked all day, and lie naked all night, on the bare boards, or benches where we saw them exhibited.

A great number of those who arrive at Rio are sent up the country, and we every day met cofilas [trains of slaves], such as Mungo Park describes in Africa, winding through the woods, as they travelled from place to place in the interior. They formed long processions, following one another in a file; the slave-merchant, distinguished by his large felt hat and poncho, brings up the rear on a mule, with a long lash in his hand. It was another subject of pity, to see groups of these poor creatures cowering together at night in the open ranchos [stables], drenched with cold rain, in a climate so much more frigid than their own.

Source: Robert Walsh, "Conditions in the Slave Market," in *A Documentary History of Brazil*, ed. E. Bradford Burns (New York: Alfred A. Knopf, 1966).

❧DOCUMENT 43❧
SLAVE CAPTAIN JOSEPH CRASSONS DE MEDEUIL ON THE EAST AFRICAN SLAVE TRADE

The illegal trade of Africans as slaves continued in eastern Africa well into the nineteenth century. As European powers made a concerted effort to monitor the slave trade in West Africa, the trade continued to flourish in the coastal waters of eastern Africa and in the waters of the Indian Ocean.

The stretch between Mozambique and Ibo is fairly thickly populated. It is there we go in search of our blacks. We trade for them at Kerimba, lbo and Mozambique, small islands detached from the coast and inaccurately marked on the map.

From Cape Delgado to Kilwa the coast is inhabited only by Moors and Arabs who take from it a prodigious number of blacks, particularly from the river Mongallo, a little-known river which flows through fertile and thickly populated country stretching a long way inland.

.... this country produces millet, indigo, superb cotton, silkier even than the cotton produced on the Ile de Bourbon, sugar cane, gums in abundance, brown cowries of the second sort which are currency at Jiddah and in Dahomey, besides elephant ivory which is very common, as are elephants, and lastly negroes—superb specimens if they are selected with care. This selection we cannot make ourselves, being at the discretion of the traders, who are now aware of our needs and who know that it is absolutely essential for us to sail at a given season in order to round the Cape of Good Hope. In addition to competition amongst ourselves the expeditions have never been properly thought out and always left to chance, and so it happens that three or four ships find themselves in the same place and crowd each other out. This would not happen if there were a properly organized body and the expeditions were planned to fit in with the seasons and the quantity of cargo and the means of using up surplus also planned, since it is not the business of seamen to concern themselves with correspondence and administration. To my knowledge, the trading that has been done in this port for the last three years, without counting traders not personally known to me, is as follows:

La Pintadet	Capt.	600	blacks	
La Victoire	La Touche	224	"	1st voyage
Les bons amis	Beguet	336	"	
La Sainaritaitte	Herpin	254	"	
La Créolle	Crassons	176	"	
La Victoire	La Touche	690	"	In his three voyages,
		230	"	3rd voyage
[omitted]	Berton	233	"	
La Grande Victoire	Michel	289	"	
La Thémis	Bertau	450	"	
La Grande Victoire	Michel	289	"	
La Créolle	Crassons	211	"	
La Thémis	Bertau	480	"	2d voyage
La Gde. Victoire	Capt. Rouilliard	250	"	
		4,193	"	

A total, to my knowledge, of 4,193, and certainly there must have been more in three years.

Source: Joseph Crassons de Medeuil, "The East African Coast, Select Documents," in *A Collection of Documents on the Slave Trade of East Africa,* ed. R. W. Beachey (London: Rex Collings, 1976).

❦DOCUMENT 44❦
CAPTAIN W. F. OWEN VISITS PORT QUELIMANE (1822)

Slave traders from Brazil often found it most desirable to acquire captives from East Africa in the early-nineteenth century. A visitor to one of the slave-trading entrepôts there described the methods used to conduct this trade.

From eleven to fourteen slave vessels come annually from Rio de Janeiro to this place, and return with four to five hundred slaves each on an average. They are purchased with blue dungaree, coloured cloths, arms, gun powder, brass and pewter, red coloured beads in imitation of coral, cutlery and various other articles. The free blacks of the country and banyans [merchants' agents] carry on the trade inland for their merchants: and the arrival of one of these people among the tribes with his pedlar's stock is the signal for the general warfare when the weak become the victim of the strong. To contain the slaves collected for sale every Portuguese house has an extensive yard or enclosure, called a barracon, generally surrounded by a lofty brick wall.

Source: W. F. Owen, "Narrative of the Voyages to Explore the Eastern Shores of Africa," in *A Collection of Documents on the Slave Trade of East Africa,* ed. R. W. Beachey (London: Rex Collings, 1976).

❦DOCUMENT 45❦
THE LOUISIANA SLAVE CODE OF 1824

Every state in the United States that had a slave population had a code enumerating the rights and responsibilities of slaves living within the state. These codes also described the legal extent to which slave-owners and their associates could discipline their slaves in order to maintain peace and security within the plantation districts.

ART. 172.—The rules prescribing the police and conduct to be observed with respect to slaves in this State, and the punishment of their crimes and offences, are fixed by special laws of the Legislature.

ART. 173.—The slave is entirely subject to the will of his master, who may correct and chastise him, though not with unusual rigor, nor so as to maim or mutilate him, or to expose him to the danger of loss of life, or to cause his death.

ART. 174.—The slave is incapable of making any kind of contract, except those which relate to his own emancipation.

ART. 175.—All that a slave possesses, belongs to his master; he possesses nothing of his own, except his peculium, that is to say, the sum of money, or moveable estate, which his master chooses he should possess.

ART. 176.—They can transmit nothing by succession or otherwise; but the succession of free persons related to them which they would have inherited had they been free, may pass through them to such of their descendants as may have acquired their liberty before the succession is opened.

ART. 177.—The slave is incapable of exercising any public office, or private trust; he cannot be tutor, curator, executor nor attorney; he cannot be a witness in either civil or criminal matters, except in cases provided for by particular laws. He cannot be a party in any civil action, either as plaintiff or defendant, except when he has to claim or prove his freedom.

ART. 178.—When slaves are prosecuted in the name of the State, for offences they have committed, notice must be given to their masters.

ART. 179.—Masters are bound by the acts of their slaves done by their command, as also by their transactions and dealings with respect to the business in which they have entrusted or employed them; but in case they should not have authorised or entrusted them, they shall be answerable only for so much as they have benefitted by the transaction.

ART. 180.—The master shall be answerable for all the damages occasioned by an offence or quasi-offence committed by his slave, independent of the punishment inflicted on the slave.

ART. 181.—The master however may discharge himself from such responsibility by abandoning his slave to the person injured; in which case such person shall sell such slave at public auction in the usual form, to obtain payment of the damages and costs; and the balance, if any, shall be returned to the master of the slave, who shall be completely discharged, although the price of the slave should not be sufficient to pay the whole amount of the damages and costs; provided that the master shall make the abandonment within three days after the judgment awarding such damages, shall have been rendered; provided also that it shall not be proved that the crime or offence was committed by his order; for in case of such proof the master shall be answerable for all damages resulting therefrom, whatever be the amount, without being admitted to the benefit of the abandonment.

ART. 182.—Slaves cannot marry without the consent of their masters, and their marriages do not produce any of the civil effects which result from such contract.

ART. 183.—Children born of a mother then in a state of slavery, whether married or not, follow the condition of their mother; they are consequently slaves and belong to the master of their mother.

ART. 184.—A master may manumit his slave in this State, either by an act inter vivos [between living persons] or by a disposition made in prospect of death, provided such manumission be made with the forms and under the conditions prescribed by law; but an enfranchisement, when made by a last will, must be express and formal, and shall not be implied by any other circumstances of the testament, such as a legacy, an institution of heir, testamentary executorship or other dispositions of this nature, which, in such case, shall be considered as if they had not been made.

ART. 185.—No one can emancipate his slave, unless the slave has attained the age of thirty years, and has behaved well at least for four years preceding his emancipation.

ART. 186.—The slave who has saved the life of his master, his master's wife, or one of his children, may be emancipated at any age.

ART. 187.—The master who wishes to emancipate his slave, is bound to make a declaration of his intentions to the judge of the parish where he resides; the judge must order notice of it to be published during forty days by advertisement posted at the door of the court house; and if, at the expiration of this delay, no opposition be made, he shall authorise the master to pass the act of emancipation.

ART. 188.—The act of emancipation imports an obligation on the part of the person granting it, to provide for the subsistence of the slave emancipated, if he should be unable to support himself.

ART. 189.—An emancipation once perfected, is irrevocable, on the part of the master or his heirs.

ART. 190.—Any enfranchisement made in fraud of creditors, or of the portion reserved by law to forced heirs is null and void; and such fraud shall be considered as proved, when it shall appear that at the moment of executing the enfranchisement, the person granting it had not sufficient property to pay his debts or to leave to his heirs the portion to them reserved by law; the same rule will apply if the slave thus manumitted, was specially mortgaged; but in this case the enfranchisement shall take effect, provided the slave or any one in his behalf shall pay the debt for which the mortgage was given.

ART. 191.—No master of slaves shall be compelled, either directly or indirectly, to enfranchise any of them, except only in cases where the enfranchisement shall be made for services rendered to the State, by virtue of an act of the Legislature of the same, and on the State satisfying to the master the appraised value of the manumitted slave.

ART. 192.—In like manner no master shall be compelled to sell his slave, but in one of two cases, to wit: the first, when being only co-proprietor of the slave, his co-proprietor demands the sale in order to make partition of the property; the second, when the master shall be convicted of cruel treatment of his slave, and the judge shall deem proper to pronounce, besides the penalty established for such cases, that the slave shall be sold at public auction, in order to place him out of the reach of the power which his master has abused.

ART. 193.—The slave who has acquired the right of being free at a future time, is from that time, capable of receiving by testament or donation. Property given or devised to him must be preserved for him, in order to be delivered to him in kind, when his emancipation shall take place. In the mean time it must be administered by a curator.

ART. 194.—The slave for years 2 cannot be transported out of the State. He can appear in court to claim the protection of the laws in cases where there are good reasons for believing that it is intended to carry him out of the State.

ART. 195.—If the slave for years dies before the time fixed for his enfranchisement, the gifts or legacies made him revert to the donor or to the heirs of the donor.

ART. 196.—The child born of a woman after she has acquired the right of being free at a future time, follows the condition of its mother, and becomes free at the time fixed for her enfranchisement, even if the mother should die before that time.

Source: State of Louisiana, "The Louisiana Slave Code of 1824," in *A Documentary History of Slavery in North America*, ed. Willie Lee Rose (New York: Oxford University Press, 1976).

⮞DOCUMENT 46⮜
A LETTER BY SIMÓN BOLÍVAR TO FRANCISCO DE PAULA SANTANDER

The liberation of many republics in Central and South America from Spanish colonial control was often followed by the abolition of slavery. Revolutionary leaders like Simón Bolívar used the promise of emancipation as a means of attracting slaves to the cause of revolutionary struggle.

Magdalena, July 8, 1826

My dear General:

Yesterday, I received your letter of May 6, and various newspapers and private communications that have kept me awake all night, not because they add anything to what I already know, but because they confirm my previous conviction that all is lost. Neither a general federation nor a local constitution can restrain these unruly slaves: particularly now that every one pursues his own ends.

I regard the Congress of the Isthmus as a theatrical play, and I view our laws as did Solon, who believed that laws only served to burden the weak without restraining the strong. While these thoughts keep passing through my mind, the newspaper writers proclaim that heroes are subject to the laws and that principles take precedence over men. What an ideology! This is to be the celestial land where laws personified will engage in combat in place of heroes, while principles, like the Fates, will direct affairs and govern man. Virgins and saints, angels and cherubin will be the citizens of this new paradise. Bravo! Bravíssimo! Let those legions of Milton march on to stem the course of Páez insurrection, and, since principles govern rather than men, you and I are no longer needed in any capacity. This is the point I have wished for in this celebrated tragedy, a thousand times repeated through the centuries, yet ever new to the blind and the stupid, who observe nothing until they are themselves affected. What leaders!

General Páez has written me, under date of April 6, and he has sent me other letters which describe the threatening situation that confronts him. All this, it seems, is the work of two or three former slaves of Morillo, who are now their liberators' masters.

I am very much pleased that the Congress has been able to meet to enact measures in the present crisis. It can rely upon all those who are dependent upon me, but not upon me personally. I want no more civil wars. I have experienced four in fourteen years, and censure inevitably falls upon both the vanquished and the victor. I repeat, all is lost if Páez continues upon his path of insurrection, for, when any object is falsely based, the slightest mishap causes its downfall. He who falls is indeed lost. I do not care to be that person. I am weary of exercising this abominable discretionary power when I am convinced, to the very marrow of my bones, that our America can only be ruled through a well-managed; shrewd despotism. We are far from emulating the happy times of Athens and Rome, and we must not compare ourselves in any way to anything European. Our origins have been of the most unwholesome sort: All our antecedents are enveloped in the black cloak of crime. We are the abominable offspring of those raging beasts that came to America to waste her blood and to breed with their victims before sacrificing them. Later, the illegitimate offspring of these unions commingled with the offspring of slaves transplanted from Africa. With such racial mixtures and such a moral history, can we place laws above heroes and principles above men? Very well then, let these ideologically minded gentlemen govern and fight and we shall again witness the beautiful ideal of a Haiti and see a breed of new Robespierres become the worthy magistrates of this fearful liberty. I repeat: all is lost; and, since everything progresses in a manner counter to my ideas and opinions, let them manage without me. Should the government or the Congress summon me, I shall go to Colombia; then, from Guayaquil, I will proclaim, in solemn tones, what I have just stated in this letter.

I think that matters cannot possibly be reconstituted as they were before, as those who know only how to continue in the Spanish fashion will doubtless desire. No possible benefit would result from mere legal reforms. It might be said that we already have too many laws, especially laws modeled after those of the Spanish liberals. So it is, but what does this signify? Where is there an army of occupation to impose order? Africa?—we shall have more and more of Africa. I do not say this lightly, for anyone with a white skin who escapes will be fortunate. The sad part of it all is that the ideologists, who are the vilest and most cowardly of men, will be the last to perish. Long accustomed to the yoke, they will bear it patiently, though imposed by their own slaves. The masterminds of this tempest—Pérez, Michelena, de Francisco, and all those other wretches—will fan the first fires of the pyre that will consume our remains. Their one reward will be that they will go last. Never has the tocsin been sounded in vain; everyone hears it, and all are preparing for combat, friend and foe alike. As the legislators did the trumpeting, their call will not be ignored, as in Caracas, where the voice of the law has gone unheeded by the inhabitants and where, instead, whoever has conscientiously attempted to comply with it has suffered punishment—a crime worthy of that heavenly land!

I am sending you the papers from Bolivia that report what took place at the installation of the Congress. I have told General Sucre that the birth and existence of Bolivia is a hymn to wisdom. Most couples have happy weddings . . . but then. . . .

I know of the arrival of the French agent.

Revenga tells me that you are anxious for him to become Minister of Finance, a choice that I approve, though I feel that everything we do today is of no value whatsoever. In England the failure of Colombia's bankers is only one out of some six hundred similar bankruptcies.

I am your devoted friend,

BOLÍVAR

Source: Simón Bolívar, "To Francisco De Paula Santander, Vice President of Colombia," in *Selected Writings of Bolivar, Volume II—1823–1830,* ed. Harold A. Bierck, Jr. (New York: Colored Press, 1951).

∽DOCUMENT 47∽
THE FIRST NEGRO NEWSPAPER'S OPENING EDITORIAL (1827)

Freedom's Journal was the first African-American newspaper to be published in the United States. In the following document, publishers Samuel Cornish and John B. Russwurm describe their purpose and intent in establishing this newspaper.

TO OUR PATRONS

In presenting our first number to our Patrons, we feel all the diffidence of persons entering upon a new and untried line of business. But a moment's reflection upon the noble objects, which we have in view by the publication of this journal; the expediency of its appearance at this time, when so many schemes are in action concerning our people encourage us to come boldly before an enlightened publick. For we believe, that a paper devoted to the dissimination of useful knowledge among our brethren, and to their moral and religious improvement, must meet with the cordial approbation of every friend to humanity.

The peculiarities of this Journal, renders it important that we should advertise to the world our motives by which we are actuated, and the objects which we contemplate.

We wish to plead our own cause. Too long have others spoken for us. Too long has the publick been deceived by misrepresentations, in things which concern us dearly, though in the estimation of some mere trifles; for though there are many in society who exercise towards us benevolent feelings; still (with sorrow we confess it) there are others who make it their business to enlarge upon the least trifle, which tends to the discredit of any person of colour; and pronounce anathemas and denounce our whole body for the misconduct of this guilty one. We are aware that there are many instances of vice among us, but we avow that it is because no one has taught its subjects to be virtuous; many instances of poverty, because no sufficient efforts accommodated to minds contracted by slavery, and deprived of early education have been made, to teach them how to husband their hard earnings, and to secure to themselves comfort.

Education being an object of the highest importance to the welfare of society, we shall endeavour to present just and adequate views of it, and to urge upon our brethren the necessity and expediency of training their children, while young, to habits of industry, and thus forming them for becoming useful members of society. It is surely time that we should awake from this lethargy of years, and make a concentrated effort for the education of our youth. We form a spoke in the human wheel, and it is necessary that we should understand our pendence [dependence] on the different parts, and theirs on us, in order to perform our part with propriety.

Though not desiring of dictating, we shall feel it our incumbent duty to dwell occasionally upon the general principles and rules of economy. The world has grown too enlightened, to estimate any man's character by his personal appearance. Though all men acknowledge the excellency of Franklin's maxims, yet comparatively few practise upon them. We may deplore when it is too late, the neglect of these self-evident truths, but it avails little to mourn. Ours will be the task of admonishing our brethren on these points.

The civil rights of a people being of the greatest value, it shall ever be our duty to vindicate our brethren, when oppressed; and to lay the case before the publick. We shall also urge upon our brethren, (who are qualified by the laws of the different states) the expediency of using their elective franchise; and of making an independent use of the same. We wish them not to become the tools of party.

And as much time is frequently lost, and wrong principles instilled, by the perusal of works of trivial importance, we shall consider it a part of our duty to recommend to our young readers, such authors as will not only enlarge their stock of useful knowledge, but such as will also serve to stimulate them to higher attainments in science.

We trust also, that through the columns of the FREEDOM'S JOURNAL, many practical pieces, having for their bases, the improvement of our brethren, will be presented to them, from the pens of many of our respected friends, who have kindly promised their assistance.

It is our earnest wish to make our journal a medium of intercourse between our brethren in the different states of this great confederacy: that through its columns an expression of our sentiments, on many interesting subjects which concern us, may be offered to the publick: that plans which apparently are beneficial may be candidly discussed and properly weighed; if worth, receive our cordial approbation; if not, our marked disapprobation.

Useful knowledge of every kind, and everything that relates to Africa, shall find a ready admission into our columns; and as that vast continent becomes daily more known, we trust that many things will come to light, proving that the natives of it are neither so ignorant nor stupid as they have generally been supposed to be.

And while these important subjects shall occupy the columns of the FREEDOM'S JOURNAL, we would not be unmindful of our brethren who are still in the iron fetters of bondage. They are our kindred by all the ties of nature; and though but little can be effected by us, still let our sympathies be poured forth, and our prayers in their behalf, ascend to Him who is able to succour them.

From the press and the pulpit we have suffered much by being incorrectly represented. Men whom we equally love and admire have not hesitated to represent us disadvantageously, without becoming personally acquainted with the true state of things, nor discerning between virtue and vice among us. The virtuous part of our people feel themselves sorely aggrieved under the existing state of things— they are not appreciated.

Our vices and our degradation are ever arrayed against us, but our virtues are passed by unnoticed. And what is still more lamentable, our friends, to whom we concede all the principles of humanity and religion, from these very causes seem to have fallen into the current of popular feeling and are imperceptibly floating on the stream—actually living in the practice of prejudice, while they abjure it in theory, and feel it not in their hearts. Is it not very desirable that such should know more of our actual condition; and of our efforts and feelings, that in forming or advocating plans for our amelioration, they may do it more understandingly? In the spirit of candor and humility we intend by a simple representation of facts to lay our case before the public, with a view to arrest the progress of prejudice, and to shield ourselves against the consequent evils. We wish to conciliate all and to irritate none, yet we must be firm and unwavering in our principles, and persevering in our efforts.

If ignorance, poverty and degradation have hitherto been our unhappy lot; has the Eternal decree gone forth, that our race alone are to remain in this state, while knowledge and civilization are shedding their enlivening rays over the rest of the human family? The recent travels of Denham and Clapperton in the interior of Africa, and the interesting narrative which they have published; the establishment of the republic of Hayti after years of sanguinary warfare; its subsequent progress in all the arts of civilization; and the advancement of liberal ideas in South America, where despotism has given place to free governments, and where many of our brethren now fill important civil and military stations, prove the contrary.

The interesting fact that there are FIVE HUNDRED THOUSAND free persons of colour, one half of whom might peruse, and the whole be benefitted by the publication of the journal; that no publication, as yet, has been devoted exclusively to their improvement—that many selections from approved standard authors, which are within the reach of few, may occasionally be made—and more important still, that this large body of our citizens have no public channel—all serve to prove the real necessity, at present, for the appearance of the FREEDOM'S JOURNAL.

It shall ever be our desire so to conduct the editorial department of our paper as to give offence to none of our patrons; as nothing is farther from us than to make it the advocate of any partial views, either in politics or religion. What few days we can number, have been devoted to the improvement of our brethren; and it is our earnest wish that the remainder may be spent in the same delightful service.

In conclusion, whatever concerns us as a people, will ever find a ready admission into the FREEDOM'S JOURNAL, interwoven with all the principal news of the day.

And while every thing in our power shall be performed to support the character of our journal, we would respectfully invite our numerous friends to assist by their communications, and our coloured brethren to strengthen our hands by their subscriptions, as our labour is one of common cause, and worthy of their consideration and support. And we most earnestly solicit the latter, that if at any time we should seem to be zealous, or too pointed in the inculcation of any important lesson, they will remember, that they are equally interested in the cause in which we are engaged, and attribute our zeal to the peculiarities of our situation; and our earnest engagedness in their well-being.

Source: Samuel Cornish and John B. Russwurm, "The First Negro Newspaper's Opening Editorial, 1827," in *A Documentary History of the Negro People in the United States, Volume I,* ed. Herbert Aptheker (New York: Carol Publishing Group, 1951).

∞DOCUMENT 48∞
EXCERPT FROM THE LIBERATOR (1831)

William Lloyd Garrison became the most famous American abolitionist because of his role as editor of the Liberator, *the most successful and longest-running abolitionist weekly in the United States. The following editorial offers a typical sample of the antislavery rhetoric that regularly appeared in the pages of Garrison's newspaper.*

In the month of August, I issued proposals for publishing *The Liberator* in Washington city; but the enterprise, though hailed in different sections of the country, was palsied by public indifference. Since that time, the removal of the *Genius of Universal Emancipation* to the Seat of Government has rendered less imperious the establishment of a similar periodical in that quarter.

During my recent tour for the purpose of exciting the minds of the people by a series of discourses on the subject of slavery, every place that I visited gave fresh evidence of the fact, that a greater revolution in public sentiment was to be effected in the free states—and particularly in *New-England*—than at the south. I found contempt more bitter, opposition more active, detraction more relentless, prejudice more stubborn, and apathy more frozen, than among the slave owners themselves. Of course, there were individual exceptions to the contrary. This state of things afflicted, but did not dishearten me. I determined, at every hazard, to lift up the standard of emancipation in the eyes of the nation, *within sight of Bunker Hill and in the birth place of liberty.* That standard is now unfurled; and long may it float, unhurt by the spoliations of time or the missiles of a

desperate foe yea, till every chain be broken, and every bondman set free! Let southern oppressors tremble—let their secret abettors tremble—let their northern apologists tremble—let all the enemies of the persecuted blacks tremble.

I deem the publication of my original Prospectus unnecessary, as it has obtained a wide circulation. The principles therein inculcated will be steadily pursued in this paper, excepting that I shall not array myself as the political partisan of any man. In defending the great cause of human rights, I wish to derive the assistance of all religions and of all parties.

Assenting to the "self-evident truth" maintained in the American Declaration of Independence, "that all men are created equal, and endowed by their Creator with certain inalienable rights—among which are life, liberty and the pursuit of happiness," I shall strenuously contend for the immediate enfranchisement of our slave population. In Park-street Church, on the Fourth of July, 1829, in an address on slavery, I unreflectingly assented to the popular but pernicious doctrine of gradual abolition. I seize this opportunity to make a full and unequivocal recantation, and thus publicly to ask pardon of my God, of my country, and of my brethren the poor slaves, for having uttered a sentiment so full of timidity, injustice and absurdity. A similar recantation, from my pen, was published in the *Genius of Universal Emancipation* at Baltimore, in September, 1829. My conscience is now satisfied.

I am aware that many object to the severity of my language; but is there not cause for severity? I *will* be as harsh as truth, and as uncompromising as justice. On this subject, I do not wish to think, or speak, or write, with moderation. No! no! Tell a man whose house is on fire, to give a moderate alarm; tell him to moderately rescue his wife from the hands of the ravisher; tell the mother to gradually extricate her babe from the fire into which it has fallen;—but urge me not to use moderation in a cause like the present. I am in earnest—I will not equivocate I will not excuse—I will not retreat a single inch—AND I WILL BE HEARD. The apathy of the people is enough to make every statue leap from its pedestal, and to hasten the resurrection of the dead.

It is pretended, that I am retarding the cause of emancipation, by the coarseness of my invective, and the precipitancy of my measures. *The charge is not true.* On this question my influence,—humble as it is,—is felt at this moment to a considerable extent, and shall be felt in coming years—not perniciously, but beneficially—not as a curse, but as a blessing; and posterity will bear testimony that I was right. I desire to thank God, that he enables me to disregard "the fear of man which bringeth a snare," and to speak his truth in its simplicity and power.

And here I close with this fresh dedication:

"Oppression! I have seen thee, face to face,
And met thy cruel eye and cloudy brow;
But thy soul-withering glance I fear not now—
For dread to prouder feelings doth give place
Of deep abhorrence! Scorning the disgrace
Of slavish knees that at thy footstool bow,
I also kneel—but with far other bow
Do hail thee and thy herd of hirelings base:—
I swear, while life-blood warms my throbbing
    veins,
Still to oppose and thwart, with heart and hand,
Thy brutalizing sway—'till Afric's chains
Are burst, and Freedom rules the rescued land,—
Trampling Oppression and his iron rod:
Such is the vow I take—so HELP ME GOD!"

Source: William Lloyd Garrison, *"The Liberator,*
Vol. I., No. 1. January 1, 1831," in *Documents of
American History,* ed. Henry Steele Commager
(New York: Appleton-Century-Crofts, 1963).

◆DOCUMENT 49◆
FREDERICK DOUGLASS AND
THE SLAVE-BREAKER (1834)

Frederick Douglass was the best-known black aboli-
tionist during the antebellum era. In the following
passage, Douglass describes the episode that led to
his decision in 1834 to flee from slavery in Maryland
and seek his fortune as a free man in the northern
states. The account was published in 1845.

If at any one time of my life, more than another, I
was made to drink the bitterest dregs of slavery, that
time was during the first six months of my stay with
this man Covey. We worked all weathers. It was
never too hot, or too cold; it could never rain, blow,
snow, or hail too hard for us to work in the field.
Work, work, work, was scarcely more than the order
of the day than of the night. The longest days were
too short for him, and the shortest nights were too
long for him. I was somewhat unmanageable at the
first, but a few months of this discipline tamed me.
Mr. Covey succeeded in breaking me—in body, soul,
and spirit. My natural elasticity was crushed; my intellect languished; the disposition to read departed,
the cheerful spark that lingered about my eye died
out; the dark night of slavery closed in upon me, and
behold a man transformed to a brute!

Sunday was my only leisure time. I spent this under
some large tree, in a sort of beast-like stupor between
sleeping and waking. At times I would rise up and a
flash of energetic freedom would dart through my
soul, accompanied with a faint beam of hope that
flickered for a moment, and then vanished. I sank
down again mourning over my wretched condition. I
was sometimes tempted to take my life and that of

Covey, but was prevented by a combination of hope
and fear. My sufferings, as I remember them now,
seem like a dream rather than like a stern reality.

Our house stood within a few rods of the Chesapeake bay, whose broad bosom was ever white with
sails from every quarter of the habitable globe.
Those beautiful vessels, robed in white, and so delightful to the eyes of free men, were to me so many
shrouded ghosts, to terrify and torment me with
thoughts of my wretched condition. I have often, in
the deep stillness of a summer's Sabbath, stood all
alone upon the banks of that noble bay, and traced,
with saddened heart and tearful eye, the countless
number of sails moving off to the mighty ocean. The
sight of these always affected me powerfully. My
thoughts would compel utterance; and there, with no
audience but the Almighty, I would pour out my
soul's complaint in my rude way with an apostrophe
to the moving multitude of ships. . . .

I shall never be able to narrate half the mental experience through which it was my lot to pass, during
my stay at Covey's. I was completely wrecked,
changed, and bewildered; goaded almost to madness
at one time, and at another reconciling myself to my
wretched condition. All the kindness I had received at
Baltimore, all my former hopes and aspirations for
usefulness in the world, and even the happy moments
spent in the exercises of religion, contrasted with my
then present lot, served but to increase my anguish.

I suffered bodily as well as mentally. I had neither
sufficient time in which to eat, or to sleep, except on
Sundays. The overwork, and the brutal chastise-
ments of which I was the victim, combined with that
ever-gnawing and soul devouring thought—"I am a
slave—and a slave for life—a slave with no rational
ground to hope for freedom"—rendered me a living
embodiment of mental and physical wretchedness.

Source: Frederick Douglass, "Frederick Douglass and
the Slave-Breaker, 1834," in *A Documentary History*
of the Negro People in the United States, Volume I,
ed. Herbert Aptheker (New York: Carol Publishing
Group, 1951).

◆DOCUMENT 50◆
POPE GREGORY XVI, IN SUPREMO (1839)

For centuries, the practice of slavery had endured
with the blessing and approval of the Roman
Catholic Church. It was not until 1839, after Great
Britain had abolished slavery throughout the British
Empire, that church leaders stated their opposition
to the African slave trade and to the practice of slav-
ery itself.

Placed at the supreme height of the Apostolate, and
although no merits of our own assisting, vicegerents

of Jesus Christ, the Son of God, who, by reason of his exceeding great charity, having been made man, hath also vouchsafed to die for the redemption of the world, we consider that it pertaineth to our pastoral solicitude that we should thoroughly endeavor to turn away the faithful from the inhuman traffic in negroes, or any other class of men.

When, indeed, the light of the gospel first began to be diffused, those wretched persons, who, at that time, in such great number went down into the most rigorous slavery, principally by occasion of wars, felt their condition very much alleviated among the Christians. For the apostles, inspired by the divine Spirit, taught, in fact, the slaves themselves to obey their carnal masters as Christ, and to do the will of God from the heart; but they commanded the masters to act well towards their slaves, and to do to them what is just and equal, and to forbear threatenings; knowing that there is a Master both of those and of themselves in the heavens, and that with Him there is no respect of persons.

Universally, however, since sincere charity to all would most strenuously be recommended by the law of the gospel, and Christ, our lord, could declare that he would esteem as done or denied to himself whatever of kindness or mercy might be done or denied to the least and to the poor, it easily ensued therefrom, not only that Christians should regard their slaves, and especially Christians, as brethren, but also that they should be more prone to present with liberty those who might deserve it; which, indeed, Gregory Nyssa indicates to have been first habitually done on the occasion of the paschal solemnities. Nor were wanting some who, excited by more ardent charity, cast themselves into chains that they might redeem others, of whom that apostolic man, our predecessor, Clement I, the same of most holy memory, testifies that he had known many. Therefore, in the course of time, the darkness of pagan superstitions being more fully dissipated, and the morals also of the ruder nations being softened by means of faith working by charity, the matter progressed so far that now, for many ages, no slaves can be held among many Christian nations. But, grieving much we say it, there were subsequently, from the very number of the faithful, those who, basely blinded by the lust of sordid gain, in remote and distant lands, reduced to slavery Indians, Negroes, or other miserable persons; or, by traffic begun and extended in those who had been made captive by others, did not hesitate to aid the shameful crime of the latter. By no means, indeed, did many, Roman Pontiffs of glorious memory, our predecessors, omit severely to rebuke, according to their duty, the conduct of those persons as dangerous to their own spiritual safety, and disgraceful to the Christian name; from which, also, they perceived this to follow, that the nations of infidels would be more and more

hardened to hate our true religion. To which refer the apostolic letter of Paul III, of the 29th day of May, 1537, given under the Fisherman's Ring to the cardinal archbishop of Toledo, and another, subsequently, more ample than the former, by Urban VIII, given on the 22d day of April, 1639, to the Collector of the Rights of the Apostolic Chamber in Portugal, in which letter they are by name most severely censured who should dare or presume to reduce to slavery the western or southern Indians, to sell, to buy, to exchange, or give them away, to separate them from their wives and children, or spoil them of their property and goods, to conduct or send them to other places, or in any manner to deprive them of liberty, or retain them in slavery, and also to afford to those who do the aforesaid things, counsel, aid, favor or assistance, upon any pretext or studied excuse, or to preach or teach that it is lawful, or in any other mode to cooperate in the premises. These ordinances of the said pontiffs, Benedict XIV, afterwards confirmed and renewed by a new apostolic letter to the Bishops of Brazil, and of certain other regions, given on the 20th day of December, 1741, by which he excited the solicitude of those prelates to the same end. Still earlier, more-over, another predecessor of ours, more ancient than these, Pius II, when, in his time, the dominion of the Portuguese was extended into Guinea, a region of the negroes, gave a letter on the 7th day of October, 1462, to the bishop of Rubi who was about to proceed thither, in which he not only conferred on that prelate proper faculties for exercising his sacred ministry in that region with greater fruit, but, on the same occasion, animadverted severely against those Christians who dragged the neophytes into slavery. And, in our times, also, Pius VII, led by the same spirit of religion and charity as his predecessors, sedulously interposed his offices with influential persons, that the traffic in negroes should at length cease entirely among Christians. These ordinances and cares of our predecessors, indeed, by the aid of God, profited not a little in protecting the Indians and other persons aforesaid from the cruelty of invaders or the cupidity of Christian merchants; not so much, however, that this holy see could rejoice in the full success of its efforts in that behalf; since, on the contrary, the traffic in negroes, although in some degree diminished, is yet, hitherto, carried on by many Christians. Wherefore WE, desiring to turn away so great a reproach as this from all the boundaries of Christians, and the whole matter being maturely weighed, certain cardinals of the holy Roman church, our venerable brethren being also called into council, treading in the footsteps of our predecessors, with apostolic authority, do vehemently admonish and adjure in the Lord all believers in Christ, of whatsoever condition, that no one hereafter may dare unjustly to molest Indians, negroes, or other men of this sort; or to spoil them of their goods; or to reduce them to slavery; or to extend help or favor to others who perpetrate such things against them; or to exercise that inhuman trade by which negroes, as if they were not men, but mere animals, howsoever reduced into slavery, are, without any distinction, contrary to the laws of justice and humanity, bought, sold, and doomed sometimes to the most severe and exhausting labors; and, moreover, the hope of gain being by that trade proposed to the first captors of the negroes, dissensions, also, and, as it were, perpetual wars are fomented in their countries. We, indeed, with apostolic authority, do reprobate all the aforesaid actions as utterly unworthy of the Christian name and, by the same apostolic authority, do strictly prohibit and interdict that any ecclesiastic or lay person shall presume to defend that very trade in negroes as lawful under any pretext or studied excuse, or otherwise to preach, or in any manner, publicly or privately, to teach contrary to those things which WE have charged in this, our Apostolic Letter. But that this, our same letter, may be more easily notorious to all, nor any one may be able to allege ignorance of it, we decree and order it to be published, as is customary, by one of our cursitors, at the doors of the church of the Prince of the Apostles, of the Apostolic Chancery, and of the General Court upon Mount Citorio, and at [the line] of the Campo di Fiora de urbe, and the copies to be fixed there.

Given at Rome, at St. Mary Major's, under the Fisherman's Ring on the 3d day of December, 1839, in the ninth year of our pontificate.

ALOISIUS CARDINAL LAMBRUSCHINI.

Source: Gregory XVI (Bartolomeo Alberto Cappellari), "Apostolic Letter of Our Most Holy Lord Gregory XVI, by Divine Providence, Pope: Concerning the Not Carrying on the Trade in Negroes," in *Letters of the Late Bishop England to the Hon. John Forsyth, on the Subject of Domestic Slavery: To Which Are Prefixed Copies, in Latin And English, of the Pope's Apostolic Letter, Concerning the African Slave Trade, with Some Introductory Remarks, etc.,* ed. John Murphy (New York: Negro Universities Press, 1969).

❧DOCUMENT 51❧
SOLOMON NORTHUP DESCRIBES A SLAVE AUCTION

Solomon Northup, a free black who was kidnapped and sold into slavery, describes a slave auction that he witnessed in Louisiana. Northup labored as a slave for 12 years until he was eventually freed because of the intervention of northern abolitionists who had learned about the circumstances of his captivity.

In the first place we were required to wash thoroughly, and those with beards to shave. We were then furnished with a new suit each, cheap, but clean. The men had hat, coat, shirt, pants and shoes; the women frocks of calico, and handkerchief to bind about their heads. We were now conducted into a large room in the front part of the building to which the yard was attached, in order to be properly trained, before the admission of customers. The men were arranged on one side of the room, the women at the other. The tallest was placed at the head of the row, then the next tallest, and so on in the order of their respective heights. Emily was at the foot of the line of women. Freeman [Theophilus Freeman, owner of the slave pen] charged us to remember our places; exhorted us to appear smart and lively,— sometimes threatening, and again, holding out various inducements. During the day he exercised us in the art of "looking smart," and of moving to our places with exact precision.

After being fed, in the afternoon, we were again paraded and made to dance. Bob, a colored boy, who had some time belonged to Freeman, played on the violin. Standing near him, I made bold to inquire if he could play the "Virginia Reel." He answered he could not, and asked me if I could play. Replying in the affirmative, he handed me the violin. I struck up a tune, and finished it. Freeman ordered me to continue playing, and seemed well pleased, telling Bob that I far excelled him—a remark that seemed to grieve my musical companion very much.

Next day many customers called to examine Freeman's "new lot." The latter gentleman was very loquacious, dwelling at much length upon our several good points and qualities. He would make us hold up our heads, walk briskly back and forth, while customers would feel of our hands and arms and bodies, turn us about, ask us what we could do, make us open our mouths and show our teeth, precisely as a jockey examines a horse which he is about to barter for or purchase. Sometimes a man or woman was taken back to the small house in the yard, stripped, and inspected more minutely. Scars upon a slave's back were considered evidence of a rebellious or unruly spirit, and hurt his sale.

An old gentleman, who said he wanted a coachman, appeared to take a fancy to me. From his conversation with Burch [Freeman's business associate], I learned he was a resident in the city. I very much desired that he would buy me, because I conceived it would not be difficult to make my escape from New Orleans on some northern vessel. Freeman asked him fifteen hundred dollars for me. The old gentleman insisted it was too much as times were very hard. Freeman, however, declared that I was sound of health, of a good constitution, and intelligent. He made it a point to enlarge upon my musical attainments. The old gentleman argued quite adroitly that there was nothing extraordinary about the Negro, and finally, to my regret, went out, saying he would call again. During the day, however, a number of sales were made. David and Caroline were purchased together by a Natchez planter. They left us, grinning broadly, and in a most happy state of mind, caused by the fact of their not being separated. Sethe was sold to a planter of Baton Rouge, her eyes flashing with anger as she was led away.

The same man also purchased Randall. The little fellow was made to jump, and run across the floor, and perform many other feats, exhibiting his activity and condition. All the time the trade was going on, Eliza was crying aloud, and wringing her hands. She besought the man not to buy him, unless he also bought herself and Emily. She promised, in that case, to be the most faithful slave that ever lived. The man answered that he could not afford it, and then Eliza burst into a paroxysm of grief, weeping plaintively. Freeman turned round to her, savagely, with his whip in his uplifted hand, ordering her to stop her noise, or he would flog her. He would not have such work—such snivelling; and unless she ceased that minute, he would take her to the yard and give her a hundred lashes. Yes, he would take the nonsense out of her pretty quick—if he didn't, might he be d—d. Eliza shrunk before him, and tried to wipe away her tears, but it was all in vain. She wanted to be with her children, she said, the little time she had to live. All the frowns and threats of Freeman, could not wholly silence the afflicted mother. She kept on begging and beseeching them, most piteously, not to separate the three. Over and over again she told them how she loved her boy. A great many times she repeated her former promises—how very faithful and obedient she would be; how hard she would labor day and night, to the last moment of her life, if he would only buy them all together. But it was of no avail; the man could not afford it. The bargain was agreed upon, and Randall must go alone. Then Eliza ran to him; embraced him passionately; kissed him again and again; told him to remember her—all the while her tears falling in the boy's face like rain.

Freeman damned her, calling her a blubbering, bawling wench, and ordered her to go to her place, and behave herself, and be somebody. He swore he wouldn't stand such stuff but a little longer. He would soon give her something to cry about, if she was not mighty careful, and that she might depend upon.

The planter from Baton Rouge, with his new purchase, was ready to depart.

"Don't cry, mama. I will be a good boy. Don't cry," said Randall, looking back, as they passed out of the door.

What has become of the lad, God knows. It was a mournful scene indeed. I would have cried myself if I had dared.

Source: Solomon Northup, "A Slave Auction Described by a Slave," in *A Documentary History of the Negro People in the United States, Volume I,* ed. Herbert Aptheker (New York: Carol Publishing Group, 1951).

❧DOCUMENT 52❧
EXCERPTS FROM LIEUTENANT BARNARD AFTER SEIZING THE PROGRESSO NEAR QUELIMANE (1843)

Occasionally, European naval vessels on the high seas stopped and searched vessels that were illegally transporting Africans as slaves to the Americas. The following account describes the wretched conditions of the Africans aboard one of the vessels that was liberated in this fashion.

. . . the slaves broke adrift and broke open the casks of aqua ardiente [brandy], which some of them drank in large quantities: others took salt water, salt beef and pork and raw fowls, in consequence of which fifty died the first night, which unfortunately was squally; to save the vessel the poor wretches were obliged to be kept below or run the risk of being washed overboard.

We saw poor sickly skeletons lying on the deck, evidently dying and much disfigured by having been trodden on or crushed underneath by the others: they could just gasp, and now and then open their lips whilst an orange was squeezed on them. The others were all covered with craw-craws and itch, and were scratching large sores all over their bodies and howling like maniacs for water. I went on the slave deck, and half the blacks were then on it, who gave their sign of welcome by clapping their hands in concert.

Source: Lieutenant Barnard, "Three Years Cruise in the Mozambique Channel for Suppression of the Slave Trade," in *A Collection of Documents on the Slave Trade of East Africa,* ed. R. W. Beachey (London: Rex Collings, 1976).

❧DOCUMENT 53❧
THE SLAVE MUST THROW OFF THE SLAVE-HOLDER, HENRY HIGHLAND GARNET (1843)

Henry Highland Garnet, a black abolitionist in the United States, believed that nothing short of insurrection could help the slaves in the southern states achieve emancipation. Such views were considered extreme by most other abolitionists of the era.

Brethren and Fellow Citizens
Your brethren of the North, East, and West have been accustomed to meet together in National Conventions, to sympathize with each other, and to weep

over your unhappy condition. In these meetings we have addressed all classes of the free, but we have never, until this time, sent a word of consolation and advice to you. We have been contented in sitting still and mourning over your sorrows, earnestly hoping that before this day your sacred liberty would have been restored. But, we have hoped in vain. Years have rolled on, and tens of thousands have been borne on streams of blood and tears, to the shores of eternity. While you have been oppressed, we have also been partakers with you; nor can we be free while you are enslaved. We, therefore, write to you as being bound with you.

Many of you are bound to us, not only by the ties of a common humanity, but we are connected by the more tender relations of parents, wives, husbands, children, brothers, and sisters, and friends. As such we most affectionately address you.

Slavery has fixed a deep gulf between you and us, and while it shuts out from you the relief and consolation which your friends would willingly render, it affects and persecutes you with a fierceness which we might not expect to see in the fiends of hell. But still the Almighty Father of mercies has left to us a glimmering ray of hope, which shines out like a lone star in a cloudy sky. Mankind are becoming wiser, and better—the oppressor's power is fading, and you, every day, are becoming better informed, and more numerous. Your grievances, brethren, are many. We shall not attempt, in this short address, to present to the world all the dark catalogue of this nation's sins, which have been committed upon an innocent people. Nor is it indeed necessary, for you feel them from day to day, and all the civilized world look upon them with amazement.

Two hundred and twenty-seven years ago, the first of our injured race were brought to the shores of America. They came not with glad spirits to select their homes in the New World. They came not with their own consent, to find an unmolested enjoyment of the blessings of this fruitful soil. The first dealings they had with men calling themselves Christians, exhibited to them the worst features of corrupt and sordid hearts; and convinced them that no cruelty is too great, no villainy and no robbery too abhorrent for even enlightened men to perform, when influenced by avarice and lust. Neither did they come flying upon the wings of Liberty, to a land of freedom. But they came with broken hearts, from their beloved native land, and were doomed to unrequited toil and deep degradation. Nor did the evil of their bondage end at their emancipation by death. Succeeding generations inherited their chains, and millions have come from eternity into time, and have returned again to the world of spirits, cursed and ruined by American slavery.

The propagators of the system, or their immediate ancestors, very soon discovered its growing evil, and its tremendous wickedness, and secret promises were made to destroy it. The gross inconsistency of a people holding slaves, who had themselves "ferried o'er the wave" for freedom's sake, was too apparent to be entirely overlooked. The voice of Freedom cried, "Emancipate yourselves." Humanity supplicated with tears for the deliverance of the children of Africa. Wisdom urged her solemn plea. The bleeding captive plead his innocence, and pointed to Christianity who stood weeping at the cross. Jehovah frowned upon the nefarious institution, and thunderbolts, red with vengeance, struggled to leap forth to blast the guilty wretches who maintained it. But all was in vain. Slavery had stretched its dark wings of death over the land, the Church stood silently by—the priests prophesied falsely, and the people loved to have it so. Its throne is established, and now it reigns triumphant.

Nearly three millions of your fellow-citizens are prohibited by law and public opinion, (which in this country is stronger than law,) from reading the Book of Life. Your intellect has been destroyed as much as possible, and every ray of light they have attempted to shut out from your minds. The oppressors themselves have become involved in the ruin. They have become weak, sensual, and rapacious—they have cursed you—they have cursed themselves—they have cursed the earth which they have trod.

The colonists threw the blame upon England. They said that the mother country entailed the evil upon them, and that they would rid themselves of it if they could. The world thought they were sincere, and the philanthropic pitied them. But time soon tested their sincerity.

In a few years the colonists grew strong, and severed themselves from the British Government. Their independence was declared, and they took their station among the sovereign powers of the earth. The declaration was a glorious document. Sages admired it, and the patriotic of every nation reverenced the God-like sentiments which it contained. When the power of Government returned to their hands, did they emancipate the slaves? No; they rather added new links to our chains. Were they ignorant of the principles of Liberty? Certainly they were not. The sentiments of their revolutionary orators fell in burning eloquence upon their hearts, and with one voice they cried, Liberty or Death. Oh what a sentence was that! It ran from soul to soul like electric fire, and nerved the arm of thousands to fight in the holy cause of Freedom. Among the diversity of opinions that are entertained in regard to physical resistance, there are but a few found to gainsay that stem declaration. We are among those who do not. Slavery! How much misery is comprehended in that single word. What mind is there that does not shrink from its direful effects? Unless the image of God be obliterated from the soul, all men cherish the love of Liberty. The nice discerning political economist does not regard the sacred right more than the untutored African who roams in the wilds of Congo. Nor has the one more right to the full enjoyment of his freedom than the other. In every man's mind the good seeds of liberty are planted, and he who brings his fellow down so low, as to make him contented with a condition of slavery, commits the highest crime against God and man. Brethren, your oppressors aim to do this. They endeavor to make you as much like brutes as possible. When they have blinded the eyes of your mind—when they have embittered the sweet waters of life—then, and not till then, has American slavery done its perfect work.

To SUCH DEGRADATION IT IS SINFUL IN THE EXTREME FOR YOU TO MAKE VOLUNTARY SUBMISSION. The divine commandments you are in duty bound to reverence and obey. If you do not obey them, you will surely meet with the displeasure of the Almighty. He requires you to love him supremely, and your neighbor as yourself—to keep the Sabbath day holy—to search the Scriptures—and bring up your children with respect for his laws, and to worship no other God but him. But slavery sets all these at nought, and hurls defiance in the face of Jehovah. The forlorn condition in which you are placed, does not destroy your moral obligation to God. You are not certain of heaven, because you suffer yourselves to remain in a state of slavery, where you cannot obey the commandments of the Sovereign of the universe. If the ignorance of slavery is a passport to heaven, then it is a blessing, and no curse, and you should rather desire its perpetuity than its abolition. God will not receive slavery, nor ignorance, nor any other state of mind, for love and obedience to him. Your condition does not absolve you from your moral obligation. The diabolical injustice by which your liberties are cloven down, NEITHER GOD, NOR ANGELS, OR JUST MEN, COMMAND YOU TO SUFFER FOR A SINGLE MOMENT. THEREFORE IT IS YOUR SOLEMN AND IMPERATIVE DUTY TO USE EVERY MEANS, BOTH MORAL, INTELLECTUAL, AND PHYSICAL THAT PROMISES SUCCESS. If a band of heathen men should attempt to enslave a race of Christians, and to place their children under the influence of some false religion, surely Heaven would frown upon the men who would not resist such aggression, even to death. If, on the other hand, a band of Christians should attempt to enslave a race of heathen men, and to entail slavery upon them, and to keep them in heathenism in the midst of Christianity, the God of heaven would smile upon every effort which the injured might make to disenthral themselves.

Brethren, it is as wrong for your lordly oppressors to keep you in slavery, as it was for the man thief to steal our ancestors from the coast of Africa. You should therefore now use the same manner of resistance, as would have been just in our ancestors when the bloody foot-prints of the first remorseless soul-thief was placed upon the shores of our fatherland. The humblest peasant is as free in the sight of God as the proudest monarch that ever swayed a sceptre. Liberty is a spirit sent out from God. and like its great Author, is no respecter of persons.

Brethren, the time has come when you must act for yourselves. It is an old and true saying that, "if hereditary bondmen would be free, they must themselves strike the blow." You can plead your own cause, and do the work of emancipation better than any others. The nations of the world are moving in the great cause of universal freedom, and some of them at least will, ere long, do you justice. The combined powers of Europe have placed their broad seal of disapprobation upon the African slave-trade. But in the slave-holding parts of the United States, the trade is as brisk as ever. They buy and sell you as though you were brute beasts. The North has done much—her opinion of slavery in the abstract is known. But in regard to the South, we adopt the opinion of the New York Evangelist—We have advanced so far, that the cause apparently waits for a more effectual door to be thrown open than has been yet. We are about to point out that more effectual door. Look around you, and behold the bosoms of your loving wives heaving with untold agonies! Hear the cries of your poor children! Remember the stripes your fathers bore. Think of the torture and disgrace of your noble mothers. Think of your wretched sisters, loving virtue and purity, as they are driven into concubinage and are exposed to the unbridled lusts of incarnate devils. Think of the undying glory that hangs around the ancient name of Africa—and forget not that you are native born American citizens, and as such, you are justly entitled to all the rights that are granted to the freest. Think how many tears you have poured out upon the soil which you have cultivated with unrequited toil and enriched with your blood; and then go to your lordly enslavers and tell them plainly, that you are determined to be free. Appeal to their sense of justice, and tell them that they have no more right to oppress you, than you have to enslave them. Entreat them to remove the grievous burdens which they have imposed upon you, and to remunerate you for your labor. Promise them renewed diligence in the cultivation of the soil, if they will render to you an equivalent for your services. Point them to the increase of happiness and prosperity in the British West Indies since the Act of Emancipation.

Tell them in language which they cannot misunderstand, of the exceeding sinfulness of slavery, and of a future judgment, and of the righteous retributions of an indignant God. Inform them that all you desire is FREEDOM, and that nothing else will suffice. Do this, and for ever after cease to toil for the heartless tyrants, who give you no other reward but stripes and abuse. If they then commence the work of death, they, and not you, will be responsible for the consequences. You had better all die—die immediately, than live [as] slaves and entail your wretchedness upon your posterity. If you would be free in this generation, here is your only hope. However much you and all of us may desire it, there is not much hope of redemption without the shedding of blood. If you must bleed, let it all come at once—rather die freemen, than live to be slaves. It is impossible like the children of Israel, to make a grand exodus from the land of bondage. The Pharaohs are on both sides of the blood-red waters! You cannot move en masse, to the dominions of the British Queen—nor can you pass through Florida and overrun Texas, and at last find peace in Mexico. The propagators of American slavery are spending their blood and treasure, that they may plant the black flag in the heart of Mexico and riot in the halls of the Montezeumas. In the language of the Rev. Robert Hall, when addressing the volunteers of Bristol, who were rushing forth to repel the invasion of Napoleon, who threatened to lay waste the fair homes of England, "Religion is too much interested in your behalf, not to shed over you her most gracious influences."

You will not be compelled to spend much time in order to become inured to hardships. From the first moment that you breathed the air of heaven, you have been accustomed to nothing else but hardships. The heroes of the American Revolution were never put upon harder fare than a peck of corn and a few herrings per week. You have not become enervated by the luxuries of life. Your sternest energies have been beaten out upon the anvil of severe trial. Slavery has done this, to make you subservient, to its own purposes; but it has done more than this, it has prepared you for any emergency. If you receive good treatment, it is what you could hardly expect; if you meet with pain, sorrow, and even death, these are the common lot of slaves.

Fellow men! Patient sufferers! behold your dearest rights crushed to the earth! See your sons murdered, and your wives, mothers and sisters doomed to prostitution. In the name of the merciful God, and by all that life is worth, let it no longer be a debatable question whether it is better to choose Liberty or death.

In 1822, Denmark Veazie, of South Carolina, formed a plan for the liberation of his fellow men. In the whole history of human efforts to overthrow slavery, a more complicated and tremendous plan was never formed. He was betrayed by the treachery of his own people, and died a martyr to freedom. Many a brave hero fell, but history, faithful to her high trust, will transcribe his name on the same monument with Moses, Hampden, Tell, Bruce and Wallace, Toussaint L'Ouverture, Lafayette and Washington. That tremendous movement shook the whole empire of slavery. The guilty soul-thieves were overwhelmed with fear. It is a matter of fact, that at that time, and in consequence of the threatened revolution, the slave States talked strongly of emancipation. But they blew but one blast of the trumpet of freedom and then laid it aside. As these men became quiet, the slaveholders ceased to talk about emancipation; and now behold your condition today! Angels sigh over it, and humanity has long since exhausted her tears in weeping on your account!

The patriotic Nathaniel Turner followed Denmark Veazie. He was goaded to desperation by wrong and injustice. By despotism, his name has been recorded on the list of infamy, and future generations will remember him among the noble and brave.

Next arose the immortal Joseph Cinque, the hero of the *Amistad*. He was a native African, and by the help of God he emancipated a whole shipload of his fellow men on the high seas. And he now sings of liberty on the sunny hills of Africa and beneath his native palm-trees, where he hears the lion roar and feels himself as free as that king of the forest.

Next arose Madison Washington that bright star of freedom, and took his station in the constellation of true heroism. He was a slave on board the brig *Creole,* of Richmond, bound to New Orleans, that great slave mart, with a hundred and four others. Nineteen struck for liberty or death. But one life was taken, and the whole were emancipated, and the vessel was carried into Nassau, New Providence.

Noble men! Those who have fallen in freedom's conflict, their memories will be cherished by the true-hearted and the God-fearing in all future generations; those who are living, their names are surrounded by a halo of glory.

Brethren, arise, arise! Strike for your lives and liberties. Now is the day and the hour. Let every slave throughout the land do this, and the days of slavery are numbered. You cannot be more oppressed than you have been—you cannot suffer greater cruelties than you have already. Rather die freemen than live to be slaves. Remember that you are FOUR MILLIONS!

It is in your power so to torment the God-cursed slaveholders that they will be glad to let you go free. If the scale was turned, and black men were the masters and white men the slaves, every destructive agent and element would be employed to lay the oppressor low. Danger and death would hang over their heads day and night. Yes, the tyrants would meet with plagues more terrible than those of Pharaoh. But you are a patient people. You act as though you were made for the special use of these devils. You act as though your daughters were born to pamper the lusts of your masters and overseers. And worse than all, you tamely submit while your lords tear your wives from your embraces and defile them before your eyes. In the name of God, we ask, are you men? Where is the blood of your fathers? Has it all run out of your veins? Awake, awake; millions of voices are calling you! Your dead fathers speak to you from their graves. Heaven, as with a voice of thunder, calls on you to arise from the dust.

Let your motto be resistance! resistance! RESISTANCE! No oppressed people have ever secured their liberty without resistance. What kind of resistance you had better make, you must decide by the circumstances that surround you, and according to the suggestion of expediency. Brethren, adieu! Trust in the living God. Labor for the peace of the human race, and remember that you are FOUR MILLIONS.

Source: Henry Highland Garnet, "The Slave Must Throw Off the Slaveholder," in *Afro-American History, Primary Sources,* ed. Thomas R. Frazier (Chicago: Dorsey Press, 1988).

❧DOCUMENT 54❧
"WHAT IS IT TO BE A SLAVE" (1846)

Antislavery rhetoric appeared in many forms during the antebellum era in the United States. The following poem, published in a labor journal, was designed to generate a sense of solidarity between the slave and the industrial workingman.

Hast thou ever asked thyself
What is it to be a slave?
Bought and sold for sordid pelf,
From the cradle to the grave!

'Tis to know the transient powers
E'en of muscle, flesh and bone,
Cannot in thy happiest hours,
Be considered as thine own:

But thy master's goods and chattels
Lent to thee for little more
Than to fight his selfish battles
For some bits of shining ore!

'Tis to learn thou hast a heart
Beating in that bartered frame,
Of whose ownership—no part
Thou can'st challenge—but in name—

For the curse of slavery crushes
Out the life-blood from its core;
And expends its throbbing gushes
But to swell another's store.

God's best gift from heaven above,
Meant to make a heaven on earth,
Hallowing, humanizing love!
With the ties which thence have birth;

These can never be his lot,
Who, like brutes, are bought and sold;
Holding such—as having not
On his own the spider's hold!

'Tis to feel, e'en worse than this,
If aught worse than this can be,
Thou hast shrined, for bale or bliss,
An immortal soul in thee!

But that this undying guest
Bears thy body's degradation,
Until slavery's bonds, unblest,
Check each kindling aspiration:

And what should have been thy light,
Shining e'en beyond the grave,
Turns to darkness worse than night,
Leaving thee a hopeless slave!

Such is Slavery. Couldst thou bear
Its vile bondage. Ok! my brother,
How, then, canst thou, will thou dare
To inflict it on another?

Source: Voice of Industry, January 23, 1846, "What Is It to Be a Slave," in *Northern Labor and Antislavery, a Documentary History,* ed. Philip S. Foner and Herbert Shapiro (Westport, CT: Greenwood, 1994).

❧DOCUMENT 55❧
THE QUEIRÓS LAW (1850)

The government of Brazil officially ended legal trading in African slaves with the Queirós Law in 1850. Despite this law, the illegal trade in African slaves continued until the 1880s when slavery itself was abolished in Brazil.

We, Dom Pedro, by the Grace of God, and the unanimous acclamation of the people, Constitutional Emperor and Perpetual Defender of Brazil, make known to all our subjects, that the General Legislative Assembly has decreed, and we have approved, the following Law:

ART. I. Brazilian vessels wherever found, and foreign vessels found in the ports, bays, anchorages, or territorial waters of Brazil, having slaves on board, whose importation is prohibited by the Law of the 7th of November, 1831, or which may have landed them, shall be seized by the authorities, or by Brazilian ships of war, and considered importers of slaves. Those which have not slaves on board, nor shall have recently landed them, shall, if appearances are found of having been employed in Slave Trade, also be seized, and considered as attempting to import slaves.

II. The Imperial Government will draw up regulations specifying the appearances which shall constitute legal presumption of vessels being destined for the Slave Trade.

III. The principals in the crime of importing or of attempting to import slaves, are: the owner, the captain or master, the mate, the boatswain, and the supercargo. The accomplices are: the crew, and those who assist in the landing of slaves on Brazilian territory, or who assist in concealing, them from the knowledge of the public authorities, or in preventing their seizure at sea, or in the act of landing, if pursued.

IV. The importation of slaves into the territory of the empire is hereby considered piracy, and shall be punished by its tribunals with the pains and penalties declared in Article II of the Law Of 7th November, 1831. The attempting and abetting shall be punished according to the rules of the Articles XXXIV and XXXV of the Criminal Code.

V. The vessels treated of in Articles I and II, and all boats employed in landing, hiding, or the fraudulent removal of slaves, shall be sold, with all the cargo found on board; and the proceeds shall belong to the captors, deducting one-fourth part for the informer, if any. And the Government, the prize being adjudged good, shall grant to the crew of the vessel making the capture, the sum of forty milreis for each African seized, which shall be distributed in conformity with the laws in that respect.

VI. All the slaves seized shall be re-exported at the cost of the State to the ports from whence they came, or to any other point out of the empire which the Government may think proper; and until this re-exportation shall take place, they shall be employed on work under the guardianship of the Government; in no case are their services to be conceded to private persons.

VII. Passports shall not be given to merchant-ships for the coast of Africa, until their owners, captains, or masters, have signed a declaration that they will not receive any slave on board of their vessels; the owner giving bond in a sum Of money equal to the value of the ship and cargo; which bond shall not be cancelled unless they prove within eighteen months that they have strictly fulfilled the conditions of their declaration.

VIII. All seizures of vessels treated of in Articles I and II, as well as the freedom of the slaves captured on the high seas, or on the coast, before landing, or in the act of landing, or immediately after landing in barracoons and depots on the coasts, or in ports, shall be tried and judged, in the first instance, by the Maritime Court, and, in the second instance, by the Council of State. The Government will fix by regulation the form of process in the first and second instance, and may create maritime judges in such ports as may be required; the judges of the respective districts serving of right as maritime judges, when appointed for that purpose.

IX. The maritime judges shall be equally competent to try and sentence the accused mentioned in the IIIrd Article. From their decisions there shall be the same right of recourse and appeal to the superior courts as in the case of responsible public functionaries. The persons named in the IIIrd Article of the Law Of the 7th of November, and who are not included in the IIIrd Article of this Law, are to be tried and sentenced in the ordinary judicial tribunals.

X. All provisions to the contrary are hereby revoked.

We command, therefore, all the authorities to whom a knowledge and the execution of the said Law belongs to execute the same, and to cause it to be executed, and thoroughly to observe that which is contained in it. Let the Department of justice cause this to be printed, published, and distributed.

Given at the Palace of Rio de Janeiro, this 4th of September, 1850, 29th of the Independence and of the Empire.
EUZEBIO DE QUEIROZ COUTINHO MATTOZO CAMARA.

Source: Pedro II, Dom (Pedro de Alcântara), emperor of Brazil, "The Queiroz Law," in *A Documentary History of Brazil,* ed. E. Bradford Burns (New York: Alfred A. Knopf, 1966).

➤DOCUMENT 56➤
FUGITIVE SLAVE ACT (1850)

Enacted as a part of the Compromise of 1850, legislation approved by the U.S. Congress and signed into law that same year, the Fugitive Slave Act was a measure that was universally unpopular throughout the northern states. Since federal law enforcement officials were expected to participate in the capture and return of runaway slaves, many northern abolitionists became actively involved in the Underground Railroad as they sought to assist fugitives who were trying to escape from slavery in the South.

Section 1
Be it enacted by the Senate and House of Representatives of the United States of America in Congress assembled, That the persons who have been, or may hereafter be, appointed commissioners, in virtue of any act of Congress, by the Circuit Courts of the United States, and Who, in consequence of such

appointment, are authorized to exercise the powers that any justice of the peace, or other magistrate of any of the United States, may exercise in respect to offenders for any crime or offense against the United States, by arresting, imprisoning, or bailing the same under and by the virtue of the thirty-third section of the act of the twenty-fourth of September seventeen hundred and eighty-nine, entitled "An Act to establish the judicial courts of the United States" shall be, and are hereby, authorized and required to exercise and discharge all the powers and duties conferred by this act.

Section 2

And be it further enacted, That the Superior Court of each organized Territory of the United States shall have the same power to appoint commissioners to take acknowledgments of bail and affidavits, and to take depositions of witnesses in civil causes, which is now possessed by the Circuit Court of the United States; and all commissioners who shall hereafter be appointed for such purposes by the Superior Court of any organized Territory of the United States, shall possess all the powers, and exercise all the duties, conferred by law upon the commissioners appointed by the Circuit Courts of the United States for similar purposes, and shall moreover exercise and discharge all the powers and duties conferred by this act.

Section 3

And be it further enacted, That the Circuit Courts of the United States shall from time to time enlarge the number of the commissioners, with a view to afford reasonable facilities to reclaim fugitives from labor, and to the prompt discharge of the duties imposed by this act.

Section 4

And be it further enacted, That the commissioners above named shall have concurrent jurisdiction with the judges of the Circuit and District Courts of the United States, in their respective circuits and districts within the several States, and the judges of the Superior Courts of the Territories, severally and collectively, in term-time and vacation; shall grant certificates to such claimants, upon satisfactory proof being made, with authority to take and remove such fugitives from service or labor, under the restrictions herein contained, to the State or Territory from which such persons may have escaped or fled.

Section 5

And be it further enacted, That it shall be the duty of all marshals and deputy marshals to obey and execute all warrants and precepts issued under the provisions of this act, when to them directed; and should any marshal or deputy marshal refuse to receive such

warrant, or other process, when tendered, or to use all proper means diligently to execute the same, he shall, on conviction thereof, be fined in the sum of one thousand dollars, to the use of such claimant, on the motion of such claimant, by the Circuit or District Court for the district of such marshal; and after arrest of such fugitive, by such marshal or his deputy, or whilst at any time in his custody under the provisions of this act, should such fugitive escape, whether with or without the assent of such marshal or his deputy, such marshal shall be liable, on his official bond, to be prosecuted for the benefit of such claimant, for the full value of the service or labor of said fugitive in the State, Territory, or District whence he escaped: and the better to enable the said commissioners, when thus appointed, to execute their duties faithfully and efficiently, in conformity with the requirements of the Constitution of the United States and of this act, they are hereby authorized and empowered, within their counties respectively, to appoint, in writing under their hands, any one or more suitable persons, from time to time, to execute all such warrants and other process as may be issued by them in the lawful performance of their respective duties; with authority to such commissioners, or the persons to be appointed by them, to execute process as aforesaid, to summon and call to their aid the bystanders, or posse comitatus [those called to assist a law officer] the proper county, when necessary to ensure a faithful observance of the clause of the Constitution referred to, in conformity with the provisions of this act; and all good citizens are hereby commanded to aid and assist in the prompt and efficient execution of this law, whenever their services may be required, as aforesaid, for that purpose; and said warrants shall run, and be executed by said officers, any where in the State within which they are issued.

Section 6

And be it further enacted, That when a person held to service or labor in any State or Territory of the United States, has heretofore or shall hereafter escape into another State or Territory of the United States, the person or persons to whom such service or labor may be due, or his, her, or their agent or attorney, duly authorized, by power of attorney, in writing, acknowledged and certified under the seal of some legal officer or court of the State or Territory in which the same may be executed, may pursue and reclaim such fugitive person, either by procuring a warrant from some one of the courts, judges, or commissioners aforesaid, of the proper circuit, district, or county, for the apprehension of such fugitive from service or labor, or by seizing and arresting such fugitive, where the same can be done without process, and by taking, or causing such person to be taken, forthwith before such court, judge, or commissioner, whose duty it shall be to hear and determine the case of such claimant in a summary manner; and upon satisfactory proof being made, by deposition or affidavit, in writing, to be taken and certified by such court, judge, or commissioner, or by other satisfactory testimony, duly taken and certified by some court, magistrate, justice of the peace, or other legal officer authorized to administer an oath and take depositions under the laws of the State or Territory from which such person owing service or labor may have escaped, with a certificate of such magistracy or other authority, as aforesaid, with the seal of the proper court or officer thereto attached, which seal shall be sufficient to establish the competency of the proof, and with proof, also by affidavit, of the identity of the person whose service or labor is claimed to be due as aforesaid, that the person so arrested does in fact owe service or labor to the person or persons claiming him or her, in the State or Territory from which such fugitive may have escaped as aforesaid, and that said person escaped, to make out and deliver to such claimant, his or her agent or attorney, a certificate setting forth the substantial facts as to the service or labor due from such fugitive to the claimant, and of his or her escape from the State or Territory in which he or she was arrested, with authority to such claimant, or his or her agent or attorney, to use such reasonable force and restraint as may be necessary, under the circumstances of the case, to take and remove such fugitive person back to the State or Territory whence he or she may have escaped as aforesaid. In no trial or hearing under this act shall the testimony of such alleged fugitive be admitted in evidence; and the certificates in this and the first [fourth] section mentioned, shall be conclusive of the right of the person or persons in whose favor granted, to remove such fugitive to the State or Territory from which he escaped, and shall prevent all molestation of such person or persons by any process issued by any court, judge, magistrate, or other person whomsoever.

Section 7
And be it further enacted, That any person who shall knowingly and willingly obstruct, hinder, or prevent such claimant, his agent or attorney, or any person or persons lawfully assisting him, her, or them, from arresting such a fugitive from service or labor, either with or without process as aforesaid, or shall rescue, or attempt to rescue, such fugitive from service or labor, from the custody of such claimant, his or her agent or attorney, or other person or persons lawfully assisting as aforesaid, when so arrested, pursuant to the authority herein given and declared; or shall aid, abet, or assist such person so owing service or labor as aforesaid, directly or indirectly, to escape from such claimant, his agent or attorney, or other person or persons legally authorized as aforesaid; or shall harbor or conceal such fugitive, so as to prevent the discovery and arrest of such person, after notice or knowledge of the fact that such person was a fugitive from service or labor as aforesaid, shall, for either of said offences, be subject to a fine not exceeding one thousand dollars, and imprisonment not exceeding six months, by indictment and conviction before the District Court of the United States for the district in which such offence may have been committed, or before the proper court of criminal jurisdiction, if committed within any one of the organized Territories of the United States; and shall moreover forfeit and pay, by way of civil damages to the party injured by such illegal conduct, the sum of one thousand dollars for each fugitive so lost as aforesaid, to be recovered by action of debt, in any of the District or Territorial Courts aforesaid, within whose jurisdiction the said offence may have been committed.

Section 8
And be it further enacted, That the marshals, their deputies, and the clerks of the said District and Territorial Courts, shall be paid, for their services, the like fees as may be allowed for similar services in other cases; and where such services are rendered exclusively in the arrest, custody, and delivery of the fugitive to the claimant, his or her agent or attorney, or where such supposed fugitive may be discharged out of custody for the want of sufficient proof as aforesaid, then such fees are to be paid in whole by such claimant, his or her agent or attorney; and in all cases where the proceedings are before a commissioner, he shall be entitled to a fee of ten dollars in full for his services in each case, upon the delivery of the said certificate to the claimant, his agent or attorney; or a fee of five dollars in cases where the proof shall not, in the opinion of such commissioner, warrant such certificate and delivery, inclusive of all services incident to such arrest and examination, to be paid, in either case, by the claimant, his or her agent or attorney. The person or persons authorized to execute the process to be issued by such commissioner for the arrest and detention of fugitives from service or labor as aforesaid, shall also be entitled to a fee of five dollars each for each person he or they may arrest, and take before any commissioner as aforesaid, at the instance and request of such claimant, with such other fees as may be deemed reasonable by such commissioner for such other additional services as may be necessarily performed by him or them; such as attending at the examination, keeping the fugitive in custody, and providing him with food and lodging during his detention, and until the final determination of such commissioners; and,

in general, for performing such other duties as may be required by such claimant, his or her attorney or agent, or commissioner in the premises, such fees to be made up in conformity with the fees usually charged by the officers of the courts of justice within the proper district or county, as near as may be practicable, and paid by such claimants, their agents or attorneys, whether such supposed fugitives from service or labor be ordered to be delivered to such claimant by the final determination of such commissioner or not.

Section 9

And be it further enacted, That, upon affidavit made by the claimant of such fugitive, his agent or attorney, after such certificate has been issued, that he has reason to apprehend that such fugitive will he rescued by force from his or their possession before he can be taken beyond the limits of the State in which the arrest is made, it shall be the duty of the officer making the arrest to retain such fugitive in his custody, and to remove him to the State whence he fled, and there to deliver him to said claimant, his agent, or attorney. And to this end, the officer aforesaid is hereby authorized and required to employ so many persons as he may deem necessary to overcome such force, and to retain them in his service so long as circumstances may require. The said officer and his assistants, while so employed, to receive the same compensation, and to be allowed the same expenses, as are now allowed by law for transportation of criminals, to be certified by the judge of the district within which the arrest is made, and paid out of the treasury of the United States.

Section 10

And be it further enacted, That when any person held to service or labor in any State or Territory, or in the District of Columbia, shall escape therefrom, the party to whom such service or labor shall be due, his, her, or their agent or attorney, may apply to any court of record therein, or judge thereof in vacation, and make satisfactory proof to such court, or judge in vacation, of the escape aforesaid, and that the person escaping owed service or labor to such party. Whereupon the court shall cause a record to be made of the matters so proved, and also a general description of the person so escaping, with such convenient certainty as may be; and a transcript of such record, authenticated by the attestation of the clerk and of the seal of the said court, being produced in any other State, Territory, or district in which the person so escaping may be found, and being exhibited to any judge, commissioner, or other officer authorized by the law of the United States to cause persons escaping from service or labor to be delivered up, shall be held and taken to be full and conclusive evidence of the fact of escape, and that the service or labor of the person escaping is due to the party in such record mentioned. And upon the production by the said party of other and further evidence if necessary, either oral or by affidavit, in addition to what is contained in the said record of the identity of the person escaping, he or she shall be delivered up to the claimant. And the said court, commissioner, judge, or other person authorized by this act to grant certificates to claimants or fugitives, shall, upon the production of the record and other evidences aforesaid, grant to such claimant a certificate of his right to take any such person identified and proved to be owing service or labor as aforesaid, which certificate shall authorize such claimant to seize or arrest and transport such person to the State or Territory from which he escaped: Provided, That nothing herein contained shall be construed as requiring the production of a transcript of such record as evidence as aforesaid. But in its absence the claim shall be heard and determined upon other satisfactory proofs, competent in law.

Approved, September 18, 1850.

Source: U.S. Congress, Fugitive Slave Act (1850; www.nationalcenter.org/HistoricalDocuments.html)

⊷DOCUMENT 57⊷
HENRY BROWN ESCAPES IN A BOX (1851)

Many slaves attempted to escape from slavery in the southern states, but few were as imaginative as Henry "Box" Brown, who literally mailed himself to Philadelphia—and to freedom.

I now began to get weary of my bonds; and earnestly panted after liberty. I felt convinced that I should be acting in accordance with the will of God, if I could snap in sunder those bonds by which I was held body and soul as the property of a fellow man. I looked forward to the good time which every day I more and more firmly believed would yet come, when I should walk the face of the earth in full possession of all that freedom which the finger of God had so clearly written on the constitutions of man, and which was common to the human race; but of which, by the cruel hand of tyranny, I, and millions of my fellow-men, had been robbed.

I was well acquainted with a storekeeper in the city of Richmond, from whom I used to purchase my provisions; and having formed a favourable opinion of his integrity, one day in the course of a little conversation with him, I said to him if I were free I would be able to do business such as he was doing; he then told me that my occupation was a money-making one, and if I were free I had no need to change for another. I then told him my circumstances in regard to my master, having to pay him 25 dollars per month, and yet that he refused to assist me in saving my wife from being sold and taken away to the South, where I should never see her again; and even refused to allow me to go and see her until my hours of labour were over. I told him this took place about five months ago, and I had been meditating my escape from slavery since, and asked him, as no person was near us, if he could give me any information about how I should proceed. I told him I had a little money and if he would assist me I would pay him for so doing. The man asked me if I was not afraid to speak that way to him; I said no, for I imagined he believed that every man had a right to liberty. He said I was quite right, and asked me how much money I would give him if he would assist me to get away. I told him that I had 166 dollars and that I would give him the half; so we ultimately agreed that I should have his service in the attempt for 86. Now I only wanted to fix upon a plan. He told me of several plans by which others had managed to effect their escape, but none of them exactly suited my taste. I then left him to think over what would be best to be done, and, in the mean time, went to consult my friend Dr. Smith, on the subject. I mentioned the plans which the storekeeper had suggested, and as he did not approve either of them very much, I still looked for some plan which would be more certain and more safe, but I was determined that come what may, I should have my freedom or die in the attempt.

One day, while I was at work, and my thoughts were eagerly feasting upon the idea of freedom, I felt my soul called out to heaven to breathe a prayer to Almighty God. I prayed fervently that he who seeth in secret and knew the inmost desires of my heart, would lend me his aid in bursting my fetters asunder, and in restoring me to the possession of those rights, of which men had robbed me; when the idea suddenly flashed across my mind of shutting myself up in a box, and getting myself conveyed as dry goods to a free state.

Being now satisfied that this was the plan for me, I went to my friend Dr. Smith and, having aquainted him with it, we agreed to have it put at once into execution not however without calculating the chances of danger with which it was attended; but buoyed up by the prospect of freedom and increased hatred to slavery I was willing to dare even death itself rather than endure any longer the clanking of those galling chains. It being still necessary to have the assistance of the storekeeper, to see that the box was kept in its right position on its passage, I then went to let him know my intention, but he said although he was willing to serve me in any way he could, he did not think I could live in a box for so long a time as would be necessary to convey me to Philadelphia, but as I had already made up my mind, he consented to acompany me and keep the box right all the way.

My next object was to procure a box, and with the assistance of a carpenter that was very soon accomplished, and taken to the place where the packing was to be performed. In the mean time the storekeeper had written to a friend in Philidelphia, but as no answer had arrived, we resolved to carry out our purpose as best we could. It was deemed necessary that I should get permission to be absent from my work for a few days, in order to keep down suspicion until I had once fairly started on the road to liberty; and as I had then a gathered [injured] finger I thought that would form a very good excuse for obtaining leave of absence; but when I showed it to one overseer, Mr. Allen, he told me it was not so bad as to prevent me from working, so with a view of making it bad enough, I got Dr. Smith to procure for me some oil of vitriol in order to drop a little of this on it, but in my hurry I dropped rather much and made it worse than there was any occasion for, in fact it was very soon eaten in to the bone, and on presenting it again to Mr. Allen I obtained the permission required, with the advice that I should go home and get a poultice of flax-meal to it, and keep it well poulticed until it got better. I took him instantly at his word and went off directly to the storekeeper who had by this time received an answer from his friend in Philadelphia, and had obtained permission to address the box to him, this friend in that city, arranging to call for it as soon as it should arrive. There being no time to be lost, the store-keeper, Dr. Smith, and myself, agreed to meet next morning at four o'-clock, in order to get the box ready for the express train. The box which I had procured was three feet one inch wide, two feet six inches high, and two feet wide: and on the morning of the 29th. day of March, 1849, I went into the box—having previously bored three gimlet holes opposite my face, for air, and provided myself with a bladder of water, both for the purpose of quenching my thirst and for wetting my face, should I feel getting faint. I took the gimlet also with me, in order that I might bore more holes if I found I had not sufficient air. Being thus equipped for the battle of liberty, my friends nailed down the lid and had me conveyed to the Express Office, which was about a mile distant from the place where I was packed. I had no sooner arrived at the office than I was turned heels up, while some person nailed something on the end of the box. I was then put upon a waggon and driven off to the depot with my head down, and I had no sooner arrived at the depot, than the man who drove the waggon tumbled me roughly into the baggage car, where, however, I happened to fall on my right side.

The next place we arrived at was Potomac Creek, where the baggage had to be removed from the cars, to be put on board the steamer; where I was again placed with my head down, and in this dreadful position had to remain nearly an hour and a half, which, from the sufferings I had thus to endure, seemed like an age to me, but I was forgetting the battle of liberty, and I was resolved to conquer or die. I felt my eyes swelling as if they would burst from their sockets; and the veins on my temples were dreadfully distended with pressure of blood upon my head. In this position I attempted to lift my hand to my face but I had no power to move it; I felt a cold sweat coming over me which seemed to be a warning that death was about to terminate my earthly miseries, but as I feared even that, less than slavery, I resolved to submit to the will of God, and, under the influence of that impression, I lifted up my soul in prayer to God, who alone, was able to deliver me. My cry was soon heard, for I could hear a man saying to another, that he had travelled a long way and had been standing there two hours, and he would like to get somewhat to sit down; so perceiving my box, standing on end, he threw it down and then two sat upon it. I was thus relieved from a state of agony which may be more easily imagined than described. I could now listen to the men talking, and heard one of them asking the other what he supposed the box contained; his companion replied he guessed it was "THE MAIL." I too thought it was a mail but not such a mail as he supposed it to be.

The next place at which we arrived was the city of Washington, where I was taken from the steam-boat, and again placed upon a waggon and carried to the depot right side up with care; but when the driver arrived at the depot I heard him call for some person to help to take the box off the waggon, and some one answered him to the effect that he might throw it off; but, says the driver, it is marked "this side up with care;" so if I throw it off I might break something, the other answered him that it did not matter if he broke all that was in it, the railway company were able enough to pay for it. No sooner were these words spoken than I began to tumble from the waggon, and failing on the end where my head was, I could hear my neck give a crack, as if it had been snapped asunder and I was knocked completely insensible. The first thing I heard, after that, was some person saying, "there is no room for the box, it will have to remain and be sent through to-morrow with the luggage train"; but the Lord had not quite forsaken me, for in answer to my earnest prayer He so ordered affairs that I should not be left behind; and I now heard a man say that the box had come with the express, and it must be sent on. I was then tumbled into the car with my head downwards again, but the car had not proceeded far before, more luggage having to be taken in, my box got shifted about and so happened to turn upon its right side; and in this position I remained till I got to Philadelphia, of our arrival in which place I was informed by hearing some person say, "We are in port and at Philadelphia." My heart then leaped for joy, and I wondered if any person knew that such a box was there.

Here it may be proper to observe that the man who had promised to accompany my box failed to do what he promised; but, to prevent it remaining long at the station after its arrival, he sent a telegraphic message to his friend, and I was only twenty seven hours in the box, though travelling a distance of three hundred and fifty miles.

I was now placed in the depot amongst the other luggage, where I lay till seven o'clock, p.m., at which time a waggon drove up, and I heard a person inquire for such a box as that in which I was. I was then placed on a waggon and conveyed to the house where my friend in Richmond had arranged I should be received. A number of persons soon collected round the box after it was taken in to the house, but as I did not know what was going on I kept myself quiet. I heard a man say "let us rap upon the box and see if he is alive;" and immediately a rap ensued and a voice said, tremblingly, "Is all right within?" to which I replied—"all right." The joy of the friends was very great; when they heard that I was alive they soon managed to break open the box, and then came my resurrection from the grave of slavery. I rose a free-man, but I was too weak, by reason of long confinement in that box, to be able to stand, so I immediately swooned away. After my recovery from the swoon the first thing, which arrested my attention, was the presence of a number of friends, every one seeming more anxious than another, to have an opportunity of rendering me their assistance, and of bidding me a hearty welcome to the possession of my natural rights. I had risen as it were from the dead; I felt much more than I could readily express; but as the kindness of Almighty God had been so conspicuously shown in my deliverance, I burst forth into the following him [hymn] of thanksgiving.

I waited patiently, I waited patiently for the
    Lord, for the Lord;
And he inclined unto me, and heard my calling:
I waited patiently, I waited patiently for the
    Lord,
And he inclined unto me, and heard my calling:
And he hath put a new song in my mouth,
Even a thanksgiving, even a thanksgiving, even a
    thanksgiving unto our God.
Blessed, Blessed, Blessed, Blessed is the man,
    Blessed is the man,
Blessed is the man that hath set his hope, his
    hope in the Lord;
O Lord my God, Great, Great, Great.

Source: Henry Brown, "Henry Brown Escapes in a Box," in *A Documentary History of Slavery in North America,* ed. Willie Lee Rose (New York: Oxford University Press, 1976).

∾DOCUMENT 58∾
REPORT BY COMMANDER WYVILL (1852)

Despite official efforts by the Brazilian government to abolish the slave trade, there is evidence that Portuguese slave traders continued to ply the waters off the coast of eastern Africa. As long as there was a market for slaves in Brazil, the trade continued.

I regret that the Portuguese authorities instead of repressing this traffic, afford every facility for its continuance. I learn that the Governor of Inhambane permitted a slaver to lie at anchor off that port for three weeks and capture 1000 slaves in December 1851, and that the Governor of Ibo connived at the trade.

SPXXXIX 1852/53,
Selected Committee Report: Q 1627

Source: Commander Wyvill, "Commander Wyvill, Commander-in-Chief at the Cape, Reported in 1852," in *A Collection of Documents on the Slave Trade of East Africa,* ed. R. W. Beachey (London: Rex Collings, 1976).

∾DOCUMENT 59∾
APPEAL OF THE INDEPENDENT DEMOCRATS (1854)

Perhaps more than any other legislative act of the antebellum era, the Kansas-Nebraska Act of 1854 polarized the political parties within the United States because it upset the status quo arrangement that had been developed by the Missouri Compromise of 1820. By calling into question the issue of slavery's expansion into the territories, the Kansas-Nebraska Act ignited a political firestorm that would eventually lead the nation to civil war in 1861.

As Senators and Representatives in the Congress of the United States it is our duty to warn our constituents, whenever imminent danger menaces the freedom of our institutions or the permanency of the Union.

Such danger, as we firmly believe, now impends, and we earnestly solicit your prompt attention to it.

At the last session of Congress a bill for the organization of the Territory of Nebraska passed the House of Representatives by an overwhelming majority. That bill was based on the principle of excluding slavery from the new Territory. It was not taken up for consideration in the Senate and consequently failed to become a law.

At the present session a new Nebraska bill has been reported by the Senate Committee on Territories, which, should it unhappily receive the sanction of Congress, will open all the unorganized Territories of the Union to the ingress of slavery.

We arraign this bill as a gross violation of a sacred pledge; as a criminal betrayal of precious rights; as part and parcel of an atrocious plot to exclude from a vast unoccupied region immigrants from the Old World and free laborers from our own States, and convert it into a dreary region of despotism, inhabited by masters and slaves.

Take your maps, fellow citizens, we entreat you, and see what country it is which this bill gratuitously and recklessly proposes to open to slavery. . . .

This immense region, occupying the very heart of the North American Continent, and larger, by thirty-three thousand square miles, than all the existing free States-including California . . . this immense region the bill now before the Senate, without reason and without excuse, but in flagrant disregard of sound policy and sacred faith, purposes to open to slavery.

We beg your attention, fellow-citizens, to a few historical facts:

The original settled policy of the United States, clearly indicated by the Jefferson proviso of 1784 and the Ordinance of 1787, was non-extension of slavery.

In 1803 Louisiana was acquired by purchase from France. . . .

In 1818, . . . the inhabitants of the Territory of Missouri applied to Congress for authority to form a State constitution, and for admission into the Union. There were, at that time, in the whole territory acquired from France, outside of the State of Louisiana, not three thousand slaves.

There was no apology, in the circumstances of the country, for the continuance of slavery. The original national policy was against it, and not less the plain language of the treaty under which the territory had been acquired from France.

It was proposed, therefore, to incorporate in the bill authorizing the formation of a State government, a provision requiring that the constitution of the new State should contain an article providing for the abolition of existing slavery, and prohibiting the further introduction of slaves.

This provision was vehemently and pertinaciously opposed, but finally prevailed in the House of Representatives by a decided vote. In the Senate it was rejected, and—in consequence of the disagreement between the two Houses—the bill was lost.

At the next session of Congress, the controversy was renewed with increased violence. It was terminated at length by a compromise. Missouri was allowed to come into the Union with slavery; but a section was inserted in the act authorizing her admission, excluding slavery forever from all the territory acquired from France, not included in the new State, lying north of 36° 30'. . . .

The question of the constitutionality of this prohibition was submitted by President Monroe to his cabinet. John Quincy Adams was then Secretary of State; John C. Calhoun was Secretary of War; William H. Crawford was Secretary of the Treasury; and William Wirt was Attorney-General. Each of these eminent gentlemen—three of them being from the slave states—gave a written opinion, affirming its constitutionality, and thereupon the act received the sanction of the President himself, also from a slave State.

Nothing is more certain in history than the fact that Missouri could not have been admitted as a slave State had not certain members from the free States been reconciled to the measure by the incorporation of this prohibition into the act of admission. Nothing is more certain than that this prohibition has been regarded and accepted by the whole country as a solemn compact against the extension of slavery into any part of the territory acquired from France lying north of 36° 30', and not included in the new State of Missouri. The same act let it be ever remembered—which authorized the formation of a constitution by the State, without a clause forbidding slavery, consecrated, beyond question and beyond honest recall, the whole remainder of the Territory to freedom and free institutions forever. For more than thirty years—during more than half our national existence under our present Constitution—this compact has been universally regarded and acted upon as inviolable American law. In conformity with it, Iowa was admitted as a free State and Minnesota has been organized as a free Territory.

It is a strange and ominous fact, well calculated to awaken the worst apprehensions and the most fearful forebodings of future calamities, that it is now deliberately proposed to repeal this prohibition, by implication or directly—the latter certainly the manlier way—and thus to subvert the compact, and allow slavery in all the yet unorganized territory.

We cannot, in this address, review the various pretenses under which it is attempted to cloak this monstrous wrong, but we must not altogether omit to notice one.

It is said that Nebraska sustains the same relations to slavery as did the territory acquired from Mexico prior to 1850, and that the pro-slavery clauses of the bill are necessary to carry into effect the compromise of that year.

No assertion could be more groundless. . . .

The statesmen whose powerful support carried the Utah and New Mexico acts never dreamed that their provisions would be ever applied to Nebraska. . . .

Here is proof beyond controversy that the principle of the Missouri act prohibiting slavery north of 36° 30', far from being abrogated by the Compromise Acts, is expressly affirmed; and that the proposed repeal of this prohibition, instead of being an affirmation of the Compromise Acts, is a repeal of a very prominent provision of the most important act of the series. It is solemnly declared in the very Compromise Acts "that nothing herein contained shall be construed to impair or qualify" the prohibition of slavery north of 36° 30'; and yet in the face of this declaration, that sacred prohibition is said to be overthrown. Can presumption further go? To all who, in any way, lean upon these compromises, we commend this exposition.

These pretenses, therefore, that the territory covered by the positive prohibition of 1820, sustains a similar relation to slavery with that acquired from Mexico, covered by no prohibition except that of disputed constitutional or Mexican law, and that the Compromises of 1850 require the incorporation of the pro-slavery clauses of the Utah and New Mexico Bill in the Nebraska act, are mere inventions, designed to cover from public reprehension meditated bad faith.

Were he living now, no one would be more forward, more eloquent, or more indignant in his denunciation of that bad faith, than Henry Clay, the foremost champion of both compromises. . . .

We confess our total inability properly to delineate the character or describe the consequences of this measure. Language fails to express the sentiments of indignation and abhorrence which it inspires; and no vision less penetrating and comprehensive than that of the All-Seeing can reach its evil issues. . . .

We appeal to the people. We warn you that the dearest interests of freedom and the Union are in imminent peril. Demagogues may tell you that the Union can be maintained only by submitting to the demands of slavery. We tell you that the Union can only be maintained by the full recognition of the just claims of freedom and man. The Union was formed to establish justice and secure the blessings of liberty. When it fails to accomplish these ends it will be worthless, and when it becomes worthless it cannot long endure.

We entreat you to be mindful of that fundamental maxim of Democracy—EQUAL RIGHTS AND EXACT JUSTICE FOR ALL MEN. Do not submit to become agents in extending legalized oppression and systematized injustice over a vast territory yet exempt from these terrible evils.

We implore Christians and Christian ministers to interpose. Their divine religion requires them to behold in every man a brother, and to labor for the advancement and regeneration of the human race.

Whatever apologies may be offered for the toleration of slavery in the States, none can be offered for its extension into Territories where it does not exist, and where that extension involves the repeal of ancient law and the violation of solemn compact. Let all protest, earnestly and emphatically, by correspondence, through the press, by memorials, by resolutions of public meetings and legislative bodies, and in whatever other mode may seem expedient, against this enormous crime.

For ourselves, we shall resist it by speech and vote, and with all the abilities which God has given us. Even if overcome in the impending struggle, we shall not submit. We shall go home to our constituents, erect anew the standard of freedom, and call on the people to come to the rescue of the country from the domination of slavery. We will not despair; for the cause of human freedom is the cause of God.

> S. P. Chase
> Charles Sumner
> J. R. Giddings
> Edward Wade
> Gerritt Smith
> Alexander De Witt

Source: S. P. Chase, Charles Sumner, et al., "Appeal of the Independent Democrats," in *Documents of American History*, ed. Henry Steele Commager (New York: Appleton-Century-Crofts, 1963).

➳DOCUMENT 60➳
MASSACHUSETTS PERSONAL LIBERTY ACT (1855)

In order to counter the effects of the Fugitive Slave Act of 1850, many of the northern states enacted "personal liberty laws" that would protect the rights of fugitive slaves within their borders and make it more difficult for slaveowners to reclaim captives.

An Act to protect the Rights and Liberties of the People of the Commonwealth of Massachusetts.

Sec. 1. [Act of 1842 extended.]

Sec. 2. The meaning of the one hundred and eleventh chapter of the Revised Statutes is hereby declared to be, that every person imprisoned or restrained of his liberty is entitled, as of right and of course, to the writ of *habeas corpus*, except in the cases mentioned in the second section of that chapter.

Sec. 3. The writ of *habeas corpus* may be issued by the supreme judicial court, thecourt of common pleas, by any justice's court or police court of any town or city, by any court of record, or by any justice of either of said courts, or by any judge of probate; and it may be issued by any justice of the peace, if no magistrate above named is known to said justice of the peace to be within five miles of the place where the party is imprisoned or restrained, and it shall be returnable before the supreme judicial court, or any one of the justices thereof, whether the court may be in session or not, and in term time or vacation. . . .

Sec. 6. If any claimant shall appear to demand the custody or possession of the person for whose benefit such writ is sued out, such claimant shall state in writing the facts on which he relies, with precision and certainty; and neither the claimant of the alleged fugitive, nor any person interested in his alleged obligation to service or labor, nor the alleged fugitive, shall be permitted to testify at the trial of the issue; and no confessions, admissions or declarations of the alleged fugitive against himself shall be given in evidence. Upon every question of fact involved in the issue, the burden of proof shall be on the claimant, and the facts alleged and necessary to be established, must be proved by the testimony of at least two credible witnesses, or other legal evidence equivalent thereto, and by the rules of evidence known and secured by the common law; and no *ex parte* deposition or affidavit shall be received in proof in behalf of the claimant, and no presumption shall arise in favor of the claimant from any proof that the alleged fugitive or any of his ancestors had actually been held as a slave, without proof that such holding was legal.

Sec. 7. If any person shall remove from the limits of this Commonwealth, or shall assist in removing therefrom, or shall come into the Commonwealth with the intention of removing or of assisting in the removing therefrom, or shall procure or assist in procuring to be so removed, any person being in the peace thereof who is not "held to service or labor" by the "party" making "claim," or who has not "escaped" from the "party" making "claim," within the meaning of those words in the constitution of the United States, on the pretence that such person is so held or has so escaped, or that his "service or labor" is so "due," or with the intent to subject him to such "service or labor," he shall be punished by a fine of not less than one thousand, nor more than five thousand dollars, and by imprisonment in the State Prison not less than one, nor more than five years. . . .

Sec. 9. No person, while holding any office of honor, trust, or emolument, under the laws of this Commonwealth, shall, in any capacity, issue any warrant or other process, or grant any certificate, under or by virtue of an act of congress [February 12, 1793] . . . or under or by virtue of an act of congress [September 18, 1853] . . . or shall in any capacity, serve any such warrant or other process.

Sec. 10. Any person who shall grant any certificate under or by virtue of the acts of congress, mentioned in the preceding section, shall be deemed to have resigned any commission from the Commonwealth which he may possess, his office shall be deemed vacant, and he shall be forever thereafter ineligible to any office of trust, honor or emolument under the laws of this Commonwealth.

Sec. 11. Any person who shall act as counsel or attorney for any claimant of any alleged fugitive from service or labor, under or by virtue of the acts of congress mentioned in the ninth section of this act, shall be deemed to have resigned any commission from the Commonwealth that he may possess, and he shall be thereafter incapacitated from appearing as counsel or attorney in the courts of this Commonwealth. . . .

Sec. 14. Any person holding any judicial office under the constitution or laws of this Commonwealth, who shall continue, for ten days after the passage of this act, to hold the office of United States commissioner, or any office . . . which qualifies him to issue any warrant or other process . . . under the [Fugitive Slave Acts] shall be deemed to have violated good behavior, to have given reason for the loss of public confidence, and furnished sufficient ground either for impeachment or for removal by address.

Sec. 15. Any sheriff, deputy sheriff, jailer, coroner, constable, or other officer of this Commonwealth, or the police of any city or town, or any district, county, city or town officer, or any officer or other member of the volunteer militia of this Commonwealth, who shall hereafter arrest . . . any person for the reason that he is claimed or adjudged to be a fugitive from service or labor, shall be punished by fine . . . and by imprisonment. . . .

Sec. 16. The volunteer militia of the Commonwealth shall not act in any manner in the seizure . . . of any person for the reason that he is claimed or adjudged to be a fugitive from service or labor. . . .

Sec. 19. No jail, prison, or other place of confinement belonging to, or used by, either the Commonwealth of Massachusetts or any county therein, shall be used for the detention or imprisonment of any person accused or convicted of any offence created by [the Federal Fugitive Slave Acts] . . . or accused or convicted of obstructing or resisting any process, warrant, or order issued under either of said acts, or of rescuing, or attempting to rescue, any person arrested or detained under any of the provisions of either of the said acts. . . .

Source: General Court of Massachusetts, "Massachusetts Personal Liberty Act," in *Documents of American History*, ed. Henry Steele Commager (New York: Appleton-Century-Crofts, 1963).

≈DOCUMENT 61≈
THOMAS EWBANK DESCRIBES A BRAZILIAN SLAVE AUCTION (1856)

In 1856, slavery was still flourishing in Brazil, and in the following account, a contemporary observer describes the conditions that were present in the slave markets of that country.

I have repeatedly passed an auction store at the corner of Ourives and Ouvidor. Today printed bills were hanging by the door. I took one and stepped in. A long table extended from near the entrance to the low box pulpit of the salesman. Behind it, a light iron railing cut off a portion of the store. The place was filled with new and secondhand furniture, old pictures, Dutch cheeses, Yankee clocks, kitchen utensils, crockeryware, old books, shoes, pickles, etc. . . .

Vendues of these things are held here daily, and once or twice a week another variety of merchandise is offered. This was the case today—an assorted invoice of colored goods, arranged on benches behind the railing. The catalogue contained eighty-nine lots, and each lot had a corresponding number pinned to it, that purchasers, on running over the list, might compare the articles with their description. These goods were living beings. Every lot was a man or woman, a boy or girl. There were fifty-three males, most of whom ranged between eighteen and thirty years of age—carpenters, masons, smiths, and country hands. One was a sailor, another a caulker and boatman. There were two tailors, a coachman, a saddler, a sawyer, a squarer of timber (one expert with the adze), a shoemaker, cooks, a coffee-carrier, and a barber surgeon, who, like most of his profession, was a musician—"No. 19, one Rapaz, *Barbeiro, bom sangrador e musico*" ["barber, surgeon, and musician"].

Of females, the oldest was twenty-six, and the youngest between seven and eight—washers, sewers, cooks, two dressmakers *muito prendada*—very accomplished. Others made skirts, dressed ladies' hair, etc. A couple were wet nurses, with much good milk, and each with a colt or filly, thus: "No. 61, one Rapariga, con muito bom *leite, com cria.*" *Cria* signifies the young of horses, and is applied to Negro offspring.

They were of every shade, from deep Angola jet to white or nearly white, as one young woman facing me appeared. She was certainly superior in mental organization to some of the buyers. The anguish with which she watched the proceedings, and waited her turn to be brought out, exposed, examined, and disposed of, was distressing. A little girl, I suppose her own, stood by her weeping, with one hand in her lap, obviously dreading to be torn away. This child did not cry out—that is not allowed—but tears chased each other down her cheeks, her little bosom panted violently, and such a look of alarm marked her face as she turned her large eyes on the proceedings, that I thought at one time she would have dropped.

"Purchasers of pots and pot-lids," said Diogenes, "ring them lest they should carry cracked ones home, but men they buy on sight." If such was the practice of old, it is not so now: the head, eyes, mouth, teeth, arms, hands, trunks, legs, feet—every limb and ligament without are scrutinized, while, to ascertain if aught within be ruptured, the breast and other parts are sounded.

The auctioneer, a tall, black-whiskered man of thirty-five, was a master of his profession, if one might judge from his fluency and fervor. A hammer in his right hand, the forefinger of his left pointing to a plantation hand standing confused at his side, he pours out a flood of words. The poor fellow had on a canvas shirt, with sleeves ending at the elbows and trousers of the same, the legs of which he is told to roll above his knees. A bidder steps up, examines his lower limbs, then his mouth, breast, and other parts. He is now told to walk toward the door and back to show his gait. As he was returning, the hammer fell, and he was pushed back within the railing. Another, who had but four toes on one foot, was quickly disposed of.

The clerk next went behind the rails and brought forward a woman—a field hand. She was stout, and seemed older than reported in the catalogue. Dressed as sparely and plainly as the men, she too was examined, and told to walk to and fro. When near the door, a bidder interrogated her, but on what I could not comprehend. His last remark was translated plainly by her raising her skirt to expose her legs. They were much swollen. Two hundred and fifty milreis was the sum she brought.

Source: Thomas Ewbank, "The Auction," in *A Documentary History of Brazil*, ed. E. Bradford Burns (New York: Alfred A. Knopf, 1966).

∽DOCUMENT 62∾
ABRAHAM LINCOLN'S "HOUSE DIVIDED" SPEECH (1858)

In one of his often-quoted addresses on the issue of slavery, Abraham Lincoln declared that "a house divided against itself cannot stand." Though not an abolitionist, Lincoln supported the free soil position, which opposed the expansion of slavery into any of the western territories of the United States.

Mr. President and Gentlemen of the Convention.
If we could first know where we are, and whither we are tending, we could then better judge what to do, and how to do it.

We are now far into the fifth year, since a policy was initiated, with the avowed object, and confident promise, of putting an end to slavery agitation.

Under the operation of that policy, that agitation has not only, not ceased, but has constantly augmented.

In my opinion, it will not cease, until a crisis shall have been reached, and passed.

"A house divided against itself cannot stand."

I believe this government cannot endure, permanently half slave and half free.

I do not expect the Union to be dissolved—I do not expect the house to fall—but I do expect it will cease to be divided.

It will become all one thing, or all the other.

Either the opponents of slavery, will arrest the further spread of it, and place it where the public mind shall rest in the belief that it is in course of ultimate extinction; or its advocates will push it forward, till it shall become alike lawful in all the States, old as well as new—North as well as South.

Have we no tendency to the latter condition?

Let any one who doubts, carefully contemplate that now almost complete legal combination—piece of machinery so to speak—compounded of the Nebraska doctrine, and the Dred Scott decision. Let him consider not only what work the machinery is adapted to do, and how well adapted; but also, let him study the history of its construction, and trace, if he can, or rather fail, if he can, to trace the evidences of design, and concert of action, among its chief bosses, from the beginning.

But, so far, Congress only, had acted; and an indorsement by the people, real or apparent, was indispensable, to save the point already gained, and give chance for more.

The new year of 1854 found slavery excluded from more than half the States by State Constitutions, and from most of the national territory by Congressional prohibition.

Four days later, commenced the struggle, which ended in repealing that Congressional prohibition.

This opened all the national territory to slavery; and was the first point gained.

This necessity had not been overlooked; but bad been provided for, as well as might be, in the notable argument of "squatter sovereignty," otherwise called "sacred right of self government," which latter phrase, though expressive of the only rightful basis of, any government, was so perverted in this attempted use of it as to amount to just this: That if any one man choose to enslave another, no third man shall be allowed to object.

That argument was incorporated into the Nebraska bill itself, in the language which follows: "It being the true intent and meaning of this act not to legislate slavery into any Territory or state, not exclude it therefrom; but to leave the people thereof perfectly free to form and regulate their domestic institutions in their own way, subject only to the Constitution of the United States."

Then opened the roar of loose declamation in favor of "Squatter Sovereignty," and "Sacred right of self government."

"But," said opposition members, "let us be more specific—let us amend the bill so as to expressly declare that the people of the territory may exclude slavery." "Not we," said the friends of the measure; and down they voted the amendment.

While the Nebraska bill was passing through congress, a law case, involving the question of a negroe's freedom, by reason of his owner having voluntarily taken him first into a free state and then a territory covered by the congressional prohibition, and held him as a slave, for a long time in each, was passing through the U.S. Circuit Court for the District of Missouri; and both Nebraska bill and law suit were brought to a decision in the same month of May, 1854. The negroe's name was "Dred Scott," which name now designates the decision finally made in the case.

Before the then next Presidential election, the law case came to, and was argued in the Supreme Court of the United States; but the decision of it was deferred until after the election. Still, before the election, Senator Trumbull, on the floor of the Senate, requests the leading advocate of the Nebraska bill to state his opinion whether the people of a territory can constitutionally exclude slavery from their limits; and the latter answers, "That is a question for the Supreme Court."

The election came. Mr. Buchanan was elected, and the endorsement, such as it was, secured. That was the second point gained. The endorsement, however, fell short of a clear popular majority by nearly four hundred thousand votes, and so, perhaps, was not overwhelmingly reliable and satisfactory.

The outgoing President, in his last annual message, as impressively as possible echoed back upon the people the weight and authority of the indorsement.

The Supreme Court met again; did not announce their decision, but ordered a re-argument.

The Presidential inauguration came, and still no decision of the court; but the incoming President, in his inaugural address, fervently exhorted the people to abide by the forthcoming decision, whatever it might be.

Then, in a few days, came the decision.

The reputed author of the Nebraska bill finds an early occasion to make a speech at this capitol endorsing the Dred Scott Decision, and vehemently denouncing all opposition to it.

The new President, too, seizes the early occasion of the Silliman letter to indorse and strongly construe that decision, and to express his astonishment that any different view had ever been entertained.

At length a squabble springs up between the President and the author of the Nebraska bill, on the mere question of fact, whether the Lecompton constitution was or was not, in any just sense, made by the people of Kansas; and in that squabble the latter declares that all he wants is a fair vote for the people, and that he cares not whether slavery be voted down or voted up. I do not understand his declaration that he cares not whether slavery be voted down or voted up, to be intended by him other than as an apt defi-

nition of the policy he would impress upon the public mind—the principle for which he declares he has suffered much, and is ready to suffer to the end.

And well may he cling to that principle. If he has any parental feeling, well may he cling to it. That principle, is the only shred left of his original Nebraska doctrine. Under the Dred Scott decision, "squatter sovereignty" squatted out of existence, tumbled down like temporary scaffolding—like the mould at the foundry served through one blast and fell back into loose sand—helped to carry an election, and then was kicked to the winds. His late joint struggle with the Republicans, against the Lecompton Constitution, involves nothing of the original Nebraska doctrine. That struggle was made on a point, the right of a people to make their own constitution, upon which he and the Republicans have never differed.

The several points of the Dred Scott decision, in connection with Senator Douglas' "care not" policy, constitute the piece of machinery, in its present state of advancement. This was the third point gained.

The working points of that machinery are:

First, that no negro slave, imported as such from Africa, and no descendant of such slave can ever be a citizen of any State, in the sense of that term as used in the Constitution of the United States.

This point is made in order to deprive the negro, in every possible event, of the benefit of this provision of the United States Constitution, which declares, that—

"The citizens of each State shall be entitled to all privileges and immunities of citizens in the several States."

Secondly, that "subject to the Constitution of the United States," neither Congress nor a Territorial Legislature can exclude slavery from any United States territory.

This point is made in order that individual men may fill up the territories with slaves, without danger of losing them as property, and thus to enhance the chances of permanency to the institution through all the future.

Thirdly, that whether the holding a negro in actual slavery in a free State, makes him free, as against the holder, the United States courts will not decide, but will leave to be decided by the courts of any slave State the negro may be forced into by the master.

This point is made, not to be pressed immediately; but, if acquiesced in for a while, and apparently indorsed by the people at an election, then to sustain the logical conclusion that what Dred Scott's master might lawfully do with Dred Scott, in the free State of Illinois, every other master may lawfully do with any other one, or one thousand slaves, in Illinois, or in any other free State.

Auxiliary to all this, and working hand in hand

with it, the Nebraska doctrine, or what is left of it, is to educate and mould public opinion, at least Northern public opinion, to not care whether slavery is voted down or voted up.

This shows exactly where we now are, and partially also, whither we are tending.

It will throw additional light on the latter, to go back, and run the, mind over the string of historical facts already stated. Several things will now appear less dark and mysterious than they did when they were transpiring. The people were to be left "perfectly free" "subject only to the Constitution." What the Constitution had to do with it, outsiders could not then see. Plainly enough now, it was an exactly fitted niche, for the Dred Scott decision to afterwards come in, and declare the perfect freedom of the people, to be just no freedom at all.

Why was the amendment, expressly declaring the right of the people to exclude slavery, voted down? Plainly enough now, the adoption of it, would have spoiled the, niche for the Dred Scott decision.

Why was the court decision held up? Why, even a Senator's individual opinion withheld, till after the Presidential election? Plainly enough now, the speaking out then would have damaged the "perfectly free" argument upon which the election was to be carried.

Why the outgoing President's felicitation on the indorsement? Why the delay of a reargument? Why the incoming President's advance exhortation in favor of the decision?

These things look like the cautious patting and petting a spirited horse, preparatory to mounting him, when it is dreaded that he may give the rider a fall.

And why the hasty after endorsements of the decision by the President and others?

We can not absolutely know that all these exact adaptations are the result of preconcert. But when we see a lot of framed timbers, different portions of which we know have been gotten out at different times and places and by different workmen—Stephen, Franklin, Roger and James, for instance—and when we see these timbers joined together, and see they exactly make the frame of a house or a mill, all the tenons and mortices exactly fitting, and all the lengths and proportions of the different pieces exactly adapted to their respective places, and not a piece too many or too few—not omitting even scaffolding—or, if a single piece be lacking, we can see the place in the frame exactly fitted and prepared to yet bring such piece in—in such a case, we find it impossible to not believe that Stephen and Franklin and Roger and James all understood one another from the beginning, and all worked upon a common plan or draft drawn up before the first lick was struck.

It should not be overlooked that, by the Nebraska bill, the people of a State as well as Territory, were to be left "perfectly free" "subject only to the Constitution."

Why mention a State? They were legislating for territories, and not for or about States. Certainly the people of a State are and ought to be subject to the Constitution of the United States; but why is mention of this lugged into this merely territorial law? Why are the people of a territory and the people of a state therein lumped together, and their relation to the Constitution therein treated as being precisely the same?

While the opinion of the Court, by Chief Justice Taney, in the Dred Scott case, and the separate opinions of all the concurring Judges, expressly declare that the Constitution of the United States neither permits Congress nor a Territorial legislature to exclude slavery from any United States territory, they all omit to declare whether or not the same Constitution permits a state, or the people of a State, to exclude it.

Possibly, this was a mere omission; but who can be quite sure, if McLean or Curtis had sought to get into the opinion a declaration of unlimited power in the people of a state to exclude slavery from their limits, just as Chase and Macy sought to get such declaration, in behalf of the people of a territory, into the Nebraska bill—I ask, who can be quite sure that it would not have been voted down, in the one case, as it had been in the other.

The nearest approach to the point of declaring the power of a State over slavery, is made by Judge Nelson. He approaches it more than once, using the precise idea, and almost the language too, of the Nebraska act. On one occasion his exact language is, "except in cases where the power is restrained by the Constitution of the United States, the law of the State is supreme over the subject of slavery within its jurisdiction."

In what cases the power of the states is so restrained by the U.S. Constitution, is left an open question, precisely as the same question, as to the restraint on the power of the territories was left open in the Nebraska act. Put that and that together, and we have another nice little niche, which we may, ere long, see filled with another Supreme Court decision, declaring that the Constitution of the United States does not permit a state to exclude slavery from its limits.

And this may especially be expected if the doctrine of "care not whether slavery be voted down or voted up," shall gain upon the public mind sufficiently to give promise that such a decision can be maintained when made.

Such a decision is all that slavery now lacks of being alike lawful in all the States.

Welcome or unwelcome, such [a] decision is probably coming, and will soon be upon us, unless the power of the present political dynasty shall be met and overthrown.

We shall lie down pleasantly dreaming that the people of Missouri are on the verge of making their State free; and we shall awake to the reality, instead, that the Supreme Court has made Illinois a slave State.

To meet and overthrow the power of that dynasty, is the work now before all those who would prevent that consummation.

That is what we have to do.

But how can we best do it?

There are those who denounce us openly to their own friends, and yet whisper us softly, that Senator Douglas is the aptest instrument there is, with which to effect that object. They do not tell us, nor has he told us, that he wishes any such object to be effected. They wish us to infer all, from the facts, that he now has a little quarrel with the present head of the dynasty; and that he has regularly voted with us, on a single point, upon which, he and we, have never differed.

They remind us that he is a very great man, and that the largest of us are very small ones. Let this be granted. But "a living dog is better than a dead lion." Judge Douglas, if not a dead lion for this work, is at least a caged and toothless one. How can he oppose the advances of slavery? He don't care anything about it. His avowed mission is impressing the "public heart" to care nothing about it.

A leading Douglas Democratic newspaper thinks Douglas' superior talent will be needed to resist the revival of the African slave trade.

Does Douglas believe an effort to revive that trade is approaching? He has not said so. Does he really think so? But if it is, how can he resist it? For years he has labored to prove it is a sacred right of white men to take negro slaves into the new territories. Can he possibly show that it is less a sacred right to buy them where they can be bought cheapest? And, unquestionably they can be bought cheaper in Africa than in Virginia.

He has done all in his power to reduce the whole question of slavery to one of a mere right of property; and as such, how can he oppose the foreign slave trade—how can he refuse that trade in that "property" shall be "perfectly free"—unless he does it as a protection to the home production? And as the home producers will probably not ask the protection, he will be wholly without a ground of opposition.

Senator Douglas holds, we know, that a man may rightfully be wiser to-day than he was yesterday—that he may rightfully change when he finds himself wrong.

But, can we for that reason, run ahead, and infer that he will make any particular change, of which he, himself, has given no intimation? Can we safely base

our action upon any such vague inference?

Now, as ever, I wish to not misrepresent Judge Douglas' position, question his motives, or do ought that can be personally offensive to him.

Whenever, if ever, he and we can come together on principle so that our great cause may have assistance from his great ability, I hope to have interposed no adventitious obstacle.

But clearly, he is not now with us—he does not pretend to be—he does not promise to ever be.

Our cause, then, must be intrusted to, and conducted by its own undoubted friends—those whose hands are free, whose hearts are in the work—who do care for the result.

Two years ago the Republicans of the nation mustered over thirteen hundred thousand strong.

We did this under the single impulse of resistance to a common danger, with every external circumstance against us.

Of strange, discordant, and even, hostile elements, we gathered from the four winds, and formed and fought the battle through, under the constant hot fire of a disciplined, proud, and pampered enemy.

Did we brave all then, to falter now?—now—when that same enemy is wavering, dissevered and belligerent?

The result is not doubtful. We shall not fail—if we stand firm, we shall not fail.

Wise councils may accelerate or mistakes delay it, but, sooner or later the victory is sure to come.

Source: Abraham Lincoln, "The House Divided Speech, June 16, 1858," in *Abraham Lincoln, a Documentary Portrait through His Speeches and Writings,* ed. Don E. Fehrenbacher (Stanford, CA: Stanford University Press, 1964).

❧ DOCUMENT 63 ❧
JOHN BROWN'S LAST SPEECH (1859)

The abolitionist John Brown was executed shortly after his failed effort to seize the arsenal at Harper's Ferry, Virginia, in 1859. Brown's reputation as a martyr to the abolitionist cause grew largely from the words spoken to the court in his final speech.

I have, may it please the Court, a few words to say.

In the first place, I deny everything but what I have all along admitted,—the design on my part to free the slaves. I intended certainly to have made a clean thing of that matter, as I did last winter, when I went into Missouri and there took slaves without the snapping of a gun on either side, moved them through the country, and finally left them in Canada. I designed to have done the same thing again, on a larger scale. That was all I intended. I never did intend murder, or treason, or the destruction of property, or to excite or incite slaves to rebellion, or to make insurrection.

I have another objection; and that is, it is unjust that I should suffer such a penalty. Had I interfered in the manner which I admit, and which I admit has been fairly proved (for I admire the truthfulness and candor of the greater portion of the witnesses who have testified in this case),—had I so interfered in behalf of the rich, the powerful, the intelligent, the so-called great, or in behalf of any of their friends,—either father, mother, brother, sister, wife, or children, or any of that class,—and suffered and sacrificed what I have in this interference, it would have been all right; and every man in this court would have deemed it an act worthy of reward rather than punishment.

This court acknowledges, as I suppose, the validity of the law of God. I see a book kissed here which I suppose to be the Bible, or at least the New Testament. That teaches me that all things whatsoever I would that men should do to me, I should do even so to them. It teaches me, further, to "remember them that are in bonds, as bound with them." I endeavored to act up to that instruction. I say, I am yet too young to understand that God is any respecter of persons. I believe that to have interfered as I have done—as I have always freely admitted I have done—in behalf of His despised poor, was not wrong, but right. Now, if it is deemed necessary that I should forfeit my life for the furtherance of the ends of justice, and mingle my blood further with the blood of my children and with the blood of millions in this slave country whose rights are disregarded by wicked, cruel, and unjust enactments,—I submit; so let it be done!

Let me say one word further.

I feel entirely satisfied with the treatment I have received on my trial. Considering all the circumstances, it has been more generous than I expected. But I feel no consciousness of guilt. I have stated from the first what was my intention, and what was not. I never had any design against the life of any person, nor any disposition to commit treason, or excite slaves to rebel, or make any general insurrection. I never encouraged any man to do so, but always discouraged any idea of that kind.

Let me say, also, a word in regard to the statements made by some of those connected with me. I hear it has been stated by some of them that I have induced them to join me. But the contrary is true. I do not say this to injure them, but as regretting their weakness. There is not one of them but joined me of his own accord, and the greater part of them at their own expense. A number of them I never saw, and never had a word of conversation with, till the day they came to me; and that was for the purpose I have stated.

Now I have done.

Source: John Brown, "John Brown's Last Speech," in *Documents of American History,* ed. Henry Steele Commager (New York: Appleton-Century-Crofts, 1963).

⮀DOCUMENT 64⮀
WILLIAM LLOYD GARRISON'S SPEECH ON THE EXECUTION OF JOHN BROWN (1859)

The following speech by the abolitionist William Lloyd Garrison served as an elegy upon the death of John Brown. Rather than viewing Brown as a "fanatical" abolitionist, Garrison viewed him as a fellow traveler who understood the difficult means that were required to rid the United States of the scourge of slavery.

. . . For thirty years I have been endeavoring to effect, by peaceful, moral and religious instrumentalities, the abolition of American slavery; and, if possible, I hate slavery thirty times more, if possible, an abolitionist of the most uncompromising character.

A word or two in regard to the characteristics of John Brown. He was of the old Puritan stock—a Cromwellian who 'believed in God,' and at the same time 'in keeping his powder dry,' He believed in 'the sword of the Lord and of Gideon' and acted accordingly. Herein I differed widely from him. But, certainly, he was no 'infidel'—oh, no! How it would have added to the fiendish malignity of the New York *Observer,* if John Brown had only been an 'infidel' evangelically speaking! But being exactly of the *Observer* pattern of theology, that fact has been a very hard pill to swallow; yet, so bent upon sustaining slavery in our land is that wicked journal, that it is pre-eminently ferocious in its spirit toward John Brown, and has been loudly clamorous for his execution, notwithstanding his religious faith.

As it respects his object at Harper's Ferry, it has been truly stated here by those who have preceded me, and by John Brown himself, whose declarations to the court have been read. The man who brands him as a traitor is a calumniator. The man who says that his object was to promote murder, or insurrection, or rebellion, is, in the language of the apostle, 'a liar, and the truth is not in him.' John Brown meant to effect, if possible, a peaceful Exodus from Virginia; and had not his large humanity overpowered his judgement in regard to his prisoners, he would in all probability have succeeded, and not a drop of blood would have been shed. But it is asked, 'Did he not have stored up a large supply of Sharp's rifles and spears? What did they mean?' Nothing offensive, nothing aggressive. Only this:—he designed getting as many slaves as he could to join him, and then putting into their hands those instruments for self-defence. But, mark you! self defiance, not in standing their ground, but on their retreat to the mountains; on their flight to Canada; not with any design or wish to shed the blood or harm the hair of a single slaveholder in the State of Virginia, if a conflict could be avoided. Remember that he had the whole town in his possession for thirty-six hours; and if he had been the man so basely represented in certain quarters, he might have consummated any thing in the way of violence and blood. But, all the while, he was counselling the strictest self-defence, and forbearance to the utmost, even when he had his enemies completely in his power.

As to his trial, I affirm that it was an awful mockery, before heaven and earth! He was not tried in a court of JUSTICE. Mark how they crowded the counts together in one indictment—MURDER, TREASON, and INSURRECTION! Of what was John Brown convicted? Who knows? Perhaps some of the jury convicted him of treason; others of murder; and others, again, of insurrection, Who can tell? There was no trial on any specific point. John Brown has been judicially assassinated. It was the trial of the lamb by the wolf—nothing less. . . .

Was John Brown justified in his attempt? Yes, if Washington was in his; if Warren and Hancock were in theirs. If men are justified in striking a blow for freedom, when the question is one of a threepenny tax on tea, then, I say, they are a thousand times more justified, when it is to save fathers, mothers, wives and children from the slave-coffle and the auction-block, and to restore to them their God-given rights. Was John Brown justified in interfering in behalf of the slave population of Virginia, to secure their freedom and independence? Yes, if LaFayette was justified in interfering to help our revolutionary fathers. If Kosciusko, if Pulaski, if Steuben, if DeKalb, if all who joined them from abroad were justified in that act, then John Brown was incomparably more so. If you believe in the right of assisting men to fight for freedom who are of your own color—(God knows nothing of color or complexion—human rights know nothing of these distinctions)—then you must cover, not only with a mantle of charity, but with the admiration of your hearts, the effort of John Brown at Harper's Ferry.

I am trying him by the American standard; and I hesitate not to say, with deliberation, that those who are attempting to decry him are dangerous members of the community; they are those in whom love of liberty has died out; they are the great lineal descendants of the tories of the Revolution, only a great deal worse. If the spirit of '76 prevailed to-day, as it did at that period, it would it would make the soil of the Commonwealth too hot to hold them. See the consistency, the vigilance, the determination of the South in support of her slave system! She moves and acts as by one impulse. Every man on her soil who is

suspected of cherishing the principles of liberty is tabooed, persecuted, and brutally outraged, especially if he be from the North. She makes clean work of it, and is consistent. On the other hand, how is it at the North? Presses which are venomously pro-slavery in spirit, and wholly Southern in their design, are every where allowed; presses which insult the good name and fame of the old Commonwealth, dishonor her illustrious dead, and contemn her glorious memories, for the purpose of 'crushing out' the spirit of freedom, and making absolute the sway of a ferocious slave oligarchy—and this they do with impunity. Now I say that if the North should, in defence of, her free institutions, imitate the example of the South in support of slavery, there would be a speedy and thorough cleaning out of our cities and towns, of those who are desecrating the ground upon which they stand. And it would be a more hopeful state of things than it is now; for this toleration is not the result, of principle, but the lack of it—it is not a noble forbearance, but a loss of vital, regard for the cause of liberty.

A word upon the subject of Peace. I am a non-resistant—a believer in the inviolability of human life, under all circumstances; I, therefore, in the name of God, disarm John Brown, and every Slave at the South. But I do not stop there; if I did, I should be a monster. I also disarm, in the name of God, every slaveholder and tyrant in the world. For wherever that principle is adopted, all fetters must instantly melt, and there can be no oppressed, and no oppressor, in the nature of things. How many agree with in regard to the doctrine of the inviolability of human life? How may non-resistants are there here to-night? There is one! Well, then, you who are otherwise are not the men to point the finger at John Brown, and cry 'traitor'—judging you by your own standard. Nevertheless, I am a non-resistant and I only desire, but have labored unremittingly to effect, the peaceful abolition of slavery, by an appeal to the reason and conscience of the slaveholder; yet, as a peace man—an 'ultra' peace man—I am prepared to say, 'Success to every slave insurrection at the South, and in every slave country.' And I do not see how I compromise or stain my peace profession in making that declaration. Whenever there is a contest between the oppressed and the oppressor,—the weapons being equal between the parties,—God knows my heart must be with the oppressed, and always against the oppressor. Therefore whenever commenced, I cannot but wish success to all slave insurrections. I thank God when men who believe in the right and duty of wielding carnal weapons, are so far advanced that they will take those weapons out of the scale of despotism, and throw them into the scale of freedom. It is an indication of progress, and a positive moral growth; it is one way to get up to the sublime platform of non-resistance;

and it is God's method of dealing retribution upon the head of the tyrant. Rather than see men wear their chains in a cowardly and servile spirit, I would, as an advocate of peace, much rather see them breaking the head of the tyrant with their chains. Give me, as a non-resistant, Bunker Hill, and Lexington, and Concord, rather than the cowardice and servility of a Southern slave plantation. . . .

Source: William Lloyd Garrison, "Speech of William Lloyd Garrison," in *Documents of Upheaval, Selections from William Lloyd Garrison's* The Liberator, *1831–1865,* ed. Truman Nelson (New York: Hill and Wang, 1966).

∾DOCUMENT 65∾
CRITTENDEN COMPROMISE (1861)

Legislators worked valiantly to achieve a compromise between the northern and southern states that would avert the American Civil War, but their efforts were in vain.

A joint resolution (S. No. 50) proposing certain amendments to the Constitution of the United States.

Whereas serious and alarming dissensions have arisen between the northern and southern states, concerning the rights and security of the rights of the slaveholding States, and especially their rights in the common territory of the United States; and whereas it is eminently desirable and proper that these dissensions, which now threaten the very existence of this Union, should be permanently quieted and settled by constitutional provisions, which shall do equal justice to all sections, and thereby restore to all the people that peace and good-will which ought to prevail between all the citizens of the United States: Therefore,

Resolved by the Senate and House of Representatives of the United States of America in Congress assembled, (two-thirds of both Houses concurring,) That the following articles be, and are hereby, proposed and submitted as amendments to the Constitution of the United States, which shall be valid to all intents and purposes, as part of said Constitution, when ratified by conventions of three-fourths of the several States:

Article 1
In all the territory of the United States now held, or hereafter acquired, situate north of 36 degrees 30 minutes, slavery or involuntary servitude, except as a punishment for crime, is prohibited while such territory shall remain under territorial government. In all the territory south of said line of latitude, slavery of the African race is hereby recognized as existing, and shall not be interfered with by Congress, but shall be protected as property by all the departments of the territorial government during its continuance. And when any territory, north or south of said line, within such boundaries as Congress may prescribe, shall contain the population requisite for a member of Congress according to the then Federal ratio of representation of the people of the United States, it shall, if its form of government be republican, be admitted into the Union, on an equal footing with the original States, with or without slavery, as the constitution of such new State may provide.

Article 2
Congress shall have no power to abolish slavery in places under its exclusive jurisdiction, and situate within the limits of States that permit the holding of slaves.

Article 3
Congress shall have no power to abolish slavery within the District of Columbia, so long as it exists in the adjoining States of Virginia and Maryland, or either, nor without the consent of the inhabitants, nor without just compensation first made to such owners of slaves as do not consent to such abolishment. Nor shall Congress at any time prohibit officers of the Federal Government, or members of Congress, whose duties require them to be in said District, from bringing with them their slaves, and holding them as such during the time their duties may require them to remain there, and afterwards taking them from the District.

Article 4
Congress shall have no power to prohibit or hinder the transportation of slaves from one State to another, or to a Territory, in which slaves are by law permitted to be held, whether that transportation be by land, navigable river, or by the sea.

Article 5
That in addition to the provisions of the third paragraph of the second section of the fourth article of the Constitution of the United States, Congress shall have power to provide by law, and it shall be its duty so to provide, that the United States shall pay to the owner who shall apply for it, the full value of his fugitive slave in all cases where the marshall or other officer whose duty it was to arrest said fugitive was prevented from so doing by violence or intimidation, or when, after arrest, said fugitive was rescued by force, and the owner thereby prevented and obstructed in the pursuit of his remedy for the recovery of his fugitive slave under the said clause of the Constitution and the laws made in pursuance thereof. And in all such cases, when the United States shall pay for such [a] fugitive, they shall have the right, in

their own name, to sue the county in which said violence, intimidation, or rescue was committed, and to recover from it, with interest and damages, the amount paid by them for said fugitive slave. And the said county, after it has paid said amount to the United States, may, for its indemnity, sue and recover from the wrong-doers or rescuers by whom the owner was prevented from the recovery of his fugitive slave, in like manner as the owner himself might have sued and recovered.

Article 6

No future amendment of the Constitution shall affect the five preceding articles; nor the third paragraph of the second section of the first article of the Constitution; nor the third paragraph of the second section of the fourth article of said Constitution; and no amendment will be made to the Constitution which shall authorize or give to Congress any power to abolish or interfere with slavery in any of the States by whose laws it is, or may be, allowed or permitted.

And whereas, also, besides those causes of dissension embraced in the foregoing amendments proposed to the Constitution of the United States, there are others which come within the jurisdiction of Congress, and may be remedied by its legislative power; and whereas it is the desire of Congress, so far as its power will extend, to remove all just cause for the popular discontent and agitation which now disturb the peace of the country, and threaten the stability of its institutions; Therefore,

1. Resolved by the Senate and House of Representatives of the United States of America, in Congress assembled, That the laws now in force for the recovery of fugitive slaves are in strict pursuance of the plain and mandatory provisions of the Constitution, and have been sanctioned as valid and constitutional by the judgement of the Supreme Court of the United States; that the slaveholding States are entitled to the faithful observance and execution of those laws, and that they ought not to be repealed, or so modified or changed as to impair their efficiency; and that laws ought to be made for the punishment of those who attempt by rescue of the slave, or other illegal means, to hinder or defeat the due execution of said laws.

2. That all State laws which conflict with the fugitive slave acts of Congress, or any other constitutional acts of Congress, or which, in their operation, impede, hinder, or delay the free course and due execution of any of said acts, are null and void by the plain provisions of the Constitution of the United States; yet those State laws, void as they are, have given color to practices, and led to consequences, which have obstructed the due administration and execution of acts of Congress, and especially the acts for the delivery of fugitive slaves, and have thereby

contributed much to the discord and commotion now prevailing. Congress, therefore, in the present perilous juncture, does not deem it improper, respectfully and earnestly to recommend the repeal of those laws to the several States which have enacted them, or such legislative corrections or explanations of them as may prevent their being used or perverted to such mischievous purposes.

3. That the act of the 18th of September, 1850, commonly called the fugitive slave law, ought to be so amended as to make the fee of the commissioner, mentioned in the eighth section of the act, equal in amount in the cases decided by him, whether his decision be in favor of or against the claimant. And to avoid misconstruction, the last clause of the fifth section of said act, which authorizes the person holding a warrant for the arrest or detention of a fugitive slave, to summon to his aid the posse comitatus [those selected to assist a law officer], and which declares it to be the duty of all good citizens to assist him in its execution, ought to be so amended as to expressly limit the authority and duty to cases in which there shall be resistance or danger of resistance or rescue.

4. That the laws for the suppression of the African slave trade, and especially those prohibiting the importation of slaves in the United States, ought to be made effectual, and ought to be thoroughly executed; and all further enactments necessary to those ends ought to be promptly made.

Source: Congressional Globe (Washington, DC: Congressional Globe Office, 1860).

◈DOCUMENT 66◈
AN ACT FOR THE RELEASE OF CERTAIN PERSONS HELD TO SERVICE OR LABOR IN THE DISTRICT OF COLUMBIA (1862)

The first legally sanctioned emancipation of slaves held in captivity during the American Civil War took place in the District of Columbia when Congress authorized the compensated emancipation of slaves who were held in Washington, D.C., in April 1862.

Be it enacted by the Senate and House of Representatives of the United States of America in Congress assembled, That all persons held to service or labor within the District of Columbia by reason of African descent are hereby discharged and freed of and from all claim to such service or labor; and from and after the passage of this act neither slavery nor involuntary servitude, except for crime, whereof the party shall be duly convicted, shall hereafter exist in said District.

Sec. 2. And be it further enacted, That all persons loyal to the United States, holding claims to service or labor against persons discharged therefrom by this act, may, within ninety days from the passage thereof, but not thereafter, present to the commissioners hereinafter mentioned their respective statements or petitions in writing, verified by oath or affirmation, setting forth the names, ages, and personal description of such persons, the manner in which said petitioners acquired such claim, and any facts touching the value thereof, and declaring his allegiance to the Government of the United States, and that he has not borne arms against the United States during the present rebellion, nor in any way given aid or comfort thereto: Provided, That the oath of the party to the petition shall not be evidence of the facts therein stated.

Sec. 3. And be it further enacted, That the President of the United States, with the advice and consent of the Senate, shall appoint three commissioners, residents of the District of Columbia, any two of whom shall have power to act, who shall receive the petitions above mentioned, and who shall investigate and determine the validity and value of the claims therein presented, as aforesaid, and appraise and apportion, under the proviso hereto annexed, the value in money of the several claims by them found to be valid: Provided, however, That the entire sum so appraised and apportioned shall not exceed in the aggregate an amount equal to three hundred dollars for each person shown to have been so held by lawful claim: And provided, further,

That no claim shall be allowed for any slave or slaves brought into said District after the passage of this act, nor for any slave claimed by any person who has borne arms against the Government of the United States in the present rebellion, or in any way given aid or comfort thereto, or which originates in or by virtue of any transfer heretofore made, or which shall hereafter be made by any person who has in any manner aided or sustained the rebellion against the Government of the United States.

Sec. 4. And be it further enacted, That said commissioners shall, within nine months from the passage of this act, make a full and final report of their proceedings, findings, and appraisement, and shall deliver the same to the Secretary of the Treasury, which report shall be deemed and taken to be conclusive in all respects, except as hereinafter provided; and the Secretary of the Treasury shall, with like exception, cause the amounts so apportioned to said claims to be paid from the Treasury of the United States to the parties found by said report to be entitled thereto as aforesaid, and the same shall be received in full and complete compensation: Provided, That in cases where petitions may be filed presenting conflicting claims, or setting up liens, said commissioners shall so specify in said report, and payment shall not be made according to the award of said

commissioners until a period of sixty days shall have elapsed, during which time any petitioner claiming an interest in the particular amount may file a bill in equity in the Circuit Court of the District of Columbia, making all other claimants defendants thereto, setting forth the proceedings in such case before said commissioners and their actions therein, and praying that the party to whom payment has been awarded may be enjoined from receiving the same; and if said court shall grant such provisional order, a copy thereof may, on motion of said complainant, be served upon the Secretary of the Treasury, who shall thereupon cause the said amount of money to be paid into said court, subject to its orders and final decree, which payment shall be in full and complete compensation, as in other cases.

Sec. 5. And be it further enacted, That said commissioners shall hold their sessions in the city of Washington, at such place and times as the President of the United States may direct, of which they shall give due and public notice. They shall have power to subpoena and compel the attendance of witnesses, and to receive testimony and enforce its production, as in civil cases before courts of justice, without the exclusion of any witness on account of color; and they may summon before them the persons making claim to service or labor, and examine them under oath; and they may also, for purposes of identification and appraisement, call before them the persons so claimed. Said commissioners shall appoint a clerk, who shall keep files and [a] complete record of all proceedings before them, who shall have power to administer oaths and affirmations in said proceedings, and who shall issue all lawful process by them ordered. The Marshal of the District of Columbia shall personally, or by deputy, attend upon the sessions of said commissioners, and shall execute the process issued by said clerk.

Sec. 6. And be it further enacted, That said commissioners shall receive in compensation for their services the sum of two thousand dollars each, to be paid upon the filing of their report; that said clerk shall receive for his services the sum of two hundred dollars per month; that said marshal shall receive such fees as are allowed by law for similar services performed by him in the Circuit Court of the District of Columbia; that the Secretary of the Treasury shall cause all other reasonable expenses of said commission to be audited and allowed, and that said compensation, fees, and expenses shall be paid from the Treasury of the United States.

Sec. 7. And be it further enacted, That for the purpose of carrying this act into effect there is hereby appropriated, out of any money in the Treasury not otherwise appropriated, a sum not exceeding one million of dollars.

Sec. 8. And be it further enacted, That any person

or persons who shall kidnap, or in any manner transport or procure to be taken out of said District, any person or persons discharged and freed by the provisions of this act, or any free person or persons with intent to re-enslave or sell such person or person into slavery, or shall re-enslave any of said freed persons, the person of persons so offending shall be deemed guilty of a felony, and on conviction thereof in any court of competent jurisdiction in said District, shall be imprisoned in the penitentiary not less than five nor more than twenty years.

Sec. 9. And be it further enacted, That within twenty days, or within such further time as the commissioners herein provided for shall limit, after the passage of this act, a statement in writing or schedule shall be filed with the clerk of the Circuit court for the District of Columbia, by the several owners or claimants to the services of the persons made free or manumitted by this act, setting forth the names, ages, sex, and particular description of such persons, severally; and the said clerk shall receive and record, in a book by him to be provided and kept for that purpose, the said statements or schedules on receiving fifty cents each therefor, and no claim shall be allowed to any claimant or owner who shall neglect this requirement.

Sec. 10. And be it further enacted, That the said clerk and his successors in office shall, from time to time, on demand, and on receiving twenty-five cents therefor, prepare, sign, and deliver to each person made free or manumitted by this act, a certificate under the seal of said court, setting out the name, age, and description of such person, and stating that such person was duly manumitted and set free by this act.

Sec. 11. And be it further enacted, That the sum of one hundred thousand dollars, out of any money in the Treasury not otherwise appropriated, is hereby appropriated, to be expended under the direction of the President of the United States, to aid in the colonization and settlement of such free persons of African descent now residing in said District, including those to be liberated by this act, as may desire to emigrate to the Republics of Hayti or Liberia, or such other country beyond the limits of the United States as the President may determine: Provided, The expenditure for this purpose shall not exceed one hundred dollars for each emigrant.

Sec. 12. And be it further enacted, That all acts of Congress and all laws of the State of Maryland in force in said District, and all ordinances of the cities of Washington and Georgetown, inconsistent with the provisions of this act, are hereby repealed.

Approved, April 16, 1862.

Source: U.S. Congress, "An Act for the Release of Certain Persons Held to Service or Labor in the District of Columbia" (1862; http://www.nara.gov/exhall/featured-document/dcact/dcproc.html).

⧼DOCUMENT 67⧽
THE EMANCIPATION PROCLAMATION (1863)

The Emancipation Proclamation is one of the most important documents in the history of the United States. Issued out of wartime necessity, Abraham Lincoln's proclamation changed forever the cause of the American Civil War, for the proclamation made the war a struggle for freedom and in so doing, elevated the purpose of the war to that of a moral crusade.

By the President of the United States of America:
A PROCLAMATION

Whereas on the 22nd day of September, A.D. 1862, a proclamation was issued by the President of the United States, containing, among other things, the following, to wit:

That on the 1st day of January, A.D. 1863, all persons held as slaves within any State or designated part of a State the people whereof shall then be in rebellion against the United States shall be then, thenceforward, and forever free; and the executive government of the United States, including the military and naval authority thereof, will recognize and maintain the freedom of such persons and will do no act or acts to repress such persons, or any of them, in any efforts they may make for their actual freedom.

That the executive will on the 1st day of January aforesaid, by proclamation, designate the States and parts of States, if any, in which the people thereof, respectively, shall then be in rebellion against the United States; and the fact that any State or the people thereof shall on that day be in good faith represented in the Congress of the United States by members chosen thereto at elections wherein a majority of the qualified voters of such States shall have participated shall, in the absence of strong countervailing testimony, be deemed conclusive evidence that such State and the people thereof are not then in rebellion against the United States.

Now, therefore, I, Abraham Lincoln, President of the United States, by virtue of the power in me vested as Commander-In-Chief of the Army and Navy of the United States in time of actual armed rebellion against the authority and government of the United States, and as a fit and necessary war measure for suppressing said rebellion, do, on this 1st day of January, A.D. 1863, and in accordance with my purpose so to do, publicly proclaimed for the full period of one hundred days from the first day above mentioned, order and designate as the States and parts of States wherein the people thereof, respectively, are this day in rebellion against the United States the following, to wit:

Arkansas, Texas, Louisiana (except the parishes of St. Bernard, Plaquemines, Jefferson, St. John, St. Charles, St. James, Ascension, Assumption, Terrebonne, Lafourche, St. Mary, St. Martin, and Orleans, including the city of New Orleans), Mississippi, Alabama, Florida, Georgia, South Carolina, North Carolina, and Virginia (except the forty-eight counties designated as West Virginia, and also the counties of Berkeley, Accomac, Northhampton, Elizabeth City, York, Princess Anne, and Norfolk, including the cities of Norfolk and Portsmouth), and which excepted parts are for the present left precisely as if this proclamation were not issued.

And by virtue of the power and for the purpose aforesaid, I do order and declare that all persons held as slaves within said designated States and parts of States are, and henceforward shall be, free; and that the Executive Government of the United States, including the military and naval authorities thereof, will recognize and maintain the freedom of said persons.

And I hereby enjoin upon the people so declared to be free to abstain from all violence, unless in necessary self-defense; and I recommend to them that, in all cases when allowed, they labor faithfully for reasonable wages.

And I further declare and make known that such persons of suitable condition will be received into the armed service of the United States to garrison forts, positions, stations, and other places, and to man vessels of all sorts in said service.

And upon this act, sincerely believed to be an act of justice, warranted by the Constitution upon military necessity, I invoke the considerate judgment of mankind and the gracious favor of Almighty God.

Source: Abraham Lincoln, "The Emancipation Proclamation," in *Documents of American History,* ed. Henry Steele Commager (New York: Appleton-Century-Crofts, 1963).

⌁DOCUMENT 68⌁
THE CIVIL WAR AMENDMENTS TO THE U.S. CONSTITUTION

The Thirteenth, Fourteenth, and Fifteenth Amendments to the U.S. Constitution, ratified in 1865, 1868, and 1870, respectively, are generally regarded as "the Civil War amendments." These constitutional changes abolished slavery in the United States and granted freed blacks civil liberties and voting rights that had been denied prior to the war.

AMENDMENT XIII (1865)

SECTION 1. Neither slavery nor involuntary servitude, except as a punishment for crime whereof the party shall have been duly convicted, shall exist within the United States, or any place subject to their jurisdiction.

SECTION 2. Congress shall have power to enforce this article by appropriate legislation.

AMENDMENT XIV (1868)

SECTION 1. All persons born or naturalized in the United States, and subject to the jurisdiction thereof, are citizens of the United States and of the State wherein they reside. No State shall make or enforce any law which shall abridge the privileges or immunities of citizens of the United States; nor shall any State deprive any person of life, liberty, or property, without due process of law; nor deny to any person within its jurisdiction the equal protection of the laws.

SECTION 2. Representatives shall be apportioned among the several States according to their respective numbers, counting the whole number of persons in each State, excluding Indians not taxed. But when the right to vote at any election for the choice of electors for President and Vice-President of the United States, Representatives in Congress, the Executive and Judicial officers of a State, or the members of the Legislature thereof, is denied to any of the male inhabitants of such State, being twenty-one years of age, and citizens of the United States, or in any way abridged, except for participation in rebellion, or other crime, the basis of representation therein shall be reduced in the proportion which the number of such male citizens shall bear to the whole number of male citizens twenty-one years of age in such State.

SECTION 3. No person shall be a Senator or Representative in Congress, or elector of President and Vice President, or hold any office, civil or military, under the United States, or under any State, who, having previously taken an oath, as a member of Congress, or as an officer of the United States, or as a member of any State legislature, or as an executive or judicial officer of any State, to support the Constitution of the United States, shall have engaged in insurrection or rebellion against the same, or given aid or comfort to the enemies thereof. But Congress may by a vote of two-thirds of each House, remove such disability.

SECTION 4. The validity of the public debt of the United States, authorized by law, including debts incurred for payment of pensions and bounties for services in suppressing insurrection or rebellion, shall not be questioned. But neither the United States nor any State shall assume or pay any debt or obligation incurred in aid of insurrection or rebellion against the United States, or any claim for the loss or emancipation of any slave; but all such debts, obligations, and claims shall be held illegal and void.

SECTION 5. The Congress shall have the power to enforce, by appropriate legislation, the provisions of this article.

AMENDMENT XV (1870)

SECTION 1. The right of citizens of the United States to vote shall not be denied or abridged by the United

States or by any State on account of race, color, or previous condition of servitude—

SECTION 2. The Congress shall have power to enforce this article by appropriate legislation.

Source: United States, "The 'Civil War Amendments' to the United States Constitution," in *Documents of American History*, ed. Henry Steele Commager (New York: Appleton-Century-Crofts, 1963).

∾DOCUMENT 69∾
THE LAW OF FREE BIRTH (1871)

Brazil made an effort to abolish slavery in stages. The Law of Free Birth emancipated children born of slave parents, but it did not end slavery itself. It was not until 1888 that slavery was abolished entirely in Brazil.

Princess Imperial, Regent, in the name of His Majesty the Emperor Senhor D. Pedro II, makes known to all the subjects of the Empire, that the General Assembly has decreed, and that she has sanctioned, the following Law:

Art. I. The children of women slaves that may be born in the Empire from the date of this Law shall be considered to be free.

1. The said minors shall remain with and be under the dominion of the owners of the mother, who shall be obliged to rear and take care of them until such children shall have completed the age of eight years.

On the child of the slave attaining this age, the owner of its mother shall have the option either of receiving from the State the indemnification of 600 dollars, or of making use of the services of the minor until he shall have completed the age of twenty-one years.

In the former event the Government will receive the minor, and will dispose of him in conformity with the provisions of the present Law.

The pecuniary indemnification above fixed shall be paid in Government bonds, bearing interest at six per cent. per annum, which will be considered extinct at the end of thirty years.

The declaration of the owner must be made within thirty days, counting from the day on which the minor shall complete the age of eight years; and should he not do so within that time it will be understood that he embraces the option of making use of the service of the minor.

2. Any one of those minors may ransom himself from the onus of servitude, by means of a previous pecuniary indemnification, offered by himself, or by any other person, to the owner of his mother, calculating the value of his services for the time which shall still remain unexpired to complete the period, should there be no agreement on the quantum of the said indemnification.

3. It is also incumbent on owners to rear and bring up the children which the daughters of their female slaves may have while they are serving the same owners.

Such obligation, however, will cease as soon as the service of the mother ceases. Should the latter die within the term of servitude the children may be placed at the disposal of the Government.

4. Should the female slave obtain her freedom, her children under eight years of age who may be under the dominion of her owners shall, by virtue of [section] 1 [above], be delivered up, unless she shall prefer leaving them with him, and he consents to their remaining.

5. In case of the female slave being made over to another owner her free children under twelve years of age shall accompany her, the new owner of the said slave being invested with the rights and obligations of his predecessor.

6. The services of the children of female slaves shall cease to be rendered before the term marked in 1, if by decision of the Criminal judge it be known that the owner of the mothers ill-treat the children, inflicting on them severe punishments.

7. The right conferred on owners by 1 shall be transferred in cases of direct succession; the child of a slave must render his services to the person to whose share in the division of property the said slave shall belong.

II. The Government may deliver over to associations which they shall have authorized, the children of the slaves that may be born from the date of this Law forward, and given up or abandoned by the owners of said slaves, or taken away from them by virtue of Article 1, 6.

1. The said associations shall have a right to the gratuitous services of the minors, until they shall have completed the age of twenty-one years, and may hire out their services, but shall be bound—

1st. To rear and take care of the said minors.

2ndly. To save a sum for each of them, out of the amount of wages, which for this purpose is reserved in the respective statutes.

3rdly. To seek to place them in a proper situation when their term of service shall be ended.

2. The associations referred to in the previous paragraph shall be subject to the inspection of judges of the Orphans' Court, in as far as affects minors.

3. The disposition of this Article is applicable to foundling asylums, and to the persons whom the judges of the Orphans' Court charge with the education of the said minors, in default of associations or houses established for that purpose.

4. The Government has the free right of ordering the said minors to be taken into the public establishments, the obligations imposed by 1 on the authorised associations being in this case transferred to the State.

III. As many slaves as correspond in value to the annual disposable sum from the emancipation fund shall be freed in each province of the Empire.

1. The emancipation fund arises from—

1st. The tax on slaves.

2ndly. General tax on transfer of the slaves as property.

3rdly. The proceeds of six lotteries per annum, free of tax, and the tenth part of those which may be granted from this time forth, to be drawn in the capital of the Empire.

4thly. The fines imposed by virtue of this Law.

5thly. The sums which may be marked in the general budget, and in those of the provinces and municipalities.

6thly. Subscriptions, endowments, and legacies for that purpose.

2. The sums marked in the provincial and municipal budgets, as also the subscriptions, endowments, and legacies for the local purpose, shall be applied for the manumission of slaves in the provinces, districts, municipalities, and parishes designated.

IV. The slave is permitted to form a saving fund from what may come to him through gifts, legacies, and inheritances, and from what, by consent of his owner, be may obtain by his labor and economy. The Government will see to the regulations as to the placing and security of said savings.

1. By the death of the slave half of his savings shall belong to his surviving widow, if there be such, and the other half shall be transmitted to his heirs in conformity with civil law.

In default of heirs the savings shall be adjudged to the emancipation fund of which Article III treats.

2. The slave who, through his savings, may obtain means to pay his value has a right to freedom.

If the indemnification be not fixed by agreement it shall be settled by arbitration. In judicial sales or inventories the price of manumission shall be that of the valuation.

3. It is further permitted the slave, in furtherance of his liberty, to contract with a third party the hire of his future services, for a term not exceeding seven years, by obtaining the consent of his master, and approval of the judge of the Orphans' Court.

4. The slave that belongs to joint proprietors, and is freed by one of them, shall have a right to his freedom by indemnifying the other owners with the share of the amount which belongs to them. This indemnification may be paid by services rendered for a term not exceeding seven years, in conformity with the preceding paragraph.

5. The manumission, with the clause of services during a certain time, shall not become annulled by want of fulfilling the said clause, but the freed man shall be compelled to fulfil, by means of labour in the public establishments, or by contracting for his services with private persons.

6. Manumissions, whether gratuitous or by means of onus, shall be exempted from all duties, emoluments, or expenses.

7. In any case of alienation or transfer of slaves, the separation of husband and wife, and children under twelve years of age from father or mother, is prohibited under penalty of annulment.

8. If the division of property among heirs or partners does not permit the union of a family, and none of them prefers remaining with the family by replacing the amount of the share belonging to the other interested parties, the said family shall be sold and the proceeds shall be divided among the heirs.

9. The ordination, Book 4th, title 63, in the part which revokes freedom, on account of ingratitude, is set aside.

V. The Emancipation Societies which are formed, and those which may for the future be formed, shall be subject to the inspection of the Judges of the Orphans' Court.

Sole paragraph. The said societies shall have the privilege of commanding the services of the slaves whom they may have liberated, to indemnify themselves for the sum spent in their purchase.

VI. The following shall be declared free:

1. The slaves belonging to the State, the Government giving them such employment as they may deem fit.

2. The slave given in usufruct to the Crown.

3. The slaves of unclaimed inheritances.

4. The slaves who have been abandoned by their owners.

Should these have abandoned the slaves from the latter being invalids they shall be obliged to maintain them, except in case of their own penury, the maintenance being charged by the judge of the Orphans' Court.

5. In general the slaves liberated by virtue of this Law shall be under the inspection of Government during five years. They will be obliged to hire themselves under pain of compulsion; if they lead an idle life they shall be made to work in the public establishments.

The compulsory labour, however, shall cease so soon as the freed man shall exhibit an engagement of hire.

VII. In trials in favour of freedoms—

1. The process shall be summary.

2. There shall be appeal ex officio when the decisions shall be against the freedom.

VIII. The Government will order the special registration of all the slaves existing in the Empire to be proceeded with, containing a declaration of name, sex, age, state, aptitude for work, and filiation of each, if such should be known.

1. The date on which the registry ought to commence closing shall be announced beforehand, the longest time possible being given for preparation by means of edicts repeated, in which shall be inserted the dispositions of the following paragraph.

2. The slaves who, through the fault or omission of the parties interested, shall not have been registered up to one year after the closing of the register, shall, de facto, be considered as free.

3. For registering each slave the owner shall pay, once only, the emolument Of 500 reis, if done within the term marked, and one dollar should that be exceeded. The produce of those emoluments shall go towards the expenses of registering, and the surplus to the emancipation fund.

4. The children of a slave mother, who by this Law became free, shall also be registered in a separate book.

Those persons who have become remiss shall incur a fine of 100 dollars to 200 dollars, repeated as many times is there may be individuals omitted: and for fraud, in the penalties of Article CLXXIX of the Criminal Code.

5. The parish priests shall be obliged to have special books for the registry of births and deaths of the children of slaves born from and after the date of this law. Each omission will subject the parish priest to a fine of 100 dollars.

IX. The Government, in its regulations, can impose fines of as much as 100 dollars, and the penalty of imprisonment up to one month.

X. All contrary dispositions are revoked.

Therefore, order all authorities to whom, &c. Given at the Palace of Rio de Janeiro, on the 28th September, 1871. 50th of the Independence and of the Empire.

PRINCESS IMPERIAL, REGENT.

THEODORO MACHADO FREIRE PEREIRA DA SILVA.

Source: Pedro II, Dom (Pedro de Alcântara), emperor of Brazil, "The Law of Free Birth," in *A Documentary History of Brazil*, ed. E. Bradford Burns (New York: Alfred A. Knopf, 1966).

❦DOCUMENT 70❦
EGYPTIAN JUDICIAL RULING ON SLAVERY AND ISLAM (1882)

During "the scramble for Africa," various European powers carved out colonial possessions on that continent. One of the stated goals of many European powers during this colonial era was the ending of the practice of slavery within Africa. In the following account, we see the difficulty often encountered when trying to reconcile different legal and cultural codes to achieve the desired result of bringing an end to slavery.

Does the Koran after all sanction this modern form of Slavery? I am inclined to think that the Mahomedan authorities who were consulted in 1877 opined that it did not, and I believe they were right. I have searched the Koran from end to end, and I find that the retention of captives taken in war and not ransomed is the only form of Slavery sanctioned by Mahomet (Koran, ch. 47, v. 4. and 5). The Prophet would have shrunk with horror from the present system, under which men, women, and children are hurried from their tropical homes, dragged in chains, driven with whips down to the sea coast, or to the river, or to the desert tracks, and finally a miserable remnant of them sold in the market at Cairo or Constantinople, "Show kindness to your Slaves." (ch. 4, 40), says Mahomet, and again "Alms should buy the freedom of slaves." (Ch. 9, 60.) But the great doctrine of emancipation itself is preached in one remarkable injunction which might well be printed in letters of gold on the walls of every Mahomemedan [sic] mosque as a preamble to an Arabic translation of the Slave-trade convention. It runs thus:

"If any one of your slaves asks from you his freedom give it him if you judge him worthy of it; grant them a little of the goods which God has granted you." (Ch. 24, v. 33).

Source: John Scott, "Anti-Slavery Reporter," in *A Collection of Documents on the Slave Trade of East Africa*, ed. R. W. Beachey (London: Rex Collings, 1976).

❦DOCUMENT 71❦
THE BERLIN ACT (1885)

The Berlin Act established the basic premises followed by European powers during "the scramble for Africa" when colonial settlements were carved out of the African continent. One of the basic assumptions associated with this era of colonial expansion was that under the trusteeship and "civilizing influence" of European culture, the practice of slavery could be eliminated throughout all of Africa. These themes are reflected in the following Introduction to the act.

In the Name of Almighty God.
Her Majesty the Queen of the United Kingdom of Great Britain and Ireland, Empress of India; His Majesty the German Emperor, King of Prussia; His Majesty the Emperor of Austria, King of Bohemia, &c., and Apostolic King of Hungary; His Majesty the King of the Belgians; His Majesty the King of Denmark; His Majesty the King of Spain; the President of the United States of America; the President of the French Republic; His Majesty the King of Italy; His Majesty the King of the Netherlands, Grand

Duke of Luxemburg, &c.; His Majesty the King of Portugal and the Algarves, &c.; His Majesty the Emperor of All the Russias; His Majesty the King of Sweden and Norway, &c.; and His Majesty the Emperor of the Ottomans, wishing, in a spirit of good and mutual accord, to regulate the conditions most favourable to the development of trade and civilization in certain regions of Africa, and to assure to all nations the advantages of free navigation on the two chief rivers of Africa flowing into the Atlantic Ocean; being desirous, on the other hand, to obviate the misunderstanding and disputes which might in future arise from new acts of occupation on the coast of Africa; and concerned, at the same time, as to the means of furthering the moral and material well-being of the native populations; have resolved, on the invitation addressed to them by the Imperial Government of Germany, in agreement with the Government of the French Republic, to meet for those purposes in Conference at Berlin, and have appointed as their Plenipotentiaries, to wit: . . . Who, being provided with full powers, which have been found in good and due form, have successively discussed and adopted . . . a General Act, composed of the following Articles.

Source: "The Berlin Act of 1885," in *Concert of Europe*, ed. Rene Albrecht-Carrie (New York: Walker and Company, 1968).

∾DOCUMENT 72∾
THE GOLDEN LAW (1888)

In 1888, the government of Brazil officially abolished slavery through an imperial decree. Brazil was the last nation in the Western Hemisphere to maintain a slave-based economy.

The Princess Imperial Regent, in the name of His Majesty the Emperor Dom Pedro II, makes known to all subjects of the Empire that the General Assembly has decreed, and she has approved, the following Law:—

Art. 1—From the date of this Law slavery is declared abolished in Brazil.

2. All contrary provisions are revoked.

She orders, therefore, all the authorities to whom belong the knowledge and execution of the said Law to execute it, and cause it to be fully and exactly executed and observed.

The Secretary of State for the Departments of Agriculture, Commerce, and Public Works, and ad interim for Foreign Affairs, Bachelor Rodrigo Augusto da Silva, of the Council of His Majesty the Emperor, will cause it to be printed, published, and circulated.

Given in the Palace of Rio de Janeiro, May 13, 1888, the 67th year of Independence and of the Empire.

PRINCESS IMPERIAL REGENT
RODRIGO AUGUSTO DA SILVA

Source: Rodrigo Augusto Da Silva, "The Law Abolishing Slavery," in *A Documentary History of Brazil*, ed. E. Bradford Burns (New York: Alfred A. Knopf, 1966).

∾DOCUMENT 73∾
FREDERICK DEALTRY LUGARD ON SLAVERY (1893)

Frederick D. Lugard was a European colonial administrator who worked to end the slave trade within Africa. The following passage reflects the intense level of racism that motivated Lugard and many of his fellow colonial administrators.

These savages do not think or act as we do. They are, in truth, like 'dumb driven cattle'. With the slave caravan they suffer uncomplainingly starvation, the scourge and all the painted horrors of so many writers. They meet a European safari, and they hide in the jungle and rejoin the Slavers. Like cattle, they will face any misery, but dread the unknown. They are brought on by us,—fed, clothed, and spoken kindly to; they bolt. Why? Perhaps they are suspicious of what all this means, and as in the dumb brute's instinct to wander which makes them go. They wander off as cattle do, regardless of state and food, of danger from lions, or danger of a cruel master, instead of a kind one. The very immediate present is the only thought, and sooner than march tomorrow to the unknown, they slip off today, and follow the caged bird's instinct, and, like it, they perish in their ill-advised liberty; but who blames the foolish bird?

Source: F. D. Lugard, "The Rise of Our East African Empire," in *A Collection of Documents on the Slave Trade of East Africa*, ed. R. W. Beachey (London: Rex Collings, 1976).

∾DOCUMENT 74∾
A MEMORANDUM CONCERNING ISLAMIC LAWS GOVERNING SLAVERY IN EAST AFRICA (1895)

Much of the slave trade that existed in East Africa in the late-nineteenth century was conducted under the auspices of Muslim slave traders. In order to understand the type of slavery that persisted in this region, it is important to consider the Muslim laws that governed the institution of slavery. The following description of these laws was written by one Arthur Hardinge.

In Zanzibar as in other Moslem countries the institution of slavery rests upon the "Sheria," or religious law, which is here, unlike that of Turkey and Egypt, the secular and municipal law also. This law has been modified in practice (1) by local custom, and (2) by the arbitrary Edicts of despotic Rulers issued under foreign pressure, and which, whilst condemned by native public opinion as illegal and contrary to the faith, and evaded whenever possible, have been enforced from time to time in a greater or less degree by the physical power of the infidel.

The following are the legal disabilities which the Mahommedan religion and law (and the two are in Zanzibar, save for the exceptions mentioned above, identical) impose upon the slave:—

(a.) He cannot own, or acquire, or dispose of private property without the permission of his master.

(b.) He cannot give evidence in a Court of justice, nor, without his master's sanction, take an oath.

(c.) He cannot, without the sanction of his master, contract a legal marriage, nor, according to most of the doctors, even with the permission of his master, have more than two wives at the same time.

(d.) He cannot sue his master before a Court of law, unless severely ill-treated by the latter. In case of such ill-treatment the Cadi may and ought to warn the master that if the complaint is repeated, and proved genuine, he will forfeit his slave. Should the slave sue his master a second time, and the charge of cruelty be established, the Cadi may order the slave to be valued and sold, and the purchase-money to be paid to the master.

(e.) He cannot sue any other person, whether free or slave, without his master's consent; with it, he is free to do so.

(f.) He cannot, without his master's permission, engage in trade, undertake a journey, or even make the pilgrimage to Mecca, nor in general claim any legal or civil right, except through and with his master's sanction.

(g.) There is no legal limitation to his master's power of punishing him, and, theoretically, I believe that he might put him to death without himself being held guilty of murder, or of any more serious offence than cruelty.

The principle of the Mosaic law which made it penal to scourge a slave to death, if he died under the lash, but not if he survived it one day (Exodus xxi, 20), on the ground that the slave was "his master's money," and his loss a sufficient penalty in itself, would appear to have been followed to a still harsher and more logical conclusion by the Mahommedan jurists; but, in practice, I imagine that in most Moslem countries, even without European pressure, the equity of the Ruler would be allowed to correct the injustice of the law, and that the severe, though not the capital, punishment of a master proved to

have recklessly killed his slave would commend itself to the popular sense of right.

A master may imprison his slave for a short term, and may give him nineteen strokes at a time as a punishment for an offence without being held guilty, by the usage of Zanzibar, of cruelty, To beat him without cause, or to inflict a really cruel beating with cause, would justify the Cadi, if complained to by the slave, and if the cruelty had been repeated twice, in ordering his master to sell him, The Ibadhis, I believe, allow the punishments which a master may inflict without committing cruelty to be somewhat more severe than is the case among the Sunnis.

(h.) Save the general prohibition described above of ill-treatment or cruelty, there is no legal limitation to the amount or nature of the work which a master may impose on his slave, whether the latter be a man, woman, or a child.

These disabilities are mitigated as follows: (a) by custom, (b) by the arbitrary power of the Sultan,

(a.) In practice slaves do hold property of their own, and are allowed by their masters to dispose of it. It is quite a common thing for a slave to have slaves of his own, and to treat the produce of their labour as his personal property. In practice, moreover, the slave is always allowed to labour two days in the week, or at least one day for himself and his family alone, and what he earns on those days is regarded by local custom as exclusively his. He is also permitted to retain a small portion of what he earns while working for his master, and once every six months he is entitled to new clothing (one shirt or white cotton gown for a man, two pieces of cloth for a woman). If his master gives him neither board, lodging, nor clothing beyond the regular half-yearly allowance mentioned above he is entitled to half his earnings, or 2 dollars or 2 1/2 dollars a month. Should his master refuse it him he can be summoned on the slave's complaint by the Cadi, and ordered to pay the slave, and, in the event of his persisting in his refusal, he can be imprisoned, not, however, be it noted, for harshness to his slave, but for contempt of the Cadi's order. If the slave gets no pay he is entitled to a portion of a room, a bed, and any food left over from his master's meals or cooked by the slaves of the house, or, in place of food, to 2 annas a day out of his earnings. If he is invalided, custom obliges the master to provide for him. Only last week I freed a slave on the ground of cruelty on the part of his master, who had turned him adrift when unfit, on account of a bad leg, to work, and who then, as soon as his leg was healed, seized and forced him to return to labour. All these relaxations and indulgences are, strictly speaking, conventional rather than legal, but they have become so stereotyped by custom that the Courts consider themselves justified in regarding a refusal to grant them as technically equivalent to cruelty, I have always myself so considered them, and have several times on that ground given their freedom to slaves who complained that they had been without reason withheld.

(b.) The Sultan, by the exercise of his authority as Hakim, or temporal Ruler, prohibits the sale of slaves. In a case of "cruelty," therefore, the slave has to be liberated without the compensation which the letter of the law gives the master. This procedure being, however, contrary to the Sheria, a Cadi would not apply it himself, but would send the parties to His Highness.

I will now proceed to describe the means by which a slave can acquire his freedom (a) by the law and (b) by the usage and positive Edicts of the Sultans, which have modified it.

According to the Mahommedan law, no authority whatever, except his master, can free a slave.

There are, so far as I know, only three exceptions to this rule:—

1. After the death of a master, two witnesses, being men of good repute, declare before Cadi that they heard the deceased verbally pronounce the slave to be free. The Cadi can then free him without reference to the claims of the heirs. Some of the jurists of the Ibadhi sect, to which the Sultan and the Zanzibar Arabs, as distinct from the Swahilis, belong, doubt the lawfulness of such manumission on mere hearsay evidence. I may observe, indeed, that the general doctrines of the sect are much less favourable to the rights of the slave than those of orthodox Mahommedanism with which they are occasionally in conflict on points of the law of slavery, and that emancipation among the lbadhis is a good deal rarer than among Sunnis.

2. A concubine who bears her master a child, if not actually freed by him on its birth, becomes *ipso facto* a free woman at his death, and cannot even during his lifetime be sold. This form of emancipation, which is known to the law as "istilad," is, of course, dependent on the master recognizing the child, which in most Mahommedan countries he is not strictly bound to do, even though he may believe it to be his; in Zanzibar he usually so recognizes it, but the "mustallida," or "umm-el-walad," as the mother is called, does not necessarily acquire absolute freedom till after the master's death. The latter cannot sell her, but he may lawfully continue, without marrying, to cohabit with her so long as she is a slave, unless he should give her in marriage to another man, in which case she must be divorced before he can again have intercourse with her, I should add that a slave concubine, not being an "umm-el-walad," cannot, if married with her master's consent, and not divorced by her husband, be sold, but her master may compel her to work for him. Her children, even if her husband is a freeman, are slaves, and their master may make them work for him, but,

like their mother, they cannot be sold. According to the Ibadhis, though the master cannot sell a concubine by whom he has had a child, her immunity ceases at his death, and she can be offered for sale by his children born of wives who inherit her as their property, and who can usually insure her being bought by her own children, the latter, though not heirs, being free. This cruel practice was prohibited for a time by Seyyid Barghash, who was himself the son of a slave, but his prohibition had, of course, no legal force.

3. A person committing certain specified sins, such as breaking the Ramadan fast, killing another Mahommedan accidentally and unintentionally ("katl-el-hatta"), and divorcing his wife by "zihar," may be ordered by the Cadi to manumit a slave, or to feed a certain number of poor persons as "tahrir," or atonement.

Exclusive of these particular modes of emancipation, there are three forms by which a master can manumit:—

1. "Atak," the verbal grant of immediate and unconditional freedom.

2. "Tadbir," a promise of freedom contingent on the master's death, and revocable by him at pleasure at any time before, it but otherwise conferring freedom immediately the master dies, not only on the slave himself, but on all his children born subsequent to the promise; and

3. "Kitabah," a written agreement to free the slave on certain conditions such as the payment in instalments of a ransom, pending the completion of which the slave, under the title of "mukaltib," enjoys a certain amount of personal freedom, but cannot by himself perform any valid legal or civil act.

Of these three modes of manumission, I believe "tadbir" to be the commonest in Zanzibar at present; "kitabah" is, I am told, a good deal rarer.

It should be remembered, in this connection, that the emancipation of slaves is a very meritorious act in the eyes of the Mahommedan religion, and that it has always been common for devout Moslems to purchase them with this specific object, a bequest of money for this purpose by will being considered peculiarly commendable.

It is a tradition that the Prophet once exclaimed: "Whosoever shall free a Moslem slave God will free every member of his body, limb by limb, from the fire of hell."

The emancipation by a stranger, such as a British Consul or other authority, of slaves purchased with this religious intention, is therefore strongly resented by their owners, as depriving them of the merits of their contemplated act, and defrauding them, so to speak, of an investment in the world to come.

To sum up, whilst the Mahommedan law generally encourages emancipation, it requires, with a very few exceptions, that it should be the master's own free and spontaneous act.

At Zanzibar, however, the principles described above, although theoretically immutable, have been undermined by the operation of modern non-Mahommedan legislation, such as the Treaty between Seyyid Barghash and Her Majesty forbidding the introduction of any slaves by sea, the Decree of Seyyid Khalifa giving freedom to all slaves entering his territory after a certain date, that of Seyyid Ali prohibiting the sale and purchase of slaves, or their acquisition by any means save direct inheritance, and the Articles in the Brussels Act permitting and directing emancipation by a variety of authorities unknown to Sacred law.

Thus both the Sultan and I myself habitually free slaves in the exercise, so to speak, of our prerogative. His highness, I believe, keeps within the letter of the law, by ordering the master in every case to free the slave himself, thus maintaining the fiction of a voluntary act, since no Arab or Swahili Hampden would ever be found to insist on legal rights, in the face of a Royal command. I of course simply grant papers of freedom, without regard either to the letter or to the spirit of the law.

It is indeed very doubtful whether emancipation granted, even by a master, under compulsion, could be regarded as legally valid in the native Courts. They would certainly not recognize emancipation by myself or the Brussels Act, and, as far as they dared, they would, if appealed to, hardly be able to help pronouncing it invalid.

Suppose, for instance, a slave freed by me contrary to the Sheria were to bring an action against his former master, and that the latter were to plead that the emancipation was illegal, and that the plaintiff was still a slave, and therefore could not sue him, the Cadi would, according to strict law, be obliged to dismiss the case, and would probably do so, if he fancied it would go no further; but if the slave were shrewd enough to threaten him with the Sultan's anger for ignoring one of his Decrees, he would most likely discover some pretext for referring the dispute to His Highness, and thus shifting on to the shoulders of the latter the responsibility of breaking the Sacred Law. One convenient and rather interesting loophole for the Cadis of the lbadhi sect is the doctrine of "takiah," or pious hypocrisy, which permits a man to commit an action forbidden by God, if necessary, to save himself, so long as he abhors it in his heart. Thus the chief lbadhi Cadi here once told me, in reply to a question which I had put to him, that it would not be sinful for him to eat pork, if commanded by a tyrant to do so on pain of punishment, and when I cited to him the examples of Daniel and other saints who had been flung to lions rather than violate God's commands to please Kings, he ingenuously remarked these holy men being endowed with the gift of prophecy, were enabled to foretell beforehand that God would not allow the lions to do them any harm.

"We, however," he added, "have no assurance, if the Sultan should put us in the fort, for applying the Divine Law without fear of man, that Allah would send an angel to release us." It is probable that the Sultans themselves, in signing and enforcing all these Edicts against the Moslem laws of slavery, in order to conciliate mighty infidel powers, have found, and will continue to find, much comfort in this pleasant and useful doctrine of "takiah."

The grounds on which slaves are now freed by the Sultan and myself are twofold: (1) illegal purchase or importation, and (2) cruelty. It frequently happens that slaves come here with complaints of one kind or another, and that it transpires on inquiry that they have either been imported since the Decree of Seyyid Khalifa, or changed masters by sale, gift, or bequest, since the Decree of Seyyid Ali—both of which, owing to real or pretended ignorance, are, I regret to say, constantly disobeyed. Complaints of cruelty are a good deal more frequent; but many of the cases brought before me are purely frivolous, and often amount merely to a blow or to a mild castigation with the stick for impertinence, laziness, assaults on other slaves, or some equally trifling matter. Once, for instance, a concubine complained to me that her master had brought home a second slave girl, and wanted either to be emancipated herself, or to be given, if her rival were not instantly dismissed, a separate house to live in with her children. On her master's agreeing to this she objected, because the house was in the country and was not in town, and she ultimately carried her point, and drove the rival concubine from the field. When, however, any case of real cruelty comes to my notice, and the slave shows either marks of severe beating, or of having been insufficiently fed, or been made to work when physically unfit, or complains of the withholding of any of the customary indulgences, I either free him myself if he belongs to the mainland, or send him, if a native of Zanzibar, to the Sultan, with a request that he may be freed, and his master punished according to the merits of the case; and His Highness has hitherto in every instance most readily carried out my wishes. I should add that the same procedure is followed in the case of slaves sold or imported contrary to the Sultan's Decree; and, further, that since 1890, under the agreement between Seyyid Khalifa and sir Gerald Portal of the 13th September, 1889, all persons, whatever their origin, born in Pemba and Zanzibar, are born free. I have not so far insisted on this last measure, for it, at present, only affects very young children; and there is always the obvious danger that some owners (I trust not very many) might reply that, if these children are not their slaves, they are under no obligation to maintain or assist their slave mothers in maintaining them. Such a contention would, of course, be most inhuman, and quite opposed to the Mahommedan religion; but it might not be easy for the Sultan or myself to appeal to the Mahommedan law in this respect, after having ourselves disregarded it in so many others. The question as to how these children's rights shall be asserted, and what compensation, if any, shall be assigned to their present masters for providing them till they grow up, will, however, become more pressing every year. My own inclination would be, whilst treating them in every other respect as absolute freemen, to apprentice them for a term of years—seven, ten, or any other reasonable period—after the age of (say) 15, to their parents' master, and thus make them pay back in useful labour the cost of their maintenance during childhood.

Source: Arthur Hardinge, "Africa No. 6 C-7707, 26 February 1895," in *A Collection of Documents on the Slave Trade of East Africa,* ed. R. W. Beachey (London: Rex Collings, 1976).

∾DOCUMENT 75∾
DECREE RESPECTING DOMESTIC SLAVERY IN GERMAN EAST AFRICA (1901)

Colonial administrators employed a variety of means to end slavery in their respective colonial regions. The following document represents efforts taken in German East Africa to end the indigenous practices of slavery that persisted in that area.

I
No one shall be placed in a condition of slavery, when he is not already in such, by disposing of himself by sale or by being sold by relations, or on account of debts or other obligations. or as punishment for adultery.

II
Every domestic slave is empowered to bring about a termination of his slavery by paying a ransom.

III
The amount of this ransom will be fixed by the competent authorities, and a document establishing his liberty is to be made out for every slave by the authorities, after the stipulated sum of money has been paid in.

IV
Every domestic slave must be permitted to work on his own account during two days of the week, or else to apply to his own uses the same proportion of the earnings of his work. So far as the rights fixed by custom in this respect are more favourable to the slave than this present Regulation, they are to remain unaltered. In case of a dispute between owner and slave on this point as on others, the matter will be decided by the other competent authorities.

V
The owner of a domestic slave is bound also to support him in old age, and to care for him during illness. This obligation is not abolished when a slave, from incapacity of old age or illness, is given his freedom.

VI
The transference of rights of ownership over a domestic slave can only take place with the consent of the slave and before the competent authorities, on whose concurrence the transaction depends. Before allowing the transference, the authorities must examine the legality of the state of slavery, besides other points, which may appear to them as important, and especially pay attention to preventing the members of one family from being separated from one another without their consent.

VII
The right of ownership over a domestic slave is forfeited when the owner is guilty of a grave lack of duty towards his slave. The competent authorities must make official inquiries into any cases of this kind which may reach their ears, and are empowered to cause the slave to be set at liberty by means of a document declaratory of his freedom, without the ex-owner having the right to put in any claim to compensation.

VIII
Infractions of the Regulations laid down in the present Decree are punishable by a money fine of up to 500 rupees, or up to three months' imprisonment—that is, as far as higher punishments are not incurred under existing laws on the subject.

IX
This decree comes into force on the day of its promulgation.

THE IMPERIAL CHANCELLOR
Count V. Bulow

Source: Count V. Bulow, "Decree Respecting Domestic Slavery in German East Africa," in *A Collection of Documents on the Slave Trade of East Africa,* ed. R. W. Beachey (London: Rex Collings, 1976).

～DOCUMENT 76～
LEAGUE OF NATIONS
SLAVERY CONVENTION (1926)

One of the efforts undertaken by the League of Nations in the decade following World War I was a campaign to end slavery worldwide.

ALBANIA, GERMANY, AUSTRIA, BELGIUM, THE BRITISH EMPIRE, CANADA, THE COMMONWEALTH OF AUSTRALIA, THE UNION OF SOUTH AFRICA, THE DOMINION OF NEW ZEALAND, AND INDIA, BULGARIA, CHINA, COLOMBIA, CUBA, DENMARK, SPAIN, ESTONIA, ABYSSINIA, FINLAND, FRANCE, GREECE, ITALY, LATVIA, LIBERIA, LITHUANIA, NORWAY, PANAMA, THE NETHERLANDS, PERSIA, POLAND, PORTUGAL, ROUMANIA, THE KINGDOM OF THE SERBS, CROATS AND SLOVENES, SWEDEN, CZECHOSLOVAKIA AND URUGUAY,

Whereas the signatories of the General Act of the Brussels Conference of 1889–90 declared that they were equally animated by the firm intention of putting an end to the traffic in African slaves;

Whereas the signatories of the Convention of Saint-Germain- en-Laye of 1919, to revise the General Act of Berlin of 1885, and the General Act and Declaration of Brussels of 1890, affirmed their intention of securing the complete suppression of slavery in all its forms and of the slave trade by land and sea;

Taking into consideration the report of the Temporary Slavery Commission appointed by the Council of the League of Nations on June 12th, 1924;

Desiring to complete and extend the work accomplished under the Brussels Act and to find a means of giving practical effect throughout the world to such intentions as were expressed in regard to slave trade and slavery by the signatories of the Convention of Saint-Germain-en-Laye, and recognising that it is necessary to conclude to that end more detailed arrangements than are contained in that Convention;

Considering, moreover, that it is necessary to prevent forced labour from developing into conditions analogous to slavery,

Have decided to conclude a Convention and have accordingly appointed as their Plenipotentiaries:

[40 names of diplomats follow; these are not included here]

Who, having communicated their full powers, have agreed as follows:

Article 1.

For the purpose of the present Convention, the following definitions are agreed upon:

(1) Slavery is the status or condition of a person over whom any or all of the powers attaching to the right of ownership are exercised.

(2) The slave trade includes all acts involved in the capture, acquisition or disposal of a person with intent to reduce him to slavery; all acts involved in the acquisition of a slave with a view to selling or exchanging him; all acts of disposal by sale or exchange of a slave acquired with a view to being sold or exchanged, and, in general, every act of trade or transport in slaves.

Article 2.

The High Contracting Parties undertake, each in respect of the territories placed under its sovereignty, jurisdiction, protection, suzerainty or tutelage, so far as they have not already taken the necessary steps:

(a) To prevent and suppress the slave trade;

(b) To bring about, progressively and as soon as possible, the complete abolition of slavery in all its forms.

Article 3.

The High Contracting Parties undertake to adopt all appropriate measures with a view to preventing and suppressing the embarkation, disembarkation and transport of slaves in their territorial waters and upon all vessels flying their respective flags.

The High Contracting Parties undertake to negotiate as soon as possible a general Convention with regard to the slave trade which will give them rights and impose upon them duties of the same nature as those provided for in the Convention of June 17th, 1925, relative to the International Trade in Arms (Articles 12, 20, 21, 22, 23, 24, and paragraphs 3, 4 and 5 of Section II of Annex II), with the necessary adaptations, it being understood that this general Convention will not place the ships (even of small tonnage) of any High Contracting Parties in a position different from that of the other High Contracting Parties.

It is also understood that, before or after the coming into force of this general Convention the High Contracting Parties are entirely free to conclude between themselves, without, however, derogating from the principles laid down in the preceding paragraph, such special agreements as, by reason of their peculiar situation, might appear to be suitable in order to bring about as soon as possible the complete disappearance of the slave trade.

Article 4.

The High Contracting Parties shall give to one another every assistance with the object of securing the abolition of slavery and the slave trade.

Article 5.

The High Contracting Parties recognise that recourse to compulsory or forced labour may have grave consequences and undertake, each in respect of the territories placed under its sovereignty, jurisdiction, protection, suzerainty or tutelage, to take all necessary measures to prevent compulsory or forced labour from developing into conditions analogous to slavery.

It is agreed that:

(1) Subject to the transitional provisions laid down in paragraph (2) below, compulsory or forced labour may only be exacted for public purposes.

(2) In territories in which compulsory or forced labour for other than public purposes still survives, the High Contracting Parties shall endeavour progressively and as soon as possible to put an end to the practice. So long as such forced or compulsory labour exists, this labour shall invariably be of an exceptional character, shall always receive adequate remuneration, and shall not involve the removal of the labourers from their usual place of residence.

(3) In all cases, the responsibility for any recourse to compulsory or forced labour shall rest with the competent central authorities of the territory concerned.

Article 6.

Those of the High Contracting Parties whose laws do not at present make adequate provision for the punishment of infractions of laws and regulations enacted with a view to giving effect to the purposes of the present Convention undertake to adopt the necessary measures in order that severe penalties may be imposed in respect of such infractions.

Article 7.

The High Contracting Parties undertake to communicate to each other and to the Secretary-General of the League of Nations any laws and regulations which they may enact with a view to the application of the provisions of the present Convention.

Article 8.

The High Contracting Parties agree that disputes arising between them relating to the interpretation or application of this Convention shall, if they cannot be settled by direct negotiation, be referred for decision to the Permanent Court of International Justice. In case either or both of the States Parties to such a dispute should not be parties to the Protocol of December 16th, 1920 relating to the Permanent Court of International Justice, the dispute shall be referred, at the choice of the Parties and in accordance with the constitutional procedure of each State either to the Permanent Court of International Justice or to a court of arbitration constituted in accordance with the Convention of October 18th, 1907, for the Pacific Settlement of International Disputes, or to some other court of arbitration.

Article 9.

At the time of signature or of ratification or of accession, any High Contracting Party may declare that its acceptance of the present Convention docs not bind some or all of the territories placed under its sovereignty, jurisdiction, protection, suzerainty or tutelage in respect of all or any provisions of the Convention; it may subsequently accede separately on behalf of any one of them or in respect of any provision to which any one of them is not a party.

Article 10.

In the event of a High Contracting Party wishing to denounce the present Convention, the denunciation shall be notified in writing to the Secretary-General of the League of Nations, who will at once communicate a certified true copy of the notification to all the other High Contracting Parties, informing them of the date on which it was received.

The denunciation shall only have effect in regard to the notifying State, and one year after the notification has reached the Secretary-General of the League of Nations.

Denunciation may also be made separately in respect of any territory placed under its sovereignty, jurisdiction, protection, suzerainty or tutelage.

Article 11.

The present Convention, which will bear this day's date and of which the French and English texts are both authentic, will remain open for signature by the States Members of the League of Nations until April 1st, 1927.

The Secretary-General of the League of Nations will subsequently bring the present Convention to the notice of States which have not signed it, including States which are not Members of the League of Nations, and invite them to accede thereto.

A State desiring to accede to the Convention shall notify its intention in writing to the Secretary-General of the League of Nations and transmit to him the instrument of accession, which shall be deposited in the archives of the League.

The Secretary-General shall immediately transmit to all the other High Contracting Parties a certified true copy of the notification and of the instrument of accession, informing them of the date on which he received them.

Article 12.

The present Convention will be ratified and the instruments of ratification shall be deposited in the office of the Secretary-General of the League of Nations. The Secretary-General will inform all the High Contracting Parties of such deposit.

The Convention will come into operation for each State on the date of the deposit of its ratification or of its accession.

In faith whereof the Plenipotentiaries have signed the present Convention.

DONE at Geneva the twenty-fifth day of September, One thousand nine hundred and twenty-six, in one copy, which will be deposited in the archives of the League of Nations. A certified copy shall be forwarded to each signatory State.

Source: League of Nations, "League of Nations Slavery Convention" (1926; http://www.yale.edu/ lawweb/ avalon/league/lea001.htm).

∾DOCUMENT 77∾
UNITED NATIONS UNIVERSAL DECLARATION OF HUMAN RIGHTS (1948)

Developed as the clearest statement of human rights of the twentieth century, the Universal Declaration of Human Rights proclaimed that "slavery and the slave trade shall be prohibited in all their forms." Fifty years after its adoption in 1948, the world community still aspires to this goal, though the actions of some nations perpetuate slavery in the modern world.

Written at the U.N. in 1948:
Preamble
WHEREAS recognition of the inherent dignity and of the equal and inalienable rights of all members of the human family is the foundation of freedom, justice and peace in the world,

WHEREAS disregard and contempt for human rights have resulted in barbarous acts which have outraged the conscience of mankind, and the advent of a world in which human beings shall enjoy freedom of speech and belief and freedom from fear and want has been proclaimed as the highest aspiration of the common people,

WHEREAS it is essential, if man is not to be compelled to have recourse, as a last resort, to rebellion against tyranny and oppression, that human rights should be protected by the rule of law,

WHEREAS it is essential to promote the development of friendly relations between nations,

WHEREAS the peoples of the United Nations have in the Charter reaffirmed their faith in fundamental human rights, in the dignity and worth of the human person and in the equal rights of men and women and have determined to promote social progress and better standards of life in larger freedom,

WHEREAS Member States have pledged themselves to achieve, in co-operation with the United Nations, the promotion of universal respect for and observance of human rights and fundamental freedoms,

WHEREAS a common understanding of these rights and freedoms is of the greatest importance for the full realization of this pledge,

Now, Therefore, The General Assembly proclaims This Universal Declaration of Human Rights as a common standard of achievement for all peoples and all nations, to the end that every individual and every organ of society, keeping this Declaration constantly in mind, shall strive by teaching and education to promote respect for these rights and freedoms and by progressive measures, national and international, to secure their universal and effective recognition and observance, both among the peoples of Member States themselves and among the peoples of territories under their jurisdiction.

Article 1
All human beings are born free and equal in dignity and rights. They are endowed with reason and conscience and should act towards one another in a spirit of brotherhood.

Article 2
Everyone is entitled to all the rights and freedoms set forth in this Declaration, without distinction of any kind, such as race, colour, sex, language, religion, political or other opinion, national or social origin, property, birth or other status.

Furthermore, no distinction shall be made on the basis of the political, jurisdictional or international status of the country or territory to which a person belongs, whether it be independent, trust, nonselfgoverning or under any other limitation of sovereignty.

Article 3
Everyone has the right to life, liberty and security of person.

Article 4
No one shall be held in slavery or servitude; slavery and the slave trade shall be prohibited in all their forms.

Article 5
No one shall be subjected to torture or to cruel, inhuman or degrading treatment or punishment.

Article 6
Everyone has the right to recognition everywhere as a person before the law.

Article 7
All are equal before the law and are entitled without any discrimination to equal protection of the law. All are entitled to equal protection against any discrimination in violation of this Declaration and against any incitement to such discrimination.

Article 8
Everyone has the right to an effective remedy by the

competent national tribunals for acts violating the fundamental rights granted him by the constitution or by law.

Article 9
No one shall be subjected to arbitrary arrest, detention or exile.

Article 10
Everyone is entitled in full equality to a fair and public hearing by an independent and impartial tribunal, in the determination of his rights and obligations and of any criminal charge against him.

Article 11
(1) Everyone charged with a penal offence has the right to be presumed innocent until proved guilty according to law in a public trial at which he has had all the guarantees necessary for his defence.
(2) No one shall be held guilty of any penal offence on account of any act or omission which did not constitute a penal offence, under national or international law, at the time when it was committed. Nor shall a heavier penalty be imposed than the one that was applicable at the time the penal offence was committed.

Article 12
No one shall be subjected to arbitrary interference with his privacy, family, home or correspondence, nor to attacks upon his honour and reputation. Everyone has the right to the protection of the law against such interference or attacks.

Article 13
(1) Everyone has the right to freedom of movement and residence within the borders of each State.
(2) Everyone has the right to leave any country, including his own, and to return to his country.

Article 14
(1) Everyone has the right to seek and to enjoy in other countries asylum from persecution.
(2) This right may not be invoked in the case of prosecutions genuinely arising from non-political crimes or from acts contrary to the purposes and principles of the United Nations.

Article 15
(1) Everyone has the right to a nationality.
(2) No one shall be arbitrarily deprived of his nationality nor denied the right to change his nationality.

Article 16
(1) Men and women of full age, without any limitation due to race, nationality or religion, have the right to marry and to found a family. They are entitled to equal rights as a marriage, during marriage and at its dissolution.
(2) Marriage shall be entered into only with the free and full consent of the intending spouses.
(3) The family is the natural and fundamental group unit of society and is entitled to protection by society and the State.

Article 17
(1) Everyone has the right to own property alone as well as in association with others.
(2) No one shall be arbitrarily deprived of his property.

Article 18
Everyone has the right to freedom of thought, conscience and religion; this right includes freedom to change his religion or belief, and freedom, either alone or in community with others and in public or private, to manifest his religion or belief in teaching, practice, worship and observance.

Article 19
Everyone has the right to freedom of opinion and expression; this right includes freedom to hold opinions without interference and to seek, receive and impart information and ideas through any media and regardless of frontiers.

Article 20
(1) Everyone has the right to freedom of peaceful assembly and association.
(2) No one may be compelled to belong to an association.

Article 21
(1) Everyone has the right to take part in the government of his country, directly or through freely chosen representatives.
(2) Everyone has the right of equal access to public service in his country.
(3) The will of the people shall be the basis of the authority of the government; this will shall be expressed in periodic and genuine elections which shall be by universal and equal suffrage and shall be held by secret vote or by equivalent free voting procedures.

Article 22
Everyone, as a member of society, has the right to social security and is entitled to realization, through national effort and international co-operation and in accordance with the organization and resources of each State, of the economic, social and cultural rights indispensable for his dignity and the free development of his personality.

Article 23

(1) Everyone has the right to work, to free choice of employment, to just and favourable conditions of work and to protection against unemployment.

(2) Everyone, without any discrimination, has the right to equal pay for equal work.

(3) Everyone who works has the right to just and favourable remuneration ensuring for himself and his family an existence worthy of human dignity, and supplemented, if necessary, by other means of social protection.

(4) Everyone has the right to form and to join trade unions for the protection of his interests.

Article 24

Everyone has the right to rest and leisure, including reasonable limitation of working hours and periodic holidays with pay.

Article 25

(1) Everyone has the right to a standard of living adequate for the health and well-being of himself and of his family, including food, clothing, housing, and medical care and necessary social services, and the right to security in the event of unemployment, sickness, disability, widowhood, old age, or other lack of livelihood in circumstances beyond his control.

(2) Motherhood and childhood are entitled to special care and assistance. All children, whether born in or out of wedlock, shall enjoy the same social protection.

Article 26

(1) Everyone has the right to education. Education shall be free, at least in the elementary and fundamental stages. Elementary education shall be compulsory. Technical and professional education shall be made generally available and higher education shall be equally accessible to all on the basis of merit.

(2) Education shall be directed to the full development of the human personality and to the strengthening of respect for human rights and fundamental freedoms. It shall promote understanding, tolerance and friendship among all nations, racial or religious groups, and shall further the activities of the United Nations for the maintenance of peace.

(3) Parents have a prior right to choose the kind of education that shall be given to their children.

Article 27

(1) Everyone has the right freely to participate in the cultural life of the community, to enjoy the arts and to share in scientific advancement and its benefits.

(2) Everyone has the right to the protection of the moral and material interests resulting from any scientific, literary or artistic production of which he is the author.

Article 28

Everyone is entitled to a social and international order in which the rights and freedoms set forth in this Declaration can be fully realized.

Article 29

(1) Everyone has duties to the community in which alone the free and full development of his personality is possible.

(2) In the exercise of his rights and freedoms, everyone shall be subject only to such limitations as are determined by law solely for the purpose of securing due recognition and respect for the rights and freedoms and others and of meeting the just requirements of morality, public order and the general welfare in a democratic society.

(3) These rights and freedoms may in no case be exercised contrary to the purposes and principles of the United Nations.

Article 30

Nothing in this Declaration may be interpreted as implying for any State, group or person any right to engage in any activity or to perform any act aimed at the destruction of any of the rights and freedoms set forth herein.

Source: United Nations, "United Nations Universal Declaration of Human Rights" (1948; www.tufts.edu/departments/fletcher/multi/texts/UNGARES217A.txt).

☙DOCUMENT 78☙
UNITED NATIONS PROTOCOL AMENDING THE SLAVERY CONVENTION SIGNED AT GENEVA ON 25 SEPTEMBER 1926

The United Nations has continued the efforts begun by the League of Nations to end slavery worldwide, as this document and the next show. Unfortunately, despite the best efforts of the international community to end the practice, slavery persists in some parts of the world at the end of the twentieth century.

DONE AT THE HEADQUARTERS OF THE UNITED NATIONS, NEW YORK, ON 7 DECEMBER 1953

The States Parties to the present Protocol,

Considering that under the Slavery Convention signed at Geneva on 25 September 1926 (hereinafter called "the Convention") the League of Nations was invested with certain duties and functions, and

Considering that it is expedient that these duties and functions should be continued by the United Nations,

Have agreed as follows:

Article I

The States Parties to the present Protocol undertake

that as between them selves they will, in accordance with the provisions of the Protocol, attribute full legal force and effect to and duly apply the amendments to the Convention set forth in the annex to the Protocol.

Article II

1. The present Protocol shall be open for signature or acceptance by any of the States Parties to the Convention to which the Secretary-General has communicated for this purpose a copy of the Protocol.

2. States may become Parties to the present Protocol by:

(a) Signature without reservation as to acceptance;

(b) Signature with reservation as to acceptance, followed by acceptance;

(c) Acceptance.

3. Acceptance shall be effected by the deposit of a formal instrument with the Secretary-General of the United Nations.

Article III

1. The present Protocol shall come into force on the date on which two States shall have become Parties thereto, and shall thereafter come into force in respect of each State upon the date on which it becomes a Party to the Protocol.

2. The amendments set forth in the annex to the present Protocol shall come into force when twenty-three States shall have become Parties to the Protocol, and consequently any State becoming a Party to the Convention, after the amendments thereto have come into force, shall become a Party to the Convention as so amended.

Article IV

In accordance with paragraph 1 of Article 102 of the Charter of the United Nations and the regulations pursuant thereto adopted by the General Assembly, the Secretary-General of the United Nations is authorized to effect registration of the present Protocol and of the amendments made in the Convention by the Protocol on the respective dates of their entry into force and to publish the Protocol and the amended text of the Convention as soon as possible after registration.

Article V

The present Protocol, of which the Chinese, English, French, Russian and Spanish texts are equally authentic, shall be deposited in the archives of the United Nations Secretariat. The texts of the Convention to be amended in accordance with the annex being authentic in the English and French languages only, the English and French texts of the annex shall be equally authentic, and the Chinese, Russian and Spanish texts shall be translations. The Secretary-General shall prepare certified copies of the Protocol, including the annex, for communication to States Parties to the Convention, as well as to all other States Members of the United Nations. He shall likewise prepare for communication to States, including States not Members of the United Nations, upon the entry into force of the amendments as provided in article III, certified copies of the Convention as so amended.

IN WITNESS WHEREOF the undersigned, being duly authorized thereto by their respective Governments, signed the present Protocol on the date appearing opposite their respective signatures.

DONE at the Headquarters of the United Nations, New York, this seventh day of December one thousand nine hundred and fifty-three.

ANNEX TO THE PROTOCOL AMENDING THE SLAVERY CONVENTION SIGNED AT GENEVA ON 25 SEPTEMBER 1926.

In article 7 "the Secretary-General of the United Nations" shall be substituted for "the Secretary-General of the League of Nations."

In article 8 "the International Court of Justice" shall be substituted for "the Permanent Court of International Justice," and "the Statute of the International Court of Justice" shall be substituted for "the Protocol of December 16th, 1920, relating to the Permanent Court of International Justice."

In the first and second paragraphs of article 10 "the United Nations" shall be substituted for "the League of Nations."

The last three paragraphs of article 11 shall be deleted and the following substituted:

"The present Convention shall be open to accession by all States, including States which are not Members of the United Nations, to which the Secretary-General of the United Nations shall have communicated a certified copy of the Convention.

Accession shall be effected by the deposit of a formal instrument with the Secretary-General of the United Nations, who shall give notice thereof to all States Parties to the Convention and to all other States contemplated in the present article, informing them of the date on which each such instrument of accession was received in deposit."

In article 12 "the United Nations" shall be substituted for "the League of Nations."

Source: United Nations, "United Nations Protocol Amending the Slavery Convention Signed at Geneva on 25 September 1926" (1953; www.umn.edu/ humanrts/instree/f2psc.htm).

SUPPLEMENTARY CONVENTION ON THE ABOLITION OF SLAVERY, THE SLAVE TRADE, AND INSTITUTIONS AND PRACTICES SIMILAR TO SLAVERY (1956)

The United Nations has continued the efforts that were begun by the League of Nations to end slavery worldwide. Unfortunately, despite the best efforts of the international community to end the practice, slavery persists in some parts of the world at the end of the twentieth century

PREAMBLE

The States Parties to the present Convention

Considering that freedom is the birthright of every human being;

Mindful that the peoples of the United Nations reaffirmed in the Charter their faith in the dignity and worth of the human person;

Considering that the Universal Declaration of Human Rights, proclaimed by the General Assembly of the United Nations as a common standard of achievement for all peoples and all nations, states that no one shall be held in slavery or servitude and that slavery and the slave trade shall be prohibited in all their forms;

Recognizing that, since the conclusion of the Slavery Convention signed at Geneva on 25 September 1926, which was designed to secure the abolition of slavery and of the slave trade, further progress has been made towards this end;

Having regard to the Forced Labour Convention of 1930 and to subsequent action by the International Labour Organisation in regard to forced or compulsory labour;

Being aware, however, that slavery, the slave trade and institutions and practices similar to slavery have not yet been eliminated in all parts of the world;

Having decided, therefore, that the Convention of 1926, which remains operative, should now be augmented by the conclusion of a supplementary convention designed to intensify national as well as international efforts towards the abolition of slavery, the slave trade and institutions and practices similar to slavery;

Have agreed as follows:

SECTION I: INSTITUTIONS AND PRACTICES SIMILAR TO SLAVERY

Article 1

Each of the States Parties to this Convention shall take all practicable and necessary legislative and other measures to bring about progressively and as soon as possible the complete abolition or abandonment of the following institutions and practices, where they still exist and whether or not they are covered by the definition of slavery contained in article 1 of the Slavery Convention signed at Geneva on 25 September 1926:

(a) Debt bondage, that is to say, the status or condition arising from a pledge by a debtor of his personal services or of those of a person under his control as security for a debt, if the value of those services as reasonably assessed is not applied towards the liquidation of the debt or the length and nature of those services are not respectively limited and defined;

(b) Serfdom, that is to say, the condition or status of a tenant who is by law, custom or agreement bound to live and labour on land belonging to another person and to render some determinate service to such other person, whether for reward or not, and is not free to change his status;

(c) Any institution or practice whereby:

(i) A woman, without the right to refuse, is promised or given in marriage on payment of a consideration in money or in kind to her parents, guardian, family or any other person or group; or

(ii) The husband of a woman, his family, or his clan, has the right to transfer her to another person for value received or otherwise; or

(iii) A woman on the death of her husband is liable to be inherited by another person;

(d) Any institution or practice whereby a child or young person under the age of 18 years is delivered by either or both of his natural parents or by his guardian to another person, whether for reward or not, with a view to the exploitation of the child or young person or of his labour.

Article 2

With a view to bringing to an end the institutions and practices mentioned in article 1(c) of this Convention, the States Parties undertake to prescribe, where appropriate, suitable minimum ages of marriage, to encourage the use of facilities whereby the consent of both parties to a marriage may be freely expressed in the presence of a competent civil or religious authority, and to encourage the registration of marriages.

SECTION II: THE SLAVE TRADE

Article 3

1. The act of conveying or attempting to convey slaves from one country to another by whatever means of transport, or of being accessory thereto, shall be a criminal offence under the laws of the States Parties to this Convention and persons convicted thereof shall be liable to very severe penalties.

2. (a) The States Parties shall take all effective measures to prevent ships and aircraft authorized to fly their flags from conveying slaves and to punish persons guilty of such acts or of using national flags for that purpose.

(b) The States Parties shall take all effective measures to ensure that their ports, airfields and coasts are not used for the conveyance of slaves.

3. The States Parties to this Convention shall exchange information in order to ensure the practical co-ordination of the measures taken by them in combating the slave trade and shall inform each other of every case of the slave trade, and of every attempt to commit this criminal offence, which comes to their notice.

Article 4

Any slave who takes refuge on board any vessel of a State Party to this Convention shall ipso facto be free.

SECTION III: SLAVERY AND INSTITUTIONS AND PRACTICES SIMILAR TO SLAVERY

Article 5

In a country where the abolition or abandonment of slavery, or of the institutions or practices mentioned in article I of this Convention, is not yet complete, the act of mutilating, branding or otherwise marking a slave or a person of servile status in order to indicate his status, or as a punishment, or for any other reason, or of being accessory thereto, shall be a criminal offence under the laws of the States Parties to this Convention and persons convicted thereof shall be liable to punishment.

Article 6

1. The act of enslaving another person or of inducing another person to give himself or a person dependent upon him into slavery, or of attempting these acts, or being accessory thereto, or being a party to a conspiracy to accomplish any such acts, shall be a criminal offence under the laws of the States Parties to this Convention and persons convicted thereof shall be liable to punishment.

2. Subject to the provisions of the introductory paragraph of article 1 of this Convention, the provisions of paragraph 1 of the present article shall also apply to the act of inducing another person to place himself or a person dependent upon him into the servile status resulting from any of the institutions or practices mentioned in article 1, to any attempt to perform such acts, to bring accessory thereto, and to being a party to a conspiracy to accomplish any such acts.

SECTION IV: DEFINITIONS

Article 7

For the purposes of the present Convention:

(a) "Slavery" means, as defined in the Slavery Convention of 1926, the status or condition of a person over whom any or all of the powers attaching to the right of ownership are exercised, and "slave" means a person in such condition or status;

(b) "A person of servile status" means a person in the condition or status resulting from any of the in-

stitutions or practices mentioned in article 1 of this Convention;

(c) "Slave trade" means and includes all acts involved in the capture, acquisition or disposal of a person with intent to reduce him to slavery; all acts involved in the acquisition of a slave with a view to selling or exchanging him; all acts of disposal by sale of exchange of a person acquired with a view to being sold or exchanged; and, in general, every act of trade or transport in slaves by whatever means of conveyance.

SECTION V: CO-OPERATION BETWEEN STATES PARTIES AND COMMUNICATION OF INFORMATION

Article 8

1. The States Parties to this Convention undertake to co-operate with each other and with the United Nations to give effect to the foregoing provisions.

2. The Parties undertake to communicate to the Secretary-General of the United Nations copies of any laws, regulations and administrative measures enacted or put into effect to implement the provisions of this Convention.

3. The Secretary-General shall communicate the information received under paragraph 2 of this article to the other Parties and to the Economic and Social Council as part of the documentation for any discussion which the Council might undertake with a view to making further recommendations for the abolition of slavery, the slave trade or the institutions and practices which are the subject of this Convention.

SECTION VI: FINAL CLAUSES

Article 9

No reservations may be made to this Convention.

Article 10

Any dispute between States Parties to this Convention relating to its interpretation or application, which is not settled by negotiation, shall be referred to the International Court of Justice at the request of any one of the parties to the dispute, unless the parties concerned agree on another mode of settlement.

Article 11

1. This Convention shall be open until 1 July 1957 for signature by any State Member of the United Nations or of a specialized agency. It shall be subject to ratification by the signatory States, and the instruments of ratification shall be deposited with the Secretary-General of the United Nations, who shall inform each signatory and acceding State.

2. After 1 July 1957 this Convention shall be open for accession by any State Member of the United Nations or of a specialized agency, or by any other State to which an invitation to accede has been addressed by the General Assembly of the United Nations. Accession shall be effected by the deposit of a formal instrument with the Secretary-General of the United

Nations, who shall inform each signatory and acceding State.

Article 12

1. This Convention shall apply to all nonself-governing, trust, colonial and other non-metropolitan territories for the international relations of which any State Party is responsible; the Party concerned shall, subject to the provisions of paragraph 2 of this article, at the time of signature, ratification or accession declare the non-metropolitan territory or territories to which the Convention shall apply ipso facto as a result of such signature, ratification or accession.

2. In any case in which the previous consent of a non-metropolitan territory is required by the constitutional laws or practices of the Party or of the non-metropolitan territory, the Party concerned shall endeavour to secure the needed consent of the non-metropolitan territory within the period of twelve months from the date of signature of the Convention by the metropolitan State, and when such consent has been obtained the Party shall notify the Secretary-General. This Convention shall apply to the territory or territories named in such notification from the date of its receipt by the Secretary-General.

3. After the expiry of the twelve month period mentioned in the preceding paragraph, the States Parties concerned shall inform the Secretary-General of the results of the consultations with those non-metropolitan territories for whose international relations they are responsible and whose consent to the application of this Convention may have been withheld.

Article 13

1. This Convention shall enter into force on the date on which two States have become Parties thereto.

2. It shall thereafter enter into force with respect to each State and territory on the date of deposit of the instrument of ratification or accession of that State or notification of application to that territory.

Article 14

1. The application of this Convention shall be divided into successive periods of three years, of which the first shall begin on the date of entry into force of the Convention in accordance with paragraph I of article 13.

2. Any State Party may denounce this Convention by a notice addressed by that State to the Secretary-General not less than six months before the expiration of the current three-year period. The Secretary-General shall notify all other Parties of each such notice and the date of the receipt thereof.

3. Denunciations shall take effect at the expiration of the current three- year period.

4. In cases where, in accordance with the provisions of article 12, this Convention has become applicable to a non-metropolitan territory of a Party, that Party may at any time thereafter, with the consent of the territory concerned, give notice to the Sec-

retary-General of the United Nations denouncing this Convention separately in respect of that territory. The denunciation shall take effect one year after the date of the receipt of such notice by the Secretary-General, who shall notify all other Parties of such notice and the date of the receipt thereof.

Article 15

This Convention, of which the Chinese, English, French, Russian and Spanish texts are equally authentic, shall be deposited in the archives of the United Nations Secretariat. The Secretary-General shall prepare a certified copy thereof for communication to States Parties to this Convention, as well as to all other States Members of the United Nations and of the specialized agencies.

IN WITNESS WHEREOF the undersigned, being duly authorized thereto by their respective Governments, have signed this Convention on the date appearing opposite their respective signatures.

DONE at the European Office of the United Nations at Geneva, this seventh day of September one thousand nine hundred and fifty-six.

Source: United Nations, "Supplementary Convention on the Abolition of Slavery, the Slave Trade, and Institutions and Practices Similar to Slavery" (1956; http://www.ifs.univie.ac.at/intlaw/konterm/vrkon_en/ html/doku/slavery2.htm).

➣DOCUMENT 80➣
BRAZILIAN GOVERNMENT RECOGNIZES SLAVE LABOR (1995)

Officials in Brazil have acknowledged that despite that nation's efforts to end the practice, certain forms of slavery persisted among various indigenous peoples.

The Brazilian Government will set up, in June, an executive group to fight slave labor in Brazil. The decision, announced late in May by the minister of Labor, Paulo Paiva, at a public audience promoted by the Commissions of Minorities, Labor, Agriculture, and Human Rights of the Chamber of Deputies, shows that the government has finally surrendered to the evidence of the existence of this kind of labor in Brazil. A report issued by the Land Pastoral Commission (CPT) called *Conflicts in Rural Areas—Brazil 1994* points out the growth of slave labor in Brazil, including the exploitation of Indian labor. This kind of crime, which was being constantly denounced by social movements and leftist parties, used to be officially regarded as an exaggeration of the actual situation. It was the society, however, that once again took concrete steps against such practice: through the National Forum Against Violence, it is launching the National Campaign against slave labor.

For over three years, CIMI [Indianist Missionary Council] has been denouncing the use of Indian slave labor. According to the entity, the sugarcane industry in Mato Grosso at one point relied on the slave and semislave labor of 7 thousand Indians belonging to the Guarani Kaoiwa, Terena, and Guarani Nhandeva peoples. Among them there were children who earned salaries corresponding to 50–60% of those received by the adults. In 1993, repeated denunciations from CPT and CIMI led that state to set up a Permanent Commission for Investigating and Inspecting Labor Conditions in Charcoal Kilns and Distilleries in the State of Mato Grosso do Sul, which is made up of 11 state secretariats and agencies, 16 nongovernment organizations and also CPT, CIMI and the State Commission for the Defense of Human Rights.

The inspection carried out in plants and charcoal kilns has become more intense and, as a result, two police investigations have been opened. In spite of all this effort, labor relations remain below human standards. The Indians are fighting for labor rights, earn terribly low salaries in relation to the rest of the country and, in most cases, work under unsafe conditions. Because they are paid according to their production, they work over 12 hours a day without any break for lunch. Social movements expect the executive group to do more than simply recognize that the crime actually exists.

Brasilia, June 8th, 1995
Indianist Missionary Council—CIMI

Source: Indianist Missionary Council, "Brazilian Government Recognizes Slave Labor," in *Newsletter,* n. 162, June 8, 1995

∾BIBLIOGRAPHY∾

General

Adshead, S. A. M. 1992. *Salt and Civilisation.* London: Macmillan.

Althusser, Louis. 1970. *Politics and History.* London: New Left Press.

Asher, R. A., ed. 1994. *The Encyclopedia of Language and Linguistics.* New York: Pergamon Press.

Babcock-Abrahams, Barbara. 1975. "A Tolerated Margin of Mess: The Trickster and His Tales Reconsidered." *Journal of the Folklore Institute* 11 (3): 147–186.

Barry, Kathleen. 1984. *Female Sexual Slavery.* New York: New York University Press.

Beaud, Michel. 1983. *A History of Capitalism 1500–1980.* Translated by Tom Dickman and Anny Lefebvre. New York: Monthly Review Press.

Beckles, Hilary. 1984. "Capitalism and Slavery: The Debate over Eric Williams." *Social and Economic Studies* 33: 171–185.

Bethell, Leslie. 1966. "The Mixed Commissions for the Suppression of the Transatlantic Slave Trade in the Nineteenth Century." *Journal of African History* 7 (1): 79–93.

Black, Kerrigan. 1996. "Afro-American Personal Naming Traditions." *Names* 44: 105–125.

Carrithers, M., et al., eds. 1985. *The Category of the Person: Anthropology, Philosophy, History.* Cambridge: Cambridge University Press.

Craton, Michael; James Walvin; and David Wright. 1976. *Slavery, Abolition, and Emancipation.* New York: Longman.

Curtin, Philip. 1969. *The Atlantic Slave Trade: A Census.* Madison: University of Wisconsin Press.

Davis, David Brion. 1988. *The Problem of Slavery in Western Culture.* Oxford: Oxford University Press.

———. 1984. *Slavery and Human Progress.* New York: Oxford University Press.

Degler, Carl N. 1976. "Why Historians Change Their Minds." *Pacific Historical Review* 45: 167–184.

Devisse, Jean, and Michael Moliat. 1979. *The Image of the Black in Western Art. Vol. 2.* New York: William Morrow.

Dow, George Francis. 1969. *Slave Ships and Slaving.* Port Washington, NY: Kennikat Press.

Drescher, Seymour, and Stanley Engerman, eds. 1998. *A Historical Guide to World Slavery.* New York: Oxford University Press.

Duchet, Michéle. 1977. *Antropologie et histoire au siècle des lumières.* Paris: Flammarion.

Dumont, Louis. 1980. *Homo Hierarchicus: The Caste System and Its Implications.* Chicago: University of Chicago Press.

Eltis, David. 1987. *Economic Growth and the Ending of the Transatlantic Slave Trade.* Oxford: Oxford University Press.

Eltis, David, and James Walvin, eds. 1981. *The Abolition of the Atlantic Slave Trade.* Madison: University of Wisconsin Press.

Engels, Friedrich. 1972. *The Origin of the Family, Private Property, and the State.* New York: International Publishers.

Engerman, Stanley. 1996. "Slavery, Serfdom, and Other Forms of Coerced Labor: Similarities and Differences." In *Serfdom and Slavery: Studies in Legal Bondage.* Edited by M. L. Bush. New York: Longman.

Fanon, Frantz. 1968. *The Wretched of the Earth.* New York: Grove Press.

Fox-Genovese, Elizabeth. 1976. *Origins of Physiocracy.* Ithaca, NY: Cornell University Press.

Fox-Genovese, Elizabeth, and Eugene D. Genovese. 1983. *Fruits of Merchant Capital.* New York: Oxford University Press.

Gilroy, Paul. 1993. *The Black Atlantic.* Cambridge, MA: Harvard University Press.

Gottlieb, Beatrice. 1993. *The Family in the Western World.* Oxford: Oxford University Press.

Guilmartin, John. 1980. *Gunpowder and Galleys: Changing Technology and Mediterranean Warfare at Sea in the Sixteenth Century.* Cambridge: Cambridge University Press.

Herskovits, Melville J. 1958. *The Myth of the Negro Past.* Boston: Beacon Press.

Honour, Hugh. 1989. *The Image of the Black in Western Art. Vol. 4.* Cambridge, MA: Harvard University Press.

Hurston, Zora Neale. 1978. *Mules and Men.* Bloomington: Indiana University Press.

Inikori, Joseph E., ed. 1982. *Forced Migration: The Impact of the Export Slave Trade on African Societies.* London: Hutchinson.

Inikori, Joseph E., and Stanley L. Engerman, eds. 1992. *The Atlantic Slave Trade: Effects on Economies, Societies, and Peoples.* Durham, NC: Duke University Press.

Jakobsson, Stiv. 1972. *Am I Not a Man and a Brother?* Uppsala, Sweden: Almqvist and Wiksells.

Kellet, R. J. 1992. "Infanticide and Child Destruction— The Historical, Legal, and Pathological Aspects." *Forensic Science International* 53: 1–28.

Klein, Herbert S. 1978. *The Middle Passage: Comparative Studies in the Atlantic Slave Trade.* Princeton, NJ: Princeton University Press.

Lovejoy, Paul E. 1983. 1986. *Salt of the Desert Sun.* Cambridge: Cambridge University Press.

———. *Transformations in Slavery.* Cambridge: Cambridge University Press.

Mannix, Daniel, and Malcolm Cowley. 1965. *Black Cargoes: A History of the Atlantic Slave Trade 1518–1865*. New York: Viking.

Marx, Karl. 1906. *Capital: A Critique of Political Economy*. New York: Modern Library.

———. 1975. "Letter to P. V. Annenkov, December 28, 1846." In *Marx-Engels Selected Correspondence*. Edited by S. W. Ryazanskaya. Moscow: Progress Publishers.

Masani, R. P. 1966. *Folk Culture Reflected in Names*. Bombay: Popular Prakashan.

Mathewson Denny, Frederick. 1987. "Names and Naming." In *Encyclopedia of Religion*. Vol. 10. Edited by M. Eliade et al. London: Macmillan.

Mauss, Marcel. 1985. "A Category of the Human Mind: The Notion of Person; The Notion of Self." In *The Category of the Person: Anthropology, Philosophy, History*. Edited by M. Carrithers et al. Cambridge: Cambridge University Press.

Maxwell, John Francis. 1975. *Slavery and the Catholic Church: The History of Catholic Teaching Concerning the Moral Legitimacy of the Institution of Slavery*. London: Barry Rose Publishers.

Meillassoux, Claude. 1991. *The Anthropology of Slavery: The Womb of Iron and Gold*. Chicago: University of Chicago Press.

Meltzer, Milton. 1993. *Slavery: A World History*. New York: Da Capo Press.

Miers, Suzanne, and Igor Kopytoff, eds. 1977. *Slavery in Africa: Historical and Anthropological Perspective*. Madison: University of Wisconsin Press.

Moers, E. 1996. *Literary Women*. London: Women's Press.

Murdock, George P. 1981. *Atlas of World Cultures*. Pittsburgh: University of Pittsburgh Press.

———. 1983. *Outline of World Cultures*. New Haven, CT: Human Relations Area Files.

Murdock, George P., ed. 1931. *The Evolution of Culture*. New York: Macmillan.

Nieboer, H. I. 1910. *Slavery as an Industrial System*. The Hague: M. Nijhoff.

Northrup, David, ed. 1994. *The Atlantic Slave Trade*. Lexington, MA: D. C. Heath.

Padgug, Robert A. 1975. "Problems in the Theory of Slavery and Slave Society." *Science and Society* 40: 3–27.

Parish, Peter J. 1989. *Slavery: History and Historians*. New York: Harper and Row.

Parry, Clive, ed. 1969–. *Consolidated Treaty Series*. 231 vols. to date. Dobbs Ferry, NY: Oceana Publications.

Patterson, Orlando. 1967. *The Sociology of Slavery*. London: McGibbon and Kee.

———. 1991. *Freedom: Freedom in the Making of Western Culture*. New York: Basic Books.

———. 1979. "On Slavery and Slave Formations." *New Left Review* 117: 31–67.

———. 1982. *Slavery and Social Death*. Cambridge, MA: Harvard University Press.

Pomeroy, Sarah B. 1995. *Goddesses, Whores, Wives, and Slaves*. New York: Schocken Books.

Rawley, James A. 1981. *The Transatlantic Slave Trade*. New York: Norton.

Rodriguez, Junius P., ed. 1997. *The Historical Encyclopedia of World Slavery*. Santa Barbara, CA: ABC-CLIO.

Schwartz, Stuart; Linda Wimmer; and Robert Wolff. 1997. *The Global Experience*. New York: Longman.

Scott, S. P. 1973. *The Civil Law*. New York: AMS Press.

Seed, Patricia. 1995. *Ceremonies of Possession*. Cambridge: Cambridge University Press.

Segal, Ronald. 1995. *The Black Diaspora*. New York: Farrar, Straus and Giroux.

Shell, Robert. 1995. *Children of Bondage*. Johannesburg: Witwatersrand University Press.

Smith, Elsdon C. 1967. *Treasury of Name Lore*. New York.

Smith, Marion. 1930. "The First Codification of the Substantive Common Law." *Tulane Law Review* 4: 178–189.

Solow, Barbara L. 1991. *Slavery and the Rise of the Atlantic System*. New York: Cambridge University Press.

Stock, Eugene. 1899. *The History of the Church Missionary Society*. London: Church Missionary Society.

Strauss, Leo, and Joseph Cropsey, eds. 1981. *History of Political Philosophy*. Chicago: University of Chicago Press.

Tibbles, Anthony, ed. 1994. *Transatlantic Slavery: Against Human Dignity*. London: Her Majesty's Stationery Office.

Van den Berghe, Pierre L. 1967. *Race and Racism: A Comparative Perspective*. New York: Wiley.

Wallerstein, Immanuel. 1979. *The Capitalist World-Economy*. Cambridge: Cambridge University Press.

Walvin, James. 1984. *Slavery and the Slave Trade: A Short Illustrated History*. Jackson: University of Mississippi Press.

Watson, Alan. 1989. *Slave Law in the Americas*. Athens: University of Georgia Press.

Wesley, Charles H. 1942. "Manifests of Slave Shipments along the Waterways, 1808–1864." *Journal of Negro History* 27 (2): 155–174.

Williams, Eric. 1944. *Capitalism and Slavery*. Chapel Hill: University of North Carolina Press.

Williamson, Laila. 1978. "Infanticide: An Anthropological Analysis." In *Infanticide and the Value of Life*. Edited by Marvin Kohl. New York: Prometheus Books.

Africa

Abdul, Sheriff. 1987. *Slaves, Spices, and Ivory in Zanzibar*. London: James Currey.

Abdul, Sheriff, and Ed Ferguson. 1991. *Zanzibar under Colonial Rule*. Athens: University of Ohio Press.

Abiola, E. Ola. 1974. *A Textbook of West African History (A.D. 1000 to the Present)*. Ado-Ekiti, Nigeria: Omolayo Standard Press.

Adefuye, Ade; Babatunde Agiri; and Jide Osuntokun, eds. 1987. *History of the Peoples of Lagos State*. Ikeja, Nigeria: Lantern Books.

Aderibigbe, A. B., ed. 1975. *Lagos: The Development of an African City*. London: University Press.

Ajayi, J. F. A. 1961. "The British Occupation of Lagos, 1851–1865: A Critical Review." *Nigeria Magazine* 69: 96–105.

———. 1965. *Christian Missions in Nigeria, 1841–1891: The Making of a New Elite*. London: Longman.

Ajayi, J. F. A., and Michael Crowder. 1985. *Historical Atlas of Africa*. London: Cambridge University Press.

Ajayi, J. F. A., and Michael Crowder, eds. 1971. *History of West Africa*. London: Longman.

Akpan, M. B. 1973. "Black Imperialism: Americo-Liberian Rule over the African Peoples of Liberia, 1841–1964." *Canadian Journal of African Studies*. 7 (2): 217–236.

Alagoa, E. J. 1970. *Jaja of Opobo: The Slave Who Became a King*. London: Longman.

Allen, Richard B. 1989. "Economic Marginality and the Rise of the Free Population of Colour in Mauritius, 1767–1830." *Slavery and Abolition* 10 (2): 126–150.

———. 1983. "Marronage and the Maintenance of Public Order in Mauritius, 1721–1835." *Slavery and Abolition* 4 (3): 214–231.

Allibert, Claude. 1996. "Métallurgie, traite et ancien peuplement du Canal de Mozabbique aux Xe–XIIe siècles. Eléments historiques pour un essai de compréhension due déb$ut du peuplement austro-africaine de Madagascar." Paper presented at Fanandevozana or Slavery. Antananarivo, Madagascar.

Allibert, Claude, and Pierre Verin. 1996. "The Early Pre-Islamic History of the Comores Islands: Links with Madagascar and Africa." In *The Indian Ocean in Antiquity*. Edited by Julian Reade. London: Kegan Paul International.

Allison, Robert, ed. 1995. *The Interesting Narrative of the Life of Olaudah Equiano Written by Himself*. Boston: Bedford Books.

Alpers, E. A. 1975. *Ivory and Slaves in East Central Africa*. London: Heinemann.

Anene, J. C. 1966. *Southern Nigeria in Transition 1885–1906*. London: Cambridge University Press.

Armstrong, James, and Nigel Worden. 1989. "The Slaves, 1652–1834." In *The Shaping of South African Society, 1652–1840*. Edited by Richard Elphick and Hermann Giliomee. Cape Town: Maskew Miller Longman.

As-Sa'di, Abderrahman ben Abdallah ben 'Imran ben 'Amir. 1964. *Ta'rikh as-Sudan*. Translated by Octave Houdas. Paris: Adrien-Maisonneuve.

Austen, Ralph. 1979. "The Trans-Saharan Slave Trade: A Tentative Census." In *The Uncommon Market: Essays in the Economic History of the Atlantic Slave Trade*. Edited by Henry Gemery and Jan S. Hogendorn. New York: Academic Press.

Ayandele, Emmanuel. 1966. *The Missionary Impact on Modern Nigeria*. London: Longman.

Bakir, Abd el-Mohsen. 1952. *Slavery in Pharaonic Egypt*. Cairo: Imprimerie de'l IFAOC.

Barboza, Steven. 1988. "The Doorway of No Return—Goree." *American Visions* 3 (3): 6–9.

Barnes, Sandra T. 1980. *Ogun: An Old God for a New Age*. Philadelphia: Institute for the Study of Human Issues.

Barnes, Sandra T., ed. 1989. *Africa's Ogun: Old World and New*. Bloomington: Indiana University Press.

Barth, Heinrich. 1965. *Travels and Discoveries in Northern and Central Africa*. London: Frank Cass.

Beachey, R. W. 1996. *A History of East Africa, 1592–1902*. London: Tauris.

———. 1976. *The Slave Trade of Eastern Africa*. New York: Barnes and Noble.

Beckingham, C. F. 1995. "The Quest for Prester John." In *The European Opportunity*. Edited by F. Fernandez-Armesto. Aldershot, Eng.: Variorum.

Birmingham, David. 1966. *Trade and Conflict in Angola: The Mbundu and Their Neighbours under the Influence of the Portuguese 1483–1790*. Oxford: Clarendon Press.

Blassingame, John W., ed. 1977. *Slave Testimony: Two Centuries of Letters, Speeches, Interviews, and Autobiographies*. Baton Rouge: Louisiana State University.

Bloch, Maurice. 1980. "Modes of Production and Slavery in Madagascar: Two Case Studies." In *Asian and African Systems of Slavery*. Edited by James L. Watson. Berkeley: University of California Press.

Boahen, A. Adu. 1987. *African Perspectives on Colonialism*. Baltimore: Johns Hopkins University Press.

———. 1975. *Ghana: Evolution and Change in the Nineteenth and Twentieth Centuries*. London: Longman.

———. 1986. *Topics in West African History*. Burnt Mill, Essex, Eng.: Longman.

Bohannan, Paul, and Philip Curtin. 1971. *Africa and the Africans*. Prospect Heights, IL: Waveland Press.

Bottignole, Silvana. 1984. *Kikuyu Traditional Culture and Christianity: Self Examination of an African Church*. Nairobi: Heinemann.

Brace, Joan. 1983. "From Chattel to Person: Martinique, 1635–1848." *Plantation Society* 2 (1): 63–80.

Bradbury, R. E. 1964. *The Benin Kingdom and the Edo-Speaking Peoples of South-Western Nigeria*. London: International African Institute.

———. 1973. *Benin Studies*. London: International African Institute and Oxford University Press.

Burns, A. C. 1929. *History of Nigeria*. London: George Allen and Unwin.

Burton, Sir Richard. 1872. *Zanzibar: City, Island, and Coast*. London: Tinsley Brothers.

Campbell, Gwyn. 1989. "Madagascar and Mozambique in the Slave Trade of the Western Indian Ocean, 1800–1861." In *Economics of the Indian Ocean Slave Trade in the Nineteenth Century*. Edited by William Gervase Clarence-Smith. London: Frank Cass.

———. 1988. "Slavery and Fanampoana: The Structure of Forced Labour in Imerina (Madagascar), 1790–1861." *Journal of African History* 29 (3): 463–486.

Carvalho, Joaquim Barradas de. 1983. À la recherche de la spécificite de la renaissance Portugaise: L' "Esmeraldo de situ orbis" de Duarte Pacheco Pereira et la littérature portugaise de voyages à l'époque des grandes découvertes. 2 vols. Paris: Fondation Calouste Gulbenkian Centre Culturel Portugais.

Clark, Andrew Francis, and Lucie Colvin Phillips. 1994. *Historical Dictionary of Senegal*. Metuchen, NJ: Scarecrow Press.

Clark, Leon E. 1991. *Through African Eyes: The Past, the Road to Independence*. New York: Apex Press.

Clark, Robert. 1846. *Sierra Leone: A Description of the Manners and Customs of the Liberated Africans*. London: Ridgway.

Clarke, Peter B. 1982. *West Africa & Islam: A Study of Religious Development from the 8th to the 20th Century*. London: Edward Arnold.

Cobbing, Julian. 1988. "The Mfecane as Alibi: Thoughts on Dithakong and Mbolompo." *Journal of African History* 29 (3): 487–519.

Collins, Robert. 1992. "The Nilotic Slave Trade: Past and Present." In *The Human Commodity: Perspectives on the Trans-Saharan Slave Trade*. Edited by Elizabeth Savage. London: Frank Cass.

Coniff, Michael, and Thomas Davis. 1994. *Africans in the Americas*. New York: St. Martin's.

Connah, Graham. 1975. *The Archaeology of Benin: Excavations and Other Researches in and around Benin City, Nigeria*. Oxford: Clarendon Press.

Conneau, Theophilus. 1976. *A Slaver's Log Book, or 20 Year's Residence in Africa*. Englewood Cliffs, NJ: Prentice-Hall.

Cooper, Frederick. 1980. *From Slaves to Squatters: Plantation Labor and Agriculture in Zanzibar and Coastal Kenya, 1890–1925*. New Haven, CT: Yale University Press.

Cordeiro, Luciano. 1971. *Diogo Cão*. Lisbon: Agencia-Geral do Ultramar.

Costanzo, Angelo. 1987. *Surprizing Narrative: Olaudah Equiano and the Beginnings of Black Autobiography*. New York: Greenwood Press.

Crowe, S. E. 1942. *The Berlin West Africa Conference, 1884–1885*. Westport, CT: Negro Universities Press.

Crowther, Samuel. 1970. *Journal of an Expedition up the Niger and Tshadda Rivers*. London: Frank Cass.

Curtin, Philip D. 1968. *Africa Remembered: Narratives by West Africans from the Era of the Slave Trade*. Madison: University of Wisconsin Press.

———. 1969. *The Atlantic Slave Trade: A Census*. Madison: University of Wisconsin Press.

———. 1975. *Economic Change in Pre-Colonial Africa: Senegambia in the Era of the Slave Trade*. Madison: University of Wisconsin Press.

Cutrufelli, Maria Rosa. 1983. *Women of Africa: Roots of Oppression*. London: Zed Press.

Daaku, Kwame Yeboa. 1970. *Trade and Politics on the Gold Coast, 1600–1720: A Study of the African Reaction to European Trade*. Oxford: Oxford University Press.

van Dantzig, Albert. 1980. *Forts and Castles of Ghana*. Accra: Sedco.

———. 1980. *A Short History of the Forts and Castles of Ghana*. Accra: Sedco.

Davidson, Basil. 1991. *Africa in History*. New York: Macmillan.

———. 1969. *A History of East and Central Africa*. London: Longman.

Davies, K. G. 1975. *The Royal African Company*. New York: Octagon Books.

Debbasch, Yvan. 1988. "L'Espace du Sierra-Leone et la politique francaise de traite a la fin de l'Ancien Regime." In *De la traite a l'esclavage*. Edited by Serge Daget. Paris: Harmattan.

DeCorse, Christopher R. 1992. "Culture Contact, Continuity, and Change on the Gold Coast: A.D.

1400–1900." *African Archaeological Review* 10: 163–196.

Dickson, Kwamina B. 1969. *A Historical Geography of Ghana*. Cambridge: Cambridge University Press.

Dike, K. O. 1956. "John Beecroft, 1790–1854." *Journal of the Historical Society of Nigeria* 1 (1): 5–14.

Diop, Cheikh Anta. 1987. *Precolonial Black Africa*. Trenton, NJ: Africa World Press.

Donley-Reid, L. 1990. "A Structuring Structure: The Swahili House." In *Domestic Architecture and the Use of Space*. Edited by S. Kent. Cambridge: Cambridge University Press.

Dorigny, Marcel. 1993. "La Société des Amis des Noirs et les projets de colonisation en Afrique." *Annales Historiques de la Révolution Française*. 293–294: 421–429.

Duff, E. C., and W. Hamilton-Browne. 1972. *Gazetteer of the Kontagora Province*. London: Frank Cass.

Duffy, James. 1959. *Portuguese Africa*. Cambridge, MA: Harvard University Press.

Duke, Marvin L. 1974. "Robert F. Stockton: Early U.S. Naval Activities in Africa." *Shipmate* (December): 22–25.

Eldredge, Elizabeth, and Fred Morton, eds. 1994. *Slavery in South Africa: Captive Labor on the Dutch Frontier*. Boulder, CO: Westview Press and Pietermaritzburg: University of Natal Press.

Equiano, Olaudah. 1995. *Olaudah Equiano: The Interesting Narrative and Other Writings*. New York: Penguin.

Ewald, Janet. 1992. "Slavery in Africa and the Slave Trades from Africa." *American Historical Review* 97 (1): 465–485.

Fage, J. D.; Roland Oliver; and Richard Gray. 1975. *The Cambridge History of Africa from c. 1600 to c. 1790*. New York: Cambridge University Press.

Fanon, Frantz. 1968. *The Wretched of the Earth*. New York: Grove Press.

Fisher, Allan, and Humphrey Fisher. 1970. *Slavery and Muslim Society in Africa; The Institution in Saharan and Sudanic Africa and the Trans-Saharan Trade*. London: C. Hurst.

Frederickson, George. 1981. *White Supremacy: A Comparative Study in American and South African History*. New York: Oxford University Press.

Friedman, Ellen G. 1983. *Spanish Captives in North Africa*. Madison: University of Wisconsin Press.

Fyfe, Christopher. 1962. *A History of Sierra Leone*. London: Oxford University Press.

Fynn, John Kofi. 1971. *Asante and Its Neighbours, 1700–1807*. London: Longman.

Gailey, Harry A., Jr. 1981. *History of Africa: From 1800 to Present*. Huntington, NY: Krieger Publishing.

Gates, Henry Louis, Jr. 1996. "Europe, African Art, and the Uncanny." In *Africa: The Art of a Continent*. Edited by Tom Phillips. New York: Guggenheim Museum.

Geary, Sir William N. M. 1927. *Nigeria under British Rule*. London: Frank Cass and Company.

Gershoni, Yekutiel. 1985. *Black Colonialism: The Americo-Liberian Scramble for the Hinterland*. Boulder, CO: Westview Press.

Gilroy, Paul. 1993. *The Black Atlantic*. Cambridge, MA: Harvard University Press.

Glasse, Cyril. 1989. *The Concise Encyclopedia of Islam*. San Francisco: Harper and Row.

Goodwine, Marquetta L. 1995. *Gullah/Geechee: The Survival of Africa's Seed in the Winds of the Diaspora*. Vol. 1, *St. Helena's Serenity*. New York: Kinship Publications.

Grace, John. 1975. *Domestic Slavery in West Africa*. New York: Barnes and Noble.

Granlund, V. 1879. *En svensk koloni i Afrika eller Svenska Afrika Kompaniets historia*. Stockholm: n.p.

Grove, C. P. 1948. *The Planting of Christianity in Africa*. London: Lutterworth.

Hallett, R. 1965. *The Penetration of Africa: European Enterprise and Exploration Principally in Northern and Western Africa University Press to 1830*. London: Routledge.

Hamilton, Carolyn, ed. 1995. *The Mfecane Aftermath: Reconstructive Debates in Southern African History*. Johannesburg: Witwatersrand University Press and Pietermaritzburg: University of Natal Press.

Harris, Joseph, ed. 1993. *Global Dimensions of the African Diaspora*. Washington, DC: Howard University Press.

Hartigan, Royal J. 1986. "Blood Drum Spirit: Drum Languages of West Africa, African-America, Native America, Central Java, and South India." Ph.D. dissertation, Department of History, Wesleyan University, Middletown, Connecticut.

Herskovits, Melville J. 1958. *The Myth of the Negro Past*. Boston: Beacon Press.

Hill, Richard. 1959. *Egypt in the Sudan, 1820–1881*. London: Oxford University Press.

Hilton, Anne. 1985. *The Kingdom of Kongo*. Oxford: Clarendon Press.

Hiskett, Mervyn. 1984. *The Development of Islam in West Africa*. New York: Longman.

Hogben, Sidney John. 1967. *An Introduction to the History of the Islamic States of Northern Nigeria*. Ibadan, Nigeria: Oxford University Press.

Hole, Charles. 1896. *The Early History of the Church Missionary Society for Africa and the East*. London: Church Missionary Society.

Holt, P. M., and M. W. Daly. 1988. *A History of the Sudan*. London: Longman.

Holt, Peter. 1970. *The Mahdist State in the Sudan, 1881–1898*. Oxford: Clarendon Press.

Hutchinson, Louise Daniel. 1979. *Out of Africa: From West African Kingdoms to Colonization*. Washington, DC: Anacostia Neighborhood Museum of the Smithsonian Institution.

Iliffe, J. 1995. *Africans: The History of a Continent*. Cambridge: Cambridge University Press.

James, L. A. Webb. 1995. *Desert Frontier*. Madison: University of Wisconsin Press.

Johnson, Douglas. 1992. "Recruitment and Entrapment in Private Slave Armies." In *The Human Commodity: Perspectives on the Trans-Saharan Slave Trade*. Edited by Elizabeth Savage. London: Frank Cass.

———. 1988. "Sudanese Military Slavery from the 18th to the 20th century." In *Slavery and Other Forms of Unfree Labour*. Edited by Leonie Archer. London: Routledge.

July, Robert W. 1992. *A History of the African People*. Prospect Heights, IL: Waveland Press.

Kelly, Kenneth G. 1997. "The Archaeology of African-European Interaction: Investigating the Social Roles of Trade, Traders, and the Use of Space in the Seventeenth and Eighteenth Century Hueda Kingdom, Republic of Benin." *World Archaeology* 28 (3): 354–364.

Klein, A. Norman. 1994. "Slavery and Akan Origins." *Ethnohistory* 41: 627–656.

Klein, Martin, ed. 1993. *Breaking the Chains: Slavery, Bondage, and Emancipation in Modern Africa and Asia*. Madison: University of Wisconsin Press.

Koslow, Phillip. 1995. *Centuries of Greatness: The West African Kingdoms*. New York: Chelsea House.

Law, Robin. 1977. *The Oyo Empire c. 1600–c. 1836: A West African Imperialism in the Era of the Atlantic Slave Trade*. Oxford: Clarendon Press.

———. 1977. "Royal Monopoly and Private Enterprise in the Atlantic Trade: The Case of Dahomey." *Journal of African History* 18: 555–577.

———. 1991. *The Slave Coast of West Africa, 1550–1750: The Impact of the Atlantic Slave Trade on an African Society*. Oxford: Clarendon Press.

Lawrence, A. W. 1963. *Trade Castles and Forts of West Africa*. London: Jonathan Cape.

Le May, G. H. 1995. *The Afrikaners*. Oxford: Oxford University Press.

Levtzion, Nehemia. 1973. *Ancient Ghana and Mali*. London: Methuen.

———. 1963. "The Thirteenth- and Fourteenth-Century Kings of Mali." *Journal of African History* 4 (3): 341–353.

Lipton, Merle. 1985. *Capitalism and Apartheid*. London: Gower Publishing House.

Littlefield, Daniel C. 1991. *Rice and Slaves*. Urbana: University of Illinois Press.

Losi, John B. 1914. *History of Lagos*. Lagos: Tika-Tore Press.

Lovejoy, Paul E. 1981. *The Ideology of Slavery in Africa*. London: Sage Publications.

———. 1983. *Transformations in Slavery: A History of Slavery in Africa*. Cambridge: Cambridge University Press.

Lovejoy, Paul, and Jan Hogendorn. 1993. *The Slow Death of Slavery: The Course of Abolition in Northern Nigeria, 1897–1936*. Cambridge: Cambridge University Press.

Lugard, Frederick D. 1968. *The Rise of Our East African Empire*. London: Frank Cass.

———. 1933. "Slavery in All Its Forms." *Africa* 6: 1–14.

McEvedy, Colin. 1980. *The Penguin Atlas of African History*. New York: Penguin Books.

Mack, Beverly. 1992. "Women and Slavery in Nineteenth-Century Hausaland." *Slavery and Abolition* 13 (1): 89–110.

Macmillan, William. 1963. *Bantu, Boer, and Briton*. Oxford: Clarendon.

McSheffrey, Gerald M. 1983. "Slavery, Indentured Servitude, Legitimate Trade, and the Impact of

Abolition in the Gold Coast, 1874–1901: A Reappraisal." *Journal of African History* 24: 349–368.

Manning, Patrick. 1990. *Slavery and African Life: Occidental, Oriental, and African Slave Trades.* Cambridge: Cambridge University Press.

———. 1982. *Slavery, Colonialism, and Economic Growth in Dahomey, 1640–1960.* Cambridge: Cambridge University Press.

Matheson, Jane D. 1974. "Lagoon Relations in the Era of Kosoko, 1845–1862: A Study of African Reaction to European Intervention." Ph.D. dissertation, Department of History, Boston University, Boston, Massachusetts.

Maxwell, Kevin B. 1983. *Bemba Myth and Ritual: The Impact of Literacy on an Oral Culture.* New York: Peter Lang.

Meillassoux, Claude. 1991. *Anthropology of Slavery.* Chicago: University of Chicago Press.

Meillassoux, Claude, ed. 1975. *L'Esclavage en Afrique precoloniale.* Paris, Maspero.

Miers, Suzanne, and Igor Kopytoff. 1977. *Slavery in Africa.* Madison: University of Wisconsin Press.

Miers, Suzanne, and Richard Roberts, eds. 1989. *The End of Slavery in Africa.* Madison: University of Wisconsin Press.

Miller, Joseph C. 1982. "Commercial Organization of Slaving at Luanda, Angola, 1760–1830." In *The Uncommon Market: Essays in the Economic History of the Atlantic Slave Trade.* Edited by Henry A. Gemery and Jan S. Hogendorn. New York: Academic Press.

———. 1988. *Way of Death: Merchant Capitalism and the Angolan Slave Trade, 1730–1830.* Madison: University of Wisconsin Press.

Miller, Randall, and John David Smith, eds. 1988. *Dictionary of Afro-American Slavery.* Westport, CT: Greenwood.

Miner, Horace. 1953. *The Primitive City of Timbuctoo.* Princeton, NJ: Princeton University Press.

Moore, Shelley. 1986. "Goree." *Crisis* 93 (6): 18–21, 56.

Mouser, Bruce L. 1973. "Trade, Coasters, and Conflict in the Rio Pongo from 1790 to 1808." *Journal of African History* 14 (1): 45–64.

Mundt, Robert. 1987. *Historical Dictionary of the Ivory Coast.* Metuchen, NJ: Scarecrow Press.

Murdock, George Peter, ed. 1931. *The Evolution of Culture.* New York: Macmillan.

Mzimela, Sipe E. 1988. *Whither South Africa: A Manifesto for Change.* New York: Martin Luther King Fellow Press.

Ndiaye, Joseph. 1989. *The Slave Trade at Goree Island and Its History.* Gorée, Senegal: Ndiaye.

Newitt, Malyn. 1984. *The Comoro Islands: Struggle against Dependency in the Indian Ocean.* Boulder, CO: Westview Press.

Nicholls, C. S. 1971. *The Swahili Coast.* London: George Allen.

Nobles, Wade. 1986. *African Psychology.* Oakland, CA: Black Family Institute.

Northrup, David. 1978. "African Mortality in the Suppression of the Slave Trade: The Case of the Bight of Biafra." *Journal of Interdisciplinary History* 9 (Summer): 47–64.

Nurse, Derek. 1980. *Bantu Migration into East Africa.* Nairobi: University of Nairobi Institute of African Studies.

O'Fahey, R. S. 1973. "Slavery and the Slave Trade in Dar Fur." *Journal of African History* 14 (1): 29–43.

O'Fahey, R. S., and J. L. Spaulding. 1974. *Kingdoms of the Sudan.* London: Methuen.

O'Meara, Dan. 1996. *Forty Lost Years: The Apartheid State and the Politics of the National Party, 1948–1994.* Athens: Ohio University Press and Johannesburg: Ravan Press.

Oliver, Ronald, and Brian M. Fagan. 1975. *Africa in the Iron Age: c. 500 B.C. to A.D. 1400.* Cambridge: Cambridge University Press.

Oliver, Roland, and J. D. Fage. 1990. *A Short History of Africa.* New York: Penguin Books.

Omer-Cooper, J. D. 1994. *History of Southern Africa.* London: James Currey.

———. 1966. *The Zulu Aftermath: A Nineteenth-Century Revolution in Bantu Africa.* London: Longman.

Paulme, Denise, ed. 1971. *Women of Tropical Africa.* Berkeley: University of California Press.

Peires, Jeff. 1989. "The British and the Cape, 1814–1834." In *The Shaping of South African Society, 1652–1840.* Edited by Richard Elphick and Hermann Giliomee. Cape Town: Maskew Miller Longman.

Perham, Margery F. 1956. *Lugard.* London: Collins.

Peterson, John. 1969. *Province of Freedom.* London: Faber.

Porter, R. 1968. "The Crispe Family and the African Trade in the Seventeenth Century." *Journal of African History* 9 (1): 57–77.

Posel, Deborah. 1991. *The Making of Apartheid, 1948–61: Conflict and Compromise.* Oxford: Clarendon Press.

Prunier, Gerard. 1992. "Military Slavery in the Sudan during the Turkiyya." In *The Human Commodity: Perspectives on the Trans-Saharan Slave Trade.* Edited by Elizabeth Savage. London: Frank Cass.

Ransford, Oliver. 1972. *The Great Trek.* London: Murray.

Reynolds, Edward. 1974. *Trade and Economic Change on the Gold Coast: 1807–1874.* New York: Longman.

Robertson, Claire, and Martin L. Klein, eds. 1983. *Women and Slavery in Africa.* Bloomington: Indiana University Press.

Rodney, Walter. 1970. *A History of the Upper Guinea Coast, 1545 to 1800.* Oxford: Clarendon Press.

Romero, Patricia. 1981. "Laboratory for the Oral History of Slavery: The Island of Lamu on the Kenya Coast." *American Historical Review* 88 (3): 858–882.

———. 1997. *Lamu: History, Society, and Family in an East African Port City.* Princeton, NJ: Markus Wiener Publishers.

———. 1988. "Slave Children." In *Dictionary of Afro-American Slavery.* Edited by Randall Miller and John David Smith. Westport, CT: Greenwood.

Ross, Robert. 1983. *Cape of Torments.* London: Routledge.

Ryder, A. F. C. 1969. *Benin and the Europeans, 1485–1897.* New York: Humanities Press.

Saumagne, C. 1934. "Ouvriers agricoles ou rôdeurs de celliers? Les circoncellions d'Afrique." *Annals d'histoire économique et sociale* 6: 351–364.

Sempebwa, Joshua Wantate. 1978. *The Ontological and Normative Structures in the Social Reality of a Bantu Society: A Systematic Study of Ganda Ontology and Ethics.* London: Macmillan.

Shell, Robert. 1994. *Children of Bondage: A Social History of the Slave Society at the Cape of Good Hope, 1652–1838.* Hanover, NH: Wesleyan University Press.

Shepherd, Gill. 1980. "The Comorians and the East African Slave Trade." In *Asian and African Systems of Slavery.* Edited by James L. Watson. Berkeley: University of California Press.

Sherlock, Phillip Manderson. *Anansi the Spider Man.* 1954. Binghamton, NY: Vail-Ballou Press.

Shick, Tom W. 1977. *Behold the Promised Land: A History of Afro-American Settler Society in Nineteenth-Century Liberia.* Baltimore: Johns Hopkins University Press.

———. 1971. "A Quantitative Analysis of Liberian Colonization from 1820 to 1843 with Special Reference to Mortality." *Journal of African History* 12: 45–59.

Slessarev, V. 1959. *Prester John: The Letter and the Legend.* Minneapolis: University of Minnesota Press.

Smith, Robert S. 1979. *The Lagos Consulate, 1851–1861.* Berkeley: University of California Press.

———. 1969. "To the Palaver Islands: War and Diplomacy on the Lagos Lagoon in 1852–1854." *Journal of the Historical Society of Nigeria.* 5 (1):3–25.

———. 1989. *Warfare and Diplomacy in Pre-colonial West Africa.* Madison: University of Wisconsin Press.

Stuckey, Sterling. 1987. *Slave Culture.* Oxford: Oxford University Press.

Sundiata, I. K. 1980. *Black Scandal: America and the Liberian Labor Crisis, 1929–1936.* Philadelphia: Institute for the Study of Human Issues.

Sutton, J. E. G. 1990. *A Thousand Years of East Africa.* Nairobi: British Institute in Eastern Africa.

Temperley, Howard. 1991. *White Dreams, Black Africa: The Antislavery Expedition to the Niger River, 1841–1842.* New Haven, CT: Yale University Press.

Temple, C. L., and O. Temple. 1965. *Notes on the Tribes, Emirates, and States of the Northern Provinces of Nigeria.* London: Frank Cass.

Thompson, Robert Farris. 1983. *Flash of the Spirit.* New York: Vintage Books.

Thornton, John K. 1992. *Africa and Africans in the Making of the Atlantic World, 1400–1680.* Cambridge: Cambridge University Press.

———. 1983. *The Kingdom of Kongo.* Madison: University of Wisconsin Press.

Trimingham, John Spencer. 1980. *The Influence of Islam upon Africa.* New York: Longman.

Turner, Lorenzo Dow. 1974. *Africanisms in the Gullah Dialect.* Ann Arbor: University of Michigan Press.

Van der Merwe, Pieter. 1995. *The Migrant Farmer in the History of the Cape Colony, 1657–1842.* Translated from Afrikaans by Roger Beck. Athens: Ohio University Press.

Vansina, Jan. 1966. *Kingdoms of the Savana.* Madison: University of Wisconsin Press.

Wallerstein, Immanuel. 1986. *Africa and the Modern World.* Trenton, NJ: Africa World Press.

Walz, Terence. 1985. "Black Slavery in Egypt during the Nineteenth Century as Reflected in the Mahakama Archives of Cairo." In *Slaves and Slavery in Muslim Africa.* Vol. 2, *The Servile Estate.* Edited by John Ralph Willis. London: Frank Cass.

———. 1978. *Trade between Egypt and Bilad As-Sudan, 1700–1820.* Paris: Institut Français D'Archéologie Orientale Du Caire.

Wilks, Ivor. 1993. *Forests of Gold: Essays on the Akan and the Kingdom of Asante.* Athens: Ohio University Press.

Wilson, Monica, and Leonard Thompson, eds. 1969. *The Oxford History of South Africa.* New York: Oxford University Press.

Worden, Nigel. 1995. *The Making of Modern South Africa: Conquest, Segregation, and Apartheid.* New York: Blackwell.

———. 1985. *Slavery in Dutch South Africa.* Cambridge: Cambridge University Press.

Worden, Nigel, and Clifton Crais, eds. 1994. *Breaking the Chains: Slavery and Its Legacy in the Nineteenth-Century Cape Colony.* Johannesburg: Witwatersrand University Press.

Wyse, Akintola. 1989. *The Krio of Sierra Leone.* London: Hurst.

Zook, George F. 1919. "The Company of the Royal Adventurers Trading to Africa." *Journal of Negro History* 4 (2): 134–231.

Ancient and Classical

Adams, Robert Mc. 1982. "Property Rights and Functional Tenure in Mesopotamian Rural Communities." In *Societies and Languages of the Ancient Near East: Studies in Honour of I. M. Diakonoff.* Edited by J. N. Postgate. Warminster, Eng.: Aris and Phillips.

Adcock, F. E. 1966. *Marcus Crassus Millionaire.* Cambridge: Cambridge University Press.

Altenmuller, Hartwig, and Ahmed M. Moussa. 1991. "Die Inschrift Amenemhets II. aus dem Ptah-Tempel von Memphis: Ein Vorbericht." *Studien zur Altägyptischen Kultur* 18: 1–48.

Andrewes, Antony. 1956. *The Greek Tyrants.* London: Hutchinson's University Library.

Annequin, Jacques. 1972. "Esclaves et affranchis dans la conjuration de Catilina." *Actes du colloque sur l'esclavage.* Paris: Les Belles Lettres.

Astin, Alan E. 1978. *Cato the Censor.* Oxford: Clarendon Press.

Austin, M. M., and P. Vidal-Naquet. 1977. *Economic and Social History of Ancient Greece: An Introduction.* Berkeley: University of California Press.

Badian, Ernst. 1958. *Foreign Clientelae.* Oxford: Clarendon Press.

Barrow, R. H. 1928. *Slavery in the Roman Empire.* London: Macmillan.

Bartchy, S. Scott. 1992. "Slavery." In *Anchor Bible Dictionary.* New York: Doubleday.

Beavis, Mary Ann. 1992. "Ancient Slavery as an Interpretive Context for the New Testament Servant Parables with Special Reference to the Unjust Steward (Luke 16:1–8)." *Journal of Biblical Literature* 111 (1): 37–54.

Beker, J. Christiaan. 1980. *Paul the Apostle: The Triumph of God in Life and Thought*. Philadelphia: Fortress Press.

Berlev, Oleg. 1965. Review of William Kelly Simpson. 1963. *Papyrus Reisner I: The Records of a Building Project in the Reign of Sesostris I*. Boston: Museum of Fine Arts. *Bibliotheca Orientalis* 22: 263–268.

———. 1987. "A Social Experiment in Nubia during the Years 9–17 of Sesostris I." In *Labor in the Ancient Near East*. Edited by Marvin A. Powell. New Haven, CT: Yale University Press.

Bierbrier, Morris. 1982. *The Tomb-Builders of the Pharaohs*. London: British Museum Publications.

Blake, William O. 1861. *The History of Slavery and the Slave Trade, Ancient and Modern*. Columbus, OH: H. Miller.

Boese, Wayne E. 1973. "A Study of the Slave Trade and Sources of Slaves in the Roman Republic and the Early Roman Empire." Ph.D. dissertation, Department of History, University of Washington, Seattle, Washington.

Bowra, C. M. 1935. *Ancient Greek Literature*. Oxford: Oxford University Press.

———. 1961. *Greek Lyric Poetry*. Oxford: Oxford University Press.

Bradley, Keith R. 1987. "On the Roman Slave Supply and Slavebreeding." In *Classical Slavery*. Edited by Moses I. Finley. London: Frank Cass.

———. 1986. "Seneca and Slavery." *Classica et mediaevalia* 37: 161–172.

———. 1983. "Slave Kingdoms and Slave Rebellions in Ancient Sicily." *Historical Reflections/Refexions Historiques* 10: 435–451.

———. 1989. *Slavery and Rebellion in the Roman World, 140 B.C.–70 B.C.* Bloomington: Indiana University Press.

———. 1994. *Slavery and Society at Rome*. New York: Cambridge University Press.

———. 1987. *Slaves and Masters in the Roman Empire: A Study in Social Control*. New York: Oxford University Press.

———. 1978. "Slaves and the Conspiracy of Catiline." *Classical Philology* 73: 329–336.

———. 1986. "Social Aspects of the Slave Trade in the Roman World." *Münsterische Beiträge zur antike Handelsgeschichte* 5 (1): 49–58.

Bradley, Michael. 1978. *The Iceman Inheritance; Prehistoric Sources of Western Man's Racism, Sexism, and Aggression*. New York: Kayode.

Brennan, T. Corey. 1993. "The Commanders in the First Sicilian Slave War." *Rivista di Filologia e di Istruzione Classica* 121: 153–184.

Brinkhof, Johannes Jacobus. 1978. *Een studie over het peculium in het Klassieke Romeinse recht*. Meppel, Netherlands: Krips Repr.

Brockmeyer, Norbert. 1979. *Antike Sklaverei*. Darmstadt, Ger.: Wissenschaftliche Buchgesellschaft.

Brown, Peter. 1967. *Augustine of Hippo*. Berkeley: University of California Press.

Bruce, F. F. 1936. "Latin Participles as Slave-Names." *Proceedings of the Leeds Philosophical and Literary Society* (Literary and Historical Section) 5: 44–60.

Brunt, Peter A. 1971. *Italian Manpower, 225 B.C.–A.D. 14*. Oxford: Clarendon.

———. 1971. *Social Conflicts in the Roman Republic*. London: Chatto and Windus.

Buccellati, G. 1991. "A Note on the Muškēnum as Homesteader." *Maarav* 7: 91–100.

Buckland, W. W. 1970. *The Roman Law of Slavery*. London: Cambridge University Press.

Burn, Andrew R. 1977. *The Pelican History of Greece*. London: Pelican.

Bury, J. B., and Russell Meiggs. 1975. *A History of Greece to the Death of Alexander the Great*. New York: St. Martin's.

Cambiano, Giuseppi. 1987. "Aristotle and the Anonymous Opponents of Slavery." In *Classical Slavery*. Edited by Moses I. Finley. London: Frank Cass.

Carcopino, Jerome. 1941. *Daily Life in Ancient Rome*. London: Routledge.

Cartledge, P. A. 1979. *Sparta and Lakonia*. London: Routledge.

Casson, L. 1989. *The Periplus Maris Erythraei*. Princeton, NJ: Princeton University Press.

Cato, Marcus Porcius, and Marcus Terentius Varro. 1934. *On Agriculture*. Translated by William Davis Hooper and Harrison Boyd Ash. Cambridge, MA: Harvard University Press.

Chamoux, Francois. 1965. *The Civilization of Greece*. London: George Allen and Unwin.

Charlesworth, M. P., ed. 1939. *Documents Illustrating the Reigns of Claudius and Nero*. Oxford: Oxford University Press.

Chevallier, Raymond. 1976. *Roman Roads*. London: B. T. Batsford.

Chirichigno, Gregory C. 1993. *Debt-Slavery in Israel and the Ancient Near East*. Sheffield, Eng.: Sheffield Academic Press.

Clarke, John. 1996. "Hypersexual Men in Augustan Baths." In *Sexuality in Ancient Art*. Edited by Natalie Boymel Kampen. Cambridge: Cambridge University Press.

Columella, Lucius Junius. 1941. *On Agriculture*. Translated by Harrison Boyd Ash. London: Heinemann.

Copalle, Siegfried. 1908. *De servorum Graecorum nominbus*. Marburg, Germany: Typis Academicis.

Cornell, Tim J. 1995. *The Beginnings of Rome*. London: Routledge.

Crombie, Ian M. 1962–1963. *An Examination of Plato's Doctrines*. 2 vols. New York: Humanities Press.

Crook, J. A.; Andrew Lintott; and Elizabeth Rawson, eds. 1994. *The Cambridge Ancient History*. Vol. 9. New York: Cambridge University Press.

Cruz-Uribe, E. 1982. "Slavery in Egypt during the Saite and Persian Periods." In *Revue Internationale des Droits de l' Antiquite* (Brussels) 29: 47–71.

Dalton, O. M., ed. 1915. *The Letters of Sidonius*. Oxford: Clarendon.

Danadamaev, Muhammad. 1984. *Slavery in Babylonia*. Dekalb: Northern Illinois University Press.

Daressy, Georges. 1915. "Une stèle de l'Ancien Empire maintenant détruite." *Annales du Service des Antiquités de l'Egypte* 15: 207–208.

David, A. R. 1986. *The Pyramid Builders of Ancient Egypt*. London: Routledge.

De Ste. Croix, Geoffrey E. M. 1981. *The Class Struggle in the Ancient Greek World*. Ithaca, NY: Cornell University Press.

Deimel, A. 1930. *Codex Hammurabi*. Rome: Pontifical Biblical Institute.

Diakonov, Igor M. 1987. "Slave-Labour vs. Non-Slave Labour: The Problem of Definition." In *Labor in the Ancient Near East*. Edited by Marvin A. Powell. Ancient Oriental Series 68. New Haven, CT: American Oriental Society.

———. 1974. "Structure of Society and State in Early Dynastic Sumer." In *Sources and Monographs: Monographs of the Ancient Near East. Vol. 1*. Los Angeles: Undena Publications.

Donadoni, S., ed. 1992. *Der Mensch des Alten Agypten*. New York: Campus.

Drinkwater, J. F. 1984. "Peasants and Bagaudae in Roman Gaul." *Classical Views* 3: 349–371.

Driver, Godfrey R., and John C. Miles. 1935. *The Assyrian Laws*. Oxford: Clarendon Press.

———. 1952–1955. *The Babylonian Laws*. 2 vols. Oxford: Clarendon Press.

Du latifundium au latifondo: Un héritage de Rome, une création médievale ou moderne? 1995. Paris: Centre Pierre Paris.

Dudley, D. R. 1941. "Blossius of Cumae." *Journal of Roman Studies* 31: 94–99.

Dumont, J. C. 1987. *Servus: Rome et l'esclavage sous la républic*. Rome: École française de Rome.

Eckstein, Arthur. 1995. *Moral Vision in the Histories of Polybius*. Berkeley: University of California Press.

Edwards, I. E. S. 1980. *The Pyramids of Egypt*. Harmondsworth, Eng.: Penguin Books.

Ehrenberg, Victor. 1973. *From Solon to Socrates*. London: Methuen.

Endesfelder, E., ed. 1991. *Probleme der fruhen Gesellschaftsentwicklung im Alten Agypten*. Berlin: Institut fur Sudanarchaologie und Agyptologie.

Etienne, R. 1972. "Cicéron et l'esclavage." In *Actes du colloque d'histoiré sociale*. Paris: Les Belles Lettres.

Eyre, Christopher. 1987. "Work and the Organisation of Work in the New Kingdom." In *Labor in the Ancient Near East*. Edited by Marvin A. Powell. Ancient Oriental Series 68. New Haven, CT: American Oriental Society.

Festugière, A. J. 1959. *Antioche paienne et chretienne: Libanius, Chrysostome, et les moines de Syrie*. Paris: E. de Boccard.

Fine, John V. A. 1983. *The Ancient Greeks: A Critical History*. Cambridge, MA: Belknap Press.

Finley, Moses I. 1973. *The Ancient Economy*. London: Chatto and Windus.

———. 1980. *Ancient Slavery and Modern Ideology*. New York: Viking.

———. 1981. "Debt-Bondage and the Problem of Slavery." In *Economy and Society in Ancient Greece*. Edited by Brent D. Shaw and Richard P. Saller. London: Chatto and Windus.

———. 1981. *Economy and Society in Ancient Greece*. London: Chatto and Windus.

———. 1984. *Politics in the Ancient World*. Cambridge: Cambridge University Press.

———. 1981. "The Servile Statuses of Ancient Greece." In *Economy and Society in Ancient Greece*. Edited by Brent D. Shaw and Richard P. Saller. London: Chatto and Windus.

———. 1960. *Slavery in Classical Antiquity: Views and Controversies*. Cambridge: Heffer.

Finley, Moses I., ed. 1984. *The Legacy of Greece*. Oxford: Oxford University Press.

Fischer, Henry G. 1958. "An Early Occurrence of *hm* "Servant" in Regulations Referring to a Mortuary Estate," *Mitteilungen des Deutschen Archäologischen Instituts, Abteilung Kairo* 16: 131–137.

Forest, W. G. 1980. *A History of Sparta 950–192*. London: Duckworth.

Freeman, Kathleen. 1976. *The Work and Life of Solon*. New York: Arno Press.

Frend, W. H. C. 1971. *The Donatist Church*. New York: Oxford University Press.

Freshfield, Edwin, ed. 1926. *A Manual of Roman Law: The Ecloga*. Cambridge: Cambridge University Press.

Friedman, David Noel, ed. 1992. *Anchor Bible Dictionary*. New York: Doubleday.

Gamsey, Peter. 1970. *Social Status and Legal Privilege in the Roman Empire*. Oxford: Clarendon Press.

Gardiner, Alan H. 1940. "Adoption Extraordinary." *Journal of Egyptian Archaeology* 26: 23–29.

Garlan, Yvon. 1988. *Slavery in Ancient Greece*. Ithaca, NY: Cornell University Press.

Garland, A. 1992. "Cicero's Familia Urbana." *Greece and Rome* 39: 163–172.

Garnsey, Peter. 1996. *Ideas of Slavery from Aristotle to Augustine*. Cambridge: Cambridge University Press.

Gelb, I. J. 1973. "Prisoners of War in Early Mesopotamia." *Journal of Near Eastern Studies* 32: 70–98.

Giardina, A., and A. Schiavone, eds. 1981. *Societe la produzione schiavistica*. Rome and Bari: Laterza and Figli.

Gordon, C. 1963. *Hammurabi's Code: Quaint or Forward Looking?* New York: Holt, Rinehart and Winston.

Gragarin, Michael. 1986. *Early Greek Law*. Berkeley: University of California Press.

———. 1995. "The First Law of the Gortyn Code Revisited." *Greek Roman and Byzantine Studies* 36 (Spring): 7–15.

Grant, Frederic C., and H. H. Rowley, eds. 1963. *Dictionary of the Bible*. New York: Scribners.

Grant, Michael, and Rachel Kitzinger, eds. 1988. *Civilization of the Ancient Mediterranean: Greece and Rome*. New York: Charles Scribner's Sons.

Gratien, B. 1995. "La basse Nubie a l' Ancien Empire: Egyptiens et autochtones." In *Journal of Egyptian Archaeology* 81: 43–56.

Grayson, A. Kirk. 1972. *Assyrian Royal Inscriptions*. Wiesbaden, Germany: Otto Harrassowitz.

Green, William. 1976. *British Slave Emancipation: The Sugar Colonies and the Great Experiment, 1830–1865*. Oxford: Clarendon Press.

Griffith. Francis L. 1898. *The Petrie Papyri: Hieratic Papyri from Kahun and Gurob*. London: n.p.

Grote, George. 1951–1957. *History of Greece*. 12 vols. Boston: J. P. Jewett.

Grubbs, Judith Evans. 1995. *Law and Family in Late Antiquity.* Oxford: Clarendon.

Grunert. 1980. "Das demotische Rechtsbuch von Hermopolis-West: Zu den Eigentumsverhaltnissen im ptolemaischen Agypten." *Das Alterum* (Berlin) 12: 96–102.

Gundlach, Rolf. 1994. *Die Zwangsumsiedlung auswärtiger Bevölkerung als Mittel ägyptischer Politik bis zum Ende des Mittleren Reiches.* Forschungen zur Antiken Sklaverei 26. Stuttgart: Franz Steiner Verlag.

Gustafson, M. Forthcoming. "*Inscripta in fronte*: Penal Tattooing in Late Antiquity." *Classical Antiquity.*

Guthrie, William K. C. 1975. *A History of Greek Philosophy.* Cambridge: Cambridge University Press.

Hammond, N. G. L. 1994. *Philip of Macedon.* Baltimore: Johns Hopkins University Press.

Hare, Richard M. 1982. *Plato.* Oxford: Oxford University Press.

Harrill, J. Albert. 1995. *The Manumission of Slaves in Early Christianity.* Tübingen, Germany: J. C. B. Mohr.

Hayes, William C. 1955. *A Papyrus of the Late Middle Kingdom in the Brooklyn Museum (Papyrus Brooklyn 35.1446).* New York: Brooklyn Museum.

Helck, Wolfgang. 1963. "Materialien zur Wirtschaftsgeschichte des Neuen Reiches III." *Abhandlungen der Akademie der Wissenschaften und der Literatur in Mainz* 2: 135–542.

———. 1984. "Sklaven." In *Lexikon der Ägyptologie. Vol. 5.* Edited by Wolfgang Helck and Wolfhart Westendorf. Wiesbaden, Germany: Otto Harrassowitz.

Hoffner, H. 1995. "Hittite Laws." In *Law Collections from Mesopotamia and Asia Minor.* Edited by M. Roth. Atlanta, GA: Scholars Press.

Holden, A. 1974. *Greek Pastoral Poetry.* London: Penguin.

Hunger, Herbert. 1955. *Die Normannen in Thessalonike.* Graz, Austria: Verlag Styria.

Huxley, George Leonard. 1962. *Early Sparta.* Cambridge, MA: Harvard University Press.

Janssen, Jacob J. 1967. "Eine Beuteliste von Amenophis II und das Problem der Sklaverei im Altem Aegypten." *Jaarbericht van het Vooraziatisch-Egyptisch Genootschap (Gezelschap) "Ex Oriente Lux"* 6: 141–147.

———. 1975. *Commodity Prices from Ramessid Period.* Leiden: Brill.

———. 1975. "Prolegomena to the Study of Egypt's Economic History during the New Kingdom." *Studien zur altagyptischen Kultar* 3: 127–185.

Jay, P., ed. 1973. *The Greek Anthology.* London: London University Press.

Jones, A. H. M. 1956. "Slavery in the Ancient World." *Economic History Review* 2 (9): 185–199.

———. 1959. "Were Ancient Heresies National or Social Movements in Disguise?" *Journal of Theological Studies,* n.s., 10: 280–298.

Jones, C. P. 1987. "*Stigma*: Tattooing and Branding in Graeco-Roman Antiquity." *Journal of Roman Studies* 77: 139–155.

Joshel, Sandra. 1986. "Nurturing the Master's Child: Slavery and the Roman Child-nurse." *Signs* 12: 3–22.

Jowett, Benjamin, trans. 1885. *The Politics of Aristotle Translated into English with Introduction, Marginal Analysis, Essays, Notes, and Indices.* 3 vols. Oxford: Clarendon Press.

Keck, Leander E. 1988. *Paul and His Letters.* Second edition, revised and enlarged. Philadelphia: Fortress Press.

Kehoe, Dennis P. 1988. *The Economics of Agriculture on Roman Imperial Estates in North Africa.* Göttingen, Germany: Vandenhoeck and Ruprecht.

Kirk, Geoffrey S. 1986. *The Nature of Greek Myths.* London: Pelican.

Kirschenbaum, Aaron. 1987. *Sons, Slaves, and Freedmen in Roman Commerce.* Jerusalem: Magnes Press.

Kuziscin, Vasilij Ivanovic. 1984. *La grande proprietà agraria nell'Italia romana II secolo a.C-I seocolo d.C.* Rome: Editori Riuniti.

Lambertz, Max. 1907–1908. *Die griechischen Sklavennamen* 2 vols. Vienna: Staatsgymnasium.

Lattimore, Richmond, trans. 1967. *The Iliad of Homer.* Chicago: University of Chicago Press.

———. 1991. *The Odyssey of Homer.* New York: Harper Perennial.

Leibovitch, Nehama. 1967. *Studies in Genesis.* Jerusalem: World Zionist Organization, Department for Torah Education and Culture in the Diaspora.

Lemche, N. P. 1975. "The 'Hebrew Slave': Comments on the Slave Law Ex. xxi 2–11." *Vetus Testamentum* 25: 129–144.

Lesky, A. 1961. *A History of Greek Literature.* London: London University Press.

Lorton, D. 1977. "The Treatment of Criminals in Ancient Egypt through the New Kingdom." *Journal of the Economic and Social History of the Orient* 20: 2–64.

MacCormack, G. 1973. "The lex Poetelia." *Labeo* 19: 306–317.

MacMullen, R. 1974. *Roman Social Relations.* New Haven, CT: Yale University Press.

Manning, C. E. 1989. "Stoicism and Slavery in the Roman Empire." In *Aufstieg und Niedergang der römischen Welt.* Edited by Wolfgang Haase. Berlin and New York: De Gruyter.

Marshall, B. A. 1976. *Crassus: A Political Biography.* Amsterdam: A. M. Hakkert.

Masson, Olivier. 1973. "Les noms des esclaves dabs la Grece antique." In *Acts du Colloque 1971 sur l'esclavage.* Paris: Belle Lettres.

Meillassoux, Claude. 1986. *Anthropologie de l'esclavage: Le ventre de fer et d'argent.* Paris: Presses Universitaires de France.

Mendelsohn, Isaac. 1949. *Slavery in the Ancient Near East.* New York: Oxford University Press.

Micolier, Gabriel. 1932. *Pécule et capacité patrimoniale: Étude sur le pécule, dit profectice, depuis l'édit "de peculio" jusqu' à la fin de l'époque classique.* Lyon: Bosc Frères.

Miller, Fergus. 1984. "Condemnation to Hard Labour in the Roman Empire: From the Julio-Claudians to Constantine." *Papers of the British School at Rome 39.* London: n.p.

Moore, J. M., ed. 1975. *Aristotle and Xenophon on*

Democracy and Oligarchy. London: London University Press.

Neeve, Pieter Willem de. 1984. *Colonus: Private Farm-Tenancy in Roman Italy during the Republic and the Early Principate.* Amsterdam: J. C. Gieben.

Neufeld, E. 1951. *The Hittite Laws.* London: Luzac and Company.

Newman, W. L. 1887–1902. *The Politics of Aristotle.* 4 vols. Oxford: Clarendon Press.

Oates, Whitney J., ed. c. 1948. *Basic Writings of St. Augustine.* 2 vols. New York: Random House.

Peet, Thomas E. 1930. *The Great Tomb Robberies of the Twentieth Egyptian Dynasty.* Oxford: n.p.

Perl, Gerhard. 1977. "Zu Varros instrumentum vocale." *Klio* 59: 423–429.

Pharr, Clyde. 1952. *The Theodosian Code and Novels.* Princeton, NJ: Princeton University Press.

Phillips, William D., Jr. 1985. *Slavery from Roman Times to the Early Transatlantic Trade.* Minneapolis: University of Minnesota Press.

Polybius. 1969. *Polybius: The Histories.* Translated by William R. Paton. London: Heinemann.

Powell, M., ed. 1987. *Labor in the Ancient Near East.* New Haven, CT: American Oriental Society.

Rawson, Beryl. 1986. *The Family in Ancient Rome: New Perspectives.* Ithaca, NY: Cornell University Press.

Reduzzi Merola, Francesca. 1990. *"Servo parere": Studi sulla condizione giuridica degli schiavi vicari e di sottoposti a schiavi nelle esperienze greca e romana.* Camerino, Italy: Jovene.

Reilly, Linda Collins. 1978. "The Naming of Slaves in Greece." *Ancient World* 1 (3): 111–113.

Rose, H. J. 1934. *A Handbook of Greek Literature.* London: London University Press.

Rostovteff, M. 1957. *Social and Economic History of the Roman Empire.* Oxford: Oxford University Press.

Roth, Martha. 1995. *Law Collections from Mesopotamia and Asia Minor.* Atlanta, GA: Scholars Press.

Sasson, J. M., ed. 1995. *Civilizations of the Ancient Near East. Vol. 1.* New York: Simon and Schuster.

Scarborough, John. 1978. "Reflections on Spartacus." *Ancient World* 1 (2): 75–81.

Scheidel, Walter. 1994. *Grundpacht und Lohnarbeit in der Landwirtschaft des römischen Italien.* Frankfurt am Main: Peter Lang.

Scullard, Howard H. 1963. *From the Gracchi to Nero.* London: Methuen.

Sealey, Raphael. 1976. *A History of the Greek City States, ca. 700–338 B.C.* Berkeley: University of California Press.

Skydsgaard, Jens Erik. 1968. *Varro the Scholar.* Copenhagen: Munksgaard.

Speiser, E. A., ed. 1964. *The Anchor Bible.* Garden City, NY: Doubleday.

Stevens, C. E. 1933. *Sidonius Apollinaris and His Age.* Oxford: Clarendon.

Stockton, David. 1979. *The Gracchi.* Oxford: Oxford University Press.

Swartley, Willard M. 1983. *Slavery, Sabbath, War, and Women: Case Issues in Biblical Interpretation.* Scottdale, PA: Herald Press.

Thompson, E. P. 1952. "Peasant Revolts in Late-Roman Gaul and Spain." *Past and Present* 2: 11–23.

Toynbee, Arnold. 1965. *Hannibal's Legacy.* London: Oxford University Press.

Van Dam, Raymond. 1985. *Leadership and Community in Late Antique Gaul.* Berkeley: University of California Press.

Van den Ploeg, J., 1972. "Slavery in the Old Testament." *Vetus Testamentum Supplement* 22: 72–87.

Van Hook, Larue, trans. 1945. *Isocrates.* Cambridge, MA: Harvard University Press.

Varro. *Agriculture.* 1981. Included in Thomas Wiedemann. *Greek and Roman Slavery.* Baltimore: Johns Hopkins University Press.

Vlastos, Gregory, ed. 1971. *Plato: A Collection of Critical Essays.* Garden City, NY: Doubleday.

Vogt, Joseph. 1974. *Ancient Slavery and the Ideal of Man.* Oxford: Basil Blackwell.

von Hagen, Victor W. 1967. *The Roads that Led to Rome.* London: Weidenfeld and Nicolson.

Walbank, Frank William. 1972. *Polybius.* Berkeley: University of California Press.

Ward, Allen Mason. 1977. *Marcus Crassus and the Late Roman Republic.* Columbia: University of Missouri Press.

Watson, Alan. 1987. *Roman Slave Law.* Baltimore: Johns Hopkins University Press.

———. 1975. *Rome of the XII Tables: Persons and Property.* Princeton: Princeton University Press.

Weaver, P. 1972. *Familia Caesaris.* Cambridge: Cambridge University Press.

Weaver, P. R. C. 1964. "Vicarius and vicarianus in the familia Caesaris." *Journal of Roman Studies* 54: 117–128.

Westbrook, R. 1988. *Studies in Biblical and Cuneiform Law.* Paris: J. Gabalda.

White, Kenneth Douglas. 1967. "Latifundia." *Bulletin of Institute of Classical Studies* 14: 62–79.

———. 1970. *Roman Farming.* Ithaca, NY: Cornell University Press.

Whittaker, C. R. 1987. "Circe's Pigs: From Slavery to Serfdom in the Later Roman World." In *Classical Slavery.* Edited by Moses I. Finley. London: Frank Cass.

Wiedemann, Thomas, ed. 1981. *Greek and Roman Slavery.* Baltimore: Johns Hopkins Press.

Willetts, Ronald. 1967. *The Law Code of Gortyn.* Berlin: De Gruyter.

Wirth, Peter. 1980. *Eustathiana.* Amsterdam: Adolf M. Hakkert.

Wiseman, D. 1962. "The Laws of Hammurabi Again." *Journal of Semitic Studies* 7: 161–172.

Wolfram, H. 1988. *The History of the Goths.* Berkeley: University of California Press.

Wood, N. 1988. *Cicero's Social and Political Thought.* Berkeley: University of California Press.

Woolley, C. Leonard. 1965. *The Sumerians.* New York: Norton.

Yavetz, Zvi. 1988. *Slaves and Slavery in Ancient Rome.* Oxford: Transaction Books.

Zeber, Ireneusz. 1981. *A Study of the Peculium of a Slave*

in Pre-Classical and Classical Roman Law. Wroclaw, Poland: Uniwersytetu Wroclawskiego.

Zilletti, Udo. 1968. "In Tema di *Servitus Poenae*: Note di Diritto Penal Tardoclassico." *Studia et Documenta Historiae et Juris* 34.

Asia

Anderson, Mary M. 1990. *Hidden Power: The Palace Eunuchs of Imperial China.* Buffalo, NY: Prometheus Books.

Biot, M. Edward. 1849. "Memoir on the Condition of Slaves and Hired Servants in China." *Chinese Repository* 18 (7): 347–363.

Bray, Francesca. 1986. *The Rice Economies: Technology and Development in Asian Societies.* New York: Basil Blackwell.

Ch'u, T'ung-tsu. 1961. *Law and Society in Traditional China.* Paris: Mouton.

Dolgopol, Ustinia, and Snehal Paranjape. N.d. *Comfort Women, an Unfinished Ordeal: Report of a Mission.* Geneva: International Commission of Jurists.

Doolittle, Justus. 1867. *Social Life of the Chinese.* New York: Harper's.

Ebisawa, Tetsuo. 1983. "Bondservants in the Yuan." *Acta Asiatica* 45: 27–48.

Feeny, David. 1993. "The Demise of Corvee and Slavery in Thailand." In *Breaking the Chains: Slavery, Bondage, and Emancipation in Modern Africa and Asia.* Edited by Martin A. Klein. Madison: University of Wisconsin Press.

Garon, Sheldon. 1993. "The World's Oldest Debate? Prostitution and the State in Imperial Japan, 1900–1945." *American Historical Review* 98 (3): 710–732.

Gernet, Jacques. 1995. *Buddhism in Chinese Society: An Economic History from the Fifth to the Tenth Centuries.* New York: Columbia University Press.

Grey, John Henry. 1878. *China: A History of Laws, Manners, and Customs of the People.* London: Macmillan.

Grousset, Rene. 1970. *The Empire of the Steppes: A History of Central Asia.* New Brunswick, NJ: Rutgers University Press.

Hicks, George. 1995. *The Comfort Women: Japan's Brutal Regime of Enforced Prostitution in the Second World War.* New York: Norton.

Hiraki, Minoru. 1982. *Choson huki nobiche yonku* (A study of slavery in the Later Choson). Seoul: Chisik Sanopsa.

Hoëvell, W. R. van. 1848. *De emancipatie der slaven in Neerlands-Indië: In de verhandeling.* Groningen.

Hong, Seung-ki. 1983. *Koryoeui kuijoksahoewa nobi* (Aristocratic society of koyro and slaves). Seoul: Iljokak.

Hopkirk, Peter. 1992. *The Great Game: The Struggle for Empire in Central Asia.* New York: Kodansha International.

Howard, Keith, ed. 1995. *True Stories of the Korean Comfort Women.* London: Cassell.

Hucker, Charles. 1978. *The Ming Dynasty: Its Origins and Evolving Institutions.* Ann Arbor: Center for Chinese Studies, University of Michigan.

Jaschok, Maria. 1988. *Concubines and Bondservants: The Social History of a Chinese Custom.* Hong Kong: Oxford University Press.

Kim, Hak-sun. 1995. "Bitter Memories I Am Loath to Recall." In *True Stories of the Korean Comfort Women.* Edited by Keith Howard. London: Cassell.

Klass, Morton. 1988. *Caste: The Emergence of the South Asian Social System.* Philadelphia: Institute for the Study of Human Issues.

Knaap, Gerrit J. 1996. "Slavery and the Dutch in Southeast Asia." In *Fifty Years Later: Antislavery, Capitalism, and Modernity in the Dutch Orbit.* Edited by Gert Oostindie. Pittsburgh: University of Pittsburgh Press.

Lasker, Bruno. 1950. *Human Bondage in Southeast Asia.* Chapel Hill: University of North Carolina Press.

Louie, Kam. 1980. *Critiques of Confucius in Contemporary China.* New York: St. Martin's.

Meijer, Marinus J. 1980. "Slavery at the End of the Ch'ing Dynasty." In *Essays on China's Legal Tradition.* Edited by Jerome Alan Cohen, R. Randle Edwards, and Fu-mei Chang Chen. Princeton, NJ: Princeton University Press.

Miers, Suzanne. 1994. "Mui Tsai through the Eyes of the Victim: Janet Lim's Story of Bondage and Escape." In *Women and Chinese Patriarchy: Submission, Servitude and Escape.* Edited by Maria Jaschok and Suzanne Miers. Hong Kong: Hong Kong University Press.

Mitamura, Taisuke. 1970. *Chinese Eunuchs: The Structure of Intimate Politics.* Rutland, VT: C. E. Tuttle Company.

Mote, Frederick W., and Denis Twitchett, eds. 1988. "The Ming Dynasty." In *The Cambridge History of China, part 1, Volume 7.* Cambridge: Cambridge University Press.

Panananon, Chatchai. 1982. "Siamese 'Slavery': Institution and Its Abolition." Ph.D. dissertation, Department of History, University of Michigan, Ann Arbor, Michigan.

Patnaik, Utsa, and Manjari Dingwaney. 1985. *Chains of Servitude: Bondage and Slavery in India.* Madras, India: Sangam Books.

Reid, Anthony, ed. 1983. *Slavery, Bondage, and Dependency in Southeast Asia.* St. Lucia, Australia: University of Queensland Press.

Salem, Ellen. 1978. "Slavery in Medieval Korea." Ph.D. dissertation, Department of History, Columbia University, New York.

Schopen, Gregory. 1994. "The Monastic Ownership of Servants or Slaves: Local and Legal Factors in the Redactional History of Two Vinayas." *Journal of the International Association of Buddhist Studies* 17: 145–173.

Sharma, Ram Sharan. 1980. *Sudras in Ancient India: A Social History of the Lower Order down to circa A.D. 600.* Delhi, India: Montilal Banarsidass.

Soh, Chunghee Sarah. 1996. "The Korean 'Comfort Women' Movement for Redress: From a Bilateral Compensation to a Human Rights Issue." *Asian Survey* 36 (12): 1226–1240.

Talib, Y., and F. Samir. 1988. "The African Diaspora in Asia." In *UNESCO General History of Africa.* Vol. 3, *Africa from the Seventh to the Eleventh Century.* Edited by M. El Fasi. London: Heinemann.

Terwiel, B. 1983. "Bondage and Slavery in Early Nineteenth-Century Siam." In *Slavery, Bondage, and*

Dependency in Southeast Asia. Edited by Anthony Reid. St. Lucia, Australia: University of Queensland Press.

Totsuka, Etsuro. 1995. "Military Sexual Slavery by Japan and Issues in Law." In *True Stories of the Korean Comfort Women.* Edited by Keith Howard. London: Cassell.

Tsai, Shih-shan Henry. 1996. *The Eunuchs in the Ming Dynasty.* New York: State University of New York Press.

Turton, Andrew. 1980. "Thai Institution of Slavery." In *Asian and African Systems of Slavery,* edited by James L. Watson. Berkeley: University of California Press.

Twitchett, Denis C. 1956. "Monastic Estates in T'ang China." *Asia Major* 5 (1): 123–146.

van Sertima, I., ed. 1985. *African Presence in Early Asia.* New Brunswick, NJ: Transaction Books.

Watanabe, Kazuko. 1994. "Militarism, Colonialism, and the Trafficking of Women: 'Comfort Women' Forced into Sexual Labor." *Bulletin of Concerned Asian Scholars* 26 (4): 3–15.

Watson, James L. 1980. "Transactions in People: The Chinese Market in Slaves, Servants, and Heirs." In *Asian and African Systems of Slavery.* Edited by James L. Watson. Berkeley: University of California Press.

Watson, James L., ed. 1980. *Asian and African Systems of Slavery.* Berkeley: University of California Press.

Wilbur, C. Martin. 1943. *Slavery in China during the Former Han Dynasty, 206 B.C.—A.D. 25.* New York: Russell and Russell.

Williams, E. T. 1910. "The Abolition of Slavery in the Chinese Empire." *American Journal of International Law* 4 (4): 794–805.

Yon'guhoe, Chôngdaehyôp, and Chôngsindae Yon'guhoe, eds. 1993. *Kangje-ro kkûllyogan chosônin kunwianpudûl* ([Forcibly drafted Korean military comfort women). Seoul: Hanul.

Australia and the Pacific Islands

Beechert, Edward. 1985. *Working in Hawaii: A Labor History.* Honolulu: University of Hawaii Press.

Journal of Pacific Studies. 1994–1995. Special Issue, *Migration and Labour.* Vol. 20.

McCall, Grant. 1976. "European Impact on Easter Island: Response, Recruitment, and the Polynesian Experience in Peru." *Journal of Pacific History* 11 (2): 90–105.

McCall, Grant; Brij V. Lal; Harold E. Davis; and H. E. Maude. 1983. "Book Review Forum: Slavers in Paradise." *Pacific Studies* 6 (2): 60–71.

Malo, David, and Nathaniel Emerson, trans. 1951. *Hawaiian Antiquities (Moolelo Hawaii).* Honolulu: Bernice Pauahi Bishop Museum.

Maude, H. E. 1981. *Slavers in Paradise: The Peruvian Labour Trade to Polynesia, 1862–1864.* Canberra: Australian National University Press.

Moore, Clive. 1992. "Labour, Indenture, and Historiography in the Pacific." In *Pacific Islands History: Journeys and Transformations.* Edited by Brij V. Lal. Canberra, Australia: Journal of Pacific History.

Moore, Clive; Jacqueline Leckie; and Doug Munro, eds. 1990. *Labour in the South Pacific.* Townsville, Australia: James Cook University.

Munro, Doug. 1993. "The Pacific Islands Labour Trade: Approaches, Methodologies, Debates." *Slavery and Abolition* 14 (2): 87–108.

———. 1990. "The Peruvian Slavers in Tuvalu: How Many Did They Kidnap?" *Journal de la Société des Océanistes* 90: 43–46.

Newbury, Colin. 1980. "The Melanesian Labor Reserve: Some Reflections on Pacific Labor Markets in the Nineteenth Century." *Pacific Studies* 4 (1): 1–25.

Richardson, J. B. 1977. "The Peruvian Barque *Adelante* and the Kanaka Labour Recruitment." *Journal of Pacific History* 12 (4): 212–214.

Scarr, Deryck. 1968. *A Cruize in a Queensland Labour Vessel to the South Seas.* Honolulu: University of Hawaii Press.

Shlomowitz, Ralph. 1996. *Mortality and Migration in the Modern World.* Aldershot, Eng.: Variorum.

Takaki, Roland. 1983. *Pau Hana: Plantation Life and Labor in Hawaii.* Honolulu: University of Hawaii Press.

Toussaint, Auguste. 1972. *Histoire des iles Mascareignes.* Paris: Berger-Levrault.

Europe

Abu-Lughod, Ibrahim. 1963. *Arab Rediscovery of Europe.* Princeton, NJ: Princeton University Press.

Actes du Congrès de Vienne. 1819. Brussels: Chez Weissenbruch.

Albuquerque, Luís de. 1987. *Navegadores, viajantes, e aventureiros Portugueses: Séculos XV e XVI.* Lisbon: Caminho.

———. 1983. *Os descobrimentos Portugueses.* Lisbon: Publicações Alfa.

Albuquerque, Luís de, ed. 1989. *Tratado de Tordesilhas e outros documentos.* Lisbon: Publicações Alfa.

Andrews, Kenneth. 1984. *Trade, Plunder, and Settlement: Maritime Enterprise and the Foundation of the British Empire.* Cambridge: Cambridge University Press.

Anstey, Roger. 1975. *The Atlantic Slave Trade and British Abolition, 1760–1810.* Cambridge: Cambridge University Press.

Anstey, Roger, and P. E. Hair. 1976. *Liverpool, the African Slave Trade, and Abolition.* Liverpool: Historic Society of Lancashire and Cheshire.

Aragão, Augusto C. Teixeira de. 1898. *Vasco da Gama e a vidigueira: Estudo historico.* Lisbon: Imprensa Nacional.

Atchebro, Dogbo Daniel. 1990. *La société des nations et la lutte contre l'esclavage 1922–1938.* Geneva: Memoire of the Institut Universitaire des Hautes Etudes Internationales.

Azevedo, João Lúcio de. 1909. *O Marquez de Pombal e a sua epoca.* Lisbon: Livraria Classica Editora.

Badinter, Elisabeth, and Robert Badinter. 1990. *Condorcet (1743–1794): Un intellectuel en politique.* Paris: Librairie Fayard.

Baker, Keith Michael. 1975. *Condorcet: From Natural Philosophy to Social Mathematics.* Chicago: University of Chicago Press.

Bamford, Paul. 1973. *Fighting Ships and Prisons: The Mediterranean Galleys of France in the Age of King Louis XIV.* St. Paul: University of Minnesota Press.

Barker, A. 1978. *The African Link: British Attitudes to the Negro in the Era of the Atlantic Slave Trade, 1550–1807*. London: Frank Cass.

Barry, Boubacar. 1988. *Le Senegambie du XVe au XIXe siecle*. Paris: Harmattan.

Baxter, Richard. 1925. *Chapters from A Christian Directory; or, A Summ of Practical Theology and Cases of Conscience, by Richard Baxter, Selected by Jeannette Tawney, with a Preface by the Right Rev. Charles Gore, D.D.* London: G. Bell and Sons.

Behrendt, Stephen D. 1991. "The Captains in the British Slave Trade from 1785 to 1809." *Transactions of the Historic Society for Lancashire and Cheshire* 140: 79–140.

Bellot, Leland J. 1971. "Evangelicals and the Defense of Slavery in Britain's Old Colonial Empire." *Journal of Southern History* 37 (1): 19–40.

Benot, Yves. 1988. *La Révolution française et la fin des colonies (1789–1794)*. Paris: Editions La Découverte.

Berding, Helmut. 1974. "Die Ächtung des Sklavenhandels auf dem Wiener Kongress 1814/15." *Historische Zeitschrift* 219 (2): 265–289.

Blackburn, Robin. 1991. "Anti-Slavery and the French Revolution." *History Today* 41: 19–25.

Blackett, R. J. M. 1978. "Fugitive Slaves in Britain: The Odyssey of William and Ellen Craft." *Journal of American Studies* 12 (1): 41–62.

Blake, J. W. 1949. "The Farm of the Guinea Trade." In *Essays in British and Irish History*. Edited by H. A. Cronne, T. W. Moody, and D. B. Quinn. London: Frederick Muller.

Bloch, Marc. 1975. *Slavery and Serfdom in the Middle Ages*. Berkeley: University of California Press.

Blum, Jerome. 1966. *Lord and Peasant in Russia from the Ninth to the Nineteenth Century*. New York: Atheneum.

Bodin, Jean. 1962. *The Six Bookes of the Commonweale*. Edited by K. D. McRae. Cambridge, MA: Harvard University Press.

———. 1986. *Les six livres de la république*. Paris: Librairie Arthème Fayard.

Bonnassie, Pierre. 1991. *From Slavery to Feudalism in South-Western Europe*. Cambridge: Cambridge University Press.

Boogaart, Ernst van den, and Pieter C. Emmer. 1979. "The Dutch Participation in the Atlantic Slave Trade, 1596–1650." In *The Uncommon Market: Essays in the Economic History of the Atlantic Slave Trade*. Edited by Henry A. Gemery and Jan S. Hogendorn. New York: Academic Press.

Boswell, John. 1977. *The Royal Treasure*. New Haven, CT: Yale University Press.

Boxer, Charles R. 1969. *The Portuguese Seaborne Empire: 1415–1825*. London: Hutchinson.

———. 1963. *Race Relations in the Portuguese Colonial Empire, 1415–1825*. Oxford: Clarendon Press.

Bridenbaugh, Carl, and Roberta Bridenbaugh. 1972. *No Peace beyond the Line: The English in the Caribbean, 1624–1690*. New York: Oxford University Press.

British Parliamentary Papers: Slave Trade. 1969. 95 vols. Shannon, Ire.: Irish University Press.

Bro Jørgensen, and A. A. Rasch. 1969. *Asiatiske, vestindiske, og guinesiske handelskompagnier*. Copenhagen: Rigsarkivet.

Bromberg, E. I. 1942. "Wales and the Medieval Slave Trade." *Speculum* 17: 263–269.

Brooks, George E. 1993. *Landlords and Strangers*. Boulder, CO: Westview Press.

Brown, Laura. 1993. *Ends of Empire: Women and Ideology in Early Eighteenth-Century English Literature*. Ithaca, NY: Cornell University Press.

Brundage, James R. 1987. *Law, Sex, and Christian Society in Medieval Europe*. Chicago: University of Chicago Press.

Brutus, Timoleon C. 1946–1947. *L'homme d'Airain: Étude monographique sur Jean-Jacques Dessalines, fondateur de la nation haïtienne*. Port-au-Prince, Haiti: N. A. Theodore.

Bull, Hedley; Benedict Kingsbury; and Adam Roberts, eds. 1992. *Hugo Grotius and International Relations*. Oxford: Clarendon Press.

Burdon, John, ed. 1931–1935. *Archives of British Honduras*. 3 vols. London: Sifton Praed.

Campbell, R. H., and A. S. Skinner, eds. 1981. *Adam Smith: An Inquiry into the Nature and Causes of the Wealth of Nations*. Indianapolis, IN: Liberty Classics.

Canavaggio, J. F. 1990. *Cervantes*. New York: Norton.

Cardellini, I. 1981. *Die biblischen "Sklaven"—Gesetze im Lichte des keilschriften Klavenrechts*. Bonn: P. Hanstein.

Certeau, Michel de. 1975. *Un politique de la langue: La Révolution française et les patois—L'enquete de Grégoire*. Paris: Gallimard.

Charles, B. G. 1934. *Old Norse Relations with Wales*. Cardiff: University of Wales Press.

Chejne, Anwar. 1974. *Muslim Spain: Its History and Culture*. Minneapolis: University of Minnesota Press.

Clarkson, Thomas. 1808. *The History of the Rise, Progress, and Accomplishment of the Abolition of the African Slave Trade by the British Parliament. Vol.1*. London: Longman, Hurst, Rees, and Orme.

Code Napoléon. 1810. Paris: Firmin Didot.

Colgrave, Bertram. 1968. *The Earliest Life of Gregory the Great by an Anonymous Monk of Whitby*. Lawrence: University of Kansas Press.

Condorcet. 1996. *Politique de Condorcet: Textes choisies et présentés par Charles Coutel*. Paris: Editions Payot et Rivages.

Cone, Carl B. 1964. *Burke and the Nature of Politics: The Age of the French Revolution*. Lexington: University of Kentucky Press.

Cooper, Anna Julia. 1988. *Slavery and the French Revolutionists (1788–1805)*. Translated from the French with an introductory essay by Frances Richardson Keller. Lewiston, NY: Edwin Mellen Press.

Cortés López, José Luis. 1989. *La esclavitud negra en la España peninsular del siglo XVI*. Salamanca, Spain: Ediciones Universidad de Salamanca.

Coupland, Reginald. 1964. *The British Anti-Slavery Movement*. New York: Barnes and Noble.

Craft, William, and Ellen Craft. 1860. *Running a Thousand Miles for Freedom, or The Escape of William and Ellen Craft from Slavery*. London: William Tweedie.

Crow, Hugh. 1970. *Memoirs of the Late Captain Hugh Crow of Liverpool*. London: F. Cass.

Crowe, S. E. 1942. *The Berlin West Africa Conference, 1884–1885*. Westport, CT: Negro Universities Press.

Daget, Serge. 1971. "L'Abolition de la traite des Noirs en France de 1814–1831." *Cahiers d'Etudes Africaines* 11 (1): 14–58.

———. 1979. "British Repression of the Illegal French Slave Trade: Some Considerations." In *The Uncommon Market: Essays in the Economic History of the Atlantic Slave Trade*. Edited by Henry A. Gemery and Jan S. Hogendorn. New York: Academic Press.

———. 1980. "A Model of the French Abolitionist Movement and Its Variations." In *Anti-Slavery, Religion, and Reform: Essays in Memory of Roger Anstey*. Edited by Christine Bolt and Seymour Drescher. Folkestone, Eng.: Dawson.

———. 1990. *La traite des noirs: Bastilles négrières et velléités abolitionnistes*. Nantes: Ouest France Université.

———. 1989. "Traites des noirs, relations internationales, et humanitarisme, 1815–1850." *Relations internationales* 60 (Winter): 413–427.

Davis, David Brion. 1966. *The Problem of Slavery in Western Culture*. New York: Oxford University Press.

de la Torre y del Cerro, Antonio, and Luis Suarez Fernandez, eds. 1952. *Documentos referentes a las relaciones con Portugal durante el reinado de los reyes católicos*. Valladolid, Spain: Consejo Superior de Investigaciones Cientificas.

De Witte, C. M. 1953–1954. "Les Bulles Pontificales et l'expansion Portuguese au XVe Siecle." *Revue d'Histoire Ecclesiastique* 48: 683–718 and 49: 438–461.

Defarri, Roy Joseph, et al., eds. 1951–1987. *The Fathers of the Church*. 70 vols. Washington, DC: Catholic University of America Press.

Dickinson, John, ed. and trans. 1927. *The Statesman's Book of John of Salisbury*. New York: Knopf.

Dickinson, W. Calvin, and Eloise R. Hitchcock, eds. 1996. *The War of the Spanish Succession, 1702–1713: A Selected Bibliography*. Westport, CT: Greenwood Press.

Diffie, Bailey W., and George D. Winius. 1977. *Foundations of the Portuguese Empire, 1415–1580*. Minneapolis: University of Minnesota Press.

Dmytryshyn, Basil. 1973. *Medieval Russia: A Sourcebook*. Hinsdale, IL: Dryden.

Dockes, Pierre. 1982. *Medieval Slavery and Liberation*. Chicago: University of Chicago Press.

Domínguez Ortiz, Antonio. 1952. "La esclavitud en Castilla durante la Edad Moderna." In *Estudios de historia social de España*. Edited by Carmelo Viñas y Mey. Madrid: CSIC.

———. 1971. *The Golden Age of Spain: 1516–1659*. New York: Basic Books.

Drescher, Seymour. 1987. *Capitalism and Antislavery: British Mobilization in Comparative Perspective*. New York: Oxford University Press.

———. 1977. *Econocide: British Slavery in the Era of Abolition*. Pittsburgh: University of Pittsburgh Press.

Duby, Georges. 1974. *The Early Growth of the European Economy: Warriors and Peasants from the Seventh to the Twelfth Centuries*. Ithaca, NY: Cornell University Press.

———. 1980. *The Three Orders: Feudal Society Imagined*. Chicago: University of Chicago Press.

Dunlop, O., and R. C. Denman. 1912. *English Apprenticeship and Child Labor*. New York: Macmillan.

Durkheim, Emile. 1970. *Montesquieu and Rousseau: Forerunners of Sociology*. Ann Arbor: University of Michigan Press.

Egilsson, Ólafur. 1969. *Reisubók*. Reykjavík, Iceland: Almenna Bókafélag.

Eichler, Eckhard. 1991. "Untersuchungen zu den Königsbriefen des Alten Reiches." *Studien zur Altägyptischen Kultur* 18: 141–171.

———. 1993. "Untersuchungen zum Expeditionswesen des ägyptischen Alten Reiches." Wiesbaden, Germany: Otto Harrassowitz.

Eisenbichler, Konrad, ed. 1991. *Crossing the Boundaries: Christian Piety and the Arts in Italian Medieval and Renaissance Confraternities*. Kalamazoo, MI: Medieval Institute Publications.

Emmer, Pieter. 1981. "Abolition of the Abolished: The Illegal Dutch Slave Trade and the Mixed Courts." In *Abolition of the Atlantic Slave Trade*. Edited by James Walvin and David Eltis. Madison: University of Wisconsin Press.

Ezran, Maurice. 1992. *L'Abbé Grégoire, defenseur des juifs et des noirs: Révolution et tolerance*. Paris: Editions L'Harmittan.

Farrar, F. W. 1907. *Lives of the Fathers: Sketches of Church History in Biography*. London: Adam and Charles Black.

Feldbaek, O. 1981. "The Organisation and Structure of the Danish East India, West India, and Guinea Companies in the 17th and 18th Centuries." In *Companies and Trade: Essays on Overseas Trading Companies during the Ancien Regime*. Edited by Leonard Blussé et al. Leiden: Leiden University Press.

Feldbaek, O., and O. Justesen. 1980. "Kolonierna i Asien og Afrika." In *Politikens Danmarks Historie*. Edited by S. Ellehfj and Kristof Glamann. Copenhagen: Politikens Forlag.

Fellows, Otis E., and Norman L. Torrey, eds. 1942. *The Age of Enlightenment: An Anthology of Eighteenth-Century French Literature*. New York: Appleton-Century-Crofts.

Ferguson, Moira. 1992. *Subject to Others: British Women Writers and Colonial Slavery, 1670–1834*. New York: Routledge.

Fernández-Pérez, Paloma. 1997. *El nuestro familiar de la metrópoli: Redes de parentesco y consolidación de lazos mercantiles en Cádiz, 1700–1812*. Madrid: Siglo XXI de España.

Field, Daniel. 1976. *The End of Serfdom*. Cambridge, MA: Harvard University Press.

Fikes, Robert. 1980. "Black Scholars in Europe during the Renaissance and the Enlightenment." *Negro History Bulletin* 43 (July–September): 58–60.

Filliot, J. M. 1974. *La traite des esclaves vers les Mascareignes aux XVIIIe siecle*. Paris: Office de la Recherche Scientifique et Technique Outre-mer.

Fonseca, Luís Adão da. 1987. *O essencial sôbre*

Bartolomeu Dias. Lisbon: Imprensa Nacional-Casa da Moeda.

Freedman, Paul. 1991. *The Origins of Peasant Servitude in Medieval Catalonia*. Cambridge: Cambridge University Press.

Freeman, Michael. 1980. *Edmund Burke and the Critique of Political Radicalism*. Oxford: Basil Blackwell.

Furneaux, Robin. 1974. *William Wilberforce*. London: Hamish Hamilton.

Gates, Henry L., Jr. 1987. *Figures in Black: Words, Signs, and the "Racial" Self*. New York: Oxford University Press.

Gaull, Marilyn. 1988. *English Romanticism: The Human Context*. New York: Norton.

Geneve [Geneva], Université de. 1975. *Chypre des origenes au moyen-age: Seminaire interdisciplinaire*. Geneva: Université de Geneve.

George, Claude. 1968. *Rise of British West Africa*. London: Houlston.

Gerzina, Gretchen. 1995. *Black London: Life before Emancipation*. New Brunswick, NJ: Rutgers University Press.

Gibson, Charles. 1971. *The Black Legend: Anti-Spanish Attitudes in the Old World and the New*. New York: Knopf.

Ginnell, Laurence. 1917. *The Brehon Laws*. Dublin: West.

Gregory, Saint. 1916. *History of the Franks*. Translated, with notes, by Ernest Brehaut. New York: Columbia University Press.

Gregory I. 1950. *Pastoral Care*. Translated by Henry Davis. Baltimore: Newman Press.

Grotius, Hugo. 1925. *The Law of War and Peace: De jure belli ac pacis, libri tres*. Indianapolis, IN: Bobbs-Merrill.

Güterbock, H. G. 1972. "Bermerkungen zu den Ausdrücken ellum, wardum und asirum in hethitischen Texten." In *Gesellschaftklassen im alten Zweistromland und in angrenzenden Gebeiten*. Edited by D. O. Edzard. Munich: Verlag der bayerischen Akademie der Wissenschaften.

Hald, Kristian. 1975. "Traellenavne." In *Kulturhistoriskt lexikon for nordisk medeltid, Vol. 19*. Malmo, Sweden: Allhems.

Hale, Lindsay Lauren. 1997. "Preto Velho: Resistance, Redemption, and Engendered Representations of Slavery in a Brazilian Possession-Trance Religion." *American Ethnologist* 24 (2): 392–414.

Hanke, Lewis. 1949. *The Spanish Struggle for Justice in the Conquest of America*. Philadelphia: University of Pennsylvania Press.

Heers, Jacques. 1981. *Esclaves et domestiques au moyen âge dans le monde mediterranéen*. Paris: Fayard.

Hellie, Richard. 1971. *Enserfment and Military Change in Muscovy*. Chicago: University of Chicago Press.

Hernaes, Per O. 1992. *The Danish Slave Trade from West Africa and Afro-Danish Relations on the 18th-Century Gold Coast*. Trondheim, Norway: Trondheim University.

Herrmann-Otto, Elisabeth. 1994. *Ex ancilla natus: Untersuchungen zu den "hausgeborenen" Sklaven und Sklavinnen im Westen des römischen Kaiserreiches*. Stuttgart: Franz Steiner Verlag.

Herzog zu Sachsen, Max. 1929. *Der heilige Theodor, Archimandrit von Studion*. Munich: Georg Muller.

Higman, Barry W. 1984. *Slave Populations of the British Caribbean, 1807–1834*. Baltimore: Johns Hopkins University Press.

Hilgarth, J. 1978. *The Spanish Kingdoms, 1250–1516*. Oxford: Clarendon Press.

Hill, G. 1972. *A History of Cyprus*. Cambridge: Cambridge University Press.

Hinde, Wendy. 1973. *George Canning*. New York: St. Martin's Press.

Hinton, Richard J., ed. 1898. *Poems by Richard Realf: Poet, Soldier, Workman*. New York: Funk and Wagnalls.

Hoare, Prince. 1820. *Memoirs of Granville Sharp, Esq*. London: Henry Colburn.

Hobbes, Thomas. 1985. *Leviathan*. New York: Penguin Classics.

Højlund Knap, Henning. 1983. "Danskerne og slaveriet—negerslavedebatten i Danmark indtil 1792." In *Dansk kolonihistorie—indffring og studier*. Edited by Peter Hoxcer Jensen. Århus, Denmark: Forlaget Historia.

Hollander, Lee M., tr. 1928. *The Poetic Edda*. Austin: University of Texas.

Holm, P. 1986. "The Slave Trade of Dublin: 9th to 12th Centuries." *Peritia* 5: 317–345.

Howell, Raymond C. 1987. *The Royal Navy and the Slave Trade*. New York: St. Martin's.

Hübner, Wolfgang. 1984. *Varros instrumentum vocale im Kontext der antiken Achwissenschaften*. Stuttgart: Franz Steiner.

Hume, David. 1987. "Of National Characters." In *Essays: Moral, Political, and Literary*. Edited by T. H. Green and T. H. Grose. Indianapolis, IN: Liberty Classics.

Hunt, Lynn. 1996. *The French Revolution and Human Rights: A Brief Documentary History*. New York: St. Martin's.

Hurwitz, Edith. 1973. *Politics and the Public Conscience: Slave Emancipation and the Abolitionist Movement in Britain*. London: Allen and Unwin.

Iverson, Tore. 1994. *Trelldommen: Norsk slaveri i middelalderen*. Bergen, Norway: Bergen University.

James, C. L. R. 1963. *The Black Jacobins*. New York: Vintage Press.

James, E., ed. 1980. *Visigothic Spain*. Oxford: Oxford University Press.

James, Francis G. 1985. "Irish Colonial Trade in the Eighteenth Century." *William and Mary Quarterly* 19 (3): 329–356.

Jenkins, Dafydd. 1986. *The Law of Hywel Dda*. Llandysul, Wales: Gomer.

Johne, Klaus-Peter; Jens Köhn; and Volker Weber. 1983. *Die Kolonen in Italien und den westlichen Provinzen des römischen Reiches*. Berlin: Akademie-Verlag.

Johnson, Merwyn S. 1978. *Locke on Freedom: An Incisive Study of the Thought of John Locke*. Austin, TX: Best Print.

Johnson, Rossiter. 1879. "Richard Realf." *Lippincott's Magazine* 3: 293–300.

Jones, Gwyn. 1984. *A History of the Vikings*. New York: Oxford University Press.

Jornadas, Americanistas. 1973. *El tratado de Tordesillas y su proyeccion*. Valladolid, Spain: Universidad, Seminario de Historia de América.

Kamen, Henry Arthur Francis. 1991. *Spain, 1469–1714: A Society of Conflict*. London: Longman Press.

———. 1969. *The War of Succession in Spain, 1700–15*. London: Weidenfeld and Nicolson.

Karras, Ruth Mazo. 1988. *Slavery and Society in Medieval Scandinavia*. New Haven, CT: Yale University Press.

Kelly, Christopher. 1987. *Rousseau's Exemplary Life: The "Confessions" as Political Philosophy*. Ithaca, NY: Cornell University Press.

Klein, Herbert S. 1978. *The Middle Passage: Comparative Studies in the Atlantic Slave Trade*. Princeton, NJ: Princeton University Press.

Kolchin, Peter. 1987. *Unfree Labor: American Slavery and Russian Serfdom*. Cambridge, MA: Harvard University Press.

La Boétie, Estienne de. 1975. *The Politics of Obedience: The Discourse of Voluntary Servitude*. Introduction by Murray N. Rothbard; translated by Harry Kurz. New York: Free Life Editions.

Laistner, M. 1957. *Thought and Letters in Western Europe A.D. 500–1000*. London: London University Press.

Lane, Margaret. 1972. *Frances Wright and the "Great Experiment."* Manchester, Eng.: Manchester University Press.

Lang, David M. 1957. *The Last Years of the Georgian Monarchy, 1658–1832*. New York: Columbia University Press.

Levi-Provençal, Évariste. 1950–1953. *Histoire de l'Espagne Musulmane*. 3 vols. Leiden: Brill.

Levi-Strauss, C. 1962. *La pansee sauvage*. Paris: Plon.

Linder, Ammon. 1977. "Knowledge of John of Salisbury in the Late Middle Ages." *Studi Medievali* 18 (2): 315–366.

Lindsay, Arnett. 1920. "Diplomatic Relations between the United States and Great Britain Bearing on the Return of Negro Slaves, 1788–1828." *Journal of Negro History* 5: 261–278.

Livermore, H. V. 1947. *A History of Portugal*. Cambridge: Cambridge University Press.

———. 1971. *The Origins of Spain and Portugal*. London: Allen and Unwin.

Lobo Cabrera, M. 1990. "La esclavitude en la España moderna: Su investigación en los últimos cincuenta años." *Hispania* 176.

Lourie, Elena. 1990. *Crusade and Colonisation: Muslims, Christians, and Jews in Medieval Aragón*. Brookfield, VT: Variorum.

Lüsebrink, Hans-Jürgen, and Manfred Tietz, eds. 1991. *Lectures de Raynal: L'histoire des deux Indes en Europe et en Amérique au XVIIIe siècle*. Oxford: Voltaire Foundation.

McNeill, John T., and Helena M. Gamer. 1990. *Medieval Handbooks of Penance*. New York: Columbia University Press.

Marshall, P. J., and G. Williams. 1982. *The Great Map of Mankind: British Perceptions of the World in the Age of Enlightenment*. London: J. M. Dent.

Marti, Evelin. 1929. "The English Slave Trade and the African Settlements." In *The Cambridge History of the British Empire*. Edited by J. Holland Rose, A. P. Newton, and E. A. Benians. Cambridge: Cambridge University Press.

Marx, Karl. 1971. *Early Texts*. Translated and edited by David McLellan. New York: Barnes and Noble.

Mattoso, Katia M. de Queirós. 1986. *To Be a Slave in Brazil, 1550–1888*. New Brunswick, NJ: Rutgers University Press.

Maxwell, Kenneth. 1995. *Pombal: Paradox of the Enlightenment*. Cambridge: Cambridge University Press.

Meer, Frederick van der. 1961. *Augustine the Bishop*. London: Sheed and Ward.

Mesa, Roberto. 1990. *El colonialismo en la crisis del XIX español*. Madrid: Ediciones de Cultura Hispánica.

Miers, Suzanne. 1975. *Britain and the Ending of the Slave Trade*. New York: Longman.

Miller, Eugene F., ed. 1987. *David Hume: Essays, Moral, Political, and Literary*. Indianapolis, IN: Liberty Fund.

Molina Martínez, Miguel. 1991. *La leyenda negra*. Madrid: NEREA.

Montesquieu, Charles de Secondat. 1977. *The Spirit of Laws: A Compendium of the First English Edition*. Edited by David Wallace Carrithers. Berkeley: University of California Press.

Moore, John S. 1988. "Domesday Slave." *Anglo-Norman Studies* 11: 191–220.

Moreau de St. Mery, Louis Médéric. 1783–1790. *Loix et constitutions des colonies Françaises de l'Amerique sous le vent, de 1550 à 1785*. 6 vols. Paris: Privately printed.

Morris, John. 1976. *Domesday Book*. Chichester, Eng.: Phillimore.

Müller, Wilhelm Johann. 1968. *Die Africanische auf der guneischen Gold Cust gelegene Landschafft Fetu*. Hamburg: Graz.

Ndamba Kabongo, Albert. 1976. *Les esclaves à Seville au début du XVIIe siècle: Approche de leurs origines et de leur condition*. Memoir of Mâitrisse. Université de Toulouse le Mirail. Microfiche. Paris: Micro Editions Hachette.

Necheles, Ruth. 1971. *The Abbé Grégoire 1787–1831: Odyssey of an Egalitarian*. Westport CT: Greenwood.

Netscher, P. M. 1888. *Geschiedenis van de koloniën Essequebo, Demerary en Berbice, van de vestiging der Nederlanders aldaar tot op onzen tijd*. The Hague: Martinus Nijhoff.

Neveus, Clara. 1974. *Tralarna i landskapslagarnas samhalle: Danmark och Sverige*. Uppsala, Sweden: Uppsala University.

Nietzsche, Friedrich. 1966. *Beyond Good and Evil*. Translated by Walter Kaufmann. New York: Random House.

———. 1974. *The Gay Science*. Translated by Walter Kaufmann. New York: Random House.

Novaky, György. 1990. *Handelskompanier och kompanihandel: Svenska Afrikakompaniet 1649–1663, en studie i feodal handel*. Uppsala, Sweden: Universitetet.

O'Brien, Connor. 1992. *The Great Melody: A Thematic Biography and Commented Anthology of Edmund Burke*. Chicago: University of Chicago Press.

O'Driscoll, Gerald P., Jr. 1979. *Adam Smith and Modern Political Economy.* Ames: Iowa University Press.

Oostindie, Gert, ed. 1996. *Fifty Years Later: Antislavery, Capitalism, and Modernity in the Dutch Orbit.* Pittsburgh: University of Pittsburgh Press.

Ott, Thomas O. 1973. *The Haitian Revolution, 1789–1804.* Knoxville: University of Tennessee Press.

Palmer, Colin. 1981. *Human Cargoes: The British Slave Trade to Spanish America, 1700–1739.* Urbana: University of Illinois Press.

Parry, J. H. 1974. *The Spanish Seaborne Empire.* New York: Knopf.

Peabody, Sue. 1996. *"There Are No Slaves in France": The Political Culture of Race and Slavery in the Ancien Régime.* New York: Oxford University Press.

Pelteret, David. 1995. *Slavery in Early Medieval England.* Woodbridge, Eng.: Boydell.

Pereira, Duarte Pacheco. 1937. *Esmeraldo de situ orbis.* London: Hakluyt Society.

Peres, Damião. 1983. *História dos descobrimentos Portugueses.* Porto, Portugal: Vertente.

Phillips, W. D., Jr. 1990. *Historia de la esclavitude in España.* Madrid: Siglo XXI de España.

Pieterse, Jan Nederveen. 1992. *White on Black: Images of African and Blacks in Western Popular Culture.* New Haven, CT: Yale University Press.

Pike, Joseph B., ed. and trans. 1938. *Frivolities of Courtiers and Footprints of Philosophers.* Minneapolis: University of Minnesota Press.

Pluchon, Pierre. 1991. *Histoire de la colonisation française: Le premier empire colonial, des origines à la Restauration.* Paris: Fayard.

Postma, Johannes Menne. 1990. *The Dutch in the Atlantic Slave Trade, 1660–1815.* Cambridge: Cambridge University Press.

Priester, L. R. 1987. *De Nederlandse houding ten aanzien van de slavenhandel en slavernij 1596–1863.* Middelburg, Netherlands: Commissie Regionale Geschiedbeoefening Zeeland.

Prytz, Kare. 1991. *Westward before Columbus.* Oslo: Norsk Maritimt Forlag.

Putney, Martha. 1975. "The Slave Trade in French Diplomacy from 1814 to 1815." *Journal of Negro History* 60 (3): 411–427.

Quarta, Pietro Luigi. 1993. "Reflexiones acerca de la leyenda negra en la historia de España." *Rivista de Studi Politici Internazionali* 60 (1): 92–100.

Raimond, Jean, and J. R. Watson, eds. 1992. *A Handbook to British Romanticism.* New York: St. Martin's.

Raphael, D. D. 1985. *Adam Smith.* New York: Oxford University Press.

Ravenstein, E. G., ed. 1898. *A Journal of the First Voyage of Vasco da Gama, 1497–1499.* London: Hakluyt Society.

Rediker, Marcus. 1987. *Between the Devil and the Deep Blue Sea.* Cambridge: Cambridge University Press.

Reich, Jerome. 1968. "The Slave Trade at the Congress of Vienna: A Study in English Public Opinion." *Journal of Negro History* 53: 129–143.

Resnick, Daniel P. 1972. "The Société des Amis des Noirs and the Abolition of Slavery." *French Historical Studies* 7 (4): 558–569.

La Révolution française et l'abolition de l'esclavage: Textes et documents. 1969. 12 vols. Paris: Editions d'histoire sociale.

Richardson, David. 1994. "Liverpool and the English Slave Trade." In *Transatlantic Slavery: Against Human Dignity.* Edited by Anthony Tibbles. London: HMSO.

Ripley, C. Peter, ed. 1985. *The Black Abolitionist Papers: The British Isles, 1830–1865.* Chapel Hill: University of North Carolina Press.

Rousseau, Jean-Jacques. 1932. *The Social Contract and Discourses.* London: E. P. Dutton.

Sandoval, Alonso de. 1987. *Un tratado sobre la esclavitud (De instauranda aethiopum salute).* Madrid: Alianza Editorial.

Saunders, A. C. de C. M. 1982. *A Social History of Black Slaves and Freedmen in Portugal 1441–1555.* Cambridge: Cambridge University Press.

Schneider, G. A. 1900. *Der Hl. Theodor von Studion.* Munster: Heinrich Schoningh.

Schouls, Peter A. 1992. *Reasoned Freedom: John Locke and Enlightenment.* Ithaca, NY: Cornell University Press.

Schutz, John A. 1950. "James Ramsay, Essayist: Aggressive Humanitarian." In *British Humanitarianism: Essays Honoring Frank J. Klingberg.* Edited by Samuel Clyde McCulloch. Philadelphia: Church Historical Society.

Schwartz, Joachim [Condorcet]. 1788. *Réflexions sur l'esclavage des nègres, par M. Schwartz, pasteur du Saint Evangile à Bienne, membre de la Société économique de B***.* New edition, revised and corrected. Paris: Froullé.

Schwarz, Suzanne. 1995. *Slave Captain: The Career of James Irving in the Liverpool Slave Trade.* Wrexham, Eng.: Bridge Books.

Scobie, Edward. 1972. *Black Britannia: A History of Blacks in Britain.* Chicago: Johnson Publishing.

Serrão, Joaquim Veríssimo. 1982. *O Marquês de Pombal: O homen, o diplomata, e o estadista.* Lisbon: Camaras Municipias.

Sethe, Kurt. 1906. *Urkunden der 18. Dynastie.* Leipzig: Hinrichs.

Shahan, Robert W., and J. I. Biro, eds. 1978. *Spinoza: New Perspectives.* Norman: University of Oklahoma Press.

Shklar, Judith. 1987. *Montesquieu.* Oxford: Oxford University Press.

Shyllon, F. O. 1974. *Black Slaves in Britain.* London: Oxford University Press.

Sigurdsson, Gisli. 1988. *Gaelic Influence in Iceland: Historical and Literary Contacts.* Studia Islandica 46. Reykjavík: Bokutgafa Menningarsjoos.

Solin, Heikki. 1971. *Beitrage zur Kenntnis der griechischen Personennamen in Rom 1.* Commentationes Humanarum Litterarum 48. Helsinki: Societas Scientiarum Fennica.

———. 1990. *Namenpaare: Eine Studie zur romischen Namengebung.* Commentationes Humanarum Litterarum 90. Helsinki: Societas Scientiarum Fennica.

Sommerville, Johann. 1992. *Thomas Hobbes: Political Ideas in Historical Context.* London: Macmillan.

Spinoza, Baruch. 1982. *The Ethics, and Selected Letters.* Edited and translated by Samuel Shirley. Indianapolis, IN: Hackett.

———. 1958. *Political Works*. Edited by A. G. Wernham. Oxford: Clarendon Press.

Stein, Robert Louis. 1979. *The French Slave Trade in the Eighteenth Century: An Old Regime Business*. Madison: University of Wisconsin Press.

Stephen, George. 1854. *Antislavery Recollections: In a Series of Letters Addressed to Mrs. Beecher Stowe, Written by Sir George Stephen, at Her Request*. London: Thomas Hatchard.

Stiller, Richard. 1972. *Commune on the Frontier: The Story of Frances Wright*. New York: Thomas Y. Crowell.

Tacitus, Cornelius. 1970. *The Agricola and the Germania*. New York: Penguin Books.

Temperley, Harold W. V. 1925. *The Foreign Policy of Canning, 1822–1827*. London: G. Bell and Sons.

———. 1968. *Life of Canning*. New York: Haskell House.

Temperley, Howard. 1972. *British Antislavery, 1833–1870*. London: Longman.

Thompson, E. A. 1969. *The Goths in Spain*. Oxford: Oxford University Press.

Thompson, E. P. 1968. *The Making of the English Working Class*. London: Pelican.

Tiainen-Anttila, Kaija. 1994. *The Problem of Humanity: Blacks in the European Enlightenment*. Helsinki: Finnish Historical Society.

Tooley, M. J., ed. and trans. 1955. *Six Books of the Commonwealth by Jean Bodin*. Oxford: Basil Blackwell.

Tremearne, A. J. N. 1913. *Hausa Superstitions and Customs: An Introduction to the Folk-Lore and the Folk*. London: J. Bale, Sons and Danielsson.

Truxes, Thomas M. 1988. *Irish American Trade, 1660–1783*. Cambridge: Cambridge University Press.

Tulard, Jean, ed., 1987. *Dictionnaire Napoléon*. Paris: Fayard.

Turley, David. 1991. *The Culture of English Antislavery*. London: Routledge.

Unger, W. S. 1958–1960, 1965. "Bijdragen tot de geschiedenis van de Nederlandse slavenhandel." In *Economisch-Historisch Jaarboek*. Vols. 26, 28. The Hague: n.p.

Venter, C. 1991. "Die Voortrekkers en die ingeboekte Slawe wat die Groot Trek Meegemaak Het." *Historia* 39 (1): 14–29.

Verlinden, Charles. 1955. *L'esclavage dans l'Europe médiévale*. Bruges, Belgium: De Tempel.

———. 1969–1970. "Medieval 'Slavers.'" *Explorations in Economic History* 7: 1–14.

———. 1963. "Traite des esclaves et traitants italiens à Constantinople (XIIIe–XVe siècles)." *Moyen Age* 69: 791–804.

Vernadsky, George. 1965. *Medieval Russian Laws*. New York: Octagon.

Vieira, António. 1951. *Obras escolhidas*. Lisbon: Livraria Sá da Costa.

Vogt, John. 1979. *Portuguese Rule on the Gold Coast 1469–1682*. Athens: University of Georgia Press.

Vogt, Joseph, and Norbert Brockmeyer. 1983. *Bibliographie zur Antiken Sklaverei*. Bochum, Germany: Studienverlag Dr. N. Brockmeyer.

Vogt, Joseph, et al., eds. 1994. *Forschungen zur Antiken Sklaverei*. Weisbaden and Stuttgart: Steiner.

Wade-Evans, A. W. 1909. *Welsh Medieval Law*. Oxford: Clarendon.

Wallis, H. 1986. "'Things Hidden from Other Men': The Portuguese Voyages of Discovery." *History Today* 36 (June): 27–33.

Walvin, James. 1973. *Black and White: The Negro and English Society, 1555–1945*. London: Oxford University Press.

———. 1992. *Black Ivory: A History of British Slavery*. London: HarperCollins.

———. 1971. *The Black Presence: A Documentary History of the Negro in England, 1555–1860*. London: Orbach and Chambers.

Ward, William. 1969. *The Royal Navy and the Slavers*. New York: Pantheon.

Warner, Oliver. 1962. *William Wilberforce and His Times*. London: B.T. Batsford.

Warrender, Howard. 1957. *The Political Philosophy of Thomas Hobbes*. London: Oxford University Press.

Watt, William Montgomery. 1967. *A History of Islamic Spain*. Edinburgh: Edinburgh University Press.

Weissman, Ronald F. E. 1982. *Ritual Brotherhood in Renaissance Florence*. New York: Academic Press.

Welchman, Jennifer. 1995. "Locke on Slavery and Inalienable Rights." *Canadian Journal of Philosophy* 25 (1): 67–83.

Wieskel, Timothy. 1980. *French Colonial Rule and the Baule Peoples*. New York: Oxford University Press.

Wilberforce, Robert Isaac, and Samuel Wilberforce. 1838. *The Life of William Wilberforce*. London: John Murray.

Wilks, Michael, ed. 1984. *The World of John of Salisbury*. Oxford: Basil Blackwell.

Willams, Eric Eustace. 1971. *From Columbus to Castro: The History of the Caribbean*. New York: Harper and Row.

Williams, Carl O. 1937. *Thraldom in Ancient Iceland*. Chicago: University of Chicago Press.

Williams, G. 1897. *History of the Liverpool Privateers and Letters of Marque with an Account of the Liverpool Slave Trade*. London: Heinemann.

Williams, Mary Wilhelmine. 1920. *Social Scandinavia in the Viking Age*. New York: Macmillan.

Williamson, James A. 1927. *Sir John Hawkins*. Oxford: Oxford University Press.

Wilson, Ellen Gibson. 1990. *Thomas Clarkson: A Biography*. New York: St. Martin's.

Wood, Michael. 1986. *Domesday: A Search for the Roots of England*. New York: BBC Books.

Latin America

Abrahams, Roger D. 1983. *The Man-of-Words in the West Indies: Performance and the Emergence of Creole Culture*. Baltimore: Johns Hopkins University Press.

Agorsah, E. Kofi, ed. 1994. *Maroon Heritage: Archaeological, Ethnographic, and Historical Perspectives*. Bridgetown, Barbados: Canoe Press.

Aguirre, Carlos. 1993. *Agentes de su propia libertad: Los esclavos de Lima y la desintegración de la esclavitud, 1821–1854*. Lima: Universidad Católica del Perú.

Aguirre Beltrán, Gonzalo. 1972. *La población negra en México: Estudio etnohistórico*. Mexico City: Fondo de Cultura Económica.

Alberro, Solange. 1988. *Inquisición y sociedad en México, 1571–1700*. Mexico City: Fondo de Cultura Económica.

Alvarez Argel, Luis Raul. 1964. *Don Diego de Almagro y el descubrimiento de Chile*. Santiago, Chile: Editorial Universitaria.

Anderson, Robert Nelson. 1996. "The Quilombo of Palmares: A New Overview of a Maroon State in Seventeenth-Century Brazil." *Journal of Latin American Studies* 28 (3): 545.

Arranz Márquez, Luis. 1991. *Repartimientos y encomiendas en la isla Española (El repartimiento de Albuquerque de 1514)*. Madrid: Fundación García-Arévalo.

Áviles Fábila, René. 1957. *Vicente Guerrero: El insurgente ciudadano*. Mexico City: Sociedad de Amigos del Libro Mexicano.

Axtell, James. 1992. *Beyond 1492*. New York: Oxford University Press.

Azevedo, Celia M. 1995. *Abolitionism in the United States and Brazil: A Comparative Perspective*. New York: Garland.

Azevedo, Fernando de. 1950. *Brazilian Culture: An Introduction to the Study of Culture in Brazil*. New York: Macmillan.

Bailey, L. R. 1966. *The Indian Slave Trade in the Southwest*. Los Angeles: Westernlore Press.

Bakewell, P. J. 1971. *Silver Mining and Society in Colonial Mexico: Zacatecas, 1546–1700*. Cambridge: Cambridge University Press.

Ballesteros Gaibrois, Manuel. 1987. *Diego de Almagro*. Madrid: Sociedad Estatal para la Ejecucion Programas del Quinto Centenario.

Bannon, John F. 1966. *Indian Labor in the Spanish Indies: Was There Another Solution?* Boston: Heath.

Barber, Ruth. 1932. *Indian Labor in the Spanish Colonies*. Albuquerque: University of New Mexico Press.

Bastide, Roger. 1978. *The African Religions of Brazil: Towards a Sociology of the Interpenetration of Civilizations*. Baltimore: Johns Hopkins University Press.

Beckles, Hilary. 1986. "'Black Men in White Skins': The Formation of a White Proletariat in West Indian Society." *Journal of Imperial and Commonwealth History* 15 (October): 5–21.

———. 1990. *A History of Barbados: From Amerindian Settlement to Nation-State*. Cambridge: Cambridge University Press.

Beckles, Hilary, and Verene Shepherd, eds. 1991. *Caribbean Slave Society and Economy*. New York: New Press.

Belaunde, Victor Andrés. 1938. *Bolívar and the Political Thought of the Spanish American Revolution*. Baltimore: John Hopkins Press.

Belgium, Erik, and Don Nardo. 1991. *Great Mysteries, Voodoo: Opposing Viewpoints*. San Diego, CA: Greenhaven Press.

Bento, Antônio, ed. 1887. *A Redempção*. São Paulo, Brazil: n.p.

Berdan, Frances. 1982. *The Aztecs of Central Mexico: An Imperial Society*. New York: Holt, Rinehart and Winston.

Bergad, Laird W.; Fe Iglesias Garcia; and Maria del Carmen Barcia. 1995. *The Cuban Slave Market, 1790–1880*. New York: Cambridge University Press.

Bethell, Leslie. 1970. *The Abolition of the Brazilian Slave Trade. Britain, Brazil, and the Slave Trade Question, 1807–1869*. Cambridge: Cambridge University Press.

Bettelheim, Judith. 1988. "Jonkonnu and Other Christmas Masquerades." In *Caribbean Festival Arts*. Edited by John W. Nunley and Judith Bettelheim. Seattle: University of Washington Press.

Bilby, Kenneth. 1995. "A Separate Identity: The Maroons of Jamaica." *Faces* 11 (8): 29.

Black, Clinton. 1958. *History of Jamaica*. London: Collins Clear-Type Press.

Blanchard, Peter. 1992. *Slavery and Abolition in Early Republican Peru*. Wilmington, DE: Scholarly Resources.

Blazquez y Delgado-Aguilera, Antonio. 1898. *El adelantado Diego de Almagro*. Ciudad Real, Spain: Establicimiento Topografico Provincial.

Bolland, O. Nigel. 1988. *Colonialism and Resistance in Belize: Essays in Historical Sociology*. Benque Viejo del Carmen, Belize: Cubola Productions.

———. 1977. *The Formation of a Colonial Society: Belize, from Conquest to Crown Colony*. Baltimore: Johns Hopkins University Press.

Bowser, Frederick. 1974. *The African Slave in Colonial Peru, 1524–1650*. Stanford, CA: Stanford University Press.

Boxer, C. R. 1962. *The Golden Age of Brazil, 1695–1750: Growing Pains of a Colonial Society*. Berkeley: University of California Press.

———. 1962. *A Great Luso-Brazilian Figure: Padre Antônio Vieira, S.J., 1608–1697*. Berkeley: University of California Press.

———. 1952. *Salvador de Sá and the Struggle for Brazil and Angola 1602–1686*. London: Athlone Press.

Brathwaite, Edward Kamau. 1974. "The African Presence in Caribbean Literature." In *Slavery, Colonialism, and Racism*. Edited by Sidney Mintz. New York: W. W. Norton.

———. 1971. *The Development of Creole Society in Jamaica*. Oxford: Oxford University Press.

Breathett, George. 1988. "Catholicism and the Code Noir in Haiti." *Journal of Negro History* 73 (1): 1–11.

Brown, Diana DeGrout. 1994. *Umbanda: Religion and Politics in Urban Brazil*. New York: Columbia University Press.

Bruce, F. F. 1936. "Latin Participles as Slave Names." *Glotta* 25: 42–50.

Buchner, John H. 1854. *The Moravians in Jamaica*. London: Longman and Brown.

Buckley, Roger N. 1979. *Slaves in Red Coats: The British West India Regiments, 1795–1815*. New Haven, CT: Yale University Press.

Burdon, John, ed. 1931–1935. *Archives of British Honduras*. 3 vols. London: Sifton Praed.

Burkholder, Mark, and Lyman L. Johnson. 1990. *Colonial Latin America*. New York: Oxford University Press.

Burns, E. Bradford. 1966. *A Documentary History of Brazil*. New York: Knopf.

Bush, Barbara. 1989. *Slave Women in Caribbean Society, 1650–1838*. Bloomington: Indiana University Press.

Bushnell, David. 1970. *The Santander Regime in Gran Colombia*. Westport, CT: Greenwood Press.

Camamis, George. 1977. *Estudios sobre el cautiverio en el Siglo de Oro*. Madrid: Gredos.

Campbell, Mavis Christine. 1988. *The Maroons of Jamaica, 1655–1796: A History of Resistance, Collaboration, and Betrayal*. South Hadley, MA: Bergin and Garvey.

Cardoso, Gerald. 1983. *Negro Slavery in the Sugar Plantations of Veracruz and Pernambuco, 1550–1680: A Comparative Study*. Washington, DC: University Press of America.

Carr, Albert Z. 1963. *The World and William Walker*. New York: Harper and Row.

Carrancá y Trujillo, Raúl. 1938. "El Estatuo Jurídico de los Esclavos en las *Postrimerías de la colonización Española*." *Revista de Historia de América* 3: 20–60.

Cassá, Roberto, and Genaro Rodríguez Morel. 1993. "Consideraciones alternativas acerca de las rebeliones de esclavos en Santo Domingo." *Anuario de la Escuela de Estudios Hispanoamericanos* 50 (1): 103–113.

Castro Pozo, Hildebrando. 1947. *El yanaconaje en las haciendas piuranas*. Lima, Peru: Cia. de Impresiones y Publicidad.

Catholic Church (Pope Alexander VI). 1927. *The Earliest Diplomatic Documents on America: The Papal Bulls of 1493 and the Treaty of Tordesillas*. Berlin: P. Gottschalk.

Caulfield, James E. 1896. *One Hundred Years' History of the Second West India Regiment*. London: Forster Groom.

Clementi, Hebe. 1974. *La abolición la esclavitud en América Latina*. Buenos Aires: Pleyade.

Cole, Hubert. 1967. *Christophe King of Haiti*. New York: Viking Press.

Columbus, Christopher. 1960. *The Journal of Christopher Columbus*. Edited by L. A. Vigneras. New York: Bramhall House.

Columbus, Ferdinand. 1959. *The Life of the Admiral Christopher Columbus*. Edited by Benjamin Keen. New Brunswick, NJ: Rutgers University Press.

Conniff, Michael L., and Thomas J. Davis. 1994. *Africans in the Americas*. New York: St. Martin's.

Conrad, Robert E. 1972. *The Destruction of Brazilian Slavery, 1850–1888*. Berkeley: University of California Press.

Cooney, Jerry W. 1974. "Abolition in the Republic of Paraguay: 1840–1870." In *Jahrbuch für Geschichte von Staat, Wirtschaft, und Gesellschaft Lateinamerika*. Edited by Richard Konetzke and Hermann Kellenbenz. Cologne and Vienna: Böhlau Verlag.

Corwin, Arthur F. 1967. *Spain and the Abolition of Slavery in Cuba, 1817–1886*. Austin: University of Texas Press.

Costa, Emilia Viotti da. 1985. *The Brazilian Empire: Myths and Histories*. Chicago: University of Chicago Press.

Courlander, Harold. *The Drum and the Hoe: Life and Lore of the Haitian People*. 1985. Berkeley, London, and Los Angeles: University of California Press.

Cox, Edward. 1982. "Fédon's Rebellion 1795–96: Causes and Consequences." *Journal of Negro History* 67: 7–20.

Craton, Michael. 1978. *Searching for the Invisible Man: Slaves and Plantation Life in Jamaica*. Cambridge, MA: Harvard University Press.

———. 1982. *Testing the Chains: Resistance to Slavery in the British West Indies*. Ithaca, NY: Cornell University Press.

Crawford, W. Rex. 1961. *A Century of Latin American Thought*. Cambridge, MA: Harvard University Press.

Crosby, Alfred W., Jr. 1972. *The Columbian Exchange: Biological and Cultural Consequences of 1492*. Westport, CT: Greenwood.

Cunha, Euclydes. 1944. *Rebellion in the Backlands*. Chicago: University of Chicago Press.

Dance, Daryl C. 1985. *Folklore from Contemporary Jamaicans*. Knoxville: University of Tennessee Press.

Davis, David Brion. 1975. "Slavery: The Continuing Contradiction." In *The African in Latin America*. Edited by Ann M. Pescatello. New York: Random House.

Davis, Wade. 1986. *The Serpent and the Rainbow*. New York: Warner Books.

Dayan, Joan. 1995. *Haiti, History, and the Gods*. Berkeley: University of California Press.

De Camp, David. 1967. "African Day-Names in Jamaica." *Language* 43: 139–147.

Dean, Warren. 1976. *Rio Claro: A Brazilian Plantation System, 1820–1920*. Palo Alto, CA: Stanford University Press.

Degler, Carl N. 1971. *Neither Black nor White: Slavery and Race Relations in Brazil and the United States*. New York: Macmillan.

Deive, Carlos Esteban. 1989. *Los guerrilleros negros: Esclavos fugitivos y cimarrones en Santo Domingo*. Santo Domingo, Dominican Republic: Fundación Cultural Dominicana.

Devas, Raymond P. 1974. *A History of the Island of Grenada, 1498–1796*. St. George's, Grenada: Carenage Press.

Dirks, Robert. 1987. *The Black Saturnalia: Conflict and Its Ritual Expression on British West Indian Slave Plantations*. Gainesville: University of Florida Press.

Donoso, Armando. 1913. *Bilbao y su tiempo*. Santiago, Chile: Zig Zag.

Drescher, Seymour. 1988. "Brazilian Abolition in Comparative Perspective." *Hispanic American Historical Review* 68 (3): 429–460.

Dunn, Richard. 1972. *Sugar and Slaves: The Rise of the Planter Class in the English West Indies, 1624–1713*. Chapel Hill: University of North Carolina Press.

"Edit du Roi, Touchant la Polices des Isles de l'Amérique Françoise: Du mois de Mars 1685." In *Le Code Noir, ou Recueil des reglemens rendus jusquà présent. Concernant le gouvernement, l'administration de la justice, la police, la discipline et le commerce des negres dans les colonies françoises*. 1980. Basse-Terre, Guadeloupe: Société d'histoire de la Guadelo University Presse.

Edwards, Bryan. 1793. *The History, Civil and Commercial, of the British Colonies in the West Indies*. London: John Stockdale.

Ellis, Alfred Burden. 1885. *The History of the First West India Regiment.* London: Chapman and Hall.

Emmanuel, Isaac S., and Suzanne A. Emmanuel. 1970. *History of the Jews of the Netherlands Antilles.* 2 vols. Cincinnati, OH: American Jewish Archives.

Fagan, Brian. 1993. "Brazil's Little Angola." *Archaeology* 46 (July): 14–19.

Falcão, Edgard Cerqueira, ed. 1963. *Obras científicas, políticas, a sociais de José Bonifácio de Andrada e Silva.* São Paulo: Grupo de Trabalho Executivo das Homenagens so Patriarca.

Fausto, Boris. 1995. *História do Brasil.* São Paulo: Editora da Universidade de São Paulo.

Fick, Carolyn. 1990. *The Making of Haiti: The Saint Domingue Revolution from Below.* Knoxville: University of Tennessee Press.

Fisher, John Robert. 1977. *Silver Mines and Silver Miners in Colonial Peru, 1776–1824.* Liverpool: Centre for Latin-American Studies, University of Liverpool.

Franco Silva, A. 1992. *Esclavitud en Andulaucia 1450–1550.* Granada, Spain: Servicio de Publicaciones de la Universidad de Granada.

Freyre, Gilberto. 1966. *The Masters and the Slaves: A Study in the Development of Brazilian Civilization.* 2d English language edition. New York: Alfred A. Knopf.

———. 1972. *A Propósito de José Bonifácio.* Recife, Brazil: Ministério de Educação e Cultura.

Fuentes Díaz, Vicente. 1989. *Revaloración del General Vicente Guerrero: Consumador de la independencia.* Chilpancingo, Mexico: Gobierno del Estado de Guerrero.

Galván, Manuel de Jesús. 1989. *Enriquillo.* Santo Domingo, Dominican Republic: Ediciones de Taller.

Garrigus, John. 1988. "A Struggle for Respect: The Free Coloreds of Pre-Revolutionary Saint-Domingue, 1760–69." Ph.D. dissertation, Department of History, Johns Hopkins University, Baltimore, Maryland.

Geggus, David P. 1989. "The Haitian Revolution." In *The Modern Caribbean.* Edited by Franklin W. Knight and Colin A. Palmer. Chapel Hill: University of North Carolina Press.

Gibson, Charles. 1964. *The Aztecs under Spanish Rule: A History of the Indians of the Valley of Mexico, 1519–1810.* Stanford, CA: Stanford University Press.

———. 1971. *The Black Legend: Anti-Spanish Attitudes in the Old World and the New.* New York: Knopf.

———. 1966. *Spain in America.* New York: Harper and Row.

Gonzalez, Nancie L. 1988. *Sojourners of the Caribbean: Ethnogenesis and Ethnohistory of the Garifuna.* Urbana: University of Illinois Press.

Goody, Jack. 1986. "Writing, Religion, and Revolt in Bahia." *Visible Language* 20: 318–343.

Goslinga, Cornelis Christiaan. 1985. *The Dutch in the Caribbean and in the Guianas 1680–1791.* Dover, NH: Van Gorcum.

———. 1979. A Short History of the Netherlands Antilles and Surinam. The Hague: Martinus Nijhoff.

Granzotto, Gianni. 1985. *Christopher Columbus, the Dream and the Obsession: A Biography.* Garden City, NY: Doubleday.

Gutierrez A. Ildefonso. 1992. "La Iglesia y los Negros." In *La Historia de la Iglesia en Hispanoamérica y las Filipinas. Siglos XV–XIX.* Edited by Pedro Borges. Madrid: Biblioteca de Autores Cristianos.

Hall, Gwendolyn Midlo. 1971. *Social Control in Slave Plantation Societies: A Comparison of St. Domingue and Cuba.* Baltimore, MD: Johns Hopkins Press.

Hall, N. A. T. 1992. *Slave Society in the Danish West Indies: St. Thomas, St. John, and St. Croix.* Johns Hopkins Studies in Atlantic History and Culture. Baltimore: Johns Hopkins University Press.

Hamilton, K. G. 1967. *A History of the Moravian Church.* Bethlehem, PA: Board of Christian Education.

Handler, Jerome S., and Frederick W. Lange. 1978. *Plantation Slavery in Barbados: An Archaeological and Historical Investigation.* Cambridge, MA: Harvard University Press.

Hanke, Lewis. 1935. *The First Social Experiments in America: A Study in the Development of Spanish Indian Policy in the Sixteenth Century.* Cambridge: Cambridge University Press.

———. 1949. *The Spanish Struggle for Justice in the Conquest of America.* Philadelphia: University of Pennsylvania Press.

Haring, C. H. 1947. *The Spanish Empire in America.* New York: Oxford University Press.

Harrell, Eugene Wilson. 1976. "Vicente Guerrero and the Birth of Modern Mexico." Unpublished thesis, Department of History, Tulane University, New Orleans, Louisiana.

Hartsinck, Jan Jacob. 1770. *Beschryving van Guiana, of de Wilde Kust, in Zuid-America.* Amsterdam: G. Tielenbur.

Hemming, John. 1984. "Indians and the Frontier in Colonial Brazil." In *The Cambridge History of Latin America.* Edited by Leslie Bethell. Cambridge: Cambridge University Press.

Henao, Jesús María, and Gerardo Arrubla. 1938. *History of Colombia.* Chapel Hill: University of North Carolina Press.

Hennessey, Alistair. 1989. "Reshaping the Brazilian Past. *Times Literary Supplement,* July 14–20, 763–764.

Higman, Barry W. 1993. "The Slave Population of the British Caribbean: Some Nineteenth-Century Variations." In *Caribbean Slave Society and Economy: A Student Reader.* Edited by Hillary Beckles and Verene Shepherd. New York: New Press.

Hoetink, H. 1972. "Surinam and Curaçao." In *Neither Slave nor Free: The Freedman of African Descent in the Slave Societies of the New World.* Edited by David W. Cohen and Jack P. Greene. Baltimore: Johns Hopkins University Press.

Holloway, Thomas H. 1989. "'A Healthy Terror': Police Repression of *Capoeiras* in Nineteenth-Century Rio de Janeiro." *Hispanic American Historical Review* 69: 637–676.

———. 1977. "Immigration and Abolition: The Transition from Slave to Free Labor in the São Paulo Coffee Zone." In *Essays Concerning the Socio-Economic History of Brazil and Portuguese India.* Edited by Dauril Alden and Warren Dean. Gainesville: University Press of Florida.

Holm, John. 1988–1989. *Pidgins and Creoles*. 2 vols. Cambridge: Cambridge University Press.

Hoog, Levina de. 1983. *Van rebellie tot revolutie: Oorzaken en achtergronden van de Curaçaose slavenopstanden in 1750 en 1795*. Leiden: Universiteit van de Nederlandse Antillen.

Hoogbergen, Wim. 1990. "The History of the Suriname Maroons." In *Resistance and Rebellion in Suriname: Old and New*. Edited by Gary Brana-Shute. Williamsburg, VA: Department of Anthropology, College of William and Mary.

Hopkins, Keith. 1978. *Conquerors and Slaves: Sociological Studies in Roman History, Volume I*. Cambridge: Cambridge University Press.

Hünefeldt, Christine. 1994. *Paying the Price of Freedom: Family and Labor among Lima's Slaves*. Berkeley: University of California Press.

IBGE (Instituto Brasileiro de Geografia e Estatística), ed. 1990. *Estatísticas históricas do Brasil*. Rio de Janeiro: Fundação Instituto Brasileiro de Geografia e Estatística.

James, C. L. R. 1968. *The Black Jacobins: Toussaint L'Ouverture and the San Domingo Revolution*. New York: Random House.

Johnson, Howard. 1995. "Slave Life and Leisure in Nassau, Bahamas, 1783–1838." *Slavery and Abolition* 16 (1): 45–64.

Kapsoli, Wilfredo. 1975. *Sublevaciones de esclavos en el Perú, s. XVIII*. Lima, Peru: Universidad Ricardo Palma.

Karasch, Mary. 1986. *Slave Life in Rio de Janeiro 1808–1850*. Princeton, NJ: Princeton University Press.

Keegan, William F. 1992. *The People Who Discovered Columbus: The Prehistory of the Bahamas*. Gainesville: University of Florida Press.

Keen, Benjamin. 1966. *A History of Latin America*. Boston: Houghton Mifflin.

Kent, Raymond K. 1970. "African Revolt in Bahia." *Journal of Social History* 3 (Summer): 334–356.

———. 1965. "Palmares: An African State in Brazil." *Journal of African History* 6: 161–175.

Kerns, Virginia. 1983. *Women and the Ancestors: Black Carib Kinship and Ritual*. Urbana: University of Illinois Press.

Kiemen, Mathias C. 1954. *The Indian Policy of Portugal in the Amazon Region, 1614–1693*. Washington, DC: Catholic University of America Press.

Kiple, Kenneth F. 1984. *The Caribbean Slave: A Biological History*. Cambridge: Cambridge University Press.

Klein, Herbert S. 1986. *African Slavery in Latin America and the Caribbean*. New York: Oxford University Press.

———. 1967. *Slavery in the Americas: A Comparative Study of Virginia and Cuba*. Chicago: University of Chicago Press.

Knight, Franklin W. 1970. *Slave Society in Cuba during the Nineteenth Century*. Madison: University of Wisconsin Press.

Landers, Sharon Bamberry. 1995. "An Exploration of the Theory and Practice of Slavery in Seventeenth-Century Brazil in the Writings of Padre Antônio Vieira." Ph.D. dissertation, Department of History, Texas Christian University, Forth Worth, Texas.

Las Casas, Bartolomé de. 1988. *Historia de las Indias*. Madrid: Alianza.

Laurencio, Juan B. 1974. *Campana contra Yanga en 1608*. Mexico City: Citlaltepetl.

Laviña, Javier. "Iglesia y esclavitud en Cuba." *América Negra* 1 (June): 11–29.

Lecuna, Vicente, comp. 1951. *Selected Writings of Bolívar*. Edited by Harold A. Bierck, Jr. New York: Colonial Press.

Levine, Robert M. 1992. *Vale of Tears: Revisiting the Canudos Massacre in Northeastern Brazil, 1895–1897*. Berkeley: University of California Press.

Lewis, J. Lowell. 1992. *Ring of Liberation: Deception Discourse in Brazilian Capoeira*. Chicago: University of Chicago Press.

Lewis, Laura A. 1995. "Spanish Ideology and the Practice of Inequality in the New World." In *Racism and Anti-Racism in World Perspective*. Edited by Benjamin B. Bowser. Thousand Oaks, CA.: Sage Publications.

Lindo-Fuentes, Héctor. 1995. "The Economy of Central America: From Bourbon Reforms to Liberal Reforms." In *Central America, 1821–1871: Liberalism before Liberal Reform*. Edited by Lowell Gudmundson and Héctor Lindo-Fuentes. Tuscaloosa: University of Alabama Press.

Lipp, Solomon. 1975. *Three Chilean Thinkers*. Waterloo, Canada: Wilfred Laurier University Press.

Lockhart, James, and Stuart B. Schwartz. 1983. *Early Latin America: A History of Colonial Spanish America and Brazil*. Cambridge: Cambridge University Press.

Lombardi, John V. 1971. *The Decline and Abolition of Negro Slavery in Venezuela; 1820–1854*. Westport, CT: Greenwood Press.

Long, Edward. 1972. *The History of Jamaica*. New York: Arno Press.

Lynch, John. 1986. *The Spanish American Revolutions, 1808–1826*. New York: W. W. Norton.

McAlister, Lyle. 1984. *Spain and Portugal in the New World 1492–1700*. Minneapolis: University of Minnesota Press.

McClendon, R. Earl. 1933. "The *Amistad* Claims: Inconsistencies of Policy." *Political Science Quarterly* 48: 386–412.

McFarlane, Milton C. 1977. *Cudjoe of Jamaica: Pioneer for Black Freedom in the New World*. Short Hills, NJ: Ridley Enslow.

McKinley, P. Michael. 1985. *Pre-Revolutionary Caracas: Politics, Economy, and Society, 1777–1811*. Cambridge: Cambridge University Press.

MacLachlan, Colin, and Jaime E. Rodriguez. 1980. *The Forging of the Cosmic Race: A Reinterpretation of Colonial Mexico*. Berkeley: University of California Press.

MacLeod, Murdo J. 1973. *Spanish Central America: A Socioeconomic History, 1520–1720*. Berkeley: University of California Press.

McNitt, Frank. 1972. *Navajo Wars: Military Campaigns, Slave Raids, and Reprisals*. Albuquerque: University of New Mexico Press.

Madariaga, Salvador de. 1952. *Bolívar*. Coral Gables, FL: University of Miami Press.

Mair, Lucille Mathurin. 1986. *Women Field Workers in Jamaica during Slavery*. Mona, Jamaica: University of the West Indies.

Manchester, Alan K. 1933. *British Preeminence in Brazil, Its Rise and Decline: A Study in European Expansion*. Chapel Hill: University of North Carolina Press.

Mariz, Cecilia Loreto. 1994. *Coping with Poverty: Pentecostals and Christian Base Communities in Brazil*. Philadelphia: Temple University Press.

Maso Vazquez, Calixto. 1973. *Juan Latino: Gloria de Espana y su raza*. Chicago: Northeastern Illinois University.

Masur, Gerhard. 1948. *Simon Bolívar*. Albuquerque: University of New Mexico Press.

Matos Mar, Jose. 1976. *Yanaconaje y reforma agraria en el Peru*. Lima, Peru: Instituto de Estudios Peruanos.

Mattos, Ilmar Rohloff de. 1987. *O tempo saquarema*. São Paulo: Editora Hucitec.

Mattoso, Katia de Queiros. 1986. *To Be a Slave in Brazil 1550–1888*. New Brunswick, NJ: Rutgers University Press.

Mavis, Campbell. 1990. *The Maroons of Jamaica*. Trenton, NJ: Africa World Press.

Mencke, John G. 1979. *Mulattoes and Race Mixture: American Attitudes and Images, 1865–1918*. Ann Arbor, MI: UMI Research Press.

Mezière, Henri. 1990. *Le General Leclerc, 1772–1802 et l'expédition de St. Domingue*. Paris: Tallandier.

Miitraux, Alfred. 1959. *Voodoo in Haiti*. New York: Schocken Books.

Mintz, Sidney W. 1974. *Caribbean Transformations*. Chicago: Aldine.

Moore, David M. 1989. "Anatomy of a 17th-Century Slave Ship: Historical and Archaeological Investigations of the *Henrietta Marie* 1699." M.A. thesis, Department of History, Eastern Carolina University, Greenville, North Carolina.

Moreau de St. Mery, Louis Médéric. 1793. *Description topographique et politique de la partie Espagnol de l'ile de Saint Domingue*. Philadelphia: Privately printed.

———. 1797. *Description topographique, physique, civile, politique, et historique de la partie Française de l'ile St. Domingue*. Philadelphia: Privately printed.

Mörner, Magnus. 1967. *Race Mixture in the History of Latin America*. Boston: Little, Brown.

Mörner, Magnus, ed. 1970. *Race and Class in Latin America*. New York: Columbia University Press.

Morrissey, Marrietta. 1989. *Slave Women in the New World: Gender Stratification in the Caribbean*. Lawrence: University Press of Kansas.

Mullin, Michael. 1992. *Africa in America: Slave Acculturation and Resistance in the American South and the British Caribbean, 1736–1831*. Urbana: University of Illinois Press.

Nabuco, Carolina. 1950. *The Life of Joaquim Nabuco*. Stanford, CA: Stanford University Press.

Nabuco, Joaquim de Araújo. 1977. *Abolitionism: The Brazilian Anti-Slavery Struggle*. Chicago: University of Illinois Press.

———. 1883. *O abolicionismo*. London: Kingdom.

———. 1880–1881. *0 Abolicionista: Orgão da Sociedade Brazileira Contra a Escravidão*. Rio de Janeiro: Brazilian Anti-Slavery Society.

———. 1975. *Um estadista do império*. Rio de Janeiro: Editora Nova Aguilar.

Navarro Azcue, Concepcion. 1986. "La esclavitud en Cuba, antes y después de las leyes abolicionistas." In *Estudios sobre la abolición de la esclavitud*. Edited by Francisco de Solano. Madrid: Consejo Superior de Investigaciones Científicas.

Needell, Jeffrey D. 1995. "Identity, Race, Gender, and Modernity in the Origin of Gilberto Freyre's *Oeuvre*." *American Historical Review* 100 (1) (February): 51–77.

Nicholls, David. 1988. *From Dessalines to Duvalier*. New York: Macmillan.

Novak, Maximillian E., and David Stuart Rodes. 1976. "Introduction." In *Oroonoko*, by Thomas Southerne. Lincoln: University of Nebraska Press.

Oldendorp, C. G. A. 1987. *A Caribbean Mission*. Edited and translated by Arnold R. Highfield and Vladimir Barac. Ann Arbor, MI: Karoma Publishers.

Olwig, Karen Fog. 1985. *Cultural Adaptation and Resistance on St. John: Three Centuries of Afro-Caribbean Life*. Gainesville: University of Florida Press.

Ott, Thomas. 1973. *The Haitian Revolution*. Knoxville: University of Tennessee Press.

Oviedo y Valdés, Gonzálo Fernández de. 1959. *Historia general de las Indias*. Madrid: Ediciones Atlas.

Palacios Preciado, Jorge. 1973. *La trata de negros por Cartagena de Indias*. Tunja: Universidad Pedagogica y Tecnologica de Colombia.

Palmer, Colin A. 1986. "The Company Trade and the Numerical Distribution of Slaves to Spanish America, 1703–1739." In *Africans in Bondage: Studies in Slavery and the Slave Trade*. Edited by Paul E. Lovejoy. Madison: African Studies Program, University of Wisconsin-Madison.

———. 1981. *Human Cargoes: The British Slave Trade to Spanish America, 1700–1739*. Urbana: University of Illinois Press.

———. 1976. *Slaves of the White God: Blacks in Mexico 1570–1650*. Cambridge, MA: Harvard University Press.

Paquet, Sandra Pouchet. 1992. "The Heartbeat of a West Indian Slave: The History of Mary Prince." *African American Review* 26: 131–146.

Parra-Pérez, Caracciolo. 1992. *Historia de la primera república de Venezuela*. Caracas: Biblioteca Ayacucho.

Parry, John H., and Robert G. Keith, eds. 1984. *New Iberian Worlds: A Documentary History of the Discovery and Settlement of Latin America to the Early Seventeenth Century*. New York: Times Books.

Patrocínio, José do, ed. 1880–1888. *Gazeta da Tarde*. Rio de Janeiro.

Paula, Alejandro F., ed. 1974. *1795. De slavenopstand op Curaçao: Een bronnenuitgave van de originele overheidsdocumenten*. Curaçao: Centraal-Historisch Archief.

Peña Batlle, Manuel Arturo. 1948. *La rebelión de Bahoruco*. Ciudad Trujillo: Impresora Dominicana.

Pla, Josefina. 1972. *Hermano negro: La esclavitud en el Paraguay*. Madrid: Paraninfo.

Pluchon, Pierre. 1989. *Toussaint Louverture: Un révolutionnaire noir d'Ancien Régime*. Paris: Fayard.

Poppino, Rollie E. 1968. *Brazil: The Land and the People*. New York: Oxford University Press.

Porter, Arthur T. 1963. *Creoledom*. London: Oxford University Press.

Prandi, R. 1991. *Os Candombles de Sao Paulo: Velha Magia na Metropole Nova*. São Paulo: HUCITEC and Editora da Universidada de São Paulo.

Price, Richard, ed. 1979. *Maroon Societies: Rebel Slave Communities in the Americas*. Baltimore: Johns Hopkins University Press.

Prince, Mary. 1987. *The History of Mary Prince, a West Indian Slave (Related by Herself)*. In *Classic Slave Narratives*. Edited by Henry Louis Gates, Jr. New York: Penguin Books.

Pulis, John W. 1997. "Bridging Troubled Waters: Moses Baker, George Liele, and the African-American Diaspora to Jamaica." In *Moving On: Black Loyalists in the Afro-Atlantic World*. New York: Garland.

———. 1998. *In the Holy Mountains: Missions, Moravians, and the Making of Afro-Christianity in Jamaica*. New York: Gordon and Breach.

Pulsipher, Lydia Mihelic. 1994. "Landscapes and Ideational Roles of Caribbean Slave Gardens." In *The Archaeology of Garden and Field*. Edited by Naomi Miller. Philadelphia: University of Pennsylvania Press.

Ragatz, Joseph Lowell. 1963. *The Fall of the Planter Class in the British Caribbean, 1763–1833*. New York: Octagon.

Ramos, Donald. 1986. "Community, Control, and Acculturation: A Case Study of Slavery in Eighteenth-Century Brazil." *Americas* (4): 419–451.

Rego, Waldeloir. 1968. *Capoeira Angola, ensaio sócio-etnográfico*. Rio de Janeiro: Graf. Lux.

Reis, Joao Jose. 1993. *Slave Rebellion in Brazil: The Muslim Uprising of 1835 in Bahia*. Baltimore: Johns Hopkins University Press.

Roberts, Peter A. 1988. *West Indians and Their Language*. Cambridge: Cambridge University Press.

Rodriguez, Frederick M. 1972. "Negro Slavery in New Spain and the Yanga Revolt." M.A. thesis, Department of History, DePaul University, Chicago, Illinois.

Ros, Martin. 1994. *Night of Fire*. New York: Sarpedon.

Rouse, Irving. 1992. *The Taínos: The People Who Discovered Columbus*. New Haven, CT: Yale University Press.

Rout, Leslie B., Jr. 1976. *The African Experience in Spanish America: 1502 to the Present Day*. Cambridge: Cambridge University Press.

Saez, J. Luis. 1994. *La Iglesia y el negro esclavo en Santo Domingo: Una historia de tres siglos*. Santo Domingo, Dominican Republic: Patronato de la Ciudad Colonial.

Sánchez, Joseph P. 1990. *The Spanish Black Legend: Origins of Anti-Hispanic Stereotypes*. Albuquerque, NM: Spanish Colonial Research Center.

Schuler, Monica. 1970. "Ethnic Slave Rebellions in the Caribbean and the Guianas." *Journal of Social History* 3 (4): 374–385.

Schwartz, Stuart B. 1978. "Indian Labor and New World Plantations: European Demands and Indian Responses in Northeastern Brazil." *American Historical Review* 83 (1): 43–79.

———. 1992. *Slaves, Peasants, Rebels: Reconsidering Brazilian Slavery*. Urbana: University of Illinois Press.

———. 1985. *Sugar Plantations in the Formation of Brazilian Society: Bahia, 1550–1835*. Cambridge: Cambridge University Press.

Scott, Rebecca J. 1993. "Explaining Abolition: Contradiction, Adaptation, and Challenge in Cuban Slave Society 1860–1886." In *Caribbean Slave Society and Economy: A Student Reader*. Edited by Hillary Beckles and Verene Shepherd. New York: New Press.

———. 1985. *Slave Emancipation in Cuba: The Transition to Free Labor, 1860–1899*. Princeton, NJ: Princeton University Press.

Sepulveda, Juan G. 1941. *Tratado sobre las justas causas de la guerra contra los Indios*. Mexico City: Fondo de Cultura Economica.

Shafer, Robert Jones. 1978. *A History of Latin America*. New York: Heath.

Sharer, Robert J. 1994. *The Ancient Maya*. Stanford, CA: Stanford University Press.

Shearer, Donald C. 1933. *Pontificia Americana*. New York: J. F. Wagner.

Sheppard, Jill. 1977. *The "Redlegs" of Barbados: Their Origins and History*. Millwood, NY: KTO Press.

Sheridan, Richard B. 1985. *Doctors and Slaves: A Medical and Demographic History of Slavery in the British West Indies, 1680–1834*. Cambridge. Cambridge University Press.

Sherlock, Phillip Manderson. 1954. *Anansi the Spider Man*. Binghamton, NY: Vail-Ballou Press.

Sherman, William. 1979. *Forced Native Labor in Sixteenth-Century Central America*. Lincoln: University of Nebraska Press.

Simpson, Lesley B. 1966. *The Encomienda in New Spain: The Beginning of Spanish Mexico*. Berkeley: University of California Press.

———. 1934–1940. *Studies in the Administration of the Indians in New Spain*. 3 vols. Berkeley: University of California Press.

Skidmore, Thomas E. 1990. "Racial Ideas and Social Policy in Brazil, 1870–1940." In *The Idea of Race in Latin America*. Edited by Richard Graham. Austin: University of Texas Press.

Smith, Theophus. 1994. *Conjuring Culture*. New York: Oxford University Press.

Spalding, Karen. 1984. *Huarochiri, an Andean Society under Inca and Spanish Rule*. Stanford, CA: Stanford University Press.

Sprague, William. 1939. *Vicente Guerrero, Mexican Liberator*. Chicago: R. R. Donnelley.

Spratlin, Valaurez. 1938. *Juan Latino: Slave and Humanist*. New York: Spinner Press.

Stein, Stanley J. 1985. *Vassouras: A Brazilian Coffee County, 1850–1900*. Princeton, NJ: Princeton University Press.

Stern, Steve J. 1993. *Peru's Indian People and the Challenge of Spanish Conquest: Huamanga to 1640*. Madison: University of Wisconsin Press.

Stevens, Henry, ed. 1893. *The New Laws of the Indies*. London: Chiswick Press.

Stevens-Arroyo, Antonio M. 1988. *Cave of the Jagua: The Mythological World of the Taínos*. Albuquerque: University of New Mexico Press.

Stinchcombe, Arthur L. 1995. *Sugar Island Slavery in the Age of Enlightenment: The Political Economy of the Caribbean World*. Princeton, NJ: Princeton University Press.

Stipriaan, Alex van. 1993. *Surinaams contrast: Roofbouw en overleven in een Caraïbische plantagekolonie, 1750–1863*. Leiden: KITLV Uitgeverij.

Stone, Michael C. 1994. "Caribbean Nation, Central American State: Ethnicity, Race, and National Formation in Belize, 1798–1990." Ph.D. dissertation, Department of Anthropology, University of Texas at Austin.

Swahn, Jan-Öjvind, and Ola Jennersten. 1984. *Saint Barthélemy: Sveriges sista koloni*. Hoganas, Sweden: Wiken.

Tannenbaum, Frank. 1946. *Slave and Citizen: The Negro in the Americas*. New York: Vintage Books. Reprinted. 1963. New York: Random House.

———. 1975. "Slave or Citizen: A Problem of Semantics?" In *The African in Latin America*. Edited by Ann M. Pescatello. New York: Random House.

Taunay, Alfredo d'Escragnolle. 1930. *O visconde do Rio Branco, gloria do Brasil da humandade*. Second edition. São Paulo: Weiszflog Irmãos.

Thomas, Hugh. 1971. *Cuba: The Pursuit of Freedom*. New York: Harper and Row.

Thompson, Vincent B. 1987. *The Making of the African Diaspora in the Americas 1441–1900*. New York: Longman.

Todd, Janet, ed. 1992. "Introduction." In *Oroonoko, The Rover, and Other Works by Aphra Behn*. London: Penguin.

Toplin, Robert Brent. 1992. *The Abolition of Slavery in Brazil*. New York: Atheneum.

Trouillot, Henock. 1966. *Dessalines, ou, La tragédie post-coloniale*. Port-au-Prince, Haiti: Editions Panorama.

Turner, Mary. 1982. *The Disintegration of Jamaican Slave Society, 1787–1834*. Urbana: University of Illinois Press.

Valtierra, Ángel, SJ. 1980. *Pedro Claver: El santo redentor de los negros. Cuarto centenario de su nacimiento 1580–24 de junio–1980*. Bogotá: Banco de la República.

Van Lier, Rudolf A. J. 1971. *Frontier Society*. The Hague: Martinus Nijhoff.

Vandercook, John W. 1928. *Black Majesty: The Life of Christophe, King of Haiti*. London: Harper.

Varona, Alberto J. 1973. *Francisco Bilbao: Revolucionario de América*. Panama City: Ediciones Excelsior.

Vianna, Hélio. 1970. *História do Brasil*. São Paulo: Edições Melhoramentos.

Vila Vilar, Enriqueta. 1977. *Hispanoamérica y el comercio de esclavos*. Seville: Escuela de Estudios Hispano-Americanos.

Villar Cordova, Socrates. 1966. *La institucion del yanacona en el incanato*. Lima, Peru: Universidad Nacional Mayor de San Marcos.

Viotti da Costa, Emilia. 1985. *The Brazilian Empire: Myths and Histories*. Chicago: University of Chicago Press.

Voelz, Peter M. 1993. *Slave and Soldier: The Military Impact of Blacks in the Colonial Americas*. New York: Garland.

Westergaard, Waldemar. 1917. *The Danish West Indies: Under Company Rule*. New York: Macmillan.

White, Jon Manship. 1971. *Cortes and the Downfall of the Aztec Empire*. New York: St. Martin's.

Whitehead, Neil Lancelot. 1990. "Carib Ethnic Soldiering in Venezuela, the Guianas, and the Antilles, 1492–1820." *Ethnohistory* 37 (4): 357–385.

Wilson, Samuel M. 1990. *Hispaniola: Caribbean Chiefdoms in the Age of Columbus*. Tuscaloosa: University of Alabama Press.

Wood, Russell A. 1984. "Colonial Brazil: The Gold Cycle c. 1690–1750." In *The Cambridge History of Latin America*. Edited by Leslie Bethell. Cambridge: Cambridge University Press.

Zavala, Silvio Arturo. 1973. *La encomienda indiana*. Mexico City: Editorial Porrua.

Zorita, Alonso de. 1963. *Life and Labor in Ancient Mexico: The Brief and Summary Relation of the Lords of New Spain*. New Brunswick, NJ: Rutgers University Press.

Zulawski, Ann. 1995. *They Eat from Their Labor: Work and Social Change in Colonial Bolivia*. Pittsburgh: University of Pittsburgh Press.

Middle East

Abd al-Rahim, A. A. 1974. *Al-rif al-misri fi al-garn al-thamin ashar*. Cairo: Matbaat Jamiat Ayn al-Shams.

Ali, A. Yusuf, ed. 1946. *The Holy Qur'an: Text, Translation, and Commentary*. Washington, DC: American National Printing.

Austin, Allen D., ed. 1996. *African Muslims in Antebellum America: Proud Exiles*. New York: Routledge.

Ayalon, David. 1977. "Eunuchs in the Mamluk Sultanate." In Myriam Rosen-Ayalon, ed., *Studies in Memory of Gaston Wiet*. Jerusalem: Institute of Asian and African Studies, Hebrew University of Jerusalem.

———. 1994. *Islam and the Abode of War: Military Slaves and Islamic Adversaries*. Aldershot, Eng.: Variorum.

———. 1979. *The Mamluk Military Society*. London: Variorum.

———. 1977. "The Muslim City and the *Mamluk* Military Aristocracy." In *Studies on the Mamluks of Egypt*. Edited by David Ayalon. London: Variorum Reprints.

Bates, Ülkü. 1978. "Women as Patrons of Architecture in Turkey." In *Women in the Muslim World*. Edited by Lois Beck and Nikki R. Keddie. Cambridge, MA: Harvard University Press.

Bon, Ottaviano. 1996. *The Sultan's Seraglio*. London: Saqi Books.

Burns, Robert. 1973. *Islam under the Crusaders*. Princeton, NJ: Princeton University Press.

Cahen, Claude. 1968. *Pre-Ottoman Turkey: A General Survey of the Material and Spiritual Culture and History, c. 1071–1330*. Translated by J. Jones-Williams. New York: Taplinger.

Clarke, Peter B. 1982. *West Africa and Islam: A Study of Religious Development from the 8th to the 20th Century*. London: Edward Arnold.

Clissold, S. 1977. *The Barbary Slaves*. Totowa, NJ: Rowman and Littlefield.

Davison, Roderic. 1963. *Reform in the Ottoman Empire 1856–76*. Princeton, NJ: Princeton University Press.

De Jong, Garrett E. 1934. "Slavery in Arabia." *Moslem World* 4 (4): 126–144.

Fisher, Alan W. 1978. "The Sale of Slaves in the Ottoman Empire." *Bogaziçi Universitesi Dergisi* 4: 149–171.

Frances, E. 1969. "Constantinople Byzantine aux XIVe et Xve siècles. Population-Commerce-Métiers." *Revue des Etudes Sud-Est Européennes* 7: 405–412.

Frend, W. H. C. 1969. "Circumcellions and Monks." *Journal of Theological Studies*, n.s., 20: 542–549.

Gibb, H. A. R., and Harold Bowen. 1950–1957. *Islamic Society and the West*. 1 vol. in 2 parts. London: Oxford University Press.

Glasse, Cyril. 1989. *The Concise Encyclopedia of Islam*. San Francisco: Harper and Row.

Hathaway, Jane. 1996. *The Politics of Households in Ottoman Egypt: The Rise of the Qazdaglis*. Cambridge: Cambridge University Press.

———. 1992. "The Role of the Kizlar Agasi in Seventeenth and Eighteenth Century Ottoman Egypt." *Studia Islamica* 75: 141–158.

———. 1994. "The Wealth and Influence of an Exiled Ottoman Eunuch in Egypt: The Waqf Inventory of Abbas Agha." *Journal of the Economic and Social History of the Orient* 37: 293–317.

Hourani, Albert. 1970. *Arabic Thought in the Liberal Age, 1798–1939*. Oxford: Oxford University Press.

Irwin, Robert. 1968. *The Middle East in the Middle Ages: The Early Mamluk Sultanate, 1250–1382*. Carbondale: Southern Illinois University Press.

Kati, Mahmoud. 1913. *Ta'rikh el-Fettach*. Translated by Octave Houdas and M. Delafosse. Paris: n.p.

Lapidus, Ira M. 1988. A *History of Islamic Societies*. Cambridge: Cambridge University Press.

Lewis, Bernard. 1990. *Race and Slavery in the Middle East*. Oxford: Oxford University Press.

Little, Donald. 1986. *History and Historiography of the Mamluks*. London: Variorum.

Mansel, Philip. 1995. *Constantinople: City of the World's Desire, 1453–1924*. London: John Murray.

Marmon, Shaun E. 1995. *Eunuchs and Sacred Boundaries in Islamic Society*. Oxford: Oxford University Press.

Meyerson, Mark. 1991. *The Muslims of Valencia*. Berkeley: University of California Press.

Murray, Gordon. 1989. *Slavery in the Arab World*. New York: New Amsterdam.

A *Narrative of the Adventures of Lewis Marott, Pilot-Royal of the Galleys of France: Giving an Account of His Slavery under the Turks; His Escapes out of It, and Other Strange Occurrences that Ensued Thereafter*. 1677. London: Edward Brewster.

Ochsenwald, William. 1980. "Muslim European Conflict in the Hijaz: The Slave Trade Controversy, 1840–1859." *Middle Eastern Studies* 16 (1): 115–126.

Palmer, J. A. B. 1953. "The Origin of the Janissaries." *Bulletin of the John Rylands Library*. 35: 448–481.

Patterson, Orlando. 1982. *Slavery and Social Death: A Comparative Study*. Cambridge, MA: Harvard University Press.

Peirce, Leslie P. 1993. *The Imperial Harem: Women and Sovereignty in the Ottoman Empire*. Oxford: Oxford University Press.

Penzer, Norman. 1936. *The Harem*. London: George G. Harrap.

Petit, Paul. 1955. *Libanius et la vie municipale a Antioche au IVe siècle après J. C.* Paris: Paul Geuthner.

Pipes, Daniel. 1981. *Slave Soldiers and Islam*. New Haven, CT: Yale University Press.

Popovic, A. 1976. *La revolte des esclaves en Iraq au IIIe/IXe siecle*. Paris: Geuthner.

Rahman, Fazlur. 1979. *Islam*. Second edition. Chicago: University of Chicago Press.

Raymond, Andre. 1973–1974. *Artisans et commercants au Caire au XVIIIe siecle*. 2 vols. Damascus: Institut Francais de Damas.

———. 1991. "Soldiers in Trade: The Case of Ottoman Cairo." *British Society for Middle Eastern Studies Bulletin*. 18: 16–37.

Risso, Patricia. 1986. *Oman and Muscat and Early Modern History*. New York: St. Martin's.

Rosenthal, Franz. 1952. A *History of Muslim Historiography*. Leiden: Brill.

Rutter, Eldon. 1993. "Slavery in Arabia." *Journal of the Royal Central Asian Society* 20: 315–332.

Shaw, Stanford J. 1971. *Between Old and New: The Ottoman Empire under Sultan Selim III, 1789–1807*. Cambridge, MA: Harvard University Press.

———. 1976. *History of the Ottoman Empire and Modern Turkey*. Cambridge: Cambridge University Press.

Soden, W. von. 1964. "Muškēnum und de Mawali des frühen Islam." *Zeitschrift für Assyriologie* 56: 133–141.

Spaulding, Jay. 1982. "Slavery, Land Tenure, and Social Class in the Northern Turkish Sudan." *International Journal of African Historical Studies* 15 (1): 1–20.

Speiser, E. A. 1958. "The Muškēnum." *Orientalia*, n.s., 27: 19–28.

Toledano, Ehud R. 1982. *The Ottoman Slave Trade and Its Suppression, 1840–1890*. Princeton, NJ: Princeton University Press.

Uzuncarsili, I. H. 1943. *Osmanli Devleti Teskilatindan Kapukulu Ocaklari*. 2 vols. Ankara: Turk Tarih Kurumu.

Vryonis, Speros, Jr. 1971. *The Decline of Medieval Hellenism in Asia Minor and the Process of Islamization from the Eleventh through the Fifteenth Centuries*. Berkeley: University of California Press.

———. 1971. "Isadore Glabas and the Turkish Devshirme." Reprinted in Vryonis, *Byzantium: Its Internal History and Relations with the Muslim World—Collected Studies*. London: Variorum Reprints.

———. 1971. "Seljuk Gulams and Ottoman Devshirmes." Reprinted in Vryonis, *Byzantium* London: Variorum Reprints.

Wittek, Paul. 1958. "*Devshirme* and *Shari'a*." *Bulletin of the School of Oriental and African Studies*. 17: 271–278.

Zygulski, Zdzislaw, Jr. 1992. *Ottoman Art in the Service of the Empire*. New York: New York University Press.

Modern

Ben, Yosef. 1985. *Greek Jewry in the Holocaust and Resistance 1941–1944*. Tel Aviv: Saloniki Jewry Research Center.

Boltz, Jennifer. 1995. "Chinese Organized Crime and Illegal Alien Trafficking: Humans as a Commodity." *Asian Affairs* 22 (3): 147–158.

Chepesiuk, Ron. 1992. "Peonage for Peach Pickers." *Progressive* 56 (12): 22–24.

Crosette, Barbara. 1997. "What Modern Slavery Is, and Isn't." *New York Times*, July 27.

Daniel, Pete. 1990. *The Shadow of Slavery: Peonage in the South, 1901–1969*. Urbana: University of Illinois Press.

Ferencz, Benjamin B. 1979. *Less than Slaves: Jewish Forced Labor and the Quest for Compensation*. Cambridge, MA: Harvard University Press.

Friedrich, Otto. 1994. *The Kingdom of Auschwitz*. New York: Harper-Perennial.

Herbert, Ulrich. 1990. A *History of Foreign Labor in Germany, 1880–1980*. Ann Arbor: University of Michigan Press.

Hilberg, Raul. 1967. *The Destruction of the European Jews*. Chicago: Quadrangle Books.

Homze, Edward L. 1967. *Foreign Labor in Nazi Germany*. Princeton, NJ: Princeton University Press.

Karim, Farhad. *Contemporary Forms of Slavery in Pakistan*. 1995. New York: Human Rights Watch.

Kerem, Yitzchak. 1986. "Rescue Attempts of Jews in Greece in the Second World War." *Pe'amim* 27: 77–109.

Krausnick, Helmut, et al. 1968. *Anatomy of the SS State*. London: Collins.

Luczak, Czeslaw. 1990. "Forced Labor." In *Encyclopedia of the Holocaust*. Edited by Israel Gutman. New York: Macmillan Publishing.

Malcolm X. 1965. *Malcolm X Speaks: Selected Speeches and Statements*. Edited, with prefatory notes, by George Breitman. New York: Merit Publishers.

Miers, Suzanne. 1996. "Contemporary Forms of Slavery." *Slavery and Abolition* 17: 238–246.

Milward, Alan S. 1977. *War, Economy, and Society 1939–1945*. Berkeley: University of California Press.

Piszkiewicz, Dennis. 1995. *The Nazi Rocketeers: Dreams of Space and Crimes of War*. Westport, CT: Praeger.

Potts, Lydia. 1990. *The World Labour Market: A History of Migration*. New York: Zed Books.

Rone, Jemera. 1995. *Children in Sudan: Slaves, Street Children, and Child Soldiers*. New York: Human Rights Watch.

Silvers, Jonathan. 1996. "Child Labor in Pakistan." *Atlantic Monthly* (February): 79–92.

U.S. Congress. 1994. *By the Sweat and Toil of Children: The Use of Child Labor in American Imports*. July 15. Report to the Committees on Appropriations. Washington, D.C.: Government Printing Office.

U.S. Congress House of Representatives. Committee on International Relations. 1996. *Slavery in Mauritania and Sudan*. Joint Hearings. March 13, 1996. Washington, DC: Government Printing Office.

Udesky, Laurie. 1994. "Sweatshops behind the Labels." *Nation* 258 (19): 665–668.

United Nations. 1953. General Assembly Official Records, Eighth Session, Third Committee, 529th meeting (November 20).

———. 1951. *The Suppression of Slavery,* Memorandum Submitted by the Secretary-General. New York: United Nations.

———. 1953. United Nations Document A/2438 (August 17).

———. 1953. United Nations Document E/2431/ Addendum 2 (August 24).

United Nations General Assembly. 1990. *"International Convention on Protection of the Rights of All Migrant Workers and Members of Their Families."* Report A/45/838. New York: United Nations.

Vigil, James Diego. 1997. *From Indians to Chicanos: The Dynamics of Mexican American Culture*. Prospect Heights, IL: Waveland Press.

Wiesel, Elie. 1990. *From the Kingdom of Memory: Reminiscences*. New York : Summit Books.

North America

Abel, Annie Heloise. 1992. *The American Indian as Slaveholder and Secessionist*. Lincoln: University of Nebraska Press.

Abrahams, Roger D. 1966. "Some Varieties of Heroes in America." *Journal of the Folklore Institute* 3 (3): 341–362.

Abzug, Robert H. 1994. *Cosmos Crumbling: American Reform and the Religious Imagination*. New York: Oxford University Press.

Acuna, Rodolfo. 1981. *Occupied America: A History of Chicanos*. New York: Harper and Row.

Adams, Alice. 1908. *The Neglected Period of Anti-Slavery in America*. Gloucester, MA: Peter Smith.

Adams, Charles Francis. 1874. *Memoirs of John Quincy Adams Comprising Portions of His Diary from 1795 to 1848*. Philadelphia: Lippincott.

Adams, John R. 1977. *Edward Everett Hale*. Boston: Twayne.

———. 1989. *Harriet Beecher Stowe*. Updated edition. Boston: Twayne.

Allen, Richard. 1983. *The Life Experience and Gospel Labors of the Right Reverend Richard Allen Written by Himself*. Edited by George A. Singleton. Nashville, TN: Abingdon.

Allen, Will W. 1971. *Banneker: The Afro-American Astronomer*. Freeport, NY: Libraries Press.

Altoff, Gerard T. 1996. *Amongst My Best Men: African-Americans and the War of 1812*. Put-in-Bay, OH: Perry Group.

American Anti-Slavery Society. 1838. *The Constitution of the American Anti-Slavery Society*. New York: American Anti-Slavery Society.

Andrews, E. A. 1836. *Slavery and the Domestic Slave-Trade in the United States*. Baltimore: Light and Stearns.

Andrews, William L. 1980. *The Literary Career of Charles W. Chesnutt*. Baton Rouge: Louisiana State University Press.

————. 1987. "Six Women's Slave Narratives, 1831–1909." In *Black Women's Slave Narratives.* Edited by William Andrews. New York: Oxford University Press.

————. 1986. *To Tell a Free Story: The First Century of Afro-American Autobiography, 1760–1865.* Urbana: University of Illinois Press.

Anthony, Katharine. 1954. *Susan B. Anthony: Her Personal History and Her Era.* Garden City, NY: Doubleday.

Antieau, Chester James. 1997. *The Intended Significance of the Fourteenth Amendment.* Buffalo, NY: W. S. Hein.

Aphornsuvan, Thanet. 1990. "James D. B. DeBow and the Political Economy of the Old South." Ph.D. dissertation, Department of History, SUNY-Binghamton, New York.

Aptheker, Herbert. 1993. *American Negro Slave Revolts.* 6th edition. New York: International Publishers.

Ashworth, John. 1965. *One Continual Cry.* New York: Humanities Press.

————. 1995. *Slavery, Capitalism, and Politics in the Antebellum Republic.* Volume 1, *Commerce and Compromise, 1820–1850.* New York. Cambridge University Press.

Atkin, Andrea M. 1995. "Converting America: The Rhetoric of Abolitionist Literature." Ph.D. dissertation, Department of English, University of Chicago.

Averkieva, Julia. 1941. *Slavery among the Indians of North America.* Moscow: USSR Academy of Sciences.

Azevedo, Celia M. 1995. *Abolitionism in the United States and Brazil: A Comparative Perspective.* New York: Garland.

Bacon, Margaret Hope. 1986. *Mothers of Feminism: The Story of Quaker Women in America.* San Francisco: Harper and Row.

————. 1980. *Valiant Friend: The Life of Lucretia Mott.* New York: Walker.

Bailey, Hugh C. 1965. *Hinton Rowan Helper, Abolitionist-Racist.* Tuscaloosa: University of Alabama Press.

Bailey, L. R. 1973. *Indian Slave Trade in the Southwest.* Los Angeles: Westernlore Press.

Bailey, N. Louis, and Elizabeth Ivey Cooper, eds. 1981. "John Laurens." In *Biographical Directory of the South Carolina House of Representatives.* Columbia: South Carolina University Press.

Baker, Moses. 1803. "An Account of Moses Baker, a Mulatto Baptist Preacher near Martha Brae." *Evangelical Magazine and Missionary Intelligencer* 11: 365–371.

Bancroft, Frederic. 1928. *Calhoun and the South Carolina Nullification Movement.* Baltimore: Johns Hopkins University Press.

————. 1931. *Slave-Trading in the Old South.* Baltimore: J. H. Furst.

Barber, John W. 1840. *A History of the Amistad Captives.* New Haven, CT: E. L. and J. W. Barber.

Barnes, Gilbert Hobbs. 1933. *The Anti-slavery Impulse, 1830–1844.* Gloucester, MA: Peter Smith.

Barnes, Gilbert Hobbs, and Dwight L. Dumond, eds. 1934. *Letters of Theodore Dwight Weld, Angelina Grimké Weld, and Sarah Grimké, 1822–1844.* New York: D. Appleton.

Barringer, James G. 1987. "The African Methodist Church: 200 Years of Service to the Community." *Crisis* 94 (June/July): 40–43.

Barry, Kathleen. 1988. *Susan B. Anthony: Biography of a Singular Feminist.* New York: New York University Press.

Bartlett, Irving. 1993. *John C. Calhoun: a Biography.* New York: Norton.

Bastide, Roger. 1972. *African Civilization in the New World.* New York: Harper and Row.

Batey, Grant M. 1954. *John Chavis: His Contributions to Education in North Carolina.* Master's thesis, Department of History, North Carolina College, Durham.

Baxter, Maurice. 1984. *One and Inseparable: Daniel Webster and the Union.* Cambridge, MA: Harvard University Press.

Bayliff, William H. 1951. *Boundary Monuments on the Maryland-Pennsylvania and the Maryland-Delaware Boundaries.* Annapolis: Maryland Board of Natural Resources.

Beals, Carleton. 1960. *Brass-Knuckle Crusade: The Great Know-Nothing Conspiracy, 1820–1860.* New York: Hastings House.

Bearden, Jim, and Linda Jean Butler. 1977. *Shadd: The Life and Times of Mary Shadd Cary.* Toronto: NC Press.

Bedini, Silvio A. 1972. *The Life of Benjamin Banneker.* New York: Charles Scribner's Sons.

Belkin, Lisa. 1989. "Freedoms Are Renewed in Recalling Deliverance." *New York Times,* June 19.

Bell, Howard H. 1969. *A Survey of the Negro Convention Movement, 1830–1861.* New York: Arno Press.

Bell, Malcolm. 1987. *Major Butler's Legacy: Five Generations of a Slaveholding Family.* Athens: University of Georgia Press.

Bennett, Robert A. 1974. "Black Episcopalians: A History from the Colonial Period to the Present." *Historical Magazine of the Protestant Episcopal Church* 43 (September 3): 231–245.

Bentley, George. 1955. *A History of the Freedmen's Bureau.* Philadelphia: University of Pennsylvania Press.

Berlin, Ira. 1974. *Slaves without Masters: The Free Negro in the Antebellum South.* New York: Pantheon Books.

Berlin, Ira, and Philip D. Morgan, eds. 1993. *Cultivation and Culture: Labor and the Shaping of Slave Life in the Americas.* Charlottesville: University Press of Virginia.

Berlin, Ira, et al. 1992. *Slaves No More: Three Essays on Emancipation and the Civil War.* Cambridge: Cambridge University Press.

Berson, Lenora E. 1971. *The Negroes and the Jews.* New York: Random House.

Billington, Ray Allen. 1953. *The Journal of Charlotte L. Forten.* New York: Collier.

Birmingham, Stephen. 1971. *The Grandees: America's Sephardic Elite.* New York: Harper and Row.

Birney, Catherine H. 1885. *The Grimké Sisters.* Boston: Lee and Shepard.

Birney, William. 1969. *James G. Birney and His Times: The Genesis of the Republican Party.* New York: Bergman.

Blackburn, Robin. 1988. *The Overthrow of Colonial Slavery, 1776–1848*. London: Verso.

Blackwell, Alice Stone. 1930. *Lucy Stone: Pioneer of Women's Rights*. Boston: Little, Brown.

Blanchard, Jonathan. Papers. Buswell Memorial Library, Wheaton College, Wheaton, Illinois.

Blassingame, John W. 1972. *The Slave Community: Plantation Life in the Antebellum South*. New York: Oxford University Press.

Blassingame, John W., ed. 1977. *Slave Testimony: Two Centuries of Letters, Speeches, Interviews, and Autobiographies*. Baton Rouge: Louisiana State University Press.

Blassingame, John W., and Mae G. Henderson, eds. 1980–1984. "Antislavery Newspapers and Periodicals." In *Annotated Index of Letters in the Philanthropist, Emancipator, Genius of Universal Emancipation, Abolition Intelligencer, African Observer, and the Liberator*, Volume 1,(1817–1845). Boston: G. K. Hall.

Blassingame, John W.; Mae G. Henderson; and Jessica M. Dunn, eds. 1980–1984. "Antislavery Newspapers and Periodicals." In *Annotated Index of Letters in the National Anti-Slavery Standard*, Volume 4 (1840–1860), and Volume 5 (1861–1871). Boston: G. K. Hall.

Bleser, Carol K. 1987. *The Hammonds of Redcliffe*. Oxford: Oxford University Press.

Bleser, Carol, K., ed. 1988. *Secret and Sacred: The Diaries of James Henry Hammond, a Southern Slaveholder*. New York: Oxford University Press.

Blockson, Charles L. 1987. *The Underground Railroad: First-Person Narratives of Escapes to Freedom in the North*. Englewood Cliffs, NJ: Prentice-Hall.

Blue, Frederick J. 1994. *Charles Sumner and the Conscience of the North*. Arlington Heights, IL: Harlan Davidson.

———. 1973. *The Free Soilers: Third Party Politics, 1848–54*. Urbana: University of Illinois Press.

———. 1987. *Salmon P. Chase: A Life in Politics*. Kent, OH: Kent State University Press.

Boller, Paul F. 1974. *American Transcendentalism, 1830–1860: An Intellectual Inquiry*. New York: G. P. Putnam's Sons.

Boskin, Joshua. 1986. *Sambo: The Rise and Demise of an American Jester*. New York: Oxford University Press.

Boston Slave Riot and Trial of Anthony Burns. 1854. Boston: Fetridge and Company.

Botkin, B. A., ed. 1941. *Slave Narratives: A Folk History of Slavery in the United States from Interviews with Former Slaves*. Washington, DC: U.S. Government Printing Office.

Boucher, Chauncey S. 1919. "The Annexation of Texas and the Bluffton Movement in South Carolina." *Mississippi Valley Historical Review* 4 (6): 3–33.

Bowman, Shearer Davis. 1993. *Masters and Lords: Mid-19th Century U.S. Planters and Prussian Junkers*. New York: Oxford University Press.

Boyd, Daniel L. 1974. "Free-Born Negro: The Life of John Chavis." BA thesis, Department of History, Princeton University, Princeton, New Jersey.

Boyd, James R. 1883. "William Still: His Life and Work to This Time." In *William Still: The Underground Railroad*. Philadelphia: William Still.

Boylan, Ann M. 1994. "Benevolence and Antislavery Activity among African American Women in New York and Boston, 1820–1840." In *The Abolitionist Sisterhood: Women's Political Culture in Antebellum America*. Edited by Jean Fagan Yellin and John C. Van Horne. Ithaca, NY: Cornell University Press.

Bracey, John. 1993. "Foreword." In Herbert Aptheker, *American Negro Slave Revolts*. New York: International Publishers.

Bracey, John H.; August Meier; and Elliott Rudwick, eds. 1971. *Blacks in the Abolitionist Movement*. Belmont, CA: Wadsworth Publishing.

Braithwaite, William. 1961. *The Second Period of Quakerism*. Cambridge: Cambridge University Press.

Brauer, Kinley. 1967. *Cotton versus Conscience: Massachusetts Whig Politics and Southwestern Expansion, 1843–1848*. Lexington: University of Kentucky Press.

Brawley, Benjamin. 1937. *Negro Builders and Heroes*. Chapel Hill: University of North Carolina Press.

Brewer, W. M. 1928. "Henry Highland Garnet." *Journal of Negro History* 13 (1): 36–52.

Bridges, C. A. 1941. "The Knights of the Golden Circle: A Filibustering Fantasy." *Southwestern Historical Quarterly* 44 (January): 287–302.

Brock, Peter. 1990. *The Quaker Peace Testimony, 1660–1914*. York, Eng.: Ebor Press.

Brock, William. 1979. *Parties and Political American Dilemmas, 1840–1850*. Millwood, NY: KTO Press.

Brodie, Fawn. 1974. *Thomas Jefferson, an Intimate History*. New York: Norton.

Brooks, George E. 1970. *Yankee Traders, Old Coasters, and African Middlemen*. Boston: Boston University Press.

Brown, Charles H. 1980. *Agents of Manifest Destiny: The Lives and Times of the Filibusters*. Chapel Hill: University of North Carolina Press.

Brown, David H. 1990. "Conjure/Doctors: An Exploration of a Black Discourse in America, Antebellum to 1940." *Folklore Forum* 23 (1–2): 3–46.

Brown, Josephine. 1856. *Biography of an American Bondman, by His Daughter*. Boston: R. F. Walcutt.

Brown, Richard H. 1966. "The Missouri Crisis, Slavery, and the Politics of Jacksonianism." *South Atlantic Quarterly* 65 (Winter): 55–72.

Brown, William Wells. 1847. *Narrative of William W. Brown, a Fugitive Slave, Written by Himself*. Boston: Anti-Slavery Office.

Brunvand, Jan Harold. 1986. *The Study of American Folklore: An Introduction*. New York: W. W. Norton.

Bumbrey, Jeffrey Nordlinger. 1976. "Historical Sketch of the Pennsylvania Abolition Society." In *A Guide to the Microfilm Publication of the Papers of the Pennsylvania Abolition Society at the Historical Society of Pennsylvania*. Philadelphia: Pennsylvania Abolition Society and Historical Society of Pennsylvania.

Burke, Edmund, and William Burke. 1835. *An Account of the European Settlements in America*. Boston: J. H. Wilkins.

Burnham, Philip. 1993. "Selling Poor Steven: The Struggles and Torments of a Forgotten Class in Antebellum America: Black Slaveowners." *American Heritage* 44 (1): 90–97.

Byerman, Keith E. 1994. *Seizing the Word: History, Art, and Self in the Work of W. E. B. DuBois.* Athens: University of Georgia Press.

Cable, Mary. 1971. *Black Odyssey: The Case of the Slave Ship* Amistad. New York: Viking Press.

Cady, Edwin H. 1966. *John Woolman: The Mind of the Quaker Saint.* New York: Washington Square Press.

Caldehead, William. 1972. "How Extensive Was the Border State Slave Trade? A New Look." *Civil War History* 18 (1): 42–55.

Calhoun, John C. 1957–. *The Papers of John C. Calhoun.* Edited by Clyde N. Wilson. Columbia: South Carolina University Press.

Campbell, Penelope. 1971. *Maryland in Africa: The Maryland State Colonization Society 1831–1857.* Urbana: University of Illinois Press.

Campbell, Stanley W. 1968. *The Slave Catchers: Enforcement of the Fugitive Slave Law, 1850–1860.* Chapel Hill: University of North Carolina Press.

Carney, Judith A. 1993. "From Hands to Tutors: African Expertise in the South Carolina Rice Economy." *Agricultural History* 67: 1–30.

Carruth, Gorton, ed. 1989. *What Happened When: A Chronology of Life and Events in America.* New York: Harper and Row.

Castel, Albert. 1958. *A Frontier State at War: Kansas, 1861–1865.* Ithaca, NY: Cornell University Press.

Cecil-Fronsman, Bill. 1992. *Common Whites: Class and Culture in Antebellum North Carolina.* Lexington: University Press of Kentucky.

Cell, John. 1982. *The Highest Stage of White Supremacy.* London: Cambridge University Press.

Ceplair, Larry, ed. 1989. *The Public Years of Sarah and Angelina Grimké: Selected Writings, 1835–1839.* New York: Columbia University Press.

Chambers-Schiller, Lee. 1994. "'A Good Work among the People': The Political Culture of the Boston Antislavery Fair." In *The Abolitionist Sisterhood: Women's Political Culture in Antebellum America.* Edited by Jean Fagan Yellin and John C. Van Horne. Ithaca, NY: Cornell University Press.

Chapell, Naomi C. 1929. "Negro Names." *American Speech* 4: 272–275.

Chapelle, Howard. 1927. *The Baltimore Clipper.* Salem, MA: Marine Research Society.

———. 1967. *The Search for Speed under Sail.* New York: Norton.

Chavis, John. Letters held in the Willia P. Mangum Papers. Library of Congress, Duke University Library, and University of North Carolina, Chapel Hill.

Chesnutt, Charles W. 1988. *The House behind the Cedars.* Athens: University of Georgia Press.

Chesnutt, Helen. 1952. *Charles Waddell Chesnutt: Pioneer of the Color Line.* Chapel Hill: University of North Carolina Press.

Chyet, Stanley F. 1962–1963. "Aaron Lopez: A Study in Buenafama." *American Jewish Historical Quarterly,* 52: 295–309.

Claiborne, J. F. H. 1860. *Life and Correspondence of John A. Quitman, Major-General, U.S.A., and Governor of the State of Mississippi.* New York: Harper.

Clifford, Deborah Pickman. 1979. *Mine Eyes Have Seen the Glory.* Boston: Little, Brown.

Coffin, Levi. 1876. *Reminiscences of Levi Coffin, Reputed President of the Underground Railroad.* Cincinnati: Western Tract Society.

Cohen, David, and Jack Greene. 1972. *Neither Slave Nor Free.* Baltimore: Johns Hopkins University Press.

Cohen, Hennig. 1962. "Slave Names in Colonial South Carolina." *American Speech* 28: 102–107.

Coit, Margaret L. 1950. *John C. Calhoun, American Portrait.* Boston: Houghton Mifflin.

Coleman, Mrs. Chapman. 1871. *The Life of John J. Crittenden.* Philadelphia: J. B. Lippincott.

Collison, Gary. 1997. *Shadrach Minkins: From Fugitive Slave to Citizen.* Cambridge, MA: Harvard University Press.

Commons, John R., et al. 1910. *A Documentary History of American Industrial Society.* Cleveland: A. H. Clark.

Coniff, Michael L., and Thomas J. Davis. 1994. *Africans in the Americas: A History of the Black Diaspora.* New York: St. Martin's.

Connelley, William E. 1918. *A Standard History of Kansas and Kansans.* Chicago: Lewis.

Cook, James F. 1995. *The Governors of Georgia, 1754–1995.* Macon, GA: Mercer University Press.

Cooley, Timothy Mather. 1837. *Sketches of the Life and Character of the Reverend Lemuel Haynes, A.M., for Many Years Pastor of a Church in Rutland, Vermont, and Late in Granville, New York.* New York: Negro University Press.

Cooper, Richard. 1985. *John Chavis: To Teach a Generation.* Raleigh, NC: Creative Productions.

Cooper, William. 1978. *The South and the Politics of Slavery, 1828–1856.* Baton Rouge: Louisiana State University Press.

Cornelius, Janet Duitsman. 1983. "We Slipped and Learned to Read: Slave Accounts of the Literacy Process, 1830–1865." *Phylon* 44 (3): 171–186.

———. 1991. *"When I Can Read My Title Clear": Literacy, Slavery, and Religion in the Antebellum South.* Columbia: University of South Carolina Press.

Cover, Robert. 1975. *Justice Accused: Antislavery and the Judicial Process.* New Haven, CT: Yale University Press.

Covington, James W. 1995. *The Seminoles of Florida.* Gainesville: University Press of Florida.

Cox, LaWanda. 1981. *Lincoln and Black Freedom: A Study in Presidential Leadership.* Urbana: University of Illinois Press.

Craven, Avery O. 1932. *Edmund Ruffin, Southerner: A Study in Secession.* New York: D. Appleton.

Creel, Margaret Washington. 1988. *A Peculiar People: Slave Religion and Community—Culture among the Gullahs.* New York: New York University Press.

Crenshaw, Ollinger. 1941. "The Knights of the Golden Circle: The Career of George Bickley." *American Historical Review* 47 (October): 23–50.

———. 1942. "The Speakership Contest of 1859–60." *Mississippi Valley Historical Review* 29: 323–338.

Crofts, Daniel W. 1971. "The Black Response to the Blair Education Bill." *Journal of Southern History* 37 (1): 41–65.

Cromwell, Otelia. 1958. *Lucretia Mott*. Cambridge, MA: Harvard University Press.

Crozier, A. 1969. *The Novels of Harriet Beecher Stowe*. New York: Oxford University Press.

Crum, Mason. 1968. *Gullah: Negro Life in the Carolina Sea Islands*. New York: Negro Universities Press.

Cullen, Charles T. 1987. *St. George Tucker and Law in Virginia, 1772–1804*. New York: Garland.

Cunliffe, Marcus. 1979. *Chattel Slavery and Wage Slavery: The Anglo-American Context, 1830–1860*. Athens: University of Georgia Press.

Cunningham, Noble. 1987. *In Pursuit of Reason: The Life of Thomas Jefferson*. Baton Rouge: Louisiana State University Press.

Curry, J. L. M. 1969. *A Brief Sketch of George Peabody, and a History of the Peabody Education Fund through Thirty Years*. New York: Negro Universities Press.

Curtin, Philip D. 1990. *The Rise and Fall of the Plantation Complex: Essays in Atlantic History*. Cambridge: Cambridge University Press.

Cushing, J. D. 1961. "The Cushing Court and the Abolition of Slavery in Massachusetts: More Notes on the Quock Walker Case." *American Journal of Legal History* 5: 118–119.

Dabney, Virginius. 1981. *The Jefferson Scandals: A Rebuttal*. New York: Dodd, Mead.

Dangerfield, George. 1952. *The Era of Good Feelings*. New York: Harcourt Brace and Company.

Daube, David. 1952. "Slave-Catching." *Juridical Review* 64: 12–28.

Davenport, Frances, ed. 1967. *European Treaties Bearing on the History of the United States and Its Dependencies to 1648*. Gloucester, MA: Peter Smith.

David, Paul, et al. 1976. *Reckoning with Slavery: A Critical Study in the Quantitative History of American Negro Slavery*. New York: Oxford University Press.

Davis, Charles T., and Henry Louis Gates, Jr., eds. 1985. *The Slave's Narrative*. New York: Oxford University Press.

Davis, David Brion. 1986. "The Emergence of Immediatism in British and American Antislavery Thought." In *From Homicide to Slavery: Studies in American Culture*. Edited by David Brion Davis. New York: Oxford University Press.

———. 1986. *From Homicide to Slavery: Studies in American Culture*. New York: Oxford University Press.

———. 1975. *The Problem of Slavery in the Age of Revolution, 1770–1823*. Ithaca, NY: Cornell University Press.

———. 1966. *The Problem of Slavery in Western Culture*. Oxford: Oxford University Press.

Davis, Hugh. 1990. *Joshua Leavitt, Evangelical Abolitionist*. Baton Rouge: Louisiana State University Press.

The Debate on the Constitution: Federalist and Antifederalist Speeches, Articles, and Letters during the Struggle over Ratification, Part One. 1993. Edited by Bernard Bailyn. New York: Library of America.

Debo, Angie. 1970. *A History of the Indians of the United States*. Norman: University of Oklahoma Press.

DeBoer, Clara Merritt. 1994. *Be Jubilant My Feet: African American Abolitionists in the American Missionary Association 1839–1861*. New York: Garland.

———. 1995. *His Truth Is Marching on: African Americans Who Taught the Freedmen for the American Missionary Association 1861–1877*. New York: Garland.

———. 1973. *The Role of Afro-Americans in the Origin and Work of the American Missionary Association, 1839–1877. Part 1 & 2*. Ph.D. dissertation, Department of History, Rutgers University. Ann Arbor, MI: University Microfilms.

Deetz, James. 1993. *Flowerdew Hundred: The Archaeology of a Virginia Plantation, 1619–1864*. Charlottesville: University Press of Virginia.

Degler, Carl N. 1978. "Experiencing Slavery." *Reviews in American History* 6: 277–282.

———. 1971. *Neither Black nor White: Slavery and Race Relations in Brazil and the United States*. New York: Macmillan.

———. 1974. *The Other South: Southern Dissenters in the Nineteenth Century*. New York: Harper and Row.

Delany, Martin R. 1852. *The Condition, Elevation, Emigration, and Destiny of the Colored People of the United States, Politically Considered*. Philadelphia: Martin R. Delany.

Dethloff, Henry C. 1988. *A History of the American Rice Industry, 1685–1985*. College Station: Texas A&M University Press.

De Voto, Bernard A. 1989. *The Year of Decision: 1846*. Boston: Houghton Mifflin.

Diehl, Lorraine. 1992. "Skeletons in the Closet: Uncovering the Rich History of the Slaves of New York." *New York* 25 (39): 78–86.

Dilday, Kenya A., and Jonathan Gill. 1996. "Food." In *Encyclopedia of African-American Culture and History*. New York: Macmillan.

Dillard, Joey L. 1971. "The West-African Day-Names in Nova Scotia." *Names* 19 (4): 257–261.

Dillon, Merton L. 1985. 1986. "Benjamin Lundy: Quaker Radical." *Timeline* 3 (3): 28–41.

———. 1966. *Benjamin Lundy and the Struggle for Negro Freedom*. Urbana: University of Illinois Press.

———. 1990. *Slavery Attacked: Southern Slaves and Their Allies, 1619–1865*. Baton Rouge: Louisiana State University Press.

———. *Ulrich Bonnell Phillips: Historian of the Old South*. Baton Rouge: Louisiana State University Press.

Donald, David. 1960. *Charles Sumner and the Coming of the Civil War*. New York: Knopf.

———. 1995. *Lincoln*. New York: Simon and Schuster.

Donald, Leland. 1997. *Aboriginal Slavery on the Northwest Coast of North America*. Berkeley: University of California Press.

Donnan, Elizabeth, ed. 1931. *Documents Illustrative of the History of the Slave Trade to America*. Washington, DC: Carnegie Institution of Washington.

Donovan, Herbert. 1925. *The Barnburners: A Study of the Internal Movements in the Political History of New York and of the Resulting Changes in Political Affiliations, 1830–1852*. New York: New York University Press.

Dormon, John H. 1977. "The Persistent Specter: Slave Rebellion in Territorial Louisiana." *Louisiana History* 18: 389–404.

Dorris, Jonathan T. 1936. *Old Cane Springs*. Louisville, KY: Standard Printing.

Douglass, Frederick. 1855. *My Bondage and My Freedom*. New York: Miller, Orton.

———. 1845. *Narrative of the Life of Frederick Douglass, an American Slave*. Boston: American Anti-Slavery Office.

Douty, Esther M. 1968. *Forten the Sailmaker: Pioneer Champion of Negro Rights*. Chicago: Rand McNally.

Drake, Frederick C. 1970. "Secret History of the Slave Trade to Cuba Written by an American Naval Officer, 1861." *Journal of Negro History* 55: 218–235.

Drake, S. 1990. *Black Folk Here and There*. 2 vols. Los Angeles: University of California Center for Afro-American Studies.

Drake, Thomas. 1950. *Quakers and Slavery in America*. New Haven, CT: Yale University Press.

———. 1938. "Thomas Garrett Quaker Abolitionist." In *Friends in Wilmington, 1738–1938*. Edited by Edward P. Bartlett. Wilmington, OH: Clinton County Historical Society.

Driver, Leota S. 1969. *Fanny Kemble*. New York: Negro Universities Press.

DuBois, Ellen Carol. 1978. *Feminism and Suffrage: The Emergence of an Independent Women's Movement in America 1848–1869*. Ithaca, NY: Cornell University Press.

DuBois, W. E. B. 1995. *Black Reconstruction in America*. New York: Simon and Schuster.

———. 1909. *John Brown*. Philadelphia: G. W. Jacobs.

———. 1899. *The Philadelphia Negro*. Philadelphia: University of Pennsylvania Press.

DuBois, W. E. B., ed. 1902. *The Negro Artisan*. Atlanta, GA: Atlanta University Press.

Dumond, Dwight Lowell. 1961. *Antislavery: The Crusade for Freedom in America*. Ann Arbor: University of Michigan Press.

———. 1959. *Antislavery Origins of the Civil War in the United States*. Ann Arbor: University of Michigan Press.

Dusinberre, William. 1996. *Them Dark Days: Slavery in the American Rice Swamps*. New York: Oxford University Press.

Earle, Thomas, ed. 1847. *The Life, Travels, and Opinions of Benjamin Lundy, Including His Journeys to Texas and Mexico; with a Sketch of Contemporary Events, and a Notice of the Revolution in Hayti*. Philadelphia: William D. Parrish. Reprinted 1969. New York: Negro Universities Press.

Eaton, Clement. 1964. *The Freedom of Thought Struggle in the Old South*. New York: Harper and Row.

———. 1957. *Henry Clay and the Art of American Politics*. New York: Little Brown and Company.

Eckhardt, Celia Morris. 1984. *Fanny Wright: Rebel in America*. Cambridge, MA: Harvard University Press.

Edelstein, Tilden G. 1968. *Strange Enthusiasm: A Life of Thomas Wentworth Higginson*. New Haven, CT: Yale University Press.

Edwards, Lillie Johnson. 1990. *Denmark Vesey*. New York: Chelsea House Publishers.

———. 1996. "Episcopalians." In *Encyclopedia of African-American Culture and History*. Edited by Jack Salzman, David Lionel Smith, and Cornel West. New York: Macmillan.

Edwards, Samuel. 1974. *Rebel! A Biography of Thomas Paine*. New York: Praeger Press.

Egerton, Douglas R. 1993. *Gabriel's Rebellion: The Virginia Slave Conspiracies of 1800 and 1802*. Chapel Hill: University of North Carolina Press.

Ehrlich, Walter. 1979. *They Have No Rights: Dred Scott's Struggle for Freedom*. Westport, CT: Greenwood Press.

Elkins, Stanley M. 1959. *Slavery: A Problem in American Institutional and Intellectual Life*. Chicago: University of Chicago Press.

Ellis, Richard E. 1987. *The Union at Risk: Jacksonian Democracy, States' Rights, and the Nullification Crisis*. New York: Oxford University Press.

Ellis, William. 1985. *Madison County: 200 Years in Retrospect*. Richmond, KY: Madison County Historical Society.

Embree, Elihu, and Robert H. White. 1932. *The Emancipator (Complete)*. Nashville, TN: B. H. Murphy.

Escott, Paul D. 1979. *Slavery Remembered: A Record of Twentieth-Century Slave Narratives*. Chapel Hill: University of North Carolina Press.

Essien-Udom, Essien Udosen. 1969. *Black Nationalism: A Search for Identity in America*. New York: Dell.

Estell, Kenneth., ed. 1994. *The African-American Almanac*. Detroit: Gale Research.

Ettinger, Amos. 1936. *James Edward Oglethorpe, Imperial Idealist*. Oxford: Clarendon Press.

Farber, Daniel A., and Suzanna Sherry. 1990. *A History of the American Constitution*. St. Paul, MN: West Publishing.

Farrison, William Edward. 1969. *William Wells Brown: Author and Reformer*. Chicago: University of Chicago Press.

Faust, Drew Gilpin. 1977. "Evangelicalism and the Meaning of the Proslavery Argument: The Reverend Thornton Stringfellow of Virginia." *Virginia Magazine of History and Biography* 85 (January): 3–17.

———. 1981. *The Ideology of Slavery: Proslavery Thought in the Antebellum South, 1830–1860*. Baton Rouge: Louisiana State University Press.

———. 1982. *James Henry Hammond and the Old South: A Design for Mastery*. Baton Rouge: Louisiana State University Press.

———. 1986. *A Sacred Circle: The Dilemma of the Intellectual in the Old South, 1840–1860*. Philadelphia: University of Pennsylvania Press.

———. 1979. "A Southern Stewardship: The Intellectual

and the Proslavery Argument." *American Quarterly* 31 (Spring): 63–80.

Fehrenbacher, Don E. 1978. *The Dred Scott Case.* New York: Oxford University Press.

———. 1987. *Lincoln in Text and Context: Collected Essays.* Palo Alto, CA: Stanford University Press.

———. 1980. *The South and Three Sectional Crises.* Baton Rouge: Louisiana State University Press.

Feldman, Lynne B., and John N. Ingham, eds. 1994. *African American Business Leaders: A Biographical Dictionary.* Westport, CT: Greenwood.

Ferguson, Leland. 1992. *Uncommon Ground: Archaeology and Early African America, 1650–1800.* Washington, DC: Smithsonian Institution Press.

Finkelman, Paul. 1994. "'Hooted Down the Page of History': Reconsidering the Greatness of Chief Justice Taney." *Journal of Supreme Court History* 1994: 83–102.

———. 1981. *An Imperfect Union: Slavery, Federalism, and Comity.* Chapel Hill: University of North Carolina Press.

———. 1996. "Legal Ethics and Fugitive Slaves: The Anthony Burns Case, Judge Loring, and Abolitionist Attorneys." *Cardozo Law Review* 17 (May): 1793–1858.

———. 1985. *Slavery in the Courtroom. An Annotated Bibliography of American Cases.* Washington, DC: Library of Congress.

———. 1989. "Medicine, Nutrition, Demography, and Slavery." In *Articles on American Slavery, Volume 15.* New York: Garland Publishing.

———. 1988. *Statutes on Slavery: The Pamphlet Literature.* New York: Garland.

Finkelman, Paul, ed. 1995. *His Soul Goes Marching On: Responses to John Brown and the Harpers Ferry Raid.* Charlottesville: University Press of Virginia.

Fisher, Ruth Anna. 1942. "Manuscript Materials Bearing on the Negro in British America." *Journal of Negro History* 27 (1): 83–93.

Fishkin, Shelly Fisher, and Carla L. Peterson. 1990. "'We Hold These Truths to Be Self-Evident': The Rhetoric of Frederick Douglass' Journalism." In *Frederick Douglass: New Literary and Historical Essays.* Edited by Eric J. Sundquist. Cambridge: Cambridge University Press.

Fitzhugh, George. 1960. *Cannibals All! or Slaves without Masters.* Cambridge, MA: Belknap Press.

Fladeland, Betty. 1955. *James G. Birney: Slaveholder to Abolitionist.* Ithaca, NY: Cornell University Press.

———. 1972. *Men and Brothers: Anglo-American Antislavery Cooperation.* Urbana: University of Illinois Press.

Fluche, Michael. 1975. "Joel Chandler Harris and the Folklore of Slavery." *Journal of American Studies* 9 (December): 347–363.

Fogel, Robert, and Stanley Engerman. 1974. *Time on the Cross: The Economics of American Negro Slavery.* Boston: Little, Brown.

———. 1974. *Time on the Cross: Evidence and Methods—A Supplement.* Boston: Little, Brown.

Fogel, Robert William. 1989. *Without Consent or Contract: The Rise and Fall of American Slavery.* New York: Norton.

Foner, Eric. 1970. *Free Soil—Free Labor—Free Men: The Ideology of the Republican Party before the Civil War.* New York: Oxford University Press.

———. 1983. *Nothing but Freedom: Emancipation and Its Legacy.* Baton Rouge: Louisiana State University Press.

———. 1988. *Reconstruction: America's Unfinished Revolution.* New York: Harper and Row.

Foner, Laura, and Eugene D. Genovese. 1969. *Slavery in the New World: A Reader in Comparative History.* Englewood Cliffs, NJ: Prentice-Hall.

Foner, Philip S. 1964. *Frederick Douglass: A Biography.* New York: Citadel.

———. 1950. *Life and Writings of Frederick Douglass.* 5 vols. New York: International Publishers.

Foner, Philip S., and Josephine F. Pacheco. 1984. *Three Who Dared: Prudence Crandall, Margaret Douglass, Myrtilla Miner—Champions of Antebellum Black Education.* Westport, CT: Greenwood Press.

Foot, Michael, and Isaac Kramnick, eds. 1987. *The Thomas Paine Reader.* London: Penguin.

Ford, Lacy, Jr. 1988. "Recovering the Republic: Calhoun, South Carolina, and the Concurrent Majority." *South Carolina Historical Magazine* 89 (July): 146–159.

Forster, C. H. 1954. *The Rungless Ladder: Harriet Beecher Stowe and New England Puritanism.* Durham, NC: Duke University Press.

Foster, Frances Smith. 1979. *Witnessing Slavery: The Development of Ante-bellum Slave Narratives.* Madison: University of Wisconsin Press.

Fox-Genovese, Elizabeth. 1991. *Feminism without Illusions.* Chapel Hill: University of North Carolina Press.

———. 1988. *Within the Plantation Household.* Chapel Hill: University of North Carolina Press.

Franklin, John H. 1943. *The Free Negro in North Carolina 1790–1863.* Chapel Hill: University of North Carolina Press.

———. 1994. *Reconstruction after the Civil War.* Chicago: University of Chicago Press.

Franklin, John H., and A. Alfred Moss. 1994. *From Slavery to Freedom: A History of African Americans.* New York: McGraw Hill.

Frederick, Duke. 1966. "The Second Confiscation Act: A Chapter of Civil War Politics." M.A. thesis, Department of History, University of Chicago, Chicago.

Frederickson, George. 1988. *The Arrogance of Race: Historical Perspectives on Slavery, Racism, and Social Inequality.* Middletown, CT: Wesleyan University Press.

———. 1981. *White Supremacy: A Comparative Study in American and South African History.* New York: Oxford University Press.

Freehling, Alison Goodyear. 1982. *Drift toward Dissolution: The Virginia Slavery Debate of 1831–1832.* Baton Rouge: Louisiana State University Press.

Freehling, William W. 1965. *Prelude to Civil War: The Nullification Controversy in South Carolina, 1816–1836.* New York: Oxford University Press.

———. 1990. *The Road to Disunion: Secessionists at Bay, 1776–1854.* New York: Oxford University Press.

Frey, Sylvia. 1991. *Water from the Rock: Black Resistance in a Revolutionary Age.* Princeton, NJ: Princeton University Press.

Fridlington, Robert. 1995. *The Reconstruction Court, 1864–1888.* Danbury, CT: Grolier.

Friedman, Lawrence J. 1982. *Gregarious Saints: Self and Community in American Abolitionism, 1830–1870.* New York: Cambridge University Press.

Friedman, Lawrence M. 1973. *A History of American Law.* New York: Simon and Schuster.

Frothingham, Octavius Brooks. 1969. *Gerrit Smith: A Biography.* New York: Negro Universities Press.

Fry, Gladys-Marie. 1975. *Night Riders in Black Folk History.* Knoxville: University of Tennessee Press.

———. 1990. *Stitched from the Soul: Slave Quilts from the Ante-bellum South.* New York: Dutton Studio Books.

Fuller, Edmond. 1971. *Prudence Crandall: An Incident of Racism in Nineteenth-Century Connecticut.* Middletown, CT: Wesleyan University Press.

Gamble, Douglas A. 1979. "Joshua Giddings and the Ohio Abolitionists: A Study in Radical Politics." *Ohio History* 88 (1): 37–56.

Gara, Larry. 1961. *The Liberty Line: The Legend of the Underground Railroad.* Lexington: University of Kentucky Press.

———. 1991. *The Presidency of Franklin Pierce.* Lawrence: University Press of Kansas.

———. 1961. "William Still and the Underground Railroad." *Pennsylvania History* 1: 33–44.

Gates, Henry Louis, Jr. 1987. "Introduction." In *The Classic Slave Narratives.* Edited by Henry Louis Gates, Jr. New York: Penguin Books.

———. 1996. "White Like Me." *New Yorker,* June 17: 66–81.

Geggus, David P. 1989. "Racial Equality, Slavery, and Colonial Secession during the Constituent Assembly." *American Historical Review* 94 (December): 1290–1309.

Genovese, Eugene. 1980. *From Rebellion to Revolution: Afro-American Slave Revolts in the Making of the Modern World.* Baton Rouge: Louisiana State University Press.

———. 1974. *Roll, Jordan, Roll: The World the Slaves Made.* New York: Pantheon Books.

George, Carol V. R. 1973. *Segregated Sabbaths: Richard Allen and the Emergence of Independent Black Churches 1760–1840.* New York: Oxford University Press.

Georgia. *The Code of the State of Georgia.* 1861. Prepared by R. H. Clark, T. R. R. Cobb, and D. Irwin. Atlanta: Franklin Steam Publishing House.

———. *The Code of the State of Georgia.* 1867. Revised and corrected by David Irwin. Atlanta: Franklin Steam Publishing House.

Georgia Writers' Project. 1940. "Drums and Shadows." Athens: University of Georgia Press.

Gerteis, Louis S. 1973. *From Contraband to Freedom: Federal Policy toward Southern Blacks, 1861–1865.* Westport, CT: Greenwood Press.

Gerzina, Gretchen. 1995. *Black London: Life before Emancipation.* New Brunswick, NJ: Rutgers University Press.

Gienapp, William E. 1987. *The Origins of the Republican Party, 1852–1856.* New York: Oxford University Press.

Gilje, Paul. 1996. *Rioting in America.* Bloomington: Indiana University Press.

Gilmore, Al-Tony, ed. 1978. *Revisiting Blassingame's "The Slave Community": The Scholars Respond.* Westport, CT: Greenwood Press.

Glatthaar, Joseph. 1990. *Forged in Battle: The Civil War Alliance of Black Soldiers and White Officers.* New York: Free Press.

Glick, Wendell, ed. 1972. *The Writings of Henry D. Thoreau: Reform Papers.* Princeton, NJ: Princeton University Press.

Going, Allen J. 1957. "The South and the Blair Education Bill." *Mississippi Valley Historical Review* 44 (2): 267–290.

Goldberg, David. 1993. *Racist Cultures: Philosophy and the Politics of Meaning.* Oxford: Blackwell.

Gomez, Michael. 1994. "Muslims in Early America." *Journal of Southern History* 60 (4): 671–710.

Goodheart, Lawrence B. 1990. *Abolitionist, Actuary, Atheist: Elizur Wright and the Reform Impulse.* Kent, OH: Kent State University Press.

———. 1982. "Tennessee's Antislavery Movement Reconsidered: The Example of Elihu Embree." *Tennessee Historical Quarterly* 41 (3): 224–238.

Gossett, Thomas. 1965. *Race: The History of an Idea in America.* New York: Schocken.

Gougeon, Len. 1995. "Thoreau and Reform." In *The Cambridge Companion to Henry David Thoreau.* Edited by Joel Myerson. Cambridge: Cambridge University Press.

Grant, Mary H. 1994. *Private Woman, Public Person: An Account of the Life of Julia Ward Howe from 1819 to 1868.* Brooklyn, NY: Carlson.

Gray, Lewis C. 1933. *History of Agriculture in the Southern United States to 1860.* 2 vols. Washington, DC: Carnegie Institution.

Green, Constance McLaughlin. 1956. *Eli Whitney and the Birth of American Technology.* Boston: Little Brown and Company.

Green, Fletcher M. 1930. *Constitutional Development in the South Atlantic States, 1776–1860: A Study in the Evolution of Democracy.* Chapel Hill: University of North Carolina Press.

Green, Richard L., ed. 1985. *A Salute to Black Scientists and Inventors.* New York: Empak.

Greenberg, Kenneth S. 1996. *The Confessions of Nat Turner and Related Documents.* Boston: St. Martin's.

Greene, Helen Ione. 1946. "Politics in Georgia, 1853–1854: The Ordeal of Howell Cobb." *Georgia Historical Quarterly* 30 (2): 185–211.

Griffith, Cyril F. 1975. *The African Dream: Martin R. Delany and the Emergence of Pan-African Thought.* University Park: Pennsylvania State University Press.

Guilds, John C. 1992. *Simms: A Literary Life.* Fayetteville: University of Arkansas Press.

Guillory, James Denny. 1968. "The Pro-Slavery Arguments

of Dr. Samuel A. Cartwright." *Louisiana History* 9 (4): 209–227.

Gummere, Amelia Mott. 1922. *The Journal and Essays of John Woolman.* New York: Macmillan.

Gunther, Gerald, ed. 1969. *John Marshall's Defense of McCulloch v. Maryland.* Stanford, CA: Stanford University Press.

Gutman Herbert G. 1976. *The Black Family in Slavery and Freedom 1750–1925.* New York: Pantheon.

———. 1975. *Slavery and the Numbers Game: A Critique of Time on the Cross.* Urbana: University of Illinois Press.

Hadden, Sally E. 1993. "Law Enforcement in a New Nation: Slave Patrols and Public Authority in the Old South, 1700–1865." Ph.D. dissertation, Department of History, Harvard University, Cambridge, MA.

Hahn, Steven. 1983. *The Roots of Southern Populism: Yeomen Farmers and the Transformation of the Georgia Backcountry.* New York: Oxford University Press.

Hall, Gwendolyn Midlo. 1992. *Africans in Colonial Louisiana: The Development of Afro-Creole Culture in the Eighteenth Century.* Baton Rouge: Louisiana State University Press.

Hall, Kermit L.; William M. Wicek; and Paul Finkelman. 1996. *American Legal History: Cases and Materials.* New York: Oxford University Press.

Hall, Mark. 1982. "The Proslavery Thought of J. D. B. DeBow: A Practical Man's Guide to Economics." *Southern Studies* 21 (Spring): 97–104.

Hamer, Philip M. 1935. "British Consuls and the Negro Seamen's Acts, 1850–1860." *Journal of Southern History* 1 (2): 138–168.

———. 1935. "Great Britain, the United States, and the Negro Seamen's Acts, 1822–1848." *Journal of Southern History* 1 (1): 3–28.

Hamilton, Alexander; James Madison; and John Jay. 1961. *The Federalist Papers.* Edited by Clinton L. Rossiter. New York: Mentor Books.

Hamilton, Holman. 1964. *Prologue to Conflict: The Crisis and Compromise of 1850.* Lexington: University of Kentucky Press.

Hanaford, Phebe A. 1883. *Daughters of America, or Women of the Century.* Augusta, ME: True and Company.

Hancock, Harold B. 1973. "Mary Ann Shadd: Negro Editor, Educator, and Lawyer." *Delaware History* 15 (3): 187–194.

Hansen, Debra Gold. 1993. *Strained Sisterhood: Gender and Class in the Boston Female Anti-Slavery Society.* Amherst: University of Massachusetts Press.

Harding, Walter. 1982. *The Days of Henry Thoreau: A Biography.* New York: Dover Publications.

Harlan, Louis R. 1972. *Booker T. Washington: The Making of a Black Leader.* New York: Oxford University Press.

Harlow, Ralph Volney. 1939. *Gerrit Smith: Philanthropist and Reformer.* New York: Henry Holt.

Harper, Ida Husted. 1899. *The Life and Work of Susan B. Anthony.* Indianapolis, IN: Bowen-Merrill.

Harrington, Spencer. 1993. "Bones and Bureaucrats: New York City's Great Cemetery Imbroglio." *Archaeology* 2: 28–38.

Harris, Julia Collier. 1918. *The Life and Letters of Joel Chandler Harris.* New York: Houghton Mifflin.

Harris, Robert L., Jr. 1981. "Charleston's Free Afro-American Elite: The Brown Fellowship Society and the Humane Brotherhood." *South Carolina Historical Magazine* 81: 289–310.

Harrison, Lowell. 1949. "Thomas Roderick Dew: Philosopher of the Old South." *Virginia Magazine of History and Biography* 57 (October): 390–404.

Harrisse, Henry. 1897. *The Diplomatic History of America: Its First Chapter 1452–1494.* London: B. F. Stevens.

Harrold, Stanley. 1986. *Gamaliel Bailey and Antislavery Union.* Kent, OH: Kent State University Press.

Hartgrove, W. B. 1918. "The Story of Josiah Henson." *Journal of Negro History* 3 (1): 1–21.

Hatch, Alden. 1969. *The Byrd's of Virginia.* New York: Holt, Rinehart and Winston.

Hatcher, William E. 1908. *John Jasper: The Unmatched Negro Philosopher and Preacher.* New York: F. H. Revell.

Haviland, Laura S. 1881. *A Woman's Life-Work: Labors and Experiences of Laura S. Haviland.* Chicago: Publishing Association of Friends.

Hayden, J. Carleton. 1971. "Conversion and Control: Dilemma of Episcopalians in Providing for the Religious Instructions of Slaves, Charleston, South Carolina, 1845–1860." *Historical Magazine of the Protestant Episcopal Church* 40 (June 2): 143–171.

Hays, Elinor Rice. 1961. *Morning Star: A Biography of Lucy Stone 1818–1893.* New York: Harcourt, Brace and World.

Haywood, Jacquelyn S. 1974. *The American Missionary Association in Louisiana during Reconstruction.* Ph.D. dissertation, Department of History, University of California-Los Angeles. Ann Arbor, MI: University Microfilms.

Heidler, David. 1994. *Pulling the Temple Down: The Fire-Eaters and the Destruction of the Union.* Mechanicsburg, PA: Stackpole Books.

Heimert, Alan. 1966. *Religion and the American Mind: From the Great Awakening to the Revolution.* Cambridge, MA: Harvard University Press.

Heitmann, John Alfred. 1987. *The Modernization of the Louisiana Sugar Industry 1930–1910.* Baton Rouge: Louisiana State University Press.

Helper, Hinton R. 1968. *The Impending Crisis of the South and How to Meet It.* Edited by George Frederickson. 1857. Reprint, Cambridge, MA: Harvard University Press.

Henig, Gerald S. 1973. *Henry Winter Davis: Antebellum and Civil War Congressman from Maryland.* New York: Twayne.

Henshaw, Henry W. 1910. "Slavery." In *Handbook of American Indians North of Mexico.* Edited by Frederick W. Hodge. Washington, DC: Bureau of American Ethnology.

Hersh, Blanche Glassman. 1978. *The Slavery of Sex: Feminist Abolitionist in America.* Urbana: University of Illinois Press.

Hickey, Donald R. 1989. *The War of 1812: A Forgotten Conflict.* Urbana: University of Illinois Press.

Higginbotham, A. Leon. 1978. *In the Matter of Color: Race and the American Legal Process*. New York: Oxford University Press.

Hilliard, Sam Bowers. 1972. *Hogmeat and Hoecake: Food Supply in the Old South 1840–1860*. Carbondale: Southern Illinois University Press.

Hine, Darlene Clark; Elsa Barkley Brown; and Rosalyn Terborg-Penn, eds. 1993. *Black Women in America: An Historical Encyclopedia*. Brooklyn, NY: Carlson.

Hinks, Peter P. 1997. *To Awaken My Afflicted Brethren: David Walker and the Problem of Antebellum Slave Resistance*. University Park: Pennsylvania State University Press.

Hinton, Richard J., ed. 1898. *Poems by Richard Realf: Poet, Soldier, Workman*. New York: Funk and Wagnalls.

Hodges, Graham, ed. 1996. *The Black Loyalist Directory: African Americans in Exile after the American Revolution*. New York: Garland.

Holmes, Jack D. L. 1970. "The Abortive Slave Revolt at Pointe Coupee Louisiana, 1795." *Louisiana History* 11: 341–362.

Holmes, Urban. 1930. "A Study of Negro Onomastics." *American Speech* 5: 463–467.

Holt, Michael F. 1978. *The Political Crisis of the 1850s*. New York: Norton.

———. 1992. *Political Parties and American Political Development from the Age of Jackson to the Age of Lincoln*. Baton Rouge: Louisiana State University Press.

Horsman, Reginald. 1962. *The Causes of the War of 1812*. Philadelphia: University of Pennsylvania Press.

Howard, John Henry. 1827. *The Laws of the British Colonies in the West Indies and Other Parts of America Concerning Real and Personal Property and Manumission of Slaves, with a View of the Constitution of Each Colony*. London: Joseph Butterworth and Son.

Howe, Marc A. DeWolfe. 1932. "Thomas Wentworth Higginson." *Dictionary of American Biography*. Edited by Dumas Malone. New York: Charles Scribner's and Sons.

Hoyt, Edwin. 1970. *The Amistad Affair*. New York: Abelard-Schuman.

Hudson, Harold Gossie. 1976. "John Chavis." In *Dictionary of Negro Biography*. Edited by Rayford W. Logan and Michael R. Winston. New York: Norton.

Huggins, Nathan Irvin. 1977. *Black Odyssey: The Afro-American Ordeal in Slavery*. New York: Pantheon Books.

Hurmence, Belinda. 1989. *Before Freedom: When I Just Can Remember*. Winston-Salem, NC: John Blair.

Hutchinson, Louise Daniel. 1981. *Anna J. Cooper: A Voice from the South*. Washington, DC: Smithsonian Institution Press.

Jacoway, Elizabeth. 1980. *Yankee Missionaries in the South: The Penn School Experiment*. Baton Rouge: Louisiana State University Press.

Jaffa, Harry. 1959. *Crisis of the House Divided: An Interpretation of the Lincoln-Douglas Debates*. Garden City, NY: Doubleday.

James, Isaac. 1954. *"The Sun Do Move": The Story of the Life of John Jasper*. Richmond, VA: Whittet and Shepperson.

Jay, William. 1853. "Introductory Remarks to the Reproof of the American Church Contained in the Recent *History of the Protestant Episcopal Church in America* by the Bishop of Oxford." In *Miscellaneous Writings on Slavery*. Boston: John P. Jewett.

Jefferson, Thomas. 1955. *Notes on Virginia*. Edited by William Peden. Chapel Hill: University of North Carolina Press.

———. 1950–. *The Papers of Thomas Jefferson*. 20 vols. Edited by Julian P. Boyd. Princeton, NJ: Princeton University Press.

Jeffreys, M. D. W. 1948. "Names of American Negro Slaves." *American Anthropologist* 50: 571–573.

Jenkins, Everett, Jr., ed. 1996. *Pan-African Chronology: A Comprehensive Reference to the Black Quest for Freedom in Africa, the Americas, Europe and Asia, 1400–1865*. New York: McFarland and Company.

Jennings, Thelma. 1980. *The Nashville Convention: Southern Movement for Unity, 1848–1851*. Memphis, TN: Memphis State University Press.

Johannsen, Robert. 1989. *The Frontier, the Union, and Stephen A. Douglas*. Urbana: University of Illinois Press.

———. 1991. *Lincoln, the South, and Slavery: The Political Dimension*. Baton Rouge: Louisiana State University Press.

———. 1973. *Stephen A. Douglas*. New York: Oxford University Press.

Johnson, Clifton Herman. 1958. *The American Missionary Association, 1846–1861: A Study of Christian Abolitionism*. Ph.D. dissertation, Department of History, University of North Carolina at Chapel Hill. Ann Arbor, MI: University Microfilms.

Johnson, Harry H. 1910. *The Negro in the New World*. London: Methuen.

Johnson, Michael P., and James L. Roark. 1984. *Black Masters: A Free Family of Color in the Old South*. New York: W. W. Norton.

———. 1982. "'A Middle Ground': Free Mulattoes and the Friendly Moralist Society of Ante-bellum Charleston." *Southern Studies* 21 (3): 246–265.

Johnson, Michael P., and James L. Roark, eds. 1984. *No Chariot Let Down: Charleston's Free People of Color on the Eve of the Civil War*. New York: Norton.

Johnson, Rossiter. 1879. "Richard Realf." *Lippincott's Magazine* 3: 293–300.

Johnson, Vicki Vaughn. 1992. *The Men and the Vision of the Southern Commercial Conventions, 1845–1871*. Columbia: University of Missouri Press.

Jones, Alfred Haworth. 1983. "Joel Chandler Harris: Tales of Uncle Remus." *American History Illustrated* 18 (3): 34–39.

Jones, Bessie, and Bess Lomax Hawes. 1987. *Step It Down: Games, Plays, Songs, and Stories from the Afro-American Heritage*. Athens: University of Georgia Press.

Jones, Howard. 1987. *Mutiny on the Amistad: The Saga of a Slave Revolt and Its Impact on American Abolition, Law, and Diplomacy*. New York: Oxford University Press.

———. 1977. *To the Webster-Ashburton Treaty: A Study in Anglo-American Relations, 1783–1843.* Chapel Hill: University of North Carolina Press.

Jones-Jackson, Patricia. 1987. *When Roots Die: Endangered Traditions on the Sea Islands.* Athens: University of Georgia Press.

Jordan, Winthrop D. 1993. *Tumult and Silence at Second Creek: An Inquiry into a Civil War Slave Conspiracy.* Baton Rouge: Louisiana State University Press.

———. 1974. *The White Man's Burden: Historical Origins of Racism in the United States.* London: Oxford University Press.

———. 1968. *White over Black: American Attitudes toward the Negro, 1550–1812.* Baltimore: Penguin Books.

Jordon, Weymouth T. 1958. *Rebels in the Making: Planters' Conventions and Southern Propaganda.* Tuscaloosa, AL: Confederate Publishing.

Joyner, Charles. 1984. *Down by the Riverside: A South Carolina Slave Community.* Urbana: University of Illinois Press.

Karcher, Carolyn L. 1994. *The First Woman in the Republic: A Cultural Biography of Lydia Maria Child.* Durham, NC: Duke University Press.

Katz, William L. 1990. *Breaking the Chains: African-American Slave Resistance.* New York: Atheneum.

Keane, John. 1995. *Tom Paine: A Political Life.* London: Bloomsbury.

Keckley, Elizabeth. 1868. *Behind the Scenes: Thirty Years a Slave and Four Years in the White House.* New York: G. W. Carleton.

Keene, Jesse L. 1961. *The Peace Convention of 1861.* Tuscaloosa, AL: Confederate Publishing.

Kehoe, Alice Beck. 1992. *North American Indians: A Comprehensive Account.* Englewood Cliffs, NJ: Prentice-Hall.

Keller, Frances Richardson. 1978. *An American Crusade: The Life of Charles Waddell Chesnutt.* Provo, UT: Brigham Young University Press.

Kelso, William M. 1984. *Kingsmill Plantations, 1619–1800: Archaeology of Country Life in Colonial Virginia.* San Diego: Academic Press.

Kemble, Frances Anne. 1863. Journal of a Residence on a Georgian Plantation in 1838–1839. New York: Harper and Brothers.

Kerr, Andrea Moore. 1992. *Lucy Stone: Speaking Out for Equality.* New Brunswick, NJ: Rutgers University Press.

Killens, John Oliver. 1970. *The Trial Record of Denmark Vesey.* Boston: Beacon Press.

Kim, Hyong-In. 1990. "Rural Slavery in Antebellum South Carolina and Early Choson Korea." Ph.D. dissertation. Department of History, University of New Mexico, Albuquerque, New Mexico.

King, Wilma. 1995. *Stolen Childhood: Slave Youth in Nineteenth Century America.* Bloomington: Indiana University Press.

Kiple, Kenneth F. 1988. "Diet." In *Dictionary of Afro-American Slavery.* Edited by Randall M. Miller and John David Smith. New York: Greenwood Press.

Kiple, Kenneth F., and Virginia Himmelsteib King. 1981. *Another Dimension of the Black Diaspora: Diet, Disease, and Racism.* Cambridge: Cambridge University Press.

Kirkham, Bruce E. 1977. *The Building of Uncle Tom's Cabin,* Knoxville: University of Tennessee Press.

Kirwan, Albert D. 1962. *John J. Crittenden: The Struggle for the Union.* Lexington: University of Kentucky Press.

Klein, Aaron E. 1971. *The Hidden Contributors: Black Scientists and Inventors in America.* New York: Doubleday and Company.

Klein, Herbert S. 1967. *Slavery in the Americas: A Comparative Study of Virginia and Cuba.* Chicago: University of Chicago Press.

Klein, Philip S. 1962. *President James Buchanan: A Biography.* University Park: Pennsylvania State University Press.

Knight, Edgar W. 1930. "Notes on John Chavis." *North Carolina Historical Review* 7: 326–345.

Koger, Larry. 1985. *Black Slaveowners: Free Black Slave Masters in South Carolina, 1790–1860.* Jefferson, NC: McFarland.

Kolchin, Peter. 1993. *American Slavery, 1619–1877.* New York: Hill and Wang.

———. 1987. *Unfree Labor: American Slavery and Russian Serfdom.* Cambridge, MA: Harvard University Press.

Korn, Bertram Wallace. 1973. *Jews and Negro Slavery in the Old South.* In *Jews in the South.* Edited by Leonard Dinnerstein and Mary Dale Palsson. Baton Rouge: Louisiana State University Press.

Kotlikoff, Laurence J., and Sebastian Pinera. 1977. "The Old South's Stake in the Inter-Regional Movement of Slaves, 1850–1860." *Journal of Economic History* 37 (2): 434–450.

Kraditor, Aileen S. 1969. *Means and Ends in American Abolitionism: Garrison and His Critics on Strategy and Tactics, 1834–1850.* New York: Pantheon Books.

Kurland, Phillip B., and Lerner, Ralph. 1987. *The Founders' Constitution.* Chicago: University of Chicago Press.

Lambert, Frank. 1994. *Peddler in Divinity: George Whitefield and the Transatlantic Revivals.* Princeton, NJ: Princeton University Press.

Lane, Ann J., ed. 1971. *The Debate over Slavery: Stanley Elkins and His Critics.* Urbana: University of Illinois Press.

Lane, Margaret. 1972. *Frances Wright and the "Great Experiment."* Manchester, Eng.: Manchester University Press.

Larison, Cornelius Wilson. 1988. *Sylvia Dubois: A Biografy of the Slav Who Whipt Her Mistres and Gand Her Fredom.* Edited by Jared C. Lobdell. New York: Oxford University Press.

Lauber, Almon Wheeler. 1969. *Indian Slavery in Colonial Times within the Present Limits of the United States.* New York: AMS Press.

Laurie, Bruce. 1989. *Artisans into Workers: Labor in Nineteenth Century America.* New York: Noonday Press.

Learned, H. Barrett. 1958. "William L. Marcy." In *The American Secretaries of State and Their Diplomacy,* Volume 6. 17 vols. Edited by Samuel Flagg Bemis. New York: Pageant Book Company.

Leonard, Ira M., and Robert D. Parmet. 1971. *American Nativism, 1830–1860.* New York: Van Nostrand Reinhold.

Lerner, Gerda. 1964. *The Grimké Sisters from South Carolina*. Boston: Houghton Mifflin.

Levine, Lawrence W. 1977. *Black Culture and Black Consciousness: Afro-American Folk Thought from Slavery to Freedom*. Oxford: Oxford University Press.

Levine, Robert. 1997. *Martin R. Delany, Frederick Douglass, and the Politics of Representative Identity*. Chapel Hill: University of North Carolina Press.

Levy, Leonard W., and Dennis J. Mahoney, eds. 1987. *The Framing of the Constitution*. New York: Macmillan.

Lewis, David Levering. 1993. *W. E. B. DuBois: Biography of a Race*. New York: Henry Holt.

Lincoln, C. Eric. 1984. *Race, Religion, and the Continuing American Dilemma*. New York: Hill and Wang.

Lindsay, Arnett. 1920. "Diplomatic Relations between the United States and Great Britain Bearing on the Return of Negro Slaves, 1788–1828." *Journal of Negro History* 5: 261–278.

Littlefield, Daniel C. 1991. *Rice and Slaves*. Urbana: University of Illinois Press.

Litwack, Leon. 1979. *Been in the Storm So Long: The Aftermath of Slavery*. New York: Vintage Books.

Lively, Donald E. 1992. *The Constitution and Race*. New York: Praeger.

Livermore, George. 1970. *An Historical Research Respecting the Opinions of the Founders of the Republic on Negroes as Slaves, as Citizens, and as Soldiers*. New York: Augustus M. Kelley.

Llowance, Mason I. Jr.; Ellen E. Westbrook; and R. C. DeProspo, eds. 1994. *The Stowe Debate: Rhetorical Strategies in Uncle Tom's Cabin*. Amherst: University of Massachusetts Press.

Lloyd, Arthur Young. 1939. *The Slavery Controversy, 1831–1860*. Chapel Hill: University of North Carolina Press.

Lloyd, Christopher. 1949. *The Navy and the Slave Trade*. London: Longmans.

Lobb, John, ed. 1971. *"Uncle Tom's Story of His Life": An Autobiography of the Rev. Josiah Henson*. London: Frank Cass and Company.

Lofton, John. 1948. "Denmark Vesey's Call to Arms." *Journal of Negro History* 33 (4): 395–417.

———. 1964. *Insurrection in South Carolina: The Turbulent World of Denmark Vesey*. Yellow Springs, OH: Antioch Press.

Logan, Shirley Wilson. 1995. *With Pen and Voice: A Critical Anthology of Nineteenth-Century African-American Women*. Carbondale: Southern Illinois University Press.

Loveland, Anne C. 1966. "Evangelicalism and 'Immediate Emancipation' in American Antislavery Thought." *Journal of Southern History* 32 (2): 172–188.

Lumpkin, Katharine Du Pre. 1974. *The Emancipation of Angelina Grimké*. Chapel Hill: University of North Carolina Press.

Luraghi, Raimondo. 1978. *The Rise and Fall of the Plantation South*. New York: New Viewpoints.

Lutz, Alma. 1968. *Crusade for Freedom: Women in the Antislavery Movement*. Boston: Beacon Press.

Mabee, Carlton. 1970. *Black Freedom: The Nonviolent Abolitionists from 1830 through the Civil War*. New York: Macmillan.

———. 1993. *Sojourner Truth: Slave, Prophet, Legend*. New York: New York University Press.

McAdoo, Bill. 1983. *Pre–Civil War Black Nationalism*. New York: David Walker Press.

McClendon, R. Earl. 1933. "The *Amistad* Claims: Inconsistencies of Policy." *Political Science Quarterly* 48: 386–412.

McCurry, Stephanie. 1995. *Masters of Small Worlds: Yeoman Households, Gender Relations, and the Political Culture of the Antebellum South Carolina Low Country*. New York: Oxford University Press.

Macdonald, Robert R.; John R. Kemp; and Edward F. Hass, eds. 1979. *Louisiana's Black Heritage*. New Orleans: Louisiana State Museum.

McFeely, William S. 1991. *Frederick Douglass*. New York: W. W. Norton.

McGowan, James A. 1977. *Station Master on the Underground Railroad: The Life and Letters of Thomas Garrett*. Moylan, PA: Whimsie Press.

McKitrick, Eric L., ed. 1963. *Slavery Defended: The Views of the Old South*. Englewood Cliffs, NJ: Prentice-Hall.

McManus, Edgar. 1966. *A History of Negro Slavery in New York*. Syracuse, NY: Syracuse University Press.

McPherson, James. 1964. *The Struggle for Equality: Abolitionists and the Negro in the Civil War and Reconstruction*. Princeton, NJ: Princeton University Press.

McReynolds, Edwin C. 1988. *The Seminoles*. Norman: University of Oklahoma Press.

Maddex, Jack P., Jr. 1979. "'The Southern Apostasy' Revisited: The Significance of Proslavery Christianity." *Marxist Perspectives* 2 (Fall): 132–141.

Mails, Thomas E. 1992. *The Cherokee People: The Story of the Cherokees from Earliest Origins to Contemporary Times*. Tulsa, OK: Council Oaks Books.

Maizlish, Stephen E. 1982. "The Meaning of Nativism and the Crisis of the Union; The Know Nothing Movement in the Antebellum North." In *Essays on American Antebellum Politics, 1840–1860*. Edited by Stephen E. Maizlish and John J. Kushma. College Station: Texas A & M University Press.

Malin, James C. 1942. *John Brown and the Legend of Fifty-six*. Philadelphia: American Philosophical Society.

Malone, Dumas, and Allen Johnson, eds. 1930. *Dictionary of American Biography*. New York: Charles Scribner's Sons.

Maltz, Earl M. 1990. *Civil Rights, the Constitution, and Congress, 1863–1869*. Lawrence: University Press of Kansas.

Manning, William, ed. 1942. *Diplomatic Correspondence of the United States: Canadian Relations, 1794–1860*. Washington, DC: Carnegie Endowment for International Peace.

Marambaud, Pierre. 1971. *William Byrd of Westover*. Charlottesville: University of Virginia Press.

Marcus, Jacob R. 1970. *The Colonial American Jew 1492–1776*. Detroit: Wayne State University Press.

Martin, Berbard, and Mark Spurrell. 1962. *The Journal of A Slave Trader, John Newton, 1750–1754*. London: Epworth Press.

Mason, Julian D., Jr., ed. 1989. *The Poems of Phillis*

Wheatley. Chapel Hill: University of North Carolina Press.

Mathew, William M. 1988. *Edmund Ruffin and the Crisis of Slavery in the Old South: The Failure of Agricultural Reform*. Athens: University of Georgia Press.

Mathews, Donald G. 1977. *Religion in the Old South*. Chicago: University of Chicago Press.

May, Robert E. 1985. *John A. Quitman: Old South Crusader*. Baton Rouge: Louisiana State University Press.

———. 1973. *The Southern Dream of a Caribbean Empire 1854–1861*. Baton Rouge: Louisiana State University Press.

Mayfield, John. 1979. *Rehearsal for Republicanism: Free Soil and the Politics of Antislavery*. Port Washington, NY: Kennikat Press.

Meade, George P. 1946. "A Negro Scientist of Slavery Days." *Scientific Monthly* 62: 317–326.

Meadows, Henry H. 1914. "The Police Control of the Slave in South Carolina." Unpublished manuscript, Emory University, Atlanta, GA.

Meier, August. 1963. *Negro Thought in America, 1880–1915*. Ann Arbor: University of Michigan Press.

Meltzer, Milton, and Patricia G. Holland, eds. 1982. *Lydia Maria Child: Selected Letters, 1817–1880*. Amherst: University of Massachusetts Press.

Mencken, H. L. 1955. *The American Language*. 4th edition. New York: Knopf.

Merideth, Robert. 1968. *The Politics of the Universe: Edward Beecher, Abolition, and Orthodoxy*. Nashville, TN: Vanderbilt University Press.

Merrill, Walter M. 1963. *Against Wind and Tide: A Biography of William Lloyd Garrison*. Cambridge, MA: Harvard University Press.

Merritt, Elizabeth. 1923. *James Henry Hammond, 1807–1864*. Baltimore: Johns Hopkins University Press.

Messmer, S. G., ed. 1908. *The Works of the Right Reverend John England, First Bishop of Charleston, Volume 5*. Cleveland, OH: Arthur H. Clark Co.

Miller, Edward A. 1995. *Gullah Statesman: Robert Smalls from Slavery to Congress, 1839–1915*. Columbia: University of South Carolina Press.

Miller, Floyd J. 1975. *The Search for a Black Nationality: Black Colonization and Emigration, 1787–1863*. Urbana: University of Illinois Press.

Miller, John C. 1977. *The Wolf by the Ears: Thomas Jefferson and Slavery*. New York: Norton.

Miller, Kelly. 1916. "The Historic Background of the Negro Physician." *Journal of Negro History* 1 (2): 99–109.

Miller, M. Sammy. 1975. "Legend of a Kidnapper" *Crisis* 82 (April): 118–120.

Miller, Randall M., and John David Smith, eds. 1988. *Dictionary of Afro-American Slavery*. Westport, CT: Greenwood.

Miller, William Lee. 1996. *Arguing about Slavery: The Great Battle in the United States Congress*. New York: Knopf.

Mills, Bruce. 1994. *Cultural Reformations: Lydia Maria Child and the Literature of Reform*. Athens: University of Georgia Press.

Mirsky, Jeannette, and Allan Nevins. 1952. *The World of Eli Whitney*. New York: Macmillan.

Mitchell, Betty. 1981. *Edmund Ruffin, a Biography*. Bloomington: Indiana University Press.

Mohr, Clarence L. 1986. *On the Threshold of Freedom: Masters and Slaves in Civil War Georgia*. Athens: University of Georgia Press.

Monaghan, Jay. 1955. *Civil War on the Western Border, 1854–1865*. Boston: Little, Brown and Company.

Monfredo, Miriam Grace. 1993. *North Star Conspiracy*. New York: Berkley Publishing Group.

Montgomery, Michael, ed. 1994. *The Crucible of Carolina: Essays in the Development of Gullah Language and Culture*. Athens: University of Georgia Press.

Mooney, James L., ed. 1991. *Dictionary of American Naval Fighting Ships*. Washington, DC: Naval Historical Center.

Moore, Glover. 1953. *The Missouri Controversy, 1819–1821*. Lexington: University of Kentucky Press.

Moore, J. Preston. 1955. "Pierre Soulé: Southern Expansionist and Promoter." *Journal of Southern History* 21 (May): 203–223.

Moore, John Hebron. 1958. *Agriculture in Ante-Bellum Mississippi*. New York: Bookman Associates.

———. 1988. *The Emergence of the Cotton Kingdom in the Old Southwest: Mississippi, 1770–1860*. Baton Rouge: Louisiana State University Press.

Moore, Wayne D. 1996. *Constitutional Rights and Powers of the People*. Princeton, NJ: Princeton University Press.

Morais, Herbert M. 1969. *The History of the Negro in Medicine*. New York: Publishers Company.

Morgan, Edmund. 1975. *American Slavery, American Freedom: The Ordeal of Colonial Virginia*. New York: Norton.

Morris, Christopher. 1988. "An Event in Community Organization: The Mississippi Slave Insurrection Scare of 1835." *Journal of Social History* 22 (3): 93–111.

Morris, Richard B. 1946. *Government and Labor in Early America*. New York: Columbia University Press.

Morris, Robert. 1981. *Reading, 'Riting, and Reconstruction: The Education of Freedmen in the South, 1861–1870*. Chicago: University of Chicago Press.

Morris, Thomas D. 1974. *Free Men All: The Personal Liberty Laws of the North, 1780–1861*. Baltimore: Johns Hopkins University Press.

———. 1996. *Southern Slavery and the Law, 1619–1860*. Chapel Hill: University of North Carolina Press.

Morrison, Chaplain W. 1967. *Democratic Politics and Sectionalism: The Wilmot Proviso Controversy*. Chapel Hill: University of North Carolina Press.

Morriss, Andrew P. 1995. "'This State Will Soon Have Plenty of Laws'—Lessons from One Hundred Years of Codification in Montana." *Montana Law Review* 56: 359–450.

Morton, Patricia, ed. 1996. *Discovering the Women in Slavery: Emancipating Perspectives on the American Past*. Athens: University of Georgia Press.

Moulton, Phillips P. "The Influence of the Writings of John Woolman." *Quaker History: The Bulletin of the Friends Historical Association* 61 (2): 3–13.

Mullin, Gerald W. 1972. *Flight and Rebellion: Slave Resistance in Eighteenth Century Virginia*. New York: Oxford University Press.

Mullin, Michael. 1992. *Africa in America: Slave Acculturation and Resistance in the American South and the British Caribbean, 1736–1831*. Urbana: University of Illinois Press.

Munroe, John A. 1979. *History of Delaware*. Newark: University of Delaware Press.

Murphy, Larry, J.; Gordon Melton; and Gary L. Ward, eds. 1993. *Encyclopedia of African-American Religions*. New York: Garland.

Myerson, Joel, ed. 1984. *The Transcendentalists: A Review of Research and Criticism*. New York: Modern Language Association of America.

Nash, Gary B. 1988. *Forging Freedom: The Formation of Philadelphia's Black Community, 1720–1840*. Cambridge, MA: Harvard University Press.

———. 1989. "New Light on Richard Allen: The Early Years of Freedom." *William and Mary Quarterly* 46 (2): 332–340.

Nash, Gary B., et al. 1994. *The American People: Creating a Nation and a Society*. New York: HarperCollins.

Needles, Edward. 1848. *An Historical Memoir of the Pennsylvania Society, for Promoting the Abolition of Slavery; Relief of Free Negroes Unlawfully Held in Bondage, and for Improving the Condition of the African Race. Compiled from the Minutes of the Society and Other Official Documents*. Philadelphia: Pennsylvania Abolition Society.

Nelson, William Edward. 1995. *The Fourteenth Amendment: From Political Principle to Judicial Doctrine*. Cambridge, MA: Harvard University Press.

Newman, Richard, ed. 1990. *Black Preacher to White America: The Collected Writings of Lemuel Haynes, 1774–1833*. Brooklyn, NY: Carlson.

Newton, James, and Ronald Lewis, eds. 1978. *The Other Slaves: Mechanics, Artisans, and Craftsmen*. Boston: G. K. Hall.

Nichols, Alice. 1954. *Bleeding Kansas*. New York: Oxford University Press.

Nichols, Charles H. 1963. *Many Thousand Gone: The Ex-Slaves' Account of Their Bondage and Freedom*. Bloomington: Indiana University Press.

Nichols, Roy F. 1948. *The Disruption of American Democracy*. New York: Macmillan.

Northup, Solomon. 1968. *Twelve Years a Slave*. Edited by Sue Eakin and Joseph Logsdon. Baton Rouge: Louisiana State University Press.

Nott, Josiah Clark. 1849. *Connection between the Biblical and Physical History of Man*. New York: Bartlett and Welford.

Nott, Josiah Clark, and George R. Gliddon. 1857. *Indigenous Races of the Earth*. Philadelphia: Lippincott.

———. 1854. *Types of Mankind*. Philadelphia: Lippincott, Grambo, and Company.

Novak, John E., and Ronald D. Rotunda. 1991. *Constitutional Law*. St. Paul, MN: West Publishing.

Nye, Russell B. 1963. *Fettered Freedom: Civil Liberties and the Slave Controversy, 1830–1860*. East Lansing: Michigan State University Press.

Oakes, James. 1982. *The Ruling Race*. New York: Knopf.

Oates, Stephen B. 1990. *The Fires of Jubilee: Nat Turner's Fierce Rebellion*. New York: Harper and Row.

———. 1970. *To Purge This Land with Blood: A Biography of John Brown*. New York: Harper and Row.

———. 1977. *With Malice toward None: The Life of Abraham Lincoln*. New York: Harper and Row.

Odum, Howard W. 1936. *Southern Regions of the United States*. Chapel Hill: North Carolina University Press.

Ogilvie, Marilyn Bailey. 1986. *Women in Science: Antiquity through the Nineteenth Century*. Cambridge, MA: MIT Press.

Oglethorpe, James Edward. 1994. *The Publications of James Edward Oglethorpe*. Edited by Rodney M. Baine. Athens: University of Georgia Press.

Olmsted, Denison. 1846. *Memoir of Eli Whitney, Esq.* New York: Arno Press.

O'Neale, Sondra A. 1985. "Challenge to Wheatley's Critics: There Was No Other 'Game' in Town." *Journal of Negro Education* 54 (4): 500–511.

Onuf, Peter. 1987. *Statehood and Union: A History of the Northwest Ordinance*. Bloomington: Indiana University Press.

Owens, Leslie H. 1976. *This Species of Property: Slave Life and Culture in the Old South*. New York: Oxford University Press.

Owsley, Frank L. 1949. *Plain Folk of the Old South*. Baton Rouge: Louisiana State University Press.

Painter, Nell Irvin. 1988. "Martin R. Delany: Elitism and Black Nationalism." In *Black Leaders of the Nineteenth Century*. Edited by Leon Litwack and August Meier. Urbana: University of Illinois Press.

———. 1996. *Sojourner Truth: A Life, a Symbol*. New York: W. W. Norton.

Paludan, Phillip Shaw. 1994. *The Presidency of Abraham Lincoln*. Lawrence: University Press of Kansas.

Pasternak, Martin B. 1995. *Rise Now and Fly to Arms: The Life of Henry Highland Garnet*. New York: Garland.

Paustian, P. Robert. 1978. "The Evolution of Personal Naming Practices among American Blacks." *Names* 26 (1): 177–191.

Payne, Charles Edward. 1938. *Josiah B. Grinnell*. Iowa City: State Historical Society of Iowa.

Payne, Daniel Alexander. 1891. *History of the African Methodist Episcopal Church*. Nashville, TN: Publishing House of the A.M.E. Sunday School Union.

Pearson, Edward A. 1992. "From Stono to Vesey: Slavery, Resistance, and Ideology in South Carolina, 1739–1822." Ph.D. dissertation, Department of History, University of Wisconsin–Madison, Madison, Wisconsin.

Pease, Jane H. 1969. "The Freshness of Fanaticism: Abby Kelley Foster." Ph.D. dissertation, Department of History, University of Rochester, Rochester, New York.

Pease, Jane H., and William H. 1975. *The Fugitive Slave Law and Anthony Burns: A Problem of Law Enforcement*. Philadelphia: J. B. Lippincott.

———. 1990. *They Who Would be Free: Blacks' Search for Freedom, 1830–1861*. Chicago: University of Chicago Press.

Pease, William H., and Jane H. 1995. *James Louis Petigru:*

Southern Conservative, Southern Dissenter. Athens: University of Georgia Press.

———. 1971. "The Negro Convention Movement." In *Key Issues in the Afro-American Experience.* Edited by Nathan I. Higgins et al. New York: Harcourt Brace Jovanovich.

Peck, Abraham J. 1987. "'That Other Peculiar Institution': Jews and Judaism in the Nineteenth Century South." *Modern Judaism* 7: 99–114.

Peek, Phil. 1978. "Afro-American Material *Culture and the Afro-American Craftsman." Southern Folklore Quarterly* 42 (2–3): 109–134.

Pemberton, Doris Hollis. 1983. *Juneteenth at Comanche Crossing.* Austin, TX: Eakin Publications.

Penick, James L., Jr. 1981. *The Great Western Land Pirate: John A. Murrell in Legend and History.* Columbia: University of Missouri Press.

Perdue, Charles L., et al. 1976. *Weevils in the Wheat: Interviews with Virginia Ex-Slaves.* Charlottesville: University Press of Virginia.

Perdue, Theda. 1979. "The Development of Plantation Slavery before Removal." In *The Cherokee Indian Nation, a Troubled History.* Edited by Duane H. King. Knoxville: University of Tennessee Press.

———. 1996. "Slavery." In *Encyclopedia of North American Indians.* Edited by Frederick E. Hoxie. New York: Houghton Mifflin.

———. 1979. *Slavery and the Evolution of Cherokee Society, 1540–1866.* Knoxville: University of Tennessee Press.

Perry, Michael. 1994. *The Constitution in the Courts: Law or Politics?* New York: Oxford University Press.

Perskey, Joseph. 1992. "Unequal Exchange and Dependency Theory in George Fitzhugh." *History of Political Economy* 24 (1) (Spring): 117–128.

Peterson, Merrill. 1987. *The Great Triumvirate: Webster, Clay, and Calhoun.* New York: Oxford University Press.

———. 1962. *The Jefferson Image in the American Mind.* New York: Oxford University Press.

Phillips, Ulrich B. 1918. *American Negro Slavery.* Gloucester, MA: D. Appleton and Company

Pinkney, Alphonso. 1976. *Red, Black, and Green: Black Nationalism in the United States.* Cambridge: Cambridge University Press.

Ploski, Harry A., and James Williams, eds. 1989. *The Negro Almanac: A Reference Work on the African American.* New York: Gale Research Inc.

Post, C. Gordon, ed. 1953. *A Disquisition on Government and Selections from the Discourse.* New York: Liberal Arts Press.

Potter, David M. 1976. *The Impending Crisis, 1848–1861.* New York: Harper and Row.

Price, Richard. 1983. *First Time: The Historical Vision of an Afro-American People.* Baltimore: Johns Hopkins University Press.

Puckett, Newbell N. 1938. "American Negro Names." *Journal of Negro History* 23: 35–48.

———. 1975. *Black Names in America.* Boston: G. K. Hall.

———. 1937. "Names of American Negro Slaves." In *Studies in the Science of Society.* Edited by G. P. Murdock. New Haven, CT: Yale University Press.

Pulis, John W., ed. 1997. *Moving On: Black Loyalists in the Afro-Atlantic World.* New York: Garland.

Quarles, Benjamin. 1974. *Allies For Freedom: Blacks and John Brown.* New York:

———. 1969. *Black Abolitionists.* New York: Oxford University Press.

———. 1968. *Frederick Douglass.* New York: Oxford University Press.

———. 1962. *Lincoln and the Negro.* New York: Oxford University Press.

———. 1961. *The Negro in the American Revolution.* Chapel Hill: University of North Carolina Press.

———. 1953. *The Negro in the Civil War.* Boston: Little, Brown.

Raboteau, Albert J. 1978. *Slave Religion.* New York: Oxford University Press.

Randell, Willard Sterne. 1993. *Thomas Jefferson: A Life.* New York: Henry Holt.

Rawick, George P., ed. 1972. *The American Slave: A Composite Autobiography.* Westport, CT: Greenwood.

Rawley, James A. 1969. *Race and Politics: "Bleeding Kansas" and the Coming of the Civil War.* Philadelphia: J. B. Lippincott Company.

Rayback, Joseph G. 1971. *Free Soil: The Election of 1848.* Lexington: University Press of Kentucky.

———. 1948. "The Presidential Ambitions of John C. Calhoun, 1844–1848." *Journal of Southern History* 14 (3): 331–356.

Realf, Richard. 1860. Testimony in "Mason Report." In U.S. Congress, Senate. *Committee Reports, 1859–60.* January 11–21: 91–113.

Ream, Debbie Williams. 1993. "Mine Eyes Have Seen the Glory." *American History Illustrated* 27 (1): 60–64.

Reidy, Joseph P. 1992. *From Slavery to Agrarian Capitalism in the Cotton Plantation South: Central Georgia, 1800–1880.* Chapel Hill: University of North Carolina Press.

Reimers, David M. 1965. *White Protestantism and the Negro.* New York: Oxford University Press.

Remini, Robert. 1991. *Henry Clay: Statesman of the Republic.* New York: W. W. Norton.

Render, Sylvia Lyons. 1979. *Charles Waddell Chesnutt: Eagle with Clipped Wings.* Washington, DC: Howard University Press.

Renehan, Edward J., Jr. 1995. *The Secret Six: The True Tale of the Men Who Conspired with John Brown.* New York: Crown.

Rhodes, Jane. 1992. "Breaking the Editorial Ice: Mary Ann Shadd Cary and the Provincial Freeman." Ph.D. dissertation, Department of History, University of North Carolina at Chapel Hill.

Richards, Leonard L. 1970. *"Gentlemen of Property and Standing": Anti-Abolition Mobs in Jacksonian America.* New York: Oxford University Press.

———. 1986. *The Life and Times of Congressman John Quincy Adams.* New York: Oxford University Press.

Richardson, Joe M. 1986. *Christian Reconstruction: The American Missionary Association and Southern Blacks, 1861–1890.* Athens: University of Georgia Press.

Richardson, Marilyn, ed. 1987. *Maria W. Stewart:*

America's First Black Woman Political Writer. Bloomington: Indiana University Press.

Richardson, Robert D. 1986. *Henry Thoreau: A Life of the Mind.* Berkeley: University of California Press.

Riddleberger, Patrick W. 1966. *George Washington Julian, Radical Republican.* Indianapolis: Indiana Historical Bureau.

Ripley, C. Peter, ed. 1992. *The Black Abolitionist Papers.* Volume 5, *The United States, 1859–1865.* Chapel Hill: University of North Carolina Press.

Rippon, John, ed., 1801. *The Baptist Annual Register.* London: Brown and James.

Roane, Spencer. 1906. "Letters of Spencer Roane, 1788–1822." *New York Public Library Bulletin* 10: 167–180.

Robert, Joseph Clarke. 1941. *The Road from Monticello: A Study of the Virginia Slavery Debate of 1832.* Durham, NC: Duke University Press.

Roberts, John W. 1989. *From Trickster to Badman: The Black Folk Hero in Slavery and Freedom.* Philadelphia: University of Pennsylvania Press.

Roberts, Rita. 1994. "Patriotism and Political Criticism: The Evolution of Political Consciousness in the Mind of a Black Revolutionary Soldier." *Eighteenth Century Studies* 27 (Summer): 569–588.

Robinson, William H. 1981. *Phillis Wheatley: A Bio-Bibliography.* Boston: G. K. Hall.

———. 1984. *Phillis Wheatley and Her Writings.* New York: Garland.

Rodriguez, Junius Peter, Jr. 1992. "Ripe for Revolt: Louisiana and the Tradition of Slave Insurrection, 1803–1865." Ph.D. dissertation, Department of History, Auburn University, Auburn, Alabama.

Roediger, David R. 1991. *Wages of Whiteness: Race and the Making of the American Working Class.* London: Verso.

Rolfe, John. 1971. *A True Relation of the State of Virginia Lefte by Sir Thomas Dale, Knight, in May Last 1616.* Charlottesville: University Press of Virginia.

Roper, John Herbert. 1984. *U. B. Phillips: A Southern Mind.* Macon, GA: Mercer University Press.

Rose, Anne C. 1981. *Transcendentalism as a Social Movement, 1830–1850.* New Haven, CT: Yale University Press.

Rose, Willie Lee. 1964. *Rehearsal for Reconstruction: The Port Royal Experiment.* New York: Bobbs-Merrill.

Rossbach, Jeffrey. 1982. *Ambivalent Conspirators: John Brown, the Secret Six, and a Theory of Slave Violence.* Philadelphia: University of Pennsylvania Press.

Ruby, Robert H., and John A. Brown. 1993. *Indian Slavery in the Pacific Northwest.* Spokane, WA: Arthur H. Clark.

Rugoff, Milton. 1981. *The Beechers: An American Family in the Nineteenth Century.* New York: Harper and Row.

Russell, John H. 1916. "Colored Freeman as Slave Owners in Virginia." *Journal of Negro History* 1 (July): 233–242.

Saillant, John. 1994. "Lemuel Haynes' Black Republicanism and the American Republican Tradition, 1775–1820." *Journal of the Early Republic* 14 (3): 293–324.

Salitan, Lucille, and Eve Lewis Perera, eds. 1994. *Virtuous Lives: Four Quaker Sisters Remember Family Life, Abolitionism, and Women's Suffrage.* New York: Continuum.

Sallinger, Sharon. 1987. *"To Serve Well and Faithfully": Labor and Indentured Servants in Pennsylvania.* Cambridge: Cambridge University Press.

Salzman, Jack; David Lionel Smith; and Cornel West, eds. 1996. *Encyclopedia of African-American Culture and History.* New York: Macmillan Library Reference.

Scarupa, Harriet. 1995. "Learning from Ancestral Bones: New York's Exhumed African Past." *American Visions* (February/March): 18–21.

Schlesinger, Arthur M. Jr., ed. 1983. *The Almanac of American History.* Greenwich, CT: Bison Books.

Schor, Joel. 1977. *Henry Highland Garnet: A Voice of Black Radicalism in the Nineteenth Century.* Westport, CT: Greenwood.

Schwarz, Philip J. 1996. *Slave Laws in Virginia.* Athens: University of Georgia Press.

———. 1988. *Twice Condemned: Slaves and the Criminal Laws of Virginia, 1705–1865.* Baton Rouge: Louisiana State University Press.

Schweninger, Loren. 1979. *James T. Rapier and Reconstruction.* Chicago: University of Chicago Press.

———. 1990. "John Carruthers Stanly and the Anomaly of Black Slaveholding." *North Carolina Historical Review* 67 (April): 159–192.

Scott, Donald M. 1979. "Abolition as a Sacred Vocation." In *Antislavery Reconsidered: New Perspectives on the Abolitionists.* Edited by Lewis Perry and Michael Fellman. Baton Rouge: Louisiana State University Press.

Scott, John Anthony. 1961. "On the Authenticity of Fanny Kemble's Journal of a Residence on a Georgian Plantation in 1838–1839." *Journal of Negro History* 46: 233–242.

Sekora, John, and Darwin Turner, eds. 1982. *The Art of Slave Narrative: Original Essays in Criticism and Theory.* Macomb: Western Illinois University Press.

Selby, John. 1977. *Dunmore.* Williamsburg: Virginia Independence Bicentennial Commission.

Sellin, J. T. 1976. *Slavery and the Penal System.* New York: Elsevier.

Sensbach, Jon. 1991. *A Separate Canaan: The Making of an Afro-Moravian World in North Carolina, 1763–1856.* Ann Arbor, MI: University Microfilms.

Sewell, Richard H. 1976. *Ballots for Freedom: Antislavery Politics in the United States, 1837–1860.* New York: Oxford University Press.

———. 1988. *The House Divided: Sectionalism and Civil War, 1848–1865.* Baltimore: Johns Hopkins University Press.

Shapiro, Herbert. 1984. "The Impact of the Aptheker Thesis: A Retrospective View of American Negro Slave Revolts." *Science and Society* 48: 52–73.

Shaw, George C. 1931. *John Chavis.* Binghamton, NY: Rail-Ballou Press.

Shewmaker, Kenneth, ed. 1990. *Daniel Webster: The "Completest Man."* Hanover, NH: University Press of New England.

Shore, Laurence. 1986. *Southern Capitalists: The Ideological Leadership of an Elite, 1832–1885*. Chapel Hill: University of North Carolina Press.

Shyllon, Folarin. 1977. *James Ramsay: The Unknown Abolitionist*. Edinburgh: Canongate.

Siebert, Wilbur H. 1898. *The Underground Railroad from Slavery to Freedom*. New York: Macmillan.

Silverman, Jason H. 1992. "Ashley Wilkes Revisited: The Immigrant as Slaveowner in the Old South." *Journal of Confederate History* 7: 123–135.

———. 1980. "Kentucky, Canada, and Extradition: The Jesse Happy Case." *Filson Club History* 54 (January): 50–60.

———. 1997. "'The Law of the Land Is the Law': Antebellum Jews, Slavery, and the Old South." In *Struggles in the Promised Land: Towards a History of Black-Jewish Relations in America*. Edited by Cornel West and Jack Salzman. New York: Oxford University Press.

———. 1985. *Unwelcome Guests: Canada West's Response to American Fugitive Slaves, 1800–1865*. Millwood, NY: Associated Faculty Press.

Simmons, William, J. 1968. *Men of Mark: Eminent, Progressive, and Rising*. New York: Arno.

Simpson, John Eddins. 1973. *Howell Cobb: The Politics of Ambition*. Chicago: Adams Press.

Singleton, Theresa. 1991. "The Archaeology of Slave Life." In *Before Freedom Came: African-American Life in the Antebellum South*. Edited by Edward Campbell, Jr., and Kym Rice. Charlottesville: University Press of Virginia.

Singleton, Theresa A., ed. 1985. *The Archaeology of Slavery and Plantation Life*. Orlando, FL: Academic Press.

Sinha, Manisha. 1994. "The Counter-Revolution of Slavery: Class, Politics and Ideology in Antebellum South Carolina." Ph.D. dissertation, Department of History, Columbia University, New York, New York.

Skipper, Ottis Clark. 1958. *J. D. B. DeBow: Magazinist of the Old South*. Athens: University of Georgia Press.

Slaughter, Thomas P. 1991. *Bloody Dawn: The Christiana Riot and Racial Violence in the Antebellum North*. New York: Oxford University Press.

Smedley, R. C. 1969. *History of the Underground Railroad*. New York: Arno Press.

Smith, Abbot Emerson. 1947. *Colonists in Bondage: White Servitude and Convict Labor in America, 1607–1776*. Chapel Hill: University of North Carolina Press.

Smith, Craig R. 1989. *Defender of the Union: The Oratory of Daniel Webster*. New York: Greenwood.

Smith, Elbert B. 1975. *The Presidency of James Buchanan*. Lawrence: University Press of Kansas.

Smith, Hilrie Shelton. 1972. *In His Image, But . . . Racism in Southern Religion, 1780–1910*. Durham, NC: Duke University Press.

Smith, John David. 1991. *An Old Creed for the New South: Proslavery Ideology and Historiography, 1865–1818*. Athens: University of Georgia Press.

Smith, John David, and John C. Inscoe, eds. 1993. *Ulrich Bonnell Phillips: A Southern Historian and His Critics*. Athens: University of Georgia Press.

Smith, Julia Floyd. 1985. *Slavery and Rice Culture in Low Country Georgia, 1750–1860*. Knoxville: University of Tennessee Press.

Smith, Page. 1976. *Jefferson: A Revealing Biography*. New York: American Heritage.

Smith, Venture. 1971. *A Narrative of the Life and Adventures of Venture Smith*. Boston: Beacon Press.

Snay, Mitchell. 1989. "American Thought and Southern Distinctiveness: The Southern Clergy and the Sanctification of Slaves." *Civil War History* 35 (4) (December): 311–328.

———. 1993. *Gospel of Disunion: Religion and Separatism in the Antebellum South*. Cambridge: Cambridge University Press.

Sobel, Mechal. 1987. *The World They Made Together: Black and White Values in Eighteenth-Century Virginia*. Princeton, NJ: Princeton University Press.

Soderlund, Jean R. 1994. "Priorities and Power: The Philadelphia Female Anti-Slavery Society." In *The Abolitionist Sisterhood: Women's Political Culture in Antebellum America*. Edited by Jean Fagan Yellin and John C. Van Horne. Ithaca, NY: Cornell University Press.

———. 1985. *Quakers and Slavery: A Divided Spirit*. Princeton, NJ: Princeton University Press.

Spain, August O. 1951. *The Political Theory of John C. Calhoun*. New York: Bookman Associates.

Spalding, Phinizy. 1977. *Oglethorpe in America*. Chicago: University of Chicago Press.

Spalding, Phinizy, and Harvey H. Jackson, eds. 1989. *Oglethorpe in Perspective: Georgia's Founder after Two Hundred Years*. Tuscaloosa: University of Alabama Press.

Stagg, J. C. A. 1983. *Mr. Madison's War: Politics, Diplomacy, and Warfare in the Early Republic*. Princeton, NJ: Princeton University Press.

Stampp, Kenneth M. 1990. *America in 1857: A Nation on the Brink*. New York: Oxford University Press.

———. 1942. "An Analysis of T. R. Dew's *Review of the Debate in the Virginia Legislature*." *Journal of Negro History* 27 (October): 380–387.

———. 1956. *The Peculiar Institution*. New York: Random House.

Stanley, A. Knighton. 1979. *The Children Is Crying: Congregationalism among Black People*. New York: Pilgrim Press.

Starling, Marion Wilson. 1981. *The Slave Narrative*. Boston: G. K. Hall.

Starobin, Robert S. 1970. *Denmark Vesey: The Slave Conspiracy of 1822*. Englewood Cliffs, NJ: Prentice-Hall.

Staudenraus, Philip J. 1961. *The African Colonization Movement, 1816–1865*. New York: Columbia University Press.

Stearns, Charles. 1969. *Narrative of Henry Box Brown*. Philadelphia: Rhetoric Publications.

Stephenson, Wendell. 1938. *Isaac Franklin: Slave Trader and Planter of the Old South*. Baton Rouge: Louisiana State University Press.

Stepto, Robert B. 1979. *From Behind the Veil: A Study of Afro-American Narrative*. Urbana: University of Illinois Press.

Sterkx, H. E. 1972. *The Free Negro in Ante-Bellum Louisiana.* Cranbury, NJ: Fairleigh Dickinson University.

Sterling, Dorothy. 1991. *Ahead of Her Time: Abby Kelley and the Politics of Anti-Slavery.* New York: W. W. Norton.

Sterling, Dorothy, ed. 1984. *We Are Your Sisters: Black Women in the Nineteenth Century.* New York: Norton.

Stevens, Charles Emery. 1973. *Anthony Burns: A History.* Williamstown, MA: Corner House Publishers.

Stevenson, Brenda. 1996. *Life in Black and White: Family and Community in the Slave South.* New York: Oxford University Press.

Stevenson, Brenda, ed. 1988. *The Journals of Charlotte Forten Grimké.* New York: Oxford University Press.

Stewart, James Brewer. 1976. *Holy Warriors: The Abolitionists and American Slavery.* New York: Hill and Wang.

———. 1970. *Joshua Giddings and the Tactics of Radical Politics.* Cleveland: Case Western University Press.

———. 1992. *William Lloyd Garrison and the Challenge of Emancipation.* Arlington Heights, IL: Harlan Davidson.

Still, William. 1883. *The Underground Railroad.* Philadelphia: William Still.

Stiller, Richard. 1972. *Commune on the Frontier: The Story of Frances Wright.* New York: Thomas Y. Crowell.

Stimson, John Ward. 1903. "An Overlooked American Shelley." *Arena* 7: 15–26.

Stuckey, Sterling. 1988. "A Last Stern Struggle: Henry Highland Garnet and Liberation Theory." In *Black Leaders of the Nineteenth Century.* Edited by Leon Litwack and August Meier. Urbana: University of Illinois Press.

———. 1987. *Slave Culture: Nationalist Theory and the Foundations of Black America.* New York: Oxford University Press.

Sutch, Richard. 1975. "The Breeding of Slaves for Sale and the Westward Expansion of Slavery." In *Race and Slavery in the Western Hemisphere.* Edited by Stanley L. Engerman and Eugene D. Genovese. Princeton, NJ: Princeton University Press.

———. 1975. "The Treatment Received by American Slaves: A Critical Review on the Evidence Presented in *Time on the Cross.*" *Explorations in Economic History* 12: 335–448.

Suttles, Wayne, ed. 1990. *Handbook of North American Indians: Northwest Coast.* Washington, DC: Smithsonian Institution.

Swerdlow, Amy. 1994. "Abolition's Conservative Sisters: The Ladies' New York City Anti-Slavery Societies, 1834–1840." In *The Abolitionist Sisterhood: Women's Political Culture in Antebellum America.* Edited by Jean Fagan Yellin and John C. Van Horne. Ithaca, NY: Cornell University Press.

Swisher, Carl. 1974. *History of the Supreme Court of the United States: The Taney Period, 1836–1864.* New York: Macmillan.

———. 1936. *Roger B. Taney.* New York: Macmillan.

Syrett, John. 1971. "The Confiscation Acts: Efforts at Reconstruction during the Civil War." M.A. thesis, Department of History, University of Wisconsin, Madison.

Tadman, Michael. 1989. *Speculators and Slaves: Masters, Traders, and Slaves in the Old South.* Madison: University of Wisconsin Press.

Tannenbaum, Frank. 1946. *Slave and Citizen: The Negro in the Americas.* New York: Vintage Books.

Taylor, Joe Gray. 1963. *Negro Slavery in Louisiana.* Baton Rouge: Louisiana Historical Association.

Taylor, Robert M., Jr., ed. 1987. *The Northwest Ordinance 1787: A Bicentennial Handbook.* Indianapolis: Indiana Historical Society.

Thomas, Benjamin P. 1950. *Theodore Dwight Weld: Crusader for Freedom.* New Brunswick, NJ: Rutgers University Press.

Thomas, John L. 1963. *The Liberator: William Lloyd Garrison.* Boston: Little, Brown.

Thomas, Karen M. 1992. "Juneteenth Remembers Slavery, Celebrates Freedom." *Chicago Tribune.* June18, final edition.

Thompson, Robert Farris. 1983. *Flash of the Spirit: African and Afro-American Art and Philosophy.* New York: Random House.

Thornton, John K. 1991. "African Dimensions of the Stono Rebellion." *American Historical Review* 96 (October): 1101–1113.

Thorpe, Earl. 1971. *Black Historians: A Critique.* New York: William Morrow.

Trefousse, Hans L. 1963. *Benjamin Franklin Wade: Radical Republican from Ohio.* New York: Twayne.

Trudel, Marcel. 1990. *Dictionnaire des esclaves et de leurs propriétaires au Canada Français.* Ville LaSalle, Quebec: Éditions Hurtubise.

———. 1960. *L'esclavage au Canada Français.* Quebec: Les Presses Universitaires Laval.

Trueblood, David Elton. 1966. *The People Called Quakers.* Richmond, IN: Friends United Press.

Truth, Sojourner. 1991. *Narrative of Sojourner Truth: A Bondswoman of Olden Time.* Edited by Olive Gilbert. New York: Oxford University Press.

Tucker, St. George, ed. 1996. *Blackstone's Commentaries.* 5 vols. Trenton, NJ: Law Book Exchange.

Tureaud, A. P., and C. C. Haydel. 1935. *The Negro in Medicine in Louisiana.* New Orleans: Amistad Research Center.

Turner, Edward Raymond. 1912. "The First Abolition Society in the United States." *Pennsylvania Magazine of History and Biography* 36: 92–109.

Tyler, Alice Felt. 1962. *Freedom's Ferment: Phases of American Social History from the Colonial Period to the Outbreak of the Civil War.* New York: Harper and Brothers.

U.S. Congress. Senate. 1856. *Report of the Decisions of the Commissioner of Claims under the Convention of February 8, 1833, between the United States and Great Britain, Transmitted to the Senate by the President of the United States, August 11, 1856.* Senate Executive Document 103, 34th Congress, 1st sess. Washington, DC: Nicholson.

Venable, Austin L. 1942. "The Conflict between the Douglas and Yancey Forces in the Charleston

Convention." *Journal of Southern History* 8 (May): 226–241.

———. 1945. "The Role of William L. Yancey in the Secession Movement." M.A. thesis, Department of History, Vanderbilt University, Nashville, Tennessee.

Venet, Wendy Hamand. 1991. *Neither Ballots nor Bullets: Women Abolitionists and the Civil War.* Charlottesville: University Press of Virginia.

Vlach, John Michael. 1978. *The Afro-American Tradition in Decorative Arts.* Cleveland: Cleveland Museum of Art.

———. 1993. *Back of the Big House: The Architecture of Plantation Slavery.* Chapel Hill: University of North Carolina Press.

———. 1991. *By the Work of Their Hands: Studies in Afro-American Folklife.* Ann Arbor, MI: UMI Research Press.

Wade, Richard C. 1964. *Slavery in the Cities: The South, 1820–1860.* Oxford: Oxford University Press.

Wagenknecht, Edward. 1965. *Harriet Beecher Stowe: The Known and the Unknown.* New York: Oxford University Press.

Waklyn, Jon L. 1973. *The Politics of a Literary Man: William Gilmore Simms.* Westport, CT: Greenwood.

Walker, David. 1829. *David Walker's Appeal to the Colored Citizens of the World, 1829–1830, Its Setting and Its Meaning, together with the Full Text of the Third, and Last, Edition of the Appeal.* New York: Humanities Press.

Walker, James. 1976. *The Black Loyalists.* New York: Africana.

Walters, Ronald G. 1978. *American Reformers, 1815–1860.* New York: Hill and Wang.

Walther, Eric H. 1992. *The Fire-Eaters.* Baton Rouge: Louisiana State University Press.

Walton, Augustus Q. 1835. *A History of the Detection, Conviction, Life, and Designs of John A. Murel, the Great Western Land Pirate.* Athens, TN: G. White.

Washington, John E. 1942. *They Knew Lincoln.* New York: E. P. Dutton.

Watson, Charles S. 1993. *From Nationalism to Secessionism: The Changing Fiction of William Gilmore Simms.* Westport, CT: Greenwood.

Watt, James. 1995. "James Ramsay, 1733–1789: Naval Surgeon, Naval Chaplain, and Morning Star of the Antislavery Movement." *Mariner's Mirror* 81 (2): 156–170.

Weatherford, Jack. 1991. *Native Roots: How the Indians Enriched America.* New York: Crown Publishers.

Webber, Thomas. 1978. *Deep Like the Rivers: Education in the Slave Quarter Community, 1831–1865.* New York: W. W. Norton.

Weinstein, Allen; Frank Otto Gatell; and David Sarasohn, eds. 1968. *American Negro Slavery: A Modern Reader.* New York: Oxford University Press.

Welch, Eloise Turner. 1976. *The Background and Development of the American Missionary Association's Decision to Educate Freedmen in the South, with Subsequent Repercussions.* Ph.D. dissertation. Ann Arbor, MI: University Microfilms.

Wells, Tom Henderson. 1968. *The Slave Ship Wanderer.* Athens: University of Georgia Press.

Welsch, Roger L. 1981. *Omaha Tribal Myths and Legends.* Chicago: Swallow Press.

Wender, Herbert. 1930. *Southern Commercial Conventions, 1837–1859.* Baltimore: Johns Hopkins Press.

Wesley, Charles. 1970. *The Fifteenth Amendment and Black America, 1870–1970.* Washington, DC: Associated Publishers.

Westwood, Howard C. 1992. *Black Troops, White Commanders, and Freedmen during the Civil War.* Carbondale: Southern Illinois University Press.

White, Deborah Gray. 1985. *Ar'n't I a Woman? Female Slaves in the Plantation South.* New York: Norton.

———. 1983. "Female Slaves: Sex Roles and Status in the Antebellum Plantation South." *Journal of Family History* 8 (Fall): 248–261.

Whitten, David O. 1981. *Andrew Durnford: A Black Sugar Planter in Antebellum Louisiana.* Natchitoches, LA: Northwestern State University.

Wiecek, William E. 1978. "Slavery and Abolition before the United States Supreme Court, 1820–1860." *Journal of American History* 65: 34–59.

———. 1977. *Sources of Anti-Slavery Constitutionalism.* Ithaca, NY: Cornell University Press.

Wiggins, William H. 1993. "Juneteenth: Tracking the Progress of an Emancipation Celebration." *American Visions* 8 (3) (June/July): 28–31.

———. 1987. *O Freedom! Afro-American Emancipation Celebrations.* Knoxville: University of Tennessee Press.

Wikramanayake, Marina. 1973. *A World in Shadow: The Free Black in Antebellum South Carolina.* Columbia: University of South Carolina Press.

Wilder, Daniel W. 1875. *The Annals of Kansas.* Topeka, KS: G. W. Martin.

Wiley, Bell I. 1938. *Southern Negroes, 1861–1865.* New Haven, CT: Yale University Press.

Wilkins, Thurman. 1988. *Cherokee Tragedy.* Norman: University of Oklahoma Press.

Williams, Carolyn. 1994. "The Female Antislavery Movement: Fighting against Racial Prejudice and Promoting Women's Rights in Antebellum America." In *The Abolitionist Sisterhood: Women's Political Culture in Antebellum America.* Edited by Jean Fagan Yellin and John C. Van Horne. Ithaca, NY: Cornell University Press.

———. 1991. "Religion, Race, and Gender in Antebellum American Radicalism: The Philadelphia Female Anti-Slavery Society, 1833–1870." Ph.D. dissertation, Department of History, University of California-Los Angeles.

Williams, Leonard F. 1972. *Richard Allen and Mother Bethel: African Methodist Episcopal Church.* Philadelphia: Historical Commission of Mother Bethel A.M.E.

Williams, Michael W., ed. 1993. *The African American Encyclopedia.* New York: Marshall Cavendish.

Williams, Russ E., ed. 1972. "Slave Patrol Ordinances of St. Tammany Parish, Louisiana, 1835–1838." *Louisiana History* 13: 399–412.

Williamson, Joel. 1980. *New People: Miscegenation and Mulattoes in the United States.* New York: Free Press.

Wilson, Carol. 1994. *Freedom at Risk: The Kidnapping of Free Blacks in America, 1780–1865*. Lexington: University of Kentucky Press.

Wilson, Ellen. 1976. *The Loyal Blacks*. New York: Capricorn Books.

Winks, Robin W. 1971. *The Blacks in Canada: A History*. New Haven, CT: Yale University Press.

Wish, Harvey. 1941. "The Revival of the African Slave Trade in the United States, 1856–1860." *Mississippi Valley Historical Review* 27: 569–588.

Wish, Harvey, ed. 1960. *Antebellum: Writings of George Fitzhugh and Hinton Rowan Helper on Slavery*. New York: Capricorn Books.

Wood, Betty. 1984. *Slavery in Colonial Georgia, 1730–1775*. Athens: University of Georgia Press.

Wood, Forrest G. 1990. *The Arrogance of Faith: Christianity and Race in America from the Colonial Era to the Twentieth Century*. Boston: Northeastern University Press.

Wood, Peter. 1974. *Black Majority: Negroes in Colonial South Carolina from 1670 through the Stono Rebellion*. New York: Norton.

Woodson, Carter G. 1968. *The Education of the Negro Prior to 1861*. New York: Arno Press.

———. 1925. *Free Negro Owners of Slaves in the United States in 1830*. Washington, DC: Association for the Study of Negro Life and History.

Woodson, Carter G., ed. 1926. *The Mind of the Negro as Reflected in Letters Written during the Crisis, 1800–1860*. Washington, DC: Association for the Study of Negro Life and History.

Woodward, C. Vann. 1971. *Origins of the New South, 1877–1913*. Baton Rouge: Louisiana State University Press.

———. 1966. *Reunion and Reaction: The Compromise of 1877 and the End of Reconstruction*. Boston: Little, Brown.

Woolman, John. 1922. *The Journal and Essays of John Woolman*. Edited by A. M. Gunmere. New York: Macmillan.

Wright, Frances. 1972. *Life, Letters, and Lectures, 1834–1844*. New York: Arno Press.

Wright, Louis B. 1940. *The First Gentlemen of Virginia*. San Marino, CA: Huntington Library.

Wright, Louis B., and Marion Tinling, eds. 1941. *The Secret Diary of William Byrd of Westover, 1709–1712*. Richmond, VA: Dietz Press.

Wyatt-Brown, Bertram. 1969. *Lewis Tappan and the Evangelical War against Slavery*. Cleveland: Case Western Reserve University Press.

———. 1982. *Southern Honor: Ethics and Behavior in the Old South*. New York: Oxford University Press.

Wyman, Lillie Buffum Chace. 1913. *American Chivalry*. Boston: W. B. Clarke.

Wyman, Lillie Buffum Chace, and Arthur Crawford Wyman. 1914. *Elizabeth Buffum Chace, 1806–1899: Her Life and Its Environment, Volume 1*. Boston: W. B. Clarke.

Yang, Liwen. 1992. "John Brown's Role in the History of the Emancipation Movement of Black Americans." *Southern Studies* 3: 135–142.

Yellin, Jean Fagan. 1972. *The Intricate Knot: Black Figures in American Literature, 1776–1863*. New York: New York University Press.

Yellin, Jean Fagan, ed. 1987. *Incidents in the Life of a Slave Girl*. Cambridge, MA: Harvard University Press.

Yellin, Jean Fagan, and John C. Van Horne, eds. 1994. *The Abolitionist Sisterhood: Women's Political Culture in Antebellum America*. Ithaca, NY: Cornell University Press.

Yetman, Norman R. 1967. "The Background of the Slave Narrative Collection." *American Quarterly* 3: 535–553.

Zaborney, John J. 1997. "'They Are Out for Their Victuals and Clothes': Slave Hiring and Slave Family and Friendship Ties in Rural, Nineteenth-Century Virginia." In *New Directions in the African-American History of Virginia*. Edited by John Saillant. New York: Garland.

Zamir, Shamoon. 1995. *Dark Voices: W. E. B. DuBois and American Thought, 1888–1903*. Chicago: University of Chicago Press.

Zikmund, Barbara Brown, ed. 1984. *Hidden Histories in the United Church of Christ*. New York: United Church Press.

Zilversmit, Arthur. 1967. *The First Emancipation*. Chicago: University of Chicago Press.